SOCIALISM AND AMERICAN LIFE

PRINCETON STUDIES

IN AMERICAN CIVILIZATION

NUMBER 4

SOCIALISM
AND
AMERICAN
LIFE

EDITORS: DONALD DREW EGBERT

AND STOW PERSONS

VOLUME 1

PRINCETON, NEW JERSEY

PRINCETON UNIVERSITY PRESS

1952

Copyright, 1952, by Princeton University Press

L.C. Card: 75-135388

ISBN 0-691-07521-2

Fourth Printing, 1970

———

*Publication of this book has been aided by a grant from the
Princeton University Research Fund*

Printed in the United States of America
by Princeton University Press, Princeton, New Jersey

To the Memory of
David Frederick Bowers

PREFACE TO VOLUME 1

THIS book was conceived in connection with two year-long student conferences conducted at Princeton University by the Program in American Civilization as part of its regular undergraduate teaching. Like all the work of the Program, the book is an attempt to cast light on important aspects of American civilization considered, not in isolation, but with reference to the other cultures which have influenced, and been influenced by, that of the United States. And it attempts to do so by cutting across the boundaries of the various fields of knowledge separated by modern specialization. This it does, not by denying the necessity for such specialized knowledge in the modern world, but by bringing together and as far as possible coordinating the knowledge and opinions of qualified experts in many different fields. A generous subvention from the Rockefeller Foundation made it possible to secure the collaboration of an unusually distinguished group of specialists who served as lecturers in the student conferences at Princeton and, on the basis of those lectures, prepared the essays in the present volume. The members of the group were carefully selected so as to combine a wide range of subject matter with representation of as many different major currents of American political and social opinion as possible. In the end the group proved to be about equally divided between those who have actually participated in socialist movements of one sort or another, and nonsocialists interested in socialism simply as a subject for study.

In addition to the essays written by these specialists, the book contains, in Volume 2, detailed critical bibliographies enlarged from those prepared under the direction of members of the staff of the Program in American Civilization for the guidance of the students enrolled in its conferences. It can be said with considerable assurance that, whatever the limitations of these bibliographies, no others of comparable range have ever before been published on this subject. Although they have been prepared with the cooperation and advice of the specialists participating in the symposium, all responsibility for opinions implicitly or explicitly expressed therein rests, not on them, but on the editors and on those other members of the staff of the Program in American Civilization who have directly shared the task of preparing the bibliographies. More detailed acknowledgments in connection with the bibliographies will be found in the preface to Volume 2.

The editors are well aware that this book can—and undoubtedly will—be criticized from several points of view. It will no doubt be criticized by conservatives on the grounds that, because several of the participants are convinced socialists of one variety or another, the book "teaches socialism." To this the editors would simply reply that socialism, whether one approves of it or not, is, after all, one of the most powerful influences in the world today; and no American can hope to consider himself educated who does not seek to understand the premises and history, the possible contributions and limitations, of the chief varieties of socialism, in comparison and contrast with the American democratic tradition.

Marxist critics will no doubt attack the book from exactly the opposite point of view, that is, on the grounds that its editors and many of the contributors are not Marxists or, indeed, socialists at all. For Marxists hold that Marxian doctrine cannot be understood by anyone seeking to investigate it "objectively," but only by those who participate to the full in Marxist action appropriate to the capitalist crisis and the revolutionary opportunities of the proletariat. To these Marxist critics the editors would reply that various shades of Marxist opinion are represented among the authors of several of the essays.

And finally, the book will be criticized—with some justice—because, like all symposia representing several shades of opinion, it necessarily lacks a single unified point of view, and because the different chapters, being by different hands, necessarily vary in the adequacy of their presentation. In answer to this the editors can only say that the subject of the relation of socialism to the various aspects of American life and thought is much too complex to be treated adequately by any one man or from any single standpoint. And while it is true that the contributors diverge widely in the *value* which they attribute to the various influences of socialism on American life, nevertheless there are also surprisingly large areas of agreement, not only as to matters of sheer historical fact but as to the *degree* to which socialism has directly or indirectly affected American life.

The two volumes are dedicated by the editors to the memory of their friend and colleague, David Bowers, who at least as much as anyone was responsible for the conception of this book as well as of the two conferences on which it is based. Had he lived he would have been one of the editors of the publication. Before his untimely death in June 1945 not only had he conducted half of the first conference and delivered the lecture on which his essay herein is based, but he prepared the original draft of large sections of the critical bibliographies. It cannot be too strongly emphasized that whatever merit this book may have is to be attributed in major part to his broad scholarship, to his great ability and intelligence.

DONALD DREW EGBERT AND STOW PERSONS, *Editors*

Princeton, New Jersey
August 1, 1951

CONTENTS · VOLUME 1

Preface   vii

Introduction: TERMINOLOGY AND TYPES OF SOCIALISM,
    by DONALD DREW EGBERT AND STOW PERSONS   1

  I. SOCIALISMS CLASSIFIED ACCORDING TO THE NATURE OF THEIR
    GOAL   6
      RELIGIOUS SOCIALISMS. SECULAR SOCIALISMS. ANARCHISM.

  II. SOCIALISMS CLASSIFIED ACCORDING TO THEIR TYPE OF ORGANI-
    ZATION   8
      COMMUNITY TYPE. PARTY TYPE. STATE SOCIALISM. COOP-
      ERATIVE TYPE. ANARCHISM.

  III. SOCIALISMS CLASSIFIED ACCORDING TO THEIR ATTITUDE TO-
    WARD PROGRESS AND CHANGE   11
      SOCIALISMS WHICH LOOK BACKWARD. SOCIALISMS WHOSE
      GOAL LIES IN THE PRESENT. SOCIALISMS WHOSE GOAL LIES
      IN THE FUTURE.

  IV. SOCIALISMS CLASSIFIED ACCORDING TO THE PARTICULAR INSTI-
    TUTIONS FAVORED AS FUNDAMENTAL TO ACHIEVING AND SUS-
    TAINING THE GOOD LIFE   15
      RELIGIOUS INSTITUTIONS. EDUCATIONAL INSTITUTIONS. ART
      AND INSTITUTIONS FAVORING THE ARTS. POLITICAL AND
      ECONOMIC INSTITUTIONS, ETC.

Chapter 1: SOCIALISM IN EUROPEAN HISTORY TO 1848,
    by E. HARRIS HARBISON   21

  I. SOCIALISM IN MEDIEVAL ECONOMY   26

  II. SOCIALISM AND EARLY MODERN ECONOMY   30
      THE DEVELOPMENT OF ECONOMIC INDIVIDUALISM AND
      UTOPIAN REACTIONS. CHANGES IN THE CHARACTER OF SO-
      CIALISM: IN SCOPE; IN OBJECTIVE; IN MOTIVATION.

  III. SOCIALISM AND THE INDUSTRIAL REVOLUTION   41
      THE AMBIGUITY OF CAPITALISM. NEW CONCEPTS. THE TRAN-
      SITION FROM "UTOPIAN" TO "SCIENTIFIC" SOCIALISM. THE
      Communist Manifesto.

Chapter 2: EUROPEAN SOCIALISM SINCE 1848,
    by HARRY W. LAIDLER   53

  I. THE *Communist Manifesto*   57

  II. SOCIALISM FROM THE FIRST INTERNATIONAL TO WORLD WAR I   60
      THE FIRST INTERNATIONAL. THE BEGINNINGS OF GER-
      MAN SOCIAL DEMOCRACY. OTHER SOCIALIST PARTIES.

III. THE GENERAL SOCIALIST VIEWPOINT AND THE THEORETICAL
BASES OF MARXISM   66

IV. THE REVISIONISTS, AND THE ORTHODOX MARXIANS' REPLY TO
THE REVISIONISTS   70
     BERNSTEIN VERSUS KAUTSKY.

V. THE FABIANS   74

VI. SYNDICALISM   78

VII. GUILD SOCIALISM   80

VIII. THE RISE OF RUSSIAN COMMUNISM   82

IX. SOCIALIST CRITICISM OF COMMUNISTS   91

X. RECENT SOCIALIST DEVELOPMENTS   92
     THE BRITISH LABOUR PARTY. SOCIAL DEMOCRACY ON THE
     CONTINENT.

Chapter 3: THE RELIGIOUS BASIS OF WESTERN SOCIALISM,
     by ALBERT T. MOLLEGEN   97

I. AMERICAN SOCIALISM IS WESTERN SOCIALISM   99

II. THE CHRISTIAN BASIS OF SECULAR UTOPIANISM   100
     BIBLICAL AND HELLENIC SOURCES. THE MIDDLE AGES. MORE'S
     Utopia.

III. THE CHRISTIAN BASIS OF SCIENTIFIC SOCIALISM   109
     MARX AND THE JEWISH-CHRISTIAN APOCALYPTIC SPIRIT.
     COMPARISON AND CONTRAST BETWEEN THE CHRISTIAN AND
     MARXIAN VIEWS.

IV. THE CHRISTIAN BASIS OF SECTARIAN COMMUNISM   112
     APOCALYPTIC SECTARIAN COMMUNITIES: THE SHAKERS AND
     THE GERMAN-AMERICAN COMMUNITIES.

V. THE CALVINIST AND UTOPIAN BASIS OF MODERN CHRISTIAN
SOCIALISM   114
     THE ONEIDA COMMUNITY AND CALVINISM.

VI. SECULAR UTOPIAN SOCIALISM   118
     ROUSSEAU AND CHRISTIANITY.

VII. THE AMERICAN SOCIAL GOSPEL AND CHRISTIAN UTOPIAN SO-
CIALISM   119
     THE SOCIAL GOSPEL: THE EPISCOPAL PATTERN AND ITS
     SPREAD. THE MERGING OF CHRISTIAN IDEALISM AND SECULAR
     SOCIALISM.

VIII. CHRISTIAN SCIENTIFIC SOCIALISM   122
     GEORGE D. HERRON. HARRY F. WARD.

IX. NEO-CALVINIST SOCIALISM   122
     THE FRONTIER FELLOWSHIP. CHRISTIANS FOR SOCIAL RE-
     CONSTRUCTION.

Chapter 4: CHRISTIAN COMMUNITARIANISM IN AMERICA,
    by STOW PERSONS   125

I. THE SPIRIT OF EVANGELICAL REVIVALISM   128
    REVIVALISM, AND PERFECTIONIST AND MILLENNIALIST
    IDEAS.

II. THE SHAKERS   132
    MOTHER ANN LEE. THE SPREAD OF SHAKERISM AND THEO-
    LOGICAL REASONS FOR IT. SHAKER SOCIAL THEORY AND
    ORGANIZATION. THE DECLINE OF SHAKERISM.

III. ONEIDA PERFECTIONISM   140
    NOYES'S EARLY DAYS AND BELIEFS; PERFECTIONISM, MILLEN-
    NIALISM, COMPLEX MARRIAGE. BIBLE COMMUNISM AND
    THE ONEIDA COMMUNITY. THE THEORY AND PRACTICE OF
    BIBLE COMMUNISM. COMPLEX MARRIAGE AT ONEIDA. MU-
    TUAL CRITICISM. NOYES'S VIEW OF HISTORY. THE SUCCESS
    AND FAILURE OF ONEIDA.

Chapter 5: THE SECULAR UTOPIAN SOCIALISTS,
    by T. D. SEYMOUR BASSETT   153

I. THE EUROPEAN BACKGROUND   156
    OWEN, FOURIER, CABET, WEITLING.

II. OWENISM IN AMERICA   161
    NEW HARMONY. OTHER OWENITE PROJECTS. OWENISM AND
    AMERICAN SOCIETY.

III. FOURIERISM AND ICARIANISM   173
    COMMUNITARIANS IN THE AGE OF JACKSON. FOURIERISM
    UNDER BRISBANE'S LEADERSHIP, 1840-1844. HISTORY OF
    THE PHALANXES. THE ICARIANS, 1848-1895.

IV. LIBERAL COMMUNITARIAN IDEOLOGY AND AMERICAN IDEAS   190
    RELIGION, PHILOSOPHY, AND THE ARTS. POLITICAL THEORY
    AND PRACTICE. SOCIOLOGICAL AND PSYCHOLOGICAL THEORY
    AND PRACTICE.

V. THE LIBERAL COMMUNITARIANS AND MARXISM   204

Chapter 6: THE BACKGROUND AND DEVELOPMENT OF
    MARXIAN SOCIALISM IN THE UNITED STATES,
    by DANIEL BELL   213

I. SOCIALISM: THE DREAM AND THE REALITY   215

II. THE MIRAGE OF UTOPIA   228

III. 1886—THE FIRST DIVIDE   233

IV. PURIST AND PURE-AND-SIMPLE   242

V. FISSION, FUSION, AND FACTION   257

VI. THE GOLDEN AGE OF AMERICAN SOCIALISM   267

VII. THE INNER WORLD OF AMERICAN SOCIALISM   293

VIII. THE DECLINE AND FALL OF AMERICAN SOCIALISM   302

IX. THE MELANCHOLY INTERMEZZO   329

X. THE CALIGARI WORLD OF UNDERGROUND COMMUNISM   334

XI. THE PLAYBOYS OF THE WESTERN WORLD   346

XII. IN DUBIOUS BATTLES   369

XIII. THE DAYS OF SERE AND YELLOW LEAF   394

Chapter 7: AMERICAN SOCIALISM AND THE SOCIALIST
       PHILOSOPHY OF HISTORY,
       by DAVID F. BOWERS   407

I. THE SOCIALIST THEORY OF HISTORY   409
       TYPES OF SOCIALISM IN RELATION TO THE SOCIALIST THEORY
       OF HISTORY: RELIGIOUS, SECULAR UTOPIAN, MARXIAN. BASIC
       PROBLEMS OF THE SOCIALIST THEORY OF HISTORY: THE
       PROBLEM OF HISTORICAL CAUSATION; OF HISTORICAL LAW;
       OF HISTORICAL ENDS.

II. THE SOCIALIST AND AMERICAN DEMOCRATIC THEORIES OF
     HISTORY   418

III. THE INTERACTION OF SOCIALIST AND AMERICAN DEMOCRATIC
      THEORIES OF HISTORY   423

Chapter 8: THE PHILOSOPHICAL BASIS OF MARXIAN SOCIAL-
       ISM IN THE UNITED STATES,
       by SIDNEY HOOK   427

I. THE PHILOSOPHICAL BASIS OF SOCIAL MOVEMENTS   429

II. BASIC PRINCIPLES OF MARXISM   432
       THE NATURALISTIC THEORY OF MAN. THE EVOLUTIONARY
       AND HISTORICAL APPROACH. ABSOLUTE DETERMINISM. THE
       PRINCIPLE OF ORGANICISM. DIALECTICS IN NATURE. DIALEC-
       TICAL METHOD.

III. AN ALTERNATIVE SOCIALIST PHILOSOPHY   448

IV. WHY HAS SOCIALISM NOT BEEN MORE SUCCESSFUL IN THE
     UNITED STATES?   450

Chapter 9: THE INFLUENCE OF MARXIAN ECONOMICS ON
       AMERICAN THOUGHT AND PRACTICE,
       by PAUL M. SWEEZY   453

I. MARXIAN ECONOMICS   456
       THE MARXIAN THEORY OF THE ECONOMICS OF CAPITALISM.

II. THE INFLUENCE OF MARXIAN ECONOMICS ON THE AMERICAN SOCIALIST MOVEMENT 460
WEYDEMEYER. SOCIALIST LABOR PARTY. SOCIALIST PARTY. COMMUNIST PARTY.

III. THE INFLUENCE OF MARXIAN IDEAS ON AMERICAN ECONOMISTS 468

IV. THE INFLUENCE OF MARXISM ON THORSTEIN VEBLEN 473

V. THE INFLUENCE OF SOCIALIST IDEAS ON AMERICAN GOVERNMENTAL POLICY 477

VI. REASONS FOR THE SLIGHT INFLUENCE OF MARXIAN ECONOMIC IDEAS IN THE UNITED STATES 483

Chapter 10: AMERICAN MARXIST POLITICAL THEORY,
by WILL HERBERG 487

I. BOURGEOIS AND SOCIALIST POLITICAL THEORY 489

II. POLITICAL TYPES OF AMERICAN SOCIALISM 490
SOCIALIST LABOR PARTY. SOCIALIST PARTY. INDUSTRIAL WORKERS OF THE WORLD. EARLY GOMPERSISM. COMMUNIST PARTY.

III. OPERATIVE IDEAS OF AMERICAN SOCIALIST POLITICAL THEORY 493
THE REVOLUTION. SOCIALISTS IN THE EXISTING ORDER. THE NEW SOCIAL ORDER.

IV. SOME CENTRAL PROBLEMS OF SOCIALIST POLITICAL THEORY 509
POWER, ORGANIZATION, FREEDOM. DEMOCRACY: TRANSITORY INSTITUTION OR ENDURING HUMAN VALUE? WHAT KIND OF SOCIALIST STATE? INDIVIDUAL—STATE—SOCIETY.

V. SOCIALIST THEORY AND AMERICAN LIFE 518

VI. NEW DEPARTURES IN SOCIALIST THEORY 521

Chapter 11: SOCIOLOGICAL ASPECTS OF AMERICAN SOCIALIST THEORY AND PRACTICE,
by WILBERT E. MOORE 523

I. SOCIALIST THEORY OF SOCIETY 526
SOCIOLOGICAL ECONOMICS. THE THEORY OF SOCIAL STRATIFICATION. SOCIALIST THEORY AND THE AMERICAN SOCIAL ORDER.

II. ORGANIZATION OF AMERICAN SOCIALIST GROUPS 546
THE SOCIALIST COMMUNITIES. MODERATE SOCIALIST PARTIES. RADICAL PARTIES.

III. AMERICAN SOCIALIST CLIENTELE 553

Chapter 12: THE PSYCHOLOGY OF AMERICAN SOCIALISM,
by GEORGE W. HARTMANN 557

I. SOURCE MATERIALS AND PROBLEMS OF METHOD 559

II. APPLICABILITY OF THE CONCEPTS OF "NEED" AND "FRUSTRA-
TION"   562

III. SOCIALISM AS A VALUE-SYSTEM OR PATTERN OF DRIVES   565
INTERPLAY OF IDEAS OF VALUE, CONFLICT, POWER.

IV. VARIETIES OF SOCIALIST "EXPERIENCE" AND BEHAVIOR   570
SOCIALISTS TO WHOM SOCIALISM IS CENTRAL VERSUS PERIPH-
ERAL. SOCIALISTS AS "HEALTHY-MINDED" VERSUS "SICK
SOULS." SOCIALISTS CONCERNED WITH COMPLETE CULTURAL
CHANGE VERSUS POLITICAL AND ECONOMIC OBJECTIVES.

V. SOCIALIST CLIENTELE   579

VI. MOTIVATION IN A SOCIALIST ORDER   583

VII. WHAT BEHAVIOR MODIFICATIONS FACILITATE OR ACCOMPANY
SOCIALISM?   586

VIII. PSYCHOLOGICAL RESISTANCES TO SOCIALISM   590

Chapter 13: AMERICAN WRITERS ON THE LEFT,
by WILLARD THORP   599

I. PROLOGUE   601

II. PROBLEMS OF THE LEFTIST WRITERS   606

III. FOUR TYPICAL LEFTISTS   610
MAX EASTMAN, JOSEPH FREEMAN, PHILIP RAHV, ISIDOR
SCHNEIDER.

IV. WHAT THREE WRITERS' CONGRESSES REVEAL   616

V. EVALUATIONS   619

Chapter 14: SOCIALISM AND AMERICAN ART,
by DONALD DREW EGBERT   621

I. RELIGIOUS UTOPIAN SOCIALISM AND ART   625
PIETISTIC COMMUNITARIANS. CALVINISTIC COMMUNI-
TARIANS.

II. SECULAR UTOPIAN SOCIALISM AND ART   630
OWENITES, FOURIERISTS, ICARIANS.

III. MARXISM: THE MARXIAN PHILOSOPHY OF ART   636

IV. MARXISM (CONTINUED): MARXIAN ART AND THE EUROPEAN
BACKGROUND   650
ENGLAND. GERMANY. SOVIET RUSSIA.

V. MARXISM (CONTINUED): ITS EFFECTS ON ART IN THE UNITED
STATES   705
DIRECT AND INDIRECT INFLUENCE.

Index to Volume 1   755

INTRODUCTION

Terminology and Types of Socialism

BY DONALD DREW EGBERT

AND STOW PERSONS

THE problem of investigating the role which socialism has played in the United States is, of course, greatly complicated by the fact that there are so many different types of socialism, most of which are referred to in one way or another in the essays or bibliographies that follow. Because these different types are not systematically brought together in any other part of this book, the introduction will be chiefly devoted to a brief analysis of the major varieties of socialism, an analysis which can also serve in part as an introduction to socialist terminology.

In this book, unless otherwise noted, the word socialism is taken to include communism in accordance with the usage prevailing today.[1] However, a brief statement concerning the origins and development of these two terms is necessary, for their relation to one another has varied somewhat at different periods of time.[2] It should first be noted that "socialist" and "socialism," "communist" and "communism," are all words of relatively recent coinage, even though most of the points of view for which they stand go far back in human history. None of them, in their modern sense, can be found before the 1820's, and they all originated in either England or France. The earliest known use of the word "socialist" in its present meaning, to denote tendencies opposed to individualism, occurred in 1827 in the *Co-operative Magazine*, published in London by followers of the socialist Robert Owen; while "socialism" seems to have originated in France where it first appeared in print in 1831. "Communist" and "communism," however, were not coined until 1840, or shortly before, being first used by members of the secret and militant revolutionary societies which flourished in Paris under Louis-Philippe.[3]

After the Owenites coined the word socialist, they used it for a few years as their own distinctive label, but in the 1840's they lost their

---

[1] Oscar Jászi, "Socialism," *Encyclopaedia of the Social Sciences*, XIV (1934), p. 188, states that socialism is the inclusive term.

[2] For the history of socialist terminology see especially the definitive article by Arthur E. Bestor, Jr., "The Evolution of the Socialist Vocabulary," *Journal of the History of Ideas*, Vol. 9, No. 3 (June 1948), pp. 259-302; also Carl Grünberg, "Der Ursprung der Worte 'Sozialismus' und 'Sozialist,'" *Archiv für die Geschichte des Sozialismus und der Arbeiterbewegung*, II (Leipzig, 1912), pp. 372-79, and Oscar Jászi, *op.cit.*, pp. 188-201. Additional bibliography is cited by Bestor, p. 277, note 95.

[3] According to Max Beer, "Communism," *Encyclopaedia of the Social Sciences*, IV, p. 81, the term communism did not appear in print before 1840, but was coined in the secret revolutionary societies of Paris between 1834 and 1839. Bestor, *op.cit.*, p. 279, states that the new term "was born" in the year 1840. According to the *New English Dictionary*, under "Communism," an Englishman named [John] Goodwyn Barmby claimed in 1848 to have invented the word in 1840 at Paris while "in the company of some disciples of Babeoeuf [*sic*], then called Equalitarians." Bestor (p. 280) says that Barmby went to Paris in June 1840 armed with a letter from Robert Owen, and arrived there just as the new French terms were being introduced; however, Bestor credits Barmby with naturalizing the words communism and communist, among others, in English.

3

monopoly of the term, which was now applied to the followers of Charles Fourier and to other socialist and reformist groups of a peaceful nature. Consequently, Karl Marx and Friedrich Engels felt it necessary to use the word communist, rather than socialist, in their *Communist Manifesto* of 1848, so as to distinguish their militant working-class movement from nonmilitant middle-class efforts at social reform including Owenism and Fourierism.[4] All these middle-class movements the *Manifesto* attacked as "utopian," that is to say, as being so ideal, so divorced from contemporary life, as to be impossible of achievement.

Thus the word communism, from its associations with the secret societies of Paris and with the *Communist Manifesto*, for a time connoted revolutionary action leading to the violent overthrow of all noncommunist forms of social organization, a usage then restricted, however, to the continent of Europe. And socialism, by contrast with communism, connoted nonviolent, constitutional, and hence gradual, reform.

After the failure of the Revolutions of 1848, the revolutionary form of socialism to which the name communism had become attached was now largely discredited. Gradually the name lost the militantly revolutionary implications which it had acquired on the Continent. At about the same time the word socialism was losing its narrowly sectarian connotations, partly as a result of the failure of the Owenite movement, to which it had formerly been restricted. As socialism thus became a more inclusive term, it tended to assimilate and replace the word communism, so that by the mid-1860's it was widely accepted as the comprehensive name for the whole movement. Whereas now the term communism was limited either to those systems which insisted that property be held in common, or to small cooperative communities which were seeking reform but which might or might not insist on completely collective ownership.

For many years thereafter the meaning of these words was to remain stable, until—shortly after World War I—the terms communist and communism were deliberately reestablished in Russia with all the militant and revolutionary connotations which Marx and Engels had given to them back in 1848. It was in March 1918 that the Russian Social-Democratic Labor Party (Bolsheviks) decided to change its name to the Communist Party, in accordance with a proposal made by Lenin nearly a year earlier mainly on the grounds that the majority of the official Social Democratic parties had betrayed socialism by supporting World War I. From that time to this the name communism has customarily been applied to the revolutionary, as distinguished from the evolutionary, form of socialism.

In Russia too, Lenin, followed by Stalin, began to use the word social-

[4] Cf. Harry W. Laidler, p. 57, note 3, herein.

ism in a somewhat special sense[5] as the name for what Karl Marx had called the first phase of communist society.[6] By this Marx meant the period after the revolution of the proletariat had resulted in public ownership of the means of production but before the proletarian state had, in Engels' phrase, withered away, a period in which each person was to receive from society according to the quantity and quality of his work. Whereas Marx's second stage of communism, which alone is what Lenin and Stalin have meant by communism, was to be a classless and stateless society in which each person would receive according to his needs.

Thus today there is considerable confusion in the use of the words socialism and communism because of their respective multiple meanings. As indicated above, socialism is used in at least three ways: as a general term which includes communism, as a special Leninist-Stalinist term to indicate Marx's first stage of communism, and sometimes as referring to evolutionary socialism alone. And communism, too, has three very different meanings: revolutionary (as opposed to evolutionary) socialism; socialism based on the holding of all property in common; and thirdly, socialism which seeks to bring about reform by means of small experimental communities.[7] All of these meanings occur in this book, as in most other general books on the subject.

Not only do the most important terms in the whole socialist vocabulary have several different meanings, but several widely accepted terms have sharply prejudicial connotations. To this day the Marxian terms "utopian socialism" (for pre-Marxian and non-Marxian socialism)[8] and "scientific socialism" (for Marxism) are generally used even by those non-Marxians who believe that Marxism is far from being scientific and even actually utopian. Because these Marxian terms have long been so widely accepted by Marxians and non-Marxians alike, they will be found throughout much of this book, but will be used descriptively and, as far as possible, without the Marxian prejudicial connotations. Only after most careful consideration did the editors reluctantly decide to retain this traditional, if highly confusing, terminology in the present volume, and then only because they

[5] For this use of the word socialism see V. I. Lenin, *The State and Revolution* (New York: International Publishers, 1932), p. 78. The original Russian edition was published in 1918.

[6] See Karl Marx, *Critique of the Gotha Programme* (New York: International Publishers, 1938), p. 10. The original German edition was published by Engels only in 1891, after Marx's death, but Marx wrote the *Critique* in 1875.

[7] Bestor, *op.cit.*, p. 301.

[8] The derogatory use of "utopian" as applied to social movements, a usage which has become so completely associated with Marxism ever since it appeared in the *Communist Manifesto*, did not, however, actually originate with Marx and Engels. Bestor, *op.cit.*, p. 287, points out that before 1848 reformers had frequently applied the term utopian to rival schemes of which they disapproved. Fourier, for example, thus used the word a number of times, always in a disparaging sense.

5

found it impossible to arrive at a new and more exact terminology completely acceptable to all their numerous collaborators.[9]

Despite the many confusions in the traditional terminology, despite the various changes in the meaning of the word socialism itself, it can at least be said that all forms of socialism have shared the belief that only through some form of collective organization, some form of collective action, can the individual come nearest to fulfilling his potentialities. Nearly all forms of socialism have maintained that this can be accomplished only through the elimination of unearned increment, and most of them have insisted upon the collective ownership of at least some of the means of production.

However, while all the various kinds of socialism do agree that the goal is the highest development of man, they disagree sharply as to what constitutes man's highest development. They disagree also as to what type of social organization can offer mankind the highest opportunities for individual development either during the period when the goal of the good life is being sought or after that goal has been reached. Moreover, they disagree as to the location of the goal in history—differ, that is, in their attitudes toward change; for while the great majority of socialists look forward to an ideal society in the future, some (perhaps wrongly called socialists) place the goal in the present, while still others look back to some event in the past as having made a communal way of life imperative. And lastly, the different varieties emphasize different institutions as basic for achieving and developing the good life.

In sum, socialisms differ fundamentally over such questions as (I) the nature of the goal, and (II) the nature of the organization of mankind best suited either for achieving the ideal society or for maintaining it when it is once achieved. They differ also as to (III) the location of the goal in history, and (IV) the nature of the human institutions considered most fundamental to historical development. While these different points of view, these different classifications, crisscross one another and overlap at many points, and while a more or less parallel development can be traced in them all, no one of them alone is adequate to identify and define the various types of socialism. But as all of them are implied at one place or another in the chapters and critical bibliographies that follow, it may be helpful to describe each one briefly here, even though in so doing it will be impossible to avoid a certain amount of repetition.

I. Socialisms Classified According to the Nature of Their Goal

As noted above, all forms of socialism and related movements agree that the goal is the highest development of the individual, while disagreeing as to the exact nature and location of this goal.

[9] For a revised terminology, at times used herein, see Bestor, *op.cit.*, pp. 301-2.

6

(1) Some varieties of socialism—notably the religious varieties, such as the Shakers, the Oneida Community, etc.—insist that the highest development of man is a spiritual one, reached only in the Christian millennial order and achieved only through God's grace; although a suitable socialist way of life here and now is usually considered to be requisite to the realization of the millennium. Some of these groups, including the Shakers and the Oneida Community among many others, have believed that the socialist way of life involves a considerable degree of withdrawal from ordinary society; while the later Christian socialists consider socialism to mean participation in the social problems of all humanity as part of the Christian life.

(2) The great majority of socialists, however, including all strict Marxists, reject the supernatural and hold the secular belief that the highest human development can and will be reached in history conceived as a unitary process, and that it can be accomplished through some specific kind of collectivistic organization.

(3) Although in many respects anarchism has much in common with socialism, in other ways it differs profoundly, especially in the ways in which it seeks its goal. Practically all anarchists agree with the secular socialists that human nature can reach its highest development in *this* world; and socialists and anarchists alike believe in an ultimate order of society which is without classes or coercion. However, anarchists are more individualistic than socialists insofar as they attach greater importance to *voluntary* social action as a means for achieving the highest development of human nature. It is this emphasis on voluntary social action which has particularly characterized well-known anarchist projects and theories such as the mutual banks of Proudhon or Kropotkin's doctrine of mutual aid.

The most profound difference between the various types of socialism, on the one hand, and of anarchism, on the other, lies in the fact that they disagree as to when the ultimate classless and stateless society should be instituted. While socialists consider that it can be achieved only after some period of transition, anarchists believe that it must be brought about more immediately. Nevertheless, anarchists themselves disagree as to the *degree* of immediacy. A few, the more completely individualistic anarchists, would institute the classless society at once. But most anarchists—including Mikhail Bakunin, Marx's influential opponent in the struggle for control of the First International—have been more closely linked to socialism in its Marxian form because they subscribe to what is known as communist anarchism. For like the Marxian communists, the communist anarchists ordinarily insist that a violent revolution must take place before the classless and stateless society can be achieved. Unlike the Marxians, however, they maintain that the classless and stateless society

7

should come about directly after the revolution; whereas Marx stated that the revolution would be followed by a period of transition in which the state would still exist but would be under the control of the proletarian class. This period Marx only occasionally referred to as the "dictatorship of the proletariat," a term heavily emphasized by his Leninist-Stalinist interpreters.

II. Socialisms Classified According to Their Type of Organization

A survey of this book reveals five chief types of organization which have been made use of by socialism and related social movements. These five types can be called respectively: (1) the community type; (2) the party type; (3) state socialism; (4) the cooperative type (including aspects of industrial unionism); and (5) anarchism, which, as suggested above, usually has certain socialistic connotations.

(1) The community type of socialist organization is best identified in relation to one or the other of two main subvarieties. One of these can be called the exclusive community because it is intended to serve the purposes of a limited group only and is not at the beginning supposed to be applied to society as a whole. While there have been literally hundreds of examples of this exclusive form of socialism in America—most of them founded in the seventeenth, eighteenth, or early nineteenth centuries— the illustrative material in this book is drawn mainly from the following communities: Ephrata, Amana, the settlements of the Rappites and the Shakers, the Oneida Community, and some aspects of Mormonism. It will be noted that all these examples have had a religious purpose, and this has also been true of most of the other exclusive communities in this country.

The second kind of community type of socialism can be described as the experimental or pilot community intended for the purpose of working out basic problems of socialism, not just for a restricted group, but with the hope of becoming the prototype and model for universal communal organization. Usually, although not always, the goals sought by these communities have been secular rather than supernatural. In the United States the most important examples of this kind of socialism—sometimes referred to in this book as liberal communitarianism—have been the communities established during the early and middle nineteenth century in accord with the ideas of Robert Owen, of Charles Fourier, or of Étienne Cabet.

(2) The second chief type of socialist organization is the party type. All the important examples of this have been based in large part on the doctrines of Karl Marx, so that none of the major examples is earlier than the middle of the nineteenth century. As the name implies they are all concerned with the socialist reorganization of society by political means

at the culmination of the "class struggle." However, the party type of organization can be either authoritarian or democratic in its point of view.

The democratic party type looks forward to achieving socialism by peaceful and gradual means rather than by sudden revolution, and in the United States can be said to represent an attempt to reconcile the American democratic tradition with Marxism. The best example of this type in the United States is the Socialist Party, which customarily has considered itself as being patriotically American as well as international in its interests.

The authoritarian variety is sometimes called by its adherents "democratic centralism." It is democratic insofar as free discussion of a given socialist problem is encouraged up to a certain point, but then discussion is declared closed, the decision is handed down from above by a small central group and is supposed to be accepted by the rank and file without question or comment. This kind of party organization, developed on a revolutionary Marxist basis by Lenin in Russia, has been best exemplified in the United States by the Communist Party. Because of its close relations with the Communist Party in Russia as well as with communists in other countries, the Communist Party in the United States has customarily prided itself on having a point of view which is ultimately international. Actually, however, the Communist Party becomes nationalistic at such times as the immediate situation seems to indicate that a temporary nationalism can best promote the ultimate world-wide triumph of communism under the leadership of Soviet Russia.

(3) State socialism can be said to represent the desire to avoid the class struggle presupposed by the party types. Here the state seeks to represent more completely the inclusive ideals of the whole existing community, ideals in terms of which a program of socialization may be gradually extended to ever wider areas of the national economy. Since state socialism minimizes the class struggle as an issue, its program can seek to appeal to the interests of various social groups, instead of being restricted to those of the proletariat alone. The British Fabian tradition as reflected in the Labour government after World War II represents this form of socialism.

It is obvious that in many countries the trend of legislation toward public control or ownership in certain economic areas might be interpreted as a tendency toward state socialism. However, such legislation is often termed state capitalism when—as in Bismarck's Germany—the intention is clearly to preserve capitalism in its most essential aspects. In such cases it is felt that the operations of capitalism itself will be reinforced through public regulation or even a limited degree of public ownership. In this volume no effort has been made to follow out the implications of this particular tendency for recent American public policy.

(4) The fourth or cooperative type of socialist organization has many different manifestations. Unlike party socialism or state socialism, these cooperative varieties tend to be suspicious of the state, so that their form of organization is basically economic rather than political. Thus they are customarily organized as cooperatives consisting of *either* producers *or* consumers independent of the state. However, these cooperative groups are considered to be socialistic only if they condemn the existing political and social order as a whole, and advocate a new social order to be accomplished by remolding human nature, human institutions, or both. This is the aim, for example, of syndicalism, of guild socialism, and of some other varieties of industrial unionism, all of which are based on organizations of producers.

In its syndicalist, or revolutionary form, this kind of producers' socialism favors direct industrial expression of the class struggle through direct revolutionary action by labor, with particular emphasis on the general strike. The best known American example of this point of view has been the I.W.W. (Industrial Workers of the World), popularly known as the "Wobblies." Largely a native development within the American labor movement, the I.W.W. has nevertheless been influenced by French syndicalism (so named from the French trade unions, or *syndicats*), and by aspects of anarchism and of Marxism. The English form of socialism known as guild socialism, which has had little influence in this country, was likewise partly inspired by syndicalism, but its doctrine was evolutionary rather than revolutionary.

In the United States, consumers' cooperatives have generally been interested in changing only the system of distribution, and insofar as they have not sought to alter the general social order they have not been socialistic. Nevertheless, certain founders and promoters of the cooperative movement have, as individuals, hoped for more radical changes of an anarchist, syndicalist, or socialist character.

(5) As previously noted, anarchists tend to fall into two categories: the extremely individualistic anarchists on the one hand, and the more numerous communist anarchists on the other. Those of the individualistic type (for example, Thoreau) are necessarily opposed to organization, and, as extreme individualists, can hardly be considered socialists. The others who (like Mikhail Bakunin and like Kropotkin) believe in communist anarchism, combine the philosophy of anarchism with the revolutionary program of Marxian communism. That is to say, like Marxian communists, they recognize the existence of a class struggle between property owners and workers, but, unlike the Marxians, they fear the state and other "coercive" political organizations as much as capitalism. Unlike the Marx-

ians, therefore, they discard political action and oppose the party type of organization encouraged by Marxism. At the same time, their belief in the class struggle and the consequent necessity for a revolt of the masses often leads communist anarchists to seek to organize the masses into industrial unions for direct economic action—leads them, in short, toward syndicalism and a syndicalist type of organization.

III. Socialisms Classified According to Their Attitude toward Progress and Change, i.e., According to the Location of Their Goal in History

In Chapter 7 herein, David Bowers has discussed in some detail how socialisms differ in their points of view toward history. However, in anticipation of his essay we may briefly note that some varieties locate their goal not within secular history but at its culmination in a divine event— the millennium. This is especially true of the religious utopian communities, nearly all of which have believed that the perfection of man—human salvation—can only be achieved after some future divine event, some divine catastrophe or revolution, and then only through God's grace. Most of them, therefore, have looked forward particularly to the second coming of Christ; although the Shakers and the Perfectionists of Oneida have been exceptional in believing that the second coming had already occurred.

Unlike the religious socialists, all other forms of socialism locate their goal of the perfection of man *within* human history; but, as already suggested, they differ as to where in human history it is to be placed. On the basis of this difference, three chief points of view can be distinguished as follows: (1) A few of these socialists who reject the supernatural consider that the goal, the ideal, has already been achieved in a specific idealized period of the past; (2) Some others, who are sometimes (perhaps wrongly) called socialists, believe that the goal lies in the present and therefore seek to maintain the status quo; (3) The great majority of the secular socialists, however, believe that it lies in the future, but are unable to agree as to just how history operates to reach the goal. Of these, some insist—along with the religious socialist communities—that history operates through catastrophe and revolution. Some maintain that it operates through evolution, while others uphold the theory of cyclical repetition. Still others believe in a combination of evolution, revolution, and repetition: indeed, Karl Marx's doctrine of the dialectic is, in a sense, such a combination. For according to the dialectic any given tendency, or "thesis," eventually gives rise to its antithesis, and after a violent struggle—the revolution—a synthesis takes place. This in turn gives rise to its own

11

antithesis, so that the whole cycle of evolution and revolution repeats itself in a new form again and again.[10]

It was largely on the basis of these three main points of view toward the location of the goal in history—in the past, the present, or the future— that Marx and his friend, Friedrich Engels, classified the chief social movements of their day in the famous *Communist Manifesto* of 1848. Because this basis of their classification has not always been generally recognized, and because it is not specifically dealt with elsewhere in this book, it is briefly summarized here.

(1) The kinds of socialism which look backward to their goal are called in the *Manifesto* "reactionary socialism," and are attacked for nostalgically seeking to revive aspects of earlier societies that are more or less collectivistic. Marx and Engels, on the contrary, subscribed to a belief in progress away from the past although within the framework of "laws" of historical development. According to these Marxian laws of history, human society can and should progress toward a climax in a classless society made possible by the triumph and temporary dictatorship of the proletariat. For this reason Marxians necessarily insist that any attempt to return to earlier societies is reactionary because it would result in postponing the proletarian revolution and the classless society. Among the examples Marx cites of such reactionary socialism is really what later became known as Christian socialism.[11] In the words of the *Manifesto*, "the parson has ever gone hand in hand with the landlord," so that to Marx and Engels even Christian socialism is simply a form of what they called "feudal socialism," meaning thereby a reactionary survival from the Middle Ages masquerading as socialism. One of the other examples of reactionary socialism cited in the *Manifesto* is the petty bourgeois attempt to revive the collectivism of the medieval guilds. This aspect of reactionary socialism was to become particularly important with William Morris, who during much of his life was regarded as a Marxist and whose ideas were destined to have a strong influence on such later forms of socialism as Fabianism and guild socialism.

(2) Those secular social movements which hold that the good life has just been attained and therefore lies in the present, Marx and Engels called "conservative or bourgeois socialism." They considered this to include all attempts of the middle class to buttress capitalism and maintain the existing state of affairs by adopting enough measures of social reform to keep the working class quiet. Under this heading Marx would put not only what is now called state capitalism, but even the state socialism of his German rival, Lassalle.

[10] For a more complete definition of the dialectic, by Harry W. Laidler, see p. 57, note 4, in this volume; also Volume 2, PART III, Topic 5.

[11] The first issue of the *Christian Socialist*, from which Christian socialism takes its name, came out in 1850 at London.

(3) The only kinds of socialism for which Marx had any respect were those that look forward to their goal, that believe in the idea of progress. Of these, however, he distinguished two types, one of which the *Communist Manifesto* somewhat scornfully called "critical-utopian socialism and communism." The other is his own brand of socialism, usually known either as communism (the name given to it in the *Manifesto*), or as scientific socialism (so called for reasons to be indicated later), or simply as Marxism.

By critical-utopian socialism Marx meant only the secular varieties of utopian socialism, because to him the religious utopian communities were not really socialistic since they did not seek to remold society as a whole in order to achieve a better life for the individual in *this* world. Even the secular utopians—whose beliefs, like those of Marx himself, partly sprang from the rational-romantic ideals of the Enlightenment— were considered by Marx mistaken in maintaining not only that man is completely free to remold history, but that the ideal society can be put into practice on a small scale at once and can be spread by education and without violence. For Marx held that man is very largely determined by the Marxian laws of history, of social development, laws which ultimately have an economic basis. In accordance with those laws and in the light of the situation then existing on the Continent, Marx was convinced that the eventual ideal (or classless) society could ordinarily be achieved only following a violent revolution. Thus in Marx's view the secular utopians were being highly unrealistic in ignoring both the laws of history and the existing social situation, and it was for this reason that he applied to them the name of utopians, by which they have since been known. Nevertheless, in the *Manifesto* Marx and Engels did praise the utopians for maintaining that class antagonisms exist and that capitalism is decomposing. And no less an authority than Lenin has pointed out that utopian socialism, particularly French utopian socialism, was one of the chief currents of contemporary thought contributing to the formulation of Marxism.[12]

For Marxians, then, Marxism is the only completely realistic philosophy of socialism, a philosophy based on Marx's own materialistic interpretation of history, and involving not only a whole economic and political theory but a thoroughgoing program for social revolution. To this philosophy Marx and his followers have given the name of "scientific" socialism because they believe that Marx discovered laws of economic and social

[12] Lenin, in *The Teachings of Karl Marx* (first published, abbreviated, in the Granat Russian Encyclopedia in 1914; complete English edition, Martin Lawrence Ltd., 1931), said that the three chief influences on Marx's thought were: (1) German classical philosophy, especially that of Hegel, who was the source of Marx's doctrine of the dialectic; (2) English classical economics, on the basis of which Marx conceived his labor theory of value (for which see Paul Sweezy, pp. 457ff. herein); and (3) French [utopian] socialism.

change of such validity that general predictions as to the forthcoming development of the fundamental economic conditions of society can be made on the basis of them, and made with the precision of natural science. Because Marxians believe that man is free to act only within the framework of these laws, freedom consists in understanding how the Marxian laws of history and the laws of nature operate, and in acting accordingly. However, since Marx's own time there have been disagreements as to his views concerning the exact degree to which man is determined by the laws of history, for Marx expressed himself differently under different circumstances. This is the source of the controversy as to whether the classless society is to occur inevitably regardless of human actions, or whether (as Marxians today usually maintain) the efforts of all good Marxians are necessary to ensure the coming of the classless society as well as to speed up its development. A certain lack of consistency among the contributors to the present volume indicates that this point has not yet been fully settled.

However, the question of the inevitability of socialism is only one of the issues which have divided socialists since Marx's day and which have caused the varieties of socialism to multiply greatly. Another chief point at issue has been the nature of the Marxist revolution—whether it must be violent (as Marx and Engels maintained in the *Communist Manifesto* and most of their other writings), or whether it can be gradual, achieved by legal parliamentary means (as Marx and Engels later admitted was then possible in a few countries with strong democratic traditions). Still other major disputes have occurred among Marxists over such problems as to when the state can be expected to wither away, or as to the relation of labor unions to socialism, or the relation of international socialism to Russian communism. To this day the question as to which faction represents the true Marxist doctrine continues, of course, to stir up violent controversies in many parts of the world.

All these disputes, among others, have had pronounced repercussions in American socialism, and one or more of them has been responsible for the splitting off of elements of the Socialist Labor Party to help form the Socialist Party, of elements of the Socialist Party to form the Communist Party, and of parts of the Communist Party to form the Trotskyist groups, as well as for other splits referred to in this book. In many cases these splits have in part resulted from the differing importance attributed to various human institutions considered most fundamental for bringing about socialism, and this brings us to our last classification.

IV. Socialisms Classified According to the Particular Institutions Favored as Fundamental to Achieving and Sustaining the Good Life

When the goal of the good life is a supernatural one and thus lies outside of history, it is, of course, the *religious* institutions and the religious aspects of life that are considered primary. For this reason, although the various religious utopian communities have regarded their communal forms of social organization as important, they have nonetheless considered them entirely secondary to salvation and therefore to religious beliefs and practices.

When the socialist goal is considered to lie in this world, sharp differences of opinion exist among the different varieties of socialism as to just which aspects of life in this world, and therefore which human institutions, are most fundamental. And while some of them believe that the reform of existing but corrupt institutions will be sufficient, others maintain that only through completely new social inventions can a new social order be achieved.

(1) To some forms of socialism it is the *educational* institutions, and the ethical-rational qualities which they stand for, which are most fundamental for achieving man's aspirations. Thus the secular utopians, such as Robert Owen and Cabet, were convinced that man is by nature both good and rational and can therefore be educated to overcome the evils of a corrupting environment and to bring society and himself to full perfection. For that matter, even most of the kinds of socialism which do not believe that education is primary have nevertheless given an important place to education as a factor in bringing about or enhancing the good life. It is for this reason that propaganda has been considered so necessary by most brands of socialism and that the arts have usually been valued by socialists chiefly for social usefulness in education and propaganda.

(2) However, in at least one important case—that of the great English socialist, author, artist, and craftsman, William Morris—*art* itself, and the social institutions which encourage the widespread practice of art, have been considered most fundamental. To Morris and to his many followers art is the expression of that joy in work which they have felt is basic for the good life and which they have believed would become universal under socialism. Meanwhile, because they attributed so many of the evils of contemporary society to industrialization and the consequent mechanization of the individual, they have sought to revive the medieval guilds as the institutions best suited to fostering the arts and handicrafts. The guild socialists took over this concept but sought to combine it with industrial trade-unionism in an effort to make it more suited to the needs of an industrialized society.

15

(3) A much larger number of socialists have held that *political* institutions are the most important of all, although they have differed among themselves as to whether control over these political institutions should be gained by legal and evolutionary means or by extralegal and revolutionary means. The German socialist Dühring, for example, emphasized politics as having decisive influence on economics and as being the determining factor also in other aspects of life.

(4) The point of view of Marx and Engels was in sharp contrast to that of Dühring, whom they attacked because they insisted that *economic* changes are ultimately responsible for all other change, including political change. It was for this reason that Engels wrote his celebrated polemic against Dühring popularly known as *Anti-Dühring*. However, the socialists who, like Marx and Engels, agree that the economic aspects of life are the basic ones, disagree as to whether production or consumption is more important. Furthermore, of those who stress the basic role of production some insist that the industrial aspects of production are the primary ones, while others emphasize the agrarian aspects, maintaining that land monopoly is the sole cause of the exploitation of human beings. Marx, of course, tended to emphasize industrial production by giving a primary role to the industrial proletariat (even though he did make an occasional bow toward the peasantry in the *Communist Manifesto* and elsewhere), and this long remained the orthodox Marxian view. Because of Russian conditions, Lenin assigned a much greater importance to the peasants, although he did not consider them socialists, while Stalin, following in Lenin's footsteps, made use of the Five Year Plan to mechanize and industrialize agricultural production. In so doing, Stalinists maintain, he made it possible to fuse the interests of the industrial working class and the peasant class so that their area of common interests becomes ever larger as they march forward together, but under the leadership of the industrial workers, toward the classless society.

(5) While most varieties of socialism place heavy emphasis on one of the kinds of institutions—such as the religious, educational, artistic, political, or economic institutions mentioned above—they usually do not emphasize this alone but give considerable secondary importance to others as well. In some kinds of socialism, two or more of these types of institutions are given an equal importance. Such is the case with the kind of socialism known as jural or juridical socialism. This, as its name implies, recognizes the primary significance of legal rights because these can guarantee both political and economic rights and thus guarantee both *political* and *economic* institutions as being equally important. For this reason the chief exponent of juridical socialism, the Austrian socialist Anton Menger, opposed Marxism for maintaining that economic theory

alone is fundamental, and he insisted that socialism should be based on three legal rights—the right of workingmen to the whole produce of labor, the right to exist, and the right to work.

Marxism itself involves an insistence on the worth of many kinds of institutions. Even though the ultimate basis of Marxism is economic, nevertheless upon that economic basis Marx erected a superstructure in which, Marxists claim, all other valid aspects of human existence are taken into account. And this, many of them say, has been particularly true since Lenin made it especially clear that economic propaganda alone is inadequate and that a general world view must be implanted in the proletariat.

Thus to Marxists the economic changes in history are looked upon as paving the way for the proletariat to seize control of political institutions, with the aid of educational propaganda in which the arts can play a part. Only when this political control has been gained and a temporary proletarian state ("the dictatorship of the proletariat") set up, can fundamental jural reform be achieved, as for example in the Russian constitution of 1936. Such juridical reform, together with reforms in other aspects of life, can in turn, they say, help to further the fundamental economic changes which eventually will make possible a classless, stateless, and therefore nonpolitical society. In the Leninist-Stalinist view, these fundamental economic changes, necessary for bringing about the classless society, can be achieved only by means of joint action by the industrial proletariat and the peasantry, whose interests are becoming identical with the mechanization of agriculture. And, according to Marxian doctrine, once the classless society has at last been achieved, the individual will finally be free to develop himself to the full so that all the finer aspects of human life will flourish as never before.

It is probably significant that Marxism, which despite its ultimate economic foundations has dealt with a greater number of other important aspects of life than any other variety of socialism, receives more attention in this volume than other forms of socialism. Its wide scope has even enabled it to appeal to many who, like William Morris, have actually been in basic disagreement with Marx's fundamental economic materialism. It is this Marxian emphasis on the social worth of so many different kinds of human institutions that has given all forms of Marxism a collective strength especially lacking in the individualistic kind of anarchism, for such anarchism is completely anti-institutional in regarding all religious, educational, artistic, political, legal, economic, and other institutions as likely to hamper the full development of the individual.

Since no one of the above classifications of the various kinds of socialism is alone adequate to delimit and define the nature of all the different

17

varieties, the essays and critical bibliographies which follow will be found to cross and recross from one of them to another, to combine and recombine elements taken from them all. Largely because of this crossing and recrossing, some repetition will be found not only within this volume but also between Volumes 1 and 2. Part of the repetitiousness, however, has deliberately been cultivated by the editors so that individual essays may be clear to those readers who are not interested in the book as a whole but only in the subject matter of a single chapter or of a single section of the bibliographies.

The first three essays herein are devoted to the European backgrounds of American socialism, religious and secular, because practically all the chief types of socialism in the United States have either originated abroad or else have sprung from ideas developed abroad at an earlier date. The first essay, by E. Harris Harbison, deals with the early history of socialism by tracing its development in Europe from the early Middle Ages to Marx. Chapter 2, by Harry W. Laidler, treats the development of European socialism in its Marxian phases from 1848 to the present. In the third chapter, A. T. Mollegen discusses the religious basis of Western socialism, including Marxism, and ends with short analyses of the varieties of American socialism which have particularly felt the influence of the Christian tradition.

Thus Mr. Mollegen's essay serves as a transition to the three chapters that follow, for not only does each of these deal with one of the three most important types of socialism as found in the United States, but the first is specifically religious in nature. These three types of socialism are generally known even to most non-Marxians by the more or less Marxian names of religious utopian socialism, secular utopian socialism, and "scientific" or Marxian socialism. The chapter on religious utopian socialism, by Stow Persons, discusses the Shakers and the Oneida Community as the two most representative and peculiarly American examples of Christian utopian—or more exactly, communitarian—socialism. In the next essay, T. D. S. Bassett studies the various forms of secular utopian socialism in this country, with emphasis on Owenism, Fourierism, and Icarianism. The last chapter in this group, by Daniel Bell, deals with all the major varieties of Marxian socialism in the United States while stressing the history of the Socialist Party.

The remaining eight essays are on various specific aspects of American socialism, beginning with two chapters on the general subject of the theoretical foundations of socialism but with special reference to the United States. In the first of these, David Bowers has investigated one major segment of socialist philosophy fundamental to all forms of socialism, namely, the socialist philosophy of history. In so doing, he links together the doctrines of both religious and secular socialism in America and thus paves the way for the essay that follows, Sidney Hook's analysis of the philosophical foundations of Marxism.

The next two chapters are directly concerned with those specific aspects of life and of socialist theory which Marx himself considered to be the most fundamental: the economic and—second only to the economic—the political aspects. Paul Sweezy discusses Marxian economics and its relation to American thought and practice, while Will Herberg considers the manifestations of Marxian political theory in American life with special reference to the Socialist Party, the Socialist Labor Party, the I.W.W., and the Communist Party.

Then follow two chapters dealing respectively with the sociology and psychology of American socialism. The sociological implications of the socialist theory of society in relation to the organization and clientele of American socialist groups are investigated by Wilbert Moore. George W. Hartmann studies socialism as a movement, or group of movements, psychologically distinctive in espousing an all-embracing plan of organization for meeting all the basic needs of every person included within its scope.

The essays conclude with consideration of literature and art—those aspects of human life which William Morris regarded as the most fundamental of all, but which most socialists have valued more for their utilitarian and educational possibilities. The relations of American socialism to American literature are studied by Willard Thorp. In the closing chapter of the symposium Donald Egbert discusses the chief varieties of American socialist art in relation to European origins and influences, and with particular reference to the indirect effects of socialism on American life. Thus the concluding essay returns once more to the European background with which this volume began and serves to give a further reminder to the reader that the subject of socialism in American life cannot be adequately understood without reference to European prototypes and parallels.

It might be noted parenthetically that no chapter on socialism and the natural sciences has been included simply because science in the United States has been so little affected by socialism. However, occasional refererences to the implications of socialism for science will be found in this book, especially in the second volume.

Volume 2, which consists of selective and critical bibliographies in the form of a series of essays, is organized in sections related to the chapters of Volume 1. However, advantage is taken of the opportunity offered by the bibliographies to summarize in them various socialist issues not specifically treated in the first volume. In so doing, an effort has been made to present the historiography of socialism more completely and thereby give greater scope and greater unity to the book as a whole. Because of the complexity and range of the problems considered in them, the bibliographies, also, have had to be prepared by several hands. Thus the entire publication has been a cooperative one—it could not have been produced without the generous help of authorities in many fields. It is the hope and belief of the editors that the wide range of opinion represented by the numerous contributors and advisers has allowed the book to achieve a kind of collective objectivity all too lacking in most writings on this highly controversial subject of socialism in American life.

CHAPTER 1

Socialism in European History to 1848

BY E. HARRIS HARBISON

E. HARRIS HARBISON is Professor of History at Princeton University. His special field is the history of the Renaissance and Reformation.

For bibliography in Volume 2 relevant to Mr. Harbison's essay, see especially PART I, General Reading, *passim*, and Topics 1, 2, 5, 6, 7.

T HE study of American socialism begins in Europe. Any understanding of socialistic thinking and practice in American life must rest upon knowledge of the part played by socialism in European history.

The connection between Europe and America in this respect is a dual one of continuity and parallel. Two human beings may act alike for two quite different reasons: first, because one influences the other; and second, because each, though isolated from the other, is confronted by roughly the same general situation. Americans have not only consciously imitated their ancestors and contemporaries in Europe, but they have often unconsciously retraced some of the steps taken by the older civilization of which they are a part. The forms assumed by socialistic thought in the United States are often to be explained as direct borrowings from western Europe. Less often but no less significantly they are to be looked upon as similar reactions to similar economic and social situations, situations which have generally arisen in Europe, particularly in Great Britain, before they have arisen in roughly similar form across the Atlantic. For almost a thousand years Europe has been a kind of laboratory of social change and experiment. Some of this experimentation has been deliberately imitated across the water, some deliberately rejected, some repeated without any consciousness that it had been performed before. America is related to Europe, in other words, both by historical continuity and by historical parallel.

Any view of socialism in European history, if it is to have value for the present study, must be three-dimensional. Rapid and cursory as such a view must be within the limits of an introductory chapter such as this, it should suggest depth and perspective.

It is not enough to trace the development of socialistic thought and practice from Plato to Marx, as many of the older accounts do, in a single dimension. It is characteristic of "socialism," as of other social theories in European history, that it cannot be understood apart from the historical fortunes of its dialectical opposite, in this case "individualism." The study of the history of individualism gives the study of socialism a second dimension. In any broad view of European history the development of a peculiar dialectical relationship between individualism and socialism was the fact of real historical significance, not the development of socialism alone. To one outside the western tradition, this developing tension between a precocious and self-conscious individualism and an answering and equally self-conscious socialism is the distinguishing mark of western European social history. The communistic thought of Hebrew prophets, Christian apostles, and Greek philosophers was an important European heritage, no doubt, but to understand modern socialism it sometimes seems more important to know the Medici and the Fugger than it is to know

23

Amos and Plato. Somewhat like the dimensions of length and breadth, individualism and socialism cannot be separated from each other in any balanced study of European social development.

Length and breadth are completed by depth. At any given point in European history the dialectical relationship between individualism and socialism was always relative to a particular existing pattern of economic relationships. To be a socialist (in a general sense of the word) meant one thing in the thirteenth century, another in the sixteenth, and still another in the nineteenth. Just *what* any reformer wished to transfer from individual to social ownership, *how*, and *why* are all questions which can only be answered by a painstaking historical inquiry into the contemporary economy. *Omnia sunt communia* is an ancient cry, but just what is comprehended in "all things," what is involved in rendering them "common," and why bother, are problems which are always relative to "the prevailing mode of production and exchange" in any century. Knowledge of the existing economy is absolutely essential to the understanding in depth of any socialistic theory or experiment.

Another preliminary question suggests itself: Where to begin? How much of European history is relevant to the subject of this volume? It has been argued by some that there is no real socialism before Marx—in which case the present chapter could be eliminated. Sombart assumes that modern socialism begins with the French Revolution and the accompanying technological revolution in Great Britain.[1] Mannheim goes back to the Protestant Reformation and the Anabaptists.[2] Bede Jarrett finds enough of importance to fill at least a slim volume on *Mediaeval Socialism*.[3] And there are always classical and Biblical scholars to insist that the subject properly begins with Plato's *Republic* and the second chapter of Acts—indeed, such is the general thesis of Chapter 3 in this book.

If one accepts the counsel of perfection already suggested, a three-dimensional study of socialism in European history must begin where "Europe" begins, i.e., somewhere about the age of Charlemagne. What came before—prophetic castigations of the unfeeling rich, Plato's communism for the classes, the Stoic natural law of human equality, primitive Christian communism—may safely be treated as part of the heritage with which Europe began. What came after, however, is all directly relevant to an examination of the interplay of individualism and socialism in the developing European society. The medieval guild, for instance, seen through a haze of nostalgic sentiment, inspired later American as well as British socialists; and it is not altogether fanciful to compare medieval and

[1] Werner Sombart, *Socialism and the Social Movement in the Nineteenth Century* (New York, 1898), chap. 1.
[2] *Ideology and Utopia* (New York, 1940), especially pp. 190-91.
[3] London, n.d. (ca. 1913).

American societies as "frontier societies" and to note the parallelisms in their socialistic experiments. The whole millennium of European history from Charlemagne to Marx has relevance for the present subject.

To grant this proposition, however, is to pose a further problem: the almost insoluble problem of selection. The bibliography of this book gives some indication of what an extensive literature has grown up on the subject of European socialism. But it scarcely suggests the still larger literature devoted to the development of capitalism and to European economic history in general. Fortunately the purpose of the present volume supplies a certain criterion of selection. This purpose is to launch a critical inquiry, to survey the ground for further scholarly cultivation, to ask the questions which may lead to new work rather than merely to summarize work already done. In the present case what will be suggested is a point of view rather than a set of conclusions, a way of considering the thin thread of socialistic thought and practice in European history to 1848 rather than a connected tracing of this thread.

This point of view may be briefly adumbrated as follows. The development of socialism in European history may be compared with the typical development of the family sense in the ordinary human being—if one admits from the start that the comparison is playful rather than realistic. The child is born into a natural group, the family, in which there is a vague distinction of "mine" and "thine" within a surrounding "ours." His personal possessions are important to him, but the really important things—food, shelter, implements of work—are actually common possessions. It is impossible to describe this arrangement as either "individualistic" or "socialistic." The child did not choose his situation and he does not reflect deeply upon it unless there is some unusual reason. Adolescence brings a change, a concentration of the self, a self-conscious separation from the family group. The passionate individualism of youth is proverbial. It spreads far beyond the sense of physical possession to intellectual independence and spiritual revolt against authority. The adolescent's desire for a room of his own is one symptom of a more general desire to mark off the boundaries between himself and all other individuals. The third stage, of return to the family through marriage, is something far different from the first entrance into the family group. It is deliberate and self-conscious, even if the emotional drives involved are as complex and contradictory as loneliness and love. The common and mutual responsibilities are far more vivid to the partners in marriage than they could be to the child, and the communal aspects of married life take on new meaning against the background of adolescent individualism and isolation. To parents the family is a "socialistic" institution in a way it can never be to children.

The comparison of this parable of the individual with the communal economy of the Middle Ages, the economic individualism of the early modern period, and the increasing collectivism of the past century is perhaps too neat. But medieval social theory has at least something of the child's naïveté about it. There is often a quality in early modern individualism which tempts historians to describe it as adolescent. And Marxian socialism has something of that sophisticated sense of the significance of each stage of past experience for the present which we have assumed that the individual has upon reentering the family through marriage. The point is that the particular character of modern collectivism, whether socialistic or otherwise, cannot be understood as a mere return to an earlier communalism nor as a mere reaction to an extreme individualism, but only as something of both.

I. Socialism in Medieval Economy

It is difficult to describe medieval economy in words sharpened by use in a later and far different age. "Individualism and socialism as ordinarily understood," A. D. Lindsay remarks, "emphasize one or other of the two aspects which in Christian teaching are inseparable."[4] And so during the Christian Middle Ages, as Tawney points out, "contrasts which later were to be presented as irreconcilable antitheses" appear as "differences within a larger unity."[5] We need to dull the sharpness of nineteenth-century words, to muddy their clearness, before we can approximate the ambiguity of medieval terms and of medieval economic practices. For this reason it is better to use clumsy technical terms with Latin roots such as *paternalism* and *communalism* to describe the economic life of the Middle Ages. Paternalism suggests a society patterned after the family in which privilege is the meed of protection; it suggests also the power for good or evil of strong-willed individuals in such a society. Communalism suggests a society which thinks and acts in terms of communities, which is held together by community mindedness; it suggests the anonymity of the individual and the constant enveloping pressure upon him of the group. Iron wills working within the silken bands of custom, tradition, and public opinion—this is a better popularization of the significant features of medieval society than the older picture of stagnation and uniformity.

In this society making a living was always a means to an end, never an end in itself, so far as conscious reflection about the matter was concerned. The end of society was salvation, not satisfaction of material wants. The weight of the Christian tradition bore heavily upon any

[4] A. D. Lindsay, *s.v.* "Individualism," in *Encyclopaedia of the Social Sciences,* vii. On terminology, see A. E. Bestor, Jr., "The Evolution of the Socialist Vocabulary," *Journal of the History of Ideas,* ix (June 1948), pp. 259-302.

[5] R. H. Tawney, *Religion and the Rise of Capitalism* (New York, 1926), p. 20.

attempt to justify profit, though it favored the dignity of labor as a means of grace.

Most medieval economic activity was communal or corporate rather than individualistic. The units of production were the agricultural manor and the urban guild. Within these units there were rights which look to us like private property rights: the peasant possessed his house, his garden, and his strips of arable land just as the artisan possessed the tools of his trade. But other rights were distinctly communal, "rights of participating in a common life," such as the peasant's rights in the common land of the manor and the artisan's rights to an equal share of the available raw materials and an equal opportunity in the carefully protected local market. Peasant and artisan were thus capitalist and laborer at the same time, and yet neither in the modern sense. The driving force of production was generally the immediate pressure of need rather than the remote attraction of profit, and the units of production were strictly regulated both from within and from without in accordance with this general motivation. There was no scope for unlimited profit-seeking in the custom of the manor, the regulations of the guild, or the contractual obligations of peasant and townsman to an overlord. Medieval minds were certainly not preoccupied about using wealth to create more wealth: "So much wine and salt came to our monastery from its estates," wrote a thirteenth-century chronicler, "that it was simply necessary to sell the surplus."[6]

Distribution was determined by custom, and custom was in turn based upon an uneasy compromise between communal need and individual greed, not upon the workings of a free market. Economic relationships were grounded upon status in the vast majority of cases until a money economy began to spread after the eleventh century. Ancient forms of community organization, spiritual functions, or military need determined status, and status generally determined economic occupation. High as the spiritual aims of medieval society were, the end of economic activity was in practice mainly to support the clergy and nobility; but it was always recognized that the producers had to be able to keep body and soul together in order to do their job. All this was expressed legally in a tangled web of custom and contract which remains today in the documents as a kind of monument to an age in which purely economic factors were never the primary basis of man's relation to man.

If it were possible to visualize the "ownership" of any given square mile of arable land in the eleventh century, some of this highly abstract analysis might take on concrete meaning. One would find no "owner" in the modern sense but rather a human chain of holders of rights, from serf through lord of the manor to overlord and king, each with certain rights in the

[6] Caesar of Heisterbach, quoted by F. L. Nussbaum in *A History of the Economic Institutions of Modern Europe* (New York, 1933), p. 32.

land or a part of it, each bound to the others in the chain by duties theoretically owed on account of rights held. It is generally true that there was almost no landowning in the Middle Ages, only land holding. "Lordship"—a right to a higher standard of living through the claim to a portion of the labor or services of other human beings—generally replaced "ownership" in the modern sense. Thus "property" was a vaguer and more ambiguous term than it is today, including rather abstract rights as well as land and movables.

The most important consequence of this situation was that there could never be any such thing as absolute unconditional ownership of private property. All ownership was "mere conditional use." The rights to land, i.e., to productive capital, were invariably confused and overlapping and they invariably implied obligations. "Theoretically," writes Jarrett, "the means of production remained in the hands of the community. The Feudal System was perhaps the nearest approach to a consistent system of communism that has ever been practised on a large scale."[7] This startling statement by one of the ablest students of the problem probably goes too far. It dramatizes the strong community sense of the Middle Ages, but it ignores the equally significant medieval emphasis upon the sanctity of private right.[8] Within the community mindedness of medieval property relationships there was a sharp sense of "mine" and "thine" which attached as clearly to contractual rights and obligations as to real and movable property. In fact, the deeper one gets into the subject, the more cautious one becomes about generalization, and the more impressed with the depth of meaning in Tawney's phrase about "differences within a larger unity." In practice there was a constant tendency of strong-willed feudal lords to turn land holding into landowning, but until the thirteenth century the bonds of legal and moral restraint held firm. Until feudalism itself was undermined, its implicit theory of property retained some relation to actual practice: common ownership and individual holding and use.[9]

The Schoolmen introduced an element of confusion by adopting Aristotle's apparently contradictory formula: private ownership, common use. Since both formulas express the point of importance, that private possession always implies public obligations, the contradiction is more apparent than real.[10] But the Schoolmen, led by Thomas Aquinas, mark a subtle transition here. Aquinas understood the rising middle class and the new world of trade. It does not seem fanciful to suppose that he wanted a

[7] Bede Jarrett, *Social Theories of the Middle Ages* (London, 1926), p. 132. See also his *Mediaeval Socialism* (New York, 1914), p. 15.

[8] See e.g., C. H. McIlwain, *The Growth of Political Thought in the West* (New York, 1932), pp. 370, 394.

[9] On this and what follows, see Jarrett, *Social Theories*, chap. 5.

[10] Jarrett, *Social Theories*, p. 144, notices this contradiction but does nothing to explain it.

theory of property which would fit trade as well as land holding. He knew that a man cannot buy and sell objects which he does not "own" in some real sense. Aristotle's theory could serve better here than the comparatively confused feudal practice, and it was not hard to reconcile with Christian ethics if one translated "common use" into Christian charity and the social obligations of wealth in general.

Since Aquinas' treatment of property was the starting point for nearly all important social thinkers of the early modern period, it is worth noting that most of his intellectual energy was expended upon the famous common-sense argument for private property as an experienced necessity, not upon an argument for communism as the ideal. Apparently the first had to be argued, the second could be assumed. If men were all good, communism would apply since it is the ideal pattern. Communism is certainly not evil, it is simply too lofty to be realized by fallen human beings, unless it be by apostles or monks. Monastic communism then is a reminder of lost innocence, a standing proof that although private property is a practical necessity if men as they are since the Fall are to live together with a reasonable amount of harmony, it is not an absolute necessity, not a rule of divine or even of natural law. It is at this point that Aquinas made creative use of Aristotle in elaborating the social utility of recognizing the right to private property by positive human law. He left no loophole here for the Waldensians, the Spiritual Franciscans, and other heretics of his day who argued like the sects of a later time that the ideal could and should be realized by human beings, that the church should return to apostolic poverty. But he was sensitive enough to the dangers implicit in the expanding commercialism of his day to insist strongly upon the common use of what was privately owned. The corollary of private property was almsgiving, and although the amount of the contribution might be limited by "inconvenience" to the giver, the "need" of the sufferer came first.

Medieval society was never so articulate about itself as it was in Aquinas just at the moment in the thirteenth century when the new economic forces which were to undermine medieval institutions were making themselves clearly felt. The Middle Ages in general had a way of keeping ideals untarnished and available for use in the fullness of time even when practice seemed impossibly far removed from them. For instance, when kings were pitiful weaklings and law a set of rules without sanction, the ideas of monarchy and constitutionalism survived for future development. In somewhat the same way but with contrary results, the Middle Ages held high an ideal communism while making practical common-sense concessions to an incipient economic individualism. It was Aquinas, a propertyless Dominican friar, who elaborated the classic medieval argument for private property. The church never entirely forgot the second chapter of Acts even while chastising those of its children who wanted to return here and now to pentecostal communism.

From this point of view, the study of medieval society as a whole—its manors and guilds, its feudal contracts and monastic communities, its feudal and scholastic theory—is more important for the later history of socialism than any myopic examination of medieval communistic sects or radical revolts like the Peasant Rebellion of 1381. It was from this common soil of the Middle Ages that both modern individualism and modern socialism were to spring. Before the close of the Middle Ages there were departures both ways from what might be called the medieval compromise on property as expressed by Aquinas, but these were not so significant as the character of the compromise itself. During the later Middle Ages the contrasts between wealth and poverty were far more vivid and brutal than they are today, the tone of life more violent, and the tendency to fly to emotional extremes more pronounced.[11] It is not hard to imagine the proud display and callous indifference to suffering on the part of the rulers of society which lay behind the English peasants' well-known cry of 1381: "Things cannot go well in England, nor ever will, until all goods are held in common and there are neither serfs nor gentlemen and all of us are one."[12] The irresponsibility of landlords was theoretically even more "radical" in the Middle Ages than the vaguely-defined communism of peasant rebels. The point of real importance is that by the later thirteenth and fourteenth centuries there were significant stirrings of discontent in the economically progressive parts of Europe—northern Italy, the Rhine valley, the Netherlands. These heralded the birth of a competitive and dynamic economy which would soon undermine the foundations of medieval society and its ideals. In a sense both the heretics and Thomas Aquinas himself were symptoms of the new stresses and strains. The history of modern socialism begins not with peasant agitators like John Ball or Jack Cade, but with the birth of this new individualistic economy.

II. Socialism and Early Modern Economy

The truly "radical" movement of the later medieval and early modern period was the growth of economic individualism, not the appearance of a few communistic books, sects, and communities. Against the background of nineteenth-century individualism, "radical" is today almost synonymous with "socialist" or "communist." Against the background of medieval communalism, "radical" (if the word had been used) would have called up most readily the picture of "landlord," "monopolist," or "usurer" in the sixteenth century. Thomas More's *Utopia* was not so radical

[11] The classic account is Johan Huizinga, *The Waning of the Middle Ages* (London, 1924), especially chap. 1.

[12] *Œuvres de Froissart*, Kervyn de Lettenhove, ed. (Brussels, 1869), ix, p. 388.

a book in its own day as Machiavelli's *Prince*. Both men had qualms about publishing, but it was the *Prince* which remained in manuscript while the *Utopia* was published and eagerly read all over Europe. It is essential to the understanding of utopian socialism to remember that when it first appeared in European history as a fairly consistent theory, it was very largely a reactionary protest against a new, "progressive," and poorly understood economic movement, an appeal to turn the clock backward. It is this nostalgic quality, this restoration mentality, which most clearly distinguishes so much socialistic thought before Marx.

The development of economic individualism was part of a broader movement in European society which textbooks are prone to call "the emancipation of the individual." Now almost a century since Burckhardt wrote his classic study of the Renaissance, in a day impressed by the dangers of emancipated individualism, some writers are apt to look at the other side of the picture and call the movement "the disintegration of medieval society." It might be more precise to describe what happened on almost every level of European society between the mid-fifteenth and the mid-eighteenth centuries as "the definition of boundaries": the emergence, fixation, and sharpening of boundaries between individuals, between classes, between nationalities, between properties and authorities. The simplest example is the emergence of geographical boundaries between political authorities, frontiers which could not possibly be drawn on a map of medieval Europe. Machiavelli's *Prince* dramatized the geographical definition as well as the moral isolation of the modern state as Donatello dramatized the autonomy of the free-standing individual in sculpture. Descartes spoke for the whole age when he argued in a famous paragraph of the *Discourse on Method* that the creations of individual genius are always more perfect than the works of many hands. The definition of authority followed the same lines. The chief aim of European monarchs during the early modern period was to reduce all the complexities of feudal relationships to the simple relationship of sovereign to subject and to absolve the royal power so far as possible from all legal and institutional restraints. Thus Bodin could define the nature of sovereignty because he could see its outlines in contemporary political practice as no medieval thinker could have seen them. The central theological problem of the Protestant Reformation—grace versus free will—was from one point of view a problem of defining boundaries left undefined and fluid in medieval theology. The fixing of frontiers previously undrawn was one of the most striking preoccupations of early modern Europe.

One of the most important aspects of this process was the sharper definition of "mine" and "thine." Beside the free-standing individual of Renaissance portraiture and the sovereign state of Renaissance political theory there appeared the absolute owner. Ownership gradually became more definable, more individual. At the same time it became more irresponsible and unconditional. In western Europe the slow growth of a money economy enabled the peasant from the thirteenth century onwards to buy his freedom from the conditions on which he held land, and in the process he lost his land. The lord in selling his right to certain services assumed absolute ownership of the land and soon forgot that land holding had ever been conditional.[13] The revival of Roman law accelerated the process by cutting through the tangle of medieval custom and demanding sharper definitions of both property and authority. By the seventeenth century there was little question in western Europe, as there would have been four or five centuries earlier, about who "owned" a particular bit of land. The landlord's title, like the stockholder's rights in a joint stock company, was capable of more precise legal definition than a vassal's fief or a master's rights in his guild. Both were now significantly more individual and more irresponsible.

It is not surprising, therefore, that during the seventeenth and eighteenth centuries the theoretical argument for private property was refined, elaborated, and grounded in a thoroughly individualistic doctrine of natural law. This was mainly the work of English writers—Hobbes, Locke, and Adam Smith—with important assistance from the French *philosophes*. By the end of the eighteenth century the three major arguments for private property—that it is a natural (or moral) right, that it is a civic (or legal) right, and that it is justified by its social utility—had all found forceful expression, both singly and in varying combinations. On the subject of property the French *Declaration of the Rights of Man* began where Thomas Aquinas could never have begun: "The right to property being inviolable and sacred. . . ."[14]

This strengthening of the practical and theoretical supports of individual ownership of property, however, was a gradual process. In general, early modern economy was an unstable phase of the transition from a feudal to a capitalistic economy. The older units of production did not disappear all at once. The manor survived in many parts of Europe and reappeared in the New World as the *encomienda*. The guilds were generally nationalized and so preserved for further subordinate usefulness. But economic activity was becoming progressively more individualistic as well as more consciously directed toward profit making: it could now properly be called "individual enterprise" in place of the earlier communal satisfaction of need. The "radicalism" of the later Middle Ages was winning out. The regulated companies and even the joint stock

---

[13] Jarrett, *Social Theories*, pp. 141-43. Cf. McIlwain, *op.cit.*, pp. 198-99.

[14] Article XVII. See W. B. Guthrie, *Socialism before the French Revolution* (New York, 1907), chap. 8.

companies preserved some of the corporate character of medieval commercial activity, but the important figures in western European economy were coming to be the improving landlord and the individual entrepreneur, acting alone or in "partnership," their attention fixed upon expanding production and increasing profit. In theory the state replaced the church and the local community as the regulator of distribution, using the devices of subsidy and prohibition, monopoly and privilege. Paternalism and communalism had grown to "mercantilism" or "étatism." But there was growing control of distribution by the unregulated market—another way of saying that distribution was steadily becoming more unplanned, more automatic and impersonal, though still regulated by the state with its own military strength in mind. In theory the end of economic activity was still outside itself—in the state now, whether dynastic or national. But in the practice of mercantilism in the seventeenth century, particularly in the Dutch Provinces and in England, it was sometimes difficult to say whether government was controlling business enterprise or vice versa. It was just at this point in the development of European economy, when the movement toward economic individualism was gathering momentum in England and yet was still restrained by political and patriotic, if not by ethical and religious, considerations, that the North American colonies were founded. Had they taken root a century or two earlier, the basic economic presuppositions of North American society would have been quite different.

The socialistic theories and experiments of the early modern period were dialectically related to the growing economic individualism which we have sketched. The complexity of this relationship is particularly evident in Sir Thomas More's famous work, published in 1516. The real significance of the *Utopia* becomes apparent when one remembers the complete lack of any such approach to social problems in the Middle Ages, and then notes the continuity of socialist criticism from More through Winstanley, Morelly, and Mably to Saint-Simon, Fourier, and Owen. Every major feature of pre-Marxian socialism is present in this, its first classic expression: the optimistic faith in human nature, the overweening emphasis upon environment and proper education, the nostalgia for lost innocence and integrity, and the exaggerated uniformitarianism which is the measure of every utopian's revulsion from rugged individualism. But something else is there in the *Utopia* which was not always to be found in its successors: a shrewd, informed, and firsthand analysis of the contemporary economy, of the actual workings of the raw new economic individualism, done by a lawyer who was equally at home in problems of government, business, and agriculture. His analysis was set down upon paper just at the moment when the corrosive effect of capitalistic practices upon medieval economic customs and ideals was first clearly felt and before there was any question whatever in the minds of ordinary folk that both justice and precedent were on the side of the critics of the new practices.[15]

Early modern socialism, as we have already pointed out, was essentially a conservative critique of a new and strange individualism felt to be excessive. But like the new economy itself, More's criticism was ambiguous. It seems to be a truism, particularly of English history, that in turning back to restore the good old days men often unwittingly moved forward. Ostensibly the only practical remedy suggested in the first book of *Utopia* is to turn the clock back: to "re-edify" the buildings and towns ruined by the expansion of sheep farming, to "suffer not these rich men to buy up all, to engross and forestall and with their monopoly to keep the market alone as please them"; in other words, to restore the best in medieval economic regulation.[16] Ostensibly the chief sources of theoretical remedy are Plato's *Republic* and Christian monasticism. But it is very significant that the kingdom of Utopia as presented to the reader exists *now*, beyond the equator. It is removed from existing European society not in time but in place. Here are human beings who escaped the Fall, so to speak, and so are untrammelled by Christian history. True, theirs is a perfectly static society, which has bored every reader possessed of an ounce of restlessness or initiative, but as a standard by which to test European society and possibly to galvanize it into reform, Utopia has a potential dynamism which the Garden of Eden had long lacked. It is just as revolutionary as it is reactionary.

In More's day the medieval assumption that communism was God's original pattern was dimmed but by no means blacked out. When More speaks in his own person in the dialogue he never questions the ultimate *rightness* of communism. Raphael is made to argue that "where possessions be private . . . it is hard and almost impossible that there the weal public may *justly* be governed and *prosperously* flourish." More's reply does not question the justice, but it does doubt the prosperity: "Me thinketh that men shall never there live *wealthily* where all things be common," because of the lack of incentive to labor. Again in the last paragraph of the book the author questions the "good *reason*" of the Utopians' way of life, but not its ultimate goodness.[17] More, in other words, expends more intellectual energy than Aquinas in arguing the theoretical validity of

[15] The most discerning recent treatment of the *Utopia*—J. H. Hexter, *The Biography of an Idea: a Study of Sir Thomas More's Utopia* (Princeton University Press)—had not appeared in print when this was written. Hexter writes, "The Utopian Discourse is the production of a Christian humanist uniquely endowed with a statesman's eye and mind, a broad worldly experience, and a conscience of unusual sensitivity, who saw Sin and especially the Sin of Pride as the Cancer of the Commonwealth."

[16] *Utopia* (Everyman ed.), p. 26.

[17] *Utopia*, pp. 43, 45, 114. Italics added.

communism, but the two agree implicitly that private property is certainly not of divine or natural law. More foresaw many of the dangers of unregulated individualism, and the playful emphasis upon uniformity in Utopia—from clothes to equal apportionment of children among families—was the measure of his fears. But he did not believe that freedom of thought need go overboard with the suppression of economic individualism, and he was not driven to the hysterical lengths of a Proudhon on the subject of private property because he was still a good Thomist. There was impressive continuity in the utopian tradition in these matters from More to Robert Owen, a continuity which is both amazing and amusing. The measure of Owen's distrust of individualism in any form was to be found in the regular architecture of his parallelograms, their standardized schools, and their children scampering about uniformly clad in "a dress somewhat resembling the Roman and Highland garb."[18] The *Utopia*, like most of its successors down to *A New View of Society*, by Robert Owen, was essentially good medieval doctrine on the ownership of property applied to and shaped by contemporary problems.

In spite of such continuity, however, there were significant changes in socialist thought as the early modern period ran its course: changes of scale, of objective, and of motivation. These may be measured not only by products of the literary imagination like the *Utopia* but also by the actual socialistic experiments of the period. Each of the great revolutions which ushered in the modern world—the Protestant Reformation, the Puritan Rebellion, and the French Revolution—produced a small but significant "left-wing" movement at the moment when the lowest classes, which had joined the middle classes in the early stages of each upheaval, began to feel disillusioned about the course taken by the revolution. Although there was not the continuity between these communistic movements that there was in the literary tradition, they were the abortive beginnings of modern socialism as a movement rather than as a theory. From the Anabaptists through Winstanley's "Diggers" to Babeuf's "Equals," there was a certain uncoordinated development which was the result of progressive changes in European economy and society as a whole rather than of any conscious building upon past experience within a socialist "movement."

The change of scale to be noted is the slow expansion of the size of communistic communities, both in practice and theory. In general this expansion lagged somewhat behind the actual expansion of viable political units from feudal principalities to national states, and far behind the rapidly growing economic interdependence of Europe.

The medieval monastic community was the model for heretical com-

[18] Robert Owen, "Report to the County of Lanark," *A New View of Society and Other Writings* (Everyman, 1927), p. 278.

munist groups in the early modern period. These groups rejected the monastic objective of separation from the world in order the better to serve God, but carried monastic practices out into the world. Between the Fraticelli of the thirteenth century, the Brethren of the Common Life of the fifteenth, and the Moravian Anabaptist communities of the sixteenth, there was a difference of degree rather than of kind. Each successive group tended to think of itself more and more as a "holy community," a light set upon a hill, a seed planted in the soil—a conviction which seemed to become more firmly held as the bonds which had drawn medieval society together progressively dissolved. There would be no need for force or even for persuasion (here the Taborites of the fifteenth century and the Münster Anabaptists of 1534 were untypical because of very special military circumstances); the gospel of holding goods in common would spread by example, the light would find reflection, the seed would reproduce itself. At most, federation of such communities was thought to be the only artificial device necessary to aid the providential process. True, there was an amazingly wide subterranean organization of left-wing groups in central Europe before and even shortly after the Peasants' Rebellion of 1525, but the communistic element within these groups soon settled into the typical "holy community" pattern.[19]

More's *Utopia* is the first evidence of significant expansion of scale. Plato's communism like St. Benedict's was for the few, whereas the Utopians' was *for all those belonging to a "national" group.* If one asks what holds Utopian society together as More presents it, the answer is not religion (there are different sects in Utopia) and certainly not enlightened economic self-interest. The social bond is what we would call patriotism: pride in common history and achievement, a sense of distinctness from other people, willingness to sacrifice everything for a way of life which is thought both unique and good. The preconditions of a workable communism in Utopia are a large degree of national isolation and exclusiveness; problems of surpluses, both of goods and population, are solved by a sort of benevolent imperialism. Utopia is described as a loose federation of cities, but actually every political, social, or economic matter of any real importance is handled on a national scale. In this respect More's book belongs to the age of national states rather than to the age of medieval localism. A century later the uses of patriotism as a social cement are even more clearly appreciated in Campanella's *City of the Sun.* The inhabitants are pictured as being consumed by love for their native land and at one point the author remarks, "When we have taken away self love, there remains only love for the state."[20]

[19] Karl Kautsky, *Communism in Central Europe in the Time of the Reformation* (London, 1897), is still a good introduction to the subject.
[20] Campanella, in Henry Morley, *Ideal Commonwealths* (7th ed., London, 1896), pp. 225-26.

By the seventeenth century English national self-consciousness was more highly developed than in More's day and it was natural for even the left-wing movements of the Puritan Rebellion to betray the influence of the national idea. Gerrard Winstanley began his "true levelling" on a hill in Surrey with a handful of followers, but he ultimately turned to Cromwell in 1651 and elaborated his *True Law of Freedom* on a national scale. The Diggers had first acted perforce as a "holy community" and trusted that their example would spread. But after their crushing defeat by the gentry and the law courts, it was impossible to think of going ahead with anything but a national program. Winstanley believed in the initiative and independence of the small community. He shared More's admiration for the London Companies, and some features of his scheme borrowed from guild organization. At the other end of the scale, his comparison of the nature of "monarchy" and of "commonwealth" had universal application. But his utopia in its final form was essentially national, coextensive with the Puritan revolutionary Commonwealth.[21]

Still another century and the national scale of left-wing activity became almost normal and inevitable. There is no trace of the holy community idea in Babeuf's conspiracy during the French Revolution. Organization was (or was intended to be) on a nation-wide scale; capture of the state was the immediate objective; and plans for the future revolved around a kind of permanent dictatorship of the proletariat in a new state. Laski remarks that the Babouvists "had practically no conception of socialism as an international force."[22] It might be added that they had no more conception of socialism as a local community affair. Their generation had forgotten that socialism was once a matter of saintly communities holding their lamps aloft in a naughty world. By the time of the French Revolution the scale of socialist activity had expanded from the community to the national state: the "light set upon a hill" had been replaced by public-service illumination.

As for the second kind of change—change of objective—there were some attempts in socialistic thought and experiment to keep pace with the slow contemporary shift from thinking primarily in terms of consumption and subsistence to thinking primarily in terms of production and profit, but these attempts were fitful and not always self-conscious. Throughout European history socialistic thought has concerned itself with distribution, but only modern socialism concerns itself seriously with problems of production.

[21] On Winstanley, see particularly G. H. Sabine's introduction to his edition of *The Works of Gerrard Winstanley* (Ithaca, N.Y., 1941).

[22] H. J. Laski, "The Socialist Tradition in the French Revolution," in F. J. C. Hearnshaw, ed., *The Social and Political Ideas of Some Representative Thinkers of the Revolutionary Era* (London, 1931), p. 228.

Monastic communism was a consumers' communism. Medieval monasteries, it is true, were often more efficient productive units than surrounding manors, but the production of a surplus above the subsistence requirement was irrelevant to the community's spiritual purpose and could be embarrassing in practice, as the previously quoted passage from a thirteenth-century chronicler suggests. Even among the Anabaptists, as Kautsky remarks, it was "a communism of the consumers, not of the producers"; "communal housekeeping, not . . . communal labor." But this communal housekeeping resulted directly in communal production on a large scale among the Hutterite Brethren in Moravia. They had come together for reasons which had nothing to do with increasing economic output, but they were soon outproducing surrounding "individual initiative" in the making of cloth, the brewing of beer, and the breeding of horses. Eventually production was developed on such a large scale that it was no longer an accessory to an originally Biblical communism, but rather the very basis of this communism.[23] The Moravian Anabaptists apparently confirmed what evidence there was from the history of monasticism that communism could outproduce individualistic compromises in certain circumstances.

This was not the normal way, however, that socialistic thought and practice achieved the transition to concern about production. Even when outproducing the surrounding economy, socialist groups never justified the superiority of their way of life by its productive capacity, so far as I am aware, until after the industrial revolution had accelerated the familiar boom and bust cycle of business activity. The transition must be sought in the slow shift of emphasis in socialist thought from "the right to subsistence" to "the right to labor."[24] The first book of More's *Utopia* gives a brilliant analysis, for its day, of some of the contemporary causes of unemployment, but in the second book the right to labor is forgotten and there is much typical concern with the duty to labor as a corollary of the right to subsistence. Production is traditional. The Utopians have not progressed in their technology nor shown any real desire to do so. Prosperity is the result of limiting wants rather than of expanding production. Bacon's *New Atlantis* is the first literary dramatization of the possibility of unlimited expansion of productive capacity through applied science, but it is almost totally unconcerned about the social problems involved. It is hard to say whether "the society of Salomon's House" as presented in the book is more a public than a private foundation, and the question is certainly not important to the author.

The importance in this respect of Winstanley's original act of cultivating the common land (April 1649) has usually been overlooked.

[23] Kautsky, *Communism in Central Europe*, pp. 12, 191-215.
[24] Cf. Guthrie, *Socialism before the French Revolution*, pp. 49-51.

However traditional he was in sketching his national utopia, this original act, in a year of hardship and unemployment for the poor in England, was perhaps the first symbolic assertion in modern terms of the right to work. Giving employment to the unemployed was closely linked in his thought with producing more food for hungry mouths by nationalizing and utilizing the commons and the confiscated lands. The voice which summoned him to his mission said, "*Work* together, eat bread together."[25] A Benedictine monk would have understood this voice, but the order of thought was now really reversed from that of monastic and early heretical communism: communal production was now the basis, not the by-product, of equal distribution. By the early nineteenth century, as we shall see, socialists were finally driven to base their case upon the inefficiency of capitalism as a system of production, upon the inability of the competitive system to provide steady work for all. Their primary objective by then was to socialize production, not to communize consumption.

The third change to be noted in the character of socialism during the early modern period was the change in motivation from the dominance of noneconomic motives (such as religion or patriotism) to the dominance of more purely economic considerations.

Men have been driven to cry *omnia sunt communia* for a great variety of reasons, but these reasons were never purely, or even predominantly, economic until the early nineteenth century. It is sometimes a temptation to assume that where the motives are religious or patriotic or noneconomic in general, it is not significant or "true" socialism one is dealing with.[26] But in view of the revival of both nationalism and Orthodoxy in Soviet Russia within the past two decades, this seems to be dangerous reasoning. It may be equally dangerous, however, to argue that "socialism is an economic system which will work only when non-economic motives—such as religion or family affection—are dominant."[27] The historical record suggests that the motives of socialists have been and still are as rich and varied as human motives in general, but that there was undeniably a fairly steady narrowing of motivation during the three centuries of the early modern era. The inspiration of early communistic experiments in European history was uniformly religious, or more specifically, Biblical. The inspiration of others was recognizably patriotic. By the mid-nineteenth century the inspiration of most socialist writings was overwhelmingly economic.

One indication of change in underlying motivation was the extent to

[25] Sabine, *Winstanley*, pp. 10-14. Italics added.
[26] Cf. H. W. Laidler, *Social-Economic Movements* (New York, 1944), p. 107: "Communism in these latter [religious] groups, however, was an incidental feature, and they had little social significance."
[27] F. J. C. Hearnshaw, *A Survey of Socialism* (London, 1928), p. 109.

which any early modern socialistic writer or group criticized contemporary Christianity *on purely social grounds.* Medieval reformers and heretics said harsh things about the wealth of the church, but there was never the slightest hint of Marx's argument that religion is opium for the people. Nor was there a trace of such an argument in the *Utopia.* The Anabaptists—"robustly material and highly spiritual" at the same time, in Mannheim's felicitous phrase[28]—did attack the social conservatism of orthodox Protestantism among other things, and this may mark the faint beginnings of such criticism. But the first clear suggestion comes in Winstanley's bitter critique of Puritanism, the "divining doctrine" which scares the common folk into looking heavenward while the clergy devour their substance here on earth. Sabine gives a subtle analysis of Winstanley's personal faith as mysticism with "a tone of secularism" about it—"secularism tinged with a religious motivation."[29] Obviously it is well not to be too dogmatic about what was religious and what secular in the motives of socialists during the early modern period. But by the time of the *philosophes* and the French Revolution, socialist criticism in France at least had emancipated itself from any religious motivation in the struggle with *l'infâme.* The motives of Morelly and Mably were broadly humanitarian and ethical, purely secular though not as yet exclusively economic.

A more definite indication of change was the measure of purely economic interpretation of society and history to be found in successive writers. The classes of medieval Europe were divided by privilege and status, those of modern Europe by the possession of wealth. To twentieth-century historians looking back over the record, the recognition of this change lagged far behind the fact. Only a few perspicacious individuals were privileged to see beneath the surface during social upheavals and to note the economic causes and class struggles. Thomas More saw more of the purely economic roots of political, social, and moral problems than anyone of his day. There is not much evidence among the left-wing sects of the sixteenth century of self-consciousness as a distinct economic class, but Winstanley's faith, borrowed from the earlier sects, that the poor and despised were to be the chosen instrument of social regeneration was "the form in which class-feeling became most definitely self-conscious in the seventeenth century," as Sabine remarks.[30] Harington saw clearly that the Puritan Rebellion represented a shift of the economic balance of power from one class to another, and Barnave saw the same thing happening in the French Revolution. But generally it was those on the individualistic side of the economic fence (like Harington) who led the way here.

[28] *Ideology and Utopia*, p. 192.   [29] Sabine, *Winstanley*, pp. 39, 48, 68-70.
[30] *Ibid.*, p. 24.

Thus together with the continuity which the history of socialism exhibited during the three hundred years between the discovery of America and the French Revolution, there was significant ambiguity and instability in its nostalgic longing to restore a pattern of primitive purity, and an important change in scale, objective, and motivation. As the eighteenth century drew to its close, the slow pace of this change was sharply accelerated by the industrial revolution.

III. Socialism and the Industrial Revolution

What Sombart calls the period of "high" or fully developed capitalism began with the agricultural, communications, and industrial revolutions of the later eighteenth century. In the hundred years before 1848, the demands of a growing imperial market combined with a revolution in the basic technology of certain manufacturing industries to thrust Great Britain far ahead of the rest of Europe in productive capacity. The main economic and social results are too familiar to need anything but briefest mention here. The essential features were the application on a grand scale of capitalism to industry, the spectacular increase in productivity, the social dislocation and disorganization which followed, the practical emancipation of capitalistic enterprise from almost all remaining political controls (religious restraints had already dropped away), and the development of a theory to explain and justify this emancipation, the theory of "laissez faire."

It is tempting to say that the industrial revolution marked the final triumph of that individualism which had been the "radicalism" of the later Middle Ages. Individuals and private groups, owning land and machines absolutely and acting with more purely economic ends in view than ever before, won a remarkable independence of action, uprooted and relocated masses of people in urban areas as a result of their economic initiative, and gradually managed to gain a large voice in the conduct of their governments. By the mid-nineteenth century these individuals and groups probably owed less legal and moral responsibility to the larger community of which they were a part (in their case the nation) than their predecessors had owed at any previous time in European history. Certainly the absolute and irresponsible character of private property rights had never been more sharply emphasized in law and popular belief. To those who drafted the great revolutionary declarations and constitutions on both sides of the water in the later eighteenth century, "property" was on the same plane as "life" and "liberty"—and to some later historians it has seemed that the greatest of these was property. When the young Engels spoke of the terrible misery of the working classes to a middle-class acquaintance in Manchester, the gentleman listened quietly and

41

replied, "And yet there is a great deal of money made here; good morning, sir."[31]

In spite of appearances, however, this was not the economic individualism of Thomas More's day. There was ambiguity at the very heart of "high" capitalism. The age which saw the triumph of individualism in law, politics, and culture was also the age which saw the development of a technology which was eventually to undermine and destroy this individualism. Before 1848 it was abundantly evident in Great Britain at least that industrial capitalism was a social power. Ownership of the machines, which were now more important than land as a means of production, carried with it the power to move men about, to regiment and organize them into factories, to determine their living conditions and cultural opportunities. Production in a Lancashire cotton mill was "social" in a sense not true of sixteenth-century communities of weavers. Nineteenth-century textile workers were called "manufacturers," makers by hand, but actually it was the "factory," a complex organization of power, machines, and human tenders, which did the making. Apart from association with machines and with each other, the individual workers could not make a square inch of cloth. This was one of the more important reasons why the early nineteenth century was permeated and fascinated by the idea of "association."[32]

Fully developed capitalism, then, was the quintessence of individualism from one point of view while from another it was a powerful socializing agency. This meant that it could be attacked from two opposite directions: from that of a utopian socialism horrified by its heartless individualism, and from that of an earlier small-scale economic individualism frightened by its crushing of the small independent farmer and artisan. The century before 1848 was a century of confusion as well as of creation in the history of socialistic thought. The reason was that men continued to live in the shadow of earlier interpretations of the conflict between economic individualism and socialism for some time after a revolutionary technology had rendered these interpretations obsolescent. In the early years of the nineteenth century nostalgic individualists and utopian socialists attacked capitalism and each other with about the same gusto. The more hardheaded and realistic attack on capitalism actually came from the individualists, and before they gave up the struggle they had taught the socialists the doctrine of class struggle and the economic interpretation of history. It is one of the curious but understandable anomalies of the period that

[31] Quoted by Edmund Wilson, *To the Finland Station* (New York, 1940), p. 139. On the triumph of individualism in early nineteenth-century Britain, see particularly the classic treatment of A. V. Dicey, *Lectures on the Relation between Law and Public Opinion in England* (2nd ed., London, 1914).

[32] See J. L. Puech, *La Tradition socialiste en France et la Société des Nations* (Paris, 1921), pp. 203ff.

socialists were educated to the socializing tendencies of fully developed capitalism mainly through the writings of individualistic critics of the new order.

Several features of the new age of iron and steam were of particular importance for the development of socialism. The first was the sheer speed of technological and social change. Belief in unchanging principles of social order, in natural law and natural rights, would be increasingly difficult in this new world of mechanical invention, quickly shifting population, and rapid urbanization. Socialism would soon have to come to terms with the fact of social change, now accelerating at an unprecedented rate. A second feature was the international character of highly developed capitalism. The industrial revolution began in Great Britain, but Britain's far-flung trade was its necessary basis; the interests of her industrialists, who were importing cotton from America and selling manufactures in Asia, had the immediate effect of making the nation more internationally minded than ever before. Socialist thought would soon have to come to grips with international as well as national problems. Thirdly, the spectacular increase in productive capacity which resulted from harnessing the expansive power of steam helped to turn the spotlight of social criticism from problems of sharing a fixed stock of wealth to problems of maintaining an accelerating production of new wealth. And finally, the increasing awareness of the purely economic factor in human existence was suggesting the belief among some that man *does* live by bread alone—or at least that his struggle for bread is more important than any past age had conceived it to be. The birth of "political economy" was an important event. As the classical theorists developed their subject, there emerged a belief in an autonomous realm of economic law which was capable of theoretical isolation and treatment as a self-contained system. Soon socialists would be compelled to turn political economists themselves and buttress their theories increasingly with purely economic argument.

From the failure of Babeuf's conspiracy in Paris during May 1796 to the publication of the *Communist Manifesto* in London in February 1848, the theater of significant socialist thought and action was Great Britain. Here the utopian tradition came to its finest flowering in Robert Owen. Here the classical political economists deftly analyzed the new economy and, thanks to workingmen's institutes and the slow spread of popular education, helped set even the lowest orders of society to thinking about rents, profits, and wages, use value and exchange value, production and distribution. Here the critics of the new order first took up the intellectual weapons forged by the defenders of capitalism and turned them upon their makers. And here it was that the German authors of "scientific socialism" found the illustrative social material if not the actual inspiration for their major theories. Above all, it was in England that the first fairly long-lived proletarian movement took place—for this was the real significance of Chartism. Since the brilliant work of Max Beer a generation ago in revealing both the richness and "recklessness" of British social thinking during the early nineteenth century, it is no disparagement of French and German thinkers to say that for a time the British were as far ahead in their intellectual adjustment to the new age as they were in their technology and business management. Beer remarks that most of the later Continental controversies about Marx's *Capital* were "in their essence fought out in the years between 1820 and 1830 in England round Ricardo."[33] He might have gone even further and said that most of the major problems and premises of modern socialism were at least adumbrated in England during the two decades which followed the end of the wars with Napoleon. Before the collapse of the Grand National Consolidated Trades Union in 1834 almost every major type of present day socialism except Marxism had appeared in England: Christian socialism, Tory socialism, socialism by gradualist political action, cooperative socialism, and syndicalism. In addition, almost every major type of modern socialist strategy, from getting the vote to staging a general strike, had either been tried or suggested.

The transition from "utopian" to "scientific" socialism did not take place overnight with the publication of the *Communist Manifesto*. It began with the appearance in 1805 of Charles Hall's *Effects of Civilisation*. "The situation of the rich and poor," wrote this obscure physician, "like the algebraic terms plus and minus, are in direct opposition to, and destructive of each other." "Civilisation" means that wealth is power, and this means exploitation of the poor by the rich, class struggle, international war. Hall's remedy was utopian: return to the land. But his diagnosis was grimly realistic.[34] Forty years later Marx and Engels felt they had purged their analysis of all nonscientific elements, but they left one notoriously utopian belief embedded in their system: the doctrine of the classless society. The transition, then, was gradual—and it is not complete today. It can be described as the culmination of changes which we have already singled out for notice in early modern socialism: the slow turn from a desire to restore society to conform with a divine or natural norm to a theory of historical evolution; the expansion of geographical scale; the increasing attention to the problem of production; and the growing emphasis upon economic argument and economic motivation.

The great utopians of the early nineteenth century were so thoroughly imbued with the doctrine of natural law that they had almost no feeling for historical development. This is particularly true of Owen, who had no more confidence that the mere passage of time would be favorable to his

[33] Max Beer, A *History of British Socialism* (London, 1920), i, pp. v, 188.
[34] Beer, *op.cit.*, pp. 126-32.

schemes than had Sir Thomas More. Neither his early followers nor the Chartists developed any real historical insight. The feudal critics of the new order were an exception, particularly the Comte de Saint-Simon. He had absorbed the great idea of the eighteenth century that time is on man's side, that civilization is a process rather than a condition. "The golden age of humanity is not behind us," he wrote, "it is to come, and will be found in the perfection of the social order." Here the apocalyptic hopes of heretical communists were transformed into historical expectations. But it is difficult to see precisely how the idea of progress influenced Saint-Simon's social theory. He periodized history as the eighteenth century had generally done in stages of knowledge, not in stages of technique and resulting social organization as Marx was to do, and so there was really no significant relationship between his historical perspective and his social analysis. The English conservative critics—Coleridge, Southey, and Carlyle—were no more successful in finding an organic relationship between their sense of historical evolution and their socialist idealism. They sensed the inevitability of change but regretted it.

The first trace of a true fusion between anticapitalist theory and the idea of historical evolution appeared in Thomas Hodgskin's *Natural and Artificial Right of Property Contrasted* (1832), but the sketch he gave of historical development was confused and fragmentary.[35] John Francis Bray's *Labour's Wrongs and Labour's Remedy* (1838-1839) was somewhat clearer, even though the background was Owenite socialism rather than anticapitalist individualism: "The present crisis is no more than a natural movement attending *the course of things*—it is but one move of *that mighty ocean of events*, the billows of which have rolled on from eternity, and will progress in unchecked power for ever."[36] The sense here shown for the significant event, for the crucial evidence of "the course of things," appeared briefly among some Chartist writings during the crisis of 1834, even Owen himself being somewhat affected by it. Perhaps some day this feeling for event may be shown to be essentially a secularized version of an earlier Puritan faith in "dispensations," but for the moment all we can say is that it appeared in England before it became of such profound significance for Marx and Engels.[37]

The scale of socialistic thinking during the early nineteenth century was still predominantly local or national, but there were strong hints that socialistic theory would soon expand to fit the scale upon which the

[35] On Hodgskin, see Élie Halévy, *Thomas Hodgskin* (Paris, 1903), particularly pp. 132-35 and 191-209; and the briefer account in Beer, *op.cit.*, pp. 259-70. While the writing of this chapter was in progress, my colleague Professor Jacob Viner graciously allowed me to plunder not only his knowledge and critical acumen, but also his books, particularly on the subject of Hodgskin.

[36] Quoted by Beer, *op.cit.*, p. 243. Italics added.

[37] See e.g., Edmund Wilson, *op.cit.*, p. 139.

capitalistic economy was operating. The idea of what Edmund Wilson calls "small seminal new worlds inside the old" received a new lease on life during the early years of the century. German pietism, issuing in communities like that of the Moravian Brethren at Herrnhut in the mid-eighteenth century, had helped to revive the holy community tradition. Owen's "parallelograms," his followers' "trade manufactories," and Fourier's "phalansteries" carried this tradition into the world of industrial capitalism with very few adjustments to its new surroundings beyond complete secularization of the idea. Fourier hoped that the principle of "association" would build local communities, then federate them in larger groups which would pyramid up to a world confederation with its capitol at Constantinople. But the stimulus to his thinking was eighteenth-century cosmopolitanism, not the logic of fully developed capitalism. He and Owen (like Thomas More) were much more concerned with eradicating competitive individualism from human nature than in socializing capital as it actually existed in their day. It seems safe to say, however, that the national scale was still the more normal scale of socialistic thought and action, as it had been with Babeuf. Socialists, like their enemies the political economists, were becoming increasingly internationally minded, but behind their hopes for "peace through work, work in peace" nearly always lurked a warm belief in the civilizing "mission" of their own nation. Both French and British socialists believed in the faith of liberal nationalism, that nations could act as larger "seminal worlds within the old." Until 1848 there were only a few hints of fusion between the philosophical universalism of the eighteenth century and the logic of nineteenth-century economic facts. Bray was one of the few who saw that the "course of things" was not confined to national channels: "The present is not a merely local movement, it is not confined to country, colour, or creed—the universe is the sphere in which it acts."[38]

In the matter of the concern of socialists with problems of production, the early nineteenth century was the decisive turning point. Not that socialists ceased to be interested in distribution. In fact, the publication of Colquhoun's *Wealth, Power, and Resources of the British Empire* in 1814 and of Ricardo's *Principles of Political Economy and Taxation* in 1817 was the signal for an outburst of both socialist and individualist criticism of the way the new wealth was being distributed. John Locke and Adam Smith had both insisted that labor was the source of value. Neither could have guessed that men with empty stomachs and literal minds would come along and interpret this to mean exclusively wage labor, not the labor of farmer, artisan, merchant, and industrialist. But this was what happened to the classic doctrine in the hands of anti-

[38] Beer, *op.cit.*, p. 243. On the general subject, see the essay of Puech cited in note 32, particularly pp. 75-76, 79-80, 203-9; and Beer, pp. 235, 313, 344.

capitalist critics after 1815, and the result was a series of rather humorless attempts to determine mathematically just how little of the full fruits of his toil the laboring man actually received. Colquhoun's figures suggested that he received about one-sixth of what he produced; John Gray thought it one-fifth; William Thompson was willing to make it about one-half; but Thomas Hodgskin agreed with William Hall that it was closer to one-eighth.[39] In any case the wage-earner was not getting what should be coming to him, and socialists in general were just as worried about it as they had been in Thomas More's day—and now for more "scientific," i.e., statistical reasons.

They were often more worried, however, by something More could hardly have understood, the problem which came to be called that of overproduction. The business cycle is traceable back to the sixteenth century, but few would dispute the importance which Beer attaches to the depression which began in Great Britain in 1816 as the first social crisis quite unmistakably caused "not by scarcity, but by overproduction." Adam Smith had argued for private property because it was a more productive system than any other. But was it? Owen and his followers saw that the competitive system was subject to recurrent spasms of unproductive idleness because of overproduction in terms of profitable demand. If profit is the only motive for production, they maintained, then new wealth will constantly be channeled into the pockets of the few, the purchasing power of the many will collapse, and production will temporarily cease. The problem, as Owen put it, was "to let prosperity loose on the country" by seeing to it that "consumption may be made to keep pace with production."[40] John Gray's solution—"that production, instead of being the effect of demand, ought to be the cause of it"—was expressed more clearly by William Thompson, another Owenite, who argued that only a system which assured the laborer of the whole fruit of his toil could continue to produce without interruptions and setbacks. One of the chief concerns of Owen's followers, therefore, was the unproductiveness of capitalism and the unemployment which resulted. The same concern was evident in the subtitle of Hodgskin's first important work: "The Unproductiveness of Capital. . . ."[41] The ground had shifted, in part at least, from arguments about distribution based on divine or natural justice to arguments about production based on utility and efficiency. Fair distribution was now a means to the end of increased production and full employment.

[39] See Beer, op.cit., pp. 248, 213, 221, 264, 129.
[40] Robert Owen, "Report to the County of Lanark," op.cit., pp. 248, 253.
[41] Beer, op.cit., pp. 212, 223; Thomas Hodgskin, Labour Defended against the Claims of Capital, or the Unproductiveness of Capital Proved with Reference to the Present Combinations amongst Journeymen [1825], G. D. H. Cole, ed. (London, 1922).

The history of the birth and growth of "economic man" has not yet been written, although Peter Drucker has written of his demise.[42] It may be, as some economists are now telling us, that he never existed at all, that the political economists of the early nineteenth century were simply investigating a new field of human behavior and never meant to suggest that the economic aspect was the whole of human life. Be that as it may, there are certain broad facts of British social and intellectual history during this period which may be cited as evidences of his existence and which are important for the history of socialism: the emancipation of commerce and industry from all religious restraints and from almost all political controls; the growing agreement among the middle classes that it was the purpose of government to foster prosperity, not of business to strengthen the state; the growing conviction of the wage-earning classes that whether they asked for the vote or took direct action, economic reform was more important than political; the belief of political economists in certain "iron laws" which were autonomous and unaffected by man-made statutes; and finally the belief of a few that the key to understanding the historical development of mankind was not divine providence, not political or military genius, but technological change, economic interest, and the struggle for existence between economic classes.

The priority in isolating the economic factor in human existence and working out an economic interpretation of history belongs to the individualists rather than to the socialists. It is of course true that Saint-Simon, Fourier, and Owen all saw quite clearly the predominant importance of the purely economic factor. But they seem to have sensed the danger to their cooperative ideal in any appeal to purely economic motives. At any rate, they never extinguished the flames of their religious or secular idealism in the waters of economic determinism. Actually it was those who expected less of human nature—the individualists—who developed the general theory that the way men make a living, the way they produce and distribute goods, shapes the social and political arrangements of any given historical epoch and colors its beliefs. Perhaps Harington and Barnave were the first to sketch this approach to history, as we have suggested. But it was Charles Hall (1805) and above all Thomas Hodgskin (1825), both relatively obscure in their day, who took seriously the underlying materialism in British thinking from Hobbes and Locke to Adam Smith and Ricardo, applied it to the brute facts of industrial capitalism as they saw them, and then sketched out the theory of class struggle as the key to history. Marx and Engels later found support for their own economic determinism in these individualistic predecessors, but the significant thing is that the economic interpretation was impressed

[42] *The End of Economic Man* (New York, 1939), particularly pp. xii, 50-58.

by the facts upon one after another sympathetic observer of the condition of the working class, as it was upon Friedrich Engels during his first visit to Manchester in 1843.[43] It was the individualists, both defenders and critics of capitalism, who developed the theory, but thanks to the authors of the *Communist Manifesto* it was the socialists who made use of it as social myth.

The publication of the *Communist Manifesto*[44] was a genuinely revolutionary event—not because it immediately touched off a social revolution (which it did not), not because it immediately changed men's minds (which it could not until it was widely read, later), nor because its major ideas were absolutely fresh and original (which they were not). It was a revolutionary document in somewhat the same sense as the *Declaration of Independence*: it summed up the accumulated knowledge and experience of generations and at the same time thrust its readers forward into the future with the confidence that the universe was on their side. It is the current fashion in historical writing to deny revolution in favor of evolution, to see continuity where contemporaries (like Marx himself) could see only revolutionary change. To follow this fashion in judging the *Manifesto* would be to deny what might be called the explosive possibilities of great summaries in the history of thought. In this sense, the broader the synthesis of all previous lines of thinking, the greater the revolutionary potentialities. Until social conditions were ripe and until Marx and Engels combined the major strands of socialistic thinking into one organic whole, socialism as action never amounted to much more than a series of abortive proletarian movements in the wake of middle-class revolutions, from the Reformation and the Puritan Rebellion to the French Revolution and the English Reform Movement of 1832. After the work of combination was done, hitherto unsuspected explosive possibilities were revealed in the European socialistic tradition.

It was the *Communist Manifesto* which gave socialism a philosophy of history and brought the ideals of utopians into organic relationship with the idea of development in time. Gone by now was any trace of nostalgia for a primitive state of nature or grace in which all things were held in common. Gone was all suggestion of restoration or return to a past age, or of voyage to a distant land. To the authors the triumph of capitalism over feudalism had become a necessary stage in the historical evolution of the classless society. In fact they showed a cool admiration for the marvelous achievements of the European bourgeoisie which balanced their

[43] See the account of Edmund Wilson, *op.cit.*, pp. 134-39.

[44] The best discussion of the *Manifesto* produced in connection with the hundredth anniversary of its publication appeared, unsigned, in the *Times Literary Supplement*, Dec. 13, 1947. This, written by Edward Hallett Carr, was republished by him in his book, *Studies in Revolution* (London, 1950), chap. 2.

hatred of its brutality—an attitude of which neither Thomas More nor Thomas Hodgskin would have been capable. For the first time the whole social problem was treated in resolutely and consistently dynamic terms, and the face of socialistic thought was turned irrevocably from the past to the future.

The long and halting tendency to expansion of scale reached its culmination in the *Manifesto*. All brethren houses, communities of saints, "phalansteries," and "parallelograms," even all national utopias, had now become utterly irrelevant in a world so tightly bound together by bourgeois finance that economic isolation of even the tiniest local community or economic autarchy of even the largest nation-state was no longer possible. Apparently it was not enough that England's leading economic thinkers in the century before 1848 had been Scots and Irishmen and therefore presumably above a narrow English nationalism. Before socialism could be universalized, i.e., brought into vivifying touch with the cosmopolitanism of the Enlightenment and the broad fact of the economic interdependence of nations, two Germans had to be uprooted from their families and their native soil and thrust into a position from which they could see what was happening in Great Britain from a perspective which was supranational. Marx and Engels "were the first great social thinkers of their century to try to make themselves, by deliberate discipline, both classless and international."[45]

It hardly needs to be pointed out that, so far as the problem of objective is concerned, the socialization of production was the main concern of the *Manifesto*, not mere equalization of distribution. In early communistic communities production had been incidental to a proper solution of the problem of distribution. Distribution was now incidental to the inevitable historical solution of the problem of production—more precisely, the problem of who was to control the means of production. The utopian indictment of capitalism as unproductive was transformed into a description of how capitalism actually produced its own grave diggers.

Finally, in the matter of motivation, Marx and Engels were the first in the European socialist tradition to push the economic interpretation of human nature and history to its logical conclusion. The idea of "ideology," first sketched for popular consumption in the *Manifesto*, effectively disposed of all previous considerations of the problem of socialistic motivation as unrealistic. Whether Marx was the main contriver of the triumph of "economic man" as Drucker argues, or whether on the contrary he was "the first thinker to expose in all its hollowness the moral inadequacy of a commercial civilization" as Harold Laski insists,[46] it is undeniable that

[45] Edmund Wilson, *op.cit.*, p. 160.

[46] Cf. Drucker, *op.cit.*, p. 52, and H. J. Laski, *Karl Marx, an Essay* (League for Industrial Democracy, 1933), p. 47. Also, Jacques Barzun, *Darwin, Marx, Wagner* (Boston, 1941), pp. 144ff.

he tended to reduce the complexity of human motivation to economic drives. The question "why socialism?" which before 1848 had been asked and answered with every conceivable kind of human motive—religious, moral, and political—became mainly a question of economics after the publication of the *Manifesto*.

The importance for America of European socialistic thought and experiment before 1848, however, does not lie solely in its summation by Marx. If we have stressed Sir Thomas More, the father of "utopian" socialism, and Karl Marx, its grave digger, it has been as symbols of the birth and decline of a tradition which nevertheless reached back of 1516 and continued after 1848. Revolutionary summation always involves distortion, and there was loss as well as gain in the magnificent simplicities of the *Communist Manifesto*. Many earlier forms of European socialism were still valid, as American reformers saw the situation, long after 1848. Furthermore, the principles and even occasionally the practices of these earlier forms have had a way of acquiring new relevance almost overnight in our contemporary world whenever the rigidities of Marxian dogma have failed to fit changing economic facts. The need for industrial decentralization revives the relevance of earlier communal experiments in the history of socialism. Overemphasis on production drives many in the twentieth century back to distribution as the more central problem. Disillusionment about ever realizing the purely economic utopias of Marx or Manchester impels many to agree with Mussolini's hysterical cry that "economic man does not exist." An ebbing faith in progress and a swelling suspicion of historical relativism even induce some among our contemporaries to search as their predecessors did for norms which are true everywhere and at all times. New relevance of old ideas may appear in the most unexpected places. Perhaps the idea of a T.V.A. as an economic "measuring rod" is not altogether unrelated to the medieval belief that communities of monks were needed to hold aloft the ideal of communism in a world of fallen men. In spite of all the revolutionary changes which followed the industrial revolution and the writings of Marx, the modern world is still in touch with the earlier socialism which has been the subject of this chapter. In subtle and unnoticed ways, whether by continuity or by parallel, the historical connections are still intact.

CHAPTER 2

European Socialism Since 1848

BY HARRY W. LAIDLER

HARRY W. LAIDLER is Executive Director of the League for Industrial Democracy. A leading member of the Socialist Party for many years, he has been the candidate of the party for governor of New York and United States senator. He is the author of numerous books and articles on social problems including *Social-Economic Movements* (1944), widely recognized as the standard work on the subject.

For bibliography in Volume 2 relevant to Mr. Laidler's essay, see especially PART I, General Reading, and Topics 3, 4, 5, 7, 8, 9, 10.

IN EARLY December 1847, a small group of workers from England, France, Germany, Belgium, Poland, and other countries met secretly in the dingy rooms of the London German Workers' Union in the British capital, on the occasion of the second Congress of the Communist League.

The outstanding figures at that congress were Karl Marx, brilliant young German intellectual of twenty-nine who a few years before had become a convinced socialist, and his closest friend, Friedrich Engels, German businessman, socialist, and military strategist. The meeting discussed the revolutionary ferment that was taking place in the Europe of those days. It likewise commissioned Marx and Engels to draft a manifesto, setting forth the principles and philosophy of the League and presenting a program of immediate and far-flung social change and a clarion call to action.

Early the next year, after impatient urgings by the officers of the Communist League, Marx and Engels fulfilled their commission, and in the first days of February, a few weeks before the French Revolution of 1848, the *Communist Manifesto* was issued. With the circulation of this historic document may be said to have been launched the modern socialist movement.

In the Europe of that day a century ago there were here and there only scattered handfuls of men and women working for a socialist society. Their numbers were temporarily augmented during the abortive political revolutions that shook the Continent in 1848, but, when the revolutionists were crushed and the reactionary regimes of the royal houses of Europe again became masters of the situation, the Communist League was dissolved: organized groups of socialists were hunted, arrested, and imprisoned, and whatever propaganda was undertaken had to be for the most part conducted underground. The working class during these days, as Engels later put it, "was reduced to a fight for political elbow-room, and to the position of extreme wing of the middle-class radicals. Wherever independent proletarian movements continued to show signs of life, they were ruthlessly hunted down."[1]

To many of the statesmen of that day, as well as to the disillusioned revolutionists, it looked as if the movement in behalf of a cooperative social order had been permanently crushed. But this movement had not died. After a decade of comparative inactivity, it began slowly to revive. In nation after nation it took root among the masses; and today, after a century of struggle, socialists and communists occupy the citadels of political power in many nations of the world. This fact is dramatically illustrated in every session of the United Nations. At the first U.N. General

[1] Karl Marx and Friedrich Engels, *The Manifesto of the Communist Party* (Chicago, 1902?), Preface, p. 4.

Assembly meeting held in New York in the fall of 1946, for instance, the session was presided over by Henri-Paul Spaak, first president of the U.N. Assembly and socialist foreign minister, later premier, of Belgium. The meetings of the Assembly were kept in smooth running order by the United Nations' secretary-general, Trygve Lie, former minister of foreign affairs of the Labor government of Norway, a socialist government. The roll of outstanding delegates of the Assembly, moreover, included representatives of the Labour governments of the United Kingdom, Australia, and New Zealand; of the communist controlled governments of the Soviet Republics and Yugoslavia; and of the coalition governments of Czechoslovakia, France, the Netherlands, Poland, India, Chile, in the cabinets of which socialists, communists, or both, were then prominently represented.

Prior to 1848 the dominant form of socialism among the comparatively small number of men and women who declared themselves adherents of the socialist school of thought had been that of utopian socialism. The utopians bitterly assailed the evils of private ownership of industry, buttressing their criticisms with the doctrines of equality, justice, and brotherhood as found in the teachings of the Old and New Testaments, of the Stoics, and of the latest humanists and rationalists. They urged various forms of community ownership of the means of production and distribution and dealt with the necessity of developing an environment under which the common man could realize his highest potentialities.

There was little conception in the writings of most of the utopians of the evolutionary and revolutionary forces at work in modern society. They failed to consider the historical mission of capitalism in increasing production and in developing the capacities of the working class to organize and assume increasing responsibilities in the life of the nation and the world. Many of them, moreover, visualized the change to a new social order coming about not as a result of economic, political, and psychological conflicts, but as a result of the discovery of the truth regarding the workings of "natural" or moral law, or else as a result of an appeal to the reason of mankind, to religious faith, or to the suggestive effects of successful experiments in communistic colonies.

Many utopians worked out in great detail a blueprint of the future society. Unfortunately the future patterns set forth by them differed considerably from each other. "And as each one's special kind of absolute truth" was "conditioned by his subjective understanding, his conditions of existence, the measure of his knowledge and his intellectual training, so the only solution possible in this conflict of absolute truths," as Friedrich Engels maintained, was that "they should grind each other down."[2]

[2] Friedrich Engels, "Socialism: Utopian and Scientific," *Karl Marx, Selected Works* (New York, n.d.), II, p. 155.

I. The "Communist Manifesto"

The *Communist Manifesto* thoroughly revolutionized socialist thought.[3] The character of the *Manifesto* was determined largely by the industrial revolution that had been going on since the middle of the previous century, with its economic dislocations, misery, and unrest; by the swift changes in status of the new working-class and capitalist groups; and by the writings of the utopians, the economists, and the philosophers of those days. Among philosophers, G. W. F. Hegel (1770-1831) with his dialectical logic influenced the thinking of Marx and Engels more than did any other.[4]

The *Manifesto* regards the history of civilization as a history of class struggles; among others, struggles between slaves and masters and between serfs and feudal lords. Under capitalism, the main conflict is one between the working class and the capitalist class. With the development of capitalism, Marx and Engels maintained, the industrial structure of capitalist countries concentrates increasingly into fewer and fewer hands, and an ever larger proportion of the smaller capitalists is hurled into the ranks of the nonowning working class. Thus the owning class, as the years advance, shrinks in numbers, while the few big capitalists become increasingly powerful.

On the other hand, the workers, with the development of capitalism, grow in numbers. Exploited by the owning class, they are able to purchase back with their wages only a part of the fruits of their labor. Be-

---

[3] A question has often been raised as to why the *Manifesto* was called "communist" rather than "socialist," since socialists have since that date regarded this important document as one of their classics. The explanation of Friedrich Engels is that in 1847 the word "socialist" was applied to those who were regarded either as adherents of various utopian schemes or as social reformers who urged mere palliatives which "professed to redress, without any danger to capital and profit, all sorts of social grievances." On the other hand, the term "communist" was then usually applied to those who "had proclaimed the necessity of a total social change." See Engels' Preface to the 1888 edition of *The Manifesto of the Communist Party* (edition cited above), p. 7. For analysis of the *Communist Manifesto* and Marxian socialism see H. W. Laidler, *Social-Economic Movements* (New York, 1944), Pt. II.

[4] Hegel maintained that change took place through the struggle of antagonistic elements and the resolution of these contradictory elements into a synthesis. The *thing* or *being* against which the contradiction operated he called the positive or thesis. The antagonist element was the negative or antithesis. To Hegel the contradiction was "the source of all movements and life; only insofar as it contains a contradiction can anything have movement, power and effect." The continued operation of the negative, he maintained, led to the negative of negation or synthesis. Marx, a "Young Hegelian," was the first to apply the Hegelian dialectic to the social sciences. To him the positive or thesis was the system of private property; the negative or antithesis, the working class or proletariat. As a result of the conflict between the proletariat (the antithesis) and private property (the thesis), we may expect to see arise a new type of industrial society (the synthesis) under which the workers would organize a classless society, where the principal means of production and distribution were owned and operated by the community for the benefit not of one class, but of all society.

cause of this and other defects of the capitalist society, periodic depressions break out. The bourgeoisie overcomes each crisis by mass destruction of productive forces, by the conquests of new markets, and the more thorough exploitation of the old ones, that is to say, by paving the way for more extensive and more destructive crises, and by diminishing the means whereby crises are prevented. "The weapons with which the bourgeoisie felled feudalism to the ground are now turned against the bourgeoisie itself." Subjected to mass unemployment during these periodic depressions and to constant exploitation, the misery of the workers increases. Labor becomes more class conscious. It begins to organize to protect its interest first in local unions, and then in national and international unions and in labor parties.

In the political field, the workers seek increasingly to form a political party of their own. Such a party is continually upset as a result of competition between the workers themselves. "But it ever rises up again, stronger, firmer, mightier. It compels legislative recognition of particular interests of the workers, by taking advantage of the divisions among the bourgeoisie itself."

"Finally," the *Manifesto* maintains, "in times when the class-struggle nears the decisive hour, the process of dissolution going on within the ruling class, in fact, within the whole range of old society, assumes such a violent, glaring character that a small section of the ruling class cuts itself adrift, and joins the revolutionary class, the class that holds the future in its hands. Just as, therefore, at an earlier period, a section of the nobility went over to the bourgeoisie, so now a portion of the bourgeoisie goes over to the proletariat, and in particular a portion of the bourgeois ideologists, who have raised themselves to the level of comprehending theoretically the historical movements as a whole. . . .

"All previous historical movements," the *Manifesto* declares, "were movements of minorities, or in the interest of minorities. The proletarian movement is the self-conscious, independent movement of the immense majority. . . ."[5]

[5] This passage has figured prominently in the later controversy between socialists and Russian communists over the question of democracy versus dictatorship. In 1875, Marx described the political transition period from capitalism to socialism as a "dictatorship of the proletariat": see Karl Marx, *Critique of the Gotha Programme* (New York, 1938), p. 18. Communists have quoted this passage as proof of the fact that Marx would approve their type of dictatorship if alive today. Socialists reply that Marx had in mind not a rule by a small minority—the inner circle of the communist party—but rule by the proletariat "as a movement of the immense majority," as the passage indicates. To strengthen their position, socialists also quote Marx as believing that "freedom consists in converting the state from an organ standing above society into one completely subordinated to it" (*Critique of the Gotha Programme*, cited above, p. 17). Opponents of dictatorship likewise refer to the statement of Engels in 1891 (in a monograph published in the *Neue Zeit*, xx) that "If anything is certain

The upshot of the class struggle in modern society, the *Manifesto* continues, is the conquest of the state apparatus by the proletariat. When that conquest is accomplished, "the proletariat will use its political supremacy to wrest, by degrees, all capital from the bourgeoisie, to centralise all instruments of production in the hands of the State, i.e., of the proletariat organised as the ruling class, and to increase the total productive forces as rapidly as possible."

The *Manifesto* then enumerates some immediate measures which might seem insufficient in and of themselves but which promise to lead to more adequate measures of social change, such as the nationalization of credit, the imposition of heavy progressive income taxes, the abolition of property in land, and free education to all children in public schools.

In conclusion, the *Manifesto* declares that the communists refuse to conceal their aims. They insist that "their ends can be attained only by the forcible overthrow of all existing social conditions. Let the ruling classes tremble at a communistic revolution! The proletarians have nothing to lose but their chains. They have a world to win. Working men of all countries, unite!"

At the time when this *Manifesto* was issued, there was no powerful political movement of the workers in any country of the world. In most of Europe, the workers' right to suffrage was severely restricted, where not denied. In 1864, sixteen years after the issuance of the *Manifesto*, for instance, Gladstone asserted that still in Great Britain forty-nine fiftieths of the working class were excluded from the franchise.[6] Trade unions were weak and, in many places, illegal; the consumers' cooperative movement was still in its infancy; illiteracy among the working class was widespread and laws for the protection of labor were few and far between. Thus it was that many men and women who, like Marx and Engels, advocated a revolutionary change in the economic system, saw little or no chance for immediate change through peaceful and democratic channels. They believed that if the working class was to "emancipate itself" from the wage system in the immediate future, it must be through some violent upheaval and extralegal seizure of governmental machinery—a belief which (as will be seen) Marx and Engels later modified.

At the time that copies of the *Communist Manifesto* were distributed, largely in secret, by the revolutionaries of Europe, there were many, including Marx and Engels, who felt that the social revolution which

---

it is that our party and the working class can triumph only under the form of the democratic republic." See Karl Kautsky, *Social Democracy versus Communism* (New York, 1946), p. 39.

[6] See J. H. Robinson and C. A. Beard, *Outlines of European History* (New York, 1912), Pt. II, p. 388. It was not until 1867 that the English workers were in possession of the franchise.

would sweep the working class into power was about to break out. Europe was seething with unrest. In France, the center of the revolutionary movement, the state under Prime Minister Guizot and King Louis Philippe had long been hopelessly corrupt. Political power was centered in the few. Taxes were high. The masses were desperately poor. Open signs of dissension were suppressed.

As a result of popular discontent, Guizot was forced to resign. No fundamental change, however, followed in the French economy, and bitter criticisms against the evils of the day continued. A huge protest meeting was staged before the Foreign Office in Paris on the night of February 23, 1848. Shots were fired and several people were killed. The next morning the entire city was in a state of insurrection. Louis Philippe abdicated, whereupon a republic was proclaimed. Other revolts broke out in Austria, Hungary, Italy, Bavaria, Saxony, Switzerland. Constitutional reforms were effected as a result of these conflicts, but soon reaction began to lift its head. In June, the Paris workers revolted against the new republican government which had begun to swing to the right. The rebels were defeated. Many were imprisoned; many transported without trial.

As for the Communist League, the members of its central committee, located in Cologne, were arrested by the Prussian police and imprisoned. The League was dissolved, and the reactionary governments of Europe began to breathe more easily again. Within a few years, however, forces which by many had been called communist, by others, socialist, began again to mobilize.

II. Socialism from the First International to World War I

In the early sixties when the United States was engaged in its tragic Civil War, at least two events took place which indicated that the socialist movement had not been destroyed by the ruthless opposition of the powers that be, but had been gaining new converts and laying the foundation of a future powerful socialist movement.

The first of these events was the birth of the First International in London in 1864. The second was the birth of the social democracy in Germany. In 1862, advanced members of the French working class decided to utilize their visit to the International Exhibition in London to enter into closer relations with the British trade union movement and the London labor leaders. Here they met George Odger, Robert Applegarth, and others who, while fighting for the reform of the British suffrage, had organized demonstrations in favor of the Northern states of the United States, of the Poles then in arms against the Russians, and of the Italians struggling to be free. After an exchange of addresses in 1863, it was decided to hold a conference in London to form an International Association of Working Men. The conference was held September 25-28, 1864, and representatives of all workingmen's societies residing in London were asked to attend a public meeting in St. Martin's Hall on September 28.

Among the noted leaders accepting the invitation was Karl Marx, who had been hard at work in London on *Das Kapital* and other socialist classics since his banishment from Paris to the British capital in 1849. Marx was called upon to deliver the inaugural address. In this he acknowledged the unprecedented growth in trade and commerce in Great Britain from the forties, when the *Communist Manifesto* was issued, until 1864; but he maintained that during these years the wealthy were growing richer while the misery of the poor was increasing. During this period, however, the common people had not been inactive. The Chartist movement had been busily at work in the legislative chambers and had, after a thirty-year fight, succeeded in getting the ten-hour day on the statute books. This was "not only a great practical success," but "the victory of a principle," for "it was the first time that in broad daylight the political economy of the middle class succumbed to the political economy of the working class." It had also contributed "immense physical, moral, and intellectual benefits . . . to the factory operatives." Cooperative factories, moreover, Marx declared, had developed during the fifties and early sixties "by the unassisted efforts of a few bold 'hands.'" "By deed instead of by argument, they have shown that production on a large scale and in accord with the behests of modern science, may be carried on without the existence of a class of masters employing a class of hands; that to bear fruit, the means of labour need not be monopolized as a means of dominion over, and of extortion against, the labouring man himself; and that, like slave labour, like serf labour, hired labour is but a transitory and inferior form, destined to disappear before associated labour plying its toil with a willing hand, ready mind, and a joyous heart." Nevertheless, continued Marx, "if kept within the narrow circle of the casual efforts of private workmen," such cooperatives "will never be able to arrest the growth in geometrical progression of monopoly, to free the masses, nor even to perceptibly lighten the burden of their miseries. . . . Cooperative labour ought to be developed to national dimensions, and, consequently, to be fostered by national means. . . .

"To conquer political power has become the great duty of the working classes. . . . One element of success they possess—numbers; but numbers weigh only in the balance, if united by combination and led by knowledge."[7] The fight for a foreign policy based on the morals and justice which should govern the relations of private individuals is also a part of the struggle for the emancipation of the workers.

[7] L. E. Mins, ed., *Founding of the First International, a Documentary Record* (New York, 1937), pp. 35-37. See also Karl Marx, *Address and Provisional Rules of the Working Men's International Association* (London, 1934).

In conclusion Marx, whose address possessed a strong Chartist flavor, laid down the rules for the International. These rules included the following:

"That the emancipation of the working classes must be conquered by the working classes themselves; that the struggle for the emancipation of the working classes means not a struggle for class privileges and monopolies, but for equal rights and duties, and the abolition of all class rules;

"That the economical subjection of the man of labour to the monopolizer of the means of labour, that is the sources of life, lies at the bottom of servitude in all its forms, of all social misery, mental degradation, and political dependence;

"That the economic emancipation of the working classes is therefore the great end to which every political movement ought to be subordinate as a means;

"That the emancipation of labour is neither a local nor a national, but a social problem, embracing all countries in which modern society exists, and depending for its solution on the concurrence, practical and theoretical, of the most advanced countries."[8]

To arrange for an international organization of labor and to serve as a vital and guiding center of working activities was, Marx maintained, the task of the I.W.M.A. (International Working Men's Association). Marx advised the workers to organize independent labor parties, to demand social reform and factory legislation, to oppose all warlike diplomacy, and to carry on a vigorous class struggle until they had become the possessors of political power and had nationalized the means of production.

The I.W.M.A. held six congresses in London and on the Continent from 1865 to 1872. The British trade unionists, who, during the first few years, were left in control of the association, endeavored to use it as a means of extending the benefits of British trade unionism to the Continent. Their attention, however, was soon turned to home affairs, and following the second Reform Act of 1867, which enfranchised large numbers of the British people, the English trade unionists left the leadership increasingly to Marx and Engels. The affiliation of many of the continental organizations turned the International congresses into arenas for the bitter discussion of revolutionary tactics. Marx and his followers urged, for the most part, parliamentary action to bring about the transformation to a socialist society, while the French, Italian, Spanish, and Russian representatives advocated either revolutionary economic action or secret conspiracies with a view to insurrection.

While differing in tactics from Proudhon, Bakunin, and their followers, Marx for some years looked upon the results of the revolutionary agitations of those days with high hopes. "Things are moving," he wrote to Engels

[8] Mins, *op.cit.*, p. 39.

in 1867 with his usual optimism; "And in the next revolution, which is perhaps nearer than it appears, we (i.e., you and I) have this powerful engine in our hands."[9]

When the Paris Commune was proclaimed on March 18, 1871, following a revolt of Paris workers against the National Assembly, many members of the International felt that the social revolution in Europe was on the way. The Commune, however, was overthrown seven weeks after its formation, and with the field for practical action cut off, sectarian and revolutionary conspiracies within the International found a fertile field.

In 1872, a congress of the I.W.M.A. was held at The Hague. A battle royal took place at this congress between Marx and Mikhail Bakunin, a leader of the anarchists. Marx vigorously opposed the proposals of Bakunin for the organization of workers in secret conspiratorial groups. He also took occasion at this historic gathering to tell the assembled delegates that Engels and he did not deny that "there are countries like England and America, and, if I understood your arrangements better, I might even add Holland, where the worker may attain his object by peaceful means." "But," he added, "not in all countries is this the case."[10]

Marx urged that the International be saved from falling into the hands of the anarchists, and, in order to prevent this from taking place, he suggested the transfer of the Association to the United States. The majority followed his advice, and the headquarters were removed to New York, where, after a comparatively inactive existence, the First International died in 1878. Marx, in the meanwhile, went back to his task of finishing *Das Kapital*.

The German socialist movement had its beginnings in the revolutionary days of 1848. "Socialism," writes W. H. Dawson, "emerged from the convulsions and the ferment of these years as a fresh goal of popular aspirations. It was socialism which remained after the earthquake, the tempest, and the fire had passed away."[11]

The fifties saw the birth and later the restriction and suppression of many German workingmen's organizations. They likewise witnessed the growth of a moderate cooperative movement of Schulze-Delitzsch, which aimed to inculcate in the working class the doctrine of "self-help" as opposed to "state help." This movement organized cooperatives to aid merchants to obtain raw materials, and also developed loan associations.

[9] *Karl Marx and Friedrich Engels; Correspondence, 1846-1895; a Selection with Commentary and Notes* (New York, n.d.), p. 227. Italics omitted.

[10] See Karl Kautsky, *The Dictatorship of the Proletariat* (tr. by H. J. Stenning; Manchester, Eng., [1919]), pp. 9-10.

[11] W. H. Dawson, *German Socialism and Ferdinand Lassalle* (London, 1891), p. 33. See also Laidler, *op.cit.*, pp. 226-27.

It appealed primarily to small tradesmen and members of the artisan class, and had little effect on the workers.

In the early sixties, a Workingmen's Association of the city of Leipzig appointed a committee to see what could be done to establish similar groups throughout Germany. A meeting was held in Berlin in October 1862. Those present represented diverse opinions regarding the course of action they should follow. Some favored the adoption of a nonpolitical platform. Others were for making their proposed association an appendage of the Progressist Party, formed in 1861 to represent a more liberal point of view than did the Conservatives and National-Liberals of that day.

In the midst of their confused discussion, Ferdinand Lassalle, brilliant orator, scholar, and lawyer, addressed the artisan association. The date of his address—April 12, 1862—has at times been referred to as "the birthday of the German social democracy."

Lassalle declared that the true function of the state was "to help in the development of the human race toward freedom." Such a state, however, could be attained only through the rule of the majority based on universal and equal suffrage. The workers, thanks to the growth of the factory system, were *potentially* the most powerful force in the state. The next necessary step was to make them *legally* the most powerful force by instituting a complete democracy. The next revolution would place the workingmen in power and would constitute a victory for all mankind.

This address made a deep impression on the delegates, while the authorities, accusing Lassalle of "exciting the non-possessing classes to hatred and contempt of the possessing classes," caused his arrest.

The following year, on March 31, 1863, Lassalle was invited by the Leipzig Workingmen's Association, followers of Schulze-Delitzsch, to appear before it. In his address he vigorously criticized the credit unions and cooperative societies proposed by Schulze-Delitzsch as mere palliatives. He enunciated the "iron law of wages"; urged that the workers organize and operate their own productive organizations, with the state advancing the capital; and, as a means of promoting such a program, declared that the working class must organize an independent political party in order to achieve political rights.

The majority of the committee of the workers' association adopted Lassalle's viewpoint; consequently, in late May 1863, Lassalle found himself at the head of the democratic movement and formed the Universal German Workingmen's Association. This Association was one of the forerunners of the Social Democratic Workingmen's Party, formed in 1869.

During the next few years a vigorous controversy was waged within the German social democracy between the Lassalleans (Lassalle himself had been killed in a duel in 1864) and the Marxists over state aided productive enterprises and other immediate demands, and over the character of labor party control. The Lassalleans favored a somewhat dictatorial form of party organization; Bebel and Liebknecht, their leading opponents, urged a democratic form.

It was not until the Erfurt Congress in 1891 that the party adopted a platform thoroughly Marxian in conception. In the meanwhile, the party had been bitterly opposed by Bismarck, then Chancellor of Germany, who instigated legislation in the late seventies which placed a ban on all socialist meetings and socialist distribution of literature.[12]

From its inception in the sixties to World War I—even during the years of the antisocialist legislation (1878-1890)—the German Social Democratic Party was regarded as the leading socialist political movement in Europe. During these years it forced Germany to adopt much social legislation, was responsible for a large amount of municipalization of industry, and was a potent force in the trade union and cooperative movements, as well as in many of the cultural movements of Germany. By 1914, the German social democracy had registered a popular vote of four and a half million and had 110 representatives in the Reichstag.[13]

Other powerful Labor, Socialist, and Social Democratic parties had also developed, before World War I, despite tremendous obstacles. The French socialists, who began to mobilize their strength in the seventies of the last century under the leadership of Guesde, were by 1914 represented in the Chamber of Deputies by 103 members, while the British Labour Party, born in 1900, was represented in the House of Commons just before the outbreak of World War I by forty-two members. Other nations had influential Labor and Socialist parties with considerable parliamentary strength. This representation in European countries in 1914 was as follows:

Country	Socialist Deputies	Country	Socialist Deputies
Austria-Hungary	82	Holland	16
Belgium	39	Italy	80[14]
Denmark	32	Finland	90
Germany	110	Norway	23
France	103	Russia	14[15]
Great Britain	42	Sweden	73

[12] This ban was continued until 1890. Bismarck sought to stop the development of the German socialist movement both by the passage of social insurance and other social reform legislation and by suppression. However, by 1890 the votes of the social democracy were triple those of 1878, and Bismarck realized that the antisocialist legislation had failed.

[13] At first, as Paul Kampffmeyer brings out in *Changes in the Theory and Tactics of the Social Democracy* (Chicago, 1908), German social democrats looked upon the election of their representatives to the Reichstag as useful primarily for propaganda purposes. Later they became convinced that socialist members of legislatures should do all they could to put legislation favorable to the masses on the statute books.

[14] Seventy-two socialists were elected on the Socialist and Socialist Reformist party tickets. Others were independent socialists.

[15] There were also ten Labor members of the Duma.

In 1889, several of the socialist parties formed the Second International, which lost its effectiveness with the outbreak of war in 1914 and with the foundation, in 1919, of the Third International.

III. The General Socialist Viewpoint and the Theoretical Bases of Marxism

From the organization of the socialist parties in Europe in the latter half of the nineteenth century to the outbreak of World War I, there were many schools of thought in the socialist movement and various differences of opinion within each school on socialist theory and practice. All branches of the modern socialist movement (which may be said to date from the issuance of the *Communist Manifesto* in 1848) were, however, fundamentally agreed on several points.

Socialists of various schools were united in the belief that democratic institutions which were gradually being established in the field of political relationships should be extended to the economic sphere. They maintained that in the early days of capitalism it was possible for large numbers of workers with a small amount of capital to become the owners of the primitive and inexpensive tools with which they worked, and of the small stores and businesses prevalent in those days. As a result, the artisan was usually able, after some years of apprenticeship, to become the master in his own economic house and to enjoy a large degree of economic democracy. With the development, however, of the great corporations, trusts, and combines, ownership and management of industry tended to concentrate in fewer hands. Production in general ceased to be of an individual nature and became collective. Each worker in the factory was responsible for the production of only a small part of the manufactured article. The average worker had no share in the ownership of the factory in which he worked: he was a "hired hand" and was employed as long as he produced a profit for his employer. Economic democracy for him had disappeared.

It was impossible, socialists declared, to turn back the wheels of economic progress and return to small individualistic production in order to restore the individualistic type of democracy formerly enjoyed. Further, the product of industry in the days of hand power was infinitely less than in an age of machinery, steam, electricity, and mass production. Only under collective production could poverty be abolished. Thus, in an age when man had advanced from individual production to collective production, the only way to assure democracy in industry for the great mass of the population was to go forward from individual to collective ownership of the means of production and distribution. Thus mankind would be able to supplement economic democracy with political democracy, and, by doing so, strengthen the forces of democracy in every aspect of the common life.

In the second place, socialists during those days were united in the belief that, to have maximum meaning to modern man, the great ethical ideals of justice, of equality, and of brotherhood had to be applied to the workaday economic life of the community.

They also believed that the conduct of human beings was greatly influenced by the conditions under which they and their fellows worked and that an improvement in economic and social environment would be accompanied, all else being equal, by the development of a finer type of human being.

Socialists were firmly convinced that society was not static but dynamic; that society had in the past evolved from one economic system to another; and that, as Marx had pointed out, the logical next step in economic evolution in the case of a developed capitalist system was an advance from private to social ownership of the principal industries of a country. There were serious evils, they maintained, in capitalistic society—evils of unjust inequality of wealth and income, of industrial and human waste, of concentration of power over the economic, political, and cultural life of the community, and of great and increasing insecurity, among others. These evils, socialists insisted, could not be abolished short of an advance to a cooperative social order.

Lastly, the European socialists of that period were likewise agreed that the transfer from private to social ownership would be brought about not as a result of the conscious efforts of the present owners of industry, but as a result of the combined economic, political, and educational activities of the plain people in countries whose economies were ripe for fundamental social change.

The three theoretical cornerstones of Marxian socialism, especially in the early days, have been the materialistic conception of history, the theory of surplus value, and the doctrine of the class struggle. Of these the materialistic conception of history (or the economic interpretation of history, as some have called it), and the class-struggle theory, formed the sociological basis of Marxism, while the theory of surplus value may be regarded as a part of the Marxian economic theory.

As part of their sociological critique, Marx and Engels contended that social changes are determined primarily by economic and material forces and the reaction of these forces on the conduct of men; and that these forces under the capitalist system bring into play a struggle between the owners of industry and the workers which can only result in the dominance of the workers, and, as has been brought out before, in the elimination of all classes and all class struggles.

Friedrich Engels in 1888 gave a classic explanation of the materialistic conception of history when he wrote:

". . . in every historical epoch the prevailing mode of economic production and exchange, and the social organization necessarily following from it, form the basis upon which is built up, and from which alone can be explained, the political and intellectual history of that epoch; that consequently the whole history of mankind (since the dissolution of primitive tribal society, holding land in common-ownership) has been a history of class struggles, contests between exploiting and exploited, ruling and oppressed classes; that the history of these class struggles forms a series of evolution in which, now-a-days, a stage has been reached where the exploited and oppressed class—the proletariat—cannot attain its emancipation from the sway of the exploiting and ruling class—the bourgeoisie—without, at the same time, and once for all, emancipating society at large from all exploitation, oppression, class-distinction and class struggles."[16]

Marx and Engels never contended that the material forces were the only forces influencing social change, although they were the dominant ones. "According to the materialistic conception of history," wrote Engels in the latter part of his life, "the factor which is *in the last instance* [my italics] decisive in history is the production and reproduction of actual life. More than that neither Marx nor I have ever asserted. But when anyone distorts this so as to read that the economic factor is the sole element, he converts the statement into a meaningless, abstract, absurd phrase. The economic condition is the basis, but the various elements of the superstructure—the political forms of the class contests . . . the legal forms, and also all the reflexes of these actual contests in the brains of the participants, the political, legal, philosophical theories, the religious views . . . all these exert an influence on the historical struggles, and in many instances determine their form."[17]

Assuming the truth of the materialistic conception of history and the conception of class conflict, Marx and Engels maintained that their application to the economic and social forces brought into play by the capitalist system of production and distribution indicated the virtual inevitability of socialism as the next step in industrial development.

In the field of *economic* theory, Marx and Engels took over the theory of value that had, during the previous century and a half, been gradually evolved by numerous French and English economists. This theory in brief was that the value of a commodity, that is to say, the quantity of any other commodity for which it will exchange, depends on the relative

[16] Friedrich Engels, Preface to the 1888 edition, *The Manifesto of the Communist Party* (edition cited above), p. 8.

[17] E. R. A. Seligman, *Economic Interpretation of History* (New York, 1907), pp. 142-43; *Sozialistische Akademiker*, Oct. 15, 1895, p. 251.

quantity of labor necessary for its production.[18] The development of the theory, before Marx and Engels, had begun with such economists as William Petty of England and Boisguillebert in France, and had ended with Ricardo of England and Sismondi of France.[19]

In estimating the amount of labor embodied in a commodity, Marx argued that it was not only necessary to consider the quantity of labor *last* employed, say, in producing a finished article, but that consideration must be given to labor previously exerted in the production of the raw material, and employed on the tools, machinery, and buildings. Consideration must likewise be given to the "quantity of labor necessary for [the production of a commodity] in a given state of society, under certain social average conditions of production, with a given social average intensity, and average skill of the labor employed."[20]

Labor power, like other commodities, he declared, has a value, and that value is determined by the *quantity* of labor necessary to produce it. Thus in the end "the value of laboring power is determined by the value of the necessaries required to produce, develop, maintain, and perpetuate the laboring power."[21]

Under the capitalist system, a worker is employed by the owner of industrial tools and machines. Suppose he was employed in adding to the value of cotton. Suppose he worked at a job for four hours and that these four hours of average labor were realized in a quantity of gold equal to $3. Then $3 would be the price, or the expression of the daily value of that man's laboring power. Over and above the four hours required to replace his wages, the worker would likely have to labor several additional hours, say four hours, surplus labor which would realize itself in a *surplus value* or *surplus produce*. If, for instance, the spinner worked eight hours, he would be paid $3 for wages, while the capitalist would receive the other $3 in the form of surplus value for which he paid no equivalent. Of course the whole of the profit is not pure gain for the capitalist. Part of the surplus goes to the landlord under the name of rent, part to a moneylending capitalist as interest, so that there remains to the industrial capitalist as such only industrial or commercial profit.

Marx did not criticize the capitalists for taking to themselves this surplus value, maintaining that this appropriation by the owning class was inevitable as long as capitalism existed. But he declared that the system which created the surplus value should be eliminated so that the workers would secure the full fruits of their labor. In fact, he contended that forces generated by the value-making processes of the capitalist order

---

[18] David Ricardo, *Principles of Political Economy*, first published in 1817.
[19] Karl Marx, *Critique of Political Economy* (Chicago, 1913), p. 56.
[20] Karl Marx, *Value, Price and Profit* (Chicago, 1908?), p. 62. Italics omitted.
[21] *Ibid.*, p. 76. Italics omitted.

would fatally weaken the profit system, and also that it was the historic mission of the workers not so much to *destroy* capitalism as to prepare themselves to take over control of the productive machinery when the capitalist controls had become so weak as to be no longer effective.

IV. The Revisionists, and the Orthodox Marxians' Reply to the Revisionists

During the decades from the enunciation of the Marxian sociological and economic theories before World War I, many socialists in different countries sought a modification of Marxian theory and practice. In Germany, where the great Marxian scholars were born and received their formal education, and where the first powerful socialist movement came into existence, a school of thought known as revisionism, a school critical of the Marxian doctrine, began to develop in the late nineties, following the deaths of Marx and Engels.[22] The center of the revisionist movement was in southern Germany—Saxony and Bavaria—where capitalist industry was slower in developing than in Prussia and where the state was more democratic. George von Vollmar, the leader of the Bavarian socialists, had always been critical of the Marxian theory that capital and land were being concentrated in ever fewer hands. He urged that socialists pay greater attention to immediate reforms than to far-flung measures of socialization, particularly if they were to win the allegiance of the farming section of the population.

The cause of the revisionists was greatly aided by the publication of *Die Voraussetzungen des Socialismus und die Aufgaben der Sozial-demokratie* (translated under the title *Evolutionary Socialism*) in 1899.[23] The author of the book was Eduard Bernstein, a former banking clerk who, having to leave Germany in 1878 on the passage of the antisocialist legislation of that year, spent the next twenty years in exile in Switzerland and England. While in England, Bernstein had come into close contact with Friedrich Engels and with the leaders of the Fabian Society, who greatly influenced his socialist thinking. As the years advanced, as capitalism continued to expand and as the revolutionary situation which Marx and Engels visualized failed to materialize immediately, Bernstein became increasingly convinced that Marxian doctrine had to be modified. He wrote a series of articles while in London for a German socialist magazine, the *Neue Zeit*, and, on returning to Germany in 1900, found himself at the head of the official opposition within the Social Democratic Party.

[22] Marx died in 1883; Engels, in 1895. See Laidler, *op.cit.*, chap. 20, for a brief description of revisionism.

[23] Eduard Bernstein, *Evolutionary Socialism* (New York, 1909).

Bernstein's six main criticisms of the Marxian doctrine were:

(1) That the collapse of the capitalist system had not taken place as soon as Marx and Engels had assumed, and was not then imminent;

(2) That, while the general tendencies of social development set forth by Marx were correct, the "Fathers of Scientific Socialism" had not correctly judged the *time* element;

(3) That the class struggle had not developed so sharply as Marx had predicted, and that, while the middle class had changed its character, it had by no means disappeared from the social scene;

(4) That concentration of industry had been spotty and had proceeded more slowly and irregularly than Marx and Engels had thought would be the case;

(5) That, under the pressure of the working class, social reaction had set in against the exploiting tendencies of capital, and that the living standards of the workers were gradually improving through the efforts of organized labor, of consumer cooperatives, of social legislation, etc., thus avoiding the need for great catastrophic changes;

(6) And finally, that greater chances for success lay in a steady advance of the working class than in violent sudden change.

Bernstein likewise took up the Marxian theoretical doctrines. He criticized the "oversimplified version" of the materialistic conception of history, which failed to recognize the influence of noneconomic factors in social evolution (a criticism that applied to many of Marx's followers rather than to Marx himself), and pointed out that, once the influence of other than economic forces was acknowledged, predictions of future developments became more difficult. The exponent of revisionism likewise criticized the use of the phrase "materialist conception" on the ground that the doctrine was not based upon philosophic materialism.

As for the labor theory of value and the theory of surplus value, Bernstein declared that they were mere abstract concepts remote from actual conditions. He likewise maintained that whether the Marxian theory of value was correct or not was immaterial to the proof of the existence of surplus value and exploitation. The existence of surplus value, he maintained, was an empirical fact demonstrable from experience and needed no deductive proof. Experience showed that one part of the community, though living in idleness, enjoyed an income out of all proportion to the ratio of its number to that of the total number of workers. The man on the street who had no acquaintance with Marx could understand this fact of life without any difficulty.

Turning to the problem of socializing industry, Bernstein contended that many small businesses were not at that time ripe for socialization and that it was beyond the ability of government as then constituted to socialize all large industries at once. Marx had, he pointed out, said little concerning the irregular character of the trend toward industrial concentration.

In the preparation for a socialized state, Bernstein further emphasized more than did Marx the importance of the consumers' cooperative movement and the trade union movement as a supplement to political action.

In the political arena, the revisionist further insisted, democratic methods must be used as a means to socialism. The idea of the dictatorship of classes, as enunciated by Marx, should be discarded. This concept belongs to a lower civilization. It was conceived at a time when people knew little or nothing of the more modern methods of passing and enforcing social legislation. Socialism, he maintained, is the legitimate heir of liberalism.

As for the immediate tasks ahead, Bernstein declared that they include the working out of an agricultural program about which Marx had said little, the encouragement of cooperatives and of municipal ownership, the formulation of a foreign policy, the removal of the existing class franchise, and the emancipation of social democracy "from a phraseology that is actually outworn." Social democracy, he concluded, must make up its mind to appear to be what it had in reality become—"a party that strives after the socialist transformation of society by the means of democratic and economic reform."[24]

The revisionist doctrines of Bernstein and his followers were hotly criticized by Karl Kautsky and others.[25] The Marxists defended the doctrine of the materialist conception of history, though admitting Bernstein's contention that the interplay of economic and noneconomic forces on human conduct made exact prophecy difficult. They split over the question of the validity of the Marxian theory of value and its importance in the Marxian system of thought. They admitted that Marx and Engels in their early writings had made mistakes in *timing* future social changes— Friedrich Engels himself had freely written about these mistakes[26]—but they declared that Marx had rightly predicted the *general direction* of economic developments.

Kautsky and the Marxists further admitted that concentration had taken place unevenly in various industrial fields, but declared that many of Bernstein's figures in his chapters on concentration were quite irrelevant. The important thing, for instance, was not the number of small industries that survived, as Bernstein seemed to argue, but the proportion of the output produced by small and by large concerns.

[24] *Ibid.*, p. 197.   [25] Laidler, *op.cit.*, chap. 21.
[26] Friedrich Engels, *The Condition of the Working Class in England in 1844* (London, 1892), Preface, especially pp. xff.

The Marxists likewise disagreed with Bernstein's contention that people rose from the working class into the middle class as a result of having a higher "middle-class income," and maintained that those receiving high wages might still be regarded as members of the working class for they still were employed and exploited by the owning group in society.

Kautsky and his followers, moreover, while maintaining in their reply to Bernstein that class antagonisms under capitalism were increasing rather than softening and that a revolutionary change would have to take place, conceived of revolution not as a violent overturn or coup d'état, but a change in the control of government from the capitalist class to the working class; a change that they hoped would be brought about by the ballot and by democratic action. Nor was it necessary for the capitalist system to collapse before such a revolution was possible. Kautsky and his followers, in fact, agreed with Bernstein and other revisionists that social reforms which warded off severe economic crises and raised the physical, mental, and ethical standards of the workers were to be encouraged as a means of bringing about fundamental social change. In general, they continued to defend "the increasing misery" theory, but they maintained that the word "misery" should be used in the psychological rather than the physical sense of that term.

As for the socialist society, Kautsky agreed with Bernstein that socialists should not have as their goal the public ownership of all industry, but a society which would best prevent exploitation and serve the interests of the common man. Under socialism, he contended, while the essential industries should be owned by the community, many services should be left to cooperatives of production and consumption, and a considerable number to private control.

"Nothing is more false," declared Kautsky, "than to represent the socialist society as a simple, rigid mechanism whose wheels when once set in motion run on continuously in the same manner.

"The most manifold forms of property in the means of production—national, municipal, cooperatives of consumption and production, and private—can exist beside each other in a socialist society; the most diverse forms of industrial organization, bureaucratic, trades union, co-operative and individual; the most diverse forms of remuneration of labor. . . . The same manifold character of economic mechanism that exists to-day is possible in a socialistic society. Only the hunting and the hunted, the struggling and resisting, the annihilated and being annihilated of the present competitive struggle are excluded and therewith the contrast between exploiter and exploited."[27]

[27] Karl Kautsky, *Social Revolution* (Chicago, 1905), pp. 166-67.

V. *The Fabians*

While the Lassalleans and the Marxists and later the revisionists and Marxists were debating socialist theory and practice in Germany, the British socialists, and particularly the Fabian socialists, were developing a theoretical basis for a faith of their own in a socialist order.[28]

In the late eighteen-forties, Friedrich Engels had prophesied that revolution was likely to occur in England in the early fifties. By the time of the next crisis, which, he thought, "must break out in 1852 or 1853," Engels maintained that "the English people will have had enough of being plundered by the capitalists and left to starve when the capitalists no longer require their services. If up to that time the English bourgeoisie does not pause to reflect—and to all appearances it certainly will not do so—a revolution will follow with which none hitherto known can be compared."[29] No sudden and violent revolution materialized, however, either in the fifties or in the decades that followed.

Engels later explained some of the reasons for the failure of his prophecy to come true. After the crisis of 1847 there had been a revival of trade in England, which had ushered in "a new industrial era," as Marx had pointed out in his address at the launching of the First International. This revival resulted from many factors, including the repeal of the Corn Laws, financial reforms, the discovery of gold in California and Australia, the increasing absorption of English manufactured goods by colonial markets, the opening up of China to western commerce, the astounding economic development of the United States, and the introduction of ocean steamers and railways which "realized actually what had hitherto existed only potentially, a world market."

As a result of these national and world forces, declared Engels, England's industrial progress from the forties to the eighties was "colossal and unparalleled," such, in fact, that in the latter period the status of 1844 appeared to be "comparatively primitive and insignificant."[30] As for the workers, during those days they had to some extent shared in the increased productivity in industry and in the monopoly position that British industry in some fields occupied. While the privileged minority of skilled workers pocketed most of the gains, "even the great mass had, at least, a temporary share now and then. And that is the reason why, since the dying out of Owenism," maintained Engels in the early nineties, "there has been no socialism in England."

The monopoly position of England, however, Engels added, will not long continue, and when the breakdown comes, the English working class will find itself generally on a level with its fellow workers abroad. "And

[28] Laidler, *op.cit.*, chaps. 17, 18.
[29] Engels, *Condition of the Working Class in England in 1844*, p. 296.
[30] *Ibid.*, Preface, p. vi.

that is the reason," he concluded, "why there will be socialism again in England."[31]

There had been other forces at work in England in the generation following the *Communist Manifesto*. Restrictions during those days were increasingly removed from trade union activities; organized labor grew in numbers and influence; legislation was passed which protected workers from some of the worst abuses of the factory system; consumers' cooperatives began to flourish; suffrage laws were liberalized; and the workers began to think increasingly in terms of independent political action, as opposed to violent upheavals, as a means of improving their condition.

During these years, moreover, with the increasing influence of the working class, leading economists of the day began to show renewed interest in the relations of labor to property. Among these economists, John Stuart Mill was the most prominent. Mill gave much attention to the question of land. "Land," he maintained, "is the original inheritance of the whole species." The individual's right to land, therefore, is not sacred. Income from land in the form of rent tends to increase, not as a result of the exertion or sacrifice of the owners, but as a result of the efforts of the community. It is thus not a "violation of the principles on which private property is grounded, if the state should appropriate this increase of wealth, or part of it, as it arises. This would not properly be taking anything from anybody; it would merely be applying an accession of wealth, created by circumstances, to the benefit of society, instead of allowing it to become an unearned appendage to the riches of a particular class." Landlords, he continued, "grow richer, as it were in their sleep, without working, risking, or economizing. What claim have they, on the general principle of social justice, to this accession of riches?"[32]

As a result of Mill's teachings and those of others, a Land Tenure Reform Association was formed in England containing in its membership many distinguished economists, while labor began to take a keen interest in national control of land and the appropriation by society of unearned increments in land values. Mill, Cairnes, and others likewise gave much sympathetic attention during this period to the socialist indictment of capitalism, as did many of the outstanding essayists of the times, among them John Ruskin (1819-1900), Thomas Carlyle (1795-1881), Charles Kingsley (1819-1875), and Frederick Denison Maurice (1805-1872).

During the generation from the late forties to the eighties while these changes were taking place in Great Britain, the writings of Marx and Engels were being read and discussed widely by German and other continental socialists. Although many of Marx's writings were available

[31] *Ibid.*, pp. xvii-xviii.
[32] J. S. Mill, *Principles of Political Economy* (several eds.), Book II, chap. 2, par. 6; and Book V, chap. 2, par. 5.

only to those Englishmen who read German and French, a considerable number of his articles and shorter pamphlets were available in English and widely read. Moreover, Marx came personally in touch with many Englishmen during his exile in London from 1849 to his death in 1883.

In 1880, two articles on Marxism appeared in one of the English monthlies, one favoring and one opposing the Marxian school of thought. In 1881, Henry Hyndman, a brilliant though dogmatic English intellectual who had read deeply of Marx, published a book, *England for All*, which embodied the main tenets of Marx on the relationships of labor to capital. Hyndman, however, aware of British prejudice against Marxism, did not mention the name of Karl Marx throughout the volume, contenting himself with a statement in his Preface that, "for the ideas and much of the matter contained in chapters two and three, I am indebted to the work of a great thinker and original writer," whose works he hoped would soon be accessible to the majority of Englishmen! This slight, by the way, caused an estrangement between Hyndman and Marx and Engels, which was never healed.

It was in the England subjected to the foregoing economic, social, and educational influences that the Fabian Society was born in 1883. At or shortly after its formation, the society attracted such distinguished men and women as Sidney and Beatrice Webb, Bernard Shaw, Graham Wallas, Sidney Olivier, and Annie Besant.

The Fabians held as their goal no mere reform program within the framework of capitalism, but sought as far-flung a goal as that of the Marxists in the days of the *Communist Manifesto*—"the reorganization of Society by the emancipation of Land and Industrial Capital from individual and class ownership, and the vesting of them in the community for the general benefit."[33] Unlike the Marxists and the revisionists, however, they made little or no mention in their original propaganda of the three cornerstones of scientific socialism—the materialistic conception (or economic interpretation) of history, the class struggle, and surplus value.

The Fabians, with Marx, saw socialism coming as a result of great social and economic forces. But, viewing the development in England in those days, they believed, with the revisionists, that socialism would come not through a coup d'état or sudden violent change, but through gradual peaceful progress as a result of the reaction of society to private monopoly, the progress of political democracy, the expansion of municipal and national ownership, and the changed attitude of the people of the country toward the individual's responsibility to the commonwealth. They laid much stress on the fact that the owner of industry had been gradually handing over his functions as manager to hired salary workers and that he was no longer as essential to the economic system as when owner and

[33] E. R. Pease, *The History of the Fabian Society* (New York, 1916?), p. 269.

manager were one. "All students of society who are abreast of their time . . . ," declared Sidney Webb in his essay on the historic basis of socialism, "realize that important organic changes can only be (1) *democratic*, and thus acceptable to a majority of the people, and prepared for in the minds of all; (2) *gradual*, and thus causing no dislocation, however rapid may be the rate of progress; (3) *not regarded as immoral* by the mass of the people, and thus not subjectively demoralizing to them; and (4) in this country at any rate, *constitutional* and *peaceful*."[34]

To Webb, as to many other leaders of socialist thought, socialism was but the further application of democracy to our common life. "There is every day a wider consensus that the inevitable outcome of Democracy is the control by the people themselves, not only of their own political organization, but, through that also, of the main instruments of wealth production. . . . The economic side of the democratic ideal is, in fact, Socialism itself."[35]

As for the economic theories of the Fabians, Bernard Shaw took the conception of economic rent held by John Stuart Mill and by Henry George, the famous American whose visit to England in the early eighties had helped to lay the foundation for the Fabian Society. Shaw argued against the private appropriation of rent. He went beyond these economists, however, and declared that there were not only rents from land due to differential advantages, but industrial rents due to advantages of sites, of machinery, and of the more favored businesses. Such rents, he argued, should not be appropriated by private capitalists as they did not result from the mental and bodily efforts of their recipients. Shaw also took issue with Marx on his labor theory of value, declaring that the exchange value of a commodity depended not on the quantity of labor embodied in it, but upon its utility.

The Fabians approached socialism not only from the historical, industrial, and economic angles, but from the standpoint of social morality. The effects of capitalism on character, they declared, were disastrous. Socialism, on the other hand, would advance social morality and give to the individual a chance for the freest and fullest development.

Finally, the Fabians analyzed, as Marx had failed to do, many of the problems that would arise under a collectivist society, and suggested ways and means of meeting these problems. Later (1920) Webb declared that the early Fabians had underestimated the importance of trade unionism, consumers' cooperatives, and municipal ownership in bringing about industrial democracy; that their practical proposals for nationalization had been too vague and general; that they had failed to give adequate atten-

[34] G. B. Shaw and others, *Fabian Essays in Socialism* (Boston, 1908), p. 30. Italics added.
[35] *Ibid.*, pp. 30-31.

tion to the international phases of socialized industry; and that they had not sufficiently applied to human relations under socialism the lessons of modern psychology. As those who have followed the later writings of the Webbs and other Fabians fully realize, the Fabians in the last generation or so have contributed greatly to an understanding of the real significance of many movements which they had neglected in their first score of years of activity.[36] In their early days, as has been suggested, the Fabians had a profound effect on the revisionist leader, Eduard Bernstein, and throughout their career they have greatly influenced the thinking and activities of the British Labour Party and the socialist movement throughout the world.

VI. Syndicalism

While the German and British socialists were developing their varied brands of socialist theory and practice, many radicals in France and some of the other countries in Europe were developing a different philosophy of social change, a philosophy referred to as syndicalism.[37]

The French syndicalists took over as one of their foundation stones the Marxian concept of the class struggle and sought ever to sharpen that concept. They agreed with Marx that a constant struggle is going on between the capitalist and the working class. That struggle is not to be deplored, but to be hailed as a creative force leading to the emancipation of the working class. It is the class struggle which is the unifying force in the battle for industrial freedom; which is developing the workers' consciousness of their intellectual and moral nature; and which is creating more appropriate forms of industrial organization.

The class struggle, syndicalists maintained, cannot be waged effectively on the political field. Political groups are weak and transient, made up of men and women of various interests brought together by a community of ideas. The state is an instrument of class rule. When a worker is elected to parliament, the bourgeoisie brings its corrupting influence on him and on the labor party, whose policies are likely to degenerate into bargaining, compromising, and collaborating with the bourgeois political parties.

It is thus for labor to work through industrial rather than political organizations. In trade and industrial unions men and women of the same general interests are brought together, and workers can enter into a "direct" struggle with their employers. Direct action may be violent or

[36] The Webbs, among other things, wrote the classic *History of Trade Unionism* (1894), prepared a monumental work on the cooperative movement and public ownership, *The Consumers' Co-operative Movement* (1924), and brilliantly analyzed the problems of a socialized society in their *A Constitution for the Socialist Commonwealth of Great Britain* (1920). Later they wrote extensively on *Soviet Communism: a New Civilisation?* (1935).

[37] Laidler, *op.cit.*, chap. 22.

nonviolent. It may consist of strikes, boycotts, the use of the union label, or sabotage, etc. Of these actions, the most important is the strike. "The strike brings the workingmen face to face with the employers in a clash of interests. . . . It further deepens the chasm between them, consolidating the employers on the one hand, and the workingmen on the other, over against one another. It is a revolutionary fact of great value."[38]

The revolutionary effect of the strike, declared the syndicalists, depends in large part on the way it is conducted. It should be conducted with militancy. Workers of other trades should be involved and individual strikes should help lay the foundation for a general strike "which will be the final act of emancipation."[39]

Like the Bolsheviks of a later period, syndicalists laid great emphasis on the importance of the small, conscious, and militant minority as leaders of the revolution. After the syndical revolution, syndicalists urged, the political state as we know it would disappear, and industry would be run by local and national trade-union federations.[40] On the whole, the French syndicalists gave little attention to the problem of how their proposed state would be organized, maintaining that the proper forms would be worked out by labor when necessity arose.

The French socialist leaders and the political socialists of other lands vigorously criticized the syndicalists for ignoring the effectiveness of parliamentary action and the necessity of retaining the political state, with its important political, social, and economic functions. They declared that if key industries were owned and run by syndicalists, rather than by the entire community, it would be possible for workers in these industries to "charge what the traffic would bear," and exploit the rest of the community. While acknowledging the value of industrial action, socialists pointed to the almost insuperable obstacles in the path of using either the strike in individual industries or the general strike for revolutionary purposes. Many socialists, moreover, condemned the syndicalists' use of sabotage on the ground that such underhanded methods of warfare had a vitiating effect on the labor movement.[41]

[38] Louis Levine, *Syndicalism in France* (New York, 1914), pp. 126-27.

[39] *Ibid.*, pp. 132-33.

[40] Syndicalists drew a good deal of their philosophy from anarchists, who urged the abolition of the state. Anarchists of that period were roughly divided into anarcho-communists and anarcho-syndicalists (both of whom would substitute for private ownership a system of community or producers' ownership), and individualist anarchists (who would not disturb present property relationships). Many anarchists accepted syndicalism as the expression of the anarchist principle in the economic field. See Laidler, *op.cit.*, p. 283.

[41] See Laidler, *op.cit.*, pp. 307-11; J. Ramsay MacDonald, *Syndicalism* (Chicago, 1912); W. W. Crook, *The General Strike* (Chapel Hill, N.C., 1931); Sidney and Beatrice Webb, *What Syndicalism Means* (London, 1912).

VII. Guild Socialism

At the time of World War I, still another school of socialist thought appeared on the European scene—the school of guild socialism. Guild socialism was a cross between French syndicalism, with its emphasis on the need for producers' control, and modern British and continental socialism, with its advocacy of public ownership of the essential industries.[42] Guild socialism made its appearance in England about twenty years after the formative period of syndicalism in France, a generation after the formation of the Fabian Society, and more than two generations following the appearance of the *Communist Manifesto*.

The guild socialist school of thought might be said to have been officially launched with the appearance in 1912 of several articles on the subject by S. G. Hobson and A. R. Orage.[43] These articles were followed three years later by the formation of the National Guilds League after the Fabian Society had refused to commit itself to the guild socialist philosophy. G. D. H. Cole was one of the chief founders of the League and, in the ensuing years, its outstanding leader.

In part, guild socialism represented a reaction against a Fabian approach which, in urging collective ownership in city and nation, had given little attention to the rights and responsibility of the worker. In part it was influenced by the Marxian analysis of the evils of the wage system; by the syndicalist championship of the producer; by the American industrial unionists' conception of a future industrial society. At the same time one could find in the movement something of "the craftsmen's challenge and the blazing democracy of William Morris; the warning of Mr. Belloc against the huge shadow of the Servile State. . . ; the insistence of Mr. Penty on the perils of industrialism and its large-scale organisation, and his recovery . . . of the significant and unique word 'guild.' "[44] During World War I, the movement was vitalized by the so-called shop-steward movement with its revolt against wartime restrictions of labor and its demand for increasing workers' control of managerial functions.[45]

In general, the guild socialists urged the abolition of the wage system and the establishment of self-government in industry through a system of national guilds made up of all workers in an industry, working in conjunction with the state or commune. While the *title to* industry should be in the hands of the state or of some other agency or agencies representing the community, the guildsmen believed that *the operation of* a particular

---

[42] See Laidler, *op.cit.*, chap. 23, for a description of guild socialism.

[43] Six years earlier, in 1906, a rather nebulous form of guild socialism had made its appearance with the formation of the Guilds Restoration Movement.

[44] M. B. Reckitt and C. E. Bechhofer, *The Meaning of National Guilds* (New York, 1918), pp. xiii-xiv.

[45] *Encyclopaedia of the Social Sciences*, vii, p. 720.

industry should be primarily in the hands of guilds representing all of the workers in an industry—manual workers, skilled craftsmen, and members of technical and managerial staffs.

While the guildsmen were opposed to enlarging the control of the state over the management of industry and many guildsmen advocated the replacing of the state by a "commune," they did not favor the drastic extralegal actions urged by the early Marxists, the syndicalists, and later the Russian communists, as a means to their goal. It was not the job of the guildsman, as Cole maintained, to work for an "early revolution, but for the consolidation of all forces on the lines of evolutionary development. . . ."[46] Cole saw, as did most socialists, the growth of trade unionism, cooperative and labor political action, as helpful approaches to more far-reaching workers' control of industry.

Guild socialism as an organized movement disappeared in the late nineteen-twenties. The reasons for this disappearance were threefold: many former guildsmen gave increasing attention to the Russian experiment; the wartime militancy of various British labor forces disappeared; the Fabians and other socialist groups incorporated some of the features of the guild school of thought in their own social thinking.

Cole, however, while rejoining the reorganized Fabian Society and becoming one of its most distinguished figures, continued to call himself a guild socialist, though in his later writings he declared that, with the coming of mass production, the conduct of industry was "necessarily a highly technical matter." It had thus, he asserted, become increasingly difficult for the average manual or clerical worker to pass worthwhile judgments on many phases of industry. On account of these developments, the case against "workers' control," he continued, was far more formidable than he had thought when he wrote his early books on the subject. However, he refused to accept the notion "that all hope of 'workers' control' must be abandoned and that we must content ourselves with the safeguard of ultimate political control over the technical autocrats of industry."[47] In his later writings, while he would have the guilds work out plans for output, prices, and conditions of employment and present them to a National Planning Commission for approval, he would also see to it that "the final authority for approving the economic plan" would be left to Parliament.[48] Cole, moreover, made it clear that the elaborate blueprints for a guild socialist society which he had formerly submitted for the approval of the public were merely meant as illustrative material and that he had no intention of indicating dogmatically, as had utopian socialists of the past, how socialism could best be applied.[49]

[46] G. D. H. Cole, *Guild Socialism* (New York, 1920), p. 168.
[47] G. D. H. Cole, *Economic Planning* (New York, 1935), p. 342.
[48] G. D. H. Cole, *The Simple Case for Socialism* (London, 1935), pp. 154-55.
[49] *Ibid.*, p. 156.

The guild socialist movement, while criticized vigorously in many respects by the majority of British socialists, had a considerable influence on socialist thought and action in Britain and throughout the world. As in the case of the syndicalist movement earlier, its influence resulted especially from its exposition of the need for avoiding bureaucratic collectivism and for seeing to it that all workers who had a function to perform in industry should have a chance to make their voices heard in the running of the industrial machine.

During the late eighteen-nineties and the early years of the twentieth century before World War I, it is thus seen that—with the growing strength of labor on the political, economic, and cooperative fields, and with labor's numerous successful efforts to improve its lot—Marxists, revisionists, Fabians, and guild socialists in the western European democracies were, on the whole, united in the belief that socialism could and should be ushered in through peaceful political, economic, and educational means, and that violent coup d'état methods of social change were becoming more and more outmoded. All these groups were, in fact, in increasing agreement with Friedrich Engels' observation, made in 1895 shortly before his death, that "the time of surprise attacks, of revolutions carried through by small conscious minorities at the head of unconscious masses, is past."[50] "The irony of world history turns everything upside down. We, the 'revolutionaries,' the 'rebels'—we are thriving far better on legal methods than on illegal methods and revolt. The parties of order, as they call themselves, are perishing under the legal conditions created by themselves."[51]

Only the syndicalists of France and the syndicalist-anarchists of Spain and other countries among the radicals urged the coup d'état methods in Western democracies as the way out, and in France the syndicalists were opposed by the strong socialist movement led by Jean Jaurès, Léon Blum, and others, who were ardent advocates of democratic social change.

VIII. The Rise of Russian Communism[52]

In Russia and some of the other eastern countries of Europe where political dictatorship was still largely the order of the day, the followers of Karl Marx were in the early twentieth century still widely divided on the tactics they should pursue in reaching their goal.

During the last quarter of the nineteenth century, anarchists and other revolutionists in Russia had battled against the tsarist government with every weapon at their command, many thousands of them suffering arrest,

50 Engels' Introduction in Karl Marx, *The Class Struggles in France* (New York, 1934), p. 25.
51 *Ibid.*, pp. 27-28.   52 Laidler, *op.cit.*, Pt. IV.

imprisonment, exile, execution. In the late eighteen-nineties, the Russian Social Democratic Labor Party had been formed to advance the cause of socialism, but this group felt that little could be done to bring about the revolution until economic conditions were ripe. They had small hope of reaching the peasants, who constituted so large a part of the population, until the big landlords had expropriated the peasants' lands.[53]

In 1903 the Social Democratic Labor Party held its second congress. The gathering showed the existence of marked differences among the delegates. One group, led by Lenin, demanded a more thorough centralization of control in the hands of the party's executive committee and more vigorous suppression of all independent activities. The other group, led by Martov, urged a more democratic party organization and greater freedom of action among local units. The first group developed into the Bolsheviks, later known as Russian communists; the second, into the Mensheviks.

In the next congress, in 1904, a bitter discussion took place between these two groups on the subject, "In case of a political revolution in Russia, what attitude should the party adopt?" The Mensheviks maintained that victory would be decisive if the next revolution in Russia resulted in the creation of a constituent assembly under the direct pressure of the people in revolt. The monarchical regime, following such a revolution, should be liquidated, but socialists should not seek to capture all power by eliminating other liberal parties from the provisional government. The Bolsheviks, on the other hand, urged a "struggle for the revolutionary dictatorship of the proletariat and the peasants, aiming at a complete social transformation on the basis of the Bolshevist platform." The Bolsheviks at this gathering won a majority and were given the name which meant "majority"; the defeated group was named "Menshevik," meaning minority.[54]

These two groups continued to function during the 1905 revolution and the massacres that followed that unsuccessful revolt. Soviets during these revolutionary days sprang up in various parts of the country, while many socialists and laborites propagandized for their cause in the Russian Duma, established shortly after the uprising.

From the 1905 revolt to the revolutionary days of 1917, the Mensheviks were the functioning majority and the Bolsheviks the minority within the fold of the Social Democratic Labor Party. The Mensheviks continued to insist that Russia must pass through the stage of capitalist development

[53] In 1901, soon after the organization of the Social Democratic Labor Party, another party, the Social Revolutionists, was formed to do work primarily among the agricultural population. The Social Revolutionists did not preclude the use of violence as a means of social change.

[54] Étienne Antonelli, *Bolshevik Russia* (tr. from the French by C. A. Carroll; New York, 1920), pp. 60-62.

before it was ready for a successful social revolution and that the next stage of Russia would be the stage of political democracy. A country is ripe for socialization, they claimed, when industry is highly developed; when a small group of private capitalists practically controls the economic interests of the nation; and when the workers are educated, organized, and disciplined as a result of that development. This, they maintained, is the teaching of Marx and the teaching of common sense.

Turning to Russia, they declared that resources and industries in that backward country were then undeveloped, her masses were uneducated, her industrial population was controlled by a small percentage of the people. The hour for social revolution had not yet struck. In this situation a bourgeois republic must follow absolutism, while socialism must follow a bourgeois republic.

The Bolsheviks replied to this argument with the contention that it was possible to jump from a primitive to a socialist economy without necessarily passing through the capitalist stage of development. This was partly due to the fact that other countries in Europe were advanced in their capitalist systems, and a revolution starting in Russia was likely to ignite a flame which would spread throughout Europe. When socialism was established in the industrially developed European countries, these socialist governments would help Russia to adapt itself to the requirements of a socialist society. Russia, further, among socialist countries, could serve as the agricultural storehouse for the industrialized part of Europe.

To attain their goal, the Bolsheviks, or communists, before and immediately following the 1917 Revolution elaborated their theory of social change. Social revolution could not be achieved, they maintained, by the peaceful means of the ballot, aided by economic, cooperative, and general educational activity. During times of peace, while the proletariat was preparing for the crisis, it was legitimate for the workers to enter electoral campaigns and to function in parliaments. In such assemblies communists could point out the class character of the state, show the futility of reforms, "demonstrate the real interests which dominate the capitalist—and 'yellow' socialist—political parties, and point out why the entire capitalist system must be overthrown."[55] However, the communists insisted that the parliamentary struggle should be regarded as "only a school, only a fulcrum for the organisation of the extra-parliamentary struggle of the proletariat"; for the essential questions of the labor movement within the capitalist order are settled by force, by open struggle, the general strike, the insurrection of the proletarian masses.[56]

[55] Statement by Zinoviev to the I.W.W., written Jan. 1920 on behalf of the Third International. See R. W. Postgate, *The Bolshevik Theory* (New York, 1920), p. 234.

[56] Joseph Stalin, *Theory and Practice of Leninism* (2nd ed., London: Communist Party of Great Britain, 1926), p. 25.

As for the particular types of open struggle to be employed in seizing power, besides temporarily using parliamentary and agitational methods, communists should organize street demonstrations, inaugurate general strikes, urge insurrection in the army and navy, and, at the proper moment, arm the proletariat. They should then seize strategic positions in the economic and political life of the country—munition plants and arsenals, the press, the means of communication and transportation, the sources of light and power, and the public buildings—and proclaim their control of the machinery of government.[57] Following the seizure of power, the old state machines would be shattered and a dictatorship of the proletariat would be set up during a transitional period which would later be followed by the disappearance of the classes and "the withering away of the state."

The Bolsheviks took every advantage of the weakness of the corrupt tsarist regime and of the inefficient and powerless capitalist class at the end of a disastrous war. They capitalized upon the desire of the industrial population for bread, of the soldiers and sailors for peace, and of the peasants for land. Following the revolution of March 1917, they mobilized the masses for the overthrow of the Kerensky regime and the setting up of the communist dictatorship. They likewise established the Third or Communist International to assist in the building of communist parties in capitalist countries and to speed up the world revolution. The international condemned "bourgeois democracy," declared that communism could be brought about only through extraparliamentary means, and urged left-wing elements in all countries to split away from the existing socialist and trade-union movements and to form communist parties and "Red" trade unions directed by central committees in Moscow.

In the second Congress of the Comintern, in August 1920, the assembled delegates were summoned to the work of "world revolution" at once. The Congress adopted the famous "twenty-one points," or conditions of admission to the Comintern. Parties wanting to join the Communist International were told that they must create illegal machines to assist them in the hour of revolution; that they must carry on systematic campaigns among trade unions, farmers' organizations, consumers' cooperatives, and other mass groups; must seek to remove from posts in the labor movement all reformist and centrist elements; must give full support to the Soviet republic; must hinder the transportation of munitions of war to the enemies of the Soviet republic; and must carry out all of the decisions of the Comintern and its committees. The manifesto maintained that communists must have no confidence in bourgeois legality, as "in nearly every country of Europe and America, the class struggle is entering upon the phase of civil war."

[57] *Ibid.,* p. 100.

As a result of the tactics pursued by communist parties, working-class organizations in most European countries were split into socialist and communist groups. Civil war broke out in Germany. Communists gained control of Hungary and Bavaria. In these countries, however, the pendulum soon swung to the right, and extreme conservative and rightist parties took the place of communist governments. In Italy, Fascist forces swept into the government.

For this swing to reaction, many students blamed the division and violent tactics of the communists. "I think it possible," declared Professor Harold J. Laski in the early forties, "that had Lenin not precipitated the fatal split in the working-class forces implied in the foundation of the Third International, certainly not Hitler, and perhaps not Mussolini, would have attained power. But the preliminary conditions of their success was that, through communist fanaticism, the organized forces of the working class were divided and hesitant when they could have been united and strong."[58]

During the latter nineteen-twenties and the early nineteen-thirties, the German Communist Party was the strongest one outside of Russia. In Germany, communists constantly attacked Social Democratic Party members as "social fascists." Many communists openly stated their belief that the destruction of German social democracy, followed by a Fascist dictatorship, were the necessary preliminaries to communism. In fact, the Central Committee of the Communist International declared in 1932 that, "The establishing of an open fascist dictatorship in Germany, by destroying all the democratic illusions among the masses and liberating them from the influence of social democracy, accelerates the rate of Germany's development toward the democratic revolution."[59] The German communists joined with the Nazis in voting against the socialist-led Prussian government. In the Berlin traffic strike engineered less than three months before nazism came into power—a work stoppage designed to stir up the population against the republic on the occasion of the approaching elections for parliament—the strike committee consisted of an equal number of communists and Nazis.[60]

After the Nazis had gained power in Germany, however, the Kremlin became fearful of the rising power of Hitler and ordered an abrupt reversal of Comintern policy. It called a convention of the Communist International—the first in seven years—and the Communist parties of the world were instructed to join with the social democrats, whom they

[58] H. J. Laski, *Reflections on the Revolution of Our Time* (New York, 1943), p. 84.
[59] *International Press Correspondence*, English edition, Vol. 12, No. 17 (April 13, 1932), p. 378.
[60] Eduard Heimann, *Communism, Fascism or Democracy?* (New York, 1938), p. 189.

had formerly called "social fascists," and other progressive forces, in united-front activities against fascism. Communists were told, however, to explain to the masses that unity was possible only on condition that "the necessity of the revolutionary overthrow of the rule of the bourgeoisie and the establishment of the dictatorship of the proletariat in the form of Soviets be recognized, that support of one's own bourgeoisie in imperialist war be rejected, and that the party be constructed on the basis of democratic centralism which ensures unity of will and action and has been tested by the experience of the Russian Bolsheviks."[61] The resolutions likewise made it clear that, though the immediate task of the proposed united fronts was to fight fascism, the more far-flung aim was that of putting communists in a position of leadership so that they might be able to lead labor to the proletarian dictatorship when the proper time came.

Meanwhile, the Soviet economy was passing through several stages of state capitalism or state socialism. From the November Revolution of 1917 (October Revolution, according to the Russian calendar) to the middle of 1918 the government inaugurated a period of "Workers' Control." During these months, while the railroads and key industries were run by the government, most industries were under government regulation, but not under government operation. The management of each factory was given over to the persons employed therein, whether to a majority or to all of the workers. The government soon found, however, that each individually controlled factory "was without knowledge, alike of what the whole community of consumers needed or desired, and of how much all the other factories were simultaneously producing."[62]

This type of control resulted in low production. As a result, the government issued a decree on June 28, 1918, placing each plant in charge of a single manager appointed by and responsible to the government itself. A new government department was also organized charged with the job of directing manufacturing and mining throughout the country, "with," as the Webbs declared years later, "the dominant object of getting produced, not what the workmen in each factory thought fit, or even what the manager might decide, but what the community needed and desired in due order and proportion. It had, in fact, been discovered by painful experience that the 'liquidation of the employer' necessarily involved the governmental planning of production."[63] The development of the Supreme Economic Council of Public Economy, authorized to organize the national economy and the finances of the state, soon followed.

The period of "Workers' Control" lasting from the November Revolution

[61] Seventh World Congress of the Communist International, *Resolutions* (New York, 1935), p. 37. Italics omitted.
[62] Sidney and Beatrice Webb, *Soviet Communism*, II, p. 608.
[63] *Ibid.*, II, p. 609.

to the middle of 1918 gave way to "War Communism" with the coming of the Civil War. Upon the outbreak of violence, many of the old factory owners and managers who had remained in Russia during the two revolutions left the country, while others remained to sabotage their plants. As a result of military necessity, the government undertook a more systematic nationalization of large industries, and, on November 29, 1920, at the height of War Communism, nationalization was decreed in the case of all plants operated by machinery and employing more than five workers, as well as in the case of handicraft industries employing ten or more workers.

From the standpoint of supplying the army with enough clothes and ammunition to win the Civil War, state administration of industry from the summer of 1918 to the end of 1920 was in general successful. But much bureaucracy, inefficiency, and waste were in evidence in the state industries, while lack of business executives was painfully felt. The task of trying to industrialize a backward agricultural country overnight and of running it efficiently had proved impossible of achievement. The result was hunger, unrest, revolts, practical breakdown of the economic system.

To prevent further revolt, the New Economic Policy was adopted. Under this policy, the government substituted the taxation of peasants for food acquisition; gave peasants freedom to dispose of their surplus commodity after the payment of government levies, and small merchants freedom to buy and sell; reorganized many state industries, and began a policy of state leasing. Many restrictions were taken off cooperative enterprises and, in a decree of July 7, 1921, all small enterprises employing less than twenty persons were exempted from future nationalization and municipalization.

In defending this course, Lenin declared that the revival of small industry was the greatest need of the hour, for small industry could flourish without large reserve stocks of fuel, food, and raw material—reserves which did not then exist in Russia.[64] Under the N.E.P., the Soviet economy was saved from collapse. Industry revived, but private merchants and small manufacturers, called Nepmen, grew in strength.

Lenin died in 1924 and Stalin gradually assumed power. Stalin soon found himself engaged in a vigorous controversy with Trotsky and others who criticized the government for failing vigorously to sow the seeds of social revolution throughout Europe and for so encouraging private industry in Russia as to lead to a probable return of capitalism. Stalin won out in the controversy, but incorporated many measures which Trotsky and others had urged in the Russian system. The N.E.P. was liquidated. In 1928 the government adopted the first Five Year Plan to speed up

[64] See Lenin, *Concerning the Food Tax.*

industrialization, and in 1930 it began a campaign for the complete collectivization of farms. From these years to World War II, the government, through its various Five Year Plans, concentrated largely on the task of industrializing Russia, with the view of providing a technological basis for higher living standards and of building up a huge war machine as a means of protection in case of another war. By 1940, the output of industry was reported by the government to be around seven times as high as in 1928, although in many instances the quality of goods produced greatly suffered.

The Russian economy, with the help of the Allies, stood the difficult test of World War II, and, following the war, most of the industries of the nation continued to be owned by the government and operated by government trusts and combines. In 1940, just before Russia entered World War II, about 600 such trusts existed, bringing under unified control many plants producing similar types of commodities or engaged in processing specific commodities from the collection of the raw material to their manufacture and sale. In general, the government appointed the directors of the trusts and these directors appointed the factory managers. Plant managers, in turn, conferred frequently with representatives of trade unions and of the communist cells in the plant concerning methods of administration, but had the final say—subject to instructions from the directors of the trust—as to how the plant should be run. Units of industry were in general charged with paying their own way.[65]

When the dictatorship was established, many communists were of the opinion that within a few years the dictatorial features of the Soviet Republic would be eliminated and Russia would join the ranks of the world's democracies. In 1936 a new constitution was formed which proclaimed the "democratic" character of the government. Despite the new constitution, however, the dictatorship of the inner circle of Communist Party leaders continued to control the destiny of the country with the democratic rights of free speech, free press, free assembly, freedom of association, and freedom of movement practically nonexistent.[66]

After World War I, when reaction followed the period of revolution, the Soviet government temporarily gave up the dream of communizing Europe through revolutionary outbreaks of the European proletariat, as has been before pointed out, and concentrated most of its efforts on the building up of the Russian economy.

Following World War II, however, when the Russian army—assisted by the arms, supplies, and manpower contributed by the Allies—defeated

---

[65] See Laidler, op.cit., chap. 28.

[66] Ibid., especially pp. 403-6; 423-30. See also J. E. Davies, Mission to Moscow (New York, 1941), especially pp. 49-50, 302-3, 400-3; A. R. Williams, The Soviets (New York, 1937), pp. 353, 378; Norman Thomas and Joel Seidman, Russia— Democracy or Dictatorship? (New York, 1939).

the Axis powers on the eastern front, Stalin saw his opportunity to use Russian military and economic power, Russian prestige and propaganda, the tragic conditions resulting from a devastating war, and the willing cooperation of the Communist parties of the various nations, to incorporate many of the eastern European countries in the Soviet Republic or to bring them within the Russian sphere of influence. As a result, by 1947, the greater part of eastern and central Europe had come directly or indirectly under communist domination, and the key industries in most of these countries had passed from private to state ownership and control. In 1949, nearly all of China came under the domination of Chinese communist armies.

Except for Yugoslavia, the policies of these communist-controlled countries were, at the beginning of the 1950's, directed by the ruling group in Russia. In Yugoslavia, following World War II, increasing friction arose between Premier Tito and the Kremlin.

Late in 1947, the Russian communists had formed the Communist Information Bureau (the Cominform) as the supreme directive and centralizing organ of communism in the world-wide struggle for communist victory. The resolutions of the Cominform made it clear that the Russian ruling group would henceforth insist that Russian policies since 1917 must be regarded as the unquestionable model for communists in other countries to follow. Communist parties in all countries except Yugoslavia agreed to follow this model. Premier Tito demanded that Yugoslavia and other countries be given freedom to choose the type of tactics that seemed best adapted to them. On June 28, 1948, the conflict between Tito and the Cominform came to a head with the publication in the Czech Communist Party paper, *Rude Pravo*, of a communiqué from the Cominform expelling the Yugoslav party from that organization. The communiqué condemned Tito and his followers for regarding the peasants, not industrial workers, as the pillars of the state, for rushing into ill-considered legislation, for developing an unorthodox form of party structure, and—of greatest importance—for being "unfaithful" to the Soviet Union.

In the ensuing convention of the Yugoslav Communist Party in late July, the delegates refused to capitulate to Moscow, and supported Tito with "unanimous enthusiasm." Since then, Russia and her satellites have boycotted Yugoslavia and constantly threatened the country with attack. The Tito government, as a result, has become increasingly oriented toward the West. "Titoism," with its belief that Communist parties outside of Russia should be free from Russian domination, has spread to other countries. Fear of its further spread has resulted in numerous purges of leaders suspected of Titoist tendencies.

IX. Socialist Criticism of Communists

While these developments have been taking place in Russia and elsewhere under the Communist Party leadership, democratic socialists in Western countries have become increasingly critical of communist theory and tactics. Many socialists have maintained since the Russian revolution that communists did a great disservice to the world by their refusal in 1917 to join with the other socialist parties in Russia in forming a coalition socialist government. These socialists point out that in the elections to the Constituent Assembly, which Lenin and the Bolsheviks favored, 36,000,000 votes were cast, of which only 4,000,000 were polled by the bourgeois parties. Of the remainder, the Social Revolutionists and Social Democrats received 23,000,000; the Bolsheviks, 9,000,000. Kautsky maintained that if the Bolshevik Party had joined in forming the government with the other socialist parties, representing the overwhelming proportion of the voting population, "the Constituent Assembly would have carried out everything in the interests of labor that was at all realizable," and "Russia would have been spared the civil war with all its horrors, cruelties and destruction," while the population would have been "accorded the greatest possible measure of freedom."[67]

The coup d'état instigated by Lenin and the communists, lacking the active support of the great mass of the people, led inevitably to the terror and the continued dictatorship with its suppression of democratic rights and its tragic repercussions throughout the world.

Other socialists, in criticizing the communists and communism, have concentrated most of their attention on the tactics of the followers of Lenin in democratic countries. The Third International in its early years insisted that Communist parties in democratic countries discard democratic methods, denounce political democracy, preach the gospel of dictatorship, divide the working-class forces on the political and trade-union fields, and direct many of their sharpest attacks against labor and social democratic parties. By so doing, charge these critics, communists greatly weakened the labor and progressive movements of many European countries and prepared the way in Germany and other lands for the triumph of fascism. Democratic socialists likewise criticize communists for their "rule or ruin" tactics, their misrepresentation of the views of their opponents, and their belief that "the ends justify the means" and that all means are justifiable no matter how reprehensible as long as they promise to advance communists nearer to their goal.[68] Since World War II, democratic socialists have bitterly attacked the ruling group in communist Russia for its "aggressive imperialist policies."

[67] Karl Kautsky, *Social Democracy versus Communism* (New York, 1946), pp. 63-65.
[68] See Laidler, *op.cit.*, chap. 29.

X. Recent Socialist Developments

While the communists—taking advantage of the insecurity and inequalities of the capitalist system and the terrible havoc caused by the two World Wars—established themselves in the citadel of power in the vast stretches of Russia and later expanded their control over other peoples in Europe and Asia, many democratic socialists of central and western Europe were playing an increasingly important part in their respective countries. On the other hand, in Italy the Socialist Party was destroyed as a result of the Fascist coup d'état in 1922. And the social democratic movements of Germany and Austria were completely submerged by the accession to power of the German Nazis and the Austrian Fascists in the early thirties, not to emerge again until the defeat of the Axis powers toward the end of World War II.

Of the Labor and Socialist parties in Europe which continued their rise to power during and immediately after the interwar period, the British Labour Party was the most outstanding. During this period, the British movement, in fact, assumed the leadership of the world political forces making for democratic socialism, a place occupied before 1914 by the German social democracy.

The British Labour Party, which had made its first impress on British legislation during the eight-year period, 1906 to 1914, emerged from the war of 1914-1918 as "His Majesty's Chief Opposition," and formed minority Labour governments in 1924 and again in 1929. In the elections held in June 1945, immediately after the defeat of Germany, Labour surprised practically everyone, including itself, by electing 393 out of 640 members of the House of Commons. Never before in history, may it be said in passing, had a democratic socialist party in a major country elected to office an overwhelming majority of the national legislature.

The party, following the election, organized the government under the leadership of Prime Minister Clement Attlee. Within the next few years, it passed legislation in the domestic field which greatly strengthened and unified the social insurance system, provided for a National Health Service, liberalized the system of labor laws, inaugurated a nation-wide program for land utilization, town building, city planning, and rehousing, and provided for the nationalization of the Bank of England, the mines, inland transportation, civil aviation, cable and wireless, electric power, atomic energy, gas, and a large part of the steel industry. In the field of foreign relations, its chief departures from the former government were made in its decrees of independence to India, Burma, and Transjordan, in the granting of self-government to Ceylon, and in measures for increased political democracy and economic well-being among the colonies.

In its program of socialization, the Clement Attlee Labour government sought to proceed to a democratic socialist society in an orderly and gradual fashion; to provide reasonable compensation to private owners for the property purchased from them; to utilize extensively the public-corporation form of public ownership; to place the management of government industries under the control of boards on which various producer, consumer, and professional interests were directly or indirectly represented; to decentralize publicly controlled industry as much as was consistent with efficiency; and to retain and strengthen democratic freedom as the country was shifting its basis from a private profit-making to a socialized economy.

During the 1945 electoral campaign, the party maintained that its ultimate purpose was "the establishment of the socialist commonwealth of Great Britain—free, democratic, efficient, progressive, public-spirited, its material resources organized in the service of the British people." "However," it continued, "socialism cannot come overnight, as the product of a week-end revolution. The members of the Labour Party, like the British people, are practical-minded men and women." It maintained that there were basic industries ripe for public ownership, while others could be left to go on with their useful work. It later declared that its public ownership program, to be carried through during a five-year period in office, would bring into the public sector about twenty per cent of the industrial life of the nation. After five years, it would present a second program for the further extension of public controls. Meanwhile, it would establish "Working Committees," consisting of representatives of the employers, workers, and government, in certain industries for which there were no immediate nationalization plans, with a view to reducing waste and promoting efficiency.

In early 1950, Prime Minister Attlee dissolved his government and called for an election. In the ensuing campaign the Labour Party promised that, if reelected, besides proceeding with the nationalization of the steel industry, it would take steps to transfer beet sugar manufacture and sugar refining and the cement industry to public ownership; would socialize cold storage facilities; mutualize industrial insurance, and expand public controls and ownership in other spheres. The result was that Labour returned 315 of its members to Parliament, a decrease of 78, although the Labour vote increased by eleven per cent. The Conservatives won 297 seats, an increase of 78.

Following the election, the Labour Party decided to slow up its program of nationalization on account of the closeness of the voting strength in Parliament and of the need for insuring the successful operation of the industries already transferred to the public sector.

In the autumn of 1950, in preparation for the next election, the party issued a further statement, *Labour and the New Society*, setting forth the objectives of democratic socialism; praising the results already achieved by the nationalized industry; urging further public ownership where such seemed necessary to protect the public interest; declaring that consumers' cooperation had a big and expanding function to perform in production and distribution, but contending also that "private enterprise has a proper place in the economy." In regard to such enterprise, the statement added that the Labour government should "aid and encourage its efficiency and enterprise. But the community has the right to see to it that it works in the interest of the nation. Britain must never again be put in pawn to big business. Private owners must never be allowed to amass great concentrations of power." Throughout the manifesto, the party emphasized the fact that "the true purpose of society is to promote and protect the dignity and well-being of the individual."[69]

The Margate Conference of the Labour Party in October 1950 showed a distinct difference of opinion as to whether the Labour government should mark time or speed ahead on its nationalization program. The Conference ended with the moderate forces preserving a majority on the executive committee.

In Scandinavia, the Social Democratic Party, during the years between the two World Wars, was in control of the Danish government almost continuously from 1924 to 1940—for five of those years as a majority party. In Sweden and Norway, the social democrats were asked to head their respective governments in 1932; and from that time to World War II, socialist Premiers Hansson of Sweden and Nygaardsvold of Norway were leaders of these governments. In the late nineteen-forties and early nineteen-fifties all-socialist governments were in control of Denmark, Norway, and Sweden.

In France, Belgium, Switzerland, Finland, and Czechoslovakia, powerful socialist parties existed during the interwar period with socialist prime ministers occasionally serving as heads of the French and Belgian governments. In France, Léon Blum, the leading socialist, headed the Popular Front government in 1936 and again briefly in 1938. During his term of office, he carried out a social reform program providing for industrial conciliation, for the forty-hour week, holidays with pay, greater government control of the Bank of France, public control of certain munitions plants, a revised taxation system, price stabilization, an enlarged public works program, and the expansion of various social services—a program which indicated the extreme changes to which liberal nonsocialist parties working with socialists in a coalition government would agree.

During the two years following World War II, socialists were called upon to serve as president and prime minister of France, as prime minister of Belgium, and as president of Austria, though representing minority parties in their respective governments. In France, a program of public

[69] British Labour Party, *Labour and the New Society* (London, 1950), pp. 3, 23, and Pt. IV.

ownership of certain of the key industries was agreed upon by several of the progressive parties. In Czechoslovakia, a decree for the nationalization of all large industries was issued by a coalition government in which communists and socialists were prominently represented. However, in February 1948, Czechoslovakia was abruptly transformed, under pressure from Russia, into a so-called "people's democracy," a dictatorship of the Soviet approved type. The government was purged of all democratic socialist and other elements refusing to follow the communist line, and on April 28 new nationalization laws were passed by the purged parliament which affected ninety per cent of the country's industrial capacity. A new constitution based on the Soviet constitution was promulgated in May.

In Germany after World War II, Social Democratic parties with a program of socialization became important factors in the non-Russian zones, while socialists in the Russian zone were placed under almost irresistible pressure by the occupying Russian troops to form a so-called Socialist Unity Party controlled largely by communists. In Italy, the Socialist Party, which had furnished some of the leading figures in the postwar coalition government, split over the issue of the united front with communists.

During the years immediately before and after World War II, an increasing number of socialist economists have given much attention to the question of how to guarantee the maintenance of freedom under a socially planned economy. Specifically they have dealt with problems of price fixing under socialism, the maintenance of the free choice of the consumer and of the mechanism for guaranteeing full employment, and have endeavored to see to it that democratic techniques are incorporated in every phase of socialized industry. They have given much consideration also to the limits of public ownership and of voluntary consumers' and producers' cooperatives under socialism, and to the types of industry that can safely be left to private enterprise subject to controls that would duly protect the interests of consumers and workers.

With the British socialists, they have looked with increasing favor on the public corporation as an instrument for ensuring an efficient and flexible type of public ownership and on the need for decentralizing the control of public industries as much as is compatible with social efficiency. They have endeavored to relate the findings of social psychology, biology, and anthropology to human motivation, particularly in the field of industrial incentives, and as a means of bringing about socialism peacefully and democratically. They have shown increasing concern regarding how to bring about effective cooperation in the battle for a cooperative social order between industrial workers, "white-collar" workers, the agricultural population, and ethical and religious forces in the community.[70]

[70] Laidler, *op.cit.*, chap. 40, and pp. 729-32.

Socialists, since World War II, have likewise emphasized increasingly the need for international organization and action. They have played a prominent role, as has been indicated, in the United Nations, have encouraged the creation of machinery for the elimination of the economic and social causes of war, and have held a number of meetings looking toward the revival of the Socialist International. In 1947, they formed the Committee for International Socialist Conferences (the Comisco) to gather and distribute information and to call conferences to discuss problems of mutual interest to European socialists. Socialist émigrés from Russian satellite countries likewise organized a loose federation—the Socialist Union of Central-Eastern Europe.

While the Communist International was officially dissolved in 1943, democratic socialists, noting the rapid and almost instantaneous shifts in foreign policy on the part of communist parties throughout the world, following the shifts in Russian policy, have contended that the spirit of the Third International, if not the structure, is still alive in the Cominform (Communist Information Bureau), an organization ostensibly established for the purpose of exchanging information among the Communist parties of Europe. They themselves, though always opposed to any centrally controlled international of the type of the Comintern, have ever welcomed an international forum of socialists for the exchange of experiences and opinions and for closer personal contacts.

In the hundred years that have passed since the issuance of the *Communist Manifesto*, it is thus seen that the socialist and communist forces have grown from insignificant bands of underground revolutionists to the most potent forces in many of the governments of Europe. Today it would be untrue to say that the advocates of capitalism in Europe are nonexistent and that private enterprise is dead. It would be short of the truth to declare that the spirit of fascism and nazism had been fully destroyed. Nevertheless, the two most potent forces in Europe today are the communists, with their advocacy of totalitarian communism—which many socialists maintain is the antithesis of socialism[71]—and the democratic socialists and their sympathizers who favor the gradual socialization of basic industries, and who insist that this go hand in hand with the strengthening of democratic institutions. For to them democracy, freedom, and socialism are indivisible.

As everyone knows, these two movements are now engaged in a titanic struggle for the capture of the soul of Europe. On the outcome of that struggle will depend the future of European civilization and the future of the world.

[71] Kautsky, *Social Democracy versus Communism*, p. 90.

CHAPTER 3

The Religious Basis of Western Socialism

BY ALBERT T. MOLLEGEN

ALBERT T. MOLLEGEN, Professor of Christian
Ethics at the Protestant Episcopal Theological
Seminary, Alexandria, Virginia, is a New Testa-
ment scholar. A founder of the Fellowship of
Socialist Christians, he has published several
articles on social problems in relation to the
Christian tradition.

For bibliography in Volume 2 relevant to
Mr. Mollegen's essay, see especially PART III,
Topics 8, 9, and General Reading; also PART II,
Topics 13, and 1, 2, 4; PART I, General Reading
(section 1), and Topics 1, 2, 5, 7; PART V,
Topic 9.

I. American Socialism is Western Socialism

THE religious basis of American socialism is the religious basis of Western civilization. It is the thesis of this chapter that socialism in Western culture is ultimately derived from the Christian religion, as is almost every important conception of human society and almost every movement for social change in the Western tradition. Perhaps nazism is the only major exception since it is a neopagan religious movement consciously at enmity with Judaistic and Christian interpretations of existence as well as with the classical Greek tradition.

The relation of conceptions of society and of social movements to their religious basis is, of course, conditioned by all of the elements which constitute history. Biblical religion is dynamic by nature and imparts its dynamism to the culture which it influences, so that there is a continuous interaction between the specifically Christian tradition and the movements of culture which are influenced directly or indirectly by that tradition.

That American socialism is only a particular formation of Western culture and is rooted in the Christian religion is indicated by a quotation from the bibliographical guide prepared for students in the seminars out of which this volume grew: "In America as in Europe, socialism falls into two chief phases known, in Marxian terminology, as utopian and scientific socialism. According to Marxists, scientific socialism is Marxism or strongly influenced by Marxism. Utopian socialism (and to the Marxist all socialism not based on Marx is utopian) can be divided into two chief varieties, one marked by its religious communism, the other secular in nature. Chronologically, in the United States as in Europe, utopian socialism has for the most part preceded Marxian socialism, while religious utopianism tended to precede the secular varieties."[1]

The religious utopian, the secular utopian, and the scientific stages of socialism reflect in the socialist tradition three stages of Western cultural consciousness which are testified to in one way or another in almost every philosophy of history since the seventeenth century. In Comte, the three stages are generalized into a philosophy of history determined by the nature of the human mind and necessitating three successive stages in each branch of knowledge: the theological or fictitious state; the metaphysical or abstract state; the scientific or positive state. The Marxian and positivist versions of these three stages are but two interpretations of the historic fact that Western man placed the trust which he had once given to God, first in human reason and second in empirical science. A

[1] P. 1 of mimeographed material for General Reading, Second Conference Session, *Types of American Socialism*, 1946-1947 Conference, Special Program in American Civilization, Princeton University.

99

Christian culture was secularized and then mechanized in its consciousness of itself. Roughly, the sixteenth century was still Christian, the seventeenth and eighteenth centuries were humanistic in a Promethean sense,[2] and the nineteenth century was empiricist in predominant trends. Since men's interpretation of reality plays an important role in history, such interpretations were factors in the rise of natural-law equalitarian democracy and of technology, both of which confirmed and developed the trends of thought which produced them.

American socialism reproduces, therefore, the career of European socialism which itself is a part of the career of Western culture. Understood on such a scale all American socialism, from the earliest Christian sectarian communities such as the Shakers to the modern Socialist and Communist parties, has a Christian basis, although the conception of that basis and the relation to it is widely varied.

To disclose that basis, Biblical religion will have to be discussed in some detail, together with the outlook of classical antiquity which has interacted with the Biblical tradition to form new combinations of the two. This will be done with special reference to the conceptions of history, and of society and its goal, which appear later in American socialism in its religious utopian, secular utopian, and then Marxian forms.

II. The Christian Basis of Secular Utopianism

The earliest Christian church in Jerusalem has been called a socialistic community and, since much of Christian socialist thought and even Marxian thought has referred to the New Testament community, it will be a good place to begin our study. The sharing of physical goods in the first Christian congregations is an indubitable fact, but it was a part of a whole complex of ideas which belonged to the original and classical Christian experience and may not be divorced from that context without distortion. Several things must be understood in order to see clearly what was the character of this alleged socialism.

Of paramount importance is the New Testament conviction that the eschatological Kingdom of God has broken into human history and that its fullness is imminent. The phrase, Kingdom of God, means the sway of the personal God over human society and physical nature in such a way that God's will is done without hindrance, opposition, or imperfection. By the first century, this conception had undergone two major transformations, the first coming from the great preexilic prophets, Amos, Hosea, Micah, Isaiah, and Jeremiah with their forerunners, and the Second Coming

---

[2] "Bacon's task, it may be said, was to prove that natural science was Promethean and not Mephistophelean." Basil Willey, *The Seventeenth Century Background* (London, 1934), p. 33. The same author's *The Eighteenth Century Background* (New York, 1941), traces the development of secularism further.

from the Apocalyptic writers such as the authors of Daniel, Enoch, and IV Ezra.

Prior to the prophetic movement, God's reign and the national power and prosperity were almost identical. The prophets proclaimed that Israel and Judah stood under the divine judgment and would be destroyed because of their idolatry. This worship of false gods expressed itself in disobedience to God's moral commands and produced an unjust society. The prophets' struggle was at one and the same time a struggle to disclose the righteous character of God (theological warfare), to recover the true worship of God (liturgical reformation), to return to the republished moral commands of God (reformation of moral theology and conversion of the people) and to conform the order of society to God's will (political and economic change, sometimes instigating political revolution, particularly in the northern kingdom). Elijah, who became the symbol for all prophecy, struggled against the Baals, their prophets and their cultus, and also against the political and economic behavior and social structures which they sanctioned. Elijah's warfare on Mount Carmel was of one piece with his condemnation of Jezebel's oriental despotism and land policy and his sanction, through Elisha, of Jehu's revolution.[3]

Late Greek religion and philosophy might describe man's dilemma as caused by his rational soul being bound to his body and hence to the material universe, but Biblical religion has a radically different dualism from the mind-matter one. It is the dualism between God and his rebellious creatures.

The prophets spoke with a united voice. "The end is come upon my people Israel."[4] "Can the Ethiopian change his skin, or the leopard his spots? Then may ye also do good, that are taught to do evil."[5] Hebrew culture-religion would be destroyed with all of its social structures, and the Palestinian soil itself desolated. But the destructions of God were but the beginnings of his new creation. Those who were turning their lives (repenting) in response to the prophetic word were the true people of God, the remnant. This remnant would survive the coming catastrophe and become the foundation and pattern of the new religious nation which would appear after the return from the Babylonian exile.

The word of the transcendent and holy God, spoken by the prophets, proclaimed God's destruction and his re-creation. The prophetic word created the new people of God even as it doomed the old societies who identified themselves with God. The prophets were vindicated by history. The catastrophes came, the judgment of God fell; the prophetic word had been the foretaste of the divine activity in history.

But the prophesied good time on earth did not appear beyond the

[3] I Kings 18:20-19:21, I Kings 21, II Kings 9.
[4] Amos 8:2. [5] Jeremiah 13:23.

catastrophes. The exiles returned, prophetic religion was codified and made the basis of the reformation of society, yet the Kingdom tarried long. Instead of the perfect sway of God in history, Judaism came, and the struggle between God and his people began again on a new and higher level but with equal intensity.

The second great transformation of the Biblical idea of the Kingdom of God occurred with the Apocalyptic writers. On the negative side, their great new message faced the inevitability of sin (rebellion against God) both in the individual person and in the great continuous social structures and movements of human history. This was said mythologically in terms of the primordial fall of mankind and of the rule of the fallen angelic powers (principalities, thrones, dominions) over history. Both man and human society were distorted and moving toward destruction by reason of the separation from God which sin had caused. But the Apocalyptic writers had an unshakable faith. God, they maintained, would assert his full sway and vindicate those who remained faithful, taking them into his new age, a new heaven and a new earth. The Apocalyptists, however, were troubled by their solution. Who were the faithful and obedient? The profoundest of these writers, the author of IV Ezra, could not say with St. Paul that none was righteous by the Law for he had no justification by faith in Christ, nor could he say that many including himself were good enough to be vindicated. When he looked upward toward God, he despaired, he became the Publican of Jesus' parable.[6] When he looked outward toward the Gentile world and the "sinners" of his own people he was tempted to be self-righteous, the Pharisee of Jesus' parable.[7] But God would reign and that soon. The Kingdom of God was very near in time and its coming would abolish all rules inimical to God's, raise up the dead, and clothe the remnant with righteousness and incorruptible bodies. The physical universe would participate in this transfiguration. In some of the apocalyptic literature, God's agent in this inauguration of the everlasting Kingdom was a heavenly figure called by Enoch "the Son of Man."

The New Testament's good news is simply that Jesus is this Son of Man, that the final and perfect age has broken into history by the mighty action of God in Christ's coming, death, resurrection and outpouring of his Spirit. Christ is both the Word and the activity of God, the Word made flesh, who has overcome the barrier of sin between man and God and opened the way from earth to heaven from the heavenly side. This good news is expressed theologically by the Christian doctrines of the Incarnation, the Atonement, and the Holy Spirit.

[6] II Esdras 7:62-69; 9:36-37; Luke 18:9-14.
[7] II Esdras 7:20-24; 7:60-61; Luke 18:9-14. The Pharisee in the parable of Jesus did not have Ezra's sorrow for the damnation of the Gentiles and most of the Jews.

The New Testament conviction is that the eschatological Kingdom has begun to come in Christ and that the church's existence is a sure sign that history approaches its final judgment and consummation. This is the first principle of the New Testament mind. The second is that the Kingdom of Christ, the community where his Lordship is acknowledged in word and deed and where his Spirit is received, is a new creation. The response to Christ, faith, is trust, allegiance, obedience, fellowship with him as Lord. Faith in Christ is love of God who sent forth Christ. "We love him [God], because he first loved us [in Christ]."[8] God's act in Christ and the response evoked by it bring God and the faithful ones together so that his Spirit is communicated to and shared by them. The faithful are bound together as human persons by the same bond by which they are bound to God, the bond of the Spirit. The community of the Spirit, "the blessed company of all faithful people," is, therefore, the Body of Christ with his mission to proclaim the good news and to incorporate all who respond into the fellowship with God and with the faithful, which is possible only through Christ. "That which we have seen and heard declare we unto you also, that ye also may have fellowship with us! yea, and our fellowship is with the Father, and with his Son Jesus Christ." And this fellowship (commonness) is in material things because it is in the divine life. "But whoso hath this world's goods [livelihood], and beholdeth his brother [fellow Christian] in need, and shutteth up his compassion from him, how doth the love of God abide in him?"[9]

If that is a word from the Asia Minor churches at the turn of the first century, the same fellowship is promised in the Roman congregation about A.D. 70 as from Christ himself: "Verily I say unto you, There is no man that hath left house, or brethren, or sisters, or mother, or father, or children, or lands, for my sake, and for the gospel's sake, but he shall receive a hundredfold now in this time, houses, and brethren, and sisters, and mothers, and children, and lands, with persecutions; and in the age which is coming everlasting life."[10] Earlier, St. Paul was zealous to see that his Gentile churches contributed to "the saints" in Jerusalem but his recommendation shows clearly that it is a voluntary weekly gift to a Christian community chest that he means.[11] The saints in Jerusalem were in need partially because they had liquidated their real estate for their community fund.[12] Their sharing exhausted their real goods because of the evangelical fervor, the family responsibility for each member, and the sense of an imminent end of "this age," which characterized their common life. That the tradition has characterized Ananias as a liar shows the voluntary nature of the sharing of real goods, although no doubt there

8 I John 4:19.
10 Mark 10:29.
12 Acts 4:32-5:11.

9 I John 1:3, I John 3:17.
11 I Corinthians 16:1-4.

was the pressure of social censure and social approval working to effect every one's participation.

This so-called socialism is really, therefore, the voluntary sharing of a community which, through Christ and by his Spirit, has begun to participate in the eschatological age of which he is the Lord. This age is transcendent in quality, imminent in time and present in first installment; that is, as an "earnest."

In relation to the world around it, the early church was a sect but it was a remnant called out of the world which was passing away only because it was to inherit the divinely transformed world which was to come. The early church was an eschatological community with the hope of imminent cosmic inheritance. "Know ye not that the saints shall judge the world?" said St. Paul to the "not many wise after the flesh, not many mighty, not many noble" who were the Christians at Corinth.[13]

In Hellenic culture another and different kind of universal commonalty was appearing. The community bond was not the Spirit of the Son of God who became incarnate, but the reason of man which found embodiment a provincial, restricting, and corrupting thing. The rational soul transcended particularity and contemplated the immaterial world of ideas or the final cause of the world. As Diogenes Laertius, perhaps with a later editor's note, says, there is an attempt of reason to rise above the particularity even of family in varied schools of Greek philosophy. "It is also their doctrine that amongst the wise there should be a community of wives with free choice of partners, as Zeno says in his *Republic* and Chrysippus in his treatise *On Government* (and not only they, but also Diogenes the Cynic and Plato). Under such circumstances we shall feel paternal affection for all the children alike, and there will be an end of the jealousies arising from adultery."[14]

In Plato's *Republic*, the philosopher-rulers alone are forbidden to own property. "The purpose is the same as that of the still more emphatic prohibition of family life, the elimination of the conflict between public duty and personal interest. . . . It is plain that the governing classes to whom the regulations are meant to apply are expected to find no gratification for the sexual impulses except on the solemn occasions when they are called on to beget offspring for the State. The extension of the duties of the guardian to both sexes of itself carries the consequence that these occasions arise only at long intervals. . . ."[15]

Zeller says of the Stoics that, while they paid great attention to the state and to domestic life in their writings, this was a secondary level of

[13] I Corinthians 6:2 and 1:26.
[14] *Diogenes Laertius*, VII, 131 (tr. by R. D. Hicks; Loeb Classical Library), Vol. II, p. 235.
[15] A. E. Taylor, *Plato* (New York, 1936), pp. 277-78.

their rational ethic. "The ideal of the Stoics, however, was not realized in any one of the existing forms of government, but in that polity of the wise which Zeno described, undoubtedly when a Cynic, but which was fully set forth by Chrysippus—a state without marriage, or family, or temples, or courts, or public offices or coins—a state not in hostility with any other state, because all differences of nationality have been lost in a common brotherhood of all men."[16] Zeller argues that, when Epictetus dissuades men from marriage and parenthood, he is not moved only by the practical consideration that society is not composed solely of "wise men" but by his deep conviction that responsibility for the state and the family confine and limit the wise man's achievement of the good life.[17] This is true also of Seneca's philosophy. Reason, as the Stoics understood it, rose above all particularities such as sexual differentiation, family ties and loyalties, and historically formed cultures. The transcendent rational world, which the wise man entered by his reason's rapport with the rational form of nature, was peopled only by the few who achieved an absolute quieting of the passions ($\dot{a}\pi\acute{a}\theta\epsilon\iota a$) by reason. In the existing world, the Stoic was a lonely figure seeking complete self-sufficiency and indifference to external good or ill fortune. This imperturbability ($\dot{a}\tau a\rho a\xi\acute{\iota}a$) seemed better accomplished in withdrawal from responsibility to society and its institutions. While it is true that modern democracy inherits its equalitarianism, derived from the Natural Law, from the Stoics, it is also apparent that this modern natural equality is held with a sense of responsibility to society which is radically different from that of the ancient Greeks.

It is also true that the equalitarianism of the Stoics was set in a different understanding of history from that which informs the modern Western consciousness. Classical Greek culture had what Tillich calls "the non-historical interpretation of history."[18] "In Greek philosophy, 'nature' is a rational category, designating everything as far as it exists by growth ($\phi\acute{v}\sigma\epsilon\iota$) or by essential necessity, not artificially ($\theta\acute{\epsilon}\sigma\epsilon\iota$) or by arbitrary thinking and acting."[19] "The great Greek historiography shows the genesis, acme, and decay of cities and nations."[20] Fate, fortune, and providence, therefore, tend to become one, for as Herodotus says, "God loves to cut short everything that overtops its kind. In this way, a great army is destroyed by a small army in certain circumstances—as, for instance, when God in his envy sends down panic upon them or thunder. Then

---

[16] E. Zeller, *The Stoics, Epicureans and Skeptics* (London, 1870), pp. 303-4.
[17] *Ibid.*, p. 306.
[18] Paul Tillich, *The Protestant Era* (Chicago, 1948), p. 16.
[19] *Ibid.*, p. 18.
[20] *Loc.cit.*

they perish, and their last state is unworthy of their first. God suffers no one to be proud except himself."[21]

Christian fellowship and Greek rational justice flowed together in the three centuries between the New Testament and Augustine, who was the father of the West's "medieval synthesis." The synthesis was a compound of tensions. First, the final eschatological age of Christianity, the Kingdom of God in its full glory, was no longer expected in a near future but was understood to be related to history somewhat in the same way as Plato's realm of ideal forms was related to material and human existence. The Kingdom's consummation, the second advent of Christ and his absolute reign, was indefinitely postponed, and the downward movement of God in Christ, the Incarnation and Atonement, was understood to be effective chiefly in elevating the faithful to the transcendent Kingdom. Second, by identification of the true church with the millennium of the Book of Revelation the highest historical possibility was realized here on earth without revolutionary changes in social structure.[22] History, for Augustine, reached its zenith in the Catholic Church and awaited the second advent of Christ with no better stage of history expected except the purification of the church and the quieting of the environing world. Third, Augustine's was the first great and powerful theology to undergird social responsibility with the mandate of Christian ethics and the motivation of Christian love of God. The City of God here in its pilgrimage uses the peace which comes of the earthly city's precarious and relative justice so that the Christian must seek to further that peace. The head of a family has his troubles in his household, the judge in the city, and the emperor in the Empire and the world. But they must wield power "because it would be worse if the bad should get all the sovereignty, and so overrule the good, therefore in that respect, the honest men may esteem their own sovereignty a felicity."[23]

For Augustine, Stoic rationalism gives a true picture of the pre-Fall world. Private property, slavery, imperialism, the state—indeed all coercion and inequality—flow from the Fall of Man and from the divine remedy which quiets the strife of the fallen world. Sin has disrupted the harmony of God's original creation but the authority of men over men with legalized coercion is God's ordering by which the original justice and peace of innocent society are precariously approximated. But above this responsible citizenship is the heavenly life which seeks the vision of God beyond all particular and material existence. Celibacy, poverty, and obedience are the normative marks of the community which is above the

[21] *Greek Historical Thought* (tr., with an intro. by Arnold J. Toynbee; New York, 1924), p. 129.
[22] *The City of God*, xx, 6-13.
[23] *Ibid.*, iv, 15 (John Healey translation).

earthly community. Social responsibility is transcended in the monastic orders, which are the best expression in history of the City of God. Augustine, and indeed all of medievalism, lives ideally in the monastery and seeks the mystical transcendence of this world which is the vision of God. This is the Kingdom of Christ in so much as it is achievable before death. The religious orders are compounded from the fellowship of the New Testament sect, which is above the world as it is within the world, and from the Greek contemplative philosopher and mystic who rises above the particularity and materiality of existence by reflection and religious vision. Their celibacy as a higher way of Christian living—not as a special discipline required by a special service, as it tends to become in the mendicant orders and later—derives from the Greeks as does their goal, *visio Dei*. Their community of property, which is a renunciation of property, is more Hellenic than New Testament in conception.

For Augustine—and the Middle Ages—there was also a secondary level of the City of God here on earth. The church was realized best in the religious orders, but it was composed also of those who were not able to obey the counsels of perfection but could only obey the precepts. The governing of society, the Christianizing of family, state, culture, and the economic order is carried on by them.

This dual ethic of the counsels and the precepts, and this realization of eschatology in the monastic and nonmonastic church, was threatened and broken through in the twelfth and thirteenth centuries. Bernard of Clairvaux, Dominic, and Francis of Assisi, revived the ascetical life but threw its zeal outward into the re-creation of the church and of the common people. Bernard was the most powerful Christian figure in the West and the mendicant orders carried their devotion and piety to the masses, with whom they lived.

The turn of the twelfth century becomes a turning point in Western consciousness. The Christianization of the pagan, begun with St. Paul, reached maturity so that new possibilities could appear. Francis of Assisi gave almost perfect articulation to this maturity of Catholic man. For Francis, all of God's creatures, human, animal, and inanimate, were caught up by God's love into one great community with their Redeemer and with one another. He preached to the birds, was brother to Sun, had Moon for sister as well as "our sister, the death of the body."[24] Catholic man was son of God by adoption and grace and akin to wind, air, and cloud, water, fire, and earth. Without a touch of pantheism, Francis sang of, and with, the harmony of creation and its adoration of its Creator. Greek *nature* ($\phi \upsilon \sigma \iota \varsigma$) had been redeemed on all its levels, and thirteenth-century man saw nature as it had never been seen before. For

[24] "The Canticle of the Sun," translated by Matthew Arnold, *Essays in Criticism, First Series* (London, 1895), pp. 212-13.

the first time in human history a culture was permeated with the Christian view of, and love of, nature. This permeation launched the Christian Renaissance and is the indispensable presupposition of the modern arts and empirical sciences. It was not an accident that Cimabue and Giotto created great frescoes in the Church of St. Francis in Assisi and played an important role in the beginnings of naturalistic painting; nor was it a chance happening that the phrase "experimental science" should come prematurely from a Franciscan friar, Roger Bacon, a contemporary of St. Thomas Aquinas. Again it was no accident that it was Joachim of Floris, a Cistercian abbot, who broke through the Augustinian identification of the millennium with the church and expected a new and third age of the Holy Spirit to begin in A.D. 1260. This new age was to be without hierarchies, ecclesiastical or secular. It was to be contemplative, the mendicant monks being normative for its life. Still again it was no accident that it was Franciscan *Spirituales* who spread the Joachimite movement, criticizing the ecclesiastical institutions from the standpoint of a divinely created but historically possible and imminent age. The monastic community of Augustine's City of God became dynamically missionary with Francis, and with the Joachimites the Franciscan life became normative for a new historical age.

The thirteenth century is the time of modern man's birth. Securely grounded in God's life by the divine descent to man in Christ and the reconciliation of the world to God effected by Christ's death, Western man was refashioned until his consciousness expressed his freedom from nature's cycle of birth and death. Mature Catholic man stood, in God, above nature and could portray it as Raphael does. Set by God as master of nature in himself and in the subhuman world, Western man could begin to observe nature as an object. The chief difference of modern empiricism from such empiricism as the classical Greek world possessed— in Aristotle, for instance—lies in the modern transcendence of nature inwardly and the return to nature as an object outwardly. This is a necessary, although by no means the only necessary, precondition for modern empirical science and the resultant technology. But more than this, the victory over natural decay and death in the human spirit delivered the conception of history from nature's cycles, and Western man entered again with hope not only into expectation of the final age to come, but also into the Christian Apocalypse's expectation of an historical good time which would replace the medieval period. This is the necessary precondition of the idea of historical progress toward an utopian goal which began to characterize Western culture from the middle of the eighteenth century onward. Describing Turgot's goal of history, Karl Löwith writes:

"This secular terminal or *eschaton* is a religious respect for personal liberty and labor; inviolability of the right of property; equal justice for everyone; multiplication of the means of subsistence; increase of riches; and augmentation of enjoyments, enlightenment, and all means to happiness. Who does not recognize in these once so novel standards of Turgot, Condorcet and Comte the traditional values of the American citizen, at least up to the depression of the thirties? It took two hundred years for the faith in increase, augmentation, and multiplication to become as doubtful as the popular identification of bigger with better."[25]

The Utopia which had begun as a no-*place* in the sixteenth century with Thomas More became for the eighteenth century a real goal in *time*. The secularization of modern man, begun in the seventeenth century, continued Christianity's optimism, and its basic ideas of man, society, and history were rationalized and transformed by the disappearance of the dimension in which the Christian doctrines of Creation, Sin, Death, Incarnation, Atonement, Church, and Last Things had set all existence.

III. The Christian Basis of Scientific Socialism

It was only in such a context that the Marxian faith could arise. "Recent writers have detected beneath the Hegelianism of Marx's triadic pattern of history (i.e., primitive communism, the class struggle, and communist society), the older apocalyptic of the Hebrew prophets and of the New Testament in which also there is a Fall and in which the present evil age issues in a catastrophe, which will usher in the Messianic age."[26]

Marx was a Jewish Christian Apocalyptist in spirit, a Hegelian in methodological thinking, and an empiricist in gathering data for his philosophy of history. He inverted the Hegelian dialectic so that Spirit does not move history, but changing economic relations which move history create the expressions of Spirit. All cultural and religious phenomena are ideologies which justify the class relationships of a given period of history. Hegel rationalized divine providence and Marx materialized Hegel's rationalization.

The Christian basis of Marxism can be seen by a simple comparison of the framework of Christian and Marxian dogma. There is a parallelism of which Marx himself was partially aware. For Marx and Engels, the Edenic period was the primitive communism of human society as it emerged from the animal world. The Fall of man came when the natural division of labor created "more than was necessary for its mere main-

---

[25] Karl Löwith, *Meaning in History* (Chicago, 1949), p. 101.
[26] Mary Frances Thelen, *Man as Sinner* (New York, 1946), p. 34. Dr. Thelen continues with a brilliant comparison of Marxian and Christian mythology similar to the one offered here.

tenance"[27] so that additional labor could be supported. Labor then acquired value and was supplied by making slaves of war captives. The Marxian Fall is like the Hegelian Fall, however, in that it is also a rise. "Without slavery, no Greek State, no Greek art and science; without slavery, no Roman Empire. But without Hellenism and the Roman Empire as a basis, also no modern Europe."[28]

The class struggle which results from this Fall is guided by an immanent dialectical principle graspable by positive science. This is the Marxian equivalent for Providence, materializing Hegel's *Geist*. History is brought to its final crisis by the breakdown of capitalist distribution and the unemployment and misery of increasing numbers of proletarians. In the fullness of time, Marx grasps the true meaning of history, sees and proclaims the proletariat's election to be the messianic people. This true and prophetic word creates in the proletariat a self-consciousness of its role so that it organizes and revolts. This catastrophe inaugurates the dictatorship of the proletariat which is the Marxian substitute for the Apocalypse's millennial reign of the martyred saints with Christ and for the Augustinian church.[29] When the dictatorship of the proletariat has socialized the economy, educated the people, and universalized the revolution, the state as a coercive institution withers away; that is, it becomes purely administrative and without coercion. This is a gradual process, the exact method and time of which is unforeseeable at the present. The final stage of communism, however, is as much a certainty for the Marxian as the eschatological Kingdom of God is a certainty for Christians.

Christians are certain by faith. Communists insist that they *know*. After the dictatorship has abolished classes, state coercion is not necessary to deal with individual excesses because such excesses will be taken care of by "the armed people itself, as simply and as readily as any crowd of civilised people, even in modern society, parts a pair of combatants."[30] Of the final stage, Lenin writes, "we know that the fundamental social cause of excesses which consist in violating the rules of social life is the exploitation of the masses, their want and their poverty. With the removal of this chief cause, excesses will inevitably begin to 'wither away.' We do not know how quickly and in what succession, but we know that they will wither away. With their withering away, the State will also *wither away*."[31] This certainty, of course, is thought to be derived from scientific understanding of society. "We are not Utopians," declares Lenin in the same paragraph.

[27] Friedrich Engels, *Anti-Dühring*, quoted in Emile Burns, ed., *Handbook of Marxism* (New York, 1935), p. 274.
[28] *Loc.cit.*
[29] The Book of Revelation 20:4, and *The City of God*, xx, 6-13.
[30] Lenin, *The State and Revolution*, quoted in Burns, *op.cit.*, p. 747.
[31] *Loc.cit.*

The religious character of this whole outlook is patently clear. It is an incredibly naive faith which unconsciously presupposes the whole Christian world view but retains only the formal structure of Christianity, accepts the utopian view of man and of historical progress, and cures man's malady by revolution, socialism, education, and material abundance.

Only two more things need to be said in general about the religious quality of Marxian socialism.

First, the faith of the orthodox communist includes an uncriticized substitute for the Christian article of faith, "I believe in the Holy Catholic Church." Since 1917, the U.S.S.R. has been regarded as the historical embodiment of the eschatological goal, "the only fatherland of the international proletariat, the principal bulwark of its achievements and the most important factor for its international emancipation."[32] In the face of the threatening Armageddon, "the struggle of the world bourgeoisie against the Soviet Russian Republic" (Lenin's language), "the international proletariat must on its part facilitate the success of the work of socialist construction in the U.S.S.R., and defend it against the attacks of the capitalist Powers by all the means in its power."[33]

This attitude toward "the fatherland" is the simple key to the right-about-faces of the Communist Party in the United States during the period of the 1930's and 1940's. And as this fact became clearer and clearer, it alienated more and more of those Americans whose sympathy for communism had a Judeo-Christian religious basis. Increasingly such sympathizers became all too aware that the policy of the American Communist Party had no direct connection with the need for social justice in this country, a need which they themselves had felt in accordance with the Sermon on the Mount or other Biblical admonitions. Instead, it became obvious that party policy was dictated from Soviet Russia on the basis of sheer expediency and in complete harmony with the prevailing Russian policy of the moment. Thus, when nazism threatened Russia, antinazism and American intervention was the policy both of the Communist Party and of the communists within the popular front movements. Before the Nazi-Soviet nonaggression pact, the immediate program was repeal or drastic amendment of the United States' Neutrality Act, all possible aid to the victim of aggression, and a complete embargo on the aggressor. After the nonaggression pact of 1939, when the American League for Peace and Democracy—a Popular Front organization composed of communist and noncommunist anti-Nazis and interventionists—applied this policy (of embargoing the aggressor and helping the victim) to the Soviet invasion of Finland, the League dissolved overnight and American Peace Mobilization soon appeared. When the war came the American

[32] Communist International Programme (1928), as quoted in Burns, op.cit., p. 1022.
[33] Loc.cit.

Communist Party in concert with the other Communist parties throughout the world proclaimed it an imperialist war originating "in the very structure of the capitalist system."[34] "Browder, in May 1941, went so far as to say, 'The new Roosevelt course is essentially for America the same direction which Hitler gave for Germany in 1933.' "[35] When the U.S.S.R. was invaded, the somersault was reversed and "the Browder policy" of unqualified cooperation with every force allied with Russia was put into effect. But by July 1945, the triple reversing somersault was complete and the groundwork was laid for the recent declarations which indicate that the American Communist Party is again obedient to the International Programme of 1928 and "inspired" to pursue the original policy "to fight with all the means in their power for the land of the proletarian dictatorship, in the event of an imperialist attack thereupon."[36]

The second and final observation about the communist relation to Christianity is that the religious idolatry of communism gives it the peculiar quality of ruthlessness which has alienated Christians, socialists, liberals, and the masses of Europe. The self-deification of the Communist Party probably exceeds any pretensions ever made by any historical group for it claims infallibility for its judgments in every realm of human life. Its interpretations of historical events, art expressions, and scientific knowledge brook no differing opinions, and wherever the party has the power its interpretations are rigorously enforced and "revisionists" or "deviationists" are liquidated.

Orthodox communism took organized form in the United States in 1919. Marxism had arrived in the middle of the nineteenth century. It was the last of the major types of socialism to take root in this country. Its relationship to its Christian basis is more remote than that of any other type of socialism in America, since in it the secularization of the Biblical view has proceeded so far as to destroy almost every vestige of its Christian substance.

IV. The Christian Basis of Sectarian Communism

At the opposite extreme from American orthodox Marxian communism are the expressedly Christian sectarian communities, one of the oldest of which is "The United Society of Believers in Christ's Second Appearing" or "The Millennial Church," popularly called "the Shakers." Schismatic offshoot from the English Quakers, a group of eight Shakers led by Ann Lee emigrated to New York state in 1774 and founded a colony. The movement had some missionary success in the early nineteenth-century Christian revivalist areas and created fifteen societies in nine states. While

[34] W. Z. Foster, *What's What about the War*, a pamphlet quoted by Martin Ebon, *World Communism Today* (New York, 1948), p. 285.
[35] Ebon, *op.cit.*, p. 286.   [36] Burns, *op.cit.*, p. 1023.

it is undoubtedly true that Ann Lee's personal attitude toward sex marked the movement with its celibate attitude, it is also true that it seems to have been influenced by the mystical pietism which in Germany stems from the impact of the medieval ideal, and especially of the mendicant orders, on the simple common people of thirteenth-century Europe. The Shakers, and such German-American communities as the Rappites and the Society of Separatists at Zoar, have a remarkable similarity of views on sex, marriage, and property, although these views are applied with differing degrees of rigor. For Ann Lee, sexual lust was the root of sin, and celibacy an absolute condition for following Christ. God was thought to include both the male and female principles so that Adam, being made in the image of God, was androgynous as were the original humans in the myth told by Aristophanes in *The Symposium*.

All Greek rationalism from Plato to the great modern Eastern Orthodox thinker, Berdyaev, is haunted by the effort to transcend the particularity which in Biblical religion is accepted as a divinely willed creaturehood, the limits of which only sin oversteps. This attempt to overcome the particularity of sexuality is often combined with the attempt to overcome the particularity of private property. Early Christian monasticism combined these two and required celibacy and poverty. Under the influence of the Biblical idea of fellowship there was a movement from the anchoritic ideal of the late third century (St. Anthony) to the community of common worship and common labor of St. Basil's monastery at Caesarea (ca. A.D. 370). Basil had seen that "the hermit has only one aim, to be self-sufficient; and this is plainly opposed to the law of love," so that "the monk ought to labor with his hands,—tend the sick, wash the feet of the saints, give pains to hospitality and brotherly love."[37] As we have seen, the mendicant orders moved outward in missionary love in the thirteenth century. The Dominicans, however, arose out of a conscious effort to discipline the great movements of lay people devoted to the monastic ideal, movements which began as early as 1090 in Germany and appeared in various forms. Often a lay group practicing community of goods settled near a monastery to become an auxiliary to the monastic community. Heretical versions of this movement such as the Cathari, the Waldenses, and the so-called Brethren of the Free Spirit, became very powerful. The Biblical and the Classical traditions, mingling as the basis of religious experience, produce almost infinite variations of doctrine and practice, some of which are extremely aberrational from the standpoint of orthodox Christianity or common sense naturalism. The late eighteenth- and early nineteenth-century religious socialistic communities in America belonged to this development and arose chiefly among groups

[37] Quoted by K. E. Kirk, *The Vision of God* (New York, 1932), pp. 265-66.

which, stirred by the currents of Protestantism and the Renaissance, were undisciplined by education in any of the normative Christian or humanist traditions.

The Shakers, Rappites, and Zoar Separatists are representative of apocalyptic sectarian communism. This is their Biblical aspect. Their communities are separated from the world with no expectation of solving the problems of the world. They expect the final end of the world in a not too distant future. The Shakers, for instance, seem to have derived their popular name from their interpretation of the shaking of their bodies by the Spirit's incoming as presaging signs of the eschatological shaking of the world which marked the Biblical description of the end. Ann Lee, the second and female incarnation of Christ, inaugurated the millennial life which is lived out in their communities so that they were also known as the Millennial Church. While they accepted the state's order and justice and obeyed it within limits, they gave no active support to it nor did they strive to improve it. They were separatists.

V. The Calvinist and Utopian Basis of Modern Christian Socialism

The perfectionism of the sectarian groups differed greatly from that of the Dartmouth graduate, J. H. Noyes, who founded "The Perfectionist Community of Oneida." As Parrington says, Noyes was a recrudescence of "the old millennial spirits, the Diggers and Levelers."[38] He manifested even less understanding of political power than did Winstanley in his appeals to Parliament and Cromwell, for in a letter to William Lloyd Garrison in 1837 Noyes renounced all allegiance to the government of the United States and asserted "the title of Jesus Christ to the throne of the World." He wrote: "I have renounced active co-operation with the oppressor [i.e., the U.S. government] on whose territories I live; now I would find a way to put an end to his oppression. . . . I cannot attempt to reform him, because I am forbidden to 'cast pearls before swine.' I must therefore either consent to remain a slave till God removes the tyrant, or I must commence war upon him, by a declaration of independence and other weapons suitable to the character of a son of God. . . . *My hope of the millennium begins where Dr. Beecher's expires*—viz., AT THE OVERTHROW OF THIS NATION."[39]

Oneida, as the first fruits of this perfectionism, as the example of, and the missionary base for, a radical revolution by religious and moral suasion, was Noyes's weapon. The rational character of his utopia reproduced in his communities the life of Plato's philosopher-rulers. Marriage was group

[38] Vernon L. Parrington, *Main Currents in American Thought* (New York, 1930), II, p. 343.
[39] *Ibid.*, pp. 343-44.

marriage with no special relationship between one man and one woman. Cohabitation was absolutely voluntary, without preliminary courtship, and requestable only through a third person. Children were reared in a community nursery and the parents neither had special rights to them nor showed special interest in them. They were the community's children. Administered with Yankee shrewdness, the communism of farming and industry was successful until, in 1880, the Oneida Community became a capitalist company, largely as a result of public pressure.

Christian asceticism in Noyes came from the Calvinist stream but reason's transcendence over particularity determines both the nature of this asceticism and the ordering of his community. Furthermore, his ideal community is not created by an apocalyptic conception of history so that it is understood to be both a prototype of, and an instrument for, universal realization. Noyes, therefore, in socialist history symbolizes the turning of classical Reformation theology into religious idealism. This fact can be elaborated briefly by saying that Luther had destroyed for subsequent Protestantism the Catholic dual ethic of the counsels of perfection for "the religious" and the precepts for the nonmonastic life in the world. Luther's restudy of the Bible led him to a new conception of the perfection commanded in the Sermon on the Mount. The love required by Jesus was impossible of achievement but the command was for all and not for those especially called to be "religious." Luther understood that God called men into the Christian life in the orders of creation, the family, the state, the social structures, etc. The divine calling (summons to faith in Christ) is answered by man in his place as father, magistrate, serf, etc. The divine calling gives divine meaning to the secular calling, *vocatio* gives meaning to vocation. Lutheranism tended, therefore, to an inward responsibility to the absolute love of Christ, which would produce despair except for the daily forgiveness of sins, which is received by faith. Life under God is intolerable except by faith alone. By faith alone is there an entrance into the divine justification of man through Christ. The outer man, however, lived groaningly in responsibility to the ordinances of life, since it is only through these ordinances that we may love one another. While the natural structures of society, the orders, are secular they are divinely ordained and are the external channels through which love is expressed. Over them the state presides as the divinely appointed guardian of order and justice. There are many passages in Luther which express this:

"Although man in his soul is sufficiently justified by faith, and has all that he ought to have, excepting that the same faith must increase into that life, yet he still remains in this bodily life upon earth, and must rule his own body, and mix with men. This is where works begin: here he must not be idle, the body must be exercised with fasting and prayer, with toil and labor, and with all moderate discipline, that it may become obedient, and conform to the inward man, and to faith. . . . However much the work of Christ was needed and has served to produce piety or salvation, so also are His other works, and the works of Christians, needed by them for salvation, since they are all services rendered freely for the good of others. . . . In like manner St. Paul, in Romans xiii and Titus iii, exhorts Christians that they should be subject to the authority of this world, not that this will make them religious, but in order that in so doing they may freely serve others, and the Government, by doing their will in love and freedom."[40]

It is easy to see that Lutheran Christianity has no tendency to social radicalism. For Luther the majesty of God's sovereignty invades human life primarily in the humility of God's Son. Christianity centers in the broken man on the Cross saving man from sin.

For Calvin, however, God's sovereignty itself is the center of the faith and the Cross is the divine strategy for setting the lives of the faithful consciously within this sovereignty's invasion of history. As Troeltsch says of Calvin, "the opposition between the legal order [of society] and its spirit of punishment and authority, its connection with the struggle for existence against the purely voluntary order of love, has been quite lost. The legal order is solely a useful member appointed by God in the up-building of rational society as already in the Old Testament. . . . The Sermon on the Mount is to be understood in the light of the Old Testament as an expression of the unchangeableness of God; Christ has added nothing to it and altered nothing, but since He has not opposed the social and legal order of the Old Testament He has confirmed it."[41]

Protestantism is Biblical. It stems from the Hebrew rather than the classical Greek tradition. It knows no dual ethic of the counsels and the precepts. But Luther knows of a contradiction between love on the one hand and the positive law of coercive power of society on the other hand. This is not a contradiction to Calvin, for whom love may use positive law and coercive power as its expressions. Calvin could not have said with Luther:

"God's Kingdom is a kingdom of grace and mercy and not a kingdom of wrath or of punishment. For it means nothing but forgiveness and protection, loving and serving, doing good, having peace and joy, etc. But the kingdom of this world is a kingdom of wrath. In this kingdom there is nothing but punishment and resistance, judgment and condemnation in order to force the evil and to protect the good. Therefore also this kingdom possesses and wields the sword. . . . The texts which speak of

[40] Ernst Troeltsch, *The Social Teachings of the Christian Churches* (tr. by Olive Wyon; New York, 1931), II, pp. 837-38.
[41] *Ibid.*, p. 888.

mercy belong to the Kingdom of God and to Christians, they do not apply to the secular law. For a Christian must not only be merciful, but he must also suffer all manner of evil, etc. But the Kingdom of this world, which is simply the servant of the Divine wrath over evil men and precursor of hell and of eternal death, . . . must not be merciful but severe."[42]

In Calvinism, Christians, standing within God's Kingdom and power, sought, without fusing church and state or controlling state by church, to bring this world under the divine sovereignty to the highest possible degree. Troeltsch rightly calls this Calvinism a kind of Christian socialism:

"Choisy, in particular, brings out the character of a 'Christian Socialism,' the united care for eternal well-being, and the moral correctness of each individual exercised by the authority of the Church and State, the common responsibility of the community for each member, the social reform and philanthropy which was carried out down to the smallest detail. . . . This Socialism is thoroughly anti-Communist, but everywhere it makes the community responsible for the individual member, and in certain instances it requires the greatest sacrifices of public and private means."[43]

There is no necessary reason for Calvinism to continue its original conservatism. Everything depends upon the Christian judgment about what social measures conform to the will of God and are possible in a particular place and time. This judgment as to possibility is deeply affected by the theological viewpoint, but it is also affected by sociological and historical knowledge and by the changes made in "the possible" by changes in society itself.

These facts make it clear why countries which were deeply influenced by Calvinism have shown the greatest social development and the greatest stamina in surviving as democracies,[44] although there are, of course, many other factors in the progress and strength of these areas of Western culture.

It was this Calvinist socialism out of which came that version of Christianity which is popularly called in America the Social Gospel. From it also there came the various forms of specific Christian socialism where *socialism* is used in the modern sense of collective ownership and operation of "the means of production." As H. Richard Niebuhr has shown, the immediate forerunners of the Social Gospel were evangelicals, and Washington Gladden, "the father of the social gospel," was nourished by the evangelical tradition.[45] Its original form is still most widely held among Methodists.

[42] *Ibid.*, p. 867.
[43] *Ibid.*, p. 903.
[44] John Baillie in *What Is Christian Civilization?* (New York, 1945) develops this point.
[45] H. Richard Niebuhr, *The Kingdom of God in America* (New York, 1937), p. 161.

VI. Secular Utopian Socialism

The nineteenth century confronted American Christianity with an active socialist movement which was completely secular in character. This socialism was imported from Europe and had a Christian basis, as we have seen, but that basis is hidden in the radically new charge of meaning which the word *nature* bears.

"In the 'historical' sense Nature means 'things as they now are or have become,' *natura naturata*; in the other ('philosophical') sense, 'things as they may become,' *natura naturans*," writes Basil Willey, and goes on to show further confusions. *Nature* may mean primitive and uncorrupted lack of artificiality or the perfected actualization of capacities. Nature may be looked at as static or as dynamic, i.e., actualizing its potentialities. In Rousseau both conceptions are held. "Thus 'philosophical' naturalism becomes 'historical' (in quite another sense) if, in your view of 'what things might become,' you contemplate a return to a lost paradise."[46]

Rousseau, like Locke and a host of others, mistook the Christian view of nature for nature-in-itself both in man and in the subhuman orders. This is the second "Fall" of Western man and it is historical, not mythological. Western man fell from his Christian manhood by denying the truth of the original Fall myth, accepting the moral character and view of life, which he had as a Christian, as the achievements of his natural reason.

If one takes Augustine's conception of the primitive state of man and dynamizes it with a doctrine of progress as natural development, omitting the Creation, Fall, Incarnation, Atonement, Church, and Eschaton, then history unfolds the capacities of original nature and the result is an evolution toward utopia as that conception appears in Babeuf, Saint-Simon, Fourier, and Robert Owen. The viewpoint will not be radically changed if it is set within a theistic, a deistic, or an atheistic context. A deist, as Louis de Bonald once said, is a man who in his short lifetime has not had time to become an atheist.[47]

If one retains some degree of Christian and historical realism, as Rousseau did, one may infer, as did the revolutionary utopians, that since evil is the product of history, history must begin again. Marx called bourgeois-capitalist society "the closing chapter of the pre-historic stage of human society."[48]

Beneath all modern socialist theories, evolutionary or revolutionary, there lies the dogma of the goodness and the perfectibility of human nature. The so-called utopian socialists, upon whom Marx poured such

[46] Willey, *The Eighteenth Century Background*, pp. 205-6.
[47] Quoted by Karl Löwith, *Meaning in History*, p. 234, n. 51.
[48] Karl Marx, *A Contribution to the Critique of Political Economy* (Chicago, 1904), quoted by Löwith, *op.cit.*, p. 35.

scorn, trusted naively in reason, education, persuasion, and voluntary progress. From a classical Christian viewpoint, however, even Marxism is utopian since it expects human sin to disappear from human nature and from history as the result of the revolutionary achievement of the socialist classless society.

VII. The American Social Gospel and Christian Utopian Socialism

American Christianity after the Civil War was almost unaware of secular socialism until its complacency was shaken by what Henry E. May calls "The Three Earthquakes."[49] The catastrophic strikes of 1877, 1886, and 1892-1894 successively removed veils from some Christian eyes. At one and the same time the churches began to be aware of secular socialism, which was a changing, fusing, separating interaction between evolutionary and revolutionary socialism, and of the social ills which socialism proposed to remedy. The awakening was almost unanimous in its critical rejection of all forms of socialism. It expressed itself in an increasing awareness of the plight of the great mass of working people, in individual Christians wrestling with the social problems from the standpoint of Christian ethics, and in a steady conversation carried on in lectures, books, and theological magazines.

In the latter part of the nineteenth century, organizations began to appear in the denominations and on an interdenominational level which concentrated on Christian social action, social education, or both.

Unexpectedly, the Episcopal Church showed the most immediate and widespread concern and gave rise to two unofficial groups which are important both for their sustained influence and for their typical character. The Church Association for the Advancement of the Interests of Labor, founded in 1887 and known as "Cail," had from the beginning the support of such men as Bishop F. D. Huntingdon of Central New York and Bishop Henry Codman Potter of New York. Early in its history, some forty Episcopal bishops were its vice-presidents. For forty years, this group, far from being radical, worked to improve the housing, the education, the health, the wages, the hours, and the working conditions of labor and promoted peaceful arbitration of labor disputes, notably by means of Bishop Potter's committee for mediation which "Cail" conceived. The Church Social Union, begun in 1890 and concentrating exclusively on awakening and educating the Church to social action, was composed of "Cail" members and similar men. These two organizations influenced the whole Church so that officially appointed commissions, official statements on social issues

[49] Henry E. May, *Protestant Churches and Industrial America* (New York, 1948), p. 91.

and, finally, what became a Department of Christian Social Relations, resulted.

This Episcopal pattern developed with denominational accents and characteristics among the Congregationalists, the Methodists, the Presbyterians, and the Baptists, so that a carefully done study of *The Rise of the Social Gospel* by Charles Howard Hopkins[50] can conclude with chapters called "Social Christianity Becomes Official" and "The Churches Federate for Social Action." The latter deals with the origin and development of the Federal Council of Churches of Christ in America.

Diverse theological and ecclesiastical traditions produced the men and movements which went into this Social Gospel reformism. Out of this diversity, however, there emerged a common theological tendency which can be called an American Social Gospel Theology. It was the predominant influence in the whole movement, unofficial and official. Viewed as a trend with many pauses and returns to early phases it may be described, without too much injustice, as the transformation of Calvinist theocracy into utopian idealism. The Kingdom of God became an ideal for actualization in future history, a society to be built by men who had caught the divine vision. Jesus was supposed to have taught this ideal and to have exemplified in his person the method of obtaining it as well as its spirit. The Christian movement, which stemmed from Jesus, was the leaven intended to leaven the whole lump of mankind. The Cross was thought of as the element of sacrifice by which progress was made toward the achievement of the historical goal. In Marxian language, this social idealism was religious utopianism and, when it was socialistic, it was utopian socialism. Marxism and other "realistic" sociological analyses could and did make valid criticisms of it. For instance, a Marxian author, himself originating in American Methodism, makes the following comment on Richard Ely, one of the early Social Gospel leaders:

"While denying that economic interest conditioned religious views and insisting, on the other hand, that religion completely transcended interest, he developed a program for working men which stressed strongly just those qualities which served the interests of the bourgeois group to which he belonged and toned down those qualities that were essential to the interests of the workers."[51]

It was inevitable for many, therefore, that Christian idealism should become increasingly realistic and merge with secular social idealism. In particular, the Christian idealist and the secular socialist repugnance to war coalesced and provided the gateway through which such men as

[50] C. H. Hopkins, *The Rise of the Social Gospel in American Protestantism, 1865-1915* (New Haven, 1940), chaps. 17 and 18.

[51] James Dombrowski, *The Early Days of Christian Socialism in America* (New York, 1936), p. 57.

Norman Thomas passed from the religious ranks to the Socialist Party. One of the most remarkable careers of this pacifist-socialist strain in American Christianity is that of A. J. Muste. Convinced by World War I that war could be ended only by concerted action on the part of internationally organized labor, he moved from the Christian ministry into the labor movement. There he was converted to the necessity of force as an instrument of social change. Deeply influenced by Marxism, his universalist idealism led him to sympathize with the Trotsky position in the Stalin-Trotsky break. Finally, disillusioned with all use of coercion, he reverted to absolute religious pacifism and returned to the church. Traversing a circle, he recovered essentially the Christian-utopia-through-suffering position which he held during World War I. His pilgrimage produced a fantastic proposal before the recent war. In his secular socialist days, Muste had regarded war as the product of capitalism, and universal socialism as the remedy for war. In an article in the *Christian Century*, December 14, 1938, he reversed this logic by arguing that the churches should become pacifist, removing the military instrument of imperialism, without which capitalism would collapse, and thereby forcing national and international economic relations into basic transformations. This was the political expression of "The Way of the Cross," the title of the article, and was Muste's Christian solution to the world crisis of 1938!

Such extremes, of course, were not general but it is clear that the same conceptions of nature, man, history, and progress-toward-utopia which informed secular socialism increasingly informed the American Social Gospel. The secularized child of classical Christianity began to secularize the parent. The extreme development of liberal theology has been described by H. Richard Niebuhr with a sharp aphorism: "A God without wrath brought men without sin into a Kingdom without judgment through the ministrations of a Christ without a cross."[52]

Niebuhr also explains why most adherents to the Social Gospel as well as Christian socialists stood with the proponents of evolutionary progress:

"Since no reconciliation to the divine sovereign was necessary the reign of Christ, in the new interpretation, involved no revolutionary events in history or the life of individuals. Christ the Redeemer became Jesus the teacher or spiritual genius in whom the religious capacities of mankind were fully developed. . . . Evolution, growth, development, the culture of the religious life, the nurture of the kindly sentiments, the extension of humanitarian ideals and the progress of civilization took the place of the Christian revolution."[53]

[52] Niebuhr, *op.cit.*, p. 193.
[53] *Ibid.*, pp. 192-93.

VIII. Christian Scientific Socialism

Some Christian socialists, including A. J. Muste as mentioned above, have been deeply influenced by Marx. Among them are George D. Herron and Harry F. Ward, who mark two stages of a route which led to an identification of Christianity with Marxism. Fundamentally this movement of thought derives from an idealism which accepts the political realism and the economic determinism of Marx. These men had seen persuasion and idealism tried, and had tried it themselves. They were driven by the logic of utopianism and of experience to the acceptance of the class struggle and to the inevitability of coercion to social change. Herron thought that religion "should continue to make use of the appeal to good will and renunciation, but it should also expect to use coercion. . . . He did not expect to get very many brethren to the altar of economic sacrifice, at least not enough to ward off the revolution."[54]

Dr. Harry F. Ward has gone through this same stage and one step beyond. His book, *The New Social Order* (1919), is described by J. Neal Hughley, after giving excerpts, in these words: "Even these numerous quotations from Ward's lyric to progress and to a coming universal enlightenment do not portray adequately the scope and depth of such social gospel faith. Only the actual reading of the text can convey a truly vivid impression of this almost mystical Condorcet-like optimism."[55] From this position Ward moved steadily from moralistic attacks on capitalism to a slightly revised Marxism and a eulogy of the Soviet by 1944. He knows, however, that the workers' inevitable victory is a matter of *faith*, and fears that American capitalism will destroy political democracy completely and establish an American fascism. Those who have found in the Soviet the beginning of the Kingdom of God on earth live today in the shadow of the great fear that a Fascist America with the atomic bomb will crush the U.S.S.R. and wipe out the hopes of mankind for an indefinite future.

IX. Neo-Calvinist Socialism

If Christian socialism has any future in America, its greatest influence will probably come from the group called the Frontier Fellowship, Christians for Social Reconstruction (formerly the Fellowship of Socialist Christians), centered around Reinhold Niebuhr, Paul Tillich, and Eduard Heimann.[56] In the past two decades, this group's theology, social analysis,

[54] Dombrowski, *op.cit.*, p. 192.

[55] J. Neal Hughley, *Trends in Protestant Social Idealism* (New York, 1948), p. 92.

[56] For the theology of these men and its application to social problems, the following works are relevant: Reinhold Niebuhr, *The Nature and Destiny of Man* (New York, 1941, 1943, 2 vols.); Eduard Heimann, *Freedom and Order* (New York, 1947); Paul Tillich, *The Protestant Era* (Chicago, 1948), especially chaps. 2, 3, 16, 17.

and interpretation of contemporary history have moved rapidly. While it is a religious fellowship and not a social action group and, therefore, has no "party line" either theological, political, or on specific issues, its general trend has been to the right theologically from liberalism, toward the center politically from the left, and it has supported the Marshall Plan policy in Europe. Without conscious intent, it has completed a circle by returning the Christian Social Gospel to its full Christian basis as a post-liberal orthodoxy. This theological position is far from the neo-orthodoxy of Continental Protestantism but its difference lies in its lack of literalization of its symbols and in its rigorously dialectical, and not simply supernaturalistic, affirmation of the relation of the transcendent to history. Most of its members belong to, or are favorably disposed to, Americans for Democratic Action.

The theology of this group with its emphasis on the transcendence of God, the continuous faith-reception of God's revelation in Christ, the sin of man, and the daemonic character of historical movements, prevents any identification of the Kingdom of God with actual or future socialist societies. These emphases also prevent any doctrinaire blueprints for the future. The majority's judgment, based on an empirical analysis of history, leads the group in a socialist direction, but the Christian criticism of power makes it aware of its concentration of political and economic power.

Perhaps with complete independence of this group, W. H. Auden has described the attitude with which it faces the future:

> Let us therefore be contrite but without anxiety,
> For Powers and Times are not gods but mortal gifts from God;
> Let us acknowledge our defeats but without despair,
> For all societies and epochs are transient details,
> Transmitting an everlasting opportunity
> That the Kingdom of Heaven may come, not in our Present
> And not in our Future, but in the Fullness of Time.
> Let us pray.[57]

[57] W. H. Auden, *For the Time Being* (New York, 1944), pp. 96-97.

CHAPTER 4

Christian Communitarianism in America

BY STOW PERSONS

STOW PERSONS is Professor of History at the State University of Iowa. During the years that the manuscript of this book was prepared, he was Assistant Professor of History at Princeton, where he was connected with the Program in American Civilization and served for a year as its Chairman. His particular field of interest is American intellectual and religious history.

For bibliography in Volume 2 relevant to Mr. Persons' essay, see especially PART II, General Reading (sections 1, 2), and Topics 2, 4; also PART III, General Reading (section 1); PART IV, General Reading (section 1); PART VI, General Reading (section 3A), and Topic 1.

T HE first American socialists were religious zealots who formed small communities in which goods were held in common. When the Marxists of the mid-nineteenth century dismissed these communitarians with the condescending epithet, "utopian," they succeeded both in fastening a persistent historical judgment upon their predecessors in the socialist tradition and in introducing a dubious distinction between the presumed "scientific" character of Marxism and the sentimental dreams of the utopians. For it is by now apparent that each movement was in many respects an appropriate reaction to the peculiar conditions of its own day, while at the same time each had its utopian elements.

The social and economic setting of early American communitarianism was an evangelical and rural society in which the theological doctrines and moral precepts of the Calvinistic tradition had already made a firm alliance with a flourishing agrarian capitalism. In such an environment the appearance of several religious sects practicing forms of communitarian socialism poses a difficult problem of explanation for the historian. Some of these sects, to be sure, were European in origin, drawn to America by the freedom of the wilderness and the relative security of a society committed by the logic of its development to religious freedom. Those sects of German origin maintained the traditions of seventeenth-century Dutch and German pietism or baptism, and by identifying their piety with an ethnic solidarity were able to sustain their communities in some instances for several generations. But for the very reason that they kept alive the mysticism of Böhme, the communitarians of Ephrata and Amana and the followers of George Rapp isolated themselves from the America of their day. In deliberately perpetuating an alien tradition these Germans were able to throw little light on an essentially American problem. Other communitarian sects, however, were purely American products, the fruit of native experience, recruiting their members from the farms and shops—and churches—of the surrounding countryside. It is from the records of two of the more successful of these indigenous sects, the Shakers and the Oneida Perfectionists, that we may perhaps gain some insight into the motives which led a small number of men and women to abandon the agricultural-commercial capitalism of their day and embrace the disciplined cooperation of the sectarian community.

Much has been written about the details of daily life in these communities. But in emphasizing quaint curiosities and picturesque features many of these accounts intensify the problem by stressing what was peculiar and ignoring the continuities which united sectarian endeavor to the life of the times. A more systematic explanation of the communitarian phenomenon has come from the European sociologists of religion. According to this theory the religious doctrines and practices which resulted

127

in sectarian socialism expressed the suppressed aspirations of submerged or frustrated people. It is pointed out that a sharp distinction was made by the sectarian between the regenerate few and the sinful world. He attempted to withdraw from the world so far as possible in order to live in strict gospel purity. Here in a community of the saints an unusual blend of paternalism and functional equalitarianism frequently culminated in various practical—or impractical—forms of community ownership of goods.

While there is much that commends itself in this social approach to the problem of religious radicalism the peculiarities of the American scene would appear to require some refinements in the theory. Those communitarian sects that recruited their members from the native American population at the beginning of the nineteenth century did not find their converts among the suppressed masses of the people, relatively speaking. Rather they found them among moderately prosperous farmers and craftsmen, the donation of whose property to the cause frequently furnished the initial investment that made communal living possible. Nor can the communitarian sects be regarded as sublimated expressions of revolt against a hostile social environment. Although the early Shakers experienced sporadic persecution, the memory of which they carefully cherished, this persecution was the consequence rather than the cause of their radicalism. Frustration of a sort there certainly was, else the sectarian communities would never have been born. But the mesh of the traditional explanation is too coarse to sift out the decisive factors which stimulated radical sectarianism. In the fluid American environment, where no fixed class, church, or social privileges determined the framework of social thought and action, subtler forces were also at work. I propose to supplement the sociological explanation of Christian communitarianism by assigning some determining force to religious ideas themselves.

American religious communism was a direct product of the great evangelical revivals of the eighteenth and nineteenth centuries. The communitarians were men already engaged in a great religious enterprise—the thirst to taste in full measure the gospel promise. Going beyond the great body of their fellow revivalists they carried to an extreme but logical development certain of the evangelical tendencies. They might almost be regarded as the ultimate expression of the evangelical Protestantism of the nineteenth century. At least it is clear that when revival fervor began to cool after mid-century the sectarian communities on the periphery were the first to feel the chill and to wither.

I. The Spirit of Evangelical Revivalism

The triumph of evangelical Protestantism in America was achieved through the agency of a series of religious revivals which lasted almost continuously for more than a century following the Great Awakening of 1734-1744. Although the institution of revivalism originated in the churches of the Calvinistic tradition it quickly proved itself to be more congenial to the spirit and teaching of such radical seventeenth-century sects as the Quakers and Baptists. In the fervent atmosphere of the revival, millennial expectations were encouraged, and heretical doctrines of direct inspiration and perfect sanctification became widespread. By the time of the Revolution, a generation after the Great Awakening, when the frontier of settlement ran through central New England and New York along the valleys of Appalachia to eastern Kentucky and Georgia, these and similar ideas were endemic to the backwoods, ready to be fused into the various brands of nineteenth-century evangelical Protestantism.

Out of the welter of sectarian and denominational activity of the time there began to emerge a new complex of religious ideas fundamentally antithetical to the Calvinism and Anglicanism which had dominated the colonial epoch. There was of course the same practical piety of sin and regeneration typical of all forms of early Protestantism. But the promise of God's redeeming grace was now understood to be extended to all who would avail themselves of it, rather than restricted to a chosen few. Such universalism presupposed free moral agency. Just as man was responsible for his sins, so he must repent and seek forgiving grace. The spectacular successes of the revivals seemed to testify to the assurance of salvation for all those who would earnestly lay hold of the means of grace. It has frequently been observed that such a doctrine was congenial to a prosperous and growing society where free men were in control of their own social destiny.

But the radical spirit of the new movement appeared most clearly in the perfectionist and millennialist ideas which had always cast a lurid light around the fringes of Protestantism and now emerged with renewed strength in the revival fervor. How was the Christian to understand the requirements of the sanctified life to which God called those who were justified by Christ's redeeming grace? Orthodox Protestants, instructed by an educated clergy sophisticated in the ways of the world and mindful of the limitations of the flesh, had always interpreted these requirements with caution and common sense. The revivalists, however, insisted upon the full measure of gospel promise. A merciful God who could forgive man his sins might justly require of the believer complete sanctification or perfection. The thirst for perfect holiness came to characterize evangelical revivalism and to determine its special problems. Perfection was defined in various ways. The Methodists thought of it as perfect love. The Disciples, following Alexander Campbell, defined it in characteristically American fashion as the liberty of the gospel in contradistinction to the bonds of the law. The more radical revivalists, with whom we are particularly concerned, understood Christian perfection to be freedom from sin.

The burden of Christian perfection in its most exacting form could scarcely be borne, even in the enthusiasm of revival, without the support of the millennial hope. The ancient Christian promise of Christ's return to earth to overthrow the wicked and reign for a thousand years with his saints provided the necessary stimulus to enable earnest believers to persevere in sanctity, expecting that the promised day was about to dawn. From the time of Jonathan Edwards to that of William Miller multitudes of Americans understood the revivals to be signs that the millennium was at hand.

A closer inspection of two areas of the frontier at the time of the Revolution will show how these ideas were fermenting, and what might develop from them. In New England the line of settlement ran through southwestern Maine, central New Hampshire and Vermont, and the hills of western Massachusetts and Connecticut. These areas had been lately settled by Baptists and Puritan Congregationalists. From 1772 to the end of the century sporadic revivals occurred in Alfred and Gorham, Maine; in Canterbury and Enfield, New Hampshire; in New Lebanon, New York; in Hancock and Brimfield, Massachusetts, and in neighboring towns.[1] A new sect appeared, the Freewill Baptists, making many converts and promoting the revival. This was a common characteristic of American revivalism, which, as a popular movement, encouraged the growth of sects free from the inhibitions of the established churches and prepared to make a popular appeal to the needs and emotions of the frontiersman. Under these circumstances the theological doctrines of orthodox Congregationalism and the Calvinistic Baptists quickly dissolved.

Under the leadership of Benjamin Randall, a former Congregationalist and convert of Whitefield, the Freewill Baptists were scattered across the New England frontier by the end of the eighteenth century.[2] They abandoned the traditional Puritan theology of predestination, particular election, and limited atonement, and embraced the evangelical revival doctrines sketched above. But they advanced to a degree of sectarian radicalism relatively rare among the revivalists. In the intensity of their simple revival enthusiasm they insisted upon the personal union of the believer with God at the moment of regeneration. They taught that the repentance which was a necessary condition of regeneration

[1] Isaac Backus, A History of New England: With Particular Reference to . . . Baptists (Newton, Mass., 1871, 2 vols.), II, pp. 278-80, 471-74; Shaker Manifesto, xv (Feb. 1885), pp. 33-34.

[2] J. M. Brewster, "The Freewill Baptists," in The Centennial Record of Freewill Baptists, 1780-1880 (Dover, N.H., 1881), pp. 9-19.

was worthless unless it entailed the complete abandonment of all sin. Nor did they believe that a person once regenerated would persevere in sanctity except through his own efforts. These rigorous tenets were sustained by the earnest expectation that the second coming of Christ was immediately at hand. No distinction was made between clergy and laity, each individual being free to testify according to his light. At their spontaneous gatherings for exhortation and singing, the emotional intensity frequently expressed itself in outbursts of dancing, which earned the Free Baptists the contemptuous nicknames, "Merry Dancers," or "New Lights."[3] Here in extreme form was the typical revival emphasis upon the need of release from sin, and the equally characteristic danger of subsequent backsliding as the excitement passed and men realized that they were again succumbing to temptation.

While this rebirth of seventeenth-century sectarian radicalism was occurring in New England a similar movement was under way at the southern end of the long line of frontier settlement. During the Revolution Scotch-Irish Presbyterians from Pennsylvania were moving southwestward along the valleys into western Virginia and North Carolina, and thence through the gaps into Kentucky, Tennessee, and the upper Ohio valley. Local revivals under Presbyterian auspices occurred in western Pennsylvania in 1778 and the years following. The institution inevitably fanned out into the Southwest with the migrants. The Presbyterians soon sensed the incompatibility of Calvinist theology with the revival spirit, and leadership in the movement passed to Baptists and Methodists. The first camp meeting was a spontaneous affair in western North Carolina, and the camp meeting quickly became a typical feature of southern revivalism. The doctrines disseminated through these agencies were similar to those of the Freewill Baptists, although somewhat less radical in character.[4]

Here again several new sects emerged to capitalize upon the revival, chiefly at the expense of the Presbyterians. The Cumberland presbytery found that on virtually all important points of doctrine it had moved out of the ambit of the Westminster Confession, and consequently it reformed itself as an independent body. The revivalist tendency to disregard precise confessional formulations found expression in Barton W. Stone's Christian Church, dedicated to the union of all Christians on a simple Bible faith. Most radical of all were the "Schismatics" or "New Lights" led by John Dunlavy and Richard McNemar, who succeeded in

---

[3] *Free Baptist Cyclopedia* (Chicago, 1889), pp. 164-68; *Shaker Manifesto*, XIII (Oct. 1883), p. 218, XV (Jan., Feb. 1885), pp. 11-12, 33.

[4] William Speer, *The Great Revival of 1800* (Philadelphia, 1872), pp. 24-49; Robert Davidson, *History of the Presbyterian Church in the State of Kentucky* (New York, 1847), pp. 165-69.

capturing most of the Presbyterian churches in Kentucky and southeastern Ohio.[5]

The doctrines of the Schismatics closely paralleled those of the northern Freewill Baptists. Their antecedents were Quaker and Arminian rather than Calvinist, although the leaders of the movement seem for the most part to have been trained as Presbyterians. In the Quaker tradition was the strong emphasis upon the sufficiency of the inner light of inspiration to certify to salvation and to assure correct doctrine. It was admitted that while regeneration should bring release from sin, this was an exceedingly difficult state to achieve, given the weakness and corruption of the natural man. Rejecting the orthodox doctrine of the regeneration of man by the imputed righteousness of Christ through vicarious suffering, the Schismatics held that man must suffer as Christ suffered in order to achieve his victory. This was, in short, an exacting doctrine of perfection in human and ethical terms. How was it possible for man to achieve it? Here again the millennialist expectation served to sustain the believer in the hope that with Christ's speedy return the devil would be chained and sin destroyed.[6] Spontaneous exhortation, singing, and dancing replaced formal services of worship. Intensity of feeling was manifest in visionary trances, "speaking in tongues," and the physical paroxysms known as the "falling" and "jerks." Revelations in trance had led the Schismatics to focus their millennial hopes on the year 1805.[7]

II. The Shakers

As the New Light revival reached its height a new sect appeared with teachings and practices peculiarly suited to appeal to the more uncompromising and enthusiastic revivalists. Joseph Meacham, a Baptist revivalist of New Lebanon, New York, hearing of a group of religious refugees living at nearby Watervliet, investigated and discovered Ann Lee and eight followers, who called themselves Shakers.[8]

The Shakers stemmed from a seventeenth-century French sect known as Prophets. Under persecution a few of them had fled to England where they merged with radical Quakers. They combined their millennialism and perfectionism with the characteristic Quaker social doctrines, but were distinguished chiefly by the practice of celibacy and the belief that in his second coming Christ would take the female form.[9] One of the group more gifted in personal qualities and visionary power than the others,

[5] J. P. MacLean, *Shakers of Ohio* (Columbus, Ohio, 1907), pp. 28-34, 37-38.

[6] Richard McNemar, *The Kentucky Revival* (New York, 1846), pp. 11-12, 30, 38-39, 48-53.

[7] *Ibid.*, pp. 61-80.

[8] *Shaker Manifesto*, viii (June 1878), p. 139.

[9] *Ibid.*, viii (Feb. 1878), p. 39; Marguerite Melcher, *The Shaker Adventure* (Princeton, N.J., 1941), pp. 5-15.

an ascetic and mystic named Ann Lee, had been recognized by the Shakers as embodying the second manifestation of the Christ spirit. She rationalized the practice of celibacy and made it the distinguishing characteristic of her following by teaching that the sexual relationship was the basic sin of the epoch which ended with the second advent. Celibacy thus became the chief symbol of triumph over sin.[10]

Much more important, however, than any practices of the Shakers was the fact that the millennial prophecy had at last been fulfilled. The Kingdom had come! A new era had dawned, bringing a new perspective from which to view both the past and the future. Of course the manner of the event scarcely satisfied those who were awaiting the descent of a King in clouds of glory, but the Shakers pointed out that such people would not have recognized Jesus of Nazareth either. The millennial Kingdom was a spiritual realm which one entered only by confessing and forsaking all sin. The Shakers themselves professed to know the joys and peace of this Kingdom. In them the millennial promise was realized. It was this claim to have entered the Kingdom that placed the Shakers in a strategic position with respect to the orthodox millennialists of their day.

Ann Lee came to America with the faithful eight in 1774, having been charged by revelation to establish the millennial church in the new world. Whether she knew enough of religious conditions across the Atlantic to know that the time was ripe for her is uncertain. She was an ignorant woman, but clearly possessed of considerable native intelligence and purity of character. In any event, the conservative American Calvinists for their part knew well the dangers which she represented, for since the days of the Great Awakening they had been accustomed to point to the French Prophets in warning of the results to which unrestrained revival enthusiasm might lead.[11]

Once contact with the American revivalists had been made, five years after their settlement on the Hudson, the Shakers threw themselves into the work and began to make converts. Meacham's New Lebanon congregation was won over in a body, and other New Lights followed. It was to the Freewill Baptists with their millennialist expectations that the appeal was first addressed. Mother Ann toured the revival areas of Massachusetts and Connecticut in 1780 and 1781. She was repeatedly mobbed, but whether for religious or political reasons is not clear. During the next two years Shaker missionaries converted many Freewill Baptists of central New Hampshire and southern Maine.[12] The conversions in the South-

[10] *Shaker Manifesto*, VIII (Mar. 1878), pp. 63-64.

[11] *The Christian History; Containing Accounts of the Propagation and Revival of Religion in England, Scotland, and America* (No. 2, Mar. 12, 1743), pp. 11-13.

[12] *Shaker Manifesto*, VIII (June 1878), p. 139, XII (Apr. 1882), pp. 75-76; *Free Baptist Cyclopedia*, pp. 453-54; Backus, *History*, II, pp. 297, 462.

west followed a similar pattern. Hearing of the New Light revival in Kentucky and Ohio the Shakers dispatched three missionaries in 1804 and three more in 1805. One of them, Issacher Bates, was said to have traveled some 38,000 miles, mostly on foot, between 1801 and 1811. In this region also Shaker successes were confined to the areas of New Light strength, namely, central Kentucky and southwestern Ohio.[13]

Why were the Shakers moderately successful in recruiting, in view of the widespread abuse, the radicalism of their social ethics, and the unnatural character of celibacy in an agricultural community where people were accustomed to marry young and where children were an economic asset? The explanation was presumably theological. Shaker doctrines so fulfilled the expectations of the radical revivalists that some of them were persuaded in spite of all the sacrifices involved.

The New Light concern for Christian perfection had tended in an ethical and practical direction. The American revivalist was becoming ever more preoccupied with release from sin. The Shakers met this need with their rigorous but concrete ethics of self-denial. Christ's Kingdom awaited those with strength to crucify the flesh. The great problem of the revivalists had been the inevitable relapse into sin which followed the waning of revival fervor. The Shakers met this issue by boldly asserting that perfection was rational, a way of life rather than a state of mind.[14] It was out of this consideration that Shaker community life developed spontaneously. Once organized, the community lent all of its weighty psychological and social sanctions to the support of the doctrine. But in the early years, when it was still cradled in frontier revivalism, Shaker perfectionism derived its major sanction from its associated millennialist teaching.

On the American frontier the typical sectarian expectation of the Second Coming was of the premillennialist variety. Catastrophic events were supposed to attend the establishment of Christ's Kingdom and the destruction of present principalities and powers. While the anticipation of these great events filled men with excitement, it was a feeling not easily sustained as time passed and daily life continued in its normal patterns. Premillennialism easily led to disillusionment unless fed by deep and continuous craving or dissatisfaction. The measure of Ann Lee's genius was her ability to transform the typical premillennial impulse into a new form which assumed new relationships to the Christian and secular communities in which it was born.

The Shakers taught that the millennium had already begun, though

[13] *Shaker Manifesto*, xiv (Nov., Dec. 1884), pp. 252-53, 277; Melcher, *Shaker Adventure*, pp. 67-70.
[14] *Shaker Manifesto*, xiii (Feb., July, Oct. 1883), pp. 37-38, 150-51, 217-20, xiv (Oct. 1884), pp. 224, 227-28.

not in the form which the premillennialists expected. Christ's second coming had been spiritual. The Christ spirit had been revealed to Ann Lee, instructing her to form a true church of believers who, upon confession and renunciation of sin, would enter the millennial Kingdom.[15] This Shaker doctrine, which may be called intermillennialism to distinguish it from the prevailing view, provided the theoretical basis for the assurance of Shaker missionaries that they had themselves entered the Kingdom through the abandonment of sin. It also satisfied the craving of at least a few of the more radical New Lights for the special revelation of divine purpose which their premillennialism had led them to expect. From Maine to Kentucky they hailed the Shaker missionaries as providential agents.[16]

Shakerism established itself as a new sect which proposed to discipline and sustain the spirit and outlook of radical revivalism. Its dependence upon the revival impulse extended even to the forms of religious ritual which it adapted to the spontaneous practices of revivalism. Those most striking features of Shaker devotional services, the dancing, marching, and singing, were in fact the ecstatic "exercises" of the revival reduced to the routine patterns of ritual. But the Shaker leaders were wise enough not to repress entirely the spontaneous individual expression of devotion. Until the middle of the nineteenth century their services were frequently characterized by outbursts of religious ecstasy reminiscent of the New Light revival.

In its late eighteenth-century context the Shaker brand of millennialism was at once reactionary and progressive. Its dependence upon special revelation and divine intervention looked back to the seventeenth century rather than toward the secular century ahead when Shakerism would come to seem a quaint anachronism. But on the other hand, although Shaker intermillennialism was the most radical type of chiliasm yet to appear in America, it was nevertheless capable of molding an outlook on life and history quite consistent with the emerging secular idea of social progress. From the vantage point of the Kingdom the Shaker apologist offered an interpretation of history that had the true nineteenth-century liberal ring. The best example is the work of one of the early New England converts, Benjamin S. Youngs, whose *Testimony of Christ's Second Appearing* was first published in 1808. The Shaker divided history into a series of epochs representing the progressive unfolding or revelation of the divine plan. To mention his treatment of the Christian era only, Youngs distinguished first the age of the primitive Christian church to whose purity of life and doctrine, he, in common with most radical

[15] *Ibid.*, VIII (June 1878), p. 139.
[16] McNemar, *Kentucky Revival*, pp. 80-83; *Shaker Manifesto*, XV (Feb. 1885), pp. 33-34.

Protestants, looked back with the deepest veneration. The primitive church had been gradually corrupted by the power of the Roman bishops, however, and there followed the long night of the reign of Antichrist. Eventually the power of Rome was broken, and as a consequence the seventeenth and eighteenth centuries witnessed the spread of tolerance, civil liberty, and equalitarian social ideas. These tendencies paved the way for the second manifestation of the Christ spirit in Mother Ann, about 1770. This event ushered in the latest epoch, a dispensation purer in many ways than that which had preceded it. The Shakers professed to adhere more rigorously than did Jesus to the principle of nonviolence. But most important, they had discovered the positive principles of peaceful social organization. The millennial epoch which was then dawning would witness the gradual spread of these principles among men.[17] God's method was progressive, his ends were to be wrought out in history. The social ethics of the emerging Kingdom were to be those of humanitarianism. Moreover, the ascetic self-denial to which the Shakers gladly subscribed tended to mask the authoritarian discipline of the system both for the Shakers themselves and for the many sympathetic observers among their contemporaries.

Shaker community life—"gospel order," as they called it—developed spontaneously out of the practical perfectionism of Shaker doctrine and practice. As the practical implications of life without sin became apparent the withdrawal from the world became inevitable. The full development of perfectionist ethics was impossible except in a community of the faithful, and once the community was formed it was justified theoretically. "To constitute a true church of Christ, there must necessarily be a union of faith, of motives and of interest, in all the members who compose it. There must be 'one body and one bread': and nothing short of this union in all things, both spiritual and temporal, can constitute a true church, which is the body of Christ."[18] There is no evidence that the Shaker venture into communitarian socialism was undertaken with any knowledge of previous communitarian theory or practice, aside from their scanty and sentimentalized information about the primitive church. The Shaker communities lay at the headwaters of the communitarian socialist tradition of English-speaking America. Thereafter, all of the religious and liberal communitarians were aware of the Shaker experience, and the more studious among them examined the "gospel order" closely.

Many of the first generation Shaker converts were substantial property owners. It became customary for less affluent believers to gather on these

[17] B. S. Youngs, *The Testimony of Christ's Second Appearing* (2nd ed., Albany, N.Y., 1810), pp. x-xxiii, Pt. II.

[18] Calvin Green and Seth Wells, *A Summary View of the Millennial Church* (Albany, N.Y., 1823), p. 51.

properties and work them jointly, although others continued to live apart, assembling for worship in the usual sectarian manner. From these practical origins the formal community pattern was developed by Ann Lee's successors, Joseph Meacham and Lucy Wright. The first community was gathered at New Lebanon, N.Y., in 1787. At the peak of development in 1826 eighteen societies were scattered through New York, Massachusetts, Connecticut, New Hampshire, Maine, Kentucky, Ohio, and Indiana.[19]

The Shakers had no formal socialist theory, strictly speaking. Their practices grew out of the daily needs of group work and worship. In that the ultimate function of authority was to maintain the law of God in all purity the system could be called theocratic. Within these limits, however, the scrupulous regard for the spiritual integrity of the individual assured an unusual degree of practical equality. This was particularly true in respect to the equality of rights and privileges enjoyed by the women. The Shakers concurred in the ancient religious doctrine that true liberty was realized in submission to the will of God. As the ideology of democracy gained wider expression during the nineteenth century Shaker theorists were obliged to qualify it. They presumed that the theocracy of the Kingdom would be both monarchical, in that God's will would prevail, and democratic, in that men would sustain it gladly. They recognized the necessary differences of function and levels of authority in any society, but preferred to sanctify every function rather than to offset inequalities with the opportunity for political expression offered by the democratic system.[20]

The governmental structure of the Shaker community was chiefly the result of the organizing skill of Joseph Meacham and Lucy Wright. Final authority was concentrated in the ministry, a self-perpetuating group chosen for superior purity and wisdom. The power of the ministry was apparently checked only by the crystallized opinion of the body of believers. It was recognized that no one had a right to anything, for the inner voice of inspiration took precedence over all external authorities. There were, however, many instances where actions contrary to the wishes of the ministry were confirmed when convincing evidence of a spiritual impulse appeared. God's governance was not limited by constitutional powers or restraints.[21]

The social unit was the family, composed of members of both sexes and presided over by Elders and Eldresses. The latter were Assistant Ministers subject to assignment to families by the central ministry at New Lebanon. The economic and other activities of the family were under

[19] *Shaker Manifesto*, xii (Dec. 1882), pp. 267-69, xiii (May, Oct. 1883), pp. 104-6, 217-20.
[20] *Ibid.*, xiv (Feb. 1884), pp. 27-28.
[21] *Ibid.*, xiii (Nov. 1883), p. 243.

the supervision of Deacons and Deaconesses.[22] The paramount importance of the family was not uncommonly stressed by communitarian socialists. It was also frequently emphasized by radical Protestant sectarians. The Shakers believed that they derived it from their theory of the dual sexuality of the Godhead. The revelation of God the Father was made through Christ. This revelation, though perfect, was incomplete. Now God the Mother had been revealed through Ann. At last the spirit of love and tenderness here embodied made the revelation complete, and by its light a truly spiritual social organization was possible. The model was of course the family, presided over by God the Father and Mother. It was a "social organization, permanently founded on the principles of equality of the sexes, virgin purity, unworldliness, the confession of sin, and community of property; the practical fruits of which are pure love, industry, meekness, unselfishness, innocence, and all good Christian qualities."[23]

Mother Ann was accustomed to admonish her followers: "Put your hands to work and your hearts to God." As an economic enterprise Shaker communitarianism was an unqualified success. Diversified craft work supplemented basic agriculture. Subsistence rather than affluence was of course the intention. Perhaps because they always remained faithful to the standards of personal asceticism the Shakers only gradually became aware of the subtle poison of corporate prosperity. In 1855 a bill proposing to limit Shaker landholdings was introduced in the New York legislature. Aware of the extent to which Believers had become preoccupied with worldly concerns the Shaker leaders signified that they would not oppose the measure, which was forthwith dropped.[24] Dependent as they were upon the surrounding society for recruits, however, it is doubtful that the deeper insight into spiritual values which might have repressed their Yankee practicality would have lengthened the life of their enterprise.

Since the success of Shakerism depended largely upon its ability to recruit its members from millennialist revivalism the drying up of that movement inevitably spelled the doom of the United Society of Believers. Adventist revivalism reached its peak in the eighteen-forties with Millerite millennialism. The Shakers urged their doctrines with the same cogency as in the earlier New Light revivals, and increased their numbers to about 6,000, the maximum enrollment of their history. But the tide turned against them quickly. The spiritualist movement which swept the country in the forties and fifties seems to have had its origin among the Shakers, and had spiritualism retained its religious affiliations it might also have fur-

[22] *Ibid.*, XIII (Nov. 1883), p. 242, XIV (Feb. 1884), pp. 27-28.
[23] *Ibid.*, XIII (June, July 1883), pp. 129-30, 148-49.
[24] Melcher, *Shaker Adventure*, p. 173.

nished fertile soil for missionary activity. But spiritualism turned in the direction of free love, anarchism, and materialism, which left the Shakers no points of contact.[25]

The secularization of spiritualism signalized the end of that type of revivalism which produced and sustained Shakerism. Revivalism in other forms has of course continued down to the present day, but without the same millennialist and perfectionist emphases. As they thus became isolated from the surrounding community the Shakers of the later nineteenth century tended to show more interest in their communalism than in their religious doctrines. This was especially true of the thinking of Elder Frederick Evans, most famous of the later Shakers. By 1874 the Society had sunk to the point of advertising in newspapers for members, offering a "comfortable home for life" to any who would embrace Shaker principles. This date may serve to signify the end of Shakerism.

Unlike their successors in the socialist tradition of both the communitarian and party types the Shakers were not particularly conscious of belonging to a larger socialist movement. Their socialized institutional organization was the spontaneous product of their religious zeal. Hence it was only gradually that the Shakers developed their critique of American life after the fashion typical of all socialist movements. As the form and discipline imposed upon Shakerism by its intermillennial doctrine gave the society stability and durability it became necessary perforce to define the meaning of Shakerism with reference to the character and ideals of the larger community which it rejected but in the midst of which it had to live. The Shakers could not ignore American democratic society; and while they criticized it, they could not, as we have already seen, reject its ideals completely. As the outside world gradually encroached upon them the Shaker leaders were forced to make extensive concessions in the form of incorporating into their eschatological system typical features of the democratic outlook. Thus at the beginning of the socialist movement in the United States the democratic ideology demonstrated what was to become its perennial capacity to drain off the radical impulses of movements of social protest by infusing them with its own principles.

Shaker sectarian theory in the early years of the nineteenth century had been rather more indifferent to the political state than hostile to it. Although they emphasized pacifism and nonparticipation in political life the Shakers were realistic enough to appreciate the conditions of religious toleration under which the sect was permitted to exist. Toleration was regarded as one of the evidences of the transitional character of republican society, foreshadowing better times to come. With the passage of the years and the stabilization of the Shaker societies the growing importance

[25] *Shaker*, I (July 1871), pp. 49-51.

of relations with the outside world was paralleled by further concessions in the ideological realm. The Shaker critique of capitalist democracy as completed by Elder Frederick W. Evans differed in detail but hardly in spirit from the proposals for social change advocated by many secular reformers. "The new heavens and the new earth" were to provide a place for secular democracy as well as for Shaker piety.[26]

The final dispensation following the seven epochs of the millennial era, as Evans conceived it, would witness the perfection of secular democracy. This would be the "new earth" promised in the revelation of St. John. Men and women would then be found to participate equally in social and political privileges; land for cultivation would be distributed by the state, and would revert to the state upon the death of the cultivator; education would be free and universal; doctors, lawyers, priests, speculators, soldiers, and customs collectors would be unnecessary; poverty, anxiety, conflict, and war would be known no more. The "new heavens" in these last times would be the Shaker societies, still living apart from the world and filled with "spiritual celibates," but to whom the citizens of the new earth would turn for moral guidance and spiritual insight.[27]

III. Oneida Perfectionism

In 1831, the so-called Finney revival, reaching out from central New York state into western New England, was responsible for the conversion of a young Dartmouth graduate of Putney, Vermont, named John Humphrey Noyes. The Finney revival represented the penetration of evangelical revivalism into the liberal wing of the Calvinist churches, coming to be known as the "New School." Noyes later testified that the millennial hope had been widely prevalent in the revival, and that he had set his heart upon it. It remained with him always. Perfectionist ideas were not current, perhaps because they had always been anathema to the Calvinists. But the logic of his millennialism led Noyes to yearn for the power to "overcome the world."[28] He gave up the study of law and entered Andover Seminary to prepare for the ministry. Finding Andover cool to his revival zeal he transferred after a year to Yale.

From his study of Scripture, Noyes, who always remained a Biblical literalist, discovered that the second coming of Christ was not an event to occur in the future, as the premillennialists assumed. It had occurred within a generation of Christ's ministry on earth, at the very beginning of the Christian era. The spiritual kingdom which Christ had then established was about to be made manifest in the material world; this was the event

[26] F. W. Evans, *Two Orders: Shakerism and Republicanism* (Pittsfield, Mass., 1890).

[27] Evans, *Shaker Reconstruction of the American Government* (Hudson, N.Y., 1888).

[28] *Confessions of John H. Noyes. Part I. Confession of Religious Experience: Including a History of Modern Perfectionism* (Oneida Reserve, 1849), pp. 2-5.

imperfectly apprehended by the revivalists. Thus for Noyes, as for the Shakers, the millennial kingdom was to undergo a progressive development. This curious form of intermillennialism was to be the foundation of all of Noyes's heresies.[29] The promise of Christian progress, together with the influence of Wesley and David Brainerd and the teaching of the liberal Calvinist, N. W. Taylor, all combined to stimulate in the eager student the hope of achieving perfect holiness.[30]

A prolonged and intense spiritual crisis followed. How could he possibly meet the demands of such an exalted standard? Certain evangelical perfectionist students had been drawn to Yale by Taylor's teaching that man had full ability to meet the demands of the divine law. Through these students Noyes came into contact with the scattered group of perfectionists, chiefly in upstate New York, who were keeping alive the ecstatic Antinomian and Quaker tradition of direct inspiration. From these perfectionists Noyes gained a realization of the importance of reposing complete faith in the regenerating power of God. He discovered the therapeutic value of transferring his sins. Eventually he experienced a second conversion, and believed himself to have been perpetually cleansed from sin. Noyes emerged from this experience with his personality transformed and his life reoriented. His affiliations with the orthodox religious community were broken, and he was barred from the Yale campus, becoming one of a little group of perfectionist zealots deplored by all sober citizens.[31]

Calvinist theologians had always taught that the regenerate person was still heir to the infirmities of the flesh. Noyes, who was trained in this tradition, now regarded it as a shabby compromise. He insisted that the second conversion completely cleansed from sin, although he was realistic enough to define freedom from sin as purity of spirit without claiming to. be beyond temptation or past moral improvement. The gift of grace released the sinner from the restraints of the moral law for the liberty of the Gospel. The truly regenerate person was no longer subject to the external laws of morality and the intellect, but to the divine leadings of the Spirit. Noyes admitted that he found this to be an extremely difficult readjustment. It required a sensitivity to and discrimination among spiritual influences which had to be painfully developed. Noyes's orthodox friends regarded him as crazy, although it is clear to us that his reliance upon direct divine inspiration represented the rediscovery of a typical feature of radical Protestant sectarianism. The "liberty of the Gospel" opened the floodgates of Noyes's imagination and intellect. It was at this period that he began to speculate upon the problems of sex, hygiene,

[29] *Ibid.*, p. 9. [30] *Ibid.*, p. 10.
[31] *Ibid.*, pp. 13-20.

disease, death, and history which preoccupied him for the remainder of his life.[32]

In the Antinomian perfectionists of his day Noyes found ready at hand potential recruits comparable to the New Light revivalists among whom the Shakers worked. They were in fact the extreme left wing of that movement. Their leaders were James Boyle, Theophilus R. Gates, and C. H. Weld, brother of the abolitionist, Theodore Dwight Weld. Noyes traveled about in Massachusetts, Connecticut, and New York attempting to wean them away from what he called their "Wesleyan legality" in favor of his doctrines of second conversion and intermillennialism. He found them relatively few in number, turbulent, and difficult to organize. They were widely and probably justly accused of fanaticism and immorality. Being orthodox premillennialists they rejected Noyes's doctrine of the Second Coming. If they were to be organized into a coherent religious body it was apparent to Noyes that they must first be disciplined. After three years of effort he admitted that he had failed to establish himself as their leader.[33] For the time being he gave up proselytizing among the perfectionists and returned to the family home at Putney to start afresh with the members of his own family and immediate neighbors.

Noyes organized a Bible class and set about teaching his theories to any who would listen. During the decade 1836-1846 he worked out the details of his doctrinal system. It closely resembled that of the Shakers. Noyes in fact admitted that but for what he regarded to be the erroneous Shaker conception of the nature of the Kingdom of Heaven he would himself have become a Shaker.[34] He shared with them the theory of the duality of the Godhead, male and female, although Noyes maintained, unlike the Shakers, that the same relationship between the sexes prevailed in Heaven as under the present dispensation. This view was consistent with the contrast, fundamental to his system, between the law which governs men in the sinful state and the liberty which is enjoyed by the regenerate. Noyes had early concluded that all acts of the unregenerate were sinful, but that for the believer all things were lawful. The notoriety which attended Noyes's career stemmed chiefly from the fact that this doctrine was applied to relations between the sexes. True to the evangelical spirit of the time Noyes's teaching bore almost no relation to the liberal Calvinism in which he had been reared. It was a mixture of Antinomian theories of direct inspiration, Quaker ideas about the cultivation of holiness, Pelagian notions of human ability, Wesleyan perfectionism, and revivalist millennialism, rounded off with unique theories of his own on many other subjects. He called the system Calvinist perfectionism merely because he

[32] *Ibid.*, pp. 20-23.   [33] *Ibid.*, pp. 48-70.
[34] *Witness*, ı (Sept. 25, 1839), p. 77.

insisted that the truly regenerate person will persevere in holiness to the end.[35]

The social implications of Noyes's central doctrine emphasizing the contrast between the legal restraint upon the unregenerate and the liberty of the believer were soon to assert themselves. The perfectionists with whom Noyes had associated in 1834 after his second conversion were widely accused of sexual immorality. Noyes himself had believed at that time that the same principle applied here as in all other outward acts, namely, "whatsoever is not of faith is sin; but for him who believeth all things are lawful."[36] The chaotic consequences of this doctrine must have become soon apparent to him, for by 1837 he was teaching that not until the Kingdom was institutionalized on earth would marriage be abandoned. In the meanwhile he favored the advice of Paul to remain celibate.[37] This advice was conditioned explicitly by Paul's assumption that the Kingdom was about to come. Yet when, during the following year, many of his Putney disciples showed signs of sympathy with the Shakers, Noyes dampened his chiliastic ardor sufficiently to marry one of his followers, Harriet Holton, and to advise the others to do likewise.[38]

The formation of a community paralleled the development of doctrine. What had been at first a family Bible-study group slowly grew to be a congregation. In 1841 a Society of Inquiry was formed, officers elected, and a small chapel erected. Stenographic reports of the discussions were published in the *Witness*, the journal which Noyes edited as a means of maintaining contact with the perfectionists of New York and New England.[39] Noyes hoped that the Society would be a germ from which would grow a "Free Church" uniting all perfectionists.[40] A similar society, modeled on the Putney group was soon formed in Newark, New Jersey. With the acquisition of property and the arrival of recruits from New York a corporation was formed, which, by a natural process of development, became a socialized community. This development was not premeditated. As Noyes later remarked, "a spirit of love led naturally to a community of goods," but community of goods, or association, to use the Fourierist term which Noyes himself employed at this time, was never more than an "incidental help to the main purpose," namely, the extension of Christ's sovereignty in the world.[41]

[35] Noyes's theological writings of this period were gathered in a volume called *The Berean: a Manual for the Help of Those Who Seek the Faith of the Primitive Church* (Putney, Vt., 1847). See pp. v-viii for Noyes's own summary.

[36] *Witness*, I (Sept. 25, 1839), p. 78.

[37] *Ibid.*, I (Jan. 23, 1839), p. 49.

[38] I Corinthians, 7:29-31; *Witness*, I (Nov. 21, 1838), p. 26, I (Sept. 25, 1839), p. 78.

[39] *Witness*, II (1841), pp. 19, 25, 26, 28, 33, 41, 42, 49, 57.

[40] *Ibid.*, II (Feb. 22, 1841), pp. 9-10.

[41] *Circular*, I (May 16, 1852), p. 105.

Ever since the time during his student days when he discovered the testimony of Scripture that the Second Coming had already occurred, and that Christ was at hand ready to join those made perfect to receive him, Noyes looked forward eagerly to the great event. The ten years of teaching at Putney had been a preparation for it. The social movements of the eighteen-thirties and forties, Millerite adventism, Fourierism, abolitionism, spiritualism, all seemed to be signs of the times pointing toward the establishment of the Kingdom. Noyes's millennial doctrine was too sophisticated to propose that Christ would return to earth in the crude physical form. Rather Christ would return as a spirit infusing believers, destroying evil, and transforming society. His coming would be like the coming of spring, which, because of its spiritual nature, would be difficult to detect as a precise event. But in the spring of 1847 Noyes felt that the moment had at last arrived. The Putney community had achieved a degree of purification which expressed itself both in community of property and in several miraculous cures of illness which indicated a power in the community to overcome death itself. On June 1, 1847, Noyes propounded the question whether it was not then time to proclaim that God had come in the Putney Association. The members unanimously resolved that the Kingdom had come.[42]

This dramatic event represented the full development of Noyes's inter-millennialism. The liberty of the Gospel enjoyed by the individual believer was now extended to the holy community. The remainder of Noyes's career was devoted to charting the social relationships of the Kingdom. Among the practices which distinguished the new dispensation (Noyes's Perfectionism) from the sinful world the most important were complex marriage, Bible communism, and mutual criticism.

In attributing central significance to the relationship between the sexes these Perfectionists were only giving expression to an interest which had always fascinated radical sectarians. But whereas the Shakers, for instance, regarded the sexual impulse as a sinful appetite to be repressed, Noyes's followers proposed to employ it deliberately as symbolic of the spiritual union of believers. One can hardly doubt that the final elaboration of Noyes's theological system was intended to rationalize the complex marriage between all of the members of the community. He taught that Spirit is a substance, with external and internal properties. Christ's hope for his followers, that they might all be one, even as he and the Father were one, provided the ultimate insight into Christian perfection. There were two forms of spiritual union similar to those of physical union: to fill and to envelop; the male and female principles. These were the great desires of the spiritual as well as of the physical life. They explained the creation of the sexes. The desire to fill and to be enveloped is male; the

42 *Spiritual Magazine*, II (July 15, 1847), pp. 65-69.

desire to be filled and to envelop is female. "Love in its highest form is the reciprocal and satisfied attraction of these two forms of desire." Thus the universal chain of relationship descended from God in Christ, through Christ in the church, to the union of believers. Marriage was the symbol and seal of this universal relationship.[43]

The complex marriage which these doctrines justified was far from being the unregulated promiscuity deplored by shocked contemporaries. It represented rather the disciplining of the sexual forces released by this radical version of the traditional doctrine of Christian liberty. The community exercised constant supervision over the relations between its members.[44] There was doubtless some justice in its claim to be the first noncelibate community in which sexual irresponsibility ceased to exist. Nor is there any evidence to indicate that the powerful forces of sex escaped from the spiritual discipline to which they were subordinated, at least as long as the religious teachings of the community retained their hold upon its members. In fact, one suspects that complex marriage was no more offensive to the Victorian conventions of the mid-nineteenth century than was the Perfectionists' insistence that sexual relations were important enough to be openly discussed and regulated in the interests of the community. But whatever the cause, the reaction of a society in which the monogamous family was the most important institution was sharp and decisive. Noyes and his disciples were driven out of Putney and the state of Vermont, seeking refuge at Oneida in the Perfectionist stronghold of central New York.

The choice of Oneida reflected the success of Noyes in his constant journalistic efforts to propagate his views among the revivalistic perfectionists in that region. The magazines which he edited circulated widely in central New York, bringing a small but steady stream of recruits to the community. To them Noyes stood for the same disciplinary force which the Shakers represented among the New Lights. By contributing their property they made possible an enterprise which for several years operated at a deficit. Oneida was at the center of the "burnt-over" region, where evangelical revivalism had been endemic for half a century, "the birthplace of many of the mightiest moral and political movements of the times in which we live," as Noyes had rather magniloquently expressed it.[45] These transplanted New Englanders, their Puritan heritage blended with evangelical revivalism and released from the restraints of the ancestral social order, were strangely alive to the appeal of ideal causes, to what later came to be called the "enthusiasm of humanity." They were prone to

---

[43] *Ibid.*, I (Mar. 15, 1846), pp. 1-4, (Apr. 15, 1846), pp. 17-19.

[44] *Hand-Book of the Oneida Community; Containing a Brief Sketch of Its Present Condition, Internal Economy, and Leading Principles. No. 2* (Oneida, N.Y., 1871), pp. 49-58.

[45] *Witness*, I (Sept. 3, 1837), p. 9.

enlist in every popular cause of the day, from dress and diet reform to spiritualism and abolition. The community at Oneida attempted to harness this idealism and make it coherent by giving it a philosophy of reform in the doctrine of perfect holiness.

The theory of Bible communism as perfected in the years after the settlement at Oneida rested upon the religious principles in which the members of the community were already well grounded. Salvation from sin once achieved was transformed into the positive attribute of universal love. The problem for social theory was to design or designate institutions in which the spirit of love would be most freely expressed. True to the perennial religious instinct the Perfectionists chose the family as the institution best expressing the values they cherished. In the Heavenly Kingdom the believer is united in Christ by love. He is also perfectly dedicated to doing the will of the Father. These qualities of love and submission were of course peculiarly characteristic of the family relationship. The social structure of the Kingdom was therefore analogous to that of the family. The members were united in love, all property was held in common, and authority gravitated spontaneously to those best suited by spirit and intellect to exercise it. The social functions of production, education, worship, and amusement were all conceived in familial terms. In the vocabulary of classical socialist theory this Christian familism might be classified as a kind of syndicalism. Noyes once observed that his form of communism could easily be extended if employers would substitute the family relationship for the prevailing labor system. Each business enterprise would simply become a family, its size depending upon its economic requirements. It would at the same time become a church and a school. In a real sense its business would be sanctified. The essential precondition was of course entire salvation from sin.[46]

The Oneida Perfectionists agreed with the Shakers that the government of the Kingdom was ultimately theocratic and immediately paternalistic. In its spiritual aspects the Kingdom was a church whose officers were appointed by God and whose authority was to be accepted by the members. From the human point of view leadership should be the reward of natural ability. Noyes realized that where authority is coterminous with ability and character the social group must be small—a family or a congregation. At the daily evening meetings for the discussion of religious and practical problems, which all members were expected to attend, unanimity of agreement reminiscent of the Quaker meeting was always sought.[47]

The repudiation of the world with its iniquitous political arrangements, which has usually characterized radical sectarianism, received

[46] *Circular*, I (June 13, 1852), p. 121, II (Dec. 11, 1852), p. 30.
[47] *Spiritual Magazine*, II (July 1, 1847), pp. 57-59; *Hand-Book*, pp. 17-36.

somewhat ambiguous expression by the Oneida Perfectionists. Like the Shakers they owed much to the society which cradled them, and although they had every reason to emphasize the depth of the chasm separating the Kingdom from the sinful world, in fact they were neither willing nor able to adopt the attitude toward the outside world which the logic of their position seemed to require. It was true that during the early years of preparation when Noyes was awaiting the advent of the Kingdom he had bitterly denounced all existing governments as symbols of the apostasy. He had written to William Lloyd Garrison (March 22, 1837) that he equated the establishment of the Kingdom with the overthrow of the government of the United States. Three years later he had made a rather feeble revolutionary gesture himself by persuading his Putney followers to repudiate their allegiance to the federal government in a formal resolution.[48] But the government remained hale and sound, and the Kingdom finally came unattended by catastrophic social revolution.

The relatively painless transition to the new dispensation compelled Noyes to abandon his earlier judgments upon the absolute corruption of the old order. The revolution once deemed necessary had proved to be an evolutionary progression. It was now apparent that American republican liberty, with its presuppositions of certain intellectual and moral standards, had prepared the way for Bible communism, a higher stage of civilization in which sin and selfishness were abolished. The achievement of perfection, which Noyes had earlier defined as the gift of grace through faith, was now found to entail a moral refinement which required changes in social relationships resulting in "entire communism."[49]

No constitution or bill of rights defined the privileges of community members, nor was any necessary. The Creator was acknowledged to be the owner of all things, and all duties and privileges were assigned by him through inspiration, direct or indirect. Noyes informed his followers that the restraints which the system imposed upon them were those required by a higher civilization, while the liberty of spirit they enjoyed was likewise impossible in the sinful world.[50] The secular socialistic communities of the mid-nineteenth century, of which Noyes was a close student, inevitably failed, in his opinion, because they failed to solve the problem of liberty and union. They had expected that the new social relationships of community would transform character; and yet they had relied upon selfish personal rights and legal justice when they expected that stock ownership and scientifically calculated wages would supply

[48] *William Lloyd Garrison, the Story of His Life Told by His Children* (Boston and New York, 1885, 1889, 4 vols.), II, pp. 145-48; *Witness*, I (Aug. 20, 1840), p. 168.
[49] *Circular*, I (Feb. 1, 8, 1852), pp. 49-50, 53.
[50] *Ibid.*, I (Nov. 30, 1851), pp. 13-14, VI (Nov. 29, 1869), pp. 289-91.

the incentive for community action. Consequently they never achieved the unity which they sought. In uniting in submission to the will of God the Bible communists found their individual desires and purposes perfectly reconciled.[51]

Complex marriage doubtless gave the Oneida community its dramatic appeal to mid-nineteenth century Perfectionists, but it was the institution of mutual criticism which disciplined and united the community. Mutual criticism was the public analysis of one's defects and virtues to which all members of the community submitted at periodic intervals. Noyes had encountered the technique when a student at Andover, and had been profoundly impressed by the zeal for moral and spiritual improvement which it had stimulated among the students practicing it. He introduced the practice at Putney in 1846 after the doctrinal foundations had been laid. At that time the purpose of criticism was understood to be the cultivation of the spirit of improvement among the members in preparation for the union with the primitive church which Noyes taught would follow the institutionalization of the Kingdom. Members were encouraged to offer themselves for criticism voluntarily. The experience was often an ordeal. But the spirit of love in which criticism was administered effectively healed any wounds that were inflicted. During the first year every member of the community submitted to criticism, and the effect was profoundly stimulating. When increasing numbers at Oneida made community criticism impracticable, committees and classes for criticism were formed.[52]

The ceremony of criticism quickly became the center of the religious life of the community. Living as they professed to be in the Kingdom every act was an act of devotion, and consequently the members attached relatively little importance to formal services of worship. The meeting for criticism served as the instrumentality for the operation of the divine spirit upon the believer. Because the Perfectionists believed in direct inspiration it was important that some such socializing agency should direct the impulses of the spirit into useful channels and prevent the anarchy which unrestrained religious enthusiasm had usually brought in its wake. Noyes himself, when present, was the guiding spirit in criticism. It was chiefly through his gifts for character analysis that he maintained his paternal control over his followers. He compared criticism to law enforcement agencies in the secular world, except for the fact that criticism, by going behind acts to character, molded conduct rather than repressed it.[53]

The theory that leadership was confirmed by inspiration and should

[51] Ibid., I (Aug. 4, 1852), pp. 154-55.
[52] Ibid., I (Mar. 21, 1852), pp. 74-75, II (June 29, July 6, 1853), pp. 258, 266.
[53] Ibid., I (Oct. 10, 1852), p. 193.

be accepted in a peaceable spirit did not always escape criticism, especially when in the frequent absences of Noyes his deputies lacked his skill and authority. Noyes conceded that there was a corrupting tendency in power itself, but he reassured the believers that human authority was a temporary phenomenon which would disappear with spiritual growth. In the Kingdom as in the classless society government would eventually wither away. But in the meanwhile he prescribed criticism as the best means to restrain the officers and protect the members. Every two or three months subordinate officials should be criticized by the community in the presence of a superior officer. Anticipating the question, who should preside over the criticism of Noyes himself, the leader blandly declared that when Christ or Paul or some member of the primitive church visited the community he would do it.[54]

Since criticism was the sovereign remedy for the "insensible diseases" commonly called character defects, it was not surprising that Noyes should prescribe it for physical diseases as well, according to his own unique theory of physiotherapy. He believed that disease originated in the spirit, attacking the bodily organism through gaps in its spiritual defenses. The therapeutic function of criticism was to find the character defect and by eliminating it close off access of disease to the body. By frugal living and by overcoming the fear of death Noyes expected that not only would sickness be prevented, but ultimately death itself.[55]

Noyes's evangelical perfectionism had the same ambiguous quality as that of the Shakers. His view of human history, though set in a religious frame of reference which at first glance seemed remote enough from the secular outlook of the mid-nineteenth century, was actually quite compatible with the progressive optimism of the period. After the removal to Oneida the Perfectionists seemed to prefer to minimize their sectarian isolation and to identify themselves as far as possible with the larger community. In their Second Annual Report of 1850 they emphasized the compatibility between republicanism and Bible communism. Both were dedicated to the advancement of reason and truth. "Republicanism then is bound by the very terms of its existence to disregard all outward limitations and partial forms of truth, and to proceed right on to the complete evolution of heaven's justice among men; or in other words, to merge itself in the Kingdom of God."[56] In the same spirit the Perfectionists expressed a lively interest in the current intellectual movements, such as

[54] *Ibid.*, II (June 25, 1853), pp. 255-56.

[55] *Ibid.*, I (Oct. 31, 1852), p. 206, II (June 4, 1853), p. 231. For examples of faith healing among Perfectionists see the *Spiritual Magazine*, I (1846), pp. 113-20, I (1847), pp. 173-75, II (1847), pp. 45-46, 62-63, 78, 145-47, 187-89, 191, II (1849), pp. 220-24, 270-72.

[56] *Second Annual Report of the Oneida Association . . . Feb. 20, 1850* (Oneida Reserve, N.Y., 1850), pp. 26-27.

mesmerism, positivism, Darwinism, and eugenics. Nevertheless, Noyes never relinquished his millennialist theology as the basic rationale of the movement, and after the Civil War these ideas would quickly acquire a distinctly dated flavor.

The achievement of material prosperity by the Oneida Community in its later years is a familiar story and need not be recounted here. The effect of this affluence upon the life of the community is difficult to assess. But it clearly made possible advanced education for the children of the community. The secular culture of the late nineteenth century which they encountered in the outside world quickly dissolved the millennialist and perfectionist theology in which they had been reared, and with it went the whole rationale of the community.

Oneida Perfectionism failed for both external and internal reasons. The intense hostility of orthodox neighbors to the institution of complex marriage need not have terminated Bible communism any more than the suppression of polygamy ended Mormonism. It was the failure to win recruits that spelled the end of the movement. Noyes had hoped to form a Free Church among his Perfectionist followers, who would organize congregations in the usual pattern. Community living need not follow at once, although Noyes assumed that it would ultimately develop out of the perfectionist precepts of the Free Churches as it had already done at Putney.[57] These Free Churches failed to materialize. The evangelical revivalism of the late nineteenth century no longer produced the fervid premillennialism which was the key to effective proselytizing by the intermillennialists. Although Noyes never lost his interest in revivals wherever they occurred, nevertheless as the years passed he became ever more deeply absorbed in the problems of communal living to the exclusion of making new converts.

That Noyes himself was a member of the last generation of intermillennialists became abundantly clear when his own children repudiated the faith. These were not the "stirpes," the offspring of the eugenics program inaugurated in 1869. The latter were too young to play any significant role in the life of the community. It was the older children who had grown up in the community who voluntarily abandoned Bible communism because its religious rationale seemed archaic.

In the Marxist vocabulary the term "utopian" was applied to those socialist movements and thinkers preceding Marx and Engels whose variously visionary, romantic, or rationalistic programs of social reconstruction reflected an immature and imperfect understanding of the needs of the proletariat and of the class struggle. To the extent that the communitarian Christians of America were the products of a preindustrial society unaware

[57] *Circular*, I (Dec 14, 1851), p. 22.

of the proletarian character of their protest we can certainly accept and apply to them the epithet, utopian. But it is difficult to find beneath their religious preoccupations the objective evidences of social oppression which the Marxian thesis requires. In fact, the communitarians were as authentic an expression of nineteenth-century rural and evangelical America as the Marxists themselves were of early industrial society in Europe, and in this sense each movement displayed its own "utopian" and "scientific" characteristics.

Both the Shakers and the Oneida Perfectionists survived to the end of the era of rural evangelical revivalism, and with the passing of that movement the communitarian enterprise perished. Since the religious communities were a product of that particular brand of revivalism the causes of its decline undoubtedly account for their demise as well. These causes may indeed have reflected the influence of industrialism in replacing the rural outlook with a new urban psychology. The effects of such a change upon the religious mind have been subtle and pervasive. Although the institution of revivalism has been able to survive in the twentieth century in part by adapting itself to an urban culture, it has undergone a radical change in spirit. The old millennialist expectation is still occasionally apparent, but it is now generally associated with a catastrophic judgment upon the world rather than with the realization of personal salvation through a romantic reconstruction of social institutions linking this world and the next. Similarly, the perfectionism of the modern chiliastic sects is merely a psychological by-product of the emotional ecstasy of conversion. The "holiness" thus achieved has little or no positive social or ethical implication. One would hardly expect a concern with social reform to emerge out of such a matrix.

In the larger sense it still remains true that the communitarian Christians inevitably failed as socialists because their socialism was subordinate to their religion. But this is to frame a judgment which the communitarians themselves would have regarded as irrelevant. They were acquainted with the short-lived efforts of their Owenite and Fourierist contemporaries of the mid-nineteenth century to form communities on a rationalistic basis, the failure of which they attributed to the absence of spiritual discipline. But there is no evidence that they ever sensed how effectively the ideology of liberal American nationalism in combination with industrialism would render the whole communitarian enterprise obsolete.

CHAPTER 5

The Secular Utopian Socialists

BY T. D. SEYMOUR BASSETT

T. D. SEYMOUR BASSETT, Assistant Professor of History at Earlham College, was from 1946 to 1948 Research Associate and Bibliographer of the Program in American Civilization at Princeton. Formerly a member of the staff of the National Archives in Washington, his special field is American social history.

For bibliography in Volume 2 relevant to Mr. Bassett's essay, see especially PART II, General Reading (sections 1, 2), and Topics 5, 6, 7, 12; also PART I, Topics 2, 6; PART III, General Reading (section 2); PART IV, General Reading (section 1), and Topic 8; PART V, General Reading (sections 1C and 2A), and Topics 5, 6, 7, 8, 9; PART VI, General Reading (section 2A), and Topics 2, 3.

ONE aspect of the ferment resulting from the territorial and industrial expansion of the United States in the nineteenth century was the repeated emergence in the North and West of small groups with new views of society. Breaking with the dominant traditions of individualism and orthodox religion, they pointed the way to heavenly or earthly happiness by establishing communities upon sectarian or humanitarian principles.

These two types—secular and sectarian—had much in common. They were both reactions against the evils of society at large. By necessity or choice, they both adopted communitarian solutions and faced the same problems of close association. The fortunes of both were subject to the larger movements of American history, which in the end overwhelmed them. They were aware of each other's little worlds, commented upon each other's fortunes in their publications, exchanged visits and occasionally members.

The differences between the two types were nevertheless profound. The establishments of the religious sects prospered more and longer, in many ways ventured further from common American patterns, and reached further back into European tradition for their justification. They were, with few exceptions, homogeneous, static, and closed systems; the secular communities were heterogeneous, dynamic, and free. A study of the secular type, in spite of the brevity of its experiments, can better illuminate American history just because of its closer relation to the dominant modes of life which it combated and the relative modernity of its philosophy.

This essay deals primarily with the three most important branches of American secular utopian socialism: Owenism, Fourierism, and Icarianism. Like the Marxians, these communitarians had a secular goal in history and on earth, and the ways they chose to approach it were without the sanction of any particular religious denomination or sect. Like other utopians they felt caught in a frustrating social environment and tried to escape it under the guidance of irrational myths—what Karl Mannheim calls symbolic substitutes for reality.[1] They were less myth-oriented than the religious utopians, but more so than the Marxians. They were socialists in the broad sense of proposing various degrees of collective ownership and activity whereby the oppressive contemporary society could be supplanted and individuals could achieve their highest potentials. Their insistence on immediate change from the prevailing conditions of American capitalism to a collective township environment was revolutionary; their strategy both inside that community and for the world at large was gradualist.

Why were some nineteenth-century Americans sufficiently frustrated to construct or accept others' constructions of blueprints for an ideal

[1] See the bibliography in Volume 2, PART I, Topic 6.

society? Most Americans for at least three generations after 1776, like the Soviet communists after their Revolution, were blatantly proclaiming that theirs *was* the ideal social state in the making; that it had the best constitution on earth; and that the mission of America was to extend the blessings of liberty throughout the world. The very pitch of their spread-eagle oratory betrayed the inferiority complex of a newcomer to the society of nations. Secular utopianism was imported between 1824 and 1849, when the strains caused by American expansion were most acute. The shocks of this period were delivered by a new industrial system which was recognized but little understood and which operated in an unevenly but swiftly broadening market area. When an old order first feels the attack of a new, the psychological pains are more alarming than at later stages. The growth of urban industrialism accelerated quantitatively during the next century, but the shocks of succeeding periods were the result of the new system's enormous size and power and the international conflicts which it aggravated. Secular utopianism and the equally ineffectual contemporary trade unionism and native agrarianism were the three movements in the North which first organized the opposition to American commercial and industrial capitalism.

The main purpose of this essay is to outline the Americanization of European secular utopian socialism. Against a background sketch of the European founders and their eighteenth-century ideas, each temporary minority movement is described in connection with the general history of the United States. The process of viewing these movements as part of American history suggests relationships with the frontier, the factory system, urbanization, political parties, the ferment of reform, and the progress of science and religion. The last section points out a number of undeveloped themes in the social theory and practice of these communitarians, notes their relation to Marxism, and evaluates the prophetic quality of their ideas.[2]

I. The European Background

The original theorists of the three major branches of American secular utopianism were Europeans born under the Enlightenment, repelled by the violence of the French Revolution, and arrested by the misery accompanying early industrialism in Great Britain and France. Robert Owen, Charles Fourier, and Étienne Cabet, in spite of the universalist terms of their utopias, wrote for an English and French public. In propounding their basic theories they were little concerned with American conditions; and when circumstances turned Owen's and Cabet's attention to the New World, they made grave mistakes in judging these conditions.

[2] The bibliography in Volume 2, PART I, Topic 2 and PART II, Topics 5, 6, includes detailed studies of secular utopianism and the general sources of this essay.

Of the three leaders, Robert Owen (b. 1771) was the first to risk his theories in practice. He had climbed the ladder of success in British cotton textile manufacture when the economic disorganization of the Napoleonic era presented a challenge. His first proposals to the upper classes (1812-1820) applied his experience as a benevolent employer at New Lanark, Scotland, to national problems, especially overproduction and deflation. Although faced with an economic problem, he proposed an educational reform on the theory that the difficulty arose from the inculcation of wrong principles and that the remedy was proper character training in a propitious environment. Owen had worked this theory out himself, with scarcely any borrowing from Fourier, who had already published his own theories. For Owen had compared notes with pioneer educators—Pestalozzi, Oberlin, and Fellenberg to whose school at Hofwyl, Switzerland, he later sent all four of his sons. Without impairing his profits, he had succeeded in changing the character of his child laborers.

The second period of Owen's development began when he realized that the upper classes were not listening to him. Undaunted, he turned to labor about 1822, and approached in much of his propaganda the equalitarianism of John Gray and William Thompson. When the agent of the Rappite community at Harmony, Indiana, presented Owen with the chance to buy a ready-made site for an experiment with his educational and socialistic theories, he threw himself into the enterprise until it failed in 1827. After an abortive plan the following year to try again in Mexico, his communitarianism subsided for eight years. Owen became the advocate of cooperatives, trade unions, and employment service during this period. His journal, the *New Moral World*, returned to the community theme in 1836, and he supported an English experiment at Harmony Hall, Queenwood (1839-1845). Withdrawing his support from this in 1844, he returned to the American forum to compete in vain with the Fourierists for four successive winters. The man who had backed a loser had little chance with Americans to win a second race. After a final formulation of his utopian theory in 1849, with many new features, he occupied the last years of a very old age with spiritualism. Owen retained throughout his life the temperament of an upper-class philanthropist constrained by the coldness of his peers to ally himself with the workingmen.

Owen's contemporary, Charles Fourier (b. 1772), consistently maintained the outlook of a petty-bourgeois critic of bourgeois society. He observed the evils of merchant capitalism from shifting residence in Lyons, Marseilles, Paris, and other French cities. At Lyons from 1790 to 1793, he gained an enduring hatred of disorder and violence from his personal experience of the Revolution. In the siege of Lyons by the Convention forces in 1793, the goods which represented his fortune were commandeered for the defense of the city, and he was briefly jailed and threatened with execution by the victorious besiegers.

Fourier seems, in contrast to Owen, to have stated his case in 1808 and to have held it faithfully until his death in 1837. From the day he first advertised that he would be at his quarters every noon to discuss with any benevolent capitalist the use of the capitalist's money for a phalanx, he returned punctually at the appointed hour. Minor shifts in the targets of his propaganda did modify his secondary ideas, as in his reversal on the Jewish question when he hoped to attract the capital of Baron Rothschild. He entertained the possibility of experimenting in the New World even less than Owen or Cabet. Unlike them, he was never propelled by circumstances to any American venture. His mature life as a bachelor was a routine planned to the smallest detail in which his time and activities were classified and fitted together with the paradoxical haphazard nicety of his writings. He kept a schedule of so many pages a day, and his writings are full of classifications; but he neither brought to the task a systematic preparation nor ended with a systematic presentation.

The youngest of the three founders, Étienne Cabet (b. 1788), had a much greater sympathy for French Revolutionary ideals, but no less an abhorrence of revolutionary violence. Cabet was born of a proletarian family in Dijon, and studied there under the revolutionary veteran and pedagogue, Joseph Jacotot. Through Jacotot's influence he was appointed a teacher in the local lycée, but soon rebelled against its regimentation. Turned lawyer, he won both status and the enmity of reactionaries by his successful defense of proscribed republicans. Without sacrificing either his personal ambition or his radical principles, he pushed himself into the ranks of republican leadership by risking his position for the unpopular cause. When the government of Louis Philippe exiled him for five years, he used his enforced idleness in London to read the literature of the utopians, the physiocrats, the *philosophes*, the Bible, and the church fathers; and to write out his ideas, especially in a history of the French Revolution and in his famous utopian novel, *Voyage . . . en Icarie*. At the same time he found in Owenism a confirmation of his central ideas. After his return to Paris in 1839, he made the Icarian platform the basis for a strong political movement in competition with the propaganda of Lamennais, Pierre Leroux, Louis Blanc, the Fourierists, and the Communist League.

Cabet stressed the need for a long preparatory stage of propaganda, but the taunts of enemies and the impetuosity of disciples provoked him to put his theories to a practical test. In January 1848, he made a disastrous arrangement for land in Texas with the Peters Company of Cincinnati. His half sections had to be settled by July 1, 1848, and they were separated by lands which the state of Texas and the Peters Company withheld. The state of Texas might be accommodating, but the speculator could not be expected to sell his intervening half sections at the cheap figure suggested in the agreement, once the Icarians were settled and helpless on the land. Apparently unaware of these obstacles and of the hardships to be encountered on the Texas frontier, Cabet launched the Icarian emigration. Before many had sailed, the insurrection of February 24, 1848, persuaded numbers of his followers that politics at home was preferable to a doubtful experiment abroad. Cabet tried to lead his party in France and promote the expedition at the same time. In the end he joined the vanguard in the United States, where they found a new location at Nauvoo, Illinois. Unlike Fourierism, the Icarian movement in Europe did not long outlive its founder.

The utopian spirit of Fourier and Cabet was somewhat paralleled among the Germans in the career of Wilhelm Weitling. Proletarian in background, circumstance, and outlook he agitated equalitarian class hatred by underground tactics in France, Germany, and Switzerland. Marx expelled him from the Communist League in the spring of 1846, apparently for his inadequate grasp of the League's strategy or its theoretical basis. He continued his propaganda alone with messianic conviction, removed to the United States, and tried to finance the Iowa socialist settlement, Communia, with the contributions of a German-American labor organization. When Communia disbanded in 1853, some of its colonists joined the Icarians. No other communitarian in the United States came as close as Weitling to securing labor support.

Many varieties of the early nineteenth-century socialism of western Europe spread not only to the United States, but flowed out in other directions from their original sources. There were Icarians scattered from Germany to Spain. The romantic Christian socialism of Leroux and Saint-Simon gained a following among the opponents of the Argentine caudillo, Rosas. Fourierism eventually spread eastward as far as Russia. Such was the broad sweep of secular utopian socialism from its Anglo-French center.

Extensive genealogical research into the sources and lineage of the social ideas of Fourier, Owen, and Cabet has generally resulted in negative conclusions. These men absorbed selectively and transformed in the light of their various experience the contemporary climate of opinion—the deist, rationalist, utilitarian, and liberal parts of their eighteenth-century heritage. They had read extensively, but not with a scholar's self-conscious awareness of their relations with preceding thinkers. Fourier was perpetually involved in the ephemeral duties of his miscellaneous businesses; Owen in his manufacturing; and Cabet in his political, legal, and propagandist activities. All were under the philosophical shadow of Descartes, Newton, and Locke. Their utopias were mechanical contrivances; Fourier even posed as the Newton of the social sciences. Directly behind their rationalism and anticlericalism stood the French *philosophes* and the English deists. Their preoccupation with educational reform and their fundamental disregard of the state owed much to Rousseau, though none explicitly rejected the state, and Owen sought continually to win its favor. His theory of deliberate inculcation was a far cry from the unfolding of the natural man proposed in *Emile*. He strongly disagreed with his industrial partner, Jeremy Bentham, yet repeatedly subjected his own value judgments to the Benthamite test of utility. Fourier denied his debt to the physiocrats and yet proposed a similar subordination of industry and commerce to agriculture. Cabet's equalitarianism would acknowledge no debt to Babeuf.

The two outstanding elements in their thought most significant for an understanding of their American influence were their natural rights philosophy and their acceptance of the Christian ethic. Large numbers in the United States thought in the same terms and would listen to appeals within this intellectual framework. Locke's natural rights to life and liberty were enshrined in the Declaration of Independence, and the federal Constitution firmly buttressed the natural right to property. The secular utopians did not depart very far from the American interpretation of the right to property in construing it as the right to equal enjoyment of the riches provided by nature and man's labor. The American deists agreed with the secular utopians' ethical Christianity, but the increasing number of Americans affected by the evangelical revivals condemned the utopians' hostility to organized religion and its orthodox theology.

On both sides of the Atlantic, the secular utopians were in the broad sense liberals. Basically they believed in the free play of reason as the universal solvent of all strife and discoverer of all the realities of nature. Their tolerance of any religion, in spite of their lively opposition to orthodoxy, was based on the firm conviction that reason would ultimately triumph over all superstition. They exalted the civil rights of free speech, free press, and free assembly for the same reason: full democratic discussion was essential for a society to function justly. They believed in the freedom of their communities to manage their own affairs without the interference of any outside power. They anticipated no just need for such interference. They believed in the free choice of jobs within the community and a world of free economic enterprise in which each community would be an autonomous enterpriser and in which liberty would increase as man developed machinery as his slave. They urged the rights of women to freedom in marriage and in society; the rights of children to free access to a knowledge of nature and of a trade that would free them from dependence. This emphasis on liberty in the abstract, however compromised in practice, is what qualified the secular utopians as basically antistatist.[3]

Their liberalism paradoxically implied an ultimate determinism. Fourier's psychology assumed that passional attraction would operate as inexorably as gravity, and Owen argued against free will. Their American followers, however, except for a few leading intellectuals, subordinated determinism to activism.[4]

II. Owenism in America

Owen's ideas were probably first introduced into the United States as early as 1817 through articles in British reviews. During the next five years, native communitarian activity centered in the New York Society for Promoting Communities, a group consisting mostly of Friends and led by Cornelius C. Blatchly, a Quaker apothecary. This activity culminated in 1822 with publications by the Society and by Paul Brown, an itinerant schoolmaster of Quaker background and sympathies who was interested in this Society.[5] Even if the original impulse came through hints from Owen, deviation began immediately. Influenced by the example of the successful Shaker and Rappite communities and by the authors' Quaker background, these first American expressions were communistic and more explicitly religious.

The Owenite movement of 1824-1828 was throughout under the strong influence of Owen himself. It failed and left few traces both because it was misguided by a man not fully acquainted with American conditions and because of those conditions. When Owen's party arrived in New York on November 4, 1824, he was welcomed by Blatchly and presented with the Society's pamphlet. Owen's first question to this small group that evening is significant. "Mr. Owen asked whether any of the leading people favored them. The President replied that on the contrary, they discountenanced the idea of communities,"[6] and referred to Thomas Jefferson's

[3] See the discussion of their antistatism below, pp. 197-200; also Mousheng H. Lin, *Antistatism—A History of Utopias* (New York, 1941), especially pp. 17-27, 39-52.

[4] The orthodox James Duncan was one of the few Americans to ask who formed Owen's character (Duncan, *Animadversions on the Principles of the New-Harmony Society* [Indianapolis, Ind., 1826], pp. 8-9).

[5] New York Society for Promoting Communities, *An Essay on Commonwealths* (New York, 1822), including Melish's account of the Harmonists, extracts from Owen's *New View of Society*, and an original essay, presumably by Blatchly, "The Evils of Exclusive and the Benefits of Inclusive Wealth"; Paul Brown, *A Disquisition on Faith* (Washington, 1822); and *An Inquiry Concerning . . . Philosophic Education* (Washington, 1822).

[6] "The Diaries of Donald Macdonald, 1824-1826," Indiana Historical Society *Publications*, xiv (1942), pp. 145-379, with an introduction by Caroline D. Snedeker (Nov. 4, 1824), p. 176. Arthur E. Bestor, Jr.'s review of this publication in *New York History*, xxiv (Jan. 1943), pp. 80-86, points out Owen's success in reaching important persons.

noncommittal letter acknowledging receipt of the *Essay on Commonwealths*. This was enough for Robert Owen. Returning an equally polite and noncommittal answer to their hinted desire for funds, he cut the interview short. Thereafter, in his whirlwind publicity campaign, although he remained on good terms with these Friends as with the vast majority of those with whom he came in contact, he made no special effort either to assist their independent efforts or to attract them to New Harmony. His brief glance at their literature must have assured him not only that they were a tiny, obscure, and, as far as known, disapproved minority, but also that the religious basis of their ideas and their communist program diverged from his.

Owen was out for big game, but in his boundless enthusiasm he talked like a presidential nominee to everyone who would listen. In the eight and a half months of his first visit in the United States he proved himself his own best public relations counsel, who could attract attention even in the face of the excitement that year over the Marquis de Lafayette, the opening of the Erie Canal, and the liveliest national election campaign in years. He spent six months of the time seeking out the prominent and influential in politics, business, religion, education, and the press. His two addresses on February 25 and March 7, 1825, before both Houses of Congress, climaxed his campaign. As a wealthy English manufacturer without "English reserve" he was able to "crash" a session crowded with affairs delayed to the last minute by the House election of the President, and harangue the politicians preoccupied with the organization of a new administration. Owen exposed his plan to an amazing number of ex-presidents, prominent politicians, men of large means, and professionals, and buttonholed the new President, John Quincy Adams, and the busy cabinet officers. The credulous way he accepted polite expressions of interest and good will as signs of understanding and approval[7] and his disregard for many of the business arrangements which would put his enterprise upon a sound footing are among the characteristics which have given the term utopian its connotation of impracticality.

Owen did not proceed, however, without learning as much as he could about Americans, about frontier conditions, and about the experiences of other American community builders. He saw for himself the Watervliet Shakers near Albany, inspected factories, toured the East from Washington to Boston, entertained alternative proposals to the one which had brought him to the New World, and finally devoted nearly three weeks to an examination of the Rappite settlement and its environs. Only then was he rightly convinced that nowhere in the United States was a more

---

[7] An apparent case in point is reported in "Macdonald Diaries" (Nov. 9, 1825), p. 309: "Mr. Owen returned quite pleased with his visit to Elias Hicks, who approves of his views."

favorable site available for an immediate trial of his social system than Harmony, Indiana. His timing was good. After his agreement on January 3, 1825, to purchase Harmony he had three or four months in which to allow the German residents to remove and recruit settlers to take their places in time for the opening of business in the spring. He did not operate alone, but delegated much negotiation to his responsible young son, William, and to others of his party and among his new adherents. He had acquired one of the few moneylending, commercial, and mill centers between Cincinnati and the French-founded settlements of Kaskaskia, Vincennes, and St. Louis, not far from the main Ohio and Mississippi River routes. The Harmony pioneers had cleared and planted much land and had reached the stage of transfer from log houses to brick and frame dwellings, with enough housing for at least eight hundred. The town, renamed New Harmony, was far enough into the frontier zone to profit by the influx of population, yet not so far as to face the worst frontier hardships, either from the wilderness or from the Indians. Owen lost no money on New Harmony as a real-estate speculation, but handed down good properties to his sons.

Nearly all the arrivals of the first season came from west of the Appalachians, and especially from the nearby settlements. After the drowning of Morris Birkbeck on June 3, many of the English emigrants at his twelve year old colony across the Illinois border joined New Harmony. The backwoodsmen knew how to make a living under frontier conditions; but a speech from Robert Owen and a few conversations were not enough to teach them the principles of the new social system. An understanding of both was needed to make New Harmony succeed. Representative of a small but dominant minority were Thomas Pears, Pittsburgh capitalist; Robert L. Jennings from Philadelphia, a former Universalist minister turned freethinker; James O. Wattles, Albion, Illinois, lawyer who had joined the Birkbeck colony after political and financial reverses in New York; the Englishwoman, Frances Wright, bent on a project for the emancipation of slaves; and William Pelham, Zanesville, Ohio, postmaster and newspaperman. These were more enthusiastic, better indoctrinated, more refined, but not equipped for the heavy manual work or even for superintending the skilled operations which would keep the hitherto profitable Rappite enterprises running. Fences and machinery needed repairs when the last of the Germans left on May 5, but it is not clear that the Rappites were responsible by the terms of their agreement with Owen. Owen departed on June 5 to continue his propaganda and sight-seeing, to attend to his British affairs, and possibly to avoid the unhealthy summer climate.

Whether the leader could have avoided all the mistakes of the first summer if he had stayed is doubtful. It is certain that in his absence until

163

the following January, income-bearing activities almost stopped. Crops and stock were not properly managed. Factions apparent at the first committee elections in the spring developed until by fall the inhabitants were living on Owen's capital, quarreling over the distribution of dwindling supplies, worrying over cramped quarters, and awaiting Owen's return as for a deliverer. Owen's signal triumph during these months was William Maclure's decision to transfer his Pestalozzian school from the Philadelphia area to New Harmony, bringing to the community a constellation of scientists. Owen's eastern associates also sent better qualified workmen by the spring of 1826, and steps were belatedly taken to weed out incompetents and dissidents. Owen's continued propaganda, however, was putting the cart before the horse, contrary to the secular utopian theories that the community movement would spread by successful example and that the best propaganda is the education of a new generation in a going community of the new order.

The addition of a school would be an asset in the long run, but it did not bring immediately the necessary skilled and sober workmen nor did it help balance expenses by attracting many outside scholars. The teachers, naturalists, and artists, and the few pupils they brought with them, were either Philadelphia intellectuals who tended to withdraw to their scientific pursuits, or urban foreigners who not only looked down on the rest but created additional factional disputes. Nevertheless the community continued as long as Maclure and Owen cooperated. Maclure, like Owen, was born in the British Isles (1763), made his fortune, developed a rational philosophy and a concern for manual labor education. He retired to become America's first geologist and a patron of science. His health and other interests allowed him to stay at New Harmony only six months out of the fifteen after his arrival in January 1826, and he was forced to judge the situation by reports chiefly from his principal teacher, Marie D. Fretageot. Misunderstandings with Owen increased to the breaking point during the spring of 1827, and Maclure left for Mexico never to return, although he maintained property and interests in New Harmony for the rest of his life.

Meanwhile, the population which still pressed upon the limit of housing throughout most of 1826 had undergone a heavy turnover. Many of the first arrivals did not stay long enough to develop a working acquaintance with each other, and the numerous arrivals of the spring of 1826 often remained strangers to the earlier, in spite of proximity and common activities. A deadening burden of red tape, required by the labor-time system of dispensing supplies and planning work, withdrew several of the most conscientious workers from more profitable pursuits, and antagonized such radicals as Paul Brown, who preferred "mutual confidence" to bookkeeping. A majority exhausted themselves, more like city folk than true farmers, in a hectic round of after-work activities. Probably the most effort was expended on the six "constitutions" discussed and amended in rapid succession during the eight months following Owen's return. Owen had no difference with Americans over the importance of democratic procedure and had faith in men's ability to talk themselves into agreement. Scarcely less important to the younger inhabitants was the ceaseless round of balls, concerts, militia and fire drills, philosophical debates, Masonic meetings, and ball games. Much of this activity evidenced a high degree of culture for the frontier, but drained the energies, attentions, and resources of the community.

The centrifugal force of this heterogeneous collection of people led to the formation of three separate communities, first of the religious westerners (Macluria or No. 2), next of the English farmers (Feiba Peveli or No. 3), and later of the school society. Finally, a group of radical "republicans" led from different motives by Paul Brown and Joseph Neef distinguished themselves as Owen's severest critics. Neef had been the first Pestalozzian teacher whom Maclure had brought to the United States. Like Brown he had arrived in the spring of 1826, and he joined Brown in a profound dislike for Marie Fretageot, his principal successor as a teacher for Maclure. After schism came departure from New Harmony, which reached such proportions by the spring of 1827 that continuance was impossible. Owen made what arrangements he could with private individuals and left early in June, to come back once more the following year, go off on a wild-goose chase in search of Mexican land in Texas, and then quit the country for fifteen years.

Other Owenite communities compare with New Harmony as a farm to a village. In the chief centers of Owen's influence—New York, Philadelphia, Pittsburgh, Cincinnati, and New Harmony—money was raised, societies organized, constitutions drawn and printed, and the property of one or two landowners in the adjacent hinterland bought on mortgage. In Pittsburgh, the society never passed the stage of organization. An example of many abortive projects was the futile attempt of Paul Brown, while at New Harmony, to persuade a property owner to provide land for a communist colony at Nevilsville, on the Ohio above Cincinnati. The only community to receive financial as well as moral support from Owen and Maclure was at Yellow Springs, Ohio, settled largely by Cincinnati Swedenborgians under the leadership of their minister, Daniel Roe. When further support was withheld, the project was abandoned soon after the close of 1826. Fragmentary evidence suggests that Philadelphia Friends were concerned with the obscure Valley Forge community, whose principles had less in common with Owen's philosophy than with John Gray's equalitarianism.

The emancipation plantation founded by Owen's former associate,

Frances Wright, at Nashoba, back of Memphis, Tennessee, was one of the few communitarian experiments to begin and end on Southern soil, and one of only three secular utopian attempts in the South. It was the embodiment of the Englishwoman's own ideas, drawing passive support from the New Harmony center rather than a group enterprise like the other secondary Owenite communities. Fanny Wright was at New Harmony during its first summer, and bought the small unimproved Tennessee site the following winter. She tried to make the farm produce enough for the slave labor to buy its freedom, but the whites were not successful overseers of the handful of Negroes and unfit for manual labor themselves. Thrice she retreated from the unhealthy site, and after the last withdrawal, arranged for the transfer of her wards to Haiti in 1830. At each setback her aims became more radical until she publicly defended miscegenation and racial equality in education and work.

Nashoba was the first secular utopian community in which reform was paramount over socialism. New Harmony harbored diverse reformers, including many opposed to slavery, but its main purpose was to inaugurate the new social system. Its constitution of May 1, 1825, had barred colored membership, although it would admit Negroes as "helpers . . . if necessary" or for training to found communities elsewhere.[8] Frances Wright had broken with the conservative Quaker abolitionism of Benjamin Lundy even before Garrison had done so, and she had broadened her attack upon society to include its educational, religious, and marital institutions.

The remaining Owenite communities are tied together by a string of transferring leaders. The seed of the Franklin Community at Haverstraw, New York, was planted by Owen's propaganda in New York City, and developed probably through his acquaintance with Jacob Peterson, the Haverstraw group's chief backer.[9] Peterson supplied most of the capital for the mortgaging of a run-down sawmill and farm property well back from the Hudson River. In the spring of 1826, Robert L. Jennings, prominent during the first year at New Harmony as Sunday lecturer, commander of militia, and an editor of the *Gazette*, and perhaps feeling overshadowed by the new arrivals of the previous months, answered the call of Peterson and other leaders and came East with his wife to help draft a properly Owenite constitution and become President of the Franklin Community. The Haverstraw colony could not face its first winter without a surplus to meet its interest payments or a winter source of income to meet current expenses, and returned the property, improved by its labor, to its former owner. Many summer soldiers of the church of reason militant quit the movement, but others more convinced, including Peterson, joined

[8] *New Harmony Gazette*, i (Oct. 1, 1825), p. 2.
[9] The identity of Jacob Peterson with the Peterson referred to in "Macdonald Diaries" (Nov. 6, 1824), p. 178, has not been established.

the Forestville Community at Coxsackie, New York. Four prominent members from Coxsackie first appear in the December 15, 1827, minutes of the Kendal, Ohio, Community, and continued in responsible positions for ten months.

The Kendal Community, at what is now Massillon, had the largest domain, the longest life, the soundest economic basis, and the most independent development of any minor Owenite project. Owenism at Kendal took fire after Josiah Warren of Cincinnati and Paul Brown, on his way to teach in Tennessee, had visited there in 1825.[10] These were no orthodox Owenite missionaries even though both became associated with New Harmony. In the spring of 1826 the "Friendly Association for Mutual Interests" was formed. It acquired over 2,100 acres from the estate of a deceased Friend for about $20,000 on mortgage. The Community operated a woolen mill, a wagon shop, and a sawmill; produced the usual goods of craft and domestic industry; built and operated a school; and maintained a lyceum and a library. There is no evidence that it prospered beyond fair maintenance for it had to raise new collateral to meet its first mortgage payment. The Coxsackie veterans were probably a disturbing element that fanned antagonisms already smoldering over petty grievances; one member blamed disease and the coldness of creditors for the final failure, but the real cause was the same story: the failure to make ends meet.

The fortunes of American Owenism were strongly conditioned by the contemporary state of American society. Times were prosperous when the Owenite communities started. Otherwise none but Owen could have raised the money or security to mortgage their chosen domains, and men of property would have been reluctant to grant mortgages. The immediate success of the Erie waterway started a canal fever; public land prices had been reduced; and people were moving west in one of the periodic surges coinciding with good times. Owen had not expected to attract many frontiersmen and anticipated that the accommodations available in 1825 would not be filled for several years. The surprising effectiveness of his superficial propaganda, coupled with prosperous times, rapidly assembled nearly a thousand people. Once at New Harmony, they could not easily leave, with previous ties broken and resources depleted, and it was hard for the benevolent Owen to deny them. Such was the paradox of their mobility. In a decentralized country with slow communications, Owen could not channel and select his recruits through an Eastern office as Cabet later did through his Paris headquarters.

[10] Wendall P. Fox, ed., "The Kendal Community," Ohio Archaeological and Historical Society *Publications*, xx (1911), pp. 176-219. P. 176, is the sole source to mention, without reference, Warren and Brown in this connection. Both men were in Ohio then, and the deviations in the Kendal system show some relation to their ideas.

For most Americans, prosperity settled the frustrations created by the depression after 1819. The remainder who answered Owen's call included those who still had not recovered from the depression and probably never would recover (poor material for any society); persons like James M'Knight who had suffered temporary reverses; and some like Paul Brown who not only felt the depression, but whose standards were such that no prosperity could hide what to them were radical evils in the social order.[11]

The dissatisfied remnant had seen the defeat of Jacksonian democracy in the election of 1824. Owenism was their protest against the aristocracy of their own towns and against the Old Guard still running state and national politics. They saw the wealthy and powerful entrenched not only in government, but running business, the churches, the schools, and by their prestige molding the very habits of the people. The flood tide of missionary orthodoxy and business expansion, some nativist hostility to the foreign-born leaders, and the absence of any strong supporting reform movement reduced the Owenite challenge to negligible proportions. The social evils it proposed to combat had not yet become menacing in the United States.

What was the difference between Owen's theory and American Owenism in theory and practice? The most striking example of divergence was the attitude of the American Owenites toward religion. All opposed with Owen any religious or rationalistic test for membership; but Owen, like the Marxians, expected socialist doctrine gradually to erode the superstitious faith of his religious adherents. They rejected his mechanist determinism, and feeling only the magnetic charm of his religious enthusiasm reinforced by his quotations of gospel ethics, held the aims of Christian socialism.

The Kendal Community, especially during its first year, illustrates this religious orientation better than the experiments more directly under Owen's influence. The preamble of its constitution begins: "The first principle and that which should never be absent from the mind is Love to the Great first cause and Creator of all things. The second is a sincere regard and love to our fellow creatures. This love should extend to every created and sensible subject." It concludes: "Such are the outlines of our principles, calculated we believe, to increase happiness, arrest the progress of vice, and lead to all those virtues and graces which the Gospel enjoins

[11] Before joining the Franklin Community, M'Knight "had experienced . . . many difficulties in ordinary life" and had failed in business (James M'Knight, A Discourse Exposing Robert Owen's System [New York, 1826], p. 8). Brown complained of having suffered because existing institutions let the rich usurp power and deny justice to the poor (Twelve Months in New-Harmony, p. 3). The querulous tone of his writings bears circumstantial evidence that he resented as a schoolmaster the prejudice of school boards against freethinkers like himself.

and we humbly commend our efforts to the blessing of its Adorable Author. We, the undersigned, do therefore, relying on the smiles of Divine Providence and renouncing all amusement and practices known to preponderate in evil, agree . . . in an Association for Mutual Co-operation. . . ."[12] Persons of many religious beliefs were members, including John Harmon and a Coxsackie transfer, Samuel Underwood, both later prominent in freethinking circles, but several of the most weighty during Kendal's first year belonged to the Kendal Preparative Meeting of the Religious Society of Friends. Matthew Macy, a Friend from Nantucket, was clerk and a trustee the first year, and thereafter withdrew from active management of the Community. Articles of the constitution refer in Quaker language to "queries" and "disownment" and Macy's minutes to "concerns" and "the sense of the meeting" (officers were elected by plurality but decisions were noted as unanimous or deferred). Owen was never mentioned until May 5, 1827, when arrangements for an Owenite school were inaugurated. No rational lecture system was substituted for normal "first day" worship until August 19, 1827, and then the one o'clock meeting "for . . . mutual instruction, information and improvement in the principles of the system of cooperation" probably did not conflict with other services.[13]

Benjamin Bakewell, a leader of the Pittsburgh Owenites, attributed Owen's antireligious bias to an extreme Calvinist upbringing, and insisted "that Christianity when undefiled and the Social System are one."[14] Although he had his doubts about Owen's soundness on the dogmas of revelation and responsibility, he had contradicted the local editor's charge that Owen flouted Bible religion.[15] His friends, Thomas and Sarah Pears, informed him that no such deism flourished at New Harmony. Mrs. Pears could no longer "see how a Christian can be a perfect Owenite," but her husband still had faith: "If Mr. Owen's principles can be practiced, we shall not be far from being the most perfect Christians of our Day."[16]

The Pears were thinking of practices jangling with professed beliefs, for deism shared predominance at New Harmony with the sects. William Pelham estimated that the Swedenborgians were most numerous in September 1825, and commented frequently on the itinerant Methodist, Baptist, and even Shaker preachers who disliked having to permit remarks from the congregation as the price of using the meetinghouse. He also mentioned the Methodist inhabitants who had for a time a resident minister. His description of a Sunday morning service reminds one of a

[12] W. P. Fox, ed., "The Kendal Community," pp. 178-79.

[13] Ibid., pp. 180-81, 186, 193-94, 196, 198, 200-2.

[14] Thomas C. Pears, Jr., ed., "New Harmony, an Adventure in Happiness; Papers of Thomas and Sarah Pears," Indiana Historical Society Publications, XI (1933), pp. 1-96 (Jan. 2, 1826), p. 51.

[15] Ibid. (Dec. 21, 1825), pp. 63-64.   [16] Ibid. (Jan. 28, 1826), pp. 61-62.

contemporary rural Quaker meeting, with the sexes separated in a bare room and with its norm of plain costume.[17]

One of the objections of the radical malcontents, at the opposite pole from the Pears and Pelham, was the same failure of social virtue in practice, and the immoral tendency of Owen's preaching. Paul Brown, their most vocal protagonist, pronounced judgment upon Owen as patron, educator, and philosopher: "The whole course of his practice and preaching has had a bad effect upon the morals of the place. . . . From the practice, all the inexperienced part of the population learned levity, duplicity, avarice, distrust, and partiality: and the preaching suggested to them that they need not be scrupulous about their conduct, for they were not blameful for their words or actions.—This pernicious doctrine, based on the rash position that 'man does not form his own character' . . . had evidently a depraving influence upon the minds and hearts of the people in all parts of the town. . . . Moreover . . . individual suffering . . . deadened the wonted sympathy of many ingenuous souls. . . . Here was no room for hospitality, generosity, charity, not even friendship, nor any of those gentle endearing social virtues which dignify while they embellish human nature. At their balls and social meetings, instead of learning affability, they learned little or nothing but pride."[18]

Brown was a harsh critic of the concerts and amusements which brightened an otherwise drab existence. He criticized not as a straitlaced pietist, because they were worldly, but as a utilitarian, because they were overemphasized and distracted members from the serious purpose of making the community work. Such were the high grounds of his objections, but their tone betrays a studious, humorless, and cranky person brought up to avoid the simple pleasures. A fanatical needler, he deluged the *Gazette* with communications (most of which they printed), and toward the end (when Owen rejected them) he lectured and conducted a wall newspaper expounding his alternatives.

The keystone of his communist theory, which he had already developed at length, was natural sympathy, the root of conscience. This benevolence, universal in man, if trained by the proper persons and institutions to the perception of the order of nature, could be relied on to judge by "common sense," "self-evidence" and "intuition" the difference between right and wrong. Mutual confidence and intimate acquaintance, derivatives of philanthropy, were the proper foundations of a community, and these alone could solve the pleasure-pain calculus to produce the greatest social and individual enjoyment in the pursuit of truth.

[17] Caroline C. Pelham, ed., "Letters of William Pelham Written in 1825 and 1826," in Harlow Lindley, ed., *Indiana as Seen by Early Travelers* (Indianapolis, Ind., 1916), pp. 360-417; pp. 370-71, 373, 377-78, 380-81, 386-88, 392, 394, 398, 404.

[18] Paul Brown, *Twelve Months in New-Harmony*, pp. 87-88.

But was this Christian? Brown had specifically identified it as such. "God . . . designed man for a social being, endued him with sympathy, whereby it becomes impossible for him to be perfectly happy in the presence of those he makes miserable. On the improvement of sympathy, rests social happiness." The Golden Rule, "sincerely advanced from natural principles [not on Biblical authority], must approximate the highest degree of perfection the enjoyment of human beings is susceptible of. For sociality [is] . . . a radical part of human nature. . . . Social virtue is the chief end of man. . . ."[19] "True christianity consists in social virtue," which Christ both taught and practiced as "a universal republican and philanthropist."[20] Brown preferred with Maclure to change society by educating a new generation to "uniform liberal sentiments," but his perfectionist deism allowed him to hope for the success of communism in his time by using adult "converts to the doctrine of the renovation . . . who are willing to return into the order of human perfection."[21] Brown believed that with much of the human material on hand when he arrived on April 2, 1826, community of property and mutual confidence could have turned New Harmony into a success.

Paul Brown was the first American secular utopian and the only American Owenite to work out a detailed and systematic social philosophy. Maclure's later work was radical but not communitarian.[22] The sources of Brown's philosophy can be gathered from his recommendation of the Stoics, the Bible, Locke, Newton, Erasmus, Darwin, John Hutchinson, and Adam Smith's *Theory of Moral Sentiments*; his familiarity with Hartley, Rousseau, and Godwin; and his condemnation of Spinoza, Hobbes, Hume, and Paine for destroying orthodox religious belief without offering anything better.[23] He constantly referred to men and institutions in mechanical terms, recognized the bad habits which "the children of this world" form by association of ideas, and denied that knowledge, or any lesser degree of assurance, which he called faith, could be a voluntary act.

[19] Paul Brown, *Philosophic Education*, pp. 233-34. God he later identified in an idyllic hymn to truth, concluding: "Truth . . . is a being which ought to attract the highest adoration, and call forth the most devout ardor of the soul of man. . . . Without it were neither enjoyment, permanence, nor safety in the society of mankind . . . metaphysical truth, is little else but the real existence of things portrayed on our understanding; it being the perfect . . . conformity of our ideas to what exists beyond them." (*Ibid.*, p. 333.)
[20] *Ibid.*, p. 273.
[21] Paul Brown, *Twelve Months in New-Harmony*, p. 42.
[22] William Maclure, *Opinions on Various Subjects* (New Harmony, Ind., 1831-1838, 3 vols.). It may be inferred from Maclure's passing reference (i, p. 146) that in October 1828 he still thought "the community system" possible if under proper management; but his emphasis, like Brown's after 1828, was on education and politics.
[23] Paul Brown, *Philosophic Education*, pp. 12-15, 93, 113, 134, 176-77, 235, 339-40, 390; *Twelve Months in New-Harmony*, p. 34.

Nevertheless, in the narrow but all-important area of motivation, he recognized enough free will to enable man to counteract almost any bad habit in himself, and become a self-governing and socially virtuous human being.

In emphasizing as central to the true social system a "liberal" education combining moral, intellectual, and vocational training, Brown and Maclure joined Owen in general adherence to the Pestalozzian school. Owen and Maclure, however, stressed the "school of industry" more than Brown. Brown, Maclure, and Neef united against Owen's preference for one school staffed by teachers for different subjects, rather than fixed groups of scholars for each master; against Owen's Lancastrian emphasis on rote learning; and against his rejection of corporal punishment. Maclure was a practicing geologist, while Brown revered theoretical science, which he defined as all knowledge, derived from both mental and empirical sources.

Although Brown's ideas did not demonstrably influence later thought, they do illustrate one type of latter-day deism. For that reason the similarities between his ideas and those of some of the communitarians are worth elaborating. He crusaded against the evangelical counterreformation, and incidentally represents a Hicksite point of view contributing to the 1828 schism in the Society of Friends, to which he had undoubtedly belonged. As late as 1839, he was still lecturing to New York freethinkers on regeneration, resurrection, the Kingdom of Heaven, ethics, and government.[24] Brown's communism resembles in many respects the mixture of Owenism and Garrisonian anarchism which characterized John A. Collins' Skaneateles Community. The preachings of the vegetarian ex-Baptist, Orson S. Murray, who viewed the times as unripe for experiment,[25] reflect a similar point of view. No evidence has yet been found, however, that the Owenites of the 1840's, discussed in the last section of this essay, had ever heard of Brown, who was living in Massachusetts only a few years before. It is strange that these American Owenites, their Associationist rivals, and the hostile public persisted in misinterpreting Owen as a communist, just as Brown had done when he went to New Harmony.

Brown's deist and communist perfectionism apparently died without heirs, but some form of liberal, Protestant, perfectionist communitarianism, expressed in other religious languages, has kept reappearing in the United States ever since. The antislavery Methodist experiment at Berea, Ohio, in 1836-1837; Collins at Skaneateles, 1843-1846; the spiritualist encampments such as the one led by John Murray Spear near Warren, Pennsylvania, 1853-1863; Alcander Longley's various communities and publica-

[24] *Beacon* (New York), III (Mar. 9, 16, 23, 1839), pp. 136, 144, 152.
[25] J. H. Noyes, "The Skaneateles Community," *History of American Socialisms* (Philadelphia, 1870), pp. 161-80; *Regenerator* (Fruit Hills, Ohio, 1846-1852), ed. by O. S. Murray.

tions, 1868-1917; and even the tiny Macedonia Cooperative Community near Clarksville, Georgia, 1937- , have partaken of the same spirit. The Yankee triangle of independent joint stock communities at Hopedale, Brook Farm, and Northampton, Massachusetts, represented most of the essential features, expressed in Universalist or Unitarian and transcendental form.[26] Even the American Fourierists, who relied on a different psychology and stopped well short of equality and communism, also exhibited a perfectionism identified with the Gospel. All these groups were liberal for they welcomed persons of any denomination. Their hope for success in history marked them as secular utopians. Had any one group of them lasted a generation, however, it might have become as much a sect as the native-born Perfectionists at Oneida.

III. Fourierism and Icarianism

Between the founding of Owenite and Associationist communities, over fifteen years intervened in the spiral course of American expansion. After the failure of New Harmony, Robert Owen turned to political and economic action and propaganda in Great Britain. At the same time in the United States, Owenites shifted to politics and propaganda aimed to attract the American workingman. This shift coincided in Great Britain with the intensification and victory of the movement for parliamentary reform and for many other reforms as well. In the United States it coincided with the victory of Jacksonian democracy and the rise of anti-masonry, a movement more directly attacking the aristocracy.

Robert Dale Owen and Frances Wright, through the *Free Enquirer*, a continuation of the *New Harmony Gazette* transferred to New York, made the key plank of their platform the same educational principles which had animated Owen's community. William Maclure placed his faith in universal suffrage to secure equal rights through public education. Paul Brown, also retaining the principles which he had elaborated in his writings and preachings since before 1819, but silent on community projects, trumpeted the class struggle. He called on the people of the United States to recognize the existence of two classes—rich and privileged, poor and oppressed—and on the majority of poor and oppressed to emancipate

[26] See R. A. Gilruth, *The Community of United Christians at Berea, Ohio, in 1836* (MS Senior Thesis in History, Princeton University, 1941); MS records of the spiritualist community at Kiantone Springs, N.Y. and Pa., in the possession of Ernest C. Miller, Warren, Pa.; Alcander Longley, ed., *Communist* (1868-1885) continued as the *Altruist* (1885-1917); Macedonia Cooperative Community *Report—1948* (Glen Gardner, N.J., 1948, 20 pp.); Adin Ballou, *History of the Hopedale Community* (ed. by W. S. Heywood; Lowell, Mass., 1897); J. T. Codman, *Brook Farm; Historic and Personal Memoirs* (Boston, 1894); and Alice E. McBee, *From Utopia to Florence* (Northampton, Mass., 1947).

themselves by voting their own kind into office.[27] This change of emphasis from the community to the national scale, and from experiment to propaganda, really involved a modification of principles which Owenites were generally unwilling to admit. Some of them took the lesson of New Harmony to mean the permanent impracticality of small-scale utopian efforts. Robert Dale Owen's socialist days were over, and inside a decade he had found his place in Jackson's Democratic Party.

The panic of 1837 created a new class of discontented, especially among the laborers whose local unions and parties had been destroyed. Now the trends of "industrial feudalism" were easier to foresee, but the current of industrialism was all the more overpowering to any shallow-draft communitarian boat that ventured against it. The depression reduced the potential personnel of community projects to an economic position that made it impossible to launch them. Pioneering remained easier individually than collectively.

Neither of the two national parties could satisfy the radical reformer, except that their general agreement to minimize the government's role gave as much freedom for community experiments as for capitalist expansion. The Whigs were a coalition suspicious of the common man but eager to win his vote for free enterprise. They had given up the Federalist theory that government belongs to those who have a property stake in society, and held throughout the 1840's a strong minority position in state and national government. They asserted that every man was both a workingman and a capitalist; that poverty had its compensations in freedom from care; and that the prosperity of rich and poor alike depended on untrammeled business, protection, and sound finance. The Democrats were also an intersectional coalition drawn together from city and country. While they relied in the Northeast on the beginnings of urban political machines and accepted the services of editors as extreme as Brownson preaching the class struggle, they still retained a large southern and western back-country following. Neither party could afford to humor the reformer with anything but glittering generalities; their national responsibilities and coalition character forbade it.

Reforms, which had quietly started during or before the first Owenite movement, stimulated by evangelical revivalism, Quaker humanitarianism, and European example, split into moderate and extremist wings in the late eighteen-thirties. The teetotalers separated from the temperance men;

---

[27] Paul Brown, *The Radical: and Advocate of Equality* (Albany, N.Y., 1834). Immediately after leaving New Harmony the repetitive author answered objections to the ideas of common property and equality in his pamphlet, *A Dialogue on Commonwealths* (Cincinnati, Ohio, 1828). His last known work, *The Woodcutter; or a Glimpse of the 19th Century at the West*, MS in the Illinois State Historical Library, Springfield, reveals him still a bitter communitarian in the late 1830's or after (see p. 38 and chaps. 23, 26, and 29 of the manuscript).

the nonresistants seceded from the American Peace Society; the abolitionists organized by Garrison divided over his violent methods and extremist propaganda; feminists redoubled their efforts after their rejection by the antislavery moderates. Other special humane concerns for the insane and the prisoner, for improvements in popular and formal education, and for better health through dress and diet reform, phrenology, mesmerism, and the water cure, appeared or developed increased momentum. Every one of these movements, like secular utopian socialism, aimed at the improvement of the condition of man on earth. Each one had for its intellectual bases the same traditional values of American liberalism to which these communitarians were devoted—individual freedom, equality of opportunity, and Christian charity. Each reformer tended to favor reform in general but to emphasize a few specific reforms as the keys to the social problem. He often used the language of contemporary science to decorate his assumptions and framed his propaganda in universalist, missionary, and millenarian terms. Among the churches a new wave of revivalism reached a peak in 1843. Its extreme expression was the Second Adventist prophecy of William Miller and Joshua V. Himes.

Into this revivalist and reformist atmosphere, Albert Brisbane introduced Fourierism. This set of theories as he presented them was well adapted to the American spirit of reform, to secular, universalist, and liberal Christianity, and to millennial revivalism. While traveling and studying in Europe from 1828 to 1834, Brisbane had sampled and rejected the theories of Hegel and the Saint-Simonians before he discovered, in 1832, what he had been looking for—Fourier's complete system of social philosophy. He took a few lessons directly from the old master and associated with the Fourierist school until his return to the United States. For the next four or five years he spread the doctrine privately while a few Fourierist New Yorkers, many of them French, started a feeble organization. In the three and a half years after September 1840, Brisbane took four steps to naturalize Fourierism. He published the most thorough exposition in English;[28] converted Horace Greeley and used Greeley's *New York Tribune* to spearhead a journalistic campaign; lectured widely and encouraged local leadership; and finally effected, in April 1844, a national organization whose control soon passed to the Brook Farm transcendentalists.[29] Most important was Brisbane's success in reaching the American reformer public through the periodical press. His first organ did not reach it, but on March 1, 1842, he inaugurated a personal paid column in Greeley's penny

[28] Albert Brisbane, *Social Destiny of Man; or, Association and Reorganization of Industry* (Philadelphia, 1840), known as *Brisbane on Association*.

[29] Brisbane's activities up to his sailing for Europe in April 1844, are described by Arthur E. Bestor, Jr., "Albert Brisbane; Propagandist for Socialism in the 1840's," *New York History*, xxviii (Apr. 1947), pp. 128-58.

daily, reprinted in the weekly edition, which for nearly nineteen months carried the glad tidings to a large American audience already predisposed to sympathy. Greeley provided free publicity thereafter, as long as the movement lasted. The articles were widely clipped and also made available in pamphlet form; and most important, enough converts had been made to support a straight Associationist weekly for five and a half years.[30] The American followers of Fourier were called Fourierists by outsiders but called themselves Associationists, rejecting—like the Shakers, Quakers, and Mormons—the popular label.

Fourierism in Brisbane's hands was the social reform which claimed to embrace and justify all the partial reforms of the day. Brisbane turned a static structure based on assumptions which American Protestants would never have accepted, into what looked like a simple, workable, and dynamic program. He vigorously pruned Fourier's imaginative vagaries, omitted every suggestion of irregularity in marriage and morals, simplified the master's complicated reasoning and cut out excessive classifications and tables. Setting out upon its Pauline mission, the American movement proposed to be all things to all men, a veritable popular front of reform. Like the Apostle, the Associationists believed that they held the key to a harmony which fulfilled the law, and in fulfilling it, could overcome the old dispensation of coercion, conflict, and death. They did not quote Fourier, as they could have, on the last victory. They referred to primitive Christianity much less than other communitarians, but were like the others and the early Christians in their enthusiastic adventism.

The emphasis at this stage was on "the practical part" of Fourier's system, as Brisbane's pamphlet announced, and that referred to current questions raised by the uneven progress of merchant capitalism and its lusty child, industrialism. The English phrenologist, George Combe, had observed in 1839 the neglect of anything he could call political economy (discounting the work of Henry C. Carey) and concluded, "The Americans appear to me to be trying all manner of social experiments, guided only by their instinctive impulses. The Union may be regarded as a vast field for the cultivation of the science of political economy *by experiment.*"[31] Brisbane's Fourierism assumed the same economic principles which were self-evident to so many Americans: that labor is the ultimate source of all wealth and that every man therefore has the right to work for his share; that this requires the equal access to land; but that man has an equal right to property as past labor. Even individualist motivation and

---

[30] Albert Brisbane, *Association; or, A Concise Exposition of the Practical Part of Fourier's Social Science* (New York, 1843); ten thousand copies printed by 1847; *Phalanx* (New York, 1843-1845); *Harbinger* (Brook Farm and New York, 1845-1849).

[31] George Combe, *Notes on the United States of North America during a Phrenological Visit in 1838-9-40* (Philadelphia, 1840, 2 vols.), I, p. 303.

corporate activity were appropriated as the essence of attractive industry, without any emphasis on their changed meaning in a communitarian context. Rather than submit an economic system to the scrutiny of theorists, the American Associationists took the greater risk of submitting their practice to observation. Hence their preliminary propaganda, a series of "before" and "after" sketches contrasting the civilized or pre-Fourierist society with the Associationist combined order of industry, was all the more persuasive to the common man. There is no clearer American innovation in the movement; Fourier himself was never willing to make the test.

Did the American phalanxes draw from all parties and beliefs as on the surface their appeal would seem to indicate? In practice it seems likely that the largest number of participants had been and continued to be passive northern Whigs. American Fourierists tended toward a sort of agrarian syndicalism which eschewed separate political action and heavily discounted the value of any kind of politics. Yet their official position was neutral rather than hostile to parties, while their theory harmonized with Whig Party policy. Associationists heartily agreed with the Democrats, who still trumpeted the evils of monopoly and speculation; and Democratic papers in turn welcomed Brisbane's articles for their criticism of existing evils. It was one thing to condemn speculation and other abuses of the Christian stewardship of property, or to call the rich and poor both victims of evils inevitable in the transition from social childhood to maturity, and another to arouse the rabble against the rich. By adopting the medium of the joint stock company and a fractional formula to reconcile the interests, Fourierists, with Whigs in general, ruled out class conflict as a solution of the social problem. They feared class violence more than the Whigs, and indeed more than American industrial conditions warranted. To wealthy capitalists they offered to match their current profits through the promised efficiency of the cooperative order. To poor workingmen they promised to match the going wage with a five-twelfths share of their surplus and the benefits of social security. All were guaranteed eventually both a superior living and an abundant life.[32]

The hypothesis that participating Associationists were largely northern Whigs may be extended to suggest that to an even greater degree they were future Republicans, with a majority of them of Yankee background.

[32] J. R. Commons and others, eds., *A Documentary History of American Industrial Society* (Cleveland, 1910-1911, 11 vols.), VII, pp. 219-22, 231-39, contains samples of Associationist reasoning on the labor question which both fit a general Whig pattern and distinguish the Fourierist variety of Whiggism from the more conservative expressions of even such reformers as Wendell Phillips. Note also, *ibid.*, p. 226, the oversimplified assertion of Herman Kriege, land reformer and editor of the New York *Volks Tribun*, characterizing Fourierists as mostly merchant capitalist Whigs, and Owenites as mostly Democratic workingmen.

The prime missionary agent during the germination period, 1842-1844, was Greeley's Whig *Tribune*. Transplanted New Englanders, like Greeley himself, congregated at the geographical centers of Fourierist excitement. Many of the Yankees in New York City, Albany, the Rochester area of western New York, sections of Ohio, and the northern frontier in Michigan, Wisconsin, and Iowa were among the most ardent reformers and the most liberal and missionary Protestants. Philadelphia and Indiana, which had been strong centers of Owenism, had their Associationists, but these were definitely in the background. Instead of a subtle influence from Quakerism, there took place an equally subtle penetration of the movement by New England ideas. Gathering force in New York and the Ohio Valley, it felt the pull of the New England renaissance but was never entirely won over to transcendentalism.[33]

The religious element in Brisbane's Fourierism was secondary and moderate. Brisbane himself had imbibed the Enlightenment from his skeptic father, his French teacher Jean Manesca, and his six years of study and travel in Europe. He successively selected from its British, French, and German sources, and finally chose the French version of Fourier. Church revivalism had touched but not captured the farmers, artisans, and small tradesmen who peopled the colonies begotten by the first Fourierist propaganda. They accepted Brisbane's social reform because its fundamental rationalism was sugar-coated with a secularized Christianity. Often unaffiliated with any denomination, or just as often loosely connected with the Baptist, Methodist, Universalist, Disciples, or Swedenborgian churches, they subscribed to an antiformalist and antidogmatic Christianity which was as "practical" as Adin Ballou's, but without the crystallized content which gave his Hopedale Community a distinct character. They believed it possible to get along in a heterogeneous group because creeds were in their opinion of little importance compared with deeds.

The exercises at the second anniversary of the Wisconsin Phalanx at Ceresco on May 27, 1846, performed by a group far removed from the intellectual center of transcendentalism, reflected a kind of nonsectarian religion similar to that represented by the traditional Independence Day ceremonies. The program started with the reading of Deuteronomy 28:1-25, which refers to the blessings promised the chosen people who keep the Lord's commandments, and the curses in store for those who violate them. It continued with a prayer, the Song of Jubilee, an oration, and such "sentiments" as "Association! In perfect accordance with the Laws of the Bible, the Laws of Nature, and the Laws of Mind"; "Labor

---

[33] See W. R. Cross, *The Burnt-over District* (Ithaca, N.Y., 1950), pp. 322-32, on the character of western New York communitarians. Quakers in this area were still attracted in the 1840's.

and Capital! Twin sisters . . ."; " 'Thou shalt love thy neighbor as thyself!' A sentence hitherto without practical meaning. . . ." And they closed with a hymn.[34]

Extreme reformers like the Garrisonians could not be fully satisfied with Fourierism. Associationists chided them in true Whig style for being "one-idea" men. They charged that to pluck the mote but ignore the beam in singling out Negro slavery from all the ills of society was not beginning reform at home. The institutions of the phalanstery would radiate throughout society and heal it.[35] This type of attack included a misrepresentation, for the Garrisonians had many causes, all lighted by a passion for liberty, equality, and brotherhood. This was to them as sound a base for general reform as Fourierist "social science." Other reform movements considered themselves equally comprehensive. Psychological reasons held back many professional reformers, whose specialty was the business of promotion, not the promotion of business. Prominent status in a separate cause would be threatened in the fusion of many causes. Some were too fanatical to expose themselves to the hard requirements of daily communal life; others such as Elihu Burritt felt that the Associationists had bitten off more than they could chew. Burritt, a living refutation of Emerson's and Hawthorne's dicta that manual and mental labor cannot be combined, already a temperance lecturer and about to enter the peace and abolition movements, preferred a more piecemeal attack upon social evils, a view more firmly identified with labor's interests.[36]

The Associationists did not achieve the united front of reform which they sought. Although the rank and file moderates and radicals from many causes joined the movement, they brought with them the often unvoiced assumption that their pet projects would be most important to the phalanx. The communities which lasted longest, and those closest to Americanized Fourierism, developed their own managing cliques usually from among the moderates, and generally prevented the dominance of invading extremists.

Brisbane kept for the most part aloof from the organization and settlement of the phalanxes. He was more like Fourier than like his new converts. Although not an egotist, and a generation removed from the necessity of trafficking for a living, he had no industrial experience and preferred speculation, both mental and monetary. Toward the end of his series in the *Tribune* he commended, with a warning, the small beginnings of 1842-1843. As these attempts were defeated he became alarmed at his unexpected success, and condemned them as false starts without enough

[34] *Harbinger*, III (June 27, 1846), p. 33.
[35] J. R. Commons, *American Industrial Society*, VII, pp. 207-19.
[36] Merle E. Curti, *The Learned Blacksmith; the Letters and Journals of Elihu Burritt* (New York, 1937), pp. 16-17, on a visit to the Northampton Association in the winter of 1843.

capital, equipment, or members. The shock of his propagandist triumph sent him back to France in 1844 for further study of Fourierist manuscripts, but he continued for a decade to write and lecture in favor of a "true test" of Association.

Association had started with two major deviations from the imported theory: a stronger but undogmatic Christian emphasis and a willingness to experiment with limited means. Several dozen colonies were planted between 1842 and 1845, and nearly all were killed in the sprout. Many of these settlements do not deserve the Associationist label, but all received some of the same stimuli. The first Fourierist frontiersmen were a score of single mechanics from Brooklyn who pooled a few hundred dollars to buy some cheap and worthless land in the Poconos. Reaching the site in November 1842, they wrestled with rocks, their ignorance of farming, and poverty until the close of the next season. Thus ended the Pocono picnic of Social Reform Unity, without a trace of Fourierism except the original impulse from Brisbane and Greeley. Sylvania, the second experiment in the same region on equally barren land, this time only five miles from the Delaware above Port Jervis, was a gathering in the spring of 1843 of families from Albany and New York Fourierist circles. This example of land mania was both inspired and supported by responsible leaders, for Horace Greeley was its treasurer. More capital was sunk, two summer seasons wasted, and more improvements went to the original owner. Other experiments in western New York and in the northern mountains of Pennsylvania, except for the Swedenborgian Leraysville Phalanx with less Fourierist connection than Social Reform Unity, had the same land mania, debt and title problems, and quarrels, and broke up usually after the first summer. One or two New York phalanxes did make some attempt at occupational groups and labor-time accounting, and the phalanxes around Rochester held a meeting which betokened the confederation of their causes.

West of the Appalachians two classes of colony appeared: those on the settled edge of the public domain and those which acquired already improved land, principally in Ohio. Pittsburgh and Cincinnati, the old Owenite centers, sent forth their groups, each bolstered by "angels" whose financial wings were incapable of sustaining heavy debt payments. These generally had fertile soil, good transportation facilities, more capitalization and equipment, made more ambitious industrial efforts, and averaged a full two years of associated life. The Trumbull Phalanx, near Warren, Ohio, endured four growing seasons and had the makings of full-scale village industry, including a woolen mill and tannery. One company, the Integral Phalanx, retreated from an Ohio failure to public land in Illinois, where frontier hardships were even more rigorous.

The purest example of the magnetic pull of the frontier was the Wisconsin Phalanx at Ceresco, now Ripon. It functioned on its own domain from May 27, 1844, until the end of 1849, and was the only phalanx to share out solvent at the end. Its original nucleus of *Tribune*-reading Yankees came from Southport (present-day Kenosha), Wisconsin. Fourierism was the Southport lyceum's discussion topic for the winter of 1843-1844. The charter members were liberals in religion and "whigs or nothing"[37] in politics. Toughened by frontier hard times, they made few practical mistakes and improved a good property. The majority had undertaken the cooperative settlement in the spirit with which the Plymouth colony survived its first years on the coastal frontier, and with which self-sufficient backwoods farmers had long helped each other out in work too much for a man alone. The Fourierist sun had tanned them, but the combined order was only skin deep. As the land filled up, the rival non-Associationist settlement at Ripon made more money, lived better, and was wresting control of the town from the Phalanx. The frontier moved north, and some members of the community, wishing to move with it, sought to stake claims in the recently opened Fox Indian reservation. Inside the domain was the real source of disintegration, which external pressures only brought to a head. Only single men liked the original rude unitary tenement. A minority became increasingly addicted to reforms which affronted the conventional. The majority knew what it wanted: to leave the community and return to the speculative free-for-all. The minority was too divided for effective opposition and continued operation of the Phalanx.

The central figure of the faithful but ineffectual minority was Warren Chase, active in the Southport lyceum, business agent and lobbyist for the Ceresco charter and lands, self-appointed publicity agent, vice-president or president through 1846, and trusted to close the business in 1850. A case study of this character provides evidence bearing on the sources of his radicalism and on the role of Ceresco in releasing his energies, developing his talents, and confirming his radicalism.

Born a bastard in New Hampshire on January 5, 1813, he had lost his father at the battle of Plattsburg in 1814, and was orphaned at five. For ten years a maltreated pauper apprentice, he escaped to kindly Universalist guardians, who encouraged his thirst for knowledge and confirmed a rationalism satisfied for a decade by the freethinking *Boston Investigator*. Unable to continue in an academy after reaching his majority, he struck out for Michigan in 1835, where the panic of 1837 caught him newly-wed and penniless. For six years his family lived from hand to mouth, plagued by hunger, sickness, and poverty, and burdened by the birth of four children; but by 1843 he had acquired through manual labor his own cabin

[37] Warren Chase, *The Life-Line of the Lone One; or, Autobiography of the World's Child* (5th ed., Boston, 1868), p. 131.

and lot in Southport. Experience as a child and a husband had wounded but not hardened his sensitive soul. War had taken his father; God and the doctors had failed to save his mother. Sadly he imagined himself the rejected of men, the Lone One, the World's Child. He had felt, with the oppressed Negro, the cruelty of bondage. A decent regard for the equal status of women would have removed the burden of shame laid upon him by so many churchgoers. The nation's dislocated economic system as it operated in the West with its bank scrip, engrossing, and usury had flattened him to the floor of subsistence. The real illegitimate was conventional society, getting something for nothing at the expense of the honest laborer.

Here was a man for whom reforming activity, and especially Association, was a therapeutic. Already the friend of women's rights, abolition, peace, and total abstinence, he took up phrenology soon after 1840. At the time of the Fourierist excitement at Southport, he began to study mesmerism and to read Swedenborg, and at Ceresco, the *Water Cure Journal.* His life had seemed a failure, with no prospect of recompense beyond the grave, but mesmerism awakened his energies, and the Phalanx was their first outlet. At Ceresco during the winter of 1845-1846 he formed a spiritualist study circle in touch with Cincinnati clairvoyants interested in the nearby Clermont Phalanx. During the following year his enemies, both within and without the community, added the brand of free lover to the mark of infidel subversive which he already bore. His election as president of the Phalanx in January 1846 was its last vote of confidence in him until he was commissioned executor of its will. He turned to politics as a radical Barnburner and Free-soiler for five years, and consistently ran ahead of his ticket, thanks in part to German immigrants in the county.

Shortly after his removal from the presidency of his Association in 1847 he had urged that the model phalanx for which Brisbane and the Brook Farmers were still holding out be built around Ceresco. The new majority was whoring after Baal, and he hoped to strengthen the ranks of the faithful. In November 1849 he sent out an appeal common to many failing communities. It was like the cry of Elijah: "We only are left; let the saving remnant concentrate with us." Chase's new plan was even less Fourierist than before. His appeal left unitary living optional and ruled out all dividends to capital, on the Fourierist ground, however, that mutual guarantees come first. Also typical of late American Fourierism, he linked continuation with a project for a Protective Union Store. When no money was forthcoming to buy out the withdrawing stockholders, he conducted a cooperative store for a season, and in June 1850 presided at the Chicago National Industrial Congress. He was satisfied to see the end. Soon he would no longer be the melancholy Lone One, for by

1853 he felt that spiritualism had truly united his home and that he was surrounded by thousands of friendly spirits in both worlds. Aided by the midwife, Ceresco, a new faith which reconciled reason and revelation had been born in Warren Chase.[38]

Back in New England the liberal Protestants had earlier found a similar faith in transcendentalism. Brook Farm and Northampton were, however, results rather than causes of this transformation. The Northampton Association (1842-1845) was perhaps the most thoroughly industrial secular utopian community in American history, centering in a silk mill and dependent on the fad of sericulture. Its connection with Garrisonism was strong and it acknowledged a limited debt to Fourierism; but its intellectuals were not as illustrious as Brook Farm's, and its independent propaganda fell with scarcely an echo.

During the winter of 1843-1844 the Brook Farm Association for Industry and Education began to move toward Fourierism. The change had the effect of reducing its transcendentalism and increasing the emphasis on transcendental religion in the national movement; for in May 1845 Brook Farm publicly committed itself to the task of continuing the press campaign of the *Phalanx* through the *Harbinger*, and during the next two years sent out its own lecturers and organizers. Brisbane had harvested the June hay; Brook Farmers cut the rowen. The spiritual career of Joseph J. Cooke illustrates the type of blade gathered into the barns of the New England Associationists. He was christened and raised by orthodox parents in Rhode Island, put to trade in adolescence, little exposed to "infidel" writers, and married to a devout Baptist at twenty-one. He was lukewarm toward his wife's religion, an indifferent churchgoer, a "Home Baptist" who read newspapers and novels on Sunday. In 1840 a Baptist revivalist moved him first to the anxious seat and then to commit his life to full-time religion. He read Brisbane's articles in the *Tribune* but dismissed them as impractical. Between 1842 and 1847 he lost his money in farming and grocery ventures, was disillusioned in his church activities by what he considered the selfish shams of church leaders, and dipped temporarily into Swedenborgianism. Not until 1847 was he convinced that "association is the embodiement of the principles of Christianity, . . ." and that the eventual perfection of its science would "eradicate all evil, and . . . bring . . . the Christian Millennium. . . ." Melville's *Omoo* confirmed his opposition to any but Associationist missionary activity.[39]

---

[38] *Ibid., passim.* For appeals to concentrate on one community see that of the Ohio Phalanx below Wheeling, in the *Harbinger*, I (June 14, 1845), p. 15; Gilbert F. Bailey of the Grand Prairie Community, Indiana, in the *Regenerator*, N.S., I (Sept. 7, 1846), p. 183; and Chase's letter dated Feb. 8, 1847, in the *Harbinger*, IV (Apr. 3, 1847), p. 258, also J. R. Commons, *American Industrial Society*, VII, pp. 263-73, quoting *Spirit of the Age* (Dec. 8, 1849).

[39] J. J. Cooke, "A Personal Experience," *Harbinger*, V (July 10, 1847), pp. 65-67; quotation on p. 67.

Although Brook Farm's leadership did not change, its primary purpose shifted from education and the mutual improvement of an intellectual clique to missionary enterprise. As a school it could expect a steady income for it was well situated, well staffed, and operated on Pestalozzian principles, increasingly popular among liberal intellectuals not at all convinced by Fourierism. As a phalanx it had few visible means of support. As a center of intellectual adventure it was excited about the whole constellation of current reforms and new ideas, but would not commit itself wholly to any "narrow" cause. Fertile in theory, it was sterile in tangible results. No new community was founded in answer to its call for its spokesmen would start with nothing less than Fourier's Model Community. To the appeals of the Ceresco, Ohio, and North American phalanxes they turned a deaf ear, although they published sympathetic reports about them. Gradual development from small beginnings was one way, but not Fourier's. Besides, how could a new administration, with fresh capital and members, get along with the leaders of the existing organizations? Some of these veterans were not even sound on questions of religion, marriage, and capital's share.

Association cannot be properly evaluated by looking only at its colonies. From one perspective, it was a turbulence beneath the crust of society with a few active volcanoes. From another, an ice floe broken off from the polar cap of preindustrial capitalism, with most of its mass beneath the surface, and inexorably melted by the warm currents of a new type of free individualistic enterprise. The Brook Farm School declined, and the *Harbinger* and lecturers usually operated, as in most publicity campaigns, at a loss. While Brook Farm was for a short period the chief agent of Association, the principal stronghold of the decentralized movement remained in New York, to which several of the leading Brook Farmers removed soon after their phalanstery fire of March 3, 1846. Those who lingered in Boston organized, in January 1847, a shortlived Religious Union of Associationists under the preaching ministry of W. H. Channing and the music ministry of J. S. Dwight, and an equally temporary cooperative boarding house.

The dissolution of Brook Farm and Ceresco at the end of the decade left only the North American Phalanx, near Red Bank, New Jersey, as the forlorn hope of American Fourierism. Founded at the climax of Brisbane's and Greeley's *Tribune* campaign in September 1843 by Albany and New York families most of whom knew farming, it had steadily improved as a comprehensive agricultural cooperative. Its annual statement for 1849 showed a total production grossing over $42,000, chiefly from truck crops, hominy, and other milling. The net profit that year, after deduction for interest on the moderate debt, was scarcely over 1 per cent, but the stockholders received 5.6 per cent. The dividends had for six years

184

averaged a little over 5 per cent.[40] Greeley and Brisbane had both lent their names to this experiment. Brisbane had helped choose the site; Greeley continued to back the community as long as it lasted. The members had struggled through five years of endless debate exploring the proper application of principles to the most trivial details, but especially to matters concerning the powers of management and the distribution of effort and proceeds. They were entering a short period of agreement and clinging as hard as they knew how to the principles of Fourier. Three types of adjustment made this temporary settlement possible and produced a more convinced membership: the withdrawal of individualist dissidents; the admission of members from the wrecks of other communities; and indoctrination by the constant discussions of the first period. Deviations from the Fourierist scheme of distribution temporarily satisfied those who were both the noisiest critics and the chief recipients of concessions. The division between the farmers and those urging an expansion of mechanical and industrial activities was smoothed over when they began to operate the mill about 1849.

Scarcely three years passed before the same issues reappeared. The membership had neither been thoroughly purged nor reinforced. There remained the dissatisfied wives whose husbands still wanted to stay and the agreeable and unskilled who found the community a tolerable refuge from the hard world. The newcomers filled the vacancies and came close to doubling the population between 1844 and 1852. The manpower for further expansion and seasonal work came mainly from hired German immigrants. The transfers from other experiments represented every shade of social reform from the Fourierism of the Phalanx to the individualist anarchism of Josiah Warren. Most of them were unskilled and increased the inefficiency of the farm. Experience with problems Fourier had neglected to mention had dulled the enthusiasm of veterans and newcomers alike.

Faultfinding with the distribution of the proceeds had probably subsided least, and with prospects of increased earnings, voices were raised again. The Phalanx had made a common mistake among cooperatives in not paying labor the going wage or first securing the workingman's rights. The wage discrepancy was widest among the most necessary kinds of skilled mechanical work. In vain the majority lectured the chronic gripers on the intangible securities that went with the wage. In vain the "second-milers," priding themselves on their self-sacrifices according to the Biblical injunction, reiterated the stock phrase of conservatives, "If you don't

[40] North American Phalanx, *Exposé of the Condition and Progress of the North American Phalanx; in Reply to the Inquiries of Horace Greeley, and in Answer to the Criticisms of Friends and Foes during the Past Year* (New York, 1853), Tables I and III in appendix.

like it here why don't you go back" to the class society which makes profit its goal and force its means? This did not satisfy the cooperator who was sure that stricter labor discipline and the independence of each branch of the business would straighten everything out; nor the drifter who was happy as long as the motto, "Labor is worship," was not too strictly enforced by social pressure; nor the unmarried artisan who could make two bits a day more on the outside and had no wife to earn another income in the kitchen or laundry. The conservatives forgot the early glowing promises that the combined order would not only beat civilization at its own game of efficiency and money-making, but would go beyond private capitalism in securing the comforts and well-being of its working members. Plain fare, cramped quarters, and hard work for inferior rewards damaged the morale of all but the most zealous, and even the leaders acknowledged the common tendency to call Association a failure if it had not served selfish ends.

It was a natural and healthy reaction to the preliminary bickering which led them to state in 1853, "An abiding confidence in work, and a diminishing faith in talk, has actuated us."[41] Work diverts some minds from the grievances multiplied by close association in heterogeneous groups and reduces the opportunities for damaging talk. Yet work alone is no safety valve without patience and discussion. The nonsectarian voluntarist group that cannot negotiate its way out of schism is bankrupt, for the minority will always leave. The North American Phalanx was economically sound enough to tolerate the inferior services rendered by its less industrious members. It was neither ideologically nor politically matured enough to deal with a variety of stubborn opinions about the direction of community development and wage scales. It had made progress, but the tendency to defend a fixed position and enforce it by a majority vote increased with the loss of faith in talking practical matters over and waiting to find a solution upon which all could unite.

The political issue which the community failed to solve was the same one which remains today unreconciled in the nation at large: the farmer-labor conflict. Within the Phalanx, something had to be done about the mill. It had been repaired for operation soon after 1843, but the men to run it had left and no milling was done for five years. When further improvements were needed in 1852 and a neighbor put too high a price on the land to be flooded, the society could not agree on a site for a new one. One group urged the construction of a steam mill at Red Bank, with water transportation to New York. This would save the expense of teaming over the sandy road to Red Bank and provide the nucleus for other steam-powered industries. The majority, interested primarily in the farm, opposed the move. George B. Arnold, a former minister and nursery-

[41] *Ibid.*, p. 8.

man and president of the Phalanx in 1852, thereupon led about thirty, many of them stockholders, to form the short-lived semicapitalist Raritan Bay Association at Perth Amboy in the spring of 1853. This group had other complaints over matters of religion and the low index of production. The stock was now held by lukewarm or hostile nonresidents, for the remaining members lacked either the money or the faith to invest in their own business. When the old mill burned in September 1854 they discovered that the fires of their faith had also burned out, and voted to dissolve.

Behind the failure of community democracy lay the situation of the Phalanx as an enclave. All sides felt handicapped in their efforts to extricate themselves from the web of American society. To succeed, they had to create a business and a spirit superior to that of the world outside, and so mixed were ideas and economics in this situation that it is difficult to ascribe a preponderant influence to either.

Their material accomplishments were notable. Their soil conservation measures had improved a farm exhausted by slave and tenant cultivation. As horticulturists and truck farmers they had made innovations, met severe competition, and rapidly increased their productivity and earnings. Few farms of that day kept anywhere near such good accounts. Few corporations as large as theirs could show more accommodating or better informed relations between owners and workmen, or had even considered the industrial democracy represented by their election of their own foremen and managers. While even the reformers in the outside world had scarcely more than started their campaign for women's rights, the Phalanx had accorded women an equal right to income for their domestic labor, such laborsaving devices for their work as were available, and an equal voice in forming its business policy.

One major accomplishment the members of the community could not claim. The Phalanx had not made more money faster than capitalist enterprise. Protest as they did that the very reason for coming to the community was to escape from a money-motivated society, their self-defense testified to their unconscious allegiance to the standards of the civilization they combated. Too many of their arguments accepted the pecuniary and individualist terms of their opponents. Ceresco had been confronted with the get-rich-quick spectacle of the frontier. North American saw the same money-madness forty miles away in New York, already the nation's chief business center. At Ceresco the divided minority had wanted to continue; in New Jersey the divided minority had had enough. In both cases, however, the seceders were united in their preference for individualism, and all ultimately came around to the conclusion which had long disturbed their thoughts and hobbled their zeal: that such world mending was premature. Few secular utopians were so disgruntled as to admit that their community days were not the happiest of their lives or to renounce the idea of progress they implied in calling their efforts premature.

On the surface they had reason to be satisfied with their own achievements and to blame others, for the Associationist movement had gone down before them. They could not look elsewhere for new capital, members, or moral support. They had slight contact with the Icarians through their subscription to the Nauvoo *Popular Tribune,* and with the Shakers and Hopedale through one or more transfers from each group, but could take little comfort in the survival of such divergent communitarians.

In 1852, Albert Brisbane and Victor Considérant, chief protagonists of the French and American Fourierists, visited the Phalanx. Considérant spent six weeks in the community to study English preparatory to a search for a place to locate a new model community, and Brisbane had volunteered as his consultant. Neither gave the Phalanx a second thought, if they had considered it at all, as an organization worthy to receive further support. While Considérant paid it a left-handed compliment by remarking that no group in Europe under such conditions would have lasted two weeks and pointed out some of their accomplishments noted above, he was convinced that their Fourierism was rudimentary. Their groups and series, the Fourierist pattern for the division of labor upon which they prided themselves, were a farce; they had no attractive industry, no socialist competition or diversity of jobs. They needed a new spark to enliven them after ten years of struggle.[42] Yet Considérant would not give them this spark, but wasted the energies of another group of French beginners, plus a few lured from the North American Phalanx, on a new trial near Dallas, Texas.

Marxians, reviewing the history of communitarian socialism, emphasized as the central flaw in utopian theory the assumption that it is possible for a community to insulate itself from the overpowering pressures of capitalism. A materialist interpretation of history requires that answer. It explains why Fourierism was the final major protest by group escape before capitalism had collectivized its social controls on national and international scales. If the interplay of ideas and conditions is more complicated, and if in the last analysis the will to act is found in some cases to have a freedom to triumph over conditions, the way must be left open for an alternative explanation. The evidence in the case of the North American Phalanx points to a narrow way by which this embodiment of the socialist ideal could secure its own survival. American capitalism was burgeoning, and the ideological resources of Fourierism were neither fresh nor distinct enough to rally the weak opposition. Continual advance was the condition of survival. The Fourierists only faintly

[42] Victor Considérant, *Au Texas* (Paris, 1854), pp. 9-17.

echoed the fixed and alien idea of the medieval holy community, to which the Shakers and German pietists were firmly anchored. Visitors who could not see the underlying stagnation frequently observed that this community, even more than other secular and liberal communities, was dynamic; but the morale which would have enabled it to keep moving had not been adequately fostered.[43] The North American Phalanx, faced with tremendous odds, died of a failure of nerve.

The French adventures of Victor Considérant and Étienne Cabet, with Owen's New Harmony, were the only communities launched on a scale of capitalization and numbers at all comparable with the model communities conceived by the secular utopians. In each case the principal living theorist came from Europe to lead the enterprise, at one time sought to locate in Texas, and gathered around him at least a nucleus of European immigrants.

The Icarians held together for forty-eight years, much longer than any other liberal community. Their leaderless advance guard wasted its substance during the summer of 1848 in a vain attempt to wrestle with the Texas frontier. The next spring, after Cabet had joined them, he authorized the purchase of parts of the Mormon town of Nauvoo, on the Illinois bank of the Mississippi above Keokuk, which the Saints had evacuated scarcely three years before. Like Owen, the Icarians were now able to launch their experiment on a developed site. In 1856 Cabet lost control of the community and led a splinter group to Cheltenham, Missouri, near St. Louis, and died the following year. The European Icarians recognized Cheltenham as orthodox and sent financial aid through the Paris office of Jean Beluze. When he abandoned them in 1863 they dispersed within a year while he joined Marx's First International.

Meanwhile the branch at Nauvoo survived the overthrow of their leader and carefully planned a gradual transfer to frontier lands at Corning, Adams County, Iowa, which the community had acquired through Cabet. A boom market for their wool enabled them to endure the first years on the prairie, but the eighteen-seventies dawned on a cautious, tenacious, and ingrown group unfitted to be the beacon light of communism for the New World. The Corning Icarians outlived the revolt of their young men in 1877-1878 and again relinquished their homes to build anew nearby. The young men without them were unable to bring their dreams to fruition on the old site. Like Fourierism, Cabetism had its temporary

[43] Contrast Considérant's more acute detection of lethargy, *ibid.*, p. 10, with Fredrika Bremer's comparison, in *The Homes of the New World; Impressions of America* (tr. by Mary Howitt; New York, 1858, 2 vols.), of the static Shakers, I, pp. 556-71, and II, p. 598, with the dynamic Associationists of the North American Phalanx, I, pp. 75-85, and II, pp. 611-24. Compare Georgianna Bruce Kirby's comment on rapid changes at Brook Farm in *Years of Experience* (New York, 1887), p. 174.

transcendentalist diversion. The clan of Pierre and Jules Leroux, brothers who had developed their own brand of humanitarian and transcendentalist Christian socialism in France before 1848, persuaded a few of the Young Icarians to join its Cloverdale colony in the Sonoma valley of California,[44] but this community rapidly repeated the story of material prosperity and moribund socialism.

The last Icarian remnant at Corning, still controlled by some of its original members, dissolved in 1895. Not bankrupt in means, it was sterile in ideas to inspire its youth and win recruits. The last Icarians might have been as celibate as the Shakers and the Rappites for all the help they would accept from their children. The struggle for survival had made them rigid conservatives, instinctively turning their backs on the world;[45] in politics, traditional Republicans since the Civil War, they were unwilling to take new risks in business, and were looking backward. After 1856 they had attracted few outsiders to their communities and none to their school. Even before 1856 hardly any native Americans had joined, and less than one-seventh were immigrants from Germany and other parts of western Europe outside of France. Here was an enclave surrounded by a wall of French custom and language, a besieged citadel after 1856, on the defensive except for an abortive renaissance in the 1870's. Fascinating as the story of a French cooperative community and the Americanization of its members, the history of Icarianism belongs in the epilogue of the narrative of nineteenth-century American communitarianism because its socialism was conquered, but never naturalized.

IV. Liberal Communitarian Ideology and American Ideas

This essay has so far sought to sketch the background of American secular utopianism and summarize its history with special attention to the American influences transforming it. In keeping with the purpose of this volume and following the general pattern of its bibliography, it should not close without suggesting tentative conclusions about the secular communitarians which merit further investigation by historians of American thought and society. These suggestions at the same time elaborate the picture of Americanization already presented.

The most obvious American twist to secular utopian theory was its

[44] The M. L. De Hay collection, deposited at the Princeton University Library, contains printed works and manuscript correspondence and treatises of Jules Leroux, including an unsigned proposal for the fusion of the Cloverdale and Young Icarian communities.

[45] "Iowa of the Early Seventies as Seen by a Swedish Traveler," *Iowa Journal of History and Political Science*, xxvii (Oct. 1929), pp. 572-81, selections from Hugo Nisbeth, *Två År i Amerika (1872-1874); Resekilgringar [Two years in America . . . Accounts of Travel]* (Stockholm, 1874), translated by Roy W. Swanson, notes the "scarcely hospitable" attitude of the Icarians.

stronger emphasis on religion. As heirs to the Enlightenment in a time and place permeated by a kaleidoscopic Protestant theology, the liberal communitarians tried to occupy a halfway house between reason and revelation. Generally recognizing the fatherhood of God and the brotherhood of man, they disturbed the orthodox by tending to assert the primacy of humanity. In this period, which they themselves considered transitional, they could not help expressing, Januslike, the widest extremes of forward and backward looking thought. The various hybrid manifestations of their religion were basic in every compartment of their theory. Seeking salvation in mundane terms, they looked for health by preventives or cures in the body politic, the body economic, the body creative, and the body social, and in the individual.

Among their number were some who indulged in the esoteric and mythical symbolism more common to such sectarian communities as Ephrata, but the liberal utopians drew from oriental sources recently discovered by the transcendentalists, or from Swedenborgianism, rather than from medieval mysticism.[46] The communitarianism which cropped out in the American Church of the New Jerusalem is exemplified by the Owenite settlement at Yellow Springs, Ohio; the Associationist activities of the pioneer dentist, Solyman Brown and his Leraysville, Pennsylvania, phalanx;[47] and by the sympathetic reception which Associationists of both transcendental and western varieties gave to the new edition of Swedenborg's writings.

More important was an attenuated and for the most part unconscious romantic echo of medievalism, particularly among Fourierists. They retained enough of the idea of the holy community, created in the image of a fixed divine order, to reject the Newtonian determinism inherent in the iron law of attraction and to assume the possibility of the colonial method. Fourierism to them was not the new legislation of a creative imagination, but a prophetic promulgation of natural and divine law which fitted other prophecies from Christ to modern times. Medieval overtones can be heard in their provisions for hierarchies of class and status; in their complaints in modern terms against usurers, engrossers, and forestallers, and against wicked enclosures of the commons of the United States; in their emphasis on the usufructuary rather than the

[46] See, for example, The Zend-Avesta, and Solar Religions (New York, 1852), by Marx E. Lazarus, one-time resident of Fourierist Brook Farm and contributor to the Harbinger; C. J. H., "A Protest; of Fourierism against the Democratic Review," United States Magazine and Democratic Review, N.S., xi (Dec. 1842), pp. 646-48, alludes to a work the author is writing on Swedenborg and Fourier, to prove that Fourierism is not atheistic but "living Christianity."

[47] J. Solyman Brown, who also taught and preached at Leraysville, had been a member of the New York Society for Promoting Communities in 1822 (see its Essay on Commonwealths, p. 4).

absolute nature of property, and on wages of labor and quality of product to be determined by guild standards and not by the market; and in a frequent idealization of the village agriculture-handicraft stage of production.[48] They picked up details of the Gothic Revival in their plans for communal architecture, and many Fourierists, particularly John Dwight at Brook Farm, turned to a concept of music and ritual as handmaids of religion. At Brook Farm one could enter rooms with a crucifix on the table or images of saints on the wall, or hear a Mozart mass resounding from the reception room, or partake in lively discussions of Roman Catholic writings. For a few members like Isaac Hecker, Charles K. Newcomb, and Sophia Ripley or visitors like Orestes Brownson, this was a stage on their pilgrimages to Rome. For the rest, it was an expression of their universalism, or a dilettante and intellectualistic diversion.

The communities were also among the incubators, as well as the manifestations, of adventism, perfectionism, and spiritualism.[49] The influence of religious enthusiasm upon the communitarian movement, most of all that whipped up by the 1843 revivals, is epitomized by a participant's comment on Brook Farmers: ". . . no Adventist ever believed more absolutely in the second coming of Christ than we in the reorganization of society on a fraternal basis."[50] Not only was Fourierism, like so many

[48] See C. A. Beard, "The Political Heritage of the Twentieth Century," *Yale Review*, xviii (Spring 1929), pp. 470-71. Other echoes of medieval communalism among the European secular utopian socialists are discussed by E. H. Harbison in Chapter 1 of the present book.

[49] See W. A. Hinds, *American Communities* (3rd ed., Chicago, 1908), pp. 397-407; J. H. Noyes, *American Socialisms*, pp. 11, 57-58, 175-79, 251-52, 277, 374-76, 564-94, 613, 615; Herbert W. Schneider and George Lawton, *A Prophet and a Pilgrim; Being the Incredible History of Thomas Lake Harris and Laurence Oliphant; Their Sexual Mysticisms and Utopian Communities, Amply Documented to Confound the Skeptic* (Columbia Studies in American Culture, No. 11; New York, 1942); Spear MSS in the possession of Ernest C. Miller of Warren, Pa.; A. B. Smolnikar, *Denkwürdige Ereignisse im Leben des Andreas Bernardus Smolnikar* (Cambridge, Mass., Philadelphia and New York, 1838-1840, 3 vols.), two additional volumes referred to as published by 1842 in J. H. Noyes, *American Socialisms*, p. 252; Smolnikar, *Secret Enemies of True Republicanism . . . Developmments* [sic] *Regarding the Inner Life of Man and the Spirit World, in Order to Abolish Revolutions and Wars and to Establish Permanent Peace on Earth, also: the Plan for Redemption of Nations from Monarchical and Other Oppresive* [sic] *Speculations and for the Introduction of the Promised New Era of Harmony, Truth and Righteousness* (Springhill, Pa., 1859), pp. 81-87, 171-204, and *The Great Encyclic Epistle . . . Occasioned by the Death of . . . Abraham Lincoln, and . . . the Capture of Jefferson Davis* (Baltimore, 1865). See also J. A. Etzler, *The Paradise within the Reach of All Men, without Labor, by Powers of Nature and Machinery* (Pittsburgh, 1833, 2 vols. in one), and the sequel, *The New World; or, Mechanical System* (Philadelphia, 1841); E. S. Bates, *American Faith* (New York, 1940), pp. 421-26; J. R. Commons, *American Industrial Society*, vii, p. 188. No connection has been established between the spiritualist, John O. Wattles, and James O. Wattles of New Harmony.

[50] G. B. Kirby, *Years of Experience*, pp. 98-99. See also the *Harbinger*, iii (June 13, 1846), pp. 15-16.

sectarian community movements, shot through with adventism, but at least two small communities arose directly out of Millerism: Celesta in the Pennsylvania Alleghenies (1863-1864) and Adonai-Shomo near Athol, Massachusetts (1861-ca. 1890). A deist perfectionism without the theological connotation of sanctification appeared at the beginning with Paul Brown and Cornelius Blatchly. Its quite different Oneida form combined, as J. H. Noyes acknowledged, with Shaker communism and received a strong impulse from the Fourierists.

Interest in spiritualism was rife among the phalanxes, particularly where Swedenborgianism had a foothold. Brisbane and both Robert and Robert Dale Owen became its devotees, the first two still retaining their communitarian theory, and the last, long since divorced from the movement, striving valiantly to remove the stigma of socialism and free thought, which marked one wing of spiritualism for a generation. The first spiritualist community was that of John O. Wattles and his Cincinnati associates, who took over part of the property of the defunct Clermont Phalanx in 1846-1847. There followed A. B. Smolnikar's Grand Prairie Harmonial Institute on the Indiana-Illinois border (ca. 1849-1853); the Harmonial Brotherhood of the leading seer, Andrew Jackson Davis (1851); a group at Mountain Cove, Virginia (1851-1853), sent by spirit communications at Auburn, New York; and another led by John Murray Spear on the state line between Warren, Pennsylvania, and Jamestown, New York (1853-1863). Thomas L. Harris, member at Mountain Cove, preached his own mixture of adventism, Swedenborgianism, spiritualism, and Universalism in the Brotherhood of the New Life at several sites in New York and California after the Civil War. Spear, a Garrisonian, prison reformer, and like Harris, an ex-Universalist, set his Association of Beneficents to exploit the "electrical" properties of Kiantone Springs for the secret of perpetual motion. Other projects at the Springs included digging for relics of prehistoric webfooted man (shades of Joseph Smith!), a national spiritualist convention in 1858, and a "Columbusonian" river expedition to New Orleans in 1859-1860, proclaiming the imminent collapse of the republic and the inauguration of world federalism. The "omniarch" (Fourier's term) who proclaimed the dissolution of the community in 1863 was John Orvis, perhaps the Brook Farm missionary.

Another religious irregular, who operated at first among the Pennsylvania Dutch but later widely deposited his pseudomystical messages like cowbird's eggs in adventist, perfectionist, and spiritualist nests, was Andreas B. Smolnikar, renegade Benedictine monk and self-styled professor of Biblical literature in Austria. He announced that Christ had appointed him on January 5, 1837, at 5 p.m. to inaugurate the universal republic, and had indicated that preparations were being made in the United States. Straightway he crossed the Atlantic, delivered his credentials in five volumes, and during the next twenty years started at least three "Peace Unions" (1844, 1850, 1859). The first focused on a trial of J. A. Etzler's marvelous stump-pulling machine in Warren County, Pennsylvania—strange alliance of materialism and mysticism—and won for Smolnikar a token recognition as a vice-president of the 1844 Associationist convention with Brisbane, Greeley, Parke Godwin, C. A. Dana, and A. M. Watson. At the age of seventy he was still interpreting current events to fit his mission.

These eccentric movements symbolized the downward penetration of new intellectual currents among common men determined to hold communication with another world on their own account, and enjoy material happiness and social harmony at the same time. The varying directories of "the general assembly of the spirit life" indicate the dual background of spiritualists, drawn on the one hand like Warren Chase and J. M. Spear from Universalist and freethinking sources (whose spirit leaders were patriot deists such as Benjamin Franklin and Thomas Jefferson), and on the other from the evangelicals who were more apt to hear the voices of humanitarian reformers.

A definite but limited connection, also, can be shown between the principles and interests of the secular communitarians and those of the Hicksite wing of the Society of Friends. This connection was especially close with the Owenites. They both sought the happiness of the rational being, pioneered in benevolent reforms of social morals, especially in education and for the equality of women, and conducted their affairs in voluntarist, corporate, functional, and unadorned fashion. Persons of Quaker background and members of the Society were prominent in varying degrees at New Harmony, the Kendal and probably the Valley Forge communities, the Northampton Association, the Prairie Home Community near West Liberty, Ohio (1843-1844), and the Clarkson Phalanx on Lake Ontario (1844).

The forward looking side of secular utopian thought on religion was not limited to its relations with new sects. The discourses of W. H. Channing and the expressions of Charles A. Spear of the North American Phalanx, John Dwight, Horace Greeley, and other leaders adumbrated many cardinal tenets of Frothingham's Free Religious Association and the Social Gospel movement. These leaders retreated from the European Owenite dismissal of sin, but held to the position that a practical solution avoiding the dogma of total depravity was to emphasize social sin and Christian institutional methods of combating it. Original sin versus human perfectibility was to them a barren theological question, with both extremes leading to despair or inaction. This bears out Mannheim's observation that utopian theory, forced into contact with reality by attempts to carry it out in practice, develops a workable compromise position. The leaders had never strayed far from the American intellectual tradition and were too pragmatic to maintain a school, as their European counterparts did, after the failure of their practical efforts. Instead, they either drifted back, disillusioned, into the main currents of individualistic thought, or attached themselves to one of the perennial new movements of native radicalism.

The secular communities were also channels through which secularization continued its gradual conquest of American society and checked the evangelical counterreformation. A preacher for the Baptist Domestic Missionary Society testified a decade after the death of the Kendal Community that Massillon, Ohio, was still a nest of infidelity,[51] and the tradition of free thought survived among other ex-communitarians. Science never lost its central place in their theory, but it was understood as knowledge gained through reason and had little of the positivist emphasis on empirical and inductive methods. W. H. Channing was aware of Comtian positivism as early as 1830 and discussed it with Theodore Parker and George Ripley, but even Comte's Religion of Humanity had little to satisfy them. Henry Edger, only incidentally a communitarian, was the only thoroughgoing American disciple of Comte.[52] Neither did the secular utopians develop any special logic to reveal the historical process, although the faintest suggestion of the dialectic appears in a confused article by the Fourierist, J. H. Pulte, illustrating Schelling's "principle of polarity,"[53] and in Brisbane's concept of inverted or antagonistic relations.

They held the eighteenth-century stage theory of history which saw progress as a series of steps or stages definitely marked off, as between childhood and adolescence. For the most part they avoided the contradiction between their frequent use of the organic analogy, which implied a cyclical theory, and their firm assurance of progress. Brisbane relegated the decline of society to a time so far in the future that it was not worth discussing or claimed that the analogy applied to the parts and not to the whole. Paul Brown distinguished between mind, capable of improvement

[51] Quoted by Gilbert Vale in the *Beacon*, III (Mar. 9, 1839), p. 136.
[52] R. L. Hawkins, *Auguste Comte and the United States, 1816-1853* (Cambridge, Mass., 1936), and *Positivism in the United States, 1853-1863* (Cambridge, Mass., 1938), pp. 104-203. Edger spent the last five months of 1851 at the North American Phalanx. See also the MS correspondence (1860-1888) in the New York Public Library, of William Frey, Russian-American Positivist and founder of the Kansas community of Cedarvale in the 1870's; and the call published in the *New York Daily Tribune*, June 19, 1867, for the organization of a New York branch of the American Association for the Promotion of Social Science, to study social science "as a POSITIVE SCIENCE," signed by Josiah Warren, the former Fourierists, Horace Greeley, Albert Brisbane, Osborne McDaniel, E. P. Grant, John Orvis, and four others. Prof. R. S. Fletcher of Oberlin College called my attention to this reference. For the proceedings of the organization meeting on July 4, see *ibid.*, July 6, 8, 1867.
[53] "The Political State of the World," *Harbinger*, III (July 4, 11, 1846), pp. 51-54, 68-71. See also below, p. 206.

until death, and organism.[54] Since Brown believed that society could be directed by philosophers, such a society need not succumb to the corruptions of the flesh. While not aware of Lamarckian evolutionary theory, they held a kind of social Lamarckism. Communities could inherit acquired characteristics, for the new social environment would favor the preservation of new character variants. At the same time, the revolutionary step of shifting to a community basis of what the Fourierists called "guarantyism," the first and limited form of the combined order, was in fact a mutation corresponding to the attainment of puberty and would lead, the Fourierists believed, to another mutation at the attainment of full social maturity in the harmonic order.

Harmony symbolized the communitarian ideal; discord symbolized the evils of the outside world. Nearly all communitarians found the fullest artistic development of the harmonic ideal in music. The secular utopians, less restrained by pietist and otherworldly standards, both practiced the art more and made greater use of the musical analogy than the sectarians. The liberal groups saw in music the prime medium for the pursuit of happiness through collective recreation and creativity. Music, so cheaply enjoyed, could be a great power for the emancipation of the common man as it had hitherto been an agency for deluding him into supporting the rulers of church and state. Music had charms to heal a troubled world. Its harmony implied group discipline and the articulation of diversity into a perfect union; its melody, individual development within a consonant framework; its rhythm, dynamic progress.

Music was to Paul Brown, Josiah Warren, and Alcander Longley a science of sound capable of being expressed mathematically and an art of manipulating an instrument and communicating socially desirable sentiments through natural or customary signs. Warren invented about 1839 a system of notation which he claimed was scientific and reasonable, and Longley, not an accomplished musical teacher or performer like Warren, substituted numbers for notes in the community songs he printed. No less rationalistic was Albert Brisbane, one of whose purposes in returning to France in 1844 was to find through the study of music (for which he was ill equipped) the key to Fourier's harmonic universe. Less in the language of reason, John Dwight spoke of "music as part of the natural language of devotion" drawing souls "nearer to each other and to God."[55]

[54] General Introduction to Social Science (New York, 1876, 2 pts. in one), Pt. I, Albert Brisbane, Introduction to Fourier's Theory of Social Organization, pp. 21-50; Harbinger, III (Aug. 15, 1846), pp. 157-58; Paul Brown, Philosophic Education, pp. 286-90.

[55] Harbinger, V (June 19, 1847), p. 29. See also William Pelham's comment, ". . . singing is taught here scientifically," in "Pelham Letters," p. 380; Paul Brown, Philosophic Education, pp. 117-18, 171-73, 175, 187, 225-26; Josiah Warren, Written Music Remodeled, and Invested with the Simplicity of an Exact Science (Boston,

Yet his was not a romantic taste; he loved the ordered classics of Handel, Haydn, and Mozart and could appreciate neither the vernacular of the Hutchinson Family nor the turbulent Wagner. Dwight eagerly accepted Fourier's exaltation of opera as the group art par excellence, wrote for the musical élite of Boston and New York, and had little of Warren's concern for freeing music from commercialism and returning it to the people. He nevertheless believed that all could come to love and perform the classics, and that "music is a universal language; it knows nothing of opinions, creeds, doctrines that divide . . . [and it keeps alive the hope for] a truly catholic and universal church" of humanity united.[56]

Music was only the most abstract and universal means of communication; the same communitarians were usually interested in the harmonization of mankind through both music and language. Starting with a linguistic concern for scientific grammar, phonetics, and spelling reform, they frequently confessed the hope for an esperanto, if not for the universalization of a modified English, which would unite all men.

Unity out of diversity (e pluribus unum), without resort to the coercive state, was the theme of the quotations on the title page of Brisbane's 1843 pamphlet, Association. "Not through hatred, collision, and depressing competition; not through War, whether of Nation against Nation, Class against Class, or Labor against Capital; but through Union, Harmony, and the reconciling of all Interests . . . is the Renovation of the World, the Elevation of the degraded and suffering Masses of Mankind, to be sought and effected." "Our Evils are Social, not Political, and a Social Reform only can eradicate them." Here is the nub of the liberal communitarians' theory—antistatist, minimizing economics, and implicitly subordinating it to sociological questions of status and psychological questions of motivation. This essay, after outlining the variations in their fundamental antistatism, will summarize their practical efforts to grapple with problems of social control and motivation, and will compare the economic analysis of capitalism, which a few Associationists made, with that of the Marxians who succeeded them. An analysis of the economic arrangements of the more extreme secular communities would be profitable, but in this essay out of scale with the minor importance which nearly all communitarians ascribed to economic problems. Depressions focused their attention on economic ills, but they chose social solutions; indeed, the term "economic" as we use it was not yet in the vocabulary. No common pattern emerges

ca. 1859), especially the unpaged preliminary remarks and pp. 1-5; and Alcander Longley, Communism . . . Also Containing a Complete System of Simple Phonography or Rapid Writing: With Several Communist Songs: Printed in a New System of Phonetic Figure Music (St. Louis, Mo., 1880), and The Phonetic Songster (St. Louis, Mo., n.d.).

[56] Harbinger, v (June 19, 1847), p. 29. For discussion of secular utopian arts see Chapter 14 herein.

from the economic expedients resorted to. Whether pure communist or individualist, communities sampled normal and radical business methods, and tried new ones such as doing without money and specific barter, or Warren's labor notes.

It may seem strange to think of the American Owenites and Associationists, normally Whigs or Democrats, as in any way connected with "anarchists." The vast majority of secular utopians insistently denied any connection with the "no government" Garrisonians, then the only thoroughly subversive element in the North. Nevertheless, they had as little use for politics as the early Christians, and when they did not bother to go back that far to justify their attitude, as little use as the pure liberal in business, who wanted only to be let alone to make money. As noted above, the Owenites were disillusioned by the failure of government to rescue them from the clutches of creditors after 1819 and by the failure of Jacksonian democracy in 1824; the Fourierists, by the demagoguery of the Whigs' 1840 campaign and the rabble-rousing of the Democrats. They hated lawyers and promised virtually to abolish the profession of law in their communities. Their very withdrawal from general society was one vote of no confidence in government, and their strong voluntarism was another.

Communitarian antistatism was implicit or overt. The majority were implicitly opposed to political action, else they would have organized parties, or at least pressure groups. At most they reentered politics only to further reforms dearest to their hearts, such as antislavery; or voted passively as they always had, or discussed a positive political program in the American language of federalism, which was incidentally Rousseau's, Fourier's, and Proudhon's. The Fourierists Parke Godwin and Charles A. Dana were, with the mutualist William A. Greene, particularly interested in Proudhon, but more for his theory of mutual banking than for his federalism.

Greeley, the Whig politician and stanch Associationist, and Owen, who tried hardest to persuade the leading state and national politicians, were the outstanding exceptions. Owen never gave up the tactic of seeking the key men, but it was this characteristic which separated the American Owenites from their foreign leader. What they grasped, particularly the Quakers among them (who were Christian anarchists), was Owen's gospel of nonviolent and rational education in a cooperative environment as the sole and sufficient means of transforming society. Owen remarked in 1844 that the disciples of Fourier were better material—and he implied, in some respects closer to his own position—than the Americans calling themselves Owenites.[57] With Greeley the case was different. Risen from printer's devil to employer, he recognized the importance of securing the

[57] J. R. Commons, *American Industrial Society*, vii, p. 167.

workingman's support for the Whig Party. Genuinely interested in Christian reform, he wished to give his party a moral justification. Although he offered money and encouragement to the Associationists and fought their journalistic battles, he was neither their theorist nor a leader in their communities. In short, he was first of all a politician who sought to square Whiggism with social reform.

Most of the independent non-Fourierist communities of the forties combined Garrisonian anarchism with American communist Owenism. They were neither more nor less "successful" than the implicitly antistatist Associations as business enterprises, experiments in uncoerced group living, and cradles of new theories. Their members tended to be active abolitionists, pacifists, and vegetarians. Partial exceptions were the three New England joint stock associations at Hopedale, Brook Farm, and Northampton, which had no trace of Owenism, and the One-Mentian Community in the Poconos (1843), which was nearest to the European Owenism of 1843 except in religion, and among the late Owenite projects the furthest from explicit antistatism. The Northampton Association (1842-1846) had strong connections with Garrison and the peace movement and lasted longer than the average American community. No sizable community of liberals except Icaria surpassed the Hopedale Community (1842-1856) in years of active life, and nowhere else was the nonresistant anarchist position so fully preached or practiced. Adin Ballou's Yankees operated under the joint stock compact of January 1841, independent of Garrison or Owen. They prescribed no theological or ritualistic test beyond belief in Christianity (although they insisted on strict ethical standards), and severed all voluntary connections with coercive government. The Marlboro Association in Ohio (1841-1845) lasted as long as any western phalanx except Ceresco and possibly Trumbull, on a basis of Pentecostal communism. One of the Brooke brothers who provided the property, an ascetic doctor, succeeded in earning a living without the use of money. John A. Collins's experiment at Skaneateles, New York (1843-1846), the nearest communitarian approach to a purely Garrisonian anarchism, ended, like Ceresco, without financial loss. Collins's free thought was Owenite and he shared a belief in full communism with Paul Brown. The virtue of the Prairie Home Community (1843-1844), peopled mostly by Hicksite Quaker farmers, was to live together amicably without an iota of formal planning or leadership. Orson S. Murray, a native Vermonter like Collins, was spreading his version of Garrison's principles at Brandon, Vermont, when Collins's antislavery caravan of 1843 passed through town and enlisted him for Prairie Home. Murray lost his press in a Lake Erie shipwreck and never joined the group; but his *Regenerator*, started in 1846, was friendly to Owenism and anarchism.

The anarchism of Josiah Warren after he left New Harmony is well known, but his nonsocialist communities built on individual sovereignty are not generally understood to fit the definition of liberal, secular, utopian communitarianism. Warren called one of his ventures "Utopia," and was among the most thoroughgoing in his emphasis on liberty and a secular goal. Unlike Thoreau, who also criticized the evils of competition and insisted on individualistic action, he was not guided by a conscience which revealed a higher law than the state's, but by the rational theory of mutual confidence and exchange held by Paul Brown to be essential to communism. Power and property have a close relationship; and so, said Rousseau and the antistatist utopians, do liberty and equality. The equity which Warren aimed to foster by individualistic means tended toward the equalization of property. Each workingman, freed from the "unnecessary" and unequal burdens imposed by the coercive state, could enjoy relatively equal access to resources when limited to what he could individually exploit and defend (for Warren was no nonresistant). The emancipated laborer could receive the full product of his labor because time-money freed him from the combined power of capital to exact profit. Equity implied the equalization of power and the achievement of as communitarian a system through individual private property as the Associationists could achieve through joint stock or the American Owenites through common property. Warren, instead of dispensing with money, like Dr. A. Brooke, adopted the system of labor notes used at New Harmony for exchange between its three communities. With other secular communitarians, he conceived of his cure with reference to an agrarian-commercial rather than an industrial economy. At Warren's Modern Times, Long Island (1851-1857), the freethinkers put into practice their doctrines of free love, and Warren and Stephen Pearl Andrews their monetary theories. Here flowered Henry Edger's lone American exposition of Comtian positivism.

Neither Ballou nor Warren carried liberty and equality further than the anarchist communitarian, James Arrington Clay, for much of his harmless life a man without a community. God as the power of love universally diffused throughout creation was central in his theology, from which he derived an ethic of nonresistance and freedom in love. For the practice of this mild but subversive doctrine in his native Gardiner, Maine, he suffered jail. He first appeared in the role of David against the institutional Goliath in 1845 at the age of thirty-one. After he emerged from prison in 1855, he shook the dust of Maine from his feet and joined the Point Hope Community at Berlin Heights, Ohio. Clay, like Warren, accepted private enterprise while rejecting capitalism. With Oneida and Shaker communism he found much to agree, but he rejected celibacy and Biblical infallibility. Steeped in the Bible, he based his principles on natural reason and intuition. A perfectionist come-outer, he sought "to join a community whose interests shall be united; where love shall take the place of gold, peace that of war, plenty of want, health that of sickness, life that of death. . . . a model kingdom of heaven."[58]

To the secular utopians the cure for society lay in raising its minimum standards, reorganizing its hierarchy according to natural abilities, and in reorienting its motivations. They nearly all urged the emancipation of women without carrying the reform to Clay's extreme. The unitary dwelling was frequently considered the mechanism for elevating woman's status from domestic drudgery, but the inmates generally did not acknowledge it for what it was—a source of dissension and unhappiness to persons unaccustomed to apartment or tenement-house living. Robert L. Jennings did admit that the Franklin Community had learned its lesson and would not have any more married couples, but only young people, who would grow up in the new social system.[59]

Doubts continually appeared as to the ability of adults to adjust to community life. Must social change begin by remolding the individual, or society? At times they expressed themselves like Marxians and described the core of education as life in a community; but after a failure, they blamed the participants' social immaturity. They tended to lean toward the individualist's answer, and depended on education not only to prepare men for the new society, but to bring the social revolution peacefully, and eventually to settle questions of status with reference to the natural aristocracy revealed by nurture. The Owenites were the first importers of the educational ideas of the Enlightenment as carried out principally by Pestalozzi, but the American movement for educational reform, once stimulated by them, went back to the European sources. The later secular utopians, borrowing from new American Pestalozzians, were able to surpass the Owenite achievement. The Brook Farm School had a superior location to New Harmony's, a more harmonious and accomplished staff and greater success. The scarcely less notable schools at Northampton and Fruitlands outclassed the common school at Kendal. Except for these embodiments of the central core of their theory, the liberal and tran-

[58] James A. Clay, *A Voice from the Prison; or, Truths for the Multitude and Pearls for the Truthful* (Boston, 1856), p. 23. Clay was convicted in 1854 for "lewd and lascivious cohabitation with an unmarried woman, in my own house" on evidence "that we slept in the same bed," but acquitted of an adultery charge after two doctors testified to the woman's virginity (*ibid.*, pp. 28-29). Commitment to an insane asylum was then suggested. See *ibid.*, pp. 25-27, 37-52, 55-56, 83-131, 195-227, 234-52, 298-99, 303, 338, 356-61, and H. K. Morrell, "Fifty Years Ago; Some of the People Who Were in Gardiner Then," unidentified newspaper clipping in Maine State Library, extracted for the author by Marion B. Stubbs, Librarian. Clay published the periodicals, *David's Sling* (Gardiner, Me., 1845), with Isaac Rowell, and the *Eastern Light* (Gardiner, Me., 1854-1855), and possibly others. He characteristically gave his publications away and refused to copyright his book.
[59] James M'Knight, *Discourse Exposing Robert Owen's System*, p. 13.

scendentalist communitarians were forced to concentrate too much on the business of survival to do it justice. No other aspect of their theory has received a more thorough confirmation in modern practice than their educational ideas.

Noteworthy as the efforts of the secular utopians were to improve the status of women in their communities and to educate all persons for maximum usefulness in a new society, the immediate health of their organizations could not be secured by these means. Social control to overcome the tendency of their heterogeneous materials to split and disperse had to be found in new internal customs, new uses for old ones, and new attitudes. Looking as they frequently did at the Shakers and other sectarian communities, they could not appropriate the sectarians' methods of securing social cohesion. They were too close to the American democratic tradition to countenance an oligarchical or autocratic leadership which held the keys of the Kingdom. They did not believe in the segregation of the sexes, and most of them opposed any radical departure from monogamy. They were not satisfied with any extensive imposition of uniformity in food, clothing, or shelter, for these things were too closely connected with ways to express and develop their individuality. On the other hand, they never reached the state of being able to realize with economic success the nonpecuniary incentives of attractive industry suggested by their own theorists: job rotation, short hours, pay differentials, and honors according to pleasantness or disagreeableness of work, healthy working conditions, and social securities superior to what the surrounding economy offered.

The secular utopians did have a common antagonism toward the outside world and a safety valve in the practice of democracy. They consequently had frequent success in the integration of maladjusted personalities and in holding together in the face of serious handicaps. Freud has pointed out that aggressiveness in small communities finds an outlet in enmity toward the outgroup. At the same time, fears for individual security are forgotten in common fears for the security of the community. Ceresco cohered partly to withstand the attacks of individualistic Ripon. The communitarian strategy in propaganda was perhaps more to make people unhappy by their criticism of existing society than to paint their utopias, although the two tactics were complementary. The sense of having escaped the hell of civilization, of being the pioneers in a movement which their idea of progress assured them would inevitably conquer; and the sense of importance in this movement gained by participation in the committees, assemblies, and elections by which the communities were managed contributed both to character integration and social cohesion. The maladjusted part of their personnel received the most help and did not often contribute enough toward community self-support. The foreigner, who would be ridiculed and pushed aside by parochial nativists, was made to feel at home and gently taught American ways. The disappointed spinster who had felt that nobody loved her became the favorite but still only a producer of flowers. Clearly, the communities could not endure with only the frustrated flotsam and jetsam of a depression, whether drifting incompetents or men as able as John Collins, who turned radical in 1837 and conservative again in the better times of 1846. The competent and healthy who were convinced of communitarian values regardless of hard or easy times had to carry the rest. Warren Chase is perhaps the best example of a man who found himself in a phalanx, but his outlook did not depend on the temporary hardships of 1837-1843. The testimony of scores of others that their happiest days were spent in the communities cannot be written off as face-saving. The returners, who had left dissatisfied but came back after a while in the cold world, the repeaters, who tried different varieties of community and were ever ready to join a new experiment, and the ex-communitarians in the native radical movement, all testify to the permanent orientation acquired or confirmed in the communities.[60]

On the debit side, the exigencies of close living probably broke or failed to integrate another group of characters. If not irreparably damaged, they were mended by such other institutions as those of the frontier or the Roman Catholic Church. The perfectionist who does not provide for intermediate satisfactions is the most susceptible to severe disillusionment when he sees his ideal remain unattainable in the stars. The secular communitarians, from Paul Brown to Brisbane, were very explicit in pointing out the satisfactions to be gained en route to perfect harmony, but not every adherent took advantage of these rest stops.

The relation of leadership to membership was one of the most fertile sources of discord. Hostile critics such as Fairchild of Oberlin and the Danish-American writer, Harro Harring, needed no evidence to convince them that community socialism was the road to serfdom.[61] If they had bothered with evidence, the discontented minorities—Paul Brown, James

[60] Sigmund Freud, *Civilization and Its Discontents* (New York, 1930), p. 90, referred to by Cavendish Moxon in *Science & Society*, xii (Spring 1948), p. 202; Warren Chase, *Life-Line of the Lone One*, p. 126; Fredrika Bremer, *Homes of the New World*, ii, pp. 619-20, on the salvaging of a spinster at the North American Phalanx; Elizabeth Robinson, "Get the people unhappy with their present condition" and the work is almost done, communication dated Mt. Pleasant, Ohio, "4th mo. 1846" in *Regenerator*, N.S., i (July 13, 1846), p. 116; *ibid.* (Sept. 9, 1846), pp. 184-85, on the career of J. A. Collins; John Gilbert, New York City, "To the Friends of Human Progression" in *ibid.* (July 27, 1846), p. 134, declaring his desire to try again after participating in three failures.

[61] James H. Fairchild, "Fourierism," *Oberlin Quarterly Review*, i (Nov. 1845), pp. 224-45, answered with eight articles in the *Harbinger*, beginning iii (July 11, 1846), pp. 77-80, and ending iii (Oct. 17, 1846), pp. 301-3; H. P. Harring, *Harro Harring's Episteln an die Fourieristen* (New York, 1844), p. 31.

M'Knight, the anti-Cabetist faction at Nauvoo, and many others—were ready to testify to the despotism they had undergone. Antistatists and liberals in general are supersensitive to encroachments upon liberty and equality, but the dominant element never intended as much leveling of status as their language implied. The opposition to leaders came also from the more orthodox in religion, such as M'Knight at the Franklin Community and the Methodists of Macluria, or from the more individualistic and industrialistic in economics, such as the Raritan Bay Association. The leaders who contributed the most financial support and propagandist and administrative effort carried unacknowledged weight. Owen and Maclure at New Harmony, Jacob Peterson at Franklin, George B. Arnold at the North American Phalanx, Abner Enoch at the Integral Phalanx, and the resident farmers at the Leraysville Phalanx were only a few of the men whose property and skills were preponderant. Although divorced by the community constitutions from formal power, they tended to exercise power informally, and at their discretion to force abandonment. Where the leaders spent too much time in propaganda or otherwise grew out of touch with the colonies, as at New Harmony, Skaneateles, Northampton, Hopedale, Red Bank, and Icaria, rival factions developed away from the common outlook which could achieve compromise and continuance. The device used at Ceresco in 1846 and Icaria in 1877 to bring in a neutral president from the outside with previous experience elsewhere in the movement was only temporarily successful.

In all the communities, the designation of radical and conservative as for or against the existing situation is too oversimplified to be useful, and the superficial identification of radicalism with maladjustment is too sweeping. The existing situation shifted rapidly; all were accounted radicals by the world, and by no means all were maladjusted. Internal parties contended for greater or less speed in approaching the ideal, for return to a solution closer to capitalism, or for a great number of specific changes scarcely connected with fundamental policy.

V. The Liberal Communitarians and Marxism

If the American secular utopians did not solve the hard problems of social control, they at least tried or suggested many of the alternatives which Marxian socialists have variously adopted. Their analysis of capitalism, based upon a priori principles and random observations, never approached the systematic, comprehensive, and more empirical treatment of Marx. His indebtedness to French and English secular utopians, as well as the long strides he took beyond them, are well known. That any of the American utopians approached his point of view is surprising, since they were looking from a very different background at capitalism in a less developed stage. The bulk of the American participants in liberal communities were religious or humanitarian enthusiasts, obsessed with land mania, and without much first-hand acquaintance with the factory system. A few leading Fourierists in the Northeast, however, went beyond the simple class-struggle formulas of American radical labor. These leaders were not infected with the frontier fever, and although they were religious, they approached religion as cosmopolitan intellectuals.

The manifesto of William H. Channing published soon after the organization of the American Union of Associationists on May 27, 1846, and articles on labor by C. A. Dana and Albert Brisbane the same year,[62] are particularly rich in parallels to Marxism. Their emphasis on liberal religion and the community method of peaceful revolution was distinct, but their central theme was the following economic indictment:

The institutions and conditions controlling the productive or laboring classes contain the keys to the economic problem and to the interpretation of history. The rights to labor and to the fruits of labor are "the two great fundamental rights of man—without which political rights become often worthless."[63] The wage system under capitalism is more advanced than the systems of slavery and serfdom before it, but it leads to the concentration of capital, the increasing misery of labor, and bloody revolution or a new feudalism in which the ruling class will reduce the whole population to the servitude already suffered by factory operatives. It is no accident that the social superstructure reflects the tyranny of capital. It corrupts and controls all branches of the state, public opinion and custom, organized religion and the professions, and even literature; and yet not because capitalists are always individually wicked, but because of the system. Although capitalism is an international alliance sweeping on to world empire in defiance of patriotism and morals, it is rent by internal conflicts as well as threatened by the class struggle. The contradiction between the forces and relations of production on the international scene produces wars while technology multiplies conditions making for peace. The contradiction at home creates poverty in the midst of overproduction and the potential plenty which machinery could pro-

---

[62] "To the Associationists of the United States," *Harbinger*, III (June 13, 1846), pp. 14-16, signed by Channing as Domestic Corresponding Secretary; Charles A. Dana, "Labor for Wages," *ibid.*, II (Apr. 25, 1846), pp. 318-19; and Albert Brisbane, "The Organization of Labor," *ibid.*, III (June 27, July 4, 25, Aug. 15, 1846), pp. 44-46, 59-62, 108-10, 157-60. Two thousand copies of Dana's pamphlet were printed by the Associationists of Cleveland and distributed free. See also the discussion of "the class issue" in *Exposé of the Condition and Progress of the North American Phalanx*, pp. 8-16, and the emphasis on "increased production, for there is not wealth enough produced, however distributed, to supply adequately human wants" (p. 16); and the letter from a Thompsonville, Connecticut, textile worker in the *Harbinger*, III (June 20, 1846), p. 30, with the editorial comment (p. 29), "Each increase in [the masses'] . . . number and each improvement in . . . machinery arms with a new weapon that power that tramples them. . . ."

[63] Brisbane, *ibid.* (June 27, 1846), p. 46; cf. (Aug. 8, 1846), p. 160.

duce. Rigid industrial discipline and oppression backed by the state; long hours, monotony, and excessive division of labor; loss of skills and self-confidence; occupational diseases and the stultification of mind and morals; the exploitation of women and children; unemployment because of the reserve army of labor created by technological improvements—all are forced upon the toiling masses whose only property is their labor. The ruling class itself turns to conspicuous consumption, sterile exercise of privilege, and parasitism. Although the employer has all the power, his philanthropy is futile, for he too is a slave of competition. Neither can labor legislation, such as for a maximum ten-hour day, have any lasting effects, and the history of labor organization is one of betrayal by its leaders. The escape from this dilemma is possible only through the abolition of individual property in land, and through the propaganda and leadership of the Associationist vanguard, which has worked out a plan for the right system to be applied first throughout the nation and ultimately the civilized world: ". . . the people must look to themselves for the vindication of their rights. . . ."[64]

The comparison must not be overdrawn. Marx himself had little quarrel with the liberal communitarians either as to the oppressive conditions under capitalism or the conditions under full socialism. On the latter score both were anarchists. But he did object to their emphasis on imagined rather than actual conditions, and more especially to their idea of the historical process and of revolution. More than the Marxians they contradicted their determinism with an idealist activism. They were more apt to solicit capital from capitalists than to speak of the people's winning their rights. "Antagonistic interests" to Associationists were not the same as the class struggle to Marxians. The concept of inverted or antagonistic relations, which Brisbane perhaps gathered from Hegel, is as close as the Associationists came to the Marxian dialectic. Labor organization for political purposes is not merely secondary, it is as futile as the syndicalists later said; and for economic purposes and ultimate revolution it is abhorrent. Brisbane, observing the lack of organization and the docility and mobility of American operatives, believed "feudal monopoly" more likely than revolution. Concentration of capital and the contradiction between the forces and relations of production can only be inferred, and these Associationists realize only the general tendency, not the increasing scale of production and the accumulation of capital. Marx is brief, but they are silent on the theory of the business cycle. Land, not the instruments of production, is emphasized in the proposed shift from individual to corporate (not communist) ownership. These Americans are more explicit than Marx in their prophecy that, in the last phase of capitalist civilization, agricultural production will be collectivized and the small

[64] Brisbane, *ibid.* (July 4, 1846), p. 62.

farmers reduced to hirelings. In other writings the Americans tended to follow the will o' the wisp of currency reform. Brisbane, Dana, and Godwin, no less than Warren, tinkered with ideas of money and banking.

Nevertheless, these Associationists of 1846 were closer to Marxism than the colonists of the preceding three years. Their 1846 campaign was more of a critical analysis than a plan, and later Associationist theory retreated almost entirely to the study of "social science" in order to reveal the historical process. The American Fourierists at this stage did show a trace of dialectical materialism and determinism in pointing to a material remedy for economic conditions to be achieved abruptly by the masses under the leadership of converted intellectuals when the time was ripe.

Marxism stirred Icaria during the 1870's. In the depression years after 1873, the community at Corning, Iowa, came alive, and looked for a time as if it would become one of the centers of the First International in the United States. Its members followed with keen interest the developing radicalism of Europe. A photograph of Bakunin hung in their common room, and a few of his disciples, as well as Marxian exiles of the Paris Commune of 1871, congregated at Corning. Its young men wanted to expand and keep abreast of the times, to industrialize and become a headquarters for communist propaganda among the Franco-American proletariat. This movement was Icaria's major attempt to plunge into the current of American life and at the same time hold to the communitarian principle of standing as a pilot project, as the most effective kind of propaganda of the deed, for American labor. After much wrangling the exiles were admitted, and after still more bickering, the Young Icarians got their chance to carry out their program, but without the steadying influence of their elders. They attracted as many native radicals and cranks as communists, and lacked even the staying power of the opposing faction. During the 1880's the Young Icarians voted for the Greenback Party rather than the Marxian Socialistic Labor Party.

One other connection with Marxism involves Icaria: the brief experience of a few later socialists at the Iowa community. In 1867, Alcander Longley, already well acquainted with two phalanxes (Clermont and North American), became a probationary member, and published at Corning the preliminary number of his paper, the *Communist*. Later, he associated with the Socialistic Labor Party in St. Louis, and wrote the utopian novel, *What Is Communism? A Narrative of the Relief Community*, a mélange of his Fourierist experience, the full communism of the American Owenites and the Icarians, and the tactics of the native cooperative movement. The story concludes, however, as no other communitarian document does, with the organization of a Communist Party. Like the Marxians, rather than the populists and Lassalleans, who put politics first, Longley makes political action the climax of the revolutionary movement after a strong nucleus has been established by the economic action and propaganda of the class struggle. Unlike the Marxians, Longley is sanguine that the communist victory will cause no counterrevolution which cannot be controlled through the courts.[65] Laurence Gronlund, also briefly an Icarian, proposed his own cooperative commonwealth and became successively attached to Bellamyite Nationalism, the Socialist Labor Party, and the American Fabian Society. Few ex-Associationists besides Longley even temporarily joined the Marxians. If still active reformers, they most often promoted the cooperative movement. John Orvis, for example, learned the Rochdale system in England and returned to organize for the Sovereigns of Industry.

At the turn of the century, the communitarian ideology was still strong among western socialists removed from urban industrialism. When the Debs-Berger minority withdrew from its temporary union with the Brotherhood of the Cooperative Commonwealth in 1898, the Marxian labor movement turned its back forever on secular utopianism. The majority proceeded with its program to capture a western state by mass migration, and planted the town of Equality, Washington (1898-1906). Two similar communities on the Puget Sound frontier were founded at Home and Burley, and all three had an anarchist tinge. After World War I, Marxians participated at New Llano, Louisiana, and in the Sunrise Community, Michigan, where the anarchist attitude was strong.

The American liberal community movement can be understood only with reference to the conditions of American life during the second quarter of the nineteenth century. It attracted Americans when it spoke their language. It failed when more powerful movements seemed to promise better material returns and to fit more closely the new urban-industrial climate of opinion. Association, the most important American expression of secular utopianism, had the benefit of shrewd native propagandists who were in tune with contemporary intellectual, reform, and religious movements. With the European founders of all three secular utopian movements, they recognized the importance of organizing on a large scale a single concentrated model experiment. Americans were too decentralized for such a union; too enthusiastic for such caution; too independent for such discipline. Neither depression-hit farmers and artisans nor transcendentalists were good community material. Among the liberal Protes-

[65] *What Is Communism?* (2nd ed. rev. and enl., St. Louis, Mo., 1890), especially pp. 13, 16, 43-65, 398-413. Longley's platform called for the expropriation of the means of production by amendments to state and national constitutions. Communist economy would be without wages, strikes, taxation, or tariffs; and would be managed "by the people of each township in country places, and of each ward in towns and cities" or subdivisions of 2,000, each autonomous, federated, and ruled by a majority, according to universal adult suffrage.

tants were those whose faith might have been sufficient defense against the assaults of the environment, as another faith had proved to be for the sectarians. But those who had faith lacked funds and those who had funds lacked faith; and no community could assemble enough men with practical skills. Most capitalists balked at yielding all their property to communism and found their share of profits under joint stock arrangements too small. Most workingmen could earn better wages outside and were not worried about security. Despite the communitarians' emphasis on the family and their promises of an economy of abundance and improved status in cooperative life, the frontier and the growing city better satisfied these major desires to establish a home, make money, and get ahead.[66]

No one needed to be without a humanitarian and an ego satisfying cause if he did not join a community. For almost every phase of American society, special interest groups existed to improve it and displace their aggressions, as the social psychologists say. They proposed changes in immigration, tariff, land and currency policy, cooperative stores, and better labor conditions. They urged women's rights, peace, and reforms in schools, prisons, and the care of the handicapped. Americans a century ago were awakening to a new interest in health and groping toward sciences which have only recently begun to be put on an empirical basis. Phrenology, mesmerism, and spiritualism guessed connections between mental and physical health; Grahamism, temperance, vegetarianism, Bloomerism, and hydropathy were preoccupied with diet, clothing, and cleanliness. The secular utopians looked kindly on all these concerns and added an emphasis on the relation between the social and architectural environment and individual health; but each health faddist preferred in the long run the circles of his own kind. All liberal communitarians honored the American symbols of equal rights and liberty and united more wholeheartedly against slavery than against any other social evil. Like the major parties, they were loose coalitions united by what they opposed rather than the tight vanguards they aimed to be. They were unable, like other reformers, to win converts in the South and for the most part were more concerned with reforms than with social reform. The rising intensity of the dominant antislavery issue diverted the liberal utopians (along with their Northern Whig and Barnburner associates, and indeed even the German-American Marxians), into the great Republican coalition of radicals and Northern businessmen, which won the Civil War. The South was easier to hate than American society at large.

[66] See T. L. Nichols, *Forty Years of American Life* (London, 1864, 2 vols.), I, pp. 407-8, for an early expression of the frontier theory of the failure of communitarianism by a disillusioned participant. *Ibid.*, I, pp. 58-69, he blames its failure on the poor quality of the personnel and emphasizes the stimuli to upward mobility provided by the lyceum and the common school system.

Is there a usable residue in the theories of the liberal utopians? Certainly not in their a priori intellectualism, with its neglect of practical or irrational obstacles; nor in the ambiguity of their dual orientation, with Rousseau, toward the Golden Age and the Rational Society, unless it be transformed into a balanced respect for tradition and scientific innovation. For the long list of their prophetic insights which have become realized commonplaces today, a just recognition is appropriate. Most enticing to many moderns is their version of the perennial Edenic dream of the garden city. Their conception looked back to the communal village of the Middle Ages, as perpetuated in Puritan Massachusetts, and ahead to the cooperative farm community emancipated by technology. Valuable too was their humanistic and democratic outlook and their earnest grappling in practice as well as in theory with the age-old problem of the one and the many.

The history of American socialism may be viewed graphically as a kind of double dialectic, involving reactions between its phases and reactions with American society. The communitarians provided one thesis, and the Marxians its antithesis. Each movement took imperfect steps to naturalize itself. Each the American people repudiated as a movement for its failure to present its case successfully on their terms, but both contributed to the social solutions which Americans partially worked out. Both retained a reliance on myth and a spirit of adventism, varying according to the times in which they were conceived. The synthesis between communitarian and Marxian utopianism has not yet taken place. Instead, several tribes of homeless radicals strike out in new directions. Among the few Marxian remnants, the Communist Party, mingling hopes and observations in true utopian fashion, points to the Soviet Union as the model community of one-third of the world. Each amorphous group bears an element of communitarian theory, refined by contact with Marxism and by current observations. All turn to problems of ethics, civil liberties, and education with renewed interest. They reject eighteenth- and nineteenth-century ideas of progress, but seek grounds for modifying the cyclical dilemma of permanent class struggle, Michels' iron law of oligarchy and Pareto's circulation of élites. Some emphasize pragmatism, positive science, and programs piecemeal in objective but national or international in scope. Others have retreated toward an antistatist voluntarism, either religious or agnostic. The mass of organized labor finds itself confronted with problems faced by the secular utopians, but which it has long avoided, concerning the broad implications of political and economic action. Some socialist Christians have reemphasized the permanent tension between "ought" and "is," which is characteristically utopian and prophetic; but they are quick to point out their simultaneous emphasis on individual sin, which the secular utopians tended to minimize. The ideas of permanent revolution and sure but broken progress toward the Kingdom of God are the chief contributions of the Judaeo-Christian tradition to all the socialism ever produced by Western civilization. Perhaps these broken pieces will coalesce to surmount a crisis, or sink with the rest of society into that chaos or refined slavery which both Marxians and pre-Marxians predicted as alternatives to socialism.

Actually, the dialectic, at best a figure of speech, fails along with other simplifications describing all conditions as following the same pattern. Society is always a mixture of different systems. The record of the century after the close of the religious wars in 1648 provides evidence that society gets along better by a recognition of laissez faire between systems than when Procrustean fanatics decree that every one must lie in a standard bed. There is room for the small socialist community even today. But since it represents the social solution most removed from the conditions of modern civilization, it can attract only a few as the expression of the kind of life which the world in its gross and compromising forms can only approximate.

CHAPTER 6

The Background and Development of Marxian Socialism in the United States

BY DANIEL BELL

DANIEL BELL, at present labor editor of *Fortune* and Lecturer in Sociology at Columbia, was formerly managing editor of the *New Leader* and of *Common Sense*. He has also been a member of the faculty of the Social Science Program in the College of the University of Chicago, and is the author of many articles on socialism, labor problems, and related subjects.

For bibliography in Volume 2 relevant to Mr. Bell's essay, see especially PART II, General Reading, and Topics 8, 9, 10, 11. Also see PART III, General Reading (section 3), and Topics 1-7; PART IV, General Reading (section 2), and Topics 4-9. Additional material can be found in PART I, General Reading (sections 2, 3), and Topics 3, 4, 5, 8.

I. Socialism: The Dream and the Reality

SOCIALISM was an unbounded dream. Fourier promised that under socialism people would be at least "ten feet tall." Karl Kautsky, the embodiment of didacticism, proclaimed that the average citizen of a socialist society would be a superman. The flamboyant Antonio Labriola told his Italian followers that their socialist-bred children would each be Galileos and Giordano Brunos. And the high-flown, grandiloquent Trotsky described the socialist millennium as one in which "man would become immeasurably stronger, wiser, freer, his body more harmoniously proportioned, his movements more rhythmic, his voice more musical, and the forms of his existence permeated with dramatic dynamism."[1]

America, too, was an unbounded dream. The utopians gamboled in its virgin wilderness. Some immigrants called it the *Goldene Medinah*, the golden land. Here it seemed as if socialism would have its finest hour. Both Marx and Engels felt a boundless optimism. In 1879 Marx wrote, ". . . the United States have at present overtaken England in the rapidity of economical progress, though they lag still behind in the extent of acquired wealth; but at the same time, the masses are quicker, and have greater political means in their hands, to resent the form of a progress accomplished at their expense."[2] Engels, who wrote a score of letters on the American scene in the late 1880's and early '90's, repeated this prediction time and again. In his introduction to the American edition of *The Conditions of the Working Class in England*, written at the height of enthusiasm over the events of 1886—notably the spectacular rise of the Knights of Labor and the Henry George campaign—he exulted: "On the more favored soil of America, where no medieval ruins bar the way, where history begins with the elements of modern bourgeois society, as evolved in the seventeenth century, the working class passed through these two stages of its development [i.e., a national trade-union movement and an independent labor party] within ten months." And five years later, his optimism undiminished by the sorry turn of events, Engels wrote to Schlüter: ". . . continually renewed waves of advance, followed by equally certain set-backs, are inevitable. Only the advancing waves are becoming more powerful, the set-backs less paralyzing. . . . Once the Americans get started it will be with an energy and violence compared with which we in Europe shall be mere children."[3]

But there still hovers the melancholy question, posed by Werner Som-

[1] Quoted in Hayim Greenberg, "Socialism Re-examined." *International Socialist Forum* (London), June 1942, p. 2120.

[2] Letter to Danielson, No. 169 in *Karl Marx and Friedrich Engels: Selected Correspondence, 1846-1895* (New York, 1934), p. 360.

[3] Letter to Schlüter, No. 222, *ibid.*, p. 497.

215

bart at the turn of the century in the title of a book, *Why Is There No Socialism in the United States?* To this Sombart supplied one set of answers. He pointed to the open frontiers, the many opportunities for social ascent through individual effort, and the rising standard of living of the country as factors. Other writers have expanded these considerations. Selig Perlman, in his *Theory of the Labor Movement*, advanced three reasons for the lack of class consciousness in the United States: the absence of a "settled" wage-earner class; the "free gift" of the ballot (workers in other countries, denied such rights—for example, the Chartists—developed political rather than economic motivations); and third, the impact of succeeding waves of immigration. It was immigration, said Perlman, which gave rise to the ethnic, linguistic, religious, and cultural heterogeneity of American labor, and to the heightened ambitions of immigrants' sons to escape their inferior status.

In the end, all such explanations fall back on the naturally-endowed resources and material vastness of America. In awe of the fact that the Yankee worker consumed almost three times as much bread and meat and four times as much sugar as his German counterpart, Sombart finally exclaimed: "On the reefs of roast beef and apple pie socialistic Utopias of every sort are sent to their doom."[4]

Other explanations have indicated equally general, and relevant, facts. Some have stressed the agrarian basis of American life, with the farmer seesawing to radicalism and conservatism in tune to the business cycle. Others have pointed to the basically geographic, rather than functional, organization of the two-party system, with its emphasis on opportunism, vacuity of rhetoric, and patronage as the mode of political discourse; hence, compromise, rather than rigid principle, becomes the prime concern of the interest-seeking political bloc.

Implicit in many of these analyses, however, was the notion that such conditions were but temporary. Capitalism as an evolving social system would of necessity "mature." Crises would follow, and at that time a large, self-conscious wage-earner class and a socialist movement, perhaps on the European pattern, would probably emerge. The great depression was such a crisis—an emotional shock which shook the self-confidence of the entire society. It left permanent scar tissue in the minds of the American workers. It spurred the organization of a giant trade-union movement which in ten years grew from less than three million to over fifteen million

---

[4] Quoted in Goetz A. Briefs, *The Proletariat* (New York, 1937), p. 193. Communist economists deny this material gain. A leading statistician, Jurgen Kuczynski, has stated that the living conditions of American labor in the last hundred years have actually deteriorated. Confronted with his own evidence that real wages had increased from 1790 to 1900, Kuczynski falls back on Lenin's theory that capitalism divided the workers into the labor aristocracy, bribed by higher wages, and the exploited masses. See Jurgen Kuczynski, *A Short History of Labour Conditions under Industrial Capitalism*, Vol. II, *The United States of America, 1789 to the Present Day* (London, 1943).

workers, or one-fourth of the total labor force of the country.[5] It brought
in its train the smoking-hot organizing drives and sit-downs in the Ohio
industrial valley which gave the country a whiff of class warfare. In the
1940's labor entered national politics with a vigor—in order to safeguard
its economic gains. Here at last was the fertile soil which socialist theorists
had long awaited. Yet no socialist movement emerged, nor has a coherent
socialist ideology taken seed either in the labor movement or in government. So Sombart's question still remains unanswered.

Most of the attempted answers have discussed not *causes* but *conditions*,
and these in but general terms. An inquiry into the fate of a social movement has to be pinned in the specific questions of time, place, and
opportunity, and framed within a general hypothesis regarding the "why"
of its success or failure. The "why" which this essay proposes (with
the usual genuflections to *ceteris paribus*), is that the failure of the socialist movement in the United States is rooted in its inability to resolve
a basic dilemma of ethics and politics. The socialist movement, by its
very statement of goal and in its rejection of the capitalist order as a
whole, could not relate itself to the specific problems of social action in
the here-and-now, give-and-take political world. It was trapped by the
unhappy problem of living *"in* but not *of* the world," so it could only act,
and then inadequately, as the moral, but not political, man in immoral
society. It could never resolve but only straddle the basic issue of either
accepting capitalist society, and seeking to transform it from within as
the labor movement did, or becoming the sworn enemy of that society,
like the communists. A religious movement can split its allegiances and
live *in* but not *of* the world (like Lutheranism); a political movement
can not.

In social action there is an irreconcilable tension between ethics and
politics. Lord Acton posed the dilemma in a note: "Are politics an attempt
to realize ideals, or an endeavour to get advantages, within the limits of
ethics?" More succinctly, "are ethics a purpose or a limit?"[6] In the largest
sense, society is an organized system for the distribution of tangible rewards and privileges, obligations and duties. Within that frame, ethics
deals with the *ought* of distribution, implying a theory of justice. Politics
is the concrete *mode* of distribution, involving a power struggle between
organized groups to determine the allocation of privilege. In some
periods of history, generally in closed societies, ethics and politics have

[5] Actually such a statistic slights the real magnitude of labor's swift rise. The non-
agricultural labor force is approximately forty-five million, so that unionization touches
one in three. Even here a further breakdown is revealing. Nearly every major manufacturing industry (except chemicals and textiles) is more than 80 per cent unionized.

[6] Cited in Gertrude Himmelfarb, "The American Revolution in the Political Theory
of Lord Acton," *Journal of Modern History*, Dec. 1949, p. 312.

gone hand in hand. But a distinguishing feature of modern society is the separation of the two; and ideology—the façade of general interest and universal values which masks a specific self-interest—replaces ethics. The redivision of the rewards and privileges of society can only be accomplished in the political arena. But in that fateful commitment to politics, an ethical goal, stated as "purpose rather than limit," becomes a fararching goal before which lies a yawning abyss that can be spanned only by a "leap." The alternatives were forcefully posed by Max Weber in his contrast between the "ethics of responsibility" (or the acceptance of limits) and the "ethics of conscience" (or the dedication to absolute ends). Weber, arguing that only the former is applicable in politics, writes: "The matter does not appear to me so desperate if one does not ask exclusively who is morally right and who is morally wrong? But if one rather asks: Given the existing conflict how can I solve it with the least internal and external danger for all concerned?"[7] Such a pragmatic compromise rather than dedication to an absolute (like bolshevism or religious pacifism) is possible, however, only when there is a basic consensus among contending groups about the rules of the game. But this consensus the socialist movement, because of its original rejection of society, while operating within it, could never fully accept.

The distinctive character of "modern" politics is the involvement of *all* strata of society in movements of social change, rather than the fatalistic acceptance of events as they are. Its starting point was, as Karl Mannheim elegantly put it, the "orgiastic chiliasm" of the Anabaptists, their messianic hope, their ecstatic faith in the millennium to come. For (as E. H. Harbison points out in Chapter 1) the Anabaptism of the sixteenth century, of Thomas Münzer and those who sought to establish at Münster the Kingdom of God on earth, proclaimed not merely that equality of souls stressed by Luther, but also equality of property. Otherworldly religious quietism became transformed into a revolutionary activism in order to realize the millennium in the here and now. Thus the religious frenzy of the chiliasts which burst the bonds of the old religious order threatened to buckle the social order as well; for unlike previous revolutions, chiliasm did not aim against a single oppression, but at the entire existing social order.

The characteristic psychological fact about the chiliast is that for him "there is no inner articulation of time." There is only the "absolute presentness." "Orgiastic energies and ecstatic outbursts began to operate in a worldly setting and tensions previously transcending day to day life became explosive agents within it."[8] The chiliast is neither "in the world

[7] *From Max Weber* (ed. by H. H. Gerth and C. W. Mills; New York, 1946), p. 9. In the same volume see also Weber's "Politics as a Vocation," pp. 119ff.

[8] Karl Mannheim, *Ideology and Utopia* (New York, 1936), pp. 190-93.

[n]or of it." He stands outside of it and against it because salvation, the millennium, is immediately at hand. Where such a hope is possible, where such a social movement can transform society in a cataclysmic flash, the "leap" is made, and in the pillar of fire the fusion of ethics and politics is possible. But where societies are stable, and social change can only come piecemeal, the pure chiliast in despair turns nihilist, rather than make the bitter-tasting compromises with the established hierarchical order. "When this spirit ebbs and deserts these movements," writes Mannheim, "there remains behind in the world a naked mass-frenzy and despiritualized fury." In a later and secularized form, this attitude found its expression in Russian anarchism. So Bakunin could write: "The desire for destruction is at the same time a creative desire."

Yet not only the anarchist, but every socialist, every convert to political messianism, is in the beginning something of a chiliast. In the newly-found enthusiasms, in the identification with an oppressed group, hope flares that the "final conflict" will not be far ahead. ("Socialism in our time," was the affirmative voice of Norman Thomas in the 1930's.) But the "revolution" is not always immediately in sight, and the question of how to discipline this chiliastic zeal and hold it in readiness has been the basic problem of socialist strategy.

The most radical approach was that of Georges Sorel with his concept of the revolutionary myth (*"images de batailles"*), a myth which functions as a bastardized version of the doctrine of salvation. These unifying images, Sorel wrote, can neither be proved nor disproved, thus they are "capable of evoking as an undivided whole" the mass of diverse sentiments which exist in society. "The syndicalists solve this problem perfectly, by concentrating the whole of socialism in the drama of the general strike; thus there is no longer any place for the reconciliation of contraries in the equivocations of the professors; everything is clearly mapped out so that only one interpretation of Socialism is possible." In this "catastrophic conception" of socialism, as Sorel called it, *"it is the myth in its entirety which is alone important."*[9]

But in the here and now, people live "in parts." "History does not work with bottled essences," wrote Acton, "but with active combinations; compromise is the soul if not the whole of politics. Occasional conformity is the nearest practical approach to orthodoxy and progress is along diagonals. . . . Pure dialectics and bilateral dogmas have less control than custom and interest and prejudice."[10] And for the socialist movements, operating on "partial" day-to-day problems, the dilemma remained.

[9] Georges Sorel, *Reflections on Violence* (3rd ed., New York, 1912), pp. 131, 136, emphasis in the original.
[10] Himmelfarb, *op.cit.*, p. 312.

219

Neither nineteenth-century American radicals nor the American socialists faced up to this problem of social compromise. The utopias that were spun so profusely in the nineteenth century assumed that in the course of evolution "reason" would find its way and the perfect society would emerge. But so mechanical were the mannikin visions of human delights in such utopias that a modern reading of Bellamy, for example, with its plan for conscript armies of labor ("a horrible cockney dream," William Morris called Looking Backward) only arouses revulsion.

The "scientific socialist" movement that emerged at the turn of the century mocked these utopian unrealities. Only the organization of the proletariat could bring a better world. But this apparent relatedness to the world was itself a delusion. The socialist dilemma was still how to face the problem of "in the world and of it," and in practice the early socialist movement "rejected" the world; it simply waited for the new. Although the American Socialist Party sought to function politically by raising "immediate demands" and pressing for needed social reforms, it rarely took a stand on the actual political problems that emerged from the on-going functioning of the society. "What but meaningless phrases are 'imperialism,' 'expansion,' 'free silver,' 'gold standard,' etc., to the wage worker?" asked Eugene V. Debs in 1900. "The large capitalists represented by Mr. McKinley and the small capitalists represented by Mr. Bryan are interested in these 'issues' but they do not concern the working class."[11] These "issues" were beside the point, said Debs, because the worker stood outside society. Thus Debs and the socialist movement as a whole would have no traffic with the capitalist parties. Even on local municipal issues the party would not compromise. The socialist movement could "afford" this purity because of its supreme confidence about the future. "The socialist program is not a theory imposed upon society for its acceptance or rejection. It is but the interpretation of what is, sooner or later, inevitable. Capitalism is already struggling to its destruction," proclaimed the Socialist national platform of 1904, the first issued by the Socialist Party.[12]

But unlike the other-worldly movements toward salvation, which can always postpone the date of the resurrection, the Socialist Party, living in the here and now, had to show results. It was a movement based on a belief in "history"; but it found itself outside of "time." World War I finally broke through the façade. For the first time the party had to face a stand on a realistic issue of the day. And on that issue almost the entire intellectual leadership of the party deserted, and the back of American socialism was broken.

[11] E. V. Debs, "Outlook for Socialism in the U.S.," International Socialist Review, Sept. 1900; reprinted in Writings and Speeches of Eugene V. Debs (New York, 1948), p. 37.
[12] Proceedings, National Convention of the Socialist Party, Chicago, Illinois, May 1 to 6, 1904, p. 308.

The socialist movement of the 1930's, the socialism of Norman Thomas, could not afford the luxury of the earlier belief in the inevitable course of history. It was forced to take stands on the particular issues of the day. But it too rejected completely the premises of the society which shaped these issues. In effect, the Socialist Party acknowledged the fact that it lived "in" the world, but refused the responsibility of becoming a part "of" it. But such a straddle is impossible for a *political* movement. It was as if it consented to a duel, with no choice as to weapons, place, amount of preparation, etc. Politically, the consequences were disastrous. Each issue could only be met by an ambiguous political formula which would satisfy neither the purist, nor the activist who lived with the daily problem of choice. When the Loyalists in Spain demanded arms, for example, the Socialist Party could only respond with a feeble policy of "workers aid," not (capitalist) government aid; but to the Spaniard, arms, not theoretical niceties, were the need of the moment. When the young trade unionists, whom the socialists seeded into the labor movement, faced the necessity of going along politically with Roosevelt and the New Deal in order to safeguard progressive legislative gains, the socialists proposed a "labor party" rather than work with the Democrats, and so the Socialist Party lost almost its entire trade-union base. The threat of fascism and World War II finally proved to be the clashing rocks through which the socialist argonauts could not row safely. How to defeat Hitler without supporting capitalist society? Some socialists raised the slogan of a "third force." The Socialist Party, however, realized the futility of that effort; in characteristic form, it chose abnegation. The best way to stem fascism, it stated, "is to make democracy work at home." But could the issue be resolved other than militarily? The main concern of the anti-Fascist movement had to be with the political center of Fascist power, Hitler's Berlin, and any other concern was peripheral.

In still another way the religious, chiliastic origin of modern socialism revealed itself—the multiplication of splits, the constant formation of sectarian splinter groups each hotly disputing the other regarding the true road to power. Socialism is an eschatological movement; it is sure of its destiny, because "history" leads it to its goal. But though sure of its final ends, there is never a standard of testing the immediate means. The result is a constant fractiousness in socialist life. Each position taken is always open to challenge by those who feel that it would only swerve the movement from its final goal and lead it up some blind alley. And because it is an ideological movement, embracing all the realm of the human polity, the Socialist Party is always challenged to take a stand on every problem from Viet Nam to Finland, from prohibition to pacifism. And, since for every two socialists there are always three political opinions, the consequence has been that in its inner life, the Socialist Party has never, *even for a single year,* been without some issue which threatened to split the party and which forced it to spend much of its time on the problem of reconciliation or rupture. In this fact lies the chief clue to the impotence of American socialism as a political movement, especially in the past twenty years.[13]

But what of the proletariat itself? What is its role in the socialist drama of history? How does the proletariat see through the veils of obscurity and come to self-awareness? Marx could say with Jesus, "I have come to end all mysteries, not to perpetuate them." His role, in his own self-image, was to lay bare the fetishes which enslave modern man and thus confute Hegel's claim that freedom and rationality had already been achieved. But like his old master he could only deal with the "immanent" forces of history, not the mechanics of social action.[14]

All political movements, Marx wrote, have been slaves to the symbols of the past.[15] But history is the process of progressive disenchantment: men are no longer bound to the river gods and anthropomorphic deities of

[13] Far beyond the reaches of this essay is the problem of the psychological types who are attracted by such a sectarian existence, types discussed in some detail in Chapter 12. Yet one might say here that certainly the illusions of settling the fate of history, the mimetic combat on the plains of destiny, and the vicarious sense of power in demolishing opponents all provide a sure sense of gratification which makes the continuance of sectarian life desirable. The many leadership complexes, the intense aggressiveness through gossip, the strong clique group formations, all attest to a particular set of psychological needs and satisfactions which are fulfilled in these opaque, molecular worlds.

[14] In *The German Ideology* Marx poses the question of how self-interest becomes transformed into ideology. "How does it come about," he asks, "that personal interests continually grow, despite the persons, into class-interests, into common interests which win an independent existence over against the individual persons, in this independence take on the shape of general interests, enter as such into opposition with the real individuals, and in this opposition, according to which they are defined as general interests, can be conceived by the consciousness as ideal, even as religious, sacred interests?" See Karl Marx, *The German Ideology* (New York, 1939), notes, p. 203. But Marx, exasperatingly, never really answered his own question! Sidney Hook, in his article on "Materialism" in the *Encyclopaedia of the Social Sciences* (New York, 1933), x, p. 219, rephrases the problem in these words: "What are the specific mechanisms by which economic conditions influence the habits and motives of classes, granted that individuals are actuated by motives that are not always a function of the individual self-interest? Since classes are composed of individuals, how are class interests furthered by the non-economic motives of individuals?" But he too left it as a question. So far, no Marxist theoretician has yet detailed the crucial psychological and institutional nexus which shows how the "personifications" or mask of class role, is donned by the individual as self-identity.

[15] "Thus Luther donned the mask of the Apostle Paul, the Revolution of 1789 to 1814 draped itself alternately as the Roman Republic and the Roman Empire," Marx wrote in *The Eighteenth Brumaire of Louis Bonaparte.* For an exciting view of the relation of Marx to myths, see the two articles by Harold Rosenberg in the *Kenyon Review,* Autumn 1948, and Autumn 1949, entitled "The Resurrected Romans and the Pathos of the Proletariat."

the agricultural societies; nor need they be bound to the abstract impersonal deity of bourgeois Protestantism. Man himself was potential. But how to realize his potentiality? The intellectual was, in part, capable of self-emancipation because he possessed the imagination to transcend his origins. But the proletariat, as a class, could develop only to the extent that the social relations of society itself revealed to the slave the thongs that bound him. Man is no more free, said Marx in *Das Kapital*, because he can sell his labor power to whom he wishes. Exploitation is implicit in the very structure of capitalist society, which in order to live must constantly expand by extracting surplus value and thus accumulate new capital. In the process, the proletarian would be reduced to the barest minimum of human existence (the law of increasing misery) and thus robbed of any mark of distinction. In the agony of alienation he would realize consciously a sense of identity which would unite him with others and create a cohesive social movement of revolution.[16] In action he would no longer be manipulated but "make" himself.

Thus the scene is set for the grand drama. Out of the immanent, convulsive contradictions of capitalism, conflict would spread. The proletariat, neither in nor of the world, would inherit the world. But History (to use these personifications) confounded Marx's prophecy, at least in the West. The law of increasing misery was refuted by the tremendous advances of technology. The trade union began bettering the worker's lot. And, in the political struggles that followed, it found that it could sustain itself not by becoming a revolutionary instrument against society, but by accepting a place within society.

In the America of the nineteenth century, almost every social movement had involved an effort by the worker to escape his lot as a worker. At times the solution was free land, or cheap money, or producers' cooperatives, or some other chimera from the gaudy bag of utopian dreams. The rise of the American Federation of Labor signaled the end of this drive for some new "northwest passage." Under Gompers, labor's single ambition was to achieve a status on a par with that of business and the church, as a "legitimate" social institution of American life. The socialists within and without the A.F.L. challenged this approach, and lost. As a

---

[16] Actually, in Marx's writings there are three distinct concepts of class, as Raymond Aron has pointed out in "Social Structure and the Ruling Class," *British Journal of Sociology*, Mar. 1950. Marx's historic analysis, as in *The Eighteenth Brumaire*, shows a subtle awareness of the complex shadings of social roles which, in action, give rise to many varied social categories and diverse political interest groups. In the conclusion to *Das Kapital*, however, Marx begins a simplified analysis of "essential" class on the basis of source of income; but the conversion of income groups into congruent categories itself faces the question of what are the mechanisms of self-awareness. Finally, as in the *Communist Manifesto*, there is the eschatological view, in which the *Götterdämmerung* of history polarizes society into two classes and awareness arises from beholding the widening abyss.

result, before World War I they found themselves isolated from the labor movement which they regarded as necessary for the fulfillment of socialism. During the New Deal and after, however, the socialists in the unions, faced with a similar dilemma, chose the labor movement. When the Socialist Party refused to go along, it lost its strength as a tangible force in American political life.

But even apart from its presumed relation to socialism, perhaps the most significant fact regarding the "consciousness" of the American proletariat is that in the past thirty years American middle-class mass culture has triumphed over capitalist and worker alike. The America of 1890, the capstone of the Gilded Age, was a society of increasing differentiation in manners and morals, the area, that is, of *visible* distinction and the one that could give rise, as in Europe, to class resentment. It saw the emergence in baroque mansion, elaborate dress, and refined leisure activities of a new *haut* style of life. By the 1920's this style was already gone. Beneath this change was the transformation of entrepreneurial to corporate capitalism, with a corresponding shift in the social type from the self-made man to the smooth, faceless manager. But beyond that it was a change in the very character of society, symbolized in large measure by the adjective which qualified the phrases "mass production" and "mass consumption." Production—apart from war needs—was no longer geared *primarily*, as it had been in the late nineteenth and early twentieth centuries, to turning out capital goods (steel, railroad equipment, tools), but to the output of consumers' durable goods (autos, washing machines, radios, etc.). The mass market became the arbiter of taste, and the style of life was leveled. In another dimension of this vast social revolution that has been taking place during the past quarter of a century, professional skill has been replacing property as the chief means of acquiring and wielding power, and the educational system rather than inheritance has become the chief avenue for social ascent. In short, a new-type, bureaucratic, mass society has been emerging, and with it, new institutions, of which the modern trade union is one. If the worker was "absorbed" culturally into the social structure of this new, bureaucratic mass society, the trade union itself finally achieved its respectability.

World War II brought a social truce and the beginnings of a social merger between the major power blocs in American life. "Labor" was living in and of the capitalist society. It was represented on government boards and was consulted on policy. The rise of totalitarianism and the beginning emergence of a garrison economy here as a response demonstrated that all social groups had a common fate if democracy fell. In this respect all other values have become subordinate. And the emergence of a garrison economy as a response to the threat of a third world war illustrated the need for some defined national interest in the form of government decision to bring the particular self-interest groups to heel. For the fast-dwindling Socialist Party the answer to this new dilemma was still a "third force," or a "neither-nor" position which sought to stand apart and outside the swirling sandstorm of conflict.[16a] Like the ostrich in the Slavic parable, they put their heads in the sand and thought no one was looking. By 1950, nobody was.

For the twentieth-century communist, however, there are none of these agonizing problems of ethics and politics. He is the perpetual alien living in hostile enemy territory. Any gesture of support, any pressure for social reforms—all of these are simply tactics, a set of Potemkin villages, the façades to be torn down after the necessary moment for deception has passed. His is the ethic of "ultimate ends"; only the goal counts, the means are inconsequential.[17] Bolshevism thus is neither in the world nor of it, but stands outside. It takes no responsibility for the consequences of any act within the society nor does it suffer the tension of acquiescence or rejection. But the socialist, unlike the communist, lacks that fanatical vision, and so faces the daily anguish of participating in and sharing responsibility for the day-to-day problems of the society.

It is this commitment to the "absolute" that gives bolshevism its religious strength. It is this commitment which sustains one of the great political myths of the century, the myth of the iron-willed Bolshevik. Self-less, devoted, resourceful, a man with a cause, he is the modern Hero. He alone, a man of action, a soldier for the future, continues the tradition of courage which is the aristocratic heritage bestowed on Western culture and which has been devitalized by the narrow, monetary calculus of the bourgeoisie. (Can the businessman be the Hero?) Such is the peculiar myth which has taken deep hold among many intellectuals. It is a myth which is also responsible for a deep emotional hatred and almost path-ologic resentment felt most keenly by the ex-communist intellectual, the "defrocked priest," toward the party. For the "Bolshevik," through the myth of absolute selflessness, claims to be the "extreme man," the man of no compromise, the man of purity. The intellectual, driven to be moral, fears the comparison and resents the claim. Thus he bears either a sense of guilt or a psychological wound.

In addition to the myth of the Bolshevik as iron-willed Hero, twentieth-century communism has made several other distinctive contributions to the theory and practice of modern politics. Like so many other social doctrines, these were never put down systematically in a fully self-

16a The "third-force" position was repudiated by Norman Thomas in 1951. He came out staunchly in favor of America's effort to repel communist aggression in Korea.
17 "The believer in an ethic of ultimate ends," wrote Max Weber, "feels 'responsible' only for seeing to it that the flame of pure intention is not quelched." Max Weber, "Politics as a Vocation," in Gerth and Mills, eds., op.cit., p. 121.

conscious fashion; yet over the years they have emerged as a coherent philosophy. Of these contributions some five can be linked schematically. These are central for understanding the history of the Communist Party in this country and are summarized here (some are dealt with in more detail elsewhere in this book, particularly in Chapter 10).

One of the major innovations of the Bolsheviks is their theory of power. Against the nineteenth-century liberal view which saw social decisions as a reconciliation of diverse interests through compromise and consensus— a theory which social democracy gradually began to accept after World War I when it was called upon to take responsibility for governments and enter coalitions—the Bolsheviks saw politics as a naked struggle for power, power being defined as a monopoly of the means of coercion. Power was thought of almost in the sense of physics, its equation being almost literally mass times force equals power. The individual, central to the liberal theory of a market society, was for the Bolshevik a helpless entity. Only the organized group counted, and only a mass base could exert social leverage in society.

But a mass requires leadership. The great unresolved dilemma of Marxian sociology was the question of how the proletariat achieves the consciousness of its role. To await the immanent development of history was to rely on the fallacy of misplaced abstraction. "Spontaneity" was not for Lenin a reality in mass politics; nor was the trade union an effective instrument. His answer, the most significant addition to revolutionary theory, was the vanguard role of the party.

Against the "economism" which glorified the role of the trade union, Lenin argued that the mere organization of society on a trade-union basis could only lead to wage consciousness, not revolutionary consciousness; against the spontaneity theories of Rosa Luxemburg he argued that the masses, by nature, were backward. Only the vanguard party, aware of the precarious balance of social forces, could assess the play and correctly tip the scales in the revolutionary direction. The classic formulation of revolutionary avant-guardism Lenin outlined in his *What Is to Be Done?* published as early as 1903.

In it he wrote that without the "dozen" tried and talented leaders, and talented men are not born by the hundred, professionally trained, schooled by long experience and working in perfect harmony, no class in modern society is capable of conducting a determined struggle. "I assert," said Lenin, "(1) that no movement can be durable without a stable organization of leaders to maintain continuity; (2) that the more widely the masses are spontaneously drawn into the struggle and form the basis of the movement, the more necessary it is to have such an organization and the more stable must it be (for it is much easier for demagogues to sidetrack the more backward sections of the masses); (3) that the organization must consist chiefly of persons engaged in revolution as a profession."[17a]

If the party were to become a vanguard, it needed discipline in action, and thus there arose the principle of party hierarchy and "democratic centralism." In theory there was full discussion of policy before decision, and rigid adherence to policy once discussion had been closed. In practice a line was laid down by the leadership which was binding on all. Lenin's promulgation of these doctrines split Russian socialism in 1903 and brought about the emergence of the Bolshevik and Menshevik factions. In the beginning Trotsky opposed Lenin's ideas, but later he capitulated. As he reveals in his autobiography: ". . . there is no doubt that at that time I did not fully realize what an intense and imperious centralism the revolutionary party would need to lead millions of people in a war against the old order. . . . Revolutionary centralism is a harsh, imperative and exacting principle. It often takes the guise of absolute ruthlessness in its relation to individual members, to whole groups of former associates. It is not without significance that the words 'irreconcilable' and 'relentless' are among Lenin's favorites."[18]

From the principle of power and the theory of party organization rose two other key tenets of bolshevism. One was the polarization of classes. Because it looked only toward the "final conflict," bolshevism split society into two classes, the proletariat and the bourgeoisie. But the proletariat could only be emancipated by the vanguard party; hence anyone resisting the party must belong to the enemy. For Lenin, the maxim of the absolute ethic meant that "those who are not for me are against me." Hence, too, a formulation of the theory of "social fascism," which in the early 1930's branded the social democrats rather than Hitler as the chief enemy, and led the communists to unite, in several instances, with the Nazis in order to overthrow the German Republic.

The second tenet, deriving from the backward nature of the masses, was the key psychological tactic of formulating all policy into forceful slogans. Slogans dramatize events, make issues simple, and wipe out the qualifications, nuances, and subtleties which accompany democratic political action. In his chapter on slogans[19] Lenin wrote one of the first manuals on modern mass psychology. During the revolution, the Bolsheviks achieved a flexibility of tactic by using such slogans as "All Power to the Soviets," "Land, Peace, and Bread," etc. The basic political tactic of all Communist parties everywhere is to formulate policy primarily through the use of

17a V. I. Lenin, *What Is to Be Done?* (New York, 1929), p. 116.
18 Leon Trotsky, *My Life* (New York, 1930), pp. 161-62.
19 V. I. Lenin, "On Slogans," in *Toward the Seizure of Power,* Vol. xxi, Book i, *Collected Works* (New York, 1932), pp. 43-50.

key slogans which are transmitted first to the party rank and file and then to the masses.[20] The consequence of the theory of the vanguard party and its relation to the masses is a system of "two truths," the *consilia evangelica*, or special ethics endowed for those whose lives are so dedicated to the revolutionary ends, and another truth for the masses. Out of this belief grew Lenin's famous admonition—one can lie, steal, or cheat, for the cause itself has a higher truth.

Communism as a social movement did not, with the brief exception of the late nineteen-thirties, achieve any sizable following in the United States. Its main appeal, then, was to the dispossessed intelligentsia of the depression generation and to the "engineers of the future" who were captivated by the type of elitist appeal just described. Within American life, its influence was oblique. It stirred many Americans to action against injustices, and left them with burnt fingers when, for reasons of expediency, the party line changed and the cause was dropped. It provided an unmatched political sophistication to a generation that went through its ranks and gave to an easygoing, tolerant, sprawling America a lesson in organizational manipulation and hard-bitten ideological devotion which this country, because of tradition and temperament, found hard to understand. But most of all, through the seeds of distrust and anxiety it sowed, communism has spawned a reaction, an hysteria and bitterness that democratic America may find difficult to erase in the bitter years ahead.

Thus within the span of a century American socialism passed from those bright and unbounded dreams of social justice which possessed the utopians and early Marxians alike to—in the deeds of one bastard faction at least—a nightmare of distrust and bitterness. The remainder of this chapter will be devoted to the history of that transformation.

II. The Mirage of Utopia

When the American colonies broke away from England they inscribed upon the back of the great seal authorized by Congress *Novus Ordo Seclorum*—we are the new order of the ages, the beginning of the American era. The American continent, with its vast lands and mighty riches, was destined to be a great social laboratory. Here the unfolding design of "God, Master Workman," would be manifest. Such a disguised deism, emphasiz-

---

[20] Compare Hitler's use of the idea of slogans: "The great masses' receptive ability is only very limited, their understanding is small, but their forgetfulness is very great. As a consequence of these facts, all effective propaganda has to limit itself only to a very few points and use them like slogans until even the very last man is able to imagine what is intended by such a word. As soon as one sacrifices this basic principle and tries to become versatile, the effect will fritter away as the masses are neither able to digest the material offered nor to retain it." See *Mein Kampf* (New York, 1940; the complete and unabridged Reynal and Hitchcock, ed.), p. 234.

ing the aspect of God as a craftsman rather than a fixed revelation, was congenial to the growth of a pragmatic temper. It was a society which, if it did not welcome, would at least abide without scorn the efforts of small bands to explore the design of the millennium. And if in places the response was hostile, there was the Icarian wilderness, stretching from Texas to Iowa, in which utopian colonies might find refuge, safe from prying eyes, to continue their chiliastic search. Small wonder then that such colonies arose in prodigal number.

Utopian socialism struck many roots in America, but few took hold. One might suppose that this early growth did nourish the later, stronger shoots of political socialism. Yet such a view is denied by Morris Hillquit, American Socialist leader and historian of the movement. "On the whole it is safe to say," Hillquit asserted, "that the early utopian theories and communistic colonies had but little influence on the formation of the modern socialist movement in the United States."[21]

Hillquit, however, viewed the connection only in terms of organizational links between the utopians and the later political movements. Himself an ideologue, he sought to establish a distinctive, "scientific" basis for political socialism. But the Hillquit interpretation is extremely narrow. In the continuing socialist definition of ethical goal, the utopian influence was obdurate. If it failed to take deep root, certainly it affected the character of the soil from which the later movements of social protest emerged. The utopian spirit was largely responsible for a flood of novels, scholarly tracts, semiliterary treatises, and other imaginative bits (catalogued by V. L. Parrington, Jr., in his *American Dreams*) which have fired the minds of millions; these utopias, particularly those of Edward Bellamy and Laurence Gronlund, exercised a strong influence on American socialism. The utopian influence was responsible, too, for the host of dazzling reform schemes which were presented by socialists all through the nineteenth century; these ranged from various money and land panaceas which, by a quick twist of the financial system, promised to change the social structure of the country, to the colonization plans, some of which popped up as late as 1897 and played an important role in the founding—and splitting—of the Debsian Social Democratic Party. Finally the utopian climate shaped the thinking of the early American labor movement and turned it to the espousal of homesteading, producers' cooperatives, and greenbackism. It was in reaction to these futile efforts that Samuel Gompers evolved his own ideas of pure-and-simple unionism. Thus even if only to combat the utopian influence, every section of American political socialism down to World War I had to come to grips with it.

Labor's earliest significant political activity in the United States began

[21] Morris Hillquit, *History of Socialism in the United States* (New York, 1903), p. 149.

in 1829 with the Workingmen's Party of New York. Quite typically, it was organized by middle-class humanitarians. However, it drew labor support and its ticket in 1829 included six workers among eleven candidates for the state assembly. The party's chief aims were the abolition of imprisonment for debt, a lien law which would allow workers to make claim on a bankrupt employer, and free public education. Apart from these immediate demands, however, it had no unified philosophy. Followers of Robert Owen were interested largely in widespread education, while machinist Thomas Skidmore proposed a plan for the renewed division of property in each generation. The party soon split, with the factions cutting across various lines. In part the split was an issue of personalities. A second crossing was between those who insisted on daily "bread-and-butter" issues against those who sought to commit the party to distant political goals, and among the latter there were quarrels over the definition of goals. Finally there were the old-line politicians, ready to step in at the first sign of electoral strength and deal with opportunistic elements. In varying degree these divisions were to recur and split the tens of labor parties that flourished briefly in the latter half of the century.

The political failure of the independent Workingmen's Party inspired some labor people to swear off politics and inspired others, particularly George Henry Evans, a former leader of the party, to a new political tack. Evans had long been convinced that the solution of the labor question lay in opening cheap western lands that would drain off excess and wage-depressing labor supply. In the 1840's Evans shaped a new political strategy—the tactic of the free-floating pressure group. If labor had its own party, he argued, it would have to present a coherent program on a wide variety of fractious issues, e.g., tariff, money, immigration, land, etc. But the Agrarian League could support men of diverse parties, as long as they would sign a preelection pledge to support the free-land plank. Evans' tactic was to become a potent argument in labor's constant debate regarding political action.

Throughout the 1840's the agrarian question and cooperative colonies absorbed the energies of the labor and intellectual groups. At this time almost all discussion of socialism hinged on the distribution of property, and in the specific sense on the land question—so much so, in fact, that in 1848 Webster's American Dictionary, as revised by Goodrich, defined both socialism and communism in terms of agrarianism: "SOCIALISM, n. A social state in which there is a community of property among all the citizens; a new term for AGRARIANISM. [See COMMUNISM]."[22]

This emphasis on land was responsible for changing the ideas of many German radicals who flocked here after 1848. One such was Herman

[22] Cited by A. E. Bestor, Jr., in "The Evolution of the Socialist Vocabulary," Journal of the History of Ideas, IX, No. 3 (June 1948), p. 263.

Kriege, a leader in Europe of the League of the Just. In the United States the theories of George Henry Evans attracted him and he founded the Social Reform Association to propagate the idea of free land. For his pains he was expelled by Karl Marx from the European socialist group. A better-known figure was Wilhelm Weitling, a magnetic individual who had been active in the secret revolutionary societies in Europe and had been a member of the émigré German workingmen's society of which Marx and Engels were the leaders. In America, his quick eye saw that the abstract theories he once held were meaningless. Here, political rights had been achieved and the problem was one of economic reform. In 1850 Weitling brought forth a plan for a labor exchange bank as a compromise between the existing order and revolution. Since property in this country was widely distributed, he gave up his early faith in the common owner-ship of all property. But because the merchant capitalist was the source of monopoly, exchange alone was to be centralized. To be sure the labor exchange bank was no new idea. It had been tried in London by Robert Owen almost twenty years before and was the favorite theme of Louis Blanc and other French socialists. The idea in simple outline was a socialized marketing plan. The weakness of Owen's scheme had been that any and all commodities were bought by the bank, but only the most use-ful were sold, leaving a huge amount of unwanted items. Weitling thought he could remedy Owen's weakness by linking producers' cooperatives to the exchange.

Weitling called a convention in 1850, the first national convention of German workmen on American soil; but the exchange bank never came to fruition. Weitling's high-handed methods, his refusal to submit to the majority when he disagreed with it, and his self-assertiveness soon antag-onized other members. So, on personal grounds the organization broke up.

In the succeeding decade the socialist "movement" was limited to German working-class centers in the large northern cities. In the early 1850's Joseph Weydemeyer, a personal friend of Marx and Engels, came to New York and sought to introduce their theories to the German workers' groups, but without much success. During the same period vague socialist doctrines were held by various German émigrés who had organized popu-lar sports unions or *Turnvereins*. However, they had little contact with or influence on the labor movement of the time.

In the early sixties unionism again was on the rise. But its course was not clear. Some voices favored straightforward economic bargaining to resist employer wage-cutting; others spoke for broader work reforms (e.g., shortening the work day) through legislative action; some wanted producers' cooperatives; still others demanded reforms in the money and credit system to curb the power of the financier; and some voices, echoing the past, called for new free land as a way of helping reduce the supply of urban labor and give the worker a chance at his own livelihood. In the next forty years, moving almost as regularly as the tides, labor turned first to political action and then to economic organization. A failure in one field would give rise to sentiment for the other and then the tide would turn again.

The first dominant tendency was toward political action, and in 1866 the National Labor Union was organized in Baltimore. (The same year, another organization, the International Workingmen's Association, among whose leaders was Karl Marx, was holding its first meeting in Geneva.) At first, the main objective of the Union, a federation led by William Sylvis of the molders, was the enactment of an eight-hour-day law. A year later, however, this question had been pushed into the background and the new pipe of Pan was money reform. Of the three-thousand-word declaration of principles adopted by the National Labor Union almost two thousand words dealt with financial reform. Labor's interests (in spite of occasional attacks leveled against "producer classes") were still primarily with those of the "producer," the farmer, and the small business-man rather than with wage and hour demands.

In 1869, Sylvis died and shortly thereafter the National Labor Union declined. Whether the organization might have held together if the dynamic Sylvis had lived is an open question. The waters were already running the other way. A labor party in Massachusetts which had scored a smashing success in 1869 foundered badly the following year. A similar loss of political interest was manifest throughout the labor movement. The revival of industry by 1870 and the disastrous failure of almost all the producers' cooperatives brought about a new interest in straightforward trade unionism. By 1872, unionism had grown strong enough to strike suc-cessfully in many cases for an eight-hour day. The new leaders of labor— Siney of the miners, Saffin of the molders, and Foran of the coopers— were primarily trade unionists.

When, following the depression of 1873 and the disintegration of a number of national trade unions, the political current came running in again, the Greenback Party was formed, and it included a number of the older leaders of the National Labor Union. The party's platform argued that cheap money would relieve industrial depressions; older references to the exploiting "producer classes," however, disappeared. Peter Cooper was nominated for the presidency in 1876 and received about 82,000 votes, largely from the rural districts.

The depression of 1873 also opened socialism as a possible road for American workers. Although socialist groups had existed for many years they had been confined largely to German émigré circles in the large metropolitan centers. Now new forces were coming in. Greenbackism was still the dominant hope of American trade-union leadership but now socialism began a bid for leadership.

III.   1886—The First Divide

The impetus to socialist political organization in the United States came from three European sources: the International Workingmen's Association (the First International) dominated by Marx; the political ideas of Ferdinand Lassalle, the founder of German social democracy; and the volatile anarchism of Mikhail Bakunin.

The philosophy of the First International was primarily economic. Through the trade-union struggle, Marx felt, the laborer would achieve the consciousness of class that would enable him to act politically and win power; the socialist state would be built on the existing trade unions and cooperative societies. For Lassalle, however, trade unionism implied cooperation between worker and employer and only direct political organization would do; the victorious state would then build a syndicalist structure as the framework of the socialist society. Not only a theoretical but a deep personal enmity existed between Marx and Lassalle, and these wholehearted, venomous hatreds carried over to their followers. In personality, the two men were poles apart. Lassalle was a fashionable dandy, at home in the archly-refined salons of European society; he was a great orator and master of a flaming rhetoric; his escapades and love affairs were notorious over the continent. Marx was not like that. He lived, poverty stricken, harassed, constantly dunned for debts, in a shabby section of London. Sickness forever plagued his large family, particularly the children. But the most galling fact was that the swarthy Lassalle—Marx viciously described him in letters to Wilhelm Liebknecht as that "Jewish nigger"—was gaining a name as the founder of the socialist movement in Germany while Marx lived isolated and ignored in drab and drafty exile.

London in the 1850's and 1860's was the center for Europe's political refugees. There was freedom, but only to study and talk rather than act. This political impotence fed emotional rancor. Marx was the most bitter of all. He feuded constantly both with the German and with the Russian exiles. The most barbed shafts, however, were reserved for the Russians. Marx felt that the Russian populist theories as expressed by Alexander Herzen and the anarchist doctrines espoused by Bakunin were romantic posturings. The chief target was the anarchist. A huge, emotionally-tortured giant, Bakunin spent most of his time dreaming up fantastic schemes to organize underground groups in Russia, where he had been imprisoned and whence he had escaped. Bakunin felt that only a violent revolution, sparked by deeds of terror, could unseat those entrenched in power. His romantic nature made him susceptible to a variety of queer

233

influences, among them that of a young Russian fanatic named Nechayev who soon ran afoul of the Russian secret police, and who in prison betrayed his friends. This episode later gave rise to Marx's scurrilous charge that Bakunin had been a police spy. Although untrue, it was effective enough to cause Bakunin's expulsion from the First International.[23]

These bickerings had their tragi-comic counterpart here in the affairs of the "International." In 1870 the declining National Labor Union had declared its adherence "to the principles of the International Workingmen's Association and expects to join the said association in a short time." It never did. The International then began chartering sections directly in the United States. But its following was only among the established German workingmen's societies. In 1857 a Communist Club had been established in New York, whose leading figure was Friedrich Sorge, a German music teacher. Another German workingmen's society had been formed in New York by some ardent Lassalleans. In 1868, feeling the time ripe for political activity, the two had merged and formed the Social Party of New York. Candidates were nominated for office but the vote was insignificant. In 1869 the Social Party reorganized as the General German Labor Association, or Section 1 of the International. The following year other sections arose and the total membership, according to a report by Sorge, reached 5,000.

But trouble soon boiled up. A group of American intellectuals, many of them Fourierist tinged, had in 1869 formed a group called New Democracy, which two years later disbanded and reorganized as Sections 9 and 12 of the International. Section 12 was dominated by two eccentric women, Victoria Woodhull and Tennessee Claflin, who published a weekly bearing their combined names. The two felt superior to the "alien" sections and began issuing manifestoes championing free love, universal language, and other "advanced" ideas. Their activities aroused great antagonism among the sober-minded German workmen. In his autobiography Samuel Gompers recalls his own emotions: "Section 12 of the American group was dominated by a brilliant group of faddists, reformers, and sensation-loving spirits. They were not working people and treated their relationship to the labor movement as a means to a 'career.' They did not realize that labor issues were tied up with the lives of men, women, and children—issues not to be risked lightly. Those pseudo-Communists played with the labor movement. This experience burned itself into my memory so that I never forgot the principle in after years."[24]

These carousings inevitably split the American affiliate of the Inter-

[23] For a picture of this period see the studies by E. H. Carr of the nineteenth-century revolutionists, particularly *The Romantic Exiles* (New York, 1933), and his biographies of Marx and Bakunin.

[24] Samuel Gompers, *Seventy Years of Life and Labor; an Autobiography* (New York, 1925), I, p. 55.

national. In 1872, the Section 12 "intellectuals" called one convention. The Germans led by Sorge called another. Both groups sent delegates to the International's 1872 Hague convention. Marx, who fully controlled the organization, recognized Sorge as the legitimate "Internationalist." At this convention the fight with Bakunin so threatened Marx's power that he transferred the office of the grand council to New York—in order to ditch it—and placed Sorge in charge. Far removed from the center of organized European labor, the International soon disintegrated.

Section 12 went on its merry japes and in due course frittered away. But factionalism was still rampant in the remaining sections. The deepening depression of 1873 brought a demand from some new members led by Adolph Strasser that the American group devote more attention to domestic problems and allow greater cooperation with nonsocialist elements in the labor movement. But Section 1, the German stronghold, stood like a stone wall and the newcomers left in disgust. Together with a number of Lassalleans they formed a new party, the Social Democratic Party of North America, and named Strasser as national secretary. The purified Internationalists (Marxians) denounced this tendency to reformism:

"[We] reject all co-operation and connection," they said, "with the political parties formed by the possessing classes, whether they call themselves Republicans or Democrats, or Independents or Liberals or Patrons of Industry or Patrons of Husbandry (Grangers) or Reformers or whatever name they may adopt."

But factionalism soon developed inside both parties. In the Social Democratic Party a split arose between the dogmatic Lassalleans, who were completely hostile to unions, and those who felt that unions should be brought into the party. In the International, quarrels between Sorge and other members developed on nonpolitical issues; as so often is the case, they devolved largely on questions of power, prestige, and position within the tiny organization. The International was rapidly breaking up. In July 1876 the International Workingmen's Association formally dissolved, an act rare in socialist annals, where an old guard hangs on and rarely surrenders.

The restlessness of the workers, aggravated by years of depression, exploded violently in 1876 and 1877. In the Pennsylvania coal fields, the Molly Maguires, the secret coal unionists, answered employer violence with murder. In 1877 a series of railway strikes swept the country and galvanized the labor movement; it took federal troops to end the disorders. For the socialists these flash fires of violence seemed to signalize the awakening of the American working class. The German Social Democratic Party, only ten years old, had won almost half a million followers. It seemed as if American labor were ready to follow in those steps.

In 1876, an attempt was made, initiated by the fast-growing Knights of Labor, to unite the trade unionists, socialists, and Greenbackers. However, the socialists would not fully accept the money-reform scheme presented by the Greenbackers and withdrew. Those remaining moved into the Greenback Labor Party. Shortly thereafter the old Lassallean (Strasser) and Internationalist (Sorge) groups reunited and formed the Workingmen's Party of the United States. Naturally, old differences were not obliterated. There were still the "trade-union" and the "political" socialists. But in the excitement of the next three years these distinctions were momentarily forgotten.

In 1876 the Workingmen's Party made election gains in Milwaukee, Chicago, and Cincinnati. By the next year, no less than twenty-four newspapers directly or indirectly supporting the party were flourishing, of which eight were in English. These successes strengthened the political faction, and in 1877 the party changed its name to the Socialist Labor Party. The election successes continued: in Chicago, where Albert R. Parsons, a socialist, was secretary of the local trade-union body, the vote in 1879 rose to 11,800, and four men were elected to the legislature. In various other cities (with the exception of Cincinnati, where the socialists and the trade unions were apart), the socialist vote also rose. By the end of the year, the Socialist Labor Party claimed a membership of 10,000 in 100 locals in twenty-five states.[25]

Eighteen hundred and seventy-eight also brought success to the Greenback Labor Party. Peter Cooper's vote in 1876 had been small and the party largely farmer-based, with a sprinkling of Eastern reformers. But the great strikes of 1877 and the open hostility of the federal government to labor brought a resurgence of workingmen's political action. Independent workingmen's parties were formed in New York, Pennsylvania, and Ohio. In several of these states alliances were entered into with the old Greenback Party, and the votes soared. In most of the organizations the active leaders were from the Knights of Labor. These successful electoral alliances, particularly in Ohio and Pennsylvania, naturally gave rise to thought of a national farmer-labor alliance, and in 1878 the National Party was formed. Although a number of veteran labor leaders such as Richard Trevelick, Sylvis' successor (who was made chairman), and Uriah Stephens, founder of the Knights of Labor, were present, the party was largely controlled by farmers, radical small businessmen, and lawyers.

[25] In California, where the Socialist Labor Party refrained from nominating candidates and "dividing the forces of the labor movement," a workingmen's party organized by a popular rabble-rouser, Denis Kearny, had become a power in the state on the basis of the slogans of "Down with the Rich," and "The Chinese Must Go." The socialist-tinged Kearny movement was able to influence the writing of a new liberal state constitution, and even captured San Francisco in 1879, but old-line politicians entered the party and it soon lost its earlier radical characteristics.

236

In the congressional election that year nearly a million votes were cast for Greenback candidates, and fourteen representatives were elected to Congress.

These astounding successes posed a problem for the Socialist Labor Party. Many members began to agitate for joint action with the money reformers. After much debate the party voted in 1880 to endorse James B. Weaver, the presidential nominee of the Greenbackers. But two dissenting wings formed: one, the trade unionists, argued against dilution of labor issues, the other, the revolutionary elements, protested against truckling to reformist elements. The party compromised, typically, by supporting only the presidential and vice-presidential candidates of the Greenbackers, while nominating candidates of its own for state and municipal offices. In Chicago, however, even such a solution was not good enough for the stiff-necked and anticompromise elements in the party, and they ran candidates against the regular Socialist Labor Party nominees, who were aligned with the Greenbackers.

Socialism's high hopes, however, were soon shattered. "Good times" had returned, and interest in greenbackism and socialism slackened. Weaver's vote fell to a dismal 300,000. Defeatism spread. In his report to the 1880 convention Philip Van Patten, the national secretary of the Socialist Labor Party, stated, "It is especially to be regretted that we had not secured the election of at least a dozen representatives in the legislature of every Northern State, since a party which has elected a number of representatives is considered tolerably permanent, while one who has not, is regarded by the public as transient and uncertain." And when socialist meetings no longer attracted the large crowds they once had, Van Patten remarked bitterly, "The plundered toilers are rapidly being drawn back to their old paths, and are closing their ears to the appeals of reason. They are selling their birthright for a mess of pottage by rejecting the prospect of future emancipation in their greed for the trifling remains of the present."[26]

Party membership fell off rapidly and in the defeat people looked for new roads. The Socialist Labor Party was reduced to an empty shell. Its membership dropped to less than 1,500, of whom perhaps 10 per cent were native Americans. Within the closed, isolated circle of socialists anarchism now burgeoned and political socialism declined. In 1883 Van Patten, discouraged by the tedious quarreling, simply walked out of the party, turning up later in a minor government post.

In 1880 the party split in two. The revolutionary wing organized its own group and in 1881 affiliated with Bakunin's anarchist International Working People's Association, the so-called "Black International." The anarchist movement, also predominantly German, was aided at the time

[26] Cited in Hillquit, *History of Socialism in the United States*, pp. 226-27.

237

by the arrival in the United States of the German agitator Johann Most. Most, a fiery orator and forceful writer, was noted for his biting wit and sharp, slashing personal polemics. A prolonged sickness in infancy had left him deformed; a cruel childhood and heavy work at an early age deepened his bitterness. He had been imprisoned a number of times in Europe for riotous speeches and had been jailed by an English court for extolling the assassination of Alexander II. Most became the acknowledged leader of anarchism in the United States and wrote most of the Pittsburgh manifesto of 1883, which united the revolutionary splinter of the Socialist Labor Party with preexisting anarchist groups.

In the prosperity of the early 1880's, the workers on the whole were apathetic about revolutionary activity. The beginnings of depression in 1883 marked a reversal of mood. The period of 1883-1885 was hard, not so much because of unemployment as because of a pressure on wages and the tightening of money. Farmers, workers, small businessmen were affected by the squeeze. Hardest hit were the unskilled and the semi-skilled workers who had been brought into the factory, and the farmers who were at the mercy of the railroads. The common outcry of these groups rose against a new Moloch—"monopoly"—and the breakup of monopoly became the great political issue of the next two decades. In this period, the Knights of Labor made sensational gains. In one year, from 1885 to 1886, membership jumped from little more than 100,000 to 700,000. The Socialist Labor Party gained new strength, too, but the anarchist movement gained in even greater proportion.

In 1885, the anarchist movement boasted about eighty organized groups and a total of 7,000 members. Chicago was the center. There the Black International had some 2,000 members, and its leaders, particularly Albert Parsons, had close ties with the local labor movement. Chicago, at the time, was the center also of a widespread agitation for an eight-hour day. By early May 1886 almost 80,000 workers were on strike for that demand. On May 3 the police fired into a large unruly crowd which was struggling with some strikebreakers of the McCormick reaper works, killing four. The anarchists immediately called for a protest meeting in Haymarket Square, a popular meeting place about two miles west of the Loop. A crowd of about 3,000 had patiently listened to long anarchist speeches when, toward the close of the rally, a bomb was hurled, killing one police officer and wounding many others. In the consequent public hysteria, eight anarchists were convicted of conspiracy to throw the bomb. Four, including Albert Parsons, were hanged, one committed suicide, the sentences of two were commuted to life imprisonment, and one was sent to prison for a shorter term. The back of the movement was broken.[27]

[27] In 1893 the three in prison were freed by Governor John Altgeld. Just the previous year, anarchism had again attracted public attention when a young firebrand,

238

The year 1886 was a momentous one for the Socialist Labor Party, too. The rapid growth of labor organization and an unfavorable court decision on a boycott case had turned the New York unions to political action. In 1886, with socialist support, the Central Labor Union of New York organized an independent labor party and nominated Henry George for mayor. Across the country similar stirrings were felt. The United Labor Party of Chicago, organized by the Central Labor Union, ran up 20,000 votes in the spring elections—before the Haymarket bomb. In eleven other states labor parties of one hue or another, with close cooperation between the labor movement and socialists, Knights, Greenbackers, and other reformers, were organized. The most important effort, however, was the George campaign in New York.

Henry George stands paramount in the authentic tradition of the great agrarian reformers of the United States. Like Henry C. Carey, who disputed Ricardo's theory of rent, he saw land as playing the decisive role in the production and distribution of wealth in the United States, and like George Henry Evans, he saw the solution to our social ills in the public control of land. Born in Philadelphia in 1837, George went to sea as a young lad, roamed the country, learned the printer's trade, and settled for a while in San Francisco, where he became the founder of the San Francisco *Evening Post*. Living on the edge of the economic frontier, George observed that where new areas were opened, land would be gobbled up by speculators, the price would soar, economic enterprise, as a consequence, would contract, and profits and wages drop. The idea of regulating land usage through a tax which would confiscate all speculative gain and allow the land to develop in accord with the needs of industry was for him the means of smoothing out the sharp edges of depression. The single-tax idea had a unique appeal: to the small manufacturer it reduced the high initial costs of starting a business; to the farmer it meant the end

---

Alexander Berkman, shot and wounded the obstinate H. C. Frick, head of the Carnegie Steel Company, during the bloody Homestead strike. But anarchism no longer commanded a following. Johann Most, by that time a bitter old man editing his droning paper *Freiheit* and frequenting the German saloons, met with a mirthless fate. In 1901, while indulging in a protracted "beer session," he thoughtlessly "filled out" an issue of his paper with a hackneyed article entitled "Murder Against Murder," which had been written in 1850 by an old German revolutionist, Karl Heinzen. Unfortunately for Most, the day after the issue appeared President McKinley was shot in Buffalo by a muddled Polish radical, Leon Czolgosz. Most immediately ordered the withdrawal of the paper from circulation, but a copy had fallen into the hands of the New York police. Although there was no discernible connection between the *Freiheit* article and Czolgosz, Most was arrested and convicted in New York courts on the vague charge of outraging public decency. The aging man was sentenced to a year in jail, but this time the strain of prison broke the gnomic anarchist, and four years later he died. Apart from the flamboyant career of Emma Goldman and some strength in the Jewish labor movement in the early 1900's, anarchism faded away completely as a political force in America.

239

of the useless land-grabber; to the urban worker it promised jobs and the end of house rent. George published his ideas in two books, the second of which, *Progress and Poverty*, published shortly after the disastrous financial crisis of 1879, caught on in spectacular fashion. In the book George extended his theory and argued that the fertility of land and its desirability as a business location or market were a result of natural and social reasons from which no single individual ought to profit. By taxing all gains from land equal to its full rental value, monopoly would be destroyed and the land thrown open for the use of those who would develop it productively.

For the socialists, the single tax was an old story. Marx had proposed as one of the transition measures included in the *Communist Manifesto* that all ground rents be paid to the state. But his proposal had never been phrased in the striking fashion of *Progress and Poverty*; the single-tax idea, coming at the apt moment it did, gained a sure-fire acceptance, even among the socialists. Marx, fearful of George's influence on the socialists in the United States—where Kriege and Weitling had already been enticed by land theories—sought to demolish the single taxer. In a letter to Sorge, he wrote:

"Theoretically the man [Henry George] is utterly backward! He understands nothing about the nature of *surplus value*. . . . [His] idea originally belonged to the bourgeois economists; it was put forward . . . by the earliest *radical* followers of Ricardo, soon after his death. I said of it in 1847, in my work against Proudhon: 'We can understand that economists like Mill (the elder) . . . Cherbuliez, Hildtich and others have demanded that rent should be paid to the state in order that it may serve as a substitute for taxes. This is a frank expression of the hatred which the *industrial capitalist* dedicates to the *landed proprietor*, who seems to him a useless and superfluous element in the general total of bourgeois production.' " After pointing out that the program had also been offered as a socialist panacea in France, Marx continued: "All these 'socialists' since Colins have this much in common that they leave *wage labour* and therefore *capitalist production* in existence and try to bamboozle themselves or the world into believing that if ground rent were transformed into a state tax *all the evils* of capitalist production would disappear of themselves. The whole thing is therefore simply an attempt, decked out with socialism, *to save capitalist domination* and indeed *to establish it afresh* on *an even wider basis* than its present one. This cloven hoof (at the same time ass's hoof) is also unmistakably revealed in the declamations of Henry George. . . . On the other hand George's book, like the sensation it has made with you, is significant because it is a first, if unsuccessful, attempt at emancipation from the orthodox political economy."[28]

[28] Letter of Marx to Sorge, June 30, 1881, in Marx-Engels Correspondence, *op.cit.*, pp. 394-96.

Despite these cogent criticisms, the Socialist Labor Party supported George because they saw his campaign as a movement of labor against capital. In fact the platform of the United Labor Party as originally drafted contained the "immediate demands" of the socialists. When George accepted the nomination, however, the platform was rewritten to emphasize the single tax, currency reform, and factory legislation.

The campaign was one of the most spectacular in the history of the United States. Pitted against George were Abram S. Hewitt, the son-in-law of Peter Cooper, nominated by Tammany, and Theodore Roosevelt, the nominee of the Republicans. The press of the city was almost unanimously and harshly aligned against George. He had the support, however, of various liberal leaders and professionals including Daniel De Leon and the famous Catholic priest Father McGlynn. McGlynn, a great hero of the Irish workers, rallied so much Catholic support for George that Tammany obtained a statement from the vicar-general of the church in which he declared that the majority of the Catholic clergy would "deeply regret the election of Mr. George to any position of influence."

Hewitt won with 90,000 votes. But George ran ahead of Roosevelt, garnering 68,000 votes to T. R.'s 60,000. The United Labor Party was now in a position to make great advances, but two events typical of the fate of labor parties occurred, robbing it of that opportunity. First, the old-line parties at the next legislature passed a series of labor laws which embodied a number of the immediate demands of the laborites. Secondly, the fissure between the incompatible single taxers and the socialists cracked open. The single taxers sought to turn the party into an all-inclusive movement, uniting all producing classes against the landlords, thus answering such critics as Hewitt, who claimed that the Labor Party was setting class against class. The socialists wanted a more radical party.

The struggle between the two continued for a year, splitting almost every club in the state. The break came when the call for the state convention in 1887 omitted all labor demands and concentrated instead on land and currency reforms. Then, on the demand of George, who charged dual alliances, the socialists were expelled. Still hoping to rally the unions, the socialists next organized a Progressive Labor Party. But the elections of 1887 proved a disappointment to all. George's total in New York City fell to 37,000; the Progressive Labor Party received 5,000 votes. Prosperity was returning and the radical voters were proving fickle, so that the labor parties in other cities shared the same fate. A year later George left his own party and supported Democratic Grover Cleveland for president. Father McGlynn, who had been excommunicated from the church for criticizing his archbishop, conducted a final campaign of the United Labor Party in 1888 and then laid it to rest.[29]

[29] Arthur Nichols Young, *The Single Tax Movement in the United States* (Princeton, N.J., 1916).

241

DANIEL BELL

For the socialists, the experience was the beginning of a decisive new phase in policy and tactics. The Henry George campaign had given them new life but had also demonstrated to their minds the futility of fusion politics. Henceforth, they were committed unswervingly to a straight class approach and a socialist ticket. It was a decision which was reinforced in the ascendancy of a new and decisive leader, Daniel De Leon.

That fateful year 1886 also marked the emergence of the American Federation of Labor. Trade unionism was being established on a new and permanent basis in American life. With the lesson of the foundering Knights of Labor in mind, it rejected the old utopian mirages; its aims were limited and practical. The relationship between the American Federation of Labor and the new socialist movement was to be crucial for the development of socialist strength in America.

On the national scene, a new industrial plutocracy was flexing its muscles in a crude and powerful way. Economically, it was exerting powerful leverage against the farmer while heavily squeezing the worker; politically, it was buying up state legislatures and exercising a dominant influence in the Republican Party; culturally, it was spawning the gilded architectural monstrosities and displaying a grossness of taste that was to turn against it both the scions of the older upper-middle classes, such as Brooks and Henry Adams, and the rising intellectual class. The consolidation of industrial capitalist power was beginning. With it, said Engels, would come the emergence of a class-conscious proletariat ready to take up the struggle. With that perspective, the socialists entered the next two decades.

IV. Purist and Pure-and-Simple

In 1893, said Oliver Wendell Holmes, "a vague terror went over the earth and the word socialism began to be heard." This was a year of violence.

In Homestead, Pennsylvania, Henry C. Frick locked out the workers of the Carnegie Steel plant and brought in the Pinkertons. Seven strikers and three strikebreakers were killed in the ensuing gunfire before the militia smashed the strike. At Homestead a craft union for the first time had faced not just an employer, but the modern industrial corporation, and had lost. It was an important symbol for American labor. On the same day that the state troops arrived at Homestead, a running battle was being fought in Idaho's Coeur d'Alene district between silver miners and company strikebreakers. The federal troops sent in by Grover Cleveland broke that strike. A year later, the workers in the "model" village of Pullman struck, and 40,000 railway men west of Chicago refused to haul the Pullman cars, virtually halting all rail traffic. It took a federal injunction and federal troops to start the trains rolling again.

242

These were the jungle years. The Supreme Court had written Herbert Spencer's social statics into the law of the land, and the iron-jawed capitalists prepared to demonstrate that the philosophy of natural rights meant their God-given authority to rule untrammeled. Social Darwinism was a congenial doctrine for the new plutocracy.

Not only did labor feel oppressed but the dirt farmer likewise felt that this was now the last-ditch stand against the money power in the East. Six months after the Chicago World's Fair the border farmers met in the windy city to organize for free silver and populism.[30] The costumes were garish, but the talk was earnest. Present at the sessions were William Jennings Bryan, Ignatius Donnelly—former congressman, adventurer, and author of a fabulous utopian novel about the lost continent of Atlantis—Jacob Coxey, James B. Weaver, and "Bloody Bridles" Waite, the populist governor of Colorado, who presided. They demanded that the government act to break the money power of Wall Street. A year later, Coxey's army was to symbolize this demand with the famous petition to Washington "with boots on."

The "masses were in motion." This seemed to be the moment that Marx had prophesied in one of his last letters, written in 1879.[31] But if the masses were growing restless, nowhere was there a movement to assume the initiative. The American Federation of Labor was cautiously skirting any radical commitments. In the West a native radicalism was beginning to congeal, but it lacked a theory and a sense of direction. In the East the sectarian and disputatious Socialist Labor Party was coming under the inflexible and iron hand of Daniel De Leon, who would only divert it further from the main stream of American labor.

In 1888, the Socialist Labor Party, exhausted by the battles of 1886, was largely an old soldiers' home, its hoary veterans bitterly disputing the tactics of past campaigns. Following the Henry George debacle, the S.L.P. again split into its two tiresomely familiar factions. The minority, around the New York *Volkszeitung*, favored abandoning political action; the majority, however, decided to run pure socialist candidates. The minute socialist vote in the New York municipal elections in 1888, however, plus the renewed emphasis of the American Federation of Labor on the need for an eight-hour day, helped the trade-union faction. In a

---

[30] Unnoticed amidst the hubbub of the fair, Frederick Jackson Turner quietly read before the sessions of the American Historical Association a paper entitled "The Significance of the Frontier in American History." The frontier was passing, said Turner. The primary pioneer stage and the second phase of pastoral life were already past. Random crop method was giving way to intensive individual farming. But beyond these loomed the factory farm and centralized production. It is doubtful whether the populists, the actors in Turner's drama, knew of his words, although to them the portents were painfully clear.

[31] See the letter to Danielson cited in footnote 2 of this chapter.

stealthily organized *Putsch* they ousted the political action leadership and eliminated all "Lassallean" theory from the party platform. The deposed group seceded and organized the Socialist Labor Party of the "Cincinnati persuasion," as it was called (taking the name of its headquarters city), a group which led a cursory existence until its amalgamation with the Social Democracy of America, the party formed by Debs and Victor Berger in 1897.

Engels, who maintained close interest in the United States, arising out of a trip to America in 1888, sorely wished the entire *"alte Genossen"* (old comrades) would disappear. To the faithful Sorge, he wrote acidly: ". . . If the whole *German* Socialist Labour Party went to pieces as a result, it would be a gain, but we can hardly expect anything as good as that. . . . I consider the decay of the specifically German party, with its absurd theoretical confusion, its corresponding arrogance and its Lassalleanism, a real piece of good fortune. . . . The Socialist laws were a misfortune not for Germany, but for America to which they consigned the last *Knoten*. I often used to marvel at the many *Knoten* faces one met with over there; these have died out in Germany, but are flourishing over yonder."[32]

Two events tended to change the character of the party. One was the immigration in the late eighties, especially from Russia and eastern Europe, which supplied new recruits to the party. These immigrants, particularly the younger Jewish intellectuals, were eager to learn American ways. They built up strong unions in a short time and became a factor in New York labor life. The United Hebrew Trades, organized in those lines of work in which Jewish workers predominated, started in 1888 with one union and two years later had 13,500 members in forty affiliates. Its organizers, among them Morris Hillquit, joined the Socialist Labor Party.[33] The second event was the advent of Daniel De Leon, who joined the party in 1890, and within a year was its undisputed leader and master.

Daniel De Leon, the most controversial figure in American socialism, was born in 1852 in Curaçao, Dutch West Indies. Although often considered Jewish, he referred to himself as a "respectable Venezuelan Catholic."[34] Sickly as a boy, he was sent to school in the European mountains and then to the University of Leyden. He entered Columbia Law

[32] *Knote* was a favorite term of derision of Marx. The word meant a diehard philistine, and derived from the old handicraftsmen of narrow and backward mentality. See Marx-Engels Correspondence, *op.cit.*, pp. 467 and 87.

[33] "When I joined the party, the net result of its Americanization efforts was represented by the publication of one English weekly," wrote Hillquit in his autobiography. "Subsequently, an 'American Section' of the party was formed in New York. In our zeal for the cause, we did not even appreciate the exquisite humor of a political party of the United States establishing a solitary 'American section' in the metropolis of the country." See Morris Hillquit, *Loose Leaves from a Busy Life* (New York, 1934), p. 44.

[34] Waldo Frank in *Commentary*, July 1947, p. 44.

School in 1872, practiced in Texas, and returned to teach international law at Columbia for six years. But the excitement of politics attracted him. He became active in the Henry George campaign, joined the Knights of Labor two years later, passed through Edward Bellamy's Nationalist clubs, and, attracted by the rigorous logic of Marxist theory, joined the Socialist Labor Party. There, his status among the German workingmen as a *Gelehrte,* a "professor," his intelligence and his ruthlessness, quickly won him the leadership of the party and the editorship of its English-language paper.

De Leon was intensely personal and his forthright ways provoked either immediate loyalty or bitter hatred. Slight-bodied and of small stature, he had a large head which, with his piercing black eyes, fine-etched features, and carefully modeled beard, gave him a commanding presence. He had a remarkable talent for elucidating simply the vagaries of abstract theory; he was also a debater with a decided flair and love for picturesque invective—a necessary talent, in those days, for political success. Under De Leon's initiative, the Socialist Labor Party nominated a national presidential ticket in 1892 which received 21,000 votes, a feeble total compared to the over one million received by General Weaver, the Populist candidate that year. Yet for the Socialist Labor Party there now was at least the exhilaration of activity.

De Leon's first political objective was to capture the trade unions. Within the American Federation of Labor the socialists persistently sought to win endorsement of socialist aims, and almost succeeded in doing so. De Leon, however, wanted to capture the declining Knights of Labor, which would be a more malleable instrument. He infiltrated the New York assembly and made a deal with the western elements to oust Terence V. Powderly, grand master of the Knights. But he failed to gain national power when the new grand master reneged on his bargain of giving the Socialist Labor Party the editorship of the Knights' *Journal,* and added insult to injury by refusing even to seat De Leon as a delegate. De Leon's answer to these failures was to create a new organization, the Socialist Trades and Labor Alliance. For him it was to be an instrument of social change, but for the half-million organized workers in the United States such a move, coming after the fratricidal war between the Knights and the American Federation of Labor, spelled dual unionism and danger. Trade unionists within the party, especially from the Jewish unions, opened attack on De Leon, but his policy was endorsed in a resolution which condemned the Knights and the A.F.L. as "buffers of capitalism against whom every intelligent effort of the working class for emancipation has hitherto gone to pieces." De Leon's trade-union policy plus his high-handed application of party discipline caused a revolt. In 1899 the faction led by Morris Hillquit and Job Harriman, known as the "Kangaroos," jumped the party and joined with Debs in forming the Socialist Party. Thereafter, the Socialist Labor Party declined. De Leon went on *in vacuo* developing his powerful theoretical schemes, jibed at and mocked, until his death in 1914.

Daniel De Leon was a mechanical giant in a doll's house. Although the political drama passed him by, he continued setting the scene in immaculate fashion for the revolution that never came. His devotion to his cause was deep and abiding. He lived in a tenement on New York's lower east side, barely meeting his needs from the small and irregular salary as editor of the Socialist Labor Party's paper, yet refusing, on moral grounds, to supplement his income by writing for the capitalist press. Despite this personal attitude, he feared the role of sentiment and moral indignation as a motive force in socialist organizations. It was a quality which he shared with Lenin.[35] "The more feeling you put into them, the surer they are to capsize and go down," he wrote. He considered his job the creation of the "scientific" principle (it was the word most employed in his vocabulary), and he prided himself that his propositions were as neat as the theorems of trigonometry. "His peculiar traits and methods," reflected Hillquit in his autobiography, "were not due entirely to his personal temperament and character. In part at least they were the logical expression of his social philosophy."[36] The modern psychological temper, however, would reverse the emphasis of the two statements.

De Leon had carefully studied Marx and had set himself the task of extending the unfinished portion of the Marxist analysis—the road to power. With a rigor unsurpassed in Marxist exegetical writing, he drew a schema that, abstractly, was a cleanly-thought-through progression from a number of Marxist premises. He argued, first, the futility of seeking higher wages and shorter hours within the capitalist system, and therefore the chimerical quality of gains through "reformist" unions. In a sharp attack on the Fabians, he pointed out that partial gains won by the workers would be eroded by the corrupting nature of bourgeois values, and in an acid metaphor drawn from the Roman struggles of the Gracchi, he predicted that the trade-union leaders, as they became established, would be absorbed into the capitalist system as "labor lieutenants." In a fully developed capitalist country, said De Leon, the concern of the

[35] The Russian Bolshevik leader held a high opinion of the American Marxist, and there is in their works a striking parallelism. Lenin's theory of "economism"—the doctrine that the workers without vanguard communist leadership would only develop trade-union, not revolutionary, consciousness—contained in *What Is to Be Done?* written in 1903, is quite similar to De Leon's harsh condemnation of the "labor lieutenants" of capitalism in his *Two Pages from Roman History*, written in 1902. De Leon's specific image of the revolutionary industrial union as the functional unit of the socialist society was given definite expression in Lenin's theory of soviets two decades later.

[36] Hillquit, *Loose Leaves from a Busy Life*, p. 46.

246

Marxist must be entirely with the program of revolution: "A political party that sets up 'immediate demands,'" he wrote, "by so much blurs its 'constant demand' or goal. The presence of 'immediate demands' in a Socialist platform reveals pure and simple politicianism—corruption, or the invitation to corruption."[37]

For De Leon, the political and economic revolution had to proceed *simultaneously*, because the victory of one without the other would invite corruption. "Suppose that at some election, the class conscious political arm of labor were to sweep the field . . . what would there be for them to do? *Simply to adjourn on the spot sine die* . . . it would be . . . a signal for social catastrophe if the political triumph did not find the working class of the land industrially organized, that is, in full possession of the plants of production and distribution, capable, accordingly, to assume the integral conduct of the productive powers of the land . . . the plants of production and distribution having remained in capitalist hands production would be immediately blocked."[38] The key to worker's emancipation was the industrial union in which the workers in each industry would combine. Production and administration would be guided by industrial-union government. All the workers who use "the identical tool" would join trade and shop branches (i.e., a craft unit). The crafts making the same product would be combined into a local industrial union and pyramided into a national industrial union. At the peak would be the industrial council of national industrial unions.

The operation of the socialist state, which Marx never attempted to describe, was envisaged by De Leon in this lulling fashion: "The parliament of civilization in America will consist, not of Congressmen from geographic districts, but of representatives of trades throughout the land, and their legislative work will not be the complicated one which a society of conflicting interests, such as capitalism, requires but the easy one which can be summed up in the statistics of the wealth needed, the wealth producible, and the work required—and that any average set of workingmen's representatives are fully able to ascertain, infinitely better than our modern rhetoricians in Congress."[39] Lenin's *State and Revolution* more than a decade later repeated this simple, functional scheme, even to the claim that the ordinary worker would be as able an administrator as any professional.

Although De Leon insisted on the radical overthrow of the existing

[37] Daniel De Leon, "Demands, Immediate and Constant," cited in *Platform of the Socialist Labor Party* (New York, 1932), a leaflet published by the New York Labor News Company.

[38] Daniel De Leon, *Socialist Reconstruction of Society* (New York, 1905), a pamphlet published by the New York Labor News Company.

[39] Daniel De Leon, cited in Arnold Petersen, *Proletarian Democracy vs. Dictatorships and Despotism* (4th ed., New York, 1937), p. 29.

capitalist institutions, he was against force. "The ballot is the weapon of civilization,"[40] he wrote, and the working class should not adopt the methods of class war, which is provoked by the capitalist, but "place itself upon the highest plane civilization has reached. . . . It must insist upon the enforcement of civilized methods."

For a number of years after the 1899 split, efforts were made to reunite the Socialist Labor Party and the Socialist Party. The Amsterdam congress of the Second International in 1904 called for the fusion of both parties. In 1908 De Leon took the initiative and suggested unity but was turned down unceremoniously by the Socialist Party executive. In January 1917, three years after De Leon's death, the last futile effort was made. Through the years, the Socialist Labor Party has remained firm and unyielding, the most consistent Marxist organization in America, a bleak cenotaph to the cold genius of Daniel De Leon.

De Leon had rigorously outlined one pole of American labor—doctrinal purity and sectarian isolation. Sam Gompers evolved another—*ad hoc* pragmatism and continual compromise. If socialism as an historically organized movement has not achieved a permanency in American life, it is largely due to the role of the American Federation of Labor.

For years Engels had warned against the isolation of the Socialist Labor Party. In a letter to Sorge in 1891, he said, "it proves how useless is a platform—for the most part theoretically correct—if it is unable to get into contact with the actual needs of the people." Yet when the American Federation of Labor was formed, the socialists for the most part were hostile to it, or sought to divert it from trade-union policies. The official leadership of the A.F.L. returned the hostility. In the heat of conflict both sides were driven to positions more extreme than either had intended.

The socialist attitude derived in large measure from a consistent misreading of the tempo of development of the American working class. Marxian theory had predicted that in the "logic of events" the working class would arrive at a self-conscious evaluation of its own position and become socialist. Every fresh stirring of labor from the National Labor Union on was hailed as a demonstration of that rising class-consciousness. The campaign of 1886, the frenetic activity of the Knights of Labor, and the burgeoning labor parties were each hailed as starting points. In that context, the formation of the American Federation of Labor, with an emphasis on the skilled worker and narrow craft organizations, which in effect were largely beneficiary societies, could only be seen as a retrogression. What the socialists failed to perceive was the crucial fact that the American Federation of Labor was the first labor group to accept its role as a permanent class within American society and to create an

[40] De Leon, *Socialist Reconstruction of Society*, p. 59.

248

institutional framework for its continued existence. The earlier labor movements sought to build enclaves within the structure of capitalist society—in producers' cooperatives, land reform, money reform, and other straws from the land of Prester John. But they did not want to be unions and accept the singular condition of unionism—the day-to-day acceptance of capitalist society.

The early leaders of the American Federation of Labor, Adolph Strasser, P. J. McGuire, and Samuel Gompers, had gone through the sectarian schools of socialist dogmatics. The interminable theoretical wranglings which constituted the curriculum had left them with a skepticism of Marxian politics as applied to the American scene, and helped to shape the here-and-now, pure-and-simple trade unionism of the A.F.L. Because the aims of the Federation were limited to the immediate problem of wages and hours, two important consequences followed. One of these was the decisive rejection, after tentative flirting, of the farmers, Greenbackers, small businessmen, and the various "antimonopoly" political campaigns; such alliances, which proved the undoing of the National Labor Union and the Knights of Labor, merely sucked the worker into the vortex of a swiftly rising political whirlwind, lifted him high, and dumped him unceremoniously when its force was spent. The second consequence was the open acceptance of the concentration of economic power as an inevitable fact of industrial capitalism. Labor could try to hedge in, but not challenge, the power of the rising new class. On the "trust issue," thus, the new trade-union movement broke with the middle-class and agrarian reformers. These two basic assumptions meant that labor would not stand outside capitalist society and challenge it, but would seek a secure place within it, and, when powerful enough, slowly transform it by demanding a share of power.

These attitudes gain vividness only when interpreted through the life history of Sam Gompers, the man who enunciated them and who, with driving force, created the American labor movement in his own stubborn and pragmatic image. Samuel Gompers is the great totem of the American labor movement, and the rules of endogamy and other taboos he set down have become the prescribed rituals of American labor. A forbidding and stubborn father, the "sons" were reared in his image, retaining all the ritual forms but, except for John L. Lewis, little of the vitality.

Born in 1850, the son of Dutch-Jewish parents, Gompers grew up in London working-class quarters, where he absorbed a sense of his own class; and at the age of thirteen came to the United States. When Gompers was twenty-three he went to work in the cigar shop of David Hirsch, a German revolutionary exile whose factory was the center of many burning theoretical controversies. Cigarmaking at that time was an easy and gregarious operation. The men sat around large tables, talking volubly as their fingers swiftly and mechanically shaped the cigars. In the shop Gompers came under the influence of Karl Ferdinand Laurrell, an ardent Marxist who had been active in the First International. Marxism then meant, however, a fierce trade unionism, as against the political biases of the Lassalleans, and Gompers was quickly won to the trade-union viewpoint. But it was the obstinate manner in which the sectarians ignored the bread-and-butter concerns of the union that soured him completely on the political socialists. At that time the cigarmakers' union faced competition from cheap, low-paid "homeworkers" who made the cigars in their tenement homes. Gompers, as the head of the union, sought legislation outlawing the production of cigars in homes. He marked for reprisal those legislators who voted against the measure and called for support of those who worked for the bill. These men were running on old-line party tickets. But the political socialists were dead-set against voting for old-party candidates, even the prolabor ones, charging that such a move might provide temporary gains for the cigarmakers but corrupt the labor movement and destroy political socialism. Even when the first tenement-house bill was enacted, the socialists refused to support for reelection Gompers' man, Edward Grosse, who had been instrumental in pushing through the measure.

But the Marxist influences left indelible traces in Gompers' philosophy. This was particularly true of the crude "economic determinism" which was characteristic of his view of society. In his autobiography, Gompers wrote sententiously, "Economic power is the basis upon which may be developed power in other fields. It is the foundation of organized society . . . economic organization and control over economic power [are] the fulcrum which made possible influence and power in all other fields. . . . This fundamental concept upon which the A.F. of L. was later developed was at that time not formulated in men's minds."[41]

This conviction underlay Gompers' philosophy of "voluntarism," which consisted, essentially, in a fear of the state. Since the state was a reflection of dominant economic power groups, any state intervention could only lead to domination by big business. Gompers, like the old Manchester liberals, wanted a "negative state." At the 1914 convention of the American Federation of Labor, one delegate asked: "Why, if you are opposed to the eight-hour work day for men by law, did you ask for a law regulating and limiting injunctions?" Gompers replied: "In the law to limit and regulate injunctions we propose to clip the power of the courts insofar as labor is concerned, and in an eight-hour law for men it is to give courts still greater power than they now have. Is there no difference?"[42]

It is an old axiom that men develop loyalties to the institutions they

[41] Gompers, op.cit., I, pp. 286-87, 223.
[42] David J. Saposs, Readings in Trade Unionism (New York, 1927), p. 397.

250

build, and tend to see events from those particular vantage points. In Gompers, we have a case study of the socialist who entered the union movement, began to see the American scene from that perspective, and changed his viewpoints as unionism in the course of its development found a respectable place in American society. For the socialists, however, life was still a triumph of dogma over experience.

Within the Socialist Labor Party, the influence of Sorge, acting as Engels' emissary, had been thrown consistently on the side of the trade-union faction. The defeat of the politicos in 1890 raised hopes that peaceful cooperation between the socialists and Gompers might be reached. But they could not agree. The issue was too fundamental. It arose out of the demand of the socialists within the A.F.L. for the revival of a separate central trades charter in New York City, for they charged the Central Labor Union with insidious Tammany Hall connections. Gompers refused, stating that the constitution of the American Federation of Labor permitted only labor unions and forbade political representation. At the 1890 convention Lucien Sanial, the socialist spokesman, argued that the Socialist Labor Party was a "bona fide" labor body, and that in Europe the socialists had organized the first trade unions and kept them free of capitalist interference. Gompers stated his case with impressive logic: if the Socialist Labor Party were admitted, he asked, why not such other parties as single taxers, anarchists, and Greenbackers? Partisan politics, he added, was a source of disruption and would split the Federation. If the Socialist Labor Party were admitted, it would be the wedge to independent political activity through the S.L.P. or a party dominated by it. Such an action would be construed as an endorsement of socialism and split the American Federation of Labor. It would keep many unions, such as the railroad unions and bricklayers, who were considering joining, from affiliating.

During this debate Gompers used a phrase which has since become famous as descriptive of the intention of the A.F.L. "Unions, pure and simple," he said, "are the natural organization of wage workers to secure their present material and practical improvement and to achieve their final emancipation." Gompers denied in the debate that he was unsympathetic to socialism, but, he said, "the working people are in too great need of immediate improvement[s] in their condition to allow them to forego them in the endeavor to devote their entire energies to an end however beautiful to contemplate. . . . The way out of the wage system is through higher wages."[43]

When Gompers was upheld by a vote of 1,574 to 496, Lucien Sanial, the

[43] Gompers, *op.cit.*, i, p. 385. See also *An Interesting Discussion at the Tenth Annual Convention of the American Federation of Labor* (1891), a pamphlet published by the American Federation of Labor.

S.L.P. representative, declared war against the "fakirs" and said that the "Socialists would cram Socialism down the throats of the American workingman."[44]

In the next three years the debate raged fiercely. De Leon argued that the rapid growth of industrial concentration would bring with it the corollary of Marx's law, the increasing misery of the working class. The American Federation of Labor was attacked as seeking to make the workers contented. In turn Gompers charged that the Socialist Labor Party cared less for the strike than for a few more votes and for newspaper circulation. The attacks became personal. De Leon wrote in the *People*: "From this fear of ruining individual prospects arises the slander of socialism on the part of such men as McGuire and Gompers . . . and all other advocates of pure and simple trade union fakism who are secretly plotting for personal advancement with either capitalism or capitalistic politicians."[45]

In 1893, the socialists came within a hair of capturing the American Federation of Labor. Led by Thomas J. Morgan, the secretary of the machinists' union, and J. Mahlon Barnes of the cigarmakers, they introduced a series of planks which demanded compulsory education and the nationalization of mines, railroads, and utilities. Plank ten called for "the collective ownership by the people of all means of production and distribution." They asked that these planks be submitted for "favorable consideration" to the A.F.L. affiliates. After a hectic debate, the phrase "favorable consideration" was deleted by 1,253 to 1,182 but the entire resolution of submission was carried overwhelmingly. The convention also voted to endorse free silver and instructed the executive council to bring about an alliance with the farmers' organizations.

During the year, a large number of unions within the American Federation of Labor voted to endorse the socialist program, and local affiliates were active in politics. But political activity proved fruitless. A report in the A.F.L.'s *Federationist* in November 1894 listed 300 members of the A.F.L. who had been candidates for office, but of whom only a half dozen had been elected. Strasser, Gompers, and McGuire came out unequivocally against plank ten of the program. They charged it would prevent the growth of the organization and discourage many unions from joining. At the 1894 convention, plank ten was defeated through a parliamentary maneuver by 1,217 to 913. The socialists took revenge on Gompers by voting for and electing the miner John McBride for president. The year that followed was the only one during the rest of his life that Gompers

[44] Quoted from N. I. Stone, "Attitude of the Socialists toward the Trade Unions" (New York, Volkszeitung Library, 1900), p. 4, in Louis S. Reed, *Labor Philosophy of Samuel Gompers* (New York, 1930), p. 80.
[45] De Leon in the *People*, August 13, 1893; October 8, 1893.

was out of office in the American Federation of Labor; and in 1895 he was returned to office once more.

Gompers had now grown quite bitter against the socialists. When De Leon launched the dual Socialist Trades and Labor Alliance—and in Gompers' lexicon dual unionism was the worst of all crimes—Gompers, who was himself no mean polemicist, poured out some vitriol of his own. In an editorial in the *Federationist*, he wrote:

"We note . . . that the work of union wrecking is being taken up by a wing of the so-called socialist party of New York, headed by a professor without a professorship, a shyster lawyer without a brief, and a statistician who furnished figures to the republican, democratic and socialist parties. These three mountebanks, aided by a few unthinking but duped workers, recently launched, from a beer saloon a brand new national organization, with the avowed purpose of crushing every trade union in the country."[46]

A few years later, when De Leon's dual unionism had split the Socialist Labor Party and his union movement was failing, Gompers wrote, ". . . this moribund concern, conceived in iniquity and brutal concubinage with labor's double enemy, greed and ignorance, fashioned into an embryonic phthisical dwarf, born in corruption and filth; and now dying, surrounded by the vultures of its progeny ready to pounce on the emaciated carcass of the corpse."[47]

By 1900 Gompers had shed the socialist influence and even most of its rhetoric. He had no ultimate aim for labor nor was he in favor of replacing private enterprise. He wanted ten cents an hour more and a half hour a day less. At first Gompers fought the socialists on differences in tactics and organizational strategy, later he fought them on the grounds of principle.

It was shortly after this that the A.F.L. took the much debated step of entering the National Civic Federation, an organization of employers, labor, and the public whose chief officers were, in seeming anomaly, Mark Hanna, the Republican political boss and McKinley kingmaker, as president, and Samuel Gompers as first vice-president.[48] Gompers' own explanation of the move indicated his new concerns. "It helped to establish the practice," he wrote, "of accepting labor unions as an integral social element and logically of including their representatives in groups to

[46] Gompers in the *American Federationist*, April 1896, p. 33.

[47] Gompers in the *American Federationist*, August 1898, p. 115.

[48] Although Gompers at this point mingled freely with the political and business greats, he would refuse dining invitations at the homes of the wealthy. In his autobiography he relates that he would often go to dinner parties at the homes of industrialists and explain to them labor's viewpoints. But he never dined there, waiting until the end of the discussion to leave and eat outside. It is unlikely that such behavior arose out of a fear of being corrupted. More likely, Gompers, self-conscious of his proletarian origins, used this device to shock his audience pleasurably and to reinforce his own arrogance.

discuss policies."[49] This was now labor's single ambition: to win acceptance as a "legitimate" social group, equal with business and the church as an established institution of American life. For Gompers, the immigrant boy, it was a personal crusade as well. He sought to win recognition for labor in all civic aspects of American life: an entry and a hearing at the White House; an official voice in the government, i.e., the Department of Labor; respectful relations with employers; representation in community agencies; etc. To become respectable—this was Gompers', and labor's, aim.

The socialist opposition to Gompers consistently iterated two themes: one, the charge of class collaboration; second, the failure to organize the unskilled into industrial unions. In 1897 the Western Federation of Miners, under left-wing socialist leadership, withdrew from the American Federation of Labor and helped form the Western Labor Union, later the American Labor Union, which sought to organize the unskilled along industrial lines and endorsed socialism. To the jealous Gompers this was another instance of the treacherous "dual unionism" of the socialists. In 1902, Max S. Hayes, a socialist leader, introduced a resolution at the A.F.L. convention fully endorsing socialism. After heated debate, the resolution was just barely defeated 4,897 to 4,171, with 387 not voting.

In the fluctuations of socialist power within the American Federation of Labor, 1902 was the peak year, after which the socialist strength declined. This is an incongruous fact, for 1902 was the beginning of rising socialist political influence in the United States. The answer to this paradox is that the socialist vote was never drawn primarily from organized labor—a fact that was one of its fundamental weaknesses.

In 1905 the revolutionary elements in the labor movement launched the I.W.W. (Industrial Workers of the World). Gompers' retort was characteristic. "The Socialists have called another convention to smash the American trade union movement. This is the sixth 'concentrated' effort in this direction in the past decade. . . ."[50] The literal charge was unfair. Although Debs was present at the founding of the I.W.W., the organization was never socialist nor did it have party endorsement—but Gompers no longer made simple distinctions. In the large, however, the charge was true. Socialism was "dual" to the A.F.L. and suffered the consequences. For Marx and Engels, the need for close kinship between socialism and the working class was integral to their theory. In America, the practice was deficient. In later years a significant wing of the Socialist Party, led by Morris Hillquit, sought to modify the party's harsh attitude toward the leadership of the A.F.L., but the differences arising from the contradictory conceptions of labor's course were too strong. The needed unity was impossible to achieve. Since this lack of unity is the basis for

[49] Gompers, Seventy Years of Life and Labor, II, p. 105.
[50] Gompers in the American Federationist, March 1905, p. 139.

one of the crucial questions to be asked regarding the failure of socialism in the United States, the problems in connection with it are worth exploring in more systematic detail.

The first problem was the socialist characterization of the policies of the A.F.L. as "class collaborationist." Shaw once remarked that trade unionism is not socialism, but the capitalism of the proletariat. In one sense this is true. But the corollary that the trade-union leader must become the "labor lieutenant" and "lackey" of the capitalist class is not the literal sequitur. The basis of this charge was that the A.F.L. sought to benefit the skilled workers at the expense of the other sections of the working class by refusing to admit industrial unions. While the socialists may have been correct in the abstract, it was Gompers who showed the keener insight into working-class psychology. In a clumsy manner, he sought to indicate his theoretical differences with the socialists in respect to class attitudes. They only had an intellectual and he a living knowledge of the workers, he felt. "I told [the socialists]," Gompers wrote, "that the *Klassen Bewusztsein* (class consciousness) of which they made so much was not either a fundamental or inherent element, for class consciousness was a mental process shared by all who had imagination."[51] The real social cement, he said, "was *Klassengefühl* (class feeling) . . . that primitive force that had its origin in experience only." And these experiences, for the average workingman, were of a *limiting* nature: the desire for better wages, shorter hours, etc. The skilled workers had accepted their role, had a "commodity" of their own, and were in a position to bargain. Most of the unskilled, many of them immigrants, had no thought of staying in an especially low-paying job, and drifted. They constituted a large reservoir which the capitalist could always use to break strikes or depress wages. Thus it was difficult to build a permanent organization of men with no particular stake in their jobs. In behalf of the skilled worker, the American Federation of Labor forged the trade agreement as the instrument for exacting a higher price for his commodity, i.e., his skill. Control of the job supply became the prime means of giving the wage worker protection. It also meant that the union became involved in the market problems of the industry. "Business unionism," is inevitable in the maintenance of the union as a stable organization. The necessity of "business unionism"—living in and of the market—is one that the early Socialist Party could not adequately understand.

A second issue was monopoly. Every major American movement of social protest in the last two decades of the nineteenth century and the first decade of the twentieth had been organized around the antimonopoly motif. Gompers felt that monopoly as an outcome of economic growth was unavoidable. Nor did he feel that it could be controlled by the state,

[51] Gompers, *Seventy Years of Life and Labor*, I, p. 383.

which itself was subservient to the powerful economic interests. "The great wrongs attributable to the trusts," he wrote, "are their corrupting influence on the politics of the country, but as the state has always been the representative of the wealthy persons, we shall be compelled to endure its evils until the toilers are organized and educated to the degree that they shall know that the state is by right theirs, and finally and justly shall come into their own while never relaxing in their efforts to secure the very best economic, social and material improvements in their conditions."[52] This statement by Gompers, before the conservative mold finally jelled, was actually in line with socialist economic theory later developed by Rudolf Hilferding in his *Finanzkapital*. The theory saw the growth of monopoly as inevitable under capitalism. It condemned antimonopoly programs as out of keeping with historical development, and in many instances approved the development of monopoly because such concentration of productive prices would make the transformation to socialism easier. The major concern of the Marxists, therefore, was political. By winning state power they would expropriate the monopolies and take over a fully developed "socialized" mode of production. Only the "social relations" had to be changed. The German unions acquiesced in the cartelization program of German industry, and the English unions early abetted the monopoly devices of British industry. In the United States, however, socialist attention was riveted largely on the trade-agreement policy and Gompers was attacked for "class collaboration." On the monopoly issue in general, the party never defined its stand squarely. In theory and in its arguments with middle-class elements, it prophesied the inevitable concentration of industry. In its politics, however, the party, largely under the influence of agrarian elements in the West, raised political slogans of an antimonopoly nature.

The third dilemma arose out of the limited program of the American Federation of Labor. To the socialists the demand for a shorter work-day and more wages was no solution to the capitalist crisis. Some ultimate goal had to be fixed lest the workers gain illusions that the trade union was a sufficient instrument for melioration. If one accepts the viewpoint that the union, by its own nature, becomes an end in itself and an integral part of capitalist society, then such a socialist theory makes sense. If, however, one regards unionism as a social force which by its own position in an industrial hierarchy becomes a challenge to managerial power and changes the locus of power in capitalism, then Gompers' strategy of focusing on the day-to-day issues was undeniably correct. This is the very problem which unionism, now an established and powerful force in the economy, faces today.

[52] Gompers in the *American Federation of Labor Convention Proceedings*, 1899, p. 15.

V. Fission, Fusion, and Faction

Out of the European dogmatism of De Leon and the native evangelicism of Debs arose the American Socialist Party—and it combined some of the backward features of both. Hillquit, although stemming from the German tradition, was intellectually flexible; but ultimately his Marxism was too constricting a yoke; Debs, who emerged from the rich American soil, was unstable temperamentally and too rigid intellectually to allow his experiences to modify his prejudices. If one adds to this the boyish romanticism of a Jack London, the pale Christian piety of a George Herron and of the large number of Protestant ministers who flocked into the Socialist Party, the reckless braggadocio of a "Wild Bill" Haywood, and the tepid social-work impulse of do-gooders interested in prison reform, vegetarianism, birth control, woman's suffrage, and other advanced notions of the day, you have as unstable a compound as was ever mixed in the modern history of political chemistry.[53]

Formally the American Socialist Party was a fusion of two schismatic groups: an eastern wing came as a faction of the De Leonite Socialist Labor Party; a western wing as a faction from the Debsian Social Democracy of America.[54] From 1895 on, the splits in the Socialist Labor Party were as regular as binary fission among the amoebas. First to go were the Jewish socialists, who under the urging of Meyer London voted to join the Debsian movement out West. Next to go was the section in Haverhill, Massachusetts. James F. Carey, local leader of the party, had been elected a member of the city council on the Socialist Labor Party ticket, but when he voted for a new armory in town, he was attacked by De Leon and joined the Social Democracy. In St. Louis, another section of the party shook loose. The final *Götterdämmerung* took place in New York. The De Leon faction was supported by the official party papers, the *People* in English, and the *Vorwärts* in German. The Hillquit group

[53] Nor is this list of the varied types that abounded in the party meant to be exhaustive. One could add puritan consciences of millionaire socialists such as Joseph Medill Patterson (once a member of the national executive committee of the Socialist Party and in later years the Roosevelt-hating publisher of the New York *Daily News*) and J. G. Phelps Stokes; the burning Jewish intensity of Meyer London; the flaming discontent of the dispossessed farmers; the inarticulate and amorphous desire to "belong" of the immigrant workers; the iconoclastic idol-breaking of the literary radicals; the rebellious free-love addicts of Greenwich Village Bohemia; the old and broken workers; and the angry, idealistic college-student generation. And more.

[54] The geographical identifications are important in Socialist Party history. The westerners, like the American public generally, feared the "New York" influence; the easterners were afraid to put the party headquarters in Chicago, where it might be subject to the vagaries of native quack-reform doctrine. In the early years of the Socialist Party, the national headquarters were first located in Springfield, Mass., and St. Louis, Mo., because of these considerations. Although the headquarters were finally placed in Chicago, these suspicions lingered, and flared again when the "New York" influence became a factor in the party split of 1935.

rallied around the daily *Volkszeitung*. In the elections to party office each side, De Leon and Hillquit, accused the other of stuffing ballots, organizing bogus clubs, and, in general, behaving in rowdy Tammany fashion. Both claimed victory and prepared to take over the party headquarters, printing presses, and offices. When each faction came to claim possession, the two arrived head-on and came to blows. The action is described in a contemporary account: "[An] act of violence on the part of Keep [a De Leon follower] was the signal for an outburst of passion seldom witnessed in any political meeting, much less in a meeting of Socialists. The delegates pummelled each other until blood was seen flowing from many wounds. Men were sprawling on the floor, others were fighting in the corners, upon the tables, chairs and upon the piano, Hugo Vogt [another De Leon stalwart] having climbed upon the latter, yelling and fairly foaming from the mouth. . . ."[55]

Two days later another pitched battle erupted. The *Volkszeitung* (Hillquit) faction, claiming legal sanction, sent a delegation of able-bodied men upstairs to the office of the *People* to claim the party property. The De Leonites, however, in good revolutionary fashion barricaded themselves in the office and stood armed with clubs, bottles, and other weapons. "Fierce did the conflict rage for fully ten minutes; blood flowed freely," reported the *People*.[56] More blood might have flowed but for the salutary intervention of the gendarmerie. Since the De Leonites held possession, the police ordered the insurrectionists to "move on," a dramatic illustration of the old revolutionary adage that property is theft. As a result of the conflict, there appeared two Socialist Labor Parties and two *Peoples*. The case was finally decided in the capitalist courts, which awarded both the name of the organization and the title of the newspaper to De Leon. The Hillquit faction, dubbed the "Kangaroos," withdrew and opened negotiations with the Debs-Berger Social Democratic Party of America, negotiations leading to the formation of the Socialist Party of America.[57]

[55] Quoted in Social Democracy of America, *Social Democracy Red Book* (Terre Haute, Ind., 1900), p. 72.

[56] Nathan Fine, *Labor and Farmer Parties in the United States, 1828-1928* (New York, 1928), p. 175.

[57] As for De Leon's Socialist Labor Party, the natural law of evolutionary fratricide continued with remorseless logic. Even after the withdrawal of the Hillquit group, split after split continued. One group of thirty-one members issued a statement charging De Leon, the national editor, with being a Robespierre. "Every member of Section New York," they stated, continuing the metaphor, "has been declared a suspect and the Jacobin Club recently issued a decree for the establishment of a Revolutionary Tribunal variously styled Committee of Inquiry, or Spying Committee or the Holy Inquisition." Heads did roll, ideologically, and in the short period of three years a number of prominent S.L.P.ers had been vicariously executed. Among these were the former editors of the *People* and *Vorwärts*, Lucien Sanial and Hugo Vogt, two of De Leon's cohorts on the famous ruling triumvirate, Herman Simpson, chief

If American socialism thus imported its quarrelsome sectarianism from European-flavored Marxism, it more than redressed the balance with a loose evangelical fervor and moralistic tone drawn from the native West. Two men, J. A. Wayland and Eugene Victor Debs, were largely responsible for that leathery "Yankeefying" flavor. Wayland, the "one hoss philosopher," published the *Appeal to Reason*, socialism's cracker-barrel weekly, which, at its height, had a Bible Belt circulation of more than 500,000 believing readers. Debs, whom Sinclair Lewis once called the John the Baptist of American socialism, was the man whose gentleness and sweet, passionate anguish touched a chord of goodness in more Americans than probably any other figure in American life after Lincoln. Both Debs and Wayland came to socialism not through Marx, but via utopianism and dizzy cooperative-colony schemes.

Wayland, a restless and shrewd Indiana businessman, had made a sizable fortune in the printing business and Colorado real estate, but, about 1891, when already middle-aged, he became a socialist by reading Laurence Gronlund and other socialist writers of the period. Wayland felt his conversion triumphantly confirmed when, as a result of his readings, he predicted a panic in 1893, and by quickly liquidating his real-estate holdings, found his fortune increasing. In 1893 he returned to Indiana and started the *Coming Nation.* Its rambling anecdotal style ("simply Ruskin turned into the language of the common people") attracted a large readership and Wayland felt bold enough to start a socialist colony at Ruskin, Tennessee, which would serve as a practical example of the cooperative ideal. A contemporary account records his cheery disillusionment. "He sent money down to a few people who were first to arrive on the ground, and one of them who was a sort of self-constituted agent kept writing for more, alleging that various work was under way. . . . When Wayland appeared on the scene he found nothing had been done, but that the pioneers were quartered at a hotel at Tennessee City, living in luxury on the money he forwarded. . . ." Before going to Ruskin, Wayland had read none of the books on the history of the American communities. But even reading of their failures would not have deterred him, he said. He had to find out by actual experience the impossibility of all-around success in such undertakings.[58]

In 1895 Wayland began the publication of the socialist *Appeal to Reason*, which, after an initial setback during the Bryan campaign of 1896, soon caught on, and in little more than three years rose to a circula-

---

editor of the Jewish *Abendblatt*, Benjamin F. Keinard, the party's candidate for mayor, Arthur Keep, and various other former De Leonite stalwarts of the 1899 battle. The membership finally shriven and doctrinal purity achieved, the Socialist Labor Party retired into a political lamasery to await the collapse of society.

[58] "A Trip to Girard," by Wayfarer, in *Social Democracy Red Book*, p. 91.

tion of almost 100,000. In 1896, the saving remnants of the Ruskin Colony group sent out a call for a nationwide convention of socialists. Out of that convention emerged a new group, socialist in goal but utopian in orientation, the Brotherhood of the Co-operative Commonwealth. With an ambitious program ("Mutualism or the Kingdom of God Here and Now") the Brotherhood divided its work into various departments: the teaching of socialism, the settlement of colonies, the establishment of industries by building and operating factories and mills, and political action.[59] A year later, the program unrealized, the Brotherhood joined with the remnants of the American Railway Union, led by Eugene Debs, to form the Social Democracy of America.

The American Railway Union, an all-inclusive organization of railway workers organized in 1893, was Debs's break with traditional unionism. Eugene Victor Debs, born in 1855 in the dusty town of Terre Haute, Indiana, had railroading in his blood from his early youth. During the transport boom created by the Civil War, Terre Haute had zoomed into a railroad town, and young Debs roamed the switching yards soaking in the romance of rail adventure. Young Eugene Victor had absorbed his romanticism from his father, Jean Daniel Debs. His two given names, in fact, were in honor of Eugene Sue and Victor Hugo, "a tradition of reason and justice," father Daniel felt, "by which men should live."[60] At the age of fifteen, with a smattering of high-school learning but with the deep imprint of Schiller's poetry and Victor Hugo's *Les Miserables* in mind, the young Debs went to work as a wiper on the railroad. A year later, a lean, six-foot lad, he became a fireman on the short but cold run between Terre Haute and Indianapolis.

Debs worked only three years as a fireman, for on the insistence of his mother he left the hazardous occupation and took a job as a clerk in a wholesale grocery. In all, Debs worked less than five years on the railroad, but the hardships of the toil remained vivid in his impressionable mind. When the struggling Brotherhood of Locomotive Firemen organized a lodge in Terre Haute, Debs, though no longer a railroad man, joined it. In a short while, Debs became a national officer of the union. At the same time he entered local politics, being twice elected city clerk of the town. As the Brotherhood grew more powerful, Debs felt that the ultimate security of the union lay in an industrial federation which would also include the unorganized semiskilled and unskilled road workers. (In this same period, Debs was reading Gronlund's *The Co-operative Commonwealth* and Edward Bellamy's *Looking Backward*.) However, the dream of a unified railway federation collapsed under the weight of jurisdictional

[59] James Dombrowski, *The Early Days of Christian Socialism in America* (New York, 1936), p. 75.
[60] Ray Ginger, *The Bending Cross* (New Brunswick, N.J., 1949), p. 6.

disputes and petty rivalries, and Debs retired from the firemen's union, devoting his energies to a publishing company and to the editing of the *Locomotive Firemen's Magazine*, a forum whose pages were open to every dissonant voice of the day.

In 1893, in the wake of the labor turmoil that had boiled over at Coeur d'Alene, Debs returned and organized the American Railway Union on an industrial-union basis. Within a year, the new union had won a sensational strike against James J. Hill's Great Northern railway, and the membership had risen to more than 150,000. In that year the total membership of the three old-line brotherhoods was about 70,000 while the American Federation of Labor had little more than 260,000.

The panic of 1893 gave rise to the discontent and national hysteria of 1894. The threatening armies of the commonwealth—Coxey's army, Fry's army, Kelly's army—had marched grimly on Washington to demand relief for the unemployed, only to end as a ludicrous tatterdemalion mob, their leaders arrested for trampling on the grass of the Capitol.[61] But on the heels of Coxeyism came the more serious Pullman strike at Chicago, a strike that catapulted Debs to national fame. It was obvious at the time that the conservatives had the jitters. A week before the strike, an "anarchist plot" to blow up the national Capitol had been exposed by the New York *Tribune*; in Paris, the French stateman Carnot had just been assassinated. The echoes of Coxey's tramping army were still reverberating. When the American Railway Union declared a boycott on Pullman cars, within three days 40,000 railroaders had walked out in a sympathy strike, bringing traffic west of Chicago to a halt. The capitalists felt that the revolution was knocking at the door. Attorney General Richard Olney, the strong man in Cleveland's cabinet, acted swiftly to break the strike. Two federal judges granted his application for "the most sweeping injunction ever issued from a Federal Court." "A Gatling gun on paper," declared the joyful General Managers Association.[62] Under the cover of the blanket injunction, the strike slipped away fast, leaving in its wake a trail of violence and destruction.

The Pullman strike made Eugene Debs a national figure, and by his own account converted him to socialism. For violating the government injunction, Debs was sentenced to six months in prison. In Woodstock jail, he was visited by noted socialists, including Keir Hardie, the founder of the British Labour Party, and Victor Berger. In this period of enforced idleness Debs read a great deal, and, according to legend, found his Damascan road. The story is told by Debs himself in an essay, "How I Became a Socialist."[63] Debs wrote: ". . . it was here that Socialism gradually

[62] Matthew Josephson, *The Politicos* (New York, 1938), p. 578.
[61] Donald L. McMurry, *Coxey's Army* (Boston, 1929), p. 119.
[63] New York *Comrade*, April 1902; reprinted in *Writings and Speeches of Eugene*

laid hold of me in its own irresistible fashion. Books and pamphlets and letters from Socialists came by every mail and I began to read and think and dissect the anatomy of the system in which workingmen, however organized, could be shattered and battered and splintered at a single stroke. The writings of Bellamy and Blatchford early appealed to me. The Co-operative Commonwealth of Gronlund also impressed me, but the writings of [the German Marxist] Kautsky were so clear and conclusive that I readily grasped, not merely his argument, but also caught the spirit of his socialist utterance—and I thank him and all who helped me out of darkness into light."

Actually, these recollections, written in 1902 many years after the fact, obscure the backsliding and involutions of Debs's march to socialism. In 1894 and 1896, after his release from jail, Debs still considered himself a populist and figured prominently in the speculations of various populists for nomination to high office. The American Railway Union, at its 1894 convention, had endorsed the People's Party and free silver. In 1896, Henry Demarest Lloyd sought to swing the People's (Populist) Party behind Debs for president instead of Bryan. Debs, however, now vacillated on the importance of the money question. In his magazine, *Railway Times*, Debs wrote that the railroads were using the currency issue in order to divert attention from the real threat of government by injunction. During the campaign, however, he declared that free silver "afforded common ground upon which the common people could unite against the trusts."[64] Debs was active in the populist campaign and worked tirelessly for Bryan, Altgeld, and Darrow. "If Bryan had been elected President in 1896," writes Ginger, "Eugene Debs might never have become a socialist."

In 1897, Debs came around to declaring that "the issue is socialism versus capitalism. . . . We have been cursed with the reign of gold long enough." Yet the same year, Debs proposed a mass migration of unemployed to the western states in order to form cooperative colonies; and, in the most politically naive fashion imaginable, he wrote to John D. Rockefeller, of all people, for help in financing the colonization scheme. "The purpose of the organization, briefly speaking," Debs wrote to Rockefeller, "is to establish in place of the present cruel, immoral and decadent system, a co-operative commonwealth, where millionaires and beggars . . . will completely disappear, and human brotherhood will be inaugurated to bless and make the world more beautiful. . . . Then the strong will help the weak, the weak will love the strong, and the Human Brotherhood

---

V. *Debs* (New York, 1948). This version is accepted without question by a number of early biographers. See David Karsner, *Debs: His Authorized Life and Letters* (New York, 1919), p. 178; McAlister Coleman, *Pioneers of Freedom* (New York, 1929), p. 151; Fine, *op.cit.*, p. 188.

[64] Ginger, *op.cit.*, p. 190.

will transform the days to come into a virtual Paradise."[65] There is no record that Mr. Rockefeller ever replied.

Debs had announced his conversion to socialism, but his thinking was still colored by colonization and western schemes. He did not join the Socialist Labor Party, feeling that De Leon's party was too narrow and boss-ridden ever to attract a popular following. Instead, under the urging of friends, particularly Victor Berger, Debs moved toward the formation of a new political party. The contrast between Debs and Berger symbolizes, in part, two dimensions of the future Socialist Party. The core of Debs's character was a deep emotionality streaked with a homely sentimentalism; his politics derived from a romantic conception of the underdog and his commitments flowed quickly to those who also subscribed to this conception. Berger, stocky and assertive, had a shrewd sense of the practical, and had the political trick, within the Socialist Party, of clothing his ideas in revolutionary phrases and his actions in the practicalities of ward and precinct politics. His métier was organization, and in tight, almost bullying fashion, he built a machine in Milwaukee which was to be the solidest rock of the socialist achievement in America. Yet his devotion to socialism was unquestionable. Born in Austria-Hungary in 1860, Berger received a university education in Vienna and soon after came to the United States. For a while he tramped through the West doing odd jobs before settling finally in Milwaukee, where he became a school teacher. In 1892 Berger became the editor of the German-language paper *Milwaukee Vorwärts* and embarked on a political career. Berger was a Marxist and convinced, therefore, that the various colonizing and utopian schemes could not succeed. He felt that a socialist movement would develop in the United States as industrialization proceeded, but that its tempo might be different from that of the movement in Europe. In 1896, the Milwaukee socialists organized a branch of the People's (Populist) Party in an effort to capture the party's convention. When that attempt failed, Berger took a leading role in the creation of a new party.

On June 15, 1897, the skeleton of the American Railway Union met in Chicago and with the tattered remnants of the Brotherhood of the Cooperative Commonwealth formed the Social Democracy of America. The convention adopted a socialist platform calling for public ownership of all monopolies and utilities, and also public works for the unemployed. But the party could not shake the ghost of colonization. Christian socialists, footloose rebels, and middle-class romantics still made up the core of the native dissident left in the United States. As the rapid industrialism brutalized the American character, these elements saw colonization as the only "practical" implementation of their need to escape from the

[65] *Ibid.*, p. 201.

aggressive, egotistical, competitive individual nurtured by capitalist society.[66]

The Social Democracy of America never even rode out one year of life. The schism was there from the start. The executive board of the new party was dominated by the "old-guard" leaders of the American Railway Union, a fact which from the beginning created hostility among other elements in the organization. This leading group, augmented by some anarchist adherents, plumped hard for colonization. The "political" faction was led by Berger. He argued that the party could win offices, and pointed to such success as the election of two aldermen in Sheboygan, Wisconsin, and the quintupling of the vote in Milwaukee. By the second convention, in 1898, the issue of colonization could no longer be avoided. During the year, a colonization commission had explored sites in Tennessee, Washington, and Colorado. Just before the convention, it announced that it had purchased 560 acres in Cripple Creek, Colorado, on which was a gold mine of "the deeper you go the richer the ore" variety. (Later the gullible commission discovered that it had bought a gold brick.)[67] The fight during the convention was bitter, the comrades reviling each other unmercifully. The political faction charged, with merit, that the colonizers had chartered "fake" locals in order to capture the convention; in turn the colonizers charged, unfairly, that the secretary of the party had mishandled party funds. When the issue finally came to a vote after three days of wretched wrangling, the colonizers won, 52 to 37. At 2:30 in the morning, the minority bolted and at that ghostly hour formed the Social Democratic Party, its leaders being Eugene Debs, Victor Berger and Frederic Heath of Milwaukee.[68] At the final voting, Debs was absent in bed in his hotel

[66] Perhaps the last great pathetic attempt in this direction was the Christian Commonwealth colony at Commonwealth, Georgia, in 1896. "They were resolved to follow an absolute love ethic of complete sharing. Their success would be a vindication of the efficacy of Christianity for solving social problems; their failure would be the failure of love." (See Dombrowski, op.cit., p. 133.) Unfortunately they failed.

During its four-year lifetime, the colony attracted between 300 and 400 persons, and in the pages of its magazine, the Social Gospel, could be found the works of Bliss, George D. Herron, Bellamy, and other leading thinkers of the Christian socialist movement in the United States.

Since this was a Christian colony, it was almost fated that it recapitulate the eternal drama of sin and betrayal. Following a heavy freeze in 1899 and subsequent damage to crops, grumbling arose over the slim rations. A member of the colony who had been cast out for falsely accusing it of favoring "free love" began to sow the seeds of dissension. Finally, twelve backsliders from apostledom sought to throw the colony into bankruptcy hoping, through the subsequent liquidation of assets, to benefit greatly. Reluctantly, the colony decided to fight the issue in the courts. "This was regarded by many as the final surrender of the principle of love, the acknowledgment after several compromises that the ethic of nonresistance was not an adequate standard for meeting the issue of a complex social situation." (Dombrowski, op.cit., p. 165.)

[67] Social Democracy Red Book, p. 67.

[68] Theodore Debs, "The Birth of the Socialist Party," New Leader, April 28, 1934.

264

room with a fierce headache. It was a pattern to be constantly repeated. With no stomach for the quarrelsome factionalism and angry invective that accompanied party conventions, Debs was to remain away during his lifetime from almost every national convention of the Socialist Party.

The new party declared itself a "class-conscious, revolutionary social organization"; its motto: Pure Socialism and No Compromise.[69] Soon after its start, it met with some local success. In Massachusetts, in 1898, it elected a mayor in Haverhill and sent two men to the state legislature. The following year, independent socialist groups in Texas and Iowa joined the party. When the Social Democratic Party met in first national convention in March 1900 at Indianapolis, it had more than 4,500 members with 226 branches in twenty-five states.

The formation of the Social Democratic Party as a purely political party, using political methods and formulating political demands, was an important turning point in the development of a socialist movement in the United States. Perhaps the most significant aspect of its platform and outlook was the inclusion of a set of "immediate issues" as the basis for the party's agitation and educational program. It was at this time that Daniel De Leon's Socialist Labor Party had scrapped all specific resolutions and planks, retaining only the statement of principles in its public declarations. "The whole string of planks," said De Leon, ". . . remind us of the infancy of Socialists, when Socialists were still impressed with the idea that we must do something immediately for the working class."[70] The Socialist Labor Party action could only narrow the party membership, since the condition of joining was agreement on a specific doctrinal view. The inclusion by the Social Democrats, on the other hand, of meliorative appeals tended to encourage almost any variety of dissident to join, and extended the basis of consequent factionalism.

The platform of the Social Democratic Party of America, adopted at Chicago in June 1898, is interesting in the light of later New Deal legislation. It declared conventionally for a system of "co-operative production and distribution." In addition, the platform demanded "national insurance of working people against accidents, lack of employment and want in old age," a "system of public works and improvements for the employment . . . of unemployed," the "reduction of the hours of labor in proportion to the increasing facilities of production," "equal civil and political rights for

[69] The colonizers, on the other hand, moved in the opposite direction, rejecting the viewpoint of class struggle and broadening their appeal to "all men." Shortly after this, their group dwindled to only a few. A small colony with 110 settlers eventually was established at the head of Henderson Bay in the State of Washington, but it soon petered out.
[70] *Proceedings of the Tenth National (1900) Convention of the Socialist Labor Party*; cited in Joseph Dorfman, *The Economic Mind in American Civilization*, III (New York, 1949), p. 236.

men and women," "the adoption of the initiative and the referendum," the "abolition of war as far as the United States are concerned and the introduction of international arbitration instead."[71] Two omissions should be noted. One was a plank on farmers. The original statement called for the leasing of public land to farmers in parcels not greater than 640 acres, and the construction of grain elevators and cold-storage buildings to be used by the farmer at cost. Doctrinaire socialists, however, charged that this program was "reactionary" (i.e., populist). The supporters of the plank pointed out that concentration of land ownership was not taking place in the rural districts as the early theorists of socialism had predicted, and that steps to aid small private farmers were necessary. After considerable debate the plank was dropped, with the result that no section on agriculture appeared at all in the party platform. The farm issue was to plague the party for the next twelve years and never was satisfactorily resolved.

The second omission was the absence of any reference to Negroes. The lack of a policy on ethnic questions—other than the vacuous statement that socialism would solve the problem—was also to play a debilitating role in the political development of the party.

It is important to note that while the Social Democratic Party (and later the Socialist Party, which took over the platform virtually intact) focused attention on *immediate demands*, it did not take stands on the *current* issues agitating the American body politic. These "immediate demands" (or palliatives, as De Leon sneeringly called them) were measures to relieve the economic want of the workers and steps to the attainment of socialism. As such they were more politically relevant than the vague promise of a socialist industrial republic which the Socialist Labor Party held out. But the party's failure to commit itself on the actual immediate issues that had to be solved in the here and now tended to isolate it from the labor movement and from the farmers. The party failed to discuss the money issue, which was a shining panacea of previous socialist and labor parties. Nor did it consider tariff and immigration, two issues which vitally affected the interests of the trade-union movement. But perhaps most curious was the fact that the party did not take a stand on the Spanish-American war and the "paramount issue" of imperialism which was to loom so large in Bryan's campaign of 1900. Senator Albert Beveridge had proclaimed his doctrine of "Manifest Destiny." "The question is elemental," he cried out. "It is racial. God has not been preparing the English-speaking and Teutonic peoples for a thousand years for nothing but self-administration. No! He has made us the master organizers of the world. He has made us adepts in government that we may administer government among savage and senile people. And of all our race He has

[71] *Social Democracy Red Book*, pp. 132, 133.

266

marked the American people as His chosen Nation to finally lead in the regeneration of the world."

However, the Socialists would not take up this challenge. Debs wrote in 1900: "The campaign this year will be unusually spectacular. The Republican party 'points with pride' to the 'prosperity' of the country, the beneficent results of the 'gold standard' and the 'war record' of the administration. The Democratic Party declares that 'imperialism' is the 'paramount' issue and that the country is certain to go to the 'demnition bow-wows' if Democratic officeholders are not elected instead of the Republicans. The Democratic slogan is 'The Republic vs. the Empire' accompanied in a very minor key by 16 to 1 and 'direct legislation where practical.' . . ." And then he wrote, as mentioned earlier herein, "What but meaningless phrases are 'imperialism,' 'expansionism,' 'free silver,' 'gold standard,' etc., to the wage worker? The large capitalists represented by Mr. McKinley and the small capitalists represented by Mr. Bryan are interested in these 'issues,' but they do not concern the working class."[72]

But were these actually "meaningless phrases" and side issues?

VI.   The Golden Age of American Socialism

Every society and every social movement has its "golden age"—its period of muscularity and vigor—where the sense of growth is sure, the surge to power seemingly irresistible, and the crest of victory the only point in the line of vision. The years from 1902 to 1912 were the "golden age" of American socialism. In that shiny decade the voice of socialism was being heard in the land. The dabbler in cold statistical facts may find this picture puzzling. At its peak, the socialist vote never reached the heights of the Greenbackers and populists. The latter even elected a large number of congressmen and some governors, while the socialists were never able to elect more than two representatives. Yet the name of Debs is historically secure in American life, while few know the name of James B. Weaver, who as a Populist candidate in 1892 received over a million votes, a total higher than any ever achieved by Debs. The salient fact was that socialism was seen as a danger to the system in a way that populism never could be. Bryan, a moralist, never challenged the fundamental intellectual creeds of capitalism. Nor did Henry George, whose single-tax scheme was perhaps the boldest attempt to reinstate an individualist America. Neither of them threatened the power position of the rising industrial capitalist, nor could the single tax or the utopian colonization schemes ever challenge the economic power of the market system. Bryan and George, when they were radical, attacked particular *groups* of privileged men; socialism threw down the gauntlet to the system of power itself.

[72] "Outlook for Socialism in the United States," *International Socialist Review*, 1900; reprinted in *Writings and Speeches of Eugene V. Debs*, p. 37.

However, for fully half a century socialism as an intellectual system had sought to gain converts in America. Yet it was only at the turn of the century that it gained force and strength. It did so for a variety of reasons: the inheritance of the populist remnants; the existence of a stable labor movement, and above all the emergence of a rising social class whose members felt themselves outside the pecuniary values of business and who found in socialism a justification of their own social position and values. This was the intelligentsia.

In his day Herman Melville saw in a melancholy way that the individual man was trapped. But the sense of evil he felt was some vague diffuse force which enveloped the spirit. At the turn of the century, the villain was tangible and real—the industrial capitalist. He became the target of all whose values were being trampled. The Jeffersonians awoke to find that the country was no longer agrarian, that private property was now monopoly, and that freedom of contract was largely a means of achieving giant combinations, which, like an octopus, reached into every nook of economic life. These men, Brandeis, Weyl, Croly, Wilson, raised anew the cry of "bigness." Others, like Henry and Brooks Adams, who had sought to achieve a sense of tradition in American life, were outraged that money alone was becoming the basis of power and status, and wept in anger at the rising plutocracy. The self-conscious emergence of a gaudy "style" of upper-class living lent bite to the mordant satire of a Veblen. At the same time, the naked self-interest displayed by the industrial capitalists gave weight to the economic interpretations of American politics being written by Charles Beard, Gustavus Myers, and J. Allen Smith. The muckrakers were finding a richly fallow field in exposing the machinations of the corporations and the corruption of the cities.

The sense of an American past was emerging in consciousness, not in the triumphant way of justifying a manifest destiny, but in the angry response of a man whose inheritance was being squandered by others. The "wine of the Puritans" had gone sour, and the rationale of god-fearing piety had become the justification of the god-posturing exploiters. At a time when "Protestant ethic" was crumbling in the area of manners and morals, it was reaching its peak in the compulsive Methodist fervor of an acquisitive Daniel Drew. The period was marked by such an explosive burst of anger and criticism as to produce perhaps the most concentrated flowering of criticism in the history of American ideas. A whole new literary generation was to mock at its pretensions and exhaust itself in aesthetic revolt.

In this fervid onslaught against American capitalism, sympathy with socialism and its aims was easy and natural. The tremendous industrial expansion had produced a new race of wealthy, and the chasm between rich and poor was deep and visible, and growing wider. It was no accident that many of the early intellectual converts to socialism were ministers and charity workers who came into contact with the poor. The ethic of Protestant individualism charged these "failures" with being responsible for their own defeats, and denied them help on the self-righteous Malthusian grounds that such charity would sap their moral fibre; to the socialists, however, these people were victims of "the system," and the system would have to be changed.

The awareness of class sharpened the *historical* sense. A class had emerged, but, as with all life, it would also pass. The theory of evolution held marked sway at this time and contributed to the impact of socialist ideas. Followers of Spencer, or Comte, or Ward might dispute as to where society was heading. But the appeal of the socialists was simple: society was heading in a rational direction because men in the nature of their social evolution were becoming more rational, were mastering nature and harnessing it to men's purposes; they would also, in the course of events, harness society and turn it to the common good rather than to the profit of a few.

Although the socialism of the early twentieth century was "scientific," people were rarely attracted to it merely by the cold, rational analysis of society. What gave socialism its impact was the moral indignation at poverty and the evangelical promise of a better world. Therefore, in the pantheon of socialist messiahs, a forward place in the American contingent must be reserved for Edward Bellamy. For it was the "indigenous, homespun made-in-Chicopee-Falls" vision of that religiously-minded New England journalist rather than the Marxian dogmatics of organized socialism which introduced the idea of socialism to millions. Bellamy's *Looking Backward*, published in 1888, preached a simple message in an engaging, lullaby style. Julian West, a young Bostonian, is mesmerized and awakens in the year 2000. Here he finds the rational life. For twenty-five years each individual is called on to serve in the "industrial army." "All persons choose their occupations in the army of industry according to natural tastes and gifts. . . . In order to equalize the attractiveness of different occupations, the hours of work in those which are more laborious or otherwise unattractive are shortened as compared with the easier and more attractive trades . . . all alike, whether men or women, strong or weak, able-bodied or defective, share in the wealth produced by the industrial army and the share of all is equal." Acquisitiveness and aggression would vanish when men had enough for all. "Soon was fully revealed what the divines and philosophers of the old world never would have believed, that human nature in its essential qualities is good, not bad, that men by their natural intention and structure are generous, not selfish." The new society was instituted not by a moral new birth of humanity but by the

269

"reaction of a changed environment upon human nature." As Bellamy naively pictured this soft regimentation—no one questioned the image of an "army" as an ideal—no decent individual could object to these simple and obvious truths.

Bellamy's book was not unique in that time. In 1884 Laurence Gronlund's *The Co-operative Commonwealth* had outlined a society based on cooperation rather than competition which would be reached by the gradual extension of state activity. And in the decade following the publication of Bellamy's book, variants on its utopian pattern were supplied by no less than nineteen other novels, the most famous of which was William Dean Howells' *Traveler from Altruria*, published in 1894.

Bellamy's new version of utopia was a staggering success. In a few years the novel sold more than 600,000 copies. The political credo of the book, the nationalization of industry, spurred the organization of a new political movement, the Nationalist clubs. By 1891 some 162 had been organized in order to spread the "principle of association," i.e., the substitution of cooperation for competition. The movement attracted almost all the socialist-minded men of the period and became in effect a way station on the road to socialism. Daniel De Leon was a Nationalist for a short period before arriving at the hardier and tougher logical doctrines of Marxism. The organized labor movement of the period was friendly and Nationalism received the endorsement of both T. V. Powderly, head of the Knights of Labor, and Samuel Gompers. P. J. McGuire, the secretary of the American Federation of Labor, formed a Nationalist club in Philadelphia. Eugene Debs, whose political views had been strongly affected by Gronlund's *The Co-operative Commonwealth*, was an enthusiastic reader of Bellamy, and in a lengthy review of Bellamy's book concluded: "Labor is organizing for such work, and those who relish good reading should read *Looking Backward*."[73] J. A. Wayland, whose famous *Appeal to Reason* was to become the most fabulous publishing venture in socialist journalism, in 1893 founded the *Coming Nation*, which fought "for a government of, by and for the people as outlined in Bellamy's *Looking Backward*."

However, it was perhaps among the clergy that the ideas of Bellamy had the most direct influence. In 1889, the famous economist and Christian socialist Richard T. Ely wrote: "We have in this country the American type of socialism, the New Nationalism. . . ."[74] A later historian of Christian socialism, James Dombrowski, wrote: "The [Nationalist] movement quickened the social consciences of multitudes within and without the Church. It gave an impetus to the cooperative movement and provided

[73] Cited in Ginger, *op.cit.*, p. 72.
[74] Richard T. Ely, *Social Aspects of Christianity* (New York, 1889), p. 143; cited in Dombrowski, *op.cit.*, p. 93.

the inspiration for the founding of many cooperative colonies. It was an important factor in the founding of the first Christian Socialist group in the United States."[75] In Boston, the Rev. W. D. P. Bliss, one of the leaders of Christian socialism, organized an American Fabian Society in 1895 and began the publication of the *American Fabian*, whose contributors included Edward Bellamy and Henry Demarest Lloyd, to spread the ideas of Christian socialism. Closer at hand, the socialists themselves acknowledged the strong influence of Bellamy. In the *Social Democracy Red Book* of January 1900, the handbook of the Debsian Social Democratic Party of America, Frederic Heath, tracing the history of socialist thought in America, wrote: "The American awakening to Socialism began with the appearance of Edward Bellamy's *Looking Backward* in 1888."

If Bellamy and other utopian messiahs had proclaimed the vision of the new society, it was the muckrakers who exposed the corruption of the old. Though the influence of these exposés may not have been so great as the extravagant claims of John Chamberlain ("Muckraking, indeed, provided the basis for the entire movement toward Social Democracy that came to its head in the first Wilson administration. . . ."), these exposés did provide a set of tangible and simplified symbols, large identifiable targets for those who had suffered reverses, lost their jobs, or had in some way been crushed by the ruthless competition for reward. In short, muckraking supplied a devil theory of history for those who could not master the complicated algebra of political economy.

The badge "muckrakers" was pinned on the magazine writers by Theodore Roosevelt.[76] Roosevelt used the term in opprobrium, but its import was deeper than he realized. Although the later sensationalism and flamboyance of the exposés, especially those by Hearst, eventually brought muckraking into disrepute, the impulse to muckraking in the writings of Henry Demarest Lloyd grew out of a deep religious quest to rake up and cast out the corruption which prevented man from donning the "celestial crown." Lloyd, a famous magazine editor and writer of his day, wrote *Wealth against Commonwealth*, published in 1894, the first comprehensive examination of a great trust in action. The son of an orthodox Calvinist minister, he was deeply interested in "social Christianity" throughout his life. During the 1890's Lloyd became interested in cooperative colonies as an ethical solution to capitalist immorality; their failures convinced him that the good society could not be achieved piecemeal. In his last years he regarded himself as a socialist and was, when he died in 1903,

[75] Dombrowski, *op.cit.*, pp. 94-95.
[76] From a passage in Bunyan's *Pilgrim's Progress*: "The man with the Muck-Rake, the man who could look no way but downward with the muck-rake in his hand; who was offered a celestial crown for his muck-rake but who would neither look up nor regard the crown he was offered but continued to rake to himself the filth of the floor."

271

on the verge of openly identifying himself as such. In his last notebook he wrote, "Christianity is the religion that was, socialism is the religion that is to be."

Wealth against Commonwealth consists largely of a "transcript of the record" taken from legislative proceedings and flavored with such tart epigrams as "Standard [Oil] has done everything with the Pennsylvania Legislature except to refine it." While the book had a solid impact on sections of the clergy and other groups interested in social reform, it never reached a mass audience. However, a technological revolution in the art of printing—the use of glazed paper from woodpulp rather than rag, and the invention of the photoengraving process—was making possible the cheap magazine and a mass audience. And a mass audience needs excitement. The formula was supplied by S. S. McClure, who found in business practices and municipal corruption the raw meat of scandal. In a few years *McClure's* had published Ida Tarbell's *History of Standard Oil*, Lincoln Steffens' series on the shame of the cities, and later, on the shame of the states. Burton J. Hendrick exposed the life-insurance companies, and other writers related the existence of prostitution and other vices to the needs of "the system." Other magazines followed the scent. Almost no industry in American life was exempt from scrutiny. In 1905 Thomas Lawson wrote his lurid stories of stock-market manipulation in *Frenzied Finance*, Charles Edward Russell pointed to the existence of a monopolistic beef trust, Ray Stannard Baker put "the railroads on trial," leading to remedial legislation in the Hepburn Act of 1906. Perhaps the largest explosion was made by Upton Sinclair's *The Jungle*. Although written as fiction, the sickening details regarding the sale of putrid and decayed meat galvanized public opinion. But Sinclair's novel went beyond the usual peeking under stones. His hero, Jurgis, exploited by the meat-packers, fleeced by unscrupulous real-estate interests, and cast out as a hobo, finds, in a modern Pilgrim's Progress, his redemption in socialism.

In a few years the muckrakers faced the same problem, because a mirror had been held up to American society and it showed a picture of Dorian Gray. The problem was: What was to be done? Many of the muckrakers themselves as well as thousands of others came to feel that the socialists possessed the answers to this question. Upton Sinclair was a socialist even when he started. Charles Edward Russell joined the Socialist Party and became one of its leaders. Steffens, more romantic and attracted to strong power figures, became interested in Christian socialism; later, attracted by the romance and power of the Russian Revolution, he became a Bolshevik sympathizer. As a muckraker, Steffens had talked of "the system," but the socialists showed him that "the system" encompassed all of society.

In general, it can be said that four factors go far to explain the rising tide of socialism in the United States at the time we are considering. One was the absorption of populist strength, especially in the West. Most of the populist elements had been folded into the Democratic Party when Bryan became its candidate in 1896, but large unassimilable blocs found their way in and later out of the Socialist Party, a fact which goes far to explain the uneven striations of the socialist vote in the decade. A second factor was the spread of factory work and the rising demand for social legislation to guard against the attendant hazards. This issue was of great appeal to socially minded and reform elements among the middle class and especially among women. Third, was the growth of socialism in Europe, particularly in Germany, the great model in those days of culture and education. This particularly influenced intellectual opinion for it seemed to confirm the Marxist prediction of the inevitable world rise of the working class. And fourth was the newly articulated American idiom in which the socialist movement spoke, at least publicly, although inner-party debates were still conducted in the private patois of socialist dialectic.

In addition to these general reasons, a structural factor played a significant role in party growth—the loose organizational and ideological make-up of the Socialist Party, which permitted the party to be different things to different men. The iron hand of De Leon had left a deep mark. Out of a deep fear of centralized control, the new Socialist Party was so organized that the individual state organizations maintained complete control of party affairs, subject only to the national constitution. And, to avoid any one paper becoming a dominant voice, the party refused until 1914 to designate an official party press which would speak authoritatively on immediate issues of the day. The same looseness prevailed on doctrine. "The international socialist program is broad enough for the widest variety of opinion as to detail, and as to the working out of principle," wrote the Reverend George D. Herron, one of the leading figures of the party, in 1900.[77] Thus agnostic and Christian, Bohemian and Puritan, could and did join the party and seek to mold it in their image. These discordant elements could only be held together by the sure promise of victory. And without victory the loosely-tied party structure would collapse.

The Socialist Party was born in a "bloomin', buzzin', confusion." In early February 1900, the dissident members of the Socialist Labor Party led by Morris Hillquit assembled in a first national convention in Rochester and tentatively nominated Job Harriman, a California lawyer, for president, and Max S. Hayes, a Cleveland printer and editor, for vice-president.

[77] George D. Herron, "A Plea for the Unity of American Socialists," *International Socialist Review*, Dec. 1900; cited in Dorfman, *op.cit.*, III, p. 236.

Actually, the Hillquit group wanted a united ticket with the Social Democratic Party. The Social Democratic leaders were hesitant, but finally a joint ticket of Debs and Harriman was named. One disputed point, the name of the combined party, remained to be settled; otherwise everything was harmonious, or so it seemed. But soon, the "buzzin'" began. In reality, each side was still too touchy and suspicious of the other's motives. At one point, the Social Democrats accused the "Kangaroos" on the provisional national committee of violating the interim agreement on the use of name. Other charges were hurled. Actually, the real fear of the Social Democrats, smarting before the fancied contempt of the didactic S.L.P.ers who would quote Marx at the drop of a resolution, was that they would lose control of the organization. Debs wrote: "For years the official organ of the Socialist Labor Party had drilled it into their members that the Social Democratic Party consisted of a lot of freaks, frauds and fakers without a redeeming feature. . . . Hundreds of them, members of the anti-De Leon party, and I speak advisedly, still rankle with that feeling. . . ."[78] The attacks became mean and personal, and almost no one, with the exception of Debs, escaped the free-flowing invective. The confusion started blooming when the Hillquit faction, meeting with a dissident (anti-Debs) section of the Social Democrats, publicly announced that unity had been achieved, took over the name Social Democratic Party, and opened an office in Springfield, Massachusetts. Throughout the 1900 campaign there was thus one ticket, but two parties.

As public interest stirred in Debs's campaign, the rivalry began to die down. Jubilation grew when Debs received nearly 97,000 votes against 34,000 for the De Leon S.L.P. ticket. Both sides now expressed a willingness to work together, and another unity convention was called at Indianapolis. But factional lines developed at this convention before the party could be fully stabilized.[79] The new divisive issue was the old problem of "immediate demands." One faction, led by A. M. Simons of Chicago, dubbed the "impossibilists" (as against the "opportunists"), argued against the inclusion of such planks in the platform because no immediate relief was possible for the working class under capitalism. Since the social revolution was only a few years away, attention to these problems would only "sidetrack" the socialist movement. The impossibilists were defeated 82 to 30 (representing a party membership of 5,358 to 1,325), but the issue was renewed at subsequent national conventions.[80] On the second issue—a resolution on farmers—the factional lines crossed in weird fashion. In the debate, a number of so-called "opportunists," including James Carey and Job Harriman, argued for a rigid class stand against the "mid-

[78] Cited in Fine, *op.cit.*, pp. 199-200.
[79] John M. Work, "The Birth of the Socialist Party," (Socialist) *Call*, March 5, 1948.
[80] Fine, *op.cit.*, pp. 204-9.

dle-class" farmer, while Simons, the impossibilist, joined Hillquit in calling for an appeal to the farmer. Finally, because farmers were not considered as members of the working class, the delegates voted to drop all reference to meliorative demands for them from the platform and to refer the problem for study to the next convention. Eugene Debs, as was to become his habit, was absent from the convention.

Debates such as these must have been bewildering to the party novitiate. And for the historian they involved schismatic niceties in relating internal party problems to the general scene. Certainly from 1901 to 1919 the public and private doctrines of American socialism often seemed to bear little relation to each other. Publicly, the socialist message was simple and compelling: economic crises were endemic in the system because the worker was not paid the full return of his labor and the capitalist could not find markets for his goods or investment; the centralization of industry, occasioned by the need to control markets, was insistently eliminating the small entrepreneur and the middle class; the growth of trusts presaged the necessary next stage in social evolution, socialism. Internally, however, the new recruit would find himself in a morass of competing factions, each talking a special jargon, each claiming to point to the correct road to socialism. He would be assaulted by "impossibilists" who told him that a fight on taxes as a political issue was meaningless because the workers did not pay taxes.[81] He would find himself involved in detailed arguments concerning industrial versus craft unionism. And, as is typical in sectarian milieus, he would be regaled with detailed bits of gossip and innuendo about the various party leaders.

Since a party's ability to meet the various challenges of the political environment depends on its internal cohesion, the flexibility of its leadership, and the responsiveness of a mature rank and file, the tortuous internal history of the Socialist Party is worth studying in some detail.

The trade-union issue was the main axis around which the major factional groupings in the Socialist Party revolved. There was the "right wing" which sought to work within the American Federation of Labor because the bulk of organized labor was in the Federation. But the right-wingers were constantly getting caught in the cross fire from Gompers on the one side, who accused them of seeking to capture the Federation for socialism, and from Debs and the left-wingers on the other, who accused them of kowtowing to the reactionary labor leaders. The left wing itself had no consistent and unifying viewpoint. It was a

[81] This was a favorite intellectual tartar of the Socialist Labor Party. Through a complicated analysis of surplus value (i.e., the extra profit gained by the capitalists), De Leon always "proved" that the practical effect of fighting taxes would only "champion the interests of the little cockroach businessman." Why worry then about taxes? the S.L.P.ers would taunt.

varying mélange, made up in part of those who were against *all* immediate reforms, of those who were for syndicalism but against political action, and of those who favored industrial unions and militant tactics instead of the "class collaborationist" policies of the American Federation of Labor. The dilemma of the leftist wing, however, was that the militant unions it created either fell apart because it didn't know how to settle down, or became "conservative" when it did. These contradictions were reflected sharply in Debs. Of a romantic nature, he would promptly fly to any strike situation that needed his impassioned prompting to sustain its willingness and morale. Yet Debs could never accept the routine and plodding course of a day-to-day trade-union situation.

One of the earliest and important fights centered about the formation of the American Labor Union. For many years, the unions in the West, particularly the strong Western Federation of Miners, had felt that they were being ignored by the American Federation of Labor. In 1898 these groups banded together and formed the Western Labor Union, which would function west of the Mississippi River. In 1901, under the prompting of Debs, the organization changed its name in order to span the continent. Against the charge of dual unionism, Debs stingingly declared: "When the American Federation of Labor . . . relegates leaders to the rear who secure fat offices for themselves in reward for keeping the rank-and-file in political ignorance and industrial slavery, when it shall cease to rely upon cringing lobbying committees, it shall have the right to object."[82] The American Labor Union endorsed socialism. "On the practical side, however," write Perlman and Taft, "it was like any other American union. The right to strike was strictly circumscribed and controlled by central authority. Likewise, its socialism notwithstanding, the temper of the West showed itself in the advocacy of Oriental exclusion as a measure of wage protection."[83] Two years after its start, the American Labor Union began to wobble; and it finally was submerged in the Industrial Workers of the World.

Within the American Federation of Labor, meanwhile, the socialists had demonstrated some continued following. At its 1902 convention a resolution urging "the working people to organize their economic and political power to secure for labor the full product of its toil and the overthrow of the wage system and the establishment of an industrial cooperative commonwealth" was defeated by 4,897 to 4,171. The socialists, however, obtained the support of the miners, carpenters, and brewery workers, and if, as the miners had urged, the resolution had ended with the word "toil," the motion probably would have passed.[84]

[82] McAlister Coleman, *Eugene V. Debs* (New York, 1930), p. 219.

[83] Selig Perlman and Philip Taft, *History of Labor in the United States, 1896-1932* (New York, 1935), IV, p. 217.

[84] J. W. Sullivan, *Socialism as an Incubus on the American Labor Movement* (New York, 1909), pp. 18-19.

This promising show of strength in the A.F.L. on the one hand, and the formation of the American Labor Union on the other, sharpened the factionalism within the Socialist Party. The resident "action committee" of the party issued a statement attacking the founders of the American Labor Union as "compromising" the party. In reply, Debs charged that certain socialist politicians "were perhaps advised that it was wiser policy to curry favor with numbers than to stand by principles."[85] The battle was carried to the executive committee, where Debs and Berger engaged in acrimonious exchanges. Debs won this first skirmish, and the national secretary of the party who had issued the statement was replaced.

The feuding carried over into the Socialist Party national convention of 1904, the first since the unity convention of 1901. In the intervening years, party membership had grown steadily, and more than 20,000 were now enrolled. This was the first convention in which major policy decisions could be assessed in the light of practical experience as a political party. But no such assessments were made. The one thing the convention did show was that factionalism and sectarian spirit had permeated so deep that some split was inevitable in the future.

At the convention the "impossibilists," concentrated in Chicago, fought against the adoption of a state or municipal program by the party. "We have [in Chicago]," said delegate Stedman, "a question of municipal transportation, and there [are] members of this party in that city who [take] the position that they would vote in favor of granting franchises to the corporations until we controlled the entire country. . . . Some members are in favor of nothing until we have recognized Socialism which would come in by a grand cataclysm."[86]

But it was the trade-union issue which produced the sharpest strain. A resolution introduced by a Wyoming delegate called for support of industrial unions and denounced the leaders of the A.F.L. for working with the businessmen in the National Civic Federation. The resolution also had the support of a dozen or so delegates, largely from the agricultural states of the West, although, or perhaps because, they opposed unions altogether. One delegate, Irene Smith of Oregon, declared in strident fashion: "The Trades Unionist is leaning upon his little crutch and until that crutch is broken entirely under him, he will have to lean upon it, whether we preach Socialism or not. . . . the moment that the Socialist Party of the United States steps out upon a clear class-conscious platform of its own and frees its skirts from all these petty movements, then we will begin to move forward and grow."[87] The majority itself had no unified view on industrial unionism, but felt that such a flat statement would amount to interference in internal union affairs. That issue, "inter-

[85] Ginger, op.cit., p. 220.   [86] Proceedings, 1904, p. 23.
[87] Ibid., pp. 178-79.

vention," was to recur constantly in socialist debates. The minority lost 52 to 107. However, as a concession to the left wing the immediate demands of the party were condensed into a single paragraph and buried in the platform. Since the Socialist Party was not a disciplined movement, the Chicago organization, dominated by the "impossibilists," was able to repudiate the national platform and conduct its own type of campaign.

Debs was again nominated in 1904, together with Ben Hanford, an ardent New York printer who created the character of "Jimmie Higgins."[88] The growth of trusts was the main campaign issue in 1904. In previous years, capitalism had been attacked for the evils of competition; now the attack had shifted to the evils of monopoly. Debs toured the country from Maine to Oregon, drawing huge crowds wherever he went, and calling up an impressive 409,230 votes, a figure which quadrupled the previous presidential total of 96,931.

Notable as the gain was, it failed to unite the party. In fact the rift between the proponents of revolutionary unionism and the supporters of the American Federation of Labor grew deeper. The rupture deepened still further when in December 1904 Debs and five others sent a secret letter to thirty radical leaders over the country inviting them to meet in Chicago in January 1905 "to discuss ways and means of uniting the working people of America on correct revolutionary principles."[89] The conference in turn called a convention out of which arose the Industrial Workers of the World.

Like a meeting of *Meistersingers*, almost every major radical voice in America was represented at the founding convention of the I.W.W. in June 1905. Present were Debs, De Leon, Lucy Parsons, the widow of the famed anarchist Haymarket martyr, and syndicalist Big Bill Haywood. However, except for the Western Federation of Miners with its 27,000 members, no major established unions were represented. The first year's results were disappointing. No unions seceded from the American Federation of Labor and even the few within the I.W.W. were dubious of its effectiveness. The socialist press, including the *Social Democratic Herald* of Victor Berger, the Cleveland *Citizen* of Max Hayes, and the *Jewish Daily Forward* in New York, all attacked the I.W.W. When Debs took steps toward a rapprochement with De Leon, his column in the Milwaukee socialist paper was dropped.

In the midst of this fierce intramural quarreling, the Moyer-Haywood-Pettibone case broke with the sharpness of a thunderclap, and during the

[88] "Jimmie Higgins," a mythical rank-and-file member, was the "common man" of the party, the unsung hero who, through rain, snow, and sleet trudged from house to house selling party newspapers, passed out leaflets on the street corner, set up the soap-box, and performed the other laborious and menial jobs of party work uncomplainingly.

[89] Ginger, *op.cit.*, p. 237.

subsequent excitement all labor factions momentarily forgot their own concerns. Governor Frank Steunenberg of Idaho, who had been elected as a populist but had turned against the miners and small farmers during the Coeur d'Alene riots of 1899, was assassinated by a bomb on December 30, 1905. On the sworn confession of a suspect, Charles H. Moyer and Big Bill Haywood, heads of the Western Federation of Miners, and George Pettibone, a Denver businessman, were charged with plotting the murder. Although the three lived in Colorado, they were whisked across the state line without extradition hearings. The kidnapping roused the entire labor and socialist movement. Samuel Gompers at the A.F.L. convention denounced the act. Debs, with flaming passion, began a nation-wide campaign to arouse support of the three. The case made Bill Haywood a national figure.

In the midst of the Moyer-Haywood-Pettibone agitation, the I.W.W. opened its second convention. In this there arose the first split. The question was on the technique of unionism. The "conservatives," dominated by the Western Federation of Miners, wanted to build stable industrial unions. The opposition, led by Daniel De Leon, Vincent St. John, and William Trautmann, called for "revolutionary activity."

"It is true," writes Paul Brissenden, "that principles and policies were involved in the feud of 1906, but they lurked obscurely in the background, while personal antagonisms—charges and counter-charges of graft, corruption and malfeasance in office—held the center of the stage. From the inception of the movement the year before a smoldering dissension developed between the poorer and less skilled groups of workers—largely migratory and casual laborers, the 'revolutionists' or the 'wage-slave delegates' as they were called in the second convention . . . and the more highly skilled and strongly organized groups called (by the other side) the 'reactionaries' or the 'political fakirs.' It might be remarked in passing that, in this ultra-revolutionary I.W.W., the 'conservatism' of the 'reactionaries' ought to be heavily discounted and the radicalism of the 'revolutionists' raised to the *nth* degree to get the true perspective. Involved with this group hostility was the trouble stirred up by various members of the two Socialist political parties."[90]

The Western Federation of Miners, without Haywood, withdrew from the I.W.W. and began slowly to set up orderly collective-bargaining contracts. "Furthermore," as Perlman and Taft point out, "the leaders had become aware that the whole social topography of the arena of their activity was undergoing a radical transformation. . . . Into this altered environment, with a 'public' of farmers and urban middle classes, Winchester rifles and dynamite no longer fitted. Their own best fighting days

[90] Paul Brissenden, *The I.W.W.: a Study of American Syndicalism* (New York, 1919), p. 136.

over with advancing middle age, the leaders, although still nominally socialists, were moving toward a conception of the role of their organization not far apart from the American Federation of Labor. . . ."[91] In 1909, the Western Federation of Miners, under Moyer's leadership, moved to rejoin the A.F.L.

Members of the Socialist Party were less prominent at the I.W.W.'s second convention. Neither Debs nor A. M. Simons, the leaders of the left wing, attended. So the dominant role was played by De Leon, and his attitude alienated those socialists who were present. But more than De Leon's attitude, the growing syndicalist antipolitical view of the organization gave the socialists pause.

After 1906, and still more after 1908, the I.W.W. became an organization of the unskilled, and conspicuously of the migratory and frequently jobless unskilled. This transformation of the I.W.W. became complete in 1908, when De Leon himself was eliminated. De Leon wanted to fight capitalism on the "civilized plane" of political action. He charged the opposition—"slum proletarians" he called them—with "veiled dynamitism." The "Overall Brigade" ousted De Leon by the simple act of denying the validity of his credentials, a stunning blow to a man who prided himself on his organizational astuteness. De Leon then formed his own group, also using the name I.W.W. (or the Detroit faction), against the "beggars" (or Chicago faction).

The Chicago I.W.W. (i.e., the St. John and Haywood group, or the "Wobblies")[92] were unconditionally opposed to political action and favored direct action and sabotage. This anarcho-syndicalist viewpoint led to the complete break with the socialists. But although Debs himself resigned from the I.W.W., he could not bring himself to attack it: instead of issuing a public statement of disavowal, as in other instances of disagreement, he simply permitted his dues to lapse.[93]

The Socialist Party's 1908 convention opened in a spirit of optimism. In four years' time the party had doubled its membership.[94] The number of locals had grown to 2,500. Yet a basic cleavage still dominated the party. Although "impossibilist" overtones were still present, the differences had crystallized again on the union issue. The imminence of a presidential

[91] Perlman and Taft, op.cit., p. 253.
[92] The origin of the name "Wobblies" is shrouded. Brissenden says the I.W.W. was so christened by Harrison Grey Otis, the editor of the Los Angeles Times, although no reason for the peculiar nomenclature is given. Mencken, in his The American Language (4th ed., New York, 1949), pp. 190-91, ascribes the name to the garbled pronunciation of the initials I.W.W. by a Chinese cook in Seattle who, unable to say W, would say I, Wobble, Wobble. From that, the name was shortened to Wobblies.
[93] Ginger, op.cit., p. 256.
[94] 20,763 in 1904, and 41,751 in 1908. Data from American Labor Year Book (1916), p. 94.

campaign worked for unity. A resolution opposing immediate demands was snowed under, and the trade-union resolution counseled a "hands off" policy. In view of the I.W.W. stand, the socialists put the party squarely behind political action. On the farm issue, the convention continued, quixotically enough, an "impossibilist" position. The resolutions committee called for the collectivization of the agricultural trusts (i.e., farm machinery, beet sugar, oil, etc.), but said, "as for the ownership of the land by the small farmers, it is not essential to a Socialist program that any farmer shall be dispossessed of the land which he occupies and tills." However, the convention rejected this report. A variety of divergent opinions commingled in opposition. Some "right-wingers" for dogmatic Marxist reasons insisted that title to land be held in the nation; others insisted that farms, as well as industry, were being trustified so that an approach favoring small owners was false. The minority report, which stated, "we insist that any attempt to pledge to the farmer anything but a complete socialization of the industries of the nation to be unsocialistic," was passed 99 to 51.[95]

The platform finally adopted was interpreted in various ways. To Haywood, "the convention . . . adopted a platform that rang clear. The class struggle was its foundation. This was the most revolutionary period of the Socialist Party in America."[96] Actually the platform was a subtle compromise written with an eye to harmonizing the clearly defined factions. The statement of principles strongly emphasized the class struggle. But the specific demands strongly emphasized reform measures, and, unlike the 1904 platform, were not incorporated in the general text but stood out independently and could be propagated independently. Each side, therefore, was free to emphasize its own slants.

Debs was named the presidential candidate again in 1908. But now for the first time other names had been placed in opposition. No reasons were given publicly and the anti-Debs campaign was uncoordinated, but it was clear that a number of elements, particularly the strongly rightwing Wisconsin party, felt that Debs was too "left." His magnetic name, however, still swayed the convention and Debs was nominated overwhelmingly.

The Socialist Party entered the 1908 campaign fully confident of a swelling vote. In a magnificent propaganda gesture, national secretary J. Mahlon Barnes proposed that the party outfit a railroad car, to be called the "Red Special," which would tour the country and carry Debs to every corner of the land. The money was raised and the Red Special set off on its run. Debs himself carried the brunt of the campaign. Ill and subject to racking bodily pains from rheumatism and lumbago, he

[95] *Proceedings*, 1908, pp. 178-91.
[96] *Bill Haywood's Book* (New York, 1929), p. 230.

spoke from five to twenty times a day for sixty-five consecutive days. Everywhere he went great crowds jammed the meeting halls: in New York more than 10,000 persons jammed the old Hippodrome to hear him. A St. Louis paper predicted that Debs would poll more than a million and a half votes and that the 1912 election would be fought on the issue of capitalism versus socialism.[97]

When the votes were counted, the Socialist Party had 420,973—almost no increase in the four-year period. The most obvious explanation was the counterappeal of William Jennings Bryan, the Democratic candidate in 1908. In 1904, the Democrats had nominated a conservative lawyer, Alton B. Parker, and Debs had been the only outlet for a protest vote. Four years later the "Great Commoner," basing his campaign on his hoarse old battle cry of monopoly and privilege, had garnered the protesters.

The disappointing vote set the party back on its heels and started the various factions quarreling among themselves to determine who was responsible for the fall. Different reasons were adduced: lack of contact with workers, lack of militancy, domination by intellectual and middle-class elements, etc.

The fight broke out into the open when A. M. Simons, now a right-winger and editor of the *Chicago Daily Socialist*, privately raised the question of the advisability of a labor party "on the English model" to supplant the Socialist Party. The letter written to William English Walling and released by him raised a storm in the party. The most galling sections of Simons' letter were his disdainful opinions of the "left." "On the one side," he wrote, "are a bunch of intellectuals like myself, Spargo, Hunter and Hillquit; on the other side a bunch of never-works, demagogues and would-be intellectuals, a veritable 'Lumpen-Proletariat'. . . . The present executive committee is more than willing to surrender their positions if real workingmen are to take their places. They do not propose to surrender to those who have never worked save with their jaws and are tearing down every organization to which they belong."[98]

For months the socialist welkin rang with denunciations and denials of the labor-party proposition. To the left wing, a labor party, taking in diverse elements, meant a dilution of the socialist program and political compromise; to the right wing, it meant a bridge to large masses of trade unionists who were still not socialist. In the midst of the controversy, the *International Socialist Review*, a voice of the left wing, queried prominent members of the party asking: "If elected to the National Executive Committee will you favor or oppose merging the Socialist Party into a Labor Party?"

[97] Ginger, *op.cit.*, p. 283.
[98] Cited by Thomas J. Morgan, in *Who's Who and What's What in the Socialist Party*, No. 2 (January 1911).

Debs's answer to the question was immediate. He wrote: "The Socialist Party has already catered far too much to the American Federation of Labor and there is no doubt that a halt will have to be called. . . . If the trimmers had their way, we should degenerate into mere bourgeois reform."[99] Hillquit's reply was guarded. He pointed out that no labor party existed, but if ". . . independent of our desires and theories [the workers] should form . . . a *bona fide* and uncompromising working class political party . . . the logical thing for our party to do would be cooperate with such a party," although not merging, in order for the socialists to continue their propaganda work.[100]

Although the issue had threatened to disrupt the party, it soon subsided. No labor party was in sight, and the debate had been a convenient occasion for the left wing to blow off steam. But even among the right-wingers the idea did not meet full support. Many right-wingers, even Fabian-minded evolutionists, wanted a pure Socialist Party as their instrument in politics; for some the reasons were sentimental; for others doctrinaire ideological reasons were involved; for still others a stake in jobs or prestige.[101]

The issue, however, became quickly academic for a more substantial reason. By 1910, the socialist tide was surging in. In one year, from 1908 to 1909, the party membership had dropped slightly, but in 1910 the membership was up to 58,011 (from 41,479) and by 1912 had made a sensational jump to 125,826.[102] Electoral victories, too, began to multiply. In 1910 socialist mayors were elected in Milwaukee, and Schenectady, New York, and in the fall of that year Victor Berger was elected as the first socialist congressman. By May 1912, the national secretary reported a total of 1,039 socialists elected to office, including 56 mayors, 160 councilmen, and 145 aldermen.[103] The victories were largely in municipalities, and apparently an outcome of exposures of municipal corruption; only 18 state representatives and 2 state senators were in office. Nevertheless, the trend to reform via socialism was seen as a good omen. Also, the socialist press had grown mightily as well: by 1912, there were 8 foreign-language and 5 English dailies, including the New York *Call*, which had been

[99] *International Socialist Review*, Jan. 1910, p. 594; cited in Jessie Wallace Hughan, *American Socialism of the Present Day* (New York, 1911), pp. 233-34.

[100] Fine, *op.cit.*, p. 300.

[101] That the issue was not solely a left-right fight, as indicated by the *International Socialist Review*, is the fact that three right-wingers named to the national executive committee in 1910 (James Carey, George Goebel, and Lena Morrow Lewis) opposed a labor party.

[102] Report of the national secretary, *Proceedings*, 1912, p. 219.

[103] *Ibid.*, p. 220.

started in 1908; in addition there were 262 English and 36 foreign-language weeklies.[104]

In 1910 the whole country was going "progressive," and the "leftist" groups, including the socialist movement, were benefiting from the general trend. If the increasing vote was a product of a national swing to progressivism, equally relevant was the fact that the socialists were also tempering their dogmatism and widening their appeal. The socialist increase in great measure was probably due to the new appeal to the small middle class. The tone was set by Morris Hillquit. In 1910 he drew up a convention report entitled *The Propaganda of Socialism*, which is the first detailed assessment of past socialist propaganda tactics in the United States and an outline of future appeals. In this important document Hillquit said:

"Our principal efforts must be directed towards the propaganda of Socialism among the workers. But they should by no means be limited to that class alone. . . . the ultimate aims of the movement far transcend the interests of any one class in society, and its social ideal is so lofty that it may well attract large numbers of men and women from other classes . . . [the workers] are by no means the only class which has a direct economic motive for favoring a change of the existing order. The vast majority of the farming population of our country . . . is mortgaged to the money-lenders, exploited by the railroads and controlled by the stock jobbers. Vast masses of the small traders and manufacturers are beginning to realize the hopelessness of their struggle against large capital concentrated in the hands of modern industrial monopolies and trusts, and in the ranks of the professionals the struggle for existence is growing ever fiercer. . . . A movement like ours, which has set out to recast the entire modern social structure, cannot afford to banish the 'intellectuals' from its ranks. A Socialist movement consisting exclusively of 'Jimmie Higginses' would be as impotent as such a movement made up entirely or overwhelmingly of 'intellectuals' would be preposterous. . . . *Within very recent years a tendency has manifested itself in some sections of our movement to limit it entirely to wage-workers, and to reject the co-operation of all persons from other classes*, no matter how sincere they may be in their professions of Socialist faith and how valuable their services may be for the cause. This is not a rational application of the Marxian class-struggle doctrine, but an absurd caricature of it."[105]

Such an attitude was viewed by the left wing as a desertion of socialist principles. In the winter of 1911 Debs charged that the party held "not

[104] As against 3 English and 6 foreign-language dailies, and 29 English and 22 foreign-language weeklies in 1910.

[105] *Proceedings of the National Congress of the Socialist Party*, 1910, pp. 63-64. Italics added.

284

a few members who regard vote-getting as of supreme importance, no matter by what method the votes are secured, and this leads them to hold out inducements and make representations which are not at all compatible with the stern and uncompromising spirit of a revolutionary party."[106] But Debs never followed up these salvos. He refused even to be a delegate to the 1912 convention, where the issue would be put to a test.

The 1910 congress of the Socialist Party had in other ways moved slowly to meet contemporary problems. The two chief issues were immigration and the farm resolution. On both, the party had adopted moderate positions. Because the American Federation of Labor favored restriction of immigration, the party moved in a similar direction. A majority resolution, written by Berger, favored the "unconditional exclusion" of the yellow peoples, but the compromise, drafted by Hillquit, denounced exclusion on the basis of race yet favored legislative measures limiting immigration of "strike breakers and contract laborers." The party also reversed its previous demand calling for the socialization of land and adopted a statement which said: "Only to a very small extent is the land now, only to a very small extent is it likely to be for many years to come, a socially operated means of production. Even to declare in any dogmatic manner that all land must eventually become social property is somewhat utopian; to demand that the ownership of all land shall be immediately socialized is to make ourselves ridiculous."[107] The importance of the resolutions lay not only in the moderate and anti-utopian conclusions but in the fact that for the first time they had been based on careful reasearch rather than on a priori dogma.

The emphasis of the Socialist Party administration on being "practical," and the determination of the left wing to halt the drift to "reformism," drew the battle lines sharply for the 1912 convention. The year before, in a distinct gain for the left, Big Bill Haywood had been elected a member of the national executive committee. Other left strivings were visible. The I.W.W., for one, was becoming involved in nationally significant strikes culminating in the giant strike at Lawrence, Massachusetts, which shut down the town's textile industry drum tight. In the midst of this agitation the McNamara case broke. Two brothers, John and James McNamara, officials of the A.F.L. Structural Iron Workers, were arrested in early 1911 and charged with bombing the Los Angeles *Times* building on October 1, 1910, a bombing in which twenty persons were killed. Industrialists cited the case as proof of labor's belief in violence, but the entire labor movement rallied to the McNamaras' defense. Debs toured the country on their behalf. The national executive committee of the Socialist Party wired the Structural Iron Workers the support of "the entire power of its 4000 organizations, and its press consisting of ten

[106] Ginger, *op.cit.*, p. 307. [107] *Proceedings*, 1910, p. 219.

dailies, over a hundred weeklies and ten monthlies (in all languages) to be used in the defense of the McNamaras. . . ." The American Federation of Labor, too, voted support of the defendants.

For the Socialist Party the Los Angeles mayoralty was directly at stake. Job Harriman, the party's candidate, had been given a 50-50 chance of being elected. Five days before the election the McNamaras suddenly pleaded guilty, and with their confession the socialist chances plummeted. Unionists and socialists hastened to disavow earlier support of the two men. But the damage had been done.

Six months after the McNamara case the Socialist Party nominating convention opened. Tensions between the "reds" and the "yellows" ran high. Some effort would be made, it was felt, to curb the growing power of the left wing. The first incident of the convention was a caricature of a decade of party strife. A day before the convention opened, the Indianapolis socialists, the hosts, appointed one of their number to make an address of welcome clad in a pair of overalls. John Spargo, a leader of the right wing and author of many of the party's expositions of socialist doctrine, protested. He declared that the proposal was undignified and would give the capitalist press an opportunity to mock. The issue swelled in importance and became a major order of business of the socialist national executive committee. The local socialists contended that "the overalls were . . . a symbol of the fact that the Socialist Party represented the workingman. . . ." Spargo proposed that if the Indianapolis socialists persisted in their "insult," the members of the national executive committee show their displeasure by leaving the hall. For a time it looked as if the national executive committee would be rent in twain over the question of a fifty-nine cent pair of overalls. On a vote, the overalls won. The incident was the subject of much heated debate and dismal prophecies were voiced on the opening day that the event foreshadowed a split in the convention, but the welcoming speaker, in mild socialist compromise, appeared in "plain, ordinary bourgeois pants."[108]

The big question at the convention was the trade-union resolution. Everyone expected a heated conflict between a majority report endorsing the American Federation of Labor and the minority urging industrial unionism. To everyone's surprise the resolution which was brought to the floor took neither position. It stated that the party had "neither the right nor the desire" to interfere on questions of "form of organization," but it also called attention to the need for "organizing the unorganized, especially the immigrants and the unskilled laborers."[109] The resolution was a skillful bit of political compromise, for each side felt its own position

[108] "The National Socialist Convention of 1912," *International Socialist Review*, June 1912, p. 808. Berger wished it known that in the pinch he voted for overalls.
[109] *Proceedings*, 1912, p. 195.

carried, while only rhetorical concessions were made to the other side. A glow of optimism prevailed, and amid the moments of good feeling Big Bill Haywood arose and said: "To my mind this is the greatest step that has ever been taken by the Socialist party. . . . as Tom Hickey has shaken hands with Job Harriman for the first time in twenty years, I feel I can shake hands with every delegate in this convention and say that we are a united working class."[110]

For a day the convention went along in this glow. A platform which ringingly reaffirmed the class struggle ("Society is divided into warring groups and classes, based upon material interests. . . . All political parties are the expression of economic class interests.") was unanimously adopted. The platform also called for a set of "immediate demands," such as unemployment relief, minimum wage scales, graduated income tax, curbing of injunction, etc. But efforts by Victor Berger to force a stand on immediate *issues*, such as a plank calling for tariff reduction, evoked little response. The sentiment of the delegates was that the Socialist Party was not concerned with the tariff one way or the other, and the plank was overwhelmingly tossed out.

The storm which seemingly had passed broke unexpectedly the following day. The committee on the constitution was reporting and came to article II, section 6, which had created a furious debate four years before. At that time, the phrase "political action" had been vaguely defined. Now the section was tightened and its meaning made unmistakably clear. It read: "Any member of the party who opposes political action or advocates crime against the person or other methods of violence as a weapon of the working class to aid in its emancipation shall be expelled from the party. Political action shall be construed to mean participation in elections for public office and practical legislative and administrative work along the lines of the Socialist Party platform." On the motion of a delegate the more fateful word "sabotage" was inserted in the section instead of "crime against the person." The McNamara case had quickened the issue.

In the debate that followed, the right-wing leaders left no doubt that they had made up their minds to drive the "Wobbly" and reckless elements out of the party. National executive committeeman Goebel reported: "I find the movement in locality after locality disorganized, I find them fighting amongst themselves. . . . Because men have come into the Socialist party and . . . advocated . . . sabotage." Victor Berger chimed in: "In the past we often had to fight against Utopianism and fanaticism, now it is anarchism again that is eating away at the vitals of our party." The opposition retorted that the issue was between progressives and "another element that stands conservative, reactionary, monkeying with old out-

110 *Ibid.*, p. 100.

worn machinery."[111] The lines were at last cleanly drawn, and on a standing vote the section on sabotage was adopted by a vote of 191 to 90.

The convention action provoked a long and bitter dispute inside the party. Haywood, not Debs, was the target of the resolution. Haywood was outspoken and direct; Debs, evasive and vacillating. In the February 1912 issue of the *International Socialist Review*, two articles by Haywood and Debs became, in effect, a debate of the issue. Haywood wrote: *". . . no Socialist can be a law-abiding citizen. When we come together and are of a common mind, and the purpose of our minds is to overthrow the capitalist system, we become conspirators then against the United States government. . . . I again want to justify direct action and sabotage. . . . the trade unionist who becomes a party to a contract takes his organization out of the columns of fighting organizations; he removes it from the class struggle. . . ."* (Emphasis added and sentence order changed.)

Emotionally Debs agreed with Haywood. "If I had the force . . . I would use it . . . but I haven't got it, and so I am law-abiding under protest—not from scruple." But politically, Debs saw the futility of such an appeal, and turned against Haywood. The American workers, he said, are law-abiding, and "direct action will never appeal to any considerable number of them while they have the ballot and the right of industrial and political organization. . . . My chief objection to all these measures is that they do violence to the class psychology of the workers. . . ." Then Debs voiced his flat objection: ". . . I am opposed to sabotage and 'direct action.' I have not a bit of use for the 'propaganda of the deed.'[112] These are the tactics of anarchist individualists and not of Socialist collectivists."

Some of the right-wing leaders felt that Debs should not be the presidential nominee. However, they could not agree on a candidate. The New York group named Charles Edward Russell, the muckraker who had joined the party in 1908. However, the Wisconsin crowd, suspicious of "New York," named Emil Seidel, the mayor of Milwaukee. But the personal popularity of Debs was still high and he won the nomination with 165 votes to 56 votes for Seidel and 54 for Russell.

Debs made his usual colorful campaign crisscrossing the country in an emotional outpouring that stirred the hearts of people. Wilson and Teddy Roosevelt were running on "reform" platforms in 1912 and while their campaigns probably drew votes from the socialists, their frenetic activity also stirred greater interest in the campaign. Debs rolled up 897,000 votes in 1912, more than doubling the vote of the last campaign. This

[111] *Ibid.*, pp. 123, 128, 130.

[112] The phrase, *"die Tat,"* "the deed," was common as an anarchist tactic of rallying the working class behind some heroic action. This was the motive, for example, of Alexander Berkman in shooting H. C. Frick during the Homestead strike in 1893. See Emma Goldman, *Living My Life* (New York, 1931), I, p. 96.

vote, almost 6 per cent of the total, was the highest percentage of a presidential vote ever polled by the Socialist Party in the United States. The anomalous fact was that while the vote increased, the party membership declined during the campaign, and as a drive opened against the direct actionists it continued to fall. In February 1913 William D. Haywood was recalled from the national executive committee of the party on a national referendum vote. Within a year, from June 1912 to June 1913, the *Party Builder* reported a loss of more than 50,000 members.[113] Some writers, for example James Oneal in his *American Communism*, deny that the expulsion of the I.W.W. elements affected the party.[114] Such a view is untenable. There is little question but that the onslaught against the left wing hit the party hard, and the great losses in membership resulted, in large measure, from the defections of the left.

In 1912 Haywood and the I.W.W. were at the height of their popularity. More than twenty-eight I.W.W. strikes took place in which nearly 1,500 persons were arrested for strike activity. In addition, the Wobblies had perfected their mass-action "free speech" technique which had begun so successfully in Spokane in 1909.[115] Most important for Wobbly fame was the strike at Lawrence, Massachusetts, and the free-speech fight in San Diego, both in 1912, which "really introduced the Industrial Workers of the World to the American public. . . . [They] made the name of this little group of intransigeants a household word, hardly less talked about and no whit better understood than the words 'socialist' and 'anarchist.' . . . Lawrence was not an ordinary strike. It was a social revolution *in parvo*. . . . It stirred the country with the alarming slogans of a new kind of revolution. Socialism was respectable—even reactionary—by comparison."[116]

Those years, too, were the years of awakening for the rebel spirits. A new intellectual generation was tearing away the caudal vestiges of puritanism. Van Wyck Brooks' *America's Coming of Age* was a call to arms urging writers to rise above the debilitating materialism that grayed American life. The *Masses*, founded in 1911, became the calliope through

[113] Cited in Perlman and Taft, *op.cit.*, p. 286.

[114] "Following this decision [i.e., the antisabotage clause], a small group left the Socialist Party, but in the following November the party received the largest vote in its history. Its membership also increased. . . . This force tendency in the Socialist Party was checked in the convention of 1912 and it rapidly declined." James Oneal, *American Communism* (New York, 1927), pp. 27-28. Oneal, one of the leading Socialist Party publicists, was employed in the national office for many years and edited the *New Leader* from 1924 to 1940.

[115] When their orators were refused the right to speak from street corners and were arrested, the Wobblies flooded the town—and the jails—with more of their number, mostly lumberjacks, sailors, and other migratory workers, until the groaning city said "uncle": in the years 1911 to 1913 there were some fifteen free-speech fights.

[116] Brissenden, *op.cit.*, pp. 281, 282, 291.

which the young rebels whistled and hooted at the effete culture of the East and the gargoyle mansions of the new crude rich in the West. To these Greenwich Village free spirits, however, the Socialist Party under its right-wing leadership was too stodgy; insurgency could ride the wild wind more easily among the less disciplined doctrines of the left. Other intellectuals found sympathy with Haywood, too. This Polyphemus from the raw mining camps of the West had dedicated himself to the organization of the unskilled, the poverty-stricken and forgotten workers. And so he had become a hero. Haywood was defended by a group of New York intellectuals who now attacked the antisabotage clause. "We know Comrade Haywood to believe in political action," they wrote, "and to have been of great service to our party in helping it to solve the difficult problems that confront the working class upon the industrial field. Instead of exaggerating inevitable differences of opinion, instead of reviving De Leonistic tactics of personal incrimination, heresy-hunting, and disruption, we should make use of the special talents of every member within our ranks, and in this way secure loyal service and cooperation. We believe in a united working class." Among the signers were Walter Lippmann, Max Eastman, Margaret Sanger, Osmund K. Fraenkel, J. G. Phelps Stokes, William English Walling, Louis B. Boudin. Independently of this statement, Helen Keller made a deep emotional plea for unity.[117]

In May 1913 the revolutionary elements made a last effort, at the national committee meeting of the party, to repeal the antisabotage clause. They pointed out that in West Virginia, where fifty-two socialists had been imprisoned in a drive by the state against the Socialist Party, a number of socialists had captured guns and used them against the police. With the clause in the constitution, they said, the party would be unable to support the West Virginia socialists. The move was defeated, however, 43 to 16.[118] In later years Haywood voiced his bitter condemnation of the party's action. "Criminal Syndicalism laws have been upheld by the United States Court. . . . It is under such a law that the Communists were tried in Michigan. . . . The many who have been persecuted can thank the traitors of the Socialist Party who adopted Article 2, Section 6 against the working class."[119]

[117] *International Socialist Review*, Feb. 1913, pp. 606, 623.
[118] *Ibid.*, June 1913, pp. 878, 879.
[119] *Bill Haywood's Book*, p. 259. One caution should be noted: Haywood's autobiography was written in Moscow in 1927 and the charge has been made that the book was doctored. Benjamin Gitlow writes: "After Haywood died the manuscript was turned over to Alexander Trachtenberg, representative of the Comintern Publishing Department in the U.S., for final revision and publication. He changed and revised the book to conform to the Party Line and had the Party okay his revisions, and then had it published by International Publishers." See *The Whole of Their Lives* (New York, 1948), p. 51. Gitlow, an ex-communist, was a high official of the Communist Party at the time of the publication of the Haywood book.

Nineteen hundred and twelve was the high mark of socialist influence in the United States. It was the turning point as well. From that year, socialist strength and influence ebbed. After 1912, the party membership fell off rapidly and regained its earlier peak only in 1919 when membership rose to 108,000 from 81,000 in the previous year. But that new membership rise itself reflected the changed character of the Socialist Party and foreshadowed its role in the next decade. In 1912, when the party reached its zenith, it had an average of 118,000 dues payers of which 16,000, or about 13 per cent, were in the foreign-language federations. In 1918 about 25,000, or 30 per cent, were members of the foreign-language divisions. In 1919, when the membership again jumped, "practically the entire increase was furnished by recent arrivals from Russia and its Border States. The membership in the foreign-language federations rose to 57,000 or 53 per cent of the total, the bulk of it was represented by Russian, Ukrainian, South Slavic, Finnish, Lithuanian and Lettish organizations."[120]

The War and the defections of many party leaders merely completed, but were not themselves the cause of, the isolation of the socialist movement from American politics. The eclipse of American socialism took place in 1912; the rest of the years were a trailing penumbra.

We can adduce five major reasons for the decline of the Socialist Party after 1912.

1. The expulsion of the left wing, accounting for a large share of the 50,000 decline in membership from mid-1912 to mid-1913. This precipitous decline, however, obscures a salient fact: the Socialist Party always had a high turnover in membership; in usual course the falling away of old members was compensated by a new recruitment, resulting in net gains. In this respect, the loss of membership in 1912 had a dual meaning: the loss itself is attributable to the stand on sabotage, an internal party matter, but this time there was no compensating gain. For an explanation of this fact we have to turn to external factors, particularly the influence of Woodrow Wilson.

2. The use of the Socialist Party, in the period from 1910 to 1912, by old-line party politicians for electoral manipulations. This created in many cases a rising illusion of socialist strength. Thus, in the Mississippi election of 1911 the genteel wing of the Democratic Party, in order to defeat Theodore Bilbo, sought to elect a socialist lieutenant-governor and did in fact swing to the Socialist Party candidate a third of the vote. In the South particularly, remnants of the old populist groups sought to use the Socialist Party as a club against the Democrats or as a means of pressuring the Democrats for an acceptable candidate.[121]

[120] Morris Hillquit, *Loose Leaves from a Busy Life*, p. 290.
[121] Arthur W. Calhoun, "Can American Politics Be Socialized?" *Politics*, Feb. 1945, pp. 48-50.

3. The rigidity of rules imposed on socialist office-holders, which proved quite irksome for many. Once in power, socialist legislators and administrators faced the problems of compromises, concessions, deals, and other problems of the "practical" side of politics. As a result, many who wanted to "get things done" soon left the party. In Schenectady, for example, Socialist Mayor George R. Lunn, a minister, joined the Democratic Party after being defeated for reelection. In North Dakota, socialists evolved the technique of the Non-Partisan League in order to utilize the primary system and capture control of one of the major parties. Although the Non-Partisan Leaguers won control of the state in a sensationally short time, they were repudiated by the party.

4. The loss of support of the agrarian groups. The greatest degree of socialist strength, paradoxically, was always among the discontented farm elements. After 1912, the farm support of the socialists fell off. One reason was the newly gained protection from government which eased the farmers' plight. The Federal Reserve Act of 1913 expanded credit, permitted national banks to loan money on farm mortgages, and allowed six months for the rediscounting of agricultural paper against three months for commercial paper. More directly, the Federal Farm Loan Bank System, created in 1916, eased the seedtime-to-harvest credit problem. A second factor was the rising farm prosperity as a result of exports to Europe. Thus the value of wheat exports more than tripled from 1914 to 1917, rising from almost 88 to 298 million dollars, while the value of meat exports rose in similar proportion.[122]

5. Finally, of unquestioned but neglected weight was the influence of Woodrow Wilson. The presence in the White House of a man who was an intellectual had great appeal to individuals who had been socialists or were close to the party, men like Walter Lippmann and the group led by Herbert Croly which founded the *New Republic*. But Wilson's appeal was more than to the intellectuals and the echoes which their voices could magnify. The light of "The New Freedom" had an incandescence which seemed to many to shine with a clearer light than that of the socialists. In his speeches, Wilson denounced the growing centralized control of finance, the choking of opportunity by monopoly, "the control over the government exercised by Big Business," and the blight of municipal corruption.[123] Wilson himself pointed out that where many socialists had been elected it was not a socialist but a protest vote that put them in office. It was Wilson's achievement to draw off the protest vote before it jelled into a solid bloc of dissent. The solid body of social legislation which he enacted in his first term drew that reform vote tightly to himself.

[122] H. U. Faulkner, *American Economic History* (New York, 1937), pp. 461, 462, 694.
[123] Woodrow Wilson, *The New Freedom* (New York, 1933), pp. 3-32.

As a result of all this, after 1912 few socialists could believe in the "inevitability" of socialist triumph in the United States. In the years thereafter this failure of belief was to pose new problems for the existence of socialism as a *political* movement in the United States.

VII. The Inner World of American Socialism

One other factor in the decline of American socialism should also be discussed—the structural weakness of the Socialist Party itself as an instrument of propaganda, social change, or revolution. An environment provides, in Toynbee's sense, the *challenge* to a social movement; the character of the party and its leadership determine its ability to respond.

Within the American Socialist Party there was rarely any effort made to think through systematically, as Lenin had, the organization of the party and the relationship of the special character of membership to other roles in the labor movement or among the broad masses of society. Actually, the organizational structure of the Socialist Party was primarily a reflex to the type of discipline in the Socialist Labor Party. Like the founding fathers of the Continental Congress, the socialists sought in "states rights" a defense against oppression. The party constitution stated that each state ". . . shall have . . . sole control of all matters pertaining to the propaganda, organization and financial affairs within such state or territory."[124] In fact, this power was so vigorously exercised that in Wisconsin, for example, no lecturer could enter the state without the permission of the state committee, and on occasion Victor Berger, the state boss, went so far as to bar Eugene Debs himself. The party acutely feared centralization and bureaucracy. An early convention was nearly rent apart on a motion to increase the salary of the national secretary from $1,000 to $1,500 a year because one faction argued that to do so would make the post so lucrative, and the salary so out of line with proletarian tastes, that bureaucracy would result. To make sure that the will of the party membership decided all issues, referenda were ordered at the drop of a resolution, and much of the party's time was consumed in holding these town meetings by mail.[125] Local autonomy was so complete, under party structure, that strong cliques could arbitrarily run city branches or state organizations, refusing to admit outsiders or possible challengers. And in such instances the national office had little power of discipline.

Under these conditions it is not hard to understand the turnover of six

---

[124] Article x, section 4, of the Socialist Party constitution, in Appendix, *Proceedings*, 1912, p. 202.

[125] At one point the referenda were coming so thick and fast that national secretary Mailly reported: "Recently two referendums were taken upon the same subject within thirty days of each other, and as a result there are now two contradictory clauses in the present national constitution." *Proceedings*, 1904, p. 58.

293

different national secretaries in the eighteen years from 1901 to 1919 and why no official served more than five years. There was no real continuity in the national office. Nor was there any full-time responsible party leadership. Debs, the titular leader, never took administrative responsibility; Hillquit was busy with a law practice in New York; Berger edited several Milwaukee papers. Thus, unlike many European socialist parties and the later Communist Party, the leaders were not functionaries.

A different type of weakness in the party was the cult of proletarian chauvinism, the practice of endowing all virtue in the man with the horny hands merely because he was a worker. "When it comes to a pick between the intellectual, the preacher, the professor, and the working man, that man who is fresh from the ranks of the working class and who in his every day life is in actual contact with the work and the struggle," declared George Goebel, a right-wing spellbinder and longtime member of the national executive committee, "I am with that man that . . . more nearly represents the working class."[126] Thus the words "middle class" and "intellectual" became cuss words, and both sides competed violently in the effort to emphasize their working-class social origins and allegiances.

The problem, like original sin, was present at the very birth of the party. In the first fierce debates between the Hillquit "Kangaroo" group and the Berger faction of Social Democracy, the most heated epithet was the charge of being middle class. Max Hayes, a Hillquit lieutenant (who proclaimed himself a printer and a proletarian), sneered at the Berger group: "The anti-unionists were marshalled by Berger a school teacher and editor, Stedman a lawyer, McCartney a preacher, Edwards another editor, Cox another lawyer, Miller another editor, London, still another lawyer; Margaret Haile, a lachrymose woman, and one or two others—all so-called academic socialists, theorists."

To which A. S. Edwards, the editor of the *Social Democratic Herald*, wryly replied: "Comment is uncalled for, except that we might direct our attention to the fact that Harriman is a lawyer and ex-preacher, Hillquit is a lawyer, Schlueter an editor, Feigenbaum an editor, Morgan a lawyer, Jonas an editor, Stone an editor, Sissman a lawyer, Benham an editor, Taft a lawyer, Lee an editor, and finally, not to continue such trivialities to too great length, Max Hayes himself an editor and a good one."[127]

When Victor Berger attacked Debs for participating in the formation of the I.W.W., Debs's angry retort was: "Berger and Heath probably never worked for wages a day in their lives, have no trade, never had on a pair of overalls and really have no excuse to be in a trade union at all."[128] The charge was untrue. Actually, Berger and Heath had been wage

[126] *Proceedings*, 1908, p. 154.
[127] Fine, *op.cit.*, pp. 201-2.
[128] Ginger, *op.cit.*, p. 241.

earners for a longer period than Debs. Debs had worked on a railroad less than five years in his early youth, and when he took the job as secretary of the firemen's union he had left the road several years before. Most of his life, after union office, he worked as a lecturer and editor.[129] In symbolic terms the motivation for these claims is obvious. Being a worker meant a proletarian (i.e., good) policy; being bourgeois meant a middle-class (or bad) policy. This distinction has been used by the communist historian Philip Foner to explain the decline of the socialist movement, through devitalization by the "bourgeois" elements.

"The Socialist movement," Foner writes, "was running at flood tide but a considerable portion of the new membership came from outside the working-class—lawyers, doctors, dentists, preachers, educators, small manufacturers and business men and an occasional millionaire. Being persuasive speakers and excellent parliamentarians they quickly rose to leadership in the Party and came to control its policies, pushing the working-class members into the background. As one socialist put it they were 'soft and shifty stuff for Socialism to build on.' "[130]

But how does one make these identifications? At times the judgment is made on the basis of *social origin*, so that working-class parentage automatically endows one with virtue; at other times, when convenient, the basis shifts to one of current *occupation*. Actually neither the left nor the right wing could claim a monopoly of working-class adherents. Most of the right-wing leaders came from working-class parents. The leadership of the left wing was largely "bourgeois" both by social origin and occupation: William English Walling was an intellectual, J. G. Phelps Stokes a millionaire, Frank Bohn a writer, Jack London a writer.[131] The

---

[129] The legend of Debs as a proletarian will not down. At the I.W.W. convention, Haywood in attacking De Leon said, "Debs was the workingman who laid down his shovel on the locomotive when he took up the work of organizing the firemen. . . . De Leon's only contact with the workers was through the ideas with which he wished to 'indoctrinate' them. . . ." By that criterion, neither Lenin, nor Trotsky, nor Stalin, not to mention Marx or Engels, would have been allowed leadership of a working-class movement.

[130] Philip S. Foner, ed., *Jack London, American Rebel* (New York, 1947), pp. 64-65.

[131] London, the modern Rover Boy of socialism, was loudest of all in his denunciation of reformism. His letter of resignation in March 1916 attacked the party "because of its lack of fire and fight, and its loss of emphasis upon the class struggle. I was originally a member of the old revolutionary up-on-its-hind legs, a fighting Socialist Labor Party." Yet London, who had gone down to Mexico during the Pancho Villa uprising, advocated the annexation of the land below the Rio Grande by the United States. And when the Socialist Party in 1917 denounced the war, London, whose socialist views were based on the Nietzschean image of a race of supermen, raged at the party. "Civilization," he wrote, "at the present time is going through a Pentecostal cleansing that can only result in good for human kind." See Foner, *op.cit.*, pp. 123, 126. To London's letter, the New York *Call* replied, ". . . the rank and file of the Socialist Party are fighting—not always an exhilarating, romantic, spectacular fight—not always the sort of fight that makes good copy for the magazines or good

International Socialist Review, the monthly voice of revolutionary socialism, said bitingly of the representation at the 1912 convention, ". . . among other representatives of the proletariat were 21 lawyers, 18 preachers and assorted real estate agents, teachers, doctors and trade unionists."[132] Yet, as Oneal points out, "self-advertised as a proletarian wing, a later survey of its members by W. J. Ghent showed that nearly 75 percent were not proletarian."[133] And as Victor Berger stated: "Our party in Milwaukee is absolutely proletarian. . . . I may say that above ninety per cent—ninety-five per cent probably—of our vote is a working class vote. We have only about two and a half lawyers in our ranks—not enough to fill the offices."[134] In the later years the growing support of socialism in the colleges and among the rebel spirits who settled in Greenwich Village usually went to the left wing of the party. A John Reed out of Harvard, a Max Eastman off the Columbia campus, were restless souls whose spiritual hunger could not be fulfilled by the prosaic right-wing program which emphasized child-labor laws, minimum wages, and other bits and pieces of social legislation, and tended to slight the revolution. Actually, if a sociological distinction regarding the factions could be made, it would be between the rebels, the romantics, the declassed and dispossessed, all leaning to the left,[135] and the reformers, social workers, ministers, professionals, and craft-union members, who supported the right wing.

The net effect, however, of this cult of proletarian chauvinism was a repetitive litany of revolutionary rhetoric and phrase mongering. A person would claim respect solely on the basis of the length of time he had been in the party, or on the basis of his proletarian origin, his devotion to the principles of orthodox Marxism, and a genuflection to the word revolution.[136] The result was a sterile and doctrinaire set of policies. The cult

---

films for the movies—but the steady, unflinching, uncomplaining, unboasting . . . fight. . . ."

[132] *International Socialist Review*, June 1912, p. 810.

[133] *New Leader*, April 28, 1934, p. 4.

[134] *Proceedings*, 1908, p. 28. The same speech was made with little variation in 1910 and 1912.

[135] " 'Meet Comrade Joseph Medill Patterson' (County Secretary Fraenkel beamed). My hackles were up at once. I resented his bourgeois overcoat. It was beautifully tailored and adorned with a luxurious fur collar. . . . I couldn't see a millionaire with Patterson's background fitting into the proletarian revolution," wrote Ralph Chaplin in his autobiography, *Wobbly* (Chicago, 1948), p. 85. It was an attitude shared by many others. Joseph Medill Patterson, later the founder of the New York *Daily News* and a bitter isolationist and Roosevelt hater, was a member of the Socialist Party and its national executive committee in 1908. Another major stockholder in the Chicago *Tribune*, millionaire William Bross Lloyd, grandson of former Illinois Governor William Bross, a founder of the *Tribune*, and son of Henry Demarest Lloyd, was a founder of the American Communist Labor Party.

[136] Perhaps the worst sinner in this respect was Victor Berger. To the extent that he was readier to compromise and adapt to immediate political realities—going even

of proletarian chauvinism reached its most absurd heights in convention debates on such issues as paying the carfare of delegates to conventions. One can in fact almost trace the evolution of socialist reformism on this question. In 1904 the party first voted to reimburse delegates for travel expenses. In 1908 the convention, on Hillquit's motion, voted to pay the sleeping-car fare for delegates, although the minority claimed that "working class money should not be spent for palace car accommodations." Finally in 1912 the convention voted to pay Pullman car allowances; the opposition could only offer the feeble motion to limit travel to second-class or tourist accommodations "because the sleeping is just as good and costs just half as much."[137]

Equally slight amidst the weightier problems of history but equally symbolic of the basic mentalities of the socialist leadership was the Gridley affair, which took up almost two days of convention time in 1904. The credentials of delegate Gridley of Indiana were challenged on the ground that he had been named to the post of civil engineer of

---

further than the official A.F.L. position in favor of Oriental exclusion and limited immigration—he became more bellicose and "left" in his rhetoric. At one point he wrote: "In view of the plutocratic law-making of the present day, it is easy to predict that the safety and hope of this country will finally lie in one direction only—that of a violent and bloody revolution, therefore I say that each of the 500,000 socialist voters and of the 2,000,000 workingmen who instinctively incline our way, should besides doing much reading and still more thinking, also have a good rifle and the necessary rounds of ammunition in his home." Cited in *Proceedings*, 1912, p. 133. Morris Hillquit tells the story of an occasion where he and Berger represented the Socialist Party at a three-day and three-night "talk-fest" organized by Robert Hunter in an effort to convert twenty-five noted reformers to socialism. Berger at one session launched into a vehement denunciation of capitalist law and proclaimed ". . . wait until we have the power. Then we shall make our own laws, and by God, we will make you obey them." As Hillquit reports: "He was red in the face. His eyes flared and he reinforced his conclusions by striking the table with his clenched fist. An embarrassed silence fell on the gathering. The discussion came to an abrupt end." Later one of the conferees anxiously sought out Hillquit, who pointed out that in a democracy a minority obeys a law until it has sufficient strength to change it, and the former majority must now obey the new law. Did not Berger say practically the same thing? "My friend thought awhile," Hillquit concludes, "then laughed, 'C'est le ton qui fait la musique.'" See Hillquit, *Loose Leaves from a Busy Life*, pp. 58-59. It was this mistaking the tone for the music that later brought Berger into conflict with the espionage laws and resulted in his subsequent expulsion from Congress and in government persecution.

[137] John Spargo, the right-wing leader, summed up the case for comfort: "Comrades there is always the proposition of the man who says that as a working class party we should in all externals represent the working class. . . . it is expressed in the notion that we ought to come in day coaches or on the bumpers underneath the cars, if we possibly can do so. . . . that is not the working class . . . view at all. . . . men who come to the convention tired and outworn and weary are not in a position to make the best resistance to the forces of capitalism which can be made. . . . Finally, comrades, this is the twentieth century. And we of the working class demand for ourselves and our class all the advantages of the twentieth century." *Proceedings*, 1912, p. 30.

Aurora, Indiana, by the capitalist parties in the town. Gridley pleaded that he held the job because of a disability incurred in the Civil War and that he had been elected to it nineteen years before the Socialist Party was formed. The duties, he added, were technical, not political. The credentials committee finally voted to seat Gridley as an individual exception, but propounded a general rule that persons elected to office by the capitalist parties be barred from the Socialist Party. A Connecticut delegate mentioned an instance where a member accepted a job as city scavenger, but the socialist local voted charges against him for taking an appointment from the Democratic Party. So intense was this feeling that when Gridley was seated the minority demanded a roll call of states and lost 28 to 58. At the same convention a protest was lodged against the seating of J. Stitt Wilson, a prominent ex-minister and a California leader, on the ground that he had sent a congratulatory telegram to Mayor Samuel Jones of Toledo on the occasion of his election. "This was such a violation of Socialist ethics," said the delegate, "that it should debar him from taking part in the deliberations of this convention."[138]

Back of these at times outlandish feelings was the fear that traffic with the two major parties would dilute or corrupt socialist ardor and thus betray socialism. It also reflected the protective mortgage of men who, having seen the light first, feared that the late-comers would rob them of their birthright. Such fears of corruption underlay, too, the rigid refusal of the socialists to participate with other parties or reform movements, even on local issues. In June 1903 when Henry Demarest Lloyd sought to enlist Debs's support for a municipal ownership campaign in Chicago, the party standard bearer replied that he did not believe that "single taxers, socialists and anti-socialist trade unionists can successfully harmonize on any question whatsoever. . . ."[139] This attitude carried over into the heated denunciation of the labor party proposal in 1909 and ended only in 1922 with the formation of the Conference for Progressive Political Action.

And yet, underneath this proletarian cult lay a queer strain of soaring middle-class, get-rich-quick fantasies. If, as Max Scheler says, moral indignation is a disguised form of envy, underneath the proletarian veneer was a hot desire for riches. One can find regularly in the pages of the *International Socialist Review*—which labeled itself "the fighting magazine of the working-class," and of which William D. Haywood was an editor— a large number of advertisements which promised quick returns through land speculation. In the June 1912 issue, a full-page advertisement proclaimed: "DOUBLING OR TRIPLING YOUR MONEY THROUGH CLEAN HONEST

[138] *Proceedings*, 1904, pp. 15, 49.   [139] Ginger, *op.cit.*, p. 258.

INVESTMENT." It stated (shades of Henry George): "Getting in ahead of the railroad and the resulting rise in real estate values is the way thousands of people have made fortunes, especially in Western Canada. The wise real estate buyers of yesterday are wealthy people today." And in the text following: "Lots in Fort Fraser B.C.—destined to be the hub of the Canadian West." Nor were these isolated instances. Similar advertisements kept appearing in the *International Socialist Review* for many years, indicating their "pulling power." (The cover of the January 1916 issue is a painting of a hungry man in the snow, the inside half-page has an ad stating that a salesman could make $300 a month selling a cream separator.)

But this type of get-rich-quick appeal was not limited to the *International Socialist Review*. It was a mania throughout the party. In 1909 the Chicago *Daily Socialist* was carrying page advertisements for gold-mine stocks, whale-oil stocks, Florida lands, and other speculative ventures. John M. Crook, a party official and employee of the Chicago *Daily Socialist*, sold stock in a floor-surfacing-machine company; Bentall, former state secretary of the party in Illinois, promoted a flying-machine company; Kaplan, a national executive committee member from Minnesota, had other stock schemes; these, as well as Dickson's Matterhorn Goldmine and Insurance and Florida land schemes, were actively promoted by the Chicago *Daily Socialist*.

But perhaps the most spectacular promotions were those of Gaylord Wilshire, millionaire socialist and publisher of *Wilshire's Magazine*, a popular muckraking magazine of the period. After selling subscriptions to his magazine, and then common stock in it by flamboyant premiums (gold watches, pianos, etc., as prizes), Wilshire—whose name today adorns resplendent Wilshire Boulevard in Los Angeles—began the active pushing of blue-sky stocks for gold mines in British Guiana and Bishop Creek, Colorado, promising a 30 per cent dividend. The manager of the Colorado mine was Ernest Untermann, the translator of *Das Kapital* and leading socialist theoretician; various leading party officials, including a leading member of the national executive committee and a noted socialist editor, actively engaged in selling *Wilshire's Magazine* and gold-mining stock. After raising several hundred thousand dollars, Wilshire's gold-stock schemes failed in December 1910.

To the degree that any one person can encompass the fantastic contradictions inherent in the history of the socialist movement—its deep emotional visions, its quixotic, self-numbing political behavior, its sulky, pettish outbursts—it is Eugene Debs, so that in summation we must return to him once more. Debs had what the theologians call charism, the inner light of grace, or, as put by a laconic southerner, "kindlin' power." "He was a tall shamblefooted man, had a sort of gusty rhetoric that set on fire the railroad workers in their pine-boarded halls . . . made them want the world he wanted, a world brothers might own where everybody would split even. . . ," wrote Dos Passos.[140] "You felt that he really cared," said Ralph Chaplin.[141] "People loved him because he loved people," wrote Oscar Ameringer.[142] He spoke with Franciscan anguish, and when he said "brother" the recognition of kinship was instant.[143]

Yet while Debs fully *realized* the messianic role of the prophet, he lacked the hard-headedness of the politician, the ability to take the moral absolutes and break them down to the particulars with the fewest necessary compromises. He lacked, too, the awareness that a socialist leader of necessity must play both of these roles, and that in this tension there arise two risks—the corruption of the prophet and the ineffectuality of the politician. But Debs never even had the strength to *act* to the hilt the role of the prophet. A shallow dogmatism gave him the illusion of an inflexible morality. "If his mind failed to grasp a direct connection between a proposed reform and socialism," writes a sympathetic biographer, "he refused to waste time with reform. Then argument became futile; he could not be swayed." This dogmatism had its roots not in an iron revolutionary will, as with Lenin, but in an almost compulsive desire to be "left" of orthodox labor opinion. Nor did this thick streak of perpetual dissidence flow from the spirit of a dispossessed rebel like Haywood. Its wellspring was a sentimental nineteenth-century romanticism. He had been named for Eugene Sue and Victor Hugo, and their concern for the underdog, as well as the naive optimism of a Rousseau, soared in him. Yet in his personal life, manner, and habits (except for a later private addiction to drink), Debs was respectable and almost bourgeois; his

[140] John Dos Passos, *The 42nd Parallel* (New York, 1930), p. 26.

[141] Ralph Chaplin, *op.cit.*, p. 84.

[142] Oscar Ameringer, *If You Don't Weaken* (New York, 1940), p. 142.

[143] Debs's home life is of interest for those who, like Harold Lasswell, see in politics a public displacement for private motives. Debs's mother had a strong influence in his life—he left railroading at her urging for the less strenuous life of clerking—but most extraordinary was his deep attachment to his younger brother. "Theodore and Gene were of one flesh," remarked his sister, "they fairly breathed through one another." Debs married late, at the age of twenty-nine, and between his wife Kate and brother Theodore there was such strong antagonism that an open break resulted between the two. Kate Debs seemed to have been so hostile to Debs's socialist activities—it threatened her sense of middle-class respectability—that novelist Irving Stone was led to call her, in the title of his fictional portrayal of the life of Debs, the *Adversary in the House* (New York, 1948). Stone's judgment regarding Kate Debs is vigorously supported by James Oneal, a neighbor of Debs and one of the right-wing leaders of American socialism. See the review of Stone's book by August Claessens, *New Leader*, Jan. 10, 1948, and the reply by James Oneal, Jan. 31, 1948. An attempt to apply Lasswell's psychoanalytic and somatotype classification of political personalities—see his *Psychopathology and Politics* (Chicago, 1930)—to Debs is made by Kathryn Rogers, unpublished M.A. thesis, University of Chicago, 1930.

wife Kate was even more so. His literary tastes were prosaic: his favorite poet was Elbert Hubbard. But in his politics, Debs wore the romanticism like a cloak—and this was his strength as well as his weakness. It caused him to shun the practical and to shirk the obligations of day-to-day political decision. His fiercest shafts were reserved for the bureaucrat and party boss; his warmth and affection for those who led turbulent and dissident careers like his own.

How these sentiments could cruelly mislead him is illustrated in his attitude toward Tom Watson, a magical name among the populists of his day. Tom Watson of Georgia was a flaming agrarian rebel. A forceful speaker and writer, he was nominated with Bryan in 1896; but Watson refused to go along with the Democrats. Watson went to Congress, attacked the monopolists, founded *Tom Watson's Magazine*, among whose contributors were Theodore Dreiser and Edgar Lee Masters, and at the turn of the century was one of the leaders of the radical South. In later years he soured. Pressed by the race issue he became a champion of white supremacy, a vigorous antisocialist, and a defender of the Old South. The logic of crabbed populism led him to a vehement attack on the Negro ("Lynch law is a good sign: it shows that a sense of justice lives among the people"). Following the Leo Frank case in 1913 (in which a northern Jew was accused of murdering a Gentile girl, and lynched after his death sentence had been commuted), Watson became the most outspoken Jew-baiter in the country. As one biographer has written, ". . . if any mortal man may be credited (as no one man may rightly be) with releasing the forces of human malice and ignorance and prejudice, which the Klan merely mobilized, that man was Thomas E. Watson."[144] Yet, when Tom Watson died, Eugene V. Debs, recently released from the penitentiary, wrote in a letter to Mrs. Watson: "He was a great man, a heroic soul who fought the power of evil his whole life long in the interest of the common people, and they loved him and honored him."[145]

Withal, the lonely figure of Debs, his sagging, pleading gauntness, pierced all who beheld him. It was perhaps because in a final sense he was the true protestant. Debs stood at the end of the long road of the reformation. He had an almost mystical—at times omniscient—faith in the dictates of his inner self. Like the Anabaptists of old, all issues were resolved by private conscience. From the priesthood of all believers he had become the solitary individual, carrying on his shoulders the burdens of humanity. That sense of loneliness—and grandeur—touched others who were equally afflicted with the terrible sense of isolation. By his standing alone, he emphasized the individual and his rights, and at best, such an attitude of "autonomy" provides a unique defense of the dignity of the

144 C. Vann Woodward, *Tom Watson, Agrarian Rebel* (New York, 1938), p. 450.
145 *Ibid.*, p. 486.

person. But in its extreme antinomianism, in its romantic defiance of rational and traditional norms, it shirks the more difficult problem of living in the world, of seeking, as one must in politics, relative standards of social virtue and political justice instead of abstract absolutes. It is but one pole—a necessary one—in creating standards of action. But as the isolated protestant refuses to join the community of "sinners," so the isolated prophet evades the responsibility of political life. The prophet, once said Max Scheler, stands on the mountain as a signpost; he points the way but cannot go, for if he did, no longer would there be a sign. The politician, one might add, carries the sign into the valley with him.

VIII. The Decline and Fall of American Socialism

The subsequent history of American socialism is the story of breakup and decline. Although 1912 was the high-water mark of the socialist vote, it also brought an uneasy awareness that the party would never be a major force in American politics. After a dozen years the party could only poll about 6 per cent of the total vote and elect one congressman. Many members raised the question: Is American capitalism more resilient than socialists have credited it with being, or are the party's policies wrong? A feeling of tiredness was evident in the party leadership. This was particularly apparent in the case of Debs, who was wearying of the constant round of speaking and writing and felt, along with the gnawing sense of advancing age, that he was increasingly unheard. Various elements felt the party was insufficiently militant. In the far West some syndicalist-minded elements dropped off wholesale; in the Ozarks the dispossessed farmers began forming the secret and military-style Working Class Union. Thus, chunks of the left wing fell away. At the other end of the scale, the New Freedom of Woodrow Wilson, if not bringing the millennium to American labor, was, at least, furnishing tangible evidence that labor could promote gains through legislative activity. Within short order, a Department of Labor of cabinet rank was created, with William Wilson, a former secretary-treasurer of the mine workers, as secretary; the La Follette bill aiding the seamen had been passed after years of pleading by haggard Andrew Furuseth; government employees won the right to join unions and lobby for measures in their behalf; the Clayton Act, although not "Labor's Magna Carta," as Gompers had grandiloquently hailed it, did curb injunctions against labor by federal courts, thus withdrawing the sword which had been held over labor leaders by the Danbury Hatters and Buck's Stove injunction cases. Not only in Washington, but also in the various states, there were being enacted industrial safety laws, workmen's compensation, minimum wage laws, apprenticeship rules, and state anti-injunction laws. In short, the minimum beginnings of social legislation and union protection were under way. Thus the Wilsonian magnet pulled at reform elements in the Socialist Party and drew them out.

Other elements were now restless too. In its heyday, the Socialist Party had attracted a varied crew of drifters, promoters, speculators, and pitchmen who had found no place in capitalist society. Many were sincere socialists, but by temperament they needed a quick ascent if they were to stay hitched to the party. When the shooting star of socialism began to fall, these freebooters soon drifted away. Nevertheless, it was through many of them that socialism continued to exert a subtle yet unmistakable influence in American life. A case in point is the career of A. C. Townley and the meteoric rise of the North Dakota Non-Partisan League, one of the truly original phenomena in American politics.

Arthur C. Townley, like so many other Americans, started in poverty and dreamed of a fortune. In his youth he engaged in various speculative land ventures, and in 1909, a failure at the age of twenty-nine, moved to western North Dakota for his biggest plunge. He leased on credit thousands of uncultivated acres, bought tractors and farm implements, again on credit, and sowed on the wild virgin soil a huge crop of flax. But the long silky plant refused to grow and Townley went bankrupt, owing $80,000. Shortly afterward he turned to socialism and became an itinerant party organizer. But socialism, too, in North Dakota was a feeble stalk. Early in 1915, a small group of socialists decided that a third party had no tangible future in the state. They decided instead to organize the Non-Partisan League, stressing only the immediate needs of the farmers, and seek to capture one of the established parties through the primaries system. "The word socialism frightens the farmer," Townley is reported to have said. "I can take the name non-partisan . . . and use it to sugarcoat the principles of socialism and every farmer in the state will swallow them and call for more. . . . The farmers are ready."[146]

Townley's words were prophetic. The League spread like a dry prairie fire. In one year it elected Lynn Frazier governor of the state.

Hostile critics have dubbed the League a socialist front;[147] but this misreads its curious role. True, most of the backstage operators were or had been well-known socialists.[148] But its appeal and strength were populist; it was literally and figuratively straight corn. Essentially the

---

[146] Rev. S. A. Maxwell, *The Non-Partisan League from the Inside* (St. Paul, 1918), p. 45.

[147] Andrew A. Bruce, *The Non-Partisan League* (New York, 1921), p. 2.

[148] Townley was the League's chief organizer. Its legal adviser was Arthur LeSeur, a former railway attorney turned socialist who was also president of the People's College of Fort Scott, Kansas, a socialist correspondence law school whose letterhead featured Eugene V. Debs as chancellor. Charles Edward Russell, the socialist muckraker, was editor of the League's paper, while Walter Thomas Mills ("the little giant"), former Methodist minister, stock promoter, and peripatetic socialist educator, wrote the League's platform.

League's grapeshot was aimed at the *middleman* and the *speculator*, the two millstones grinding the farmer. The one—the processor in Minneapolis—controlled the price of grain storage; the other, by his speculative activities, forced up the price of land. The League program called for the state ownership of grain elevators, flour mills, etc.; state inspection of grain; hail insurance; rural credit banks; and the exemption of farm improvements from taxes. Its demands were thus simply those of a specific interest-group.

What the socialists contributed to the program was the rhetoric, the strategy, and the organizational technique. Townley's latent flair for promotion found a dazzling outlet. (The basic idea was a simple one and later to be copied by the Klan and many other rural and neighbor-based organizations.) Working farmers in each county were designated as organizers, assigned sales territory, and given a high commission for each man recruited. Paradoxically, it was the model-T Ford which in great measure made this scheme possible. With his little jalopy the farmer, rather than the outside organizer, could easily make the necessary calls to his neighbors, who knew and trusted him, and return in time to do his own chores. In less than a year, the League enrolled 50,000 members. Dues were high, but Townley promised results. The scheme of the direct primary allowed him to make good. By voting as a tight bloc, the League was able to capture the Republican Party and, in a traditionally G.O.P. state, win the election. It was one of the most notable examples of pressure-bloc manipulation in United States politics.

The old-line socialists in North Dakota resented the League: they feared it spelled the end of the party. And they were right. In 1912, the Socialist Party vote for governor was 6,834. Shortly after the formation of the League it sank to 2,615 and finally failed to place on the ballot altogether.

However, the Non-Partisan League soon came to an abrupt end. In 1921, the regular Democrats and Republicans combined their forces and succeeded in recalling Governor Frazier. Shortly thereafter, the Townley movement itself waned. The reason was peculiarly an agrarian one. Because farmers usually are short of cash, they were accustomed to pay dues by postdated checks. The result was that the farm depression in the early twenties drove the Townley movement into bankruptcy.

As a practical experiment in protest politics, the North Dakota Non-Partisan League was a striking innovation. In immediate terms, it reached its goals. It set up a state-owned mill and elevator, instituted crop insurance, etc. Its success in North Dakota stimulated the movement toward farmer-labor political action which began after World War I, and its tactic was copied in the thirties by Upton Sinclair's E.P.I.C. movement, and in some measure by the Political Action Committee in the forties.

In final assessment, however, the Non-Partisan League was less a progressive achievement than a demonstration of the retrogressive, crabbed, narrow, and xenophobic nature of agrarian socialism come to its logical conclusions. In the two decades following, the Non-Partisan League reorganized and sent a number of "progressives" to Congress, including Frazier, Nye, Lemke, and later Langer. What the end of the road turned out to be, however, can be seen in the career of William Lemke, one of the first political bosses of the League. A bull-headed Fargo lawyer, Lemke was born in poverty, and in his youth migrated to Mexico, where he engaged in various unsuccessful land speculations. Returning to North Dakota, he entered League politics. In 1932, after the revival of the League, he was elected to Congress and served until 1940, returning in 1942 and retaining a seat until his death in 1950. With the typical political narrowness of the small-town mind, his enemy was always called by the vague, amorphous name, the "interests." Politics in this view is always a "plot" and the devil, in this instance, the bankers, particularly the "international bankers." It was no accident that in 1936 Lemke, the populist, finally became the presidential candidate of Father Coughlin's Social Justice ticket, and that his appeal was a strange compound of crank money reform, free silver, isolationism, and other appeals to anxious and distressed petty-bourgeois elements. The blackish reactionary dye in populism had suffused through the cloth.[149]

If the populist pressure for immediate reform led some socialists to the tactic of the North Dakota Non-Partisan League, the strain of adventurism and agrarian violence led others to the Green Corn Rebellion and the destruction of the socialist movement in Oklahoma. Because the rebellion illustrates the other side of the populist aspect of American socialism, it is a story worth explaining.

Sparsely settled Oklahoma may not have had a working class, but it did have, in the most literal sense of the word, a proletariat—a dispossessed propertyless group with little visible means of support. These rural "proles" were an "aggregation of moisture, steam, dirt, rags, unshaven men and slatternly women and fretting children,"[150] tenant farmers who were little more than serfs to the cash crop demanded by the landlords. Many had settled as early as 1894 when the Cherokee strip had been thrown open; others had been members of Debs's American Railway Union who after defeat and blacklist had wandered into the area. Like most of the South and West, Oklahoma had been swept by populism. But, recalcitrant to the last, Oklahoma's populists had not softened and gone with Bryan into the Democratic Party. They were ridden by an

[149] See Daniel Bell, "The Grass Roots of American Jew Hatred," *Jewish Frontier*, June 1944, pp. 15-22.
[150] Oscar Ameringer, *op.cit.*, p. 229.

all-consuming hatred of their lot—the bare and uncertain living which a thin topsoil could provide.[151] This resentment was fueled by a stomping revivalism whose periodical outbursts provided relief for pent-up feelings and stifled emotions. The volatile mixture that resulted found its outlet in socialism.[152]

It was the adaptation to this religious temper that gave Oklahoma socialism its peculiar flavor. The new gospel was spread through the medium of week-long encampments, similar in form to the old-style evangelist camp meetings. Thousands of families would come from miles around, arriving in old buggies, chuck wagons, and buckboards, pitch their tents, cook, eat, and sleep on the camp grounds. A typical encampment would be opened with a rousing horseback parade, followed by a pickup mixed chorus which sang socialist versions of old populist songs to the tune of well-known religious melodies. Then followed the fire and brimstone oratory, often by noted socialist spellbinders such as Gene Debs, Kate Richards O'Hare, and Walter Thomas Mills. So went the week with a tumultuous round of singing, concerts, speeches, campfires, and memories to last for the next few months of dreary labor.

At its height, the socialist vote in Oklahoma was close to one-third of the total vote. Six socialists sat in the state legislature and the party elected numerous county officers. Proportionately, Oklahoma was the strongest socialist state in the country. But most of these socialists were "reds," and therefore against the reformist "yellows" who led the national party. Tad Cumbie ("the gray horse of the prairies"), the leader of Oklahoma's intransigeants, always flaunted a flaming red shirt at party conventions in order to show his convictions.[153] Because the official Socialist Party was considered too tame, the left-wingers organized two secret societies, the Working Class Union and the Jones Family. The members met at appointed rendezvous, gathered arms and dynamite, and waited for a moment to demonstrate that direct action could gain their

[151] "A poor man ain't got no chance in this country," raved George Hadley, looking over his untidy acres. "I've worked like a nigger all my life and look what I've got. I should 'a been rich by now and by God I will be if ever we get any justice in this country." Such was the mood of one socialist, as reported by Angie Debo in her *Prairie City*, a composite but authentic reconstruction of Oklahoma life. Angie Debo, *Prairie City* (New York, 1944), p. 131.

[152] "Pressure was upon them. . . . They were looking for delivery from the eastern monster whose lair they saw in Wall Street. They took their socialism like a new religion. And they fought and sacrificed for the spreading of the new faith like the martyrs of the old faith." Oscar Ameringer, *op.cit.*, p. 263. Ameringer, famous socialist editor and wit, had been a party organizer in Oklahoma and his salty memoirs are an invaluable sourcebook for the flavor and color of the period.

[153] At the 1912 convention Victor Berger likened the simon-pure leftists to the Hebrews who on journeys carried bundles of hay so as not to sleep on spots contaminated by Gentiles. The next day Cumbie appeared with a tiny bundle of hay pinned to his shirt.

ends. In the spring of 1917, these secret societies, which had spread through Arkansas as well, claimed 34,000 members.[154] When the United States entered World War I and the draft act was passed, the night riders moved into action. With Tad Cumbie as commander-in-chief, they proposed, like Daniel Shays of old, to secede from the Union. They thought they could halt Oklahoma's participation in the war by seizing the banks and county offices, controlling the money and the press of the state. Several "armies" did take the field and, raiding at night, burned down some railroad bridges, cut telephone lines, and destroyed some pipelines. Because they subsisted on barbecued beeves and Indian green corn, the insurrection was called the Green Corn Rebellion.[155] The rebellion, which involved in all some two thousand farmers, including Negroes and Seminole Indians, collapsed early in August 1917 when 450 of the rebels were rounded up by the militia. Three persons were killed and eighty-six convicted and sent to the penitentiary. Though not a single official of the Socialist Party was connected with the Green Corn Rebellion, thousands of socialists were arrested; other thousands fled to the Winding Stairs mountains of adjacent Colorado, Arkansas, and Texas to escape arrest.[156] Shortly after the trial of the ringleaders, an emergency convention disbanded the Oklahoma Socialist Party. The move was taken to prevent the government from linking the overt acts in Oklahoma to Victor Berger, who was then on trial in Chicago for violating the "Espionage Act."

To this wartime opera bouffe, a tragicomic footnote needs to be appended. The war had discredited the Socialist Party, and its leaders sought a new approach. Spurred by the example of North Dakota, Oscar Ameringer and others in 1921 organized the Farmer-Labor Reconstruction League, and nominated for governor J. C. ("Our Jack") Walton. A flamboyant character, Walton was the mayor of Oklahoma City and a cardholder in the railroad unions. His campaign was typical. He flayed the "interests" and spoke out, although side-tongued, against the Klan. This was the Indian summer of progressivism. In the Senate were Frazier and Nye of North Dakota, Shipstead and Johnson of Minnesota, Norris and Howell of Nebraska, Brookhart of Iowa, and La Follette of Wisconsin. Oklahoma was not one to lag behind. The League captured the Democratic Party, and "Our Jack" was swept into office in 1922 by a 60,000 plurality.

[154] *Oklahoma: a Guide to the Sooner State* (Norman, Okla., 1941), p. 48.

[155] Another version fixes the name as resulting from the coincidence with the annual green-corn dance of the Shawnee Indians, as well as the staple item of Indian green corn or "tomfuller." See the novel by William Cunningham, *The Green Corn Rebellion* (New York, 1935).

[156] Charles D. Bush, *The Green Corn Rebellion* (University of Oklahoma Graduate Thesis); cited by Ameringer, *op.cit.*, pp. 347-49, 353-54.

The farmer-laborites waited for reforms to start. Instead disquieting rumors reached their ears. "Our Jack" was seen playing golf in "tasseled knickers and silver-buckled sport shoes" on a Muskogee links, surrounded by oil derricks; worse still, remarks Ameringer, a caddy was carrying his bag! Appointments promised to farmer-laborites failed to materialize. Soon after, "Our Jack" traipsed off to Cuba with lobbyists for the oil-cement-asphalt-utilities "interests" and on his return began to build an elaborate house. A year later Walton capped this betrayal by openly joining the Klan. It was the end of socialist politics and influence in Oklahoma. Populism, of a sort, finally won out when trumpeting "Alfalfa Bill" Murray was elected governor of the state in 1930 on the Democratic ticket. But Alfalfa Bill was a far cry from old populist idealism. Like Tom Watson of Georgia he had traveled a familiar course. Beginning against the "interests" he ended as a rancorous isolationist and bigoted nativist. It was a shriveled ending for a grass-roots American radicalism.

But above all these—the defection of the left, the slipping away of the reform elements, the loss of populist support—the final gust that shattered the old Socialist Party was the whirling sandstorm of the European war. For years the international socialist congresses had blustered that a European working class would not permit a general world war to erupt. But war had come and the European socialist parties broke on the reefs of national patriotism: the German socialists supported the Kaiser, and the Russian socialists the Tsar; English socialists rallied behind the King, while French socialists, after the tragic assassination of their powerful antiwar leader Jean Jaurès, responded to the Marseillaise. Only the Italian socialists, a tiny handful of English pacifists around Ramsay MacDonald, and small groups of left-wingers, notably the Russian Bolsheviks, maintained the classic socialist position. American socialists, three thousand miles away from the conflict, were confused. Officially, the American party opposed both the war and American preparedness, but influential individuals began doubting the party's stand; others became disillusioned by the unexpected and shattering failure of European socialism.

To shore up the crumbling walls Debs in 1914 appealed for solidarity of all the left-wing forces. Once more he called for the merger of the United Mine Workers and the Western Federation of Miners to form "a revolutionary industrial organization"; and in the political field he urged the reunion of the Socialist and Socialist Labor Parties.[157] The old phrases were there, but by now they were meaningless.

By 1915 the party membership slipped to below 80,000 from the high of 125,000 in 1912. Membership rose after 1915, but it was an alien

[157] E. V. Debs, "A Plea for Solidarity," *International Socialist Review*, Mar. 1914, reprinted in *Writings and Speeches of Eugene V. Debs*, p. 372.

element, the foreign-language federations, which largely accounted for the gain; and these new groups began to dominate the party. The once vigorous socialist press began to disintegrate. By 1916 there were only two socialist dailies alive (as against five in 1912), the ineffectual New York *Call* (with a pale circulation of 15,000) and the Milwaukee *Leader* (circulation 37,000). Significantly the number of foreign-language socialist dailies rose from eight to thirteen. In the weekly field the toll was greatest. Of the 262 periodicals that flourished in 1912, only 42 remained.

It would not be too rash to say that the Socialist Party of 1917 bore little resemblance to the heterogeneous movement which had made so vigorous a dent in American life in the first dozen years of the century. Three major factors account for this difference and are explored below: a radical shift had taken place in the geographical centers of party electoral strength; a decisive transformation had taken place in the composition of the party membership; and almost the entire intellectual leadership of the party had decamped to support America's role in the war.

Before 1912 socialist strength was concentrated largely in the agrarian and mining areas of the West and Southwest. In the next years this support decreased while the strength of the Socialist Party increased proportionately in the Northeast and urban areas, particularly in New York. By 1920, in fact, New York contributed more than one-fifth of Debs's total of more than 900,000 votes, although in previous campaigns New York had never provided more than 10 per cent of the socialist total.[158] The reasons for the decline in the West have been partially enumerated. The rising strength of the Socialist Party in the urban East, and particularly in New York, was due in greatest measure to the high tide of European, and particularly Jewish, immigration. These new immigrants—again particularly the Jewish group—provided the sinews which sustained the American Socialist Party until 1932.

For a variety of historical reasons, the Jewish immigrants from eastern Europe were inclined to support radical movements. Like Carl Schurz and the German Forty-Eighters, they had participated actively in revolutionary movements in their own countries and fled because of oppression. On coming here they retained much of their radical fervor, and, as with Schurz and the German Republicans, it was only after a period of accommodation that the European enthusiasms were tempered. A goodly number of immigrants were younger men and women of education who were of necessity forced to enter the garment shops as workers. But the sweatshop conditions to which older workers had resigned themselves

[158] This was both a relative and an absolute shift, i.e., the Socialist Party vote had decreased in its old strongholds yet the new role of New York as the number one center of socialist strength was not merely a displacement of other centers but a rise in total vote as well.

stirred these young firebrands to action. In 1909, beginning with the waistmakers' strike and with the Triangle Dress Factory fire, which shocked the community into awareness of the miasmic factory conditions, unionism took hold. In less than five years, the International Ladies' Garment Workers, the Amalgamated Clothing Workers, the Furriers, and the Millinery Workers unions had won contracts and a permanent footing. With their rise came a young and new leadership that was almost wholly socialist in inclination; and the new unions became the financial backbone and chief organizational props of the Socialist Party. Besides these unions the new Jewish immigration also created a powerful fraternal and insurance organization known as the Workmen's Circle, and this also became an important source of socialist financial strength. Started in 1905 with less than 7,000 members, it grew within a decade to a membership of 52,000 with assets exceeding $625,000.

A word also needs to be said concerning the distinctive role in the American socialist movement played by the *Jewish Daily Forward* and its controversial editor, Abraham Cahan. At its height the *Forward* had a remarkable circulation of 250,000 and it was undoubtedly the most influential paper in the Jewish community of New York. The *Forward* made its unique mark because it was a Yiddish newspaper among a Yiddish folk. The early Jewish intellectuals had become separated from the Yiddish masses by their disdainful refusal to speak Yiddish. The *Forward* mirrored and articulated the pathos and deep self-pity, the despair and indignation of a bewildered immigrant folk. Characteristically, the *Forward* won its first popular support and ousted its dominant rival, the Socialist Labor Party *Abendblatt*, when it took an undogmatic and even "antisocialist" stand on two crucial issues. The *Abendblatt* attacked the Spanish-American War and, along with other doctrinaire socialist papers, refused to be roused by the Dreyfus case in France. But hatred of Spain was deep in Jewish consciousness, and Dreyfus himself was a Jew. On both issues the Jewish mass feelings were aroused and the *Forward* followed its tribal instincts.

Probably in few other instances has a newspaper had so great a cultural influence on a community. The *Forward* bound together the Jewish community and made it socialist.[159] In doing so, the *Forward* replaced the rabbi, although synagogue modes of discourse were adopted. Propaganda was carried on by *De Proletarischer Magid* (the proletarian preacher) and the lessons were called the *Red Sedre* (the weekly portion of the *Torah*). The first walking delegate, said the *Forward*, was Moses, because he led the strike against the Egyptian overseers. For many years the *Forward* exercised a decisive, and at times arbitrary, voice in the affairs of the Jewish unions, and in the period from 1920 to 1932 was the most powerful influence in the Socialist Party.

[159] Melech Epstein, *Jewish Labor in the U.S.A.* (New York, 1950), pp. 318-34.

With the successful rise of Jewish labor, fostered as this was by the *Forward*, the Socialist Party was able for the first time to elect a congressman from New York in 1914 when Meyer London carried the lower east side. For years New York had been an embarrassingly weak spot in the socialist armor because of the depredations of William Randolph Hearst, quondam reformer. "The ability of Hearst," said the New York *Call* in 1909, "to cut heavily into the Socialist vote every time he chooses to be a candidate for office must be a source of bitter humiliation to every sincere Socialist." However, the new immigration created a solid base of socialist votes which could not be swayed by the reform breezes.

The immigration as a whole was responsible for a remarkable change in the composition of the membership of the Socialist Party. After 1915 the number of party members began to rise steadily until, by 1919, it was back to almost 110,000. This new growth was due almost entirely to the foreign-language groups. Starting in 1908, the Socialist Party had begun the organization of foreign-language federations in order to reach the foreign-speaking voters. In actual practice the federations were really small national socialist parties attached to the American organization but responsive largely to the passions and concerns of the land of their origin. By 1919, at the new peak of the party, over 53 per cent of the members—a majority—were members of foreign-language federations. In 1912, these federations had constituted less than 12 per cent of the total membership. The growth in the federations was less a product of conditions in America than of enthusiasm for events in Europe. For example the Slavic federations in the Socialist Party (Russian, Ukrainian, South Slavic, Lithuanian, Lettish) almost doubled their membership in the four months following December 1918, and by April 1919 constituted a decisive bloc of 20 per cent of the party membership—a fact which was instrumental in the emergence of present-day American communism.

The third factor which transformed the character of the Socialist Party was the loss of almost the entire body of intellectuals, publicists, public figures, union leaders, etc., as a result of World War I. In fact, except for Hillquit, Berger, and Debs, not one major "name" remained in the ranks of American socialism after the war.

These defections had been foreshadowed in 1916 when the Socialist Party vote plummeted. Old and tired, Debs had refused to run. No party convention was held that year, and a national referendum nominated a journalist, Allan Benson, for president. But with the war issue casting so large a shadow, many socialists felt that their trust would reside better in Wilson and that their votes should not be wasted. Consequently, a number of prominent socialists openly supported the Democratic ticket. Among these were William English Walling, the intellectual leader of the left wing who had attacked the German social democrats for

311

voting the Kaiser's war credits; Ernest Poole, whose novel *The Harbor* had been one of the great successes of radical fiction; Ellis O. Jones, a professional humorist;[160] Mother Jones, famed union organizer and heroine of the coal fields; and John Reed and Max Eastman of the *Masses*. This enthusiasm for Wilson was strengthened by Max Eastman's report of an interview at the White House between the President and a group of *Masses'* editors. According to Eastman, Wilson represented "our popular sovereignty with beautiful distinction." And reflecting possibly the solidarity which the intellectuals felt with the professor in the White House, Eastman remarked that Wilson was "a graciously democratic aristocrat." The Woodrow Wilson Independent League, formed by these intellectuals, helped swing away much of the liberal vote from the socialists. Benson's total of about 590,000 votes represented a decline of about a third from the high point of 1912.

When the United States declared war in April 1917, the intellectuals and the union leaders continued to follow Wilson. For them, the greatest danger was German militarism; if the Kaiser won, they saw no hope for world peace. The roll call of bolters is impressive. Among those who left the party were: John Spargo, editor of the *Comrade* and the leading popularizer of socialist ideas in America who was also the theoretician of the right wing; William English Walling, perhaps the most provocative mind in American socialism and the theoretician of the left wing; A. M. Simons, editor of the Chicago *Daily Socialist*, and author of *Social Forces in American History* and *Farmers in American History*, the first attempts to see U.S. history in Marxist terms; Charles Edward Russell, the noted muckraker whom the right wing had nominated against Debs in 1912; William J. Ghent, a perceptive writer whose neglected book, *Our Benevolent Feudalism*, had in 1906 pictured with remarkable accuracy the emergence of fascism as a reaction to the socialist threat; Allan Benson, the party's presidential candidate in 1916; George D. Herron, the leader of the Christian socialist movement in America whose mother-in-law, Carrie Rand, had on his request set up the Rand School in New York; Upton Sinclair and Jack London, the two literary firebrands who had started the Intercollegiate Socialist Society; Carl D. Thompson of Wisconsin, who had sought the Socialist presidential nomination in 1916; State Senator W. R. Gaylord, the party's public spokesman in Wisconsin; Ernest Untermann, who had translated Marx's *Das Kapital* and was one of the theoreticians of the party; Robert Hunter, noted social worker whose exposés of the consequences of poverty had attracted national attention; Henry Slobodkin, one of the founders of the party; J. Stitt

[160] Among the numerous paradoxes in socialist history, shortly after Pearl Harbor, Mr. Jones—now pro-Nazi and an anti-Semite—was convicted on July 11, 1942, of sedition and sentenced to five years in prison.

Wilson, mayor of Berkeley, California, and a leading Christian socialist; Chester M. Wright, editor of the *Call*; Lucien Sanial, Gompers' old foe; Arthur Bullard, well-known writer; Frank Bohn, theoretician of syndicalism; J. G. Phelps Stokes, millionaire leftist, and his fiery wife, Rose Pastor. This capitulation of almost the entire Socialist Party intelligentsia was not unique. Almost the entire leadership of American progressivism had followed Wilson too, among them John Dewey, Clarence Darrow, and the prophets of the *New Republic*, Herbert Croly, Walter Weyl, and Walter Lippmann.[160a]

In addition to the intellectuals, the trade unions which formed the progressive and socialist bloc within the American Federation of Labor joined Gompers in support of the war. The coal miners, machinists, even the International Ladies' Garment Workers, all backed the American Alliance for Labor & Democracy. The final blow, perhaps, was the loss of the *Appeal to Reason*. The famous *Appeal*, the most popular success in socialist publishing, the paper to which Debs had contributed for many years as an associate editor, changed its name to *The New Appeal* and endorsed Wilson.

When news of the European war reached the United States, the national executive committee of the Socialist Party issued a statement on August 12, 1914, extending the sympathy of the party "to the workers of Europe in their hour of trial," and stating that "The workers have no quarrel with each other but rather with their ruling class." In December 1914, the party issued an antiwar manifesto putting forth a socialist analysis of the nature of the war. While the immediate causes of the war were stated as "thoughts of revenge . . . imperialism and commercial rivalries . . . secret intrigue . . . lack of democracy . . . vast systems of military and naval equipment . . . jingo press . . . the fundamental cause was the capitalist system." This position was endorsed in a referendum vote by a large majority in September 1915.

For a party leadership that had been attacked as middle-class, soft, and compromising, these were strong words. How are they to be explained? One viewpoint ascribes the antiwar stand of the Socialist Party to the high proportion of German, Jewish, and foreign-language elements in the party.[161] Another points to the party's distance from the scene and

160a Max Eastman opposed the war, and together with other editors of the *Masses* was indicted under the Espionage Act. During the trial, Eastman was won over to support of the war when, following the Russian Revolution, President Wilson virtually endorsed the Soviet peace program. See Hillquit, *Loose Leaves from a Busy Life*, pp. 222-33.

161 See, for example, Charles Edward Russell's autobiography, *Bare Hands and Stone Walls* (New York, 1933). Russell reports (p. 288) a conversation related to him about Victor Berger in which Berger stated: "You know, I have always hated the

consequent lack of involvement. Both of these carry a degree of truth. But equally relevant is the fact (obscured by the taunts of "yellow" and "reformist" made by extremist elements) that the American Socialist Party was heavily a doctrinaire socialist party, more so than most of its European counterparts because of its lack of commitments to the labor movement. With none of the strings of responsibilities which held the European socialists, the party, reacting by formulas, branded the war "imperialist" and then stood apart from it.

War was declared on April 6, and the following day the emergency convention of the party opened in St. Louis to announce its opposition. The antiwar statement that was adopted restated the classic Marxist analysis of war.[162] The manifesto proposed a seven-point program of opposition calling for demonstrations, petitions, opposition to conscription, and ". . . the extension of the campaign of education among the workers to organize them into strong, class-conscious and closely unified political and industrial organizations to enable them by concerted and harmonious mass action to shorten this war and establish lasting peace. . . ."

The St. Louis declaration was written by Morris Hillquit, Algernon Lee, and Charles Ruthenberg—a strange combination of two "right-wingers" and an extreme leftist. Wrote Hillquit later, "We worked on it earnestly and tensely, carefully weighing every phrase and every word, but determined to state our position without circumlocution or equivocation, to leave nothing unsaid."[163]

Although the intellectuals had deserted the party, in the two months following the adoption of the manifesto party membership jumped more than twelve thousand. Because the Socialist Party was the only one that was antiwar, it found new and surprising support for its stand, especially in the northern industrial and foreign-language centers. Thus, in 1917 the Socialist Party vote reached new spectacular heights in the municipal elections of that year. In New York, where Morris Hillquit ran for mayor, newspapers speculated freely on a possible victory, although four years before Charles Edward Russell had received less than 5 per cent of the votes. The threat was real enough for Hillquit's opponents—John F.

Kaiser, but when I see the world taking arms against him I feel that I must seize a rifle and take my place in the ranks and fight for him."

[162] "The capitalist class of each country was forced to look for foreign markets to dispose of the accumulated 'surplus wealth.' . . . The mad orgy of death and destruction which is now convulsing unfortunate Europe was caused by the conflict of capitalist interests in the European countries. . . . Our entrance into the European war was instigated by the predatory capitalists in the U.S. who boast of the enormous profits of seven billion dollars from the manufacture and sale of munitions and war supplies and from the exportation of American food stuffs and other necessities."

[163] Hillquit, Loose Leaves from a Busy Life, pp. 165-66.

314

Hylan, a nonentity picked by William Randolph Hearst; reform Mayor John Purroy Mitchell, who four years earlier had beaten a divided Tammany; and William F. Bennett, a Republican hack—to level their fire chiefly against him rather than at each other. Hillquit openly took an antiwar stand, and declared he would not support the Liberty Loan. Over the city, particularly in working-class districts, the nightly street-corner meetings reached a fever pitch. In a furious speech Theodore Roosevelt denounced Hillquit as cowardly, pacifist, and pro-German and climaxed an impassioned speech with "Yellow calls to Yellow." On election day Hillquit received 145,332 votes (an increase of nearly 500 per cent): 22 per cent of the city's voters (31 per cent in the Bronx) had voted Socialist. In addition, the party sent ten assemblymen to Albany, seven aldermen to City Hall, and also elected a municipal-court judge.

Nor was the New York vote an isolated event. In Chicago the party received nearly 34 per cent of the vote, carrying five wards (as against 3.6 per cent in the previous election). In Buffalo the Socialist vote was over 25 per cent of the total, and throughout Ohio significant totals were registered in every major city—Dayton, 44 per cent; Toledo, 34.8 per cent; Cleveland, 19.3 per cent; Cincinnati, 11.9 per cent. A survey by Paul Douglas of the 1917 vote in fourteen cities showed that the Socialist Party had polled an average of 21.6 per cent of the entire vote, a total which, if projected nationally, would have meant four million votes. The war thus gave the Socialist Party a new tone and purpose; it minimized the differences of left and right, in the first year at least, and the fever glow which resulted gave an illusion of ruddiness and new health.

The 1917 elections were the only means of socialist protest during the war. Soon thereafter, the government moved swiftly to crack down on the party. The chief instrument was the so-called Espionage Act, passed in June 1917, which forbade obstruction to recruitment, insubordination in the armed forces, etc. A year later the act was drastically widened to include such offenses as "profane, scurrilous and abusive language" about the government and constitution, "or saying or doing anything" to obstruct the sale of government bonds or the making of loans by the United States. Moreover, the Post Office Department was given the power to exclude from the mails all matter violating the provisions of the act. The Post Office acted swiftly. In short order the *American Socialist*, the official weekly of the party, the Milwaukee *Leader*, the New York *Call*, the *Jewish Daily Forward*, the *Masses*, Frank O'Hare's *Social Revolution* (formerly the *National Rip-Saw*), the *International Socialist Review*, and several German, Russian, and Hungarian socialist dailies, all had their mailing rights suspended. The only avenue open for expression was the public platform, and this, too, was soon pulled out from under.

315

Antiradical hysteria had begun with the Tom Mooney campaign. At a preparedness-day parade in San Francisco in July 1916 a bomb exploded, killing eight and wounding forty. Shortly afterward, Warren K. Billings and Tom Mooney, a radical labor leader, were arrested. An anarchist paper, the *Blast*, edited by Alexander Berkman (who had shot H. C. Frick at Homestead) was raided. Mooney came to trial in January 1917 and was sentenced to death. World-wide protest, including demonstrations in Moscow, caused Wilson to intervene and the sentence was commuted to life imprisonment. During the Mooney hysteria Wilson ordered the investigation of the I.W.W. On September 5, 1917, simultaneous raids took place in more than a dozen cities, and 166 members of the I.W.W., including Haywood, were indicted for violation of the Espionage Act. All the members of the general executive board, the secretaries of the industrial unions, the party editors, and anyone of slight standing in the organization were picked up. As new leaders replaced those imprisoned, these too were arrested. "If the government had set out not only to render the I.W.W. ineffective during the war but also to prevent its resurgence, it could not have performed its tasks with more thoroughness and completeness."[164]

The government sought to wreck the Socialist Party as well. In September 1917 the national office in Chicago was raided, and in February 1918 the chief officers, including Adolph Germer, the executive secretary, J. Louis Engdahl, editor of the *American Socialist*, the party's national publication, William F. Kruse, of the Young People's Socialist League, Irwin St. John Tucker, former head of the party's literature department, and Victor Berger were indicted. In Ohio, the leaders of the party— Charles Ruthenberg, Alfred Wagenknecht, and Charles Baker—were sentenced to one-year terms for opposing conscription. Across the country hundreds were indicted.

In the period following America's entry into the war, Gene Debs was strangely silent. He had refused to attend the St. Louis convention, although urgently requested to come by Ruthenberg. He discontinued his lecture tours. The conscription act, the Liberty Loan, the subsidies to England and France went by without protest. One biographer has implied that Kate Debs sought to deter him; Debs himself may have thought any gesture hopeless. "He still longed for peace; but he had no program. He was lost."[165] After the Russian Revolution had broken tsarist autocracy (now making plausible the slogan of a war for democracy), and Wilson had declared his war aims, many of the socialists wavered. Max Eastman and Floyd Dell, although on trial as editors of the *Masses* for antiwar propaganda, came out in support of the war. The seven socialist aldermen in New York declared themselves in favor of a Liberty Loan

[164] Perlman and Taft, *op.cit.*, p. 421.
[165] Ginger, *op.cit.*, pp. 345-48.

drive. Meyer London, the only socialist in Congress, left-handedly supported Wilson's war aims by declaring that they were similar to socialist objectives. It was at this point that Debs first began to stir. Happiest when in the opposition, he began to attack this trend in the party. In May 1918 Debs issued a statement on socialist policy, his first word in thirteen months. Stating his unqualified opposition to the war and attacking the majority socialists in Germany, he proposed another convention because the St. Louis manifesto contained "certain propositions . . . which are now impossible." After fifteen months of inactivity Debs began a speaking campaign. But the federal government took no notice and "Debs became increasingly angry. . . . Although he . . . vehemently denounced the President, nothing happened. Half of his beautiful plan [either to free socialist prisoners or get himself jailed] was being spoiled by the callous indifference of the law-enforcement officials. This was the final insult," writes biographer Ray Ginger.[166]

Finally, at Canton, Ohio, the government took notice. Actually, little that Debs said in a two-hour speech was devoted to the issues of the war. He did—for the first time—lash out at those who had deserted the party. "They lack the fiber," he said, "to endure the revolutionary test."[167] In his peroration Debs touched once on the war. On the charge of using "profane, scurrilous and abusive" language, he was arrested for violating the amended Espionage Act. The Cleveland trial was a stage which the Debs of old utilized to the fullest measure. In the hushed, tense courtroom, Debs made his own plea to the jury. His whole life was at stake and in moving sentences he summed up his credo. The ruling class, he said, was helpless against "the rise of the toiling and producing classes. . . . You may hasten the change, you may retard it; you can no more prevent it than you can prevent the coming of the sunrise on the morrow." Before the sentencing Debs made an address which included the oft-quoted ". . . while there is a lower class, I am in it; while there is a criminal element, I am of it; while there is a soul in prison, I am not free."[168] He was sentenced to ten years in prison, and sent to Atlanta.

Except for Hillquit, who had been hospitalized for tuberculosis,[168a] almost every major Socialist Party official was indicted during the war. Berger and the national officers were convicted, but two years later, while still out on bail, their convictions were set aside by the Supreme

---

[166] *Ibid.*, p. 354.

[167] The Canton, Ohio, speech in *Writings and Speeches of Eugene V. Debs*, p. 421.

[168] Statement to the Court, *ibid.*, p. 437.

[168a] Hillquit asserts that his large mayoralty vote in 1917 won him "immunity," for the government feared that an indictment "might antagonize a considerable body of people in New York" (Hillquit, *Loose Leaves from a Busy Life*, p. 234). In the summer of 1918, however, when he was preparing to defend Debs and Berger, Hillquit learned of his ailment. He spent two years in a sanitarium, thus missing the intense fratricide of the 1919 split.

Court. All told, about two thousand persons were tried under the wartime Espionage Act.

The February Revolution that overthrew the Tsar in 1917 was a lightning bolt that cleared the air. The rumbling noise of the following November was the apocalyptic thunderclap. The first *word* signaling the new world revolution had been spoken, incongruously, in the rest room reserved for the Tsar at the Finland station in Petrograd. Returning in April from Switzerland, Lenin said: "I am happy . . . to greet you as the advance guard of the international proletarian army. . . . The war of imperialist brigandage is the beginning of civil war in Europe. . . . The hour is not far when, at the summons of our Comrade Karl Liebknecht, the people will turn their weapons against the capitalist exploiters. . . . In Germany, everything is already in ferment! Not today, but tomorrow, any day, may see the general collapse of European capitalism. The Russian revolution you have accomplished has dealt it the first blow and has opened a new epoch. . . ."[169]

Lenin's remarks had been completely unexpected. His old rivals, the Mensheviks, had come to the Petrograd station to greet him. His party central committee, including Stalin, was in favor of an alliance with the other socialist parties. Lenin rejected this course. His single aim now was power, and the Bolshevik Party, the instrument he had fashioned, had to be ready for its seizure. The same night, in the marble corridors of Kshesinskaya Palace, once the house of the Tsar's ballerina-mistress and now the headquarters of the Bolshevik Party, Lenin spoke for two hours filling his audience with "turmoil and terror." In hoarse accents he denounced any policy of collaboration; he mocked the agrarian reforms of the provisional government; he denounced its war policy. The aim was clear: the peasants must seize the land, the workers the factories, all support to the provisional government must cease. "We don't need any parliamentary republic. We don't need any bourgeois democracy. We don't need any government except the Soviet of Workers', Soldiers', and Peasants' Deputies!"[170]

In November, fired by Lenin's inexorable will, the Bolsheviks seized and held power. Within a year, Europe caught fire. A socialist government was established in Finland. A revolution began in Hungary. The Kaiser abdicated. The Austrian emperor fled. The Romanovs were shot. It was the most dramatic moment in European working-class history since the Paris Commune less than fifty years before. To Europe's socialists it meant still more. Here were not the meek and humble but the revolutionary and disinherited claiming the world. For more than forty years

[169] Cited in Edmund Wilson, *To the Finland Station* (New York, 1940), p. 471.
[170] *Ibid.*, p. 475.

318

European socialism had been lumbering along, growing fat, talking of eventual victories through parliamentary elections; here in one swift surgical stroke, the body of European capitalism was pierced, and was collapsing like a stuffed strawpiece. What equally captured the minds of socialists everywhere was the dazzling spectacle of power seized by men who had been obscure individuals, mocked and derided when they had suggested those "absurd" and "utopian" theories of insurrection. As recently as 1915 Lenin's name had been known to but few European socialists (his reply to an article by Rosa Luxemburg was rejected as unclear by the *Neue Zeit*, the venerable theoretical organ of Marxian socialism). He was almost completely unknown in the United States: when he wrote a letter to the Socialist Propaganda League of Boston, an extreme left-wing antiwar organization composed largely of Slavic members, they ignored it and apparently threw the letter in the wastebasket. The *International Socialist Review* in 1915 reprinted the antiwar manifesto of the Zimmerwald conference, an effort by left socialists to proclaim their opposition to war. But Lenin's name passed unnoticed. Trotsky and Bukharin, however, were both known in New York, where they had come in 1916. Socialists had met with them, argued with them, measured their own ability against theirs; and many felt that if Trotsky, an obscure journalist, could rise to become the Marshal of the Red Army, their own stars were not far off in the heavens.

All American socialists now rushed to acclaim the Bolshevik victory. A few moderate voices, such as that of the veteran Russian socialist editor, Dr. Sergius Ingerman, were howled down. James Oneal, in a speech on November 7, 1919, the second anniversary of the Bolshevik Revolution, mocked the critics: ". . . they say there has been violence in Russia. Some violence in a revolution! Just imagine! Do they think a revolution is a pink tea party . . . every great revolution . . . [has] been accompanied with more or less violence, and it is impossible to dispense with it."

Everyone rushed to become a Bolshevik—the right wing as well as the left! The right wing even announced its readiness to join the new Third International. But a new left wing had arisen in the Socialist Party, and it would have none of the old leaders, no matter how strong the new protestations of revolutionary faith. The taint of reformism, they said, would not wear off these new wearers of Lenin's mantle. They sneered at Hillquit's "'splendid' Mayoralty campaign for cheap milk." "A Babbitt of Babbitts is Hillquit, the ideal Socialist leader for successful dentists," wrote Trotsky later, recalling his experiences in America during the war.[171]

[171] Leon Trotsky, *My Life* (New York, 1930), p. 274. Trotsky scorned the U.S. socialists: "To this day, I smile as I recall the leaders of American socialism. Immigrants

The left of 1918 was completely unlike the left of 1912.[172] The latter had been a motley collection, loosely organized, of populists, untutored syndicalists, rebels, etc. The new left wing was led by a group of tough-minded young men, many of them fresh out of metropolitan colleges, who found in the Bolshevik Revolution what a left wing had long lacked— a program around which to organize.

The emergence of the left wing in American socialism owes much to the presence here of the Russian émigrés who had been deported from France. One of the earliest meetings leading to the formation of the left-wing caucus was held in Brooklyn in the winter of 1916-1917. About twenty persons were present, including Leon Trotsky, Nikolai Bukharin, and Alexandra Kollontay of the Russians, and Ludwig Lore, Louis C. Fraina, and Louis B. Boudin of the American Socialist Party.[173] Trotsky and Fraina attacked the American Socialist Party for not resisting conscription more strongly and for not resorting to sabotage. "We intended to organize the left-wing under the direction of Comrade Trotsky and Madame Kollontay," wrote Katayama, a leading Japanese communist then in exile here, "but the Russian Revolution called them back." The group which met in Brooklyn later issued an organ called *Class Struggle*, which became the official left-wing voice within the Socialist Party. Meanwhile, an independent left wing had started in Boston, where a group of Slavic socialists formed the Socialist Propaganda League and published the *New International*. When the left wing captured control of the party in Boston, they changed the name of the periodical to *Revolutionary Age*.

who had played some rôle in Europe in their youth, they very quickly lost the theoretical premise they had brought with them in the confusion of their struggle for success" (p. 274). And yet, unconscious of the irony, Trotsky tells of his own living here: "We rented an apartment in a workers' district, and furnished it on the instalment plan. That apartment, at eighteen dollars a month, was equipped with all sorts of conveniences that we Europeans were quite unused to: electric lights, gas cooking-range, bath, telephone, automatic service-elevator, and even a chute for the garbage. These things completely won the boys over to New York" (p. 271).

[172] The mood of the young left at the time is caught in an incident related by the former communist writer, Joseph Freeman, in his autobiography. During the 1917 campaign Columbia students found it difficult to get a Columbia professor to sponsor Hillquit because of the expulsions of Dana and Cattell for their antiwar views. Freeman called Hillquit, who said: "Go to my friend Professor Seligman." Freeman was taken aback. Seligman for years had been attacked by socialists as "archreactionary" and as the "chief economic apologist of capitalism." Seligman readily agreed, saying he and Hillquit were friends who for many years had sought inconclusively to convince each other about socialism. "Personal intimacy between the champion of our cause and the apologist for capitalism was beyond our understanding," Freeman wrote. "Was it possible that the leaders of both sides did not take seriously the ideas they professed?" Joseph Freeman, *An American Testament* (New York, 1936), p. 110. Freeman's memoirs is one of the best accounts of the attraction of communism for the young intellectual.

[173] Sen Katayama, "Morris Hillquit and the Left-Wing," *Revolutionary Age*, Vol. 2, No. 4 (July 26, 1919), p. 4.

The Russian Federation of the Socialist Party became the idol of the left wing. Quite naively, its members were looked upon as the only ones who understood bolshevism, apparently through some mysterious osmosis of the language. Actually, the majority of the large membership of the Federation (which now constituted one-fifth of the party) had joined within the past year and knew little of bolshevism or socialism. But the leadership of the Russian Federation, ambitious for power, encouraged this illusion, quoted and misquoted Lenin from the Russian, and acted as the papal delegates of bolshevism. The strength of the left was concentrated in the foreign-language federations, in Michigan and Ohio (whose leaders were Charles Ruthenberg and Alfred Wagenknecht) and in New York, which now contained the bulk of party membership. Except for Ruthenberg, the leadership of the new opposition were almost completely new to the Socialist Party and virtually unknown. In a real sense, the left wing was a Young Turk movement. Programmatically, there was at this time little difference between the wings. But the left was in the position of asserting: "You were wrong before, it is now our turn." If the old guard had been willing to share power, the shape of the split would have been different.

In February 1919 a formal left-wing caucus was started in New York to capture power in the party. The left-wingers held a convention, quite aptly, in the Odd Fellows Hall, on St. Mark's Place in New York's east side, and adopted a document which came to be known as the Left Wing Manifesto. The manifesto, drafted by Louis Fraina, was written with the oracular self-consciousness of taking up where Marx's *Communist Manifesto* had left off. It reviewed the events of the past and condemned the right-wingers for "sausage socialism." The revolutionary sentiment among American workers, it proclaimed, was growing. "The temper of the workers and soldiers, after the sacrifices they have made in the war, is such that they will not endure the reactionary labor conditions so openly advocated by the master class. A series of labor struggles is bound to follow—indeed, is beginning now. Shall the Socialist Party continue to feed the workers with social reform legislation at this critical period? Shall it approach the whole question from the standpoint of votes and the election of representatives to the legislatures? Shall it emphasize the consumers' point of view, when Socialist principles teach that the worker is robbed at the point of production? . . ." The manifesto then turned to the immediate tasks ahead. It called upon the American people to organize Workmen's Councils as the instrument for the seizure of power and the basis for the proletarian dictatorship, which is to replace the overthrown government; workmen's control of industry to be exercised by industrial unions or soviets; repudiation of all national debts, with provision to safeguard small investors; expropriation of banks; expropriation of the railways and the large (trust) organizations of capital; the socialization of foreign trade.[174] In addition, the manifesto called for a disciplined party structure, a press and educational institutions owned by the party, and the centralization of party propaganda to avoid private opinions. It was thus a carbon copy, slightly smudged, of Bolshevik manifestoes during the Russian Revolution.

The left-wing convention set up an executive committee to carry the campaign to other states. "With the exception of Larkin, Lindgren and myself," said Ben Gitlow, "the rest of the members of the executive committee [there were six others] were entirely unknown in the Socialist Party and had never before acted in a leading capacity in the movement."[175]

"An astounding state of affairs resulted," said a report of the old national executive committee. "Veterans and pioneers of the movement, who had served the party in many ways for ten, twenty and thirty years, suddenly found they had no rights within the party but to pay dues. Members of the Left Wing, some of them never having joined the Socialist Party, some of them having only a card of the Left Wing, some of them being members only a few weeks, usurped all rights within the party organization."[176]

Although the left-wing leaders were relatively unknown, they had the new magic of Lenin's name behind them. A powerful factor was Lenin's letter to the American workers which was published in *Class Struggle* in December 1918, and a month later in the *Liberator*, the intellectual magazine which had replaced the *Masses*.[177] No revolution, said Lenin, ever had a smooth and assured course. Those who cried out against the horror of the Russian civil war were "sickly sentimentalists." The class struggle in revolutionary situations always provoked counterreaction and terror, and limitations of democracy were the necessary midwives of the revolution. Lenin appealed to the revolutionary traditions of America including the "war of liberation" against the English and the Civil War. Denying any absolute standards of morality and using a *tu quoque* argument, Lenin argued that the bourgeoisie had used terror in its own struggles against the feudal elements, citing 1649 and 1793. Yes, said Lenin, the revolution made mistakes. It had not suddenly turned men into saints, but the 'dead, rotting, polluted, decayed' corpse of the bourgeoisie

[174] Reprinted in *Revolutionary Radicalism, Report of the Joint Legislative Committee Investigating Seditious Activities Filed April 24, 1920, in the Senate of the State of New York*, I, pp. 706-14. This report, in four volumes, generally known as the Lusk Report (and hereafter so cited) after the committee's chairman, is an invaluable source book of socialist and communist documents during the years of World War I.

[175] Benjamin Gitlow, *I Confess* (New York, 1940), p. 27.

[176] Quoted in Fine, *op.cit.*, p. 345.

[177] Reprinted as a pamphlet by International Publishers, New York, in 1934.

could not be put into a coffin without mistakes. Only through mistakes can one learn. The letter was widely cited and used to good effect.

In March 1919 the Third International was born. Under the slogan of "Back to Marx," it adopted the name Communist, as Marx had, to distinguish itself from the social democracy. Rosa Luxemburg, who headed the German *Spartakusbund*, the left wing of German socialism, felt that the creation of the International was premature. She argued presciently that if an International came into existence when the revolutionary movement in the West was still weak, it would mean that the center of gravity of world communism would be Moscow, not Berlin. Hence, the German delegate, Hugo Eberlein, went to Moscow in March 1919 with instructions to oppose the founding of the International. Thus in the founding document of the Communist International, the signature of Germany, key to the advance of communism in Europe, is missing.[178]

One of the first acts of the new International was to order splits in every Socialist Party in the world. The revolution is sweeping Europe, declared the Comintern, and a resolute left-wing movement is necessary to speed it along. In the United States the left wing grew steadily. It seemed as if it would shortly win control of the party. No convention had been held since April 1917 in order to avoid exposing party members to persecution and imprisonment. As a result, the old Hillquit-Berger leadership was still in control. In the spring of 1919 a national referendum was held to elect new officers. The left wing won twelve of the fifteen seats on the national executive committee. For the now crucial post of international delegate, John Reed defeated Victor Berger, and for the equally important post of international secretary, the correspondent with other socialist parties, Kate Richards O'Hare beat Morris Hillquit. Quite coolly, however, the old administration charged election fraud, set aside the vote, and appointed a committee to investigate the election and bring in a report to the party convention in August. It then proceeded systematically to eliminate the left wing. In May, the old national executive committee suspended the seven left-wing foreign-language federations (Hungarian, Lettish, Lithuanian, Polish, Russian, South Slavic, and Ukrainian) thus sloughing off one-third of the party membership. It expelled outright the Michigan state organization for rejecting parliamentary methods. A month later, it eliminated the Massachusetts state body, and in August expelled the Ohio organization. When the Socialist Party convention opened on August 30, 1919, the right wing had saved its hold on the party name and machinery, but had lost two-thirds of the membership. It found official rationalizations for its actions, but the real reason for this summary procedure was the feeling of the old leaders that

[178] E. H. Carr, *Studies in Revolution* (London, 1950), p. 184.

no group of intruders, merely by virtue of signing a party card, was going to take over a party they had spent their lives in building. The left wing had acted, meanwhile, to consolidate its forces. A national conference was called in New York on June 21. But immediately the fatal amoebic process took hold, and the conference split. The sessions opened while the Lusk committee raids were going on, and the conference was forced to move from one hall to another and conduct its meetings in semisecrecy, thus adding to the heavy conspiratorial feeling which inspired the delegates. Although the conference had been called to map plans for the capture of the Socialist Party, an impatient and substantial minority led by Harry Waton pressed for the immediate formation of a communist party. The Russian Federation and the other Slavic groups also favored this step. Most of the American-branch delegates opposed the step and won. Waton shouted "Betrayers!" and bolted to set up the first communist splinter group in the United States.[179] The left wing set up a national council (including Charles Ruthenberg, Louis Fraina, James Larkin, Ben Gitlow, and Bertram D. Wolfe), but the Russian Federation refused membership, and in June, together with the Michigan state organization, issued a call for a convention in Chicago on September 1, 1919, for the purpose of organizing a communist party. In August the majority of the national council, including Fraina, Ruthenberg, and Wolfe, decided that capturing the Socialist Party was impossible, and joined the Russian Federation in sponsoring a communist party. Gitlow and Reed, however, headed a faction which held the fort on the old tactic.[180]

The Socialist Party convention opened in Chicago on August 30, 1919. Various delegates from the Gitlow-Reed faction sought entry but were "screened" by convention manager Julius Gerber and bounced with the help of the Chicago police. When the convention opened, the old leadership elected Seymour Stedman as chairman over Joseph Coldwell, 88 to 37. Thereupon the minority bolted, and with the clamoring Gitlow-Reed faction moved downstairs and formed the Communist Labor Party. Two days after the Socialist convention opened, and a day after the Communist Labor Party was formed, the delegates from the Slavic Federation, the Michigan state organization, and the Fraina-Ruthenberg group met and organized the Communist Party of America, the subsequent history of which will be traced later in this chapter.

However, the Socialist Party was still not out of the factional woods.

[179] In later years, Waton renounced Marxism and organized the Spinoza Institute of America, which during the thirties and forties met regularly in the Labor Temple on New York's Fourteenth Street, where Waton conducted classes and regularly debated with members of various left-wing splinter groups.

[180] See *The American Labor Year Book*, 1919-1920, Pt. 6, pp. 414-17.

The major problem at the 1919 convention was the relationship of the Socialist Party to the international socialist movement. Some efforts had started at Berne to revive the war-torn Second International. In the spring the party had sent James Oneal abroad to observe, and his recommendations of May 7, 1919, rejected affiliation with the Berne conference because it admitted the German "social patriots."[181] At the convention, after the left wing was completely ousted, the majority resolution opposed immediate endorsement of the Third International and called for a new, all-inclusive world body. A minority resolution called for immediate adherence to the Comintern. Both sides agreed, however, that "no party which participates in a government coalition with parties of the bourgeoisie shall be invited." Such was the temper of the "reformist" Socialist Party in 1919! Both resolutions were submitted to referendum, but the *minority* resolution carried by a vote of 3,457 to 1,444—a striking indication of the calamitous decline in party membership and the revolutionary mood of the socialist remnant. Shortly afterward the Socialist Party's application for affiliation was forwarded to Moscow. In other actions as well, the party showed that it was moving left. For the first time the Socialist Party took a stand that it had never dared to take before and unqualifiedly endorsed industrial unionism. Hillquit, who was unable to attend, went even further and in tones reminiscent of the early Debs called for amalgamation of the industrial bodies into one working-class union.

By 1920, the new found revolutionary temper of the party was cooling somewhat. In the spring of 1920 the five socialist assemblymen had been expelled from the state legislature because their pledges of party membership were deemed incompatible with their oaths of office. Hillquit moved, therefore, to rewrite the party bylaws and program.[182] As a result, a new minority led by Alexander Trachtenberg and Benjamin Glassberg, both Rand School teachers, left the party, charging that Hillquit was kowtowing to "Albany" and was seeking to "paint the Socialist Party as a nice, respectable, goody-goody affair. . . ."[183]

On the issue of affiliation with the Comintern, the majority weaseled. It voted to affiliate with the Third International provided "no formula such as 'The Dictatorship of the Proletariat in the form of Soviets' or any other special formula for the attainment of the Socialist commonwealth be imposed . . . as condition of affiliation. . . ." A revolutionary minority,

---

[181] Lusk Report, *op.cit.*, i, pp. 531-36.
[182] A section calling for the expulsion of a party member in public office who voted for war appropriations was dropped. A proviso requiring members of party committees to be citizens was passed. Two provisions of the St. Louis war program, one calling for resistance to conscription and the other calling for repudiation of the war debts, were also dropped.
[183] Lusk Report, *op.cit.*, ii, p. 1778.

led by J. Louis Engdahl, which had not bolted, again called for immediate adherence to the Third International. A third resolution, by Berger, opposed any international organization for the time being. Both the majority (Hillquit) and the minority resolutions were again submitted to a referendum; this time the majority carried by the slim vote of 1,339 to 1,301. The Socialist Party also retreated from the fiery statements of 1919. It redefined its aims as seeking ". . . to secure a majority in Congress . . . to attain its end and by orderly constitutional methods, so long as the ballot box . . . [is] maintained." Debs was once more nominated for the presidency even though—in jail and far removed from the scene—he was unable to campaign. He had always maintained his affiliation with the party.

In August of 1920, the Comintern once and for all settled the issue of Socialist Party affiliation. It issued twenty-one points which it demanded that each party obey as a condition of affiliation. The effect of these conditions was to tie securely each national party to Moscow's orders. The Communist International, said Zinoviev, was not a hotel where each member party could pick and choose its course.[184]

In November 1920 the Socialist Party application was rejected. The minority Engdahl-Kruse group then bolted. A month later the Finnish Federation withdrew.

By the quixotic whim of political fate, at a time when the flame of American socialism was guttering, Debs polled 919,799 votes, the highest total of votes in the two decades of American socialism. There was no money and there was little campaigning. But it was a personal vote, a gesture of homage to a gallant individual, a protest against the inept Democratic and Republican choices, and a protest against the government's brutal repressions of 1919. Although Debs did not follow the party quarrels closely, he reacted sharply to the twenty-one points. "The Mos-

[184] Among the twenty-one conditions were these: (1) all propaganda to be of Communist character, and the party press to be centralized under the control of the Central Committee; (2) removal of all "reformist" and "centrist" elements; (3) creation of a parallel underground apparatus and preparation for immediate revolution— "In nearly every country in Europe and America the class struggle is entering upon the phase of civil war. In such circumstances the Communists have no confidence in bourgeois legality"; (7) the repudiation of [and here the Comintern was specific] Turati, Kautsky, Hilferding, Hillquit, Longuet, MacDonald, Modigliani [It is interesting to note that except for the Italians, these men were not reformists, but the representatives of orthodox Marxism and its recognized interpreters. These men, not the reformists, were the ones Moscow feared.]; (12) acceptance of the principle of democratic centralism; (16) all resolutions of the Comintern to be binding on the constituent parties; (17) adoption of the name Communist.

When Zinoviev was asked what he would do if one of the center socialist parties (particularly the Hilferding group in Germany, which was wavering) accepted the twenty-one conditions, he replied, "We would find a twenty-second." See Ruth Fischer, Stalin and German Communism (Cambridge, Mass., 1948), pp. 141-43.

cow program wants to commit us," he said, "to a policy of armed insurrection. . . . [It is] ridiculous, arbitrary and autocratic."[185] In other ways, too, Debs reacted against the Bolsheviks. Emotionally sympathetic to their revolution, he was critical of its methods and recoiled from its ruthlessness. Although the communists today seek to canonize Debs, he expressed himself from the beginning against the continued use of terror by the Bolsheviks. He was angered at what he thought was the unnecessary murder of the Tsar, and when in June 1922 the socialist revolutionaries were put on trial, he cabled to Moscow a strong protest against their possible execution or "the unjust denial of their liberty."[186]

By 1921, the Socialist Party had almost turned its back on communism. The Jewish and Bohemian federations had left. The last adherents of the committee for the Third International had also gone. At the June convention, for the first time in its history, the party lifted its ban on cooperation with other radical and liberal groups. It now talked of a labor party in which it would find a place, and voted to join the Conference for Progressive Political Action. There was, however, little left. On paper the Socialist Party claimed 10,000 members; it was a paper membership.

There is a simple human tendency to try to read the present backwards into the past. For that reason, and because the communists shrilly cried reformism, there is a tendency among historians to obscure the fact that the Socialist Party in the period from 1919 to 1921, purged as it was of the communists, had in fact succumbed to the Bolshevik aberration, and that Hillquit, the arch-symbol of the "right," had come out vigorously as favoring revolutionary action. Nor was this wholly rhetorical. Hillquit prided himself on being an orthodox Marxist, in this respect following Kautsky, and was in those years a believer in the possible necessity of force in defending a socialist revolution against the capitalist class. Following the 1919 split, Hillquit wrote in the *Call* on September 22, 1919: "The division was not brought about by differences on vital questions of principles. It arose over disputes on methods and policy, and even within that limited sphere it was largely one of emphasis rather than fundamentals."[187] Hillquit's differences with the left lay primarily in his estimate of American conditions and his objection to the mechanical and slavish copying of bolshevism's illegal work, which he felt unnecessary in the United States. In his analysis of the failure of the Second International he applied an economic determinist analysis and concluded: "It was the economic organization of the European workers, and the pressure of their

---

[185] James Oneal, *American Communism* (New York, 1927), p. 104.
[186] David Karsner, *Talks with Debs in Terre Haute* (New York, 1922), pp. 171-73.
[187] Lusk Report, *op.cit.*, I, p. 557.

immediate economic interests (as understood by them) that broke the solidarity of the Socialist International . . . not parliamentarism. . . ." And, in an analysis which reflects both Lenin and De Leon, he continued: "The fundamental weakness of the organized labor movement has been that it was a movement of a class within a class, a movement for the benefit of the better-situated strata of labor—the skilled workers. . . . They had certain 'vested interests' in the capitalist regimes of their respective countries." Such a condition creates, he said, craft rather than class solidarity and deflects the worker from the ultimate goal to concern with immediate benefits. "In such conditions, the parliamentary activities of labor's political representatives cannot but reflect the narrow economic policies of their constituents." Turning to the present, he said, "In countries like Germany, in which the struggle for mastery lies between two divisions of the Socialist movement, one [the independent socialists, led by Haase, Dittmann, and Hilferding] class-conscious and the other opportunist [led by Ebert and Scheidemann], one radical and the other temporizing, the support of the Socialist International must . . . go to the former."[188]

Hillquit later gave these ideas theoretical expression in a remarkable little book called *From Marx to Lenin*, published in New York in 1921. Although criticizing the Communist International because "it is essentially Russian in structure, concept and program," Hillquit defended the idea of the dictatorship of the proletariat and of soviets, which he regarded merely as "occupational representation." "The Dictatorship of the Proletariat contrary to widespread popular assumption is not the antithesis of Democracy. In the Marxian view the two institutions are by no means incompatible. . . . it is frankly a limited form of democracy but it is a higher form than the democracy of the bourgeoisie because it means the actual rule of the majority over the minority while the latter represents the rule of a minority over the majority."[189] Thus, the socialist picture from 1917 to 1921 is not a simple one of "left" vs. "right" but a complete shift of the *entire* socialist movement to a frame of reference completely outside the structure of American life. By opposing World War I (I am not passing judgment but analyzing consequences) the Socialist Party cut itself off from the labor movement and created a widespread distrust of itself among the American people. In its rush to embrace a policy which bordered on adventurism, the party isolated itself completely from the main streams of American political life. When, in 1921, it had come back to even keel, it was by then a broken shell.

[188] The New York *Call*, May 21, 1919; quoted in Lusk Report, *op.cit.*, I, pp. 524-30.
[189] Morris Hillquit, *From Marx to Lenin* (New York, 1921), pp. 57, 59.

IX. The Melancholy Intermezzo

Nineteen-nineteen—for one brief moment the revolution flared, like a pillar of fire, and then guttered, leaving the American radical movement sitting among the gray, dry ashes. Nineteen-nineteen—almost every issue of the *Nation*, the *New Republic*, and the *Dial* carried articles with "revolution" in their titles. The specter that haunted Europe for sixty years was no longer distant but immediately overhead. It seemed, too, that America might have to face the same ghost. The war had produced a set of social tensions that could not be released gently. The uprooting of hundreds of thousands of persons, the patriotic sentiments that had been whipped to a high frenzy, all churned American society into an emotional jag which sought relief in violence or vicarious outlets.

The measure of recognition that labor achieved during the war evaporated quickly. The cost of living was soaring and wages lagging. Unemployment was rising and employers becoming more demanding. The result was an eruption of mass strikes on a scale never before seen in American society. Four days after the armistice, the Amalgamated Clothing Workers called a general strike which sent 50,000 tailors into the streets of New York. In January 1919 the city's longshoremen and harbor workers called a general strike that stopped all harbor traffic. The next month the entire labor movement of Seattle walked out in a general strike shutting the city down tight for five days: street cars stopped running; theaters and barber shops closed; labor guards patroled the streets; garbage wagons and funeral cars could proceed only with permits from the strike committee—it was a vignette of the Paris Commune. Over the border in Winnipeg a general strike was smashed by government forces with the deportation of the strike leaders. And across the United States there spread a demand for an eight-hour day which brought a general strike to strife-torn Lawrence, Massachusetts. The fever spread rapidly: New England telephone workers, New York actors, printing pressmen, longshoremen, railway shopmen and switchmen, in Boston even the policemen, the "armed minions" of the capitalist state, walked out, frightening the town and bringing Governor Calvin Coolidge in quickly with the state troops to break the strike. Some 367,000 workers challenged United States Steel, the great behemoth of American industry, in a strike which ran four months before being crushed by the iron hand of Judge Elbert Gary. A threat by John L. Lewis to call a national coal strike was halted only when a federal court injunction tied up strike benefit payments, and when Woodrow Wilson had denounced the proposal. More than 4,160,000 workers were out on strike that year. It seemed as if the revolution were coming.[190]

[190] J. B. S. Hardman, "Postscript to Ten Years of Labor Movement," *American Labor Dynamics* (New York, 1928), pp. 9-14.

Nineteen-nineteen was also a year of reaction. Woodrow Wilson's attorney general, A. Mitchell Palmer, led the pack in a series of "Red Raids" to exorcise the revolutionary threat. Palmer warned that 60,000 subversive radicals were loose in the country, and obtained 6,000 warrants for the arrest of dangerous aliens. On January 2, 1920, Palmer's men swooped down and in simultaneous raids in thirty-three cities netted 2,500 suspected radicals. In many cases, individuals were held incommunicado, persons were picked up without warrants, agents-provocateurs infiltrated radical sects and prodded the groups to violence. In New York, the five socialist assemblymen were ousted from Albany. In all, four thousand persons were arrested, one thousand ordered deported. Throughout the land, roving bands of vigilantes and ex-servicemen added to the hysteria by raiding I.W.W. headquarters, foreign-language clubs, etc., and beating up anyone found there. Xenophobia was rampant and found endorsement in a magazine article by the new vice-president, Calvin Coolidge. The hysteria against foreigners boiled up so that no one considered it odd that two Italian anarchists, Nicola Sacco and Bartolomeo Vanzetti, were arrested in May 1920 and charged with murder during an ordinary payroll robbery.

The outrages mounted so high that in the same month a group of lawyers headed by Charles Evans Hughes issued a report on the illegal practices of the U.S. Department of Justice stating: "We cannot afford to ignore the indications that, perhaps to an extent unparalleled in our history, the essentials of liberty are being disregarded. . . . [We know of] . . . violations of personal rights which savor of the worst practices of tyranny."[191]

In this atmosphere American industry launched its union-busting campaign under the slogan of the American Plan. By the autumn of 1920 the country was covered with a network of open-shop organizations. Fifty open-shop associations were active in New York State alone. In every industry the drive was carried on. By 1923 unionism had less than 3,620,000 members, as compared to more than 5,000,000 in 1920.[192]

Nineteen-nineteen was also the year that labor took a plunge into national independent political action. The impulses behind this move were varied. Many socialist trade unionists, forced out of the Socialist Party by the left wing, were looking for new paths; the railroad brotherhoods, who had fared well when the government took over the roads during the war, endorsed the Plumb Plan for government ownership, and sought to implement this move through political action; other unions, in reaction

[191] Chief Justice Charles Evans Hughes, *Two Addresses Delivered before the Alumni of the Harvard Law School*, Cambridge, June 21, 1920; cited in G. Louis Joughin and Edmund M. Morgan, *The Legacy of Sacco and Vanzetti* (New York, 1948), p. 211.
[192] Leo Wolman, *Ebb and Flow in Trade Unionism* (New York, 1936), p. 26.

to the events of 1919, endorsed public ownership of basic industries as a desirable goal. And, as if in prevision of what an alert labor movement could do, the solid success of the farmers' movements raised hopes that a *native* political appeal would enlist the voters where the socialists had failed. In Chicago, long the home of independent parties (one had been formed in 1851), the American Federation of Labor took the lead and organized the Labor Party of Cook County. In April 1919 it polled a sizable 50,000 votes for John Fitzpatrick, local A.F.L. head, for mayor. Satisfied with this showing, Fitzpatrick continued to take the initiative and in November 1919 called a national conference in Chicago out of which emerged the American Labor Party. Though new born, the party felt ready to enter the 1920 presidential campaign and named a ticket headed by Max Hayes, the veteran socialist leader who had left the Socialist Party after Ruthenberg had captured the Ohio movement, and Duncan MacDonald, head of the Illinois Federation of Labor, a miner and also a former Socialist Party member. In July 1920 the new Labor Party merged with the Committee of Forty-Eight, a group of liberals and ex-Bull Moosers headed by Amos Pinchot, and created instead the Farmer-Labor Party. This new coalition nominated for president a lawyer of Utah, Parley Christensen (one of the forty-eighters), and Max Hayes for vice-president. The Socialist Party refused to consider a joint slate and nominated Debs. Although the Farmer-Labor Party started from scratch and with a set of political unknowns, it managed to roll up a creditable 300,000 votes. The following year it won the official endorsement of the United Mine Workers. In 1922, seeking to broaden its base, the Farmer-Labor Party sent out an appeal to labor unions and leftist political parties to join. The socialists refused, but the communists, reversing their sectarian tactics, set out to capture the new party. When the convention opened on July 3, 1923, the genuine farmer-labor delegates found themselves outnumbered by a flood of disguised communist delegates. It was the first demonstration of the successful use of the front technique. A motley array of organizations claiming to represent workers sought credentials: sports clubs, workers' choral societies, vegetarian outfits, etc. (Sample: The Lithuanian Workers Vegetarian and Chorale Singing Society.) Fitzpatrick repudiated the conference, but the communists took over and built the first of its many "Potemkin Village" fronts, naming this one the Federated Farmer-Labor Party. The net effect of this Pyrrhic victory, however, was to send a chastened and bitter Fitzpatrick back to the Gompers fold and to destroy the tolerance of the Chicago Federation of Labor for the communists.

Meanwhile, the Minnesota Farmer-Labor Party, proceeding on its own, sought to push national independent political action. In June 1924 it called a national conference to launch a national Farmer-Labor Party. Again the communist cohorts arrived in depth and captured the party; the genuine farmer-laborites withdrew in dismay.

The large national unions, meanwhile, had kept aloof from the political efforts centering in Chicago and Minnesota. A number of them, however, favored coordinated political action on a national scale, and in February 1922, on the initiative of the railway brotherhoods, set up the Conference for Progressive Political Action (C.P.P.A.). The garment workers joined, and other unions endorsed the conference. The socialists, who had remained aloof from previous attempts, now expressed their interest. The basic idea of the C.P.P.A., however, was to follow the tactics of the North Dakota Non-Partisan League and nominate reliable candidates on old-party tickets. It would name labor candidates only when circumstances made it impossible to capture an old-party nomination. From the start the socialists sought to turn the movement into a full-fledged labor party. A motion to that end was defeated in December 1922 by the close vote of 64 to 52. Clashes between the socialists and the laborites continued, and an especially sharp conflict on the issue arose in New York in 1923. In the normal course of such events the friction among the incompatible groups would have been sufficient to disrupt the conference. But two incidents after 1922 served to hold the movement together. One was the spectacular postwar success of the British Labour Party in its replacement of Lloyd George's rapidly fading Liberal Party, a success giving rise to the hope that a repetition was possible here. The second was the Harding Ohio-gang scandals, in which William G. McAdoo, "labor's friend," was "smeared with oil." It is likely that if the Democrats had nominated McAdoo, there would have been no third-party campaign in 1924. But when the G.O.P. named Calvin Coolidge and the Democrats nominated a safe and respectable Wall Street lawyer, John W. Davis, the unions felt no alternative was possible. La Follette, aging and eager to run, clinched the decision.

If the socialists had hoped that the La Follette campaign would open the way to a firmly based Labor Party, the election events showed, as Hillquit put it, that the campaign was only an "intermezzo." The socialists and the farmer-labor groups came to the 1924 convention fully prepared to organize a permanent new party. But La Follette was against one; so were the large unions. La Follette was nominated beforehand in order to avoid the formal issue from the floor and the embarrassing attempt to organize a third party. Hillquit challenged the procedure, but the free railroad passes of the members of the Brotherhood accounted for the good attendance and the socialists were beaten.[193] Hillquit then pleaded that the progressives nominate supporting tickets in various states, pointing out that only on that basis could an effective campaign be carried on.

[193] David McKay, *The Progressive Movement of 1924* (New York, 1947), p. 119.

But even this motion was defeated. The unions endorsed La Follette but remained nonpartisan in the congressional and local campaigns. In New York the Socialist Party put La Follette at the head of its ticket and ran Norman Thomas for governor. But Thomas got only traditional socialist union support because Al Smith was running against Theodore Roosevelt, Jr., and the unions feared to jeopardize his chances. Hillquit's prediction that the lack of supporting tickets would immobilize the La Follette campaign in many states proved true. But the unions were caught in the "practical" dilemma and could find no way out. Gompers and the American Federation of Labor endorsed La Follette, the first such act in their history, even though they warned that they were not supporting any third party, only the man. Although officially supported by the American Federation of Labor, the moral and financial support from the organization was small, and it dwindled to nothing by election day. Some unions bolted. The pressmen, led by George Berry, supported Davis. Hutcheson of the carpenters and Lewis of the miners supported Coolidge.

The communist-dominated Farmer-Labor Party nominated Duncan MacDonald and William Bouck, and then sought to make a deal with the C.P.P.A. for a common ticket. However, neither La Follette nor any of the unions would have anything to do with the farmer-laborites. Suddenly, on Moscow's order, the communists reversed their position, dumped the bewildered MacDonald and Bouck, abandoned their dummy organization, and nominated William Z. Foster and Benjamin Gitlow on the Workers Party ticket.

In the election La Follette polled a disappointing 4,826,471 votes, or approximately 17 per cent of the total. In the apathetic nation only half the eligible voters had turned out to vote. La Follette had carried Wisconsin, run well in North Dakota, and had carried the city of Cleveland, but little else. His strength, as one historian of the campaign analyzes it, was drawn largely from the farmers (to the tune of 2,530,000 votes). Of the remainder, a million votes had been contributed by the socialists and a million came from labor.[194] Officially, La Follette was credited with 3,797,974 votes from the Progressive Party, 858,264 from the socialists, and 170,233 from farmer-laborites.

When the C.P.P.A. met in February 1925 it was a defeated and dispirited organization. The socialists pressed for the continuance of the movement, but the unions opposed any new third-party venture and the conference was liquidated. "Time and common cause," writes McKay, "would never quite overcome this basic weakness in the progressive movement. The labor men always suspected the Socialists; the latter, in turn, reciprocated the distrust."[195]

An era was drawing to a close. One year after the campaign, La Follette

[194] *Ibid.*, p. 221. [195] *Ibid.*, p. 73.

was dead. A year later Debs passed away. The critics were writing off the Socialist Party as well. In *Current History* for June 1924 David Karsner wrote of "The Passing of the Socialist Party," while two years later in the same magazine William J. Ghent wrote the party's epitaph.[196] The Socialist Party, he argued, was the victim of the nationalism of the war and the lessened interest in social progress that came in the twenties. In 1928 the vote of 267,835 for Norman Thomas seemed to confirm the gloomy predictions; it was the lowest vote the party had received since 1900. Socialism was at ebb tide.

X. *The Caligari World of Underground Communism*

If in 1919 the United States had a whiff of class warfare, to the communists this whiff was a heady potion. To them it was the wind that heralded the apocalypse. "Workers, the United States seems to be on the verge of a revolutionary crisis. The workers, through their mass strikes, are challenging the State. . . . Out of these mass industrial struggles must issue the means and the inspiration for the conquest of power by the workers. BOYCOTT THE ELECTIONS," declared the *Communist World*, the organ of the new Communist Party, in its first issue on November 1, 1919.[197]

With "victory" so near on the horizon, it was almost inevitable that the communist movement would split into innumerable sects, each claiming to possess the political formula for victory and denouncing others as an enemy greater than the capitalist class—for the competitor could only "mislead" the ready-to-be converted and so take them down the political primrose path.[198]

In September of 1919 two communist parties opened their conventions in Chicago. The one, calling itself the Communist Party, opened its sessions at the "Smolny."[199] No sooner was Louis Fraina elected chairman

---

[196] W. J. Ghent, "The Collapse of Socialism in the United States," *Current History*, May 1926, pp. 242-46.

[197] Lusk Report, *op.cit.*, p. 758.

[198] The sociology of sects has rarely been explored. We know that sects arise most frequently in periods of disorganization when the crust of convention has cracked, and cosmic and apocalyptic answers find more ready acceptance. In such periods, also, there is a tendency for the sects to divide and become two, typically more bitter toward each other than toward the "world" which they formerly united in opposing. The religious experiences also suggest the analogy that in the moments before salvation, or ecstasy, one must achieve *purity*, hence such rituals as absolution, purification baths, etc. The literature on the Hellenistic, Oriental, and Christian mystery sects is vast, beginning with the fount, Sir James Frazer's *Golden Bough*. For a formal sociological analysis see Georg Simmel, "The Secret and the Secret Societies," in *The Sociology of Georg Simmel* (tr. and ed. by Kurt H. Wolff; Glencoe, Ill., 1950), and Ellsworth Faris, "The Sect and the Sectarian," *Papers and Proceedings . . . American Sociological Society*, xxii (1927), pp. 144-58.

[199] The headquarters of the Russian Federation of the party, so named in imitation of the Bolshevik Party headquarters in Petrograd where the revolution had started.

than the convention broke into three factions. One was the Slavic bloc, another the Michigan state delegation (with which the Slavic bloc had united in June), and the third the Fraina-Ruthenberg group from the left-wing national conference. Formally the disagreements arose over phraseology and tactics. The Michigan delegates were suspicious of the Slavic bloc's phrase "mass action" in the party's declaration—fearing it meant approval of insurrection—and sought a commitment to "political action." The Ruthenberg wing wanted unity with the Gitlow-Reed communist group, but the Russians of the Slavic bloc feared they would be outvoted in a larger party. Finally Ruthenberg and the Russians reconciled their differences, and the Michigan delegates bolted to form a third communist party. The Communist Party platform called for "mass action" to destroy the bourgeois state[200] and to ensure its replacement by the dictatorship of the proletariat. The platform affirmed its purity by declaring that the party would not collaborate with the Socialist Party, Labor Party, Non-Partisan League, People's Council, Municipal Ownership League, etc., and would name candidates only for the legislature, shunning all nomination for executive offices.

The rival Communist Labor Party had its troubles, too: it had to face the damning charge of containing "centrists," i.e., unreliable petty-bourgeois elements. A small group of delegates, including Louis B. Boudin and Ludwig Lore, had refused to accept the extreme positions of bolshevism. Boudin, with a reputation as a foremost Marxian scholar, worried the Communist Labor Party leaders with his pronouncement that their program was un-Marxian and in violation of the *Communist Manifesto*. The issue was dissipated, however, when Gitlow informed Reed, who was to answer Boudin: "Don't worry, I have the Communist Manifesto with me and I have just the quotation you need to show up Boudin."[201] "Exposed" thus as "diluting" the revolutionary content of the program, Boudin fled the convention, and Bolshevik purity was maintained.

The Michigan delegates who bolted formed the Proletarian Party in June 1920 with branches in Detroit, Rochester, and Buffalo—the first communist "splinter" party in the United States. The Proletarian Party, under the leadership of John Keracher, survived down through the depression, and spurted briefly in the 1930's, principally in Detroit. It was effaced, however, when a number of its active members rose in the United Auto Workers' hierarchy and found themselves, of necessity, going along in support of the Political Action Committee and the Democratic Party.

In the winter following the conventions each of the parties exhausted its energies in attacks on the other. The Communist Party, composed in

---

[200] Interestingly enough, in revolutionary rhetoric at this time the phrase "the state" replaced the older "ruling class."
[201] Gitlow, *op.cit.*, p. 52.

the main of foreign-language groups, derided the Communist Labor Party as "desiring to be a revolutionary proletarian party without the proletariat," since nearly 60 per cent of the wage workers were of foreign birth. The Communist Labor Party declared that its opponent held a philosophy of revolutionary splitting—that is, "the more you split, the 'clearer' and stronger you become." It recalled that Nick Hourwich, the leader of the Russian Federation, had explained that "in order to have a group of uncompromising leaders competent to lead the working class when the final crisis comes, you must constantly 'split and split and split.' You must keep the organization small and constantly bring about situations within the party that will result in splits." In this way the membership would be refined so that a small group would be "clear" and thus determine who was "not clear."[202] The position, while a caricature, was a logical extension of the tactic of Zinoviev, the head of the Third International, in splitting every European socialist party and creating new "purified" parties to carry through the revolution. This logic was matched by the German communists (Spartacists), under the leadership of August Thalheimer, who refused in 1920 to support the general strike called by the German trade unions against the rightist Kapp *Putsch*, on the ground that these were both "counter-revolutionary wings."[203]

However "logical" the tactic may have been, it did have the mathematical consequence of reducing the membership of the communist parties, and scaring away thousands of others. Before the September 1 cleavage in the Socialist Party, the left wing had approximately 60,000 members (about a tenth of whom belonged to the nonforeign-language sections). After the splits, and the Department of Justice raids of November 1919, the two communist parties had less than 13,000 members.

In May 1920, following a letter from Zinoviev, the two parties met in secret convention and fused into the United Communist Party. Retreating from the flamboyant proclamations of the previous six months, the new party abandoned the idea of mass action as the means of freeing wartime political prisoners still in jail, although it declared that "the working class must be prepared for armed insurrection as the final form of mass action by which the workers shall conquer the state," and declared that the

---

[202] For those who worried about splits, a communist magazine was reassuring. It justified the numerous splits on the basis of a biological analogy. "The law of life in biology is division of cells and so it is the law of social science," the editor observed. "The more active divisions, the larger the great body of trained men and women at the crisis." There are those who lament that "the past year has witnessed more division than at any time in the history of the movement," he continued, but this should really not be a matter of discouragement. "Don't worry about division; rather fear the opposite," was his conclusion. See the *Western Worker*, Oakland, Calif., May 20, 1921; cited in Oneal, *op.cit.*, p. 77.

[203] Ruth Fischer, *op.cit.*, p. 126.

state was the coercive organ of the ruling class and that democracy was the empty privilege of periodically voting to confirm this rule.[204]

This "retreat" was not to the liking, however, of a substantial faction at the unity convention, which forthwith bolted and called itself the Communist Party. This faction attacked the new party as insufficiently revolutionary, as led by "adventurers and charlatans," and denounced the platform which "reeked with '*the bourgeois capitalist horror of the destruction of property and lives.*'" It denounced the United Communist Party also for considering force "*as a purely defensive measure—not as an offensive measure* for which the Communists must consciously prepare." It further mocked the new party for its lack of theoretical clarity in "the use of the term 'soviet rule under a working-class dictatorship' [which] shows a fundamental lack of understanding, [for, as everyone knows,] the Soviet Government is a form of proletarian dictatorship."[205] The bolters claimed 8,000 members, almost all of whom were of the Slavic federations, while the new United Communists had less than 3,500 members.[206] Despite the low estate of the membership of the United Communist Party, and perhaps because of its high élan, Zinoviev regarded it as the destined instrument of the revolution. He ordered the new party "immediately to establish an underground organisation even though it is possible for the Party to function legally . . . [in order to] direct revolutionary propaganda . . . and, in case of violent suppression of the legal Party organisation, [to permit] of carrying on the work."[207]

Moscow could not allow the two warring sects to continue their feud, and in 1921, under the watchful eye of a Communist International representative, a partial working unity was restored. But by 1921 the tide of world revolution had receded, and it left stranded in its backwash a number of minor sects each of which desperately sought the northwest passage—or portage—to the revolutionary seas. One of the first was the Industrial Communists, who organized in November 1919 in Terre Haute, Indiana. Their program (a garish blend of De Leon's industrial-union republic and Lenin's soviets) declared that modern society revolved around six basic industries and that the revolutionary party, in its organization, had to be a microcosmic reflection of this fact; thus the assumption of power would automatically produce industrial communism.[208]

[204] Lusk Report, *op.cit.*, II, p. 1882.
[205] Oneal, *op.cit.*, p. 91.
[206] Picayune as these doctrinal formulations may seem, they were, to the parties concerned, as serious and meaningful as that, say, of the Dunkers whose religious sect split on the issue of multiple foot-washing, one party insisting that each person should wash the feet of only one other, while their opponents contended that each should wash the feet of several, as a condition of salvation.
[207] Lusk Report, *op.cit.*, II, p. 1907.
[208] De Leon's Socialist Labor Party went through this period with its doctrinal

A year later they changed their name to the Proletarian Socialist Party, and in two years' time faded into the Rummagers' League. This group, disillusioned by party organization, became an educational society with its announced purpose to "rummage the field of history and science so as to develop the keenest intellects possible."[209] After issuing one number of its magazine, the *Rummager*, the group, to paraphrase Trotsky, was swept into the dustbin of sectarian history. By 1921 other spores emerged. These included, among others, the Committee for a Third International, headed by J. Louis Engdahl, which had left the Socialist Party in 1920; and the Workers Council, which was sympathetic to the Committee for a Third International but refused to accept the Comintern declaration that "the class struggle in almost every country in Europe and Asia is entering the phase of civil war." "By the end of 1921," summarizes Oneal, "no less than twelve communist organizations had been formed, of which eight were of a political character and intended to function as political organizations. Of these . . . seven had either died or merged."

By the end of 1921 a number of the underground communist parties had begun chafing at their burrowed existence. The United Communist Party sent up a periscope in the form of the American Labor Alliance. Shortly thereafter, the New York communists tentatively moved toward legality by forming the Workers League, which nominated Ben Gitlow for mayor, and even formulated a set of immediate demands, a step that had been repudiated two years before. Other straws were in the wind. In October, Max Eastman, the strongest intellectual supporter of the communists, attacked the underground parties for ignoring reality.

By the end of the year a number of open groups converged and in December 1921 formed the Workers Party, headed by James P. Cannon. This new party seemingly united all of the aboveground communists except the Proletarian Party. However, in February 1922 a new group, called the Workers Defense Conference of New England, emerged with a new party called the United Toilers of America. The constituent organizations (the Ukrainian, Lettish, and Polish Publishing Associations, and the Women's Progressive Alliance) made it clear that it was the creation of those underground groups of communists who believed that the organization of the Workers Party was a "betrayal" of the masses. The situation is best explained by an account of the bizarre underground maneuverings written by one of the former participants, Ben Gitlow.

"The underground Communist Party was affiliated with the Third or Communist International, but the Workers Party was not. Among the

---

purity untouched. A fastidious party by now, it scorned the Marxian illiteracy of the communists who would not learn De Leon's formulas intact and accept the Socialist Labor Party as their teacher and leader.

[209] Oneal, *op.cit.*, p. 109.

members in the movement, the underground Communist Party was known as the 'Number One' organization, while the Workers Party was the 'Number Two' organization. A large section of the underground Communist Party split away from the underground movement, feeling that the Workers Party was given too much autonomy and that its program was no more than a remote approach to the Communist program. Regarding the Workers Party as a dilution of Communist principle and a step leading toward the dissolution of the Communist movement, this group which called itself the United Toilers and was nicknamed by Lovestone the 'United Toilets,' published in its official paper, *The Workers Challenge*, edited by Harry M. Wicks, the most violent and vituperative polemics in America.[210] I should say that ninety-nine percent of the United Toilers membership came from the foreign-language federations; they were chiefly Russians, Letts, Ukrainians and Lithuanians with a handful and a sprinkling of English-speaking members.

"It soon became very clear to me that the deciding factor in the situation was Number One, the underground Communist Party, where the internal struggle was over the question of its relations with the Workers Party, or in the broader sense, its attitude toward legal public activity. On this issue Number One was divided into three main caucuses. The largest of these was the so-called Goose Caucus. . . .[211] The name 'Goose Caucus' originated in the course of a stormy debate, when William F. Dunne, exasperated by Jakira's unceasing and persistent stuttering interjected, 'Jakira, you make me sick; you cackle like a Goose,' and Amter, springing to the defense of his fellow factionalist, retorted, 'But the geese saved Rome and we shall yet save the Party,' while Lovestone, counter-attacking with ridicule, shouted back, 'All right then, from now on you're the Goose Caucus.' The name stuck.

"The Goose Caucus looked with suspicion and contempt on those members of Number Two who were not at the same time members of Number One, fought against the immediate liquidation of the underground movement, hoping in time, as soon as the changed situation in the country warranted it, to transform Number One into a legal party espousing the Communist cause.

"The chief opponents of the Geese were the Liquidators (a name bor-

[210] [Special mention should be made of the vituperative rhetoric employed by extreme revolutionary sectarians in their debate. One example from the above-named publication: "That asinine assumption of humanity and pusillanimous purveyor of putrid punk that calls himself managing editor of the official organ of the Workers Party. . . ." At one point, V. I. Lenin, no mean polemicist himself, called this left-wing communism "an infantile disorder." It was a shrewd thrust, with a psychoanalytic overtone beyond the intent of the author. D.B.]

[211] [Its leaders were L. E. Katterfeld, secretary of the party, Abraham Jakira, leader of the Russian Federation, Alfred Wagenknecht, Israel Amter, and Edward Lindgren.]

rowed from the situation in Russian Social Democracy after the revolution of 1905) who allied themselves with the non-members in Number Two, using them as political leverage for wresting control of Number One from the Geese. The Liquidators were led by Jay Lovestone, Charles E. Ruthenberg, James P. Cannon, William Z. Foster and Earl Browder.[212]

"Between these two chief contending forces were the Conciliators, who hoped to gain control by pleading unity and by holding the balance of power between the two extreme factions. While the Liquidators sought to have the Workers Party supersede the Communist Party in effect, the Conciliators recognized it as merely the legal front of Number One."[213]

The underground comedy ended finally in uproarious burlesque. In August 1922 the secret Communist Party held a convention in the woods near Bridgman, Michigan, to settle the question of legality. Three nuncios had been sent by the Comintern to guide the decisions toward open activity. Stealthily the communists converged on the wooded lakelands. Elaborate precautions against detection had been taken. The delegates traveled in small squads of two to five members, each with a captain; the routes were so laid out that the delegates would not converge in large numbers and thus arouse suspicion. Better known communists changed trains a half dozen times to throw possible shadowers off the track. Finally the squads gathered at Bridgman, a small ramshackle town of a few houses, where each stranger stuck out like a drugstore neon sign on Saturday night. The convention opened, the delegates gamboled and frolicked gaily on the lake front. And dancing with them was a Department of Justice agent with the Hollywood monicker of "K-97." When the rites had gone far enough, other agents, who had hidden in the trees, crashed the festivities and rounded up the cultists. Since it was almost as difficult to camouflage the Department of Justice watchers as it was the communists, the underground leaders heard the noise and fled. Before the hurried escape, however, all the party records, including membership lists, were buried conveniently in the presence of K-97, and later deposited in government archives.

[212] [Foster, at that time, was a member of the Workers Party, and only secretly of the underground Communist Party.]

[213] Gitlow, op.cit., pp. 132-34. From the depths of his later disillusion, Gitlow comments: "But it is really a waste of time to discuss principles in reference to this controversy, for principles played a subsidiary role; they were merely verbose rationalizations to cover up the main consideration—to gain control of the Party apparatus." The currently fashionable reduction of all political motives to a power drive does violence both to the complexities of human delusions and the peculiar hold of doctrinal pieties among men whose lives are caught up in compulsive missions. Such individuals may be driven to desire power, but such urges can be seen without contradiction and more meaningfully as a desire to make incarnate their own visions as well as to obtain the satisfactions of deference and respect from others. Ideological fanaticism, i.e., the conviction that only the knowing believer has the absolute key to the truth, is a more complex phenomenon than the hedonistic impulse to power.

Before its abrupt end the convention had voted by a narrow margin to continue the Goose Caucus line for an underground existence. But the government raid had made such cloak-and-dagger masquerades a joke, and early in 1923 the communists came up for air.

The Workers Party that emerged from the bramble patch was an emaciated, hollow-chested, feral case. It claimed 20,000 members; other estimates put the figure closer to 13,000.[214] Ninety per cent of the membership, however, was in the foreign-language federations, which led a life of their own separate from the American scene. "If we were to read the nine dailies and twenty-one weeklies of the Workers' Party carefully, one would get the complete picture of all European countries, but a very incomplete picture of political life in America," wrote John Pepper, the Comintern "Rep" (i.e., representative) in 1923.[215] The caption of the article was "Be American," and in that direction the Communist Party now sought to turn. The factionalism, however, remained. It was to continue for six years.

Two major groups had coalesced in the communist movement by 1923. One was headed by William Z. Foster and his two lieutenants, Earl Browder and James P. Cannon. The other was led by Charles Ruthenberg and the Hungarian communist John Pepper; their chief aid was Jay Lovestone.

William Z. Foster, born in 1881, had achieved a reputation as a skillful trade-union organizer. At an early age he had gone to work, and by twenty, diagnosed as consumptive, he headed West. There he was drawn into socialist work, and through his activity in logging camps passed into the I.W.W. He disagreed, however, with the Wobblies' dual unionism; and a trip to Europe brought an acquaintance with the theories of the French syndicalists and the promulgation of his famous tactic of "boring from within."

Foster argued that withdrawal of the radicals from existing unions merely isolated them and that the workers would not turn from unions which ministered to their needs, even ineffectively. Hence the necessity of an organized core for joining and capturing the American Federation of Labor.[216] Foster sought to swing the Wobbly convention of 1911 to his new tactic, but failed. He then formed the Syndicalist League of North America, and later the International Trade Union Educational League, in order to train "cadres" for work in unions. Foster, however, exercised only a small though potent influence in the Chicago labor movement. During the war the militant Foster was quiet. He sold Liberty

[214] See Oneal, op.cit., p. 145; Gitlow, op.cit., p. 158.
[215] Oneal, op.cit., p. 145.
[216] David Saposs, Left Wing Unionism (New York, 1926), pp. 48-49; William Z. Foster, American Trade Unionism (New York, 1947), pp. 14-15.

Bonds and some left-winger accused him as well of "having sold out to the officialdom because he abstained from propagating revolutionary doctrines and even conveyed the impression of having forsaken them."[217] In 1918, however, Foster, then a general organizer for the Brotherhood of Railway Carmen, launched a skillful organizing drive among packinghouse workers, and a year later was put in charge of the great steel organizing drive and strike. The two campaigns gave him his reputation in the labor movement. In 1920, inspired by the mass strikes, Foster revived the Trade Union Educational League and dreamed of ousting the aging Gompers.

Formally, Foster never joined the communist underground; at least he always denied his membership. Actually, he was a highly-placed party member who had reported to the Bridgman convention in Michigan but had left before the raid. The Trade Union Educational League was financed by the Profintern, the Red trade-union international. Foster was one of those who vigorously fought the continuance of an underground communist movement. He felt that a legal, disciplined party concentrating on trade-union work would, within a short period of time, be able to bore from within the American Federation of Labor and win control. This was Foster's chief and unyielding goal. It was to this task that he sought to commit the communists.

Foster's chief factional opponent, the real founder of modern communism in the United States and the man who eagerly sought the laurel of "America's Lenin," was a cold, power-minded man named Charles Emil Ruthenberg. Born in Cleveland in 1882, of German-Lutheran stock, Ruthenberg had held various white-collar jobs until he joined the Socialist Party. In 1909 at the age of twenty-seven he became a socialist organizer in Cleveland, and continued as a functionary in the radical movement until his death. Conservative in dress and bearing, calm and deliberate in manner, aloof and restrained socially, he was a puzzle to the more volatile, quarrelsome, frenetic individuals that the left wing attracted. But behind this tightly controlled and faceless exterior was a romantic and conspiratorial nature and a recklessness both personal and political. During World War I, Ruthenberg stacked guns in the Socialist Party cellar and sketched plans for a socialist seizure of the city hall that never materialized. A few years later, while a communist prisoner in Sing Sing, he conceived a plan for a mass escape by having an armed band arrive during visiting hours, surround him, shoot its way out, and escape to Russia to await the outbreak of revolution here. Such was the enigma of Ruthenberg.

The issue between the two factions was the communist attitude toward the labor-party movements burgeoning in the early twenties. No clear-cut

[217] Saposs, *op.cit.*, p. 49.

lines were ever really established, for at one time or another both the factions, while warily circling around each other, momentarily adopted the other's position. But consistency is of little virtue in radical politics, not for Emerson's reason of the open mind but because in most instances the decisive element in winning power is less the nature of the political position than its timing. One step backward to gain two steps forward was Lenin's formulation.

In 1921, with the defeat of the world revolution and the economic crisis in war communism, Lenin proclaimed a one-step retreat. This was signaled in a pamphlet *Left-Wing Communism; an Infantile Disorder*, a tract aimed both at the egalitarians and syndicalists (the "workers opposition" group) in Russia who called for worker control of industry, and at the extreme elements in world communism who opposed parliamentary action. In England, Moscow directed the Communist Party to enter the British Labour Party. In the United States, John Pepper directed the infiltration into the Farmer-Labor Party movements. Thus began, in 1923, the famous tactic of the "united front," the disciplined attempt to capture and control mass groups which held progressive aims.

Foster, at first, was cautious on the Labor Party question but soon made a *volte-face* and became its most ardent advocate. He went so far, in fact, as to call for the endorsement of La Follette. Ruthenberg was quiet on this point. But the entire policy was vigorously opposed by Ludwig Lore, who headed an independent current of thought and was the leader of the German communist sections.

Into this scrabble, Moscow dropped a brick. Foster's policy was declared wrong. Lore's *position* was declared right, but Lore himself was declared an opportunist. Such decisions may make no logical sense, but are extremely intelligible in the dialectic of power struggle. The Ruthenberg-Pepper bloc had been close to the Zinoviev-Stalin faction in the Russian Communist Party (largely through Pepper's connection with Zinoviev, the chairman of the Communist International). Lore, however, judging issues on their abstract and ideological merit, had voiced some support for Trotsky's ideas. Hence he had to be punished. Foster immediately declared his allegiance to Stalin, whom he perceived as the rising force. He reversed his position, denied responsibility for the formation of the Federated Farmer-Labor Party, denounced a labor party, and sought to throw the blame on Pepper for the debacle of the 1924 campaign. Hastily, Foster also dissociated himself from Lore, who had been a member of his caucus.

Since 1923, the Foster faction had held a majority in the Communist Party. Now it set out to consolidate its power. But it did so not by appealing to the membership but by sending emissaries to Moscow. "From Moscow, the contending caucus headquarters received cables, letters, documents, instructions, advice on policy. As soon as cables, or letters, were received by the contending caucuses, the caucus machinery went into immediate operation. Secret caucus meetings were called. The mimeograph machines were flooded with ink, and caucus bulletins went out to every nook and corner of the party. Besides, the caucus spies were kept very busy during those exciting days. They shadowed their factional opponents, penetrated their caucus meetings, rifled letter boxes to get their hands on caucus documents, and at the same time, while covering their tracks as best they could, collected evidence for a case on the 'illegal' factional activities of their opponents."[218]

The only point both factions could agree upon was the witch hunt against Lore. The issue came to a head at the 1925 convention. The Foster caucus was in the majority, but fearing a *Putsch* by their opponents they barricaded the national headquarters in Chicago and guarded the presses of the *Daily Worker*. However, the issue was not to be settled in that fashion. Moscow had created a "parity" commission, with a Russian general, Gusev (or Green as he was called), as chairman. In the midst of the convention, Moscow spoke. A telegram arrived stating curtly:

"Under no circumstances must majority suppress Ruthenberg group, because it has finally become clear that the Ruthenberg group is more loyal to the Communist International and stands closer to its views. . . . Ultimatum to majority that Ruthenberg must remain as secretary and Lovestone a member of the Central Executive Committee. Ultimatum to majority, to refrain making removals, replacements and dispersions against minority. Ruthenberg group must retain co-editorship Daily Worker. . . ."[219]

Ultimatum to majority, and Foster capitulated. From that date on, though factional fights continued, they no longer had meaning in terms of the American Communist Party. The members were simply Janissaries carrying out, at the outposts, the orders from the center at Moscow. Thus, in 1925, the Russian yoke on the American Communist Party was securely fastened. Lore, of course, was expelled. In a tearful speech, he pledged his allegiance to communism and concluded, "Nothing you will do will make a reformer of me, less of a revolutionist than I am today."

In 1927, Ruthenberg died and was succeeded by Lovestone. Factional activity had become more intense, yet no longer represented any real fight for the allegiance of the party membership but only a series of heresy hunts. In 1928 James P. Cannon and Max Shachtman were expelled for supporting Trotsky's position at the sixth world congress of the Comintern. The issue was "left sectarianism," or Trotsky's position of intensifying industrialization, collectivizing the peasantry, and spurring the revolutionary currents in China and Germany. The lead against Trotsky

[218] Gitlow, *op.cit.*, p. 236.   [219] *Ibid.*, p. 276.

was taken by Nikolai Bukharin, the president of the Comintern. The following year, Bukharin bit the dust. This time the crime was "right-wing deviationism," or being soft on the peasant question, opposing rapid industrialization, etc. In short, Stalin, sitting in the center of the seesaw, had cleverly shifted his weight until both his major opponents rolled off. Unfortunately for Jay Lovestone, he had sided with Bukharin *too* enthusiastically in the 1928 proceedings. Foster, seeking his opportunity, secretly wooed Stalin and got a pledge of support. It made little difference that Foster had almost no following in the American Communist Party. In the elections to the 1929 convention of the American party he had carried less than 20 per cent of the membership. On Stalin's orders, however, the rival factions were called before a commission of the Comintern, and Lovestone and Gitlow were removed from the party leadership. Fearing such a move, the two "right-wingers" had left orders with their lieutenants, Jack Stachel and Robert Minor, to seize the party property in case of an adverse decision. Secretly, however, both Stachel and Minor had sold out to Stalin, and these instructions were ignored. Gitlow and Lovestone were held in custody in Moscow while the Foster group sped back to reorganize the party. Many of the leading Lovestone followers, such as Mother Bloor and Max Bedacht, capitulated. Lovestone and Gitlow both were expelled and began the melancholy careers of heading a splinter party, calling themselves the C.P.O., Communist Party Opposition. Because Foster, however, had been *unduly* active in promoting factionalism, the wily Stalin "broke" him, too, by naming his subordinate, Earl Browder, the new general secretary of the party. After 1929 the American Communist Party was the pliant tool of Stalin. And it was in this role that it entered the fateful period of the depression.[220]

[220] In view of their subsequent history, it may be of interest to name briefly the leaders of the original factional lines in American communism and note their future careers. In 1924 the leaders of the *Foster* caucus were William Z. Foster, Earl Browder, James P. Cannon, Alexander Bittelman, William F. Dunne, Ludwig Lore, and Juliet Stuart Poyntz. Aligned against them were Charles Ruthenberg, John Pepper, Jay Lovestone, Benjamin Gitlow, Jack Stachel, and Max Bedacht.

Of the latter, Ruthenberg died a natural death. John Pepper was recalled to Moscow and disappeared in the later purges. Jay Lovestone continued as a Communist Party oppositionist until December 1940, when his group voted to dissolve and he took a prowar stand. In 1947 he became secretary of the American Federation of Labor's Free Trade Union Committee, where he directs strategy against the world-wide communist trade-union movement. Ben Gitlow, isolated and ignored for many years, turned up in the late forties as a professional anticommunist, working for various exposure groups such as the Broyles Committee of the Illinois Legislature, the American Legion, etc. Jack Stachel rose as the silent power figure in the Communist Party and was indicted in 1950 by the U.S. government as one of the eleven-man executive committee of the Communist Party. Max Bedacht was for many years executive secretary of the International Workers Order, the communist fraternal organization, and was expelled in 1946, in the post-Browder upheavals, for factionalism.

Of the Foster group, Earl Browder was from 1929 to 1945 the general secretary of

XI. The Playboys of the Western World

In early 1920 Warren G. Harding had called for "normalcy, not nostrums." Perhaps it was politically timely, but as a tag of the gargoylish decade to come the phrase was singularly inept. The twenties were, if anything, a period of smugness (on the part of the business community) and self-hate (on the part of the intellectuals). This was the great age of "nothing sacred" selling, and the age of derisive disdain for a mass-consumption culture.

These were the ballyhoo years. Business proclaimed the "new capitalism," and sought to prove it by selling shares of stock to its employees. The Harvard Business School established an annual advertising award, thus "conferring academic *éclat*" on the well-turned sales phrase. The Scriptures became the great source of sales aphorisms. *Moses, Persuader of Men* was the title of an inspirational pamphlet (issued by an insurance

---

the Communist Party until he was abruptly dumped when an article written by the French communist leader, Jacques Duclos, branded Browder as having swung *too* far to the "right" in his optimism regarding postwar Russian-American cooperation. Since then he has published various pamphlets attacking the Communist Party leadership and has vainly sought vindication in Moscow. With Browder's expulsion, William Z. Foster realized his long-cherished ambition of leading the American communist movement. Although named national chairman in 1945, Foster at this point was a figurehead, the real power in the party residing in the hands of Jack Stachel and various secret Comintern "Reps." James P. Cannon, expelled for Trotskyism, has remained faithful to those beliefs and today heads the Socialist Workers Party. Alexander Bittelman was for many years the commissar of the Jewish section of the Communist Party. In 1951 he was indicted under the Smith Act, and an order for deportation to Russia was pending. William F. Dunne was expelled in 1946 for arguing that the Communist Party had not gone left far enough after removing Browder. Together with Harrison George, another former editor of the *Daily Worker*, Dunne sought to form his own splinter communist group. The fate of Ludwig Lore was the most tragic of all. For many years an "independent" communist, Lore gradually became anti-Stalinist and in the late 1930's wrote a daily column for the *New York Post* which was highly critical of the Russian regime. Yet (according to the evidence of Hede Massing, the former wife of Gerhart Eisler, the Comintern "Rep" in the U.S., and herself a courier for the G.P.U.) Lore, all that time, was secretly employed as a G.P.U. agent, reporting to the Russian secret service! Lore, a romanticist, had unwillingly been expelled from the Communist Party. It has been a common tactic of the Comintern to demand of those expelled from the Communist Party that they undertake secret tasks for the G.P.U. as proof of their continued devotion. Others besides Lore have been so accused. Complete mystery still surrounds the fate of Juliet Stuart Poyntz, an associate of Lore. After her disgrace, Miss Poyntz broke all her old friendships and went underground. A few years later she completely disappeared. Carlo Tresca, the anarchist editor who himself was assassinated in 1943, made highly vocal accusations that his friend Juliet Poyntz had entered G.P.U. service and upon her attempt to break away had been spirited away to Russia and executed.

Louis Fraina, the first chairman of the Communist Party, dropped out of sight in 1920 after journeying to Moscow to take a Comintern assignment. He left the communist movement and reappeared in the United States in 1925 under the name of Lewis Corey. Today a professor of political economy at Antioch College, Corey is the author of several notable economic studies and a valiant anticommunist.

company, with a foreword by Dr. S. Parkes Cadman, the eminent Brooklyn minister): ". . . one of the greatest salesmen and real-estate promoters that ever lived . . . a Dominant, Fearless and Successful Personality in one of the most magnificent selling campaigns that history ever placed upon its pages." And under the sure touch of Bruce Barton (in the best-selling nonfiction title for 1925 and 1926, *The Man Nobody Knows*), Jesus was no longer a humble carpenter, but "an outdoor man and a great executive. . . . He picked up twelve men from the bottom ranks of business and forged them into an organization that conquered the world. . . . [His parables were] the most powerful advertisements of all time. . . . He would be a national advertiser today."[221] Verily, as *Fortune* said, advertising was the handwriting on the wall, the sign in the sky, and the bush that burnt regularly every night.

Standing outside the gates, the intelligentsia mocked all this in full-throated voice. Babbitt and booboisie passed into word currency. The expatriates flocked to Paris in droves: a civilized life is impossible to live in America, Harold Stearns proclaimed, and the dung and roses school flowered in Branch Cabell; the "lost generation" found a symbol in Scott Fitzgerald and its historian in John Dos Passos; Nineveh had its counterpart in Babylon (Long Island), and the lust of Caligula in the ruthless drive of the "Big Money."[222] It was a mad, careening society. It shot up to the edge of the precipice at a dizzying pace, teetered for an instant, and toppled over with a splintering crash.

By 1932 gluttony had been replaced by hunger:

Item: "CHICAGO, April 1, 1932. Five hundred school children, most with haggard faces and in tattered clothes, paraded through Chicago's down town section to the Board of Education offices to demand that the school system provide them with food."

Item: "BOSTON, June 3, 1932. Twenty-five hungry children raided a buffet lunch set up for Spanish War veterans during a Boston parade. Two automobile loads of police were called to drive them away."

Item: "NEW YORK, January 21, 1933. Several hundred jobless surrounded a restaurant just off Union Square today demanding they be fed without charge. . . . Police riot squads arrived to find the manager stabbed. . . ."[223]

By 1932 the barricades were going up all over America—if not in fact, at least in metaphor. A free-floating anxiety was diffused across America. And in the van was the free-floating intellectual. For him, there was only one perspective ahead—revolution. "I went to New York to hear the semi-scientific captains of industry say in words and facial expressions

---

[221] Cited by Frederick Lewis Allen, *Only Yesterday* (New York, Bantam ed.), p. 205.
[222] See Alfred Kazin, *On Native Grounds* (New York, 1942), pp. 189-363, for an account of the period.
[223] From contemporary press accounts cited in Mauritz Hallgren, *Seeds of Revolt* (New York, 1933), pp. 167, 169.

that they did not know what had happened or what was to be done about it," said Lincoln Steffens. "Nobody in the world proposes anything basic and real except the Communists."[224] And ". . . now we are all rummaging in our trunks wondering where in hell we left the liberty cap—'I know I *had* it'—and the moujik blouse, . . ." muttered F. Scott Fitzgerald.[225]

There were salient reasons for the intellectual—accepting Schumpeter's rough definition, as those "who wield the power of the spoken and written word"—to veer so quickly to the left. In America the intellectual had matured in a hothouse of moral disapproval of capitalism: America was "mechanistic"; capitalism was characterized by the "cash nexus" rather than an aristocracy of talent; capitalism was anti-heroic—"the stock exchange," writes Schumpeter, "is a poor substitute for the Holy Grail." Bourgeois norms of conduct, rationalistic, prudent, impersonal, and anti-quixotic, oppose the genteel tradition of the Western world, i.e., the code of the gentleman, the ideal of bravery, the myth of the hero, the emphasis on uniqueness. While the intellectual, seeking to transmit that tradition, takes over the aristocratic bias and contempt for the prosaic bourgeois world.[226]

Aristocratic attitudes provided humanistic goals, but no program of action. Marxism did. It had an intellectual system to order the flux of events (i.e., the "laws of history," the material roots of culture, class analysis of society, etc.), a set of powerful predictions (stunningly confirmed in the collapse of world capitalism), and a set of utopian goals. It also had, in the accents of Leninism, the heady language of power, the myth of the invincible Bolshevik hero, the apocalyptic "Kairos" of history, as well as some tangible evidence, in the walled-in enclave of Russian society, that communist planning was maintaining full employment and optimism at the moment of joblessness and fear in the West.

Yet it was not only the intellectual but the Christian moralist and declassed professional as well who found this wave of the future appealing. Teachers without students, lawyers without clients, doctors without patients, above all a student generation that feared its education would be wasted, all sought hope in going left. But in going left, they went, as Koestler later put it, east to Moscow. The world, as they saw it, was anything but gentle, and harsh measures were necessary. "Becoming a socialist right now," wrote Dos Passos in 1932, "would have just about the same effect on anybody as drinking a bottle of near-beer."[227] "I, too,

---

[224] Quoted in "Communism and the American Intellectuals," by Granville Hicks in *Whose Revolution?* (ed. by I. D. Talmadge; New York, 1941), pp. 81-82.
[225] "Echoes of the Jazz Age," Nov. 1931, in *The Crack-up* (New York, 1945), p. 14.
[226] See "Manners, Morals and the Novel," by Lionel Trilling in *The Liberal Imagination* (New York, 1950). Also see "The Sociology of the Intellectual," by Joseph Schumpeter, in *Capitalism, Socialism and Democracy* (New York, 1942).
[227] Quoted in Granville Hicks, *Small Town* (New York, 1946), pp. 221-22.

admire the Russian Communist leaders," wrote Edmund Wilson in 1932, "because they are men of superior brains who have triumphed over the ignorance, the stupidity and the short-sighted selfishness of the mass, who have imposed upon them better methods and ideas than they could ever have arrived at by themselves. As a writer I have a special interest in the success of the 'intellectual' kind of brains as opposed to the acquisitive kind."[228]

There was, in the excitement of the early thirties, a frosty, tingling sense, almost with cobblestone in hand and Phrygian cap on head, of history being "made." It was a bravura and romanticism that sought to gird itself in the hard angular armor of realism. Yet this mood of steely resolve was also masochistic and immolating—for the intellectual gained a deep satisfaction from vicarious identification with the bull-figures of power. The mood is most sharply reflected in a letter received by Granville Hicks in the summer of 1932. His friend wrote: "It is a bad world in which we live, and so even the revolutionary movement is anything but what (poetically and philosophically speaking) it 'ought' to be . . . from one angle, it seems nothing but grime and stink and sweat and obscene noises and the language of beasts. But surely this is what *history* is. It just is not made by gentlemen and scholars . . . by the Norman Thomases and the Devere Allens and the John Deweys. Lenin must have been (from a conceivable point of view) a dreadful man; so must John Brown, and Cromwell, and Marat, and Stenka Razin, and Mahomet, and all the others who have destroyed and built up. So will our contemporaries in the American movement be. I believe we can spare ourselves a great deal of pain and disenchantment and even worse (treachery to ourselves) if we discipline ourselves to accept proletarian and revolutionary leaders and even theorists for what they are and must be: grim fighters in about the most dreadful and desperate struggle in all history—*not* reasonable and 'critically-minded' and forbearing and infinitely far-seeing men. . . . at this stage . . . everything gives way before the terrible social conflict itself: that the power of imperialism must be fought at every turn at every moment with any weapon and without quarter; that the consciousness of the proletariat—its sense of power and its anger—must be built up by every possible device; and that, meanwhile, the kinds of things we are interested in must take their place, where they belong, out of the thickest dust and along the rim of the arena."[229]

It was a mood which lent itself easily to the justifications of deception, ruthlessness, and terror. It was an attitude toward revolution that Earl

[228] "The Case of the Author," in Edmund Wilson, *The American Jitters* (New York, 1932), pp. 310-11.

[229] "Communism and the American Intellectuals," by Granville Hicks, in *Whose Revolution?* p. 84.

Browder once expressed as the "omelet theory"—just as one had to break eggs to make an omelet, one had to break heads to make a revolution. So deep was this genuflection before the altar of revolution, so complete this dedication to the "historical mission of the proletariat," that in the course of the next decade a whole generation of intellectuals found themselves castrated—and gladly accepted their eunuch roles.

Between the romantic image of the communist conjured by the intellectuals and the grubby reality of the sectarian party lay a vast gulf. It is, perhaps, a striking illustration of how compelling a myth can be that the intellectuals ignored the disparity between illusion and actuality. "We did not understand the fine points of Marxist doctrine over which the party fought with the Trotskyites and other factions," recalled Granville Hicks, "and we were not interested in them. It was enough for us to believe that Marxism was in general right and that the Communist Party was in general Marxist."[230]

In 1932 the Communist Party was in the vortex of the "third period" or ultrarevolutionary phase of the party line.[231] The seven years of the "third period" are perhaps the most significant in the history of communism. These were the years of Stalin's consolidation of power and the years of the rise of Hitlerism—to which the "third period" tactics contributed in so large a measure.

The "third period" coincided with the emergence of the first Five Year Plan in Russia. Trotskyism had been defeated, and in wily fashion, Stalin now moved to adopt the "left" posture both to undercut Trotsky's support and to eliminate his erstwhile "right-wing" allies.[232] Abroad, the

230 *Ibid.*, p. 86.

231 Roughly speaking, seven twists or "periods" can be distinguished in communist tactics since the formation of the Comintern in 1919. Except for the first, the motives for these changes in the party line stem from the needs of the Russian Communist Party and reflect Russian political conditions. The first period, from 1919 to 1921, was the episode of world revolution. Zinoviev boasted in the first issue of the magazine *Communist International* of May 1919 that "within a year . . . the whole of Europe will be Communist. And the struggle for Communism will be transferred to America, perhaps to Asia, and to other parts of the world." This was the period of insurrections in Hungary and Bavaria, of Lenin's military adventurism in the Red Army invasion of Poland, of attempted *Putsche* in Germany, of underground organization in the U.S.A., etc. The second period, opening in 1921 and characterized by the N.E.P. (New Economic Policy) in Russia, was a retreat from the excesses of Russian "war communism"; it accepted the stabilization of world capitalism, evinced friendliness to the British Labour Party, and flirted with farmer-labor movements in the U.S. Except for a brief "left" turn, this tactic continued until 1928, when the "third period" began. In 1935 the "Popular Front" opened, and shut with a bang in the Nazi-Soviet pact of 1939. In June 1941, following Hitler's invasion of Russia, the communists again became cooperative with the democracies, a phase that lasted until 1945 when new aggressive tactics were followed.

232 Although the "third period" fitted exactly the mood of the depression period, it had been formulated, actually, in February 1928 at the plenary sessions of the

distinguishing feature of the "third period" was the designation as the main enemy not capitalism, or even fascism, but the socialist parties everywhere. Since fascism was the last stage of capitalist decay, it was a transient society, communist theorists declared. Thus it could be disregarded as a serious factor in the onward march of communism. The socialists, however, their rivals in the working class, had to be "exposed." Here is what the communist spokesmen said: "The Social-democrats, in order to deceive the masses, deliberately proclaim that the chief enemy of the working class is Fascism," declared D. Z. Manuilsky in 1932.[233] On the eve of Hitler's victory, the Comintern leader, S. Gusev, once the communist "Rep" in the United States, declared in the official Comintern publication: "It may seem that in Germany, at the present time, for example, the chief social bulwark of the bourgeoisie is Fascism, and that therefore we should deal the chief blows against Fascism. *This is not correct.*"[234]

This was the fatal theory of "social fascism." With the rationale, as declared by O. Piatnitsky, that "*nach Hitler kommt uns,*" the communists joined with the Nazis to destroy the German Republic. In July 1932 they helped the Nazis to paralyze Berlin in transport strikes; in the Prussian *Landtag*, the communists supported a Hitlerite motion to oust the socialist administration of Otto Braun.[235]

Although the victory of nazism shook the American intellectuals, only a few had the political sophistication to understand the enormously tragic consequence of communist policy.[236]

Communist International and formally adopted at the sixth world congress of the Communist International in the summer of 1928. "This third period," stated the resolution of the congress, "renders inevitable a new phase of imperialist wars between the imperialist nations, of wars waged by them against the U.S.S.R., or wars of national liberation against imperialism and imperialist intervention, of gigantic class struggles. Accentuating all international contradictions, accentuating the internal contradictions in the capitalist countries, unleashing colonial movements, this period inevitably leads, through the further development of the contradictions of capitalist stabilization, to the further shattering of capitalist stabilization." The communists, thus, were to adopt the revolutionary crouch and prepare to spring.

[233] D. Z. Manuilsky, *The Communist Parties and the Crisis of Capitalism*, p. 112, a pamphlet cited in George Marlen, *Stalin, Trotsky or Lenin* (New York, 1937), p. 119.

[234] S. Gusev in the *Communist International*, No. 19 (Oct. 15, 1932), p. 674; reprinted in *The Next Step, Report of Twelfth Plenum E.C.C.I.*, p. 9, a pamphlet issued by the Workers Library Publishers, New York. Emphasis added.

[235] "On the basis of our class policy we must in the new situation apply the strategy of the 'main fire' against Social Democracy *more than ever before. . . .* Nothing has changed as far as this principal orientation of ours is concerned," declared Ernst Thälmann, leader of the German Communist Party in the (British) *Labour Monthly*, Sept. 1932, pp. 586-90. For the communist theoretical exposition that fascism is the last stage of capitalism, see R. Palme Dutt, *Fascism and Social Revolution* (New York, 1934). For a detailed analysis of this period see S. William Halperin, *Germany Tried Democracy* (New York, 1946), pp. 444, 459, 508.

[236] A notable exception was Sidney Hook, who in an article, "The Theory of Social

The "third period" of American communism—the early depression years —was characterized by aggressive policies of organizing unemployment demonstrations, exacerbating strikes, promoting ex-servicemen's leagues, and even creating, in imitation of the German communists, a military arm, replete with uniforms, called "Red Front." The A.F.L. unions were labeled "social fascists" and the communists busily proceeded to organize rival or "dual" unions.[237] The new line on unionism was laid down by Stalin himself in an address before the American Commission of the Communist International.[238] In September 1929 the Trade Union Unity League was organized and proclaimed its central slogan as "class against class." One of its chief objectives was the "mass violation of all injunctions against labor."[239] In the next few years dual unions were set up in the clothing, textile, coal, restaurant, shoe, and marine industries. Except for a small but widely publicized coal strike in "Bloody Harlan," Kentucky, some small textile strikes, a number of skirmishes with police, and an unholy alliance with gangsters in the food industry,[240] the net result of five years of communist dual unionism was control of the fur industry in New York and a towering anticommunist bitterness throughout the labor movement of the country.

In the political field, "third period" communism lashed out bitterly at Roosevelt. The New Deal was a capitalist ruse to snare the workers.

Fascism," *Modern Monthly*, July 1934, pp. 342-52, spoke out against this policy. Thereafter, Hook was labeled a "'Trotskyite.'"

[237] In the twenties, the communist policy of "boring from within" had led, particularly in the needle trades and in the mine workers, to bitter clashes with the established leadership. In 1926 the communists gained control of the New York cloakmakers' union, one of the two large divisions of the International Ladies' Garment Workers' Union, and upon the orders of the party called a strike that ran a disastrous six months before being settled on unfavorable terms. The International Union intervened, charged that $3,500,000 had been squandered, and in a bitter fight ousted the communist leadership from the union. For an account of this episode see Joel Seidman, *The Needle Trades* (New York, 1942), pp. 153-86; also David Schneider, *The Workers Party and the Trade Unions* (Baltimore, 1928), chap. 5.

In the coal-miners' union during the twenties the communists supported the efforts of John Brophy and Powers Hapgood against the high-handed and arbitrary rule of John L. Lewis. However, when the two were most sorely in need of aid, the communists, following the new dual union line, pulled out of the United Mine Workers and organized the rival National Miners Union. Foster reluctantly went along with the new policy. Saul Alinsky, an "unauthorized" biographer of Lewis, quotes Powers Hapgood as the source for saying that Foster was unhappy about the new dual union line: see Saul Alinsky, *John L. Lewis* (New York, 1949), p. 58. For a communist version of the story of the National Miners Union see Anna Rochester, *Labor and Coal* (New York, 1931). For a history of the interunion struggle see McAlister Coleman, *Men and Coal* (New York, 1946).

[238] House Committee on Un-American Activities, *Un-American Propaganda Activities* (1940), Address by Stalin, May 14, 1929, in Appendix I, p. 877.

[239] *Labor Fact Book I* (New York, 1931), pp. 136-37.

[240] For an account of these machinations see Sidney Lens, *Left, Right and Center* (Hinsdale, Ill., 1949), pp. 239-46.

Roosevelt was merely the Bruening[241] of American capitalism. The party went so far as to castigate Roosevelt as a Fascist. The chief resolution of the party's 1934 convention declared: "The 'New Deal' of Roosevelt is the aggressive effort of the bankers and trusts to find a way out of the crisis at the expense of the millions of toilers. Under cover of the most shameless demagogy, Roosevelt and the capitalists carry through drastic attacks upon the living standards of the masses, increased terrorism against the Negro masses, increased political oppression and systematic denial of existing civil rights. . . . The 'New Deal' is a program of fascization and the most intense preparations for imperialist war . . . the Roosevelt regime is not, as the liberals and the Socialist Party leaders claim, a progressive regime, but is a government serving the interests of finance capital and moving toward the fascist suppression of the workers' movement."[242] As late as February 1935, the Communist Party manifesto was headed: AGAINST THE "NEW DEAL" OF HUNGER, FASCISM AND WAR![243]

Except for its success in attracting an important section of the intellectual fringe and the student youth, the Communist Party never achieved a wide mass following in America during the depression years. Its influence in the labor movement was nil, its political strength feeble; Foster's vote for president in 1932 was only 103,151, and the party hailed as a great victory the election of a mayor in a tiny hamlet of Minnesota, the only communist mayor in American history. In 1930, at the beginning of the depression, the party claimed 8,000 members. Two years later, after bitter winters of unemployment, "Hoovervilles," hunger riots, etc., the membership reached only 12,000. Actually considerably more had enrolled, but the new recruits, particularly proletarians, found the involved dialectics, the mysterious jargon, the heavy-handed discipline, and the highly verbal disputatious atmosphere of the party such tough sledding that they bolted almost as fast as they were recruited. The *Party Organizer*, the trade journal for party functionaries, complained in 1932 that membership turnover or "fluctuation" was "as high as 75 percent. . . . In the last registration we found that only 3,000 members had been in the party as much as two years." By 1934, the Communist Party had recruited 47,000 new members; but only 12,000 stuck, bringing the membership to a total of 24,000.[244]

[241] Heinrich Bruening, the last democratic chancellor of Germany and the leader of the Centrist party.
[242] "Draft Resolution, Eighth Convention Communist Party U.S.A.," pp. 21-22, in the pamphlet *13th Plenum* which also contains "Theses and Decisions of the Thirteenth Plenum of the E.C.C.I." The pamphlet was issued by the Workers Library Publishers, New York, in March 1934.
[243] In the magazine *Communist International*, Feb. 1935.
[244] Figures cited in Eugene Lyons, *The Red Decade* (New York, 1941), p. 74.

Although communism *never* won a mass following in the United States, it did have for many years a disproportionate influence in the cultural field. At one time, from 1936 to 1939, through the fellow travelers in the publishing houses, radio, Hollywood, the magazines, and other mass media, it exercised influence on public opinion far beyond the mere number of party members.

In 1932 a sizable group of prominent literary figures publicly endorsed William Z. Foster for president. Among them were Sherwood Anderson, John Dos Passos, Edmund Wilson, Matthew Josephson, James Rorty, Sidney Howard, Sidney Hook, Newton Arvin, Granville Hicks, Erskine Caldwell, Malcolm Cowley, Langston Hughes, Robert Cantwell, and Waldo Frank[245] (none of whom are communist sympathizers today; almost all had renounced communism by 1939). It was the first time that such a respectable group of American writers espoused a communist cause. These writers were the spring tide of the flood that followed. A literary generation, depression-barred from Paris, where their expatriate elders had gone, now turned to the revolution. Out of their cavortings emerged "proletcult" and "agitprop"—two words, yet to find their way into Mencken, which signified the first "made-to-order" art in American creative life. "Proletcult," short in communist parlance for proletarian culture, and "agitprop," a similar truncation for agitation propaganda, represented a synthetic effort of middle-class intellectuals to *create* "the" worker, and to use art as a "class weapon." Within a short space of three years a new literature, theater, and dance exploded on the American scene. Jack Conroy, William Rollins, Myra Page, Clara Weatherwax, Robert Cantwell, Albert Halper, Edwin Seaver, Edward Newhouse, Grace Lumpkin, Fielding Burke, all wrote novels which ended on the triumphal note of the downtrodden exploited worker striking off his chains and joining the Communist Party. The Theatre Union produced "Sailors of Cattaro," "Stevedore," and "Black Pit," which struck the same note. The Group Theatre put on "Waiting for Lefty" and discovered Odets. Other groups sprang up—the Workers Laboratory Theatre, Theatre of Action, the Theatre Collective. The small magazines flourished—the *Anvil, Partisan Review, Left, Left Front, Dynamo, Left Review, Blast, New Theatre, New Dance.*

And yet, it all sank, almost without a trace. While literary commissar Mike Gold proclaimed "socialist realism," these cardboard cutouts moldered in the first rains.[246] The "Popular Front," which replaced the revolu-

[245] *Investigation of Un-American Propaganda Activities in the United States: Hearings before a Special Committee on Un-American Activities of House of Representatives on H.R. 282,* Vol. 1, Aug. 12-22, and 23, 1938, pp. 379-80.

[246] Writers like Richard Wright, James T. Farrell, John Dos Passos, and Edmund Wilson, who rebelled at using political yardsticks to measure literary values, were driven out of the communist literary world.

tionary line, threw "agitprop" into the discard; the folk song and folk art replaced "proletcult."[247] If little of substance remained from this cultural spasm, the party did learn a tangible political technique: how to *organize* members of the intelligentsia and manipulate their prestige through "front organizations." And the penetration of the cultural field and the myth of Russia as a progressive state bore fruit in the Popular Front, the flowering of communism in American life.

The serious miscalculation regarding the strength of German fascism, Hitler's popular support as demonstrated in the free Saar plebiscite, and the rise of Austrian fascism in 1934 were the hammer blows that shattered the hard "third-period" policy. In its stead came the Popular Front, a soft policy that aimed at coalitions with "bourgeois" governments, at communist support of militarization in their homelands, and at a program of "collective security" among the democratic nations against fascism.[248] The first step was Russia's entry into the League of Nations, which only a few years before a resolution of the sixth congress of the Communist International had branded as "an imperialist alliance in defense of the 'robber peace' of Versailles. . . ." The 180 degree turn was completed at the seventh world congress of the Communist International, held in

---

[247] The depression and its effect of thwarting professional and artistic ambitions does not alone explain the peculiar attraction of communism for the American intellectuals. The other major fact was the lure of the Russian utopia. Russia offered not only "planning," full employment, but most important, the myth of the "new man," purposeful, idealistic, socially rather than profit motivated, engaged in communal creative enterprise rather than in competitive conspicuous-consumption endeavors. In 1933 E. C. Lindemann, a noted social philosopher, argued that human nature is changing in Russia. "There is solidarity. . . . There are other goals which have thus far served to release energies and to promote faith." See E. C. Lindemann, "Is Human Nature Changing in Russia," *New Republic*, Mar. 8, 1933; cited in Eugene Lyons, *op.cit.*, pp. 105-6.

During these years, American intellectuals flocked to Moscow, spent a month or two on guided tours, and returned to report their "first-hand observations." Efforts of more experienced observers to point to the growing conformity in all phases of Soviet life were met either with incredulity or condescending remarks about tender-mindedness. American cultural circles almost completely ignored Max Eastman's book, *Artists in Uniform*, published in 1934, detailing the history of R.A.P.P., the Russian Association of Proletarian Writers, which dictated the propagandistic content of literary production. Eastman's book for the first time told of the suicides of the famous poets Esenin and Mayakovsky, as well as the silences of Isaac Babel and Boris Pilnyak, the most original writers in Russia. Eulogists of the Soviet state, however, such as Walter Duranty, Maurice Hindus, Anna Louise Strong, Harry F. Ward, received wide hearings.

[248] Quite coolly, the rear door to a German agreement was always left open by Soviet Russia. In May 1933, six months after Hitler had come to power, when the German communist movement had been smashed, and when a world-wide anti-Nazi boycott had been started, Russia signed a commercial agreement with the Hitler government. For a general account of Soviet-Nazi trade relations in 1933-1934 see Konrad Heiden, *Der Fuehrer* (New York, 1944), pp. 700-1.

Moscow July 25 to August 20, 1935 (the last public congress, incidentally, of the world communist movement).[249] The opening address by Wilhelm Pieck struck the keynote. ". . . we communists will fight wholeheartedly to retain every ounce of democratic freedom in company with those who have held in some degree to the principles of bourgeois democracy . . . we are ready to defend the remnants of parliamentarianism. . . . If German fascism attacks the national independence and unity of small independent states in Europe, a war waged by the national bourgeoisie of these states will be a just war in which proletarians and communists cannot avoid taking part."

The report by Dimitrov, the hero of the Reichstag-fire trial[250] and the new secretary of the Comintern, outlined the Popular Front policy. It called for united fronts with the Social Democratic parties and the reformist trade unions, and insisted that in elections these should "participate on a common platform and with a common ticket of the anti-fascist front." In the United States, the communists dissolved the "dual unions" and began wooing the Socialist Party. For a time they energetically pushed the organization of a farmer-labor party; when this effort threatened to interfere with support for Roosevelt, however, the communists discouraged the move. In 1936, although formally nominating Earl Browder for president, the Communist Party actually supported and worked for the election of Franklin D. Roosevelt.[251]

[249] The major speeches and resolutions of this congress were published in November 1935 by Workers Library Publishers in a series of pamphlets. The major ones are: *Resolutions; Freedom, Peace and Bread*, by Wilhelm Pieck, which reviews the intervening years; *The United Front against Fascism and War*, by Georgi Dimitrov, which outlines the Popular Front tactic; *The Fight against War*, by M. Ercoli (Togliatti), which indicates the collective security tactic.

[250] Was Dimitrov actually a hero? Ruth Fischer, former general secretary of the German Communist Party, claims that Wilhelm Pieck, Communist Party chairman, and Maria Reese, a communist Reichstag deputy and intimate friend of Ernst Torgler, chief of the communist Reichstag deputation and a codefendant with Dimitrov, "independently, both told me, the same story: that before Dimitrov stood up in the courtroom to make his courageous peroration, he knew of the secret arrangement between the G.P.U. and the Gestapo that he would leave it a free man." These stories were told her, Miss Fischer says, "while the trial was running its course." See Ruth Fischer, *Stalin and German Communism* (Cambridge, Mass., 1948), pp. 308-9.

[251] "Early in 1936, the Communist Party officially participated in a national conference of Farmer-Labor Party forces, called in Chicago by the Farmer-Labor Party of Minnesota, under the leadership of the late Floyd B. Olson, governor of the state, who had played the dominant role in the rise of his party to power. That conference decided, with the concurrence of the Communists, that the situation was not ripe for the launching of a national Farmer-Labor Party, because the progressive and labor movements were inevitably going to support President Roosevelt for reelection in their overwhelming majority. The Communist Party, while retaining grave reservations toward Roosevelt, whose previous course had been at least ambiguous, agreed that the main task in 1936 was to defeat reaction at all costs, as represented by the Liberty League and the Republican Party, and that its own course should

The turn in line was quite opportune. In November 1935 the heads of eight unions in the A.F.L. formed a Committee for Industrial Organization in order to organize the country's great mass-production industries. A year or so later, when a number of these unions were suspended from the A.F.L., the C.I.O. began its vast organization drives. From 1936 to 1939, "industrial valley"—the long Ohio River and Great Lakes manufacturing areas including Pittsburgh, Buffalo, Cleveland, Toledo, Detroit, and Chicago—was a smoking swath, with the flash fires of unionization spreading in steel, auto, rubber, glass, packing, and other major industries. The C.I.O. needed experienced organizers by the hundreds, and the communist and socialist movements were the most likely sources. In addition, the communists and socialists assigned men by the score to go into factories, establish a political base, and organize caucuses within the growing unions in order to gain control.

Within two years the communists were able to control more than a dozen C.I.O. unions. Additionally, in the national office, Lee Pressman exercised enormous influence as general counsel. Len De Caux, another fellow traveler, edited the *C.I.O. News* and controlled C.I.O. publications. At their height, the communists controlled the United Electrical, Radio and Machine Workers Union, the West Coast longshoremen, maritime union, transport union, fur workers, the Mine, Mill and Smelter Union, and a host of smaller unions including cannery, state, and municipal workers, and communications, etc. In addition, the communists had sizable beachheads in the strategic auto union as well as in the packing and newspaper unions. Among union leaders who were communists or followed the line at this time were Harry Bridges, Joe Curran, Mike Quill, Reid Robinson, James Matles.

Nor were the communists in the political dilemma of the socialists in regard to support of Roosevelt and the Democratic Party candidates. In accordance with the new line, communist unionists went along easily with the C.I.O. policy of support of the New Deal, and in New York State the communists entered the American Labor Party, which had been organized in 1936.[252]

Some of the communist success in the labor field was due in no small measure to communist infiltration of New Deal administrative agencies,

---

be directed toward cementing progressive unity while maintaining its own complete independence. The Communist Party conducted its 1936 election campaign, organized at its Ninth Convention, under this general orientation, with considerable success, which won it a host of friends and sympathizers, and opened many doors to future collaboration with sections of broadest labor and progressive movements." So reported Earl Browder, "Remarks on the 20th Anniversary of C.P.U.S.A.," in the *Communist*, Sept. 1939, p. 801.

[252] For a biting but accurate account of these communist influences, see Ben Stolberg, *The Story of the CIO* (New York, 1938), pp. 145-56.

the scope of which was revealed only a dozen years later. At one time, for example, the communists exercised an influential voice in the National Labor Relations Board, where Nathan Witt was general counsel and Edwin S. Smith was one of the three-man board.[253] The decisions of the N.L.R.B.—and particularly its bias against the craft unions in the definition of a legal bargaining unit—helped the nascent C.I.O. considerably and established precedents which carry down to this day. The *extent* of communist influence, as revealed in the Mundt-Nixon-Wood-McCarthy exposures in 1950 is, I believe, somewhat exaggerated. Such influence was, however, *intensive* in the several agencies where communist cells were able to gain a strategic position and to seed the agencies with their followers. This was particularly true of the Department of Agriculture and the N.L.R.B. in the late thirties, and the Treasury Department and the Board of Economic Warfare during World War II.[254]

During the Popular Front, Browder put forth the slogan "Communism is Twentieth Century Americanism." It was a bold move to gain respectability. "Third period" symbols such as the regular "Lenin-Liebknecht-Luxemburg" memorial meetings were discarded; strict class interpretations of United States history, such as Jack Hardy's *The American Revolution* and Anthony Bimba's *History of the American Working-Class*—first-rate curios of Marxist historiography—were stored in the closet. In fact even Marx and Engels were stashed away. The new heroes were Tom Paine, Thomas Jefferson, and Abraham Lincoln. Party his-

[253] Witt was named by Whittaker Chambers, and later by Lee Pressman, as a secret Communist Party cardholder in testimony before the House Committee on Un-American Activities. Edwin S. Smith, after leaving the N.L.R.B., worked for various communist-front outfits and in 1948 became the director of the National Council for American-Soviet Friendship.

[254] The fullest account of the communist elite underground in Washington is contained in the testimony of Whittaker Chambers before the House Committee on Un-American Activities, August 3, 1949, and contained in a forthcoming volume, *Witness* (New York, 1951). Chambers, a former editor of the *Daily Worker*, went "underground" in 1932 and was liaison between the communist Washington apparatus and Soviet espionage. Other disclosures were made by Elizabeth Bentley, a minor courier in the Soviet espionage service, and Louis Budenz, the former managing editor of the *Daily Worker*. Of the dozen or so named by Chambers, two—Alger Hiss, former secretary-general of the San Francisco Conference which founded the United Nations, and Harry D. White, former under-secretary of the Treasury—vehemently denied the accusations. Two others, Julian Wadleigh, an economist in the Department of State, and Lee Pressman, a lawyer in the Department of Agriculture before joining the C.I.O., admitted membership in the Communist Party; Wadleigh further admitted stealing government documents for Russian espionage. The others refused to answer before congressional committees on the ground of self-incrimination. Hiss was convicted of perjury; Harry White died shortly after his appearance before a House investigating committee. Two accounts of the Hiss case are Alistair Cooke, *A Generation on Trial* (New York, 1950), and Ralph de Toledano and Victor Lasky, *Seeds of Treason* (New York, 1950); the former limits itself to the transcripts of the trials alone, the latter includes extracts of the House Committee testimony of Chambers.

torians ransacked their writings and triumphantly emerged with quotations which proved the eternal struggle of the "people" versus the "reactionaries."

The greatest triumph of communist propaganda in the U.S. was the creation of the papier-mâché front organizations. These fronts sought to hook famous names and exploit them for communist causes by means of manifestoes, open letters, petitions, declarations, statements, pronouncements, protests, and other illusions of opinion ground-swells in the land. The viciousness of the front technique was that it encouraged a herd spirit whereby only "collective opinion" carried weight; and if a critic dared challenge a tenet of Soviet faith, he was drowned out by the mass chorus of several score voices. As Eugene Lyons put it: "Did rumor-mongers charge that a horrifying famine had been enforced by the Kremlin to 'punish' forty million Soviet citizens in an area as large as the United States? Half a hundred experts on nutrition and agronomy, all the way from Beverly Hills to Park Avenue penthouses, thereupon condemned the capitalists and Trotskyites responsible for the libel, and the famine was liquidated."[255]

The corruption of the front technique was that many poor dupes, imagining that they were the leaders of the great causes, found themselves enslaved by the opium of publicity and became pliable tools of the communist manipulators behind the scenes. In other instances upper-class matrons and aspiring actresses found in the communist "causes" a cozy nonconformism to replace their passé conventions. The ultimate betrayal was of the masses of front members who gained a sense of participation which they sadly discovered to be spurious when the party line changed and they found that they themselves were victims of party manipulations.

The master of the front technique was Willi Münzenberg, a flamboyant German entrepreneur who had set up many such enterprises in Germany. His greatest success was the organization of an antiwar movement starting in 1932 (a movement whose blueprint was followed almost to the letter eighteen years later in the communist "Stockholm" peace petitions). In the spring of 1932 the French writers Henri Barbusse and Romain Rolland "sent out" a call for a world congress against war, which met in August that year. Subsequently, miniature congresses were held in each country and leagues against war and fascism organized throughout the world. The first national chairman of the American league was a former minister and school teacher in Java, a communist sympathizer within the Socialist Party, Dr. J. B. Matthews.[256] But shortly thereafter,

[255] "When Liberalism Went Totalitarian," by Eugene Lyons, in *Whose Revolution?* p. 122.
[256] Dr. Matthews grew bitter at the left-wing movement when in 1935 employees at Consumer Research, of which Matthews was an officer, called a strike and then

DANIEL BELL

Dr. Matthews, an erratic individual who flirted with many revolutionary groups, was dumped, and in his place Dr. Harry F. Ward, a professor of Christian ethics at the Union Theological Seminary, was made national chairman. In 1937, during the collective security line, when the communists turned prowar, the name of the organization was changed by a semantic sleight of hand to the American League for Peace and Democracy (being "against" war is pacifist, while being "for" peace allows one to decry aggression and call for security measures which might lead to war). At its height, the new league claimed the affiliation of 1,023 separate organizations—women's clubs, religious societies, youth groups, sports associations, etc.—with a total membership of seven and a half million. Allowing for duplications and double counting, the number was still sizable. The league published millions of pieces of propaganda, sent speakers into hundreds of other groups, lobbied in Washington, and carried on many other activities.

Two other springboards for communist influence were the American Student Union and the American Youth Congress. The "youth movement," particularly in Europe, was peculiarly a product of the postwar disillusionment. With the crumbling of older mores and with the economic disintegration of the middle class, a bitter cry arose against the "tired elders." These young "armed Bohemians," as Konrad Heiden called them, the footloose, cynical-romantic, disoriented, déclassé elements from the trenches, flocked in the postwar years to the tough-minded, antihumanitarian, nihilistic, and revolutionary movements of fascism and communism.

In the United States, the traumatic shock of the depression aroused the youth, and youth organizations proliferated. Although the American Student Union at its height never had a membership higher than 20,000 (of the million or so college youth), it claimed the intellectual core of the student body.[257] Members of the A.S.U. went into the professions, government, and trade-union bodies. Because it was the seed bed for the future intellectual elite of the country, the communists worked hard to capture it.[258]

---

organized a rival, Consumers Union. In 1939 Matthews became research director, under Martin Dies, of the House Committee on Un-American Activities, and was largely responsible for its successes. After leaving the Committee, he became a consultant for the Hearst press on communism. See J. B. Matthews, *Odyssey of a Fellow-Traveler* (New York, 1938).

[257] James Wechsler, *Revolt on the Campus* (New York, 1935).

[258] The American Student Union was born in December 1935, fusing the socialist Student League for Industrial Democracy and the communist National Students League. In the original merger agreement, the posts in the new organization were divided evenly between the socialists and communists. The first national chairman and national secretary, George S. Edwards and Joseph P. Lash, were socialists. As the communists moved toward a prowar policy, a rift between the two political groups developed. The pacifist "Oxford Pledge," the feature of the springtime college "peace

Simultaneously with the formation of the A.S.U., the communists and socialists were able to capture the fledgling American Youth Congress, which had been organized by some well-meaning liberals. Hundreds of youth organizations, particularly those of religious denominations, flocked to affiliate, especially when the Youth Congress gained the patronage of Mrs. Eleanor Roosevelt and was instrumental in setting up the National Youth Administration, a junior W.P.A. for student and unemployed youth. At its height, in 1939, the American Youth Congress claimed to represent 513 organizations with a total of 4,700,000 members. Allowing for the inevitable duplications and double counting, the residue was still high.

In the League of American Writers[259] communism gained a medium for enlisting the culture makers of American society. What gave communism its gilded appeal was Spain. The gallant cry of *No Pasaran*, coming soon after the labor movements of central Europe had been shattered so easily, gave a strong emotional lift to anti-Fascist sentiment in the United States. (Although the communists in Spain were only a tiny party and the brunt of the fighting was carried on by the socialists, anarchists, and P.O.U.M., a left-socialist party concentrated mainly in Catalonia, the Loyalist cause in the United States was virtually appropriated by the communists. And it was utilized to the full to enlarge their scope of influence.) The gritty sectarianism of proletcult gave way to the Popular Front in literature. The change was symbolized by the second congress of the League of American Writers, held in June 1937. Among those participating were Ernest Hemingway, Archibald MacLeish, Carl Van Doren, Vincent Sheean, Upton Sinclair, and others of equal repute. Although Waldo Frank, the league's first president, had signed the call to the second congress, he was strangely absent from its proceedings. In the interim he had suggested that some impartial investigation of the Moscow trials was in order, and he was unceremoniously dropped. In his place appeared, without public election, Donald Ogden Stewart, a Hollywood film writer noted for his slick and polished treatments of urbane comedy. The symbolism of the changeover was striking.

But Spain—and the Moscow trials—also drove a strong wedge in the communist influence among the intellectuals. In the unhappy Iberian country, the communists demanded control of press and propaganda, command over several armies, and the right to maintain their own secret police as a price for Russian arms and support. Finally, the intransigeant

---

strikes" (on the anniversary, April 7, of America's entry into World War I), was dropped. The majority bloc, composed of the communists and Lash's followers—who favored the collective-security program—finally reduced the socialists to an impotent minority.

[259] The League of American Writers grew out of the John Reed clubs in 1935. At the start, the league was affiliated with the International Union of Revolutionary Writers.

socialist premier, Largo Caballero, was pushed out and replaced by Juan Negrín and Alvarez Del Vayo, who were ready to accede to communist demands. As communists moved into strategic position, a reign of terror against political opponents broke out in the Loyalist camp. A P.O.U.M. "uprising" was provoked in Barcelona, and the leader of the movement, Andrés Nin, was shot; Mark Rein, the son of the Menshevik leader Raphael Abramovitch, was kidnapped and disappeared. Camillo Bernieri, an anarchist leader, was murdered. The international brigades, under the command of the French communist leader André Marty, eliminated all noncommunists from command. John Dos Passos returned in July 1937 and told part of the story in the magazine *Common Sense*. The radical *Modern Quarterly* and the socialist *New Leader* carried other bits and pieces. Only after the Loyalist cause was irretrievably lost were other parts of the story fitted together.[260]

The Moscow trials shook the sanity of the political intellectuals of the world. In the years 1936 to 1938 almost the entire palace guard of Old Bolsheviks were ruthlessly shot. Names that for years the world had known as the makers of the revolution were now branded as secret Fascist agents, even at the beginning of the revolution. Most puzzling of all were the "confessions." Kamenev and Zinoviev, Lenin's coworkers in exile, who, with Stalin, had formed the *troika*, the ruling triumvirate of Russia in 1925; Bukharin, leading party theoretician and Stalin's ally in 1927-1928; Rykov, the former premier; Radek, brilliant publicist—all stood up and repeated the same weird tale.[261] Besides these, almost the

[260] The most complete account of the Barcelona uprising is contained in "Class War in Republican Spain," by Anita Brenner, *Modern Monthly*, Sept. 1937. Luis Araquistain, former Spanish ambassador to France and a socialist leader, has told the full story of Stalin's role in Spain in a series of articles for the *New York Times*, May 19, 21, and June 4, 1939. A sketch of the events of the civil war is in Gerald Brenan, *The Spanish Labyrinth* (New York, 1943), pp. 316-32. A fictional but accurate account is in Ernest Hemingway's *For Whom the Bell Tolls*, with its savage and thinly-veiled portrait of Marty as the commissar.

[261] Many explanations of the confessions have been advanced, ranging from torture to drugs. Two brilliant fictional accounts of the trials, Arthur Koestler's *Darkness at Noon* and Victor Serge's *The Case of Comrade Tulayev*, interpret the Moscow confessions as the readiness of the Old Bolsheviks to accept "the logic" of opposition— having "thought" of opposition, the consequences were inexorable even if the action never developed. As "Bolsheviks" they should have and might have acted if the opportunity so presented itself. And, having been proved wrong "objectively" by history, they confessed. A devastating story of one person's experience is the Shipkov confessions (*New York Times*, Mar. 5, 1950). Michael Shipkov, a clerk in the U.S. embassy in Bulgaria, was arrested and was told to confess. After a week of torture, Shipkov decided to confess, feeling that the torment would stop. But it didn't. Confession is not the end. Such is the subtle nature of modern terror that the subject cannot be allowed to signal the end of his own torture. To do so would give him some control, some partial dominance of the situation. One must rob the individual of all choice, even the right to choose death on one's terms. The function of terror is to instill a sense of helplessness, to destroy the self and atomize the individual. To

entire general staff of the army, headed by the famed Marshal Tukhachev-sky, were secretly shot after being accused of conspiring with the Nazis although two of the eight generals executed were Jews. It was as Trotsky graphically put it: "Of Christ's twelve apostles, Judas alone proved to be a traitor. But if he had acquired power, he would have represented the other eleven apostles as traitors and also all the lesser apostles, whom Luke numbers at seventy."[262]

The trials provided the first occasion for a counteroffensive by the growing number of anticommunist intellectuals. John Dewey headed a commission of inquiry, which journeyed to Mexico to hear testimony from Trotsky and compile an independent record of the trials. The suggestion, even a mild one, by fellow travelers that some independent investigation ought to be pursued was met by immediate hostility, and the questioner, as in the case of Waldo Frank, was immediately cast out.[263] The two volumes issued by the Dewey commission, the second of which carried as its title *Not Guilty*, precipitated wild melees.[264] The fellow travelers circulated a round-robin letter of protest, initiated by Malcolm Cowley, Robert Coates, Stuart Davis, Marc Blitzstein, and Paul Strand. This letter was signed by "nearly 150 prominent American artists, writers, composers, editors, movie actors, college professors, and Broadway figures," according to the *Daily Worker*, and stated that the trials "have by their

---

be able to choose is the measure of some degree of freedom; therefore the pain stops not on the command of the victim but of the executioner. A comprehensive summary of the various theories on the reasons for the purge cycle in Russia is contained in the excellent *Russian Purge and the Extraction of Confession*, by F. Beck and W. Godin (New York, 1951).

[262] Leon Trotsky, *Stalin* (New York, 1941), p. 416. For a series of exciting vignettes of many of the executed Old Bolsheviks, see Alexander Barmine's *One Who Survived* (New York, 1945), a neglected but brilliant personal history of the postrevolutionary period by a former Red Army general and diplomat.

[263] Frank records his disillusionment over the trials in an extraordinary bit of self-revelation: ". . . could the vision within Marxism not be deepened? Not be made *true?* This was my hope, and my strategy. In my journal of those days I wrote: 'I collaborate with the revolutionists not expecting them to understand me: the bad logic of their dogmatic empiricism prevents that. But I must serve and understand *them:* and part of my service is to let them exploit me.' . . . The Moscow Trials were convincing that this hope had failed. . . . They called the old comrades and cowar-riors *vermin:* and insisted that all their friends throughout the world must do likewise. . . . They destroyed, not only the lives of these men, but their pasts. . . . They defiled their own world. They defiled man. And every inquirer at home they jailed or shot, and every questioner abroad they befouled with cesspool language." Waldo Frank, *Chart for Rough Water* (New York, 1940), pp. 43-45.

[264] The two volumes are *The Case of Leon Trotsky* (New York, 1937), a transcript of the proceedings in Mexico, and *Not Guilty, Report of the Commission of Inquiry* (New York, 1938). The latter was signed by John Dewey, chairman, John Chamberlain, Edward Alsworth Ross, Benjamin Stolberg, Carlo Tresca, for the American committee.

sheer weight of evidence considered a clear presumption of guilt of the defendants."[265]

By 1939 the warfare among the intellectuals flared into open, deadly battle. The widespread communist influence in publishing houses, book clubs, magazine reviewing, meant that many an anticommunist author was either ignored or ganged up on, while procommunists were petted and built up. Opposed to the communists was the new Committee for Cultural Freedom, initiated by Sidney Hook and headed by John Dewey.[266] The committee issued a statement, signed by 140 Americans, which excoriated those who denounced suppressions of intellectual freedom under fascism but failed to note and speak out against similar denials in Russia. To blast the Committee for Cultural Freedom, the communists began gathering signatures for the biggest rainbow of names yet unfolded in this surrealist universe. They rounded up 400 individuals, writers, college professors, social workers, artists, and issued an open letter which denied "the fantastic falsehood" that Russia could have anything in common with Germany and called the purveyors of such lies "fascists and their allies" who were seeking "to prevent a united anti-aggression front." The letter was released August 14, 1939. Little more than a week later Ribbentrop and Molotov signed the Soviet-Nazi nonaggression pact.[267]

How could the Communist Party, a garish political group with no real roots in American life, exercise such a wide influence in the intellectual and professional strata of American life? An intellectual is one who, almost by definition, seeks to understand and express the *Zeitgeist*. Unlike the scholar, who starts from a given set of objective problems and seeks to fill in the gaps, he begins with his personal concerns, and in the groping for self-consciousness creates intuitive knowledge about the world. The depression and the threat of fascism were the great personal concerns which forced the intellectuals to reconsider their place in the world. At no time in American life, except for a brief period in 1912, had the intelligentsia been recognized as a cohesive social group and given a platform for political articulation: this the communists provided. They

[265] Cited in Eugene Lyons, *The Red Decade*, pp. 246-48.

[266] Among other noted members: Herbert Agar, Sherwood Anderson, Carl Becker, Thomas H. Benton, Percy Bridgman, John Chamberlain, George S. Counts, Elmer Davis, Max Eastman, Irwin Edman, Morris L. Ernst, Dorothy Canfield Fisher, Harry D. Gideonse, Sidney Howard, William H. Kilpatrick, Sinclair Lewis, Eugene Lyons, Wesley Clair Mitchell, Harry A. Overstreet, John Dos Passos, Ralph Barton Perry, James Rorty, George N. Shuster, Norman Thomas, Dorothy Thompson, Ferdinand Lundberg. A goodly number of these anticommunists, it might be noted, had been members of the League of Professional Groups for Foster and Ford seven years before (see note 245).

[267] For full lists of the individuals signing the Committee for Cultural Freedom statements and the opposing open letter, see Eugene Lyons, *The Red Decade*, pp. 345, 349.

gave the intellectuals a status and recognition which they had previously been denied; and to this the intellectuals responded.

In the development of communist intellectual influence in the thirties, and carried over into the next two decades, a strange cycle is apparent. The earliest converts were the literary individuals concerned with the problem of self-expression and integrity—Dos Passos, James Farrell, Richard Wright, Sherwood Anderson, Edmund Wilson. As these became aware of the dishonesty of the communist tactic, a new group appeared, the slick writers, the actors, stage people—in short, "Hollywood"—for whom "causes" brought excitement, purpose, and, equally important, "answers" to the world's problems. The wheel turned and picked up the college professors, the ministers, and lastly the scientists. In the later years the proportion of ministers among the sucker lists of communist fronts was probably higher than any other group. Bewitched by the communist myth, unable to believe evil, attracted by the opportunity to do good, the ministers moved blissfully about, unaware of the shadowy figures behind them. In the latter half of the forties, scientists for the first time began appearing in greater number on communist "innocent" or fellow-traveling fronts, attracted, apparently, not by the utopian and Christian elements in the communist appeal, but by its tough-mindedness and power role. No studies of this fascinating sociological problem have yet been attempted; they are sorely needed.

A number of intellectuals and innocents were also attracted by one or other of the various splinter groups. And certainly no account of the revolutionary Marxist movements in the thirties would be complete without some attempted description of the numerous sects which proliferated during this time. From the vantage point of more than a decade later some of their antics seem exceedingly comic; given their premises, the problem of the "correct" strategy to be pursued in time of revolutionary flux was exceedingly serious. The churchmen who gathered at Nicaea in A.D. 325 to formulate what later became the Nicene Creed had their textual differences regarding the road to salvation. Similarly, the weightiness of "the word" had an equal relevance in revolutionary movements, and the texts of Lenin were scrutinized with all the hermeneutical care that the epigoni gave to the gospels in the first centuries after Christ.

The period of the thirties offered, in the minds of the Marxists, numerous revolutionary situations. It was the task of the "vanguard party" to make the correct assessments and through the correct tactics and slogans give fire at the right moment to the revolutionary moods of the masses. (Revolutions are like births, Trotsky once said. The forceps cannot be applied prematurely.)

There was in the evolutionary history of sects a distinct *rite de passage* (more scientifically formulated as the Law of Faction Formation and Fission). The original splinter groups emerged in the late twenties from the Communist Party. The main factional progeny of the thirties came from the Trotskyites—they who claimed the seal of purity and had the effulgent brilliance of the creator of the Red Army to sustain them. But even Trotsky alive could not guarantee unity; in fact, Trotsky alive was more likely to be the source of splits since it was a great lift to the revolutionary ego of the new sectarian leaders to have jousted with one of the original creators of the Russian Revolution.

The Trotskyites, a band of a hundred or so, were expelled from the Communist Party in 1928. Since they will be discussed at greater length later in this chapter, suffice it to say here that for the first few years they remained a "faction" within communism, rather than a general party participating in political life. Because he disapproved of this policy, Albert Weisbord, a leader of the Passaic textile strike of 1926, headed one of the first splinter groups. After flirting with the Trotskyites for several years, Weisbord conclusively broke all relations and on March 15, 1931, formed the Communist League of Struggle.[268] In the heraldic announcement of its birth, he wrote: "Not an isolated sect, but a two-fisted hard group of communists is what we are forming." Its seven years of existence were lean; each one ended with the loss of another member, with Weisbord the lonely survivor at the end.[269]

A second splinter party was formed by B. J. Field, who achieved a limited prominence in the New York hotel strike of 1934. Disagreeing sharply with the Trotskyite trade-union tactics (he thought he was bigger than the party, Cannon declared), Field led out a group of eight and united with two Lovestoneite dissidents, Ben Gitlow and Lazar Becker (who in May 1933 had formed the Workers Communist League), to create the Organization Committee for a Revolutionary Workers Party.[269a] The two ex-Lovestoneites did not tarry long in the O.C.F.A.R.W.P., however, but joined the Socialist Party, and Field settled down with the

[268] For much of the ephemeral information of the obscure sects, historians of the socialist movement must be grateful to Max Shachtman, who, anticipating their needs, gathered most of the fugitive data and published it in an article "Footnote for Historians," *New International*, IV (Dec. 1938), pp. 377-79.

[269] In 1937 Weisbord retired from revolutionary activism to revolutionary contemplation and published a huge two-volume work, *The Conquest of Power* (New York, 1937). In the late 1940's Weisbord, his views tempered, became an A.F.L. organizer in New England and Chicago.

[269a] When charged with having ignored the Trotskyites during the strike, Field replied: "I could not get in contact with you even if I wanted to; you haven't even got a telephone in your office." Cannon, the leader of the party, said, "That was true . . . we had no telephone. That deficiency was a relic of our isolation . . . when we had no need of a telephone because nobody wanted to call us up, and we couldn't call anyone. Besides, up till then, we couldn't afford a telephone." James P. Cannon, *The History of American Trotskyism* (New York, 1944), p. 132.

League for a Revolutionary Workers Party. As with similar paramecium organisms, however, such splits are impossible without attempts at fusion, and Field continued in his efforts. He proceeded to negotiations with Weisbord, but these broke down, Field concluding indignantly that "it is impossible to see how such a group with such policies and leadership can contribute anything toward building a genuine revolutionary International." Field tried his luck with the "Italian Left Fraction of Communism" (a three-man group who subscribed to the theories of Amadeo Bordiga, a flaming Italian ex-Trotskyite), the members of which had just previously worn themselves out in fruitless negotiations with Weisbord. In January 1936 Field announced that "eight fundamental questions of the revolutionary movement were discussed and complete political agreement has been arrived at." Mysteriously, however, despite complete political agreement, unity was not forthcoming. Nevertheless, Field still kept trying and two months later sought unity with the Oehler group (see below), but the seed bore no fruit. In May 1936 his membership became restive and Field lost the "Fieldites"; the majority outvoted Field and voted to rejoin the Trotskyites.

The largest of the splinter groups was the Revolutionary Workers League, led by Hugo Oehler, Tom Stamm, and Rosario Negrete, whose differences with the Trotskyite Workers Party arose out of the "French Turn." This was a maneuver, ordered by Trotsky in late 1934, to enter the Socialist parties throughout the world and steer them in a leftward direction. The Oehlerites feared the dilution of their revolutionary purity and bolted.[270] The Revolutionary Workers League was formed in November 1935, but immediately defections, expulsions, and splitlets took place. In November 1937, at the historic third plenum of the R.W.L., Oehler and Stamm had a great falling out. The latter insisted that Trotskyism had degenerated in 1928; the former placed 1934 as the year of the original sin. In addition, differences had cropped up on the trade-union question, on Spain, democratic centralism, and sundry other issues. Stamm upped and left, but claimed the same name for his group of the Revolutionary Workers League. Both organizations elected their comrade Negrete, who at the moment was languishing in a G.P.U. jail in Spain, as a member of their respective executive committees; when he returned to the United States he was greeted at the docks by two delegations, each with banners proclaiming the name of the organization and the an-

[270] The chief publications of the Revolutionary Workers League were the *Fighting Worker*, an agitational newspaper; the *Marxist*, formerly the *Fourth International*, which was the theoretical organ; and *International News*, an organ of the provisional International Contact Commission for the New Communist (4th) International. *International News* was issued jointly with the Leninist League of Scotland and the Red Front of Germany.

nouncement that he had been elected to both. (Negrete chose the Oehlerites.)

The idea of schism proved contagious and there soon began a new split in the Revolutionary Workers League led by Karl Mienov, who formed the Marxist Workers League.[271] The initial issue of the inevitable theoretical organ, *Spark* (named in honor of Lenin's prerevolutionary magazine *Iskra*, the title of which meant "spark" in Russian), proclaimed that "to be wrong on the Spanish war means to open the door wide open to social-patriotism in the coming world imperialist war.... We are proud that we split from such a centrist group."[272] However, Mienov's group was not immune to the law of faction formation and fission. Mienov himself held that Trotskyism could not be reformed but must be smashed; the minority dissented. A third "faction," a single individual named Stanford, held a unique political position. "I don't like Mienov," he wrote in *Spark*. Appalled by this caprice, Mienov retorted: "What sort of principled position is this . . . we can gauge Comrade Stanford's sincerity, however, by the fact that rather than give out leaflets for the revolution, he prefers to study for exams at Brooklyn College." Mienov, Apocrypha relate, now alone, soon developed schizophrenia and split with himself.

One other Oehlerite split-off deserves mention, the Leninist League, formed at the beginning of 1938. "While definitely anti-gynaicocratic," observes historian Shachtman, "and taking no formal position on exogamy or endogamy, it is based fundamentally on the primitive gens in so far as one must be a blood relation of the immediate family, or at least related to it by marriage, in order to qualify for membership. This has the unfortunate effect of somewhat reducing the arena of recruitment, but it does guarantee against contamination."[273]

This by no means exhausts the number of the Trotskyite splinter groups of the period, or the growth of anarchist sects, deviants from the Socialist

[271] Not to be confused with the Marxist Workers League, a previous splinter from the R.W.L. which lasted three weeks before its two members rejoined the Trotskyites. Nor is there much space here for Trotskyites and ex-Trotskyites who renounced Marxism altogether and went syndicalist, as did Joseph Zack (Kornfeder), who started the One Big Union Club and the Equalitarian Society.

[272] Mienov favored a "defeatist" versus a "defensist" position, two terms that were central to Lenin's strategy. The latter meant critical support of a regime, such as Lenin gave to Kerensky in the July days when the Kornilov armies threatened to overthrow the February Revolution; the former meant sabotaging the home government (turning the "imperialist war into a civil war") in order to precipitate a revolution. Oehler advocated that workers in Spain be defensists; Mienov was a defeatist.

[273] Shachtman, *op.cit.*, pp. 378-79. George Marlen, the totem of the Leninist League, was perhaps the most indefatigable collector of the sins of other parties. He published a book, *Earl Browder, Tool of Wall Street*, with a subtitle, *Stalin, Trotsky or Lenin*, which is a vast compendium of quotes by all the fathers of the revolution on the problems of strategy and tactics.

Labor Party, and other political spores that so profusely filled the air in this period.[274] With the coming of World War II, the sects began to decline. An effort to unite the League for a Revolutionary Workers Party, the Revolutionary Labor Group, and the Marxist Workers League failed.[275] Gradually, all these groups faded into oblivion. During the same period the Socialist Party, too, was fading, and its decline will be traced in the pages that follow.

XII. In Dubious Battles

In 1932 the Socialist Party polled 903,000 votes for Norman Thomas. It was by previous standards a respectable total and many felt that socialism was again on the march. But factional discord, like the curse on the House of Atreus, was an ineradicable heritage, and in the next eight years the savage fratricide ripped the party to shreds.

This new conflict was, in one sense, a repetition of the old immigrant-nativist division. The Socialist Party in 1928 had a paper membership of 7,000 concentrated largely in New York. What influence it had depended upon the good will of a few trade-union leaders who, from conviction or nostalgia, still held party cards. But the party had no mass following in these unions nor was it consulted about union policy; it had become a "poor relation" and was so treated. The burdens of the presidential campaign were borne almost completely by a small devoted group of old-timers in New York and the money came largely from the *Jewish Daily Forward* and the small needle-trades unions. This aging group of leaders, clustered about Hillquit, dominated the party.

There was in loose opposition another group, centered around Norman Thomas, which sought to broaden the party's appeal by concentrating on the middle-class and educated groups. In December 1928 Thomas and his lieutenant, Paul Blanshard, along with such nonsocialists as John Dewey, Oswald Garrison Villard, and Paul Douglas, launched the League for Independent Political Action, which they hoped would provide a common platform for progressive and reform elements. The "old-guard" socialist leadership felt this was a move to "liquidate" the party or change its name. When, in 1931, John Dewey invited Senator George W. Norris to "help give birth to a new party, based upon the principles of planning," the old guard, like hard-shell Baptists, reasserted their fundamentalist beliefs. "The Socialist Party is a party of the working-class," a resolution of the New York City convention declared. "[Leaders like Norris] . . .

[274] A sober and detailed examination of some of these movements is contained in William Isaacs, *Contemporary Marxian Political Movements in the U.S.* (MS Ph.D. thesis, New York University, 1939).
[275] "Report of Negotiations—RLG, LRWP, and MWL," p. 15 in *Power*, theoretical organ of Marxist Workers League (mimeographed, New York), Vol. 2, No. 1, May-June 1940.

would shift the leadership" from workers "into the hands of political leaders who have minor differences with the parties of capitalism, a policy which Socialists cannot approve."[276] This division was reflected in the social composition of the two groups. The old-guard leadership was largely European-born and/or self-educated, and—although its main leaders were lawyers—it defensively emphasized the "working-class" character of its origin and thinking. The opposition was of professional or middle-class parentage, college educated, ministerial, pacifist. Its main strength was drawn from such institutions as the League for Industrial Democracy (the successor to the Intercollegiate Socialist Society) and the magazine *The World Tomorrow*, a religious periodical whose editors were Norman Thomas, Devere Allen, and Kirby Page. There was, in addition, a personal factor. Norman Thomas, having been the party's standard-bearer in 1928, sought to become, in fact as well as in name, the spokesman of the party. With the sorry lesson of Debs in mind, he was resentful and suspicious of Morris Hillquit, who, he felt, merely wanted him as a figurehead.

Another conflict was one between generations. The old guard were party members of twenty to twenty-five years' standing. Even though many were now furiously pursuing their own professional careers and the years of high prosperity had dampened their ardor and expectations, they were still self-conscious and articulate about their many years of sacrifice for the cause. The youths who began flooding the party in the depression years—membership rose to 15,000 by 1932[277]—resented the "mortgage" on party leadership held by the old guard. They resented more the slack and tired attitude of the local leaders. Although a solid core of experienced and thoughtful men like Morris Hillquit, Algernon Lee, and Louis Waldman steered party policy at the top,[278] most of the local chairmen and organizers had acquired their posts by the mechanical process of attrition and seniority. Many of these second-string leaders looked with fear on the rising tide of new membership with its restless demand for activity. There was, unfortunately, no "middle generation" to bridge the gap.

The younger generation called themselves the "Militants." They issued a strident manifesto attacking "the apologists of gradualness," and demanded that the party "press for a relentless drive for political power instead of reform."[279] The coolness of the old guard toward the Soviets

[276] Quoted in James Oneal, *Some Pages from Party History* (a pamphlet printed by the author, New York, 1935), p. 10.

[277] Report of Clarence Senior, national secretary, to the 1932 national convention in Milwaukee, mimeographed.

[278] Victor Berger and Meyer London, the party's two ex-Congressmen, had both died in tragic street accidents in 1929.

[279] *A Militant Program for the Socialist Party of America*, No. 1, Dec. 1931 (a pamphlet issued by the Program Committee: Theodore Shapiro, Robert Delson,

was further proof to them of the lack of revolutionary temper and tough-mindedness of the party leadership. "The Russian dictatorship," the Militants declared, "was a necessary instrument for the industrialization of Russia. . . ."[280]

To the old guard this talk echoed the manifestoes of 1919. They feared these young tyros would capture the party, and sneered at their parlor radicalism. The younger Militant, wrote James Oneal bitterly, "is all too common. He . . . comes from the middle-class and professional families. Six months or a year in the party and he becomes a 'theoretician' swaggering with erudition. One immediately understands that the Socialist movement began when he joined it. He discusses problems with the gusto of one who has digested everything written since the days of Marx. He is an expert on 'tactics.' In fact this is his speciality. He solves problems of the class war here and abroad with the ease that he flicks his ashes from his cigarette."[281]

The fight came to the surface in May 1932 when the Militants joined the Thomas liberals and the "sewer socialists" of Milwaukee[282] in an incongruous alliance to depose Morris Hillquit as national chairman of the party and to name instead Milwaukee's mayor, Dan Hoan. In the heated debate some ugly charges boiled up. Hillquit's adherents charged "the Thomas alliance with bringing the issue of race and sectionalism into the party under the guise of 'Americanism.'" They stated that "a 'whispering campaign,' emphasizing the fact that Mr. Hillquit was a Jew and that the party should be rid of foreign elements, had been carried on . . . in an attempt to unhorse Mr. Hillquit as leader of the party."[283] Thomas and his chief lieutenants, Paul Blanshard and Heywood Broun, denied the charge. So too did B. Charney Vladeck, an executive of the *Jewish Daily Forward*, a Thomas supporter.

McAlister Coleman), p. 8. When one of the Militant leaders presented the group's viewpoint in the *American Socialist Quarterly*, the editors, dyed-in-the-wool Marxists, commented: "It is difficult to learn from Comrade Shapiro's article just what the militants demand. Suppose they were to get control of the party. What changes would they bring about? They are against reformism. Very well, what does reformism mean to Comrade Shapiro?" See "The 'Militant' Point of View," by Theodore Shapiro, and editor's comment, "Is This Militancy?" *American Socialist Quarterly*, Vol. 1, No. 2 (Apr. 1932), pp. 29-44.

[280] *A Militant Program*, p. 12. Among the endorsers were Devere Allen, Jack Altman, Murray Baron, Andrew J. Biemiller, Paul Blanshard, Franz Daniel, Arnold Freese, Maynard Kreuger, J. B. Matthews, and Upton Sinclair. Subsequently, this view of Russia changed radically and these socialists were among the first to appreciate and point out the danger of Russian imperialism to the world. By 1940 all these men, with the exception of Kreuger and Freese, had left the Socialist Party. Freese, who was elected mayor of Norwalk, Conn., in 1948, resigned in 1950.

[281] Oneal, *op.cit.*, p. 19.

[282] So dubbed by Hillquit to indicate their provincial concern with municipal problems to the exclusion of others.

[283] Dispatch to the *New York Times*, May 24, 1932, p. 1.

On such taut issues, truth bounces quite erratically and is difficult to pin down. This much is true: behind some of the attacks on Hillquit was an attitude characteristic of typical Mid-western provincialisms that "New York is not America." Some others felt, for opportunistic reasons, that the shaggy, shambling Dan Hoan would be a more presentable party symbol than the precise, intellectual Hillquit. In effect, Thomas' bumbling effort to create an "American" party, by which he meant an orientation to the American temperament, was given the worse possible interpretation by the touchy old guard. This saw-toothed issue left crosscuts that never healed.[284] In the final vote Hillquit retained office, 105 to 80; in terms of party membership, however, the division was a closer 7,526 to 6,894, a margin which the old guard knew was too slim to maintain.

Little of this internal feuding was reflected in Thomas' 1932 presidential race. His campaign pledges, after the usual obeisances to social ownership of major industries, spelled out a hard-headed series of meliorative demands, including five billions for immediate relief, five billions for roads, reforestation and slum clearance, unemployment insurance, old-age pensions, government aid to small homeowners, the five-day week, government employment agencies, minimum wage laws, and similar measures that were to become incorporated within the next few years in the New Deal program.

The advent of the New Deal and the events in Europe from 1932 to 1934 accentuated the divergent trends in the Socialist Party. Seeking to capitalize on the impact of the campaign and the restless discontent of the country, the socialists organized in May 1933 a Continental Congress of Workers and Farmers. They hoped it would lead to a new radical party. Despite an impressive list of labor sponsors—including Sidney Hillman, David Dubinsky, and Emil Rieve (who served as chairman)— the venture petered out. For the dulcet voice of Roosevelt was being heard in the land. Norman Thomas could mock: "After all *any* President would have to do *something* in 1933. What Roosevelt did was temporarily to stabilize capitalism with a few concessions to workers that are poor copies of Socialist immediate demands." And the Socialist Party could snap: T.V.A.—"state capitalism"; N.I.R.A.—"state paternalism"; C.C.C.— "looks like forced labor"[285]—but the labor leaders were falling under Roose-

---

[284] Hillquit himself felt it to be an anti-Semitic bias. In accepting the nomination he declared: "I am here to charge that efforts have been made to introduce the [racial] issue and not on this floor alone. I know the issue of Americanism. I have known it for many years." "Mr. Hillquit," continued the *Times* dispatch, "said he 'apologized' for having been born abroad, being a Jew and living in New York, 'a very unpopular place.'" See *ibid*.

[285] Norman Thomas, *The New Deal: a Socialist Analysis*, pamphlet published by the Socialist Party, Chicago, Dec. 1933, p. 3, emphasis in original; editorials in the *New Leader*, April 22, May 6, June 17, 1933.

velt's spell. The major fact was that the unions were quick to take advantage of the N.R.A. to organize. The almost bankrupt International Ladies' Garment Workers' Union shut down the dress industry in a shrewdly timed general strike and in one week quintupled its membership of forty thousand. Generalissimo John L. Lewis in a series of lightning moves captured the coal fields. In less than six months, the A.F.L. had gained 1,300,000 new members. The socialists were predicting a dire future, but the union leaders were too busy with their immediate problems to listen.

Other defections were taking place. Paul Blanshard, Thomas' floor whip at the 1932 convention, joined the La Guardia campaign in New York less than a year later. In his letter of resignation, he charged the Socialist Party with failure to elect a single alderman in "the natural stronghold of American Socialism," and declared that Roosevelt's program of "managed capitalism" had taken from the socialists the initiative in economic change.[286] The La Guardia administration also claimed three of the bright research men of the Socialist City Affairs Committee, which had uncovered the municipal corruption that had led to the Seabury exposés. Although they sought to remain in the party, the unhappy Thomas asked "almost as a personal favor" that the three, because of the political implications of their public move, resign.[287] The growing public bureaucracy took increasing drain of the Socialist Party. In some cases, socialists who took jobs in Washington resigned from the party in order not to jeopardize their new careers, in other instances the individuals kept silent. Whatever the case, the effect was to immobilize these people politically and weaken the party.

Movements in these years such as Technocracy, the Utopian society, Share-the-Wealth, Townsend, E.P.I.C. also took their toll. Upton Sinclair's experience was an important case in point. After twenty-five years of untiring socialist evangelism, the veteran propagandist decided that socialism was alien to the middle-class mentality of America. In September 1933 he joined the Democratic Party and wrote two pamphlets, *I, Governor of California*, and *How I Ended Poverty in California*. In these two tracts he sketched a simple scheme for putting the unemployed to

---

[286] *New Leader*, Sept. 30, 1933, pp. 5-6. Just nine months before, Blanshard, in a speech to the Student League for Industrial Democracy, had vividly sketched a picture of *Socialopia* on the day after the revolution. The picture, as reported in *Time*: "An international government, speaking an international language would control all battleships, airplanes, munitions and currency. In the U.S. state lines would vanish and the President and Congress would be replaced by a national Socialist planning board. . . . The State would enforce birth control. Working mothers would leave their young in a communal nursery in each apartment house." *Time*, Jan. 9, 1933.

[287] Private communication from Norman Thomas to Maslow, White, and Rosner, Dec. 19, 1933.

work in cooperative self-help units, and outlined an appealing reform program which included tax exemption for the small homeowner and $50 a month for the aged over sixty. The ideas caught on like wildfire and Sinclair suddenly found himself heading a political crusade, E.P.I.C., whose initials were drawn from the title of his second tract. Within six months the astonished pamphleteer found that he had won the Democratic nomination for governor (with 436,000 votes over George Creel's 288,000) and was being touted for victory in November. The frightened movie industry, banks, and railroads in full fury opened a vicious smear campaign. Advertisements mocked Sinclair's faddism, faked newsreels showed "widows" trembling over their loss of savings if Sinclair won, movie stars were pressured to speak out against him, the studios threatened to leave the state. After one of the dirtiest political campaigns on record Sinclair was beaten. But he had rolled up an astounding 879,000 (against Governor Merriam's 1,138,000). Sinclair's quick and spectacular rise, like that of the Non-Partisan League before him, showed that socialists could utilize the primary system to great political advantage. But the lesson went unheeded. The socialists denounced him for replacing orthodox socialism with panaceas, and for wrecking the party in California.[288]

But the Militants and the young intellectuals around Norman Thomas had no eye for the American scene. To them, these shapeless movements of discontent were tokens, like the flight of swallows before a storm, of the panic of the petty bourgeoisie. Their attention was riveted on Europe, because, as Marxist theory foretold, the fate of capitalism there foreshadowed the course of capitalism here.

The European events, particularly the collapse of German social democracy, pushed the Militants to the left. The movement of Bebel and Kautsky had been the shining example for right-wing socialism everywhere. Its membership was in the millions, its trade unions and cooperative societies mighty and wealthy, it exuded the air of solidity and strength. Yet it surrendered to Hitler without a shot. The lessons, said the youngsters, were clear. The German socialist movement failed because it did not disturb the economic power of the old capitalist class and it had failed to uproot the deeply embedded cultural and ideological traditions of junkerism and Prussian authoritarianism.

The rise of Hitler heightened anxieties that the rise of a mass Fascist movement here was only a matter of time.[289] Even if capitalist America

[288] Oliver Carlson, A Mirror for Californians (Indianapolis, 1941), pp. 291-302.

[289] See, for example, the symposium, "Will Fascism Come to America?" by Stuart Chase, Charles A. Beard, Theodore Dreiser, Norman Thomas, Horace M. Kallen, Waldo Frank, V. F. Calverton, in the Modern Monthly, Sept. 1934. Said Thomas: "No one can doubt that the raw material of Fascist construction or destruction lies all around in America. It simply lacks the occasion and the man to put together the

did not go Fascist, it would plunge into another war in order to escape its "contradictions" and "economic crisis." In order to stave off or combat these threats, the Militants also demanded united action with the communists. The "activism" of the communists, their tough-minded discussions of "seizing power," their learned quotations from Lenin on "tactics," their dogmatic predictions about the "course of history" had impressed many of the younger socialists. (In fact, at one point the national chairman of the Young People's Socialist League and a large segment of its national executive committee resigned *en bloc* and announced their allegiance to the Young Communist League.) But the main impulse behind the demand was the lesson of disunity in Germany and the ease with which Hitler had destroyed both communists and socialists. The united front issue came up in April 1933 when the national executive committee of the Socialist Party barely defeated, by a vote of six to five, a motion to set up a committee to meet with the Communist Party. In arguing for the motion Norman Thomas declared: "I cannot too strongly urge the adoption of this proposal. I have recently been traveling rather extensively in New England and elsewhere and know that in our own party and outside of it we shall suffer very considerable harm if we can be made to appear to be blocking any kind of united action. Frankly I am skeptical whether the Communists will undertake united action on honorable terms. But for the sake of our own members, especially our younger people, it must be made obvious that it is they who sabotage our united front, not we who disdainfully reject it."[290]

Yet if any single event served to crystallize a revolutionary wing (or two or three) in the Socialist Party, it was the Dollfuss *Putsch* in February 1934. Red Vienna, with its great municipal socialist housing projects, had long been the pride of world socialism. And "Austro-Marxism," whose great theoretician was Otto Bauer, was the inspiration of revolutionary socialism the world over. The Austrian Socialist Party, unlike its slothful German sibling, had been a vigorous party of action. Its powerful youth movement, whose symbol was the three arrows, was a model for socialist youth organizations everywhere. Its trained military corps, the *Schutzbund*, was a citizens' militia, ready to fight. But the sudden onslaught by

---

pieces of the Fascist picture. . . . The reason why . . . there has been no strong Fascist movement as yet in the United States is the fact that neither the dominant owning class [n]or its lower middle class allies and dupes have as yet felt the necessity of using Fascism to protect for a little while longer their profit system and their property rights" (p. 462).

[290] Letter to the members of the national executive committee on April 13, 1933, from Clarence Senior, the national secretary, reporting on results of the mail ballot on the motion, together with the comments by various members. Although formal action was rejected, the Socialist Party shortly afterward officially joined the Communist Party in the "United States Congress against War" and worked with it for several months until vitriolic attacks by the communists forced it to withdraw.

the *Heimwehr*, supplied with arms and mortars by Mussolini, caught the socialists off guard. In a week the *Heimwehr* was able to isolate and cut up the socialist detachments.

The gallant Austrian struggle stirred the American socialists. This was atonement for the feckless surrender of German social democracy; this was the answer to the communists who had mocked the socialist reformists. To hail their Austrian comrades during the Vienna fighting, the socialists called a mass meeting in Madison Square Garden. But to the consternation and disgust of the entire radical movement, the communists, in "third-period" style, stormed the Garden, threw chairs from the balcony, and completely disrupted the meeting. Thus, for a while, ended the united front.

Following the Austrian events the left wing opened a drive to capture control of the party. The Militants, for the first time, outlined a set of organizational and programmatic goals. They called for a "disciplined, centralized organization that can control its membership and its institutions"; by this they meant a party-owned press, direct control of the state organizations, and jurisdiction over local election campaigns. They demanded that "socialist fractions" be set up in unions in order to work for party-outlined policies. More sharply than ever before their program was etched with revolutionary acid. They called, with thundering phrases, for turning the imperialist war into a civil war; they declared their readiness, if necessary, to use extraparliamentary means to win power; they warned that a "workers dictatorship" might be needed to defend socialist victories.[291]

Even this program, however, was not sufficiently "left" for a new group that called itself the Revolutionary Policy Committee. In a resolution on the "Road to Power," the R.P.C. declared: "We make no fetish of legality . . . no institution or instrument set up by the capitalist class [i.e., parliamentary democracy] can be depended upon to establish the Workers Republic. Therefore the working-class state will be an entirely new type

[291] In May 1934 the revised Militant program declared: "The National Executive Committee should intensify the work of the party in the unions (particularly in the war, chemical and transportation industries) in order to induce them *to call a general strike in case of war* . . . the struggle against war is part of the struggle to overthrow capitalism, and . . . *if an imperialist war does break out we should make every effort to turn it into a class war.*" See *Towards a Militant Program for the Socialist Party of America*, pamphlet, May 1934, p. 35, italics in the original. This was the sharp mood engendered by the rise of fascism in Europe and the fear of its emergence here. Within the short space of four years, the views of almost all the Militants changed completely: the reactionary character of the Soviet regime revealed itself more fully in the subsequent "confession trials" and purges; at the same time, the American socialists began to appreciate more fully the democratic resiliency and traditions of American society. By 1939 the rash and adolescent rhetoric had been repudiated completely.

of state based on workers' councils, historically suited to serve as the organs of liberation."[292]

Actually the R.P.C. was a weird mélange of revolutionary romanticists and secret Lovestoneite agents. Its first head was that irresponsible adventurer J. B. Matthews; its secretary, a former theological student, Francis Henson. For a while the R.P.C. functioned as a party within a party. It had a national executive committee, maintained an R.P.C. magazine, met regularly in caucus, etc.

Despite the European events, the old guard's position had not changed. In its theory, the old guard had never been "revisionist"—that is, it had never held the gradualist, evolutionary socialist doctrines of the German Eduard Bernstein. Instead, it subscribed to Kautsky's orthodox doctrine that armed force might be necessary to defend the state power won by a legitimately achieved socialist majority. In practice, however, the old guard had completely abandoned any ideas of revolution and shied away from doctrines of force. Its European counterparts had entered "coalition" governments with bourgeois parties; it believed almost entirely in reform and slow, peaceful means as the road to socialism.[293] But the old guard was at serious disadvantage. The "tides of history" were running against it. Equally damaging was the death in October 1933 of Morris Hillquit. Hillquit was the last major link with the American socialist past and with European socialist thought. While Debs had been the voice and Berger the windmill of action, Hillquit had been the intellectual nestor of American socialism. In a party which was tossed constantly by the winds of passing theoretical fads, he was one of the few who anchored their doctrine in a solid knowledge of Marxist thought. In a movement subsisting largely on emotion, his forte was logic. His oratory, never flamboyant or rhetorical, won his audiences by the clear-cut schematism of his well-ordered mind. But his dryness of wit, his coolness of temper, his reserve of manner kept most of the membership at a distance. He was a man who among most inspired respect rather than love; the obverse, in this regard, of Debs.

Hillquit's heirs were Algernon Lee and Louis Waldman. Lee, born in Dubuque, Iowa, in 1873, and the director of the Rand School since 1909, became the party theoretician. A cultivated personality and a precise thinker (a Yankee talmudist, Ben Stolberg called him), he was a colorless speaker—a great handicap in a movement with so high a premium on oratory—and a man of procrastinating habits. On the other hand, Wald-

[292] An Appeal to the Membership of the Socialist Party, Mar. 1934, a pamphlet issued by the Revolutionary Policy Committee.

[293] In the fall of 1933, in fact, Abraham Cahan, the editor of the Jewish Daily Forward, speaking at the dressmakers' victory celebration in Madison Square Garden, extended an invitation to Roosevelt to join the Socialist Party.

man, one of the five socialist assemblymen expelled from Albany, was a dynamic speaker and a highly charged personality, but his explosive ego made him the special target of left-wing attacks. Neither of the two had Hillquit's great gifts as a compromiser, Hillquit's magnetism or his personal authority, both within and without the party. Although competent individually, the two together proved an old theorem that the sum of the parts was not equal to the whole.

The showdown came at Detroit in 1934. While Thomas was not one of the Militants, he joined with them to rewrite the party's declaration of principles. The new version was written largely by Devere Allen, a Gandhian pacifist. Yet it incorporated most of the flaming phrase-mongering of Militant rhetoric. The Socialist Party, stated the declaration, "will meet war and the detailed plans for war already mapped out by the war-making arms of the government by massed war resistance. . . . It unhesitatingly applies itself to the task of replacing the bogus democracy of capitalist parliamentarianism by a genuine workers' democracy. . . . If the capitalist system should collapse in a general chaos and confusion, which cannot permit of orderly procedure, the Socialist Party, whether or not in such case it is a majority, will not shrink from the responsibility of organizing and maintaining a government under the workers' rule."[294]

The old guard stood aghast. This was the communist incubus emerging full-size. "Anarchistic, illegal, Communist," Waldman cried. The debate continued on a heated, exaggerated plane. Devere Allen retorted, "To remain legal [in the next war] would be to brand forever the socialist movement with the mark of shame." He declared that once the new declaration was adopted, the workers of the nation would flock into the Socialist Party. "Do we want to abandon the democratic method in the attempt to gain power in the United States?" asked Jacob Panken. "We know the workers are on the march," shouted Andrew Biemiller. "We do not agree with Comrade Waldman," he continued, "that the workers are playing a slow and steady game. That is no longer true. Each week brings us fresh evidence. It is upon this general philosophy that this [drafting] committee proceeded."[295]

After three hours of heated debate in this vein, the left wing carried the day 99 to 47 (by weighted membership 10,822 to 6,512). It also swept into office a coalition national executive committee and named Leo Krzycki, a vice-president of the Amalgamated Clothing Workers, as national chairman. The fissure in the party had widened.

In retrospect, it is difficult to understand what the declaration exactly

---

[294] "Declaration of Principles," on p. 6 of special supplement, *American Socialist Quarterly*, July 1934, containing full stenographic report of the debate on the declaration.
[295] *Ibid.*, pp. 9, 16, 47, 53.

meant. Less than a month after the convention Thomas began backing away from the shrill phrases. "It neither says nor implies that American capitalist democracy is as yet equivalent to Fascism," he declared, and he ascribed the old guard's opposition as a "rationalization of [its] bitter disappointment . . . at losing to a large degree [its] control over Party machinery."[296] In later years Thomas regretted much of the wording, especially the phrase "bogus democracy."[297] Because some panicky party members feared that the wording of the revolutionary declaration might result in jail sentences, as predicted by Waldman, the declaration was submitted to a picked committee of lawyers to find out whether it was legal to be a revolutionist. They replied that it was.

The passage of the Detroit declaration unloosed a civil war in the Socialist Party and many members welcomed the party strife. "Capitalism," after all, was an abstract enemy, speaking on street corners was dull, arguing with unconvinced workers, tedious. Here the struggle was real, the enemy tangible, and most important, victory promised organizational power. For a year and a half guerrilla warfare raged in the party to the exclusion of almost all other problems. Meetings of the branches and of the city central committees became battles planned weeks in advance. Letters, telegrams, and communiqués would call members to caucuses; debates at meetings would rage fiercely for hours and spill over into the neighboring cafeterias until the small hours of the morning. Youngsters boned up eagerly on Marx, Lenin, Kautsky, and tirelessly locked phrases over long windy resolutions on "the road to power." All world history was ransacked for glittering metaphors, while in the corridors petty gossip would zestfully circulate regarding one or another party leader. Spies were planted in the opposing ranks and membership lists were packed. The barricades of Petrograd were being repeated in New York, especially one evening when the old guard abruptly raided the Yipsel offices in the Rand School and snapped new locks on the doors. Nor was this a mimetic combat. Capitalism was doomed; the only problem at hand was to capture the Socialist Party, issue the correct manifestoes, and victory would be assured.

The old guard came alive with a vigor that surprised even itself. It set up two factional newspapers[298] and issued a stream of pamphlets, booklets, and monographs. The Militants responded by issuing the *Socialist Call*, and setting up a *Call* Educational Institute to rival the Rand School.

[296] Norman Thomas, "What Happened at Detroit," *World Tomorrow*, June 28, 1934, p. 321.

[297] *Hammer and Tongs*, supplement to the *Call*, April 23, 1947, p. 9.

[298] The *Socialist Sentinel*, published by the Interstate Conference, and the *Socialist Voice*, published by the Committee for the Preservation of the Socialist Party.

Although the Detroit declaration had carried by a referendum vote of 5,933 to 4,872,[299] the conflict did not end.

Each side pointed to the 1936 convention. The old guard threatened a split if it lost. But the Militants were light-hearted. They felt that with the old guard barnacles scraped away, the ship of socialism would move more lightly, swiftly. The strike wave of 1934—the San Francisco general strike, the pitched battles in Toledo, the fifteen-state walkout in textiles, the citywide truck drivers' strike in Minneapolis—"has no near parallel in American labor history," declared a Militant leader.[300] Reinhold Niebuhr, from his *bénitier*, invoked a philosophy of history: "The right wing of our party . . . has not . . . learned a single lesson from events. . . . It meets the genuine disillusionment of young and vigorous elements in the party merely by repression and mouths the old platitudes about democracy. Its insistence that socialists must always remain within the bounds of legality is a perfect revelation of spiritual decay in socialism. No revolutionary group of whatever kind in history has ever made obedience to law an absolute obligation. . . . The touching devotion of right-wing socialism to legality and the constitution is proof either of inability or unwillingness to profit from the clear lessons of recent history or it is merely a convenient ideological tool for suppressing new life in the party."[301]

Outside party activity was almost at a complete standstill. (In 1934 Thomas received 129,000 votes for United States senator and Charles Solomon 79,000 for governor in New York City, a sharp drop of 30 per cent.) Many left the party in disgust. In New York alone, more than one thousand persons dropped out, and in the period from September 1934 to September 1935 membership dropped over the country from 22,943 to 16,270.[302]

"I find myself having less and less desire to attend the Cleveland convention," wrote James D. Graham, president of the Montana State Federation of Labor and a member of the national executive committee; ". . . this quarreling and bickering among ourselves is very depressing."[303] Similar sentiments were expressed by Dan Hoan. Neither of the two was a Militant; they had both gone along on the feeling against New York, and now felt dismayed.

The 1936 convention of the Socialist Party opened on June 1 in Cleve-

[299] *New Leader*, Oct. 27, 1934.
[300] Paul Porter, "The Meaning of the Labor Upsurge," *American Socialist Quarterly*, Dec. 1934, p. 3.
[301] Reinhold Niebuhr, "The Revolutionary Moment," *ibid.*, June 1935, p. 9.
[302] Figures computed from national office reports. Since the first total was probably inflated by purchase of extra dues stamps by both sides in order to increase convention strength, the loss in real members was probably not so high. Since party membership records were based only on the number of dues stamps sold, the figures at any point must be taken with caution.
[303] Letter to Norman Thomas, May 6, 1936.

land's gargantuan Municipal Auditorium. Giant pictures of Marx, Debs, Berger, and Hillquit decorated the hall, but most visible was the thick pall of "split." Waldman had warned a few weeks before the convention that if the Detroit declaration were not rescinded, the right wing would form a new party. But Thomas was prepared. "Personally I do not believe that a mere defection of Old Guard groups in New York, Massachusetts or even Pennsylvania or Connecticut is so terribly serious," he wrote in a private memorandum to his aides. "To some extent it may help us. Our great loss will come anyway on account of the Roosevelt sentiment and many of the votes that our right-wing friends think they can control would have gone to Roosevelt anyway. . . . It will be our own fault if we do not play up Waldman's announcement before and during the convention to our own help."[304]

On the first day both a left-wing and a right-wing delegation from New York appeared and demanded to be seated. The convention voted immediately to seat the Militants. Someone struck up the *Internationale* and the delegates rose and sang. A delegate pointed to Waldman and Lee. The two rightists had remained seated. A howl of rage broke from the convention. Amid the general uproar, few heard Waldman's tight-lipped answer: "I will not rise to sing a song of solidarity with a group that has just expelled us and split the Socialist Party."

For a second time since 1901 a major division had run its course in the American Socialist Party. With the New York old guard went the Connecticut organization of Jasper McLevy, large blocs in Massachusetts and Pennsylvania (although the Reading organization remained), the Finnish Socialist Federation, the largest of the foreign-language blocs, and the Jewish socialists—in all about 40 per cent of the membership. The old guard retained, too, the party institutions, such as the powerful Workmen's Circle, one of the financial mainstays of the party, the *Jewish Daily Forward*, radio station W.E.V.D., the Rand School, the *New Leader*, and various summer camps. More important, the trade-union officialdom in the International Ladies' Garment Workers, the Millinery Workers, and the Amalgamated Clothing Workers went with the right wing. Dan Hoan, who had fought a split, reluctantly remained with the official Socialist Party.

Yet many socialists were quite optimistic. "Many friendly critics of the party think that this split will destroy whatever prospects of future usefulness the party may have had," wrote Reinhold Niebuhr. "They are in error. . . . The vital forces of the party are not with the [old guard]. . . . In New York there is already a remarkable burst of new energy in the

[304] Letter dated May 11, 1936.

party since the hand of the Old Guard has been removed from the wheel of power."[305]

Mr. Niebuhr probably mistook the glare for the heat; it was not new energy, but new fireworks and noise. In late 1935 Norman Thomas had proclaimed the doctrine of the "all-inclusive party." He invited into the Socialist Party all independent, unaffiliated, affiliated, and dependent radical homeless, the splinter groups, factions, fractions, droplets, and kibitzers. He hoped in this fashion to achieve a "unity" of left-wing forces against fascism. Gitlowites, Zamites, Fieldites, Trotskyites, Lovestoneites all streamed into the party, and each group of intellectual pitchmen set up its own stand. A host of previously isolated one-ring circuses was now operating under one huge billowing tent. And the result was bedlam.

In the next three years, the Socialist Party was torn apart in as many directions as there are on the compass. Some fragments moved toward the communists. In the spring of 1936 exploratory talks were held between spokesmen for the Socialist and Communist parties. Present at these private sessions were Earl Browder and Jack Stachel for the communists, and Norman Thomas, Max Delson, Jack Altman, and Frank Trager for the socialists. They discussed a common ticket in the 1936 elections and "joint fraction work" in the trade unions.[306] Although the first never materialized, the second did. Jack Stachel and Rose Wortis for the communists, and Frank Trager and Herbert Zam for the socialists, worked out a merger of a communist and a socialist-led union in the white-collar field which produced the United Office and Professional Workers Union. In the unemployed field the socialist-communist alliance gave rise to the Workers Alliance, headed by the socialist David Lasser; in the colleges previous moves toward unity produced the American Student Union, headed by socialist Joe Lash. (In these, as well as other organizations, the socialists eventually either were forced out or, like Lasser and Lash, remained for the time being as captives of the communists.) United-front demonstrations on the Spanish issue were held with the communists in July 1936, and later the two groups worked together for a while in the North American Committee to Aid Spanish Democracy. Shortly before the 1936 party convention, Browder proposed a joint presidential ticket of Thomas and Browder. It is doubtful whether the idea would have been accepted; in any event, the tempo of the "Popular Front" soon pushed the communists over toward covert support of Roosevelt.[306a]

[305] Editorial, "The Conflict in the Socialist Party," *Radical Religion* (later *Christianity and Society*), Winter 1936.

[306] No "minutes" of these negotiations were ever kept. Their existence was vouched for to the writer by a participant.

[306a] The united front, it should be emphasized, was a sincere effort of the socialists

Roosevelt too made serious inroads. The New Deal had rescued a number of unions which had been on the rocks. It had given encouragement to the nascent C.I.O., particularly in its organizing campaign against big steel. Labor sought to repay that aid in the 1936 campaign. In New York, Roosevelt strategists, particularly Frances Perkins, wanted to capture 100,000 socialist and needle-trade voters who traditionally avoided the old-party lines. Hillman and Dubinsky wanted to vote for Roosevelt, but not on the Democratic ticket. Together with Waldman they launched in New York State the American Labor Party.

The A.L.P. put the Socialist Party in a dilemma. One group of socialists headed by Jack Altman feared that the right wing had pulled a coup and that the Socialist Party would be isolated. Many socialists in the C.I.O. felt that a campaign by Thomas would compromise their activity in the unions. Powers Hapgood and Franz Daniel, two members of the national executive committee—once extreme leftists, but both now C.I.O. officials—privately urged that the 1936 campaign be soft-pedaled. As the campaign developed, some of the leading Militants defected and joined the American Labor Party.

Organizationally, the party was weak. In 1936, for the first time since its growth in 1929, the party publicly admitted a sharp net loss of members.[307] In the 1936 campaign, Thomas centered his fire completely on Roosevelt. "The 'New Deal' like the 'Old Deal' has failed," the 1936 national platform declared. "Under the New Deal, more vicious attacks have been made on our civil liberties than at any period since the days immediately following the World War. . . . big business has been given almost unheard-of powers. . . . Twelve million men and women are still jobless. Hunger and destitution stalk the land. . . . Under both the 'Old Deal' and the 'New Deal' America has drifted toward insecurity and war—the logical results of capitalism."[308] The talk fell on deaf ears. The Thomas vote nationally plummeted to 187,500; in New York State he received 86,000 votes while the American Labor Party rolled up 238,000.

---

to create wide anti-Fascist unity. For the communists, as the socialists later learned to their sorrow, it was only a tactic to gain eventual control of united-front organizations.

[307] "No single explanation can be found for the loss," reported national secretary Clarence Senior. "In some states there was desertion to some of the patent-medicine remedies, Long, Coughlin or Sinclair. . . . In one, the type of evangelistic campaign put on in 1934 brought in droves of new members who did not realize what they were doing and soon dropped out. . . . Difficulties in the relationship with the Farmer-Labor Party caused a fall in Minnesota. . . . Oregon withdrew from the party for fear members would run afoul of the criminal syndicalist law." Mimeographed report to the national convention, May 23, 1936.

[308] *For a Socialist America* (1936), National Platform, Socialist Party leaflet.

In June 1936 there were two factions in the Socialist Party. One was expelled and then there were three: the old Militant group, the Clarity caucus, and the Appeal group; the last of which was a thinly woven scrim for the Trotskyites who entered the Socialist Party en bloc in June.

The old Militant group, the balding Young Turks of yesteryear, had opposed the right wing because of the latter's lethargy. They had hoped that, with the sources of inertia removed, the party would leap swiftly ahead. Now they found themselves isolated. In New York, an American Labor Party had been formed. The Wisconsin socialists were entering the Farmer-Labor Political Federation, a combination in that state of the La Follette progressives and the Milwaukee socialists. In Illinois and Detroit municipal labor parties were being organized. The old Militants wanted to move in that direction. They favored a mass labor party, cautiously approved of the Popular Front, and·haltingly endorsed collective security as against any kind of revolutionary defeatism. The old Militants were led by Jack Altman, the party secretary in New York, a past master of factional infighting, and Paul Porter of Wisconsin, a serious-minded student of socialism who had sought, in proposals like the commonwealth plan, to break away from the old stereotypes of socialist planning.

The Clarity group, composed in part of the Militant caucus, the Revolutionary Policy Committee[309] and the driftwood of the left, repeated the clichés of revolution. ("The backbone of the capitalist state is made up of the army and burocracy. . . . These instruments of permanent reaction make a purely peaceful transition to power extremely unlikely. . . . A parliamentary majority for the working-class is improbable, and in America almost impossible. . . . [These] parliamentary campaigns must be part of a general preparation of the masses for revolutionary struggles on the extra-parliamentary front.")[310] The Clarity group, in Leninist fashion, counterposed a "revolutionary vanguard" party to a mass labor party, opposed the Popular Front and damned collective security as "merely leading the working class into support of a new imperialist war." The leaders of the Clarity group were Herbert Zam, a sectarian field marshal with a worker's baton in his knapsack, Gus Tyler, a brilliant but mercurial dialectician, and the Delson brothers, Max and Robert, two intense young lawyers.

The Trotskyites were the Pharisees of the revolution. Expelled from the Communist Party in 1928, they wandered in the wilderness for five years, almost in unconscious imitation of what Toynbee called the etherialization of leadership—the group suffers privation and the leader

[309] The rest of the Revolutionary Policy Committee withdrew and followed Lovestone in seeking to infiltrate the American Labor Party and the C.I.O.

[310] "Where We Stand," editorial statement in Socialist Clarity, Mar. 1, 1937, p. 3.

withdraws to return renewed in strength. After its expulsion, the Trotskyite group had decided to remain a faction within communism rather than "turn its face to the masses" and seek new recruits. "Let us not delude ourselves with the idea we can go to the great unschooled mass now," wrote James P. Cannon, the historic leader of American Trotskyism. "The road to the masses leads through the vanguard and not over its head." In 1933, the revolutionary moment arrived. Their ranks weeded of the impatient, the dilettante, and the unstable, the Trotskyites stood in the crucible, ready for the fire. "By the end of 1933," Cannon wrote, "we felt confident that we were on the way to the reconstitution of a genuine Communist Party in this country. We were sure that the future belonged to us. A lot of struggles were yet ahead of us but we felt that we were over the hill, that we were on our way. History has proved that we were right in those assumptions. Thereafter things moved very rapidly and continually in our favor. Our progress from that time on has been practically uninterrupted."[311]

Whatever "progress" the group did make was largely by cannibalism. The first victim was the American Workers Party, a small but promising indigenous radical group led by a Dutch-born preacher named A. J. Muste. In the tradition of the proletarian preacher Muste had gone among the workers, and after ten years of pastorates emerged in 1919 as the leader of the famous Lawrence, Massachusetts, textile strike. Thereafter, he devoted himself full time to the labor movement, becoming in 1921 dean of Brookwood Labor College at Katonah, New York, the seed bed for many of the top labor organizers in the United States today. Muste gathered around him a group of brilliant labor intellectuals like David Saposs, the economist, and J. B. S. Hardman, former leader of the Jewish socialists. In 1929, these men formed the Conference for Progressive Labor Action in order to stimulate labor thinking.

With the depression, the emphasis of this group turned to action. In a few cities, notably Toledo, Allentown, and other industrial centers in the Ohio Valley area, they organized unemployed leagues with notable success. The group gained national attention when in the spring of 1934 it led the spectacular Auto-Lite strike in Toledo, one of the first of the new-style militant strikes which flashed through the Ohio Valley in the next five years.

In 1933, the C.P.L.A., in response to the industrial ferment, decided to organize the American Workers Party. In its nondogmatic approach to the American worker, the party attracted a number of quixotic and independent spirits including, besides Muste and Hardman, Sidney Hook, James Burnham, Ludwig Lore, and Louis Budenz. The responsibility of being a radical party, however, turned their attention to the need of

[311] James P. Cannon, *op.cit.*, p. 117.

"theory." The theme of "unity" was also in the air. Trotsky's analysis of the criminal nature of the "social fascist" theory struck many as acute. So when the Trotskyites proposed unification of the two groups, a majority of the American Workers Party agreed. Hardman opposed the move and retired from active politics; Budenz also opposed unity, but he reentered the Communist Party.[312] In 1934 the two groups fused and formed the Workers Party. Although the Muste group was larger, the Trotskyites were more compact and soon played the dominant role.

Under Trotsky's orders, the Workers Party soon sought entry into the Socialist Party (the tactic known in radical history as the "French turn" in honor of the first infiltration maneuver into the French Socialist Party). A number of Trotskyites, feeling this to be a dilution of revolutionary purity, bolted the Workers Party and formed the Revolutionary Workers League. Muste, exhausted by these gyrations, simply retired from political activity.[313]

The Trotskyites entered the Socialist Party, as Cannon stated candidly, in order to supply leadership to the confused and leftward moving masses. The socialists, however, were somewhat unappreciative of the honor. In his elegant prose, Commissar Cannon told of the reception and voiced his complaints:

"The negotiations with these *papier-mâché* heroes were a spectacle for gods and men. I will never forget them. I believe that in all my long and . . . checkered experience, which has ranged from the sublime to the ridiculous, and vice versa, I never encountered anything so fabulous and fantastic as the negotiations with the chiefs of the 'Militants' caucus in the Socialist Party. They were all transient figures, important for a day. But they didn't know it. They saw themselves in a distorting mirror, and for a brief period imagined themselves to be revolutionary leaders. Outside their own imagination there was hardly any basis whatever for their assumption that they were at all qualified to lead anything or anybody, least of all a revolutionary party which requires qualities and traits of character somewhat different from the leadership of other movements. They were inexperienced and untested. They were ignorant, untalented, petty-minded, weak, cowardly, treacherous and vain. And they had other faults too. . . . Our problem was to make an agreement with this rabble to admit us to the Socialist Party. In order to do that we had to negotiate. It was a difficult and sticky job, very disagreeable. But that did not deter

[312] Where subsequently he became managing editor of the *Daily Worker*, and in 1945 a returnee to his Catholic faith and one of the chief witnesses in the government's indictment in 1950 of the American Communist Party.

[313] A few years later he renounced Marxism and became the executive director of the Fellowship of Reconciliation, a pacifistic Christian socialist organization which preached Tolstoyan love and Gandhian *satyagraha*.

us. A Trotskyist will do anything for the party, even if he has to crawl on his belly in the mud. We got them into negotiations and eventually gained admission by all sorts of devices and at a heavy cost. . . . We received no welcome, no friendly salute, no notice in the press of the Socialist Party. Nothing was offered to us. Not one of the leaders of our party was offered so much as a post as branch organizer by these cheap-skates—not one. . . . If we had been subjective people standing on our honor, we might have said, 'To hell with it!' and walked away. . . . [But] we just said to ourselves: that is blackmail we are paying for the privilege of carrying out an historically important . . . task. . . . When, a little later, the leaders of the Socialist Party began to repent of the whole business; wishing they had never heard the name of Trotskyism . . . it was already too late. Our people were already inside the Socialist Party and beginning their work of integrating themselves in the local organizations."[314]

Having integrated themselves, the Trotskyites dialectically proceeded to the task of disintegration. They took over the *Socialist Appeal*, a paper published by a small band of Trotskyite scouts who had cased the terrain before the full invasion; they also set up a newspaper in California, arranged for meetings of the Trotskyite "plenums" and, in short, set up shop as a fullfledged faction.

The tumult of the earlier years was a thin-throated noise compared to the din that now ensued. Mimeograph machines clicked overtime. Meetings of fractions, caucuses, committees, blocs, splintlets took place every day and night in the week. By this time, the only ones left to debate were the party "pros" (party officials, functionaries of allied organizations such as the Workers Defense League, Workers Alliance, etc.), some remaining union officers, a sprinkling of teachers and lawyers, and the students; these debates became the substance of their days. Other party members dropped away like leaves in the October wind.

The chief issues in dispute were the labor party and Spain. For the Trotskyites a "correct" policy on Spain was the *sine qua non* of the revolutionary policy; there the "road to power" was being laid. All arguments were refracted through the experiences of the Bolsheviks in the days between February and October. Should one be a "defeatist" (i.e., place the social revolution above the civil war and set the defeat of the "bourgeois and Popular-Front" coalition as the first task), or be a "defensist" (i.e., place defeat of the enemy as the first order)? The Trotskyites wanted to set up Spanish soviets as the only means of rallying the people. They argued that Socialist Party aid should not go to the Loyalist government—as it was doing in part, through participation in the North American Committee to Aid Spanish Democracy—but to left-wing forces such as the Catalan P.O.U.M. which had a social revolutionary program.

[314] Cannon, *op.cit.*, pp. 224-26, 232.

The old Militants favored support of Largo Caballero, the leader of the socialist left wing and then the premier of the government. The Clarity group, however, carried the day by committing the party to a resolution which "advanced the notion of a social program simultaneously with a civil war." "Here for the first time," wrote Gus Tyler, "the party comes out in favor of workers', soldiers' and peasants' committees as the basis of a Socialist government."[315]

This program was not good enough, however, for the Trotskyites. Moreover, it was time to leave. Trotsky now felt that, as the German debacle had discredited the Second and Third Internationals, the defeat of the Loyalists would show the need for a Fourth International which could carry the banner of revolution across Europe. The Spanish P.O.U.M., the small Independent Labor Party of England, the dissident communist Brandler-Thalheimer group of émigré German communists were all moving in that direction. The Trotskyites wanted to get there first and, since the American group was the biggest Trotskyite faction in the world, the new line was to break loose from embarrassing "centrist" entanglements. Consequently, the Trotskyites began a series of provocations. Finally in August 1937, little more than a year after they had entered the Socialist Party, they were expelled. Soon afterward, they organized the Socialist Workers Party. The Trotskyites had gained measurably by their infiltration.

They came in with a few hundred members and walked out with more than a thousand. They had the entire socialist youth organization in tow; they had made marked gains in New York, disrupted the Illinois party, and left the California organization a shambles. If the Trotskyite experience left any positive results within the Socialist Party, these were, first, a complete political inoculation against the communists, and second, the end of the witless policy of an all-inclusive party.

Following this violent emetic, the Socialist Party was viscerally weak. The stolid and respectable Pennsylvania Dutch socialists of Reading, unable to stomach the factional diet, had joined the Social Democratic Federation. The Wisconsin socialists, hoping to build a national farmer-labor movement through their alliance with the La Follettes, talked of leaving. Only the New York and Michigan organizations maintained any degree of viable political strength.

The question of the labor party, however, disrupted the New York and Michigan socialists. In New York, the Altman-Laidler bloc, representing the trade-union and middle-class reform elements still in the party, argued for support of the American Labor Party. Thomas was inclined to go along. He was the Socialist Party's nominee for mayor of New York, but withdrew in November 1937, although the party did not publicly support

---

[315] Gus Tyler, *Save the Socialist Party from the Wreckers,* mimeographed statement (1937, but undated).

La Guardia. (The American Labor Party received 480,000 votes that year in New York City.) By a narrow vote of eight to seven, the national executive committee endorsed this policy. The Clarity forces were bitter. "The real forces behind this narrow victory for the opponents of the National Convention line," they charged, "was [sic!] the irresponsible bullying of Thomas. His constant implied threat in the open, and much more in private, to make this party decision one as between him or his loss gave some NEC members the choice of ratifying a fait accompli, or losing Thomas. The real blackjack for the petty trade union burocracy in the party was Norman Thomas."[316]

The labor-party issue dominated the 1938 convention of the Socialist Party, which opened in April, in Kenosha, Wisconsin. By this time the party membership had sunk to 7,000, or a plunge of 66 per cent from the high-water mark of 21,000 in 1934; it was even below the all-time low of 7,800 reached in 1928. Of this 1938 membership, two-thirds were concentrated in Wisconsin, New York, and Pennsylvania.[317]

Although reduced to this tiny number, the convention majority tenaciously refused, against the urgings of Thomas and Hoan, to endorse the outright entry of the Socialist Party into labor parties, such as the A.L.P. in New York and the Farmer-Labor Political Federation in Wisconsin. The majority, led by Maynard Kreuger of the University of Chicago, argued that unless the socialists affiliated as a federated bloc and retained the "right to run Socialist Party candidates against any capitalist candidates" endorsed by the labor groups, the party would lose its identity. After about five hours of vociferous debate, the majority won by a weighted membership vote of 3,414 to 3,163. On foreign policy, the socialists condemned collective security, charged that the New Deal was making war plans which would "fasten on American life a virtual fascist dictatorship," and urged the lifting of the embargo on Loyalist Spain. The line, shaped by Thomas, called for "people's boycotts" and qualified support of neutrality legislation. This was the first beginning of the "isolationist" line in Socialist Party foreign policy. (No attention was paid to the fact that this policy contradicted the party's attitude toward the application of the neutrality laws in the case of Spain.)

After the 1938 convention, the influence of the Socialist Party in the labor movement—aside from some strength among the auto workers—sank to almost zero. Leading socialists who held C.I.O. posts found themselves absorbed by trade-union problems to the exclusion of all others, and, out of political necessity, committed to the support of Roosevelt and the New Deal. Important figures such as Leo Krzycki, the former na-

[316] *The Struggle for Revolutionary Socialism Must Go On!* mimeographed statement of the Clarity group on the present situation in the party (1937, but undated), p. 3.
[317] National office report to the national convention, April 21, 1938, mimeographed.

tional chairman, Powers Hapgood and Franz Daniel, former members of the national executive committee, John Green, president of the shipyard workers, and a host of minor C.I.O. functionaries, quietly dropped away. Only one enclave of socialist strength remained, Michigan, but this too was shattered by New Deal pressure, C.I.O. discipline, and factional union politics.

Within the United Auto Workers, a showdown was shaping between president Homer Martin on the one hand and a "Unity" caucus on the other. Martin (a former Missouri Baptist minister with an other-worldly fervor, but a this-worldly, erratic, and unstable temperament) was tutored by Jay Lovestone, and surrounded by Lovestone's assistants, Francis Henson and Irving Brown (both of whom had been leaders of the socialist Revolutionary Policy Committee). The "Unity" caucus was a strange mélange of communists, aggressive union politicians, and for a while, Walter Reuther, who, nominally a socialist, was acting on his own. Their trump card was the John L. Lewis and communist alliance and the confidence that the national C.I.O. would back them.

The Socialist Party was in a dilemma. On ideological grounds, particularly because of his antiwar stand, Thomas tended to favor Homer Martin. The Michigan socialists, for union reasons—charging that Martin was a poor union leader who maintained unsavory alliances with reactionary southern know-nothing elements in the union—opposed him; but they were unhappy about allying themselves with the communists. As a logical move, the socialists approached Martin to form a harmony caucus which would fight both the communists and the reactionary elements. Martin was willing, but the scheme was finessed by Lovestone. Reuther, to the joy of the socialists, finally broke with the communists and launched an independent caucus. Hillman and Lewis, not averse to building balances of power, privately encouraged him. As a price, however, they insisted he resign from the Socialist Party. They pointed out that Frank Murphy needed full labor support for reelection as governor of Michigan, and Reuther would have to support Murphy.[318]

The Murphy issue symbolized the full dilemma of the Socialist Party in relation to the unions and the New Deal. In a letter to Norman Thomas,

[318] This was not the first time that such exactions were levied. In 1936 the auto workers convention, prodded by the socialists and with the mute consent of the communists, defeated a proposal to endorse Roosevelt for reelection. When Lewis' representative, Adolph Germer (the wartime national secretary of the party), heard this he raged: "Communists and socialists have taken over the convention, and are voting not as auto workers, but according to their political views." Lewis informed the delegates, after being prodded by a perturbed White House, that unless they supported Roosevelt a mine-workers contribution of $100,000 for organizing would be withheld. With this pistol at its head the U.A.W.—in the five minutes before adjournment—voted unanimously to support Roosevelt. See Irving Howe and B. J. Widick, *The U.A.W. and Walter Reuther* (New York, 1949), pp. 52-53.

George Edwards, the Socialist Party caucus leader in the auto union (and later president of the Detroit City Council), summed up the issue that had been wracking the party for two months: "We are now faced with a very difficult situation on the political field. Our party here is growing in the unions in membership and influence. But our progress is jeopardized by the complex situation in the current political campaign. Some of the leading unionists cannot refrain from giving some support to Murphy without sacrificing their own positions. This handicaps the party's campaign and even endangers the party organization at a time when there is a splendid chance to build the party and draw in many new elements from the entire labor movement here."[319]

The socialists in Michigan also proposed that Walter Reuther be allowed a "friendly resignation" from the party (i.e., without public notice or blast). The idea disturbed Thomas. Said he, ". . . the more I think of it, the less I like it. It will not be understood as completely friendly. It will lessen our influence and prestige and the only reason that you now seem to think it necessary is that he may have to support Murphy in some fashion. Aren't we going to be in some serious position if we have to let go every good union man who, according to your own doctrines, is obliged to support a non-Socialist candidate?"[320]

The Michigan socialists worked out a typical compromise. As union men and within the union they supported Murphy; among the socialists they supported Socialist Party candidates. This double bookkeeping was censured by the national party, and the Michigan socialists finally ran a candidate for governor against Murphy. Their candidate's vote was feeble, and the party suffered.

In New York, too, that year the socialists ran a gubernatorial candidate, despite the pleas of many union men to endorse Herbert Lehman. One reason was the refusal of the American Labor Party to admit the socialists on other than an individual membership basis. An important secondary consideration was that the party's place on the ballot depended, according to electoral law, on the vote for governor. Not only would the socialists have had to agree not to run a socialist but they would have had to endorse the A.L.P.'s "old-party" capitalist candidate; this the party would not do. Thus, the doctrinaire stand on the election issues of 1938 completed the socialist isolation from the labor movement.

By the spring of 1939, the Socialist Party was collapsing. There was almost no functioning national office, whole branches dropped away because of the continued factionalism, the party dues-paying membership in New York was averaging only 150, while only 300 persons had reg-

[319] Letter from George Edwards to Norman Thomas, Sept. 24, 1938.
[320] Letter from Norman Thomas to Ben [Fischer] and Tucker [P. Smith], Aug. 19, 1938.

istered.[321] But the old battles were still being fought. The right wing, to the extent that there still was an organized grouping, had returned to a viewpoint in no way different from that of traditional social democracy. Its spokesman, Paul Porter, rejected the Leninist conception of the party, and the role of disciplined cadres which had dominated left-wing thinking for a decade. He argued that socialists could function within "the present democratic system" and that the Socialist Party had no future in independent electoral action. Unity negotiations were opened with the Social Democratic Federation and continued in desultory fashion. But unity was impossible because of differences on the war question. The Reading, Pennsylvania, organization, because it was pacifist by inclination, did rejoin the Socialist Party.

The outbreak of war completed the destruction of the Socialist Party as a political entity. When Hitler's armies marched across Poland the party declared that "our first duty to the ideal of democracy, as well as to the interests of 130,000,000 men, women and children, is to keep America out of war. . . . Only in an America at peace can the masses make democracy work so well that it can inspire our brethren in the rest of the world to new faith in it."[322] But there was no prescription this time, as so readily in the past, on how the Polish proletariat or the French workers or British labor should act.

World War II exposed socialist thinking as the politics of irresponsibility. The socialists wanted Hitler to lose, and the Allies to win, but "it was not our job to say so," as one leading member declared. The effort to escape the dilemma of "in but not of" the world reached the most absurd heights in the party discussion on the Finnish issue. There was full sympathy for Finland in her efforts to defend herself against Russia, but concern lest any support aid the Allies or Hitler. At the meeting of the national executive committee in December 1939, these were the motions discussed and acted upon:

"We support sending of money and supplies from working class organizations here to working class organizations in Finland. (Carried)

"We support cancellation of the Finnish debt. (Carried)

"We do not raise the slogan of 'Arms to Finland.' (Carried)

"We oppose withdrawal under present conditions of [the] American ambassador to [the] U.S.S.R. (Carried)

"No reference to government policy in [the] statement. (Motion withdrawn because of actions above.)

"Full moral, financial and material support to Finnish workers." (De-

[321] Letter from Arthur G. McDowell, acting executive secretary, to Jack Altman, April 4, 1939.
[322] Socialist Party statement, released Sept. 11, 1939.

feated after Allard, in reply to questions, said that "material" included arms.)

Robert Delson, a member of the national executive committee, stated: "I vote for the motion as a whole with very serious misgivings as to whether there is any group in Finland to which we can give aid, since there is no evidence that the working class is carrying on an independent struggle."[323]

The 1940 Socialist Party convention, which opened in Washington on April 6, continued this tortuous line of reasoning. Its statement on war declared that "the fact that Hitler is the opponent does not make the Allied war a fight for democracy." It maintained that the defeat of Hitler would have meaning only if a working-class revolution followed, and charged that the Allies were discussing the "restoration of the monarchy or removal of Hitler with maintenance of domestic fascism in the Reich." In the logic of this analysis it declared: "The American working class . . . must aid the working class in the warring powers and particularly the heroic underground movements that have carried on for years despite the terror. It can render that aid only if it remains free from dictatorship itself—by keeping America out of war and out of the conditions that create dictatorship." The heart of the resolution declared that America's entry into the war would mean a dictatorship at home. It centered its fire, therefore, on military defense measures and affirmatively called for "the continuance of independent working class action through the medium of the workers' boycott of German and Japanese goods." It declared for economic neutrality and said "we condemn America's economic participation on the side of the Allies just as we condemn Russia's economic participation on the side of Nazi Germany."[324]

This resolution had not been adopted without much pulling and hauling. A "sizable" pacifist group had developed in the Socialist Party, the remnants of the revolutionary wing were still shrill, the right-wing group wanted limited aid to the Allies. Only the personal authority of Thomas held the pieces of wreckage together.

Soon after the convention, however, Hitler began his invasion of Norway and his blitzkrieg across France. For many, the politics of irresponsibility were shed. They had never expected Hitler to win and the terrifying realization that he might do so forced them to dispense with the luxury of their illusions. One prominent left-winger, who in a letter of May 1939 had stated: "In case of war . . . I am for an underground movement especially among those who remain in key industrial areas," now urged "all-out effort" to help the Allies. Half of the *Call* editorial

[323] Minutes, national executive committee, Milwaukee meeting, Dec. 9, 1939.
[324] *Proceedings, National Convention of the Socialist Party, April 6-8, 1940,* mimeographed (Washington, D.C.), pp. 3-6.

board spoke out for full economic aid to Hitler's opponents. The Wisconsin state convention voted overwhelmingly to ask the party to reconsider its stand. Altman and the right-wing group in New York joined the Committee to Defend America by Aiding the Allies. Thomas pleaded that these men leave the party quietly, rather than make a fight for their point of view, since any new factional struggle would end the party and leave no antiwar voice in America.[325]

The quickening pace of the war hastened the disintegration of the Socialist Party. When Norman Thomas testified against the bill for lend-lease aid to Britain, a group of socialists, including Reinhold Niebuhr, Alfred Baker Lewis, Jack Altman, and Gus Tyler released a statement opposing him.[326] Little more than a month later, three members of the national executive committee, Paul Porter of Wisconsin, Leonard Woodcock, party secretary in Michigan, and Arthur McDowell, former labor secretary, resigned, charging they had been gagged. Both the leaders of the Militants as well as of the Clarity group were now prowar. Only Thomas remained. Although his own position was probably at this time in the minority, Thomas was able to keep control of the party and steer it on an isolationist course because of the inability of a scattered opposition to organize. Instead they resigned.

Probably the low point of party influence was reached in May 1941 when Norman Thomas, his moral opposition to the war so complete, joined Charles Lindbergh and Burton K. Wheeler at an America First Committee rally at Madison Square Garden. Until this point there had been the ludicrous dilemma of exempting oneself from all public-policy responsibility by calling for "workers action" instead of capitalist government action, and seeking to mobilize public opinion on government policy. Now Thomas spoke out solely in terms of affecting government policy. He argued that the possibility of a "complete Anglo-American victory . . . [is] exceedingly slim," and "if we are to talk negotiated peace, why not begin a peace offensive now?" But when he spoke, Thomas spoke alone; behind him lay only the charnel house of American socialism.

XIII. The Days of Sere and Yellow Leaf

Among the radical, as among the religious minded, there are the once born and the twice born.[327] The former is the enthusiast, the "sky-blue healthy-minded moralist" to whom sin and evil—the "soul's mumps and measles and whooping coughs," in Emerson's phrase—are merely transient episodes to be glanced at and ignored in the cheerful saunter of

[325] Letter from Norman Thomas to Jack Altman, June 5, 1940.
[326] New York Times, Jan. 23, 1941.
[327] I use the distinction coined by Francis W. Newman and elaborated by William James in his The Varieties of Religious Experience.

life. To the twice born, the world is "a double-storied mystery" which shrouds the evil and renders false the good; and in order to find truth, one must lift the veil and look Medusa in the face. The trauma of the twice born, like the regenerative rites of Demeter, is a phase in the cycle of self-consciousness. Every political generation has expressed this anguish, from Milton's *Ready and Easy Way*, the disillusioned outcry of his loss of faith in Cromwell by one of the greatest of all Christian humanists, to Dostoevsky's *The Possessed* whose biting picture of Shigalovism is the most savage prophecy of the fate of egalitarian movements. The generation of the 1930's passed through the looking glass of illusions in the years from the Moscow trials to the Nazi-Soviet pact. "What is the opposition?" asks Silone's Uliva in *Bread and Wine*. "Another bureaucracy that aspires to totalitarian domination in its turn. . . . a totalitarian orthodoxy which will use every means, from cinema to terrorism, to extirpate heresy and tyrannize over individual thought."

The Nazi-Soviet pact, which exposed the moral pretensions of the communists, was a winter blast shattering the "sky-blue" optimism of the once-born enthusiasts. The *Nation* and the *New Republic*, two of the chief supporters of the Popular Front, recoiled in genteel horror. Vincent Sheean, the latter-day John Reed of communist romanticism, published a series of articles denouncing Stalinism as the "Thermidor," the counter-revolution that betrayed "October." Louis Fischer voiced the doubts that he had suppressed for years. Granville Hicks resigned rather than parrot the stupid explanations given him. Heywood Broun, the day after the pact, wrote, "the masquerade is over." In England, Harold Laski, John Strachey, Victor Gollancz, and others stepped out of the parade. The communist hacks answered back. "Why do many intellectuals retreat at sharp turns in history?" asked V. J. Jerome, the party's cultural commissar. They are, he said, "impotent subjectivists . . . Don Quixotes. . . ."[328] Chief hatchetman Mike Gold, never very happy amidst the bourgeois respectability of the Popular Front, unloosed his scatalogical adjectives: ". . . these Mumfords, MacLeishes and Franks," he shouted, "may go on spouting endlessly their torrents of 'spirituality,' all the large, facile, greasy abstract words that bookmen, like confidence men, are so perfect in producing. [But] . . . Where are they going after rejecting liberalism? Not to Communism surely, but toward the other pole, toward fascism." "Intellectuals," said Gold, recalling an earlier essay of 1937, "are peculiarly susceptible to Trotzkyism, a nay-saying trend."[329]

Some communists retreated to a theory of class morality. "History"

[328] V. J. Jerome, *Intellectuals and the War* (pamphlet, New York, 1940), pp. 16, 23.
[329] Michael Gold, *The Hollow Men* (New York, 1941), pp. 73, 122.

was the final arbiter and all values were sacrificed to the expediency of the party in fulfilling its "tasks." Others, less hard-bitten, secretly cherished the hope that the Soviet Union "really" was anti-Fascist, but biding its time. Events quickly disproved that illusion. All over the world, communists began sabotaging the war against Hitler. In September of 1940, during the dangerous days of the buzz bombs over the channel, the communists called a "peace conference" in London. In the United States communists pulled crippling strikes in the tank-producing Allis-Chalmers plant at Milwaukee and the plane-producing North American Aviation factory in Inglewood, California. The Communist Party declared in its election program that ". . . the Roosevelt Government . . . shares the responsibility for inciting war in Europe, in Scandinavia and in the Baltic."[330]

The party fronts were quickly transformed. The League for Peace and Democracy became the American Peace Mobilization, and it raised as its slogan, "The Yanks Are Not Coming."[331] Around the gates of the White House the communists began a "perpetual peace vigil." On the morning of June 22, 1941, it magically vanished.

After the Nazi invasion of Russia, the communists became the exemplars of patriotism. They eagerly adopted a no-strike pledge and actively sought to discourage other unions from striking (as when Harry Bridges kept his local Montgomery-Ward warehousemen on the job when other mail-order workers walked out in Chicago). They soft-pedaled the Negro issue, called for speedup in the factories, and mobilized their entire propaganda apparatus to exert pressure for a second front in Europe. By 1944, following the conferences of great powers at Teheran, the communists dissolved the Communist Party and became the "educational" American Communist Political Association.[332] But Browder, in his enthusiasm for the new capitalism, had stepped a little too far. Little more than a year later, in April 1945, he was denounced by Jacques Duclos, leader of the French Communist Party, for a "notorious revision

[330] *Party News*, Pre-Convention Number. Issued by the National Committee, Communist Party, for Members of the Communist Party (April 1940), p. 7.

[331] On Memorial Day, May 30, 1941, Vito Marcantonio, the vice-chairman of the American Peace Mobilization, spoke over a nation-wide radio hook-up. He began: "As a member of the United States House of Representatives, I have fought the Administration's imperialist program of armaments, conscription, war and dictatorship from the very beginning. At times I have had to vote alone. I have not opposed it partially. I have opposed it in its entirety. Therefore, I now make answer to the President's fireside speech of last Tuesday night, which proclaimed the shooting and bloodshedding and dictatorship phases of the Wall Street-Downing Street Axis scheme for war, empire and dictatorship." Reprinted as *Marcantonio Answers F.D.R.* (June 1941), a pamphlet published by the American Peace Mobilization.

[332] "Teheran and America," statement of the National Committee Plenary Meeting Issue, *Communist*, Feb. 1944, pp. 99-101.

of Marxism,"[333] and shortly after, reviled and scorned, he was cast from the party. The communists now tacked sharply toward the "third-period" line.[334] When the Russians began stirring up the Greek guerrilla E.A.M. in what had tacitly been acknowledged at Teheran as a British sphere of influence, the communists began their cry against Anglo-American imperialism. Following the rejection of the Marshall Plan and the communist coup in Czechoslovakia in February 1948, the cold war was on in earnest.

Since 1946 communist influence in the United States has diminished, although tardy public understanding of the past history of communist penetration has been whipped into almost a panic by Senator McCarthy and other right-wing Republicans. By 1950 the decline in communist influence was so huge that the total membership of party-controlled unions was less than 5 per cent of the numerical strength of organized labor. Except for the battered United Electrical Workers and the west-coast longshoremen, none of these unions were in vital defense areas; on the other hand, the communists had been beaten decisively and cleaned out of the auto workers, the maritime unions, the transport workers, and strategical areas of industrial concentration. In the political field, the communist effort to build a new political party behind Henry Wallace failed miserably when the Progressive Party obtained little more than 1,000,000 votes in 1948; shortly after the outbreak of communist aggression in Korea, Wallace, O. John Rogge, and other noncommunist progressives repudiated the communists, leaving them, for the first time in fifteen years, with no major political or labor figure to front for them. In the intellectual field the only figures who remained were Howard Fast, a writer of slick historical novels,[335] and Paul Robeson, the Negro singer. The government's indictment and conviction of the eleven-man party "politburo" on the grounds of sedition sent the party reeling even further. The membership base of the party, which from 1935 on was largely middle class, began to disintegrate.

[333] *Daily Worker*, May 24, 1945.

[334] But not sharply enough for an inveterate group of revolutionists who had growled at Browder's cozying up to the National Association of Manufacturers. They too were expelled. In the Communist Party being "premature" about a change in the party line is as fatal as being too late. The communist "purge" of 1945 was the first since 1929 and rivaled in numbers the expulsions of the twenties, although it achieved little prominence because no factional bloc was involved. Among those expelled: writer Ruth McKenney and her husband Bruce Minton, Harrison George, editor of the west-coast *People's World*, Max Bedacht, former general secretary of the party, William F. Dunne, former editor of the *Daily Worker*, Bella Dodd, New York State legislative representative, Sam Darcy, district organizer of Philadelphia, and a top group of officers of the National Maritime Union.

[335] One of which, *The American*, a fictionalized version of the life of John Peter Altgeld, was charged by Harry Barnard as infringing on his biography, *Eagle Forgotten*. Fast settled out of court for an undisclosed sum while Fast's publishers reprinted the Barnard book.

In 1950 the communist movement stood revealed before the American people not as a political party but as a conspiracy, and that conspiracy was being driven out of American life, not always with scrupulous regard for civil liberties.[336] Its operations had revealed to easygoing Americans the meaning of an expansionist ideological force of a magnitude previously unknown in history. To the twentieth-century political experience it had contributed two notable innovations: the "front technique," one of the great political inventions for manipulation in the mass society; and the creation of a disciplined political army, in mufti, stirring disaffection from within.

Withal, there remains the problem of explaining the tremendous emotional hold that communism has on tens of thousands of persons (and the curious liberal mentality which regards with understanding a conversion to communism yet views with disdain the ex-communist, seeing him as a pariah, or as Koestler strikingly put it, as the defrocked priest). The answer lies, perhaps, on a mythopoeic and psychological level. For the convert to communism there is the seductive myth "of humanity's salvation through the rebellion" and "the triumph of the unfortunate," and beyond that, "acquiescence in the mysterious and imperative law of history, resignation to a future deemed even more inevitable than glorious, subservience to the masters of the world."[337] These frame, for the average communist, a set of satisfactions: those that arise from a life of dedication and submission to discipline; a sense of conspiracy and

[336] For a detailed description of the conspiratorial nature of American communism and its complete subordination not only to the Russian political line but to Moscow's espionage demands, see Louis F. Budenz, *Men without Faces* (New York, 1950); Hede Massing, *This Deception* (New York, 1951); and the forthcoming volume by Whittaker Chambers, *Witness*.

[337] Raymond Aron, "Politics and the French Intellectual," *Partisan Review*, July-Aug. 1950, pp. 588-99. See too a fascinating psychoanalysis of a communist by Dr. Henry Lowenfeld, "Some Aspects of a Compulsion Neurosis," *Psychoanalytic Quarterly*, Jan. 1944. "At about the age of eighteen he joined the Communist Party," Dr. Lowenfeld writes (on. p. 9), "and made it the focal point of his life, serving it with a self-sacrificing faithfulness which contrasted sharply with his otherwise oversceptical, defensive attitude. In his conviction of the scientifically unquestionable correctness of the theory he found an inner security in the chaos of reality. He became a part of a great and powerful movement to which he could abandon himself in complete devotion. In identifying himself with the proletariat, the small and the weak, now large and powerful, he found a tremendous prop for his ego. . . . At the same time he considered himself a member of a modern intellectual aristocracy, with a feeling comparable to that of the religious zealots or the nobility in other periods, which further relieved his sense of smallness [his basic anxiety].

"This extensive sublimation performed the same function of preventing anxiety as did the oceanic feeling or religious faith in other individuals and in other cultural periods. . . . The end of the great figures of the Russian Revolution during the Moscow trials played an important rôle in his loss of faith. Thus his political theories no longer gave him assurance and security in the chaos but instead led him into new conflicts which finally contributed decisively to the outbreak of his neurosis."

martyrdom; an identification with "names" who espouse party causes; an air of being "informed," because one has a set of answers and a fund of organized information (drilled in incessantly at party meetings and through party literature) which one's friends do not possess; a feeling of "purpose" in a world where most people's energies are dissipated in a set of violent but aimless quests. As Ortega y Gasset said in a remarkably prescient passage twenty years ago: "Whatever the content of Bolshevism be, it represents a gigantic human enterprise. In it, men have resolutely embraced a purpose of reform, and live tensely under the discipline that such a faith instils into them. . . . If Europe, in the meantime, persists in the ignoble vegetative existence of these last years, its muscles flabby for want of exercise, without any plan of a new life, how will it be able to resist the contaminating influence of such an astounding enterprise? It is simply a misunderstanding of the European to expect that he can hear unmoved that call to new *action* when he has no standard of a cause as great to unfurl in opposition."[338]

The Socialist Party in the past decade has been alive only because of Norman Thomas. Much as he would have liked to lay down the party burdens (he once sought to build Maynard Kreuger as the party spokesman), he could not; the identification was too complete. As the character of a social movement is often symbolized in its patristic surrogates, so Norman Thomas amazingly sums up the many contradictions of the Socialist Party. A communist critic once sneered at Norman Thomas for entitling his study of poverty in the United States as *Human Exploitation* rather than *Capitalist Exploitation*. The critic had a point, for what arouses Thomas is the emotional and ethical, not the analytical and sociological. Intellectually Thomas knows that "the system" is to blame; but such abstractions have rarely held meaning for him. His interest has always been the personal *fact* of injustice, committed by people; and while socialism might remove the impersonal "basic" causes, he was always happiest when he could *act* where the problem was immediate and personal. In courageously speaking out against the sharecropper terror in Birdsong, Arkansas; in combating martial law in Terre Haute, Indiana; in exposing the Klan in Tampa, Florida; in uncovering the municipal corruption of Jimmy Walker's New York; in defying the anti-free-speech ordinances of Jersey's Boss Hague—in all these instances, Thomas' voice has rung out with the eloquent wrath of an Elijah Lovejoy or a William Lloyd Garrison.

These impulses came naturally to Norman Mattoon Thomas. Religion, orthodox Presbyterianism, was the center of his boyhood home. His father

[338] José Ortega y Gasset, *The Revolt of the Masses* (New York, 1932), pp. 199-200.

was a minister, as was his Welsh-born grandfather. He was raised in a strict Sabbatarian code, but the harshness of his ancestral Calvinism was modified by the kindness of his parents. "My father who believed theoretically in eternal damnation," wrote Thomas, "would never say of any one that he was damned."[339]

Thomas, born in Marion, Ohio, in 1884, was a sickly little boy who grew tall too fast, became an awkward, skinny kid, shy with his peers and talkative with his elders, and who found his main satisfaction in reading.[340] Norman was the eldest of six children and the family was busy always with household chores and other activities of small-town middle-class life. Of the parents Emma Mattoon was the more outstanding personality and "father was content to have it so." In thinking back on his boyhood in the small Ohio town, Thomas remarked: "What a set-up for the modern psychologically-minded biographer or novelist. A study in revolt born of reaction from Presbyterian orthodoxy and the Victorian brand of Puritanism in a midwest setting. The only trouble is that this isn't what happened."

With the financial help of an uncle, Thomas satisfied a boyhood dream and entered Princeton, graduating in 1905 as class valedictorian. Entering the ministry was a more or less destined fact. But in the age of genteel faith in progress, acceptance of the old orthodoxies seemed out of place. As with many socially-minded ministers of the day, the modernist and liberal gospel of Walter Rauschenbusch had its appeal. But it was the filth and poverty of the cold-water flats of the Spring Street slums on New York's west side that turned Thomas actively to social reform. And it was World War I and the influence of the Fellowship of Reconciliation, a religious pacifist organization, that made him a socialist. "God, I felt, was certainly not the 'God and Father of Our Lord Jesus Christ' if his servants could only serve him and the cause of righteousness by the diabolic means of war." Thomas' stand took him from the ministry into politics and journalism. (Rather than endanger the financial support his church received, he resigned the pastorate.) A tall handsome man with strongly-etched patrician features, rich resonant voice, and fine American credentials, he quickly became an outstanding leader in a party depleted of public figures. In 1924 he was nominated for governor of New

[339] Thomas has made some autobiographical references in his *As I See It* (New York, 1932). The above quotation as well as some description of Thomas' beliefs are from an unpublished memoir which Thomas wrote for his family in 1944 and to which this author had access.

[340] "I was naturally left-handed," Thomas writes, "but I had to learn to write with my right hand. Father even tried to make me throw a ball with my right arm. Nowadays, all sorts of psychic disturbances are supposed to result from this insistence on right-handedness. As far as I know I escaped. I don't think the faulty process was even responsible for my socialism. But I do suppose it added to my lack of manual skill."

York; four years later—because the two veteran party leaders, Morris Hillquit and Victor Berger, were European-born and because Dan Hoan was busy being mayor of Milwaukee—Thomas was nominated for the presidency.

As a party leader, Thomas had two serious flaws. For one, he strikingly distrusted his own generation and surrounded himself almost entirely with considerably younger men who stood in an admiring and uncritical relation to him. The other was a profound fear of being manipulated, so that every political attack was taken personally. Thomas was intent on being party leader. Often a situation would develop—particularly in the late thirties—when, if party policy tended in a direction other than his, Thomas would threaten to resign (otherwise how could he speak on an issue with pure conscience?). Yet many of Thomas' decisions were made not with an eye to the political results but to the moral consequences, as he saw them. Moreover, by background and temperament, Thomas was concerned largely with issues rather than ideas. In a party whose main preoccupation has been the refinement of "theory" at the cost, even, of interminable factional divisions—Thomas' interest in specific issues often meant shifting alliances with different factions while maintaining aloofness from the jesuitical debates that gave rise to these groups. Thus in the late thirties, Thomas was with the right wing on the labor-party issue, and shifted to the pacifist and left wing on the war problem. Thomas was probably most unhappy during the early and middle thirties when, as a professed non-Marxist, he was involved in the conflicts of fifty-seven varieties of claims to revolutionary orthodoxy.

As a man whose instincts are primarily ethical, Thomas has been the genuine moral man in the immoral society. But as a political man he has been caught inextricably in the dilemmas of expediency, the relevant alternatives, and the lesser evil. As a sophisticated modern man, Thomas has been acutely aware of his ambiguous role, and feels he has made the political choice. "One is obliged," he wrote in 1947, "to weigh one's actions in terms of relative social consequences . . . and the tragedy is that no choice can be positively good. . . . Positively [the pacifists] had nothing to offer in the problem of stopping Nazism before its triumph could not only enslave but corrupt the world. Nothing that is, except for a religious faith in the power of God, a faith stronger if it could include a belief in immortality. It was something but not enough to affirm that the method of war was self-defeating for good ends. It was not enough to say 'if all Americans would act like Gandhi' we should more surely defeat avowed fascism. Possibly, but since almost no Americans would thus act the question remained of the lesser evil." Thomas did learn the lesson of the lesser evil: instead of being an absolute pacifist, however, he became an indecisive one. When the Franco rebellion broke

401

out, Thomas gave up his religious pacifism, but was led to an ambiguous distinction whereby he supported the right of individuals to volunteer and fight, but not "American official intervention by war which would involve conscription." After Pearl Harbor, Thomas came out in "critical support" of the United States government, a position which consisted in the first years largely of ignoring foreign policy and speaking out against injustices on the home front. The Socialist Party itself adopted a formula sufficiently elastic and ambiguous to permit pacifists, antiwar socialists, and prowar socialists to continue together inside the party.[341]

In 1944, the party almost touched bottom, with Thomas receiving only 80,000 votes. The death of Roosevelt in 1945 and the severe New Deal congressional setback in 1946 raised the hopes of some socialists that labor would form a third party. A few individuals began trickling back into the Socialist Party and in 1948 some socialists hoped that a large Thomas vote would stimulate new left-wing political activity. But labor could not afford the luxury of "protest" voting and Thomas received a disappointing 140,000 votes. In 1949, the socialist vote in the New York mayoralty elections fell to an unbelievable low of under 5,000. By 1950, Thomas was ready to give up the political ghost. At the Socialist Party national convention he urged that the party give up all electoral activity and become an educational organization. But a combination of pacifists, left-wingers, and municipal isolationists from Reading and Bridgeport combined to defeat the motion. Shortly afterward the Connecticut state organization left the party when Jasper McLevy was censured for accepting the electoral support of the outspokenly reactionary businesswoman Vivien Kellems. Although some socialists believed, almost to the extent of a faith, that a correct resolution would set the party aright, even such a faith could not, as once before in history, raise this Lazarus from the dead.

After fifty years what had the Socialist Party accomplished in America? It had ruled many American cities, and three of them, Milwaukee, Reading, and Bridgeport, carry an indelible socialist stamp.[342] Many generations

[341] A situation which provoked the comment from Dwight Macdonald: "This failure to split on the war issue has always seemed to me an indication of a certain lack of political seriousness in all the S.P. factions." "Why I Will Not Support Norman Thomas," *Politics*, Oct. 1944, p. 279.

[342] Why was socialism more successful in these cities than others? In the first two, there was an identity of leadership of the labor movement and the Socialist Party. More important, there was a basic ethnic homogeneity which allowed the socialist movement, whose leaders were of similar ethnic backgrounds, to develop. "James Maurer, and most of his colleagues," reports an historian of the Reading movement, "were Pennsylvania-Germans and were conversant with the prejudices, the 'stubbornness,' the virtues, and weaknesses of this group." (See Henry G. Stetler, *The Socialist Movement in Reading, Pennsylvania* [Storrs, Conn., 1943], p. 144.) Of

had been influenced by its ideas. In the last twenty years a depression-matured generation, without profession and hope, had received a schooling in the socialist movement which permitted them to achieve high place as trade-union leaders and staff technicians, government administrators, political scientists, and propagandists. The "progressive" unions in American life, the garment workers, clothing workers, auto workers, textile workers, and many others, had a leadership that in a general way was socialist in spirit. The socialists who had left the party during the war were instrumental in creating the Union for Democratic Action and later the Americans for Democratic Action, which in 1950 had become the leading political voice of liberalism in America. Many of these quondam socialists (almost the entire leadership of the Wisconsin socialists, for example) had entered the Democratic Party, and several of them, such as Andrew Biemiller of Milwaukee and George Rhodes of Reading, had been elected to Congress. These have been the "organizational" fruits. In the form of a set of ideas, socialism has, as a pale tint, suffused into the texture of American life and subtly changed its shadings.

In 1885, an optimistic Andrew Carnegie could, in "A Talk to Young Men," advise how surely to become a success: "There is one sure mark of the coming partner, the future millionaire; his revenues always exceed his expenditures. He begins to save early. . . . A rare chance will soon present itself for investment. The little you saved will prove the basis for an amount of credit utterly surprising to you. . . . [What your] seniors require . . . is the man who has proved that he has the business habits which create capital, and to create it in the best of all possible ways, as far as self-discipline is concerned, . . . by adjusting his habits to his means. Gentlemen, it is the first hundred dollars saved which tells. Begin at once to lay up something. The bee predominates in the future millionaire."

Sixty-five years after his talk, the Carnegie Mansion, one of the last remaining large private mansions on Fifth Avenue, became the new center for Columbia University's School for Social Work. How does one

---

Milwaukee, the story is told of the 1932 election where the socialists won three out of four city-wide offices. When asked to explain the loss of the fourth, an old German socialist explained: "You see, our candidate's name was Bennowicz. If we had had someone with a good American name like Schemmelpfennig we could have won." In Milwaukee and in Bridgeport, however, many of the party's successes are due to the characters of Dan Hoan and Jasper McLevy. Milwaukee actually has never been completely socialist. In the election years that span the period of socialist rule, 1910 to 1940, although Dan Hoan was elected to office fifteen times (three as city attorney and twelve as mayor) the city invariably elected a council that was more than half nonsocialist. (See J. T. Salter, *The Pattern of Politics* [New York, 1940], pp. 135-59.) Both Dan Hoan and Jasper McLevy have been able city executives who after elections often found their greatest support in the good-government and upper-class wards of the city.

measure the contribution of a specific social movement to so great a change? Certainly, the Malthusian morality, with its insistence that social welfare robs the individual of his moral fibre, has an archaic flavor today. "As a Socialist candidate for Mayor of New York in 1925, I advocated a municipal housing program," Norman Thomas recently stated, "but in those days I would not have tried to get the kind of federal housing subsidy that Senator Taft proposed two decades later. The housing program that has been carried out in recent years would have been considered utopian in 1925."[343] Nor did Thomas dream that many of the planks in his first presidential platform, in the campaign of 1928, would have become law or accepted party policy within two decades. Among them were extension of public works, old-age pensions, public unemployment insurance, a shorter work day, government insurance against weather damage to crops, adequate flood control, the right to organize, Puerto Rican autonomy, Philippine independence, and recognition of Russia. In other words "to the considerable extent that capitalism has delivered more than seemed possible a generation ago," Thomas concluded, "it has done so by accepting things it used to denounce as Socialism."

And yet these welfare concepts, also, grew out of the American soil. It was only because we placed so high a premium on individual worth that we began to accept the idea—reminiscent of frontier communal responsibility—of the social obligations to the individual. (What is social *insurance* if not the sharing of risk and reward?) In this sense the welfare ideals of America in the middle of the twentieth century certainly differed from the collectivization tendencies in other parts of the globe which subordinated the individual and deified *group* concepts.

American society at the middle of the twentieth century was evolving in a far different direction from that predicted by Marxist sociology. There were not in America an "Army," "Church," "Large Landowners," "Bureaucracy," "Bourgeoisie," "Petty Bourgeoisie," and "Proletariat"— the staple ingredients of European social politics which in different combination accounted for the social forms of Germany, Spain, France, and Britain. How could one apply standard political categories to explain the "social role" of a Franklin D. Roosevelt? Should he be called a Tiberius Gracchus who deserted his class to become a people's tribune; an Athenian Solon whose political reforms deflected the revolutionary surge of a propertyless mass; a Louis Napoleon, manipulating first one class and then another while straddling all in order to assure his own Bonapartist rule? Or how does one define the actual political reality presented by the contrast images of industry and labor in that the one proclaims

[343] "Norman Thomas Re-Examines U.S. Capitalism," *Fortune*, Sept. 1950, p. 76.

that this is a "laboristic" society and that "Washington" is leading us off to socialism, the other declares that businessmen are running the administration and labor has no voice.

The old simplistic theories no longer hold. We seem to be evolving toward some form of technical-military-administrative state, especially as the pressures of a permanent war economy bring into focus a priority of needs which are national in character and override the demands of any particular interest group. The growth of a federal budget from four billion in 1930 to more than forty billion in 1950 (apart from the wartime peak budget of over ninety billion in 1944) was an unplanned and crescive fact, and yet these new enormous magnitudes are of decisive import in shaping the economy. Along the way, the nascent state capitalism has had to enlarge its social budgets and provide for the welfare of large masses; quondam socialists, now in high positions in labor and government, have tended to instill a sense of social responsibility. But it is not primarily a social welfare state which has developed. In the dimly-emerging social structure, new power sources are being created and new social divisions are being formed. Whatever the character of that new social structure may be—whether state capitalism, managerial society, or corporative capitalism—by 1950 American socialism as a political and social fact had become simply a notation in the archives of history.

If a cenotaph ever were to be raised for American socialism, I would nominate for inscription one story and one remark which sum up the adventures of the Socialist Party as an American political movement:

The Rabbi of Zans used to tell this story about himself:

In my youth when I was fired with the love of God, I thought I would convert the whole world to God. But soon I discovered that it would be quite enough to convert the people who lived in my town, and I tried for a long time, but did not succeed. Then I realized that my program was too ambitious, and I concentrated on the persons in my own household. But I could not convert them either. Finally it dawned upon me: I must work upon myself, so that I may give true service to God. But I did not accomplish even this.

Hasidic Tale

He who seeks the salvation of souls, his own as well as others, should not seek it along the avenue of politics.

Max Weber

CHAPTER 7

American Socialism and
the Socialist Philosophy of History

BY DAVID F. BOWERS

DAVID F. BOWERS was Associate Professor of Philosophy at Princeton University and a member of the Program in American Civilization at the time of his death in June 1945. He had already delivered a lecture on the subject of this essay before the undergraduate conference of the Program, and his carefully detailed lecture outline has been transcribed into essay form by his friend and colleague, Donald Drew Egbert. However, so detailed was Professor Bowers' outline that in very large part this essay is written in his own words.

Professor Bowers' books include the volume, *Foreign Influences in American Life*, which he edited for the Program in American Civilization in 1944, and had he lived he would have been an editor of this book.

For bibliography in Volume 2 relevant to Mr. Bowers' essay, see especially PART III, Topic 2, also Topics 1, 3, 4, 5, and General Reading; PART IV, Topics 8, 9, 12.

THE socialist philosophy of history is not only the most distinctive aspect of socialist theory, but is so completely central that almost everything else in the theory of socialism can be derived from it. For socialist philosophy is nothing but a certain way of looking at history, and one from which issues not only the socialist ethic, the socialist aesthetic, and the socialist cosmology, but also, in the more immediately practical sphere, its philosophy of politics and of economics. The present essay will be focused primarily on this socialist view of history, and will consider it in relation to three questions fundamental to the understanding of socialism in general and of American socialism in particular. These questions are: What are the basic assumptions of socialism and what role have they played in American socialism? How do these assumptions compare with their analogues in the philosophy of American democracy? And lastly, to what extent have the two sets of doctrines, socialist and democratic, historically influenced each other?

I. The Socialist Theory of History

First then, what do the socialist assumptions about history include? At a glance it may seem almost impossible to make a simple and clear statement that will cover the philosophies of all different socialists and groups of socialists. Even the most casual survey reveals that the socialist philosophy differs widely not only between individuals but especially between the fundamental types of socialism such as the religious socialisms of the eighteenth century and earlier, the secular utopian socialisms of the nineteenth century, and the Marxian socialisms of our own day. Thus, where the world view of the early religious communists has been poetic, symbolic, and theistic, looking upon history as a kind of morality play in which gods and devils have battled endlessly for the souls of men, the world view of the secular utopians has been rationalistic and humanitarian, envisaging history as a kind of endless struggle between ignorance and vice on the one side, and reason and virtue on the other. In contrast to both of these, history for the Marxian has primarily been the relentless march forward of an impersonal system of production mediated by class conflict.

Moreover, even the emotional overtones of these three fundamental types of socialism are different. Where the religious utopian has seen himself on an heroic scale as a protagonist in a titanic struggle between elemental powers, the secular utopian has been able to fancy himself as a rational benefactor of the human race and the prototype of what all mankind was eventually to become. The Marxian, however, if he is consistent, must envisage himself as merely the anonymous representative of a class, and thus as the indispensable but personally insignificant instrument of the proletariat in its march to the abolition of all classes as such, a march guided—in the Leninist view—by the Communist Party.

Finally, so great have been the differences between these chief varieties of socialism that we can even see a dialectical pattern in their development, a pattern which becomes progressively more materialistic as we move with the passage of time from one kind of socialism to another. For where the religious utopian has formulated the great issues of history in supernatural terms, and the secular utopian in moral terms, the Marxist has formulated them in economic and material terms. Similarly, whereas man in the first scheme has been made the subordinate of God, and in the second something close to the equal of God, in the third, or Marxian view, he is subjected once more to a force beyond his control—this time, however, not to God but to the mechanism of economic power.

Nevertheless, in spite of all these major differences between the varieties of socialism there is a certain common denominator, a common thread which binds them together, a common hue which tinges them all. As one would naturally expect of creeds directed to social reconstruction, all forms of socialist theory are preoccupied with such additional questions about history as the following: (1) What type of factor primarily determines the course of history? (2) Does this course of history fall into a unified pattern? (3) If so, at what goal, if any, does this pattern aim? Or, to put it more positively and in philosophic terms, every variety of socialist theory is interested in: (1) *the problem of historical causation;* (2) *the problem of historical law;* and (3) *the problem of historical ends.* And within limits they all seek to solve these problems in identical ways.

Consider, first, the problem of historical causation. Here again, at first glance, disagreement rather than agreement seems to rule. Thus, where the religious socialists, because of their theistic emphasis, have located the causal factors *outside* of history, the secular utopians, who have usually maintained both the existence of divine providence and the efficacy of the human will, have located these factors only *partly outside* history. The Marxians, on the contrary, have tended to locate them wholly *within* history, and specifically in economic institutions. Similarly, whereas both religious and secular utopians alike have defined these causal factors as characterized by purpose (whether divine or human), the Marxians rule out purpose as a primary category of explanation and explain all history ultimately in terms of economic forces.

However, although the three fundamental types of American socialism differ as to the location and the character of these determining forces, they all agree that the agency or tool *through* which the forces work is a specifically selected group or class of people who in a sense have represented the will of history in its more naked form. Some, moreover, agree

410

that it is the particular mission of the group to uncover, engage, and ultimately destroy the adversaries of history—to destroy those individuals or groups who blindly or deliberately block the forward march of history, individuals or groups whose total impact is considered to be not only chthonic and regressive, but actually wicked. For these are the forces of the antichrist, the forces of evil.

Different varieties of socialism have, of course, clothed these assumptions in different words and have described the chosen group in various ways, assigning it different degrees of initiative and of merit. To Marxists, the chosen group is the industrial proletariat, while the adversary is the capitalist. The position of both the chosen and the adversary is determined by their respective relations to the system of production, so that both of them lack initiating powers of their own and are mere links in the causal nexus of the production system. Similarly, to religious communists the actions of the chosen group (a group picked by God himself) and of the adversary (who is Satan and his forces) are also both determined; but here they are determined by their predesigned role in the drama of salvation. Each of them, therefore, is an element in the divine purpose. To the secular utopians, on the contrary, the chosen people are those who, through their utopian views and by means of their own wills, are enabled to overcome their adversary, the ignorant, by means of persuasion, and therefore in a bloodless victory.

But whatever the reason for this emphasis on an elect group in combat with the adversaries of history, and however differently the emphasis is interpreted, it does constitute a thread running through all socialist thought and accounting for many of the striking characteristics of socialism. It accounts for the persistently high morale of socialists under persecution, for the ability of socialist leaders to demand and receive the utmost in self-sacrifice from their individual followers, as well as for the moral fervor of socialists which, as is well known, rises at times to a peak which has scarcely been equaled save by the Hebrew prophets. However, this is not the only thread that runs throughout the socialist philosophy of history.

If we turn to the socialist treatment of the problem of historical law, that is to say, to the question whether history follows a unified pattern, we discover other common elements. For example, almost all socialists, again by virtue of their interest in social reconstruction, tend to believe that in the long run history possesses but a single *direction*, and that *upward*. This belief is opposed to the view which prevailed among the ancient Greeks that history is cyclical, that it repeats itself endlessly and purposelessly. In relatively modern times, also, versions of this cyclical view have been defended by Vico (d. 1744), by Schopenhauer (d. 1860), and

411

by Spengler (d. 1936), among others. In contrast to it, socialists ordinarily assume that history, like its matrix time, never completely reverses itself, and that each new historical situation has elements of novelty never before experienced. This socialist assumption is also opposed to the thesis of those historical pessimists, such as Henry Adams, who have envisioned history, like the physical universe, as in the process of running down and as therefore constantly moving at an ever accelerating rate in the direction of chaos.[1] For the socialist view customarily construes history as essentially progressive, as a curve, a spiral,[2] or zigzag, which even though it may at times lag and admit recessions, still ends at a point higher than at which it began.

This is no less true of the religious utopians who anticipated Christ's second coming, or of the secular utopians who predicted a final state of perfect human harmony, than it is of the present-day Marxians who look forward to the classless society. The most obvious exceptions to this generalization that history tends to be progressive are those socialists of the Saint-Simonian school, and in particular Fourier and Saint-Simon himself, who took seriously Condorcet's suggestion that the life of society obeys the same law of birth, maturity, and decay which governs individual life; and who therefore concluded that social decline is in the end inevitable. Yet even in such exceptional cases, this catastrophe was set so far in advance—by Fourier no less than 55,000 years hence—with so many years of human progress intervening, that its pessimistic implications were to a large extent forgotten.

Not only have most socialists inclined toward the view that history follows a course upward, but they have also maintained that this course tends to fall into distinct epochs or periods which succeed one another according to a definite rule. There are many examples of this tendency in socialist philosophy, of which perhaps the most familiar is the Marxian attempt to periodize history into five stages: barbarism, or primitive communism; the slave economy of antiquity and notably of ancient Greece and Rome; feudalism; capitalism; and proletarian communism.[3] The Marxist assumes that each of these epochs stands to the others in a necessary sequence as expressions of different stages in the evolution of modes of production, with each one leading into another as a result of the class

---

[1] Henry Adams, *The Degradation of the Democratic Dogma* (New York, 1919).

[2] Although Vico had upheld a cyclical theory of history, he did not consider the corresponding periods in his cycles to be really homogeneous. Consequently, his doctrine could be readily adapted by socialists and others to the conception of progress as a spiral movement.

[3] See especially Karl Marx, Preface to "A Contribution to the Critique of Political Economy" (originally published 1859) in *Selected Works* (New York, 1936?), I, p. 347; and Friedrich Engels, *The Origin of the Family, Private Property and the State* (Chicago, 1902), originally published in 1884. Also see Vernon Venable, *Human Nature, the Marxian View* (New York, 1945), pp. 99-103, 114-15.

antagonisms and the social revolution generated by the contradictions of a system of production.

This kind of periodizing is found in earlier forms of socialism as well as in Marxism. Among the early religious communists it was a common practice to divide history into so-called "dispensations" differing in the degree to which they reveal to mankind the true nature and disposition of God; and the order of these dispensations was necessarily considered to be according to God's hidden purpose. The Shakers, who worked out this eschatology more elaborately than did any other group, divided history into three great periods.[4] Of these the earliest was the Patriarchal Dispensation, from the fall of Adam to the birth of Christ. During this era God had left man to work out his own salvation, a task in which man had failed. The second period was the Dispensation of Christ's First Appearing, which lasted from the ministry of Jesus to the ministry of Mother Ann Lee. In this period the foundations of the true church and of salvation were laid out, but the children of light were beset on all sides by the forces of antichrist under the guise, first, of the Catholic Church and, later, of Protestant churches. The third epoch, or Dispensation of Christ's Second Appearing, was marked by the ministry of Ann Lee and the ushering in of the promised millennium in which God's nature and purpose are fully revealed. And this was to lead ultimately to the utter rout of the forces of antichrist.

Equally elaborate accounts of the periodization of history were worked out by the secular utopians. There was, however, this major difference: the secular utopians rooted the changes from epoch to epoch in the evolving capacities of man, and particularly in human reason, rather than in either the will of God, emphasized by the religious utopians, or in the compulsives of the changing economic process, like the Marxians. For example, Saint-Simon attempted to divide history into periods based on movement away from those ideologies and institutions founded on superstition, and toward ideologies and institutions founded on science.[5]

What is important to note concerning all these different efforts at periodization are the following assumptions which they hold in common. All three of them assume that the pattern of history, and therefore of the law governing its development, admit of a radical discontinuity between its various stages: history is, in short, catastrophic. In "orthodox" Marxism this takes the form of assuming that change from epoch to epoch is accompanied by violent social revolution. And while the catastrophic event between epochs was less pronounced in secular utopianism, which tended

---

[4] See B. S. Youngs and others, *The Testimony of Christ's Second Appearing* (several editions but first published in 1808 at Lebanon, Ohio); and Calvin Green and S. Y. Wells, *A Summary View of the Millennial Church* (Albany, N.Y., 1823).

[5] Georges Weill, *Saint-Simon et son œuvre* (Paris, 1894), chap. 3.

to subscribe to the doctrine of continuous progress in a relatively straight line, nevertheless the concept of abrupt change does enter in. And in Fourierism this concept of discontinuity took the highly radical form of assuming that social revolution is actually accompanied by abrupt changes in physical nature. Thus to Fourier the goodness of nature itself depended on the goodness of man, and the degree of natural evolution on the degree of human evolution; because the Fourierist "millennium," marked by the achievement of human perfection, was supposed to be accompanied by a physical change in the ocean from brine to a liquid having a most agreeable acid taste[6] not unlike lemonade.

It is true that the degree of discontinuity in history has varied with the different philosophies of the chief varieties of socialism. Nevertheless, they all have held that history is discontinuous to the degree that each historical era, when fully matured, has a distinct complex of ideas and institutions, as well as an over-all quality and value of its own not found in any other period. Moreover, they all have assumed that the sequence of these discontinuous epochs, the order in which they occur, is determined independently of the will of man even when man himself is assumed to be the chief beneficiary of the sequence, or, for that matter, the instrument through which it works. They have all assumed, in short, that the order of history is basically impersonal, with its coordinates, its direction, laid down by a power outside human control. And all of them have also assumed that this ordering of past epochs is not only independent of man but is itself noncapricious and nondeviating. The planned purpose of history is predetermined, admitting no fundamental novelty at any stage of its unfolding, and so constructed that its final stages reveal nothing not implied in its beginnings.

One obvious example of this unaberrant ordering of epochs is, of course, the attempt made by the religious utopians to construe history as the unvacillating and fixed unfolding of divine purpose. Another obvious example is the Marxian attempt to trace thought and desire back primarily to the individual's economic class, and beyond this to the impersonal workings of the particular productive system which itself is but one stage in an economic process developing in accordance with the Marxian laws of history. Even the secular utopians, who should have rejected this conception of successively ordered epochs—especially in view of their own tendency to root all historical change in the evolving capacities of man, rather than in God or in matter—actually failed to do so. This can be seen in their conception of the evolution of man as a kind of abstract process governed by providence rather than by the rational decisions of any particular man or group of men, with the result that, for such human-

[6] Charles Gide, introduction to Selections from the Works of Fourier (tr. by Julia Franklin; London, 1901), p. 14.

istically oriented socialists, history in the end became a monolithic impersonal process.

Thus the socialist conception of history reveals a strong disposition not only to read into history an eternal struggle between a saving few and an unregenerate many, but, paradoxically enough, to set that struggle very largely within an inhuman framework. For the framework is one that is almost wholly turned in upon itself, fixed in its sequences. And almost its only unmechanical trait is the fact that its development is saltatory, that its motion apes in a remote way the fits and starts, the jerks, of life itself.

This ascription of such an essentially fixed and inhuman framework to history has given rise to some of the most striking features of socialist thought. It is this, for example, which has made possible the strange grafting of socialism on the romantic dialectic of Hegel, because the Hegelian dialectic likewise ascribes such a framework or law to history. And it is out of this, also, that has grown the socialist doctrine of the inevitability of socialist victory, and—perhaps even more important—the socialist tendency to claim a special insight into history distinct from and independent of ordinary methods of knowledge. For a law of history which predicates necessary connections between discontinuities—which predicates, that is, a continuity between what are essentially independent entities—is one that cannot be discovered or explored by ordinary methods of empirical observation. Consequently, in asserting the existence of such a law, the socialist philosopher has usually been driven to claim either a special vision from God (as did the religious utopians), or an intuitive grasp of first principles (as did the secular utopians), or else a special logical method (such as the dialectic of the Marxians).

But most important of all, the ascription of this kind of framework to history enshrines in the very heart of the socialist philosophy a fundamental dichotomy or tension at both the metaphysical and psychological levels, a tension growing out of the contrast between the framework of historical law and the drama of conflict it is to enclose. For, metaphysically, where the drama, the struggle between purely human forces, suggests a universe that is "open," plastic, adventurous, and above all one in which human effort and values count, the framework gives us a universe which is "closed," rigid, self-contained and impervious to human control. Similarly, at the psychological level, where the drama arouses courage, resolution, and all the emotions appropriate to moral struggle, the framework suggests that all this effort is a little silly, and it therefore instills inertia, passivity, and above all a sense of confidence without a sense of responsibility. It is this tension, between the struggle of the elect group with its adversaries and the inhuman framework within which the struggle is set, which gives peculiar meaning to the socialist solution of the problem of ends in history, the last of the socialist doctrines to be examined here. For the heart of this solution is an attempt to resolve the tension between the drama of history and the setting of history through a premise that in the end the setting will, in spite of its present intractability, be revealed as merely a stage prop after all.

In essence the socialist solution to the problem of historical ends consists of three assertions. One of these is that the goal of history is the intellectual, moral, and physical perfecting of the individual. Another is that realization of the goal will be brought about, and indeed can only be brought about, by some form of collectivized society. According to the third, this goal will actually be reached within a definite period of time. Let us consider each of these propositions in turn.

It is often surprising to those unfamiliar with the details of socialist theory to find that socialism, which to Americans popularly connotes the repression of individuality, should in the end stand for the individualistic ideal. However, there can be no doubt whatever that this is the case. There has been nothing, for example, which the religious socialist, as an inheritor of the tradition of evangelical Christianity, has prized so highly as the salvation of his own soul. Nor has there been anything which the secular utopian, as an heir of the French Revolution, has held so important as individual liberty. Such were the beliefs which have motivated most of those who have subscribed to these two forms of socialism. And even the Marxians cannot be excluded here, because in defining the goal of the classless society they too have always, and with sincerity, defined it as a society in which each individual is to achieve a maximum opportunity for the realization of his own potentialities as a person. Marxists often forget this ideal in their frequently ruthless use of individuals and their disregard of human rights, but the ideal nevertheless remains a real part of their ideology. In short, socialism—at least in theory—holds just as tenaciously to the individualistic ideal as does its arch foe, capitalism, which also often forgets its ideal.

Where the socialist ethic differs, of course, from that of capitalism and, in so differing, constitutes a socialist protest against the capitalist ethic, is in the further insistence that the individual can realize his highest potentialities only within the context of a highly integrated economy. Socialists have developed this doctrine in different ways, but they have usually defended it in terms of two general assumptions, each of which is the corollary of the other. The first assumption is that economic or material power, as long as it is vested in a single individual or group of individuals short of the community as a whole, must inevitably corrupt the prevailing social system (as Marx believed) and perhaps also the individual wielder of power (as other forms of socialism have held). And the other assumption is that, once freed from the necessity of taking

416

thought about his own private economic wants, the individual is morally transformed so that thereafter he will both see and act in accordance with the common good. Or, to put it in another way, once freed from direct responsibility for his own private economic well-being, the individual will always act automatically in cooperation with others to procure the good of all individuals in the community.

This, of course, is a highly oversimplified account both of the collectivist ideal and of its many different socialist interpretations. In particular, it fails to do justice to the conceptions of the early religious socialists, all of whom acknowledged other corrupting influences besides the love of money and of the worldly power that money confers. They further insisted that, even when all such influences have been removed, spiritual progress still requires a special act of divine mercy. The above account also fails to do justice to the secular utopians who tended to attribute all human vice to the privative conditions of ignorance and superstition.

Yet even in this oversimplified statement of them, the socialist assumptions do have at least a symbolic value in expressing, albeit in largely economic terms, the fundamental conviction of all idealistic theories of human nature, including the socialistic theory. This fundamental conviction is that man is by nature perfectible, but that contact with the material world contaminates his purpose and fractures the social harmony in which he would otherwise live. If such contact could only be removed or neutralized, all selfishness, all sin, all ignorance—indeed all vice and unhappiness whatsoever—would vanish.

The ancestry of this conviction is both too remote and too protean in form to trace here. For the purposes of this essay it is sufficient merely to point out two facts. First, all that the collectivist ideal adds to this conviction is a recipe for neutralizing the contaminating contact with the material world. Thus the logic behind every expression of socialist collectivism, whether among the utopians or the Marxists, is the assumption that, if only the concern for and control over material goods is vested exclusively in the community, the power of material things to corrupt will be nullified; and this will be true for society as a whole and—most non-Marxian socialists insist—for the individual as well. The second fact is that, although in assigning to history the goal of human perfection the socialist resolves the tension between the drama of history and its framework in favor of the drama, nevertheless by this new device of vesting absolute economic power so largely in the impersonal community, he in a sense reverses his previous resolution of the tension. For now the drama of human conflict is made an adjunct of the setting with its framework of impersonal law.

The same disposition to favor the setting in the end is also apparent in the third component of the socialist belief about the goal of history, namely, that the goal is realizable in a finite length of time. This belief has been most explicit in the religious utopian faith that Christ's second coming is imminent or has already occurred, and also in the doctrine of the early Marxists that an international revolution of the proletariat is just around the corner. It implies that the goal of history, together with the individual and social ideal which gives that goal its content, is a fixed and static thing. This follows from the fact that, barring a miracle, only a static goal is, by its nature, realizable in time. For a goal or ideal that is constantly expanding runs beyond our grasp like quicksilver, changing form and meaning and desirability even as we approach it so that inevitably it exists only and always in the future. The socialist goal, in being realizable, must therefore remain static; and in remaining static it is also antihuman, because a static goal implies either a limit to the possibility of human development or, as already suggested, the need for a miracle in attaining it. In either case the result is the same because both are antihuman: in the first instance man's potentialities are restricted, and in the second he is made dependent upon forces outside himself. Once more the framework of history, rather than its protagonists, emerges as the dominant force.

In sum, we find that all socialist philosophies of history tend to reflect the same general set of assumptions. These assumptions are to the effect that history is in essence a struggle, not, however, between men as at first sight might seem to be the case, but fundamentally between intractable forces controlling the combatants from behind the scene. And these controlling forces are ordinarily assumed to be arranged and opposed in their development in terms of a preordained logic of their own. To put the general theory so baldly tends to reduce it, of course, to a mere caricature of itself. But such a black and white type of statement does have a certain advantage if we desire to study the theory within its specifically American context, as we shall now seek to do.

II. The Socialist and American Democratic Theories of History

The socialist theory outlined above is a fair summary, I believe, of the poles around which American socialist thought has tended to revolve, even if it is not what American socialists have always accepted in practice. The main lines of this philosophy of history were early established in America by such religious communist sects as the Shakers, and were later reinforced by the popular Owenite and Fourierist agitation of the 1820's, 1830's, and 1840's. Still later, they were given their current, or Marxian, interpretation; and this took place especially during two specific periods of time—namely, 1890 to 1912 and 1927 to 1939—in which American speculative or philosophic interest in Marxism reached a peak.

However, the spread and influence of the socialist theory of history in the United States, even among American socialists themselves, has been qualified in a number of ways. The general intellectual soil in America was for many years not ready to receive the seeds of new philosophies of history. Moreover, there was in the United States no great interest in philosophic theory after the eighteenth century, and certainly little in the philosophy of history until the latter part of the nineteenth century, when attention was focused on the subject through the influence of the Darwinian theory of evolution.

This is not to say, of course, that Americans were not *conscious* of history and of the role that America herself played in modern history: such consciousness was only natural to a nation born out of a revolutionary situation. Nor is it to say that there was no interest whatever in the philosophy of history. Books like Samuel Miller's *Brief Retrospect of the Eighteenth Century* (1803) and similar "retrospects" often raised questions in which the philosophy of history was involved. Furthermore, there was even speculation on the idea of progress in such volumes as Alexander Kinmont's *Lectures on the Natural History of Man and the Rise and Progress of Philosophy* (1839) or the *Considerations upon the Nature and Tendency of Free Institutions* (1848) by Frederick Grimké, who studied American democracy in relation to the progress of civilization. The men who wrote these and similar books were all scholars, yet even among scholars speculation in the field of the philosophy of history was usually very thin in this country for a long time. If the historical speculation in America growing out of the American Revolution is compared with the European speculation growing out of the French Revolution, a profound difference is at once apparent. Where American speculation—as seen, for example, in the writings of Freneau, Barlow, and Emerson, among others—is lyric, self-conscious, and focused both in idea and fact solely upon America, contemporary European speculation—represented by such figures as Condorcet and Comte—sought to be scientific, objective, and also concerned with universal history. It was not until the late nineteenth century, in the works of Lester F. Ward, William Graham Sumner, and Henry and Brooks Adams, that an American concern with the problems of history as a theoretical problem really emerged. And what was true of American thought in general was also true of American socialist thought in particular.

This lack of interest on the part of American socialists shows up in a number of ways. Among them is the fact that no really major contributions to the socialist philosophy of history were made by American socialists before the emergence, during the last twenty-five years or so, of the Max Eastman-Sidney Hook school of revisionist Marxism. It is true that some interest in the problem had existed earlier. For example, it

419

existed in the vast pamphlet literature of the early religious utopians defending, among other things, their millennialist view of history. It existed also in the expositions of the Fourierist philosophy of history by such writers as Albert Brisbane and Parke Godwin; and in the early defense of historical materialism by such American Marxists as Sorge, Daniel De Leon, and Louis Boudin. Yet most of this discussion rarely rose above the level of mere exposition and added little that was new to European expressions of the socialist philosophy of history. One of the few notable exceptions was the monumental work of Shaker eschatology written by Youngs and Green and entitled *Testimony of Christ's Second Appearing* (1808). But although its originality and detailed grasp of world history were so great as to arouse the interest and commendation of Thomas Jefferson, this book had little influence outside the Shaker communities.

It can be said with truth that American socialist thought failed until recent years to make any major contributions to the socialist philosophy of history, or, for that matter, to socialist theory in general. Even during the nineteenth century, insofar as American socialism was theoretically oriented at all, it was almost solely concerned with the more practical types of problems in economics, politics, and social ethics. Here, it is true, a certain amount of originality was to be found. This relatively practical point of view was well exemplified by such religious utopian groups as the Mormons and the Perfectionists of Oneida, both of which were busy with the problem of formulating defenses for their heterodox sexual mores; while such other groups as the Rappites or as the Community of the True Inspiration at Amana, Iowa, expended what little zest for theory that they had in pouring out admonitory ethical and social precepts with the practical intent of sustaining their austere modes of life.

The later American socialist groups were also concerned with various more immediately practical problems, but, in contrast to the religious communities, their interests were predominantly economic. This is well illustrated by the early Marxists in the United States who, preoccupied as they were with the immediate problems of the time, with organizing or capturing the labor movement, read almost nothing of Marx save *Das Kapital* and thus tended to stress only the economic aspects of Marxian doctrine. It is significant that the most original American contributions to Marxian thought at that period were not at all in the realm of the philosophy of history, but were to be found in the ethical defense of socialism as a social ideal, a defense propounded in the works of such popular writers as John Spargo, and still more in Daniel De Leon's brilliant foreshadowing of what later emerged in Russia as the soviet theory of social organization.

However, even though American socialists thus for a long time had no particular theoretical interest in the problem of history (a fact which, among other things, tended to reduce the effectiveness of socialist theory for helping to stabilize and direct the American socialist movement), this lack of interest was at least partly offset by certain characteristics peculiar to the American environment. For what little socialist theory of history there was in this country was greatly favored by certain similarities between it and what might be described as the American democratic attitude toward history, at least as the American democratic attitude was expressed at the popular or semipopular level. These similarities resulted, of course, from the common heritage of both socialism and American democracy in the Christian tradition and in the natural law philosophy of John Locke, a heritage which, although strong in both cases, I shall not try to trace here.

Let us consider briefly what some of the more important elements in this common heritage are. In the first place, although American thought, unlike orthodox Marxism, has not usually conceived of history in terms of a violent struggle save temporarily at the peak of Darwinian influence in the 1880's and 1890's, the concept of history centering around the activities of a chosen people has not been foreign to the American tradition. This concept was introduced into the New England colonies as early as the seventeenth century through the Puritans' belief that they constituted a select group especially chosen by God to be a leaven among nations and to establish in the "irradiant wilderness" a new City of God. And this same notion, as Ralph Gabriel has shown, was later generalized to apply to the American people as a whole.[7] It appeared first as a sense of the mission of America to convert by example all other nations to the democratic way of life, and subsequently in the less attractive form of the imperialistic doctrine of "manifest destiny."

Moreover, there is a certain similarity in the framework assigned to history by each of the two views, socialist and American democratic alike. American thought has generally assumed history to be progressive, as in the socialist theory also. And American thought—at least in its earlier phases—has also tended to assume that this trend upwards is not attributable to man alone but at least in part to the beneficent influence of a providence, however vaguely conceived, working independently of man.

Such similarities as these afforded a point of entry for socialist theory into American thought and helped that theory to gain a foothold in the American tradition. However, in other respects socialism and American democracy have, of course, differed very sharply. In terms of the figure of speech used earlier, they have differed in the fact that American democracy has definitely subordinated the impersonal setting of the drama of history to the human drama itself, and in viewing history in this way,

---

[7] Ralph Gabriel, *The Course of American Democratic Thought* (New York, 1940), especially pp. 22-25, 339-56.

421

American democracy has envisaged quite a different outcome to the drama than was anticipated by socialism. For where socialism, both religious and materialistic, has tended to emphasize the importance of the nonhuman factors within history, whether in the shape respectively of God or of the economic machine, the democratic faith in America was early oriented toward, and has increasingly developed, a radically humanistic attitude. Thus in its purest form it assumes that the chief figure in history is man, that the universe is neither prevailingly hostile nor prevailingly favorable to human history, but that in any case man has the power (provided he uses it intelligently and imaginatively) to improve his fortunes and lot on earth continuously. The democratic attitude toward history has consequently been essentially practical and self-reliant rather than theoretical and dependent. It is skeptical of trusting its ambitions to fate or circumstance, of placing undue confidence in historical prophecy. It regards theories of history, as it tends to regard all theory, not as constituting possible absolute truths interesting in themselves, but as at best instruments or hypotheses useful in solving immediate problems. In other words, the typical representative of the American democratic tradition tends to place confidence only in his own immediate observation and experience, whereas the typical socialist is much more likely to turn either to tradition or to an esoteric logic like the Marxian dialectic for an analysis of historical situations.

This necessarily means that the American democratic conception of the goal of history, as distinct from its cause and motion, must differ from that of the socialist. Because, according to democratic theory, the outcome of history depends wholly on man, and because in that theory the appraisal of man's potentialities is very high, American democratic thought generally tends to reject the notion that human development is limited, or at least to reject the possibility of knowing in advance when and how that development will be limited. In place of believing, as does the socialist, that history will come to a neat climax or conclusion, the democratic humanist tends to envisage the drama of history as continuing endlessly and as ever moving from higher to still higher climaxes.

Finally, and most familiarly, the American democratic view has generally rejected the belief that this future development of man depends upon a collectivized economy. It rejects this not only from distaste for a priori theorizing, but because such a belief runs counter to the American emphasis upon individualism not only as a goal, as in socialism, but as a method or way of life for reaching that goal. It is this point of view which is so well exemplified by William James's "importance of individuals" or by Emerson's "self-reliance."

In summary, the American democratic view as here roughly indicated contrasts with the socialist view on three essential points. It differs from socialism in its faith that man is thoroughly capable of controlling historical development, and in the corollary faith that such control depends on the use of man's practical intelligence. It also contrasts with socialism in holding that there is no single climactic to human progress but, instead, that progress will continue indefinitely. And third, the democratic faith that the mainspring of progress lies in individual rather than collective effort is directly opposed to the socialist view. These are the points, then, at which the two ideologies stand in sharpest opposition, and there now remains only to investigate the effects which each of these views has had upon the other in the United States.

III. The Interaction of Socialist and American Democratic Theories of History

It is undeniable that the two ideologies—socialist and American democratic—have converged sufficiently to exert considerable influence upon each other. Certainly, also, there can be no doubt that American socialist thought has been highly colored and modified by the American environment. Looking at the facts historically we can note that with few exceptions neither the religious utopian nor the secular utopian view of history has been able to hold out long in its American context, and all the examples of these two types of socialism have eventually declined and perished. Even Marxian socialism, which has probably taken deeper root here than any of the other socialist movements, has also undergone serious modification in the United States, despite valiant efforts, aided by encouragement from outside the country, to preserve its own ideology in pure form.

Almost as soon as Marxism was introduced into this country it began to fall prey to conscious or unconscious attempts at revisionism. Indeed, for every defender of Marxist theory in its purity, such as De Leon and Boudin, there have been a dozen who—like Eugene Debs, Morris Hillquit, and Norman Thomas—have been little concerned with theory and have not only been prepared to compromise with American democratic practice and theory, but have done so at almost every point. The result has been a gradual but steady process of democratization in the American sense of the word. Although this process has been temporarily arrested from time to time, particularly during the early years of the Russian revolution, it has been marked by the weakening or complete disappearance of such important Marxian doctrines as those of the inevitability of socialism, of the class struggle, of the dialectical method, and of the dictatorship of the proletariat. So that today among large groups of socialists little is left of the original Marxian view save the ideal of collectivism. Symptomatic of this change, for example, has been the Sidney Hook revisionism of the early

1930's which—following the lead of William English Walling's deviation of 1913 and Max Eastman's deviation of 1925—sought to graft Marxism on American instrumentalism and argued that Marxism is not a bona fide theory of history at all but a mere methodological framework useful for economic and social analysis. Yet at that time Hook (whose beliefs were later to evolve in what he now considers to be the logical post-Marxian direction) argued that his view was really not revisionist but represented what Marx himself had actually believed.

If we now turn to the history of American democratic theory we find a similar metamorphosis in process. It is true that the democratic faith in man's power to control his own destiny, the faith in experiment and in an open malleable future permitting indefinite human progress, still remains, and in fact has been intensified and clarified by such leaders of the instrumentalist school as John Dewey, who has done the most to articulate and popularize the radical humanism referred to above. The change has centered, not in this aspect of American thought, but rather in the American attitude toward individualism. The average American is no longer so certain as he once was that individual effort is in all cases superior to collective effort. And as our legislative record for the past fifty years proves, we have gradually moved in the direction of increased governmental control. In fact, if we look at this record attentively, we discover that the spirit animating it has insensibly changed from that of regarding the state as a mere organ for maintaining civil peace to that of insisting that the duty of the state is to promote the public welfare in any sphere in which improvement is desirable and in which it has been demonstrated to the satisfaction of the majority that private enterprise has failed.

It would, however, be a mistake to suppose that this change is wholly attributable to the influence of socialist agitation. Nevertheless, the latter has undoubtedly been important. It is probable that we have not yet begun to appreciate the lasting influence of such works as Edward Bellamy's utopian novel, *Looking Backward* (1888), of semisocialist movements such as the single-tax movement, and even of the Socialist Party agitation in the decade before World War I or of the Communist Party agitation in the 1920's and 1930's. However, this socialist influence cannot be measured in its direct effects alone. It must be measured also in terms of its effects achieved through individuals who have gone in and out of socialist party ranks and have later come to occupy key positions in American labor and government.

There are at least two other factors which must be taken into account. One of them is the idea of the social service state, collectivistic by implication, which was introduced from Germany as early as the 1880's by young graduate students in politics, economics, and philosophy who at

424

that time started a fashion for enrolling in German universities for post-graduate work. These men brought back with them a knowledge of and, in many cases, an enthusiasm for the social service reforms then being enacted by Bismarck, even though such reforms really represented a conservative reaction to the threat of socialism in Germany. From these young graduates, some of whom later became leading American scholars, the idea of the social service state was gradually disseminated through college classrooms into wider vistas of American life.

The other main factor influencing the rise of the collectivistic ideal in American practice is, I believe, simply the dynamic of the capitalistic system itself, its ability, that is, to regulate itself in the interest of either its own or the public good. And the lesson which, obviously enough, is implied by this, is that private ownership beyond a certain point of concentration must be curbed through collective public action.

These influences are just as difficult to trace in detail as the influence of socialism itself, and no effort will be made to trace them here. For the purposes of this essay it is merely necessary to note that, whatever the reasons for the phenomenon, the convergence of socialist and democratic theory is plain. Just as American socialism has tended to surrender its own larger philosophic framework for that of radical humanism, and has come to insist merely that even a radical humanist program implies some degree of collectivism, so in turn American democratic thought no longer adheres so stubbornly to its earlier stereotyped formulation of individualism.

Whether this tendency to convergence will proceed further in the future no one can safely prophesy. It may well do so simply because the democratic trend toward a controlled form of modified collectivization has seemingly become an established element in our social tradition, and because the uncertainties of the postwar years are in some respects apparently helping to further the process. And it appears highly probable that the socialist inclination toward democracy will become even more pronounced, for the force of Marxism both as a revolutionary movement and as a systematic theory of history seems to this writer almost wholly spent. As a revolutionary movement it has failed almost everywhere save in Soviet Russia itself, and in countries under direct Russian military dominance, or, like China, directly adjacent to Russia. Even in Soviet Russia, Marxism has now entered upon the stage of consolidation in which the purely Marxist revolutionary fervor has already been largely replaced by other interests and considerations. It would appear that, as a philosophy, Marxism has little more to say to us because of its limitations: like the philosophy of Herbert Spencer its generalizations were too closely geared to nineteenth-century conditions so that its application in other contexts now seems obviously limited.

CHAPTER 8

The Philosophical Basis of Marxian Socialism
in the United States

BY SIDNEY HOOK

SIDNEY HOOK is Professor of Philosophy at New York University. Among his many writings are several standard works which contain both sympathetic and critical discussions of various currents of Marxism, including *Towards the Understanding of Karl Marx* (1933), *From Hegel to Marx* (1936), *Reason, Social Myths and Democracy* (1940), and *The Hero in History* (1943). A democratic socialist and widely known as a leading American opponent of the current Russian regime, his own philosophy is summed up at the end of this essay.

For bibliography in Volume 2 relevant to Mr. Hook's essay, see especially PART III, General Reading (section 3), and Topics 1, 2, 4, 5, 6; PART I, General Reading (sections 3B and 3D), and Topics 3, 4, 8, 9; PART II, General Reading (section 3), and Topics 8, 9, 10, 11; PART IV, *passim*.

THE relationships between philosophical doctrines and social movements are extremely complex. It is questionable whether there exists for socialism, as for democracy, any set of ideas which can be legitimately regarded as *the* philosophical basis. And it is just as questionable whether any set of ideas can be regarded as *the* basis of any widespread social movement. The rise and spread of social movements, especially in their beginnings, may be more plausibly explained in terms of historical needs and interests. This remains true even when it is admitted that the ideas which accompany such movements, and in which needs and interests find a rational expression, on occasion influence the subsequent development of the movements they seek to justify.

I. The Philosophical Basis of Social Movements

What is meant by a philosophical "basis" of a social movement is a set of ideas about the nature of things which have some controlling influence, as premises or assumptions or necessary presuppositions, upon the characteristic social doctrines of the movement. It seems necessary, as an introductory task, to distinguish with reference to our theme among three kinds of relationships between philosophical ideas and social doctrines, on the one hand, and social actions or allegiances, on the other. They are (1) logical, (2) psychological, and (3) historical.

(1) Concerning logical relationships, it is demonstrable that for socialism, as for democracy, there is no way by which one can validly deduce what the structure of society *should be* from any set of metaphysical or theological premises about the nature of "reality" unless the latter already contains implicit value judgments. One might suspect this from the fact that we can find many convinced socialists who subscribe to the most heterogeneous philosophical and theological views. The very distinction between religious, utopian, and scientific socialists indicates this as well as the philosophical differences between socialists like Jaurès, Karl Liebknecht, Eduard Bernstein, Max Adler, Otto Bauer, Dietzgen, Plekhanov, Lenin, Bogdanov, Shaw, Bertrand Russell, and John Dewey. It is sometimes alleged that unless a socialist holds one or another philosophical view of the universe he cannot *consistently* affirm belief in his socialist principles. But this never gets beyond the stage of allegation and reveals an innocence of the ways philosophers have of squaring their beliefs about "reality" with their beliefs about what is socially desirable.

An unprejudiced examination of the *arguments* for socialism, i.e., for collective ownership and democratic control of the basic instruments of social production, rather than for some other system of society, reveals that they usually rest upon *empirical* considerations that are quite neutral to

429

whatever beliefs are entertained about the "ultimate" nature of things.

(2) That there is some connection between the psychological character or type of person a man is and the kind of philosophical ideas and social ideals he holds is probably true. But these connections are so specific to the particular individual and therefore so varied, that no generalization thus far advanced seems valid. The socialist movement is composed of individuals of all types of personality and of all degrees of intelligence. Individuals of the most diverse personalities hold similar views about the social process, while others who seem to have similar patterns of personality diverge widely in their conceptions of social fact and social value. The history of ideas is replete with illustrations of men who have fathered doctrines which have influenced liberal and progressive social movements but who have themselves been extremely conservative in their personal outlook and affiliations. Bacon and Hobbes, and to some extent, Hegel, are cases in point.

(3) There remain the historical and social-psychological connections between philosophical ideas and social movements. These connections cannot plausibly be reduced to either logical or personal connections. Nonetheless they are not mystical. Certainly, all doctrines are born in the minds of individuals. But their subsequent social career is independent of them. They can be adopted at their time of origin or in later periods to rationalize social and political needs and to justify social programs quite foreign to the intent of their progenitors. Philosophies that influence social doctrines find expression in institutions, laws, and traditions, or are directed against them. When we speak of historical and social-psychological connections between philosophical ideas and movements, it is the impact of ideas upon institutionalized life which must be considered, and the way in which the needs and interests of different social groups at the time are affected by these ideas. The psycho-genetic history of ideas must be distinguished from their social history even when they are related. The first concerns itself with the causes of the discovery of ideas by any particular individual—an extremely complex and difficult problem; the second, with the causes for the acceptance, development, and rejection of ideas in a given culture at a given time, and may be fruitfully pursued even where we know little or nothing about how or why any particular individual germinated some ideas rather than others.

In this essay I shall concern myself with the philosophical ideas of those ' socialist groups in America who have regarded themselves as "Marxist" or "scientific." In my opinion, these are the only groups which may legitimately be regarded as constituting a social movement with definite political goals and a continuing tradition. This movement lays claim to a unifying philosophy that, despite political differences, presumably colors its basic theory and practice. And it is the only socialist movement in American life which still has some contemporary relevance.

The philosophies of the religious utopian socialist groups in America are as diverse as the respective theologies from which they presumably derived justification for the socialist ordering of things. Insofar as it is possible to consider them under one rubric, they share a philosophy of supernaturalism which is compatible with any theory of social organization. An adequate study would require a consideration of the specific theological views of the different religious socialist communities and an analysis of the way in which the religious leaders of these communities conceived of the connection between their theological and social principles.

The same is true of the secular utopian socialists—the Owenites, the Fourierists, the Bellamy Nationalists, and the brilliant figures associated with the Brook Farm experiment at Roxbury, Massachusetts. In many respects their philosophical views were very diverse. Fourier's cosmic "law of attraction," the basis of his philosophical system, was not accepted by the followers of Owen and Bellamy, and not even by many American Fourierists. Owen's belief that man is a perfectly plastic organism and that he can be completely molded by his environment was rejected by the Fourierists, who made much of the innate capacities of men. Nor were Owen's later views on religion and Christianity more acceptable. Bellamy himself held to a kind of spiritualistic idealism but this had no influence upon the Nationalist groups whose organization his writings inspired. The transcendentalism of the group of thinkers associated with Brook Farm found few echoes in other utopian communities.

American utopian socialism was really a complex of many different strands of thought and action—abolitionism, humanitarianism, feminism, liberal Unitarianism, and populism. Unlike Marxism, it did not distinguish itself clearly from any of the democratic reform movements in the nineteenth century. Unlike Marxism, it had no single or distinctive theoretical source. What it represented is perhaps best typified in the life and work of Horace Greeley, "the Yankee radical," who was receptive to any idea that promised immediate or ultimate improvement of the lot of the American workers and farmers.

One of the distinctive features of the Marxist philosophy is the international character of its fundamental ideas. It does not profess to be American except in the sphere of its application. The result has been that although all ideologies in America have, in a sense, been importations, the Marxist ideology has seemed to be more "foreign" than most, even where it repeated or amplified doctrines that were indigenously American in inspiration. There does exist one variant in modern socialist thought developed by a few individuals which may be regarded as a synthesis of

Marxist ideas with a characteristic American philosophy but it has not influenced any large political organizations. Toward the close of this essay something will be said of this variant in American socialist thought.

A consequence of the international character of Marxist or "scientific" socialist philosophy is that its primary theoretical source material has been almost exclusively drawn from the writings of outstanding socialist writers no matter what their national origin. Marx and Engels, and Kautsky, Labriola, and Ferri in lesser measure, were the chief sources before World War I to which were added Lenin, Bukharin, and Trotsky after the Russian Bolshevik Revolution. Insofar as philosophy can be distinguished from the theory of history, there was not much concern with it before the Russian Revolution among Marxist political groups. After the Russian Revolution the "philosophy of dialectical materialism" was regarded more seriously by those organizations which took their orientation from the dominant thought patterns of the Soviet Union. Few Americans have made any original contributions to the philosophy of socialism, especially to the Marxist variety of socialism. Originality was something to be deplored as a sign of possible heterodoxy.

For purposes of exposition I shall organize my discussion of the philosophical assumptions of Marxian socialism in America around six of its basic principles. These principles are overlapping, not all avowed Marxist groups accept all of them or interpret them in the same way, but they are "basic" in the sense that every other principle of importance professed by Marxists can be deduced from them or regarded as an application of them. They are: (1) a naturalistic theory of man; (2) an evolutionary, historical approach to all things, especially culture and history; (3) the doctrine of absolute determinism; (4) the belief in organicism; (5) the dialectical view of cosmology and ontology; and (6) the doctrine that "the dialectical method" is the most reliable method of reaching the truth.

II. Basic Principles of Marxism

(1) *The naturalistic theory of man.* Marxian socialist thought in the United States, as elsewhere, regards man as part of nature, subject to natural laws, whether these laws are regarded as laws of "matter" or "energy." The marvelous complexity of the human creature, especially his capacity to react with and upon his environment, is not denied but Marxists assert that this complexity does not involve a radical dualism between nature and supernature. All of man's creative activity is limited by objective conditions which he does not create. Everything that can be known about him is known by the use of the same fundamental methods —not techniques—that are employed in knowing the world which is continuous with him. It is sometimes implied in popular expositions of

Marxism that this approach to man and the world is a logical necessity—as if the denial of this claim were inconceivable or self-contradictory. But the more intelligent formulations recognize that this constitutes a *program* and *proposal* whose reasonableness is manifested by the historical evidence of its success in accumulating knowledge, and the failure of any alternative approach to explain, predict, or control events.

This is the nub of the philosophical materialism, or naturalism, of Marxian socialism and is the basis of its theoretical opposition to belief in any form of supernaturalism, to any assertion that gods or devils exist, that the soul is a substantial entity and survives the body, that the cosmic order is a moral order, and that meanings and purposes can be found outside the context of human need and behavior. Its practical opposition to supernaturalism stems from the historic allegiances between dominant forms of religion and the social status quo. And it stems also from the effect of religious traditions, which preach acceptance of man's lot, no matter how bitter, on the ground that what is most precious about him, the integrity of his soul, cannot be affected essentially by the mere compulsions of the material and social environment. Both motives account for the radical secularism of American socialists in education and culture, their efforts to keep church and state separate, and their attempt to make religion in fact, as well as in doctrine, a private affair. At the same time a rather simplified conception of the role of religion in social life has prevented them from recognizing the strength of indigenous American forces, some of them religious, which have made for cultural secularism, and from combining with those forces. On the whole the Marxian socialist movement in America has had only peripheral contacts with "free thought" and "rationalistic" movements. It has been rather suspicious of organized efforts of "militant atheism," not only because such a tack would increase the difficulty of winning adherents among the masses still susceptible to religious influences, but because of its own Marxian dogma that religious belief would gradually wither away of itself once the radical insecurities of man's social and economic existence were removed.

The naturalism, or materialism, of the socialist movement made it very receptive to the advances reported by the sciences, especially the physical sciences. In presenting this material to its members and sympathizers, it made use of the language current at the time, which was couched in the idiom of nineteenth-century mechanistic materialism. The German immigrants, who at the beginning were most receptive to Marxist ideas, still had memories of the materialism of Moleschott, Büchner, Feuerbach, and Vogt. And although they were aware of the fact that Engels had scorned the popularization of these writers as "vulgar" materialism, they were not too clear about the ground for his judgment. Up to the time when the repercussions of the Russian Revolution reached American shores, the socialist movement in this country took a naive and uncritical satisfaction in the triumphs of science. After the Russian Revolution and as a consequence of familiarity with the doctrines of Lenin, American communists adopted a more critical attitude toward attempts to interpret developments in modern science along allegedly idealistic lines. Denunciations of pragmatism, positivism, and operationalism as reactionary movements allied to clericalism became de rigueur among orthodox communists. Every shift in the Russian Communist Party line toward philosophical issues was religiously studied and followed.

Marxist naturalism, or materialism, differed from traditional materialism in its avoidance of the reductionist fallacy according to which man is "nothing but" a complex aggregate of material particles, or electrical charges. Natural though man may be, he differs from other natural things as an organism, and from other organisms as a man. These differences can be most tersely expressed in the definition of man as a social, rational, symbol using, and instrument making animal. Human history is the record of the activity of associated men in pursuit of their ends. This history is just as legitimate a subject matter for scientific inquiry as any other, and the degree of our understanding of it may be measured by the number and significance of the laws and generalizations reached about the historical behavior of human beings under determinate social conditions. Historical laws may be valid, even if they cannot be deduced from more comprehensive nonhistorical natural laws, just as no one disputes the validity of certain biological laws (e.g., in genetics) because they cannot be deduced logically from physico-chemical laws.

Man's sociality is the source both of his morality and individuality. These are natural properties, not in the sense that they are part of his biological endowment, but in the sense that they develop out of social life, reflect customary modes of feeling as well as customary judgments of approval or disapproval, and finally express individual choices, rational or irrational, between alternative patterns of action. Moral judgments are historically and culturally "bound," and human responsibility, although a genuine fact of experience, is limited by the degree of freedom of action which man's conditioning environment and intelligence makes possible.

From this approach there follows the denial of natural evil or natural goodness in man. Human beings abound in natural limitations out of which evil may develop. But so may good. If what develops can legitimately be read back as a potentiality, then according to scientific socialism man is *both* naturally good and evil. From these ideas also follows its refusal to counterpose the social to the individual. They are polar categories. The "individual" marks off the distinctive pattern, in which a certain combination of social traits is manifested by an individual organism reared within a given set of traditions and institutions. This pattern, because it fuses different traits, may reveal new and creative qualities not repeated in other individuals. The crisis of man is always a crisis of his social institutions which cannot be met merely by a spiritual "revolution within" but must be met by a social revolution which transforms both social institutions and individuals.

Nonetheless the literature of socialism in America especially at the turn of the century and up to the Russian Revolution shows that although a genetic primacy is given to the social as the matrix of the individual, a moral primacy is given to the individual. The incubus of an unplanned capitalist economy is to be removed in order to liberate the individual's full powers of growth. The activity of the state is to be directed to bringing into existence those conditions which will maximize both abundance and personal freedom. Industrialism was distinguished from capitalism and regarded as part of the normal environment of modern man. The anarchist ideal of a community without a state was rejected, not on psychological grounds, but as incompatible with the proper functioning of an industrial economy.

The naturalistic conception of man as held by American socialists was vaguely formulated and defined more by its negations than by detailed positive features. In the minds of many socialists it was tied up with a general movement toward social enlightenment and personal emancipation from taboos derived from religious traditions. It was assumed without any logical warrant, and in the face of some actual evidence to the contrary, that whoever subscribed to a naturalistic philosophy would be progressive in social outlook and prepared to support the substance of the socialist program.

(2) *The evolutionary and historical approach.* The historical approach to all things natural and social in the Marxist philosophy was pre-Darwinian. Its antecedents were Hegelian and derived from Marx's analysis of cultural life. In fact, all of Marx's characteristic doctrines had been formulated by him before the publication of Darwin's work. But both Marx and Engels hailed with enthusiasm Darwin's hypothesis about the origin of species as providing an underpinning for their social philosophy. First of all it naturalized the human factor in history, particularly human intelligence, furnished an alternative explanation of the evidences of design, and therewith undermined one of the most plausible props of supernatural belief. Secondly, it suggested itself as a heuristic principle in interpreting historical and social phenomena of all kinds. The absolute constancy of any institutional form could now be regarded, even in advance of the detailed empirical evidence, as an illusion of perspective.

The acceptance of the evolutionary outlook on nature and society in the American socialist movement was strongly reinforced by the writings of John Fiske, Lester F. Ward, and especially Herbert Spencer, whose evolutionary cosmic philosophy enjoyed a great vogue among socialists despite his apotheosis of a competitive society.[1] The idea that man and his nature had evolved lent support to the hope that his nature would continue to evolve along progressive lines. The unchangeability of human nature, which was one of the stock arguments against the possibility of socialism, could now be met not merely with an expression of faith, but with a mass of evidence that men had not always been moved by the same motives which operated under capitalism. The development of human nature was integral with the development of human culture, with man's social institutions, and especially with the way in which man *works*. For the specific Marxian hypothesis was that under the conditioning influences of geography and biology, man evolves not by revolutions in his modes of thought, but by changes in the modes of production, which are the ultimate determinants of important changes in property relations, government, family life, religion, art, and science. Man, so to speak, historically humanizes himself by his labor rather than by his leisure even when the latter becomes the subjective goal of his labor.

In consequence an intense theoretical interest developed in the *origins* of social institutions—the origin of the state, the origin of the family, the origin of private property in the instruments of production. In this field American socialists were proud of the fact that an American thinker had independently contributed some of the foundation stones to the structure of their social philosophy. Lewis Morgan's *Ancient Society*[2] had been acclaimed by Marx and Engels as providing evidence for the theory of historical materialism and the view that the laws of social development are universal. Engels had written a popular book on social origins[3] based primarily on Morgan's work. Both Morgan's and Engels' studies became part of the canonic literature of the socialist movement.

Nothing testifies so eloquently to the uncritical character of the theoretical beliefs of the American socialist movement as the tenacity with which the anthropological doctrines of Morgan and Engels were held in the face of mounting evidence of their untenability. What was more amazing, the important anthropological contributions of the modern American school of anthropology—Boas, Goldenweiser, Kroeber, and Lowie—which had logically pulverized the artificial schemes of the social evolutionists, were completely disregarded, and their critique of the

---

[1] For bibliography on the interest in and acceptance of evolutionary doctrine by socialists, see especially Volume 2, PART III, General Reading (section 3), and also Topic 2.

[2] L. H. Morgan, *Ancient Society; or, Researches in the Lines of Human Progress from Savagery, through Barbarism to Civilization* (New York, 1877).

[3] Friedrich Engels, *The Origin of the Family, Private Property and the State* (tr. by Ernest Untermann; Chicago, 1902), originally published in 1884.

racialistic myths, which had enormous practical significance for agitational activity, was ignored. Up to a short generation ago, the party schools of all Marxist organizations were still teaching their anthropology out of Morgan and Engels.

The exact relevance of these excursions into anthropology to the socialist program had never been established. It was assumed that the historic questions, whether or not private property existed in primitive societies or whether or not their family form evolved from matriarchy to patriarchy, had some bearing upon the desirability or necessity of the socialist organization of society. But no one indicated how or why. Logically all that was required was to show the social possibility of the kind of changes advocated by the socialists—that the history of man and society was such that the present order of things could not be regarded as eternal. But enough was known about the history of Western culture, by Marxists and non-Marxists alike, to make apparent that the complex of social institutions which characterized capitalism had developed out of earlier forms. And as for the claim that private property in the instruments of production had always existed in one form or another, a single illustration of a primitive collectivistic society would have sufficed instead of the dogmatic claim that *all* primitive societies were originally collectivistic.

In accepting the theory of social evolution, American socialists were careful to dissociate themselves from the doctrines of the social Darwinians, who from the same evolutionary premises as those held by the socialists drew social conclusions that justified the existence of the capitalist system. The social Darwinians applied the concepts of "the struggle for existence" and "the survival of the fittest" to social life and argued that the existing power relationships and distribution of wealth were the result of the same ineluctable laws that accounted for the development of the human species. Any attempt to transform society along equalitarian lines was deemed romantic foolishness. The socialists were quick to point out that the concept of the "struggle for existence" applied primarily to struggles between different species and not between individual members of the same species, that species develop as much because of cooperation between members of species as because of struggles with other species, and that existing struggles within the human species could by no stretch of the imagination be interpreted as expressions of biological struggles. In modern society the qualities required to achieve membership in the ruling group were not muscular or intellectual skill, but the lucky accident of birth into families that possessed capital and of the chances of the economic market, which no one could control.

In their concrete analysis of the social scene, the socialists relied upon the historical concept of the "class struggle" rather than upon biological evolutionary laws. Men and societies develop through both cooperation and struggle. There are all sorts of struggles among men, but the most important ones—in the sense that they enter decisively into all the others—are the struggles which flow from economic class divisions. These divisions in turn derive from the way in which men earn their living and distribute the total social product. So long as any group possesses a monopoly of the instruments of production, class struggles will rage, taking peaceful or violent form depending upon the degree of consciousness that prevails among those who are exploited in the process of production and upon the attitude of the owning classes toward social change.

It was predicted that a new era in human history would begin with the collectivization of the instruments of production. For therewith class struggles, save for vestigial opposition inherited from the past, would disappear and human development would proceed by cooperation—a cooperation that had been frustrated by the automatic mechanisms of a class society. Men would *plan* their economies and create a rational world befitting their rational nature. The American socialists did not envisage any more than socialists elsewhere the possibility of class struggles existing in a collectivistic society, or of any type of social system supervening upon capitalism other than that of socialism. The economic struggle was the "final" social struggle. Man as an indefinitely perfectible creature would still struggle with *personal* problems—for this was the law of growth—but there would be no social problem as we understand it today. Unemployment, insecurity, war, and poverty would vanish like the bubonic plague and the other horrors of antiquity.

On the whole American socialists made intelligent use of the concept of the class struggle in interpreting the current political scene, particularly during the period—which lasted until recently—when to suggest the existence of classes in America was regarded as faintly subversive. They also applied rather crudely, but still effectively, the class-struggle approach to American history, which conventional historians had treated almost exclusively in legal, military, and political terms. They discovered in Madison and the *Federalist* an indigenous anticipation of the Marxist doctrine of the class struggle. The march of American democracy was considered a by-product of the march of American capitalism: the War of Independence in relation to the needs of colonial merchant capitalism; the Civil War a result of the conflict between two social systems, with victory going to the industrial North not because of its higher morality but because of its more developed system of production.

This tendency to interpret democracy merely as an ideological manifestation of capitalism contradicted the glorification of democracy as a way of life in the popular propaganda of the socialist movement. It played into the hands of those who argued that a planned society, by destroying capitalism, would destroy the whole heritage of democratic freedom. And it also made it easier for the communists to convert the Marxist notion of a working-class democracy into a dictatorship of the party.

One of the fundamental weaknesses of the undiscriminating historical approach of Marxism was its failure to recognize programmatic and moral *alternatives* which were equally compatible with existing historical situations. The historical past was too often accepted as a "judgment" even when, inconsistently enough, it was deplored. A lost cause was a bad cause except as a premonitory indication of a subsequent phase in the pattern of historical necessity. There was no need to speculate about the *positive* institutional features of socialism because the historical situation of the future would take care of them of itself. One could predict on historical grounds what socialism would cancel or negate, viz., the evils indigenous to capitalism, what it would *not* be. But few socialists felt any concern over the question whether there were any indigenous possibilities of evil under socialism, and whether they might be as bad as, or worse than, those of capitalism.

(3) *Absolute determinism.* At the basis of all class struggles, according to Marxist theory, is the conflict between the *forces* of production and the *social relations* of production. The relationship between these two concepts has never been exactly defined, but according to most interpretations the development of the forces of production, although stimulated or retarded by the social relations of production, has a determining significance for the evolution of society. Man's rational and creative nature irrepressibly expresses itself in new techniques, skills, and inventions. When these developments are hampered by legal property relationships to a point where basic human needs are frustrated, a social revolution occurs which changes the social structure and liberates the forces of production from their legal fetters. In the past, private property in the instruments of production played a progressive role in that it made possible a great expansion in these instruments and techniques of production. It no longer does so in the present. In the future only a collectivistic organization of society can enable the forces of production to come into their own and be rationally controlled in and for the interests of all members of society.

This process is presented as an historical and social law which *must* culminate, in virtue of ever increasing class struggles, in the victory of the proletariat and socialism. Orthodox Marxism, or what passes as such, in both its evolutionary and revolutionary expressions, takes this *must* seriously as something literally inescapable and inevitable.

The evolutionary Marxists, of whom, for all his opposition to piecemeal social reform, Daniel De Leon may be regarded as typical, conceived of the development of capitalism as the process of an inevitable gradual growth into socialism. The technological prerequisites of socialism would be built up within the legal shell of capitalism. While this was being accomplished, the proletariat and its allies would achieve such a concentration of political and industrial power that the social revolution could be peacefully achieved by constitutional means. After that, the socialist state would be organized industrially and brought into a more functional relation with the economy.

The revolutionary Marxists of the Leninist persuasion accepted the view that technologically capitalism prepares the way for socialism. But they maintained that the political phase of the social revolution could be accomplished only by force and violence, that the existing state machinery must be shattered before being replaced by the dictatorship of the proletariat, which is "substantially" the dictatorship of the Communist Party.

The consequence of this belief in inevitability was not a fatalistic resignation to events, for the class struggle was considered inevitable, too. But it made the theory and practice of orthodox Marxism fundamentally unintelligible. It reinforced faith in the outcome of things independently of the empirical evidence. When it was pointed out that the destruction of capitalism and the successful construction of socialism depended on proper leadership, proper organization, and education on the part of the communists, and that victory was therefore conditional on a number of problematic factors, the answer invariably came that in time it was also inevitable that the communists would succeed in performing properly their true functions of leadership. Since, then, the victory of socialism was inevitable, it made little difference in the long run what particular means were used to bring it about—an attitude hardly conducive to political responsibility. It made nonsense of the popular propaganda which often pictured the world as confronted by a choice between "socialism and barbarism." It imposed upon its believers, independently of the evidence, the dogma that any social development which was not socialism *had to be* merely a phase, and a passing phase, of capitalism. The nature of fascism was already determined long before it had any chance to reveal itself—it was simply another kind of capitalism. When the middle classes showed no sign of disappearing, instead of modifying their view that society must inevitably polarize itself into two classes, capitalist and proletariat, the believers in inevitability claimed that capitalism had not yet run its course. If, in face of the strong opposition of capitalist interests, the state adopted social legislation which enabled labor to organize itself on a national scale, this did not invalidate the doctrine that the state is inevitably the executive committee of the ruling economic class. It only showed that the state was acting out of fear and making concessions. That the power to compel the state to make concessions indicated a substantial measure of control over the state was denied or ignored. Everything that transpired in the world was either a necessary step forward to socialism or merely a temporary setback.

Hardly an issue arose in relation to which contradictions did not appear in the Marxist position—contradictions that were reconciled in a devout rapture that "history was on our side." Monopolies were regarded as an inevitable outcome of capitalist competition—and denounced. Agitation to curb the growth of monopolies was regarded as a Canute-like effort to sweep back the waves of economic progress—and supported. The failure of the American working class to take to the ideals of socialism was explained as the result of its relatively high standard of living, which some day would inevitably be destroyed. Its lack of any political class consciousness was attributed to the duplicity of its leaders, who "headed the working-class movement only to behead it," at the same time as it was asserted that political class consciousness inevitably arises in the course of sustained class struggles, which are themselves inevitable.

The theoretical literature of American Marxism on occasion shows an awareness of the difficulties entailed by combining the dogma of inevitability with exhortations to workers to do this or that lest something dire result. These difficulties were feebly met by the view that, although socialism is inevitable, human beings can bring it about a little sooner or a little later depending upon their knowledge or ignorance, bravery or cowardice. These latter traits at any rate are not inevitably determined by the development of capitalism. Logically, however, this involves an abandonment of the dogma of inevitability, for *in principle*, if something we do or leave undone affects the time at which a certain phenomenon appears, there may be other things we do or leave undone that have an *additional* effect upon the time. The cumulative result of all these effects may extend the time indefinitely. The possibility that events outside the social system, like earthquakes, floods, and drought so sustained as to produce famine, might interfere with the "inevitable" development of the social system was ignored—quite properly on practical grounds but improperly on theoretical grounds.

A deceptive analogy is sometimes drawn by Marxists between the inevitability of the death of the individual organism, which occurs sooner or later depending upon human efforts to prolong or shorten life, and the inevitability of socialism. Even if no question were raised about the inevitability of the death of the individual organism, the proper comparison would be to the inevitability of the death of a social system. But this is not sufficient. For the social philosophy of orthodox Marxism teaches not merely the inevitability of the death of capitalism but the inevitability of the *birth* of socialism, in which the victory of the proletariat culminates. And biologically it would be absurd to speak of the inevitability of any new birth or life. Nor does the biological analogy warrant any belief in the inevitability of the death of capitalism because of the well-known difficulties in considering cultures as organisms.

Another theoretical difficulty generated by the doctrine of inevitability is the interpretation of the historical significance to be accorded to heroic figures, good or bad, in history[4]—including men like Marx, Lenin, and Stalin. Strictly, the dogma of historical inevitability entails the view that no man in history is indispensable for any great historical event, that if any particular man celebrated for his historical eventfulness had not lived, some one else would have done his work. Depending upon their favorite hero, however, Marxists, like all other human beings, glorified the work of outstanding individuals. To save the dogma, they were compelled either to maintain that the biological existence of their heroes was socially inevitable or that the social need for a great man bestowed the title of greatness upon some favorably situated individual—mystical notions that seemed queer in the context of a "scientific" social philosophy.

The most fateful of the consequences of the belief in inevitability was its tendency to paralyze the nerve of moral responsibility. Political life abounds with temptations to use dubious means to advance political causes. And a view which sanctifies in advance the use of any means—for the good end, socialism, is sure to be realized "sooner or later"—makes it easier to yield to these temptations with an easy conscience. Among the arsenal of weapons employed in the class struggle by the American Stalinists, for example, who are stanchest in their belief in the inevitability of socialism, are slander, demagogy, organized physical terror, and even attempts at assassination of their political opponents among working-class groups. These practices, of course, do not flow from the belief in inevitability, for the latter is equally compatible with any kind of behavior, including the highest forms of moral integrity. But such a belief—by suggesting that moral values are historically irrelevant, that they are merely epiphenomenal expressions of class and party triumphs—causes those who are possessed by it to strive for victory at any price, even when that price is so high that it destroys the "all-sanctifying" goal.

Not all avowed Marxist groups in America subscribe to the dogma of inevitability, and the Socialist Party, under the influence of Norman Thomas, has been mildly critical of it. In its most innocent form, in pre-World War I days, the dogma was part of the more general theory of social evolution, which assured people who by training and habit were morally decent that society would float lazily to the harbor of their dreams.

(4) *The principle of organicism.* This principle and the two that follow characterize not all Marxian socialist groups in America but only the so-

---

[4] For a detailed discussion of this problem see Sidney Hook, *The Hero in History, a Study in Limitation and Possibility* (New York, 1943).

called Leninist groups, more particularly the Communist Party and its peripheral cultural organizations. They are principles that came to the fore in one wing of the Marxist movement after the Russian Bolshevik Revolution.

According to the principle of organicism, not only is socialism inevitable but the transformation of the entire cultural life of man is inevitable because all phases of culture are interrelated: they react on and interact with each other. But concerning the form and content of that future culture, it is safe to predict only that it will be vastly different from the culture mankind has known until now. This follows from the fact that, in the future classless society, the determining condition of culture will no longer be the mode of economic production but the rational and spontaneously creative nature of man. The "kingdom of freedom" will be marked not by the absence of all necessity but by the absence of *economic* necessity. In other words, the principle of historical materialism is itself historical and presumably will not operate in a classless society.

It does operate, however, in a most emphatic way in existing capitalist society and furnishes the Ariadne thread to the tangled complex of cultural phenomena. Whether or not other phases of culture influence the operation of the mode of production, the latter directly or indirectly influences *everything* else. This was not hard to believe in the fields of politics, law, education, and the more practical reaches of social disciplines like economics and finance. And some detailed and piecemeal studies of the political and social scene from this point of view proved quite illuminating. But in respect to art, music, literature, philosophy, science, and religion, wholesale interpretations of the most dogmatic kind became the order of the day. A "crisis" anywhere was related to *the* "crisis" of the economic order, whether or not the terms represented the same or entirely different notions. Even "the crisis of modern science," in this view, reputedly reflected the "crisis of capitalism." Whether it was abstract art that was under discussion, or objectivist poetry, functional architecture, atonal music, the modern novel, the theory of relativity, psychoanalysis, or logical empiricism, the theme would be introduced by the phrase, "It is not accidental that . . ." or its equivalent. And what was not accidental was asserted to be more or less determined (with emphasis on the "more" varying with the writer's political orthodoxy) by the economic crisis of capitalism and the confusions and struggles for power resulting from it.

A number of fundamental confusions vitiated these attempts to establish an organic connection between capitalism as an economic system and whatever cultural manifestations flourished in capitalist society. The first was an identification of a descriptive analytical approach with a normative political demand. It was one thing to frame and test the hypothesis that all cultural activity "reflected" the mode of production and the class struggles that developed therefrom. It was quite another to insist that all cultural activity had to be *evaluated* from the standpoint of the class struggle—whether it "reflected" the class struggle or not. Most of the practitioners of Marxist cultural criticism did the latter under the illusion that they were doing the former. The confusion extended to elementary definitions. For example, "the proletarian novel" was defined not only as one which gave an imaginative account of the life experiences of the proletarian under the impact of capitalism; it was also defined, in the words of one professorial communist, as "a work written from the standpoint of dialectical materialism," which by definition was the standpoint of the Communist Party.

The very term, "reflected," was never submitted to analysis. It was used so broadly that it embraced works of art and literature that seemed diametrically opposed in spirit. Everything could be brought under it. For example, "escapist" art, literature, and music would be condemned because they didn't reflect the class struggle. But since in "escaping reality" they were also taking a stand that had consequences, they "reflected" the class struggle after all. No Marxist critic of the period ever stated the criteria by which it could be ascertained when a work of art did *not* directly or indirectly "reflect" the class struggle. Since any work of art either took or did not take a "stand" on dominant social issues, it became a tautologically true proposition to assert that literature "reflected" society. But this tautology was wielded as a club to impose political uniformity. In reply to the protest against the attempt of the Communist Party to put all artists in uniform, the *New Masses,* one of its official organs, declared that *all* artists wore uniforms, whether they were aware of it or not, and that their only decision concerned the color of uniform they chose to wear.

Underlying these confusions was not only the desire to impose a political regimentation on the creative writer, thinker, and artist but the theoretical difficulty to which I have already alluded above. When pressed, orthodox Marxists would concede that to some extent the development of the arts and sciences had an autonomous character which could not be explained in social or economic terms. Following Engels they would also admit that there was a *reciprocal* interaction between the mode of economic production and law, science, religion, etc. This meant then that not in all cases could the economic factor be regarded as the independent variable whose changes necessitated changes in the cultural superstructure. Had the implications of these admissions been taken seriously, it would have become a purely empirical matter to discover whether, in respect to the emergence of a new cultural form or discovery, the social-economic factor or factors autonomous to the field in which the event was located were decisive. The empirical evidence, however, showed that most of the cultural tendencies which were blithely characterized as expressions of "the

444

crisis of capitalism" could be accounted for by alternative explanations, especially in the arts and sciences. It also became clear that the conception of reciprocal causation shattered the philosophical monism of orthodox Marxism since it allowed for the possibility that political and legal factors might redetermine the direction in which the economic system was moving. In the period of war and fascism, the political and ethical attitudes taken toward the ideals of democracy might have more influential social effects than the current situation with respect to production and unemployment.

(5) *Dialectics in nature.* Not only is culture interrelated, but since in the last analysis culture and society are also parts of nature, one must recognize, according to orthodox dialectical materialism, the interrelations between nature, society, and history. The process of "eternal development" and "dialectical self-movement" is universal and holds for everything that is or may be conceived. The dialectical development of society is only a *special* case of the general dialectical movement of the cosmos. The first cannot consistently be affirmed without affirming the second; and the denial of the second logically entails the denial of the first.

It may seem incredible that any political party presumably devoted to the practical task of revolutionizing society should make the belief in these metaphysical propositions part of its official credo, and on occasion, prerequisites of membership in good standing. Nonetheless at one period in its history, following the Russian lead, the American Communist Party declared through authoritative spokesmen that belief in the objectivity of dialectic in nature was of the essence of Marxism.

Perhaps the dominant motive behind this affirmation, aside from the desire to conform to the pattern set by the Russian party philosophers, was the desire to secure, in William James's phrase, that "sumptuosity of security" which orthodox religion provided by its theology. Since socialism was inevitable, and since its inevitability followed from the dialectic pattern which was a specific application of the more general laws of dialectic, the dialectical nature of the cosmos provided to a certain extent the *guarantee* of the victory of socialism. Socialism was destined to triumph not only over the machinations of reactionaries and the counterrevolution of fascism, but despite the vicissitudes of the natural elements themselves. Life might be doomed on this planet but not before socialism had come into its own.

The criticism that this involves an objective teleology incompatible with a naturalistic starting point has been vehemently denied. Nonetheless it is difficult to find a term which more accurately designates the view that nature both supports human effort and is friendly to it. Not only is history on our side but nature is, too.

The doctrine that nature and society are interrelated conceals a nest of ambiguities. It may mean nothing more than the commonplace that physical laws condition the existence of society in the sense that without certain permissive physical conditions societies cannot flourish. This means at most that nature limits the number of social systems that are possible but does not determine which possibility is to be realized. The doctrine may also mean that the social organization which nature permits may in turn modify certain features of its natural environment. It is also sometimes interpreted to mean that what is discovered about nature depends upon the kinds of social interests which prevail, that the development of science "reflects" certain social needs and cannot be accounted for in terms of scientific tradition and intellectual curiosity alone. Finally, it may mean that all science, natural as well as social, is "a class science." The range of meaning extends from assertions that are elementary truisms to those that are fantastic absurdities, and orthodox Marxists have maintained all of them.

(6) *Dialectical method.* Scientific method cannot give any guarantees of inevitability. Neither can it proceed on the assumption that *all* things are interrelated. Every statement it makes concerning the relations between things, every experiment it undertakes, presupposes that at least some other events and processes are indifferent to the truth of its findings. From the standpoint of dialectical materialism this represents a kind of metaphysical bias or shortcoming of the ordinary scientific approach which must be corrected by the use of dialectical method and logic. The critical feature of this logic is the recognition of the universality and objectivity of contradiction, including nature, and the interrelatedness of all things.

From this, together with the official doctrine that all dialectical materialists must be communists and vice versa, some extremely interesting consequences flow. These consequences are nothing less than a theoretical justification for a party line in all fields from art to zoology. The citations of the argument are drawn from a brochure on *Dialectical Materialism and Communism* by L. Rudas of the Marx-Engels-Lenin Institute, and widely circulated at one time by the American Communist Party, and from an article by the same author in that party's official organ, the *Communist.*

"Without dialectics there can be no scientific picture of the world . . . without dialectics there is no correct method for investigation of an individual case or a single region."[5]

"All the *correct* results in mathematics, physics and elsewhere are *dialectical results* even if their authors do not know that they are applying

[5] L[adislaus] Rudas, *Dialectical Materialism and Communism* (3rd rev. ed., Labour Monthly Pamphlets No. 4; London, n.d.), p. 8.

the dialectical method. They would arrive, however, at much more correct results if they would apply the dialectical method *consciously*."[6]

"The pre-requisite for understanding dialectical materialism is a decisive break with the traditional mode of thought, the *revolutionising of thinking*, and also the conscious fight for the higher communist social order in the ranks or at least under the leadership of the revolutionary [Communist] Party."[7]

"Plechanov and even Bukharin were not in a position to give an unexceptionable exposition of dialectical materialism, in the last resort also because they did not have an unexceptionable line in politics."[8]

From these premises it follows logically that none but those who are enrolled in the Communist Party or who follow its leadership can properly interpret the findings of the arts and sciences in virtue of their superior grasp of the dialectical method. Further, none but those who have an unexceptionable line in politics, i.e., who agree with the position of the Politburo (Stalin), can properly interpret the dialectical method. Since reality is dialectical in structure, only the dialectical method can convey the truth about it. Therefore only those who follow the lead of the Communist Party can come closest to the best truth available about reality or any phase of it.

The imposition of a party line in all subjects, according to those who hold this position, is not arbitrary or authoritarian. It is in the interest of the objective truth, which coincides with proletarian class truth, which in the last analysis is a *party* truth. It helps, not hinders, the advance of science, art, and human welfare. Whatever else the determination of a fact depends on, it also depends on a political perspective; the intellectual worker like the industrial worker should therefore be grateful for having a political officer at his elbow to guide and correct him. "Objectivism," which teaches that truth is international, that it transcends national, class, or party barriers, is denounced as a heresy in all fields of inquiry. Because it denies the principle of "partisanship" and "the class nature of truth," "objectivism" is taxed with having ultimate counterrevolutionary effects.

Here, in outline, we have a rationalization in advance of the most ruthless system of intellectual terror and suppression imaginable. All that is required to put it into operation is political power, as in the Soviet Union.

I have already stated that these philosophical ideas were not systematically developed. They operated in the background and were brought for-

---

[6] L. Rudas, "The Meaning of Sidney Hook," *Communist*, Vol. 14, No. 4 (Apr. 1935), p. 348. Italics in original.
[7] L. Rudas, *Dialectical Materialism and Communism*, p. 2. Italics in original.
[8] *Ibid.*, p. 3.

ward to combat any revision or criticism of orthodox Marxism. Nor did all groups who called themselves Marxists subscribe to them, even groups as orthodox as the Socialist Labor Party or certain sections of social democracy before World War I. However, these ideas were, and still are, an integral part of the philosophical ideology of the American Communist Party. Occasionally they are soft-pedaled in the interest of facilitating the conversion of the hesitant, but no one in the fold is permitted to criticize them or even to question them.

III. An Alternative Socialist Philosophy

From time to time individuals within and without political Marxist movements have attempted to formulate an alternative philosophy more adequate to the humanistic and scientific ideals of democratic socialism. They have drawn not only on Marx but on indigenous American thinkers like William James, John Dewey, and Thorstein Veblen. They have sought to prune the philosophy of socialism of all its metaphysical and theological elements and relate it to current developments in the social and historical sciences. This alternative philosophy may be most conveniently expounded by contrasting briefly its interpretation of the six leading principles discussed above with the position of the orthodox Marxists. The earliest representative of this tendency is perhaps William English Walling. Independent of him, Harry Laidler, Lewis Corey (in his later writings), Norman Thomas and Reinhold Niebuhr (except for item [1] below), and the present writer may be mentioned as exemplifying this trend of thought.

(1) This variant of American socialism is naturalistic in the sense that it puts its faith in scientific method as the only valid method of reaching truths about the world. "Matter" for it is not any particular kind of substance but "the subject matter" of the physical sciences. Its theory of meaning is operational and its theory of truth is predictive or experimental. It rejects the traditional mind-body dualism and interprets mind as the symbol-using activity of the organism in a social context.

(2) It accepts the facts of historical change on which the theory of social evolution is based but rejects the belief in the universality of any pattern of social development. It believes that knowledge makes a difference, and therefore emphasizes the activity and moral responsibility of man in *helping* to redetermine the direction of historical change. It denies that there is a law of progress but asserts the *possibility* of human "progress"—which it interprets as a value term.

(3) It regards the belief in inevitability as a superstition but recognizes that there are limiting tendencies in historical change which in any historical situation may restrict possibilities of action to a narrow alternative. It mediates between the view that anything is historically possible

at any time and the view that the societies are carried by irresistible waves from the crest of fulfillment to the trough of destruction. It allows for the presence of chance events in the historical process.

(4) Instead of embracing cultural organicism, it is frankly *pluralistic* in its causal analysis. Everything exists in some connection but not all connections are relevant to each other. Whatever connections are alleged to exist must be established by piecemeal analysis. The mode of economic production has primacy only for some cultural features and only with respect to some problems. Unless these are specified it makes no more sense to say that economics is "more important" than law, or science, or religion than it does to say that the heart is "more important" than the kidneys or the brain or the intestinal tract. For example, from the fact that capitalist democracies like Great Britain and the United States allied themselves with a totalitarian collectivistic economy like Russia against Hitler's crusade for world domination instead of abetting him in his invasion of Russia, it argues that political factors may have a greater influence on world affairs in the present juncture than the mode of economic production.

(5) It regards the cosmology and ontology of dialectical materialism as completely irrelevant to the program of achieving socialism, and in their own right as a series of unverifiable fantasies, intellectually irresponsible in theory and deadly mischievous in practice.

(6) It denies the validity of "dialectical" logic and affirms the sufficiency of the rational and empirical methods of science to cope with truth on every level.

To these propositions should be added its uncompromising devotion to democracy in every sector of organized social life, and its contention that without political democracy no other kind is possible. It is committed to the belief that the experimental method of science can be fruitfully applied to value conflicts. It consequently is opposed to the use of violence in human affairs but does not make a fetish of pacifism. It asks us to explore the possibility that, despite the differences which divide men confronted by specific problems in specific historical situations, their basic needs are sufficiently alike to permit negotiation of these differences. It would proceed by treating all proposals to resolve social and moral problems as hypotheses to be critically considered in the light of their causes and consequences. Where no consensus can be established, it entertains the hope that the objective reciprocal interests of men will be sufficiently strong to provide a basis of cooperation which will tolerate or compromise these differences which cannot be negotiated. To the extent that even this is not possible, to that extent a universal objective morality is not possible. But the limits of universal objective morality cannot be prejudged in advance.

449

In this alternative philosophy the leading ideas of American experimental pragmatism and naturalism are combined with Marxian realism and its historical and economic insights, in order to realize the highest traditions of American democracy. No political mass movement has so far arisen to give practical and programmatic expression to this philosophy of democratic socialism. Several tendencies within the American Socialist Party and the Social Democratic Federation are sympathetic to it but they are not numerically strong. It has sometimes been alleged that the New Deal was a social expression of this tendency but there is little evidence that the New Deal was inspired by any coherent set of ideas except the preservation of free enterprise and the extension of social security to cushion the economy against shocks. It is safe to predict, however, that if democratic socialism has a future in the United States some variant of this alternative philosophy will be accepted as an expression of its basic ideas.

IV. Why Has Socialism Not Been More Successful in the United States?

It remains to ask why, despite the reasonableness of the socialist argument even in this comparatively enlightened form, it has not made much headway. This is part of the still larger question why the American working class, despite the intensity of its economic class struggles, has been so lukewarm to socialist ideas of any kind. Certainly, the orthodox Marxist analysis does not apply here, for in virtue of the maturity of the productive forces in the United States, and until recently the absence of any territorial empire to exploit, one would have expected a riper socialist consciousness in America, which is conspicuously lacking. And whatever socialist consciousness does exist, does not vary concomitantly with the economic indices of prosperity and depression.

The explanation of this phenomenon, it seems to me, must be found on the social-psychological plane. Perhaps the most illuminating hypothesis in this connection has been advanced by Leon Samson,[9] an obscure American Marxist who combines irresponsible fantasies with some deep insights. According to Samson, socialism made little headway because the philosophy of Americanism was itself a kind of "substitutive" or "surrogate" socialism. Socialism promised a classless society in the future. Americanism taught that the citizens of the United States already enjoyed it in the present. Socialism looked forward to equality of opportunity. Americanism celebrated it not only as part of "the American Dream" but boasted that its evidences were everywhere at hand. Socialism promised a release of productive forces. Americanism pointed to the country's rising standard of

[9] Leon Samson, *Toward a United Front: a Philosophy for American Workers* (New York, 1933), especially chap. 1.

450

living: there were no limitations upon economic productivity, except temporary ones. Socialism preached the gospel of freedom and equality. These were the familiar shibboleths of the mythology of Americanism, reinforced by legend, history, and actual fact. At every point socialism encountered the obstacle of a prior faith which was so much like it in aspiration, promise, even in phrasing, that to substitute the first for the second seemed to be pointless. Americanism, fortified by the popular doctrine of progress, seemed to contain what was sensible in socialism without its mystical enthusiasm and cultural extravagances.

This is plausible enough for the period up to the great depression. But as the years of economic crisis and decline wore on, why did not the socialist philosophy take deeper root? Here it seems to me the spectacle of the Soviet Union, a police state based on total cultural terror which boasted that its economy was socialist, had an enormous influence in prejudicing American workers against anything that was labeled socialist or that involved centralized planning on a grand scale. An allegedly class-less society in which free and independent trade unions did not exist, which depended to a large extent on forced labor, and which lacked an operating Bill of Rights including the right to strike, made no appeal even to American workers on relief. To this day American communism, by and large, is not a working-class movement but a movement of periph-eral sections of the middle classes in the interest of a foreign power dedicated to the destruction of politically democratic regimes every-where. With the emergence of a politically democratic socialist order in Great Britain, the political perspective in America may change. The economic struggles of the American working class, which will persist under capitalism, may lead it to consider socialist solutions more seriously than in the past even though it rejects the term "socialism."

It may very well be that the ideals of a democratic socialist welfare economy will gradually influence the large and loosely organized con-ventional political parties, partly through the activities of small inde-pendent educational groups working within or without, partly through the climate of opinion which these groups help to generate. It may be that a unified American labor movement will seek some day its own political expression, in which case it is likely to make its own the philosophy of democratic socialism without the compromising terminology and the superfluous theoretical baggage. It is safe to predict that no matter what historical variant develops, if democratic traditions and institutions are preserved in the face of the current world-wide totalitarian crusade against them, they will acquire a more socialist content.

CHAPTER 9

The Influence of Marxian Economics
on American Thought and Practice

BY PAUL M. SWEEZY

PAUL M. SWEEZY, formerly a teacher of economics at Harvard, writes from a Marxist point of view. He is the author of *The Theory of Capitalist Development* (1942), widely regarded as a standard account of Marxian economics in English. Mr. Sweezy's latest book, *Socialism* (1949), is an introductory survey of Marxian and post-Marxian socialism.

For bibliography in Volume 2 relevant to Mr. Sweezy's essay, see especially PART IV, General Reading (section 2), and Topics 1, 2, 3, 6, 10, 11; PART I, Topic 5.

SOCIALIST ECONOMICS can mean several things, and in any discussion involving the subject it is important to be clear which meaning or meanings are intended. First, the term can mean the economic ideas of the various utopian socialists. No attempt will be made to deal with them in this essay. This is not because they do not play an important part in American intellectual history, but because their significance is so largely noneconomic: they are primarily symptoms of certain social attitudes and aspirations rather than contributions to the understanding of economic reality or the shaping of public policy.

Second, the term can be applied to a kind of reformist doctrine which otherwise-orthodox economists have not infrequently supported. In England, socialist economics in this sense has had a long and significant history. The so-called Ricardian socialists—such men as William Thompson and Thomas Hodgskin—used classical economics to indict capitalist society. The early Fabians drew much of their inspiration and their economics from John Stuart Mill. And in our own time, such eminent representatives of economic orthodoxy as Professor Pigou have on occasion pronounced in favor of socialism.[1] In this country, however, socialist economics of this variety has played a negligible role and will be given little attention in what follows.

Third, socialist economics can mean the theory and practice of a functioning socialist economy. For three decades now a socialist society has been in operation in the Soviet Union, and it is clear that its influence on the rest of the world, including the United States, has been considerable.[2] Unquestionably the impact of Soviet economics on American thought and practice would be an interesting and rewarding subject of investigation. The present writer, however, is not equipped to undertake such a study, and in this essay problems relating to the Soviet Union will come in for consideration only to the extent that they are relevant to the main theme.

Finally, socialist economics can mean the economic theories which are associated with the name of Karl Marx, and it is primarily in this sense that the term is used in the following discussion. Before investigating the influence of these theories on American thought and practice, however, we shall do well to attempt a preliminary outline of their nature and content. This is the more important since in this country what has passed as Marxism has often borne at best a rather attenuated relationship to the teachings of the master.

[1] In his *Socialism vs. Capitalism* (London, 1937).
[2] Cf. the brilliant sketch by E. H. Carr, *The Soviet Impact on the Western World* (New York, 1947).

455

I. Marxian Economics[3]

In the Marxian view, economics is one aspect of a general theory of history and society. Society is conceived of as in a constant state of change which is the product of the interaction of innumerable human beings. In their social action, however, human beings do not behave as isolated individuals. Their ideas, motives, and aims are molded by the concrete circumstances in which they live. Those who are similarly circumstanced, materially and socially, tend to act in a similar fashion. Groups determined in this way—the classes of Marxian theory—are hence the chief actors on the stage of history; their strivings and clashes create the movement which is the essence of social reality.

This approach contains certain implicit injunctions to the student of society. If he would understand what happened in any part of the world during any given span of historical time, he must first investigate the concrete circumstances of the time and place. These include especially— though not exclusively—the physical environment, the techniques of inter- course between man and nature, and the structure of relations between man and man. The investigator will find a certain social system disposing over certain technical means and existing in a given physical environment. His task will then be to discover how these various factors interact to sustain the life of society and to produce a comprehensible pattern of change. In other words, he will have to identify the social system which is relevant to his inquiry and construct a theory of its functioning and development. Having done so, he will be in a position to order and interpret the various documents and records which constitute the raw material of historical knowledge.

This, in a very general way, is the procedure of Marxism. It means that there is a different theory for each historical epoch. The particular epoch which Marx himself was most interested in may be called the "European present"; hence it came to pass that most of Marx's writings, including practically all of his more narrowly economic writings, were concerned with the dominant social system of contemporary western Europe, namely industrial capitalism. Marxian economics, as the term is generally under- stood, is therefore one part of a theory of one particular social system. It is important to emphasize this both because it distinguishes Marxian from orthodox economics and because it implies that there can be, and pre- sumably some day will be, other types of Marxian economics, e.g., Marx- ian economics of feudalism and Marxian economics of socialism.

Let us now inquire more closely into the kind of Marxian economics which has exercised an influence in this country, namely Marxian eco- nomics of capitalism. In accordance with what was said above, the start-

[3] For a fuller exposition and analysis, see P. M. Sweezy, *The Theory of Capitalist Development* (New York, 1942).

ing point of a theory of capitalism must be the determination of its basic environment, techniques, and social structure. Assuming geographical conditions and technical knowledge favorable to the development of industry, there remains the problem of social structure. What are the essential classes in a capitalist system, in the sense that if they did not exist the system would no longer be capitalist? How are they related to one another? To what motives and aims, and hence to what types of social behavior, does this set of relationships give rise? When these questions have been answered we shall be in a position to understand the driving forces and to analyze the forms of capitalist development.

It is clear from the very name of the system that one class essential to its existence is the capitalist class, those who own the instruments of production and set them in motion with a view to acquiring profits. But instruments of production do not run themselves; hence alongside the capitalist class, there must also be a working class. These two classes are sufficient to define a capitalist system. All others—landlords, interest receivers, independent peasants and craftsmen, etc.—may be absent, singly or in combination, without impairing the capitalist character of the system as a whole. Hence the theory of capitalism should first be developed on the assumption of a system from which all but the essential classes have been excluded.

The next step, then, is to analyze the relationship between the capitalist and his workers. Clearly, it is an exchange relationship—the capitalist exchanges money for labor power—and as such is a species of a larger genus. It is in this way that we arrive at the actual starting point of Marxian economics, the theory of exchange value. As is well known, Marx took over and adapted to his own ends the classical (Ricardian) theory according to which the value of a commodity is determined by the quantity of labor required to produce it. When applied to the commodity labor power, i.e., to the relationship between capitalist and worker, this theory leads naturally to the conception of surplus value as the difference between the value produced by the worker and the value consumed by the worker.

The value-form of the relation between capitalist and worker is of decisive importance in determining the character of capitalism as a whole. From the point of view of the capitalist, the purpose of buying labor power—in other words, of performing his function as a capitalist—is simply to acquire surplus value. All other possible motives (for example, the acquisition of consumable goods) are subordinated to this primary aim. Thus it comes about that success, prestige, and power in the capitalist system are tied to surplus value: other things being equal, he who has the most surplus value stands highest in the social scale.

But how does the capitalist maximize his intake of surplus value? One method is by adding this year's surplus value to next year's capital so that next year even more surplus value can be produced. This process is known as the accumulation of capital, and it implies the expansion of production. Another method is by producing more efficiently and hence more cheaply; in this way each capitalist hopes to gain at the expense of his less efficient rivals. Thus we see that in essence capitalism is an expanding system with an inherent tendency to greater efficiency and productivity. It follows that from a Marxian point of view, capitalism on the one hand, and such concepts as stability and equilibrium on the other, are in principle antithetical; the deepest differences between Marxian and orthodox economics can be traced to this source.

The heart of Marxian economics consists in a detailed analysis of the process of capital accumulation. Evidently this analysis cannot be reproduced, even in outline, in a brief sketch such as this. It must suffice to set down certain of its main conclusions, remembering all the time that these conclusions are the end products of a chain of reasoning which reaches back uninterruptedly to the most abstract theory of exchange value. In general terms, one can say that these conclusions bring to light and give formulation to what Marxists call the "contradictions" of capitalism.

First, the accumulation of capital expands the demand for labor power and hence tends to raise wages at the expense of surplus value. Capitalists meet this threat by introducing laborsaving machinery. The effect is to throw workers out of employment, to create what Marx called an "industrial reserve army," which tends to drag wages down and to guarantee to capitalists a satisfactorily cheap and docile labor force. Thus, in the Marxian view, unemployment is a necessary and (from the capitalists' standpoint) beneficent feature of the system. This position contrasts sharply with that of many modern economists, especially the Keynesians, who look upon unemployment as a remediable flaw in the make-up of the capitalist order.

Second, the accumulation of capital tends to depress the rate of profit. At a certain stage in the fall of the rate of profit capitalists temporarily cease or curtail their accumulating activity. The result is a crisis followed by a depression, during which wages are reduced and capital values deflated. In time, profitability is restored and accumulation picks up again. This explains why capitalist development follows the peculiar form of alternating cycles of prosperity and depression.

Third, as a capitalist economy matures and grows wealthier, its power to accumulate grows more than proportionately (since capitalists' consumption claims a smaller and smaller share of total surplus value). This means that producing power tends to expand at an increasing rate. Consuming power, on the other hand, is kept in check by the system's

458

natural tendency to hold down wages plus the capitalists' drive to accumulate rather than consume. Thus there is no rational relation between the growth of producing power and the growth of consuming power; in fact there is an increasing tendency for the former to grow out of all proportion to the latter. This is perhaps the fundamental contradiction of capitalism; it explains Marx's aphorism in *Capital* that "the real barrier of capitalist production is capital itself."

Fourth, the effort of capitalists to acquire surplus value at the expense of their competitors leads to a steady enlargement of the average scale of production since, generally speaking, the larger capitals both are more efficient and wield greater bargaining power than the smaller. Moreover, those which get ahead in the race tend to swallow the laggards. As a result of this double process, monopoly spreads and eventually comes to dominate the decisive branches of production. Monopoly intensifies the contradictions of capitalism which are already there and adds new ones of its own making; especially, it leads to the concentration of control over the life processes of society in the hands of a small circle of big industrialists and financiers.

Finally, the capitalist class of each country makes use of the power of the state, which it ultimately controls, in order to overcome the contradictions enumerated above and to expand the field for profitable accumulation. This leads at times to concessions to workers which are designed to keep them from turning revolutionary. But the ultimate recourse of every capitalist country is always to attempt to solve its problems at the expense of the rest of the world. This leads to all the multifarious phenomena of tariffs, export subsidies, international cartels, colonial expansionism, imperialist rivalries, and eventually war itself. Thus the efforts to overcome the contradictions of capitalism succeed only in transferring them to a new and more destructive plane.

In the final analysis, therefore, the contradictions of capitalism cannot be overcome except through the abolition of the system which gives rise to them. In the words of Lenin, "they testify to its historical-transitional character [and] explain the conditions and causes of its downfall and its transformation into a higher form."[4] This higher form, of course, is socialism, which, under the leadership of the working class, will build a rational and ultimately classless society on the material foundations inherited from capitalism.

The foregoing sketch, fragmentary though it is, should suffice to demonstrate the important point that Marxism makes no sharp distinctions between the various social sciences. In order to explain the basic principles of Marxian economics we had to begin with a theory of history and end with a theory of modern imperialism and the transition from capitalism

[4] *Sämtliche Werke*, III (Vienna and Berlin, 1929), p. 21.

to socialism. This being the case, it is naturally out of the question to attempt to isolate the influence of Marxian economics as distinct from the influence of Marxian social science in general. Thus, while we shall emphasize what everyone would regard as economics, we shall find that it is neither desirable nor feasible to avoid questions which some might regard as properly belonging to the fields of history, sociology, or political science.

II. The Influence of Marxian Economics on the American Socialist Movement

The most obvious place to look for the influence of Marxian economics is in the various socialist movements which have come into existence since Karl Marx and Friedrich Engels first put their ideas in systematic form in the late 1840's. Such an influence made itself felt in this country already in the early eighteen-fifties through the agency of the refugees of 1848 and has been a leading factor in American socialism ever since.

As Daniel Bell has mentioned briefly in Chapter 6, an important figure in the early propagation of Marxian ideas in America was Joseph Weydemeyer (1818-1866), who had been closely associated with Marx and Engels before emigrating to the United States.[5] Weydemeyer arrived in New York late in 1851 and immediately set to work to convert German-American workers to Marxism. A short-lived journal which he published in 1852, *Die Revolution*, will always be remembered for having brought out the famous "Eighteenth Brumaire of Louis Bonaparte," which many consider to be Marx's outstanding historical essay. Toward the end of 1852 Weydemeyer founded the *Proletarierbund*, which helped to lay the foundations of trade unionism among German workers. He was the leading figure in the later (1853) *Arbeiterbund* and was largely responsible for the fact that its organ, *Die Reform*, was one of the theoretically clearest and best-rounded labor papers of the period not only in the U.S., but anywhere. According to Schlüter, a series of "Economic Sketches" published by Weydemeyer in *Die Reform* "in which he treats the fundamentals of political economy in terms of Karl Marx's teachings is still worth reading today."[6]

There is an unbroken thread connecting these earliest efforts to propagate Marxian doctrines on American soil with the Socialist and Communist parties of our own day. After Weydemeyer left New York for the West in 1856 a small nucleus of faithful forty-eighters formed themselves into

[5] The following summary of the beginnings of Marxian socialism in the U.S. is based upon Hermann Schlüter, *Die Anfänge der deutschen Arbeiterbewegung in Amerika* (Stuttgart, 1907), Pt. 4. It was written before announcement of a new biography of Weydemeyer: Karl Obermann, *Joseph Weydemeyer: Pioneer of American Socialism* (New York, 1947).

[6] Schlüter, *op.cit.*, p. 149.

a *Kommunistenklub*, one member of which was Friedrich A. Sorge (1826-1906). Sorge had come into contact with Marx and Engels in London in 1852 and remained one of their most loyal associates and closest friends to the very end.[7] The *Kommunistenklub* suspended activities during the Civil War but resumed again in the middle sixties, and it was its members, above all Sorge, who took the lead in developing a branch of the First International in the United States. When the headquarters of the International were moved to New York in 1872 Sorge became the general secretary. The International was effective in planting the seeds of Marxism, especially among German-American workers, and its dissolution may be said to mark the beginning rather than the end of a genuine socialist political movement in the United States. In 1874 the Social-Democratic Workingmen's Party was formed, and this became the Socialist Labor Party in 1877. The Socialist Labor Party, despite the fact that it never had a large membership, played a significant role in the industrial and political turmoil which marked the last quarter of the nineteenth century.[8] It was undoubtedly due to the S.L.P. that proletarian socialism in this country, unlike its British counterpart, acquired and retained a Marxian character.

The Socialist Party, formed in 1901 following a split in the Socialist Labor Party, was officially a Marxist party from the outset. It was a member of the Second International (founded in 1889) and was much under the influence of the German Social Democratic Party, which at that time, as the largest socialist party in the world, enjoyed tremendous prestige in the international movement. As is well known, the Socialist Party grew steadily in the years before World War I, reaching its peak in terms of both membership and voting strength in 1912. Let us attempt to assess the quality of the Marxism of the Socialist Party in its years of greatest prosperity.[9]

[7] Marx and Engels were in constant correspondence with Sorge, and it was to him that Engels unburdened himself in a letter written the day after Marx's death.

[8] See, for example, C. M. Destler, *American Radicalism, 1865-1901* (New London, Conn., 1946), especially chaps. 8, 9, and 10. There is a need for much more detailed research on the left-wing movements of this period.

[9] The following discussion is based mainly on two sources. (1) The first source is the files of the monthly *International Socialist Review*, which was founded in 1900. The Socialist Party had no official organs, but the *International Socialist Review* was clearly modeled after the *Neue Zeit* (official theoretical journal of the German party), which it resembles somewhat in the way that a provincial weekly newspaper resembles a metropolitan daily. From 1900 to 1908 the *International Socialist Review* was under the editorship of A. M. Simons and retained the character of a medium for the discussion of socialist principles. The editorship changed hands in 1908, with Charles Kerr (head of the socialist publishing house of the same name) taking over; and in 1910 the *Review* was transformed into a popular illustrated magazine. Its usefulness for our purposes ends with this change. (2) The second source is Jessie Wallace Hughan's *American Socialism of the Present Day* (New York, 1912, but published the year before under a different title), which analyzes the Socialist Party with

Outwardly the Marxism of the Socialist Party was pure and undefiled. Not only did all the leaders proclaim themselves Marxists, but there was no avowed "revisionism" in the American movement as there was in the German. Thus in a sense the American party was more rigorously orthodox than the leading party of international socialism. Beneath the surface, however, things were very different. The absence of a revisionist movement in the Socialist Party reflected not an absence of revisionist spirit but rather a lack of interest in theoretical questions on the part of the practical politicians who controlled the party. In the eyes of such people discussion of theoretical issues was a waste of time and energy. Their Marxism consisted primarily of a simple economic determinism plus the doctrine of the class struggle. These ideas could be easily presented to a working-class audience and were therefore useful for purposes of propaganda and agitation. According to Miss Hughan, the insistence "upon sound theory as a prerequisite for sound action" was confined to "a certain section among New York Socialists," whose chief representative was Louis B. Boudin;[10] and she added it as her own opinion that "it can hardly be gainsaid that in their refusal to lay stress upon theory the majority of the American party are in accord with the spirit of Marx as shown in his own life and in such utterances as his letter on the Gotha program."[11] Actually, it would be hard to imagine anything less in accord with the spirit of the man whose main lifework was *Capital*. One can only conclude that the Marxism of the "majority of the American party," including most of its leaders, was, to say the least, a rather peculiar brand.

Alongside its practical politicians the Socialist Party of course had its theorists, most of whom wrote at one time or another for the *International Socialist Review*. It would be unfair to judge their work too harshly. They lacked the support which a strong tradition of native radical thought would have given them; they were isolated from and for the most part ignored by professional scholars and intellectuals; finally they were attempting a very difficult task, namely, to adapt to American conditions and interpret to American readers a highly complex and subtle body of social doctrines. And yet, when full allowance has been made for all these difficulties and handicaps, one must still admit that the intellectual achievements of the old Socialist Party are far from impressive. There is only one work which, aside from historical interest, is worth reading today, namely, Louis B. Boudin's *The Theoretical System of Karl*

---

particular reference to the extent to which it was an authentic Marxist movement and to the differences between the left ("revolutionist") and right ("constructivist") wings of the party. Miss Hughan, a member of the party thoroughly familiar with the relevant literature, from which she quotes freely, may be taken as a reliable guide to theoretical currents inside the American Socialist Party at its height.

[10] Hughan, *op.cit.*, p. 81.
[11] *Ibid.*, p. 82.

Marx (1907).[12] This is a very able book, at once an exposition of Marxism (with primary emphasis on economics) and a rebuttal of its critics. Boudin's refutation of Böhm-Bawerk[13] is the most effective ever written in English. Moreover, he shows a keen appreciation of the central function of Marxian economics, which is, in the words of Marx himself, "to lay bare the economic law of motion of modern society" and not, as most American socialists seem to have thought, to provide ammunition for political propaganda. Boudin was the first American Marxist to give proper weight to the theory of economic crises; and though the doctrine of underconsumption which he expounded is based on faulty reasoning, it is sufficiently correct in its outcome to enable him to throw new light on the latest stage of capitalist development especially as it was then manifesting itself in America. No writer before or since has shown a better understanding than Boudin of the paradoxical role of waste—in the form of excessive selling costs, imperialist adventures, wars, etc.—in maintaining demand and hence in keeping capitalism on its feet.

All in all, then, Boudin's book was one of the outstanding Marxist works produced anywhere in the early years of the present century, and one would think that it might have laid the foundation for an important American Marxist school. Nothing of the sort happened, however. Apparently American socialists were incapable of understanding Boudin; he remained a relatively isolated figure, more appreciated abroad than at home. Other theorists of the period were for the most part poorly trained and lacked outstanding talent. A. M. Simons, editor of the *International Socialist Review*, was a pioneer in the task of applying Marxism to the interpretation of American history, but it cannot be said that his work was of superior quality. Ernest Untermann, author of a book entitled *Marxian Economics* (1907), which is more confusing than enlightening, was a heavy German schoolmaster type whose chief service was to translate Volumes 2 and 3 of *Das Kapital* into English. William English Walling, who studied under Veblen at Chicago, acquired a considerable reputation as a theorist, but his work is erratic and bears the marks of the dilettante. Morris Hillquit, long the political leader of the party and its representative on the executive committee of the Second International, was undoubtedly the most widely known spokesman of American socialism. His main theo-

---

[12] This was first published as a series of articles in the *International Socialist Review* beginning in the issue of May 1905.

[13] E. v. Böhm-Bawerk, *Karl Marx and the Close of his System* (English translation, London, 1898). The most authoritative Marxian answer to Böhm-Bawerk is Rudolf Hilferding, *Böhm-Bawerk's Marx-Kritik* (Vienna, 1904). (In 1949 these two works were republished by Augustus M. Kelley, Inc., of New York, in a single volume with an introduction by the present writer.) Neither Boudin's nor Hilferding's counterattack, however, seems to have made the slightest impression on orthodox economists, who have gone on repeating Böhm-Bawerk's arguments ever since as though they were the last word on the subject.

retical work, *Socialism in Theory and Practice* (1909), was singled out—not unfairly—by two learned German writers as an example of the "superficial popularization of socialism which spread throughout the working-class movement at the beginning of the twentieth century and which, despite Marxist phraseology, retained none of the real content of Marxian socialism."[14] But there would be little point in prolonging the list. It is only necessary to note that the names which have been mentioned are those of the most prominent theorists of the Socialist Party; alongside them there were others whom it would be kinder not to drag from the obscurity to which the passing of the years has consigned them.

Before leaving the old Socialist Party, it may be useful to attempt a sort of synthetic reconstruction of the accepted economic theory of the movement. The doctrine of surplus value was regarded as the foundation stone of socialist economics not because it forms the starting point of the analysis of capital accumulation but rather because it was thought to "prove" that the working class is exploited under capitalism.[15] Exploitation, in turn, taken together with a theory of the direct determination of behavior by economic interests, explained the class struggle. Value theory was dropped at this point and a set of parallel and essentially unrelated theories was used to help explain the behavior of capitalism and the inevitability of socialism. Crises are the result of (1) the planless anarchic character of capitalist production; and/or (2) the fact that workers are unable to buy back the whole of their product. These forces produce unemployment and desperate competition among workers for available jobs; the exploitation and misery of the workers tends to become steadily greater. On the other side of the picture, the technical superiority of large-scale production causes a continuous centralization of capital along with the economic ruin of the middle class. Finally, according to Miss Hughan, American Marxists were in agreement on the following: "The revolution is inevitable, as a result of the technical forces of concentration of capital and massing of labor, and the ideological forces arising from the proletarization of the middle classes and the increasing exploitation of the workers."[16] The main split in the party was over the question of what kind of "revolution" it would be. The left wing believed that some day matters would come to a head and the proletariat would be more or less obliged to take over, probably against the violent resistance of the capital-

[14] "Sozialismus und Kommunismus," by Carl Grünberg and Henryk Grossman, *Wörterbuch der Volkswirtschaft*, Ludwig Elster, ed. (4th ed., Jena, 1931), III, p. 326.
[15] It may be noted in passing that no competent Marxist would accept this view today. That the working class is exploited follows directly from the obvious fact that there are other classes in society which are able to live in idleness. This, however, is not peculiar to capitalism; it is equally characteristic of slavery and feudalism. The theory of surplus value simply lays bare the specific *form* which exploitation assumes in capitalist society.
[16] Hughan, *op.cit.*, p. 114.

ists; while the right wing happily imagined that the revolution was already under way and saw evidence of it every time a municipal government installed a new free rest room.

It would take us too far afield to attempt a critique of these views; to appreciate their oversimplicity and superficiality it is enough to compare them with the brief sketch of Marxian economics presented at the beginning of this paper. Thus we see that while a majority of American socialists, including many leaders of the Socialist Party, were not interested in theory, those who were, with few exceptions, accepted a version of Marxism which is little more than a caricature. Needless to say, the party as a whole was utterly unprepared for the storms and catastrophes which lay immediately ahead, and it is not surprising that the war, the debacle of the Second International, and the Russian Revolution shattered the old socialist movement beyond hope of revival.

In terms of its influence on the country as a whole, however, there can be no doubt that in the decade and a half before World War I the Socialist Party—through its influence in organized labor, its vigorous electoral campaigns, its numerous successes in state and municipal politics, its extensive press, etc.[17]—succeeded in popularizing the idea of socialism much more effectively than had any of its predecessors. By 1914 every politically literate person in the country must have acquired at least a rudimentary conception of socialism; and the name, if not the principles, of Karl Marx had become familiar to a large number of Americans.

As noted above, the events of the war years dealt a crushing blow to the Socialist Party from which it never recovered. There were a few signs of a comeback during the early years of the Great Depression, but the rally was a reflection of the times rather than of any inner vitality. The New Deal, which seemed to offer a new and more promising outlet for the energy of social reformers, dealt the coup de grâce to the Socialist Party, which thenceforth continued to exist, along with the Socialist Labor Party,[18] as a sort of political museum piece. There can be no doubt, I

[17] Readers today need to be reminded of the extent of socialist activities at that time. In 1912 the Socialist Max Hayes got about one-third of the votes in a contest against Samuel Gompers for the presidency of the A.F.L.; in the same years Debs got approximately 900,000 out of a total of about 15 million votes cast in the presidential election which sent Wilson to the White House—this would have been equivalent to a vote of about 3 million in the 1944 election; the first Socialist Congressman (Victor Berger) was elected in 1910; Socialist municipal officials were no longer a rarity; the party controlled 5 English dailies, 8 foreign-language dailies, 262 English weeklies, 36 foreign-language weeklies, 10 English monthlies, and 2 foreign-language monthlies. L. M. Hacker and B. B. Kendrick, *The United States since 1865* (3rd ed., New York, 1939), p. 430.

[18] Those who never heard of the Socialist Labor Party, or thought that it disappeared years ago, may find the comparison far-fetched. Yet it is worth remembering that in the presidential election of 1944, Norman Thomas, perennial candidate of the Socialist Party, received less than twice the vote of Teichert, the Socialist Labor Party candidate (80,518 as against 45,336).

believe, that the Communist Party, ever since its founding in the early 1920's, has been both the most important and the most interesting factor in American socialism.

It goes without saying that the Communist Party, like all the parties which belonged to the former Third International, is a Marxist party. Moreover, the very fact that its spokesmen commonly use the term Marxism-Leninism indicates that the Communist Party adheres to the doctrines of Karl Marx as interpreted and extended by Lenin. Lenin's most important theoretical achievements can be put into three categories. First, he revived and restated the political teachings of Marx and Engels, which had been forgotten or grossly distorted in the period of the Second International. *State and Revolution* (1918) is the chief, but by no means the only, work in this category. Second, he wrote extensively on the theory and practice of revolution with particular reference to the conditions of Russia. In this field he was highly original and relied very little on Marx. Third, he extended the Marxian theory of capitalist development to take account of the most important new phenomena which appeared between the Franco-Prussian War and World War I. *Imperialism* (1917) is the decisive work here; it is primarily concerned with what would usually be called economic problems; but like most Marxian works, it makes no attempt to separate the economic from the social and the political.

The prestige and authority of Lenin—and after him of Stalin—have been so great in the American Communist Party that there has been very little that could properly be called discussion of basic theoretical problems among American communists. The works of Lenin and Stalin, and to a certain extent of other Soviet theorists, have been translated into English and circulated among the party membership. There has been hardly any attempt to go beyond them or to take up problems with which they do not deal. The work of party theorists has therefore been more in the nature of interpretation and exegesis than of independent thinking. At the same time, the enunciation of party principles has been left almost entirely in the hands of the top political leadership which has been selected for reasons other than mastery of socialist theory.

It would not be correct to say that the Communist Party has had no theory or that, like the old Socialist Party, it has underestimated the importance of theory. What is true, however, is that it took over Marxism in the form which Russian experience has given to it and so far has contributed little of its own either by way of addition or adaptation to American conditions. From the standpoint of American communists, this procedure has had both advantages and disadvantages. Lenin is the most reliable interpreter of Marx; moreover his insight into the characteristics of "the highest stage of capitalism" is unsurpassed. Because the Communist

466

Party has tried to adhere to Leninism in matters of basic principle, it has—at least so it seems to me—rarely misjudged the nature of the historical period in which we live,[19] and it has remained a genuine socialist party. (This, incidentally, has earned it the undying hatred of that numerous group in this country who can forgive socialists everything but a sincere devotion to socialism.) On the other hand the absence of a habit of, or capacity for, independent theorizing has had its disadvantages too.

This has come out clearly in questions of both international and national policy. On the former, the party has tried to keep in step with the Soviet Union and with other Communist parties; but where—for obvious "reasons of state"—the Soviet Union has chosen to keep quiet about its views and intentions, such guidance has been lacking and the party has floundered' about more or less helplessly. This is the only way to explain the fact that the Communist Party neither foresaw the possibility of the Soviet-German pact nor understood its significance when it came. In questions of national policy it lies in the nature of the case that local parties must for the most part make their own way. If they try to do this by applying strategy and tactics which have been worked out under very different historical and social conditions, it can hardly be expected that they will have much success. And yet this is what the American Communist Party did, at least until the Seventh World Comintern Congress in 1935, and it goes far to account for the party's failure in twenty-five years of intensive activity to consolidate its position with the American working class and to grow into a mass socialist party. Since 1935, and especially since the war, Communist parties outside the U.S.S.R. have ceased to think exclusively in terms of Soviet experience; but at least as far as the American Communist Party is concerned, this has not yet been followed by a theoretical reorientation in terms of American history and American social structure.

Before leaving the American socialist movement we must ask what the Communist Party has accomplished in the way of familiarizing the country with the doctrines of Marxism-Leninism. This is a very difficult problem because of the complications introduced by the Russian Revolution. There is no doubt at all that before World War I the Socialist Party was the main channel through which socialist and Marxist ideas made their way into the United States. By comparison, other channels were of quite minor importance. One cannot say the same of the Communist Party in the twenties and thirties, however. Socialism became a very real, even if to many an unpleasant, fact after 1917. Writers, publishers,

[19] The one important exception was the "Teheran" period when the Communist Party, under the leadership of Earl Browder, entertained some very extraordinary notions about the postwar world.

schools, universities—in short the whole intellectual apparatus of modern society—could no longer ignore the subject, and the person with any interest in such matters could find material with which to satisfy his curiosity. This applies especially to the Soviet Union and its leaders, but in learning about them one can hardly avoid learning about the theory and practice of socialism.[20] Thus the fact—and it undoubtedly is a fact—that well-educated Americans are familiar with, say, the Leninist theory of imperialism and are even to a certain extent influenced by it in their own thinking by no means proves that they have all been exposed to communist propaganda. To assume that it does would be to underestimate the complexity of the problem and to overestimate the effectiveness of the Communist Party. Nevertheless the writer has the impression, for what it is worth, that in proportion to its size the Communist Party has been remarkably successful in spreading a knowledge of the ideas for which it stands. This success has been achieved partly through the normal channels of political education and agitation: party press, political meetings, election campaigns, etc. In addition, the party has unquestionably been wise to invest resources in International Publishers, which has made itself indispensable to socialists and antisocialists alike by being virtually alone in the field of publishing the classics of socialism. Finally, there is a factor which is obviously impossible to evaluate quantitatively but which must have been very important, namely, the tremendous amount of free publicity which the Communist Party has received through such agencies as the press and legislative committees. Of course, this publicity has been hostile and intended to discredit the party in the eyes of the American people, and no doubt it has often had that effect. But at the same time it has brought the party to the attention of far more people than it could have hoped to reach by its own efforts, and in this way it must at times have stimulated a great deal of curiosity and indirectly laid the basis for a considerable extension of the party's range and influence.

III. The Influence of Marxian Ideas on American Economists

For purposes of exposition we can distinguish between direct and indirect influences on the one hand, and between positive and negative influences on the other. With this in mind let us consider the influence of Marxian ideas on American economic thinking. (In this connection, Veblen is such a special and at the same time such an important case that we shall reserve him for separate treatment in the next section.)

[20] Stalin once spoke of the "very existence of the Soviet republics" as "a great piece of agitation against capitalism and imperialism." Joseph Stalin, *Marxism and the National Question* (New York, 1942), p. 92. He might have added that it has certainly been the most powerful spreader of Marxist and socialist ideas. On this whole subject see Carr, *The Soviet Impact on the Western World*.

One need have little hesitation in saying that the direct and positive influence of Marxism on American economists has been slight. Remembering that we are excluding Veblen for the moment, we are probably justified in saying that there are very few outstanding American economists whose ideas have been significantly shaped by Marxism.[21] Judged by his two most important books, Professor R. A. Brady of the University of California is one.[22] Professor Leo Rogin, of the same institution until his death in 1947, was perhaps another.[23] That they are exceptional cases, however, is strongly suggested by the following facts.

(1) During the middle nineteen-thirties interest in Marxism was fairly widespread in the U.S., and the American Economic Association decided to devote the opening session of its annual meeting in 1937 to "The Significance of Marxian Economics." Professor Rogin was one of the main speakers. Professor Wassily Leontief, who acquired his knowledge of Marxian doctrines before coming to this country and is in any case certainly no Marxist, was the other. The two persons selected to discuss the main papers were Professor John Ise and Professor J. J. Spengler, neither of whom, to judge from the published report of the proceedings, could be regarded as having been significantly influenced by the theories under discussion. The present writer attended the session in question and does not recall any significant contributions from the floor.

(2) During 1944 and 1945 there took place in the pages of *American Economic Review* a controversy about whether a certain article in a Soviet publication[24] indicated that present-day Russian economists have or have not abandoned the original economic theory of Marx. Professor Rogin was one of the participants. Others were Carl Landauer, a German-trained economist; Paul Baran, likewise German-trained; Raya Dunayevskaya, the Russian émigrée translator of the Soviet article; Oscar Lange, a Pole who was then at the University of Chicago but who subsequently represented his country on the Security Council of the United Nations;

---

[21] For present purposes we must exclude from the category of American economists those whose fundamental ideas were formed before they came to this country. This would rule out, e.g., Professor J. A. Schumpeter whose *Theory of Economic Development* (tr. by Redvers Opie; Cambridge, Mass., 1934) at least in what the Germans call its *Problemstellung* shows a strong Marxian influence. Though Professor Schumpeter taught at Harvard for nearly twenty years and became an American citizen, the book in question was written long before he came to the United States, and he did not alter its underlying thesis in his subsequent writings.

[22] *The Spirit and Structure of German Fascism* (New York, 1937) and *Business as a System of Power* (New York, 1943).

[23] See his two articles, "The Significance of Marxian Economics for Current Trends of Government Policy," *American Economic Review*, Vol. 28, No. 1, Supplement (Mar. 1938), pp. 10-16, and "Marx and Engels on Distribution in a Socialist Society," *American Economic Review*, xxxviii (Mar. 1945), pp. 137-43.

[24] Translated and published under the title, "Teaching of Economics in the Soviet Union," *American Economic Review*, xxxiv (Sept. 1944), pp. 501-30.

and Brooks Otis, a teacher at Hobart College who is not a professional economist. This certainly suggests a lack of either interest or competence in problems of Marxian economics on the part of American-trained economists.

(3) For the past ten years *Science & Society* has appeared as a scholarly review inviting as contributors "not only those who have already accepted and applied Marxian principles to their researches, but also those who are exploring its possibilities." One would normally expect a Marxian review to be rather heavily weighted on the economic side; yet such has not been the case with *Science & Society*. On the contrary, it has been consistently weaker both quantitatively and qualitatively in economics than in such fields as history, literary criticism, psychology, philosophy, and art. Moreover—and this is perhaps even more symptomatic—the economist who has made the most distinguished contributions to the pages of *Science & Society* is not an American at all but the leading British Marxian economist, Maurice Dobb.

If we understand by the direct negative influence of a theory the extent to which it meets with attempts at refutation, we shall find that in this respect also Marxism has evoked only a faint response among American economists. This is in sharp contrast to Germany, where anti-Marxism has long been a serious concern of academic social scientists. The reason for the difference is clear: anti-Marxism is hardly an independent phenomenon but rather tends to develop in direct proportion to the strength of Marxism itself.

Probably the most distinguished critique of an important Marxian theory by an American scholar was E. R. A. Seligman's *The Economic Interpretation of History* (1902), which has undoubtedly done more than any other work to introduce the main principles of historical materialism to American social scientists. Seligman's presentation is fair and by no means unsympathetic;[25] at the same time, however, he advances certain criticisms, based chiefly on an alleged underestimation of the importance of cultural phenomena, which have become more or less standard with the great majority of American social scientists.[26]

Since the publication of Seligman's book, there has been a thin but

[25] Cf. the following: "The economic interpretation of history, in emphasizing the historical basis of economic institutions, has done much for economics. On the other hand, it has done even more for history. . . . Whether or not we are prepared to accept it as an adequate explanation of human progress in general, we must all recognize the beneficial influence that it has exerted in stimulating the thoughts of scholars and in broadening the concepts and the ideals of history and economics alike" (p. 159).

[26] Though Seligman himself was an economist, the main significance of *The Economic Interpretation of History* is in the field of historiography, which necessarily lies outside the scope of the present chapter. For this reason no attempt is made to pursue the subject further.

more or less steady trickle of anti-Marxian works. Professor J. E. LeRossignol has contributed a total of three,[27] none of which can be said to be specially noteworthy for penetration or originality. V. G. Simkhovitch's *Marxism vs. Socialism* (1913) is, as the name may suggest, an attempt on the part of a nonsocialist to save the socialists from Marxist error. O. D. Skelton's *Socialism: a Critical Analysis* (1911) is conscientious though for the most part not original.[28] M. M. Bober's *Karl Marx's Interpretation of History* (1927), is more than the name implies since it includes a fairly comprehensive critique of the economic theories of *Capital*.[29] It reflects the arguments of such standard anti-Marxian works as that of Böhm-Bawerk. H. B. Parkes seems to have been lacking in prophetic insight when he chose to call his book *Marxism: an Autopsy* (1939); for the rest, the work contains a considerable number of misinterpretations of Marxist theory. Finally, the latest in the anti-Marxist series to come to the attention of the present writer is J. K. Turner's *Challenge to Karl Marx* (1941). Mr. Turner was perhaps a little rash to take on so formidable an opponent.

The foregoing list is doubtless not exhaustive, but it is at any rate representative of American anti-Marxism. On the whole, it can be called relatively thin stuff. One can only conclude that the best minds in American economics have been as little interested in refuting Marx as they have been in learning from him.

The indirect influence of socialist ideas and movements here and abroad on American economic thought has certainly been considerable. At the same time, it is extremely difficult to pin down; such indirect influences form a part of the general climate of opinion which shapes people's minds and thoughts without their being aware of it. Here we shall only note certain general trends which are at least partly attributable to the rise and spread of socialism from the middle of the nineteenth century onward. In doing so, however, we must not be supposed to be claiming anything like an exclusive causal relationship. The fact is that the very conditions in industry and society which produced modern socialism also produced other political and intellectual currents which were in part independent and in part related, both as cause and as effect, to socialism. It would take a much more elaborate study than can be attempted here to disentangle these various elements in a highly complicated process.

In an informative article,[30] Professor Haney once pointed out that so-

---

[27] J. E. Le Rossignol, *Orthodox Socialism: a Criticism* (New York, 1907); *What Is Socialism?* (New York, 1921); and *From Marx to Stalin* (New York, 1940).

[28] Skelton was a Canadian.

[29] A second revised and enlarged edition of Bober's book was published in 1948. For an estimate of the new edition, see the present writer's review in the *Journal of Political Economy* for June 1949.

[30] L. H. Haney, "Der Einfluss des Sozialismus auf der Volkswirtschaftslehre," *Archiv für die Geschichte des Sozialismus und der Arbeiterbewegung*, III (1913), pp. 460-80.

cialist ideas began to make themselves felt in the works of American economists in the 1880's. This was partly the result of socialist propaganda; partly it was due to the fact that younger scholars returning from studies in Germany began to circulate new ideas about society and social problems which had hitherto had no currency in America.[31] Perry's *Elements of Political Economy* (1st ed., 1865), the most popular text of its day, supported laissez faire quite in the spirit of Bastiat. But Newcomb's *Principles* (1885) already devoted consideration to the subject of socialism, and Walker's *Political Economy* (1887) might be called the first modern textbook in the field. Walker shows an awareness of the dangers of wage cutting, speaks of the great mass of exploited workers in Europe as an undoubted fact, and puts forward various criticisms of the status quo which a few years before would have been regarded as rank heresy. Haney was certainly justified in concluding that "the extension of the scope of economics attributable to the influence of socialism thus brought into the open the connection which exists between ethical, legal, and political judgments on the one hand and those of a purely economic nature on the other."[32]

From this time on, economists felt increasingly obliged to discuss such questions as the justice—and the justification—of the existing economic order. Dimly, and perhaps unconsciously, they were being driven to a realization that they were in fact dealing with a *social system* and not with an aspect of the God-given order of nature. Beginning with Ely's *Outlines of Economics* (1893) it became standard practice for economics textbook writers to devote a chapter or part of a chapter to the subject of socialism. Moreover, the dogma of laissez faire gradually lost its authority as the legitimacy of government intervention was conceded in one case after another. How far this change in attitude had proceeded in the years before World War I can best be judged by comparing Perry's *Elements* (1865) with Taussig's *Principles* (1st ed., 1911), which held its place as by all odds the most distinguished American textbook for two full decades.

A parallel development, which is at least in part a reflection of Marxian ideas, is suggested by the passage quoted above from Seligman's *Economic Interpretation*. Economists became aware of history at about the same time that historians were becoming aware of economics. Beginning

[31] In this connection, the autobiography of Richard T. Ely, *Ground under Our Feet* (New York, 1938), is of interest. Ely returned from Germany in the summer of 1880 to become one of the leaders of the younger generation of economists. The titles of several of the sections of chapter 4 are revealing of the new spirit: "A Crust Had Formed over Political Economy," "We Rebels Protest against Laissez Faire and Orthodoxy," "Our Statement of Principles Was Not a Creed," and "Dunbar Did Not Understand: We Were Concerned about Life." Ely's *French and German Socialism in Modern Times* (New York, 1883) was probably the first attempt at an objective and impartial account of socialist doctrines to be published by an American scholar.

[32] Haney, *op.cit.*, p. 472.

in the eighteen-eighties with such books as Ely's *The Labor Movement in America* (1886) and Taussig's *A Tariff History of the United States* (1888), economists devoted increasing attention to the origins and historical development of the institutions with which they were dealing. It would be wrong, however, to overestimate the importance of this trend in American economics. It started out promisingly, but its fruit turned out to be the rather stale specialty known as "economic history." Economics departments tended more and more to recognize the importance of history by equipping themselves with one or two economic historians; when this had been done, the rest could go back with a good conscience to being as unhistorical as ever.

IV. The Influence of Marxism on Thorstein Veblen

This is not the place to discuss Veblen's position in the intellectual history of the United States. It is sufficient to note that he was one of the outstanding figures of his period and that probably no American social scientist has exercised so great an influence as Veblen has, especially in the fields of art and literature. No one has better summed up Veblen's impact on his contemporaries than Maxwell Anderson when he wrote in a letter to the *Dial*: "I once asked a friend if he had read *The Theory of the Leisure Class*. 'Why no,' he retorted, 'why should I? All my friends have read it. It permeates the atmosphere in which I live.'"[33]

The claim would hardly be made today that Veblen was a Marxist, and there are probably not many who would go so far as to classify him as a socialist. Nevertheless, the writer believes that the weight of the evidence indicates that Marxism was one of the decisive factors shaping his thought and that for the last forty years of his life he was at least a good deal more sympathetic to socialism than he was to the order of society under which he lived. If this is so, it means that Veblen has a unique place among top-ranking American economists in this as in other respects.

Veblen was not one to discuss himself, still less his intellectual debts. It follows that if one wants to trace the latter one must rely on the evidence of his writings plus the biographical information which has been painstakingly compiled by Dr. Dorfman. Opinions based on sources of this kind are, of course, likely to vary; and it is necessary to point out that there is no general agreement among students of Veblen as to the relative importance in the genesis and development of his ideas of the various intellectual influences to which he was exposed. One recent writer has even gone so far as to express the opinion that though Veblen saturated his mind with the speculation of his time "his own thought was entirely

[33] Quoted in Joseph Dorfman, *Thorstein Veblen and His America* (New York, 1945), p. 422.

original."[34] One suspects that even Veblen would have hardly regarded this as a compliment. Dr. Dorfman has been more cautious, setting down a wealth of facts but leaving their interpretation largely to the reader. The following analysis must therefore be taken as tentative and subject to revision in the light of additional evidence or further discussion.

We may first summarize some of the most important points of similarity between Veblen's ideas and those of Marx. Veblen's interpretation of history was undoubtedly a variety of economic determinism. Like Marx and Engels, he accepted the theory of a prehistoric society of primitive communism. Like them, too, he believed that the crucial transformation came with the development of private property, which divided society into mutually hostile classes. Class, and class conflict—under a variety of designations—are central concepts in practically all of Veblen's writings. In societies based on private property, the acquisition of wealth was regarded by Veblen as an end in itself, in fact as a decisive motivation of human conduct. As pointed out in our introductory sketch of Marxian economics, this thesis underlies Marx's theory of capital accumulation, which in turn is the heart of his analysis of capitalism. Veblen drew as a logical corollary his theory of leisure-class consumption as a method of advertising wealth. Marx had already stated a similar doctrine, though he did not elaborate upon it.[35] (Incidentally, the fact that Marx stressed accumulation while Veblen stressed conspicuous consumption—two sides of the same coin—is characteristic of their differing interests and temperaments.)

It could be argued, and quite correctly, that each of these similarities between Marx and Veblen can be found between Marx and one or another of Veblen's contemporaries. The fathers of American sociology all conceived of society in class terms;[36] while such historians as Turner, Parrington, and Beard were in varying degrees economic determinists. Moreover, Lester F. Ward, for example, understood very well the relation between private property and the pursuit of wealth, which "becomes a means of attaining pleasure, and this new desire finally becomes an end in itself: 'the supreme passion of mankind.' "[37]

The decisive point, however, is that the similarities between Marx and the others stop here, while this is not the case as between Marx and Veblen. There are a number of doctrines which are rightly regarded as peculiarly Marxian in the sense that they distinguish their author as the

[34] C. A. Madison, *Critics & Crusaders* (New York, 1947), pp. 311-12.

[35] Cf. the statement: "The more his [the capitalist's] wealth grows, the more he falls behind his ideal [acquiring ever more wealth] and becomes wasteful for the sake of displaying his wealth." Marx, *Theorien über den Mehrwert* (Stuttgart, 1905-1910), I, p. 378.

[36] See C. H. Page, *Class and American Sociology: from Ward to Ross* (New York, 1940).

[37] Quoted by Page, *ibid.*, p. 38.

474

THE INFLUENCE OF MARXIAN ECONOMICS

real founder of the modern socialist movement. Some of these relate to the specific "laws of motion" of the capitalist economy—e.g., the theory of surplus value and the theory of the industrial reserve army[38]—and of these there is little trace in Veblen. But there are two of a more general nature which likewise fall in this category: first, the theory of the historically transitory nature of class society, and specifically of capitalism; and second, the theory of the inevitability of socialism as the next stage of historical development.[39] It seems to the writer undeniable that both of these ideas are persistent elements of Veblen's thought.

This is not meant to imply that Veblen said either of these things in so many words. In the early days he was very anxious to remain in academic life, and he cultivated the art of being evasive on any point which might be regarded as a direct attack on the status quo. In later years, when caution was less important, his method of expressing himself had become so firmly fixed that he covered even his most savage thrusts with a protective coloring of indirection and aloofness. Moreover, Veblen, lacking the stimulation of Marx's political activism and given to gloomy forebodings about the future, gave to the theory of the inevitability of socialism a characteristic twist of his own. He never doubted the transitory nature of capitalism ("business enterprise," "the price system," etc.), and he seems to have been equally convinced that socialism must come *if society is not to fall into a new dark age*.[40] But as time went on the latter eventuality seemed to him increasingly likely. The gist of his thought on this whole question can best be indicated by quoting short passages from Dorfman's entirely reliable summaries of *The Theory of Business Enterprise* (1904) and *Absentee Ownership* (1923). In the earlier book Veblen concluded, according to Dorfman's summary, that "mankind is faced either with another regime of status and the dark ages, or with the full development of the industrial republic and machine technology. 'Which of the

---

[38] See above, pp. 457-58.

[39] See above, p. 459. Compare also with the following passage from a letter from Marx to Weydemeyer in 1852: ". . . no credit is due to me for discovering the existence of classes in modern society nor yet the struggle between them. Long before me bourgeois historians had described the historical development of this class struggle and bourgeois economists the economic anatomy of the classes. What I did that was new was to prove: (1) that the *existence of classes* is only bound up with *particular, historic phases in the development of production*; (2) that the class struggle necessarily leads to the *dictatorship of the proletariat*; (3) that this dictatorship itself only constitutes the transition to the *abolition of all classes* and to a *classless society*." (Emphasis in original.) *Karl Marx and Friedrich Engels, Correspondence 1846-1895, a Selection with Commentary and Notes* (New York, 1935), p. 57.

[40] Incidentally, one could argue that this view is compatible with Marxism. Cf. the statement in the *Manifesto*: "The history of all hitherto existing society is the history of class struggles. . . . Oppressor and oppressed stood in constant opposition to one another, carried on an uninterrupted, now hidden, now open fight, a fight that each time ended, either in a revolutionary reconstitution of society at large, *or in the common ruin of the contending classes*." (Emphasis added.)

475

two antagonistic factors may prove the stronger in the long run is something of a blind guess; but the calculable future seems to belong to the one or the other.' In either case business enterprise is a transient matter, no more than a biological sport."[41]

By the 1920's Veblen was noticeably more pessimistic, though the fundamental idea is unchanged. To quote again from Dorfman: " 'In a long run, of course,' said Veblen, 'the pressure of changing material circumstances will have to shape the lines of human conduct, on pain of extinction. . . . But it does not follow that the pressure of material necessity, visibly enforced by the death penalty, will ensure such a change in the legal and moral punctilios as will save the nation from the death penalty.' Of this the present condition of civilized nations is evidence. Whether the people come through this period of 'enforced change alive and fit to live, appears to be a matter of chance in which human insight plays a minor part and human foresight no part at all.' "[42]

If it is correct that this aspect of Veblen's thought distinguishes him sharply from his contemporaries and puts him in the Marxian camp on matters of absolutely vital importance, then the question arises as to whether Veblen could have been directly influenced by Marxism or whether we must conclude that he arrived at these views independently. We can safely rule out alternative sources of intellectual influence; indeed this is the reason why the doctrines of the historical relativity of class societies and the inevitability of socialism are so crucial for the purposes of this inquiry. A quick glance at Veblen's biography should be enough to settle the question.

We do not know when Veblen first became interested in socialist or Marxist writings, but we do know that he was reading Lassalle and Bellamy in the 1880's; we know that his second published work (the first after he decided to become an economist) was entitled "Some Neglected Points in the Theory of Socialism" (1891); we know that of the sixty-odd items in his bibliography during the fifteen years he was at the University of Chicago, more than one in five is directly identifiable from its title as being concerned with socialism or Marxism (usually both); we know that he began to teach a course on socialism in 1892 and that he continued to teach it on and off throughout his academic career; we know that when he began to think of writing a book in 1895 his first impulse was to write on socialism before he finally settled on *The Theory of the Leisure Class*;

[41] Dorfman, *op.cit.*, p. 235.

[42] *Ibid.*, p. 468. The required changes, in Veblen's view, would include elimination of the "footless nonsense of absentee ownership" and the substitution of an "unsanctified workday arrangement for the common use of industrial ways and means" (p. 469). This is, of course, merely a Veblenian version of the common definition of socialism.

476

we know that he entertained the highest opinion of Marx;[43] and we know that just before he went to Stanford in 1906 he wrote two essays for the *Quarterly Journal of Economics* under the title "The Socialist Economics of Karl Marx and His Followers," which, as Dorfman says, "are the outcome of fifteen years' teaching of socialism and thinking in its terms," and which show a knowledge of the literature of Marxism which is so far ahead of that of any of his contemporaries in the United States that there is simply no ground for comparison.[44]

In view of all this, it is difficult to avoid the conclusion that Veblen was directly and deeply influenced by Marxism. On this showing, he was not only the great exception among the leading American social scientists of his own generation; he was also the channel through which essentially Marxian ideas reached and influenced intellectual circles which were too prejudiced or too timid to judge Marx on his scientific merits. There is some truth in the dictum of the American socialist, R. R. La Monte, that "Veblen is not great as a rival of Marx, but as an expounder of Marx, a developer of Marxian theories."[45]

V. *The Influence of Socialist Ideas on American Governmental Policy*

We must now address ourselves to the question whether socialist economics, in the sense of this chapter (or in any rational sense for that matter), has exercised a significant influence on the development of American governmental policy. The assertion is so frequently made from the platform and in the press that this or that measure is socialistically (or communistically) inspired that it might seem a foregone conclusion that the answer would be in the affirmative. The writer feels, however, that such a view is totally misleading if not actually false. What is undoubtedly true is that the growth of socialism as a world-wide movement has made people more conscious of and receptive to the need for social reforms in this country as well as elsewhere. Further, it is arguable—though it would be difficult to prove—that fear of socialism has sometimes played a part in the calculations of American politicians and legislators in the sense that it has moved them to sponsor reforms which they would have otherwise opposed—just as, for example, Bismarck fathered the German system of social security in order to take the wind out of the social democratic sails. But it is a very different thing to claim that American governmental policy has been in important respects inspired by socialist ideals or

[43] According to one of his students (Howard Woolston), "He often implied if he did not say: 'Read Marx. Uncover the roots of the problem.'" *Ibid.*, p. 250.

[44] This paragraph is based on Dorfman, *passim*. For exact references to the essays by Veblen cited in the paragraph, see the bibliography in Dorfman.

[45] *International Socialist Review*, v (June 1905), p. 726.

methods. Moreover, we shall try to show that for such a claim there is little solid evidence.

This is not to argue that the charge of socialist inspiration is always made dishonestly, though this is no doubt often the case. Not infrequently, the question is one of definition. If socialism is defined in sufficiently broad terms to include practically any form of state action in the economic sphere,[46] it is of course not difficult to find plenty of evidence of its existence and influence in the United States. If one attempts to follow up such definitions, however, one is led either into hopeless confusion or to the most violent paradoxes: avowed socialists and bitter antisocialists, Republicans and Democrats, Alexander Hamilton and Franklin D. Roosevelt, must all be judged "socialists." Obviously findings of this sort, however sincerely arrived at, have no analytical value.

For our purposes it is necessary to examine briefly the various kinds of governmental policies which might conceivably be thought to reflect the influence of socialist economics. We can distinguish five categories of state action in the economic sphere: (1) action designed to protect or further the vested interests of property owners either sectionally or as a whole; (2) action designed to prevent what is felt to be intolerable abuse of monopoly power; (3) action designed to maintain employment and stabilize the economy as a whole; (4) action designed to ameliorate the conditions of workers and other low-income groups within the framework of the existing social order; and (5) action calculated (consciously or unconsciously) to alter that framework itself and to further or facilitate the achievement of a socialist society.

It is clear that governmental measures which fall in the first category have nothing to do with socialist economics except that the latter may help to explain them. It is also clear that throughout American history a large part of the economic legislation of federal and state governments has been of this description: e.g., tariffs, land grants to railroads and other forms of subsidy to private industry, fair-trade laws, N.R.A. Codes, agricultural price maintenance, regulation of the sale of corporate securities, and so forth.

Measures falling in the second category have likewise been common since the 1870's and simply reflect a demand on the part of consumers of all kinds for protection against excessive exploitation. There is nothing

[46] Such definitions have frequently been advanced by recognized social scientists, and they are probably even more widely accepted by journalists and popular writers. Two examples may be cited: "Socialism is any device or doctrine whose aim is to save individuals from any of the difficulties or hardships of the struggle for existence and the competition of life by the intervention of 'the State.'" William Graham Sumner, as quoted in Page, op.cit., p. 103. "Socialism is that policy or theory which aims at securing by the action of the central democratic authority a better distribution, and in due subordination thereunto a better production, of wealth than now prevails." James Bonar in the *Encyclopaedia Britannica,* 13th ed.

socialistic either in their inspiration or in their purpose. The best known examples are the antitrust laws and the regulation of railroads and public utilities. In practice, of course, regulation has turned out to be concerned with protecting investors at least as much as consumers and might therefore as appropriately be included under (1).

Measures falling in the third category may perhaps be said to have originated in a very tentative way with the founding of the Federal Reserve System on the eve of World War I, but they are for the most part a product of the New Deal period. It is now a widely recognized obligation of the government to do something—just what is by no means agreed— to combat depressions and to maintain at least a reasonably high level of employment. Insofar as this has a theoretical as distinct from a purely pragmatic origin it clearly stems from Keynesian and not from Marxian economics. Socialists naturally do not disapprove of concrete stabilization measures, such as public works or other forms of government spending in time of depression, but they flatly reject the view that the contradictions of capitalism can be eliminated by any program of the Keynesian type.

Measures falling in the fourth category have always been supported by socialists and certainly have the sanction of Marxian economics. We may cite as examples: progressive income taxation, regulation of hours and conditions of work, establishment of minimum wages, protection of workers' right to form trade unions and bargain collectively, and the various forms of social insurance and assistance. The United States, as is well known, has a large body of legislation of this general description, much of it enacted during the period of the New Deal. Here, then, is a field of governmental policy which might have been influenced by socialist economics. In fact, however, the aim of ameliorating the lot of low-income groups within the framework of the existing social order is in no sense peculiar to socialists; it is shared to the full by bourgeois radicals and liberals. Indeed, for liberals this is the essence of their economic program, while for socialists it merely provides the issues around which to organize the masses for the final achievement of socialism. One cannot conclude, therefore, that just because a certain reform has the support of socialists its passage is evidence of socialist influence. Moreover, the whole political history of America, and more particularly of the New Deal, certainly indicates that the driving force behind meliorative reform movements has come in overwhelming measure from nonsocialist liberal sources.[47]

The fifth category of state action listed above, namely action designed to alter the framework of the economic system, includes by definition only

[47] Concerning the absence of Marxian influence on the New Deal, see Rogin, "The Significance of Marxian Economics for Current Trends of Government Policy," *op.cit.* For the pre-World War I period, see W. E. Walling, *Socialism as It Is* (New York, 1912), especially Pt. 1 and Pt. 2, chap. 4. This book contains a useful analysis of nonsocialist reformism.

such measures as are consciously approved and supported by socialists. It follows that where we find examples of this kind we have strong prima facie evidence of socialist influence. Nor is this conclusion vitiated by the fact that political parties and governments frequently attempt to convey the impression of favoring or promoting such changes without actually providing their substance. For pseudosocialist no less than genuine socialist measures attest to the presence and importance of socialist influence. Thus that Hitler called his party "National Socialist" and tried to portray its policies as socialist can be explained only in terms of the long-standing socialist organization and aspirations of the German working class, just as—on a different level—the nationalization of large-scale industry throughout eastern Europe since the war reflects not only the influence but also the power of socialist parties.

In the United States, however, no national or state government and neither of the major political parties has ever pretended to aim at the replacement of the existing economic system by another; at most they have promised to remedy its abuses. Moreover, no large-scale program of government ownership of industry—except as a strictly temporary wartime emergency measure—has ever been adopted, and since the days of the old Socialist Party none has been seriously proposed. (In recent years, even the Communist Party has shifted its program for socialization of industry from the category of immediate to that of ultimate goals.) We are left, then, with a certain amount of municipal ownership of public utilities plus one unique type of federal project, of which the Tennessee Valley Authority is the oldest and best-known example, as possible products of the influence of socialist economics on American governmental policies.

Public ownership of local utilities is common in the field of water supply (approximately 90 per cent of the total); decidedly the exception in electric power (7 per cent) and urban transport; and virtually non-existent in gas and telephones.[48] In some few cases where it exists, the influence of socialists—whose program as a matter of course includes extension of municipal ownership of utilities—may have helped to bring it about.[49] But in the vast majority of cases, neither socialist economics nor socialist politics has had any bearing on the issue. It is hard to generalize where particular local conditions have played so important a role; nevertheless, it is probably safe to say that waterworks have usually come into public ownership because of their intimate relation to such problems

[48] John Bauer, "Public Ownership of Public Utilities in the United States," *Annals of the American Academy of Political and Social Science*, CCI (Jan. 1939), p. 50.

[49] It is noteworthy, however, that even in Milwaukee, where the Socialist Party held the mayoralty uninterruptedly from 1916 to 1940 and consistently campaigned for public ownership, all of the traditional utilities except water supply have remained in private hands.

of local government as health service and fire protection, while the origin of public ownership in other lines will commonly be found in abuse of monopoly privileges by private companies. Where cases of the latter kind occur—and they have, of course, been notoriously common in American history—the issue of public ownership tends to be identified with that of clean government and to attract the support of people whose only claim to radicalism consists in a dislike of graft and corruption.[50] A decision for public ownership taken under such conditions evidently is not motivated by socialist aims and normally gives rise to a form of municipal enterprise which is conducted according to regular business principles.[51]

The T.V.A.,[52] however, presents a more complicated problem than municipally-owned public-utility plants. It is undeniable that T.V.A. is not an ordinary governmental operation, nor is it the kind of economic enterprise which capitalist governments normally undertake. Private capital has never played a role in T.V.A.; it does not aim to make profits; the purposes which it does pursue are in the broadest sense social, including as they do not only navigation, flood control, and the maximum extension of electricity use, but also the physical and cultural development of the area which it serves; and yet the core of its activities can be called economic in the strictest sense of the term.[53] In all this there are un-

[50] Cf. the statement of former Mayor Hoan of Milwaukee: "One main step in the direction of better local government is to join forces with those who would change from private to public ownership of utilities. The change eliminates the most fruitful and the most persistent source of corruption." D. W. Hoan, *City Government: the Record of the Milwaukee Experiment* (New York, 1936), p. 47.

[51] Even the National Association of Manufacturers, usually quick to smell a "socialist rat," does not maintain that public ownership of utilities in the United States has been a socialistic experiment. "Having the government step into such fields as road building, schools, the post office, and in some instances public utilities," says the N.A.M.'s Economic Principles Commission, "has been in the hope that such centralized direction and control would confer greater benefits than were being obtained under private ownership. They have been examples of attempts to increase the non-monetary income of the American public, rather than attempts to undermine the driving motivation that comes from a system of individual enterprise." And the marginal summary accompanying the paragraph in which this passage occurs states: "Government regulation and public enterprise have not been accepted as steps toward a socialized economy." *The American Individual Enterprise System*, I (1946), p. 11.

[52] What is said of the T.V.A. applies, with appropriate modifications, to kindred projects like the Bonneville Power Authority and the proposed Missouri Valley Authority.

[53] It is true that T.V.A. is officially regarded as primarily a navigation and flood control project, and that these functions have been traditionally handled by regular government departments. This is to be explained in terms of constitutional requirements, however, and can hardly be regarded as accurately portraying the motivation and objectives of the undertaking. It is very likely that there never would have been a T.V.A. except for the electric power possibilities and implications of the plan, and in this sense the latter may be rightly said to constitute its chief purpose. See E. S. Mason, "Power Aspects of the Tennessee Valley Authority's Program," *Quarterly Journal of Economics*, L (May 1936), pp. 377-414.

doubtedly striking resemblances to socialist economic policy as it has developed in the Soviet Union and is now developing in the countries of eastern Europe which are under the control of socialist parties.

And yet one must be careful not to push the comparison too far. T.V.A.'s genuine planning lies almost wholly in the field of controlling and harnessing the water resources of the Tennessee River basin. Here it works out specific coordinated plans which are acted upon and brought to completion. In social and economic matters, however, it can do little more than experiment with new ideas and attempt to secure the cooperation of various governmental and private agencies in putting them into practice. This sort of thing is often called "planning" in this country, and of course it may accomplish much good; but it is important to realize that it has little in common with planning either in the engineering sense or in the sense in which the term applies to a socialist economy.[54] Moreover, in its all-important power program, T.V.A. has adopted, under strong pressure to be sure, the policy of fixing rates not only to cover separable costs but also an allocated portion of the capital costs of multipurpose installations. One can go so far as to say that the voluminous and bitter polemics which have surrounded this question of cost allocation bring out clearly, even if often indirectly, the underlying differences between production for profit and production for community ends. The solution which seems to have been adopted is not altogether satisfactory to anyone, but there can be no doubt that in principle it represents a victory for the traditional capitalist view.[55] Finally, no well-informed observer would maintain that those responsible for founding T.V.A. and molding its policies—such men as Franklin D. Roosevelt, George W. Norris, and David E. Lilienthal— were at any time significantly influenced by socialist economics.[56]

[54] Stalin stated the essential difference very clearly as follows: "Admittedly they [i.e., under a capitalist system] too have something akin to plans. But these plans are prognosis, guess-plans which bind nobody, and on the basis of which it is impossible to direct a country's economy. Things are different with us. Our plans are not prognosis, guess-plans, but *instructions* which are *compulsory* for all managements and which determine the future course of the economic development of our *entire* country. You see that this implies a difference of principle." Quoted by Alexander Baykov, *The Development of the Soviet Economic System* (Cambridge, Eng., 1946), p. 424. It is to be noted that private companies, and also T.V.A., plan their internal affairs in Stalin's sense. The difference, therefore, is not that such planning is absent under capitalism but that it is carried on by a large number of independent units. T.V.A. cannot be regarded as a step away from this system.

[55] For the main issues involved see Mason, *op.cit.*, and J. C. Bonbright, "Ratemaking Policies of Federal Power Projects," *American Economic Review*, Vol. 36, No. 2, Supplement (May 1946), pp. 426-34.

[56] The attempt to prove a direct socialist parentage for T.V.A. has only to be made to reveal its weakness. See F. L. Collins, *Uncle Sam's Billion-Dollar Baby: a Taxpayer Looks at the T.V.A.* (New York, 1945). According to Collins, T.V.A. is a sort of socialist conspiracy which was put over on the "innocent" Senator Norris. The "proof" is that socialists have long advocated public ownership and large-scale federal power

In the writer's opinion, it follows from the above that T.V.A. cannot properly be regarded as a socialistic experiment. Its significance rather lies in another direction. The situation which existed in the electric power industry in the early thirties was in many ways unique. The shortcomings of regulation by state commissions were painfully obvious; in rural areas only about one farm in nine enjoyed the benefits of electricity; the financial scandals of the holding-company era had been fully documented in an exhaustive Federal Trade Commission investigation and dramatized by the collapse of the Insull empire; finally, the severity of the depression created an atmosphere favorable to bold and unorthodox action. Here was an unprecedented opportunity for liberals, and in T.V.A. they took good advantage of it. There is nothing in the *conception* and *methods* of T.V.A. which is not a logical application of twentieth-century liberal ideology; and the fact that its *purposes* are akin to those of socialism merely reflects the common parentage and close historical connection between liberalism and socialism. What is unusual about T.V.A., and hence easily gives rise to misinterpretation, is that it displays the positive aspects of liberalism in actual operation and not just on paper. Is it not a compliment to socialism, and to the example of the Soviet Union, that when progressivism is translated from theory into practice it immediately acquires a socialist label?

VI. Reasons for the Slight Influence of Marxian Economic Ideas in the United States

The foregoing analysis of the influence of socialist economics on American thought and practice is sketchy and incomplete. The writer, lacking a professional grounding in American history, has felt constrained to stick to terrain more or less familiar to an economist and to avoid generalizations of a kind which an historian might feel justified in making. Nevertheless, such as it is, it does indicate that the influence of socialist economics, both ideologically and practically, has been very limited in the United States. At a time when socialism, particularly in its economic aspects, has become a dominant issue in much of the rest of the world, one cannot help wondering what explains the apparent imperviousness of our own country to an historical movement of such vitality and scope. The writer may therefore be forgiven if he closes with a few undocumented reflections on a question so full of implications for our own future and even for the future of civilization itself.

The ultimate reasons for the small extent of the influence of socialist economics in the United States are, of course, to be found in the general

developments—which is, of course, true—and that an article in a Socialist Party paper during the mid-twenties specifically mentioned Muscle Shoals and used the words "authority" and "yardstick." Any evidence of connecting links is missing.

course of American history: the absence of a feudal past obstructing the development of capitalism; the presence of rich stores of untapped natural resources; the pace and scope of geographic, demographic, and industrial expansion; and above all the fluidity of class lines and the remarkable ease of vertical mobility. The fundamental importance of these underlying conditions and trends is widely recognized, and nothing needs to be added on the subject here. There are, however, certain other factors, not unrelated to these to be sure, which have received rather less attention than they deserve. Of the latter, attention may be briefly directed to the following: (1) the attitude of American colleges and universities; (2) the character of the American labor movement; and (3) the timing and impact of the two world wars. The first affects mainly the ideological aspect of the question; while the second and third affect both the ideological and the practical political aspects.

(1) American higher education has developed almost from the outset under a system of external government by boards of trustees made up for the most part of clergymen, businessmen, and lawyers, that is to say of individuals representing the most conservative elements in the community. As a consequence, American colleges and universities have been consistently hostile to all forms of unorthodox thought or behavior. Moreover, this hostility has reached its apex in questions relating to the social sciences. Veblen's career is only the most dramatic illustration of the subordination of American higher education to values which are at best irrelevant to the proper purposes of an institution of learning. Here was one of the country's outstanding social scientists, anxious for a university career to the point of refraining from open criticism of the existing social order and taking no part at all in politics, who yet remained all his life a sort of academic outcast because his ideas were radical and his marital relations somewhat irregular.

The conservatism and timidity of American colleges and universities is, of course, a familiar story which hardly needs repeating, but it is necessary to emphasize that this has been a tremendously important factor in minimizing the influence of socialist economics in this country. It is not only that socialist ideas have rarely been favorably or even intelligently presented as a part of the academic curriculum; indeed, this is not the most important aspect of the matter. Of far greater significance is the fact that the road to an academic career has been virtually barred to all radically inclined social scientists. For obvious reasons, this has been enough to discourage all but a very few from entertaining, or at least giving utterance to, ideas displeasing to the powers that be.[57] No

[57] This mechanism of control, which American capitalism has developed to a high degree of perfection, can be most easily seen at work in the case of those members of the academic community—to mention names would be invidious—who, having

one knows, and there are no data for an objective survey, how much headway socialist economics might have made in colleges and universities if younger men setting forth on academic careers had felt free to follow their ideas wherever they might lead. But one who is familiar with American graduate students may put his estimate rather high.

(2) It may be said that higher education in other capitalist countries has hardly been more hospitable to socialist ideas than in the United States and yet in some these ideas have gained a wider currency and exercised a much deeper influence. The proposition is of doubtful validity —English universities, for example, are certainly more independent and tolerant than American—but it does serve to direct attention to the role of other institutions, and especially those of the labor movement, in fostering or checking the spread of socialism.

In this connection, the case of Imperial Germany is particularly instructive. Before World War I German universities were on the whole extremely conservative upper-class institutions which did much to combat socialism and hardly anything to advance it. And yet intellectually German socialism was the admitted leader of the world movement. Partly this is to be attributed to what must be regarded as an historical accident, that the founders of modern socialism happened to be Germans. But it is to an even greater extent due to the character of the German labor movement, to the existence of an avowedly socialist party closely linked to a large and powerful trade union federation. The result was that there were all sorts of jobs—as functionaries, editors, teachers, etc.—open to socialist intellectuals; the latter had a solid base from which to carry on their scientific and cultural work.[58]

In contrast, the American labor movement has been dominated by an intensely practical type of business unionism which has always rejected political affiliations and scorned the cooperation of intellectuals. There has been some change in this regard since the founding of the C.I.O., but

---

started out as radicals and made no progress, have conveniently changed their views and risen to positions of honor and responsibility.

[58] That they still felt keenly their exclusion from the universities, however, is indicated by the following: "Marxism," wrote Rudolf Hilferding, the leading social democratic economist, in 1909, "is often reproached with having neglected the advancement of economic theory, and this reproach certainly does not lack a measure of objective justification. But it must be admitted all the same that this neglect is only too easily explained. As a result of the endless complexities of the phenomena which it investigates, economic theory surely belongs to the most difficult of scientific undertakings. The Marxist, however, is in a special position; excluded from the universities which assure the necessary time for scientific research, he is forced to pursue scientific work in the time left over from political struggles. To expect of active participants in the political arena that their contribution to the building of science should proceed as rapidly as in the case of those who can pursue their labors in peace would be unjust if it did not bear witness to a respect for their ability." *Das Finanzkapital* (Vienna, 1923), p. ix.

even the left-wing unions still conform in the main to the traditional American pattern. As labor gets more deeply involved in politics no doubt new expedients will be tried and new alignments will emerge, but so far one can say that American labor has been hardly more hospitable to socialist economics than American colleges and universities. As we saw above in discussing the American socialist movement, the relatively small Socialist and Communist parties have not been able by themselves to compensate for such serious handicaps.

(3) Finally, a factor of a different kind would appear to warrant more study and thought than have commonly been devoted to it, namely, the peculiar impact of the two world wars on American development. It is arguable, though of course it is impossible to prove, that both in 1914 and again in 1939 American capitalism was headed for a severe crisis which might have been the beginning of fundamental political realignments. If the depression which was due about the time World War I broke out had run its course and if Wilsonian liberalism had demonstrated its incapacity to cope with the situation, the history of the twenties might have been very different from what it was. But the war intervened and completely changed the national and international setting. The United States came through enriched and the most powerful country in the world. Instead of the bankruptcy of liberal reformism, the twenties brought a few years of high prosperity followed by the bankruptcy of big-business Republicanism. When the great depression came, liberal reformism took a new lease on life and, under the leadership of the late President Roosevelt, went on to its greatest triumphs.

But by the late thirties the New Deal had lost its momentum and was visibly disintegrating. In the absence of an international crisis the Republicans would probably have come to power in 1940 with nothing to offer but old slogans and some new faces. Once again, however, war came to the rescue of American capitalism, bringing in its wake unparalleled wealth and power and postponing the day of reckoning. History thus repeats itself, though he would indeed be bold who would prophesy the length of the return engagement.

CHAPTER 10

American Marxist Political Theory

BY WILL HERBERG

WILL HERBERG, Research Director of the New York Dressmakers' Union in the International Ladies' Garment Workers' Union, is a former Marxist who held leading positions in the Communist movement until the end of 1929. At that time, he broke with the party and for some years thereafter edited an independent socialist weekly, *Workers Age*. He has since become known as an exponent of what he describes in his essay as neoliberal and theologically grounded socialism. Mr. Herberg has written many articles on social, political, and theological questions. A book by him on theology will be published in 1951, and he is preparing another on the relations of theology to the social sciences.

For bibliography in Volume 2 relevant to Mr. Herberg's essay, see especially PART II, Topics 8, 9, 10, 11; PART IV, General Reading (section 2B), and Topics 4, 5, 7, 9, 10, 12; PART V, Topics 1, 2, 4, and General Reading (section 3B).

I. *Bourgeois and Socialist Political Theory*

SOCIALIST political theory, in America as elsewhere, differs from bourgeois political theory in one crucial respect. Bourgeois politics accepts the present social order as essentially normal and, in basic features at least, regards it as in some sense final. Socialism, on the other hand, must necessarily look upon the present order as at best merely transient, bound ultimately to give way to the good society of the future. As a consequence, bourgeois political theory can never be anything more than the political theory of an established order operating as a going concern; it is static, while socialist theory is gripped in a dialectic tension between a present that is actually existent but merely provisional and a future perfect and ultimate but yet to be born. Not even the most gradualist or "opportunist" form of socialism can quite destroy this tension, but not even the most "progressive" form of bourgeois doctrine can quite capture it.

This crucial difference in theoretical orientation has its immediate political consequences. Bourgeois politics, even when radical, is essentially affirmative: its aim is to reform, improve, and consolidate the existing order. Socialist politics, however, even at its most "moderate," is essentially negative and oppositional; its true constructive role socialism reserves for the upbuilding of the new social order that is to supersede capitalism. Both work for tomorrow, but in a very different sense: for the one, tomorrow is but today perfected through progress; for the other, it is today negated and transcended in a future that marks the consummation of history.

Not every form of socialist theory, certainly not every form of American socialism, exhibits this distinctive feature in all its clarity; the admixture of nonsocialist ideology is often strong enough to obscure it from the cursory glance. Yet this polarity between the transitory, essentially "unreal" present and the "true" society of the future is to be found at the basis of all socialist theory and provides a fruitful approach, as well as a significant conceptual framework, for classifying and analyzing the many varieties of socialist theory that have left their mark in the history of American political ideas. From this point of view, socialist theory and policy may be regarded as compounded of two elemental strains, the "realistic" and the "utopian," never completely at one with each other. "We stand ready as socialists; we will not give up one iota of fundamental principle. . . . But in the meantime, we are a political party; we are no sect or church preaching the soon-coming of the Lord." In these words, uttered by an outstanding socialist spokesman at the very birth of the Socialist Party,[1] is revealed the full depth of the predicament from which socialist thought can never hope to escape.

[1] James McCartney, then a member of the Massachusetts state legislature, at the

II. Political Types of American Socialism

Before turning to an examination of the operative ideas of American socialist political theory from the viewpoint just formulated, it might be well to describe briefly the main types of American socialism[2] as they have become embodied in distinct organizations and movements in recent decades. It is not the purpose to provide a complete typology; the aim rather is to set up significant points of reference for the analysis of theory and doctrine that is to be the chief business of this paper.

Socialist Labor Party. The oldest of existing socialist organizations is the Socialist Labor Party which came into being in 1877. Its early years were filled with a succession of tempestuous crises, but by the end of the first decade of this century, it had already begun to take on the peculiar political physiognomy which it still retains. Ideologically, it represents the doctrinaire ossification of a curious American variety of socialist orthodoxy. Daniel De Leon, its revered leader, whose philosophy and style of leadership have left so indelible an impress on the character of the party,[3] was accustomed to boast that the Socialist Labor Party was uniquely American in its successful adaptation to the "advanced" stage of American economic and political development. However that may be, it is indeed a fact that the characteristic philosophy of this party, which unites a doctrinaire parliamentary politicalism *prior to*, with a doctrinaire syndicalism *after* the revolution, has hitherto been confined to its own ranks in this country and to a few short-lived offshoots in other English-speaking lands. As a political force, the party is of virtually no significance today but its singular doctrine renders it of interest to the student of socialist political theory.

Socialist Party. The Socialist Party, formed in 1901 and still active politically though split into two wings, may be regarded as a standard socialist movement with crosscurrents of diverse ideological tendencies determining its changing political aspect. It has always had a strong component of orthodox social democracy, of which Morris Hillquit was perhaps the best exemplification and which is today largely embodied in the Social Democratic Federation. Gradualist reform socialism, both of the municipal and trade-union varieties, has constituted another important element: Victor Berger, Dan Hoan, and Jasper McLevy may be

socialist unity convention in 1901. See Nathan Fine, *Labor and Farmer Parties in the United States* (New York, 1928), p. 207.

[2] This study is largely confined to developments in the twentieth century. The general conclusions, however, may be taken to cover the earlier period as well.

[3] A careful study of the various leader types (Gompers, De Leon, Debs, Haywood, Norman Thomas, et al.) and styles of leadership in the American socialist movement in relation to the social composition and political psychology of the organizations involved would prove most instructive.

taken to represent the former, and such men as Mahlon Barnes, Max Hayes, and Benjamin Schlesinger the latter. The more characteristically American radicalism of William D. Haywood and Eugene Victor Debs, with a strong touch of syndicalism in its make-up, played an influential part in former years and still has its representatives among old-timers. Nor has European-type leftism been unknown, whether of the quasi-communist, "Austro-Marxist," or British Independent Labour Party varieties. This great diversity of views, reflecting wide differences in background and outlook, has given the Socialist Party a position of central importance in the study of American socialist political theory.

Industrial Workers of the World. Unless the term is to be taken in an impossibly narrow sense, American socialism must be made to include the Industrial Workers of the World, or I.W.W. Formed in 1905, this group no longer counts for much in the industrial picture but is important for our purposes because it arose as a belated expression of American frontier radicalism under circumstances that compelled it to assume a syndicalist form and ideology.

Early Gompersism. Just as one cannot omit the radical-syndicalist I.W.W. in a representative picture of American socialism, so must one include the "conservative syndicalism" that characterized the ideology of the American Federation of Labor in the first decades after its formation in 1886. The early philosophy of Samuel Gompers, with its stress on proletarian direct action and its marked distrust of government and politics, shows definite affinity to basic syndicalism. It differs from the more familiar radical variety of syndicalism in very much the same way as the gradualistic socialism of Eduard Bernstein differed from the revolutionary socialism of his orthodox opponents. Both Bernstein and Gompers extolled the actual movement as "everything" and stressed the value of day-to-day reforms; yet both acknowledged that beyond the immediate purposes of the movement lay the ultimate goal, the "emancipation of labor."[4] For the German, however, the "movement" was social democracy,

---

[4] The early pronouncements of Samuel Gompers clearly reveal the Marxist inspiration of the ideology of the American Federation of Labor and its affinity to essential socialism: "It requires but little study to come to the conclusion that the ownership and control of wealth, of the means of production, by private corporations, which have no sympathy or apparent responsibility, is the cause of the ills and wrongs borne by the human family" (*Report of Proceedings of the Thirteenth Annual Convention of the American Federation of Labor Held at Chicago, Ill., December 11th to 19th Inclusive, 1893*, p. 11).

"Economic organization and the control over economic power are the fulcrum which makes possible influence and power in other fields. Control over the basic things of life gives power that may be used for good in every relationship of life." (Quoted by Nathan Fine, *op.cit.*, p. 127.)

"Marx did not beguile himself into thinking the ballot was all-powerful. . . . He grasped the principle that the trade union was the immediate and practical agency

whereas for the American it was trade unionism. That made the former a gradualist *socialist*, the latter a gradualist or "conservative" *syndicalist*. A reinterpretation of old-line "pure and simple" trade unionism from this point of view promises fruitful results.

Communist Party. When the Communist Party was first formed in 1919, it represented an attempt to organize independently the ultrarevolutionary sentiment that had grown strong in the Socialist Party, particularly among its foreign-born members, under the influence of the Russian Revolution. It thus arose as politically an offshoot of Russian bolshevism. When somewhat later the American communists joined the Communist International, the party became more directly an outpost of the Russian Revolution and an agency of the leading group of Bolsheviks who dominated the Soviet government and the Communist International alike. Such the Communist Party has remained to this day; the dissolution of the Communist International in 1943 made not the slightest difference in actual relations.

Precisely because the American Communist Party has been an instrument of the Russian Bolshevik leaders almost from the day of its formation, it has undergone a number of basic changes in political character since 1919 in line with the far-reaching changes in Bolshevik policy and party regime. For two or three years after 1919, during the "heroic" period of the Russian Revolution, the American Communist Party, still underground, strove to serve as an instrument of world revolution; its official ideology was orthodox Leninism. From 1923 to 1929, Russian communism was torn apart by a series of bitter intraparty struggles, out of which Stalin emerged as undisputed master. The American Communist Party, like the communist organizations of other countries, reflected the various stages of this struggle as well as its outcome;

---

which could bring the wage-earners a better life" (*Seventy Years of Life and Labor* [New York, 1925] i, p. 83).

"The trade unions, pure and simple, are the natural organizations of the wage-earners to secure their present material and practical improvement and to achieve their final emancipation" (*Report of Proceedings of the Tenth Annual Convention . . . 1890*, p. 16).

The last statement was given official sanction in one of the resolutions of the 1890 convention at Detroit: "We affirm the trade union movement to be the legitimate channel through which wage-earners of America are seeking present amelioration and future emancipation" (*ibid.*, p. 20).

The preamble to the constitution adopted in 1881 by the Federation of Organized Trades and Labor Unions, the immediate predecessor of the A.F.L., affirmed the class struggle in clear Marxist terms: ". . . a struggle is going on in the nations of the civilized world between the oppressors and the oppressed of all countries, a struggle between capital and labor, which must grow in intensity from year to year and work disastrous results to the toiling millions of all nations if not combined for mutual protection and benefit." With slight modifications, this preamble remains to the present day as the first paragraph of the constitution of the A.F.L.

its ideology was an emerging Stalinism with secondary right-left variations corresponding to the changes of direction in the Russian factional fight. Since 1930, the American Communist Party has functioned as the instrument of Soviet foreign policy, veering with the sharp turns of Russian diplomacy. It has ceased to have any definite political principles. Everything has become subject to change without notice; the only fixed point—and that has been immovable—is unswerving allegiance to Soviet interests as defined by Joseph Stalin. It has thus in my opinion lost all importance for the study of American socialist political theory.

The earlier Bolshevik radicalism, however, has been continued, with some modifications, in the Trotskyist movement in this country, largely in the Socialist Workers Party.

These, then, are the organizations and movements to which reference will chiefly be made in the following analysis of socialist political philosophy.

III. Operative Ideas of American Socialist Political Theory

The revolution: juncture of the two orders. The fundamental category of socialist political theory is the *revolution*—the point of juncture between the two social orders, between this world and the world to come. Revolution is the event or process through which the merely transient actuality of capitalism is replaced by the ultimate perfection of socialism, the earthly city of exploitation and oppression by the heavenly city of brotherly harmony.

In orthodox or normative socialism, the revolution is conceived as a unique cataclysmic event through which the party wins dominant power and thus opens the way for the establishment of the new order. The revolution is, of course, prepared for by the structural changes within the old order which capitalism, according to socialist theory, is supposed to bring about. Capitalism, in fact, destroys itself. The "inner contradictions" of the system not only produce the proletariat as "gravedigger"; they also generate the conditions that make it necessary and possible for the proletariat to perform its revolutionary mission. Here economic analysis and political doctrine meet: indeed, the term "revolution" has sometimes been used, rather confusedly, to designate the long-term economic changes that prepare the ground for the climactic event. But, properly speaking, it is this climactic event itself which is the revolution, and this event is necessarily of a political character since it relates to the transfer of power in society; it may be either constitutional or insurrectionary depending upon the means by which the power is obtained. In gradualist ("reformist") conceptions, the unique cataclysmic event is dissolved into a gradual process of the accumulation of power or into a succession of social reforms which in their totality constitute the revolution achieved.

493

In its daily practice, gradualist socialism approaches bourgeois liberalism, but this similarity should not obscure the wide difference in ultimate perspective.

However it has conceived the revolution, socialism has always held that it would be brought about by the proletariat waging relentless class war against the bourgeoisie. The Marxian conceptions of the proletariat as the dynamic force in society and of the class struggle as the motive power of history are absolutely integral to modern socialism. Differences there may be as to how the proletariat is to be defined or as to what its relations with other classes should be, but the doctrine of the revolutionary role of the proletarian class struggle has in one form or another been a central dogma in all authentic socialist movements.

American socialism has largely run true to form in these respects. Although gradualism has always had influential spokesmen, such as Morris Hillquit, American socialists have, until recent years, generally tended to think of the revolution as a single, well-defined event in the future. The revolution, however, was to be achieved peacefully by the proletariat through a disciplined, self-conscious utilization of the democratic ballot. Up to the Russian Revolution, the Socialist and Socialist Labor parties agreed on this, despite the fact that the former had a strong semisyndicalist wing which joined with the I.W.W. in urging direct action on the economic front. The Russian Revolution, however, worked a drastic change in the viewpoint of American socialism. It not only for a time suppressed all talk of gradualism in socialist ranks but it also shifted the emphasis to extralegal and insurrectionary means in the winning of power. In the Communist Party, this emphasis hardened into dogma with the formulation of the definitive Leninist viewpoint in the theses of the second congress of the Communist International (1920). In Socialist Party ranks, the issue remained for some years a source of discord contributing to the intraparty struggle and the split of 1936. Ten years later a complete reversal of sentiment had taken place, again largely under the influence of the "dialectic" of the Russian Revolution. Today, very few American socialists, outside the radical Trotskyist and semi-Trotskyist groups, think of the revolution in the simple cataclysmic terms that did service for decades. Something very close to the old, much-abused gradualism has become current, though the change has not been adequately documented in official pronouncements. There is even some doubt as to the unique revolutionary role of the proletariat; talk of a "coalition" of all "functional groups" in society as the bearer of socialism is becoming more articulate.[5]

[5] See Harry W. Laidler, *Social-Economic Movements* (New York, 1944), chap. 40, "Recent Programs for Reconstruction and a Socialized Society," and Lewis Corey, *The Unfinished Task* (New York, 1942).

In American socialist writing, it has not been unusual to try to vindicate the idea of socialist revolution in terms of the American revolutionary tradition. The two, however, have little to do with each other. The American, or rather the Anglo-American, revolutionary tradition is essentially the assertion of the right of revolutionary resistance to "tyrants," that is, to governments that overstep their proper limits and invade the "inalienable" natural rights of the citizen. Revolution, in this sense, has nothing whatever to do with any historical dialectic. But the revolution of which socialism speaks is conceived as the "locomotive of history." It is essentially the new class, the proletariat, seizing power, as the agent of history, in order to inaugurate the new social order. Except for the fact that they both involve some sort of disturbance in the political status quo, there is no real connection between the two conceptions. It is, in fact, by contrasting one with the other that the true significance of either can best be brought out.

Socialists in the existing order. On the hither side of the revolution is the existing order, capitalist society. The socialist's attitude to the existing order is fundamentally ambiguous: in the final analysis, he stands *outside* of capitalist society, or rather (as Daniel Bell also points out in Chapter 6), he is *in* but not *of* it. In the socialist view, the existing order is already written off; it may linger on for a few decades, but it has already been condemned and consigned to destruction by history. The socialist's true commitment, his true allegiance, is elsewhere. Though living in the world of today, his real citizenship is in the socialist kingdom of the future, already prefigured in the international socialist movement. Socialist policy within the existing order must therefore, in principle at least, necessarily be an "interim" policy: essentially provisional, detached, and negative. Everything is staked on the revolution.

Gradualist socialism has naturally been rather uncomfortable with this "other-worldly" orientation. It has striven to be more affirmative, but insofar as it has remained socialistic, never quite wholeheartedly. The true socialist faith, hope, and interest are necessarily fixed upon the world to come.

The spiritual alienation of the socialist from the existing order has survived all revisions of political philosophy and doctrine. It has been as strong and well marked in America as elsewhere. It has survived, at least in sentiment, the Roosevelt New Deal, which incorporated so many socialists into the governmental machinery, and World War II, which no socialist, unless he were a pacifist, could really make up his mind to oppose. In one form or another, it is the enduring mark of the socialist outlook.

The dominant institution of the existing order is the state, and the state, in standard Marxist doctrine, is the "instrument of the ruling class." On this all shades of American socialism have agreed[6]—from the S.L.P. to the communists, from the I.W.W. to the old-line, "pure and simple" trade unionists. Where they have differed is in their views on what to do about the state. The orthodox socialist position, prevalent in the Socialist and Socialist Labor parties and registered in the various communist programs, is that the ruling class must be "overthrown" and the state "captured" through the revolution; until that is achieved, the existing state remains the enemy. Reformist socialism, on the other hand, has insisted that it is possible to "permeate" gradually the existing state and in this way neutralize its capitalist character. In practice, there has usually been little difference between the two views since both permitted participation in parliamentary elections and other forms of political activity.

An altogether different attitude has traditionally been taken by syndicalist and anarchist groups in this country. In their view, the state cannot be either captured or won over; it must be "abolished," destroyed. Political activity in the ordinary sense cannot therefore enter into truly revolutionary strategy: the genuine revolutionary turns his back upon the state as an implacable enemy and a vicious parasitical growth upon society. It is curious to note how similar—aside from the revolutionary flourishes—was the attitude of original, pure and simple unionism. The early leaders of the American Federation of Labor were convinced that the government was hostile to the workingmen and that little could be expected from it. They might attempt to exert political pressure in order to remove obstacles in the way of the free functioning of trade unions but they never looked to the government to achieve their purposes for them. At bottom, they distrusted government and relied only on the power they could accumulate through organization on the economic field.[7] The authentically syndicalist cast of their thought cannot possibly be overlooked.

[6] The following characterization of the state and other "bourgeois" institutions, contained in the 1912 platform of the Socialist Party, would, until not so very long ago, have been endorsed by virtually every section of the socialist and labor movements: "The capitalist class, though few in number, absolutely controls the government—legislative, executive and judicial. This class owns the machinery for gathering and disseminating news through its organized press. It subsidizes the seats of learning—the colleges and schools—even religious and moral agencies."

[7] Compare the following two pronouncements, the first by William D. Haywood, "revolutionary" leader of the I.W.W., the second by Samuel Gompers, "conservative" leader of the A.F.L.:

"I don't go into the halls of parliament to make laws to govern the working class. . . . Just think: the miners went into session in their union hall and passed an eight-hour law. . . . And that law has proved to be court-decision proof. It's never been

Closely connected with the attitude toward the state is the problem of the road socialism must take in order to win power. Orthodox socialism in America has always stressed the democratic procedures prescribed by law and custom, primarily participation in local, state, and national elections. This conception of capturing the state by electing a socialist Congress and a socialist President very soon became fixed dogma for the Socialist Labor Party and was largely taken for granted by the non-syndicalist sections of the Socialist Party until the Russian Revolution.[8] The syndicalists, on the other hand, since they "denied" the state and abjured political activity, took a very different line. The revolutionary syndicalists of the I.W.W. dreamed of the ultimate overthrow of the capitalist system; the gradualist syndicalists of the A.F.L. strove to emancipate labor through a continuous struggle for "more, more, here and now." Both, however, placed their ultimate reliance on direct action, on industrial organization, on the strike and sabotage.

The divergence between orthodox socialism and syndicalism on this question is illustrated in American annals by two episodes of more than ordinary interest. When in 1905 the Industrial Workers of the World was formed with the support of Debs, De Leon, the Western Federation of Miners, and others, its preamble specifically described the class struggle as taking place "on the political as well as on the industrial field." De Leon's picture was quite clear: the Socialist Labor Party, by winning elections, would make the revolution, capture the state, and then—*abolish* it. Meanwhile, the Industrial Union organization, such as it was hoped the I.W.W. would become, would "take and hold" the industries of the nation and operate the new Industrial Republic. This was De Leon's idea but it was not the notion of Bill Haywood, Vincent St. John, and other syndicalists. They saw no reason for any political party whatever, not even for a socialist party. They thought that the revolutionary I.W.W. could accomplish both tasks together—overthrow the state through direct action (general strike) and then run the new order as an industrial commonwealth. Within a year, the battle was out in the open. In 1906 and 1908 serious splits took place in the I.W.W.; in the end the political reference was cut out of the preamble. The I.W.W. became a purely

---

declared unconstitutional by any supreme court. . ." (*International Socialist Review*, Feb. 1912, p. 466).

"Marx did not beguile himself into thinking the ballot was all-powerful. He grasped the principle that the trade union was the immediate and practical agency which could bring the wage-earners a better life" (*Seventy Years of Life and Labor*, I, p. 83).

[8] On this, all except syndicalists and anarchists agreed—until the coming of the communists. The following passage from the famous article II, section 6, added to the constitution of the Socialist Party by its 1912 convention, gives the normative attitude of pre-1917 American socialism on the strategy of revolution: "Political action shall be construed to mean participation in elections for public office and practical legislative and administrative work along the lines of the Socialist Party platform."

syndicalist, antipolitical organization and De Leon went his way to set up his own Socialist Labor Party industrial union.

Within the Socialist Party, a very similar battle had to be fought out. The formation and early struggles of the I.W.W. had strengthened the syndicalist elements in the Socialist Party. Haywood, Frank Bohn, and their friends—with the partial approval of Debs—were preaching straight syndicalism: direct action, sabotage, force and violence. The more thoughtful leaders of the party were seriously disturbed, and at the 1912 convention in Indianapolis they procured the passage by a huge majority of an amendment to the party constitution rendering liable to expulsion "any member of the party who opposes political action or advocates crime, sabotage or other methods of violence as a weapon of the working class to aid in its emancipation."[9] On the basis of this decision, Haywood was recalled from the national executive committee of the party early the next year.

Thus both the Socialist Party and the Socialist Labor Party decisively effected their separation from syndicalism, each in its own way. The emergence of doctrinaire communism in 1918 and 1919 brought about a radical change in the situation. The communist strategy of proletarian revolution, as laid down in the writings of the Russian Bolsheviks and the theses of the Communist International, sought to combine all forms of mass activity—political as well as direct action—for the revolutionary objective. But one thing it insisted upon as a fixed dogma: the revolution could not be accomplished peacefully, without force and violence. American socialists had generally conceived the triumph of socialism as a peaceful, constitutional, and democratic process. True, there had been warnings that if "the capitalists try to steal the elections or refuse to recognize the verdict at the polls," the workers might have to use force to bring them to their senses,[10] but this was altogether different from making proletarian insurrection a matter of fundamental principle. Amidst the political convulsions that followed World War I, the communist position gained in plausibility and won the support of large numbers of socialists and syndicalists. The recession of the revolutionary wave, however, had its effects, and despite the flurry of "revolutionism" in the Socialist Party in the early 1930's, the insurrectionist dogma has virtually dropped out of

[9] The 1908 convention of the Socialist Party had already amended the constitution to the effect that "any member of the party who opposes political action as a weapon of the working class to aid in its emancipation" would be "expelled from membership in the party," but this provision had not proved adequate. The passage on "crime, sabotage, or other method of violence" was thereupon added. The section was repealed at the St. Louis convention in 1917, under the influence of the prevalent radicalism.

[10] Victor Berger is credited with this remark, which fell in with the thinking of most socialists. Daniel De Leon, however, relied on his Industrial Union to block a capitalist rebellion.

the political theory of all but the Trotskyites. It still, however, remains a part of the communist program.

Because the true concern of the socialist is fixed on the world to come, the problem of living and working in this world becomes a very perplexing one. In harmony with its basic orientation, orthodox socialism can engage in but one really legitimate form of activity in the existing order—preparing for the revolution. In strict logic, therefore, "immediate" or "partial" demands—that is, demands that fall short of the socialist goal and may thus be granted within the framework of the capitalist system—can have no place in the socialist program. In fact, since 1900 the Socialist Labor Party has had but one demand in its election platforms: *the surrender of the capitalist class.*[11] But few other groups have managed to be so consistently self-denying.[12] Generally, ways have been found of justifying "immediate" demands as instrumental to the great goal. In the Socialist Party, such demands have been variously justified as helping to attract, mobilize, and train the masses, as serving to "expose the capitalist system," as creating improved conditions for revolutionary propaganda, and most curiously, even as a kind of socialist philanthropy.[13] Most of these arguments have also been used by syndicalists and communists, although the communist rationale of the "everyday struggle" has usually been cast in more "realistic," less humanitarian terms than is common in noncommunist circles.

However useful these justificatory devices may be for their purpose, they obviously cannot do away with the fact that in advancing "immediate" demands socialists are, in fact, affirming the present order and placing some degree of confidence in it. Between total repudiation in

[11] The phrase has varied but the principle is unalterable: ". . . the *only* issue, socialism or capitalism" (Platform of the Socialist Labor Party, 1944).

[12] In 1904, the Socialist Party convention did reduce its "immediate" demands to a single paragraph in its platform, but in 1908 a full program was restored.

[13] The following words of George Goebel at the 1901 socialist unity convention illustrate the various types of argument for "immediate" demands: "I don't care what kind of Kingdom of Heaven I am going to have; I am going to look after the poor devil alongside of me and do everything in my power to help him regardless of the Kingdom of Heaven he is going to have. . . . If I can get a man's mind along the line of municipal ownership and show him that there are good things in the movement after all, I have brought that man into the Kingdom. . . . You may talk as much as you please of the philosophy of poverty bringing men into socialism; my experience is that the man who works the fewest hours and gets the best wages and has the most money for books, is the man I have the best chance with."

At this same convention, A. M. Simons denounced such demands as "the sidetracking of the socialist movement, the turning aside of the forces of revolution," and Charles Saunders delivered himself of the following: "I stand for no immediate demands, or for only one immediate demand, and that is a complete surrender of the capitalist class. . . . Personally, I believe we cannot get anything from the capitalist class. . . . Even though we elect a whole city, it would make no difference to you or me as a workingman. Our conditions would be just the same."

principle and partial affirmation in practice, there is a gulf that is not easily bridged by any variety of socialism that remains close to its revolutionary origins.

Gradualism, indeed, is able to present its "immediate" demands with greater consistency, because to gradualism, whether of the socialist or trade-union variety, these "immediate" demands in their totality actually constitute the transition to socialism.[14] But in thus committing itself to positive work within the old order, gradualism leaves very little concrete meaning to the idea of the revolution. Neither, in fact, quite escapes the dilemma, which is inherent in the nature of socialism as an "otherworldly" movement forced to live and work in this world.

The very same dilemma is met on another level in connection with labor unions. Labor unions are, at bottom, but the organizational expression of "immediate" demands on the economic field. "Conservative" labor unions frankly avow this fact and "revolutionary" unions try to conjure it away with radical phrases, but the fact remains that *to the degree that they function as labor unions* they are both alike institutions of capitalism working within the framework of that system to improve the conditions of their members.

Daniel De Leon drew the logical consequences of the fundamental orientation he had given his party. For purposes of running the Industrial Republic of the future, the Socialist Labor Party would build its own industrial organization. But this organization would not waste its time fighting for "sops" and "stopgaps" in the form of improved conditions under capitalism. Labor unions that did take such things seriously were simply "capitalist organizations" and their leaders "labor lieutenants of the capitalist class."[15] In 1900, the Socialist Labor Party adopted a rule

---

[14] The difference between the orthodox and the gradualist positions on "immediate" demands can best be appreciated by comparing the viewpoint embodied in the 1908 platform of the Socialist Party with that of Morris Hillquit in his book, *Socialism in Theory and Practice* (New York, 1909), written about the same time.

The platform of the Socialist Party puts forward some twenty "immediate" demands as "measures calculated to strengthen the working class in its fight for the realization of [its] ultimate aim and to increase its power of resistance to capitalist oppression," and concludes: "Such measures of relief as we may be able to force from capitalism are but a preparation of the workers to seize the whole power of government in order that they may lay hold of the whole system of industry. . . ."

Hillquit (*op.cit.*, p. 102) sees the matter in a very different light. To him, "immediate" demands are *transition* demands—that is, "measures that are expected to effect this eventual transformation [from capitalism to socialism]."

[15] This classical phrase, so much admired by Lenin, still expresses the attitude of the Socialist Labor Party to labor unions. The resolution on strikes adopted by its national executive committee in May 1940 declares: ". . . among the subsidiary causes [which now reduce the workers to the status of wage slaves and which inescapably block their every attempt to throw off the yoke] stand out prominently the outworn craft unions and the reactionary so-called mass-organizations known as the

barring officers of "pure and simple" trade unions from its ranks and forbidding its own members to accept office in such organizations. The I.W.W. position was fundamentally the same except that in true syndicalist fashion it arrogated to itself the functions of both a revolutionary socialist party (to overthrow capitalism) and of a socialist industrial union (to administer the new social order). A certain amount of genuine trade-union activity, it is true, was carried on by the I.W.W. at the heyday of its existence in the years just before the outbreak of World War I, but this activity was always peripheral and was regarded as merely guerrilla warfare in the revolutionary class struggle.

Such revolutionary consistency found some echo in the Socialist Party among those elements who sympathized with the I.W.W., but by and large the party could not reconcile itself to turning its back on economic organizations embracing hundreds of thousands, and later millions, of bona fide proletarians. Its utter faith in the primacy of the economic and in the revolutionary role of the proletariat made that impossible.[16] The rationale that was developed to make sense of "immediate" demands in a revolutionary program was therefore extended to cover support of nonrevolutionary labor organizations in the revolutionary class struggle. But the situation has always been a difficult one, becoming virtually impossible when the unions, in pursuit of some legislative purpose, back "capitalist" (i.e., old-party) candidates in elections.

If a case of some plausibility can be made out for socialist support of "conservative" trade unions, it is much more difficult to justify socialist cooperation with nonsocialist *political* movements, no matter how liberal or progressive. On the principle of the class struggle, orthodox socialism must insist on uncompromising independence, on the categorical rejection of all "class collaboration." When to this consideration is added the reluctance of socialism to recognize overtly the propriety of "positive" work within the old order, it will be easily understood why the Socialist Labor Party has always rejected cooperation with nonparty groups and why, until 1921, no official approval could be obtained from the Socialist Party for such enterprises.[17] Where subsequently American socialism did

---

C.I.O. and kindred bodies. And last but not least, there stand as enemies of labor's emancipation from virtual economic serfdom the corrupt labor leaders."

[16] At the 1904 convention of the Socialist Party, the anti-trade-union resolution of the "impossibilist" faction received just a third of the votes (52 out of 159). This anti-union tendency never quite disappeared from the Socialist Party, but in later years it took the form of support of the "revolutionary" I.W.W. against the "reactionary" A.F.L.

[17] Local socialists had supported or participated in "progressive" and labor political movements before but not with national party approval. In 1907, the socialists refused to back the resolution for a labor party introduced at the A.F.L. convention. In 1908, they reversed themselves and backed such a proposal. By 1913, however, they had changed again.

permit cooperation with nonsocialist groups—for example, participation in farmer-labor or progressive movements—it was due either to the influence of gradualism or to the seepage of communist ideas of the "united front."[18]

For the communists, once they were forced by Lenin out of their early "ultraleftism," the question of "working in the unions" and cooperating with noncommunist organizations has been exclusively one of power strategy. In their official pronouncements, the American communists have never made any bones about admitting that a fundamental purpose of the "united front" tactics is to "expose the reformist leaders and win over the reformist masses." Until 1935, the "united front" was restricted to the working class and other "toiling" groups (such as peasants); in that year, however, in response to the fundamental change in Soviet foreign policy, the "Popular Front" idea was adopted and the coalition extended to embrace all sections of the population, even big capitalists, who were friendly to the Soviet Union. Since then, the scope of the "Popular Front" has varied with changing circumstances, but its constituting principle—"appeasement" of Soviet Russia—has remained the same. In any case, the power strategy of the communists makes it impossible to appraise communist policy in terms of the principles set forth in this chapter.

The quandary in which consistent socialism finds itself as a result of having to live and work in an order which is already condemned by history becomes truly unbearable in times of national excitement and war. At bottom, it will be remembered, socialism stands outside the national community, since the latter is a community of the existing order. To the national solidarity of capitalism it opposes the "international class solidarity of the proletariat" as the prefiguration of the fraternal harmony of the world socialist order of the future. In principle, therefore, revolutionary socialism cannot but be antinational, however much it may claim to be the exponent of the "higher" or "truer" welfare of the nation. Only to the degree that it is gradualistic in character, and therefore capable of envisioning its goal in terms of the piecemeal reconstruction of

---

According to the decision of the 1904 convention of the Socialist Party, no state or local organization could "under any circumstances fuse, combine or compromise with any other political party or organization," not even by refraining from making nominations, but this rule was repeatedly disregarded.

[18] The Socialist Party today favors building and participating in an independent "third" party but it does "not expect any serious 'new party' developments to take place on anything other than a basically socialist program" ("Political Policy Statement of the NEC," *Call*, May 28, 1947). The Social Democratic Federation is part of the Liberal Party in New York. Both distinctly repudiate communist "united front" tactics.

the national economy, can socialism with any consistency affirm the national interest and see any value in national solidarity.

This general attitude toward the nation governs in principle the socialist attitude to wars in which the nation is engaged. To orthodox socialism, the only "just" war—that is, the only war socialists can support and participate in—is the class war. This was the position of the great majority of American socialists during World War I,[19] although it was rather obscured in the equivocal pronouncements of the Socialist Party leadership. The Socialist Labor Party, in line with strict De Leonism, branded the war as the "product of capitalism" and washed its hands of the entire matter. However, the I.W.W., and later some of the future communists in the Socialist Party, carried the theoretical "rejection" of the war to the point of active revolutionary struggle against it.

Already in World War I, it was obvious that the theoretical socialist attitude to war was in practice considerably modified by a number of factors of varying weight. In the first place, there was the upsurge of patriotic emotion that accompanied America's entry into the war; large numbers of socialists, as Americans, could not escape its influence and soon converted their socialism into a creed of the "higher Americanism." Other socialists, more sophisticated in a Marxian sense, made learned arguments as to the duty of determining one's attitude by considerations of the "objective consequences" of the victory of one side or the other. Still others agreed in opposing the war but did so on pacifist grounds rather than for reasons of the revolutionary class struggle.

All of these "deviations" from the orthodox position, particularly the persuasive doctrine of "objective consequences," reappeared in far more vigorous form during America's participation in World War II. The Socialist Labor Party, of course, had nothing to add or subtract. But the

---

[19] "We therefore call upon the workers of all countries to refuse support to their governments in their wars. The wars of contending national groups of capitalists are not the concern of the workers. The only struggle which would justify the workers in taking up arms is the great struggle of the working class of the world to free itself from economic exploitation and political oppression. . . ."

This passage from the majority report of the committee on war and militarism at the emergency convention of the Socialist Party in St. Louis in April 1917 clearly states the orthodox socialist attitude. (The majority report was adopted by an overwhelming vote.) It also conveys very effectively the profound feeling of alienation characterizing the socialist's attitude to the existing order. All the more significant, therefore, is the fact that very much the same position was taken by the "conservative" Samuel Gompers almost on the eve of World War I. In *Labor in Europe and America* (New York, 1910), Gompers wrote: "[Workers] will forever refuse to kill one another merely because authority has put them in different uniforms. . . . They intend to resist stubbornly any reckless heads of state that may set out to employ them as mere counters in a clash of force over questions which are alien to their own great interest in social justice. On this point, 'the workingman has no country' " (pp. 276-77).

After the United States entered the world conflict in 1917, Gompers became one of the most vigorous proponents of the war.

overwhelming majority of other socialists—the right-wing Social Democratic Federation in its entirety and the great majority of the members of the left-wing Socialist Party—supported the war, though generally with a few saving reservations. Only the Trotskyites and some remnants of the I.W.W. held to the old-line revolutionary antiwar position, but the only actual opposition to the war came from groups of pacifists, primarily of religious inspiration.

Communism, which in this country took over the tradition of revolutionary opposition to war, maintained its theoretical intransigence until the middle 1930's when the new Soviet foreign policy brought to the fore the possibility of a war in which Stalin would be allied with some of the bourgeois powers. Leninist doctrine thereupon underwent rapid and radical modification so as to permit communist support of the bourgeois allies of the U.S.S.R. in such "mixed" wars. In effect, communist policy soon lost all grounding in principle and became avowedly no more than a reflection of the vicissitudes of Soviet diplomacy.

Even before the war against Hitler had wrought such havoc with traditional socialist thinking on war, nationalism, and the bourgeois state, the New Deal had brought vast ideological confusion in socialist ranks. Almost overnight, socialists, who had been proclaiming for years that any government under capitalism must be a capitalist government fundamentally inimical to the workers and that nothing good could be hoped for from the old capitalist parties, became enthusiastic supporters of the Roosevelt regime, many—yes, many "Militant" socialists—even accepting appointive office under it in some of the New Deal agencies that were springing up in Washington. No more shattering blow to socialist morale—based as it was on the *mystique* of intransigent class struggle—could be imagined. It left socialist principle in a state of utter chaos from which the movement has by no means yet recovered.

The engine of revolution in socialist theory is the proletarian class struggle and the vehicle as well as instrument of this struggle is the *movement*. All—socialists and syndicalists, gradualists and revolutionaries—have agreed on seeing the movement as at once a militant crusade to usher in the new society and a prefiguration of the future society within the present social order: as at once, so to speak, both the Saving Remnant and the beginnings of the Kingdom of Heaven. Wide differences, however, have existed as to the character and composition of the movement and particularly as to what part, if any, the party is to play within it.

In answer to the question "Who makes the revolution?" a large number of American socialists—including the I.W.W., left-wing elements in the Socialist Party, and most of the early communists—insisted that the dynamic factor was a revolutionary elite, the "conscious minority" in the frank syndicalist phrase, the "majority of the class-conscious prole-tariat" in the somewhat misleading communist formula. The predominant feeling, however, has always been that the revolutionary act would some-how be the work of the masses, of the "vast majority of the producers." By and large, it may be said that the more radical the sentiment, the more it has inclined toward some form of elite doctrine; only gradualism, in fact, has been able to give much concrete meaning to the "mass" theory through its conception of the revolution as the accumulation of piecemeal reforms achieved through the democratic process.

Syndicalists of the "revolutionary" I.W.W. as well as of the "conserva-tive" A.F.L. variety deny the necessity of a proletarian party and identify the movement with the industrial organization (labor unions). Non-syndicalists, however, have had the problem of relating party to move-ment. Until the rise of communism, the more or less general position was the one that had been developed by official German social democracy, the theory of coordinate "arms," according to which the party and the unions—sometimes the cooperatives were added—were independent but cooperating aspects of one all-embracing movement. This communism denied in toto. The party, in Leninist doctrine, was the "vanguard of the vanguard"—that is, the vanguard of the proletariat, which was itself the vanguard of the toiling masses. Indeed, it was the party that brought the idea of socialism to the proletariat, which of itself was held capable of rising only to the level of trade unionism. Consequently, the party had to exercise guidance and control over the movement through a network of party cells in all nonparty organizations. By a still further extension of the vanguard doctrine, the party leadership came to be regarded as the "vanguard of the vanguard of the vanguard," completing an authoritarian hierarchy with the "toiling masses" at the base and the party direction at the top. What this doctrine has meant for the regime and practical activ-ities of the Communist Party it is hardly necessary to relate. It may be of some importance to point out, however, that the Leninist "vanguard" theory has left its mark far beyond the bounds of official communism. The Trotskyites are openly committed to it and so in effect are a number of anti-Stalinist socialists who would be shocked if they knew the source of their views. It is a doctrine that fits in well with the pretensions of party interest.

Standing apart from the general stream of socialist thought on the rela-tion of party to movement has been the unchanging position of the Social-ist Labor Party. According to De Leonite teaching, which is, of course, normative in the S.L.P., the party and the Industrial Union have distinct, separate, and *successive* functions: the party works within the old order to capture the state and then, as its first act in power, abolishes itself and the state—whereupon the Industrial Union, built up under capitalism, comes forward to take over and run the new society.[20] Such a conception, it should be noted, rules out in advance any aspect or activity of the movement that cannot be included under either the party or the Industrial Union; there is neither need nor room for anything outside of these.

The new social order. On the other side of the revolution is the new world of socialism. Socialist theory, in America as elsewhere, has differed widely in its conception as to how the new social order was to be ushered in and established. The I.W.W. still speaks of the new order being erected "within the shell of the old." This formula was present in the original preamble of the I.W.W. constitution adopted in 1905 and represented the viewpoint not only of the syndicalists but of the Socialist Labor Party and considerable numbers in the Socialist Party as well. When De Leon and the I.W.W. theoreticians spoke of the embryo of the new order growing within the womb of capitalism, they referred specifically to the Industrial Union structure which they were building up along "scientific" lines.[21] Less dogmatic socialists included in the embryonic new order every form of government undertaking or cooperative venture they could think of; some in their enthusiasm even claimed large-scale trustified industry for the new order on the ground that such enterprise was already "objectively socialized." All, however, agreed in thinking of the revolution as primarily a clearing away of the obsolete capitalist framework so as to allow the matured collectivist setup free play—or, to use an image once popular in socialist propaganda, the revolution was the breaking of the shell of the egg to permit the newborn chick to emerge.

This concept, of course, implied that no real transition period from the old society to the new was required, or rather that this transition had already taken place within capitalism. On the morrow of the revolution, the new socialist order would be fully matured and ready to go forward in full swing. Many socialists, however, made a distinction between the conditions necessary for the *political* triumph of socialism and the conditions required for a firmly established socialist *economy.* They envisaged a longer or shorter transition period during which the political power

[20] This pattern of revolution, constructed by Daniel De Leon over forty years ago, is still held as basic party doctrine by the Socialist Labor Party and is presented in almost the very words of the master. See the resolution on strikes, referred to above, and the platform of the Socialist Labor Party for 1944.

[21] The manifesto of the founding convention of the I.W.W. in 1905 explained that the organization was to be "builded as the structure of socialist society, embracing within itself the working class in approximately the same groups and departments of industries that the workers would assume in the working class administration of the Cooperative Commonwealth."

of the socialist state would be utilized to build, extend, and secure the new collectivist institutions. With the Russian Revolution, this doctrine of postrevolutionary socialist construction became normative to communism and is more or less taken for granted in traditional socialist thinking today.

Collectivism is, of course, the keynote of the new social order. As I shall have occasion to point out more specifically below, orthodox socialism has always looked upon collectivism as not merely a new form of economic organization but as the veritable ethos of the society of the future, permeating the domains of economic, social, and spiritual life—a kind of higher existence as compared with the "selfishness" of "individualism." Warning voices against this collectivist *mystique* were never absent but only recently has the personalist, pluralist emphasis in socialism become a dominant theme.

The new social order was usually referred to by socialists as the Co-operative Commonwealth or the Industrial Republic. By the latter term it was intended to indicate that under socialism there would be no need for a political state since there would no longer be any classes or class oppression; the only direction society would require would be economic planning and administration. It seemed obvious to those possessed of an unquestioning faith in economic determinism that once economic injustice had been eliminated, an ideal state of spontaneous cooperation and un-coerced harmony could easily be achieved. Classes would disappear with the disappearance of capitalism; the state, even if not abolished outright, would soon "wither away"; a classless, stateless society would be ushered in, bringing with it peace, plenty, and untroubled happiness for ever and ever.[22]

All this was authentic socialist doctrine bearing the imprint of Marx and Engels themselves. It appealed to the ardent utopianism of the idealistic men and women who made up the rank and file of the movement and it received authoritative formulation in the pronouncements of socialist spokesmen. But it never went unchallenged. More critical minds raised a warning voice against the delusive optimism implied in these utopian visions and urged a more cautious political realism and a profounder view of human nature. "The modern state," Morris Hillquit concluded[23] after a gesture of formal endorsement of the classic Marxist doctrine, "exhibits

---

[22] No account is here taken of the distinction sometimes made between "socialism" and "communism" as earlier and later stages in the development of the new social order. Marx himself (*Critique of the Gotha Programme*) speaks of the "first" and "higher" phases of "communist society"—meaning by the former the condition of society "as it has just issued from capitalist society," by the latter the completion of the transitional process. In any case, the usage distinguishing between socialism and communism in this manner was almost unknown in America before the advent of communism. (For discussion of the history of the words *socialism* and *communism*, see the introduction to this volume.)

[23] Hillquit, *op.cit.*, pp. 98-100.

many features that seem to indicate . . . adaptability and vitality. The state, which came into being solely as an instrument of class repression, has gradually, and especially within the last centuries, assumed other important social functions, functions in which it largely represents society as a whole, and not any particular class of it. Even the element of coercion cannot be entirely absent in a socialist society, at least not as far as the human mind can at present conceive." But even Morris Hillquit was deeply affected by the prevailing climate of opinion in the socialist movement. He recognized that "socialism does not imply a state of universal harmony," as most socialists believed and preached, since "there will always be some infractions of the accepted canons of social morality." Yet he, too, believed that these infractions would be only sporadic: "There will be no universal economic motive for such infractions. They will cease to be the rule in human conduct and will become the exception."[24] For Hillquit, as for almost all of his fellow socialists, the only conceivable universal motive of antisocial conduct was economic!

In the minds of most American radicals, the idea of the stateless, classless society to be ushered in by socialism has generally been identified with the American ideal of equality. Yet the two are actually very different, reflecting profound differences in historical context and social aspiration. The American ideal of equality, generated out of the conditions of frontier life in a new unfettered world, has come to mean primarily equality of opportunity and the rejection of all distinctions not due to personal achievement. Socialism, on the other hand, arose in an established order of hardened class lines and has aimed at wiping out classes altogether and achieving a homogeneous community without internal differentiation. Striving, effort, "getting ahead" with a free field for everyone to rise according to his merit, are the distinctive marks of the American idea; security, freedom from care, and absence of contention characterize the socialist utopia. The goal, in the one case, is unimpeded class mobility; in the other, it is the elimination of classes. But since they both oppose established privilege and both resent existing prerogatives, it has not been difficult for the two to be confounded and merged in the thinking of American socialists.

Viewing as a whole the socialist scheme of historical development from competitive capitalism through revolution to the new social order of fraternal harmony, it is impossible not to see in this pattern a secularized version of the Judeo-Christian vision of the transfiguration of the world into "a new heaven and a new earth" in the Messianic age at the end of time. Socialism cannot be properly understood simply in terms of its own claim to be a strictly "scientific" doctrine working within the objective conditions of social development. Whatever may be the scientific relevance

[24] *Ibid.*, pp. 63-64.

of some of its insights and teachings, socialism as such is essentially one of the great secular religions of our time. Its dynamism, its faith, and its mythology it has taken over largely from the continuing religious tradition of Western civilization,[25] although in doing so it has reduced reality to the two-dimensional plane of socio-economic existence and thus lost sight of the self-transcending dimension of human life that characterizes man as a spiritual being. The desperate plight into which socialism has fallen in the course of the past three decades is at bottom the result of the utter collapse of the socialist ersatz religion under the impact of the crisis of our time.[26]

IV. Some Central Problems of Socialist Political Theory

It will be useful to supplement the above sketch of the chief operative ideas of socialist political theory with a brief discussion of some of its more crucial problems in the context of our recent experience.

Power, organization, freedom. Socialism, and American socialism particularly, has been almost entirely oblivious to the perils, ambiguities, and corruptions of power. The abuse of power being, in the socialist view, essentially a concomitant of *class* politics, it might naturally be expected to disappear with the abolition of classes and class privileges. Even Hillquit, for all his realism and political sophistication, could assert as a matter of obvious truth that "under socialism, there can be no party politics, in the present sense, and whatever abuses may develop in the administration of the state or the industries, can be *only* [my italics] casual, based on inexperience or error of judgment of the community or on personal incompetence, malice or ambition of the responsible officers. . . ."[27]

The syndicalists, it is true, inveighed against "politics" but their criticism was largely verbal since they too imagined that politics was a peculiarly capitalist disease which would disappear in their ideal society administered by the Industrial Union. With their simple faith in economic determinism, socialists and syndicalists alike failed to realize how deeply the power drive is rooted in the nature of man, much deeper than the superficial layers of economic interest through which it manifests itself in a commercial society; nor could they understand that power creates its own interest and feeds insatiably upon itself.

They failed, too, to see that the collectivism they were advocating might very well result in still further concentrating economic power and vesting it, together with the political power of society, in the hands of a group of

[25] See Will Herberg, "The Christian Mythology of Socialism," *Antioch Review*, III (Spring 1943), pp. 125-32.
[26] See Will Herberg, "The Crisis of Socialism," *Jewish Frontier*, XI (Sept. 1944), pp. 22-31.
[27] Hillquit, *op.cit.*, p. 33.

"managers" or administrators. Or rather they did not see why such an outcome should be viewed with any particular foreboding. Was not government by experts the enlightened, the "scientific" way of administering the affairs of society?

If socialism has been oblivious to the perils of power, it has been utterly blind to the ambivalence of organization. It has completely failed to understand the fundamental point made by John Dewey[28] that, while in the modern world, "individuals can be free only in connection with large-scale organizations . . . such organizations are limitations on freedom." The bureaucratic authoritarian potential inherent in organization has been almost entirely ignored by socialist thinkers: bureaucracy, like the abuse of power, has generally been taken to be the result of capitalist class rule and therefore intrinsically impossible in the future socialist order or in the movement which is its prefigurement. If there is one thing on which all sections of American socialists, laborites, and radicals have agreed, including even the "anti-authoritarian" anarchists, it is the worship of organization as the one appointed vehicle of salvation. A few "individualistic" intellectuals have on occasion raised their voices in dissent, but hitherto to very little effect.

In short, American socialism, like socialism everywhere, has held freedom, justice, and all the other social virtues to be sufficiently guaranteed by the abolition of capitalist private property and the inauguration of the new Cooperative Commonwealth. This naive confidence in the all-sufficiency of economic reform is, of course, rooted in the unshakable faith in the primacy of the economic that constitutes the first principle of the socialist creed. All social ills are, in the last analysis, held to be due to the iniquitous economic setup of society. Once the revolution has wiped out economic injustice, these ills will of course disappear, for with the removal of the cause the effects must go. In short, the state of unconditioned perfection, which in the Judeo-Christian vision comes at the *end* of history, socialism has placed *within* history and has therefore rendered itself incapable of understanding or grappling with the evils and shortcomings that are bound to arise in any society, even in the socialist utopia ushered in by the revolution. The socialist who, like Morris Hillquit, feels that the abuse of power under socialism can never be anything more than "casual," the labor leader who cannot understand why anyone should be disturbed at the consolidation of trade-union bureaucracy, and the sincere communist who quite simply writes off the most gruesome horrors of the Soviet regime as merely "transitional" phenomena, all illustrate the moral peril involved in trying to escape the relativities of history *within history* by absolutizing the relative. Socialism, in its aspect as secular religion, is particularly prone to this peril.

[28] John Dewey, *Freedom and Culture* (New York, 1939), p. 67.

Democracy: transitory institution or enduring human value? American socialists have generally taken democracy for granted, yet their attitude to it has been fundamentally ambiguous. In part, this has been due to the radical ambiguity inherent in the very concept of democracy; in part, however, it may be traced to the extreme sociological relativism that informs socialist thinking even on the popular level.

Democracy may be taken to mean the equalitarian mass state, the absolutism of popular sovereignty against which no individual or minority can conceivably claim any rights. But democracy may also be taken to mean a liberal, limited-power state, guaranteeing civil and political liberty, protecting the rights of individuals and groups against predatory minorities and oppressive majorities alike. The latter is the conception that has dominated Anglo-American liberalism and may be traced to Locke and earlier seventeenth-century English political thinkers; the former, stemming from Rousseau, has dominated French and Continental democratic thinking and finds its ultimate embodiment in the totalitarian mass state.

Until recently, when American socialists spoke up on behalf of democracy, it was popular absolutism they had in mind. Aside from the syndicalists, who exalted the "conscious minority" (elite) as the active force in all progress, American socialists almost without exception proclaimed themselves champions of the popular mass state. Their criticism of the existing order was basically that the economic class privileges involved in capitalist private property thwarted genuine popular sovereignty on the political field and rendered American "bourgeois" democracy a good deal of a sham. Only under socialism, where "there will be no separate economic classes with fixed and conflicting interests," Hillquit asserted,[29] "will the state represent the citizens" and be truly a "democratic state." Even those who, like the Socialist Labor Party, insisted that under socialism the state would utterly disappear, shared this general viewpoint. Only socialism could bring "real" democracy: only under socialism would the will of the people really prevail.

Committed so uncritically to the cult of popular absolutism, socialism could not look with favor upon any of the institutions that Anglo-American political experience had developed to restrain the omnipotence of the state and to protect individuals and minorities from the intolerance of majorities. The various constitutional devices limiting the powers of government and setting up systems of checks and balances were denounced by socialists as instruments of capitalist rule and reactionary

[29] Hillquit, *op.cit.*, p. 131. Startling as it may seem at first sight, this statement of the "opportunist" Hillquit is not so very different—except for its restraint of language—from the "revolutionary" affirmation of the "Militant" program adopted by the Socialist Party convention in 1934, which speaks of "replacing the bogus democracy of capitalist parliamentarism by a genuine workers democracy."

restraints on the popular will.[30] This hostile, antiliberal attitude was particularly marked among the more radical elements, but its influence can be traced even among such conservatives as the spokesmen of "pure and simple" unionism.

In denouncing the liberal conception of the limited-power state as merely a device of capitalist class rule, the socialists drew heavily on the then fashionable "economic interpretation" of the American Constitution and more generally upon the radical relativism implicit in Marxism. The constitutional state, the parliamentary system, as well as all of the liberal-democratic institutions and values, were they not after all no more than the political reflex of competitive capitalism? As such, they were not only thoroughly bourgeois in character but also mere transitory historical phenomena, bound to pass away with the passing of capitalism. Thus Marxist "historical materialism" combined with a quasi-religious cult of popular absolutism to devaluate in socialist eyes those very institutions and practices to which socialism owed its virtually unrestrained freedom of political agitation.

In recent times, however, primarily in response to the rise of a totalitarianism called socialist in Soviet Russia, a new appreciation of liberal democracy has arisen in the ranks of American socialists. In fact, it would not be too much to say that with those American socialists who are responsive to the lessons of experience—here one must exclude for different reasons the communists, the Socialist Labor Party, and the syndicalists of the I.W.W.—socialism has been virtually transformed into a neoliberal doctrine. Despite anything Marxism may have to say to the contrary, liberal-democratic concepts and values, even certain traditional bourgeois-democratic institutions, are held to have a significance that transcends the particular society that gave them birth and to be relevant to all societies striving to achieve freedom within social order, even to the socialist society of the future.[31]

[30] Thus the 1908 platform of the Socialist Party called for the abolition of the Senate, the deprivation of the Supreme Court of its right to pass on the constitutionality of legislation, the election of federal judges for short terms by popular vote, etc.—all in order to promote direct rule by the people.

[31] In the course of the recent unity negotiations between the Socialist Party and the Social Democratic Federation, agreement was reached on a statement on "Democracy and Socialism" which may be taken as expressing the view prevailing among American socialists today: ". . . the united party must be unequivocally democratic in principle and policy. . . . It must declare that democracy is an essential condition to the attainment of the socialist ideal. . . . Democracy means not merely majority rule but also protection of the rights of minorities and individuals. . . . Democracy is nowhere perfect and complete but insofar as it exists in any country, it provides the means for its own further development."

The entire statement may be found in "Hammer and Tongs," internal discussion supplement of the *Call* for April 23, 1947.

See also Corey, *op.cit.*, p. 293: "The democratic state is inseparable from parlia-

What kind of socialist state? The problem of democracy is closely connected in socialist thinking with the question as to what kind of state, if any, would prevail in the coming social order. The Socialist Labor Party and the I.W.W., it will be recalled, deny that such a question has any meaning since, in their view, the state as an institution is abolished just as soon as socialism triumphs politically, the administration of society being handed over to the Industrial Union. But the reality of the distinction may be doubted and we are still left with the question as to the nature and structure of the institution that will administer the public affairs of the future society.

In standard Marxist doctrine, a transition period is envisaged between the revolution and the definitive establishment of socialism. In this period, it is understood, a political state will be necessary to protect the revolution against attack and to effect the economic transformation. As the process of transformation proceeds, the old political functions of the state will disappear one after the other so that when the transition is completed, the state as such will have "withered away" and the affairs of society will be carried on through spontaneous and uncoerced cooperation.

This view was familiar to the more informed American socialists from the writings of Marx, Engels, Bebel, Kautsky, and other teachers, but it was rarely taken literally in any but the most rigidly doctrinaire circles. Many socialists agreed with Hillquit in regarding the socialist state as not merely a transition regime but in some sense a permanent political structure.

This problem was never formulated very precisely in American socialist thinking, to some extent because of the vast semantic confusion over the term "state." A much clearer difference of opinion developed over the sort of regime that the future socialist state, whether temporary or permanent, would require. Could the "old state machinery" of political democracy be "taken over"—of course in an improved and purified form— or would a "new type of state" have to be established in conformity with the revolutionary and proletarian tasks it would be called upon to accomplish? Until the Russian Revolution, this question meant whether the regime would be political or industrial in character. If entirely the latter, as the Socialist Labor Party and the syndicalists contended, the old political machinery would be useless and society would be run by a network of economic institutions. Most American socialists, however, thought of the tasks of the transition period as both political and industrial and therefore conceived of the future socialist state as primarily

---

mentary government with its system of checks and balances on arbitrary political power. Their breakdown, submergence and destruction mean an end to the politics of freedom and democracy."

513

a political democracy (parliamentarianism) modified so as to make it capable of handling its new "industrial" functions.

The Russian Revolution changed the entire complexion of the problem. It was now no longer a question of political versus industrial regime; the opposition now was between the socialist state as parliamentary democracy and the socialist state as an authoritarian class dictatorship. The Bolshevik position, which soon came to prevail in radical socialist circles in America, called for the "smashing of the old state machinery" and the establishment of the "dictatorship of the proletariat."

This fateful phrase had occurred several times in the writings of Marx and Engels without making much of an impression on American socialist thinking. Many had interpreted it as virtually identical with a parliamentary democracy following a socialist policy, while the Socialist Labor Party was certain that, for America, it meant, if anything at all, the De Leonite doctrine of the Industrial Republic.[32] But from 1917, the dictatorship of the proletariat came to mean one thing and one thing only—the Soviet power, or as it was generally referred to, the Soviet system.[33]

In revolutionary socialist teaching, the Soviet system as the dictatorship of the proletariat involved several things, often confounded: (1) the revolutionary social and economic purposes of the regime; (2) the arbitrary, dictatorial character of the regime, free from all restrictions of law or convention; (3) the elimination of all parliamentary-democratic forms and the concentration of absolute power into the hands of councils (soviets) of workers', soldiers' and peasants' deputies; (4) the direction

[32] Hillquit (op.cit., p. 103) apparently took "proletarian dictatorship" to refer not so much to the character of the state as to the violent methods by which the socialist state might in some countries have to be established. For the Socialist Labor Party view see the preface (1922) to the party's edition of Marx's The Gotha Program: "To the extent that the 'proletarian dictatorship' elsewhere may be required to meet the emergency created by a successful military insurrection or collapse of capitalism, to that same extent the Industrial Union fills the need here" (p. 9).

[33] Lenin's Soviet system is fundamentally different from De Leon's Industrial Union. The former is a political state established for the transition period; the latter is an economic apparatus intended as permanent administrative machinery of a new order in which there would be no administration that was not economic. In every other way, too, the two were utterly different: Lenin thought only in terms of violent insurrection, De Leon rejected such methods and pinned his faith on the "civilized weapon" of the ballot; Lenin advocated presenting "immediate" demands and "working in" nonrevolutionary organizations, De Leon rejected both; Lenin made much of the peasants (farmers) as an auxiliary to the proletariat, De Leon counted only on the industrial workers; Lenin was extremely flexible in tactics, De Leon utterly rigid; and so on. The effort to make De Leon out as somehow kindred to Lenin is based on a few careless remarks by the latter, inflated and misrepresented by enthusiastic journalists. (See the excerpts on page 56 of the Socialist Labor Party's edition of Marx's The Gotha Program.) Lenin and De Leon did have one thing in common: they both claimed to be orthodox Marxists—but their orthodoxies were worlds apart.

514

of the total affairs of society by the "party of the proletariat," all other parties being outlawed as the expression of nonproletarian interests; and (5) the corporative structure of the new social order, in which the various functions of society were to be exercised by "autonomous" public institutions (in fact, agencies of the state). It is easy today to see how all of these things add up to a thoroughgoing collectivistic totalitarianism, after the disastrous development of the Russian Revolution has revealed the inner logic of the doctrine. But in the years following World War I, this was by no means obvious. In many ways, the Bolshevik interpretation of the "dictatorship of the proletariat" was in line with familiar socialist teaching. Had not the best socialist theoreticians insisted that parliamentary democracy was really *bourgeois* democracy and therefore both ephemeral and fraudulent? Did not Hillquit himself point out[34] that "modern party politics is . . . a manifestation of the capitalist mode of production and of the economic struggle of the classes and must disappear with the abolition of the present economic order"? Despite the opposition of the right-wing social democrats, who were influenced both by Kautskyan polemics and by the ruthless persecution of the centrist and right-wing socialists at the hands of the Bolsheviks in Russia, something very near to the Leninist conception of the "dictatorship of the proletariat" became current in American socialist thinking. As late as the early 1930's, the "Militants" and other left-wing elements who dominated the Socialist Party championed views closely related to the Leninist teaching. In the communist movement, of course, the Leninist doctrine in all its rigor early became standard dogma and has remained such to this day among the Stalinists and Trotskyists alike.

Before the Russian soviet system indelibly colored all socialist thinking on the new social order, there was a wide variety of views among American socialists on the structure of the future state. All more or less agreed that with the revolution there would begin a process of systematic supersession of the political functions of the state by the functions of economic management; in Engels' phrase, "the government of persons [would be] replaced by the administration of things."[35] The state, reflecting this fundamental social process, would be dual—politico-economic—in character. "The socialist parliament," Hillquit teaches,[36] following Benoit Malon and other European socialist writers, "will remain bicameral—the political chamber taking the place of the lower house and the economic chamber that of the upper house. . . ." "Under socialism," he adds, "the industrial activities of the government are bound to increase and the political activities to diminish." More recent socialist thinking—influenced,

---

[34] Hillquit, *op.cit.*, p. 33.
[35] Friedrich Engels, *Socialism, Utopian and Scientific* (Chicago, 1908), pp. 128-29.
[36] Hillquit, *op.cit.*, pp. 141-42.

no doubt, by the New Deal—has tended to emphasize the role of semi-autonomous agencies and authorities in the apparatus of socialist administration without radically changing the basic concept.[37]

This doctrine of a mixed politico-syndical regime under socialism, bearing a strong resemblance to modern corporativist teaching, was sometimes supplemented by a characteristic faith in the bureaucrat. "The most important work of legislation and administration," Hillquit suggests, following Wilhelm Liebknecht, "will be performed by committees of experts instead of parliaments."[38]

The dual type of state—with territorial representation of the people as citizens and syndical representation as producers—was rejected by the Socialist Labor Party and the I.W.W. Both took the straight syndicalist position that under socialism men would be essentially producers so that a system of syndical corporativism through an all-embracing Industrial Union would be all that was called for.

The tendency of American socialism, though not necessarily its theory, has been largely centralist. The Marxist tradition, it is true, is ambiguous, including a highly centralist Jacobin as well as a decentralist Commune motif. In a rather simplified form, this double emphasis runs through American socialist theory.

Socialism in this country has generally been impatient of the marked anticentralist note in American political life. It has regarded such centrifugal elements as regionalism, states' rights, and our federalist tradition in general as mere relics of the past, particularly annoying as obstacles to social progress. Its own program of reform within the old order has been centralist in tendency, more out of an ingrained prepossession than out of deliberate intention.

On the other hand, in the socialist plan of the future society, some stress has usually been laid on elements making for administrative decentralization and even for devolution of function.[39] Yet for all that, the socialist state remains unitary, even when the state is the Industrial Union structure envisaged by the De Leonites. Until recently, guild socialism and anarcho-syndicalism, neither of which has ever had much influence in this country, were alone in showing much concern over the authoritarian perils of socialist centralism. Lately, however, a distinct

[37] Among "techniques of importance in building the structure of the new society," Norman Thomas (*We Have a Future* [Princeton, N.J., 1941], p. 134) lists "the device of the state (i.e., public) corporation, already in successful use in a number of fields." The Tennessee Valley Authority he recognizes as "an approximation of a socialist approach to a great economic problem" (*After the New Deal, What?* [New York, 1936], p. 18). See also his *The Truth about Socialism* (New York, 1943), pp. 16-17.

[38] Hillquit, *op.cit.*, pp. 142-43. Recent neoliberal socialism, however, is far more suspicious of rule by bureaucratic experts. See Corey, *op.cit.*, pp. 293-96.

[39] Hillquit, *op.cit.*, pp. 32, 134-35.

pluralistic note has been struck in American socialist thinking with the renewed emphasis on liberal democratic values.[40]

Individual–State–Society. In theory, socialism has always made a sharp distinction between state and society. Both Marx and Engels rejected the idealistic identification of the two and insisted that the state was simply a special (political) agency of society. But in practice, this all-important distinction was frequently blurred and the confusion gradually infected theory as well.[41] In America as elsewhere "social responsibility" soon came to mean the responsibility of the state, and the "duties of society" to be conceived as capable of fulfillment only by the government. A distinct note of organicism that would have horrified Marx began to creep into socialist teaching, to such an extent that Hillquit could actually speak of the state[42] as representing not only "the collective mind and attainments of all past generations but also the collective intellect, will and powers of its present living, feeling and thinking members." "The individual man is the child and creature of the state and tied to it with every fiber of his existence," was his conclusion. Even the doctrinaire syndicalists who "rejected" the state were guilty of the same tendency, for their rejection was in effect simply of the parliamentary ("political") form of the state; in their ideal social order, society was identified with an all-inclusive corporative-syndical structure, more pervasive but no more spontaneous or voluntary than the ordinary state. Again it was not until the rise of a neoliberal trend in socialism in recent years that an earnest effort was made by socialist thinkers to delimit and define the place of the state in social life.[43]

[40] As representative of the new pluralist decentralist emphasis see *Democracy Is Not Doomed* by Judah Drob and Travers Clement, an official publication of the Socialist Party: "Centralization is a great enemy of democracy" (p. 12). "There must be the development of diversified forms of organization, the decentralization of authority and the authorization of local and regional agencies for doing things that are local and regional" (p. 23).

Corey, *op.cit.*, in chaps. 17 and 18, develops this new approach in detail. See also Norman Thomas' works referred to above, particularly *We Have a Future*, chap. 7.

[41] "For the purposes of the present discussion," Hillquit says at the opening of his section on "The Individual and Society" (*op.cit.*, p. 18), "the terms [society and state] are here employed interchangeably."

[42] *Ibid.*, pp. 21, 24. Yet Hillquit himself found it necessary to criticize the "extreme sociocratic views" of other socialist writers (p. 23). Such an extreme organismic position was advocated by Ramsay MacDonald, then leader of the British Independent Labour Party, whose writings had wide influence in this country: "The state organization should be regarded as being of an organic type. . . . In the eyes of the state, the individual is not an end in himself but the means to 'that far-off divine event toward which the whole creation moves.' . . . The state represents the political personality of the whole. . . . It thinks and feels for the whole" (*Socialism and Government* [London, 1909], chap. 1).

[43] See Corey, *op.cit.*, chap. 18.

Reflecting its organismic leanings, American socialist thinking has been distinctly antipersonalist in its direction, despite the fact that the official ultimate goal of socialism has from the very beginning been the liberation of man. Socialists have only too readily acknowledged the totalitarian claims of society over the individual. They have taken it for granted as the fundamental article in the "progressive" creed that collective activity is intrinsically better than individual effort and that "individualism" is the cardinal sin. Sharing the ethos of modern "social consciousness," they have tended to regard individual self-reliance or personal autonomy in any form as a kind of "antisocial" defiance of society to be tolerated only where the latter has not yet found it necessary to take over the activity involved. Anarchists have been quite as enthusiastic as the more conventional socialists in championing the claims of the collectivity, for although anarchists "deny" the state, they, like the others, adore society.

Nowhere outside the totalitarian states did the total absorption of the individual in the group go as far as in the well-organized socialist movement of former years. It was German social democracy that first began the "politicalization" of everyday life and the "coordination" of the social activities of the masses. A vast network of special organizations—socialist fronts—was painstakingly built up, from trade unions and cooperatives to Socialist Sunday Schools for children, all part of the movement and all controlled by the party. No social interest was ignored, no corner of life overlooked.

In this country, of course, socialism was much weaker and could not boast of so grandiose an achievement of organization. But the spirit was the same: "Everything in and through the movement—nothing outside the movement." It was only when some of the more thoughtful socialists began to see how thoroughly totalitarian this formula really was—how, indeed, it became the very formula of totalitarianism once the movement became the state, that is, once the revolution had been accomplished—that a genuine socialist challenge to the conventional "social-mindedness" was raised. The neoliberal trend in contemporary American socialism is also strongly personalistic in emphasis.[44]

V. Socialist Theory and American Life

American socialist theory shows relatively few signs of the impact of the specific conditions of American life. The main body of socialist thought in this country has always been almost entirely European in origin; American influences have been rather secondary and incidental despite the frequent efforts of American socialists to "Americanize" their doctrine.

[44] See Will Herberg, "Personalism against Totalitarianism," *Politics*, II (Dec. 1945), pp. 369-74; also his "Crucial Question," *Commonweal*, XLIII (Feb. 22, 1946), pp. 473-76.

The central core of standard socialist doctrine is essentially international. It arose in the context of nineteenth-century European life and was brought to America as a ready-made intellectual product; it never lost the marks of its European origin.

American bourgeois political philosophies are, of course, also largely of foreign origin; but the teachings of Hobbes and Locke, of Montesquieu and the *philosophes*, of the nineteenth-century liberals and nationalists, were soon assimilated and thereafter developed as native growths. The foreign influence in socialist ideology came relatively late and was never thoroughly assimilated into a distinctively American socialist philosophy. Noteworthy American socialist thinkers there have always been, but the direction, idiom, and content of the writings of even the most independent of these bear the unmistakable imprint of Marx, Engels, Kautsky, and Lenin. Indeed, the most influential works of socialist education in this country have been the writings of these European ideologists.

The basic teachings of socialism were not merely of European origin; they were brought to this country and propagated by successive waves of European immigration. An analysis of the ideas current in American labor and socialist circles in terms of their provenance would prove most revealing. It would show how deeply the intellectual development of the socialist movement was affected by the interplay of diverse German, Russian, British, and French influences. The social forces of American life made themselves felt, of course, but only by assuming the garb and idiom of standard socialist ideology.

Yet certain important effects of American life on socialist thought can be traced. The early achievement of political democracy in America encouraged two very different kinds of attitude among socialists. On the one hand, it nourished naively "reformist" notions as to the all-sufficiency of universal suffrage for the salvation of society; on the other hand, upon the inevitable disappointment of such hopes, it led to a sweeping disparagement of parliamentarianism and "formal" democracy. Democratic demands naturally played no such role in American socialist agitation as they did in Europe.

The advanced stage of American industrial development has also had a noticeable influence on socialist theory. Socialism, in American thinking, has been conceived as simply a matter of "taking over the trusts"— that is, of transferring the ownership and control of centralized, trustified industry from private corporations to the "public" (state).[45] It has appeared, therefore, entirely a question of the radical reconstruction of existing property relations rather than as the construction of a new socialist economy. The Socialist Labor Party and the I.W.W., it will be remembered, carried this view to its logical if somewhat implausible extreme by insisting that the *only* act of the revolution would be to abolish

[45] Cf. Laidler, *Social-Economic Movements*, pp. 658ff.

the state and to let the Industrial Union, carefully built up in advance, take over society.

Deliberate attempts to "Americanize" socialist theory by recasting it along more familiar American lines have not been unknown although they have proved of relatively little significance. Eugene Victor Debs, Oscar Ameringer, and others infused a strong native populistic strain into the socialism of their time. William English Walling in 1913 and Sidney Hook much more impressively some two decades later tried to restate Marxist theory in pragmatist terms.[46] Technocratically-minded people inside and outside the socialist movement strove in the years of the great depression to launch a socialism of Veblenian inspiration. But all to little practical effect. A revision of traditional socialist thinking is under way today but it is no more specifically American than the old-line Marxism of yesterday.

Perhaps the deepest and most significant effect of the American spirit upon socialism in this country is the distinctively optimistic tone that has characterized American socialism in contrast to the profound cultural pessimism of European radicalism. Buoyancy, hopefulness, and a rather unsophisticated trust in the future have distinguished American socialist expression as they have distinguished American political expression generally. Whether the events of the past three decades have worked a change in the temper of America, socialist and nonsocialist alike, it is still too early to tell.

In their own right as an independent factor in politics, the role of the various groups here considered—aside from the American Federation of Labor—has been rather slight. Before World War I, a number of municipal administrations fell under socialist control, the party elected some score of state legislators and local officials as well as one or two congressmen; Milwaukee, Reading, and Bridgeport continued this tendency into recent times. But by and large, it would be fair to say that no socialist organization in this country has ever been sufficiently significant itself to play a part of any consequence in American political life.

Yet the indirect influence of socialism has been far from trifling. Through socialist participation in third-party and labor-party movements, particularly since 1922, American politics has been in many ways significantly affected by radical groups which otherwise have maintained a largely peripheral existence. In the La Follette campaign of 1924 and in the New York American Labor and Liberal parties, for instance, socialists have exerted a tangible influence on "practical" politics. Communist infiltration and "front" activities have had an even wider sphere of operations, but here again their activities can hardly be appraised in terms of traditional socialist tactics.

[46] William English Walling, *The Larger Aspects of Socialism* (New York, 1913); Sidney Hook, *Towards the Understanding of Karl Marx* (New York, 1933).

Far more important has been the general effect of socialist thought on American social and political life. It would not be too much to say that socialist agitation and propaganda have constituted the single most influential factor in the advance of American social reform. Untiring socialist criticism of existing conditions has invariably served as the main force in opening the way for reform legislation. In fact, every important economic and social reform that has been enacted into law in the past half-century was first raised as an "immediate" demand in some socialist program, whereupon it was invariably ridiculed as utopian and denounced as un-American. However peripheral may have been the role of American socialism in "practical" politics, it cannot be denied that the socialist movement has been pioneer and trail blazer in the field of social and economic reform.

Yet even here there is a certain ambiguity that cannot be ignored. In carrying on its valiant and unceasing fight for social reform, American socialism has contributed greatly to the promotion of the paternalistic "social-service" state. Every extension of governmental intervention in economic and social life it has hailed as a triumph of "social responsibility." By thus identifying the "social" (or "public") with the "governmental" and constantly insisting on public action to remedy social ills, socialism has helped exalt governmental intervention into an infallible panacea and thus to fortify the trend toward the omnicompetent state with totalitarian claims upon every aspect of human life. Recent socialist thinking has shown an awareness of this pitfall.

VI. New Departures in Socialist Theory

Nearly all of the problems raised in the course of this chapter have in one way or another been found to involve the same radical ambiguity in the meaning of socialism: *Is it libertarian and personalistic in its implications or does it all add up to a program of regimented totalitarianism?* Collectivism, which is the economic groundwork of socialism, would seem to possess a double potential: on the one hand, it is necessary to assure a wider area of genuine freedom under modern industrial conditions; on the other, it makes for the further devaluation of the individual and his subjection to society and the state. Until the Russian Revolution, this inherent ambivalence in the socialist idea was ignored or lightly disposed of by most socialist thinkers. Such an attitude was no longer possible after the rise of Soviet and Nazi totalitarianism, each claiming to be the true embodiment of the socialist idea. A systematic reexamination of the fundamental principles of socialism—not merely economic and political but philosophical as well—became urgently necessary if the movement was ever to regain its morale and intellectual self-respect. As a result of this process of radical revaluation, which is still under way, two new tendencies in socialist thinking have emerged in recent years which give promise of the ultimate rehabilitation of American socialist thought.

The first of these is what one might call *neoliberal socialism*. Neoliberal socialism is predicated on the principle to which modern socialism as such owes its original inspiration—that it is the aim and purpose of socialism to enhance the effective freedom of the individual. Only, instead of taking freedom for granted as the automatic consequence of economic collectivism, neoliberal socialism understands that "freedom has to be planned as well as abundance or we shall have neither"[47] and that in planning freedom under collectivism the traditional values and institutions of liberal democracy are of the most vital and immediate relevance. In fact, neoliberal socialism can best be defined as an attempt to combine a limited or controlled collectivism with a strong emphasis on personalism, pluralism, and constitutional-democratic freedom. Nonparty socialist economists such as Lewis Corey and Abba Lerner, philosophers such as Sidney Hook, public men such as Norman Thomas represent this tendency; it may be regarded as dominant in the public expression, if not always in the party thinking, of both the right-wing Social Democratic Federation and the left-wing Socialist Party.[48]

Going beyond the neoliberal departure though sharing its libertarian stress, a number of outstanding theologians and social philosophers have recently endeavored to develop a *theologically grounded socialism*. Theologically grounded socialism represents an attempt to root socialism in a more adequate understanding of man's nature and life in society than has been possible for the secularistic philosophies of recent decades. Its effort is to incorporate the valid insights of Marxism, stripped of its materialism, utopianism, and moral relativism, in a profounder and more comprehensive social philosophy deriving its dynamic and its basic conceptions from the religious affirmations of the Judeo-Christian tradition. It is not Christian socialism in the usual sense for it does not regard socialism as the contemporary equivalent of the Christian witness. Rather does it attempt to see the goals and tasks of socialism, historically conditioned as they are, within the framework of an ultimate faith transcending and yet pertinent to all the relativities of life and history. Its leading spokesman in this country is Reinhold Niebuhr.[49]

[47] Bertram D. Wolfe, "Marx—the Man and His Legacy," *American Mercury*, LXV (Sept. 1947), pp. 368-74.

[48] The two socialist weeklies, the *New Leader* (Social Democratic Federation) and the *Call* (Socialist Party), express this tendency. It is also represented in variant forms in such independent radical journals as *Partisan Review, Politics, Modern Review*, etc.

[49] *Christianity and Society*, issued quarterly by the Fellowship of Socialist Christians, represents this trend. The writings of Reinhold Niebuhr and Eduard Heimann may be consulted. See also Will Herberg, "The Ethics of Power," *Jewish Frontier*, XII (Mar. 1945), pp. 19-23; and his "Democracy and the Nature of Man," *Christianity and Society*, XI (Fall 1946), pp. 12-19.

CHAPTER 11

Sociological Aspects
of American Socialist Theory and Practice

BY WILBERT E. MOORE

WILBERT E. MOORE is Professor of Sociology, and also Research Associate of the Office of Population Research, and a member of the Program in American Civilization, in Princeton University. The author of several books, his *Industrial Relations and the Social Order* (1946) has particular bearing on the field of his present essay.

For bibliography in Volume 2 relevant to Mr. Moore's essay, see especially PART V, General Reading and Topics; also PART IV, *passim*; PART II, Topics 8, 9, 10, 11, 12.

I T IS sometimes held that sociology as a field of learning has appeared late and slowly at some of the older private colleges and universities in the United States because of a common confusion between its name and "socialism." Whatever may be the merits of this particular line of interpretation, there may be more to the confusion than the mere similarity of name. The fact is that socialism, of whatever brand, offers a theory of society and that the problem of its relations to sociology as the "science of society" is intrinsic. It is not a question of tracing out implications at several removes from the original theory, or of discovering influences that are necessarily vague and difficult of proof. A socialist theory of the nature of the social order that claims to rest upon analysis of empirical evidence is also by definition a sociological theory. Logically its relevance is direct and largely independent of questions as to whether particular sociologists were or were not influenced by particular kinds of socialist movements.

There are indeed two principal points at which socialism challenges sociological analysis. The one has just been indicated: socialism as a theory of society and of social organization. The other relates to socialism as a movement, as an organization with an internal structure presumably having some relation to the appropriate organizational theories and with some discoverable relation to the society of which it is (however reluctantly) a part.

The duality of the challenge is clearly illustrated in "scientific" socialism. It is frequently difficult to distinguish Marx the analyst from Marx the propagandist, or Marxism as a theory and Marxism as a social movement. And although the distinction is useful and even necessary for purposes of analysis, major features of both aspects of socialism are relevant to sociological inquiry.

The organization of this essay reflects this duality. The first section is devoted to a sociological appraisal of socialist theory, with incidental attempts to indicate direct and indirect influences of the latter on the body of sociological principles. The second section is devoted to a somewhat sketchier review of socialist organizations and how they fit into a nonsocialist American society. In this connection, some attention will be given to the socialist clientele and to problems of how membership in socialist movements affects the member's relations with the existing social order.

The foregoing comprehensive program will be carried out in rather unequal detail in the pages that follow. It will be necessary to limit the presentation partly on grounds of expediency in terms of time and space, partly on grounds of ignorance. Much of the material that would be useful for a thoroughgoing appraisal of American socialism as a social movement does not exist in any accessible form, or at all. Much of the remainder is fragmentary, scattered, and difficult to interpret. It follows that this essay not only presents less than is sociologically known on its subject but also presents as hypotheses more than is known as verified information.

I. Socialist Theory of Society

Socialism in any of its forms always represents a theory of social or societal organization. However, in this respect there is a marked difference between the position of religious or secular utopian socialism on the one hand and "scientific" socialism on the other.[1] The utopians, strictly considered, and to a large extent the anarchists and syndicalists have only negatively and by implication a theory of the *existing* social order. Moreover, the theory of how their eventual "millennium" or utopia proceeds or develops from the existing order is either not explicit at all, or is commonly phrased as freeing human nature from restrictive bonds or actively changing human nature through conversion.

From the standpoint of sociological theory, therefore, utopian socialism is open to analysis only with respect to the projected result, the ideal society. This result is presumably subject to appraisal in terms of known principles of social structure. However, the Marxian position provides a social theory of the preexisting form and the intermediate process as well as of the millennial end product. It is accordingly amenable to empirical as well as purely analytical test whether such and such a situation does exist as distinct from whether a different situation could exist. The latter question is not without scientific interest, but the attempt to achieve a forthright answer is naturally somewhat hazardous. In any event, it provides a more limited basis of discussion than does a formula that claims to rest upon a scientific appraisal of an actual set of social conditions. The focus of the present treatment is therefore almost exclusively on the Marxian position.

By a sort of analytical abstraction, there are four principal fields of sociological inquiry to which Marxian theory is especially relevant: (1) the theory of social change, particularly with respect to "economic determinism" or "historical materialism"; (2) the theory of culture, especially with respect to ideologies and knowledge; (3) the sociological theory of economics, that is, the institutional and organizational features of economic activity; and (4) the theory of social stratification.

Since, despite inconsistencies and ambiguities, the Marxian theory as a whole is remarkably integrated, such a division does some violence to

[1] In some other respects the distinction is likely to break down under dispassionate analysis. Thus, for example, all socialists share a belief in an eventual "millennium" or utopia, and, although this is likely to be denied by orthodox followers of Marx, subscribe to certain ethical principles which are held as being not subject to question.

the Marxian position. In fact, it is not possible to discuss the theory from any of these points of view without some reference to the others. However, the primary focus of attention may shift from one to another aspect of the theory.

The discussion here will be mainly confined to the last two of the four fields indicated. These are selected because in the current sociological literature they have been treated less often and less satisfactorily than in the case of the first two.[2] Moreover, it appears on casual comparison that there has been less direct influence of the Marxian tradition on sociological theory itself in these fields and therefore that some degree of independent critical appraisal is afforded at the strictly theoretical level of discussion.

Sociological economics. If socialism of any brand presents a theory of society, a central element in that theory is necessarily concerned with the appropriate methods of organizing the production and distribution of economic goods and services. The "appropriate" methods are those that presumably lead to the socialist ideal of the good society, that help to usher in the millennium. Thus socialist theory is directly concerned with the relations between economy and society, and in opposition to theories that make of the economy an autonomous unit to be analyzed and judged independently of the social order of which it is the instrument. The socialist rejects, on either theoretical or normative grounds, the theory of economic individualism and the mechanical, atomistic conception of economic relations that is a prominent feature of classical and neoclassical economic doctrine.

This point of view is worked out most explicitly in the Marxian theory, precisely because it is at least as much concerned with analysis of the economic system that tends to minimize the social elements in the economic sphere (roughly, "capitalism") as it is with exposition of a social order that would set the matter right. In "scientific" socialism, economic production is recognized as social in the process as well as in the product.

[2] For a concise secondary presentation of the Marxian theory of social change, see Sidney Hook, *Towards the Understanding of Karl Marx* (New York, 1933), especially chaps. 9-13. For critical treatment from the standpoint of sociological theory, see Pitirim A. Sorokin, *Contemporary Sociological Theories* (New York, 1928), pp. 514-46; Sorokin, *Social and Cultural Dynamics*, IV, *Basic Problems, Principles and Methods* (New York, 1941), pp. 155-96, 302-21; R. M. MacIver, *Social Causation* (Boston, 1942), pp. 113-20; Wilbert E. Moore, "Sociology of Economic Organization," in Georges Gurvitch and Wilbert E. Moore, eds., *Twentieth Century Sociology* (New York, 1945), chap. 15, especially pp. 455-62.

The Marxian position on the role of ideologies and systems of knowledge as aspects of culture related to social organization is compared with several other theoretical positions by Robert K. Merton in his essay on "Sociology of Knowledge," in Gurvitch and Moore, *op.cit.*, chap. 13.

Perhaps the easiest approach to Marxian "sociological economics" is to determine what Marx considered to be the "economic factor" in social organization and social change.[3] The economic factor, according to Marx, is made up of three elements: conditions of production, forces of production, and relationships of production.[4] Of these he placed chief emphasis on the last as in a sense the embodiment or realization of the other two. The elements may be examined in turn as they relate to the social character of economic activity.

(1) The conditions of production, according to Marx, are those aspects of the nonsocial environment that are of use and importance to the productive order: natural resources, population in its quantitative aspects as a labor reservoir and minimum source of demand, and climate. As "conditions" their relevance for a given productive system is static; any variation in their significance is determined in every case by the prevailing state of technology, the system of economic distribution, the socially established training facilities for the potentially productive population, and the range and direction of the ends espoused by the system.

(2) The forces of production, according to the Marxian exposition, are chiefly to be found in the prevailing technology, plus the available skills and "traditions and ideologies." Taken in conjunction with the conditions of production, these forces constitute in the broadest sense the resources upon which production may depend. If limited to technology, however, the term "forces" implies a more dynamic role in determining the structure of a system than the essentially passive and instrumental character of technical knowledge could explain.[5] The ends to be pursued, the

[3] Marx's "sociological economics" is so basic to his whole appraisal of capitalism as a system and to his criticism and comments on theories and events of his time, that the brief outline of the elements significant for the present discussion represents a synthesis made up from various sources. For further elaboration, one should consult Karl Marx and Friedrich Engels, *Manifesto of the Communist Party* (Chicago, 1906); Marx, *Capital* (Chicago, 1906, 3 vols.); Marx, *Value, Price and Profit* (Chicago, n.d.); Marx, *A Contribution to the Critique of Political Economy* (New York, 1904), especially "Author's Preface" and "Appendix." Of secondary works, the following are perhaps most useful: Sidney Hook, *Towards the Understanding of Karl Marx* (New York, 1933), especially chap. 14, "Marx's Sociological Economics"; Joseph A. Schumpeter, *Capitalism, Socialism and Democracy* (New York, 1942), Pt. i, "The Marxian Doctrine"; Paul M. Sweezy, *The Theory of Capitalist Development: Principles of Marxian Political Economy* (New York, 1942). For a Marxian criticism of sociology, see Karl Korsh, "Leading Principles of Marxism: a Restatement," *Marxist Quarterly*, i (Oct.-Dec. 1937), pp. 356-78.

[4] Whatever else may be said about the Marxian theory of social change, it cannot be said from a close examination of Marx's work that by the economic factor he meant a naive economic determinism. Indeed, the extension and complexity of the economic factor makes critical appraisal of historical materialism extraordinarily difficult, and there is an understandable tendency for proponents of the view to shift grounds among the three elements (each of which is in fact a complex functional group of elements).

[5] A number of currently popular theories of social dynamics single out of the Marxian system the emphasis on technological development and thus adhere to a

interests to be served, must either be assumed or explicitly included in the analytical system. The Marxian theory actually does both by assuming the primacy of materialistic goals and by explicitly identifying those whose materialistic interests take precedence in a given system.

(3) It is, then, on the relationships of production that primary attention must be fixed. These are the relationships between persons in the productive system that determine the locus of direction, ownership, and control. As applied to capitalism, fundamental importance was attached to the facts that some ordered and others obeyed, that some owned the "means and instruments of production" and others, owning only their own labor, served them, and as a consequence that some received large monetary returns and others small. This became for Marx the central starting point not only of the economic analysis, but of the theory of social classes as well.

The relationships of production form, according to Marx, the basic structure upon which social organization rests, and the focal point of cultural elements. Legally, these relationships are expressed in the laws of property. Here, however, a difficulty in interpretation arises, namely, the assumption of "economic" primacy and the problem of its definition or identification. Thus Marx held that the laws of property were simply a "reflection" of the existing relationships, taken as given. Seemingly one could with as much reason maintain that the productive relationships are simply a reflection of the institutions of property, taken as given. Actually, Marx or Engels, his chief collaborator, did not deny, and, with reference to specific questions and events, forthrightly admitted a close functional correspondence between other aspects of social organization and the economic organization, and even that normative systems and ideologies would in concrete cases modify the productive structure.[6]

The way in which this seeming inconsistency with a strict historical materialism was resolved was by emphasis on fundamental verities and on chronology. The original Marxian position, informed in the German historical and idealistic tradition,[7] was abstract and dealt with fundamentals, with essential characteristics. Thus, deviations from the formulation could be admitted with reference to particular times and places, but

---

sort of "fetishism of machines" (an inherently expanding technology independent of social values and oblivious to the interests of inventors or the organizations of which they are a part) somewhat analogous to what Marx refers to as a "fetishism of commodities," to which the discussion returns below. Isolated passages in Marxian writings lend themselves to this kind of oversimplification, but the theoretical system as a whole does not. For criticism of the current theories, see Moore, "Sociology of Economic Organization," *loc. cit.*

[6] See Merton, *loc. cit.*

[7] See Talcott Parsons, *The Structure of Social Action* (New York, 1937), chap. 13, "The Idealistic Tradition," especially pp. 488-95.

the fundamental character of the relationship would assert itself in the long run. In these premises, any merely empirical criticism could be met with the admonition, "Wait a while." Thus the explanations, answers to queries, and exchanges of views abound in such revealing phrases as "in the last instance," the "decisive factor," "dominant influence," and the like.[8] These arguments tend to put the matter beyond empirical proof or disproof and to rest upon an act of faith or intuition.

However, of more immediate interest is an alternative solution that is at least equally intrinsic to the Marxian position. It consists of wedding all of those structural and normative elements most closely interdependent with production and exchange to the "economic factor" itself and then doing nothing by way of internal inquiry that might dissolve the union.

In a sense, Marx, the radical or extremist, stands midway between classical economic theory and modern sociological theory of economic relations. The Marxian economics emphasizes the social relationships and structural forms .that pervade the production and distribution of goods. Although abstract in other respects, the Marxian position in this instance is far more accurate and "realistic" than that represented by classical economic theory.

Whereas the classical theory assumed a particular institutional structure without adequate attention to the significance of its historical relativity, Marx made of that structure an intrinsic characteristic of a particular system of production.

Whereas the classical theory tended to view the whole economic system as a relationship among things in the wholly impersonal operation of the "market" (including the "labor market"), Marx insisted with devastating accuracy upon the relationships between persons that lay behind the theoretical façade. Thus, he made clear the inherent power relationship involved in the differential control of capital goods, a point consistently obscured by the theories of "private" property.[9] Similarly, he drew attention to the difference between a division of labor effected by the impersonal competition of independent producers and the division of labor effected by the administrative authority of the capitalist or manager within the productive establishment.[10] This point also was obscured by the preoccupation of economists with the abstract entrepreneur rather than with the laborer or with the enterprise as a cooperative system.

There is even in the Marxian analysis an emphasis upon the tendency of an elaborate division of labor to seek in the worker a single talent or

[8] See *Karl Marx and Friedrich Engels: Correspondence, 1846-1895; a Selection with Commentary and Notes* (New York, 1936).

[9] See Wilbert E. Moore, "The Emergence of New Property Conceptions in America," *Journal of Legal and Political Sociology*, Vol. 1, No. 3-4 (Apr. 1943), pp. 34-58.

[10] See Marx, *Capital*, I, chap. 14.

skill to the exclusion of the other talents and interests of the whole man—
a paradoxically individualistic note in the formulations of avowed collectivists. This is a point from which much of the current research and
theoretical development in "industrial sociology" takes its bearings, with
specific reference to the unreality of the "logic of economics" in social
relations.[11]

Marx's departure from the classical formulation is crystallized in his
discussion of the "fetishism of commodities." He writes, "A commodity
is therefore a mysterious thing simply because in it the social character
of men's labour appears to them as an objective character stamped upon
the product of that labour; because the relation of the producers to the
sum total of their own labour is presented to them as a social relation,
existing not between themselves, but between the products of their labour. . . . There is a definite social relation between men, that assumes, in
their eyes, the fantastic form of a relation between things. . . . This I
call the Fetishism which attaches itself to the products of labour, so soon
as they are produced as commodities, and which is therefore inseparable
from the production of commodities."[12] This "fetishism" is, according
to Marx, characteristic not only of the participant in the productive system, but of the mechanical models of the "bourgeois" economists as
well.

Here a rather extended "aside" may be appropriate. Marx's discussion
of the "fetishism of commodities" raises a problem of interpretation of an
order somewhat different from historical or philosophical questions as
to "what Marx really meant." It is essentially a problem in the role of
ideas or ideologies in social organization, and is in this instance peculiarly
relevant to the sociological theory of economic organization.

"Capitalism" in socialist theory, and in other discussions also, has at
least three distinguishable aspects: (a) a system of economic production
and exchange; (b) a theory of how the system operates; and (c) a set of
normative principles maintaining that the system of a right ought to work
according to the theory. Now Marx, true to his position with respect to
the functional or causal importance of the "economic factor," tends to
regard the theory and the ideology alike as dependent variables, as parts
of the "superstructure." Indeed, he tends at times to regard the two
"nonmaterial" aspects of capitalism as the same thing. No one who has
observed the emotional tone of the supporters of the theory of laissez faire
and its associated conceptions, or the attempts of the courts to make the
uncomfortable facts of economic activity conform with abstract principles,

---

[11] See, for example, F. J. Roethlisberger and William J. Dickson, *Management and
the Worker* (Cambridge, Mass., 1939); Wilbert E. Moore, *Industrial Relations and the
Social Order* (New York, 1946).

[12] Marx, *Capital*, I, p. 83. See also the discussion in Sweezy, *op.cit.*, pp. 34-40.

can deny the empirical support for the view that classical economics is at least occasionally the "theology" of capitalism.[13]

However, Marx, owing to his rather "integral" view of economic phenomena, not only fails to make explicit the analytical distinction between theory and ideology, but confuses the ideology and the structure to which it refers. In a sense, he accepts the classical theory as a valid exposition of the nature of economic relations under capitalism and condemns it as an ideology along with the system that it reflects or supports. Thus, the capitalist economy is atomistic and impersonal not only in classical theory, but in fact. Marx writes: "This Fetishism of commodities has its origin . . . in the peculiar social character of the labour that produces them. . . . The categories of bourgeois economy consist of such like forms. They are forms of thought expressing with social validity the conditions and relations of a definite, historically determined mode of production, viz., production of commodities. The whole mystery of commodities, all the magic and necromancy that surrounds the products of labour as long as they take the form of commodities, vanishes therefore, so soon as we come to other forms of production."[14] Here Marx seems to depart from his own analytical position, which emphasizes the sociological elements in *any* economic relations, and to consider it necessary to change the system in order to modify the theoretical exposition of its operation.[15]

The extended parenthesis on the "fetishism of commodities" has not

[13] See Hook, *op.cit.*, p. 189, where the author writes, "It is not only in Samuel Butler's satiric Utopia that human beings are the instruments of production used by machines for the manufacture of bigger and better machines. That is what they are in the practice and theory of commodity-producing societies. This is what Marx means when he calls bourgeois society a 'fetishism of commodities' and the orthodox 'science' of political economy, its theology."

See also Moore, *Industrial Relations and the Social Order*, pp. 35-42, 499-504.

[14] Marx, *Capital*, I, pp. 83, 87.

[15] Two explanations of this curious theoretical position may be suggested. They are not necessarily mutually exclusive alternatives. First, Marx was trained in the German idealistic and historical tradition, with its emphasis upon the historical relativity of all social scientific knowledge. (See Parsons, *op.cit.*, chap. 13.) To this point the discussion in the text returns below. Second, as noted earlier, it is always difficult to segregate Marx the analyst from Marx the exponent of a particular set of values, those associated with socialism. Thus, it being necessary to condemn capitalism, it becomes expedient to accept as valid the mechanistic theory of the operation of the system.

This second explanation is partially confirmed by the analogy of a quite different difficulty. Marx and the Marxians provide, on occasion, a sociologically acceptable explanation of the structural sources of individual motives and actions. The individual in a complex structure to a large degree acts as he must act in that situation. The capitalist can do no other: "It's the system." But this explanation has a limited appeal as a rallying point, for the "mobilization of affect." It is accordingly more common in the propaganda ("class education") to brand the capitalists as exploiters and bloated plutocrats and thus impugn their morals while personifying the expected conflict.

been entirely tangential to the point from which this discussion started: the intermediate position of Marxism with respect to classical economics on the one hand and modern sociological theory on the other. For the theoretical difficulties that appeared in the question of the validity of classical theory are pervasive in the Marxian analysis. They may be summarized as (a) the assimilation of institutions and values to the system of production, and (b) the limitation of all principles to a particular historical context.

If Marx, unlike the classical theorists, placed emphasis upon the differential allocation of property rights, the modes of division of labor, and the social character of exchange, he considered them as intrinsic to a particular productive system and thus a part of the complex that Marx viewed rather as an element or a factor. Modern sociological theory directs attention to the functional relationships *within* the complex. If norms and institutions have the status of completely dependent variables, then there is nothing further to understand. If they have a measure of independent variability, then the Marxian position is oversimplified in rather important respects.

Since scientific theory claims some relevance to empirical fact, an empirical test is in point. Such an approach indicates that the institutions of property, division of labor, and exchange are prior to any given entrant into the economic system, and to a certain extent prior to the system as a whole. Nor is this simply a persistence of archaic forms subject to modification in terms of economic interests. There are pressures for modifications of institutions in accordance with economic interests, but since these interests are, even in Marxian terms, dichotomous and in fact multifarious, the modifications can only be claimed to represent *the* dominant interest by assuming the point to be proved. That is, it is necessary to assume the primacy of a given set of productive relationships, and specifically that the state is the "executive committee" of the exploiting class.

The institutions relevant to economic activity are undergoing constant modifications, some of which are of a rather sweeping character, and these changes redefine the relationships of production. In American experience it is only necessary to refer to the impressive changes in the economy wrought by the legalization of collective bargaining, the narrowing of the conditions and terms of employment, the special limitations on the employment of women and children, the regulation of the kinds and qualities of commodities that have legal access to the market, and a multitude of similar changes.[16] Moreover, these changes are not simply

[16] See Moore, "The Emergence of New Property Conceptions in America," *loc.cit.*; Moore, *Industrial Relations and the Social Order*, chap. 12, "Wastes of Labor Resources," and chap. 23, "Social Controls of Industry."

a representation of the shifting balance of economic pressures. Such an interpretation misses the whole functional significance of institutions as normative complexes: they serve to regulate the internal relations of associations (including productive enterprises) in such a way as to achieve a working balance among associational interests (including far more than the economic) and conformity with the general value system of the society.

The sociologist proposes annulment of the forced marriage of the social structure and the productive system on other grounds as well. Marx's interpretation is always historically relative, as should be expected from the intellectual tradition from which he is a deviant only in limited respects. He accordingly rejects universally valid principles, except in the special case of the dialectical evolution growing out of the class struggle. If this means that a scientific principle is stated under the conditions to which it applies, this is an acceptable limitation. But this is somewhat different from the categorical rejection of repeatable conditions.

The power element in differential control over production, the inherent necessity of management or direction, the intrinsic character of the division of labor in industrial production, and the segmental character of personal participation in complex associations—these are more significant principles than Marx claimed. There is no theoretical or empirical basis for thinking that they are confined to the capitalist mode of production. The introduction of collective ownership does not remove differential control over production or the efficiency of occupational specialization; it simply changes, in admittedly important ways, the procedure by which the managers gain their right to manage and the sanctions for failure to do so effectively in terms of the given situation.

Although thinking of society as a system composed of functionally interdependent elements makes sense and constitutes a useful frame of reference for analysis, the nature and limits of the interdependence are subjects for inquiry and not to be assumed as following deductively from known changes in one element. Society is a looser system than a simple mechanical model or an organism. The Marxian theory of economic organization, by assuming an almost organic integration of social systems and a virtually unique historical occurrence of functional relationships, barred the type of analytical approach that attempts to discover universal principles, limits of variability, repeated processes, and the dynamic relations among societal elements. While opening the window upon the social elements in a particular economic system, it slammed the door upon a general theory of society.

The theory of social stratification. The Marxian theory of social classes stands in sharp contrast to the "sociological economics" with respect to the detail with which the theory has been worked out. Although the "class struggle" was central to the Marxian view of social change and presumably an inherent element in the capitalist mode of production,[17] there is more assertion than exposition and analysis in Marx's own writings, and more argument over method and program than over stratification theory itself among the disputing Marxian sects. Most of Marx's writings are indeed "about" class relations and the class struggle, once his position is assumed.[18] But that position is peculiarly abstract, as the following summary will show.

The "relationships of production" form, according to Marx, the basic structure upon which social organization rests, and the focal point of cultural elements. This is the basic formulation not only of the "sociological economics," but of the stratification theory as well. For Marx was primarily interested in *one* relationship which he thought took precedence over all the multitudinous interdependencies involved in the division and specialization of labor. That relationship was the one obtaining between the capitalists, who owned the means and instruments of production, and the proletarians, who owned only their own labor. These relations are expressed in things, but are actually between persons. The instruments owned by the capitalist (machinery of production) simply reflect the dominance and control exercised over the laborer.

Social class, to Marx, was an aggregate of persons playing the same part in production, that is, standing in the same relation to other persons in the same productive system. It is thus the different functions in the productive process that are basic to class differentiation. Such a characterization of social class leads to certain fundamental questions of various degrees of generality: (1) What is meant by the "same" part in production, or the "same" function in the productive process? (2) What then are the distinguishing criteria of class membership, and how can these be judged? (3) What characteristic differences, of significance for the social structure, follow from class membership so defined? That is, is this simply a statistical aggregate, with one common feature, or with a number of common features, or a genuine social group with definite internal relationships and common values? The answers to these and

[17] In the writings of Marx and Engels, see especially the *Communist Manifesto*, the author's preface to Marx's *A Contribution to the Critique of Political Economy*, and Marx's prefaces to the earlier editions of Vol. 1 of *Capital*. A fairly orthodox elaboration of the theory is that of Karl Kautsky, *The Class Struggle* (Chicago, 1910). See also Abraham Edel, "The Theory of Classes; a Logical Analysis," *Marxist Quarterly*, i (Apr.-June 1937), pp. 237-52.

[18] Thus Sweezy writes, "Almost the entire remainder of the first volume of *Capital* [after Pt. i on "Commodities"] is devoted to the capital-labor relation in its 'isolated' and 'purified' forms." *Op.cit.*, p. 18; italics omitted.

related questions will not only elucidate the Marxian analysis, but indicate its inadequacies as well.

Since the relationships of production upon which Marx placed primary emphasis were those between capital and labor, this is the clue to his reference to those playing the same part in production, for he did not mean *precisely* the same part in view of a complex division of labor. Thus in a modern cotton textile mill the spinners and weavers clearly do not play the same part in the production of cotton cloth, nor can they in any precise sense be said to perform the same function. Yet these, together with most of the other persons in this particular productive unit, and of all other productive units, constitute a single class. For they all stand in roughly the same position in regard to the owners of the instruments of production; all are subject to the authority of the capitalist, and none has control over his work—to say nothing of production in general. In other words, for Marx the *single important functional division* in production is that between the owners of capital and the propertyless laborers, whose labor is exploited by the capitalist.

The emphasis upon this single line of distinction between persons in productive enterprises presumably gives a clear-cut criterion for judgment of class position. Put simply, one either owns the machines or one serves them. Although the purpose of the productive process is presumably to produce goods and commodities, its unofficial function is to control wage labor, which has no access to productive instruments except as specified by the owner. In other words, this is an *exploitative* system in the full evaluative meaning of the term. The capitalists and proletarians do not form two classes which are simply higher and lower, respectively, but the dominance of the former is based on and used for the control and exploitation of the latter.[19]

Class membership and class distinctions, according to the Marxians, are therefore not based on occupation as such, since those of many occupations may stand in the same position in reference to the single line of demarcation which is claimed to be fundamental. Thus both the skilled mechanic and the unskilled sweep-up man turn out to be proletarians under the skin. Moreover, class is not to be judged in terms of wealth, although there is some correspondence between wealth or its absence and class position. The Marxian emphasis is on production, with

[19] The view that in the nature of the capitalistic system the upper (capitalistic) class "exploits" the lower (proletarian) class is justified by Marx by the "labor theory of value" and the "theory of surplus value." Put simply, and therefore a little unfairly, the contention is that the source of all value is in the labor expended, but that in the capitalistic system the laborer does not receive this full value. The employee is paid in wages only part of the value of the product (which his labor has exclusively established), and the capitalist appropriates the remainder or "surplus." See *Capital*, especially Vol. 1.

distribution presumably based on the productive system. Wealth, then, is not so much a point of concern to the revolutionary follower of Marx as is the power which made the accumulation of wealth possible.

It is true that Marx recognized the existence of more than two classes, defined even in his terms. His first formulation was that there were three principal classes—capitalists, landlords, and laborers. Others were to be regarded as vestigial remnants, or intermediary types. Even the landlords he thought of as remnants of a decadent system of production, who would either become allied with the capitalists or forced down into the proletariat. The Marxian emphasis is always dynamic, not static. If there were not concretely just two classes, that was because the superior competitive power of capitalistic production had not yet been fully realized. If there still existed a petty bourgeoisie of owners of small shops and tradespeople, these would either succeed in gaining full capitalistic position, or, more likely, be forced into the proletariat.[20] This is the doctrine developed in the *Communist Manifesto* that in the course of time the competition inherent in the capitalistic system would reduce the cleavage between classes to the single one noted: the owners versus the exploited.

In summary, then, a social class according to Marx is to be objectively defined in terms of the relationships of production. Specifically, the distinction which is regarded as of transcendent importance is that between the owners of the means and instruments of production, who are thereby in a superordinate position, and the "users" of the productive instruments, who have no control over their productive activities and are therefore in a subordinate position.

Marx and the Marxians do not stop with the "objective" definition of social classes, however, for they also maintain that class interests, culminating in an inevitable class struggle, follow from differences in objective position. This makes of the class something more than a statistical aggregate; it becomes an actual or potential social group by recognition of common interests and cooperative action for their achievement. Whether "class consciousness" follows automatically from the objective position, or needs fostering by the propaganda of education and active agitation, is a matter of significant doctrinal controversy that cannot be explored here.[21] It is perhaps sufficient to note that it is possible to subscribe both to the doctrine

---

[20] Marx discusses numerous classes in his *Revolution and Counter-Revolution* (Chicago, 1912), Sec. I, "Germany at the Outbreak of the Revolution." Even here, however, he groups them into three divisions: the capitalists and their allies, the proletarians both industrial and rural, and the intermediate petty bourgeoisie. In Sec. XVIII of the same work, on "Petty Traders," he indicates the vacillating role played by these intermediate groups in the German Revolution of 1848. See also Marx, *The Class Struggles in France (1848-1850)* (New York, 1934).

[21] See Merton, *loc.cit.*

of inevitability and to the necessity of agitation by differences in time reference. It is thus possible for the more enlightened to help the process along; this becomes a special application of the slogan, "Eventually, why not now?"

Since the Marxian analysis deals with "essences" and with dynamics "inherent" in a system, a merely empirical demonstration at a particular moment selected by the critic is not required. Any critical approach to the Marxian theory of social class must first recognize the form in which the model is cast. It is necessary to understand that the Marxian analysis is *abstract*. It seeks to find the "essential" characteristics of a system and not the empirically observable totality. Thus Marx did not concern himself with a functional theory of social stratification in general, or even with social differentiation within modern society. There is no direct attention to leadership, to inequalities of position within specialized organizations, or to the role of technical or functional superiority and inferiority in social systems.[22] It is also necessary to understand that the Marxian class theory is peculiarly relative with respect to the class system associated with any given system of production, and peculiarly universal with respect to the role of class struggle in the dialectical process of evolutionary change in all societies everywhere.

However, understanding a position does not force the scientific critic to appraise it exclusively on its own grounds, for one may also question whether the formulation contributes materially to scientific knowledge or whether other theories encompass more of the empirical reality and thus require fewer assumptions or fewer relevant conditions difficult to find in nature. Moreover, no Marxian would attempt to dodge an ultimate empirical test; on the contrary, the theory is claimed to have predictive value and to lead to a program of social action. It is therefore appropriate to subject the theory to both analytical and empirical scrutiny, and even, in view of the alleged inner dynamics of the productive system, to use contemporary facts as relevant to hypotheses now a full century old.

The Marxian concentration on modern industry and commodity production, strictly speaking, as setting the pattern of the capitalistic mode of production has shortcomings that were admittedly true a century ago and remain true today. Part of the process Marx saw and foresaw has gone on apace, especially the increased capitalization not only of industry proper but also of agriculture, and the associated increasing scale of operations and tendency toward concentration of economic power. But the bulk of the agricultural population remains outside the strict Marxian formula, and indeed by any classification of strata based on occupation and type of eco-

---

[22] See Kingsley Davis and Wilbert E. Moore, "Some Principles of Stratification," *American Sociological Review*, x (Apr. 1945), pp. 242-49.

nomic relationship the rural system of stratification lies somewhat apart from that characteristic of urban populations. Moreover, despite a very high business mortality, the petty trader as a type has shown a very considerable ability to survive.

The role of trade in the economic system is in fact a key to a weakness of the Marxian doctrine that is "essential" even at the Marxian level of abstraction. For the theory is centrally concerned only with the production of commodities, and not directly with the distributive system or with the "production" of a multitude of services, of which distribution is one. This leaves various important occupational groups in a somewhat anomalous position with respect to the division between capital and labor.

In addition to independent and tenant farmers and independent merchants, given special treatment by Marx, two very considerable groups lie outside the Marxian scheme. (1) The expansion of governmental and industrial bureaucracy has given rise to a roughly delimited occupational group often called "white-collar workers." Ranging from leading executives to minor clerical workers, these people stand in no determinate relationship to the "means and instruments of production" according to the Marxian dichotomy. Actually, their generalized function is managerial, and their "interests" even under Marxian assumptions may well be closer to the financial interests of capitalists than to the interests of propertyless proletarians, because capitalist ownership in the Marxian sense may be fractured into segments, of which managerial control is one. Certainly their *expressed* interests as judged by their social affiliations, goals, and symbols of status, are not proletarian. (2) A further group that scarcely fits the Marxian scheme at any point is the increasing number of professionals in modern society. Some of these, it is true, such as "company" doctors, corporation lawyers, and a majority of the heterogeneous group of technologists known as engineers, are closely affiliated with financial and industrial organizations. But these fall more nearly into the bureaucratic or managerial group than they do into either of the approved Marxian categories. The number of nonindustrial physicians, lawyers, clergymen, teachers, and lesser professionals is large, and their proportion in the employed population is increasing.[23] The relationship of those rendering professional services in the community to the system of commodity production is certainly not to be determined on the basis of a dichotomy between capitalists and proletarians. Although cynical individuals, Marxians or otherwise, may hold that these individuals are "used" by the capitalists to palliate and delude the masses, even if this were

[23] The following table summarizes the changing occupational structure of the

true it would not account either for the venality of the professionals or for the gullibility of the proletarians.

These broad occupational groups indicate the difficulty of defining classes in terms of "relationships of [*commodity*] production." Actually, the process of economic development, which at the time Marx was writing was shifting from primary (agricultural and handicraft) to secondary (manufacturing) production, has since shifted increasingly from secondary to tertiary (service) production in the most advanced industrial economies.[24]

On the other hand, the relationships of production *within* industry are subject to change along non-Marxian lines. It was noted with reference to the Marxian "sociological economics" that the treatment of norms and institutions as dependent variables obscured the way in which the power of the employer might be limited and the character of the organization modified. This is perhaps most readily illustrated with reference to legislation on wage standards and working conditions, social insurance and security, and similar external controls on the nature of the contract of employment. The problem of social legislation has in fact been of considerable importance in the theory of socialist action. At the one extreme a rigid orthodoxy indicated opposition to all such palliative measures on grounds that they provided an illusory but organizationally effective substitute for a proletarian revolution. At the other extreme, the "revisionists" maintained that by supporting all such measures the revolution was being accomplished by degrees. An intermediate and for the most part predominant view advocated support of such measures as immediate gains, no doubt partly because belief in and work for a nebulous future revolution requires a more fundamental act of faith than can generally be

---

United States, although limiting the comparison to broad occupational groups in this way obscures the secular trend toward ever-increasing occupational specialization.

Proportional Distribution of Occupational Classes in the Classified Employable Population, 1880 and 1940*

Occupational Class	1880 (%)	1940 (%)
Professionals	4.2	7.1
Proprietors and Officials	5.1	7.9
Farmers (Owners and Tenants)	26.8	10.6
Low-Salaried Workers	3.3	16.6
Wage Earners	33.1	39.8
Servants	6.7	11.0
Farm Laborers	20.8	7.0

* Quoted from Wilbert E. Moore, *Industrial Relations and the Social Order*, p. 486, where sources are indicated.

For an attempt to bring these occupational shifts within a Marxian scheme, see Lewis Corey, "American Class Relations," *Marxist Quarterly*, i (Jan.-Mar. 1937), pp. 134-43.

[24] See Colin Clark, *The Conditions of Economic Progress* (London, 1940).

expected of the hoped-for mass following, but with continued insistence that this was not enough. Only the revisionists, however, seem to have recognized the truly independent variability of the normative structure within which an economy operates. These changes in the relationships of production, which have at least *limited* the exploiting power of employers, have come about largely by the actual or threatened political power of workers operating through the organs of the state as distinct from the productive system.

The amendment to the Marxian theory illustrated by the social and labor legislation of the types just indicated is, however, much less fundamental than that required by other changes. Two complex and not wholly separate changes are of especial importance for the theory of social classes.

The first of these major changes has been the modification, expansion, and diversification of the law of property. Property, it will be recalled, is in Marxian theory the "reflection" of the prevailing relationships of production. However, aside from the problem of independent variability, the Marxian conception is grossly oversimplified. The analysis provided by "scientific" socialism stops with the recognition of the distinction between consumers' and producers' (capital) goods, and the private or public control of the latter. But the Marxists tend to accept the rather simple notions of property implicit in the classical economic doctrines. There is no recognition of the multiplicity of property rights in the same thing, or scarce value, or the potential divisibility of those rights.[25] This means, for example, that in the modern legal structure of the corporation, "management" has to a marked extent been substituted for "capital" in the power structure of industry, and that even where tight financial control is maintained by close groups of stockholders the control rests upon quite different proprietary rights than those assumed by the ordinary notions of "private" property.[26] As a result, it is frequently more than a little difficult to identify the capitalist who is the presumed enemy of the proletariat; moreover, the dispersion of stock ownership makes possible the purchase of capital shares by individuals who occupationally serve the machine, and at least in the formal sense confuse the class issue completely.

It may be noted in passing that the tying of class alignments to the formal system of capital ownership makes possible the achievement of the classless society by legislative fiat, perhaps supplemented by the necessary time and pressure to remove "false" class consciousness. It was

[25] For a general statement on the nature of property and the changes in property law evident in modern economies, see Moore, "The Emergence of New Property Conceptions in America," *loc.cit.*

[26] *Ibid.*

earlier observed that Marx wrote more truly than he knew of the power implicit in control over productive wealth, for he limited the observation to presocialist economies. Thus socialization of ownership presumably destroys the power of one class over another since the instruments of production are henceforth owned in common. Under these assumptions there are no classes, by definition.[27] This line of argument accents the earlier observation that the Marxian theory of social class is not a general theory of social stratification, as differentiation and marked inequalities of position patently prevail even under a socialist regime.

The second of the major and complex changes in the relationships of production is the extensive bureaucratization of the industrial structure. One effect of this trend has been the great increase in the number and proportion of "managerial" employees noted above. While mechanization and rationalization have perhaps increased the production worker's subservience to the machine, the emphasis on *division* of labor neglects the correlative process of *diversification* of labor illustrated by the growing importance of research, design, planning, expediting, negotiating, selling in specialized markets, and the like. Since many of these specialties represent a roughly "horizontal" extension of functions rather than a neat system of vertical ranking, interests common to particular occupations tend to outweigh interests common to many occupations having the same relative rank. Even where questions of higher and lower, of authority and subordination, come to the fore, as they will in any complex formal organization, the significant feature of the bureaucracy is the rather large number of distinct layers intervening between the lowest worker and the highest executive. Thus the emphasis on a single division oversimplifies the actual and potential cleavages that pervade the whole structure. As noted elsewhere, ". . . careful analysis indicates the increasing importance of collective relations within the large cooperative system. The significance of independent unionism and collective bargaining has not been entirely missed in this connection, but . . . the virtually exclusive attention to this cleavage has obscured the fact that the union is not the only group in the system that has its own goals that may or may not coincide with the cooperative goals of the productive system. The bureaucratic structure is not dichotomous; it is fissionable."[28]

The appearance of powerful unions, the growth of collective bargaining, and the sporadic outbreaks of industrial conflict are themselves liable to serious misinterpretation. These processes and events seem precisely to represent the fundamental cleavage that is central to the Marxian

[27] See Mildred Fairchild, "Social-Economic Classes in Soviet Russia," *American Sociological Review*, IX (June 1944), pp. 236-41.

[28] Wilbert E. Moore, "Current Issues in Industrial Sociology," *American Sociological Review*, XII (Dec. 1947), pp. 651-57.

doctrine. However, through collective bargaining and the development of parallel management and union bureaucracies, the unions may become an internal aspect of organization within the enterprise and modify its structure and operation.[29] Industrial disputes and their settlements may be viewed as a slow and occasionally painful process of redefining the power relationship, of questioning more or less successfully the traditional "prerogatives" of management. At the level of abstraction typical of the Marxian analysis, the "inner dynamics" of the present state of industrial relations in the advanced economies appears more nearly a sort of "syndicalization by accident" than a developing class struggle between capitalists and proletarians.[30]

Socialist theory and the American social order. The sociological critique of "scientific" socialism attempted in the preceding pages has dealt with some leading theoretical issues either in terms of established sociological principles or in terms of the course of industrial development characteristic in greater or lesser degree of modern industrial economies in general. It may be useful at this point to summarize some of the peculiar features of American culture and society particularly relevant to the Marxian theory of social class.

Whatever may be said for the scientific accuracy of the Marxian exposition as a theory of social development, the theory has received a much greater grossly empirical verification in Europe than in the United States. With the exception of Spain and Portugal, virtually the entire European continent is currently governed by parties or coalitions that represent in some form the Marxian socialist tradition. In the United States, on the other hand, no branch of socialism has ever held a position of political dominance or enjoyed more than an extremely modest following. Since the United States is by no means less industrially advanced than Europe, this fact alone would seem to indicate that the success or failure of the socialist doctrine in practice has been somewhat independent of the validity of the theory of capitalist development. Of itself, the exceptional case is of sufficient importance to provide a crude confirmation of the theoretical considerations advanced in criticism of the Marxian position.

[29] This point was noted also by Daniel Bell and Will Herberg in the lectures which they delivered before the Program in American Civilization at Princeton University.

[30] The Marxian thesis does, however, imply a fundamental sociological principle that once a conflict becomes crystallized the number of contending parties reduces to two. But as long as the open and disruptive disputes are sporadic and highly variable with respect to specific issues and the way and degree of their effect upon those not initially involved, allegiances tend to shift. This is clearly true in contemporary America even with respect to those whose "objective" position "ought" to make their stand clear-cut. In this respect, racial and even ethnic cleavages are likely to be more fundamental than economic ones.

543

The question may be raised once more as it relates to the present discussion:[31] Why is there no socialism in America? Since undisciplined interpretation after the fact, that is, superior historical hindsight, is notoriously difficult of proof, some caution is indicated. It is accordingly suggested that the relevant evidence may be viewed as consistent with the general answer; the existence of alternative opportunities.[32] Aside from the facts that industrialization in America started before the land was fully settled and the frontier thus provided at least some indirect relief, and that industrialization itself was rapid and built upon an expanding domestic market and thus afforded many opportunities in industry and trade, there is the important fact that the form and some of the content of political democracy was established early. The extension of the franchise certainly had two effects of significance for the fate of socialism: first, unlike most of the socialist movements in Europe, it was unnecessary to adopt a revolutionary program in order to get political representation; second, operation through the established organs of government made possible the modification of the economic order by external pressure.

Occupational mobility and the lack of rigid inheritance of social status have tended to support what may be called the "mythology of the class-less society," or, in its more sophisticated form, the "mythology of the open-class society." Frontier communities tended to idealize (although not necessarily to practice) equalitarianism and the absence of social barriers. In the older industrial centers there grew up the doctrine that since opportunities were open and equal, each person occupied that status which he of a right ought to occupy.[33]

On the other hand, critical examination has pointed to the notable inequalities of opportunity and to the evidence on reduced range and

[31] The present summary is in essential agreement with that of Daniel Bell in Chapter 6, "The Background and Development of Marxian Socialism in America." It is introduced here with specific reference to the Marxian theory of social class and the "inevitable" appearance of class struggle.

[32] This frame of reference begs some questions of more than incidental importance. Notably, it assumes a dynamic orientation of the individual or the group toward the acquisition of the "universal means" represented by wealth and power. Or, in other words, it assumes that the individual will not be "contented with his lot." Although made a universal principle of motivation by the classical economists and, somewhat more ambiguously, by the Marxians, it shows a considerable cultural variability, as Marx himself recognized with respect to feudalism. It is most evident precisely in industrial societies, although variable in form and degree even there. The "culturally induced discontent," traced by Weber partly to the religious ideology of Calvinism, is of considerable functional importance for the kind and degree of occupational specialization demanded in modern economies. See Max Weber, *The Protestant Ethic and the Spirit of Capitalism* (tr. by Talcott Parsons; London, 1930); Moore, *Industrial Relations and the Social Order*, pp. 49-66.

[33] This view is succinctly enunciated by William Graham Sumner in his *What Social Classes Owe to Each Other* (New Haven, 1934, first published in 1883).

extent of occupational mobility within the single career.[34] It is not un-commonly asserted that the fluid society ended around the turn of the century or World War I, and that the present situation reveals the increasing rigidity of "class" lines.

Several points are worthy of comment with respect to the "alternative opportunities" previously mentioned. First, the changing structure of the economic system has meant a shift in the pattern of individual opportunity from successful entry into business as a merchant or manufacturer to a successful career in the bureaucratic structure, where merit is judged by superiors and not by the impersonal operation of the market. Second, as the demand has grown for managers and staff specialists with a high degree of technical skill, the line of ascent has shifted partly to the system of formal education. This has not eliminated differences in opportunity in view of the expense of higher education, but the direction of change has been toward extension rather than contraction of facilities in terms of merit. Third, as individuals in the lower ranks of labor or otherwise in poor bargaining positions have become disappointed with their individual chances for success, they have taken collective action through trade unions, professional associations, political pressure groups, and the like.[35] Although this phenomenon seems to give superficial support to the socialist theory, it is in fact one of the most powerful barriers to effective socialist organizations, as previously noted.

The foregoing exposition should not be taken as denial of evidence of differences of interests among "classes," recognized in crucial instances of dispute and expressed in voting and other forms of overt behavior.[36] It is suggested, however, that cleavages are sharpest over particular outstanding issues, whereas in other instances allegiances run less to cleavages than to multiform fractures, and in still other instances divide on grounds largely extraneous to generalized social rank. For the most part, the socialist claim to a "class-conscious" allegiance is much too narrow to encompass the common and differential interests found in the heterogeneous contemporary community. American society is by no means undifferentiated in the sense of elaborate distinctions of positions in terms of authority and rewards, or even unstratified in terms of the existence of

[34] The evidence is summarized and discussed in Moore, *Industrial Relations and the Social Order*, pp. 486-96.

[35] Incidentally, it should be noted that these groups, constituting new bureaucratic organizations, provide individual occupational opportunities outside the previously established structures. It is, moreover, possible for individuals to shift from positions of union leadership into managerial positions in industry.

[36] See, for example, Alfred Winslow Jones, *Life, Liberty, and Property* (Philadelphia, 1941); Robert S. Lynd and Helen Merrell Lynd, *Middletown in Transition* (New York, 1937); H. Dewey Anderson and Percy E. Davidson, *Ballots and the Democratic Class Struggle* (Stanford University, Calif., 1943); Richard T. Centers, *The Psychology of Social Classes* (Princeton, N.J., 1949).

broad strata along a general and somewhat arbitrary vertical scale. But the latter is likely to be somewhat less significant than the former, except where stereotyped reactions are appropriate in terms of broad issues. What is being suggested here is that the broad issues are not necessarily regarded as more fundamental, for the individual's primary orientation is to the multiplicity of distinctions that lie closer to hand.

American socialism, then, has operated in a largely hostile environment. It has had powerful competitors for the allegiance of workers, while the latter have been a part of a "class" system peculiarly unfavorable to the theory of socialist recruitment and class cleavage. How this has affected the organization and clientele of American socialist groups is examined in the second section of this essay.

II. Organization of American Socialist Groups

If, as earlier observed, every brand of socialism has a theory of society, either present or future, it must also have a theory of organization and role in society until the millennium is achieved. Every American socialist, whether religious or secular, utopian or "scientific," is something of a pilgrim or missionary in a hostile and heathen world. The two concluding sections of this essay will attempt to review, in an abbreviated and summary form, a few outstanding types of American socialist groups in terms of their relation to the larger society and the implications of that relation for internal organization and allegiance of clientele.

The types of American socialist organizations will be considered under the following three headings: the socialist communities, moderate socialist parties, and radical parties.

The socialist communities. In spite of important differences in ideology and theory of organization, the early American community experiments in socialism or communism have certain general similarities. In general, they represent a retreat from the broader society either as chosen people turning their backs on sin or as apostles of a new order leading others in the paths of righteousness by example and persuasion.[37] With the exception of the Oneida Community, the communities were in a

[37] See Harry W. Laidler, *Social-Economic Movements* (New York, 1944), pp. 100-9; L. L. Bernard, *Origins of American Sociology* (New York, 1943), pp. 59-112; Dorothy W. Douglas and Katharine Du Pre Lumpkin, "Communistic Settlements," *Encyclopaedia of the Social Sciences*, IV, pp. 95-102; Lillian Symes and Travers Clement, *Rebel America: the Story of Social Revolt in the United States* (New York, 1934), Pt. I. See also two early but still standard works: J. H. Noyes, *History of American Socialisms* (Philadelphia, 1870); Charles Nordhoff, *The Communistic Societies of the United States* (New York, 1875). For a succinct summary of problems of social control in such communities, see R. M. MacIver, *Society: a Textbook of Sociology* (New York, 1937), pp. 347-51.

sense a rejection of industrialism in favor of a simpler and presumably freer agricultural existence.

The socialist communities, established *de novo* rather than by transforming established patterns, were able to put to effect in microcosm their several theories of the good society. In this they had the advantage of establishing a closely integrated system of norms and social controls rather than attempting by political control to remake the rest of society or leave it untouched.

Again with the exception of the Oneida Community, the socialist communities wanted to maintain their separate and deviant mode of social organization by economic self-sufficiency, and indeed by every available mode of physical and social isolation from the influences of the sinful or unreasonable society. Mere intolerance on the part of outsiders was of course not necessarily disruptive, and indeed tended to solidify the groups. The fact that dissidents could leave the group rather than stay and contribute to its disruption also had some stabilizing effect. The essential difficulties were for the most part less spectacular. They revolved around the difficulty of existing in a society but not of it. If the communitarian socialists may be regarded as retreating from the ordinary fabric of social relations, they were also in a certain sense in rebellion against it. Lacking complete economic self-sufficiency, political sovereignty, or the means of cutting off the influence of ideas and attitudes hostile to the community ideals, the communities suffered sharp failure or slow attrition. They were in fact possible only in a still largely agrarian economy less tightly centralized in economic and political life than the modern industrial society. When supported by strong religious ideals, they showed indeed a very considerable tenacity in adverse circumstances. They were, however, not equipped to combat the force of secularization and the growing importance of a pervasive economic and social interdependence. The rigidity of the organization of the communities, adopted as a protection against disturbance from within, resulted in lack of flexibility in adapting to outside influences that asserted themselves with growing insistence.

Moderate socialist parties. Those socialists who hope to achieve the "cooperative commonwealth" by democratic political action constitute a second organizational type that raises problems of relations with the broader society quite different from those faced by the socialist communities. The political socialist emphasizes the use of part of the institutional structure (the democratic franchise) to change another part (the control of economic production). He is neither a retreatist nor, strictly speaking, a rebel.[38]

[38] See Robert K. Merton, "Social Structure and Anomie," *American Sociological Review*, III (Oct. 1938), pp. 672-82.

The socialists with an evolutionary political program are faced with the continuous problem of compromise with principle. Attempting to work within the social structure while working for its transformation, the party must meet the recurrent issue as to where to begin the battle. Since the ideal society includes a number of potentially separable goals, those within the party who are especially interested in fostering one part of the program may come into conflict with those who believe in the special virtue or expediency of other parts of the program (for example, the recurrent problems of nationalism and pacifism, or immediate improvements in the lot of workers as compared with emphasis on public ownership).

As an association rather than a community, the socialist party has only a modest claim to the allegiance of its members or control over their behavior. Although the American Socialist Party, in common with other socialist organizations, defines its membership in terms of actual participation at least to the extent of regular payment of dues, the fluctuations in rank-and-file membership tends to be extreme and the actual participation in the affairs of the party below the executive group pretty nominal. In other words, organization as a party introduces the principal organizational characteristics of the major parties, despite a differing theory of membership and participation. In fact, below the administrative officers and staff the organization tends to be even looser than that of the major parties, since in the absence of actual political power there is no opportunity to retain allegiance through "machines" or distribution of patronage. Moreover, continued political failure tends to discourage adherents. It thus becomes necessary to develop a set of explanations or rationalizations for continued organization. Aside from the extreme Marxian doctrine of inevitability, which the moderate parties do not share, the rationalizations tend to be either that the doctrines are ethically right, whatever their immediate success, and continued allegiance is a moral duty, or that the minority party serves a function as a party of protest by standing in the vanguard of social reforms, subsequently adopted by major parties owing in part to the socialist activity.

Since the moderate program calls for gradual transformation of the economy through perfectly legal instrumentalities, the casual party member or especially the election adherent is not required to make any radical break with his ordinary life pattern. He may support the socialist movement temporarily as a protest, and may play along a number of other prospects upon which he counts for greater success. The limited and vacillating character of his support is the price the organization pays for moderation, for not demanding and being in no position to demand sacrificial devotion.

It is only the party leaders who are confronted with rather far-reaching personal decisions, who as champions of a cause constantly being lost in immediate terms must make of the party something more than a mere special-interest association. The Cause must necessarily provide their main focus of attention not only because it constitutes their occupation, but because as a form of "social deviation" genuine sacrifices are entailed.[39] It is thus not surprising that concern for intraparty affairs, debates over organizational doctrine that are likely to have little efficacy however they are decided, and a general conservatism and ritualistic concern for preservation of the organization tend to characterize the moderate socialist parties.

Radical parties. The radical parties all stand explicitly in actual or potential rebellion against the existing order. For the prevailing goals and means they would substitute new ones. Compromise is therefore kept to a minimum, although still necessary for earning a living, keeping out of jail as far as possible, and especially, gaining the support of the masses they profess to lead. But as a conflict organization seeking to remake the social order, an act of faith, a conversion, is even more requisite than in the leadership of the moderate parties. The party or movement becomes a way of life by which other contacts, associational memberships, and personal activities are judged or determined. As expressed in an organizational handbook of the American Communist Party, "A professional revolutionist is a highly developed comrade, trained in revolutionary theory and practice, tested in struggles, who gives his whole life to the fight for the interests of his own class. A professional revolutionist is ready to go whenever and wherever the Party sends him. . . . If the class struggle demands it, he will leave his family for months, even years. The professional revolutionist cannot be demoralized; he is steeled, stable. Nothing can shake him. Our task is to make every Party member a professional revolutionist in this sense."[40] For the inner circles, at least, the party takes on the character of a closed community. As such, it has some undoubted appeal to the frustrated. Controversy and potential martyrdom provide a high emotional pitch, while success within the party offers some reward for the faithful. It is commonly asserted that the real rebel has no sense of humor; like many overstatements, it is based on a certain amount of valid evidence, as revolution is fairly serious business.

The organization of the radical party is determined by the revolutionary

[39] For discussion of a comparable case, see Alvin W. Gouldner, "Attitudes of 'Progressive' Trade-Union Leaders," *American Journal of Sociology*, LII (Mar. 1947), pp. 389-92.

[40] J. Peters, *The Communist Party: a Manual on Organization* (New York, 1935).

character of its goals and consequent conspiracy against the existing order, and, in the case of the American Communist Party, the international character of the movement and the predominant influence of the policies espoused by the Soviet Union. This second influence means that the doctrine as a whole, and the organizational doctrine in particular, has little relevance to American conditions. The "party line" is set elsewhere and to a marked extent reflects controversies and decisions of which the American group has no part. Thus the considerable amount of faith and discipline[41] requisite to any revolutionary program is made even more necessary by lack of relevance to local conditions. This does not mean that the line is wholly inflexible and does not change; rather, that the changes are determined outside the national or local organization and require unquestioned obedience or involve factionalism and disciplinary action.

The specific character of the relations of the American Communist Party with the American social order have in fact undergone marked changes and rapid reversals: underground activity versus the legal party; work with other "left" and progressive groups in a united front versus sharp condemnation of all deviants from strict party line as class traitors and functionaries of the bourgeoisie; dual unionism versus "fractions" within established unions ("boring from within"); condemnation of "imperialist war" versus support of "war against Fascist aggressors." The line changes under "changed conditions," but this is not to be confused with the sharply condemned "right opportunism," which implies a compromise with principle rather than a matter of organizational expediency. However, since organizational means presumably have some relation to revolutionary ends, it becomes difficult for the observer to find the objective distinction between the party's opportunism and the kind that it condemns. As the party line may become "right opportunism" after the line has changed, it is apparently also difficult for the party member to be completely sure of the distinction.

The formal structure of the Communist Party is of interest for the way it illustrates the significance of the revolutionary ideology and the necessity of tight discipline in a group engaged in conflict with established institutions. The theoretical structure is a hierarchy built up from local and regional units. In terms of the most general (and nominally most authoritative) unit at each level, the progression is from the shop or street unit (nucleus), through the section convention, the district convention, and the national convention, to the world congress of the Communist

[41] In this respect, see the recommendations for treatment of intraparty "spies" in *ibid.*, pp. 121-22.

International (until this was formally dissolved during World War II).[42]

At each of these levels, however, there is a committee that meets more frequently, and a bureau that carries on the day-to-day activities of the organization. Thus, leaving out the now unofficial relations with the International, the "structure of the Communist Party in order of responsibility" is:

> "Unit Bureau
> Unit Membership Meeting
> Section Bureau
> Section Committee
> Section Convention
> District Bureau
> District Committee
> District Convention
> Political Bureau of the C.C.
> Central Committee
> National Convention."[43]

This formal structure is complicated by such appended and affiliated organizations as the Young Communist League, dual union organization such as the temporarily established Trade Union Educational League and the Trade Union Unity League, and the "fractions" within trade unions and other organizations that attempt to gain elective positions and make them responsible to the party rather than to the electoral constituents. It also does not cover the detailed organization of the committees and bureaus at the higher levels, with their functionally specialized commissions, or the operation of agents not directly responsible to the official party. More important than these organizational complications, however, is the mode of relationship between the levels and the nature of the formal leadership. The structure is set in motion by the application of "democratic centralism."

"Democratic centralism" as explained by the Communist Party consists of pyramidal representation, starting from the nucleus and proceeding through the three higher levels of the national organization.[44] This is the "democratic" phase of the organization. The "centralism" consists in the fact that decisions and policies of higher units are binding on lesser units, and complete compliance with majority decision is demanded.

"Democratic centralism" departs from the ordinary conceptions of

[42] *Ibid.*, pp. 36-102; an organizational chart follows p. 64. See also M. Jenks, *The Communist Nucleus: What It Is—How It Works* (New York, 1928); files of the monthly *Party Organizer.*

[43] Peters, *op.cit.*, p. 44.

[44] Under "exceptional" circumstances, such as underground operations, the process of co-option, that is, appointment from above, may be necessary.

551

political democracy ("spurious bourgeois democracy") in several important respects. First, strict numerical proportionality of representation is not assumed, as some nuclei or divisions or sections may have greater weight owing to their strategic importance, that is, the importance of the industries or unions in which they are influential, the groups emphasized by current organizational policy, and so on. Second, the minority may not question the decision of the majority. Decisions are binding down the line, and initiative for questioning current policy must always come from the top. Agitation to convert the minority into a majority constitutes "factionalism" and cannot be countenanced in a revolutionary party claiming to *lead* the masses and not confuse them by discussion within the party. Lastly, there can be no question concerning the "fundamentals" of the Marxist-Leninist-Stalinist line, but as a matter of fact the line of the moment is declared to be fundamental and once declared everyone must engage in self-criticism and public confession of error in following the previous line. This preserves the solidarity of the true believers, but tends to lose the confidence of sympathizers and to mystify completely the masses that the party presumes to lead.

The internal organization of socialist groups in general, but especially of those marking the sharpest conflict with the existing order, tends to forms of ritualism paradoxical among innovators or rebels. The quarrels within and between socialist parties are almost wholly over means: means of getting into power, and, less importantly, means of exercising power once gained. The articles of faith therefore are primarily concerned with prescribed forms, which become endowed with the emotional fervor presumably aroused by the goals. This accounts for part of the behavior customarily viewed with considerable astonishment. Thus various factions of socialists and communists appear much more concerned with condemnation and defeat of other factions than with the official enemy—the capitalist class. "Utopians," "yellow socialists," "social fascists," "Trotskyites," "Lovestoneites," and other heretics from the true faith (that is, as embodied in a particular rite) are roundly condemned by any other given brand of orthodoxy. The two most inclusive designations for departures from the Communist Party line are "left deviationism" and "right opportunism."

The ritualism and sectarianism are given ultimate confirmation by attachment to special verbal symbols, represented not only by epithets and by special terms for the activities within the group (such as "agitprop" for agitation and propaganda), but also by citation of standard texts and their reinterpretation in view of changed policies. Virtually every speech or pamphlet of the communists opens and closes with quotations from one of the major prophets (Marx, Engels, Lenin, and Stalin) or, more rarely, from the current head of the national party as minor prophet ex officio.

The irony of this ritualism among strict Marxians is that "scientific" socialists, who are therefore "historical materialists," go busily about affirming in action what they deny in words, namely, the organizational functions of values, sentiments, and symbolic behavior. For the functions of the ritual are clear and are especially important precisely for those who seek to replace one institutional and normative network for another; the ritual is a security device in a hostile world. The rebel may be able to view the accepted norms more objectively than does the conformist; rarely does he treat his own deviant norms with the same objectivity.

III. American Socialist Clientele

In the final paragraphs of section i of this essay, the somewhat exaggerated question was raised, "Why is there no socialism in the United States?" In view of the discussion at that point of "alternative opportunities" and of the organizational problems reviewed in the second section, the more interesting and significant question would appear to be, "Why are there *any* socialists in the United States?" Put somewhat differently, What is the clientele of the American socialist groups?

Like many interesting questions, this one is more easily asked than answered. The answer must naturally vary with the particular type of socialism and even with the particular group. However, the evidence with respect to any group is considerably less than conclusive. Partly by implication from the previous discussion and partly by *ad hoc* interpretation, some guesses may be hazarded.

The early socialist communities were made possible, it was noted, by the temporary possibility of isolation, the lack of close economic and political centralization that grew up with urban industrial development. This tells little of the characteristics or motivations of their constituents. It is suggested that in addition to the religious ideology so evident in some of the communities, for the most part they were established when experimentation was the order of the day, when the future form of the social order had not taken on such a sacrosanct character as it subsequently acquired.[45] As the new industrial society was already taking form, America provided an alternative not available in England or Western Europe: land and the opportunity to establish new agrarian communities. Since a measure of opposition to industrialization appeared wherever the industrial revolution got under way, this particular American circumstance appears of some importance. This is especially true as

[45] This point has been suggested by Willard Thorp with reference to the early development of socialist or socialist-oriented literature in America.

many of the schemes were not home grown at all, but were originally set forth in terms of the European scene.

European traditions brought by immigrants, including the refugees from the abortive revolutions of 1848, were also influential in the moderate socialist parties. The affiliated foreign-language groups provided one of the most dependable and numerically stable elements in the American Socialist Party.[46] Their socialist allegiance was clearly in terms of old-world ideas and conditions, given superficial validity in the American scene by the exploitation practiced on immigrants of all political persuasions or none. As for native American adherents, whether as members or merely as voters, it has been suggested that the evolutionary democratic program represented those wishing to express a protest without an overly sharp break with American traditions and political procedures. As to the exact social or "class" origins of socialists, little can be established other than the comparative materials in Stetler's study of Reading, Pennsylvania, and other socialist cities.[47] These materials confirm the predominantly "lower-class" source of support for socialist city administrations and candidates for state and national offices. But this evidence is clearly inconclusive.[48] If lower economic or occupational position is for the most part a necessary cause of socialist affiliation, it is clearly not a sufficient cause. Available evidence supports no principle dissociated from the unique historical circumstances in each instance.

With respect to membership in the Communist Party or electoral or other support, even less objective data are available. As a revolutionary group, out of public favor and frequently on the wrong side of the law and of the good opinion of employers and congressional committees, the communists have not uniformly made membership a matter of public information. At the time, late in World War II, that the party became briefly the Communist Political Association, less than half of the total membership could be classified as "industrial workers" and a much smaller proportion as workers in "basic industries," by whatever definition

[46] In the first decade of this century the American Socialist Party was still largely native American in membership. In 1908, before the affiliation of most of the national language federations, 71 per cent of the dues-paying membership was reported to be native born. (See Nathan Fine, *Labor and Farmer Parties in the United States, 1828-1928* [New York, 1928], p. 324.) The affiliation of the foreign-language groups before World War I added to the party's numerical strength, but not to its standing with native American workers. The greater part of the foreign-born socialists were lost to the communist and other left groups after the split of 1919.

[47] Henry G. Stetler, *The Socialist Movement in Reading, Pennsylvania, 1896-1936* (Storrs, Conn., 1943).

[48] For a different conclusion, see that of George W. Hartmann in Chapter 12 herein.

of the latter that the party uses.[49] That this is viewed by the party as a weakness is evident in frequent statements of leaders that intensive work must be done among the actual workers in the factories—the true pro-letariat—lest the party's true character be threatened by too high a pro-portion of sympathetic intellectuals.

As a matter of fact, it is not wholly clear just what the party's aspirations are by way of membership. Many programs call for organization of all workers, for becoming a truly mass party. Other statements seem to emphasize the role of the party as the organized spearhead of the revolu-tion, the vanguard of workers, who do not need to reach the stage of political maturity implied by party membership, but only the stage required to follow party leadership.

In the American situation the Communist Party faces a peculiar dilem-ma. The labor unions have grown up largely independent of political parties, and for the most part have no special political philosophy. As a party seeking to lead the workers, the communists attempt to attract the most "advanced" and especially the most influential labor leaders. But the appeal of the communists is clearly greatest among those who have the least to lose by rebellion, and therefore perhaps the least to offer to the success of rebellion. And it is this clientele that must be sought if larger numbers and nearer approximation to the status of a mass party are to be attained.

Inference would indicate, and party brochures partially confirm, that the communist adherents include disproportionate numbers of urban Negroes, foreign-born unskilled workers, and "unattached intellectuals"

[49] The percentages of members of the party in various categories as of January 1944 was as follows, according to the data published by the party:

Categories	Per Cent
Industrial Workers	46
Basic Industry Workers	27
Trade Unionists	52
Negroes	14
Women	46
Housewives	43
Professional & White Collar	25

These data, somewhat confusing because the categories are not mutually exclusive, are also claimed to understate the proportions in the first three groups owing to the exclusion of 10,000 members in the armed services. See John Williamson, "Perspectives on the Functioning of the Communist Political Association," *Communist*, XXIII (Sept. 1944), pp. 521-32, at p. 522. Earlier figures indicated that part of the explanation for the "minority" position of the proletariat in the party is the heavy representation of office and professional workers in the New York unit, which is also the largest territorial unit. In New York the professional and white-collar workers accounted for 43 per cent of the membership in 1942, and by excluding the New York unit the industrial workers represented a bare majority in the party (51 per cent). See John Williamson, "Strengthen the War Effort by Building the Party," *Communist*, XXI (May 1942), pp. 324-35.

(although the number of these has certainly decreased). The party's numerical strength or weakness seems to be one indication of the number of possessed and desperate men in search of social salvation.

As the foregoing paragraphs imply, too little is known concerning the social determinants in adherence to socialist schemes of reform. If socialism is a challenge to the existing material order, it is also a challenge to the social scientific order. This essay has attempted to recognize the challenge if not to meet it. If one can assume the steady progress of learning, the impatient critic may be put off with an orthodox Marxian answer: "Wait a while."

CHAPTER 12

The Psychology of American Socialism

BY GEORGE W. HARTMANN

GEORGE W. HARTMANN is Chairman of the Department of Psychology at Roosevelt College of Chicago. Long active in peace movements, he is a prominent member of the Socialist Party and has been the Socialist candidate for lieutenant-governor of New York State and for mayor of New York. The author of books on educational and Gestalt psychology, he is also co-editor of the volume, *Industrial Conflict; a Psychological Interpretation* (1939).

For bibliography in Volume 2 relevant to Mr. Hartmann's essay, see especially PART V, General Reading and Topics; also PART IV, *passim*; PART II, Topics 8, 9, 10.

IF IT could be produced, a full and accurate account of the many specifically psychological factors or aspects involved in past and present socialist movements would be a genuine advantage to both "psychology" and "socialism." Psychologists, or at least those more restricted specialists known as *social* psychologists, would gain in precisely the same way that they now benefit from any sustained application of their characteristic techniques to the determination of the distinctive phenomena displayed by *any* definite category of human beings—such as Negro school children with IQs above 130, juvenile delinquents in the Boston area, military leaders, etc. Socialists similarly might benefit from, first, the increased self-understanding that emerges whenever "private" or group motivational patterns are recognized; second, anticipating the responses of non- or antisocialists to representative socialist stimuli; and, third, grappling more deeply and therefore more effectively with some of the psychological barriers that seemingly block or delay the attainment of a socialist culture. Finally, social scientists as a professional body—at least those who are obviously neither technical psychologists nor convinced or practicing socialists—would presumably profit from the availability of such behaviorally-centered material as a source of suitable illustrations for whatever preferred explanatory principles their various theoretical systems employ or require.

I. *Source Materials and Problems of Method*

Useful and desirable as such a contribution in the field of scholarship would undoubtedly be, one must recognize the formidable difficulties that prevent its straightforward achievement. There is an ancient insight to the effect that *one can understand only that which one loves*; and to the degree that all mental processes are interrelated, it may be that the converse of this proposition is also true. What this observation implies at a minimum in this context is that a psychological description of socialist thinking, feeling, and acting will clearly differ in some significant respects if made by a specialist who is favorably disposed in general to the orientation he is analyzing or if presented by an expert who is either "neutral" or in some measure antagonistic to this position and its implications. This effect must be recognized whether it arises for technically sufficient or inadequate causes or whether it appears on the pro or the con side of the issues considered.

The existing sketchy and therefore unsatisfying essays in this area demonstrate that quite plainly. What we have so far are largely rival versions prepared as it were by counsel for the plaintiff and counsel for the defendant, respectively. Those which attempt to deal with the problem from the standpoint of judge or jury are not only rarer but also (perhaps inevitably) drabber and less vital expositions. Just because an authentic psychological analysis concerns the innermost or deepest levels of personal experience, it is conceivable that a sympathetic interpretation will provide a truer and more faithful picture of the reality portrayed than an antipathetic one—for does it not penetrate layers of response that are inaccessible to any other approach?

It is a commonplace that one "knows" (in all senses of that term) one's friends far better than one's enemies. Students and others find more arguments in behalf of the outlook they support than the one they oppose, and by actual empirical count they use more words in the former than in the latter case. Equally trite but just as relevant is the fact that the best chemistry textbooks, for example, are written by those who like chemistry. The contrast and similarity between the merit and the quality of the interpretations of the religious life made by James (who was benevolently inclined thereto) and by Freud (who sharply "rejected" it) provide another pertinent example. At any rate, analyses of movements are apparently more likely to exhibit breadth and depth when there is vigor of acceptance or rejection than when there is little concern, one way or the other, about their substance. In the absence of such "arousal," both thought and its expression suffer in intensity.

These preliminary methodological considerations, with which every thoughtful analyst of great social issues has at least some rough familiarity, are peculiarly applicable to the content of this chapter. The psychology of socialism necessarily deals with many of the major values of human existence; and "values," by definition, are not purely cognitive experiences but strongly and typically saturated with affective and motor attributes. Thus contemporary field studies in applied sociology and anthropology have relied frequently upon the reports of "participant-observers." These recognize that the full reality would not be conveyed if the characteristic feelings and "irrational" impulses of the persons or groups concerned were merely described and not evaluated. In some measure, all profound experiences must be appreciated by way of the heart as well as via the head.

Facts alone are not the sole subject matter of psychology, for facts are values and values are basic facts of our common nature. Since the human organism (including the scholarly or academic variety) is primarily a value-seeking creature and not just a receptor of stimuli, it follows that the process of psychologizing the phenomena of socialism becomes an unusually severe although not insuperable test of one's capacity for "dispassionate objectivity." The entire system of values of the investigator and of the one being investigated inevitably interact. If these harmonize, even in part, then one result emerges; if they clash, another appears. Paradoxical as it sounds, it would not be objective to fail to give due weight to these vital "subjective" influences.

A lesser obstacle to a true (but not to a *truthful*) or complete portrait is not the *general* limitation outlined above, but the *specific* disadvantage that there are relatively few socialist psychologists or psychologically-minded socialists who are equipped to work on this problem, although both categories are commoner today than a generation ago. It seems reasonable to believe that as the members in both classes grow, the psychology of socialism itself as a separate body of systematized knowledge will increase in scope and precision. The socialist psychologist, by comparison with his liberal or conservative or strictly "nonpolitical" professional colleague, is characteristically more strongly motivated to inquire into the forces associated with the presence of the pattern of behavior designated as "socialism." In addition, his organizational or personal "contacts" (whether many or few, strong or weak) evidently furnish a sounder basis for description to the degree that an "insider" in any area is better prepared for that task than any "outsider." On the other hand, just because of this ego involvement or group identification, the socialist psychologist is in danger of succumbing to faulty emphases, overlooking aspects that are salient to others, or in one way or another operating within a perspective or "frame of reference" so exclusively his own that it is not convincingly communicated to others. There are epistemological advantages of some sort in looking at a phenomenon from the "outside," so to speak, as well as from the "inside."

Socialists themselves share the general advance in psychological comprehension which seems to have been made by all literate mankind in recent decades. Popular journalism, a personality-centered public school system, and other familiar agencies and influences have made the average layman today much more aware of the simpler and commoner "mental mechanisms" than his father or grandfather was. Some of this advance is certainly deceptive, being little more than the pseudosophistication involved in substituting a newer technical or scientific terminology for older literary formulas, but there is probably a genuine residuum of progress represented by clearer insights produced by the widespread use of mental tests of all types, improved personnel practices in industry, the extension and use of guidance and counseling procedures in many institutions and professions, etc. Consequently, while the mid-twentieth century is far from being a full-blown psychological era, it is much more that than any previous period in human history.

The average socialist reflects this general elevation in the plane of public enlightenment concerning subtleties in intrapsychic data and interpersonal relationships, and in a few areas probably adds a little more of his own. This "plus" usually arises out of his more or less conspicuous status and activities as a minority member of a nonsocialist community. The presence of any acute sense of difference (whether that be chiefly temperamental or attitudinal) readily fosters speculation as to why the majority is not like the minority and vice versa. Innumerable false interpretations of this basic situation appear, but some of them are good "leads" even for the most competent and critical specialist and a few are literally the best hypotheses and theories currently available. In this field, the line between primitive common sense and the ways of authentic science is less sharply drawn than in technically more developed fields with an extensive tradition of detailed or specialized skills. As one would expect, the chief deficiency of this lay socialist analysis of "the Human Nature problem" as it is commonly labeled, is that it lacks the machinery and often the will for systematic checking of hunches via pertinent statistics, longitudinal growth or case studies, mass experimentation, and the other devices by which verification proceeds in the hands of technicians. Yet as a source of basic ideas, without which research cannot start, it would be folly to neglect the folk wisdom embodied in some of the conceptions held by this variant of the "man in the street."

II. Applicability of the Concepts of "Need" and "Frustration"

Historically and psychologically, the socialist movement in all its varied manifestations in time and place is but one of the many means men have used to assure better and more satisfying lives for themselves. Logically formulated, as soon as individuals accept life itself as something worthwhile in the minimum sense that it provides the opportunity for having value-evoking experiences, then the struggle for these ends becomes also the search for the prerequisite means to their fulfilment. Beginning with the stark and banal datum of a plurality of persons living together for a limited period on the earth's surface, our basic psychological problem becomes that of explaining how some of these creatures act as though the "socialist solution" is the best method so far evolved for meeting the major recurrent needs of the race.

There seems to be no better explanatory principle at hand to account for this special striving in a particular direction than the notion of "unmet needs." A thirsty man needs water; a tired one wants rest; a lonely person wishes to have friends; the frightened child grows calm when affection and security are provided; a nation sickened by war longs for peace. Whatever will dependably restore the disturbed equilibrium of the biological system or in any way foster its well-being is a "value" to it. God in the role of "Providence" presumably discharges this comprehensive function within the context of religious imagination; a socialist world order so organized as to reduce to a minimum the chronic frustration of normal needs is the nearest contemporary secular equivalent. It is only because men ultimately prefer plenty to poverty, freedom to slavery, health to sickness, beauty to ugliness, etc., that the quest for socialism makes sense. However, this basic attraction of living tissue to certain positive goods and concomitant aversion to hurtful or negative situations is the psychobiological basis of not only socialist behavior but of *all* behavior. Wherein then does one find that peculiar configuration of forces responsible for the socialist personality?

Certainly it is not to be found in the ordinary or unqualified phenomena of frustration *as such*, central as these undoubtedly are, in all forms of social conflict. No human being can live throughout even a single day without encountering some thwarting, minor as it may be. Few of our extended purposive activities flow with unimpeded smoothness. In the healthy organism of high morale—which unfortunately is probably not the statistically average man today or at any time—these blockages may be overcome by: employing more effort than was originally contemplated; enduring whatever is not gravely burdensome; reshaping one's aims by dropping without too much regret some items as unattainable; substituting some appropriate or convenient second-best response; and so on. But all these adjustment devices can be used efficiently only if, on balance, the individual's chief demands on life are being reasonably fulfilled. If the frustration approaches catastrophic dimensions, as in some sudden change in the individual's relation to a key group, then these equilibrating mechanisms often fail and "emotional stability" disappears or is gravely impaired.

The defect of the simplified frustration hypothesis is that all people— socialists, nonsocialists, antisocialists—experience thwarting and therefore the mere fact of having been blocked in some of one's aspirations is a nondifferentiating factor. It is more pertinent to ask: *Which* personality wants have failed of satisfaction—the id's, the ego's, the superego's, or the enlarged ego's (to use Tolman's classification)? The frustration must be either of especial intensity or, more likely, of a certain *quality*; and the probabilities are that both the quality and the intensity are dependent variables of the constitution and the life history of the person affected. For example, severe thwarting may make a great artist—or even a great man—out of one individual, a criminal of another, a futile neurotic of still a third, and so on according to the matrix or system in which it appears. Like all explanatory concepts that explain too much, this one is in danger of not supplying the specific emphases that account for the particular phenomenon with which it is concerned.

One form of frustration not sufficiently stressed as the basis of the socialist disposition is that which occurs when one sees another individual frustrated and is unable to do anything to help even though eager to do so. This type of thwarting tends to be of a peculiarly poignant sort since it calls forth the acute sense of needless tragedy and injustice in community living. Experiences possessed of such depth dimensions may

563

dispose the person so affected to grope for a set of conditions under which a similar blocking of a decent impulse to give aid to one in trouble cannot take place. But even such a relatively high-level form of behavior does not necessarily have a uniquely socialist outcome. The initiating trauma with its power to mold subsequent attitudes and acts may provide the motive power for other kinds of reform, sometimes allied—like pacifism or currency and taxation proposals—and sometimes opposed—like nationalistic irredentism, evangelical denominationalism, etc. Socialists must possess (among other attributes) some slight sense of responsibility for the course of human events or they would not be socialists, but since not all persons with a "social conscience" are socialists, the establishment of this relationship alone does not tell the full story.

Contemporary applied psychology has been forced by an abundance of clinical and related evidence to make the notion of need central to most of its "working" hypotheses. A fad arises and its apparently complete irrationality is penetrated by asking: What need or needs does it satisfy in those who follow it? A new magazine is launched: What needs of sponsors, editors, contributors, and readers are realized through its existence? Again, a social movement gains momentum, and both frightened and amused spectators inevitably ask: What do the participants get out of their association in the way of positive emotional satisfactions which were not already available through existing institutional forms?

From this standpoint, *socialism is distinctive in that its psychological essence lies in its espousal of an all-embracing plan of organization for meeting the basic needs of the persons included within its scope.* Its conscious aim, by contrast with nonsocialist systems, is to inventory and catalogue the major wants of mankind and then to plan the structure and functions of the whole economy around them. All people require an optimum amount of nutrition; *ergo*, the collectivity, whether a demonstration "colony," a vast empire, or even a unified world state, ultimately assumes the responsibility for seeing that such food is provided to all citizens. In principle, every evolving need (no matter how subtle or elaborate, provided it is common to enough members) can be most efficiently met by the advanced pattern of cooperation which socialism represents and advocates.

Socialism thus construed differs from earlier and existing types of group life mainly in its claim to be able to *satisfy better more wants of more people.* It either does that or yields to some rival design which can maximize values in that respect. Obviously all societies must meet some of the minimum wants of the population or they could not survive. All of them seemingly have hitherto been so arranged intentionally or otherwise that the needs of temporarily favored groups have been comparatively fully met while the less favored have been deprived in either a few or many respects. Every identifiable social institution and each recognizable mode of group action as described either by the historian in dealing with past cultures, or by one or the other variety of social scientist in portraying contemporary systems, does ultimately rest upon the capacity to produce experiences of value to certain personalities. In the minds of many, socialism—unlike the comparatively more haphazard economies antedating it—implicitly aims at the largest possible dependable flow of crucial values to the greatest number of individuals. Such a state of material and spiritual abundance with its minimum of frustration is deemed to be the inevitable outcome of that distinctive way of producing and distributing goods and services of all kinds to which the adjective "socialist" applies.

III. Socialism as a Value-System or Pattern of Drives

Tentatively it seems possible to structure all the phenomena of social psychology by means of a triangular scheme employing the three key ideas of (1) value, (2) conflict, and (3) power. Basic to all understanding of individuals and groups (not to mention such higher scientific achievements as prediction and control) is some perception of the values implicitly regulating the behavior to be explained. Almost as elementary is the recognition that values commonly are in conflict: imperfect integration of goals or loyalties exists in every bosom and in every culture, so that we witness both the perennial spectacle of clashing individual wills and the antagonisms of rival groups. The third component of the trinity is the reality of *power* or the process whereby one value or complex of values is subordinated or arranged with respect to others, either directly or primarily within the nervous system with its hierarchy of dominant and lesser motives, or indirectly, secondarily, and symbolically through the status relations of typical individuals (the bearers of values) to each other in the community structure. This determination of position in the prevailing subjective or objective scheme may be made either peaceably or violently, but dynamically there evidently ensues a resolution in terms of the strongest forces currently operative. Since they are ultimately rooted in living tissue and therefore possess related properties, specific values (e.g., the desire for a fur coat) usually pass through phases of birth, growth, decline, and death; although it is probable that certain general or "abiding" values (e.g., the quest for justice), like the species or germ plasm that manifests or reacts to them, actually possess comparative immortality and are thus "eternal" in Münsterberg's sense if not in Plato's.

The interplay of these factors is seen with particular clarity in the complex of forces leading either to triumph or defeat of the socialist movement or trend in our culture. Thus, the (1) *values* of socialism or, for that matter, of its past, present, and future adversaries, (2) *conflict* with each other over a period of time throughout some extended area like a nation-state and (3) are resolved in terms of the respective *power* resources each commands. This formal explanatory scheme is undoubtedly oversimplified and it does look suspiciously like the much abused "thesis-antithesis-synthesis" of Hegelian dialectic; yet there is some reason for holding that despite its sketchiness it correctly reports the inherent pattern or "logic" present in both the dynamics of group life or human nature and the course of history. Without using the precise terms of our trinity, notice how the famous multiple definition of socialism in the *Encyclopaedia of the Social Sciences* incorporates them by implication: "first, a condemnation of the existing political and social order as unjust; second, an advocacy of a new order consistent with social values; third, a belief that this ideal is realizable; fourth, a conviction that the immorality of the established order is traceable not to a fixed world order or to the unchanging nature of man but to corrupt institutions; fifth, a program of action leading to the ideal through a fundamental remolding of human nature or of institutions or both; and sixth, a revolutionary will to carry out this program."[1]

Like any other attitudinal complex, socialism grows out of some matrix. From one point of view, it is simply a peculiar combination or focusing of ingredients supplied by preexisting sources principally: general tendencies toward "humanitarianism"; the specific implications of Christianity or other ethically-advanced religions; the evolution of democracy and "free institutions"; and the scientific or experimental approach to man and his works. Let these strong presocialist traditions within the culture fulfill the promise inherent in them and from their mature interaction socialism in one form or another "inevitably" appears. Such a statement of the case, while probably correct enough, may be too broadly phrased to yield that definiteness in comprehension properly preferred.

From the Gestalt standpoint, socialism is a complex behavioral "figure" imbedded in an equally elaborate "ground." Like all perceptual figures it could not be seen or in any way responded to unless it were somehow differentiated from, and contrasted with, the accompanying ground. This means that socialist personalities and societies require for their identification some measure of variation from their nonsocialist surroundings. As socialist practices become dominant, socialism presumably will lose the sharply outlined figure status it now possesses and acquire a more diffuse ground function, that is, it becomes the "frame" of action itself and not just some configured event projected against and occurring within another frame. Paradoxically as it may seem, this process of lower-

---

[1] Oscar Jászi, "Socialism," *Encyclopaedia of the Social Sciences*, xiv, p. 188.

ing relative awareness is presumably what occurs whenever a once hotly contested style of living triumphs, is "accepted," and ultimately quietly taken for granted.

If, as the historical record shows, there are socialist ideas, emotions, and activities in a dissident minority of individuals long before they characterize the behavior of a dominant majority, what are the "mental mechanisms" responsible for them in the first place? What experiences evoke them?

No better or shorter answer to this inclusive question is possible than to say that the drive to socialism is a realistically based protest against the persistence of some unsatisfying state of public affairs. But the revulsion produced by awakened discontent is not the only force acting—there is also the positive pull of a potentially more agreeable future situation, which may really be the stronger decisive force. This need to close that gap between the familiar "what is" and the more desirable "what might be" supplies the fundamental dynamism to all socialist effort. The same spirit which impels individuals to beautify or to order their local environment is operative in the socialist when engaged in his reorganizing endeavors on a larger scale.

The fact that socialism is rooted in unrest and discontent, "divine" or otherwise, should surprise no one; for does not dissatisfaction of some shade familiarly provide the driving power for improvement in any phase of life? Existents that elicit a wish to "keep them as they are" usually embody values that one hopes can be made permanent rather than transitory; thus beautiful objects must be protected against destruction by fire or breakage, youthfulness and strength may be prolonged by "security" and healthful living, etc. But realities which depress, injure, disturb, or annoy in any degree whatsoever are to be reduced or abolished whether they are such gross evils as the obliteration bombing of great cities with their noncombatant population or minor ills like overcrowded transport vehicles.

Not infrequently the urge to maintain and the urge to transform coalesce when there is a conscious endeavor to hold certain civilized gains while one struggles to enlarge the scope of old values and to foster the birth of new ones. In this respect, the energies that find a focus in socialist striving appear to be in keeping with some more comprehensive psychobiological law of growth. If growth—any growth, but particularly growth in directions indicated by powerful gradients—is denied, the individual or social organism fails to develop "orthogenically" and a host of distressing consequences may ensue. Healthy growth conceivably can occur in both socialist and nonsocialist ways, but at a given historical stage of development like the present the probability that socialism represents the life-affirming forces in society is seen as exceptionally strong by those susceptible to its appeals. It may even be that some critical right-angle turn in man's evolution is required by the objective death-avoiding demands of the world situation as, for example, in the impressive general acceptance by a nation of "free enterprisers" of the imperative necessity for socializing and internationalizing control of atomic energy. No more significant departure from the psychological presuppositions of conventional capitalism can be found. In a somewhat less dramatic but nonetheless significant way, the widespread popularity of the T.V.A. may result from the final grudging acknowledgment by most former and persistent adversaries of the apparently incontrovertible demonstration that "unified resource development anywhere helps everyone everywhere."

Emphasis on strong, albeit often hidden, motivational elements of the nature just described springs from a different approach than that which disparagingly asserts that socialism's sole utility is the emotional outlet its symbols allow to the pent-up "inferiority complex" of the masses. Even if that were all that occurred, such a function would be helpful in reducing uncomfortable tensions, for something is clearly wrong or at least undesirable in a society where most persons suffer from feelings of inferiority. Some persons when they first discern the indisputable fact that socialism appeals to the fundamental needs for emotional and economic "security" imagine that with *this* explanation they have explained the phenomenon "away," i.e., have shown it to be without any sound basis, whereas actually a movement so grounded is psychologically as firmly based as any social institution can be.

The use of the term "security" to describe one of the basic demands that men make upon life has become such a fuzzy clinical commonplace in the last two decades that a reexamination of the idea is long overdue. Warren's *Dictionary of Psychology* defines it in the narrow Adlerian sense as "a state in which conquest is guaranteed without struggle," a conception much more limited in applicability to realistic adult living than the older less technical notion of "freedom from acute fear or chronic anxiety." A person feels secure (justifiably or not) if he is living under environmental conditions that apparently contain no threats he cannot readily master and insecure if he is actually or imaginatively in danger of being overwhelmed by superior uncontrollable or hostile forces. The search for security is probably identical with the fundamental value of "autonomy," that is, the impulse to be the master of one's own destiny and not the helpless victim of unmanageable circumstances. Implicit therein is also the feature of correct or objective orientation to the demonstrable realities of experience, for without this the organism undergoes some degree of disorganization or involuntary reorganization to which the subjective sense of insecurity is related.

A socialist system would be tested by its capacity to increase the range and depth of dependable favorable relations between its members. From such a condition of mutual help, emotional security would flow in much the same natural way that a pleasant fragrance emanates from a flowering plant. The emptiness of soul that accompanies inevitable separation by death from loved ones, the bitter pangs of unrequited affection, and many other stimuli to unhappiness would certainly remain to plague mortal man; but the currently numerous unnecessary and avoidable ills which we inflict upon each other because a scarcity economy and undemocratic folkways persist would presumably vanish. That such a state of affairs is in large measure attainable within certain patterns of group life (such as distinguished the experimental colonies of the last two centuries on this continent) may be inferred from the impressive description which L. E. Deets gives of the Hutterite religious communal society in the Midwest:

"We in our culture who verbalize endlessly about peace and unity seem to find it impossible to sense the simple, earthy idea of esthetic appreciation and enjoyment of social harmony as an ultimate end in itself. Material goods, acquisition of personal power, and the ego-satisfaction of getting ahead of the other fellow are not end-values in the Hutterite culture. The Hutterite does not need them. No psychic compulsions drive him to seek them. Since his culture is free from most conflicts, he is not forced into rivalry to escape anxiety or feelings of insecurity and helplessness. He does not feel compelled to try to build an economic wall of security around himself in the form of material wealth. He is so mentally healthy that he does not require status gained by having others of lower class status under him—and no one has higher status than he, since the society is practically classless. He is not neurotic; he has few conflicts and little to fear."[2]

The psychological contrast between this idyllic picture of rural bliss and the chronic difficulties of the harassed *kleiner Mann* of urbanized industrial Western civilization is sharp enough without adding further details. Socialism at its best (which may not be the same as socialism in actual practice) is committed not only to recapturing some of the values lost when the agricultural way of life became in a sense a minority privilege, but more important, to adding those values technology has made possible for the first time in human history. This systematic difference between the tribal prototypes of socialist or cooperative man and competitive man is clearly visible in the following coherent patterns:[3]

[2] *Human Nature and Enduring Peace*, Third Yearbook of the Society for the Psychological Study of Social Issues, Gardner Murphy, ed. (New York, 1945), p. 344.
[3] Modified from Margaret Mead, *Cooperation and Competition among Primitive Peoples* (New York, 1937), p. 511.

Major Behavioral Emphasis:	Cooperation	Competition
Social Structure:	Power over persons relatively un-exercised	Depends on individual initiative
Chief Value:	Faith in an ordered society or universe	Property for individual ends
Prestige Basis:	Weak emphasis on status	Single scale of "success"; hierarchy
Personality Structure:	High individual security	Ego strongly developed

Within these over-all configurations, the nature of the typical mature selves found there would differ markedly. It must never be forgotten that *socialism is ultimately as much a program for personality modification* (betterment or improvement) *as it is a proposal for economic transformation.* The latter feature may be more prominent, but it is no more important or essential to the systematic position than the former. The part-whole relations stressed by modern field theory give special prominence to these reciprocal effects, for a substantial alteration in one aspect will inevitably evoke major modifications in others.

The tabular opposition roughly outlined above has the disadvantage of implying a sharper dichotomy than the facts of continuity justify. For example, socialism certainly is not inconsistent with, but strongly reaffirms, such old ethical norms as kindness, honesty, courage, diligence, cheerfulness, rationality, etc. Since it is one of the more rigorous and fundamental manifestations of the democratic spirit, it requires that ultimate power in the state or community be genuinely vested in the majority of the people with permanent constitutional guarantees of full civil liberties to all minorities. Much, if not most of its positive content, harmonizes with the loftiest expressed ideals of general Western or specifically American culture. This conservative or traditional aspect of socialism encourages individual identification since personal behavior may then faithfully reflect the "best" in the entire collective situation, thus providing the ideational framework for more satisfying adjustments in the making. In this as in some other vital respects, the continental or global diffusion of socialism may well follow the rules for the diffusion of any other culture trait. In 1934 the Central Conference of American Rabbis declared that "all basic economic enterprises should be socialized and democratized" thereby indicating that the absorption of the key socialist principle had made considerable headway by that date.

IV. Varieties of Socialist "Experience" and Behavior

In his famous *Varieties of Religious Experience*, William James analyzed many autobiographical documents of individuals known for their religious interests, and emerged with the conclusion that religion in one or another form supplies that minimum of direction and meaning without which certain personalities are in danger of disintegrating. Functionally, the socialist creed appears to play a similar role in giving to many lives a unifying center about which lesser loyalties are grouped. This does not imply that without a socialist tinge to their beliefs such persons would totter on the brink of emotional collapse; but it does declare that the goals and values associated with the position are more satisfying than older or alternative objectives, with the result that a self, either actually or potentially mildly or deeply divided, is now more coherently organized. Acceptance of such a position and participation in its associated activities enables the individual to operate on what he feels is a higher level than would otherwise be the case.

This emphasis suggests a rough-and-ready classification of many different categories of socialist personalities to supplement the general picture outlined in Section III above. For example, we can distinguish between: (1) socialists to whom socialism is central rather than peripheral in their careers; (2) socialists who are generally well adjusted versus those who are comparatively "sick souls"; (3) socialists concerned with complete cultural change contrasted with those limited to political and economic objectives.

The propriety of the first distinction is readily seen if one compares the place of socialism in the lives of such highly endowed persons as Angelica Balabanoff and Norman Thomas—or acknowledged leaders of high or low degree in the movement generally—with its position in the total activity stream of some indignant workman or discreet professor who sporadically votes the "straight" Socialist ticket in those election years when the other parties appear unusually obnoxious. In the former case, the depth of involvement in the commitment to the socialist cause is so marked that it approaches the complete sacrifice of "life, fortune, and sacred honor" to the triumph of the aims championed. It is not just part of the person's life that is affected, but almost literally the whole thereof. Here the sacrificial intensity of motivation is not only stronger but far more sustained than with the casual follower who finds socialism "acceptable enough" but who refuses to risk or even to offer anything substantial to bring it about. The latter may be just a fair-weather friend and "contributor" or may actually share emotionally both major victories and defeats; in any event, participation and identification are passing rather than lasting features of his conduct. A value which approaches the absolute and one which is a "marginal utility" obviously are imbedded in different strata of the ego that contains them. In the one case, one does all that one's energies allow; in the other, the process stops short with an adoption of verbal formulas.

Similarly, the propriety of the second grouping advanced above appears to be supported by common observation. The very titles of certain autobiographies, such as James Maurer's *It Can Be Done* and Oscar Ameringer's *If You Don't Weaken,* are neat reflections of that peculiar sturdiness of spirit revealed by men with high morale preserved throughout a life of bitter and unceasing struggle. The old farmer who was "converted" in his youth by Eugene Debs and vowed to remain loyal to the ideals of "the greatest man since Jesus Christ," the British miner who would no more question the goodness of socialism for all laboring men—or for that matter, all men—than a devout theist doubts the reality of God, and the urban mechanic who has achieved a real sense of solidarity with all nonpropertied laborers everywhere are less eminent but equally genuine examples of the optimistic "sane" outlook.

Needless to say, pessimistic socialists whose hearts are heavy with a sense of loss are found side by side with their more cheerful comrades. They are often disillusioned middle-aged or elderly folks who are convinced that "some form of socialism" is the answer to the great questions of the age, but who openly doubt that the average man is either bright enough or decent enough to bring it about before a series of universal catastrophes undiscriminatingly descend upon all. They look upon socialism as the one chance in a million which might save the race, but, like somber-hued theologians, they proclaim their loss of faith in mankind. They feel that the cause has been lost so far as the present generation is concerned and that the best one can hope for is that a remnant will preserve the faith until more favorable conditions in some dim future permit it to flourish again. Refugees from persecution abroad or victims of illiberal practices at home understandably exhibit this pattern of despair more often than those who have not undergone such acute suffering. It also seems to occur with more than average frequency among those who as adolescents and youths were strongly inspired to work for "socialism in our time" but who have become debilitated by "battle fatigue" as a result of the prolongation and immensity of the struggle.

Another differentiation within the socialist population which is plainly perceptible marks off those who view socialism as concerned with *all* of group life and those who deliberately restrict its applicability to the narrower political-economic sphere. To convey suitably these opposed emphases on the scope or breadth of the applicability of the doctrine, one could label one the latitudinarian (or "totalitarian"!) and the other the sectarian (or partial) approach, although unfortunately these meanings are easily reversed. It is a grave misfortune that so useful a linguistic and ideological term as "totalitarianism" now has the significance of an all-inclusive despotic tyranny whereas it could profitably and neutrally have been employed to characterize an internally harmonious culture operating on the same principles throughout all its institutions. A "total democracy," for example, would be totalitarian in this purely descriptive or nonpejorative sense.

In any event, despite the "word trouble" one encounters here, there are socialists who stress the *whole* fabric of community life, and also those to whom the vital and only important *part* (for their purposes) is the economic and political area and who therefore view it as illegitimate to extend socialist concepts to inherently nonsocialist problems of art, the educative process, family relations, religion, etc. The former include a primary concern for the character and personality not only of socialists but of all individuals within their version of the good life; the latter, while not denying its importance, are disposed to hold that this problem of personal quality and behavioral excellence will largely take care of itself as soon as the requisite forces making for such superior growth are "released" by an appropriate reconstruction of society. A certain form of materialism or "economism" in Eucken's sense appears to bound their horizon; by contrast, the others seem to have a touch of the spiritual or mystical. But for the fact that it would probably complicate matters, one could speak of one as the "secular" or deterministic and the other as the "transcendental" or voluntaristic kind of socialist. The latter displays a broadly humanistic bent and is prone to stress socialism as a form of elemental moral obligation arising from insight rather than viewing it exclusively as a natural or social necessity resulting from the inevitable adjustment to changing relations and conditions associated with the advance of "technology."

Paired contrasts of the sort just supplied could be extended almost indefinitely, for there is a sense in which it is true that there are as many different varieties of socialism as there are individual socialists. Personality always introduces its distinctive variables of emphasis and tempo into every organized group effort to move in approximately the same direction by essentially similar means. Temperamental, constitutional, and life-history factors largely account for the fact that one socialist wishes to go rapidly rather than slowly toward the goal, one includes room for some features of presocialist systems which another repudiates, one will engage in compromises while another remains unyielding, and so on.

The presence of this wide range of responses, however, should not destroy one's perception of the essential unity of the socialist *Anschauung* any more than one's awareness of the extensive differences in dogs makes one confuse them as a group with cats. There are men in general, there are individuals in particular, and there are also types or classes of men which are identifiable on the basis of one or another criterion of separateness. In most respects, socialists are clearly like "men in general" since that is the large parent population from which they are selected; but in some important or even key respects, they display significant behavioral differences besides the major one in belief which gives them their name. Hypothetically, the two most important may be expressed as follows: (1) Socialists as a body manifest *"closure"* tendencies with respect to community trends in more acute and accentuated form than the average man; (2) They are more consistent in their public attitudes than the average man.

Since *closure* is one of the major technical concepts which Gestalt theory has introduced into modern psychology, some elaboration of its general meaning must be made before we apply it to the specific problem under discussion. The term is authoritatively defined in Warren's *Dictionary* as "one of the principles of psychophysical organization, whereby the course of behavior and its segregated wholes (actions, perceptions, memories) tend to become complete or closed forms; also, the process whereby changing, incomplete systems attain a final stability." Illustrations of this mental mechanism or force is the strong tendency to "round out" unfinished processes, such as inserting the fourth side of a square when the three sides are plainly indicated, responding almost compulsively with the "required" answer of the word *Harrisburg* (if one has this particular bit of geographical knowledge) in such an informational problem as "The capital city of Pennsylvania is _____," or such as intending to change one's tie or shirt only and continuing to undress further because the preliminaries of a total act carry one along by some sort of psychic momentum. Examples of closure are almost endless and appear to be found wherever the various parts of any natural organized unity clearly reflect the dominance of that dynamic *whole* of which they are *parts*.

This generalized completion tendency is a universal human or even organismic property; its particular socialist application consequently is found in the distinctive quality of the closure phenomena found in such personalities. Man is always under some tension, but different goals beckon with varying urgencies and they are far from being equally realizable. The nonsocialist may be presumed to have a great practical advantage over the socialist in being able to achieve a larger proportion of his personal or group objectives and is therefore less under a sense of strain resulting from much "unfinished business"; just because his pattern of aims does *not* include the conscious advancement of a socialist order he typically is in the more favorable position of the person with $n-1$ things to do compared with the man who has accepted $n+1$ obligations.

This would be quantitatively true if the final states sought by the two types here contrasted were equal in their demands on the energies and emotions; but how much more is the difference in the inner conditions intensified when the difficulty of attainment is added as a complicating factor? The desire for a new car or even a house is comparatively easily met when matched against the desire to have international democratic socialism prevail throughout the world. The "unclosed configuration" in the latter instance is of such spatial and temporal magnitude that any organism sensitized thereto is bound to have a higher level of closure readiness waiting to discharge itself along appropriate paths of social change than one to whom the reorganization of the community pattern is not a "problem" and in whom therefore no requisite preparatory state is found.

It does not seem unreasonable to postulate greater dynamism in regard to cultural transformation on the part of the median socialist if one relates this to simpler manifestations of the same underlying disposition. Impatience, for instance, is a personality trait of hyperkinetic individuals under strong inner pressure to reach certain ends; this frequently leads to a short circuiting of the intervening steps because they seem psychologically less real than the ultimate goal on which most of one's psychic energies are concentrated. The man "in a hurry" to get somewhere is likely to shift from first to third gear in starting his automobile and to use second gear only when he must. Indeed, the development of the "automatic" or fluid gear shifting mechanism seems to have been the inevitable result of some principle of economy or law of least effort governing the literal *motor* behavior of the driver!

Something like this probably functions in the socialist mind reacting to the numerous inconsistencies and imperfect integration that all historical societies contain. An eventual unity is felt and implied even though not fully operative in the immediate situation. Consider the problem of the thorough and uniform democratization of all phases of organized or group living to which the American culture seems to be committed. Observation of the current scene from this standpoint might reveal roughly the following varying degrees of attainment in selected aspects: (1) As a *political* democracy the U.S. is 60 per cent democratic; (2) In matters of *social* democracy the U.S. is 40 per cent democratic; (3) With respect to *economic* democracy the U.S. is 20 per cent democratic.

This attempt at quantification may be rejected as involving variables and estimates too crude to be serviceable; but more relevant psychologically is the fact that if some people view them as highly meaningful and approximately correct, then the sense of a gap which demands bridging readily arises. The significant thing, too, about the closure tendency is that anything less than 100 per cent fulfilment keeps it in vigorous action and that the drive toward consummation is intensified with the narrowing of the distance that remains to be covered, just as the reader may discern in himself a more powerful urge to produce a "whole" circle when 90 per cent of the perimeter is given than when an arc of no more than 15 per cent of the total is presented. Even apart from the presumptive operation of this "law" or basic force in the human nervous system, there is an understandable difference in both sensitivity and response between those who feel their country is already as democratic as possible (i.e., a "closed" or stable system that has ceased to evolve in *this* aspect), and those who are convinced it has traversed but a fraction of the necessary distance.

Another illustration of this process may be found in the sharp contrast that socialists (because they are "set" to perceive such things?) see, and therefore characteristically emphasize, between the alleged principle for distributing the national dividend and the actual methods by which differences in income result. Psychologically, one of capitalism's strongest claims has been the contention that people are paid by society in proportion to their contribution to its welfare. If individual differences are real, it seems but just that pecuniary rewards in general should run approximately parallel to the amount of economic or allied service rendered, at least after a certain humanitarian minimum regardless of "merit" has been established.

While it is hard to test satisfactorily the positive value of the increment the commonwealth receives from each person's participation in its institutional activities, and hence certain variable errors in the "disbursing" operation must be expected, there is little doubt that the *capacity* to make such contributions appears in the population in accordance with the familiar Gaussian probability curve. Intelligence apparently follows this rule and so do the frequency tables for almost every distinguishable and measurable mental and physical trait of the human personality. While it is much truer to assert that people are paid for the value of the peculiar *combination* of traits they make available for certain "business" purposes rather than for their absolute standing in any single component item, such permutations likewise notoriously follow the bell-shaped or symmetrical frequency curve. Consequently, if people in any economy, capitalist or otherwise, were really paid in accord with the demonstrated scarcity of their particular psychological pattern, the curve for the distribution of the national income should also follow the so-called "normal" curve.

But it does not. It is well known that income is subject to an unusual "concentration" of wealth, a fact which appears objectively in a sharply skewed curve with most incomes heaped somewhere toward the lower end, a long tapered tail for a diminishing number of incomes of relatively great size, and a marked difference between the median or modal income and the arithmetical mean, the latter being substantially larger because of the differential weighting exerted by the bigger incomes, etc.

This departure of the income curve from the more commonly encountered norm is evidently attributed to a "constant error" or distorting influence produced by such institutional arrangements or social "forces" as inheritance, monopoly (in the form of legally sustained privileges), in-group advantages in investment and speculation, concentrated control of productive resources, the fact that lower incomes are largely set by the values dominating the controlling or paymaster fraction in the "upper brackets," etc. In other words, the income curve is essentially an expression of social power—which is also typically concentrated rather than diffused randomly—and not a faithful reflection of everyone's general utility for which suitable measures are not yet available.

The socialist's reaction system does rest upon some strong and persistent sense of tension between "what is" in the way of contemporary economic realities and "what ought to be" in terms of resulting psychological demands. On page 794 of the *Federal Reserve Bulletin* for July 1947 it is reported that the highest 10 per cent of America's "spending units" then received 32 per cent of the country's total money income as compared with the bottom 10 per cent, who secured but 1 per cent thereof! This sharp contrast in the size of various groups' shares in the national dividend (which countless Lorenz curves with their steep positive acceleration show as a stable characteristic of all major national economies for at least a century) may induce feelings of equanimity or mild interest in the scholar and indifference or pride in some successful businessmen— but to the socialist it is a source of continuing mental discomfort if for no better or deeper reason than the fact that his more pronounced egalitarian disposition makes him respond that way.

This sense of distress with what is keenly felt as an unjust state of affairs solicits and sustains corrective tendencies of various sorts which give a characteristic stamp to the conative life of the socialist personality. The fact that he is usually and humorously much clearer about what is patently wrong with the present pattern than what would be demonstrably right about some future alternative probably means that he still has much to learn. Strict income equality (such as prevailed in some experimental colonies and which George Bernard Shaw provocatively championed) is less generally supported as the way out than an alternative involving a guaranteed high minimum with a maximum perhaps no greater than twice the average. In any case, the size of the "spread" between extremes would be markedly reduced, all figures rising with total productivity increases just as they have hitherto tended to do.

Still another related way in which some form of closure makes itself felt in socialist thought is the conviction that a genuine economy of abundance is the natural terminus of the machine age. A steady flood of needed goods and services is what technological advances imply—a stream so great in fact as literally to make "plenty" available for all. But the flow is regularly cut off long before that happens. Periodic crises like wars and depressions are tantalizing, to say the least, for having allowed the multitude to glimpse the promised land, the nonsocialist governors of this expanding technology then make decisions which compel mankind to continue to trudge needlessly and wearily through an economic wilderness for another generation or more. The race might have much, but is forced to get along with so little because waste, destruction, and deliberate perversion or confining of vast productive powers keep consumption within such limits of scarcity as will permit some profit or "unearned increment" to go to the owning group.

Such an analysis, regardless of the factual accuracy of the beliefs here described, reflects the essential structure of socialist thinking. Guided by some compulsive indication that events are naturally headed in a certain approved direction, there is intense annoyance (if one may so understate the situation) when it is recognized that institutional barriers such as are collectively symbolized by "capitalism" stand in the way of the frictionless attainment of some otherwise inevitable end. Denied closure satisfaction through an early consummation of various processes, the socialist must reconcile himself to the spectacle of a world society apparently willfully remaining poor when it has in its hands the means for abolishing poverty.

The higher degree of consistency of attitude which we have attributed to socialists is not difficult to document and can be supported by a variety of evidence. Inconsistency as a formal attribute of any individual set of beliefs is a commonly encountered phenomenon. To believe that "America spends far too little upon her army and navy" and simultaneously to accept the proposition that "Under the conditions of modern warfare, international and civil wars inevitably destroy more human and social values than they preserve or create," is to affirm two positions which are at least disharmonious in spirit. Nonetheless reactions similar in the compartmentalization which they imply are of such frequent occurrence as to represent normal rather than deviant behavior. In one study by the writer[4] more than three out of four teachers held that such fundamental values as individual liberty and initiative would decline under socialism, and yet 50 per cent championed public operation and management of the nation's coal mines. Comparable percentages supported the nationalization of other major industries. This disconcerting adherence to essentially incompatible approaches to large public questions may not unfairly be considered typical of the average or consciously nonsocialist contemporary American. Perhaps uncertainty concerning the effect upon

[4] G. W. Hartmann, *The Teacher and Society*, W. H. Kilpatrick, ed. (New York, 1937), p. 194.

various aspects of life of complete versus partial socialization underlies this state of affairs.

The ideational unity of the average socialist's opinions is rarely if ever perfected, mainly because of the magnitude of the concepts to be organized and his uneven adaptation to new events and added knowledge about group life. Nonetheless, the views which he finds congenial exhibit a fairly pronounced consistency with each other presumably because they are *accepted only after passing some rough test of conformity to the general socialist framework.* A socialist who favored making all highways toll roads would be as much a freak as the professed modernist or functional architect who included ornate Gothic fenestration in an exterior design where this does not "belong." Just as eclecticism appears to make poor art and dubious science, so it destroys the possibility of building a community in accordance with definite principles of organization. Adoption of the planning viewpoint as such appears to lead to the elimination of much inconsistency in thought and behavior just because there is some standard or criterion by which uncertainties may be resolved.

That consistency in the domain of the applied social sciences is a higher and more pervasive value among socialists than among most other groups appears from the use and emphasis this notion implicitly receives in much of their polemical literature. The government operates the post office for all—why can't it supply clothing to all? It insures and pensions soldiers—why not all civilians? The public schools of America are almost completely socialized in the sense that they are maintained by community funds and presumably run on a nonprofit basis for the benefit of all—then why not deal with the health and medical needs of people in similar fashion? If a T.V.A. is so demonstrably beneficial to the particular area wherein it operates, why shouldn't every river valley in the continent eventually be subject to the same high level of technical resource management? Or, more generally, if a little socialism has proved to be valuable, why wouldn't more of it be still better?

V. *Socialist Clientele*

The selective nature of the analysis and exposition so far followed runs the danger of portraying prosocialist individuals as a little better than they actually are. Certain undeniable and salient qualities such as social sensitivity, reformist drive, and coherent convictions may seem more valuable when viewed in piecemeal fashion than when more fully judged in relation to their genesis, content, and presumptive consequences. Some correctives therefore must be introduced not so much for the purpose of demonstrating the "human, all too human" failings of comparatively high-minded souls (no more superfluous undertaking can be imagined) as for achieving something approaching a balanced picture of the motivational forces actually at work among politically aroused personalities.

Without reflecting in any way upon the possibility or desirability of socialism itself, observation of the behavior of many followers of this doctrine reveals them to share the familiar shortcomings of their non-socialist opponents. Quarrelsomeness, a hypercritical approach, obstinate attachment to explanations rendered untenable by new evidence of altered conditions (a curious "conservative" defect in a "radical" group!), a disposition to mock honest and sincere blunderers, stereotyping or "labeling" persons or movements in disregard of their complex fullness, exploiting another's good will in the name of a tenuous comradeship—these and allied evidences of human imperfection are regularly encountered in contemporary socialist meetings that open as a quiet little church of true believers. It has even been remarked by some socialists, annoyed with these and other limitations of themselves and their fellows, that the greatest obstacle to socialism is the average socialist: were he an unquestionably superior personality, the appeal of socialism would be strengthened by the spread of the opinion that none but top-quality people are identified therewith.

However, the fact that the average Quaker has been a moral aristocrat for about three centuries while Quakerism itself has not gained numerically in relation to other denominations of Christendom suggests that the issue of the "acceptance" of a viewpoint is affected by much more than the demonstrable merit of some or all of its representatives. What they stand for must have some vital meaning to others—and not just to themselves. The good man may be respected without being believed or imitated; a more vulnerable personality who typifies current folkways may win devotion despite admitted "character" weaknesses so long as he effectively champions other major values of influential groups. Indeed, there is some reason for believing that the average person feels mildly uncomfortable in the presence of someone of exceptional intellectual or moral excellence—a phenomenon which bars *rapport* and apparently underlies the disposition to accept social leadership from those who are a little, but not too much, above the middle level of the group as a whole. According to Leta Hollingsworth, an IQ difference between leaders and followers of more than 30 points appears to be too much for the "masses" to span appreciatively. The best teaching, for example, seems to occur when there is an "optimum gap" between the instructor and his class rather than a maximum difference in either attainment or endowment.

Considerations such as these make highly relevant the question whether socialists as a group are better, worse, or the same as the general population in any distinguishable human quality. Are they brighter, duller, or identical? Are they richer or poorer? Are certain body types commoner among them than among others? If a composite portrait were available, in what respects, if any, would it depart from the norm?

These are all interesting and probably important scientific questions, but it is regrettable that exact statistical information on most of these points does not exist. Self-study of the membership by organizational secretaries could readily answer some of these questions, but whatever psychological interest has arisen has usually focused on less quantitative problems. Fortunately, there is some material ordinarily buried in miscellaneous reports concerning the "psychology of radicalism and conservatism" which indicates the probabilities of real differences in some significant features.

Whatever test data we have on comparative abstract or verbal intelligence suggests that prosocialist subjects tend to score a little higher than other political groups. Back in 1924, Henry T. Moore[5] reported that the mean intelligence percentiles of Dartmouth College students during that presidential campaign year varied as follows:

La Follette supporters	67.0	(average percentile rank)		
Coolidge	49.7	"	"	"
Davis	48.4	"	"	"

This strongly implies that the Socialist-Progressive coalition candidate then appealed most to that relatively select group of college men whose capacity for symbol manipulation placed them in the upper third of their classes. At Harvard the median scholarship of the La Follette backers was one-half letter grade higher than the college as a whole, suggesting that the minority political preference of the "intelligentsia," i.e., the more bookish or academically inclined, was fairly general.

Many findings in social and political psychology are limited by temporal and spatial factors, but for at least a generation within the American culture the attitudinal relationship identified above has persisted. In 1932, Garrison noted that among Southerners, 33.3 per cent of the A students were listed as "conservative" compared to 52.6 per cent who were classed as "radical"; only 3.9 per cent of the D students were radical but 59.6 per cent were conservative![6] Despite the looseness and restricted applicability of these and similar findings, one is justified in holding that whenever progressivism and liberalism assume quasi-socialist forms they tend to do so in the minds of relatively more literate undergraduates.

[5] See H. T. Moore, "Innate Factors in Radicalism and Conservatism," *Journal of Abnormal and Social Psychology*, xx (Oct. 1925), pp. 234-44.

[6] Gwyn Moore and K. C. Garrison, "A Comparative Study of Social and Political Attitudes of College Students," *ibid.*, xxvii (July-Sept. 1932), pp. 195-208.

Comparable evidence below the college level or among the general public is less clear-cut, but the limited data imply the existence of a similar relation. The Young People's Socialist League (largely high-school youths) appears to be composed mainly of bright articulate youngsters with a distinct interest and aptitude in the social sciences as a group. In certain special-purpose organizations, for instance labor unions, such a socialist notion as is involved in viewing "workers as a potentially dominant class" is more widespread among officers and leaders than among the "rank-and-file" members.[7] So far as the mass of voters go, there may be some faint indication that the correlation persists in the fact that Reading, Bridgeport, and Milwaukee, the only large American communities with Socialist administrations in recent years, stand average or better in Thorndike's provocative index of community "goodness," which he attributes primarily to the mental and moral qualities of their inhabitants.[8]

If the data point plainly to the conclusion that socialists are at least equal to, and probably a little better than, nonsocialists in native alertness and educational achievement, then what can one say about their economic and social position, which might on a priori grounds be expected to have some low but positive correlation with these variables? There is an old and popular assumption that poverty and personal misfortune turn a man into a socialist and that the acquisition of wealth and power leads him to abandon that position. That plenty of such cases can be cited is undeniable, but no necessary "rule" to that effect can be substantiated.

In a national survey in 1936, the writer[9] made the amusing and somewhat unanticipated discovery that Socialist public-school teachers (i.e., persons who acknowledged that they had voted for Norman Thomas in 1932) had a median salary of $1,950, Republican teachers $1,750, and Democratic teachers $1,550. Within this fairly homogeneous professional group, therefore, the Socialists appeared to hold a favored or even privileged position. The figures just cited were apparently not attributable to any concentration of "radical pedagogues" in the larger northern cities with higher salary schedules, for the same relative order was maintained in New York. What few clues we have indicate that there is less resistance to socialist concepts among those with higher *earned* incomes than among those with smaller so-called *unearned* revenues from inheritance, property possession, etc., suggesting that the *source* rather than the *amount* of income may be decisive. At any rate, the notion that socialists are largely

[7] See G. W. Hartmann and Theodore Newcomb, eds., *Industrial Conflict* (New York, 1939), pp. 313-38.

[8] Cf. E. L. Thorndike, *Your City* (New York, 1939).

[9] Hartmann, *The Teacher and Society*, p. 219.

economic incompetents who rationalize their business incapacity by assaults on the rules of a game they are unable to play is untenable.

It is something else to agree that successful "business" as ordinarily transacted in the industrial and commercial world demands emotional or attitudinal adaptations which many socialists find utterly uncongenial. For example, the subjective price required to win an occasional or regular financial advantage over other persons seems like a denial of brotherhood to individuals who find some of the realities of the everyday world too sordid for them to participate in those common methods of earning a living or "getting ahead." They therefore consciously and intentionally "escape" into, or find inspiration in, a vision of a more orderly theoretical world where exploitation is absent and human relations are friendlier and happier; along with this they experience a strong compulsion to transform the real current economy they know, but reject, into the image of the ultimate ideal system that is so much more acceptable.

Part of the difference between socialists and others may therefore be sought in qualitatively and quantitatively different "levels of aspiration." Ordinarily, success raises one's expected plane of achievement, while failure tends to lower it; the size and direction of the gap between aim and realization serves to measure the amount of contentment or satisfaction resulting from the effort. Thus, anticipating a million votes and getting 100,000 is a blow; predicting 80,000 but receiving 90,000 is a joyous thrill. The socialist's aspiration level, by its very definition, is anything but modest; the demanding nature of the tensions to which he has exposed himself are such that whatever demonstrated gains occur seem petty in terms of the magnitude of the ambitious quota left unfulfilled.

VI. Motivation in a Socialist Order

The common assumption that the "profit motive" must be appealed to if the work of the world is to be done does not do justice to the multi-motivational nature of even the most meagerly endowed human being. Men are active basically because they are alive. And much of their energy flows in the direction of economically useful production without the stimulation or the direct lure of additional pecuniary gain: such obvious examples may be cited as the activities of the housewife and mother in rearing a family, or the many unpaid services to others which even the most commercially minded find themselves performing without any assurance that the concrete advantages of the auditor's asset of customer good will must result.

Experience and experiment combine to make suspect all attempted reductions of complex group or "institutional" behavior to a single motive. Workers in war industries were activated by more than the simple inducement of higher pay; their identification with the conflict through relatives in combat service, "moral" attitudes toward war and peace in general, and even amateur strategic estimates of the urgency of the struggle affected output. That the intricate social relationships of home, factory, office, and field may elevate or depress both the performance and the earnings of individuals at all levels is one of the most solidly established findings of industrial and clinical psychology.[10] Contrary to what journalistic apologists and critics often assert, one can no more properly attribute a "prime mover" role to the quest for profits even in a capitalist culture than one can make the "hunger motive" the underlying force in all that man did in precapitalist times. An interest may be powerful and fundamental in animating conduct without being the sole determiner thereof.

There can be little question that normal men usually and consciously seek "benefits" for themselves in the sense of ultimately avoiding ills and achieving desirable experiences. A modified hedonism may thus be made conformable to the facts of psychology even though ignorance of consequences, the subtlety and difficulty of choices involving degrees of goodness or badness, the puzzling phenomena of the unconscious, and the ethical validity of conscience and the sense of duty all unite to urge cautious discrimination in using so comprehensive a principle.

"Benefits," however, are rarely "profits" in the orthodox economist's sense of the word: i.e., the monetary difference or surplus income available to the entrepreneur after all other expenses of operating the enterprise have been paid. Moreover, comparatively few persons are in the role of "enterprisers"—instead their "gains" come in the form of added real wages plus whatever social income is indirectly and increasingly returned in the form of public parks and similar community services. At best, therefore, the profit motive operates strictly only within that fraction of the population cast in the role of "business leaders"—and particularly that still smaller fraction of a fraction which is neither in the salaried corporation bureaucracy or managerial staff but actually possesses and wields the power to make policy decisions at the highest level in terms of costs and returns on invested capital. Even members of such a financial elite are not so single purposed in outlook as to sacrifice every consideration to the one implicit controlling aim of maximum profits. Many directors and trustees derive more pride from being on the governing board of the largest or most influential organization than on the most "profitable" in the narrower sense and by their preferences weight an enterprise in the former direction rather than in the latter. There are many other loyalties and prejudices to which even "profiteers" sometimes deliberately give priority in place of purely monetary acquisitiveness.

[10] Cf. *Civilian Morale*, Second Yearbook of the Society for the Psychological Study of Social Issues, Goodwin Watson, ed. (New York, 1942), especially pp. 273-401.

On the whole, much of the worry as to what will keep the industrial machine functioning in a socialist society deprived of the pattern of incentives labeled personal "profit" seems bootless; indeed analysis reveals it to be largely an artificial problem. Men who are politically free appear to work just as hard and just as efficiently in nonprofit institutions such as schools, hospitals, churches, the judicial establishment, government experiment stations, etc., as they do in private profit organizations. It is a psychological error to assume that motivation is unchangeable and that here is one aspect of individual response or adjustment not subject to the laws of learning. The codes of ethics already adopted by various professions, with their emphasis on the vocational competence and responsibility of the practitioner and the rights of the client, could be extended via educational means in one form or another to all occupations in a socialist economy; in fact, the full professionalization of business may be possible only under such a system. The complex of plant and services constituting the T.V.A. is almost unthinkable as a private enterprise today; and the rule that denationalization is next to impossible once nationalization has been operating in any field is sufficient indication that whatever new motives are involved in such agencies or projects are both stronger and more satisfying than the ones they replaced. Given a commonly accepted and fairly concrete goal for *the economy as a whole*, work efforts can be as meaningfully stimulated without immediate individual economic reward as is now the case with smaller social segments where favorable conditions for high achievement exist.

Stigmatizing the administrative or other personnel of such publicly controlled organizations as "bureaucrats" is irrelevant or malicious name-calling as long as they have a useful community function to perform and are as well qualified as their critics to discharge this duty. Where officialism continues to mean a narrow, formal, or rigid routine—a routine disregarding individual requirements and unimaginatively and timorously following precedent because it would rather do the wrong thing in the "right" or prescribed way than the right thing in the wrong or different way—, then the appropriate remedy lies in a further extension of the democratic process whereby procedures can be periodically reviewed and "freshened" by joint consultation between agency members and their particular publics. The felt rewards of such active participation in economic self-government and direct control of one's destiny are similar in kind and variety to those personality gains which result from full political freedom. It is not unreasonable to hold that the motivational pattern which *democratic* socialism (there is no other kind!) aims to foster meets most of the tests of functional maturity and "autonomy," and that by comparison a competitive economic structure based on struggle appears primitive, infantile, or adolescent in development. The parallelism between individual and collective developmental stages is unusually close on this point. Cooperation or mutually helpful group planning in almost any institutional form is a more advanced cultural growth stage than simple universal rivalry for common necessities, and while there is a real danger that socialism may wrongly assume children to be adults, the reverse opinion and practice appears to be psychologically and morally a much greater peril.

VII. What Behavior Modifications Facilitate or Accompany Socialism?

The brevity of the discussion in the immediately preceding section should not blind one to the fact that the far-reaching change in the cultural fabric ultimately envisioned by a full-bodied socialism requires equally profound shifts or advances in popular attitudes. The presocialist liberalism to which the average American is sensitive evidently arose in Judaea and Hellas about 600 B.C. and centered vaguely in some sort of reflection on the possibilities of so controlling interpersonal relations that more and better satisfactions could be experienced by more people. Over the centuries, the application of this spirit has slowly and with infinite pain led to the conceptual differentiation and championing of such cardinal desiderata as justice, kindness, independent thought, protection against arbitrary political power, freedom from economic exploitation, and adjustment to individual needs and capacities. Sloganized eventually in the incomparable trinity of the French Revolution—liberty, equality, fraternity—and modernized with some gain in precision by contemporary translation into peace, plenty, and freedom, these extensive values are still further condensed, systematized, and implied by the one comprehensive term of "democracy" or "socialism." A major danger in these verbalizations is that uttering them may be made a substitute for efforts to achieve them and that saying the acceptable thing creates the illusion of its concrete presence.

There is strong reason for believing that no one of the ideals listed above can be fully realized without more or less simultaneously realizing all the rest since they appear to be interdependent objectives. Not a single one can be sacrificed in the hope of reaching or retaining one or more of the others without the eventual loss of all. Organically, they belong together; they spring from the same sources and point toward the same inclusive goals. That is why a socialist ceases to be such—in whole and not just in part—as soon as he condones or engages in inhumane conduct; thinks exclusively or primarily in "in-group" terms like nationalism or race; accepts competition as the road to economic well-being; is deliberately nonscientific or antiscientific in disregarding the findings of any form of research; and tolerates or endorses despotic authority whether this be dictatorship in home, school, factory, union, party, church, club, or any other form of human association. The polar opposites of all these five evils are indispensable minima for inspiring authentic socialist behavior.

These may seem like exceptionally severe and rigorous standards and yet the close integration of aims and methods implied in the evolution of the concept of socialism is itself the source of these stern criteria. In a highly significant article, Victor Serge declares that "psychological problems have acquired a practical importance in both domestic and foreign affairs that is at least equal to that of the immediate economic factors"— a position which historians, economists, politicians, and of course psychologists would probably all endorse. "When political decisions are to be made, the character of the people who make them is a determining factor. . . . Ideology draws upon character and in turn sustains it."[11] No plainer and truer statement could be made. The kind of socialism one gets depends heavily upon the principles and personalities of those who shape it just as a specialized socialist scheme of things in turn will mold the natures of those who grow up in that milieu.

Arriving at a socialist position is clearly a matter of learning and maturation in conformity with certain appropriate predispositions such as average intelligence and general good will toward the rest of mankind. An individual so equipped will be able to recapitulate within his own life span a sample of the tremendously complex intellectual and moral evolution of mankind, especially that portion which culminates in the socialist ideal. As far as one can tell from a few type situations, most persons can learn (with varying degrees of proficiency) to become socialists in the same sense that most people can learn to read or write their own names: that is, they must be "ready" to assimilate that particular experience. Both are adaptations to specific challenges which elicit the reactions designated after a longer or shorter period of neural reorganization occurring in a "prepared" organism.

Socialists appear normally to become such by the process of "conversion." It is unfortunate that this overdramatic term has a purely religious connotation to many, but it may be used correctly to mark a radical shift from opposition to (or, more often, ignorance of) a given world view to adherence, or the reverse. All such cases of conversion involve "insight," a technical word meaning a form of adaptive response in which the appropriateness of what one does is seen to follow directly and necessarily from the requirements of the situation or problem. Although a man can ordinarily be "converted" only after a prolonged and varied series of antecedent experiences which produce the requisite

[11] See Victor Serge, "Socialism and Psychology," *Modern Review*, May 1947, pp. 194-202.

preliminary sensitization, the shift itself when it finally occurs is usually quite rapid and "wholesale" or complete rather than partial or piecemeal in nature. The mixed intellectual and emotional reconstruction involved in socialism is often brought to a head by an impressive speech, a persuasive look, a convincing friend, or more spontaneously by inner groping for an answer to such riddles as "Why misery in a scientific age?" In any case, the important phenomenon is that the adoption of a socialist standpoint comes typically not by a steady accretion of little fragments; on the contrary, the system even when roughly outlined in its essential totality is perceived as a unit and vigorously approved. It is like suddenly finding the solution to a difficult and resistant puzzle.

The fact that a high degree of certainty and conviction parallels this process frequently puzzles the observer who does not share this assurance and skeptically suspects a pseudosolution. Yet this inner sense of rightness accounts in part for the persistence and vitality of *any* belief. The "rightness" is not exclusively an ethical persuasion, but is reinforced by the same sort of technical or objective confidence which an engineer has in a doubly-checked set of calculations. For example, to the socialist it is just as clear that (other things being equal) the social ownership and democratic management of the steel industry will eventually mean more and better steel products at less cost than under private manufacture, as it is plain that a 36-inch yardstick is longer or more extended in space than a 12-inch footrule. To him this point is no more arguable than the immediate "intuitive" deliverance of the visual-cortical mechanism, which informs one than a pen is to the right and not to the left of the inkwell, or similar elementary space perceptions. The socialist thus structures his world because the "facts" as he interprets them leave him no option—he is in a sense "coerced" by them, although he admits he finds this compulsion agreeable and not repugnant, a receptive hospitality which awakens the suspicions of others. The organization of ideas which results is for him the essential substance of truth (of goodness, too, and possibly even "beauty") in social affairs.

Since the final adoption of a socialist position usually occurs with relative rapidity (even though the "incubation" period preceding the decision may be quite prolonged), the social significance of this phenomenon of "terminal acceleration" may lie in the support it gives to at least one interpretation of the so-called "revolutionary," as opposed to the "evolutionary," process of societal change. Progress of a fundamental sort in group life may well occur by jerks or "mutations" rather than by smooth imperceptible transitions.[12] Because of the desirability and necessity of popular consent to large-scale or major alterations in the community framework, and because power relations redistribute themselves most

[12] Cf. G. W. Hartmann, "The Gestalt View of the Process of Institutional Transformation," *Psychological Review*, LIII (Sept. 1946), pp. 282-89.

clearly after a crisis or "showdown," important and grand changes in control must wait until enough people signal that they are "ripe" for such a move. If there is a favorable convergence of inner and outer conditions such that within a concentrated short period the socialist movement receives enough additional recruits to swing an effective majority, then the occasion arises for either a sharp angular turn in the direction of governing policies or for a pronounced acceleration of selected trends.

The mental or spiritual revolution which permits a swift but peaceful and orderly economic reconstruction (the only kind worth having) of the basic pattern of national existence appears to result from the more or less simultaneous emergence of the same "insight" in the great mass of the citizenry. This educative process is ordinarily and correctly thought to require plenty of time—but when it does culminate in a burst of decisive collective action, a new level of behavior is permanently established. Symbolic of this natural sequence on a miniature scale is the apparently futile effort of Jasper McLevy as a Socialist municipal campaigner. For twenty years he argued in vain with his fellow inhabitants of Bridgeport, Connecticut, until they elected him mayor in 1932, and they have continued him in office ever since. On a larger and more basic scale the situation of the labor governments of Scandinavia, New Zealand, Australia, and possibly even of Great Britain (although it is too early for assurance here), illustrate the same phenomenon. Despite occasional electoral reverses, actual advances in socialization are rarely undone.

This observation supplies some small support for the hypothesis that a socialist program meets the needs of most individuals better than the alternative programs of community management which it replaces. Voters do not invariably indicate their wishes with optimum clarity, but on the whole and despite sharp electoral fluctuations during the past century, the curve of popular approval has moved upward both for specific socialistic propositions or restricted "experiments" and for the general pattern of a "cooperative commonwealth." Like all political oscillations involving fluctuating amounts of partisan support, this unmistakable trend may be compounded as much out of aversion to "pure" capitalism as out of love of socialism as such. To the degree that the "mixed" economies of the present day reveal a declining tendency for one system and a rising proportion of the other, the inference seems warranted that the electorate expects greater comparative satisfaction from the new form and actually experiences this. Unless one denies any connection between subjectively-held values and demonstrated group trends, how else will one account for the steadily expanding area of socialization in the Western world throughout the first half of the twentieth century? Of course, some things are done not from desire but because one must; yet until a better test of happiness exists, the overt choices that are made must be taken to show where the greater good (or the lesser evil) seems to be found.

589

VIII. Psychological Resistances to Socialism

In a recent editorial in a socialist periodical devoted to summarizing the numerous statistics pointing to a steady concentration of economic power in the hands of fewer organizations, two sample items appeared: (1) One-tenth of 1 per cent of all American corporations own 52 per cent of the total corporate assets; and (2) in 1937, 1 per cent of the shareholders of the 200 largest nonfinancial corporations accounted for almost two-thirds of the outstanding common stock. These figures were followed by a challenge—"Are you really free when others own the basis of your life?" The assumption, of course, was that no one is free so long as living and working depend on "paying tribute" to somebody else: i.e., while a "few" control everything we need and use, including the very job one must have in order to continue to live.

Ardent socialists are often nonplussed by the failure of many of their audience to exhibit the same excitement or to draw the same conclusions from incontrovertible data. In the above instance, there seems to be something paradoxical about a man who has no control over the prices of the goods he must have to maintain himself, whose income depends heavily upon the whims of an employer, and who nevertheless considers himself "free." Yet paradox or not, that is exactly what happens since a defensible awareness of being free in *some* essential respects so colors his awareness that he genuinely believes himself to be free in *all*. The fact that he may be hemmed about by bonds which are invisible to him because his perceptions are insufficiently acute may explain but does not weaken the practical effect of the "illusion."

Proponents of socialism have erred frequently both in overestimating and in appealing too exclusively to the rationality of the common man (and of themselves). In a sense this is a "good" or constructive error, for even though one knows that people are neither entirely logical nor reasonable, treating them as though they were provides at least the opportunity for bringing these qualities of their natures into play, whereas working mainly with existing prejudices will merely deepen the grip of the irrational. It is not only complimentary to assume that a person is abler or better than he actually is, but pedagogically it does tend in some fashion to elevate the individual to that plane. Moreover, any planned effort to capitalize upon prejudices collapses when the socialist movement by its very nature is precluded from calling upon such powerful aids as racial, religious, or nationalistic biases. This self-denying ordinance means that socialism must battle for control of the popular mind without the advantage of many of the most powerful weapons of social conflict. Plenty of available biases nonetheless remain, such as a mental set of rejection (not always fairly or benevolently motivated) of the personalities and actions of conservative public figures, or an unanalyzed revulsion against merchants and customers involved in the sale of $10,000 fur coats or bracelets at a time when millions are chronically hungry, or a pro-employee and anti-employer orientation regardless of the merit of the particular labor dispute, etc.

Although the unity of the organism is reflected in our inability to distinguish sharply between intellectual processes and affective states, everyday practice shows it is possible to characterize certain mental operations as those which are more and those which are less rational in emphasis. This commonplace difference formed the basis of a field experiment designed and executed by the writer in connection with the regular campaign for state offices held in November 1935 in the city of Allentown, Pennsylvania. The essence of the problem was to see whether the number of votes cast for the socialist "head of the ticket" would be greater when electioneering leaflets of a heavily emotionally-toned nature were used than when argumentative and inferential appeals were applied.[13]

Following the conventional pattern of scientific inquiry, 5,000 copies each of the two leaflets reproduced below were distributed the week before the balloting in two different groups of precincts as nearly alike as the necessity for working with legally established political districts allowed; a third area was reserved as a "control." No other formal party effort to win adherents was engaged in since it was agreed to devote all of the slim resources available to this "project"; the few free radio talks which had occurred earlier presumably affected the entire city uniformly.

Text of the "Rational" Leaflet

You've heard of intelligence tests, haven't you? Well, we have a little examination right here which we are sure you will enjoy taking, even if you didn't care much for school when you were a youngster. The beauty of this test is that you can score it yourself without any teacher to tell you whether you passed or failed.

This is how it works. First read each one of the seven statements printed below. If you *approve* the idea as it stands, *underline* the word AGREE; if you *disapprove* of the idea, underline the word DISAGREE. Simple, isn't it? All right, then. Get your pencil ready. All set? Go!

1. We would have much cheaper electric light and power if this industry were owned and operated by the various governmental units for the benefit of all the people. AGREE—DISAGREE.

2. No gifted boy or girl should be denied the advantages of higher education, just because his parents lack the money to send him to college. AGREE—DISAGREE.

3. The Federal Government should provide to all classes of people

[13] Cf. G. W. Hartmann, "A Field Experiment on the Comparative Effectiveness of 'Emotional' and 'Rational' Political Leaflets in Determining Election Results," *Journal of Abnormal and Social Psychology*, xxxi (Apr.-June 1936), pp. 99-114.

opportunity for complete insurance at cost against accident, sickness, premature death and old age. AGREE—DISAGREE.

4. All banks and insurance companies should be run on a non-profit basis like the schools. AGREE—DISAGREE.

5. Higher income taxes on persons with incomes of more than $10,000 a year should be levied immediately. AGREE—DISAGREE.

6. The only way most people will ever be able to live in modern sanitary homes is for the government to build them on a non-profit basis. AGREE—DISAGREE.

7. Many more industries and parts of industries should be owned by and managed co-operatively by the producers (all the workers) themselves. AGREE—DISAGREE.

Have you answered them all? Fine. Now go back and count the number of sentences with which you AGREED. Then count the number with which you DISAGREED. *If the number of agreements is larger than the number of disagreements, you are at heart a Socialist*—whether you know it or not!

Now that you have tested yourself and found out how much of a Socialist you really are, *why don't you try voting for the things you actually want?* The Republicans and Democrats don't propose to give these things to you, because a mere look at their records will show that they are opposed to them. Do you get the point?

Text of the "Emotional" Leaflet

Allentown, Pennsylvania

DEAR MOTHER AND FATHER: November 1, 1935

We youngsters are not in the habit of giving much thought to serious things. You have often told us so and we admit it.

But while we like to play football and have a good time dancing and cause you a lot of amusement as well as worry with our "puppy loves," we sometimes think long and hard. You ought to know what many of us young folks are quietly saying to ourselves.

Our future as American citizens looks dark. We want jobs—and good jobs, too—so that we can help in the useful work of the world. But we know that many of our brightest high-school and college graduates find it absolutely impossible to get any kind of employment. We also know that this condition is not temporary, but that it will last as long as we stick to harmful ways of running business, industry and government.

We want to continue our education, but we haven't the heart to ask you to make that sacrifice. With Dad working only part-time on little pay and Mother trying to make last year's coat and dress look in season, we feel we ought to pitch in and help keep the family's neck above water. But we can't. The world as it is now run has no use for us.

Many of our teachers know what is wrong, although we can see that most of them are afraid to say what they really think. Luckily, the text-books and school magazines keep us in touch with new ideas, and we have learned how to read between the lines of the ordinary newspaper. Please don't be frightened if we tell you what we have decided!

We young people are becoming Socialists. We have to be. We can't be honest with ourselves and be anything else. *The Socialist Party is the only party which is against all wars*—and we have learned from our history courses what awful wars have taken place under both Republicans and Democrats. We refuse to be slaughtered (like Uncles Bob and Charles were in 1918) just to make profits for ammunition manufacturers.

The Socialist Party seeks to create a world in which there will be no poverty. In our science classes we learn how power machinery and other modern inventions make it possible for all of us to have enough of all the goods and services we need. Yet look at our town with its unpainted shacks, suffering parents, half-starved children! We might have every-thing, but we continue to live on next to nothing.

It is all so unnecessary. You have had to lead a poor workingman's life, because you and most of the workers and farmers of this country have regularly voted for either the Republican or Democratic parties, between which there is no real difference. These old machines are not for us.

The youth of 1935 want to Build a Better America, in which there will be no poverty, no fear of unemployment, no threat of war. We ask you to follow the lead of the Socialist Party this year because that is the most direct way for you to *help hasten the day when Peace and Plenty and lasting Prosperity will be the lot of all men.* Good parents such as you desire these things for us. But we can never have them as long as you are controlled by your old voting habits.

We are profoundly earnest about this. Our generation cannot enjoy the beauty and justice of the *New America* if you block our highest desires. There was a time when you too were young like us. We beg you in the name of those early memories and spring-time hopes to *support the Socialist ticket in the coming elections!*

YOUR SONS AND DAUGHTERS

The crucial finding was that when compared with the vote a year be-fore, the Socialist increase in the "emotional" wards was 50.00 per cent, in the "rational," 35.92 per cent, and in the "control," 24.05 per cent. This clear *differential* gain was wholly in harmony with the order of predicted results and appears to be a gratifying confirmation of the general hypoth-esis. Postelection interviews confirmed the greater impressiveness and retention value of the more "sentimental" approach, for proportionately many more recalled receiving an "open family letter" than remembered the pamphlet or folder of "questions."

While there is nothing surprising about this outcome to either the practical politician or the theoretician of human motives, there seems to be no escape from the decision that the emotional political appeal is a better vote-getting instrument than the rational approach, at least in the sense in which these terms describe the essential difference between the two leaflets reproduced above. The sentimental open letter integrates itself easily with such strong permanent central attitudes as parental affection and the desire for a "better life." It employs a familiar literary form, is concrete in imagery, "breathes sincerity," and is not obviously or even basically untrue. It is interesting because it digs deeply into the inner personality and links socialism with some vital needs.

The "intelligence test," on the other hand, is straightforward, matter of fact, and unexpectedly maneuvers the reader into an acknowledgment that he is more of a socialist than he realizes. The seven propositions which appear in this appeal were items then favored by a definite majority of sample Pennsylvania populations. Hence, the high probability of obtaining a preponderance of "agrees" from a new random selection. Otherwise, they would have been too risky to use. Save for a faint inferiority feeling which this form may create, these features are positive advantages, although they evidently did not outweigh the factors of strength in the other leaflet. Thus the ancient educational maxims of the Herbartians are vindicated anew in the field of political psychology! Those ideas will be most readily assimilated by the voter which fit in with his present "apperceptive mass," which are joined with some prepotent wants, which meet him on his own level and lead him on from where he is.

A parallel series of studies could be built about many similar questions that have been raised about ways and means of increasing the efficiency of socialist educational or propagandistic efforts. Is it better, for example, to stress the short-term or the long-term aims or advantages of socialism? There is some reason for believing that men obey a kind of psychic gravitational law—the attraction of a goal is proportional to its "value" and inversely proportional to the spatio-temporal "distance" between the organism and the objective. Specifically, the socialist movement has frequently been outbid by more flexible or opportunistic programs which have been able to promise (and apparently deliver) more immediate concrete advantages by adapting some minor phases of the socialist position without accepting the essentials. The temptation to the hard-pressed worker to take a penny now in lieu of a dollar in his old age is understandably great. What little direct experimental evidence we have points in the same direction.[14]

A related investigation used the same general method outlined in the Allentown inquiry, but changed in these content respects: the presidential

[14] Cf. G. W. Hartmann, "Immediate and Remote Goals as Political Motives," *ibid.*, XXXIII (Jan. 1938), pp. 86-99.

year of 1936 was involved, another city (Altoona, Pennsylvania) supplied the "facilities," and the leaflets now being tested for relative effectiveness carried messages centering about definite "immediate demands" vs. "general ultimate objectives." The obtained results—53 votes for the congressional candidate of the Socialist Party in the "immediate" wards, 54 in the "remote," and 53 in the controls—suggest not so much an equivalent effect in this context as a complete lack of influence on ballot-box behavior. Apparently when the leaflets reached the public, a hesitant or undecided mental condition no longer existed and consequently they lacked any directive power upon what ensued. The best interpretation seems to be that these stimuli arrived after the social field had been closed and that they lacked the intensity necessary to reopen the issue for this population.

Because proximate ends appear to be more impelling, resistance to socialist efforts frequently takes the form of deferring consideration of such proposals until "the next election," the next generation, or even the next century. This point of view seems to be representative of an acknowledgment that *eventually* socialism will prevail, but that present emergencies make it imperative to keep working a little longer with the "old system." Part of this attitude is probably motivated by a practical time perspective and a conformity reaction to contemporary majority opinion, as in the shrewd remark of a conservative campaign manager back in 1910, "The day the American people indicate unmistakably that they want socialism, the Republican Party aims to have the honor of giving it to them."

Among the many psychological obstacles which have hampered the advance of socialism in America, the language or "communication" factor as it appears in the use of characteristic names, labels, and symbols is one of the most interesting. As far as political behavior goes, a rose by any other name does *not* smell just as sweet. Because of the possibility of intimate emotionalized associations between a sign and the thing signified, reactions to persons, organizations, practices, or proposals of any kind are powerfully influenced by the words used to describe them. The minority and novel status which socialism has usually held within the American culture has made it peculiarly vulnerable in this respect.

To illustrate: For many years prior to 1934, Upton Sinclair, the prolific author, had run as a *Socialist* candidate in California for such offices as governor and United States senator, never receiving more than 60,000 votes. When in 1934 he suddenly made the "experiment" of campaigning as a *Democratic* candidate on the E.P.I.C. or "End Poverty in California" issue, he received almost a million votes. Sinclair's philosophy so far as it involved an advocacy of major collectivistic ends and means had not changed in any essentials, but for the public the *content* of his ideas was far more acceptable under one *form* than under another. A partial explanation of the spectacular difference in the amount of support given to a position is that verbal associations act like clothing which may enhance or diminish the personal attractiveness of the wearer. One may lament the inability of the average spectator to make the obvious and appropriate discrimination, but the phenomenon itself is undeniable.

Defamation or injury to reputation (which often directly involve bodily and property damage) occurs when malicious falsehoods are disseminated, intentionally or otherwise. Libel and slander typically involve the use of "actionable words" which tend to lower an individual's standing by accusations connecting him in some way with dishonorable deeds or intentions. Such charges, even if but half-believed by those among whom they circulate as "rumor," may cause intense suffering and cripple or inhibit normal activity. In a somewhat impersonal way, a cause or movement may similarly be hurt by gross misrepresentations. Thus, to publish "There is as much difference between social legislation and Socialism as there is between the common-sense advancement of the ideas of peace and the selfish or cowardly brand of treason that is known as pacifism"[15] is a not too roundabout way of implying that a socialist is a traitor! If to such hints are added the more direct charges that "Socialism is not only essentially un-American, but it is essentially undemocratic"[16] and "Socialism is essentially un-Christian,"[17] it is not surprising that the ordinary reader-citizen so authoritatively indoctrinated will come to view with scorn so contemptible a tendency. The emotional coloring thus applied or "smeared" onto an ideology and its advocates has some extraordinary consequences.

In one study, 65 per cent of a sample of 168 rural voters, 55.5 per cent of whom themselves endorsed a series of what by all historical and economic criteria would be called socialistic proposals except that the name itself did not appear, favored refusing licenses to teach in the public schools to persons who believe in socialism![18] Many evidently want the substance of socialism, but do not want it called by that horrid word.

A simple experiment will demonstrate the tremendous power of these "verbal norms" to warp a group's reaction to institutional changes. Ask any fairly large group to rank the twenty-two political party names listed in the table below in the order of their liking for these names; they are to assume that all the platforms are the same. In one application of this technique, the following results appeared:

[15] W. S. Myers, *Socialism and American Ideals* (Princeton, N.J., 1919), p. 20.
[16] *Ibid.*, p. 36.
[17] *Ibid.*, p. 47.
[18] G. W. Hartmann, "The Contradiction between the Feeling-tone of Political Party Names and Public Response to Their Platforms," *Journal of Social Psychology*, vii (Aug. 1936), pp. 336-57.

The Relative Hedonic Value of Different Party Names
(Based upon the Ratings of 140 "Urban" Voters)

Party	Crude mode	Mean	rank	Median	rank	S.D.	% of 1st mentions
Commonwealth	13	13.2	(15)	13.5	(15)	2.48	0
Communist	22	21.4	(22)	21.45	(22)	1.45	0
Conservative	17	17.4	(20)	18.77	(19)	1.99	0
Constitution	15	14.2	(17)	14.78	(16)	1.74	0
Democratic	2	2.31	(1)	2.71	(1)	1.13	25.6
Farmer-Labor	3	3.00	(2)	3.13	(2)	2.06	5.7
Federalist	12	12.4	(14)	13.02	(14)	1.38	0
Independence	11	11.28	(12.5)	11.86	(12)	3.97	0
International	16	14.08	(16)	14.9	(17)	3.5	0
Labor	4	5.76	(3)	4.9	(3)	2.4	0
Liberal	11	11.20	(11)	12.19	(13)	2.84	2.8
Liberty	10	11.09	(9)	10.87	(10)	2.95	0
National Welfare	11	11.28	(12.5)	11.55	(11)	2.84	0
Patriots	2	6.03	(4)	6.11	(5)	4.74	0
Peoples	7	7.16	(6)	6.49	(6)	1.40	5.7
Progressive	8	9.63	(8)	7.77	(7)	5.77	0
Prohibition	17	16.01	(19)	17.48	(18)	2.2	0
Radical Reform	19	18.09	(21)	20.39	(21)	3.96	0
Republican	1	7.97	(7)	8.12	(8)	4.11	37.1
Socialist	20	11.11	(10)	9.87	(9)	3.63	22.8
Technocratic	21	15.9	(18)	19.1	(20)	3.6	0
Workers	5	6.68	(5)	5.32	(4)	5.9	0

Since some of these party names are current and real, some obsolete or vestigial, and some fictitious or "unborn," a summary of the special forms of distribution followed by the special designations is enlightening:

Types of Frequency Curves Obtained for Different Party Labels

Normal probability curve	Positive-J curve	Negative-J curve	Bimodal
Commonwealth	Communist	Democratic	Conservative
Constitution	International	Farmer-Labor	Prohibition
Federalist	Radical Reform	Labor	Socialist
Independence	Technocratic	Republican	
Liberal		Workers	
Liberty			
National Welfare			
Patriots			
Peoples			
Progressive			

Inspection of these columns shows that most "unreal" or inactive political labels, unless definitely affected by special praise and blame, follow the Gaussian curve: i.e., they tend to heap up in the middle (at 8 to 12, say) of the available range of ranks from 1 to 22. Party names with a "black eye" hover near the bottom around the twenty-second place as revealed by the so-called "positive-J curve." Familiar, institutionalized, or well-entrenched labels exhibit the "negative-J" form, which means that group preferences cluster about the top ranks. The bimodal category in which "Socialist" appears is peculiar in having the characteristic "camel's back" profile indicating peaks at rank 2 and at rank 18 and a sharp dip toward the base at the center around rank 10.

The meaning of this is clear: the term "Socialist" is something toward which people find it hard to be neutral—they are either strongly for or decidedly against it. The operation of this all-or-none type of attitude in the community obviously reflects a sharp division of opinion and loyalties about this key symbol. It is probable that this bimodal relation represents an historic half-way station in developing from a stage of fairly complete *rejection* as typified by the positive-J slope to the pretty thorough *acceptance* as a standard ingredient in the culture indicated by the negative-J slope. This directional component suggests the presence of great vitality or dynamism in the word, regardless of the actual proportion in the population who may at any moment be attracted or repelled thereby; in any case, very few appear to be indifferent to it.

In the light of the considerations presented in this section and throughout the entire chapter, one conclusion seems inescapable—the course of socialism in modern times is progressively less a function of technology and economic events, but increasingly shaped by factors in the realm of psychology, logic, ethics, and education. The puzzling mystery of its triumphs and defeats is ultimately traceable to those still dimly understood natural forces that govern our behavior as individuals and as groups.

CHAPTER 13

American Writers on the Left

BY WILLARD THORP

WILLARD THORP, Professor of English at Princeton University, was the founder of the Program in American Civilization at Princeton in 1942, and since then (with the exception of a single year) has been its Chairman. The author of several books on English and American literature, he is co-editor of the *Literary History of the United States* (1948).

For bibliography in Volume 2 relevant to Mr. Thorp's essay, see especially PART VI, General Reading, and Topics 1 through 8 with occasional references also in 10.

I. Prologue

AMERICAN literature has been in the main a democratic literature closely allied to the shifts and changes of American
society. For this reason, since socialism in various forms was
continuously talked about and experimented with from the
time our national literature began to emerge, one would expect to find it reflected in that literature. And so it was.

Most of the "literature" by socialists or about socialism has hardly been
literature in the sense of having much artistic significance. This is true
of nearly all the "literature" produced in religious socialist communities
such as Ephrata and the settlements of the Rappites and Shakers; it
is true also of the writings of John Humphrey Noyes of Oneida. Nor
did such writings usually aspire to be art—their purpose was ordinarily
either theological or propagandistic, and only very rarely were they
intended to have literary quality.

For these reasons the writings of the religious communitarians will be
neglected here. For similar reasons, the writings of the secular utopians—
such as the American followers of Owen and Fourier—will also be passed
over in this essay, even though they are often interesting and important
as social documents.

I shall start instead with the great authors of our Golden Day, men
who were vitally interested in social problems but nonetheless rejected
the socialist answer. Thus it was with Emerson. Yet while Emerson
refused to join the community at Brook Farm (he was seldom a "joiner")
there are many passages in his work which show how deeply he had
pondered the social thinking of those who had ventured at West Roxbury—and whose venture finally led them to Fourierism. Thoreau, too,
had thought deeply about social problems even though, philosophical
anarchist that he was, he could not have been expected to applaud the
efforts of his friends who talked of Fourier and Brisbane, of phalanxes and
phalansteries. The measure of his resistance to their ideas can be seen
in his remarkable review of J. A. Etzler's *The Paradise within the Reach
of All Men, without Labor, by Powers of Nature and Machinery* (the
review was published in 1843). Thoreau had many reasons for being
horrified by Etzler's proposal for making an Eden of America by harnessing its power resources, but what dismayed him most was Etzler's
contention that this could be effected only through cooperation. The
vision he conjured up of a vast cooperative society evoked one of
the strongest expressions of Thoreau's anarchistic individualism: "Nothing can be effected but by one man. He who wants help wants everything else. . . . We must first succeed alone, that we may enjoy our

601

success together. . . . In this matter of reforming the world, we have little faith in corporations; not thus was it first formed."

Cooper's rejection of socialism was motivated by his strong sense of property and his notion of an educated elite, fitted by training and sense of responsibility to govern the state. When in 1847 he created a kind of utopia in his novel *The Crater*, he made it very plain that this fictive society was not socialistic during the period of its flourishing. Nor did Melville, writing political allegory two years later, in his *Mardi* of 1849, adopt socialism as the means by which his ideal state, Serenia, was brought into being. Some of its features have a socialistic cast, but Melville makes it clear that "in all things, equality is not for all. Each has his own. . . . Such differences must be. But none starve outright, while others feast. By the abounding, the needy are supplied. Yet not from statute, but from dictates born half dormant in us, and warmed into life by Alma [Christ]."

Not even from Hawthorne, among these pre-Civil War writers, do we get any wholehearted acceptance of socialism. He had put his savings into Brook Farm and lived there in 1841, but he soon found that communal labor was not productive of creative thoughts and asked to be released from his obligations. His *Blithedale Romance* (1852), though he took pains in its preface to declare that the characters are fictitious, is nevertheless a beautifully ironic study of his association with the reformers at West Roxbury. In spite of his protestations of respect for the "cultivated and philosophic minds" who took an interest in the enterprise, the novel illustrates Hawthorne's conclusion that "no sagacious man will long retain his sagacity if he live exclusively among reformers and progressive people."

Thus, while one finds that most of the leading American writers before the Civil War thought and wrote, of necessity, about the socialism of their time, their reaction to it was negative. It could hardly have been otherwise in view of the fact that individualism and self-reliance were for them the most admirable of human traits.

The literary situation between 1865 and 1910 is more involved and more confused. The dominant strain in American writing was Idealism, and such writers as Aldrich and Stedman who upheld the standard of the Ideal had no truck with socialistic ideas nor even with reform. Another group of writers—Mark Twain is the most conspicuous example—found little to criticize in the business practices of the day and were welcome guests in the homes of tycoons like Carnegie and H. H. Rogers. At the same time a few American writers of distinction had at last been converted to socialism—of some kind—and became propagandists for it in their work. Most notable of these are Edward Bellamy, W. D. Howells, and Jack London.

Bellamy's *Looking Backward* (1888) enjoyed an enormous popularity. Its ideas produced a nation-wide social movement (the Nationalist clubs) and its influence reached Europe. Why it should have been so widely read can be explained. For one thing its Marxism is so completely denatured and Americanized as to be scarcely apparent. Moreover, Bellamy was a liberal Christian and the strong ethical content of his book veiled its economic radicalism. Howells' conversion to socialism came late and was the result of his gradual moving to the left, in which direction he was impelled by his admiration for Tolstoy, the C. B. and Q. strike of 1888, the Homestead strike of 1892, and the distress he felt at the time of the trials of the anarchists for their alleged implication in the Haymarket affair. Howells' *A Traveller from Altruria* (1894) is a landmark in American socialist writing but it is more interesting as a satire on American middle-class standards than as a forward-looking program for social action made palatable as fiction. The case of the third of these writers, Jack London, is, as Huck Finn said of *Pilgrim's Progress*, "interesting but tough." He boasted that he was a socialist and he gave generously to the cause, but he got what socialism he had through personal contacts and desultory reading, and his naturalism (with its ugly implications of Nordic superiority) was always at war with it. Yet because of London's immense popularity, books in which his socialistic bias is most evident— *The People of the Abyss* (1903), *The War of the Classes* (1905), *The Iron Heel* (1908), *Revolution* (1910)—probably did more to spread ideas of socialism in this country than have the writings of any other American author. And years after his death they were to enjoy an immense popularity in Soviet Russia.

No discussion of socialism in American literature during the years between 1865 and 1910 would be complete without mention of a fascinating burst of utopian fiction in the eighties and nineties. A few American utopian novels are to be found before this period but the publication of about fifty such novels in those twenty years is a phenomenon of considerable significance. Allyn B. Forbes, who surveyed these works (in *Social Forces*, December 1927), has noted several remarkable facts about them. All of them conceive of society in economic terms and many can be called socialistic, yet none of them advocates the attainment of the utopian goal by means of force. Strangely enough, too, the terms socialism and communism do not appear in any of them. Aside from Bellamy, Howells, and Ignatius Donnelly, their authors are so little known as to be almost anonymous. It is significant, also, that very few of them were issued by the large and respectable eastern publishing houses. In a sense they constitute a kind of underground literature and their influence is for that reason difficult to assess.

As we move into the twentieth century, we begin to find writers who definitely allied themselves with the socialist movement and who speak with principles and platforms in mind. Outstanding among these is Upton Sinclair. A new pattern, typical of episodes in the careers of many leftist writers of the 1920's and 1930's, is seen in the circumstances of the composition of Sinclair's best-known novel, *The Jungle* (1906). He was on assignment from the socialist *Appeal to Reason* when he made his far-reaching investigation of conditions in the stockyards of Chicago and his goal was the writing of a serial for that magazine which would use fiction to arouse sympathy for the proletariat.

One stage more had to be reached. The socialist movement needed a literary magazine in which intellectuals who had been converted to the movement could appeal to their own kind and attempt, as best they could, to reach the working-class audience. This magazine came into existence in 1911 when Max Eastman and Piet Vlag formed the *Masses* (1911-1918). Associated with them were Floyd Dell and John Reed. Socialism at last had a journal to which writers could rally; one can say that there was at last a school of socialist writing in America.

This, in outline, is the course of American socialistic literature for the hundred years before 1920, the date which is the starting point for the rest of this essay. There are two reasons why I have chosen to devote most of this chapter to certain careers and events of but two decades, 1920 to 1940. In the first place a filling out of the synopsis just given here of the years before 1920 would yield interesting but on the whole fairly negative results. That is to say, there were few American writers before 1920 who had so wholeheartedly committed themselves to some variety of socialism that they wrote with this commitment as their chief motive. My second reason for focusing so much of this chapter on two decades of American writing will require a few paragraphs of elaboration.

In the magnitude and brilliance of its accomplishment American writing from 1920 to 1940 can be compared only with one earlier period, the years between 1840 and 1860, when most of the major work of Emerson, Thoreau, Hawthorne, and Melville was produced. The writers of the second American Renaissance were sensitive to the materialistic blight of the Prosperity Decade and even more sensitive to the horrors of the years of depression which followed the stock-market crash of 1929. Even those who, like T. S. Eliot in *The Waste Land* (1922) and Ernest Hemingway in *The Sun Also Rises* (1926), seemed to reflect most despairingly the disillusionment of their generation were, it is now clear, moral writers for whom the loss of certainty and faith was the chief motivating force. It is true that many of them seemed to turn their backs on America and its problems when they took flight to London or Paris or the Riviera; but, as later events proved, they were not so much fleeing

604

from an America in whose values, or lack of values, they could no longer believe, as searching for a new faith.

Other writers of the period—Theodore Dreiser, for example, in *An American Tragedy* (1925) and James T. Farrell in *The Young Manhood of Studs Lonigan* (1934)—revivified the mode of naturalism and anatomized, more profoundly than such predecessors as Hamlin Garland and Frank Norris had done, the newest diseases of American life. Some, who swung in the orbit of H. L. Mencken and Sinclair Lewis, satirized without mercy the provincialism, religious sectarianism, caste snobbery, and smart business ethics of the American Babbitts and "patrioteers" who flourished under the rule of Harding and Coolidge.

Without doubt the most powerful of all the literary currents during these twenty years was the leftward movement of the novelists, poets, playwrights, and critics. In one way or another, for a longer or a shorter time, nearly every writer of the period was drawn to the movement even if only to rise up and denounce it. Some old socialists like Upton Sinclair were lifted on this great tide, along with Bohemians like Floyd Dell and Edna St. Vincent Millay, young radicals like Michael Gold, Joseph Freeman, and Isidor Schneider, academic writers like Robert Herrick and Robert Morss Lovett. What drew this diverse company leftward was the persecution of liberals and radicals alike under the notorious Attorney-General Palmer; disgust with the deep corruption of American life which the scandals of the Harding administration revealed; the frustration which all of them suffered at the time of the execution of Sacco and Vanzetti; later on, the spectacle, in 1930, of a nation on the brink of ruin; then the fear of fascism and another "imperialist war."

But by far the strongest reason for the turn to the left which the writers made was the fact of the Russian Revolution and the consequent triumph of communism in the Soviet state. Before these events took place writers who believed in socialism could only hope for the time when it would be put into practice. Now the great day had arrived. Socialism was no longer a theory; for millions of people it had become a way of life. From 1919 until Trotsky was expelled from Russia in 1929, international communism was the bright dream. The Russian Revolution was only the beginning; the other revolutions would follow soon, and for America, the day was not far off. Those who believed in the Marxian gospel saw clearly the signs of disintegration as one congressional investigation after another laid bare the venality of American capitalism.

In the early twenties Lenin was revered by American radicals as a kind of Washington of his people, and Marx was studied religiously, but Trotsky was the best known of the communists. He embodied the vigor and eloquence of the ideal revolutionary and he was, as well, the articulate apologist, polemicist, and historian of the Revolution. The hero worship

605

accorded Trotsky accounts for much of the early enthusiasm of the leftist writers in America and for the strength of the lost cause of which he became the center between 1929 and 1940, the year of his death. Trotsky's expulsion from Russia, consequent upon Stalin's capture of the Communist Party, split the writers on the left in every country, but nowhere more than in America. Of the scores of quarrels and issues which all along disturbed the leftist movement none was so devastating.

II. Problems of the Leftist Writers

For the leftist writer during these years there was a constant guide in what was called "the party line." One's orthodoxy was determined by the zeal and consistency with which one bent a novel or a play to this line. In times when the Communist Party was eager to have a legion of "fellow travelers" the party line was not much in evidence. When the cycle revolved, and orthodoxy rather than wide support was desired, writers were told firmly in the pages of the *New Masses* what was required of them in ideology and in technique. To ascertain precisely how the party line for America was determined in any given week, whether in the Kremlin or by the Comintern or by party headquarters in New York, would be beyond the detective prowess of any scholar. But the fact remains that often the first question asked about a writer in these years was how near or how far from the party line he stood at the moment. In their enthusiasm as converts, writers began, as converts do, with a brave show of orthodoxy. Some contrived, year in and year out, to follow the sinuous changes of party doctrine, political and aesthetic; others, and this was the usual case, fell from grace, suddenly or gradually. If a writer's lapse was notorious, there was a whole vocabulary of abuse available to those who wished to punish him. He would be told that he had become, overnight, a "Bohemian" or a petty bourgeois or a Trotskyite or a wrecker or a revisionist or a formalist or that he was guilty of sectarianism or leftism—whatever the words for heretic and heresy were at the moment.

Thus there was a constant coming and going, shifting and changing; there were asseverations of zeal for the revolution followed by recantations; there were letters full of accusation or of a sweet reasonableness designed to bring the erring one back into the fold. Farthest from the lengthening, twisting line were writers like Hemingway and MacLeish though their political sympathies were at one particular time close enough to current orthodoxy to make them willing to publish in leftist magazines or cooperate in the Popular Front in Spain. Probably the interval during which the largest number of American writers were in some degree sympathetic with the Left was the year 1936. Early in that year Moscow officially recognized demonstrations in behalf of the Spanish

Loyalists and it sent military aid to them after the outbreak of war in July. A mere listing of the names of contributors to the *New Masses* between March 1936 and February 1937 will show how eager it was to include any degree of politically conscious writing. Among the poets are Genevieve Taggard, Marguerite Young, Kenneth Fearing, Rolfe Humphries, Archibald MacLeish, Edna Millay, Muriel Rukeyser, James Agee, Paul Engle, W. R. Benét, Horace Gregory, and Malcolm Brinnin. Among the novelists one finds Upton Sinclair, Theodore Dreiser, Sherwood Anderson, John Dos Passos, Josephine Herbst, and Edward Newhouse. The dramatists include Paul Peters, George Sklar, Albert Maltz, and John Howard Lawson. Of the journalists one notes also several who could not and certainly would not appear today in *Masses & Mainstream*, Herbert Agar, for instance, Joseph Freeman, and Vincent Sheean.

It is difficult to discover even a handful of writers who have followed the party line from the twenties down to the present time. To do so required an ideological and technical agility which only Marxian athletes like Michael Gold and Isidor Schneider have been able to maintain year after year. Schneider was contributing to the *New Masses* in the early thirties and is in mid-1951 an editor of *Masses & Mainstream*. Gold, who seems still to be in favor, was one of the original editors of the *New Masses* when it was founded in 1926.

The political hazards in this obstacle course have been many. The first, on which a number of stalwarts stumbled, was the expulsion of Trotsky from Russia. Those who left the cause when their hero fell continued to hope, with a lessening fervor, for revolution and a revolutionary literature, but they believed that in Russia Stalin had betrayed the revolution; there the cause was utterly lost. Among the writers who dropped away at this juncture Max Eastman was probably the most eminent.

The next great obstacle was the series of trials of the "Old Bolsheviks" which began in August 1936 and lasted on into 1938. Among the leaders then tried for a variety of crimes against the Soviet state were men who had become minor heroes to the leftist writers in America. The methods employed in the trials, particularly the mystifying (and suspect) confessions of the accused, disturbed Americans to whom this kind of undemocratic procedure in the courtroom was both strange and shocking.

A blow with even greater consequences was delivered by the Russo-German nonaggression pact of August 1939. From the beginning of Hitler's rise to power in Germany the Communist Party in America had forewarned of the consequences which would follow—an imperialistic war against Russia, in which the American Fascists might succeed in involving this country. Many writers had become fellow travelers at the time of Russia's intervention in the Spanish War, while the United States stood aloof watching German and Italian planes bomb into submission a people struggling to maintain a republican form of government. Then, only two years later, Russia reversed her policy and shook hands with the devil himself, Adolf Hitler. This incredible act could not be explained away. From this point on, American leftist writers began to realize how difficult, if not impossible, it was going to be to accommodate Stalinism to the individualistic and moralistic traditions of American democracy. Indeed, it is not too much to say that the Russo-German pact all but destroyed the literary front which the Communist Party had so carefully labored to build up in America.

During these politically difficult years there were, as well, difficult literary issues to argue about. "Incorrect" decisions in these matters were more easily atoned for than political deviations, but many a writer grew weary of the constant theorizing and broke away, to pursue his own course, guided by his own aesthetic. The primary question was what a Marxian analysis of literature might establish as the aims and duties of the writer.[1] Some of the more individualistic spirits attempted to argue that Marx and Engels had said little about literature or art which could serve as a guide to communist aestheticians. They maintained, moreover, that Lenin and Trotsky did not require the regimentation of writers who wished to be revolutionaries. Such heretical talk became serious when Trotsky was branded as a traitor.

Even for those who took Marxism-Leninism as their constant guide in literary theory there were questions which needed intensive study. Must a writer also be a party worker? How "political" must he be? To what audience should the leftist writer in America attempt to appeal? Some replied that the workers alone were to be kept in mind by novelists and poets because the workers would in time accomplish the revolution and their education through art and literature was a matter of paramount importance. Others maintained that before the revolution could take place the petty bourgeoisie would have to be won over to the cause. Since most American leftist writers came from that class they would be, by nature, particularly adept in addressing it and winning it to the revolution.

A further question of great moment was whether the idea of the revolution should dominate a writer's work. How much attention could one give to the individual, his private woes and domestic life, when

[1] Of the scores of attempts to develop a Marxian aesthetic one of the most thorough was Philip Rahv's "The Literary Class War," in the *New Masses* for August 1932. Rahv has long since left the Stalinist camp, and the theories set forth in this article would be repugnant to him now. See below, p. 612ff., for a discussion of Rahv's apostasy.

eventually all individuals would have to submerge themselves in the revolutionary cause? Some believed that since the revolution had been accomplished in Russia, Russian writers could be permitted more freedom in their choice of subjects than their American colleagues. They were able to depict the glorious results of a revolution in fact, the changes it had wrought in men's lives, the hopes it had aroused for an abundantly satisfying life. But in America life was still grim and the strategies required for bringing on the revolutionary situation must be ever in the minds of those whose writing served as guide and consolation to the proletariat.[2]

Critics and literary historians in the leftward movement were eager to rewrite the history of American literature. They wanted to claim for their cause Tom Paine and Jefferson, Emerson, Thoreau, Whitman, Howells, Bellamy, Jack London, and Dreiser. No one was more zealous in this reassessment than Granville Hicks, whose *The Great Tradition: an Interpretation of American Literature since the Civil War* (1933; rev. ed., 1935) was the most successful effort to provide a Marxist analysis of our literary heritage. Beside it one can put Bernard Smith's *Forces in American Criticism* (1939). By the time V. F. Calverton published his *Liberation of American Literature* (1932) he had lost his standing as an orthodox Marxist though he still maintained that his particular heresy was the true Marxist approach to literature and society.[3] This effort to bring the liberal and radical writers of the American past into the Marxist camp still goes on. Samuel Sillen, editor of *Masses & Mainstream*, has, for example, in two recent books, acclaimed Bryant and Whitman as men who carried forward the revolutionary tradition.[4]

[2] In this connection see an illuminating article by Charles Humboldt, "Communists in Novels," *Masses & Mainstream*, I (June 1949), pp. 12-31, and II (July 1949), pp. 44-65. From this article one gathers that at least until that time (1949) an ideal American communist had to be a tough fighter, able to stand alone without family or the too frequent consolations of sex, patient under discipline, a good representative of the working classes, tactful in dealing with potential supporters, tolerant with slower thinkers than himself. Errors of which writers depicting communists have been guilty are: passing off idealized labor leaders or anarcho-syndicalists as good party workers; failure to show how thoroughly a communist is tested in his activities; "glorification of free-wheeling will power" (Richard Wright's *Native Son*); conjuring up a "super-revolutionary mystique of violence to frighten the bourgeoisie"; and displays of "individual opportunism and tastelessness."

[3] Early in 1933, Calverton was given a most thorough going-over, with this book as the initial point of attack, in a long article by David Ramsey and Alan Calmer ("The Marxism of V. F. Calverton," *New Masses*, Jan. 1933, pp. 9-27). Calverton's accumulated sins were many, chief among them being his adherence to Trotsky and to the American renegade from true communism, Lovestone. It is interesting to note that as late as 1929-1930 Calverton was a contributor to the *New Masses* and that his books were favorably reviewed there during those years.

[4] *Walt Whitman: Poet of American Democracy* (New York, 1944), and *William Cullen Bryant* (New York, 1945).

Of all the literary issues we have been discussing, none has been more disputed than the degree of freedom to be accorded the writer in the selection and treatment of his materials. In times of greatest party leniency the writer was told that it was enough if he exposed the evils of a decadent capitalist society and showed that there was at least a little revolutionary idealism fermenting in the hearts of the workers and the intelligentsia. When the turn came and discipline was again to be enforced, the prescriptions became very specific indeed.[5] The issue was always a touchy one, for even the most doctrinaire member of the Communist Party has been bound to maintain that artists in Russia are freer than artists anywhere else—because, of their own volition, they write as the needs of the Soviet state inspire them to write. This is why, presumably, Max Eastman's *Artists in Uniform* (1934) has been so much reviled by Stalinists. In that work Eastman set out to show not only that orthodox Stalinist aesthetics were an absurd set of abstractions but also that in Soviet Russia excellent writers had been silenced, humiliated, driven to ridiculous recantations, and even to suicide. The title of the book became a slogan for those who believed, as Eastman by that time did, that a communized literature in any country would be a dismal failure.

III. Four Typical Leftists

The tribulations of the leftist writer who attempted to stay close to the party line or who had to make the great decision to abandon it entirely are well illustrated in four typical careers, those of Max Eastman, Joseph Freeman, Philip Rahv, and Isidor Schneider.

Mr. Eastman from 1913 to 1917 was editor of the socialist *Masses*; today he is a "roving editor" of the *Reader's Digest*. The long and rambling route he traveled between these two extremes is the easiest of the four careers to follow because he has put his signature to at least thirty books. With John Reed and others Eastman founded the *Masses* and endured the two trials—for opposition to World War I—to which the magazine was subjected. (The first ended in a jury disagreement; the second, in

[5] The contortionist's skill required of critics on the far left is well illustrated by the varying treatments given John Steinbeck's *In Dubious Battle* when it appeared in 1936 (he was then in favor) and in an article thirteen years later. Walter Ralston's review in the *New Masses* (Feb. 18, 1936) was wholly laudatory. Steinbeck's novel had been "properly hailed as an important addition to the American proletarian novel," and John Chamberlain was wrong in querying whether the "organizers [in the novel] use the workers as 'just so much revolutionary clay.'" By 1949 *In Dubious Battle* had become, in the view of Charles Humboldt (*Masses & Mainstream*, June, p. 18), a mere political travesty in which "the action staggers from incident to incident like a desperate comic strip." Mac is no communist at all but an anarcho-syndicalist, an old "Wobbly" in disguise, and Jim's "revolutionary authority" has the "face of a stormtrooper."

acquittal.) From 1918 to 1922 he edited the *Masses'* successor, the *Liberator*. When the *New Masses* was founded in 1926 his name was on the masthead as a contributing editor, yet his thinking and writing about Russia and Marxism were already leading him into the company of the recusants on whom the party has conferred, as one critic of Stalinism said, the "Order of Enemies of Mankind." In 1925 Eastman published *Since Lenin Died,* a book which was both a defense of Trotsky, then in trouble with the central committee of the Communist Party, and an attack on the maneuvers of Stalin to secure the power of the state for himself. As time went on Eastman became more and more skeptical of present-day Marxism as a "science" (a serious heresy); he held that Lenin, the true empiricist, was actually in rebellion against Marxism. In the September 1933 issue of the *New Masses* Joshua Kunitz read Eastman out of the company of revolutionary writers. "Max Eastman's Hot Unnecessary Tears" presented him as typical of "the tired petty-bourgeois radical who stands bewildered amidst the deafening clashes of two opposing worlds."

In book after book Eastman continued his crusade to vindicate Trotsky and vilify Stalin, but his position was not static. By the decade of the forties he began to look more like a champion of free enterprise than a "petty-bourgeois radical." In *Russia and the Crisis in Socialism* (1940),[6] he asked socialists for answers to two questions: Is it not free enterprise under capitalism which has made our democratic freedom possible? and Is not a state bureaucracy in the classless society of a socialist state certain to exploit the working class "more efficiently than the private capitalist can"? The preservation of the status quo was now the first of all issues to the one-time editor of three magazines which looked forward to the coming revolution.[7]

Joseph Freeman, one of the founders of the *New Masses,* has also been since 1939 inscribed among the "Enemies of Mankind." Yet his *An American Testament* (1936) seemed orthodox enough at the time it appeared. R. M. Lovett reviewed it with high praise in the *New Masses* for October 27, 1936. It was also favorably noticed in the New York and the London *Daily Worker.* Whatever Stalinists have subsequently said about this work, it stands as a valuable record of how a young man of Russian background, growing up in New York in the days just before World War I, moved farther and farther to the left and became eventually one of the leading spokesmen for communism. No other autobiography we have gives so clear a picture of the bewildering shifts and changes

[6] See chapter 13: "What to Do Now," pp. 248-49.
[7] Mr. Eastman's most succinct repudiation of his Marxist past will be found in his foreword to Benjamin Gitlow's *The Whole of Their Lives: Communism in America; a Personal History and Intimate Portrayal of Its Leaders* (New York, 1948).

among the leftist writers from 1917 to 1927, at which point the narrative ends.

Schooled at Columbia, working for a time for capitalist newspapers, the young Freeman had one foot in Bohemia and the other in the revolutionary camp. He experienced, like many of his generation, the dualism which impelled a writer simultaneously toward Beauty (which meant pure art) and toward Justice (which meant the revolution). In Russia, which he visited in 1926-1927, enraptured with what he saw, Freeman learned how to resolve this dualism. There could hardly have been in 1933-1934, when he was writing *An American Testament*, a more devoted young American leftist, and so he continued to believe himself to be until 1939. In the August issue of the *Communist International* of that year there appeared a devastating attack on Freeman by P. Dengel in an article entitled "Book Reviewing Is a Serious Matter." He began by reprimanding communist publications for the harm they had done to the cause in recommending books which "pretend to be pro-labor and even 'revolutionary' but which in reality contain more or less doses of disruptive poison in more or less concealed form." The only such work which Dengel cites is *An American Testament*. Thus his article was in reality an attack on Freeman only. Freeman, so he says, had been conditioned by his association with Greenwich Village intellectuals and by the problems of his petty-bourgeois youth. Even in his years in Russia, furthermore, he showed himself to be an underhanded defender of the Trotskyites.

Evidently Dengel's attack was the signal for the dropping of Freeman by the Stalinists. The *New Masses* continued to list him as a contributing editor until October 24, 1939, but no writing of his appeared in the magazine after July 18. At the time of the publication of his novel *Never Call Retreat* (1943) Samuel Sillen placed him beyond the pale among the renegades—Silone, Koestler, Dos Passos, Edmund Wilson, and Louis Fischer.[8] Young writers once looked up to Freeman; now, wrote Sillen, he is saying to them in effect, "Citizens, I lied." His novel is dominated by the "image of the revolution turning against itself." In it one finds "another anti-Red Testament by an ex-Red." Freeman's latest novel, *The Long Pursuit* (1947), would indicate that he has put his radical past entirely behind him and closed it off. The book is concerned solely with the bickerings and lecheries of a group of U.S.O. performers at the European front during World War II.

Philip Rahv lingered for a much shorter time than Freeman close to the party line. At present, as one of the editors of *Partisan Review* (with which he has been associated since its founding in 1934) he is about as far from Communist Party orthodoxy as one can imagine. Eastman and Freeman continued, after their apostasies, to call themselves leftists but

[8] *New Masses*, May 4, 1943, pp. 24-26.

Rahv is not so much above the battle as far removed from its heat and noise. In his recent collection of critical essays, *Image and Idea* (1949), there is scarcely a political opinion to be found.

"The Literary Class War," Rahv's "diploma piece" for the *New Masses* (August 1932) was a determined attempt to define the function of the Marxist critic and to demonstrate how Marxism might be applied to such traditional concepts of aestheticians as the Aristotelian doctrine of katharsis. With the expected zeal of a convert Rahv was very strict with deviationists and said sternly that the fellow traveler should, of course, be assimilated into the revolutionary movement if possible, but that if his bourgeois roots are too strong, "he should be neatly and rapidly dispatched on the road back." This pronouncement was severely dealt with by A. B. Magil in the *New Masses* four months later.[9] Comrade Rahv's piece, he said, was a "weird compound of truth, half-truth and pure rubbish." He had failed to recognize the importance of some of the experimental movements in the literature of the time, even though the Kharkov congress of revolutionary writers (held late in 1930) admitted their value. Furthermore, Comrade Rahv needed to be censored for being so rough with fellow travelers. But his greatest error was in making demands of leftist writers which not even the Communist Party in America imposed on its members.

Magil's attack had little apparent effect on Rhav's standing as a revolutionary writer. He continued to contribute to the *New Masses* and his *Partisan Review* was for a time sufficiently orthodox. The *Review* in its inception (1934) carried the legend "A Bi-monthly of Revolutionary Literature / Published by the John Reed Club of New York." After its early issues it moved away from the extreme left, and it is significant that in the second stage of its evolution, beginning with the issue of February 1936, the designation "A Bi-monthly of Revolutionary Literature" was dropped from the masthead. Stage three begins in December 1937 after a period of suspended publication lasting from October 1936. A marked change in policy had taken place.

With a little knowledge of what had been going on behind the scenes, one can understand what caused this change. The editors, William Phillips and Philip Rahv, had grown increasingly restive under the "Communist attempt to set up a monopoly of radical ideas." They deprecated the way in which the *New Masses* ignored the "difference between good and bad writing." But it was the Moscow trials which finally convinced them that Stalinism was "not the agent but the enemy of democratic socialism."

At the second congress of American writers (held in the summer of 1937) Rahv and Phillips, together with Fred Dupee, who had once been on the staff of the *New Masses*, announced their break with the policies of

[9] December 1932. The title of Magil's article is "Pity and Terror."

the Communist Party. In the session on criticism, aided by Mary McCarthy and Dwight Macdonald, they attacked the Stalinist domination of the group. The record of this attack, as reported in the official account of the congress, is so cryptic that it is no record at all: "The notes on the critics' session indicated that none of the topics proposed for discussion was discussed, but that the time was consumed in an attack upon the congress by a small group of six which culminated in Dwight Macdonald's remark that he was against the united front and 'for Trotsky.' These attacks were, of course, attacked, and the meeting seems to be typified by the answer of Mr. Hicks to Joseph Freeman's question, 'Can I say one word about criticism?' 'No, Joe,' replied Mr. Hicks, 'that's one thing we can't discuss.' "[10]

To those in the know, therefore, the editorial statement in the first issue of the revived *Partisan Review* came as no surprise. It declared the magazine's responsibility to the revolutionary movement in general, but disclaimed its obligation to any of the movement's organized political expressions. The tendency of social writers in America to identify themselves with the Communist Party was deplored. The *Partisan Review* would henceforth be independent, for its editors had learned that the totalitarian trend in the leftist movement could not be combated from within. From this point on the magazine was open to contributors whom the Stalinists despised, and, after the departure of Dwight Macdonald from its councils in the summer of 1943, it retained scarcely any political content whatsoever.[11]

As Rahv moved to the right he became increasingly disillusioned about the whole American literary tradition. *Image and Idea* shows that he can find little to praise among past or present American writers.[12] He turns increasingly to European writers who have been able, as the Americans have not, to convert a wide range of experience into conscious thought. Whereas in the past the national life largely determined the nature of our literature (in which Rahv finds little that is good), international forces have now begun to exert a dominant and beneficent influence. Only by submission to them will American writers cure themselves of such sins as amateurishness, obscurity, irresponsibility, swollen rhetoric, and self-parody. Inevitably, Rahv compiled his *Discovery of Europe* (1937), an anthology of selections from the record left by various American writers who felt profoundly the experience of Europe. It is in Europe, he believes, that the background and quality of an American

[10] Henry Hart, ed., *The Writer in a Changing World* (New York, 1937), p. 225.
[11] See "In Retrospect: Ten Years of *Partisan Review*," by William Phillips and Philip Rahv (*The Partisan Reader* [1946], pp. 679-88), for an account of the relations between the *Partisan Review* and the "revolutionary movement" in America.
[12] See particularly "The Cult of Experience in American Writing."

writer are tested as they are tested nowhere else; "going to Europe thus becomes a cognitive act, an act of re-discovery and re-possessing one's heritage." But there is, evidently, no need for these pilgrims to visit Mother Russia!

Most of the writers of any stature who moved to the left eventually committed some heresy and took themselves out of the movement, but Isidor Schneider, our fourth typical case, has stayed in favor with the Stalinists from the early thirties at least until mid-1951. It is instructive to study the career of such a faithful defender of the cause, a career probably unique in the annals of the literary movement on the left.

Schneider contributed, during the past sixteen years, almost 250 reviews, poems, lead articles, and special columns to the *New Masses* and *Masses & Mainstream*. As the handiest man among the magazine's handymen he took on a wide variety of assignments: the telling off of such deserters from the cause as Edmund Wilson, Waldo Frank, Arthur Koestler, and Lewis Mumford; the reviewing of all kinds of literary works, from the reactionary to the avowedly party-line. He was always considered a learned man by his colleagues, and his reviews do indeed show an unusual degree of information and are markedly conscientious. In surveying his career, one notices that—wisely, one supposes—he never indulged in the elaborate theorizing about the Marxist approach to literature which was so often fatal to leftist writers when the party line changed abruptly and they found themselves caught with dangerous heresies in their possession. Instead, Schneider propagandized continuously for such general, and therefore safe, ideas as the decadence of modern capitalist literature, the demand that the leftist writer understand what is required of him, the wide opportunity offered the literary artist who embraces Marxism. Even when he felt called on, as a practicing novelist and poet, to praise older masters like Henry James, Schneider was careful to point out their errors and the waste of talents devoted to a dying society. It would seem that he has been happy in the movement and that he has suffered no doubts when political events here or in Russia demanded an about face. His recent novel, *The Judas Time* (1946), deals with American Marxists who fail to measure up to the discipline which is required of them: the unsure, the venal, the Judases who turn renegade and learn how to make a good living from the business of betrayal. In two critiques of this novel Charles Humboldt[13] registered his regret that Schneider took a negative approach and did not depict even one communist with the virtues he would, by nature, possess. One can imagine that for Schneider security in the cause was surer just because he was not too positive and assertive. It was never possible for

[13] *New Masses*, Apr. 29, 1947, pp. 24-26; *Masses & Mainstream*, July 1949, pp. 48-49.

615

any of his fellows to accuse him of petty-bourgeois individualism or sectarianism or leftism. His errors were those of the most cautious of his colleagues and were quickly dropped and forgotten as soon as they were pointed out by the highest authority.[14]

IV. What Three Writers' Congresses Reveal

The rapidity with which dogma could become error for the writer on the left may be realized by examining what was said and what went on in three writers' congresses held in New York in the thirties. The first two were fully reported in books edited by Henry Hart: *American Writers' Congress* (1935) and *The Writer in a Changing World* (1937). The complexion of the second work differs markedly from that of the first.

The general tenor of the sessions in the first congress was the necessity for writers to ally themselves with the workers and to play their part in bringing on the revolution. Greetings were presented from revolutionary writers abroad. Louis Aragon described the peace of mind which had come to him in moving from dada to the Red Front. Matthew Josephson reported that Moscow had become an oasis of culture and that for Russian writers the "march of the social revolution in their country has been associated with the highest romance and a kind of modern heroism." Moissaye J. Olgin presented a glowing account of the first all-Union congress of Soviet writers, inspired by Stalin and chaired by Gorky. He wished his speech to constitute a message to this first congress of American revolutionary writers from their comrades abroad. Earl Browder assured the members of the group, the majority of whom were not communists, that the Communist Party had no desire to control writers, to put them "in uniform." "We are all soldiers," he said at the conclusion of his speech, "each in our own place, in a common cause. Let our efforts be united in fraternal solidarity."

Although some of the speakers, Malcolm Cowley for example, took care to point out that they were not, and probably never would be proletarian writers, and Dos Passos, in his piece on "The Writer as

[14] In the *Partisan Review* for March 1938, Mr. Herbert Solow (who has been editor of *Fortune* since 1945) made a revealing survey of the later standing, among the orthodox, of the contributors to the *New Masses* during 1926-1927. The title of his study is "Minutiae of Left-Wing Literary History." His figures show that the more articles one contributed and the more influence one exerted in the magazine the greater were his chances of becoming sooner or later one of the "Enemies of Mankind." Of the 106 writers who contributed only one article during these two years only six were, in 1938, so branded. Of the ten who contributed five or more articles, three were later in disfavor. Of the six editors, two were by 1938 in outer darkness. The article is especially interesting in what it reveals about the shifting attitude of the *New Masses* toward such writers as Hemingway, Sandburg, MacLeish, Thomas Mann, and Gide, whose eminence the editors of the magazine respected and whom they wished to claim for the cause whenever it was possible to do so.

Technician" spoke up for the writer's freedom, the theme of revolutionary writing was developed by Waldo Frank, Jack Conroy, Kenneth Burke, Granville Hicks, Edwin Seaver, Isidor Schneider, and a half dozen others. The discussions which proceeded from the papers seem to have been amicable. Almost the only dissenting voice was that of John Chamberlain, who as a guest called for more moral conflict in proletarian novels. The last business of the congress was the formation of a League of American Writers, of which Waldo Frank was to be chairman, and, at the suggestion of James T. Farrell, the congress concluded its final session by singing the *Internationale*.

The second congress, two years later, adjourned with the remark from Donald Ogden Stewart, new president of the League of American Writers, that it was late and he was hot and thirsty. There is no record that the *Internationale* was sung. It would seem that in all the sessions the theme of revolution was deliberately played down. In the prepared speeches and the discussions there was little talk about the obligations of the writer to the great day coming. The call for the congress had listed six aims which the (to be) revived League of American Writers should set for itself. They are mild indeed compared with the activities demanded of the writers by the first congress. The strongest is the fifth and it merely demands that writers "defend the political and social institutions that make for peace and encourage a healthy culture." The avowed communists present were following dutifully the change in the party line. Because of the threat of fascism and the outbreak of the Spanish Civil War, the Communist Party at this moment sought a Popular Front with democratic forces everywhere. This second congress was in fact a Popular Front affair and the cause which took the place of the earlier zeal for a proletarian literature was the battle for freedom being made by the Spanish Loyalists. This cause brought MacLeish, Hemingway, and Martha Gellhorn into the congress. The big public meeting held in Carnegie Hall was largely concerned with the dangers of fascism and the importance of the Spanish Civil War. It was at this session that Hemingway made one of his few public speeches—on "The Writer and War."

Those who were managing the congress had some difficulty in preventing obstructionists from turning the arguments away from Fascist war and the Popular Front. Mr. Harry Roskolenko wanted to know, for example, why Trotsky's *Literature and Revolution* had been removed from public circulation in the U.S.S.R. Mr. H. W. L. Dana answered him by stating that the book was now out of date since writing was going forward so rapidly in Russia. Mr. Roskolenko raised other inconvenient issues in other sessions. The few Trotskyites who crashed the meetings were probably not mollified by Joseph Freeman's assurance that the

617

"question of socialism has neither been shelved nor abandoned." Workers and farmers, liberals and progressives, communists, socialists, and all others must now unite in a "People's Front against fascism and for the defense of democracy and culture." Freeman's words must have caught the sense of the meeting, for it is recorded that "the applause was overwhelming."

The literary Popular Front had shown few premonitory signs of its imminent disintegration when the third American Writers' Congress convened at the New School for Social Research, June 2-4, 1939. Babette Deutsch, Frances Winwar, and some others had resigned from the organization, "protesting communist domination,"[15] but the roster of important figures in the literary world who sponsored or spoke at the congress was impressive. Dreiser, Hemingway, and Kenneth Burke contributed articles to the official program.[16] Dr. Eduard Beneš, Thomas Mann, Louis Aragon, Leland Stowe, Langston Hughes, and Vincent Sheean appeared and spoke. According to the record, "the complete unity of the Congress on the question of democratic culture versus fascist reaction made it possible for the delegates to devote their principal efforts toward improving their creative work and widening their spheres of influence."[17]

This harmony was not to persist for long. Even as the congress was listening to exiled German writers speak of the terrors of the Nazi regime, negotiations were under way for the Russo-German pact, which was signed barely three months later. The Popular Front for writers could not survive this blow. Many members of the League of American Writers who had maintained, like Van Wyck Brooks, that Russia, despite errors, had made a "valiant effort to bring about a just social order," now found themselves trapped. The communists, they saw, were running the League. There was nothing for them to do but resign. During the week in which the official record of the third congress, *Fighting Words* (1940), was published half a dozen members withdrew from the League's executive board. There had been a series of resignations before this, including those of the honorary president Thomas Mann and four of the ten vice-presidents. When Malcolm Cowley reviewed *Fighting Words* for the *New Republic* (August 12, 1940) he took that occasion to make public his own letter of resignation from the League. Of the 800 members, 100, including a third or more of the elected officers, sent formal resignations and many others quit by the simple process of not paying their dues.

[15] My authority for this statement is Eugene Lyons, *The Red Decade* (New York, 1941), p. 321.
[16] Published as a special issue of *Direction* for May-June 1939.
[17] "Third American Writers' Congress," in *Direction*, July-August 1939, p. 4.

This was the end.[18] The disintegration of the Popular Front in literature was swift and complete. Some who had participated as writers but not as communists found during the war that the armed forces and the F.B.I. believed they could not be trusted to file a document in a government office or carry a bazooka. When the war was over and committees hot on the trail of "un-American" activities were holding investigations before klieg lights and microphones, many writers whose "disloyalty" had consisted in attending a writers' congress or two discovered that they were guilty by association. By 1950 no one could say where the American political left was located. Writers were no longer trying to find it so that there they might take their stand.

V. Evaluations

It has not been the concern of this chapter to survey the full extent of American leftist writing or to assess its achievement. The aim has been, rather, to show how writers were drawn into the leftward movement, especially in the years between 1920 and 1940, to see what the problems were which concerned them there, and what effect the constantly changing political situation had upon authors who were trying to be, in some sense of the word, "revolutionary." But what has been said will present a distorted picture unless there is some evaluation of the contribution to American culture made by the thousands of novels, plays, poems, short stories, and critical articles, by the attacks and counter-attacks which constitute the record of this unique episode in American literary history.

In the first place it should be remembered that the movement was extensive and pervasive. It would be difficult indeed to name a writer who was not affected by it. Even a negative response did not mean indifference. Those who resisted and refused to be drawn in—Robert Frost and the Southern Agrarians, for example—spoke up against it in anger or dismay.[19]

In noting the positive effects one should put first the documentary

[18] On June 6-8, 1941 (two weeks before Germany invaded Russia), a fourth congress—an Artists' and Writers' Congress—met in New York under the auspices of the League of American Writers, the American Artists' Congress, and the United American Artists (C.I.O.). The names of the speakers (among them Alvah Bessie, Samuel Sillen, and Representative Vito Marcantonio) indicate that the Popular Front no longer existed. The delegates passed a resolution against the European war as "a brutal, shameless struggle for the redivision of empires—for profits, territories, markets." By August the League had deserted this stand and was calling for the utmost aid for Great Britain and the Soviet Union. Only two of the speeches made at the congress were printed in the *New Masses*, though it had planned to present several of them. One can imagine that their tone would not have been in harmony with the new tune the magazine was required to sing after Hitler struck at Mother Russia.

[19] See Robert Frost's "Build Soil—a Political Pastoral," and Lyle H. Lanier's "A Critique of the Philosophy of Progress," in *I'll Take My Stand* (1930).

value of even the least considerable, artistically speaking, of the proletarian plays and novels of the thirties. In them one discovers social attitudes which were new among American writers. Occasionally, too, one stumbles on valuable accounts of segments of American society which no other writing has attempted to record. Some of the novels of this kind rise above the level of documentation and may survive as literature—such novels, for instance, as Michael Gold's *Jews without Money* (1930), Grace Lumpkin's *To Make My Bread* (1932), and Robert Cantwell's *The Land of Plenty* (1934).

And the positive achievements at still higher levels of writing were not inconsiderable. If their authors had not at some time in their careers taken their stand on the left, we should not have had Steinbeck's *In Dubious Battle* (1936) and *The Grapes of Wrath* (1940), Dos Passos' *USA* (1937), Farrell's *Studs Lonigan* (1938), Hemingway's *For Whom the Bell Tolls* (1940), Richard Wright's *Native Son* (1940), Odets' *Waiting for Lefty* (1935), and Lillian Hellman's *Watch on the Rhine* (1941). The "revolutionary" writing of the thirties was the matrix which shaped the early poetry of Kenneth Fearing and Muriel Rukeyser. One of Archibald MacLeish's finest volumes of verse, *Public Speech* (1936), indicates in its title alone his desire to bring poetry to a wide audience and to make it, in his meaning of the word, "responsible."

A few writers who came to repent them of their leftist literary sins have never recovered from the disillusionment and bitterness of that recantation. In their writing they persist in refighting old wars, and one often catches a tone of vindictiveness which betrays the fact that the break was not so clean and final as they supposed. On the other hand there are several writers—the names of Malcolm Cowley and Newton Arvin come readily to mind—who are abler and wiser critics for having journeyed to the left and come home again. They have still a sense of the writer's responsibilities to more than his art. They reject the new-modish belief that the artist in America is a pathetic alien in an irredeemably materialistic society. They do not indulge in any neo-Freudian nonsense about the morbid origins of artistic creation and the fruitful sickness of the artist.

To those who once used, without prostituting, their art in the cause of the miners of Harlan County, of Sacco and Vanzetti, of the Loyalists in Spain such perverse theories of the artistic process are of little moment—no matter how far from the party line they may have now decamped.

CHAPTER 14

Socialism and American Art

BY DONALD DREW EGBERT

Donald Drew Egbert, Professor of Art and Archaeology, and of Architecture, in Princeton University, has been connected with the Program in American Civilization since the year of its founding (1942). Trained both as architect and as historian of art he has written books and articles on American art as well as in several other fields of art history.

For bibliography in Volume 2 relevant to Mr. Egbert's essay, see especially Part VI, General Reading, and Topics 1, 2, 4, 9, 10, 11, 12; also Part I, Topics 8, 9; Part II, General Reading, and Topics 1, 2, 3, 4, 5, 6, 7, 9, 10.

THAT the visual arts are by no means irrelevant to the socialist way of life has been recognized in one way or another by all the chief varieties of socialism: indeed, the arts raise so many problems vital to socialism that they could scarcely be ignored. For example, not only are works of art the products of a given social environment but they are also the peculiarly unique products of exceptional individuals, and raise with particular immediacy the difficult problem of the place of the gifted individual in a collectivized society. Furthermore, all types of socialism look forward hopefully to some kind of change for the better, to some kind of progress, either in this world or—as some forms of religious socialism would have it—in a future world. This belief in progress inevitably gives rise to questions concerning the relation of progress in the arts to progress in other aspects of society and civilization—questions such as whether modern art, like modern technology, has surpassed that of the ancient world or of the Middle Ages. Then, because socialists look forward so eagerly to future change, they seek ways of bringing the change about as rapidly as possible, which, in turn, usually involves propaganda and the problem of the relation of art to propaganda. And there is still another way in which the idea of progress gives the arts a special relevance where socialism is concerned. For the special sensitivity and insight of the artist make art a kind of mirror in which change is not just reflected, but even dynamically foreshadowed: as Leon Trotsky once phrased it, "Art, don't you see, means prophecy. Works of art are the embodiments of presentiments. . . ."[1]

Thus in many ways the history of art can cast direct light on socialist beliefs and actions. It is true that, in order to study socialism through the medium of art, works of art will have to be treated in this essay primarily as historical and social documents, with the result that their significance as *art* will be insufficiently evaluated. Nevertheless, regarded simply as documents in this partial way, works of art do offer a most revealing means for investigating the presuppositions upon which socialist thought is based, as well as the effects of those presuppositions on socialists and nonsocialists alike. The very fact that most forms of socialism have usually considered art as secondary to religious, political, or economic problems makes socialists likely to reveal themselves through their arts less self-consciously, and therefore with unstudied truthfulness. This secondary position accorded to art also makes it all the more useful for investigating the *indirect* effects of socialism, and it is the indirect and often unconscious influences exerted by socialists which have perhaps most deeply affected American life.

In studying now the relation of art to socialism in more detail, it will

[1] Leon Trotsky, *Literature and Revolution* (tr. by Rose Strunsky; New York, 1925), p. 110; also see p. 137.

623

first be advisable to point out briefly the characteristics common to the arts of all forms of socialism everywhere. After that, the characteristics of the arts of each of the important types of American socialism—religious utopian socialism, secular utopian socialism, and Marxism—will be discussed in turn, with emphasis placed on the art of architecture simply because it is the art which by its very nature involves practical social problems to an especially high degree.

All types of socialism share the implication that some collectivistic mode of life, usually based on common ownership, offers the best possibilities for freeing every man from the material worries that cramp his development—a way of life in which, in theory at least, equality, fraternity, and humanity are customarily stressed. As might be expected, therefore, those arts are emphasized which are either especially useful to the group as a whole (such as housing or craft arts), or which particularly encourage group participation on an equal basis (such as the community singing that once led John Humphrey Noyes, head of the Oneida Community, to recognize music as another path to communal sharing).[2] Largely because of the emphasis placed on social utility in art the socialist artist is usually expected to be a craftsman-mechanic trained in several useful arts with no distinction drawn between fine and applied art, which is the reason why the Shaker craftsmen-artists were actually called mechanics.[3] Since the socialist artist is required to subordinate individualistic self-expression, "art for art's sake," to social usefulness, he has at times even been required to remain anonymous.[4] Often he is encouraged to collaborate with other artists in joint aesthetic enterprises: for years the leading cartoonist of Soviet Russia was not a single individual but three men, known collectively as the Kukryniksi, who have customarily worked together on a single drawing. And in many socialist societies, including Soviet Russia, the artist is expected to submit at regular intervals to the collective criticism of his fellows.

Because all forms of socialism look forward to a future event or events as part of their belief in progress, they each subscribe to a belief in some particular goal, some specific "millennium," toward which the world or society is held to be moving. This millennium is customarily prophesied by the founder or leader of the particular group, so that the nature of the given millennium necessarily depends to a considerable degree upon

[2] R. A. Parker, *A Yankee Saint, John Humphrey Noyes and the Oneida Community* (New York, 1935), p. 244.

[3] E. D. Andrews and Faith Andrews, *Shaker Furniture* (New Haven, Conn., 1937), pp. 21, 29, etc.

[4] One of the Shaker Millennial Laws is: "No one should write or print his name on any article of manufacture, that others may hereafter know the work of his hands." Quoted by Andrews, *op.cit.*, p. 44.

the character and background of the prophet himself. As the goal of the group primarily determines what it considers worthy of expression in art, the preferences and background of the prophet-leader directly influence its arts: Karl Marx's admiration for the art of ancient Greece, for example, has colored Marxist aesthetics ever since. Moreover, the belief in a millennium to come means that among the arts to be encouraged are those considered by the prophet and his followers as the most useful for aiding existence until their millennium has been achieved. In other words, the specific way of life selected for a given socialist community will necessarily affect its art and architecture.

In the last analysis, of course, it is the nature of the specific millennium, or goal, and the way in which it is sought that determine the type of ideology to which a given socialist group subscribes. The spiritual goals of all varieties of religious utopianism clearly distinguish them from both secular utopian and scientific socialism, while the romantic idealism of the secular utopians in many respects contrasts sharply with the materialism of the Marxists. It is the effects of these different goals upon the visual arts which will primarily be considered in the pages that follow.

I. Religious Utopian Socialism and Art

In discussing, now, the characteristics of the art of the religious utopian socialist groups, for the sake of simplicity the illustrations will be drawn from only six of the innumerable communities which have existed in this country at one time or another from the seventeenth century to the present. Three of these six groups (that at Ephrata, Pennsylvania, that at Amana, Iowa, and the group known as the Rappites) were all founded by German immigrants. The other three (the Shakers, the Oneida Community, and also the Mormons, who, however, tended toward socialism in some respects only) were more "native" American in origin even though the first Shakers migrated from England. Nevertheless, despite diverse origins and backgrounds, the arts of all six of these groups have had many characteristics in common in addition to those already mentioned as common to all varieties of socialism everywhere.

Since all of these religious utopian communities were founded on a basis of Christian morality they could naturally be expected to show, as they do, a fear of any kind of art or art theory that is in any way pagan or "worldly." All of them sprang from extremely austere forms of Protestantism, and such arts as they permitted have therefore been marked by a conscious simplicity which represents an attack on vanity, on inequality, and on idolatry, particularly "popish" idolatry. The special emphasis given to the commandment, "Thou shalt not make unto thee any graven image," has often resulted in banning all pictures, and especially portraits. Such a ban long prevailed among the Shakers, and was explained by a Shaker elder in the following words: "We prohibit pictures of individual members because, 1st, of their tendency to idolatry; 2d, the liability of causing personal vanity; 3d, the consequent disunity which might result from preferences given to individuals thus noticed."[5]

Their Protestant belief in the direct equality of individuals in the sight of God as well as their Protestant reliance on the Bible encouraged these religious groups to adopt an equalitarian, communistic way of life largely based on the communism of the Apostles, and led them to allow only those arts which could encourage such a way of life. It should be noted, however, that whereas for other varieties of socialism a communistic way of life was a primary tenet from the beginning, most of these religious groups, on the contrary, only gradually adopted communism, and did so only because it made survival in this world easier. In other words, their communism instead of being an end in itself was really incidental to Christian salvation even though once it had been adopted it was justified on the grounds of precedents found in the Bible. Such communism, therefore, could affect the arts only in a secondary way, and both communism and art were considered entirely secondary to religious belief.

Pietistic communitarians. Before investigating the relation of American religious utopian socialism to art in more detail, two varieties of this kind of socialism must be distinguished, the first pietistic, the second Calvinistic, in origin. Because the pietistic communities, unlike the Calvinistic groups, heavily emphasized the inward devotional and emotional aspects of religion in which direct personal communication with God was the supreme desire, such communities tended to be unworldly, nonrational, and even anti-intellectual—characteristics reflected in their arts. Almost without exception these pietistic utopians originated either out of German pietism (as in the case of Ephrata, Amana, and the Rappites) or else out of a fusion of evangelical revivalism with Quaker pietism (as in the case of the Shakers). As might be expected, therefore, the arts of the pietistic communities of German origin show much German influence: for example, the high roof and flat-topped dormers of the Sisters' House at Ephrata (Fig. 1), built in 1743 and framed without spikes or nails, like Solomon's temple, are clearly survivals from late medieval German architecture. Whereas the Shaker meetinghouses (Fig. 2), with their side entrances and lack of a steeple, just as clearly belong to that simplified version of the Anglo-American architectural tradition which the Quakers had developed for their meetinghouses.

Each of the pietistic groups looked upon itself as a body of elect

[5] W. A. Hinds, *American Communities and Cooperative Societies* (second revision, Chicago, 1908), p. 47.

individuals equal in the sight of God and specially chosen by him for salvation, while the rest of the world was considered inevitably destined for damnation. On this account the body of the elect voluntarily sought to withdraw as completely as possible from contact with the wicked world: one of the twenty-one rules of conduct at Amana was ". . . do not waste time in public places and worldly society, that you be not tempted and led away."[6] Because of their efforts to avoid contact with the outside world, such communities—at least in the case of the German pietist groups—were usually not so interested in actively seeking converts, and for this reason, in contrast to practically all other varieties of socialism, made little use of propaganda and hence of art as propaganda.

In withdrawing from the world they tended to shun all worldly strife; usually, also, they shunned sex and family life and abhorred worldly fashions of all sorts. Their pacifism, so marked in the case of the Shakers, helped to discourage the use of art for any aggressive kind of propaganda for fear of conflict with the outer world. And the celibacy common to most of these groups, Amana and the early Rappites being notable exceptions, inevitably affected the design of their buildings because the sexes had to be segregated. In some cases, as at Ephrata, they were segregated in separate buildings (Fig. 1); in others, as in the Shaker communities, the dwellings were customarily divided into two completely separate parts each with its own entrance (Fig. 3). Since these communities frowned upon worldly fashion, their architecture and other arts, unlike those of other varieties of socialism, were both extremely simple and extremely traditional in style. The Millennial Laws of the Shakers emphasized that "Odd or fanciful styles of architecture may not be used among the Believers";[7] and this simplicity and traditionalism have always made it notoriously difficult to date a Shaker building (Figs. 2 and 3) or piece of furniture (Fig. 4) on style alone. For fear of worldliness, moreover, the pietistic socialist communities abjured nearly all arts except those immediately useful and necessary either for simple everyday existence, such as architecture and the household arts, or for communal worship in some very simple Protestant and evangelical way. Characteristic of their religious arts are the illuminated hymnbooks of Ephrata and of the Shakers (Fig. 5), and also the religious dances of the Shakers (Fig. 6), who danced like David before the Lord and thereby came to play an important part in American evangelical revivalism. For their hymnbooks the Shakers developed a simplified musical notation based on letters of the alphabet (Fig. 5), a notation intended to encourage all members of the Shaker community to participate in singing on an equal basis. As a result of such emphasis

[6] B. M. H. Shambaugh, *Amana That Was and Amana That Is* (Iowa City, Iowa, 1932), p. 244.

[7] Quoted by E. D. Andrews and F. Andrews, *op.cit.*, p. 18.

627

on both simplicity and social usefulness in art, a very direct and functional expression was often quite consciously sought. The Shakers, for example, held that "Anything may . . . be called perfect which perfectly answers the purpose for which it was designed."[8] And they had a proverb, "Every force evolves a form,"[9] a proverb remarkably similar in spirit to the slogan of twentieth-century functionalism, "Form follows function."

Because their withdrawal from the surrounding world compelled the pietistic communities to be self-sufficient, they had to raise all their own necessities of life. They necessarily followed an agricultural way of life, which appealed primarily to a peasant or farmer clientele; actually the communities of German origin were made up almost entirely of peasants who had emigrated from Germany, while the Shakers drew their converts mostly from American farmers. Such manufacturing as was done grew almost entirely out of agriculture—as, for example, the woolen industry of Amana or the handmade brooms for which the Shakers were noted—and was customarily based on handicraft. Indeed, these communities were hardly able to survive under anything other than an agrarian existence. Elder Frederick Evans, most widely known of all the Shaker leaders, once said, "Whenever we have separated from this rule [that Shaker communities must be founded on agriculture] to go into manufacturing we have blundered."[10] Consequently, the arts of these primarily agrarian communities were almost always limited to the handicrafts of peasant and farmer, while their architecture was based on that of the farmhouses and country villages from which their members had come. For this reason their settlements (Fig. 7) were often laid out in the same naively utilitarian and informal way as the farming villages on which they were modeled; and in this reflected the anti-intellectualism of the founders as well as their fundamental conservatism in everything but their peculiar religious doctrines. Occasionally, however, the leader of the group himself imposed a regular plan on the community, as in the case of the Rappite settlement at Harmony, Pennsylvania, which was laid out by John Rapp in regular blocks. But even here, in spite of axial regularity in plan, the final effect of the village was one of relative informality (Fig. 8).

Calvinistic communitarians. To be sharply distinguished from the pietistic communities are the other religious utopian socialisms that developed not out of pietism, but out of radical Calvinism. Among the most important of them in this country were the Oneida Community, and also the Mormons who in some respects were organized on a collectivistic basis and at times made efforts—such as the Second United Order—to encourage more complete socialization. The Calvinistic heritage of such

[8] *Ibid.*, p. 17. [9] *Ibid.*, p. 22.
[10] Quoted by Shambaugh, *op.cit.*, p. 156.

communities as these led them to emphasize the importance of the "calling" of each individual in this world so that, in contrast to the pietistic groups, their members were expected to participate in worldly activities, albeit in an austerely Calvinistic manner. For this reason business, industry, and the arts related to them were encouraged by Oneida and to a lesser degree by the Mormons, rather than just the agricultural arts of the pietistic communities. The Oneida Community eventually achieved world-wide fame for the silverware and animal traps that it manufactured so profitably. And significantly enough, John Humphrey Noyes, founder and leader of the Oneida Community, urged all socialist groups owning a "domain" to "sell two-thirds of that domain and put the proceeds into a machine shop,"[11] a point of view appealing much more to the nonagrarian middle class, from which Oneida drew so many of its members, than did the agrarianism of the pietistic communities.

Although, unlike Oneida, the Mormons in Utah necessarily had a rural rather than an industrial setting, their Calvinistic heritage is doubtless reflected in the fact that they have always been noted for their financial acumen. Yet in spite of their rural setting, the encouragement which they gave to some arts was at least as strong as that given by the Oneida Community; and in the end the Mormon artistic contribution was to surpass that of Oneida because of the greater extent, wealth, and duration of Mormon society.

Certainly, both of these communities had a much more worldly point of view than any of the pietistic groups, and this greater worldliness undoubtedly helped them to participate in more different kinds of art, with greater emphasis on being up-to-date, even though Calvinistic austerity did usually prevent any ornamental elaboration. While, as noted above, the villages of the pietists were rarely designed in any geometrically formal way, Salt Lake City (Fig. 9), founded by the Mormons in 1847, was laid out by Brigham Young in the regular and financially "practical" gridiron plan that any up-to-date real-estate development of the period was expected to have, although with considerably wider streets. The same up-to-dateness can be seen in the buildings of the Mormons and of the Oneida Community, especially after these groups had obtained a certain amount of wealth, and with it more awareness of worldly fashions. Thus the early Mormon temple at Kirtland, Ohio, completed in 1836, was a naive mixture of the late Georgian and the newer Greek Revival and Gothic Revival styles. The slightly later temple at Nauvoo, Illinois (Fig. 10), erected between 1841 and 1846, was designed in a considerably more sophisticated version of the Greek Revival style, though still with a somewhat Georgian cupola. Within a few years, however, the Greek Revival was dying out, a change promptly

[11] *Loc.cit.*

629

reflected in the Mormon temple begun at Salt Lake City in 1853 (Fig. 11) and designed in the now dominant Gothic Revival style. By the time the main building of the Oneida Community (Fig. 12) was built in 1860-1871, fashion had changed once more, and now an up-to-date Victorian Mansard style was employed. Yet all of these buildings, diverse as they seem, are characteristically American, as might be expected of communities whose members, unlike so many of the pietistic utopians, were nearly all native-born Americans.

Unlike the pietistic communities, too, these Calvinistic ones made use of architecture—as their large and impressive community buildings show—to demonstrate their leadership and success in worldly affairs, to serve as a kind of propaganda. Nor did their members hesitate to indulge in many forms of art frowned upon by the pietistic groups, provided that these arts either could be made to yield a financial profit for the community or else could encourage a communal spirit. The drama, for example, which the pietists looked upon as a snare of the devil, was for both Brigham Young and John Humphrey Noyes (Fig. 13) a favorite art because it required collective participation. Individualistic expression in art was correspondingly frowned upon as too often failing to deal with the real issues of life, as being, in Noyes's words, "an enemy to earnestness."[12]

It should be remembered that whereas the pietistic utopians were nearly all celibates who had withdrawn *voluntarily* from the world, such groups as the Oneida Community and the Mormons were compelled to withdraw from everyday society by the strong opposition of their neighbors to their unusual and noncelibate sex mores. Needless to say, these sexual customs affected architectural design. The plan of Salt Lake City (Fig. 9) with its many separate houses reflects the Mormon emphasis on the family as the unit of society, while at the same time Brigham Young's own large and complicated house (Fig. 14) gives architectural expression to the complicated organization of the Mormon family under polygamy. In sharp contrast, the single enormous communal dwelling at Oneida (Fig. 12) by its very architecture suggests the denial of ordinary family life implicit in Oneida's "complex marriage," or, as the enemies of the Community called it, "free love."

II. Secular Utopian Socialism and Art

Like the various forms of religious utopian socialism both pietistic and Calvinistic, the many and varied secular utopian socialist communities in this country also have had many fundamental characteristics in common, characteristics reflected in their points of view toward the

---

[12] Quoted in Parker, *op.cit.*, p. 236. Nevertheless, the works of the highly individualistic William Blake were much admired at Oneida: see *ibid.*, p. 237.

arts. The three most important groups of secular utopians, from whom our illustrations herein will be drawn, were followers respectively of Robert Owen (d. 1858), of Charles Fourier (d. 1837), and of Étienne Cabet (d. 1856), the last of whom was the author of that celebrated utopian novel, *Voyage . . . en Icarie* (1840), from which his followers took the name of Icarians. While our discussion of secular utopianism and its art will be based primarily on the beliefs which these three leaders held in common, it must be remembered that in many respects they differed sharply with one another and that the beliefs of each were by no means completely accepted by all of his followers.

Owen, Fourier, and Cabet were all inspired, directly or indirectly, by the rational-romantic ideals earlier reflected in the Enlightenment and in the French Revolution, so that they all tended to stress equality and fraternity and were absolutely certain that man is indefinitely perfectible. As the word "secular" indicates, these utopians looked forward to a millennium in *this* world achieved through rational processes of education and social reform, so that when the evils of society had at last been overcome by socialism, each person would be free to develop his potentialities to the full.

Like all such utopians, Owen, Fourier, and Cabet subscribed to the romantic belief that "natural" man is good but is made evil by ignorance resulting from unfavorable environmental conditions. Conversely, in believing that man is rational and indefinitely perfectible, they maintained that he can be redeemed by a favorable environment in which the arts could play a part, and to them the most favorable environment was that offered by a communal existence under conditions of relative equality which, in turn, necessarily affected their architecture. Convinced that such an environment can be brought about through proper exercise of human reason without any supernatural aid whatsoever, the secular utopians were frequently not interested in religion and were often atheists, as in the case of Robert Owen, or—still more frequently—were deists who looked upon God as merely the great watchmaker who had created the universe and set it in motion but whose services were no longer needed. Even those who had religious inclinations were likely to be disenchanted Protestants or spiritualists, so that they too had little or no interest in religious art.

Their utter confidence that man is a fully rational being and that human nature is completely malleable led them to the optimistic belief that all men would hasten to adopt socialism once its benefits had been rationally explained and demonstrated, once mankind had been properly educated. Thus educational propaganda (which had been minimized by the pietistic utopians for whom human nature could be modified only by God's grace) became extremely important here, so that those arts which could best be used for such propaganda were heavily stressed. It was because of this confidence in the complete efficacy of precept and example for convincing and changing the human mind that the leading secular utopian socialists wrote in such detail describing their own particular projected communities, often illustrating their descriptions with elaborate drawings of the proposed community buildings (Figs. 15 and 17). And for the same reason, whenever possible these men sought to establish actual communities as examples and models of the socialist way of life, examples which, it was thought, would inevitably convert to socialism every rational human being who saw them.

The belief of these utopians that social equality is fundamental to the good life is reflected in many ways in the specifications set down for their socialist settlements. It appears, for instance, in one of the three basic rules which Étienne Cabet proposed for his ideal community of Icaria, namely, "that we admit only those pleasures which every Icarian can enjoy equally."[13] And it appears also in the insistence of most of the utopian leaders that their settlements should be organized on the basis of great communal dwellings, generally with equal, or nearly equal, apartments like those of the polygonal socialistic "palace" (Fig. 16) illustrated in 1848 in the *Harbinger*, a Fourierist publication. The *Harbinger* stated that this "palace" was inspired by the octagonal type of house invented by Orson Squire Fowler, the celebrated phrenologist who earlier in 1848 had published a book entitled *A Home for All; or, the Gravel Wall, and Octagon Mode of Building*. Although Fowler said that, because he believed in separate family dwellings, he himself was far from advocating Fourierism, he was nevertheless a friend of Horace Greeley and others interested in the doctrines of Fourier. It is thus not surprising that in his book he carefully mentioned that his octagonal type of plan was well suited to Fourierist communities because it could house several families even more efficiently than a single one. And since Fowler particularly stressed social usefulness in architecture, since he was chiefly interested in the problem of economical housing (and for such housing had developed his "gravel wall," an inexpensive kind of concrete construction), in several respects his book strongly appealed to socialists.

But although a communal, multifamily kind of housing was desired by most utopian socialists, housing ordinarily planned with equality in mind, it should be noted that there was considerable variation in the degree and kind of equality recommended. In contrast to Owen and the Fourierists who proposed communities based on a single great communal structure (Figs. 15 and 17), Cabet would allow as many separate homes as there were households. Yet the interiors of the Icarian houses were

[13] [Étienne] Cabet, *Voyage en Icarie* (3rd ed., Paris, 1845), p. 272.

all to be laid out in the same way (although varying in size with the size of the particular family), and the exteriors of all dwellings on the same street were to be alike.[14] Indeed, in Icaria a prize was even offered for the best scheme for a model house with standardized parts, a scheme to which all houses were expected to conform. Such relatively complete equality in housing clearly reflects Cabet's insistence on equality in the distribution of all goods.

In most respects both Owen and Fourier were a good deal less equalitarian in spirit than Cabet although, unlike him, they both desired communal housing. While it is true that Owen's views varied considerably at different periods in his life, at the beginning and end of his career he firmly believed that the individual producer should have "a fair and fixed proportion of all the wealth which he creates."[15] Correspondingly, he usually stated that there would be four distinct economic classes within his ideal community, and in one early proposal published in September 1817, he promised the upper classes that "their accommodations of all kinds will be in proportion to the capital they can at first advance or may hereafter acquire." And even though he wanted to house all classes in apartments within large communal buildings, or "parallelograms," he ordinarily separated the quarters of the different classes. Thus in the project of September 1817 Owen actually segregated them in different villages, while in one of his last great projects, issued in 1841, the four classes were to occupy different sides of the same parallelogram.[16]

Fourier, too, was far from being an equalitarian for he was primarily interested in reforming capitalist methods of production rather than doing away with them entirely. He basically sought *justice* in the distribution of wealth rather than absolute equality. In his description of a "phalanx," or ideal Fourierist community, he therefore did not propose to have equally priced apartments for all, although he insisted that the costly and inexpensive apartments were to be intermixed. Nor did he require everyone to eat together even though he, like Owen and most other utopians, did emphasize community dining rooms.

In all these utopian projects the arts were usually considered important insofar as they could help to educate mankind to socialism and thereby help to bring about an environment in which man could develop his personality to the full: in short, the arts were approved primarily on the basis of social utility. Usefulness, the secular utopians believed, must come before beauty, a point of view well exemplified by another

[14] *Ibid.*, pp. 67, 22, and 46.

[15] Robert Owen, "Report to the County of Lanark" (1820), in *A New View of Society and Other Writings* (New York, 1927), p. 262.

[16] For Owen's changing views on equality see A. E. Bestor, Jr., *Backwoods Utopias* (Philadelphia, 1950), pp. 78-93.

of the three fundamental rules which Cabet laid down for Icaria, "that the agreeable be sought only when we have the necessary and the useful."[17] However, both Cabet and Fourier insisted that once the necessities of life had been achieved, their communities must be decorated with paintings and sculpture[18] in order to create the best possible environment for developing well-rounded, and therefore socially minded, human beings.

This ideal environment, in addition to being beautified by the artistic handiwork of man, must also—these utopians felt—be one which permits man to live close to "nature," a Rousseauistic point of view reflecting their romantic heritage. Their problem, however, was to harmonize this rustic impulse with their profound concern for "attractive industry." Because they felt that country life and agricultural pursuits were necessary aspects of a well-rounded existence, they proposed that their individual communities, ideal and actual, should be restricted in size and located either in the country or in a suburban setting (Figs. 15 and 19, also 17 and 20) away from the more sordid aspects of industrial civilization. And it was largely because Owen and Cabet both considered the American frontier to offer a suitable natural setting that both of these men came in person to the United States to establish their own model communities in what is today the Middle West.

Yet in spite of insisting on a "natural" environment, the secular utopians did not reject machinery and industrialization as the pietists had tended to do. On the contrary, like Marxians later, they tended to glorify the machine provided that it was not permitted to dominate mankind; for the machine could free men from drudgery and thereby allow them much more time for achieving a fuller personal development. Because of this, Étienne Cabet extolled the advantages of mass production, or, as he described it, fabrication "in enormous masses mechanically," while Owen said that "mechanism may be made the greatest of blessings to humanity" instead of "its greatest curse."[19]

Such mechanization of industry under suitable human control was regarded by most secular utopians as an important factor in progress toward a universal socialist society. This progress, they believed, could and should be steady and continuous, so that to them the process of socialization was to be a peaceful one, despite the fact that it might well develop rapidly because mankind, being rational, would soon see its advantages. Since there would be no violent break with the past, no bloody

[17] Cabet, *op.cit.*, p. 272.
[18] Cabet, *op.cit.*, p. 47. Fourier had recommended that "aptitude for the fine arts" be one of the qualifications of those admitted to Fourierist communities: see Julia Franklin, *Selections from the Works of Fourier* (London, 1901), p. 141.
[19] Cabet, *op.cit.*, p. 137, where he was referring to the manufacture of hats; and Robert Owen, "Second Address," Aug. 21, 1817, quoted by Bestor, *op.cit.*, p. 75.

revolution, they were ready to make use of any past styles of art which could be considered worthwhile for human culture even though these past styles would presumably be put together in new and original ways to express the progress that was taking place. In other words, these utopians encouraged eclecticism in art. Cabet said that in the capital of Icaria there were to be "all the varieties of architecture. Here, you would believe that you were at Rome, in Greece, Egypt, India. . . ."[20] As might be expected, also, the eclecticism of the secular utopians often reflected their pride in keeping up with the most "progressive" styles of the day. Until the 1820's, the various projects of Robert Owen were designed in the prevailing Georgian style. However, his model for an ideal socialist community at New Harmony, Indiana (Fig. 15), a model designed for him in 1825, was mostly Gothic Revival with some touches of Greek Revival, and thus combined two of the newest fashions in architecture. At the same time, the various elements borrowed from these styles of the past were all freely treated and were assembled in untraditional ways in order to suggest that such a socialist community, while making use of the past, had now progressed beyond it.

Thus the art and architecture of the secular utopians were supposed to symbolize and exemplify the progress which man could achieve by proper exercise of his reason. So completely did the leaders believe in the powers of the intellect that they sought to arrive a priori at rational principles of social organization good everywhere and for all time. Some leaders did not hesitate to impose their own principles on their followers with considerable dogmatism so that subordinates who violated the leader's principles were often subject to rigid censorship in art as in other matters. Cabet, for example, as president of the Icarians at Nauvoo, Illinois, carefully reserved for himself the power to censor all their theatrical performances,[21] in spite of the fact that in his theory, as expressed in *Voyage en Icarie*, decisions were all to be made by a committee of experts.

Complete faith in reason also often led these utopians to urge a "scientific" approach to art. Josiah Warren—once a member of Robert Owen's New Harmony colony and a participant in many other utopian experiments—developed a new system of music notation which he believed would enable music to be played or sung with scientifically exact fidelity to the composer's intention. And he hoped his method would give the art of music a wider social appeal by making scores easy to read.

This utter confidence of the secular utopians in abstract reason often resulted in an extraordinary mixture of practicality with extreme impracticality, a mixture well illustrated by their idealized architectural projects. On the one hand such projects were considered to exemplify

[20] Cabet, *op.cit.*, p. 47.
[21] Jules Prudhommeaux, *Icarie et sa fondateur, Étienne Cabet* (Paris, 1907), p. 336.

the practical economies which could result from cooperative living; and with such economies in view Owen and Fourier both insisted that the community buildings should be centrally grouped, the various parts being connected by enclosed passageways. But while Owen arranged his "parallelograms" on the four sides of a square (Fig. 15), the ideal Fourierist phalanstery was conceived by Fourier's chief follower, Victor Considérant, as a single great palace with symmetrical wings (Fig. 17), an arrangement not unlike the far from economical palace of Versailles. Needless to say, the shortlived colony which Considérant (who became an American citizen) founded at Reunion, Texas, in 1855 was not like this.

The fact that these various projects are all characterized by rigidly geometrical and symmetrical planning clearly indicates that their designers were not nearly so practical as they thought. For such symmetry could only be achieved by largely disregarding those specific practical problems which would inevitably arise with different sites and climates. And this, combined with the general fancifulness and the enormous scale of the projects, shows that the designers, despite their vaunted rationalism, were actually romantic—if often inspired—visionaries, which is of course the reason why Marx scornfully called them utopians. Despite their glorification of socialism, their praise of cooperation, they were really romantic individualists too often incapable of subordinating their own temperaments to the good of the community as a whole. For this reason, among others, the settlements founded by them could hardly hope to approximate the ideal ones so glowingly described and illustrated in their writings. The contrast between the community which Robert Owen actually established at New Harmony, Indiana, in a village bought from the Rappites (Fig. 19), and the projected edifice in which he promised to house the community eventually (Fig. 15), clearly shows how very different the actuality was from the ideal.[22] And a similar contrast is evident if a Fourierist ideal phalanx (Fig. 17) is compared with the North American Phalanx, the most successful Fourierist community actually established in this country (Fig. 20). Indeed, most of the secular utopian communities collapsed chiefly as a result of the disappointment which this contrast between the ideal and the reality brought to those who participated in the experiment.

III. Marxism: The Marxian Philosophy of Art

Because Marxism has affected American art to a much greater degree than has utopian socialism, its influence will be investigated here in much

[22] Owen promised to erect the ideal edifice on the higher land commanding the Wabash River about three miles from the village of New Harmony. Although some work was actually done at the proposed site, the value of the project was primarily propagandistic: see Bestor, *op.cit.*, pp. 128-30.

more detail. However, it should not be forgotten that the influence of the utopians has to a considerable degree been felt through Marxism itself, for although utopian socialism has been scorned by all varieties of Marxism, nevertheless, as Lenin pointed out, secular utopian socialism was one of the main sources of Marx's thought. Like the utopians, Marx believed in a kind of millennium—in his case, a revolution of the proletariat followed by a classless society. Like them, also, Marx emphasized collectivism, humanitarianism, and equalitarianism insofar as he sought to abolish all classes in society. All of these aspects of his thought have greatly affected the Marxist point of view toward the arts; yet the fundamental contributions to socialist theory and practice made by Marx himself were destined to affect the arts even more than those that grew out of utopianism. Chief among these contributions were Marx's economic and historical materialism, his emphasis on historical and social organicism and on the dialectical process, and his doctrine of a class struggle eventuating in a classless society after the triumph of the proletariat in its revolution. Although Marx never found time to develop a detailed philosophy of art based on these doctrines, he was much interested in the arts and in the late 1850's had even made some annotations for a projected work on aesthetics. In the absence of this work, his philosophy of art has to be investigated on the basis of his general philosophy in relation to the occasional and brief statements about art made by himself or by his friend and colleague, Friedrich Engels.

That Marxism is a form of philosophical materialism is clearly indicated by Engels' statement: "The material, sensuously perceptible world to which we ourselves belong is the only reality. . . ."[23] Marxians believe that man, like animals and insects, is a product of nature and is subject to the laws of nature including those of the geographical environment. However, unlike animals and insects, "man produces independently of physical needs"[24] and throughout recorded human history has exchanged the products of his labor with other men. He thus is a social being, so that for Marxians reality for mankind is primarily a *social* reality with, in the last analysis, an *economic* basis. And the economic conditions resulting from the prevailing mode of production ultimately exert a determining influence on the processes of human life—on the intellectual processes, including those of art, as well as on social and political processes.[25] Art, then, being characterized by intellectual processes, is a

[23] Friedrich Engels, "Ludwig Feuerbach and the Outcome of Classical German Philosophy," in Karl Marx, *Selected Works* (New York, 1936?), I, p. 435.

[24] Karl Marx, "Ökonomisch-philosophische Manuskripte aus dem Jahre 1844," *Marx-Engels Gesamtausgabe*, Pt. I, Vol. 3, p. 88; translation from *Literature and Art*, by Karl Marx and Friedrich Engels (New York, 1947), p. 14.

[25] See Karl Marx, Preface to "A Contribution to the Critique of Political Economy," *Selected Works*, I, p. 356.

637

form of ideology, and consequently works of art differ from purely material goods although equally determined by the prevailing mode of production. Thus, in the Marxian view ancient Greek society, for example, necessarily had a very different kind of art from that of twentieth-century capitalism because, in the last analysis, the mode of production under the slave economy of ancient Greece was so different from that of industrial capitalism. As Friedrich Engels phrased it, "Political, juridical, philosophical, religious, literary, *artistic* [italics mine], etc., development is based on economic development. . . ." He was careful to add, however, "It is not that the economic position is the *cause and alone active,* while everything else only has a passive effect. There is, rather, interaction on the basis of the economic necessity, which *ultimately* always asserts itself."[26] In other words, art, though determined by economic development, can itself affect other aspects of life, and—being a means of communication and a form of ideology—can help motivate men's minds in bringing about social change.

Since for Marxists the processes of human life, including those of art, are in the last analysis determined by the prevailing economic situation, they therefore are not determined by God (as the religious utopians had believed) or by the human reason (as the secular utopians maintained). As a consequence, religion is considered to be merely the opium of the people,[27] so that religious art is to be frowned upon. And human reason, so all-powerful to the utopians, is believed to be free to operate only within the confines of the laws of nature and of human society. In Engels' words, "Men make their history themselves, [but] only in given surroundings which condition it and on the basis of actual relations already existing. . . ."[28] Hence freedom consists, according to Engels, in "the recognition of necessity," because "necessity is blind only in so far as it is not understood."[29] Man is free, then, insofar as he understands how the laws of nature and society operate, and he can plan human goals, including artistic goals, accordingly.

Marx believed that he had himself discovered the law on which all

[26] Friedrich Engels, letter to Heinz Starkenburg, Jan. 25, 1894, in Karl Marx, *Selected Works,* I, p. 392.

[27] This well-known statement is from Marx's "Contribution to a Critique of Hegel's Philosophy of Law," first published in 1844. It is often forgotten that when Marx stated that religion is the opium of the people, he added that it could not be made superfluous without removing the disease of society which encouraged the use of this opiate.

[28] Engels, letter to Starkenburg, *op.cit.,* p. 392.

[29] The translation followed here is from V. I. Lenin, "The Teachings of Karl Marx," in Emile Burns, *A Handbook of Marxism* (New York, 1935), p. 540. Lenin was quoting from Engels' *Herr Eugen Dühring's Revolution in Science* (usually known as *Anti-Dühring*), first published in German (Leipzig, 1878). This Marxist and Leninist concept of freedom derives, of course, directly from Hegel.

social change is based, namely, that social change occurs inevitably and necessarily with changes in the mode of production. All human history, including the history of art, develops, he maintained, in accord with this economic law of the motion of society. Consequently, if man understands this law, he can so act as to accelerate (or hinder) human progress. And for Marxians, progress consists primarily in advancing toward the goal of the classless society.

Because of their belief in progress, Marxians are frequently interested, at least to some degree, in encouraging new artistic media and progressive artistic techniques which may help in achieving this Marxian goal. However, the question at once arises as to whether politics, law, science, philosophy, art, etc. (all of which, be it remembered, are for Marxians primarily determined by the prevailing mode of production), are all progressing simultaneously and uniformly in the march toward the classless society. Here the problem is complicated further by the early education and preferences of Marx himself, because as a university student he had spent considerable time in studying the literature and art of classical antiquity and had come to the conclusion, to which he always subscribed, that Greek art is the greatest art to date, or as he called it, "in certain respects . . . the standard and model beyond attainment."[30] Marx therefore had to relate this belief to his seemingly contrary one that in other respects—such as the organization of society, scientific knowledge, etc.— mankind today has progressed far beyond the Greeks; and this he did in the following way. "It is well known," he said, "that certain periods of [the] highest development of art stand in no direct connection with the general development of society, nor with the material basis . . . of its organization. Witness the example of the Greeks as compared with the modern nations or even Shakespeare."[31] For although, like Engels, Marx insisted that all development is grounded upon economic development, he also said, "In considering . . . transformations [in the economic foundation and hence in its superstructure] the distinction should always be made between the material transformation of the economic conditions of production which can be determined with the precision of natural science, and the legal, political, religious, *aesthetic* [italics mine] or philosophic—in short ideological forms. . . ."[32]

Clearly, then, Marx believed in the nonuniformity of historical development, so that for him artistic progress does not have to parallel economic progress, or social progress, or scientific progress, etc.;[33] and in this he

[30] Karl Marx, *A Contribution to the Critique of Political Economy* (tr. from second German ed. by N. I. Stone; New York, 1904), pp. 311-12.
[31] *Ibid.*, pp. 309-10.
[32] *Ibid.*, Preface, p. 12.
[33] *Ibid.*, pp. 309-12.

differed from the secular utopians, who customarily implied that progress is uniform in all fields. Marx could therefore regard Greek art as the finest in history while also maintaining that capitalism, because it is nearer in time to the classless society, is a far more advanced form of social organization than the slave economy of ancient Greece. Yet despite the advanced social organization of capitalism, "capitalist production," said Marx, "is hostile to certain branches of spiritual production, such as art and poetry."[34] In sum, although capitalistic society has gone beyond previous societies in economic development, and still further beyond them in the science and technology which have aided its economic development, Marx believed that it cannot hope to equal certain earlier forms of art. Capitalist technological supremacy, for example, is of no use for aiding modern man in a vain attempt to equal the epic poetry of the Greeks: "Inasmuch as we have so far surpassed the ancients in mechanics, etc., why [should we] not also create an epic poem?"[35] asked Marx sarcastically.

Since for Marx artistic progress does not have to parallel economic progress, it is clear that he did not regard works of art as economic commodities. Indeed, he accounted for the decline of art under capitalism on the grounds that "all the so-called higher forms of labor—intellectual, artistic, etc.—have been transformed into commodities [by bourgeois capitalism] and have thus lost their former sacredness."[36] Under capitalism, he said, "even the highest forms of spiritual production are recognized and forgiven by the bourgeoisie only because they [i.e., artists, men of letters, etc.] are represented and falsely labeled as direct producers of material wealth,"[37] so that works of art are admired for what they will fetch rather than for their quality as art. In other words, capitalism is accused of stressing quantity and exchange value instead of the quality and use value that ought to be emphasized, that will be emphasized in the classless society, and that had even been recognized to some degree in societies previous to capitalism, notably those of classical antiquity and of the Middle Ages. As Marx phrased it, "In most striking contrast with this [capitalistic] accentuation of quantity and exchange-value, is the attitude of the writers of classical antiquity, who hold exclusively by quality and use-value."[38] Similarly, though to a lesser degree, "Among the

[34] Karl Marx, *Theorien über den Mehrwert* (2nd ed., Stuttgart, 1910), I, p. 382; translation from Mikhail Lifshitz, *The Philosophy of Art of Karl Marx*, Critics Group Series No. 7 (tr. by Ralph Winn; New York, 1938), p. 78.

[35] *Loc.cit.*

[36] Karl Marx, "Arbeitslohn," *Marx-Engels Gesamtausgabe*, Pt. I, Vol. 6, p. 472; translation from Lifshitz, *op.cit.*, p. 80.

[37] Marx, *Theorien über den Mehrwert*, I, p. 385; translation from Lifshitz, *op.cit.*, p. 78.

[38] Karl Marx, *Capital*, I (Chicago, 1909), p. 401.

craftsmen of the Middle Ages there is still to be observed a certain interest in their particular work and in their skill, which was capable of rising to some degree of artistry," in contrast to "the modern worker, who is indifferent to his work."[39]

Thus, according to Marx, the precapitalistic emphasis on quality and use value, which characterized the ancient and medieval societies, produced workmen and artists who as men were better rounded and therefore happier than they could possibly be under capitalism, and who, as a result, were able to produce better works of art. For Marx insisted that in antiquity and under feudalism, despite slavery and serfdom, individuals still retained some real community ties, and had not yet been desocialized and depersonalized as they later became under the inhuman and mechanistic spirit of capitalism.

But although Marx maintained that in early periods of history the workers were able to have a sense of workmanship and artistry impossible in capitalist society, he also felt that Greek art and, to a lesser degree, medieval art represent the social childhood of man, the time when mankind was still in a relatively immature state. So even though he considered ancient art superior to any other, it should be emphasized that he did not seek to turn the clock back by attempting to revive the conditions of precapitalist society. Believing firmly that the laws of history, aided by human action, foreordained progress toward the triumph of the proletariat and the classless society, he insisted that the future should surpass the past, that the social maturity of mankind should surpass its childhood. Said Marx, "A man can not become a child again unless he becomes childish. But does he not enjoy the artless ways of the child and must he not strive to reproduce its truth on a higher plane? . . . Why should the social childhood of mankind, where it had obtained its most beautiful development, not exert an eternal charm as an age that will never return? . . . The Greeks were normal children. The charm their art has for us does not conflict with the primitive character of the social order from which it had sprung. It is rather the product of the latter, and is rather due to the fact that the unripe social conditions under which the art arose and under which alone it could appear can never return."[40]

Nevertheless, paradoxically enough, Marx held that the very decline of art, which he saw in capitalist society, does in a major sense represent progress even from the standpoint of art itself, because the decline of art is one of those many evils of capitalist society which are helping to pave the way for the revolution and for the classless society. And the classless

[39] Karl Marx and Friedrich Engels, "Die deutsche Ideologie," *Marx-Engels Gesamtausgabe*, Pt. i, Vol. 5, pp. 41-42; translation from Lifshitz, *op.cit.*, p. 80.
[40] Marx, *A Contribution to the Critique of Political Economy*, pp. 311-12.

society, by taking advantage of the methods of production developed under capitalism and adapting them to a new social order, will be marked by enormous new productive possibilities in art as in everything else. Only in this classless society, Marxians believe, can the full development of the productive powers of society and the creative powers of the individual human personality be achieved, powers which have been inevitably cramped under capitalism.

As all students of Marxism know, the cornerstone of Marx's economic doctrine is the labor theory of value, the theory that the value of a commodity must depend solely on the amount of socially necessary labor time expended in producing it. Although Marxians do not consider works of art to be commodities, they do say that art and labor are closely related: in fact, following Engels, they hold that art originated out of labor during the early period of history when human society first reached the stage of trade and industry, and that the skilled hand is actually the product of labor. Moreover, as the production of commodities requires the planned labor of workmen, so the production of works of art, they say, requires the planned and therefore conscious labor of artists. For this reason only human beings can produce art, because, as Engels remarked, "The further men become removed from animals . . . the more their effect on nature assumes the character of a premeditated, planned action directed towards definite ends known in advance."[41] Or as Marx himself expressed it, "But what distinguishes the worst architect from the best of bees is this, that the architect raises his structure in imagination before he erects it in reality."[42] Unlike animals or insects "man . . . creates according to the laws of beauty,"[43] laws which nevertheless are in the last analysis relative to the prevailing mode of production.

In recognizing that artists are not direct producers of material wealth, of commodities, Marx recognized also that the worth of works of art, unlike that of other products of human labor, should *not* ordinarily depend on the amount of socially necessary labor time required for producing them. Unlike other workmen, the artist usually does not work for a fixed wage, and unlike other products of human labor, works of art are ordinarily unique, so that there can be no real criterion of comparability between two works of art. In this respect they differ from commodities, for if commodities are to have value there must be some criterion of comparability between them on the basis of which they can be exchanged. To Marx therefore the very uniqueness of a work of art meant

[41] Friedrich Engels, *Dialectics of Nature* (New York, 1940), p. 290.
[42] Marx, *Capital*, I, p. 198.
[43] Marx, "Ökonomisch-philosophische Manuskripte aus dem Jahre 1844," *Marx-Engels Gesamtausgabe*, Pt. I, Vol. 3, p. 88; translation from *Literature and Art*, p. 15.

that it customarily does *not* have a value, but merely a price; and he was convinced that under capitalism this price depends either upon the whims of millionaires or upon artificial scarcity deliberately caused by a dealer or by the artist himself—an unsocial state of affairs of which he thoroughly disapproved. Furthermore, as indicated above, he believed that under capitalism works of art are treated—wrongly—as if they were commodities.

Only in a few rather exceptional cases can a standard of comparability exist between works of art so that, according to Marxian doctrine, only in exceptional cases can art have a value instead of just a price. For example, such a standard does exist with certain kinds of art, such as prints, which, by the very nature of the medium, are more or less mass-produced. Some Marxists point out that it can exist also in those instances, comparatively rare in capitalist society, under which the artist is paid a fixed wage like other workmen, as occurred with the American artists who worked for the W.P.A. during the depression of the 1930's.[44] For here the wages of the artists could be compared and, on that basis, a value could be arrived at for the works of art produced.

Like Marx's economic and historical materialism, his belief in the concept of organicism has also involved special problems for art. Marx held that nature is an organic whole which resembles a living organism insofar as it is more than the sum of its parts, including its human parts. Then, because he regarded human society as a kind of natural phenomenon, he, like Comte, considered that all the parts of society are organically interrelated and that the whole again is more than the sum of its parts. Since Marx thought that the social organism evolves according to definite laws of history, the concept of social organicism is closely connected with the concept of evolution. Consequently, the idea of process and development is fundamental to Marxism: Engels spoke of "the great basic thought that the world is . . . to be comprehended . . . as a complex of *processes*. . . ."[45] And because the social development of the world, fostered by the efforts of all good Marxians, is held to be proceeding toward the Marxian goal of the classless society, the Marxist believes not only in process but in progress as well.

All this has profound implications for Marxian art. As part of the Marxian concept of organicism, the human individual is considered to be subordinate to society, for the social organism is more than the sum of its individual parts. Marxists therefore frown upon individualistic self-expression in art, upon "art for art's sake," or, to put it more accurately, they believe that the artist should achieve self-expression by devoting

[44] See W. J. Blake [Blech], *Elements of Marxian Economic Theory and Its Criticism* (New York, 1939), pp. 434-36, 554, and 557 for a summary discussion of Marxian theory of price and value in works of art.
[45] F. Engels, "Ludwig Feuerbach," in Karl Marx, *Selected Works*, i, p. 453.

himself and his art to social action in order to help bring the goal of the classless society ever nearer. Only in the classless society, they say, can the all-sided development of individual personality become complete, and only then, too, can the arts reach new levels of excellence transcending even those of Greek art, so greatly admired by Marx himself.

In contrast to this future classless society, all class societies (that is to say, all societies since primitive man) and especially industrialized capitalist society, are considered to suffer from profound evils caused by the narrow specialization resulting from the division of labor. Wrote Marx and Engels, "The exclusive concentration of artistic talent in certain individuals, and its consequent suppression in the broad masses of the people, is an effect of the division of labor. . . . With a communist organization of society, the artist is not confined by the local and national seclusion which ensues solely from the division of labor, nor is the individual confined to one specific art so that he becomes exclusively a painter, a sculptor, etc. . . . In a communist society, there are no painters, but at most men who, among other things, also paint."[46]

In short, Marxians maintain that the division of labor, especially in its capitalist phase, has produced individually specialized artists who are therefore neither socially minded nor well-rounded men. This has given rise, they hold, to an evil regionalistic and nationalistic chauvinism in art, an evil distinction between the artist and the masses, between production and consumption, between work and enjoyment, between intellectual and manual labor, between aesthetic significance and utility, between high art and folk art, and between fine arts and crafts. Unlike the narrowly specialized artists of capitalism, Marxian artists are expected to participate in the life of the masses as well as to design many different kinds of things—and are expected to deal with both applied and fine art while obliterating any distinction between them. Moreover, their works must have social significance, must be socially organic and functional, and therefore must in the last analysis reflect the social conditions which are produced by the particular economic and natural environment. Like all socialist art, then, Marxian art tends to be functionalistic in spirit (although, it must be reiterated, by no means all functionalistic art is socialist).

The concept of progress which grows out of this Marxian concept of organicism is very different from that held by the secular utopians, who believed that man is progressing continuously and in a relatively straight line. For Marxians insist that progress, in art as in everything else, takes place in accord with the Hegelian dialectic, or law of motion, according to which any given tendency, or "thesis," inevitably gives rise to a

<hr />

[46] Marx and Engels, "Die deutsche Ideologie," *Marx-Engels Gesamtausgabe*, Pt. I, Vol. 5, p. 373; translation from Lifshitz, *op.cit.*, pp. 92-93.

countertendency, or antithesis, and eventually to an unavoidable conflict between them ending in a synthesis, whereupon the process begins again. In other words, Marxians look upon dialectics as—in Lenin's words—"the study of the contradiction within the very essence of things,"[47] so that "development is the 'struggle' of opposites."[48] Such conflict of opposites is considered inevitable whenever changes in the social structure, in social relations (which basically are relations of production), fail to keep up with changes in the forces governing the mode of production. And conflicts of this sort mean that progress can occur only in an irregular zigzag manner once described by Lenin as "a development . . . in spirals, not in a straight line; a development in leaps and bounds, catastrophes, revolutions. . . ."[49] In spite of its irregularity, however, all parts of the process are regarded as organically interrelated, like all natural phenomena. As Stalin has said, "dialectics does not regard nature as an accidental agglomeration of things, of phenomena, unconnected with, isolated from, and independent of, each other, but as a connected and integral whole, in which things, phenomena are organically connected with, dependent on, and determined by, each other."[50]

Because of their belief in a zigzag kind of progress Marxists are willing at times to turn sharply away from the past, to have a revolution in art as in everything else; so that Marxist art is often markedly anti-traditional and thereby emphasizes the present rather than the past. This is in harmony with the statement of Marx and Engels in the *Communist Manifesto*: "In bourgeois society . . . the past dominates the present; in communist society the present dominates the past." Yet because all parts of the dialectical process of development are organically connected, the past is organically related to the present. Indeed, the past casts light on the present because, according to the doctrine of historical materialism, the present grows out of the past and is very largely determined by it; therefore the Marxist must understand and make use of his knowledge of past art in creating the art of the present. Thus tradition is regarded as one of the inescapable determinants of art. As Lenin said, ". . . one can become a Communist only when one enriches one's mind with all the wealth of knowledge created by mankind";[51] and again, "Proletarian culture must be the result of a natural development of all the stores of

---

[47] V. I. Lenin, *Philosophical Notebooks*, Russian ed., p. 263; translation from Joseph Stalin, "Dialectical and Historical Materialism" (1938), *Leninism* (London, 1940), p. 595.

[48] V. I. Lenin, *Selected Works*, XI, pp. 81-82; translation from Stalin, *loc.cit.*

[49] V. I. Lenin, "The Teachings of Karl Marx," in Burns, *op.cit.*, p. 542.

[50] Stalin, "Dialectical and Historical Materialism," *Leninism*, p. 592.

[51] Lenin in his speech to the third congress of the Komsomol on Oct. 2, 1920, *Works* (Russian ed.), XXV; translation from Jack Chen, "The Graphic Arts in the U.S.S.R.," *Studio*, Vol. 127, No. 611 (Feb. 1944), p. 38.

knowledge which mankind has accumulated under the yoke of capitalist society, landlord society and bureaucratic society."[52]

The all-important role which Marx ascribed to the proletariat in bringing about progress toward the revolution and then toward the classless society likewise has major implications for art. The very existence of a proletariat implies the existence of a highly industrialized civilization to produce it, and since to Marxists, art, like everything else, is ultimately an expression of the economic organization of society for production, the question arises as to how art must express and reflect the productive relations of an industrialized society. Needless to say, because Marxism glorifies the proletariat as the class which will bring about the classless society against the opposition of the bourgeoisie, bourgeois subject matter in art is necessarily rejected as inimical to the masses, and only those kinds of art are stressed which best answer the needs of the proletariat itself. One of its most important needs is, of course, adequate housing, but it is interesting to note that on this question there has been a sharp split among the various factions of Marxism. The "orthodox," or theoretically revolutionary, Marxist usually takes the position expressed by Engels in *The Housing Question* (1872) that new housing for the proletariat is to be rejected *before* the revolution, for fear that by thus ameliorating the condition of the masses their zeal for bringing about a revolution will be lessened and the revolution thereby postponed. In the meantime, the only kind of additional housing to be countenanced is housing seized from wealthy capitalists by the proletariat. However, aside from the revolutionary Marxists, practically all recent kinds of socialists—including the evolutionary or gradualist Marxians (who, as their name implies, oppose a violent revolution), the state socialists, the Christian socialists, etc.—have supported the cause of more adequate living quarters for the masses even before the proletariat has triumphed.

All Marxians believe that economic change is inevitable and inevitably brings changes in all other aspects of life, including the artistic aspects. Consequently, principles of composition in art are held to be ever changing and relative to the period and place even though they ever more closely approximate absolute truth as mankind progresses.[53] And while Marxians do maintain that an absolute standard exists, they hold that in any specific instance it can only be approximated, for it is the sum total of all relative truths. This relativism (which, according to Engels,

[52] Lenin in *ibid.*; translation from Jack Chen, *Soviet Art and Artists* (London, 1944), pp. 77-78.

[53] For the Marxian concept of the nature of absolute truth see especially Engels, *Herr Eugen Dühring's Revolution in Science* (New York, 1939), pp. 94-105; and V. I. Lenin, *Materialism and Empirio-Criticism* (New York, 1927), pp. 103ff. The latter is Volume 13 of *Collected Works of V. I. Lenin.*

is necessarily even more pronounced in the historical sciences, including the history of art, than in the natural sciences)[54] implies that human nature is ever changing. And in this the Marxian point of view contrasts sharply with more absolutistic philosophies of art, notably with those of all the various kinds of academicism which stem from the classic tradition. For the academic artist, believing that human nature never fundamentally changes, holds that good art must be based on general principles of design considered to be valid universally and for all time.

Marxians also maintain that, like the principles of composition prevailing at a given time, the artist's personal style is basically determined by his environment—not just by the geographical environment, but also, and primarily, by the social environment. And this manifests itself in the class structure which eventually results from such environmental conditions, and basically from the prevailing mode of production, the prevailing division of labor. As Marx and Engels once said with reference to Raphael, an artist is "conditioned by the technical advances made in art before him, by the organization of society and the division of labor in his locality, and finally, by the division of labor in all countries with which his locality maintained relations. Whether an individual like Raphael is able to develop his talent depends entirely upon demand, which in turn depends upon the division of labor and the consequent educational conditions of men."[55]

That a particular great artist such as Raphael happens to arise at a specific time is held to be a matter of chance, although if he had not existed, a substitute would necessarily have been demanded and eventually found. In the words of Engels, already quoted in part: "Men make their history [including their art history] themselves, [though] only in given surroundings which condition it and on the basis of actual relations already existing, among which the economic relations . . . are still ultimately the decisive ones. . . . That such and such a man . . . arises at that particular time in that given country is of course pure accident. But cut him out and there will be a demand for a substitute, and this substitute will be found, good or bad, but in the long run he will be found."[56]

Because Marxians believe that the "good" man and the "happy" man is he who helps to move history forward, they consider that the good

[54] See Engels, *Herr Eugen Dühring's Revolution in Science*, pp. 97ff. Engels remarks (p. 98), for example, that the natural sciences are called the exact sciences because "*certain* results obtained by these sciences are eternal truths, final and ultimate truths." But he adds, "As time goes on, final and ultimate truths become remarkably rare in this field."

[55] Marx and Engels, "Die deutsche Ideologie," *Marx-Engels Gesamtausgabe*, Pt. I, Vol. 5, p. 372; translation from Lifshitz, *op.cit.*, p. 92.

[56] Engels, letter to Starkenburg, Jan. 25, 1894, in Karl Marx, *Selected Works*, I, pp. 392-93.

artist is inevitably a propagandist of the deed. It must not be forgotten that, although Engels said, "political, juridical, philosophical, religious, literary, artistic, etc., development is based on economic development," he added, "But all these react upon one another and also upon the economic base."[57] Thus, although the artist is ultimately conditioned by the given economic and social situation, his art in turn reacts upon that situation and inevitably plays a role of social action which can help or hinder progress. In short, all art is propaganda for good or bad and is considered good only if it helps to bring about the Marxian goal of the revolution of the proletariat followed by the classless society. Art must therefore be useful for training the leaders of the revolution (and Marxian communists sometimes restrict the word propaganda to this meaning). But it must also be suited to the needs of the masses and to their understanding, and in addition must spur them to action—must serve, in short, the purpose of "agitation" as well as education. In the process of arousing the masses, morality and truth, like everything else, are to be considered as basically relative to the particular economic and social situation. "We maintain," said Engels, ". . . that all former moral theories are the product, in the last analysis, of the economic stage which society had reached at that particular epoch,"[58] a doctrine implicit also in Lenin's statement that communist morality "is entirely subordinate to the interests of the class war. . . ."[59] Consequently, to non-Marxians the Marxian seems to act as if the end justified the means in art as in other aspects of life; whereas Marxists themselves would prefer to say that the end cannot be separated from the means because the two are dialectically interrelated and interpenetrated.

Since good propaganda is considered to be that which best educates the masses, as well as the leaders of the revolution, in their historic social role, and which therefore spurs the proletariat to action, Marxians give particular emphasis to those artistic media which best lend themselves to propagandizing the masses. It is for this reason that Marxians stress the kinds of art which can most easily be seen and understood by large numbers of people, such as newspaper cartoons, murals, great buildings, monumental sculpture, the drama, motion pictures, mass parades, and pageants. Frequently monuments and buildings are made enormous, both to be seen more easily and to impress the masses by sheer size. And

[57] Engels, *ibid.*, p. 392.
[58] Engels, *Herr Eugen Dühring's Revolution in Science*, p. 105.
[59] Lenin in his speech to the third congress of the Komsomol on Oct. 2, 1920, *op.cit.*; as translated somewhat freely in René Fülöp-Miller, *The Mind and Face of Bolshevism* (New York, 1929), p. 278. What Lenin literally said was ". . . our morality is subjected entirely to the interests of the class struggle of the proletariat. Our morality is derived from the interests of the class struggle of the proletariat." See G. S. Counts and Nucia Lodge, *The Country of the Blind* (Boston, 1949), p. 22.

also, as might be expected, the varieties of art considered as the most important of all are usually those which best lend themselves to mass production and distribution, and which—like the motion picture, or like newspaper and poster art—can therefore reach the largest possible audiences.

These, then, are the general characteristics usually found in Marxist art everywhere. And no matter where or by whom a particular Marxist art form was originated, if successful it has usually spread widely and rapidly because of the international spirit of Marxism. This spirit (which Marxians believe had already been foreshadowed and made possible by the growth of great international cartels and monopolies under capitalism) is reflected in such statements of Marx and Engels as: "With a communist organization of society . . . the artist is not confined by . . . local and national seclusion. . . ."[60] By this internationalism the different currents of Marxist art—currents which have varied in character both with the particular variety of Marxism and with the country of their origin—have been encouraged to intermingle and become modified by one another in many different ways. Not only has Marxist internationalism encouraged the spread of Marxist art into countries where Marxism is strong, but even where it is weak. And at times it has also helped to spread the forms of Marxist art where there is no *direct* Marxian influence at all. For frequently the *forms* of Marxist art, quite apart from its *content*, have been admired and imitated by internationally minded nonsocialists, or by other nonsocialists who for one reason or another have ignored or forgotten the original Marxian content of those forms. And at such times, as has often been the case in the United States, the Marxian forms have usually been much modified by the non-Marxian environment.

In order, therefore, to comprehend, first, the different manifestations of Marxian influence—direct or indirect—on American art, and, second, the modifications in them resulting from the American environment, the previous history abroad of those aspects of Marxist art which have affected art in the United States will be indicated briefly. Most of them have originated in countries where Marxism was not so swallowed up in trade-union movements as it was, for example, in France under syndicalism. Most of them, indeed, have originated in England, or Germany, or Soviet Russia; and for the sake of relative brevity, though at the risk of great oversimplification, our survey of developments abroad will be almost entirely restricted to those countries.

This means, of course, that various important questions more or less related to socialism—such as the contributions to modern housing made by the Swedish cooperatives—will have to be omitted. Even when thus

[60] For reference see note 46 herein.

abbreviated, the subject is still so complex that probably no one author can hope to treat it with the completeness that a specialist would desire; yet even a relatively superficial survey, to be of any use at all, must deal with so many facts as to become necessarily hard reading for the layman. However, in spite of such difficulties, an attempt to discuss this European background must be made here because otherwise the relations of Marxian socialism to American art and life simply cannot be understood.

IV. Marxism (continued): Marxian Art and the European Background

England. In considering the origin and development of the varieties of postutopian socialist art and art theory which have exerted the most influence on American art, we shall turn first to England, because the first great socialist leader who gave a primary place to the arts was the celebrated English author, poet, artist, and medievalist, William Morris (d. 1896). Morris was chiefly inspired by the ideas of John Ruskin, who in many respects was a Christian socialist in everything but the name and who taught drawing for a time in the Workingmen's College in London founded by the noted Christian socialist, Frederick Denison Maurice. Like Ruskin, Morris was led toward socialism chiefly by his interest in the Middle Ages. Originally a liberal (he was treasurer of the National Liberal League in 1879), Morris increasingly felt that the medieval social organization, with its spirit of cooperative effort as expressed in the medieval guilds, had integrated art and society and was far superior to the laissez-faire capitalism of his own day. Even though he realized the impossibility of returning to the conditions of the Middle Ages, to him medieval society was—comparatively, at least—an ideal society, a kind of utopia, and one which in many ways he deliberately sought to recall. His utopian spirit is reflected also in his famous romances of reform, including *The Dream of John Ball* (1888), named for a celebrated medieval leader of the lower classes, and *News from Nowhere* (1891).

However, Morris was much more than just a utopian. Among other things, he was greatly interested in the ideas of Henry George, the American exponent of the single tax; and as befitted one who had originally been destined for the church, there were also elements of Christian socialism in his thought. He himself stated that he was "a good deal influenced by the books of Charles Kingsley," the famous Christian socialist, poet, and novelist. Toward the end of his life he came under the direct influence of Marxism, for in 1883 he became a member of the Marxian [Social] Democratic Federation in England, which had been founded only a little over a year before. He withdrew from this in

1885—together with Karl Marx's daughter, Eleanor Marx Aveling—to found the Socialist League; and when this organization was taken over by anarchists, he founded the Hammersmith Socialist Society. Yet Morris' concept of socialism—though not that of most of his associates in these groups—simply called for the realization of a society of fellowship, of cooperation, in which everyone would be guaranteed complete equality of condition by the community.

Because in Morris there came together so wide a variety of the chief social and artistic movements of his day, his influence, artistic and otherwise, was many-sided and was able to spread to many different places for very different reasons and with diverse results. For one thing, Morris' medievalism made him a very prominent figure in the Gothic Revival in art. In connection with his attempt to revive the medieval guild system, Morris sought to revive handicraft as a means of restoring the well-being of the individual worker dehumanized by the machine age. Through handicraft and applied arts, he felt, the workman could become once more a self-respecting personality instead of merely a human tool; and at the same time the products of the worker's hands would themselves be much improved in quality. Besides, the separation between fine arts and applied arts, a separation also deplored by Ruskin, would be abolished.

It is obvious that Morris' criticism of the evils of industry under capitalism, as well as the ultimate social goals which he sought, had much in common with those of Karl Marx; however, like Ruskin, Morris called primarily for the *moral* reform of the evils of the industrial revolution and capitalism rather than the *economic* reform which Marx demanded and which Marx thought would bring moral reform in its train. Largely for this reason Morris had great difficulty in bringing himself even to read Marx's works. Moreover, Morris refused to subscribe to the Marxian doctrine of class struggle; and insofar as he sought to revive the medieval guilds and their handicraft, he was, in the Marxian view, both reactionary and utopian. For while Morris was not totally unmindful of the material contributions resulting from the industrial revolution (he once praised the iron steamship as the cathedral of the nineteenth century), it is true that to a considerable degree he and many of his followers did seek to turn the clock back, and in this respect differed sharply from the more completely forward-looking Marx.[61]

[61] For Morris' praise of the iron steamship see Lewis Mumford, *The Condition of Man* (New York, 1944), p. 336. Somewhat similarly Ruskin had praised the old wooden naval vessels: "Take it all and all, a ship of the line is the most honorable thing that man, as a gregarious animal, has produced" (quoted in Mumford, *Technics and Civilization* [New York, 1934] p. 208). Ruskin, too, did not completely reject the machine: he recognized the utilitarian advantages offered by machine power even though he tended to reject the steam engine, which had done so much to make

651

Morris' influence on the arts of design came chiefly from his revival of handicraft; in fact he was the leading figure in the whole "arts and crafts" movement which was destined to have a tremendous vogue throughout the Western world. Because this represented a reaction not only against the dehumanization of the craftsman by industrialism but also against that Victorian overelaboration in art resulting in part from the misuse of the new machine tools, it tended to foster a straightforward functionalism in art, especially in the applied arts. This functionalism is well illustrated by the simple forms and direct use of materials characteristic of the Morris chair, named after William Morris although not actually invented by him. Although Morris was not an architect himself (despite some training under a Gothic Revivalist, George Edmund Street), he was also to exert enormous influence on architecture through a house—Red House, Bexley Heath in Kent (Fig. 21)—which was built for him in accordance with his ideas by an architect friend, Philip Webb. This clearly reflects Morris' interest not only in a free handling of medieval design according to a native English folk tradition, but also in honest craftsmanship and in the straightforward use of regional materials and methods.

Many of Morris' ideas were shared by artists associated with the famous Pre-Raphaelite Brotherhood with which Morris himself had close connections. This was partly fostered by the Gothic Revival; and it had considerable influence on art in the United States. One of the founders, in 1861, of Morris' cooperative arts-and-crafts firm—Morris, Marshall, Faulkner and Company—was the painter, Ford Madox Brown, who is sometimes called the source of the Pre-Raphaelite movement. Madox Brown not only liked to paint pictures of workingmen but acknowledged that, somewhat like Morris, he too had "twinges" of socialism.

As all forms of socialism tend to stress social utility in art, it is not surprising that Morris and the arts and crafts movement have had so much influence on the arts of several varieties of socialism. In England, for example, many of Morris' doctrines were taken over by the two most influential socialist groups, the Fabian Society and the guild socialists. The Fabians (who consider Morris as their ideological ancestor even though he himself regarded them as too materialistic) have been especially noted for their influence on literature—as everyone knows, George Bernard Shaw was one of the leading Fabians. But they have also had considerable effect on the arts of design, a subject to which several of

---

England ugly, in favor of the more "natural" wind and water power. Similarly, in chapter 15 of *News from Nowhere*, Morris assumed a new kind of power, not unlike electricity, which eliminates smoke. Through this power "all work which would be irksome to do by hand is done by immensely improved machinery," even though "in all work which it is a pleasure to do by hand, machinery is done without."

the most important Fabian tracts have been devoted. One of the best known of these, written by the architect Arthur Clutton-Brock who had recently published a book on the work and influence of Morris, is entitled *Socialism and the Arts of Use* (1915), a title which again reflects the utilitarian and functional spirit typical of so much socialist art. The same spirit is reflected also in many of the writings of Herbert Read, today perhaps the most widely known English art critic. Read for a time strongly supported guild socialism, and, as he himself says, has been influenced by the ideas of Morris and John Ruskin as well as by some of the doctrines of Marx, of the syndicalist Sorel, and of Kropotkin, the Russian anarchist, among others.[62]

Fabians and guild socialists alike have played a particularly important part in modern city planning, and especially in connection with the development of the garden city, for two of the best known of all garden-city designers were Fabian followers of William Morris. These two were Raymond Unwin and A. J. Penty, the latter of whom also eventually became a founder of guild socialism. The garden-city movement, which later was to spread to the United States, was initiated in 1898 when Ebenezer Howard published in England his famous pamphlet, *Tomorrow: a Peaceful Path to Real Reform*, reissued in 1902 under the title of *Garden Cities of Tomorrow*. Howard himself was always as much concerned for free enterprise as for social control. However, the principles of the garden city—its location surrounded by countryside, its informally functional plan, its belt of greenery and many parks, its organization as a cooperative restricted in size and density and possessing a local industry segregated from the residential section (Fig. 22)—offered one answer to that complete isolation of city life from country life under capitalistic industrialism which had been so bitterly deplored by Marx, as well as by Morris, because it produced one-sided human beings. It is therefore not surprising that a Soviet project for rebuilding Moscow, prepared in 1935, called for one, but only one, of the most characteristic features of the garden city, namely, a greenbelt of forest.[63]

Nevertheless, Ebenezer Howard had been led to his conception of the garden city not by Marxism, but by the combined influence of Edward Bellamy's American utopian novel, *Looking Backward* (1888), of the cooperative movement (of which the English utopian socialist, Robert Owen, was the chief founder), and of the English medieval village, recently glorified anew by the Gothic Revival and particularly by William

[62] See Herbert Read's autobiography, *The Innocent Eye* (New York, 1947), especially pp. 140-42 and 240.

[63] The proposal was finally rejected, however, as "a rightest counterrevolutionary attempt to weaken the city by separating the proletariat from the technology both physically and morally": see Percival Goodman and Paul Goodman, *Communitas* (Chicago, 1947), p. 35.

Morris. From Morris also came the concept of decentralization so fundamental to the garden city: in *News from Nowhere* Morris—rejecting Bellamy's mechanistic centralization—had visualized the ideal London of the
future as an agglomeration of villages separated by woods, fields, and
gardens.

All of these influences are reflected to some degree in the two famous
English garden cities, Letchworth and Welwyn (Fig. 22). Letchworth,
founded in 1903, was planned by Howard's disciples, Raymond Unwin
and Barry Parker, while Welwyn, begun in 1919, resulted from Howard's
own initiative. Through Unwin, the influence of the garden city was to
be felt everywhere in modern suburban real-estate developments, of
which, however, both Howard and Unwin sharply disapproved. Much
of the best English planning for the period after World War II also stems
from Howard's ideas, notably the Greater London Plan of 1944 and the
Town and Country Planning Act of 1947.[64]

Germany. Like English socialism, German socialism too has made important contributions to modern art and architecture. Some of them have
originated in Germany itself, some have reflected the influence of the
English arts and crafts movement, and others have shown the influence
of Soviet Russian art; for the central position of Germany tended to make
it a kind of clearinghouse for the ideas and artistic developments of all
Europe.

In architecture, many of the chief German contributions have been
made in connection with housing for the poorer classes erected by state
or municipal authorities. Such housing developed in Germany on a large
scale long before it did in England, in Russia, or in the United States,
because Germany and several neighboring countries under German influence possessed a long tradition of housing built by municipal governments, a tradition going back to the Middle Ages. In the nineteenth
century this tradition was given a new impetus by the exaggerated
deification of the state fostered by such German philosophers as Fichte
and Hegel, the first of whom particularly emphasized the planning
function of the state. All of this helps to account for the fact that the
first important program for state socialism was formulated in Germany
by Marx's rival, Ferdinand Lassalle, and also that state capitalism on a
large scale was first developed there by the conservative Bismarck, who
sought to buttress the status quo by adopting a few conciliatory socialist

[64] For the influence of Howard and Unwin see especially the preface by F. J. Osborn
to Osborn's edition of Ebenezer Howard, *Garden Cities of Tomorrow* (London, 1946).
Also see Dugald Macfadyen, *Sir Ebenezer Howard and the Town Planning Movement* (Manchester, Eng., 1933), and James Dahir, *Communities for Better Living*
(New York, 1950).

measures. Although Bismarck's program did not include housing, it did help to foster an atmosphere of social reform in which even many nonsocialists eventually became willing to support public housing as well as other aspects of the socialist program. But it was when German socialism grew particularly strong during the early twentieth century, and especially during the period of the Weimar Republic, that the greatest developments in public housing were made in Germany, developments destined to influence American housing, notably under the New Deal. As might be expected, it was during this general period also that the influence of artists stimulated by William Morris' arts and crafts movement, and later by Soviet Russian art, aroused particular interest in Germany.

No single "socialist style" has ever developed in Germany largely because German socialism has so often been torn by dissension, with major conflicts between the state socialism of Lassalle on the one hand and Marxism on the other, between the revolutionary socialism of the "orthodox" Marxians and the evolutionary socialism of the revisionists, and between social democracy and the Russian forms of communism. Nevertheless, although no one socialist style in art has prevailed in Germany, certain tendencies affecting the arts and common to all or nearly all forms of German socialism can be pointed out.

Thus, for the reasons noted above, nearly all varieties of socialism in Germany long supported housing erected at public expense. The single exception was the strictly revolutionary Marxist group, which took the view of Engels that if the condition of the workers was much improved before the revolution, their eagerness for bringing about a revolution would be abated. Surprisingly enough, the German socialists who favored new housing usually argued for the one-family dwelling until well after the walk-up apartment and row house had developed for hard economic reasons during the Weimar Republic. And this fact suggests that political and economic radicals are often conservatives in those other fields of thought and action which they do not consider so fundamental.

Practically all of the different varieties of German socialism could be affected in various ways—although often for different reasons—by the doctrines of William Morris and the English arts and crafts movement. For instance, Morris' medievalism could appeal to those German Christian socialists who, like the followers of Bishop von Ketteler of Mainz, were also seeking to revive the guild system. And it could appeal to the nationalistic tendencies of those who supported the concept of a specifically German state socialism because the medieval revival could, if desired, be given a specifically Germanic and Wagnerian cast. At the same time, the arts and crafts movement (though not so much the medievalism of

Morris) could attract the various Marxist factions within German socialism because they believed that it offered a remedy for certain evils of the capitalist system including—for art—the separation between fine art and craft art, between the artist and the masses, between intellectual and manual labor, and between work and enjoyment. Many German Marxists, therefore, were much interested in the arts and crafts movement, but often gave it a conscious up-to-dateness in harmony with the Marxian emphasis on the present and the future, on the machine and mass production, rather than with Morris' attempt to revert to the handicrafts of the medieval guilds.

However, Morris' influence in Germany was not restricted to socialists. In many respects, and especially in its protofunctionalism, his point of view was also accepted by many Germans who were not socialists or political radicals, but who were nonetheless considered artistically radical because they subscribed to a native German tradition of functionalism in art, a tradition perhaps best exemplified by the writings of the German architect and aesthetician, Gottfried Semper (d. 1879). Semper— a liberal who was forced to flee from Germany because, with his friend Richard Wagner, he had taken an active part at Dresden in the Revolution of 1848-1849—has been called by the English critic Herbert Read, "the historical materialist in the sphere of art."[65] For Semper explained structure in art as derived from the nature of the use to which the work is to be put, from the nature of the material, and from the nature of the tools and methods employed.[66] In very similar phraseology William Morris avowed a "principle of structure that evolves its forms in the spirit of strict truthfulness, following the conditions of use, material, and construction."[67] It was therefore easy for the ideas of Morris and Ruskin to be assimilated by the followers of Semper and, conversely, for Semper's doctrines to spread among some of Morris' contemporaries in England[68] and elsewhere.

One of the pupils of Semper's son, for example, was the great Dutch

[65] Herbert Read, *Art Now* (2nd ed., New York, n.d.), p. 41.

[66] Gottfried Semper, *Der Stil in den technischen und tektonischen Künsten* (Munich, 1878), I, p. 7.

[67] Quoted in W. C. Behrendt, *Modern Building* (New York, 1937), p. 61.

[68] Nikolaus Pevsner, *Academies of Art* (Cambridge, Eng., 1940), p. 253, cites the influence of Semper on Owen Jones, the Welsh architect and decorator. Semper, while in exile for participating in the Revolution of 1848, lived for a time in London and played a part in organizing the world's fair of 1851, the Great Exhibition at the Crystal Palace. Henry Cole, the chief organizer of the Exhibition, was the leader of a group which included Owen Jones and which sought to reform design in England by proper use of the machine rather than by reacting against the machine as did William Morris. Cole himself spoke of Semper as the man from whom "our manufacturers would be likely to obtain great help." See Siegfried Giedion, *Mechanization Takes Command* (New York, 1948), pp. 350-60.

architect, H. P. Berlage, who was a Marxist but who regarded Ruskin as "the father of modern art."[69] Nevertheless, Berlage criticized Ruskin as a mere scholar who did not participate in social action through the practice of art, and he maintained that only practicing artists and architects, such as Semper, could really direct modern art upon its right path.[70] Yet like Ruskin (and like Morris, also) Berlage insisted upon the social utility of art while maintaining that, of all previous forms of art, those of the Middle Ages could best serve as the right foundation for the art of modern times.[71] And as a Marxist, he sought to justify in terms of historical materialism his return to a modernized version of the forms of medieval architecture,[72] for he felt that only the Middle Ages had previously possessed that communal spirit of working together which to him was characteristic of the twentieth century as a century of socialism.[73] He therefore insisted that the twentieth century demanded a "pure art of utility,"[74] a functionalistic art comparable to the architecture of the Middle Ages (Fig. 23). Berlage was not only the first great leader of the whole modern movement in Holland, but through his writings, his buildings, his city planning, and housing for workers (especially as exemplified in Amsterdam South, the planning of which in part reflects the influence of the medieval town), he became particularly influential in Germany. And via Germany many of his ideas were spread to other countries.

A still greater influence was exerted in Germany by the theories and works of Henry van de Velde, a famous Belgian architect, designer, and craftsman. Van de Velde, who began his career as a neo-impressionist painter, had suffered a complete physical and nervous collapse in 1889 and, while recuperating, had felt himself strongly drawn to socialism, especially in its more individualistic aspects. At this time, therefore, he spent much time reading the works of the anarchists Kropotkin and Stirner, of the "Christian anarchist" Tolstoy, and of Nietzsche, the highly individualistic glorifier of the superman. He also admired the writings of Edward Carpenter, an English socialist who was stimulated by Thoreau's *Walden*, by the Christian socialism of his friend F. D. Maurice, and especially by the somewhat more Marxian socialism of Hyndman and William Morris. Hence when an artist friend called Henry van de Velde's attention to the writings of William Morris himself, the way had been prepared: they were, Van de Velde felt, exactly what he had been seeking

[69] H. P. Berlage, *Gedanken über Stil in der Baukunst* (Leipzig, 1905), p. 22.

[70] Berlage, *loc.cit.* Together with Semper, Berlage mentioned Viollet-le-Duc, the French Gothic-Revivalist and rationalist architect.

[71] Berlage, *op.cit.*, p. 40.

[72] Henri de Man, *Psychology of Socialism* (New York, 1927), p. 246. Marx, however, presumably would not have approved of this return to medieval forms.

[73] Berlage, *op.cit.*, p. 48.

[74] H. P. Berlage in *Tweemaandelijk Tijdschrift*, II (1896), pp. 233-34.

all along. For previously he had been worried by the fact that in socialism there seemed to be no adequate place for the skill of the individual. Now at last in the writings of William Morris he had found a kind of socialism in which the individual, as artist, plays the leading role. And from now on, like Morris and like John Ruskin (the two men who, he later said, had most influenced his art),[75] Van de Velde insisted that the so-called fine arts must be applied to life—must, in short, become applied arts, for in this way the individual artist, while working for beauty, could also work to restore nobility to all mankind. This philosophy of art led Van de Velde, like Morris before him, to turn away from painting to the crafts and, in Van de Velde's case, toward architecture as well. In 1894-1895 he designed, in accordance with the principles of Morris, a house for himself at Uccle in Belgium equipped throughout with furniture, wallpaper, metal work, etc., made from his own designs. More than Morris and Ruskin, however, Van de Velde came to feel that the unintelligent use of the machine, rather than the machine itself, was to blame for the horrors of contemporary industrialized society. And gradually he even came to regard machinery itself as beautiful, recalling his childhood fascination with the engine rooms of steamers at Antwerp—a fact which may serve to remind us not only that Morris had spoken of the iron steamship as the cathedral of the nineteenth century, but that the famous French writer, Edmond de Goncourt, disparagingly referred to Van de Velde's own work as the "Yachting Style."

What De Goncourt called the "Yachting Style" was generally known as *Art Nouveau,* or *Jugendstil*—contemporary terms which clearly indicate that the movement was regarded as artistically radical.[75a] Not only was Van de Velde the chief founder of Art Nouveau but he was mainly responsible for spreading it (and thus the influence of William Morris and the English arts and crafts movement) throughout the Continent. And he became particularly influential in Germany, where from 1902 until 1914 he was director of the Arts and Crafts School at Weimar, a school destined to form part of the celebrated *Bauhaus* after World War I. Years later, with two other architects he designed the Belgian pavilion at the New York World's Fair of 1939-1940.

In addition to Berlage and Van de Velde, a third foreign artist whose influence profoundly affected German design was the French architect Tony Garnier. Garnier was born at Lyons, which ever since 1848 had

[75] Henry van de Velde, *Die Renaissance im modernen Kunstgewerbe* (1901), p. 23. For Van de Velde's life see especially K. E. Osthaus, *Van de Velde* (Hagen, 1920), and Henry R. Hope, *The Sources of Art Nouveau* (unpublished Ph.D. thesis, Harvard University, 1942).

[75a] It is significant that another Belgian founder of the Art Nouveau style, Victor Horta, was the architect of the *Maison du Peuple* (1899), headquarters of the Social Democratic Party in Brussels. Horta, too, was an avowed follower of Morris.

1. Ephrata, Pa., Sisters' House (1743).

2. New Lebanon, N.Y., Shaker meetinghouse (1824).

3. New Lebanon, N.Y., North Family dwelling.

4. New Lebanon, N.Y., South Family, Shaker furniture in the brethren's retiring

5. New Lebanon, N.Y., page from a
Shaker hymnal (1839).

6. Watervliet, N.Y., Shaker dance in the second meetinghouse.

7. Amana, Iowa, an old view of the village.

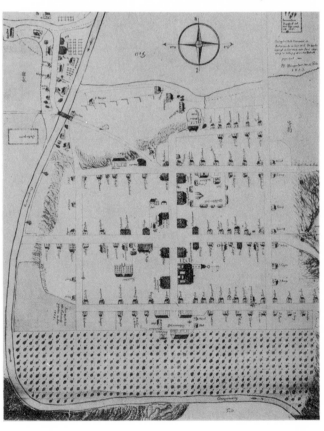

8. Harmony, Pa., plan of the Rappite settlement in 1833.

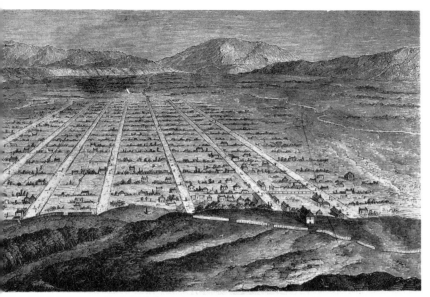

9. Salt Lake City, Utah, early view.

CAPITAL AND BASE

10. Nauvoo, Ill., Mormon temple (1841-1846).

11. Salt Lake City, Utah, Mormon temple (1853-1893).

12. Oneida, N.Y., the Mansion House (1860-1871) of the Oneida Community.

13. Oneida, N.Y., the Mansion House, assembly room.

14. Salt Lake City, Utah, an old view of Brigham Young's residence (1853-   )
showing the Lion and Beehive houses with the church office between.

15. Robert Owen, project (1825) for a communal settlement at New Harmony,

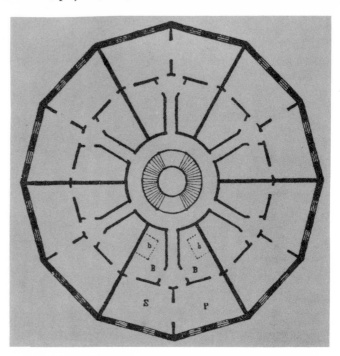

16. Project for a socialistic "palace," from the
Harbinger, Nov. 11, 1848.

17. Victor Considérant, project for a Fourierist phalanx.

18. New Icaria (near Corning, Iowa) the community of the Old Icarians (1879-   ).

19. New Harmony, Ind., in the time of Robert Owen.

20. Red Bank, N.J., the North American Phalanx in 1850, from a painting made from a daguerreotype.

21. Bexley Heath, Kent, Red House (1860) by Philip Webb for William Morris.

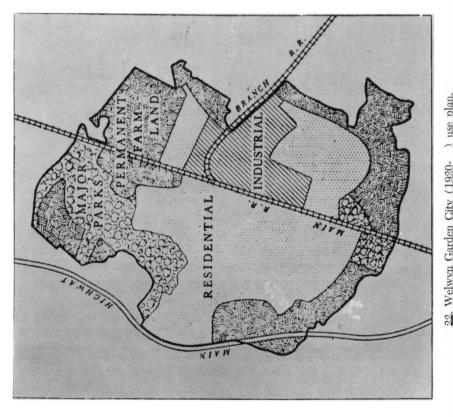

22. Welwyn Garden City (1920-   ) use plan.

23. Amsterdam Stock Exchange (1898-1903)

24. Project for the station of *Une Cité industrielle* (1901-1904) by Tony Garnier.

25. "The Communists Fall—and the Exchange Rises" by George Grosz, from his *Das Gesicht der herrschenden Klasse* (1921).

26. Weimar, memorial (1921) to those killed in the Kapp *Putsch*, by Walter Gropius.

27. Berlin (near) monument to Karl Liebknecht and Rosa Luxemburg (1926, now destroyed) by Mies van der Rohe.

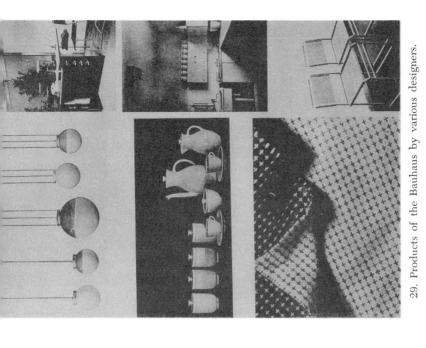

29. Products of the Bauhaus by various designers.

28. Dessau, Bauhaus workshops (1925-1926)
by Walter Gropius.

30. Berlin, Siemensstadt, housing (1929) by Walter Gropius.

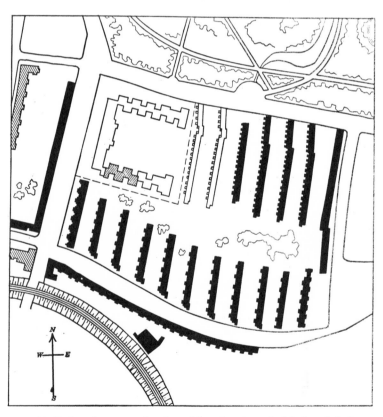

31. Berlin, Siemensstadt, plan of housing (row in black at left is
that by Gropius illustrated in Fig. 30).

33. Relief construction, *Guitar* (1913) by Picasso.

32. Nickel sculpture (1921) by Moholy-Nagy.

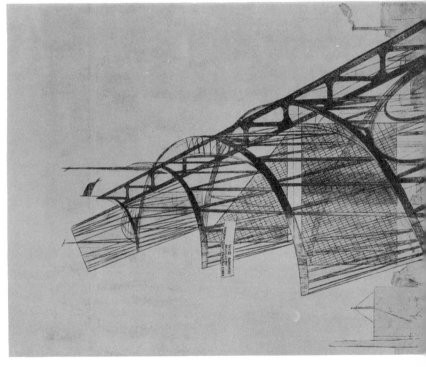

36. Moscow, Transport Workers' Club (1929) by Melnikov.

37. Moscow, apartment house (1928) by Ginzburg
and Milinis.

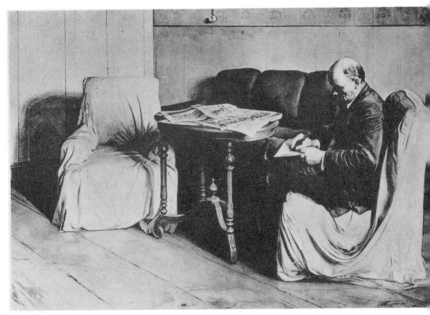

38. *Lenin at the Smolny Institute* (1931) by Isaac Brodsky.

39. *Worker and Woman Collective Farmer,* by Vera Mukhina, on
the Russian pavilion, World's Fair of 1937 at Paris.

40. Kiev, House of the Government of the Ukrainian Republic (ca. 1933).

41. Moscow, Palace of the Soviets, model by Yofan,
Helfreich, and Schuko.

42. Kiev, winning project (1947) for the Kreshchatik Street, by Vlassov (second from left), Elizarov, and Zavarov.

43. Moscow, All-Union Agricultural Exposition of 1937, part of the pavilion of the Uzbek Republic.

45. *Russian Peasants*, etching by Eugene Higgins.

44. *The Belated Kid* (1857) by William Morris Hunt,
Collection Museum of Fine Arts, Boston.

SONNETS FROM THE PORTUGUESE

I THOUGHT once
how Theocritus had
sung
Of the sweet years,
the dear and wished
for years,
Who each one in a gra-
cious hand appears
To bear a gift for mor-
tals, old or young:
And, as I mused it in
his antique tongue,

I saw, in gradual vision through my tears,
The sweet, sad years, the melancholy years,
Those of my own life, who by turns had flung
A shadow across me. Straightway I was 'ware,
So weeping, how a mystic Shape did move
Behind me, and drew me backward by the hair;
And a voice said in mastery while I strove:—
"Guess now who holds thee?"—"Death," I said.
But there
The silver answer rang: "Not Death, but Love."

THE LYF OF ADAM.
THE SONDAY OF SEPTUAGESME BEGYN-
NETH THE STORYE OF THE BYBLE, IN
WHICHE IS REDDE THE LEGENDE AND
STORYE OF ADAM WHICHE FOLOWETH.

IN the begynnyng god made & created
heuen and erthe. The erthe was ydle
and voyde and couerd with derknes.
And the spyryte of god was born on
the watres. And god said ¶ Be made
lyght, & anon lyght was made. And
god sawe that lyght was good, and
dyuyded the lyght fro derknes, and
called the lyght day & derknes nyght.

AND thus was made lyght with heuen & erthe
fyrst, & euen and mornyng was made one day.
¶ The seconde day he made the firmamente,
and dyuyded the watres that were vnder the
firmament fro them that were aboue, & called
the firmament heuen. ¶ The thyrde day were
made on the erthe herbes and fruytes in theyr kynde. ¶ The
fourth day god made the sonne and mone and sterres &c.
¶ The fyfth day he made the flisshes in the water and byrdes
in thayer. ¶ The sixthe day god made the beestis on the erthe,
eueryche in his kynde & gendre. And god sawe that all thyse
werkes were good and said ¶ Faciamus hominem &c. Make
we man vnto our similitude and ymage. Here spack the fader
to the sone & holy ghooste, or ellis as it were the comune voys
of thre persones, whan it was sayd make we, and to oure, in
plurel nombre. Man was made to the ymage of god in his
sowle. Here it is to be noted that he made not only the sowle
without the body, but he made both body & sowle. As to the
body he made male and female. ¶ God gaf to man the lordship and power vpon alle lyuyng beestis. Whan god had
made man it is not wreton. ¶ Et vidit quod esset bonum,
quia in proximo sciebat eum lapsurum. For yet he was not
parfyght til the woman was made, and therfore it is red, it is
not good the man to be allone.

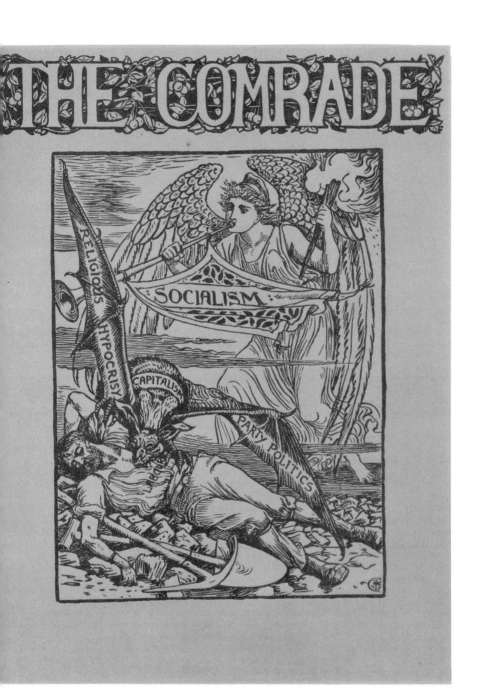

48. "The Capitalist Vampire," by Walter Crane, from the *Comrade*, October 1903.

49. "From the Depths," by William Balfour Ker, illustrating John Ames Mitchell's *The Silent War* (1906).

50. *Backyards, Greenwich Village* (1914) by John Sloan, Collection Whitney Museum of American Art, New York.

51. "Having Their Fling," by Art Young, from the *Masses*, September 1917.

52. "Cain," by Robert Minor, from the *Liberator*, April 1918.

53. *The Senate* (1935) by William Gropper, Collection Museum of Modern Art, New York, gift of A. Conger Goodyear.

54. *Lenin* (1933, now destroyed) by Diego Rivera, Rockefeller Center, New York.

55. *Russia*, detail of fresco (1930-1931) by José Clemente Orozco, New School for Social Research, New York.

56. *Bartolomeo Vanzetti and Nicola Sacco* (1931-1932) by Ben Shahn, Collection Museum of Modern Art, New York.

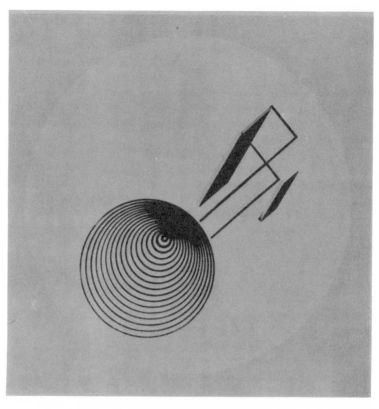

58. *Abstraction* (ca. 1922) painting by El Lissitsky.

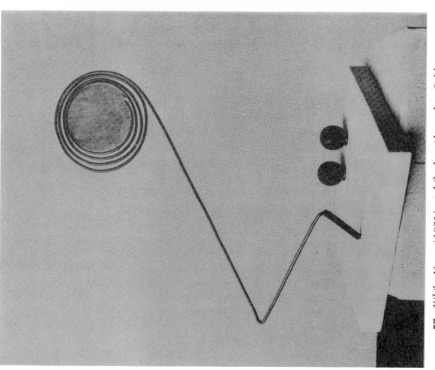

57. *Kiki's Nose* (1931) stabile by Alexander Calder.

59. (a) *T.V.A. Worker and Family* and (b) *Pleading the Gold Case* (1935) by Henry Varnum Poor, Department of Justice Building, Washington, D.C.

60. Brooklyn, Williamsburg Housing (1936-1937).

61. Greenbelt, Md. (1935-   ).

been a chief French socialist center, and was raised in a socialist family. He himself had socialist leanings described by a recent biographer as resembling the mild socialism of a Saint-Simon or a Fourier.[76] Although trained at Paris in the highly traditional and academic École des Beaux-Arts, where he won the highest student honor, the Grand Prix de Rome, Garnier partly rebelled against his academic training. Interested in the social problems raised by the expansion of industry, between 1901 and 1904 he made designs for a whole imaginary *cité industrielle* (Fig. 24) in the new and unacademic material of reinforced concrete, designs published in 1917. In 1905 the Radical Socialist (i.e., liberal) mayor of Lyons, Édouard Herriot, commissioned Garnier to redesign a large part of Lyons along the lines of his project for an industrial city. Both the work at Lyons, which was published in 1919 in a book with a preface by Herriot, and especially the project for the *cité industrielle*, aroused much interest among modern architects in postwar Germany as well as in France, and eventually throughout the world. In this way Garnier became one of the chief founders of modern architecture.

Thus in Germany the native radical movement in the arts, stemming particularly from Semper, could be encouraged in part by the socialism of Morris and Marx and of foreign artists such as Berlage, Van de Velde, and Garnier, though without being by any means completely socialist in either origin or development. Insofar as this movement sought to develop a new or revived respect for the personality of the craftsman-artist, and insofar as it tended to stress the nonseparation of fine and applied art as well as a straightforward "functional" expression in the arts, it appealed to socialists. Likewise its anti-academic "realism" appealed to many more or less radical German artists and architects who, disillusioned by World War I and its immediate aftermath, were turning to the left in art or politics or both. Among them was the artist Käthe Kollwitz, whose work was later to be admired by many Americans, and who, without ever being a member of the German Communist Party, became one of its venerated "People's Artists." Among them also was George Grosz, a painter and draftsman world-famous for his satirization of the German bourgeoisie, who was then sympathetic to communism (Fig. 25) and is said to have worked for the Spartacist group of left-wing communists. In the 1920's Grosz—who left Germany for the United States in 1933—was the leader of a group of artists to whose work was applied the term, *die neue Sachlichkeit* (i.e., the new objectivity, the new realism), a term which the inventor once said was intended to "apply as a label to the new realism bearing a socialistic flavor."[77]

---

[76] Giulia Veronesi, *Tony Garnier* (Milan, 1948), p. 10.

[77] Quoted by A. H. Barr, Jr., in Museum of Modern Art, *German Painting and Sculpture* (New York, 1931), p. 13, note. The term, *Neue Sachlichkeit*, was coined

However, it must be emphasized that this radical movement in the arts, stemming in part from Semper and reinforced by *die neue Sachlichkeit*, appealed not only to socialists but also to many nonsocialists who were interested in solving in an "objective" functional way various economic, social, and artistic problems which had been raised by the industrial revolution but which had come to a head in Germany after World War I. In other words, at that time in Germany it was easy for many socialists and many nonsocialists, Marxians and many non-Marxians, to use the same art *media* and *forms*, although often with a very different *content*.

All this is well illustrated by an association of artists called the *Novembergruppe*, founded in Berlin in the autumn of 1918 and named for the month of the republican revolution. On November 9, the Kaiser had fled from Germany and the social democrats had formed Workers and Soldiers Councils which fostered a general strike and brought about the appointment as chancellor of Friedrich Ebert, vice-president of the Social Democratic Party. The members of the Novembergruppe (which soon included most of the leaders of modern art in Germany) called themselves "revolutionaries of the spirit," insisting that a revolution in the arts should accompany the postwar political and social revolution, and urging the closest possible interrelation between art and the people. In 1919 the Novembergruppe founded a Workers Council for Art which issued a questionnaire on the subject of the relation of the artist to society, and investigated among other things the duty of a socialist state to support art, the problem of housing, the relation between fine arts and industrial arts, and the production of works of art collectively. One hundred and fourteen painters, architects, sculptors, critics, and art historians sponsored the questionnaire. Among the sponsors—many of them simply artists with little or no interest in politics—was Walter Gropius, the architect who was the first director of the newly founded Bauhaus. And several other artists who became members of the Bauhaus staff were connected with various activities of the Novembergruppe, including the architect Mies van der Rohe and the painters Kandinsky, Klee, and Feininger.

The Bauhaus, destined to be the chief focus of the various currents of modern art in Germany during the 1920's, in some respects and in a nonpolitical way continued the spirit of the Novembergruppe. As we have mentioned, the Bauhaus replaced the Arts and Crafts School at Weimar, directed since 1902 by Henry van de Velde, one of the founders

---

by Dr. G. F. Hartlaub in 1923: see Fritz Schmalenbach, "The Term *Neue Sachlichkeit*," *Art Bulletin*, Vol. 22, No. 3 (Sept. 1940), pp. 161-65. The art movement known by this name had been started in 1920 by Grosz and another German painter, Otto Dix. That Grosz worked for the Spartacists is stated by Marcel Ray, *George Grosz* (Paris, [1927]), p. 33.

of the continental arts and crafts movement known as Art Nouveau, or Jugendstil, a movement then considered to be highly radical. After Van de Velde withdrew from the Arts and Crafts School at Weimar in 1914, it was at his suggestion that Walter Gropius, a native German architect, was eventually selected to succeed him. In 1919 under Gropius' leadership the Arts and Crafts School was combined with the Grand Ducal Academy of Pictorial Art and the two were reopened as one establishment with the name of the Staatliches Bauhaus. Under Gropius and his successors the Bauhaus became the most widely known progressive art school not only in Germany, but in the whole world, and at a period when the social democratic governments dominant in so many German municipalities during the Weimar Republic were indirectly helping to foster modern architecture by their large building programs.[78] Because of the Bauhaus' artistic radicalism, it met increasing opposition in conservative Weimar, and in 1925 moved to the industrial city of Dessau, where it was soon housed in a new building erected from Gropius' designs, a building (Fig. 28) which immediately acquired a reputation as one of the most famous monuments of modern architecture.

All political activity was officially banned at the Bauhaus by Gropius.[*] Artistically, however, as a focus of modern movements in art, the Bauhaus was far left of center, so that its principles appealed to many socialists and communists as well as to many others who were simply anticonservative. Gropius himself—justly described by pupils as a liberal—was not a political socialist or communist. But as one whose avowed precursors include Ruskin, Morris, and Van de Velde[79] he has always been interested

[78] The Social Democrats, in power in many municipalities, held about half the cabinet posts in the Weimar Republic during the early years, and thereafter were in the minority; see the table in Ruth Fischer, *Stalin and German Communism* (Cambridge, Mass., 1948), p. 125.

[*] The author is most grateful to Walter Gropius for his kindness in reading over, while this volume was in press, the pages dealing with the Bauhaus. Every effort has been made to take his comments and corrections into account, but it is only fair to him to say that he disagrees with a number of the author's major conclusions as well as with the presentation of some of the more factual material. He feels, and rightly, that the picture here given of the Bauhaus is not a balanced one. The Bauhaus was a focal point for most of the currents of modern art, of which the majority had nothing whatever to do with socialism. But some had either been developed by socialists or were admired and made use of by socialists. It is only these which are being investigated in this chapter.

[79] Walter Gropius, *Idee und Aufbau des Staatlichen Bauhauses Weimar* (Munich, 1923), p. 2. Here Gropius acknowledged as his precursors not only Ruskin, Morris, and Van de Velde, but also Peter Behrens and the *Werkbund*. Behrens, in whose office Gropius, and also Mies van der Rohe, worked for a time before World War I, was such an admirer of Van de Velde's ideas that, like Van de Velde, he too had given up painting to become an architect. The Deutscher Werkbund was founded in 1907 as a result of an impassioned public lecture by Hermann Muthesius, then superintendent of the Prussian Board of Trade for Schools of Arts and Crafts. From 1896 to 1903 Muthesius had been attached to the German embassy in London for

in architecture as an essentially social art, so that the prevailing philosophy of art at the Bauhaus during his directorship can be described as more or less collectivistic, though only in a nonpolitical and non-Marxist way. In a recent letter Gropius himself has written: "The Bauhaus was more than an art institute. We were seeking to find a new way of life. The main tendency with which everyone was imbued was to stress the point that in this world of economic expediency the human being should be again the focus. That is to say, that all the economical and industrial issues are to be subordinated to the life requirements of men. In consequence of this many of the members of the Bauhaus were interested in social improvements but the main tendency was very much anti-Marxist."

In 1928 Gropius withdrew from the Bauhaus because of the ever increasing opposition of the Nazis, and was succeeded as director by one of the teachers, an architect named Hannes Meyer who, to Gropius' surprise, eventually proved to be a communist. After but two years Meyer was dismissed, and then went to the Soviet Union where he resided for some time.[80] He was replaced by Mies van der Rohe, whose philosophy of architecture is similar to that of Gropius and who remained in charge until the Bauhaus closed its doors in 1933 after the Nazis came to power.

Thus for only two years, while Hannes Meyer was director, could the Bauhaus be described as at all "communistic" in tendency in any political sense of the word. Actually the staff of the Bauhaus represented a wide diversity of political opinion, yet the difficulties put in the way of Gropius and Van der Rohe by those who—like the Nazis—wrongly identified the artistic radicalism of the Bauhaus with political radicalism, were enormous: "I hardly believe you can imagine the amount of troubles we had to go through," wrote Van der Rohe recently to the author of this chapter.

---

the purpose of carrying on research in English housing. He became a strong supporter of the English arts and crafts movement and of English architecture in the tradition of Ruskin and Morris, though Muthesius placed more emphasis on machine production. Demanding a "pure and perfect utility" and a new *Maschinenstil* (which he felt were lacking in Art Nouveau), he called for realism and objectivity in art— "a reasonable *Sachlichkeit*." He thus foreshadowed the somewhat different *Neue Sachlichkeit* which was to develop in German painting after World War I largely under socialist influences. For Muthesius and the Werkbund see Nikolaus Pevsner, *Pioneers of Modern Design* (New York, 1949), pp. 15-17.

[80] On the authority of Mr. Arthur Voyce, who adds that Meyer was an influential figure in Soviet architectural circles during the early years of his stay in the U.S.S.R. There Meyer was for a time on the teaching staff of the Academy of Architecture, contributed a number of articles to Soviet architectural magazines, and as late as 1935 was elected a member of the board of governors of the Moscow "House of Architects." He later went to Mexico. Walter Gropius has told the writer that he himself recommended Meyer for the directorship of the Bauhaus, not being then aware of Meyer's communistic leanings.

As mentioned above, Gropius was admittedly stimulated by some of the ideas of the socialist William Morris without being a socialist himself, a fact which clearly indicates that one artist can be stimulated by another without necessarily adopting the whole political and economic creed of his mentor. Moreover, it must be remembered that artists are frequently given commissions by clients to whose political philosophy they do not subscribe. For example, Gropius—though not a socialist—was commissioned by a social-democratic official of the Ministry of the Weimar Republic to design a monument to those killed in the rightist and nationalistic Kapp *Putsch* of 1920, and this was erected at Weimar in 1921 (Fig. 26). Four years later Mies van der Rohe—not a communist—was commissioned as architect of the monument (Fig. 27) erected near Berlin in 1926 in memory of Rosa Luxemburg and Karl Liebknecht, the two communist leaders shot by German officers following the Spartacist uprising of 1919.

Obviously sheer accident can often play a large part in the commissioning of works of art. Yet the fact that socialist and communist clients commissioned these two works supports the view that—other things being equal—political radicals are more inclined than conservatives to be sympathetic to radicalism in other fields, including the radicalism of artists. And this is frequently the case even if the artistic radicals— like Gropius and Van der Rohe—are not interested in specifically political radicalism at all. In other words, the belief in progress so characteristic of socialism in general and of Marxian socialism in particular, usually leads the Marxian to be sympathetic to the most advanced forms of art unless there are special reasons (for example, the anti-Westernism of Russia under Stalin) for attacking such art. And this is true even despite the fact that many political radicals (including Stalin himself) are relatively conservative in their artistic tastes, a conservatism which in these cases usually results from lack of background and training in the arts and which persists simply because Marxism gives such primacy to economic and political, rather than artistic, problems.

All of these points are well illustrated by the story of Mies van der Rohe's Luxemburg-Liebknecht memorial. To the present author Van der Rohe has written concerning that monument: "Everything was accidental from the beginning to the end. But let me tell you the facts.

"One of the first houses I built was for Hugo Perls in Berlin. Mr. Perls sold his house in the early twenties to a Mr. Edward Fuchs. Mr. Fuchs had a huge collection of Daumiers and other artists. He told friends of mine he would like to build a wing onto his house as a gallery for his collection and for this he would like to talk to me. A few days later a friend of mine told me he was going to Mr. Fuchs' for dinner. I asked him if it would not be an opportune time for me to meet Mr. Fuchs. This meeting was arranged.

"After discussing his house problems Mr. Fuchs then said he wanted to show us something. This developed to be a photograph of a model for a monument to Karl Liebknecht and Rosa Luxemburg. It was a huge stone monument with Doric columns and medallions of Luxemburg and Liebknecht. When I saw it I started to laugh and told him it would be a fine monument for a banker.

"He must have been very much disturbed by this remark because the next morning he called me and said that as I had laughed at the monument he had shown, he would like to know what I would propose. I told him I hadn't the slightest idea what I would do in his place, but as most of these people were shot in front of a wall, a brick wall would be what I would build as a monument. Fuchs could not imagine how a brick wall could be used as a monument but told me that if I had an idea he would be interested in seeing it. A few days later I showed him my sketch of the monument which in the end was built.

"He was still skeptical about it and particularly so when I showed him the bricks I would like to use. In fact, he had the greatest trouble to gain permission from his friends who were to build the monument."

Despite the large element of sheer accident in this story, it is significant that the communist followers of Liebknecht and Luxemburg finally commissioned not a design in the classical tradition based on principles considered good for all time, but one which so completely represents a belief in the idea of progress. As all students of architecture know, Mies van der Rohe and Walter Gropius are among the leading architects who have reacted sharply against the eclecticism, or imitation of past styles, which was dominating architectural design in the early years of the twentieth century. Consequently, in thus seeking to free building from historical reminiscences and achieve a basic and straightforward modern architecture (albeit partly under the stimulation, conscious or unconscious, of that movement in modern art known as cubism), they were among the chief founders of what has since become known as the "International Style." This is a name they strongly dislike, for they insist that they had no intention of establishing a new "style" but were merely seeking to return to architectural fundamentals. Yet because so many of the fundamentals that these men agreed upon can be basic for architecture everywhere, they do transcend national boundaries so that the name, International Style, has become generally accepted for this kind of architecture. And this in spite of the fact that its originators (most of whom prefer the term "the new architecture") firmly believe that good buildings must always be designed to meet specific conditions of climate and site.

Because of the nonnationalistic and consciously "modern" character of the International Style, because of its direct and "realistic" expression of the inherent qualities of new materials and techniques somewhat in the manner of *die neue Sachlichkeit*, this kind of modern architecture could easily be seized upon by many Marxists as a suitable expression of the international spirit of Marxism as well as of its conscious contemporaneity and belief in progress. As already noted, even at the Bauhaus itself the forms of this new architecture could be regarded by Hannes Meyer as to some degree infused with a Marxian content during the two years (1928-1930) of his directorship. And, as will be indicated in more detail later, the International Style was also briefly accepted in Soviet Russia until a more nationalistic point of view became dominant under Stalin.

On account of the ease with which the International Style lent itself to the international spirit of most varieties of socialism, nearly all of its leaders have at one time or another been called socialists or communists whether they actually were or not: indeed, it was primarily for the purpose of avoiding such accusations that political activity was banned at the Bauhaus by Gropius and later by Mies van der Rohe. Yet in spite of the sincere efforts of these men to be nonpolitical, when the Nazis came to power in 1933 the International Style was so antithetic to the exaggerated nationalism fostered by the Nazis that the Bauhaus was accused by them of being "degenerate" or "bolshevistic,"[81] and was eventually compelled to close its doors. For Hitler attributed "degenerate art" to the influence of the Jews, arguing that "the house with the flat roof is oriental—oriental is Jewish—Jewish is bolshevistic."

As early as 1924, when he wrote *Mein Kampf*, Hitler had attacked all modern art as "bolshevistic," probably because in Germany the influence of Russian artists was then strong. Despite the injustice of Hitler's attack (for the Russian artists in question had left Soviet Russia because Lenin disapproved of their art), from that time on those who have fostered modern art have often been subjected to the same accusation of "bolshevism," and not merely by the Nazis alone. For example, Le Corbusier, another leader of the International Style (who received part of his architectural training in the same architectural office—that of Peter Behrens—as did Gropius and Mies van der Rohe), has frequently been called "communistic," an accusation rightly denied by his chief biog-

[81] A. H. Barr, Jr., in Herbert Bayer, W. Gropius, I. Gropius, eds., Museum of Modern Art, *Bauhaus, 1919-1928* (New York, 1938), pp. 7-8.

rapher.[82] Nevertheless, it is true that some of Le Corbusier's followers, unlike the master himself, really have been communists, including the able Brazilian architect, Oscar Niemeyer, whose work has been much admired in the United States and who—like Le Corbusier—was chosen as one of the architects for the United Nations buildings in New York.[83]

But even though such leaders of the modern movement in architecture as Gropius, Mies van der Rohe, and Le Corbusier themselves are not Marxists, they are socially and internationally minded and in important respects continue the tradition of the socialist William Morris, so that some of their principles of *art* are not dissimilar to some of those held by many Marxists. Like Marx as well as Morris, the Bauhaus constantly emphasized cooperation between craftsmen and urged that distinctions between the fine arts and crafts be abolished. As Gropius said, "Today they [the visual arts] exist in isolation, from which they can be rescued only through the conscious cooperative effort of all craftsmen. . . . Architects, sculptors, painters, we must all turn to the crafts."[84] In emphasizing the crafts Gropius was distinctly in the tradition of Morris, although where Morris sought to revive the crafts for their own sake, Gropius sought rather to use them as laboratories for modern industry. Like Morris, and like Semper and Van de Velde, Gropius insisted upon straightforward expression of materials in a functional way, but, much more than Morris, stressed modern machine-produced materials and industrialized methods of design and construction (Fig. 29). "The Bauhaus," he said, "believes the machine to be our modern medium of design and seeks to come to terms with it."[85]

At this time an independent emphasis on "machinism" in the arts was being made by the postwar art movement known as "dada," a movement which had connections with communism in Germany.[86] While the

[82] Maximilien Gauthier, *Le Corbusier ou l'architecture au service de l'homme* (Paris, 1944), pp. 175-98. Gauthier also points out (p. 223) that, in 1930 at Moscow, Le Corbusier spoke of "the sacred respect for individual liberty," and thereby made enemies who regarded this as a profession of bourgeois faith held to be Trotskyist. Meyer Schapiro in an essay, "Nature of Abstract Art," *Marxist Quarterly*, Vol. 1, No. 1 (Jan.-Mar. 1937), p. 97, points out that one of Le Corbusier's slogans was, "Architecture or Revolution." In other words, according to Schapiro, Le Corbusier urged technological reform in architecture through housing, etc., with the purpose of resolving the conflict of classes and thereby *preventing* the Marxist revolution.

[83] *Life*, Vol. 22, No. 21 (May 26, 1947), p. 35. As a communist, Niemeyer was later refused admission to the United States when invited to lecture at Yale University. He had previously been one of the two Brazilian architects selected to design the Brazilian pavilion at the New York World's Fair of 1939-1940.

[84] Quoted in H. Bayer, W. Gropius, I. Gropius, eds., *op.cit.*, p. 18, from the First Proclamation of the Weimar Bauhaus.

[85] *Ibid.*, p. 27.

[86] A. H. Barr, Jr., ed., Museum of Modern Art, *Fantastic Art, Dada, Surrealism* (3rd ed., New York, 1947), pp. 23, 25-26.

Bauhaus staff did not join the dadaist group, the preoccupation of dada with "the machine" made some of the dadaists not unsympathetic to some aspects of the work done at the Bauhaus. It should be noted, however, that although the machine, industrial production, and functional expression were stressed at the Bauhaus, Gropius came to feel that the term "functionalism" (which he equated with *die neue Sachlichkeit*) was too materialistic and one-sided in its connotations[87]—in other words, Gropius, like Morris, stands for a degree of idealism that is non-Marxian.

Like most varieties of socialists, as well as like many nonsocialists, the staff of the Bauhaus was particularly interested in achieving a functional solution to the humanitarian and social problem of adequate housing for the masses. The particular architectural answer to this problem made under the Weimar Republic, and largely developed at the Bauhaus itself, was the row house oriented to the sun which permitted all the inhabitants to have an equal or almost equal amount of sunlight—a scientific arrangement for health that could and eventually did appeal also to socialistic and democratic equalitarianism. Moreover, the Bauhaus was largely responsible for further developing the superblock type of housing. The extra-large city block, but with single-family houses, had early been proposed in a pamphlet entitled *Nothing Gained by Overcrowding*, published in 1912 by Raymond Unwin, the Fabian socialist city-planner. In the 1920's it had to some degree been used in connection with the apartment housing built for the workers of Vienna by the social democratic city government. In the superblock, distances between streets are much greater than in the ordinary city block so that, by reducing the number of streets, much more of the ground area can be devoted to greenery and gardens between buildings. Like the garden city this kind of housing could therefore be accepted with approval by all but the most revolutionary Marxists because it offered an answer to that separation of city and country which Marx blamed on capitalism. Particularly influential for many socialists interested in housing, as well as for many liberals, were the row houses at Siemensstadt (Figs. 30 and 31) designed by the nonsocialist Walter Gropius, and erected as middle-class housing under the auspices of a public-utility agency in 1929, the year after Gropius had left the Bauhaus.

Since the general approach to art for which the founders of the International Style stood was in certain respects (but in certain respects only) similar to that of many Marxians, the influence of the Bauhaus could also affect some Russian communist art. Consequently, Hannes Meyer, the Swiss communist who succeeded Gropius as head of the Bauhaus, was one of several foreign architects attracted to Russia by the hope of

[87] Walter Gropius, *The New Architecture and the Bauhaus* (London, 1935), p. 19.

designing International Style buildings there. However, as already suggested, the influences also went the other way: some forms of Russian art had influenced the Bauhaus. In 1922 a great exhibition of the works of artists from the Soviet Union had been held in Berlin and had created a sensation, and at this exhibition the variety of modern Russian art known as constructivism had been particularly prominent. Although constructivism will be considered at greater length later in this chapter in connection with both Russian and American art, it might be noted here that it glorifies modern technology and the machine age—for it had developed in Russia particularly after the Bolshevik Revolution of 1917 and partly as an expression of the desire of revolutionary Russia for immediate industrialization.

By the time of the exhibition at Berlin, however, constructivism had already fallen into some disfavor in Russia primarily because Lenin considered it, with other varieties of modern art, essentially unsocial since it was too abstract and thus too difficult for the masses to understand. But as the Bauhaus, like the Russian constructivists, was interested in emphasizing modern materials, modern methods of construction, and machine-age art, it is not surprising that a few months after the exhibition of modern Russian art at Berlin, constructivism—together with the Russian variety of cubism known as suprematism—was introduced into the Bauhaus by a new teacher, László Moholy-Nagy, who had seen the exhibition of Russian constructivist art in Berlin. For Gropius had become dissatisfied with one of the two men giving the course in basic design at the Bauhaus, because this teacher had "mazdaznan" leanings—that is, he subscribed to an individualistic form of mysticism which Gropius felt was bringing a harmful sectarian spirit into the school. Early in 1923, therefore, Gropius called Moholy-Nagy to collaborate with Josef Albers in giving the course.

Moholy-Nagy, a young Hungarian of exceedingly wide-ranging interests, had been greatly stimulated by the many new developments in the art of Europe after World War I. Especially interested in Russian suprematism and constructivism, he had been one of those responsible for calling a Constructivist Congress at Weimar in 1922. He was also greatly influenced by the Dutch post-cubist movement called De Stijl, particularly as exemplified by the works of Piet Mondrian, and was not unsympathetic to dadaism, although he never became part of the movement. Elements from these currents, and especially from constructivism, now played a part in the pedagogical method which Moholy-Nagy did so much to develop at the Bauhaus. By this method he sought to acquaint students with the revolution in art made possible by modern materials and techniques (Fig. 32). In this way some forms derived from

668

various currents which originally had possessed certain socialist and revolutionary connotations were fostered not only at the Bauhaus itself, but wherever the influence of the Bauhaus spread.

Although Moholy-Nagy thought of himself as something of a revolutionary, he did so in a highly individualistic way. After World War I he had offered himself and his art to the communist regime in his native Hungary at the time when Bela Kun had led a temporarily successful revolution on the Bolshevik model. But Moholy-Nagy had been rejected by the Communist Party in Hungary partly because of the landholding status of his family, and still more because the Hungarian communists, like Lenin, frowned upon the use of nonrepresentational painting and sculpture as revolutionary weapons.

On his part, moreover, Moholy-Nagy was dissatisfied with Marxian communism because he wished to sweep away all historical art forms and therefore felt that the Marxian historical materialism was insufficiently revolutionary. He also felt that Marxism paid insufficient attention to the individual, and accordingly protested that creative individuality had been excluded from the Hungarian Revolution. Nor could he agree with the Marxian emphasis on the glorification of the proletariat. Because of this fact, when he began to admire constructivism—which he praised as the art of our century, a century characterized by technology, the machine, and socialism—he also praised it for being "neither proletarian nor capitalistic . . . without class or ancestor."[88]

Thus the great influence of the Bauhaus has indirectly helped to foster the spread of art forms derived in part, but only in part, from artistic movements which at one time or another have possessed some socialist or communist implications. These forms (though not necessarily their original socialist content) constitute an important element not only in much modern architecture, painting, and sculpture, but in practically all contemporary "industrial design" throughout the world. And they have particularly affected art in the United States, for after Hitler came to power in Germany, Moholy-Nagy, Gropius, Mies van der Rohe, Josef Albers, and other leading members of the staff of the Bauhaus including Herbert Bayer, Marcel Breuer, and the painter Lyonel Feininger were among the many German artists who migrated to the United States. Here they have exerted an enormous influence which will be discussed later in this chapter.

Soviet Russia. As the whole world knows, under the leadership of Lenin and Stalin Russia has made major contributions to Marxian theory

[88] Sibyl Moholy-Nagy, *Moholy-Nagy* (New York, 1950), p. 19, quoting an article published by Moholy-Nagy in 1922. From this biography most of the facts concerning Moholy-Nagy herein have been taken.

and practice. Many of these have to some degree affected the arts not only in the Soviet Union itself but in most other countries as well, including the United States. In order to understand the Marxian elements as they have affected some aspects of American art and art criticism, it will be necessary to devote what may at first glance seem to be an undue amount of space to tracing and illustrating the chief artistic developments within Soviet Russia itself. For the major twists and turns in Marxian art and art theory everywhere since 1917 have been directly or indirectly, positively or negatively, inspired by events in Russia and by the resulting world-wide changes in the Communist Party line. And since American forms of Marxian art and art criticism, including the theories of the various opponents of the party line as well as of its exponents, are thus in nearly all cases but second-hand versions of specific Russian developments, they can only be understood in the light of what has happened in Russia itself. Yet one might add that, because so few Americans, including Communist Party members, understand Russian, the direct influence of Soviet Russian art theory has been felt in the United States primarily through the medium not of the original Russian sources, but of translations into English. Not only the basic writings of Lenin and Stalin but even the day-to-day changes in the economic and political party line, on which the line for art depends, reach the officials of the American Communist Party almost entirely by way of publications printed in the English language.[89]

It goes without saying that any investigation of the Russian contribution to Marxian theory and practice, in art as in everything else, must begin with Lenin himself. Of the contributions specifically made by Lenin to the materialistic philosophy of Karl Marx, and thence to the theory of art, perhaps the most significant has been his insistence on the importance of practical action for bringing about the revolution of the proletariat and carrying it on to a successful conclusion in the classless society. To Lenin more than to Marx, an armchair Marxist was no Marxist at all, because, much more than Marx and Engels, Lenin was himself a practicing professional revolutionary in addition to being a theoretician. Under his leadership and inspiration, therefore—and still more under that of Stalin, also a practicing revolutionary from early youth—Soviet Russia could be expected to give, as it increasingly has, an extra importance to that practical utility and "realism" in art which

[89] According to L. F. Budenz, *Men without Faces* (New York, 1950), p. 83, where he gives a list of the publications on which the line of the American Communist Party is based. Budenz states that the chief source followed at present by the American party-liners is the *New Times*, the English-language supplement of *Trud*, a Moscow newspaper.

appeal both to the materialist and to the "practical" man of action everywhere.

With Lenin's guidance also, and even more with that of Stalin, the doctrine that power and leadership must be concentrated within a Communist Party was highly developed, and thereby added to Marxism the concept of "democratic centralism," which has had profound effects on Soviet art as on all aspects of Soviet culture. Thus in Soviet Russia, and wherever else the artist is subject to the power and influence of a Communist Party under Russian dominance, he is expected, of course, to follow the party line. Anything that smacks of individualistic self-expression, of "art for art's sake," is anathema. Instead, works of art that can serve as propaganda to help carry out the decisions of the party and of its leaders are demanded of all artists. Like everything else in Russia, art too has become increasingly subject to the careful centralized planning considered imperative in order to keep the party in complete control and to enable communism to develop in a single country "encircled" by capitalist enemies. And such planning has necessarily helped to curtail the artist's opportunities for expressing himself in any individualistic way.

The present Soviet Russian point of view toward art, the point of view now required of all communists throughout the world who follow the Communist Party line, has had a slow and stormy development largely because neither Marx nor Lenin ever developed a complete aesthetic. Both Marx and Lenin applied themselves primarily to problems of economics and to the political and social problems arising out of the economic situation simply because, in the Marxian view, these are basic for understanding all other human problems. But although neither of them was ever able to devote much time to art and art history, both were greatly interested in these subjects. Marx's early study of ancient art has already been mentioned. And Lenin once bemoaned his lack of artistic knowledge in the following words: "What an attractive field the history of art is. How much work there for a communist. . . . I regretted very much that I have never had and never shall have the time to occupy myself with art."[90]

As neither Marx nor Lenin had formulated an organized and detailed philosophy of art, for a few years after the Bolshevik Revolution of 1917 there existed in the arts no clear party line which could be followed by communists, whether in Russia or in other countries, including the United States. Since Marx and Lenin had both so clearly approved the study of art, although as a subject second to economics and politics, it

[90] A statement made by Lenin in 1905, quoted by A. Lunacharsky, "Lenin and Art," *International Literature*, No. 5 (May 1935), p. 68.

was to be expected that eventually—on the basis of the relatively few statements about art made by Marx, Engels, Lenin, and a few recognized materialist philosophers such as Chernyshevsky—a Marxist aesthetic would be developed in Soviet Russia. Yet even after a party line had developed in art, the official aesthetic was to remain relatively unsystematized for some time. As recently as 1946 the president of the U.S.S.R. Academy of Architecture could state, "So far we have [in Russia] no systematized work on the theory of architecture, throwing light on the principal phenomena of current architecture and the history of architecture as treated from the viewpoint of scientific thinking, from the viewpoint of Marxism-Leninism."[91] Only of late, largely as a result of a speech made in August 1947 by Zhdanov, secretary of the Central Committee of the Communist Party—a speech in which he urged Soviet thinkers in many fields to promote ethics and aesthetics more vigorously— have concerted official efforts been made to formulate a thoroughgoing Stalinist aesthetic. Thus, the aesthetic now prevailing in Russia assumed its present form only gradually, and only after bitter political and ideological struggles had been fought within the Marxist ranks not merely in Russia itself, but throughout the world.

These ideological conflicts revolved especially about three major groups of problems. One of these had to do with the relation of the new communist culture, especially in Soviet Russia, to the cultures of the past. Because the Bolshevik Revolution represented so sharp a break with the past, many artists insisted that only new and revolutionary art movements could express its revolutionary spirit, movements representing a reaction against all earlier historical styles, and especially against the eclecticism which had characterized "bourgeois" art since the middle of the eighteenth century. Of these more revolutionary artists, some maintained that new art *forms* should be emphasized at all costs, even as ends in themselves, with the result that this point of view became known to its opponents as formalism. Others insisted that new *techniques* should be emphasized as ends, and for this reason the machine was glorified both as the product of new technical developments and as making possible additional new techniques. Because machines are designed for sheer functional utility, these artists held that a work of art must be just as functionally useful as a machine. Insofar as these functionalists maintained that form mechanically grows out of function, they tended to neglect specifically Marxian content in art, so that eventually they were accused by more "orthodox" Marxians of a kind of formalism. And formalists and mechanistic functionalists alike could be attacked not only for neglecting Marxian content, but for cutting themselves off too

[91] *Architectural Chronicle*, No. 11 (Nov. 1946; published by the U.S.S.R. Society for Cultural Relations with Foreign Countries, Moscow), p. 2.

completely from the culture of the past, out of which, according to Marxian theory, the present has dialectically developed. Furthermore, both were to be accused of stressing novelty in art to such a degree that their works of art could not be understood by the masses of the proletariat.

This leads to a second series of problems about which the doctrinal struggle raged involving the interrelations between communist culture, and the masses, the party, and the state before it has withered away. Included among these are such questions as to what the role of the party should be in fostering and controlling art, or as to the kind of art which is to prevail during the dictatorship of the proletariat until a classless society can be achieved. Related to this, also, is the dispute as to whether the proletariat is to be limited to the industrial working classes, or whether the collectivized and mechanized peasantry can be considered as a kind of agricultural proletariat, and therefore whether peasant art can become a form of socialist art.

A third major ideological conflict has concerned the relation of the culture of Soviet Russia both to contemporary culture elsewhere and to the regional cultures within the Soviet Union. This has proved to be of particular importance for it has raised the whole problem of the relation of Soviet Russian nationalism to Marxist internationalism, and of the expression of such nationalism and internationalism in the arts.

These various ideological problems crystallized only gradually with the result that for a few years after the "October" (Bolshevik) Revolution of 1917, there was a period of relatively free experiment in art and art theory. During this period the various prerevolutionary art movements, both conservative and antitraditional, continued side by side, with each of them now loudly claiming to possess the one true Marxist and Soviet Russian content. However, once the immediate threat of White Russian armies and of foreign intervention had been met, the Russian communist leaders finally began to have more time to devote to art and its problems; and soon clashes within the Communist Party arose over the question as to just what kind of art was best suited to the Russian Marxist ideology.

The more traditional artistic currents which had continued in Russia from the art of the prerevolutionary period included, among others, the general European classic tradition of the Renaissance and post-Renaissance, a tradition first introduced on a large scale into Russia by Peter the Great as part of his program of westernization. After the October Revolution, however, this cosmopolitan academic tradition was for some time frowned upon by many because of its associations with imperial Russia. Similarly, the still older and more national traditions of

Byzantine art and also of primitive Russian art, both of which had been revived in the nineteenth century as part of the nationalistic spirit of the time, were considered unsuitable by the communists largely because both had frequently been used for religious as well as national architecture under the tsars. Also more or less traditional, though more recent in origin, was the "realistic" current which had become strong in Western art in the mid-nineteenth century as an expression of the naturalism and materialism so characteristic of the period. This literalistic kind of realism had grown so powerful that to a considerable degree it had been adopted by the academic tradition in Russia, as elsewhere, and in Russia especially by the Academy at Petrograd. Because it fitted in very well with Marx's materialistic philosophy, realism was the one prerevolutionary movement in art which could most easily be approved by the Russian communists. And they could approve it all the more easily because one of the chief founders of realism in art, the French painter Courbet, had been a leading figure in the Paris Commune of 1871, while that great early realist in literature, the French novelist Balzac, had been Karl Marx's favorite novelist.

In conflict with such older traditions, and also with one another, were various more "modern" trends which at first in Soviet Russia were often lumped together under the generic name of futurism, or cubo-futurism. Within this category fell all the various versions and mixtures of the more abstract varieties of modern art, mostly imported but modified to suit Russian needs. Thus cubism (stressing geometrically abstract simplification and dislocation of nature's forms), expressionism (which often greatly distorts the forms of nature for purposes of expression), Italian futurism (glorifying mechanism and dynamism in art), and functionalism (with its literal expression of materials and use) all contributed in varying degrees to the various art movements within Russian futurism. Because Russian futurism took its name from Italian futurism, it might be noted here that the latter was founded before World War I as a revolutionary and antibourgeois movement in art based directly on the Marxian-Nietzschean theories of the French syndicalist Sorel. Marinetti, its artist-founder, became a close friend of Mussolini, then a left-wing socialist; and Mussolini himself once said, "What I am I owe . . . to Georges Sorel."[92] Eventually, of course, Italian futurism was to become the semi-official Fascist theory of art in Italy, with Marinetti still its chief theoretician, but this was mainly after futurism had declined in Russia.

The most important art movements within Russian cubo-futurism during the period of the revolution or shortly thereafter were those Russian varieties of late cubism known as suprematism and—still more important—

[92] Quoted in E. H. Carr, *Studies in Revolution* (London, 1950), p. 163.

constructivism. Constructivism had been developed by Russian artists on the basis of "constructions" made by the Spanish-French painter Picasso as early as 1913 toward the end of his cubist period (Fig 33). However, the constructivists did not regard themselves as cubists even though they admitted that their art derived from cubism. They looked upon cubism as destructive, as a kind of revolutionary art which had disintegrated the old unified world of art. Living as they did in a Russia faced with the need for rebuilding after being almost disintegrated by revolution and civil war, the constructivists proposed to be constructive, to establish a new and unified art the very unity of which would aid in fostering a new and unified world-wide society by strengthening the emotions which make men disposed to work together and build anew. Moreover, the constructivists saw many analogies between science and art, and some Russian constructivists claimed to express by their dynamically mechanistic art the special need of revolutionary Russia for rapid progress in science and technology through industrialization. Many of them also maintained that their emphasis on dynamic movement in art was an expression of the Marxist, and particularly the Leninist, belief in revolutionary action. Interestingly enough, the importance which they gave to expressing the need for industrialization led them to admire American capitalistic technology and industrial efficiency. Similarly Mayakovsky, one of the most famous Russian futurist poets, glorified Chicago in the following words: "Chicago: City, Built upon a screw! Electro-dynamo-mechanical city!"[93]

The most widely known example of constructivism in architecture is the project for a monument to the Third International (Fig. 34) designed in 1919 by Tatlin, a Russian architect. Tatlin, who recommended "the monument of the machine" as the best architectural expression of revolutionary Russia, of industrialization, and hence of the proletariat, said that his monument to the Third International was an attempt to found "a dynamic-monumental architecture."[94] In the lower part of the steel framework of this structure, 1,300 feet high, there was to be a cubiform legislative chamber for the congresses of the Third International which would rotate once a year, and above this a pyramidal administrative chamber rotating once a month. A spherical section at the

[93] Quoted in Fülöp-Miller, op.cit., p. 23. Stalin once called Mayakovsky "the best, the most talented poet of our Soviet era," in Pravda (Dec. 7, 1935); cited by Jean Fréville, ed., Sur la littérature et l'art: V. I. Lénine, J. Staline (Paris, 1937), p. 100. For the theory of constructivism see especially the essay by Naum Gabo, one of the founders of constructivism, entitled "The Constructive Idea in Art," in J. L. Martin, Ben Nicholson, and N. Gabo, eds., Circle; International Survey of Constructive Art (London, 1937), pp. 1-10.

[94] Fülöp-Miller, op.cit., pp. 99-100.

top, rotating once a day, was to be devoted to instruments of propaganda including a radio station, cinema, etc.

In architecture, the International Style (as it was later named), which was becoming predominant in western Europe after World War I, was soon imported into Soviet Russia, where it has ordinarily been looked upon as a kind of constructivism. As already suggested, the International Style could appeal to Marxists in many ways. For one thing, its nonnational character could appeal to many who believed in the international spirit of Marxism, a spirit particularly strong in Russia in the period following the revolution, as the founding of the Communist International (or Comintern) in 1919 so clearly indicates. And not only were the practitioners of the International Style usually more practical than most constructivists, but their emphasis on new techniques could appeal to the mechanistic functionalists in Russia at the same time that their emphasis on the new abstract forms growing out of cubism was appealing to the formalists. Among the several leading foreign architects of the International Style who eventually were commissioned to design Soviet buildings were the communist, Hannes Meyer, and the noncommunist Le Corbusier (Fig. 35),[95] while many native Russians also worked in much the same style. The Transport Workers' Club at Moscow (Fig. 36), designed by the Russian architect Melnikov in 1929, represents a continuation of Russian constructivism but combined with some influence from the International Style; and here the glorification of the machine has led the architect to compose his whole building in the form of part of a gear wheel, even though a gear wheel has no direct connection whatsoever with the function of the building.[96] An apartment house in Moscow (Fig. 37), designed in 1928 by the Russian architects Ginzburg and Milinis, still more clearly reflects the influence of the mechanistic aspects of the International Style and specifically of Le Corbusier. It well exemplifies Le Corbusier's famous dogma that "A house is a machine for living in," a dogma in entire harmony with the Russian revolutionary emphasis on mechanization and industrialization.

At a relatively early date, however, considerable opposition to such emphatically "modern" tendencies as these was already in existence in Soviet Russia. Indeed, not long after the Bolshevik Revolution, some of the leading Bolsheviki had already come to consider the modern movement in art as too individualistic in temper, too separated from the masses,

[95] Among other leading architects of the International Style who worked in Russia at this period were Erich Mendelsohn, Bruno Taut, and Lurçat. However, most of these architects, including Hannes Meyer, arrived in Russia when the International Style was falling into disfavor, with the result that they designed relatively few buildings in that style.

[96] See Talbot Hamlin, "The Development of Russian Architecture—II," *Magazine of Art*, Vol. 38, No. 5 (May 1945), p. 182.

and hence fundamentally bourgeois rather than proletarian. A new movement toward a consciously proletarian culture was started by a group calling itself Proletcult, but this soon was relegated to a secondary role (though the name was revived early in Stalin's regime) partly because the Bolshevik leaders then felt that culture and art cannot be created to order and independent of the past. Thus Lenin himself insisted that modern socialism originated out of the heads of members of the bourgeois intelligentsia; that the seeds not only of socialism but of modern techniques—including artistic techniques—had therefore been sowed not by the proletariat, but by the bourgeoisie under capitalism, or even in still earlier periods of human history.

In 1920 Lenin said, "It is impossible for us to solve the question of proletarian culture without a clear understanding . . . of [all] that culture which was created in the course of humanity's development; it is only by remaking this that proletarian culture is possible. . . ."[97] His disapproval of those modern movements in art which were seeking to cut themselves off from the past is reflected in his statement: "I cannot value the works of expressionism, futurism, cubism, and other isms as the highest expressions of artistic genius. I don't understand them. They give me no pleasure."[98] For although, like all Marxists, Lenin prided himself on looking forward rather than back, in subscribing to the Marxian laws of historical development he maintained that art, like all aspects of culture, is dialectically and organically rooted in the past. He therefore felt that the modern trends in art were seeking to break too completely with history. "We must retain the beautiful . . . even though it is 'old.' . . . Why worship the new as the god to be obeyed, just because it is 'the new'?"[99] And because "it would be a great mistake to believe that you can be a communist without assimilating all human knowledge, of which communism itself is the result,"[100] he considered museums to be highly important and strongly urged their preservation during the revolution.[101] However, it should be emphasized that Lenin did not worship the past for its own sake but for its contributions to the present: as he once remarked, "It is not enough to assimilate all the knowledge that has come down to us, we must also examine it critically from the point of view of its usefulness to us. . . ."[102]

As a materialist Lenin inclined not only toward utility but also toward

[97] Quoted in Arthur Voyce, *Russian Architecture* (New York, 1948), p. 125, from *Collected Works of Nikolai Lenin*, xxv, p. 387.
[98] Klara Zetkin, *Reminiscences of Lenin* (New York, 1934), pp. 12-13.
[99] *Ibid.*, p. 12.
[100] Lenin in his speech to the third congress of the Komsomol on Oct. 2, 1920; as translated (freely) in Fülöp-Miller, *op.cit.*, p. 234.
[101] Fréville, *op.cit.*, p. 149, quoting Lunacharsky in *Iskoustvo* (Jan. 1929).
[102] Lenin, speech to the third congress of the Komsomol on Oct. 2, 1920; translation from Fülöp-Miller, *op.cit.*, p. 234.

realism in art and this suited his personal preferences, which were relatively conservative. According to his colleague Lunacharsky, Lenin "loved the Russian classics, liked realism in literature, in painting and so on."[103] Furthermore, not only did Lenin himself not understand "expressionism, futurism, cubism, and other isms," including constructivism, but he was convinced that the masses could not understand them either, a fact which made him consider such movements entirely unsuited to Marxist art. To him works of art were valuable insofar as they belong to the masses and are understood by the average man. "Art belongs to the people," he said. "It must have its deepest roots in the broad mass of workers. It must be understood and loved by them. It must be rooted in and grow with their feelings, thoughts and desires."[104] And Lenin considered artists unwilling to produce this kind of art, artists who insisted on producing more abstract kinds of art, to be altogether too individualistic and socially undisciplined. To him they were "specialists" cut off from the masses, who arrogantly assumed the right of speaking in the name of the working class and took advantage of the turmoil of the revolution to present as novelties their petty-bourgeois ideas.[105] Their abstract art seemed to him to deny the significance of the material world of nature and of human society which he believed to be the sole reality. Yet in also holding that art must play an active part in fostering the development of the classless society, Lenin further seemed to imply that works of art should be more than mere passive, mechanical, or photographic reproductions of the existing world. And since art must thus be socially significant, the still further implication seemed to be that artists who fail to produce such art should be led to do so by the Communist Party itself.

For these reasons, even though in 1920 Lenin had stated that "Every artist, and everybody who wishes to, can claim the right to create freely according to his ideal, whether it turn out good or not," he added, "But of course we are Communists. . . . We must consciously try to guide this development. . . ."[106] And in the same year he had issued a manifesto condemning all left-wing communism as "an infantile disorder."[107] Although this manifesto was an essay on Marxist strategy and tactics written primarily to uphold a new party line in problems concerning German communism, parliamentarianism, and trade unions, it was taken seriously for all other aspects of Russian life. A split therefore occurred among the more modern artists including the constructivists, some of whom, such

[103] Lunacharsky, "Lenin and Art," op.cit., p. 68.　　[104] Zetkin, op.cit., p. 13.

[105] See Fréville, op.cit., p. 111. In 1920 Lenin sharply reproved the Proletcult (founded in 1918, and the center of these "petty-bourgeois" tendencies) for neglecting the class struggle.

[106] Zetkin, op.cit., p. 12.

[107] V. I. Lenin, "Left-Wing" Communism: an Infantile Disorder (first published June 1920; 1st English ed., London, 1934).

as Tatlin, decided to devote their art solely to the revolution, while others held that art should be carried on independently of the revolution and for art's own sake. Those artists who believed in the independence of art left Russia, and their number was swelled by the fact that state subsidies to artists were reduced with the introduction of the New Economic Policy in 1921. A few of these émigrés, such as David Burliuk, came to the United States, but by far the largest number—including such well-known figures as Kandinsky, Gabo, Pevsner, and Lissitsky—then went to Germany where several of them joined the Novembergruppe in Berlin. As has already been mentioned, in 1922 a great exhibition of the works of modern Russian artists, including these men, was held in Berlin, and its influence greatly affected the whole modern movement in Germany, particularly at the Bauhaus. In that very year, the painter Kandinsky (who as a pioneer expressionist is said to have been the first artist to paint a purely abstract composition)[108] accepted Gropius' invitation to join the faculty at the Bauhaus, and there he remained for a decade. It was in the next year that Moholy-Nagy, a teacher at the Bauhaus, developed a pedagogical method based in part on Russian constructivism. Moreover, in 1923 Lissitsky (Fig. 58) collaborated for a time with Mies van der Rohe, later head of the Bauhaus. In 1920 Lissitsky had also collaborated in forming a western European constructivist group with Théo van Doesburg, the Dutch artist whose "neoplastic" variety of cubism is sometimes said to have influenced the whole Bauhaus group, although this has been vigorously denied by no less an authority than Walter Gropius. Certainly during his visit to Weimar, where the Bauhaus was then located, Van Doesburg—who had strong socialist leanings and who had joined the dadaist movement for a time—highly praised the work of the Russian modernists.[109] And he once described the evolution of modern art as ". . . towards the abstract and the universal . . . which has made possible the realisation, by a common effort and a common conception, of a collective style."[110]

[108] A. H. Barr, Jr., Museum of Modern Art, *Cubism and Abstract Art* (New York, 1936), p. 64. According to T. H. Robsjohn-Gibbings, *Mona Lisa's Mustache* (New York, 1947), pp. 84-86, Kandinsky was influenced by still earlier abstractions painted by Theosophists. It should be added that, though a Russian by birth, Kandinsky had lived in Germany from 1896 until the outbreak of war in 1914 when he returned to Russia. After the Revolution, in 1918 he taught at the Academy of Fine Arts in Moscow and worked with the art section of the People's Commissariat of Public Education. In 1918 he was appointed director of the Museum of Pictorial Culture, and in 1920 professor of scientific aesthetics at the University of Moscow. When abstract art was officially discouraged in 1921, he returned to Germany.

[109] On the authority of Professor Helmut von Erffa, then a student at the Bauhaus.

[110] Théo van Doesburg, "Vers un style collectif," *Bulletin de l'effort modern*, Vol. 1, No. 4 (1924), p. 16; quoted by R. J. Goldwater, *Primitivism in Modern Painting* (New York, 1938), p. 132.

Largely through modern German art and especially through the influence of the Bauhaus, the *forms* of Russian constructivism (though usually not its original Russian revolutionary *content*) were to have considerable effect on modern art in the Western world, including that of the United States. In Russia itself, however, following the departure of so many leading futurists and constructivists because of Lenin's disapproval, art soon became less abstract. Although in 1923 most of the remaining futurists formed a Left Front ("L.E.F."), maintaining that there could be no coalition between them and the art of the past, the Russian Communist Party sharply attacked this point of view in a resolution on literature issued July 1, 1924, which stated that the party "must fight against all frivolous and contemptuous estimates of the cultural heritage of the past." And a year later, in June 1925, another resolution of the Central Committee of the party spoke of the "infinitely more varied forms" in which the class nature of art (as contrasted with politics and economics) is manifested. As a result of this resolution a certain freedom was to be permitted in Soviet art for the next four years or so.

Of all the varieties of modern art, the International Style in architecture was for a time the most successful in surviving the party's disapproval, despite its abstractly cubistic elements. For architecture, much more than painting or sculpture, is necessarily a social art; moreover, the leaders of the International Style have always been particularly interested in social aspects of architecture. In addition, the emphasis which the International Style, in theory at least, has always placed on practical function could help make its architecture more understandable to the masses than most kinds of modern art. On this account it was then acceptable to Russian Marxism, which in the mid-1920's tended to subscribe to a mechanistic philosophy. Only when, under Stalin, the Russian revolutionary internationalism began to be accompanied by a philosophy of art that was more nationalistic, as well as both less mechanistic and less abstract, did the International Style die out in Russia.

Because Lenin believed so firmly that art should arouse the masses, he insisted that art must serve a social and party purpose as propaganda—or, as Leninists sometimes phrase it, must be devoted to moral education. As early as 1905 he had stressed the importance of literature in party propaganda when he wrote, "The socialist proletariat must establish the principle of party literature. . . . Down with non-partisan writers!"[111] And he later included the visual arts when he said, "What I have in mind

---

[111] Lenin in "Party Organization and Party Literature" (1905), *Works* (Russian ed.), vIII; translation from Joseph Freeman, "Past and Present," in J. Freeman, J. Kunitz, L. Lozowick, *Voices of October* (New York, 1930), p. 24.

is something I should call propaganda by monuments."[112] According to Lenin himself, he got the idea of using art and poetry for propaganda from Campanella's *City of the Sun*, a seventeenth-century description of a utopia in which the author mentioned the use of frescoes to serve, said Lenin, "as vivid lessons to the young in natural sciences and history" and "to awaken their civic consciousness"—to play, in short, "a vital part in the education and upbringing of the new generation." "But," added Lenin, "our [Russian] climate is hardly suitable for the fresco[e]s dreamed about by Campanella. That is why I speak primarily of sculptors and poets."[113] Thus Lenin advocated using for propaganda not only literature, but sculpture, and—in warm countries—frescoes, that is to say, murals painted on wet plaster. He also stressed the importance for propaganda purposes of great inscriptions, of newspapers, and especially of the motion picture. "Of all the arts," he said, "the most important for Russia in my opinion is the film";[114] and, ". . . among the instruments of art and education, the cinema can and must have the greatest significance. It is a powerful weapon of scientific knowledge and propaganda."[115] The theater was praised by Lenin not only for its propaganda value, but especially for its ability "to rest hard workers after their daily work."[116]

As everyone knows, with Lenin's long illness ending in his death in 1924, a bitter struggle broke out in Russia between several factions within the Communist Party, a struggle destined to have a profound effect on art and art theory not only in the Soviet Union itself but everywhere the influence of Russian communism has been felt, including the United States. From the point of view of Stalin and his followers, the various factions tended to fall into four main political groups: the Stalinists themselves as the center, the Left opposition or "deviation," the Right deviation, and the nationalist deviation.[117] Because the doctrines of each of the four groups have had some important implications for Marxist art and art theory everywhere, it will be found necessary to summarize them here. Those of the opposition groups will be summarized first in the light of their conflict with Stalinism, a conflict resulting in Stalin's victory over his chief opponents before 1930, followed by the wiping

[112] Lunacharsky, "Lenin and Art," *op.cit.*, p. 66.

[113] *Loc.cit.* In this connection it is worth recalling that some Fourierists, too, had desired to make use of large murals which were to depict modern industry and to be placed in railroad stations and public buildings: see Meyer Schapiro, "Courbet and Popular Imagery," *Journal of the Warburg and Courtauld Institutes*, IV (1941), p. 183.

[114] Lunacharsky, *Lenin and the Cinema* (Russian ed.); see Fréville, *op.cit.*, p. 149; translation from Kurt London, *The Seven Soviet Arts* (New Haven, 1938), p. 270.

[115] Joseph Freeman, "The Soviet Cinema," in *Voices of October*, p. 220; quoting Lunacharsky on Lenin.

[116] Quoted by Max Eastman, *Artists in Uniform* (New York, 1934), p. 127.

[117] See Stalin, "Report . . . to the Seventeenth Congress of the C.P.S.U.(B.)," *Leninism*, p. 515.

out of all opposition in Russia in the great purges of the thirties. In the course of relating the history of this violent political warfare the reasons for many of the characteristics of the Stalinist ideology, in art as in everything else, will become manifest. For many of those characteristics originated in some immediate need for somehow countering the ideologies and actions of the opposing groups. An account of the doctrines of those groups in relation to their struggle with Stalin will therefore help pave the way for a systematic discussion of Stalinist doctrines in art.

In considering now the art theories of the various "deviations," and especially those of the Left and Right opposition, the discussion necessarily becomes highly confusing because, in jockeying for power, the Left, the Right, and the Stalinists at times were all opposed to one another in a three-way conflict, but at other times were joined together, two against one, in a series of dubious and changing alliances. The result has been that their respective ideologies, usually in sharp opposition to one another, have nevertheless sometimes overlapped so that they have not always been entirely distinguishable. Moreover, as the party line of the Stalinists has changed, they have called their various opponents by the particular names which seemed most useful at the moment: thus at times opponents regarded as political Leftists have simultaneously held certain views on art considered to be Rightist. As Stalin himself once remarked, "We have always said that the 'Lefts' are also Rights, only they mask their Right-ness behind Left phrases."[118] In short, the Stalinists have never hesitated to change or even to reverse their definition of what constitutes Left and Right whenever the historical situation has made it seem advisable to do so—with, from the viewpoint of non-Stalinists, unfortunate or even stultifying effects for art, art theory, and artists alike. In this connection, however, it must be remembered that the frequent changes in the party line, which to a non-Marxian so often seem to indicate a lack of consistency, are justified by Stalinists on the Marxian grounds that truth is almost entirely relative to the particular economic-political situation prevailing at a given time.

In spite of all this confusion, the specific ideologies of the Left and Right opposition can usually be identified with the respective philosophies of Leon Trotsky and Nikolai Bukharin (both of whom, incidentally, had visited the United States, where in 1917 they worked together in New York for a Russian radical paper, *Novy-Mir*). Both became celebrated theoreticians as well as politicians, and by their writings, in which they both frequently referred to the arts, they greatly influenced artists and art critics wherever the various types of Russian communism spread.

[118] *Ibid.*, p. 526.

However, although Trotsky and Bukharin were usually identified respectively with the Left and Right opposition, such was by no means always the case. In 1924, for example, Trotsky was accused by Stalin, Zinoviev, and Kamenev of bourgeois, and therefore Rightist, tendencies. But late in that same year Stalin found it necessary to formulate, with Bukharin's help, the doctrine of "socialism in one country." This encountered the opposition of Trotsky's principle of "permanent revolution" according to which socialism, even to keep alive, must not merely be reinforced by far-reaching economic measures in Russia but must spread as an international movement, a movement based on the idea that a revolution in one country must at once be extended to the next. In attacking this principle Stalin accused Trotsky of Leftism. Early in 1925 he compelled Trotsky to resign as Commissar of War; in 1926 he had Trotsky expelled from the Politburo, in 1927 from the Communist Party, and two years later from the Soviet Union. Correspondingly, in 1925 Ludwig Lore was expelled from the American Communist Party for Trotskyism; then, in 1928 another purge of the American party took place when James Cannon, Max Shachtman, and about fifty others were likewise expelled as Trotskyists. For six years the Trotskyist Cannon group regarded itself as a faction within the Communist Party, then established its own party, which later split and gave rise to several communist parties with slightly different party lines in art as in everything else.

Following Trotsky's decline in power, Bukharin began to fall out with Stalin and to become the leader of the Right opposition within the party— that is to say, he began to insist that the Soviet Union must proceed much more slowly toward complete socialization than Stalin believed advisable. Yet in the years immediately following the October Revolution, Bukharin had been leader of a group called Left Communists; later, as editor of *Pravda*, he had for a time been the chief theoretician of Stalin against Trotsky. Obviously, therefore, he was not regarded by Stalin as a Rightist at all times or in all respects any more than Trotsky was always looked upon as Leftist.

Turning now to Trotsky's theory of art: his belief that communism could not possibly succeed in a single, industrially backward country surrounded by capitalistic nations, as Russia then was, had led him to hold an internationalistic, and thus Leftist, point of view in art as well as in economics and politics. For this reason, Trotsky approved of Tatlin's constructivist project for a monument to the Third International (Fig. 34), remarking that "Tatlin is undoubtedly right in discarding from his project national styles. . . ."[119] For this reason also, Trotsky approved of the International Style in architecture (then not yet known by that

[119] Trotsky, *Literature and Revolution*, p. 246.

683

name) and the corresponding modern styles in the other arts. To him the dynamic forms of futurist art, Leftist in seeking to break completely with traditional techniques and modes of expression, offered an excellent expression of the dynamism and chaos of the Russian Revolution; and he implied also that the architecture of the revolutionary period should be built in the modern materials of metal, concrete, and glass.[120] Trotsky felt, however, that the relatively peaceful period of the New Economic Policy (1921-ca. 1928)—which he regarded as a temporary retreat back to capitalism, and therefore as a regrettable lull in the revolution— could be better expressed by the calmer, more conservative forms of a modernized classicism. In Trotsky's own words: "If Futurism was attracted towards the chaotic dynamics of the Revolution . . . then neo-Classicism expressed the need of peace, of stable forms. . . ,"[121] a point of view not unlike that adopted by Stalin only a few years after he had driven Trotsky from Russia.

Unlike Lenin and Stalin, Trotsky had devoted much time to the study and criticism of literature and art; besides his well-known book of criticism, *Literature and Revolution*, originally published in 1923,[122] he had written, among other things, a monograph on Constantin Meunier,[123] the Belgian sculptor whose favorite subject was the laboring man. While Trotsky, like other Marxists, believed that art should in the last analysis serve social ends, he also firmly maintained that it should be judged not by its social usefulness, as Lenin had implied, but by its own law, the law of art. For that reason he held that art should be censored only with the greatest care, and that it should not be directly controlled by the Communist Party. Wrote Trotsky, "Artistic creation has its [own] laws—even when it consciously serves a social movement";[124] and again, "Art must make its own way and by its own means. The Marxian methods are not the same as the artistic. . . . The domain of art is not one in which the Party is called upon to command. It can and must protect and help it, but it can only lead it indirectly."[125]

Because of such statements and because of his interest in the more radical kinds of modern art and architecture, Trotsky was accused by the Stalinists of the deadly sin of "formalism." He was accused, in short, of

[120] Trotsky implied this in praising Tatlin's attempt "to subordinate the entire design to a correct constructive use of material," which is "the way that machines, bridges and covered markets have been built, for a long time": Trotsky, *op.cit.*, p. 246.

[121] Trotsky, *op.cit.*, p. 113.

[122] This important work is often said to have been published in 1924; however, in "Art and Politics," *Partisan Review*, Vol. 5, No. 3 (Aug.-Sept. 1938), p. 3, Trotsky himself gives the date of his book as 1923.

[123] According to Louis Lozowick, "Soviet Painting and Architecture," in *Voices of October*, p. 265.

[124] Trotsky, "Art and Politics," *op.cit.*, p. 10.

[125] Trotsky, *Literature and Revolution*, p. 218.

encouraging art that is abstract, or that is mechanical or experimental for its own sake, art in which the form or the technique is itself the end rather than a vehicle by which suitable socialist subject matter is given a socialist content. The Stalinists therefore increasingly maintained that Trotsky and his followers, in separating form in art from social content, were divorcing theory from practice and thus had become "idealists" who, in believing that mind, ideas, can exist without matter, were *ipso facto* not true Marxian realists. To put it another way, the Trotskyists were accused of holding that there are abstract ideal principles of formal design which are good for all time and independent of the Marxian laws of economic and social change. Insofar as Trotsky fostered art that was thus "idealistic" as well as radical, he was regarded as a Leftist. However, confusingly enough, art in which form is separated from social content in this way was also considered by the Stalinists to be characteristic of decadent bourgeois culture, and therefore as Rightist in tendency. Consequently, although usually regarded as a leader of the Left, on several counts Trotsky was eventually accused of *both* Leftism and Rightism.[126]

Somewhat similarly, buildings like the Transport Workers' Club at Moscow (Fig. 36), at times considered Leftist because of their abstract forms and radical structure, were also attacked as representing experiment for its own sake. They were thus considered expressions of formalism[127] whose designers were to be frowned upon as specialists tainted with bourgeois (and therefore Rightist) individualism and experimentalism, as well as with Leftist radicalism and idealism.

Actually, Trotsky himself had attacked formalism in his book *Literature and Revolution*. At the same time, however, he had denied the possibility of a specifically proletarian culture, had spoken of futurism as a necessary link in the history of art, and had praised aspects of constructivism. He had said, "The wall between art and industry will come down,"[128] and for this reason was also held guilty by the Stalinites of succumbing

---

[126] For the attack on Trotsky as both an "idealist" of the Left and a "mechanist" of the Right, see G. A. Wetter, S.J., *Il materialismo dialettico sovietico* (Turin, 1948), pp. 198-208.

[127] The architect of the Workers' Club at Moscow was a member of a group of architects called ASNOVA (i.e., Association of New Architects) which was founded in 1923. This constructivist group subscribed to "idealistic"—and therefore Rightist–formalism. It was attacked by a later group called VOPRA (i.e., All-Russian Society of Proletarian Architects). VOPRA was founded in 1929 to champion a proletarian class architecture, and its members claimed to be more orthodox in their allegiance to the Communist Party. This group was dominant during the first Five Year Plan when the emphasis on proletarian culture was particularly strong. See B. Lubetkin, "The Builders," *Architectural Review*, Vol. 71, No. 426 (May 1932), pp. 203-7; and Voyce, *op.cit.*, pp. 134ff.

[128] Trotsky, *Literature and Revolution*, p. 249.

to the claim, early made by constructivist members of the far Left, that art must be a science, an industry. Some of the more extreme Leftists had even gone so far as to hold that a painting is actually nothing but a "machine" for generating certain predetermined human reactions, and that artists should be engineers of form and color.[129] This, the Stalinists maintained, was an attempt to replace the artist with the engineer by making technique and sheer function an end in itself. Indeed, it amounted, the Stalinists said, to a denial that there is any such thing as art; whereas they insisted that art as such not only exists but can and should be an effective weapon in the hands of the proletariat, a weapon of which the Left was seeking to deprive the workers.

The mechanistic aspects of the Leftist point of view in some respects had even more in common with the philosophy of Bukharin, as expressed in his *Historical Materialism* (1922), than with that of Trotsky; yet as long as Bukharin supported Stalin they were widely accepted by many Stalinists as part of the official Communist Party line. They were, moreover, particularly important for art not only because Bukharin himself was a painter,[130] but because Lenin, in his dying statement, had called him "the greatest and most valuable theoretician." However, when Bukharin began to oppose Stalin about 1927, he was increasingly attacked for having interpreted Marx's materialism as a kind of mechanistic determinism. Such statements as "society . . . has much in common with a mechanism,"[131] and, "social phenomena determine at any given moment the will of the various individuals,"[132] clearly indicated, the Stalinists said, that Bukharin believed man to be completely determined by the laws of nature and of social development, and therefore by the environment. This implied, his accusers maintained, that the laws of history, of social development, act automatically so that progress toward the classless society is automatic and inevitable, proceeding in accord with a mechanical process which man can neither accelerate nor retard. In other words, the mechanists were making man merely the *agent* of history instead of a *creator* of history within the framework of society and

---

[129] Chen, *Soviet Art and Artists*, p. 58.

[130] Lenin's wife, Nadezhda Krupskaya, describes in *Memories of Lenin* (New York, [1930?]), II, p. 112, how she and Lenin first met Bukharin in 1912. The Lenins were at Cracow when they heard about a social democrat "named Orlov [Bukharin], who was making beautiful paintings of the Zakopane Mountains" not far from Cracow. He came to call on the Lenins, and Krupskaya says that when they asked about his paintings, he "took a number of splendid paintings by German artists from his bag and we examined them with great interest. Vladimir Ilyich [Lenin] liked pictures very much." Bukharin's theories of art as social expression were partly inspired by the writings of the German Marxist critic, Wilhelm Hausenstein, author of *Die Kunst und die Gesellschaft* (Munich, 1917).

[131] Nikolai Bukharin, *Historical Materialism* (New York, 1925), p. 88.

[132] *Ibid.*, pp. 40 and 42.

of nature—and thereby were denying Engels' statement that "Men make their history themselves. . . ."[133] Thus the works of man, including works of art, were being reduced by the mechanists to nothing but sheer mirror reflections of the natural and social environment unmodified by human mind or will. This mechanistic point of view (which implicitly denied the value of the Communist Party as the leading agent in bringing about the international triumph of communism) could and did encourage both a photographic kind of literal representation in painting and sculpture, and a literalistic and mechanistic functionalism in architecture.

But while such literal and mechanistic functionalism in architecture was particularly characteristic of radical artists of the Left, such literal naturalism in the representational arts was more characteristic of conservative artists of the old academic tradition in Russia which, like the academic tradition everywhere, had already assimilated the nineteenth-century naturalistic current in Western art. Hence Bukharin's philosophy, which in its mechanistic aspects was approved by many Leftists, could in other respects be considered as suited to conservatives of the Right. And in a sense this same split is reflected in his political career because, as already mentioned, although originally a leader of the Left Communists, he eventually became a leader of the Right opposition to Stalin.

In 1927 Bukharin began to oppose Stalin's proposal for the Five Year Plan, primarily because it called for the collectivization and eventual communization of the peasantry, while he had always maintained that the peasants were really inert survivals from older forms of society and thus "lack several elements necessary to make them a communist class,"[134] a view similar to that held by Trotsky. The peasants, Bukharin believed, would automatically have to pass through the stage of capitalism before they could become communists. He therefore maintained that meanwhile it was necessary to consolidate an individualistic and private (and thus capitalistic and Rightist) peasant economy—a point of view which could have important implications for folk art. He also insisted that capitalism outside of Russia was as yet unripe for revolution, arguing that by means of monopolistic organizations capitalists had become stronger everywhere, and that within nations these monopolies were fusing with the state apparatus. The result was that the Stalinists, who identified state industry with socialism, attacked him as believing that capitalism could evolve peacefully into socialism and therefore as abandoning the Leninist concept of revolution. Furthermore, like Trotsky although for different reasons, Bukharin was accused by Stalin of believing that complete socialism is impossible in a single country. And

[133] Engels, letter to Starkenburg, *Karl Marx, Selected Works*, I, p. 392.
[134] Bukharin, *op.cit.*, pp. 289-91.

when in 1928 Bukharin sought the aid of Kamenev and Zinoviev (who, after supporting Stalin against Trotsky, had attacked Stalin as an upholder of state capitalism, and then combined with Trotsky), Bukharin himself was accused of joining forces with the arch-foe Trotsky.

Stalin, who had ever increased in power since his election as general secretary of the Communist Party in 1922, showed by his close control of the Sixth World Congress of the Comintern in 1928 that he was now able to dominate Russian policy. He completely gained the upper hand over his last great enemy, Bukharin, early in 1929. In the same year Jay Lovestone and Benjamin Gitlow were removed from the leadership of the American Communist Party and expelled with their friends as Bukharinists and Right deviationists. Whereupon they founded their own small party with its own line, a party which also was to undergo splits, with each faction having its own ideology supposed to cover all aspects of life, including the arts.

Following the political defeat of Bukharin and his friends, the ideas for which they had stood were soon defeated also, a defeat which had direct and international repercussions in Marxian art. The failure of their efforts to uphold a Rightist peasant economy, a failure marked by the destruction of the richer peasants and by the collectivization of agriculture, was accompanied by a reaction leading to a renewed glorification of the industrial proletariat and the class struggle. And the newly collectivized peasants, because of their new farm machinery, were now considered by the Stalinists to be in the process of industrialization, and therefore in the process of developing a point of view like that of the proletarian class—a fact which now made them worthy subjects for Stalinist art. Moreover, the renewed emphasis on the proletariat now brought about a revival of the proletarian culture movement, although in a quite different form. Its revival was formally signalized by a Congress of Proletarian Culture held at Kharkov late in 1930, an international congress attended by delegates from the United States under the leadership of Michael Gold, writer and editor of the *New Masses*. The slogan of the Congress, based on a statement of Lenin, was that "art is a weapon" in the class war, a weapon to be used only under "the careful yet firm guidance of the Communist Party."

About this time, also, the mechanistic philosophy of which Bukharin had been the chief supporter was likewise finally defeated in Russia when, in 1929, a group of philosophers and scientists who subscribed to a form of mechanistic determinism not unlike that of Bukharin himself were worsted in a philosophical controversy. Almost simultaneously, a sharp attack was directed against all forms of art which could be considered mechanistic.

For this reason some Stalinists now began to disapprove of the works of certain conservative academic artists (already long under attack by the more abstract artists of the Left) for their "photo-naturalism," that is to say, for their mechanically literal reproductions of nature. Even Isaac Brodsky (Fig. 38), although he had been one of Lenin's favorite artists, was nevertheless accused by some Stalinists and Leftists alike of being a "photo-naturalist."[135] And practitioners of this photographically realistic kind of painting were now often criticized as "passive observers of life"[136] who therefore denied the Marxist-Leninist doctrine that within the fixed framework of the Marxian laws of historical development man is not only free to create history, including art history, but bears a responsibility to do so. Nevertheless, the fact that Brodsky, in spite of considerable Stalinist criticism, was appointed director of the Academy at Leningrad in 1932 clearly indicates that Stalinist art was itself beginning to reemphasize the academically literalistic kind of realism which Lenin had preferred and which remains characteristic of art under Stalin to this day.

Just as in theory (though not nearly so much in practice) the followers of Stalin attacked "photo-naturalism" as deterministic, so also they attacked the mechanistic determinism of those "vulgar sociologists" who—exaggerating Bukharin's thesis that "the social sciences have a *class* character"[137]—sought to adhere to the view that every man, and therefore every artist, is completely and mechanically determined by his economic class.[138] This point of view (which, as we have noted, had for a time been the dominant one in Russia) had tended to limit Soviet art to proletarian subjects. Consequently, after its supporters were defeated about 1931 by the exponents of the revised Stalinist line in a series of philosophical and artistic debates, a somewhat wider range of subject matter in the arts was made possible. And on April 23, 1932, a government decree abolished all proletarian art groups, so that once more the Proletcult movement declined in Russia.

The attack on mechanism which marked the defeat of Bukharin particularly affected architecture, and it was at this time that the mechanistic functionalists, who had been very influential in Russian architecture during the late twenties, were reproved for their mechanism with particular sharpness. As a result, the kind of architecture represented by the apartment house in Moscow (Fig. 37), designed in 1928 by two leaders of the functionalistic school, Ginzburg and Milinis, now fell into disfavor.[139]

[135] Chen, *Soviet Art and Artists*, p. 54.   [136] *Ibid.*, p. 53.   [137] Bukharin, *op.cit.*, p. xi.
[138] For the "vulgar sociology" controversy see John Somerville, *Soviet Philosophy* (New York, 1946), pp. 118ff.
[139] The architects of this apartment house were members of a group called SASS (i.e., Section of Architects of Socialist Construction), founded as OSA in 1925. The

As this type of architecture had been especially inspired by the works of Le Corbusier, it is not surprising that the whole International Style, in which he was so important a figure, was now also attacked as mechanistic. This attack first became manifest on a large scale in connection with the great architectural competition for the design of the Palace of the Soviets at Moscow. Now the many projects submitted by leading architects of the International Style were all rejected by the committee in charge, which stated in 1931: "Buildings are not machines, and naked functionalism is an insult to humanity. Buildings today, and the Palace of the Soviets above all, must express the fact that man is master of machines and not their slave or servant."[140]

The International Style was vulnerable on several other grounds. For one thing, it had originated not as a national style in proletarian Russia, but under the leadership of "bourgeois" architects in such "bourgeois" countries as Germany, Holland, and France, and therefore could be regarded as a Rightist style. Also it could be assailed by the Stalinists (along with all other kinds of art in which cubistically abstract forms appeared) for its formalism, that is, for glorifying abstraction in art at the expense of "practical" realities, for divorcing theory from practice, and thus for being "idealistic." Largely because of this supposed idealism the International Style now suffered a final defeat. For at this time, 1930-1931, the Stalinists were engaged in rooting out the last major traces of philosophical "idealism," an end achieved when Stalinist philosophers overwhelmed in debate a group of "idealist" philosophers.[141] The final triumph of Stalinism was reflected in a resolution of the Central Committee of the Communist Party, passed on June 25, 1931, which called for unremitting warfare on two fronts in the field of philosophy, warfare against mechanism and idealism simultaneously. This change in the party line meant, of course, that the architects of the International Style, such

---

members of the group had seceded from ASNOVA (see note 127) and, at a conference of OSA in 1928, had adopted a platform of constructivism-functionalism because they believed in a baldly functionalistic and mechanistic kind of building in which architecture tended to become identified with engineering. This they considered to be the best architectural expression of dialectical materialism. When—in connection with the triumph of Stalin over Bukharin and Trotsky—the group called VOPRA was founded in 1929, it attacked SASS as too mechanistic, just as it attacked ASNOVA as too idealistic and formalistic. Twenty years later, Moises Ginzburg (who, while a member of SASS, was one of the architects for the apartment house mentioned above) was to be attacked by the magazine *Soviet Art* for being the father of "cosmopolitanism" in architecture and of the enthusiasm for "capitalistic architecture": see the *New York Herald Tribune*, May 1, 1949, p. 10.

[140] Quoted by Robsjohn-Gibbings, *op.cit.*, p. 213.

[141] For these controversies see Somerville, *op.cit.*, pp. 213-28. Also see the more detailed account of the triumph of Stalinist dialectical materialism over both idealism and mechanism in Wetter, *op.cit.*, pp. 149ff.

as Hannes Meyer, former head of the Bauhaus, were now unable to design International Style buildings in Russia. Meyer himself eventually gave up and went to Mexico where Trotsky also was to receive asylum.

Thus, following the defeat of both the Left and the Right—of idealistic formalism and of mechanism, now also considered formalistic—a revised Stalinist party line was in process of crystallization. And this was already becoming manifest in changes in the leadership of Communist parties throughout the world: in 1930, for example, the year after the defeat of Bukharin, Earl Browder was made head of the American Communist Party for the purpose of putting the new line into effect. For several years it was to be a line which in a sense revived the revolutionary and proletarian spirit of the years immediately following the revolution, but with a new centralization of power which allowed even less freedom than before in the arts as in all other aspects of life.

Yet although both the Left and the Right had been defeated ideologically and artistically as well as politically, the question of nationalism and of nationalistic "deviations" had not been entirely settled, partly because of ever changing conditions in foreign relations. It is true that as early as 1924, in opposition to Trotsky, Stalin had developed and thereafter maintained the doctrine that socialism could be successfully achieved in one country alone. For his authority he had again and again cited certain statements by Lenin (which his opponents countered with other statements of Lenin), and especially Lenin's remark made in 1915 that "the victory of Socialism is possible, first in several or even in one capitalist country, taken singly."[142] However, despite Stalin's continued insistence that it was possible to bring about the victory of socialism in a single country—Russia—he did not begin to place much emphasis on a specifically Russian nationalistic spirit until well after his victory over his chief opponents, Trotsky and Bukharin. But then, in 1931 a final official signal for the beginning of a new nationalism within revolutionary Marxian internationalism was given by Stalin himself. For in that year a letter from Stalin was published in *Proletarskaya Revolyutsiya* under the title "Some Questions Concerning the History of Bolshevism." In this he attacked "Trotskyism" (now considered as including *all* opposition, whether of the Left, the Right, or of evolutionary Social Democracy) as "the vanguard of the counter-revolutionary bourgeoisie which is fighting Communism, fighting the Soviet government, fighting the building of Socialism in the U.S.S.R."[143] The emphasis here on Bolshevik history, on "the Soviet government" and on "the building of Socialism in the U.S.S.R.," now clearly reflected the nationalistic spirit which has

[142] See, for example, Stalin, "On the Problems of Leninism" (1926), *Leninism*, p. 158.
[143] Stalin, "Concerning the History of Bolshevism," *ibid.*, p. 398.

pervaded Stalinism to this day and which has had a profound effect upon Russian art and art theory.

After the advent of Hitler to power in Germany in 1933, however, it became necessary to modify this Russian nationalism somewhat by a willingness to join with other nations, including "bourgeois" nations, in opposing fascism. In January 1934 at the Seventeenth Congress of the Communist Party, Stalin first spoke out publicly against the Nazi doctrine as representing "a triumph for the idea of revenge in Europe." At the same congress he attacked as "a departure from Leninist internationalism" all deviations toward nationalism, whether "the deviation towards Great-Russian nationalism" or "the deviation towards local nationalism."[144] He insisted that nationalism is reactionary in spirit and represents bourgeois attempts to undermine the Soviet system by turning to capitalism: he specifically accused the Ukrainian nationalists of having stirred up the peasants to resist collectivization. This antinationalism in the speech meant, of course, that overt nationalism and regionalism in art, including folk art, was still restricted within Russia.

Nevertheless, in the very same speech Stalin—while reporting that "deviations" of all kinds had finally been defeated and scattered—stressed the necessity for Russian patriotic unity, and thereby foreshadowed the encouragement of a still greater all-Russian spirit of patriotism. As a consequence, a great patriotic campaign began a few months later in the Soviet press, signalized especially by an editorial in *Pravda* for June 9, 1934, which fervidly urged love of country and even used the long disused word "fatherland." Yet in September 1934 Russia entered the League of Nations; in May 1935 a mutual defense pact was signed with France, and the period of the Popular Front had begun, a period in which an increasing Russian nationalism was combined with readiness for joint international action against fascism.[145] One result of the Popular Front was that the last traces of the Proletcult movement (which had retained considerable importance outside of Russia, especially in the United States), now had to be abandoned, for its glorification of proletarian culture implied an emphasis on international class warfare hardly reassuring to those "bourgeois" nations with which Soviet Russia wished to collaborate in opposing nazism.

In order to help guarantee Russian unity in the face of the Nazi threat and at the same time to consolidate his personal position still further,

[144] Stalin, "Report . . . to the Seventeenth Congress of the C.P.S.U.(B.)," *ibid.*, p. 525. For a good brief discussion of nationalism and Soviet patriotism in art and literature, see Rudolf Schlesinger, *The Spirit of Post-War Russia; Soviet Ideology 1917-1946* (London, 1947), pp. 149-59.

[145] A summary of these events is contained in Eugene Lyons, *The Red Decade* (Indianapolis, c. 1941).

Stalin now wiped out all of his chief political opponents in the great purges of 1936-1938. Zinoviev and Kamenev, with several former Trotsky-ists, were tried and executed as traitors in 1936; several more leading ex-Trotskyists, among others, in 1937; and Bukharin and others in 1938. Two years later Trotsky was assassinated in Mexico by what most people believe was a Stalinist agent. These political purges were accompanied by a new campaign against formalism and leftism in art, a campaign that began in January 1936 when *Pravda* made a violent attack on the music of Shostakovich, which was called "un-Soviet, unwholesome, cheap, eccentric, tuneless and Leftist."[146] And *Pravda* soon followed this with an attack on the modern movement in architecture, which it described as "monstrous trick architecture."[147] In December 1937 *Pravda* accused the great theater director, Meyerhold, of formalism, largely on the grounds that seventeen years before he had dedicated one of his productions to Leon Trotsky.

Thus, in the fifteen years or so between Lenin's death early in 1924 and the completion of the purges, Stalin and his followers destroyed all opposing ideologies within the Soviet Union itself, even though the influence of his opponents has in some respects persisted outside of Russia. In the process of killing off opposing ideologies, Stalin and his followers had to begin to formulate, on what they maintain is a Leninist basis, their own interpretation of Marxism, their own systematic ideology which includes an ideology for art. By 1939, not long after the purges were over, Stalin's victory was at last so utterly complete that he finally felt free to say in public that Marx and Lenin, like ordinary mortals, sometimes made mistakes, with the implication that Stalin had become at least their equal.

Now that the effects of the various deviations have been indicated and the rise of Stalin to complete power traced, we are in a better position to discuss more systematically the positive effects on art of Stalinism itself, and this with particular reference to the period of Stalin's dominance. For however much one may disapprove of Stalinism, it cannot be denied that the Stalinists have made many important contributions and additions to the Marxian theory of art, and these have affected not only the arts of

[146] *New York Times*, Feb. 15, 1936, p. 17. This editorial in *Pravda* attacking Shostakovich was one of two, both written by Zhdanov according to Juri Jelagin, *Taming of the Arts* (New York, 1951), pp. 151-52. After this attack upon him, Shostakovich remained in official disfavor until after the highly successful première of his Fifth Symphony in December 1937. According to Jelagin (p. 162), this was the first time that official disfavor (rather than dismissal or arrest) was used by the Soviet government as a means for bringing pressure on creative artists to compel them to adjust their work to the party line.

[147] Dwight Macdonald, "The Soviet Cinema: 1930-1938, Pt. 2," *Partisan Review*, Vol. 5, No. 3 (Aug.-Sept. 1938), p. 46.

Russia itself but the official party line for art in every country in which a Communist Party exists.

As has already been mentioned, perhaps the most basic Stalinist doctrine, and the first to develop, is the doctrine that socialism can be successfully achieved in one country alone. Nevertheless, it must not be forgotten that Stalin, unlike the national "deviationists," has also customarily maintained that the Russian point of view must in the end be international if it is to be successful: as he said in 1927, the October Revolution "is not merely a revolution 'within national limits.' It is, primarily, a revolution of an international, world order. . . ."[148]

Remember also that Stalin makes an important distinction in terminology between socialism and communism, a distinction in which he follows Lenin. In the *Communist Manifesto* Marx and Engels had used the word communism rather than socialism simply because the latter then meant to most people the "utopian" socialism which Marx was attacking rather than his own "scientific" socialism. But Lenin and Stalin came to mean by socialism what Marx once called the first stage of communism,[149] that is, a transitional period in which each individual receives according to work performed, and in which the state still exists. And by communism they have meant Marx's second stage of communism, namely the classless society in which the state will, as Engels said, have "withered away," and in which each person will receive according to his needs. Hence Stalinists consider that the Soviet Union is today a socialist society rather than a communist one. And they believe that it became a fully socialist society only following the industrial and agricultural revolution produced by the first Five Year Plan (1928-1932). Not until 1935, however, did Molotov make the official announcement that Russia had become a socialist country.

But although Russia is now considered to have achieved socialism, the official view is that communism, as contrasted with socialism, will not be possible until the Soviet Union has the support of the workers in all countries and until the workers have triumphed in at least a majority of countries. For only then will the capitalist countries be "encircled" and the Soviet Union guaranteed against all possibility of capitalist intervention. As to just when this communism, with its international and classless society, will be achieved is still a matter of discussion. To many non-Stalinists some of Stalin's more recent statements seem to indicate that he now believes that the state will never wither away completely.[150]

---

[148] Stalin, "The International Character of the October Revolution" (1927), *Leninism*, p. 197.

[149] Karl Marx, *Critique of the Gotha Programme* (New York, 1938), p. 10.

[150] For example, L. F. Budenz, ex-member of the American Communist Party, in *This Is My Story* (New York, 1947), p. 162, says that Stalin, "in *The History of*

However, the Five Year Plan which was announced in March 1946 still apparently regarded communism as its ultimate ideological objective, and one which, it was calculated, will be reached in some fifteen or twenty years *if* the industrial revolution proceeds at an accelerated pace.[151]

All of these developments in the party line have had important meaning for art. Thus, Stalin's combination of nationalism with an international "socialism" gave rise to his insistence that the culture of Russia must be "national in form and socialist in content."[152] To the kind of art which results from this he himself gave the name "socialistic realism," a name he is said to have first used late in 1932 when a group of writers promised him that they would not make formalistic experiments but would hold high the flag of realism. "Say rather of socialistic realism," replied Stalin.[153]

By this kind of realism (which very largely reflects Stalin's own tastes) is meant art suited to the period of socialism, to the period which Marx called the first stage of communism. Such art is expected to have both national and international connotations and to be realistic enough for the masses to understand it without being just a transcript of nature. Furthermore, by definition it must be socially useful, socially dynamic, and educational; consequently—Stalinists insist—it can be produced only by socially-minded artists, each of whom is participating in the daily activities and emotions of the community as a whole.

A good example of socialistic realism is the sculptured group of two figures entitled *Worker and Woman Collective Farmer* (Fig. 39) which surmounted the Russian pavilion at the World's Fair held in Paris during 1937. This, executed in the highly modern material of stainless steel, was

---

the Communist Party of the U.S.S.R." discarded "the 'withering away' theory as outworn." At the party congress in 1939, Stalin said, "We go forward [from Socialism] to Communism. Will the state be retained by us also in the period of Communism? Yes, it will, if the capitalist encirclement is not liquidated." And after Tito made a speech late in June 1950 reporting that in Yugoslavia (in contrast to Russia) the state had already begun to wither away, Stalin replied with a statement in *Bolshevik* on August 1, 1950 in which he repeated that there could be no withering away of the Russian state so long as it is encircled by noncommunist enemies: see the *New York Herald Tribune* for Aug. 2, 1950, p. 12, and Aug. 4, p. 14.

[151] In 1949, at the celebration of the twenty-fifth anniversary of the death of Lenin, the editor of *Pravda* stated in a speech that the achievement of [complete] communism in the Soviet Union no longer is a remote possibility, although three more Five Year Plans may be necessary to "provide complete safety and ability to meet any emergency." See the *New York Herald Tribune*, Jan. 22, 1949, p. 5.

[152] Stalin, *Problems of Leninism* (10th Russian ed.); quoted in Fréville, *op.cit.*, p. 133.

[153] London, *op.cit.*, p. 139. According to Jelagin, *op.cit.*, p. 75, the new Soviet theory of socialist realism in art and literature was first formally introduced by Maxim Gorky in a speech before the First Convention of Soviet Writers in the fall of 1934.

intended to reflect the new class structure of the Soviet Union, a class structure achieved when, with the completion of the first Five Year Plan, all the "exploiting" classes are considered to have been eliminated, leaving the two working classes of industrial workers and peasants triumphant. Here an industrial worker and a peasant are depicted advancing dynamically side by side, respectively bearing aloft the hammer of industry and the sickle of agriculture to form the Soviet Russian symbol. In this way the artist has sought to symbolize the Stalinist belief that, with the successful mechanization of agriculture, the interests of industrial worker and peasant are now merging as the two march forward together—though with the worker as leader—toward the classless society of complete communism. Only a few months earlier Stalin had stated in promulgating the new constitution for the U.S.S.R. that the first phase of communism had now been achieved, that the working class was no longer a proletariat, and that the peasantry had been integrated into the socialist economy.

All this is symbolized in a style that is a somewhat "realistic"—though "modernized"—version of the Western and international classic tradition which had dominated official art in imperial Russia from the time of Peter the Great. The return to this Russian version of the "classical" tradition was encouraged by the fact that in literature the Russian "classics" were mostly realistic and mostly written by authors who, from Pushkin to Gorky, had been notably progressive in their social views. Actually, Vera Mukhina, the able sculptress of the *Worker and Woman Collective Farmer*, had been trained in the Western classic tradition at Paris before World War I under the celebrated French sculptor, Bourdelle. It can be said with truth that socialistic realism has often implied a return to the more or less classic forms of the prerevolutionary official tradition in Russian sculpture and architecture, forms now, however, made slightly more abstract and hence "modern" to suggest the forward-looking spirit of Marxism. Thus by means of largely traditional and international elements Stalinist Russia has sought to achieve an art which can express a Marxian content, but infused with Soviet Russian nationalism as well as internationalism.

The kind of socialist realism represented by Mukhina's sculpture has sometimes actually been called classical realism. One of the first and best known architectural examples of this classical realism (as it was later named) had been the accepted design for the Palace of the Soviets in Moscow (Fig. 41), which in its original form was prepared in 1931. Although the building was under construction when Hitler attacked Russia, its materials were largely used for defense and it was never erected. The model shows the somewhat simplified and freely-handled classic forms characteristic of so many public buildings (Fig. 40) and other works, including the famous subway in Moscow, which were built in the years shortly before or immediately after World War II. In the design for the Palace of the Soviets, these classical forms are applied to an exceedingly tall structure obviously intended to outdo all American skyscrapers in order to symbolize the great advances in modern technology made by the Soviet Union. And the whole is topped by a statue of Lenin in action, pointing dynamically forward and upward to express dynamic Marxian progress through human action. Stalin, in his role as the direct heir of Lenin, once stated, "Leninism . . . creates a special Leninist style in work. . . . It has two specific features: (a) the Russian revolutionary sweep and (b) American efficiency."[154] The model of the Palace of the Soviets clearly seems to be intended as an expression of such Leninism in architecture during the first Five Year Plan when one of the popular slogans was, "Let us catch up and overtake America." It is significant that a similar style was used for the Russian pavilion at the New York World's Fair of 1939-1940, a building designed by Yofan, chief architect of the Palace of the Soviets and also the architect, in 1933, of Stalin's personal country house on the Black Sea.

The Stalinists justified this return to a somewhat classic style partly on the grounds that it could be considered as continuing the national all-Russian tradition for public buildings and public art found in Russia ever since the time of Peter the Great. They also believed it justified because Marx regarded Greek art as in some respects "the standard and model beyond attainment," and because the art of the Greek city states was a democratic form of public art even though Greek society rested on a regrettable basis of slavery. Moreover, they upheld the use of Roman classic forms on the ground that the Romans had in some respects developed the ideals of Greece by building enormous public-utility works. Thus the spirit of ancient Greece and Rome was sometimes invoked in Stalinist Russia as the inspiration for a kind of proletarian renaissance.[155]

On September 25, 1948, however, a modification in the party line for architecture, and in this classical style, was foreshadowed by an article in *Pravda* attacking "pseudo-Parthenons" and "the excessive use of columns." The same article also contained a sharp reproof for those Soviet architects who were imitating American architecture. The author of the article—Vlassov, chief architect of the city of Kiev—stated that all such "formalism" had crept into Soviet architecture because certain architects "forgot that in the field of architecture there is going on a

---

[154] Stalin, "Foundations of Leninism" (1924), *Leninism*, p. 84. In the same lectures (p. 2), he had previously defined Leninism as "Marxism of the era of imperialism and of the proletarian revolution."

[155] Voyce, *op.cit.*, p. 149.

battle of Socialist realism against bourgeois formalism."[156] This new architectural line was but part of a great postwar cultural purge which paralleled the increasing split between the Soviet Union and its satellites on the one hand, and the Western world on the other, while also reflecting a movement away from the wartime patriotic glorification of Russian history under the tsars. For during World War II not only had anti-Westernism in Russia been less pronounced in deference to Russia's "bourgeois" and "capitalistic" allies in the struggle (with the result that the Communist International and the American Communist Party had been "dissolved" in 1943 and 1944 respectively); but within the Soviet Union nationalist traditions, even including tsarist traditions derived from western Europe, had been fostered to encourage patriotic unity against the German invader. Now, however, the reaction setting in against bourgeois traditionalism and against the capitalism of the Western world was resulting in a new emphasis on Communist Party spirit, on the class struggle, and on the glorification of Mother Russia. It was this shift in the line which brought about the changes in the American Communist Party after the French communist Duclos returned from a trip to Moscow and attacked Earl Browder in April 1945 for having supported the wartime alliances by forecasting "long-term class peace in the United States" and for having dissolved the American Communist Party in 1944. Duclos' attack was published in the *Daily Worker* on May 24, 1945, with the result that Browder was not only replaced by William Z. Foster as titular head of the Communist Party when it was reconstituted in the summer of 1945, but in February 1946 was expelled from the party as a "right opportunist." And corresponding changes took place in the art theory and practice of the American Communist Party, as of Communist parties everywhere, particularly after the Cominform (Communist Information Bureau) was founded in October 1947 as a kind of revival of the ostensibly dissolved Comintern and as an answer to the Marshall Plan, which had been first proposed the previous June.

Even though the change in the party line had been foreshadowed before the end of World War II by such events as the attack on Browder, it was given final and public approval in a speech made by Stalin on February 9, 1946. In this speech Stalin not only publicly attacked his wartime allies by assailing contemporary "monopoly capitalism," but he upheld the unquestioned superiority of all things Soviet. Even though he said nothing whatsoever about the arts, this had been the clear signal

[156] See the *New York Herald Tribune*, Sept. 26, 1948, p. 1. Specifically, Vlassov was attacking a project for the reconstruction of Yalta. In the following spring the reconstruction of Stalingrad was also criticized before the All-Union Congress of the Young Communist League as reflecting "survivals of formalism": see *ibid.*, Apr. 3, 1949, p. 9.

for a purging of the entire cultural apparatus within the Soviet Union in order to bring cultural affairs into line with the new nationalistic spirit and the new antibourgeois foreign policy.[157] And with this came renewed insistence on the principle of "partisanship," a principle based on the Marxian doctrine that there can be no such thing as complete objectivity and impartiality because the viewpoint of each individual is necessarily affected by his class allegiance. Within this class loyalty Lenin had developed the principle of party loyalty; and now Stalin gave still more emphasis to the importance, for all good Marxists everywhere, of allegiance to Soviet Russia.

The cultural purge formally began on August 14, 1946, with a resolution of the Central Committee of the Communist Party sharply reproving two literary journals of Leningrad for forgetting that literature must be devoted to the interests of the people and of the state. A week later, Andrei Zhdanov, the secretary of the Central Committee, interpreted this resolution in long speeches before the Leningrad branch of the Union of Soviet Writers, and before the leading members of the Communist Party in Leningrad, in which he attacked "bourgeois culture" and "art for art's sake" while calling for a reemphasis on Lenin's doctrine that "literature must become Party." An abridged version of these speeches was published the following December in *Political Affairs*, the theoretical organ of the American Communist Party, as a sign to party members that the cultural line had changed.

On August 26 and September 4, 1946, the Russian Central Committee promulgated two similar "resolutions on ideology," dealing now with the drama and with the motion picture. These were eventually followed by others treating still other major aspects of cultural activity, including music, genetics, and humor. And on the basis of these resolutions of the Central Committee wide-ranging changes were also made in areas of culture not specifically covered by the resolutions and not restricted to the Soviet Union itself.

For example, the new line for art could be seen in an article in *Pravda* published on August 10, 1947, attacking the art of Picasso despite the fact that Picasso had joined the French Communist Party three years before. In this article the celebrated cofounder of cubism and the father of so many other varieties of abstract art, was assailed—together with Matisse—in the following words: "It cannot be tolerated that side by side with socialist realism we still have existing a co-current represented

---

[157] For a detailed account of these cultural purges see Counts and Lodge, *op.cit.*, on which the account herein is chiefly based. And for an unfavorable review of that book by an American sympathetic to the Stalinist point of view, see Sidney Finkelstein, "Soviet Culture: a Reply to Slander," *Masses & Mainstream*, Vol. 3, No. 1 (Jan. 1950), pp. 51-62.

by worshipers of bourgeois decaying art who regard as their spiritual teachers Picasso and Matisse, cubists and artists of the formalist group."[158]

Two weeks later, on August 25, 1947, a reform of the party line in philosophy and aesthetics began with a speech by Zhdanov at a conference of philosophers and theoreticians called together by the Central Committee of the Communist Party at the instigation of Stalin himself. In this speech (soon translated in *Political Affairs* for the guidance of American party-liners) Zhdanov blamed the chief of propaganda of the party for succumbing to bourgeois philosophical thought, and at the same time urged Soviet "scientific and creative cadres" to seek "to promote more vigorously . . . ethics and esthetics."[159]

A few months after this, the purge of Soviet music began when, on February 10, 1948, the Central Committee issued a resolution accusing the composers Shostakovich, Prokofyev, Khachaturyan, and Myaskovsky, among others, of subscribing to a "formalistic anti-popular tendency," and of writing music reeking "strongly of the odor of the contemporary, modernistic, bourgeois music of Europe and America which reflects the decay of bourgeois culture. . . ."[160]

On the basis of the Central Committee's resolution concerning music a corresponding purge of painting and sculpture took place late in May 1948; and on February 10, 1949, the new line was also established in art criticism when nine Soviet writers were assailed in *Pravda* as "homeless cosmopolitans" who "lack a healthy love of country." Meanwhile, the purge of architecture had begun on September 25, 1948, with the publication in *Pravda* of the article by Vlassov already referred to. The kind of architecture thereafter approved can be seen in Vlassov's own design for the rebuilding of part of Kiev destroyed in the war (Fig. 42), even though this design was submitted by Vlassov early in 1947 before he had promulgated the new architectural line in *Pravda*. For he was no doubt chosen as the exponent of the new line because his recent work, such as

[158] *New York Herald Tribune*, Aug. 12, 1947, p. 15, some editions only.

[159] *New York Herald Tribune*, Aug. 26, 1947, p. 1, reporting Zhdanov's action of the day before. The speech was translated in full in the April 1948 issue of *Political Affairs*, pp. 344-66, under the title "On the History of Philosophy." See also p. 672 herein. Likewise see B. Meilakh, "It Is High Time to Take Up Questions of Esthetics," *Literaturnaya Gazeta*, May 22, 1948; translation in *Soviet Press Translations*, issued by the Far Eastern Institute, University of Washington, Vol. 3, No. 20 (Nov. 15, 1948), pp. 633-35. Meilakh's article was a final signal for the purge in aesthetics.

[160] Counts and Lodge, *op.cit.*, p. 162. For an excellent account of the purge in music see Alexander Werth, *Musical Uproar in Moscow* (London, 1949). In view of the frequent and particularly heavy attacks on instrumental music it is worth noting that Stalin dislikes it, according to Jelagin, *op.cit.*, p. 298. The music purge had been preceded by a conference of musicians called by the Central Committee of the Communist Party in 1947 and, as usual, addressed by Zhdanov. For his speech see Andrei A. Zhdanov, *Essays on Literature, Philosophy, and Music* (New York, 1950), pp. 76-96.

this at Kiev, was thought well suited to exemplify the shift in doctrine.

Certainly, in this design the earlier official classicism inherited from tsarist architecture, and ultimately derived from a purely west European tradition, has already been modified so as to be both more Eastern and more "modern" in character. Strictly classic elements have now been partly replaced by elements (such as towers not unlike some in the Kremlin itself) which recall the Muscovite baroque of the seventeenth century, and thus a Russian style that is Eastern rather than completely Western. But these features have been combined with some elements not unlike the expelled International Style of modern architecture in an effort to suggest once more that Marxism looks forward rather than back and that it possesses international connotations even though these are now largely subordinated to specifically Russian characteristics. And although, as part of this "progressiveness," American skyscrapers are still imitated in Russia, the Soviet authorities now claim that the Russian examples are more advanced than the American prototypes, which, they say, sway in the wind, squeak, and crack.[161]

In addition to this official Stalinist style whose changing character in architecture has just been traced, it must be remembered that there is still another form in which socialistic realism has been expressed—namely, folk art. In the Stalinist view, folk art—which is often created collectively rather than by an individual—has both international and national implications, either of which can be emphasized with changing conditions and hence changes in the party line. On the one hand, folk art can be regarded as having international implications because it is considered to possess the germinating power out of which all great art everywhere arises. It is likewise international insofar as all folk art, all art of the masses and of the common man, does tend to have some characteristics that are much the same everywhere: its content, like that of homely proverbs, is much the same regardless of national boundaries. Yet folk art in Russia can also be considered national in spirit in that it expresses the traditions of some specific nationality or region within the Soviet Union. And perhaps more important than all these other reasons for the justification of folk art in Russia is the simple fact that Stalin is known to be very fond of Russian, Georgian, and Ukrainian folk songs.

Certainly Lenin and Stalin themselves have been largely responsible for encouraging folk art in Soviet Russia. Lenin—who even before the Bolshevik Revolution had considered the problem of national minorities to be of major importance—admired "folk literature as a veritable creation of the people."[162] Because Stalin, as a native of Georgia, was a member

---

[161] See the *New Yorker*, Sept. 16, 1950, p. 19, quoting *Vechernyaya Moskva*.
[162] See Bontch-Brouévitch's discussion of Lenin's views on poetry in *Na literatournom Postou* (1931), No. 4; quoted in Fréville, *op.cit.*, pp. 148-49.

of one of the national minorities, in 1913 Lenin had selected him as the Marxist-Leninist spokesman on the right of oppressed peoples to self-determination; and with the revolution, Lenin saw to it that Stalin was made Commissar of Nationalities. Nevertheless, by 1918 Stalin came to feel that Lenin, in opposing "imperialistic chauvinism" on the part of dominant nations, was giving too much importance to minor nationalities and to their right of self-determination. Stalin now insisted that the principle of self-determination be used merely as a means in the struggle for socialism, and subordinated to the principles of socialism itself. Stalin therefore attacked "local chauvinism" and tended to reject the idea of maintaining the integrity of a multinational state by means of cultural autonomy. By 1920, however, he had modified his views somewhat and now advocated regional autonomy, when effective both economically and culturally.[163] As a consequence he helped to pave the way for giving regional and folk art a recognized place as approved forms of socialist realism.

During the late 1920's some of the more self-consciously proletarian musicians and artists began to introduce into their work elements of Russian folklore as well as of the folklore of the Asiatic peoples of the Soviet Union. But it was only after the abolition of the proletarian art groups in 1932 that folk art could really begin to achieve a position of primary importance. When in February 1944 a somewhat greater measure of nominal autonomy was granted to the various republics within the Soviet Union, each being authorized to have its own foreign ministry and army, an even greater importance could be placed upon local forms of art. However, as a result of the increased emphasis placed by Stalin on "Mother Russia" in his speech of February 9, 1946, which so clearly marked the postwar change in the party line, the folk art of minorities within the Soviet Union has since been much less stressed, and artists of the various minor nationalities have been warned again and again not to succumb to local "bourgeois nationalism." Instead they are now expected to follow the leadership of the specifically Russian people who alone of all the peoples within the Soviet Union have recently been assigned a new role of superiority, especially since a purge—aimed at "distortions of ideology" in folk art—began in 1951.

A characteristic example of socialist realism expressed in terms of the regional folk traditions so popular in the Russian art of the late 1930's and early 1940's is the pavilion of the Republic of Uzbekistan (Fig. 43) built in 1937 at the All-Union Agricultural Exposition in Moscow. Designed

[163] See B. D. Wolfe, *Three Who Made a Revolution* (New York, 1948), pp. 397-400, I. Deutscher, *Stalin, a Political Biography* (New York, 1949), pp. 181-85, and E. H. Carr, *The Bolshevik Revolution, 1917-1923* (London, 1950), p. 384.

in the regional, more or less Persian, style characteristic of central Asia in general and Uzbekistan in particular, the plan of the central motif is nevertheless in the form of a star to suggest the Soviet symbol and thereby achieve an all-Russian content which transcends the purely local tradition.

It is this content which differentiates the folk art of socialist realism from that of the nationalist deviation so sharply attacked by Stalin. For while Stalin believes that local historical traditions are to be fostered, he insists that they must not assume exclusive and anti-Soviet forms. The Stalinists also insist that folk and national art must not hesitate to employ new technical developments—even technical developments originating in capitalist countries—and thereby become somewhat international in spirit. However, according to the official doctrine as stated by Stalin himself all primarily nationalistic forms of expression, including folk art, will eventually be abandoned "when the proletariat has conquered throughout the entire world, and socialism has entered into customs [everywhere],"[164] thus at last making possible the perfect internationalism of the classless society.

Meanwhile, as long as nationalism and the state exist, Soviet artists are to be carefully controlled by the Soviet State under the leadership of the Communist Party to make sure that works of art meet the specifications of socialistic realism. For ever since the Stalinists gained complete control in Russia, the artist, like the literary man, has been expected to do all his work under the "careful and yet firm guidance of the Communist Party."[165] This ever increasing demand for conformity by artists probably became inevitable when—particularly after the ending of the New Economic Policy—the state became the sole middleman between artist and client.

As early as 1918 an Artists' Union had been established in Russia,[166] but, significantly, it was in 1929—the year after Trotsky's expulsion and the year of Bukharin's defeat—that an Artists' Cooperative was established under the control of the state and hence of the party.[167] Through this artists sell their work at prices determined by a committee of the artists themselves, and not, as the Russians delight in proclaiming, by capitalistic dealers or by the whims of capitalistic millionaires. In the spring of 1930 a plan was announced for the development of the theater, the cinema, sculpture, and painting whereby five years of normal development were to be officially telescoped into the remaining three and a half years of the Five Year Plan,[168] and an International Bureau of Revolu-

[164] Stalin, *Problems of Leninism* (10th Russian ed.); quoted in Fréville, *op.cit.*, p. 133.
[165] Eastman, *op.cit.*, pp. 15-16, quoting the circular sent out in 1932 by the organization bureau of the International Association of Proletarian Writers.
[166] London, *op.cit.*, p. 48.   [167] *Loc.cit.*
[168] Macdonald, *op.cit.*, Pt. I, in *Partisan Review*, Vol. 5, No. 2 (July 1938), p. 44.

tionary Artists was founded in the same year to guide and control communist artists in other countries. When in 1932 the completion of the Five Year Plan made it perfectly clear that Stalin had triumphed over all opposition in Soviet Russia, an official decree directed the reorganization of the entire structure of the artistic and literary societies under still closer government control. As a result, all the existing societies—whether conservative, centrist, or radical—were liquidated, and each professional group was reorganized into a central federation: thus were soon founded the Federation of Soviet Architects and the great Artists' Creative Union.[169] In 1936, which was the first year of the great purges, a Central Committee on Arts was also established[170] in order that the organization of artists and their ideology might be even more carefully supervised by a kind of totalitarian ministry of the arts. All this means that today not only the content of art, but to a very considerable degree the methods of achieving that content, are laid down for the artist. The architect Alabyan, then president of the U.S.S.R. Academy of Architecture, said in 1946, "The architect who is not guided in his entire activity by the policy of the Communist Party and the Soviet Government and who stands to one side of it, can hope for no creative progress."[171]

While the attention paid to art by the government and party has meant that Russian artists are favored in many ways, woe to the artist who fails to follow modifications in the party line! In the spring of 1949, when a reorganization of the Academy of Architecture took place as part of the general postwar attack on what was called "bourgeois cosmopolitanism" (that is, the allegedly pro-Western, pro-American, and general cosmopolitan outlook of many artists, scientists, and critics), Alabyan, then acting vice-president of the Academy, was removed from his post. He was accused of having supported the harmful activities of "cosmopolitans" for many years and of failing to safeguard the official line in regard to the "development of the study of architecture."[172]

Thus, while the Soviet artist is, financially speaking, well taken care of by the state, this holds true only if he joins the approved organizations and carefully follows the line laid down by the Central Committee of the Communist Party and hence by the Soviet government. Even some American artists and art critics sympathetic to Stalinism feel that the artistic results under this policy of rigid centralization have not been

[169] Voyce, op.cit., p. 136; and Jack Chen, "Soviet Painting," Studio, Vol. 127, No. 611 (Feb. 1944), pp. 61ff.

[170] Jelagin, op.cit., p. 76.

[171] Architectural Chronicle, No. 11 (Moscow, Nov. 1946), p. 19.

[172] New York Herald Tribune, May 1, 1949, p. 10, quoting Soviet Art. Alabyan—together with several other architects, including Yofan, one of the designers of the Palace of the Soviets, Moscow—had already been attacked in Pravda for displaying bourgeois cosmopolitanism: see the New York Times, Mar. 22, 1949, p. 16.

satisfactory to date, although they, unlike practically all non-Stalinists, insist that great improvement is eventually almost inevitable. Regardless of merit, however, it is a fact that the artists' organizations of Soviet Russia, mostly founded in connection with the increasing centralization of power under Stalin, have served in some degree as models for groups of artists in many other countries, even including (as will be seen) the United States.

V. Marxism (continued): Its Effects on Art in the United States

Like most earlier forms of socialism, all the major varieties of post-utopian socialism in the United States have in large part been imported from abroad and can only be understood in the light of their foreign origins. Nevertheless, in the process of importation these forms of socialism, and the arts to which they have given rise, have almost always been modified to some degree by American conditions. It is these American manifestations, and the reasons for them, that will now finally be considered.

For a long time—indeed, from the first appearance of Marxism in this country until just before World War I—Marxism and other socialisms influenced by Marxism had relatively little effect on the arts. The average American socialist of that period still more than most other Americans tended to regard art as a kind of unessential gilding on the practical realities of everyday life, and as having no really fundamental or even significant interaction with social problems. This point of view was much more pronounced among American socialists than among those of Europe because American Marxism at the beginning was more completely a workingman's movement primarily interested in day-to-day economic questions. Until World War I and especially until the Russian Revolution of 1917, the United States—in contrast to England and the Continent—had very few intellectuals who were directly interested in Marxism, and these few were usually regarded with the greatest suspicion by their fellow socialists. Most of them were writers, rather than artists or architects, who had become attracted to some aspects of Marxism through an earlier interest in utopianism and Christian socialism, as in the case of William Dean Howells, or else, like Jack London, Upton Sinclair, and Ernest Poole, had become conscious of social problems during the "muckraking" era. There were, however, a few artists with leanings toward Christian socialism, most of whom were inspired by the writings of John Ruskin; but these men rarely displayed their socialism in their art. Fairly typical is the case of W. J. Linton, the well-known American wood engraver who was a native of England and a friend and disciple of Ruskin, and whose socialism was expressed not in his engravings, but in the tracts and booklets which he wrote and printed at his own Appledore Press.[173]

Probably the first well-known American artist to present "the lower classes" in a deliberately sympathetic vein was William Morris Hunt (1824-1879). Some of Hunt's work (Fig. 44) was directly inspired by that of Millet, the French painter of peasant life of whom Hunt said, "When I came to know Millet, I took broader views of humanity. . . ."[174] And although Hunt was not actually a socialist, some of his work also shows the influence of Courbet,[175] the greatest founder of realism in painting, who had very close connections with French socialism. For Courbet was a close friend of Marx's contemporary and rival, the celebrated socialist-anarchist Proudhon; and, as previously mentioned, Courbet himself participated in the Paris Commune of 1871.

With the spread of naturalism as a literary and artistic movement, an increasing number of American artists began to depict realistic scenes of everyday life among the poorer classes in the cities. Chief of these was Eugene Higgins, who said that the paintings of Millet and the writings of Victor Hugo had largely molded his life: he actually identified himself with Jean Valjean, the hero of Hugo's *Les Miserables*. Higgins also said, "I am painting for men like Gorky," referring to Maxim Gorky, the Russian socialist writer who later was to become the leading literary figure of Soviet Russia; and Higgins himself occasionally depicted Russian subject matter (Fig. 45). In 1907 an article on Higgins was included among the several articles on art which the prominent American socialist, John Spargo, wrote for the *Craftsman*, an American periodical established in 1901.[176] The subtitle of Spargo's article referred to Higgins as "an American artist whose work upon canvas depicts the derelicts of civilization as do the tales of Maxim Gorky in literature." Spargo's own interest in art was partly based on the ideas of William Morris: in 1908 he published a book entitled *William Morris; His Socialism*.

The title of the *Craftsman* itself clearly reflects the influence of Morris, and through Morris, of postutopian socialism. In the first issue of the magazine the editor, Gustave Stickley, spoke of his aim "to extend the principles established by Morris." Stickley was the leading figure in the United Crafts of Eastwood (now Syracuse), New York, a group which not only published the *Craftsman* but designed and built

[173] F. J. Mather, Jr., "The Century and American Art," *The Century, 1847-1946* (New York, 1947), p. 164.

[174] Martha Shannon, *Boston Days of William Morris Hunt* (Boston, 1923), p. 40.

[175] C. H. Sawyer, "Naturalism in America," *Courbet and the Naturalistic Movement*, George Boas, ed. (Baltimore, 1938), pp. 116-17.

[176] For Spargo's article, from which the information herein on Higgins was taken, see the *Craftsman*, Vol. 12, No. 2 (May 1907), pp. 135-46. The *Craftsman* was published from 1901 through 1916.

a simplified kind of furniture inspired chiefly by the simple functional forms of William Morris' own furniture. The influence of the arts and crafts movement was likewise reflected in the similar forms of the Spanish "mission" furniture popularized by Elbert Hubbard and the Roycrofters at East Aurora, New York. Hubbard had visited Morris in 1892 and had been much affected by his artistic doctrines, though not by his socialism.

Morris' emphasis on craftsmanship, combined with his medievalism, also had a profound effect on the work of American artists and architects of the later Gothic Revival, and particularly on American typography of the period. The early typography of Goudy, for example, and that of the Gothic Revivalist architect, Bertram Grosvenor Goodhue, clearly reflect the style of Morris (cf. Figs. 46 and 47), but, as in the case of Elbert Hubbard, the socialist content of Morris' art is largely lacking. Thus, in 1922 Goodhue wrote, "Before the [First World] war I thought of myself as an internationalist, without giving the word any socialistic or radical meaning. . . ."[177]

It was especially through the medium of the *Comrade,* an American socialist periodical published in New York from 1901 to 1905, that the influence of William Morris and his followers was popularized in American book art. For among the able artists contributing to that magazine was the well-known English illustrator, Walter Crane (Fig. 48), who had been converted to socialism by Morris' essay *Art and Socialism,* and had already become widely known among American socialists on a trip to this country in 1891-1892. On this trip (during which he had published in the *Atlantic Monthly* for January 1892 an article entitled "Why Socialism Appeals to Artists") Crane had expressed particular admiration for one of Goodhue's designs.[178] Even though the *Comrade* was compelled to suspend publication after less than three years, it had an enduring effect on the technique of American illustration, an effect reinforced by later socialist periodicals. It is significant that such socialist influence has been so largely restricted to the art of drawing, because drawing is a medium which easily permits large-scale reproduction and thus can become easily available to the masses, whereas painting and sculpture have often been regarded by socialists as "fine arts" dominated by the upper classes in capitalist societies.

The *Comrade* was absorbed by the *International Socialist Review,* founded in 1900, which in turn ceased publication in 1918 during World

---

[177] C. H. Whitaker, *Bertram Grosvenor Goodhue, Architect* (New York, 1925), p. 40. However, Ralph Adams Cram, the noted Gothic Revivalist architect who was for many years Goodhue's partner, tells (in *My Life in Architecture* [Boston, 1936], pp. 20, 26, 46-47, etc.) of the enormous influence the social as well as the artistic ideas of William Morris and Ruskin had upon young American artists in the 1880's and 1890's.

[178] Whitaker, *op.cit.,* p. 16. The design admired by Crane was a magazine cover.

War I. Like most socialist periodicals this magazine displayed little interest in the arts aside from an occasional cartoon or propagandistic illustration in its later issues, and aside from a special department of literature and art conducted for only two years (1908-1910) by John Spargo who earlier had been editor of the *Comrade*.

In the period of "muckraking," interest in social problems became widely spread even among nonsocialists in this country, and several artists who later were to be famous for their work in socialist periodicals first became known for their contributions to muckraking magazines. At this time, for example, the old *Life*, then a humorous magazine under the editorship of John Ames Mitchell, showed considerable interest in problems of a social nature. Among the artists from whom Mitchell accepted drawings was Art Young, later to achieve renown primarily as a contributor to the *Masses* and other socialist periodicals. Moreover, Mitchell himself wrote a book, *The Silent War* (1906), dealing with the class struggle, and this was illustrated by William Balfour Ker (Fig. 49), who in the years just preceding World War I did much illustration for magazines of social protest, including the *Masses*.

With the *Masses*, founded in 1911 as an artists' and writers' cooperative by a group which included both radicals and nonradicals, the influence of socialism in general and of Marxism in particular greatly increased, and a much larger segment of Americans became aware of socialist content in art. Nevertheless, then and later no consistent socialist aesthetic ever developed in the United States, mainly because of the constant splitting and realigning of the numerous socialist groups. Even at a comparatively late date, relatively few members of the Marxist groups were much interested in the visual arts because there still were relatively few "intellectuals" among American Marxists, and also because neither Marx nor Lenin had ever found time to develop an aesthetic. Then, Lenin himself rejected modern "isms" in the arts only a short time after the Bolshevik Revolution, and in this was followed by Stalin, with the result that among American Marxists any interest in radically new developments in literature and art has until recently been chiefly restricted to the followers of Trotsky, reflecting Trotsky's own interest in them. Yet even among the American Trotskyists—who, it will be recalled, were all expelled from the American Communist Party in 1928—considerably more attention has been paid to literature than to the visual arts.

Aside from a few individuals, only recently have American Stalinists, and thus the American Communist Party, begun to urge the need for a consistent aesthetic, in harmony with developments in Russia itself. By background and training Stalin had originally been primarily a practicing revolutionary, rather than a theoretician, in partial contrast to such

708

prominent opponents as Trotsky and Bukharin; consequently, for a long time—in this country as elsewhere—Stalin attracted to his following fewer intellectuals than did those opponents. However, in the process of victoriously combating the philosophies of Trotsky and Bukharin, including their philosophies of art, the Stalinists devoted themselves increasingly to the theoretical aspects of Marxism, and eventually developed a general aesthetic of their own largely based on Stalin's own tastes. But this aesthetic, as we have seen, became victorious in Russia only after Stalin's victory over his chief enemies in 1929, and actually remained relatively ill-defined until after World War II.

In this country, in the years immediately following Stalin's triumph—and at first under the influence and guidance of the revived Proletcult movement in Russia—a very large number of party-line "cultural" organizations and periodicals were soon established, including, among many others, the John Reed Club, the Workers Dance League, the Workers Music League, and Theatre Collective. Particularly important was the John Reed Club, founded in 1929 as the American affiliate of the International Union of Revolutionary Writers, with branches in most large cities. Each of the principal branches had its own periodical of literature and art, the best known being the *Partisan Review*, which was founded as the organ of the New York branch in 1934 but remained under communist auspices only until 1936.

Although the various cultural organizations founded as part of the Proletcult movement exerted considerable influence between 1930 and 1935 (the year in which they either disbanded or obediently shifted their interest from revolutionary proletarian culture and class warfare to the Popular Front against fascism), the scope of these organizations was limited insofar as they tended to restrict their membership to the "proletariat." Writers and artists might be admitted to the "proletariat" because of their value as propagandists for proletarian culture, but members of other professions were ordinarily excluded, so that communist influence in American culture was necessarily somewhat restricted. With the change in the Russian line to support the Popular Front, however, and with the consequent deemphasizing of class warfare, pronounced official efforts could eventually be made to seek the support of Americans in those other professions formerly considered unduly antiproletarian in spirit. Therefore, in September 1938 William Z. Foster published in the *Communist*, then the party's theoretical organ, an article entitled "The Communist Party and the Professionals." In this he emphasized the importance of making use of carefully selected professional men willing to "display a thorough readiness to accept Party discipline"; and insisted that in view of the many "potentialities for service by Communist professionals, any tendencies in our Party to underestimate the importance of these elements should be combatted." Thus in the late thirties, up to the Soviet-Nazi pact of 1939, communist influence in the professions and in American culture in general was particularly strong. However, the fact that at this time the party line was stressing the importance of opposing fascism by means of a Popular Front with non-Marxian parties meant that any specifically Marxian art and art theory was deemphasized.

It was only after the end of World War II that the heaviest official emphasis was to be placed by communists on "art as a weapon" in the class struggle. This old slogan of Proletcult was revived once more in 1946 to accompany the cultural purges, first publicly signalized by Stalin's speech on February 9 of that year. For, with the breaking up of Russia's wartime alliance with "bourgeois" countries against Hitler, revolutionary communism and class warfare had been deliberately revived, and new purges—artistic as well as political—had become necessary because of the sharp change in the party line.

On February 11, 1946, the very day that Stalin's speech first appeared in the New York *Daily Worker*, that newspaper began to publish a series of six articles by Samuel Sillen under the general title of "Which Way Left Wing Literature?" and with such subheadings as Art and Politics, Art as a Weapon, Ideology and Art, and The Path before Us. Taking the form of an attack on an article in the current *New Masses* (written by Albert Maltz and entitled "What Shall We Ask of Writers?"), Sillen's series laid down a firm line for literature and art which was promptly supported in the Communist Party press by such wheelhorses as Mike Gold and A. B. Magil. And when *Mainstream*, a new party-line cultural periodical began publication early in 1947, Sillen was made its editor and later became editor of its successor, *Masses & Mainstream*.

Two months after Stalin's speech of February 9, a still more authoritative indication that art was now to be much more thoroughly emphasized by the party line was made by William Z. Foster (who in the summer of 1945 had replaced Earl Browder as leader of the reconstituted American Communist Party in order to put the whole new postwar line into effect). For on April 18, 1946, Foster was the chief speaker at a symposium in New York on "Art as a Weapon," a symposium jointly sponsored by the *New Masses* and the *Daily Worker*. In an article published in the *New Masses* five days later, Foster wrote ". . . there must be a clear understanding that 'art is a weapon' in the class struggle. Not only is art a weapon, but a very potent one as well."[179] And now he stressed the relative importance of *national* cultures, as opposed to internationalism, in harmony with the changing Russian foreign policy.

[179] W. Z. Foster, "Elements of a People's Cultural Policy," *New Masses*, Vol. 59, No. 4 (Apr. 23, 1946), p. 6.

In the following year a formal and definitive statement of the whole new cultural line was published in a pamphlet entitled *Culture in a Changing World, a Marxist Approach*, written by Victor J. Jerome, chairman of the cultural commission of the American Communist Party. This statement, the pamphlet said, was "based on the text of a major address delivered . . . at a Marxist cultural conference held in New York in June, 1947, under the sponsorship of the magazines, *Mainstream* and *New Masses*" (although, strangely enough, the two magazines and the *Daily Worker* had apparently carried no report of the address). The statement praised the line established by Samuel Sillen's articles in the *Daily Worker* over a year earlier. For the further guidance of party-liners, Jerome's pamphlet was reviewed favorably and at great length by Samuel Sillen himself in the March 1948 number of *Political Affairs*, the theoretical magazine of the American Communist Party, of which Jerome is editor.

In his pamphlet, as Sillen said, Jerome firmly laid down the postwar Stalinist line that socialist "reality in art involves partisanship." And in characteristic Stalinist fashion Jerome called for a two-fold struggle "simultaneously . . . against the vulgar, mechanico-materialist view" and "against the idealist disruption of reality in art . . . by its absolutizing of form" (i.e., by its formalism).

Thus for the first time strong official attempts were now being made by the American Communist Party to arrive at a complete Stalinist aesthetic by slavishly following—as usual—the postwar line laid down in Soviet Russia. As already noted, in Russia itself the development of a detailed official aesthetic had previously been hampered by the primacy given to economic and political problems, by the bitter internal controversies, by purges, and by the fear of capitalism and nazism. During World War II such an aesthetic had again been somewhat held back by the need to avoid discord with Russia's wartime allies; but at the same time the war had brought to those allies an increased interest in all things Russian including Soviet art and art theories.

For all these reasons, most of the few important books on art theory written or published by Americans sympathetic to Stalinism are of recent date. Late in 1945 there was issued by International Publishers—apparently in recognition of the survival of wartime interest in Russia and thus in Stalinist Marxism—an American edition of an able little book entitled, *Marxism and Modern Art; an Approach to Social Realism*. This, written by F. D. Klingender, an English critic sympathetic to the Stalinist point of view, had originally been published in England in 1943. However, most of the books on Marxist art which have recently been published in this country reflect the dutifully increased interest in art among Stalinists and their sympathizers since Stalin gave a new importance to art by his signal, early in 1946, for the postwar revision of Russian culture. Among the most important of these works are the volume of selections from the writings of Marx and Engels entitled *Literature and Art* (1947), Sidney Finkelstein's *Art and Society* (1947), and Louis Harap's *Social Roots of the Arts* (1949)—all issued by International Publishers. The head of this publishing house is Alexander Trachtenberg, whom one former member of the Communist Party has called "the Red cultural commissar for America."[180]

Of all the books on art criticism published in this country in connection with this new Stalinist emphasis on art, the best is Finkelstein's *Art and Society*, issued when the author was music critic of the *New Masses*, and with a title borrowed from a well-known essay by Georgy Plekhanov, a celebrated father of Russian Marxism and acknowledged teacher of Lenin. Finkelstein's book is perhaps the ablest and most complete exposition of a theory of art sympathetic to Stalinism ever published anywhere. To non-Stalinists the book may serve to demonstrate the difficulty which those who sympathize with Soviet Russia have in keeping up with the party line, for in it the author highly praised the work of Picasso (who three years earlier had joined the French Communist Party) seemingly just before *Pravda* launched, in August 1947, a sharp attack on Picasso's art as bourgeois and formalist.[181] While *Art and Society* was not published until October 1947, the book was presumably too far along in the press for any revisions to be made after the *Pravda* article had appeared in print.

At first it seemed as if Finkelstein would escape unscathed: the reviews of his book in the American communist press were almost entirely favorable. However, well over two years later, on May 15, 1950, the *Daily*

---

[180] Budenz, *Men without Faces*, p. 239. Trachtenberg was one of twenty-one leaders of the Communist Party indicted in June 1951 for conspiring to advocate or teach the violent overthrow of the government: see the *New York Herald Tribune*, June 21, 1951, pp. 1, 11, 12.

[181] However, famous foreign artists sympathetic to Russia are frequently lauded by Stalinists outside of Russia, and their reputations made use of, even though their art is in disfavor within the Soviet Union itself. This has evidently become the case with Picasso: hence the issue of *Masses & Mainstream* for March 1948 could contain (pp. 6-20) a laudatory article "Picasso at Work," by Louis Parrot. It might be added that in March 1950 Picasso was refused a visa by the Department of State when he sought to visit Washington as head of a European delegation to bring a world peace petition addressed to Congress. The Department of State said that the members of the delegation were stooges for the Partisans of Peace, which it called a communist-line organization: see the *New York Herald Tribune*, Mar. 4, 1950, pp. 1 and 6. As part of his contribution to the communist "peace" campaign, Picasso drew a dove of peace which was widely publicized. It was caricatured by a French anticommunist artist in an even more widely publicized poster of an armored dove, decorated with the Soviet symbol of the hammer and sickle, and labeled "La colombe qui fait boum" (The dove that goes bang).

Worker suddenly published an article by one Barnard Rubin entitled "Serious Errors in Finkelstein's 'Art and Society.'" In this—suprisingly—the book was now attacked as anti-Semitic, and also as "formalistic" because it had praised such "corrupt darlings of imperialism's culture" as T. S. Eliot and James Joyce by venturing to suggest that the writings of Eliot and Joyce could be used as models by progressive cultural workers.

Three days later the *Daily Worker* published Finkelstein's recantation written in the usual abject style of a party-liner attacked in a Russian-type purge (thereby, in the Stalinist view, demonstrating the "self-criticism" which in Russia is supposed to be replacing the class antagonisms of capitalist society). Finkelstein now admitted that his book suffered from a "classless" point of view toward the arts as a consequence of which he had wrongly confused primitive art and folk art, had wrongly interpreted the term "realism," and had failed to distinguish adequately between those national movements based on bourgeois approaches to art and those founded on a true working-class approach. Most humbly Finkelstein accounted for his errors by saying that he had originally written the book before World War II, and that when he had returned from military service he had not succeeded in rewriting it properly. This, being interpreted, means that he had not been successful in taking account of those shifts in the Russian policy and in the party line which had occurred since he wrote the original draft.

In spite of Finkelstein's recantation, from May until August 1950 articles and letters attacking his book appeared frequently in the *Daily Worker*. One letter was written by Louis Harap, author of *Social Roots of the Arts*, but Harap evidently made a bad mistake in thus seeking to demonstrate his orthodoxy for the *Daily Worker* a few days later printed a sharp letter from Samuel Sillen, editor of the party-line monthly, *Masses & Mainstream*, pointing out that Harap's book shared some of Finkelstein's errors.

The discussion in the *Daily Worker* was wound up on August 7 and 8, 1950, by two articles written by no less an authority than V. J. Jerome. As the party's spokesman in cultural matters, Jerome summed up the attack by pointing out that Finkelstein had clearly succumbed to "right-opportunist errors." But Jerome evidently felt that there were some alleviating circumstances and that the discussion had only succeeded in confusing many party-liners, because he called for a "thoroughly critical review" of the book as the next step. This "thoroughly critical review" duly appeared in the September 1950 number of his own magazine, *Political Affairs*. While this review (entitled "Art and Class," and written by Harry Martel and Marvin Reiss) recognized that Finkelstein had made some important contributions, it reiterated that "his work reveals a dominant tendency to a non-class approach," a "formalist" tendency to emphasize "bourgeois esthetics" and novelty, an improper treatment of realism, and a failure to recognize that bourgeois modern art obliterates "national art" and does so "in the cosmopolitan, 'international' bourgeois art jargon which is the same in New York, Hollywood, Paris, or London." He had, in short, failed "to show that the 'innovations' of the 'modernists' are merely the decadent shimmer of moribund capitalism." Significantly, however, the review concluded that "In the world-battle for peace and progress, the Communist Party recognizes that the artist is a key figure." Thus, at long last the importance of the artist was now fully accepted by the American Communist Party.

But if Finkelstein's book—notwithstanding all these delayed assaults leveled against it by the party—is outstanding in quality among writings on art by American party-liners, it seems all the better by comparison with the art criticism written by other American Marxians. For most of this has appeared in the form of articles which present not only second-hand but often inadequate versions of some phase of Russian Marxist art theory, whether of the current orthodox party line or some "deviation." And most of these articles have appeared in relatively obscure periodicals read chiefly by the fanatic few of the particular Marxist sect. Because the art theories contained in such periodicals so directly reflect, in secondary form, the Russian prototypes already discussed, no attempt will be made to treat them in detail here. Suffice it to say that most of the better-grade art criticism sympathetic to Stalinism has appeared in the pages of the *Partisan Review* in its brief Stalinist period (1934-1936), in the *New Masses* (1926-1948), and especially in *Masses & Mainstream. Dialectics: a Marxist Literary Journal*, edited by Angel Flores and published in New York by the Critics Group during the late 1930's, contained occasional articles on art from a similar point of view; and the Critics Group also issued at this time a number of important Russian Marxist documents on art, including a translation of Plekhanov's *Art and Society* (1937), and of Mikhail Lifshitz's *The Philosophy of Art of Karl Marx* (1938). In spite of the fact that during the Popular Front the party line regarded serious Marxian inquiry of this sort as "sectarian" (i.e., as too likely to stir up trouble between Soviet Russia and its non-Marxian allies in opposing fascism), the Critics Group managed to publish *Dialectics* until 1939.

Some of the best of all the Marxian art criticism written in this country has been printed in periodicals sympathetic to Trotskyism, notably the *Partisan Review* during the Trotskyist phase which occurred immediately after its revival in 1937. Valuable articles also appeared during the middle 1930's in the *Modern Monthly*, an independent periodical that published all those shades of leftist—including Trotskyist—opinion which were not Stalinist and not social democratic. The "Right deviationist" group, led by Jay Lovestone, paid less attention to the arts than did the American Trotskyists. Nevertheless, from the time that his faction was expelled from the Communist Party in 1929 until it voted to disband late in 1940, its members tended to uphold the doctrines of Bukharin concerning the unripeness of capitalism for revolution, doctrines with implications for art as well as for economics and politics.

Thus all the major points of view and all the chief changes in the party line which have been represented in the art theories and criticism of Soviet Russia itself have had protagonists in the United States. But because the writings of these protagonists have mostly been restricted to periodicals of small circulation, their direct influence on the actual practice of art has ordinarily been restricted to relatively small groups.

However, in addition to actual members of such groups there has long existed in the United States a much larger body made up of liberals, or even radicals, of various shades of opinion who have been interested in the arts, and whose opinions and theories have frequently been more or less colored—often unconsciously, and in widely different ways—by those of the various Russian factions and their American representatives. Because less subject to any party line, both the art theory and the practice of such liberal-radicals have tended to be more original. Most of them have had strong equalitarian, humanitarian, or collectivistic inclinations, often derived from earlier American currents of thought, but which have made them sympathetic to some aspects of Marxism and have frequently led them to collaborate with Marxians. Many have been artists stirred to social protest against capitalism partly, at least, by their first-hand knowledge of the difficulties and injustices which beset the artist within a primarily business and industrial civilization. Some of these artists had also served as staff artists on newspapers and in this way had become very much aware of everyday social problems and injustices. This was particularly true of several members of the group of artists known as "The Eight," formed in 1908 under the leadership of Robert Henri. This group became·known to its detractors as the "Ash-can School," because several of its members—notably John Sloan (Fig. 50) and George Luks—particularly liked to paint scenes of lower-class urban life. It is significant that George Luks had already been the subject of a laudatory article in the *Craftsman*[182] written by the well-known socialist John Spargo, and that John Sloan was later to become art editor of the *Masses* and a member of the Socialist Party.[183] Significantly, also, Robert Henri, the leader of the

[182] *Craftsman*, Vol. 12, No. 6 (Sept. 1907), pp. 599-607.
[183] According to Max Eastman, *Enjoyment of Living* (New York, 1948), p. 549.

group, was not unsympathetic to philosophical anarchism. From 1912 to 1918 he taught art at the Modern School of the Ferrer Center where for a time his celebrated pupil, George Bellows, and his friend, John Sloan, also taught. The Ferrer Center was the headquarters of the Francisco Ferrer Association, named for Francisco Ferrer Guardia, a Spanish anarchist and libertarian educator who had been executed at Barcelona in 1909 for allegedly leading a military rebellion.[184]

The socially radical spirit of such men as these was in part, at least, the result of their artistic radicalism, for they all sharply opposed academic traditions in art while upholding modernism of one sort or another. Indeed, it was largely friends of Henri and members of "The Eight"—especially Arthur B. Davies—who were chiefly to be responsible for putting on the celebrated Armory Show, held at the 69th Regiment Armory in New York in 1913, which first introduced Americans to the modern movement in art on a large scale.

Artistic radicalism of this kind has often made some American artists willing to collaborate with Marxists in attacking capitalism largely because they looked upon conservative art as a product of a philistine civilization which happened to be capitalistic. In contributing their services as illustrators or cartoonists to periodicals of social protest, many

[184] Leonard D. Abbott, "Francisco Ferrer and the Modern School," *Critic & Guide* (Girard, Kan.), Oct. 1949, pp. 10-12; and information generously furnished by Mr. Abbott, Carl Zigrosser, and Manuel Komroff. Among the sponsors of the Ferrer Center, which attracted many leading radicals and libertarians, were Mr. Abbott, the anarchists Emma Goldman, Alexander Berkman, and Hippolyte Havel, Hutchins Hapgood, and the muckraker socialist, Charles Edward Russell. Ferrer's followers also established a colony at Stelton, N.J., and published a periodical, the *Modern School*, to which Rockwell Kent and other now noted artists contributed, and of which Carl Zigrosser was at one time editor. The Ferrer Association in New York started at 6 St. Mark's Place in the fall of 1910. In October 1911 it moved to 104 East 12th Street, and a year later to 63 East 107th Street where it reached the peak of its activities. There were classes in various subjects. Will Durant taught in the children's school and gave evening talks in philosophy. Leonard Abbott lectured on literature; and Clarence Darrow and Joseph McCabe were also lecturers. Speakers at the Saturday night discussions included Alexander Berkman, Emma Goldman, Elizabeth Gurley Flynn, W. E. Walling, Lincoln Steffens, Hutchins Hapgood, Upton Sinclair, Edwin Markham, Hubert H. Harrison, Christian Brinton, and Harry Kemp. Mr. Abbott states that Henri began his art class at East 12th Street in the winter of 1911-1912 and continued it until the New York association broke up in 1918. Bellows taught at East 12th Street and at East 107th Street where Sloan also taught. Henri's class, with a model, was held two evenings a week and supervised alternately by himself and Bellows. The class was radical only in involving no systematic teaching: Henri and Bellows merely criticized the students' drawings when criticism was desired, a procedure commonplace today but then considered revolutionary. The following artists frequented the class at some time or other: Man Ray, Manuel Komroff, Ben Benn, Helen West Heller, Paul Rohland, Harry Wickey, and Adolph Wolff. The Ferrer Association came under increasing attack during World War I because of its pacifist tendencies. In the summer of 1915 the children's school was moved to Stelton, and in 1918 all activities in New York ended. Some of them were transferred to Stelton where the children's school still functions.

of them have simply been registering a protest against conservatism. In most cases, being artists, they have been temperamentally too individualistic to accept the Marxian creed in its entirety: Marx's emphasis on liberty as the goal of the class struggle has appealed to them, but not the Marxian belief in impersonal "scientific" procedure toward that goal.

This was the case with most of the more prominent artists who at one time or another contributed to the *Masses*, relatively few of whom were actually practicing political socialists. Among the contributors were well-known painters and draftsmen such as its art editor, John Sloan, also Eugene Higgins, Robert Henri, George Bellows, Arthur B. Davies, Glenn Coleman, Maurice Becker, Hugo Gellert, H. J. Glintenkamp, Boardman Robinson, and Stuart Davis; the sculptors, Jo Davidson and Mahonri Young, who submitted drawings; and various able cartoonists including Art Young and Robert Minor. With the help of such highly competent artists, the *Masses*—which is said to have marked the first appearance of "realism"[185] in an American magazine—was the best illustrated periodical in the country, at least until 1916 when John Sloan and four other staff members resigned in a dispute with Max Eastman,[186] the editor since 1913.

Before this dispute took place, the *Masses* had already begun to oppose American participation in World War I: in fact, of all the contributing artists, George Bellows was the only important one who actively supported participation. As a result of its antiwar stand, in 1917 the *Masses* was finally forced to cease publication when seven members of the staff were accused of obstructing the draft. These seven—including two artists, Art Young and H. J. Glintenkamp—were indicted under the so-called Espionage Act, and most of the group—including Art Young—were twice brought to trial. "Exhibit F" at the trial was a cartoon by Art Young entitled *Having Their Fling* (Fig. 51) in which he depicted his idea of the forces responsible for the war by showing bankers and clergymen dancing wildly in a shower of gold to the music of the devil's orchestra of cannon. Only after two juries had disagreed were the defendants finally freed, and by a very narrow margin.

Among those who deplored the attack on the *Masses* and who likewise opposed the entry of the United States into World War I were the members of the staff of a literary and artistic journal called the *Seven Arts*. This periodical had a wide influence in spite of its very brief life (it was published only from November 1916 until October 1917 when its financial sponsor refused to support the antiwar stand of the editors). Most of the

185 Eastman, *op.cit.*, p. 411.
186 *Ibid.*, pp. 548-56; also J. J. Sweeney, Museum of Modern Art, *Stuart Davis* (New York, 1945), pp. 11-12.

staff—which included Van Wyck Brooks, Randolph Bourne, Waldo Frank, and the unpolitically-minded music and art critic, Paul Rosenfeld—were socialists or liberals who, like Ruskin and Morris rather than Marx, were interested both in craftsmanship and in the arts as forces for achieving the good society. The dominant figure of the group was the socialist Van Wyck Brooks, among whose chief idols were William Morris and John Ruskin.

One young American much influenced by the *Seven Arts* was Lewis Mumford, destined to become a leading American critic of the arts, an international authority on housing and city planning, and a widely known liberal. At the age of twenty Mumford had been profoundly affected by the writings of the Scottish bio-sociologist and city planner, Patrick Geddes, whom Mumford himself had described as "a scientific interpreter of Ruskin." Because of his Ruskinian point of view derived from Geddes, Mumford was also attracted by the similar ideas of Van Wyck Brooks and other members of the *Seven Arts* group. Indeed, when the *Seven Arts* ceased publication it merged with the *Dial* of which Mumford became associate editor in 1919. Significantly enough Mumford's first book, *The Story of Utopias* (1922), was written, the preface tells us, at the suggestion of Van Wyck Brooks and under the influence of the ideas of Patrick Geddes. The stimulation of Geddes' ideas also led Mumford to become one of the founders of the Regional Planning Association of America after World War I, and to publish several important books on city planning, and on social and cultural history.

After the *Masses* stopped publication in 1917, several attempts were made to establish successors. Art Young, one of the defendants in the famous trial, was responsible for at least two of these. He first sought to establish a monthly magazine of artistic satire, entitled *Good Morning* (1919-1921), and when that failed, Young tried again with the likewise unsuccessful *Art Young's Quarterly*.

The chief successor of the *Masses* was the *Liberator*, founded in 1918 under private control[187] but under joint socialist and liberal auspices. This took up pretty much where the *Masses* had left off. Many of the artists who had contributed to the *Masses* also worked for the *Liberator*, including Young, Bellows, Robinson, and Minor (Fig. 52), who in 1918 went to Russia as the *Liberator's* foreign correspondent;[188] but now an increasingly important part was also played by younger artists, especially

[187] According to Eastman, *Enjoyment of Living*, p. 415, note 1, the *Liberator* was founded under the joint ownership and control of Eastman and his sister. Eastman, who was the first editor, resigned in 1922.

[188] He also represented the *New York World* and the *Philadelphia Public Ledger*: see Benjamin Gitlow, *The Whole of Their Lives* (New York, 1948), p. 70.

William Gropper (Fig. 53). In 1922 the *Liberator* became a completely communist-line periodical and almost immediately began to pay less attention to art except for extremely propagandistic and party-line cartoons. Two years later it ceased publication when it merged with two other left-wing periodicals to form the *Workers Monthly*.

In 1926 the *New Masses* was established by a partly different group of writers and artists, and, until lack of funds compelled it to close down early in 1948, was for most of its life a periodical sympathetic to revolutionary communism of Stalinist persuasion, even though shortly after its founding the editorial board had decided that the magazine would not be one "of communism or Moscow, but a magazine of American experiment."[189] Among the many artists who at one time or another contributed to the *New Masses* were John Sloan and Hugo Gellert (two of the six editors in the first days of the magazine), also Glenn Coleman, Adolf Dehn, Waldo Frank, Miguel Covarrubias, Art Young, Gropper, Maurice Becker, and Louis Lozowick. Of these artists several were outspoken radicals, notably Becker, Gropper, Louis Lozowick, and Hugo Gellert,[190] the last of whom painted a series of murals in the cafeteria at 30 Union Square, the building which in 1927 had become the headquarters of the *Daily Worker*.[191] Several of the contributors to the *New Masses* drew direct inspiration from European leftist art of the period. For example, the art of the then antibourgeois German satirist George Grosz (Fig. 25) seems to have had direct influence on the thin linear style and satirical subject matter of Adolf Dehn. It has also apparently helped to inspire some of the subject matter of William Gropper,[192] who is particularly fond of satirizing American "bourgeois" legislators (Fig. 53). The art of Soviet Russia early had an especially profound effect on Louis Lozowick, who had been in Berlin in 1922 and had seen the great exhibition of modern Russian art held in that year.[193] Because of Lozowick's leftist views and because he was one of the first American artists to depict industrial scenes, his work was much admired in the Soviet Union, and an exhibit of his drawings was held in Moscow in 1928.[194]

[189] Joseph Freeman, *An American Testament* (New York, 1936), pp. 381-82. The *New Masses* was reorganized in 1928 under the editorship of Michael Gold, "and now for the first time an attempt was made to create a popular literary magazine with an explicitly Marxist policy," according to Bernard Smith, *Forces in American Criticism* (New York, 1939), p. 369.

[190] M. W. Brown, *American Painting* (1913-1929), (unpublished Ph.D. thesis, New York University, 1949), p. 275.

[191] Benjamin Gitlow, *I Confess* (New York, c. 1940), pp. 307-9.

[192] Brown, *op.cit.*, pp. 276-77.

[193] While in Berlin, Lozowick talked with many modern artists: see László Moholy-Nagy, "Abstract of an Artist," *The New Vision; and Abstract of an Artist* (New York, 1946), p. 74. A few years later Lozowick published a book on Russian painting since the October Revolution entitled *Modern Russian Art* (New York, c. 1925).

[194] Brown, *op.cit.*, p. 372.

Lozowick, Becker, and Dehn were among nearly fifty artists, writers, architects, and educators who, during the presidential campaign of 1932, issued a statement calling for the formation of committees throughout the country to furnish "support in the national elections of the Communist Party and its candidates, Wm. Z. Foster and James W. Ford." According to the *Daily Worker* for September 14, 1932, the statement signed by the fifty said "that the only effective way to protest against the chaos, the appalling wastefulness, and the indescribable misery inherent in the present economic system is to vote for the Communist candidates," a point of view that many of the signers have long since repudiated. This was the first time in this country that the communists had made such direct use of writers and artists for immediate political purposes, employing now a technique of mass pressure said to have first been developed in this country by the I.W.W. in an effort to obtain amnesty for jailed "Wobblies" in 1923.

However, it is important to note that relatively few of the artists contributing to the *New Masses* in its early period were active communists or fellow travelers. Even though the editorial policy of the *New Masses* was always sympathetic to communism and closely followed the Communist Party line, one former party member on the staff wrote that of fifty-six artists and writers grouped around this periodical in the early days, only two were actually members of the party and less than a dozen were even sympathetic to it.[195] As time went on, those artists who were neither party members nor fellow travelers increasingly fell away. Some withdrew their names from the long list of contributing editors (a list carried until the magazine suspended publication as a monthly in September 1934), while others failed to do so although inactive. Of the few remaining well-known artist contributors, nearly all were to turn away from the *New Masses* in 1939 when it supported the Russo-German pact.

After the pact the *New Masses* gradually declined in circulation until, in January 1948, it appeared for the last time as a weekly, although two months later it was to be combined with another periodical and resurrected as a monthly under the title *Masses & Mainstream*. The last issue of the *New Masses* had contained an open letter from twelve Russian communist writers addressed to their colleagues in the United States, the gist of which was: Whose side are you on? In the third issue of *Masses & Mainstream*, thirty-two American writers, painters, and musicians published their reply. Said they: "We want to share . . . responsibility with you. . . . On this May Day we grip your hand. . . ." Among the signers

---

[195] Freeman, *op.cit.*, p. 379. Although Freeman's statement was published as late as 1936, it apparently applies only to the early days of the *New Masses*.

were Sidney Finkelstein, the critic, and such well-known American painters as Philip Evergood, Raphael Soyer, and Max Weber.[196] It might be added that Evergood, Weber, and Soyer, along with Hugo Gellert, Gropper, Louis Lozowick, Stuart Davis, and Joe Jones, had been among the nearly 150 signers of a letter which was prominently published in the *New Masses* and praised by the *Daily Worker* for April 28, 1938, as upholding "the verdicts in the recent Moscow trials of the Trotzkyite-Buckharinite traitors." The letter was an answer to the commission of inquiry headed by John Dewey which had investigated the Moscow trials, had interviewed Trotsky in Mexico, and had absolved him from the Moscow verdict that he had conspired with other defendants and with Fascist nations to overthrow the Soviet government and to assassinate its leaders. Weber, Gellert, and Gropper together with Art Young, Maurice Becker, Rockwell Kent, and several other artists were among the 400 signers—some of them neither communists nor fellow travelers—of a letter published in the *Daily Worker* on August 14, 1939, denying that "the U.S.S.R. and the totalitarian states are basically alike." This letter (a reply to charges leveled by John Dewey's Committee for Cultural Freedom) was published just nine days before the Nazi-Soviet pact.

It must be emphasized, however, that many of the American artists who have joined in signing statements like those cited above have kept their art largely separate from their political views even when those views have coincided with the party line. For instance, this has been the case with Max Weber. In spite of a record of frequent sympathy for Soviet Russia and for aspects of the party line as supported by such periodicals as the *New Masses* or *Masses & Mainstream*, so little has this been reflected in the subject matter of his paintings that he has been chided in the columns of *Masses & Mainstream* itself.[197]

Most of the artists who, unlike Weber, have more completely subordinated their art to Marxism or to a Marxian party line have usually expressed themselves by means of the cartoon. For example, several able cartoonists have contributed to the *Daily Worker*. Among them have been Art Young, Robert Minor, Abraham Redfield, Fred Ellis, and Jacob Burck, most of whom have worked in a simple and forceful lithographic style apparently inspired by that of Minor, a style which has also in-

[196] *Masses & Mainstream*, Vol. 1, No. 3 (May 1948), p. 6. The Russian letter had appeared in *Literaturnaya Gazeta* for Sept. 20, 1947. Another English translation is in *Soviet Press Translations*, Vol. 2, No. 21 (Dec. 15, 1947), pp. 287-89. Finkelstein and Evergood, at this writing (June 1951), are contributing editors of *Masses & Mainstream*, as is William Gropper. Weber was chairman of the Manhattan Committee of Artists for Wallace in 1948. Raphael Soyer's brother, Moses Soyer, was art editor of the *New Masses* in 1944-1946.

[197] See W. T. Burger, "Max Weber," *Masses & Mainstream*, Vol. 2, No. 4 (Apr. 1949), p. 87.

fluenced leading cartoonists on "capitalist" papers.[198] Minor himself—the only artist of the original *Masses* group to become a founder of the American Communist Party—gave up cartooning some years ago because, as a convinced member of the party, he came to believe that direct participation in communist political and economic activities is more important than cartooning for bringing about the revolution of the proletariat. Among many other activities, he has served in Moscow as the representative of the American Communist Party to the Communist International; was imprisoned for several months in 1930 for participating in a "hunger demonstration" in New York's Union Square, a demonstration calling for a general strike; and went to Spain in 1937 to oppose Franco in the Spanish Civil War. He has also run on the Communist ticket for various political offices, including governor of New York and United States senator. After Earl Browder was jailed for passport fraud in 1939, Minor was made acting secretary of the American Communist Party, usually considered the most important party post. Although Minor fell into disfavor with Moscow and with the party in 1945, when Browder was demoted and later expelled, he is still listed in *Who's Who in America* as an editor of the *Daily Worker*, and in 1950 on the occasion of his sixty-sixth birthday the *Daily Worker* reported that he "was honored by the Communist Party with the warmest greetings."[199]

The fact that Minor gave up art in favor of political and economic activity reflects the comparative lack of interest in the arts characteristic of Stalinists everywhere until after World War II. As already noted, of all the socialist and communist factions, the Trotskyist groups have from their beginnings been particularly interested in the theory and criticism of art because of Trotsky's own interest in such matters. And because Trotsky, unlike Lenin and Stalin, considered that the more abstract forms of modern art could express the spirit of the Marxist revolution, American Trotskyists have lent their support to modern movements in art which were long opposed by Lenin and Stalin and which therefore have also been generally opposed by American Stalinists.

One particularly important factor in spreading, even among nonsocialists, modern art forms that originally, at least, were regarded by some artists as possessing socialist or communist connotations, has been the influence of artists who came to this country from abroad. It will be remembered, for example, that when leftism in art—including futurism,

198 According to Freeman, *op.cit.*, p. 304, the style of Minor (who once was a cartoonist on the *St. Louis Post-Dispatch* and the *New York World*, among other papers) influenced Fitzpatrick of the *Post-Dispatch* and Rollin Kirby, formerly of the *World*.

199 *Who's Who in America* (1950-1951), and the *Daily Worker*, July 17, 1950, p. 5. For an account of Minor's extraordinary career, see Gitlow, *The Whole of Their Lives*, especially pp. 70-82, 323-25.

constructivism, and the other "isms"—felt the weight of Lenin's disapproval in 1920, many artists who were not willing to devote their art entirely to the revolution left Russia. One of the artists who migrated from Russia about this time made his way to the United States via Siberia. This was David Burliuk, who, according to his biography in *Who's Who in America*, regards himself as the founder of Russian futurism.

But since those artists who have left Soviet Russia have almost invariably been those *unwilling* to devote themselves to the revolution, the strongest Marxian influences on American painting have not come directly from Russia itself. They have come, indeed, from Mexico, mainly as a result of the influence of the communist painter, Diego Rivera. Rivera—together with Siqueiros, also a communist, and with José Orozco, a Mexican revolutionary who sympathized with some aspects of Marxism—was chiefly responsible for a great revival of mural painting in fresco. This began on a large scale in 1922-1924 with the frescoes executed in the National Preparatory School at Mexico City by a group of leading radical artists, a group which included Siqueiros, Rivera, and Orozco. Fresco as a medium could be particularly approved by all communists because, it will be recalled, Lenin had praised it as so well suited to Marxist propaganda in warm countries; but it was also approved by many noncommunists interested in its expressive possibilities for modern art. Although none of the leading Mexican artists executed major works in this country until 1930, the influence of this revival of fresco had already reached the United States. Among the first Americans to use the medium was Boardman Robinson, previously a contributor to the *Masses* and the *Liberator*, who painted his first frescoes in 1927.

Because the Mexican fresco painters have so greatly affected art in the United States, the story of the two most influential communists among them, Siqueiros and Rivera, is worth noting here in more detail. In 1922 Siqueiros, the most violently revolutionary of all the Mexican artists, was a leader in founding what became known as the Revolutionary Syndicate (i.e., Union) of Technical Workers, Painters, Sculptors, and Allied Trades, of which Rivera and Orozco were also members. This was in part inspired by Spanish syndicalism and Russian communism. Siqueiros early joined the Mexican Communist Party, in 1923 was elected a member of its executive committee, and soon became an ardent Stalinist. He first came to the United States in 1932, and at Los Angeles executed in automobile paint (as a new and revolutionary material expressive of the industrial age) a series of murals in a workers' settlement. So revolutionary and inflammatory was the content of these paintings that he was shortly compelled to leave the country. In 1934, however, he held a successful exhibition in New York, returned to New York early in

1936 as a delegate to the first American Artists' Congress, and at that time was "active more or less officially as court artist to the Communist Party until he left in 1937 to join the Government [Loyalist] military forces in Spain."[200] On May 24, 1940, he is said to have led the band of Mexican communists who, disguised as policemen, made an abortive attempt to assassinate Trotsky three months before he was murdered.[201]

In contrast to Siqueiros, who has had comparatively little influence in this country outside of communist circles, Rivera for a time had a tremendous vogue with many North American "capitalist" patrons to whom his beliefs, and hence the content of his art, were really anathema. And this was true also of the Mexican revolutionary Orozco.

Rivera, who had joined the Mexican Communist Party in 1922 and, with Siqueiros, had been made a member of its executive committee the following year, first entered the United States in 1930. After a trip to Russia in 1927-1928 he had fallen out with the Stalinists and had become an ardent follower of Trotsky. For, as Rivera said later, he too believed in "complete freedom for art";[202] and this point of view was opposed by the Stalinists as art for art's sake. It was Rivera who in 1936 secured asylum for Trotsky in Mexico, and Trotsky once praised Rivera as the greatest of all the interpreters of the October Revolution.[203] Certainly Rivera never concealed the fact that he believed in violent revolution: for example, in 1932 he wrote in an American periodical, "I want to be a propagandist of Communism. . . . I want to use my art as a weapon."[204] And in a manifesto which he issued in 1938 jointly with André Breton, the French poet and founder of surrealism, Rivera stated: "We believe that the supreme task of art in our epoch is to take part actively and consciously in the preparation of the revolution."[205]

It is significant that this manifesto was issued by Rivera,. then a Trotskyist, in collaboration with a surrealist because many of the chief surrealists, under Breton's leadership, in theory frequently supported Marxist communism. Like Marxism, surrealism seeks to discredit bourgeois ideology, which it does by attempting to destroy all existing conservative and academic conceptions in art. Thus Dali, the celebrated surrealist painter—who first visited this country in 1934, moved here to live in

200 L. E. Schmeckebier, *Modern Mexican Art* (Minneapolis, 1939), p. 162. See also Elliot Clay, "Siqueiros: Artist in Arms," *Masses & Mainstream*, Vol. 4, No. 4 (Apr. 1951), pp. 60-73.

201 Gitlow, *The Whole of Their Lives*, p. 343. See also L. A. Sánchez Salazar and Julián Gorkin, *Murder in Mexico* (London, 1950), *passim*.

202 André Breton and Diego Rivera, "Manifesto: Towards a Free Revolutionary Art," *Partisan Review*, Vol. 6, No. 1 (Fall 1938), p. 51.

203 Trotsky, "Art and Politics," *op.cit.*, p. 7.

204 Diego Rivera, "The Revolutionary Spirit in Modern Art," *Modern Quarterly*, Vol. 6, No. 3 (Autumn 1932), p. 57.

205 Breton and Rivera, *op.cit.*, p. 52.

1940, and has had an immense vogue which has especially affected American advertising art—once said, "The whole Surrealist faction is rapidly evolving towards a complete acceptance of the Communist cultural platform."[206] However, insofar as surrealists woo the irrational by seeking to express the individual's subconscious existence, rather than—like Marx —the realistic aspects of social existence including conscious action in a material world, surrealism is not accepted by Stalinists. In fact, when once the surrealists offered their services to the Soviet Union, Stalin promptly declined the offer as "impractical," whereupon Breton and most other surrealists became Trotskyists although a few other prominent surrealists (including Tristan Tzara, founder of the earlier art movement known as dada) became active Communist Party members in their respective countries.[207] Yet even if in theory many surrealists are communists of one variety or another, in actuality they tend toward a kind of anarchistic individualism which they inherited from dadaism, a movement in which Breton as well as many other surrealists had participated and which, as already noted, had communistic connections.[208]

But to return to Rivera and his vogue in the United States even among anti-Marxist circles: in 1929, the year before Rivera first came here, he had been awarded a gold medal by the relatively conservative American Institute of Architects. Two years later the Arts Commission of Detroit, of which Edsel Ford was chairman, awarded him a commission for a series of frescoes in the Detroit Institute of Fine Arts. Much controversy was aroused by these and still more by the frescoes soon commissioned for Rockefeller Center in New York. A portrait of Lenin (Fig. 54), which Rivera insisted on placing in a fresco at Rockefeller Center in 1933, caused the Rockefeller management to interrupt the work, pay off the artist, and eventually to have the fresco destroyed, thereby stirring up a tremendous furor in the art world.[208a]

One of Rivera's assistants at Rockefeller Center was the American

---

[206] Quoted by T. H. Robsjohn-Gibbings, op.cit., p. 225. Dali was later attacked by the surrealist leader André Breton as having revealed Fascist tendencies by painting a portrait of one of Franco's ambassadors: see Wallace Fowlie, Age of Surrealism (Denver, Colo., 1950), p. 106. Breton, a former member of the French Communist Party who eventually underwent a sharp revulsion against communism, came to the United States during World War II.

[207] Robsjohn-Gibbings, op.cit., pp. 192-93. In its emphasis on the subconscious, surrealism has, of course, Freudian implications. While Freudianism had some supporters in Russia until the middle 1930's, it has since been completely rejected as bourgeois doctrine: see Joseph Wortis, Soviet Psychiatry (Baltimore, 1950), especially pp. 71-102 and 120.

[208] See Barr, Cubism and Abstract Art, p. 17; also Herbert Read, The Politics of the Unpolitical (London, 1943), p. 129.

[208a] With the proceeds from this fresco, Rivera painted a Marxist version of American history in the Lovestoneite New Workers' School in New York.

artist Ben Shahn, who had attracted the attention of Rivera by a series of paintings of Sacco and Vanzetti (Fig. 56). Shahn himself had become interested in socialism partly through the Sacco-Vanzetti case itself and, earlier, by reading Ernest Poole's novel of social reform, *The Harbor*.[209] Drawings by Shahn appeared in early issues of *Masses & Mainstream*.

According to many opponents of communism, some of the boldest attempts made by communists or their sympathizers to influence Americans by means of art have been made through the medium of the motion picture, which, it will be recalled, Lenin had praised as the most significant and powerful weapon of propaganda. In the 1920's Charlie Chaplin was only the most prominent of several movie actors accused of sympathy for radical causes. In 1930 a considerable uproar was aroused by the fact that the great Soviet Russian director, Eisenstein, signed a contract with Paramount Pictures at $3,000 a week. Six months later, after a violent campaign against Eisenstein in which he was repeatedly assailed as a "Red Dog," the famous director was dismissed by Paramount without being allowed to begin a picture. All he had accomplished was to prepare two scenarios— one of them made from Theodore Dreiser's *An American Tragedy* with the hearty approval of the author, who much later was to become a communist himself. After the Paramount episode, Eisenstein conceived the idea of making a picture in Mexico and obtained the backing of Upton Sinclair, the famous socialist writer. Sinclair raised the money, took charge of editing the immense amount of film sent back from Mexico by Eisenstein, and had it condensed into a motion picture issued in 1933 under the title of *Thunder over Mexico*. This was disapproved by Eisenstein, whose supporters maintained that Sinclair had carefully edited out all revolutionary implications.

Perhaps the largest amount of public discussion over the question of communism in Hollywood was stirred up during the autumn of 1947 when several actors, directors, and others in the motion-picture industry testified before the Committee of the House of Representatives on Un-American Activities that communists or fellow travelers were dominating the Screen Writers' Guild. Various members of the Guild were brought before the Committee, and several of them were cited for contempt of Congress on refusing to state whether or not they were or had been members of the Communist Party, and were eventually jailed. One of them was Albert Maltz who had been made a scapegoat among American party-liners in February 1946 because he had the bad luck to write for the *New Masses* an article entitled "What Shall We Ask of Writers?" just before Stalin signaled for the post-war cultural purges.

[209] J. D. Morse, "Ben Shahn: an Interview," *Magazine of Art*, Vol. 37, No. 4 (April 1944), pp. 136-37. Sacco and Vanzetti were anarchists.

In 1951 the Committee on Un-American Activities likewise subpoenaed a number of prominent actors and other important figures in the film industry. Some of them—including actors Larry Parks and Sterling Hayden—testified that they were former members of the Communist Party but had broken off their communist connections.

Also well known in Hollywood was Hanns Eisler, the German-born composer against whom a writ of deportation was issued early in 1948 when he was accused of having joined the German Communist Party in 1926. Eisler (whose brother, Gerhart Eisler, was denounced by the Committee on Un-American Activities as the number-one communist agent in the United States and was later to jump bail and flee as a stowaway on the Polish motor ship *Batory*) had come to this country in 1940. He had soon made a reputation for his motion-picture scores and other music, and according to various ex-communists was prominent in spreading communist propaganda in the musical world.[210] Charged with being an undesirable alien, Hanns Eisler left the United States while his case was pending.

Such direct, or allegedly direct, connections as the above between Marxism and the arts in America have, however, been relatively limited in number and influence. As everyone knows, there are fundamental differences between Marxism and the American tradition, differences which so far have prevented Marxism from having a very wide appeal in this country, certainly in any direct way. Not the least of these differences is the characteristic American insistence on the political freedom of the individual now, and not just later in some future classless society. And this emphasis on individual freedom now (which if anything has more in common with aspects of anarchist theory than with Marxism) has usually had a particular appeal for artists, who almost by definition are exceptional individuals more or less individualistic by temperament. Consequently, Americans in general and American artists in particular, even those who feel that adequate economic freedom from want is lacking in this country, are likely to resent the kind of political and social regimentation which Marxians themselves ordinarily consider to be inherent in Marxism until the Marxian goal of the classless society has been achieved, and which is so pronounced in the "democratic centralism" of the Communist Party.

[210] *New York Herald Tribune*, Feb. 13, 1948, p. 21. Hanns Eisler wrote the music for the dramatization of Gorky's *The Mother*, which played in New York in 1935 and which has been called "unadorned Communist propaganda" by Ruth Fischer, *Stalin and German Communism*, p. 615. According to Budenz, *Men without Faces*, p. 241, Eisler had "served since 1935 as head of the International Music Bureau, connected with the Communist International, the purpose of which was to spread pro-Soviet allegiance among musicians, musical critics and composers the world over."

But although the *direct* effects of Marxism have been relatively limited in American art taken as a whole, there have been important factors helping to spread the *indirect* influence of Marxist, and especially of Russian Marxist, art in this country. In some cases this indirect and often unconscious influence has resulted from efforts within the American democratic tradition to meet the threat of Marxism by seeking to overcome various economic problems of capitalist society which have aroused the sharpest Marxist criticism, problems which in some cases, according to some critics of capitalism, have been better solved in Soviet Russia. Much art of social protest in the United States has been of this nature.

In other cases, the indirect impact of Marxism on non-Marxist art in America has been made possible by the fact that there are certain characteristics common to Marxism and the American democratic tradition which therefore encourage similar tendencies in the arts. Thus, both Marxism and American democracy, in theory if not in practice, tend to emphasize the virtues of a classless society, although the one stresses economic equality in the ownership of the means of production, the other political equality combined with equality of economic opportunity. Largely as a result of this jointly equalitarian spirit, in both cases (though much more so in Russia) the artist is under heavy pressure from the society in which he lives to conform to the prevailing mores. Moreover, both Marxism and the American tradition share an optimistic belief in progress and in the special importance of industrial and technological progress. Both, therefore, have tended to glorify the engineer and the manager of industry as "practical" men of action, rather than the "impractical" artist, and have tended also to regard art which does not serve some directly utilitarian purpose as irrelevant to "real" life. Like most working-class and middle-class people of our twentieth-century industrial civilization, the average proletarian Russian and the average middle-class American have both generally preferred relatively literal and "realistic" storytelling in art. It was no doubt largely for this reason that the superlatively realistic acting of the Moscow Art Theater not only was enthusiastically received when its troupe came to the United States in 1923, but has brought that Theater special recognition from the Soviet government under Stalin.

Besides the characteristics common to Marxism and the general American democratic tradition which have indirectly made it easier for some aspects of Marxist art to influence art in America, there are also, of course, Marxist characteristics which for several different reasons have appealed to special groups in the United States, many of them not socialist or communist sympathizers. Thus the high degree of contemporaneity, of "modernness," emphasized by much Marxist art—for example, by Soviet futurism and constructivism in the years immediately following the Revolution of 1917, and by the early Soviet films such as Eisenstein's *Potemkin*[211]—has had an appeal not only to American faddists and cultural snobs, but at the same time to many sincere artists, critics, and collectors interested in new means of expression often quite apart from any Marxist content. Then, too, the international spirit of this early Soviet art and of that of the Trotskyists has attracted many Americans with a cosmopolitan point of view, including many sincere and well-educated people who believe that true culture, true civilization, must transcend national boundaries. The Marxian emphasis on the common people has been sympathetically received by many democratic Americans, including many artists, some of them communists or socialists and some not, who have come to believe that most American art has lost touch with the everyday realities of American life. This point of view, for example, was characteristic of John Sloan and other members of the group of artists known to their detractors as the "Ash-can School": it is clearly reflected in the subject matter of Sloan's painting, "Backyards, Greenwich Village" (Fig. 50), executed in 1914 when Sloan was art editor of the *Masses* as well as a member of the Socialist Party. The tendency to regard art as a form of social expression rather than solely the product of an individual temperament achieved its widest currency in the United States during the great depression of the 1930's. It is the point of view reflected in the then widely popular "social-protest" painting of such artists with leftist sympathies as Gropper, Philip Evergood, and Mervin Jules. It was reflected also in the attitude of Stuart Davis toward his seemingly abstract paintings. And to a somewhat lesser degree it could be seen in the subject matter of works by Henry Billings, Moses and Raphael Soyer, and many other socially conscious painters of the period. In those days, indeed, it was the point of view accepted by many average Americans who had no real interest in Marxism *per se* but whose attention had been newly focused on economic and social problems by the depression.

Thus it must be remembered that aspects of Marxist art have appealed to many Americans and to American institutions for reasons that are not necessarily Marxist at all. Among such American institutions may be cited the Museum of Modern Art and the New School for Social Research in New York. The New School, for example, in 1930-1931 helped to popularize the Mexican fresco painters by giving wall space to Orozco (who, as noted above, was in sympathy with many aspects of Marxism)

---

[211] *Potemkin* was first shown in New York during the autumn of 1926. It (together with Pudovkin's *Mother*) had been highly praised by Mary Pickford and Douglas Fairbanks when they returned from a trip to Russia in the previous summer. Only one or two minor Russian films had circulated earlier in the United States. See J. Freeman, "The Soviet Cinema," in *Voices of October*, p. 217.

for his mural, *Russia* (Fig. 55), depicting Lenin, Stalin, and other Soviet leaders. Yet at the same time the authorities of the New School had Thomas Benton, the aggressively American regionalist, paint his murals of New York life entitled *City Activities*; so that the New School, although somewhat left of center in its approach to many educational and social problems, could scarcely be accused of being deliberately "communistic" or "socialistic" in any political sense.[211a]

More important has been the New York Museum of Modern Art, which since its founding in 1929 has necessarily been concerned with all new art movements, including those of Soviet Russia as well as others influenced by Soviet Russia. But the Museum of Modern Art has been interested primarily in new artistic *media* and *forms* rather than in any one specific kind of content, so that in most of its exhibition catalogues all mention of the political sympathies of even the most politically minded artists has been omitted. Because of its focus on modern art forms, particular attention has had to be paid to the more abstract and expressionistic kinds of art, including surrealism and including also the International Style in architecture, which was actually given its name by members of the Museum's staff.[212] Among the examples of recent art exhibited at the Museum have been many derived from, or influenced by, those varieties of early Soviet art which Lenin and Stalin condemned as too abstract and as therefore lacking in proper Marxist content. Thus, one of the American artists most favored by the Museum has been Alexander Calder, noted for his "mobiles" and "stabiles" constructed in wire and sheet metal. Yet the mobile, or construction that moves, was invented not by Calder, but by the Russian constructivist Naum Gabo, who, inspired by the constructions of Picasso, had executed as early as 1920 a moving construction which he called *Kinetic Model*.[213] The close relation between the forms of some of Calder's earlier works and this kind of Russian constructivism seems particularly obvious if *Kiki's Nose* (Fig. 57), one of Calder's stabiles (or nonmoving constructions) made in 1931, is compared with the painting *Abstraction* (Fig. 58), executed by the Russian constructivist Lissitsky about 1922.[214] But although some of Calder's

[211a] It is true that Benton's work was included in an exhibition on "The Social Viewpoint in Art," organized by the John Reed Club of New York in 1933, a fact suggesting that his regionalism was then not so pronounced as it later became.

[212] P. C. Johnson, Museum of Modern Art, *Mies van der Rohe* (New York, 1947), p. 43. It was so named by H.-R. Hitchcock and Johnson at the insistence of Alfred H. Barr, Jr. Barr and Johnson were (and are) members of the Museum's staff.

[213] See Ruth Olson and Abraham Chanin, Museum of Modern Art, *Naum Gabo; Antoine Pevsner* (New York, 1948), p. 18; also J. J. Sweeney, Museum of Modern Art, *Alexander Calder* (New York, 1943), p. 33. The latter rightly points out that Calder developed the mobile further than Gabo.

[214] Calder was trained as an engineer and thus not unnaturally tended to be sympathetic to the constructivists' glorification of "the Machine." In his mobiles Calder

works (especially before he came under the influence of the surrealist Miró) do show the influence of some elements of constructivism, this does not mean that they therefore necessarily reflect a Russian Marxist content. For that matter, it will be recalled that Gabo, the originator of mobiles (who with his brother, Antoine Pevsner, was given a special exhibition at the Museum of Modern Art in 1948), had left Russia with those constructivists who were *not* willing to devote the subject, form, and content of their art solely to the revolution.

While special attention has been devoted by the Museum to many abstract tendencies in modern painting and sculpture and to that related movement in architecture which it named the International Style, it has, of course, by no means restricted itself to these. For one thing, like the New School for Social Research, it has helped to encourage that modern revival of relatively realistic mural painting in fresco which, though it happened to originate with Mexican communist and revolutionary artists, spread far beyond revolutionary circles and was accepted by many who had no connection whatever with socialism or communism. The Museum has similarly shown much interest in the arts of South America simply for their contributions to modern art. The fact that—along with the works of numerous South American noncommunist artists—the Museum of Modern Art, like other American museums, has exhibited the paintings of the Brazilian communist Candido Portinari[215] is thus essentially irrelevant, the more so because Portinari's communism has not been very specifically expressed in his art aside from his interest in subjects dealing with the laboring man.

The Museum of Modern Art has also encouraged interest in folk art, partly because folk art, like other "primitive" arts, has been glorified by admirers of abstraction for its expressive simplification and distortion of the forms of nature. Thus the Museum's approach to folk art is very different from that of Stalinist Russia, where this point of view would be attacked as "formalistic." Moreover, in Stalinist Russia, in contrast to the United States, a distinction is drawn between primitive art and folk art because Marxians look upon primitive art as the product of a prehistoric classless society, whereas folk art, they say, is produced in societies

---

also reflects the influence of Mondrian, the Dutch De Stijl painter: he was led to enter the field of abstract art by a visit to Mondrian's Paris studio in 1930. See Sweeney, *op.cit.*, p. 28, and the *Museum of Modern Art Bulletin*, Vol. 18, No. 3 (Spring 1951), p. 8.

[215] The exhibition was held in 1940. In 1941 Portinari painted four frescoes on the walls of the Hispanic Foundation of the Library of Congress at Washington, frescoes paid for with funds appropriated by the Brazilian government and the Office of the Coordinator of Inter-American Affairs headed by Nelson Rockefeller. Portinari was one of the leading Brazilian communists who fled to Montevideo early in 1948: see *Time*, Jan. 19, 1948, p. 40.

with class divisions and will therefore disappear when the forthcoming classless society is achieved. Nevertheless, in both the United States and Soviet Russia, folk art can to some degree be admired as an expression of the "common man" everywhere as well as an expression of regionalistic nationalism. The great exhibition of folk art held at the Museum of Modern Art in 1932 was entitled *American Folk Art: the Art of the Common Man in America, 1750-1900.* And it is significant that this exhibition, which foreshadowed the revival of folk art under the New Deal, was held during the depths of the depression when interest in the problems of the common man was being partly, if indirectly, aroused by Marxist criticism of capitalism as the cause of those problems. In the years that followed, also, the Museum helped to foster certain kinds of art (notably those connected with public housing and large-scale planning) by means of which the New Deal was seeking to solve some of the economic and social problems that had come to a head during the depression, problems that in some cases had been encountered also in Soviet Russia.

Everyone knows how under the New Deal the federal government, and to a lesser degree the state governments, undertook a much greater responsibility for the welfare of citizens of lower than average income. Although the question is still occasionally debated as to whether the New Deal was "socialism," most authorities now seem to agree than in Franklin D. Roosevelt's view the New Deal was engaged not in fostering socialism but in tiding capitalism over a series of crises—that it was, indeed, not a single over-all plan but a series of extemporizations[216] in the form of state capitalism. Certainly the Communist Party had at first sharply opposed Roosevelt, and continued to do so after the American recognition of Soviet Russia in 1933. Late in 1935, however, the Communist Party reversed itself and began to support the New Deal, including its art projects, in harmony with the changing Russian foreign policy. For with the Seventh World Congress of the Communist International, held at Moscow in July 1935, the new Russian policy of a Popular Front against fascism had finally been defined.[217] Once this shift in the party line had taken place, the American Communist Party—though under attack from the Special House Committee for the Investigation of Un-American Activities as set up in 1938 under the chairmanship of Martin Dies—continued to support Roosevelt until October 1939. In that month its leader, Earl Browder, was arrested for passport fraud, some two months after the Nazi-Soviet nonaggression pact. Following the Nazi attack on

216 For example, this view of the New Deal was expressed by Miss Frances Perkins, Roosevelt's Secretary of Labor, in a speech before the Program in American Civilization, Princeton University, Mar. 8, 1950.

217 The policy of the Popular Front had, however, been tentatively formulated as early as 1933. See Gitlow, *The Whole of Their Lives*, pp. 257-58.

Russia, Roosevelt again received communist support, but this was once more withdrawn from the Democrats after World War II.

Yet even though the New Deal was originally opposed by American communists, its emphasis on social welfare, as opposed to individualistic laissez faire, had early helped to pave the way for some indirect Marxist influence in this country largely because many of the problems of the New Deal were somewhat similar to those already met by Soviet Russia. In particular, Russia had already developed a very concentrated organization for centralizing both the national and social aspects of planning on a huge scale. Such planning—which in Russia was based on the Marxian doctrine that man differs from other animals in consciously planning to achieve social goals[218]—had commenced when Lenin formed a state planning commission as early as 1920, but had greatly increased in importance with the Five Year Plans, the first of which began in 1928. Since the New Deal felt the necessity of developing a much greater amount of large-scale planning than had ever before been known in this country, the Russian example doubtless was something of a spur to the United States as well as to many other countries hit by the depression.[219]

When bitter controversy arose over the degree of centralization that might be permitted in the United States, at first the tendency under the leadership of the more radical elements within the New Deal was for a considerable amount of centralization. As time went on, however, partly as a kind of reaction against the ever increasing centralization of power that was taking place in Soviet Russia under Stalin, it gradually became evident that the American planners who in the long run received the approval of large numbers of their countrymen were those who held that neither large-scale planning nor its administration should be too completely centralized. The Tennessee Valley Authority, for example, with its vast engineering and architectural works, was finally carried through successfully under the direction of David Lilienthal, who believes in a multiple economy in which centralized planning under government auspices is restricted to a limited number of certain kinds of problems, and who even then urges that the administration of all plans be decentralized.[220] And Robert Moses, New York City's great planner of parks and parkways who has had so profound an effect on American landscape and highway design, has always insisted that regional and local decentralization of governmental authority in planning is necessary if the American democratic tradition is to be preserved.

[218] For a summary of Marx's views on planning, see especially Vernon Venable, *Human Nature: the Marxian View* (New York, 1946), particularly p. 78 and pp. 155ff.
[219] For the relation of socialism and of Soviet Russia to planning, see Edward H. Carr, *The Soviet Impact on the Western World* (New York, 1947), pp. 20ff.
[220] D. E. Lilienthal, *T.V.A.—Democracy on the March* (New York and London, 1944), chaps. 14, 15, 18.

During the New Deal, as part of its large-scale plans for combating the depression, the federal government, with the encouragement of President Roosevelt himself, first faced the problem of enabling artists to survive by giving them government commissions.[221] Late in 1933 the Department of the Treasury set up a relief program under which nearly 4,000 needy artists executed some 700 murals in public buildings as well as over 15,000 other works of art before the project closed in the following summer. The Treasury then launched a somewhat different project aimed less at relief than at the decoration of public buildings by the most competent artists available. Meanwhile, the Federal Art Project of the Works Progress Administration was established in 1935 to take over relief for other artists, enrolling at its peak over 6,000 persons. Before it came to a close in 1939 the members of the project had developed an enormous Index of American Design, had conducted free art classes averaging 60,000 students a month, and had painted many additional murals in public buildings, besides carrying on numerous other activities.

Because the Mexican fresco painters, and especially the communist Diego Rivera, had begun to have a great vogue in this country just before the New Deal began, it is not surprising that the influence of these men was felt in many of the mural paintings executed under the various New Deal projects, most of them by artists who were not socialists, communists, or fellow travelers. The influence of the Mexicans sometimes manifested itself directly in the use of the revived fresco technique, and less directly in helping to foster subject matter with more conscious "social significance," more criticism of economic and social conditions, than had previously been found in American art. Fairly typical examples of this socially-conscious subject matter—although particularly well executed—are the murals which Henry Varnum Poor painted in 1935 under the second art project of the Department of the Treasury for the Department of Justice Building in Washington (Fig. 59). In one of them entitled *T.V.A. Worker*, the chief figure is depicted with a kind of halo, apparently because he is engaged in working on a great social project and is therefore considered to be especially worthy of canonization by mankind. Whereas in the companion mural, *Pleading the Gold Case*, the lawyer who pleads for the retention of the gold standard is represented as thin-lipped and sharp-faced presumably because he was believed to place the value of gold above that of humanity.

One mural sponsored by this second phase of the Treasury Department's program aroused particular controversy. This was one of the two

[221] The original suggestion is said to have come from Roosevelt's friend and former schoolmate, the artist George Biddle, who had been impressed by hearing that the Mexican government had hired Rivera, Orozco, and other artists to paint murals in public buildings at mechanics' wages.

murals painted by Rockwell Kent for the Federal Post Office Building in Washington, and installed in 1937. Part of the painting, the subject of which was the delivery of mail to Puerto Rico by airplane, depicted a colored woman holding a letter on which was an inscription in a strange language. When eventually the language was recognized as Eskimo, the inscription was translated by the Arctic explorer Stefansson as follows: "To the peoples of Puerto Rico, our friends. Go ahead, let us change chiefs. That alone can make us equal and free." Whereupon Kent was accused of urging revolt.[222]

Not very long thereafter, in 1939, an investigator for the Committee on Un-American Activities stated before it that Kent was a communist, presumably because Kent was known to be a member of a considerable number of organizations usually considered as part of the Communist Front.[223] Kent promptly wrote to Martin Dies, the chairman of the Committee, maintaining that he was not a member of the Communist Party, that his opinions and public actions had never been influenced by the party and that he had never held or advanced views to any degree inconsistent with our American democracy.[224] It would seem, therefore, if Kent's own repeated statements are accepted, that he is one of the considerable number of American artists who sympathize with many of the social aims of Marxian communism, but who are too individualistic ever to conform completely to the rigid control of the Communist Party. Yet, among other activities, he has been a contributing editor of the *New Masses*, served as chairman of a conference supporting the *Daily Worker* in April 1945, and was president of the International Workers Order, a fraternal insurance agency founded in 1930 which has been described as "organized by Communists and . . . under the control of Communists from the beginning. . . ."[225]

It was natural for many of the artists who participated in the art projects of the New Deal, especially those who worked for the W.P.A., to develop a new interest in the point of view of the workingman, for

[222] See Rockwell Kent, *This Is My Own* (New York, 1940), p. 307.

[223] In 1949 and in 1951 the House Committee on Un-American Activities listed Kent as having been "affiliated with at least eighty-five Communist-front organizations": see the *New York Times*, Apr. 19, 1949, p. 6, and the *New York Herald Tribune*, Apr. 5, 1951, p. 39.

[224] Kent, *op.cit.*, pp. 356-57.

[225] See Budenz, *Men without Faces*, pp. 211 and 191. In April 1951 Kent, as president of the International Workers Order, was a witness before the New York Supreme Court in a suit brought by the State Insurance Department in an effort to have the I.W.O. dissolved on the ground that it was communist dominated: see the *New York Herald Tribune*, Apr. 4, 1951, p. 19, and Apr. 5, p. 2. Late in June 1951 a justice of the New York Supreme Court ordered the "dissolution and liquidation" of the I.W.O. as a "political front for a revolutionary group": *ibid.*, July 1, 1951, section 2, p. 3.

like workingmen and unlike most artists, W.P.A. artists were paid according to a fixed scale of wages. Understandably, therefore, they too formed trade unions to protect their common interests, and in some cases these trade unions and similar organizations of artists were no doubt partly inspired by prototypes which existed in Mexico and also in Soviet Russia, and which there had been founded under the auspices of members of Communist parties. Among the most prominent of the American organizations were the Artists' Union, which was established in 1933; the United American Artists, which became an affiliate of the C.I.O.; and the American Artists' Congress, founded in 1936 to combat war and fascism and to defend the individual artist's civil rights through collective action.[226] The Artists' Union for three years (1934-1937) published a magazine, *Art Front*, to which such well-known radical artists as Gropper, Lozowick, and Maurice Becker contributed, and of which Ben Shahn and Stuart Davis were editors. Not only did communists found some of the artists' organizations of this kind, but within some of them they greatly helped to encourage the spread of proletarian subject matter already popularized among leftist artists by the John Reed clubs. Moreover, in some cases communists made every effort to take over artists' organizations, and members who declined to follow the party line were driven out. For example, several leading members of the American Artists' Congress, including the painters George Biddle and Niles Spencer, the sculptor William Zorach, and the critic-historians Lewis Mumford and Meyer Schapiro, resigned from the congress because they refused to approve the Russian attack on Finland.[227] As a result of occasional episodes of this kind, many conservatives and some middle of the roaders became convinced that not only the artists' organizations founded during the New Deal but the art projects of the New Deal itself were all helping to lead directly to the triumph of communism in the United States. Thus, shortly after the House Committee on Un-American Activities had reported in January 1939 that "a rather large number of the employees on the Federal Theater Project are either members of the Communist Party or are sympathetic to the Communist Party," Congress cut off all appropriations, and the project was forced to close.

In addition to penetrating many of the art organizations under the New Deal, American communists and their sympathizers also often supported

[226] H. M. Kallen, *Art and Freedom* (New York, 1942), II, pp. 895-96.

[227] *Art Digest*, Vol. 14, No. 15 (May 1, 1940), p. 14. The American Artists' Congress and the United American Artists joined with the League of American Writers in running an Artists' and Writers' Congress which met early in June 1941, and which passed a resolution condemning the European war as "a brutal shameless struggle," two weeks before Germany invaded Russia. A few weeks later most of these organizations were calling for the utmost aid to Soviet Russia.

the efforts of American minorities, and particularly the Negro minority, to achieve equal rights in the arts as well as in other aspects of American life. This was part of a large-scale attempt to win Negroes to communism, and during the early years of the depression was carried on under the slogan "Self-Determination for Negroes in the Black Belt" in accordance with a program laid down in 1928 by the Sixth World Congress of the Comintern. In 1925 communists had been responsible for organizing the American Negro Labor Congress, later called the League of Struggle for American Rights. In 1936 they had helped to establish the National Negro Congress. This was captured completely by the communists in 1940, but by 1947 was dissolved, according to some authorities because the communists had decided to devote their full attention to infiltrating and capturing the National Association for the Advancement of Colored People—an attempt which failed.

As long as the revolutionary slogan, "Self-Determination in the Black Belt," prevailed, American communists often sought to foster revolutionary Negro art. However, in 1935 the communist line changed as part of the change in world communist strategy. For now, with the Popular Front against fascism, the communists subordinated the idea of revolution to that of democratic resistance to fascism. In American Negro affairs this meant that the party line now for a time supported the position of the National Association for the Advancement of Colored People, which had formerly been attacked as "reformist." Following the Nazi-Soviet pact, moreover, the communists ceased to emphasize the importance of the American Negro and Negro art because of the Nazi notions of race. And even after Nazi Germany attacked the Soviet Union in 1941 all agitation for Negro rights (and, correspondingly, for Negro art) continued to be played down, but for a different reason. For now the communists feared that self-conscious militancy on the part of American Negroes would destroy national unity: at a time when the primary goal of the Soviet Union was to win the war, other aims had to be postponed. But once World War II had ended and postwar tensions began to increase between Russia and her wartime allies, the communists once more revived the program of "Self-Determination in the Black Belt," and in 1951 even moved their national party headquarters to Harlem. Again some attempt was made to foster Negro art.

One of the most important Negroes won over to sympathy with Soviet Russia and important aspects of the party line was Dr. W. E. B. Du Bois, the educator and writer who eventually became a contributing editor of the *New Masses* and *Masses & Mainstream*. A founder of the National Association for the Advancement of Colored People (in which he was a major figure until asked to resign in 1948), Dr. Du Bois had begun to urge as early as 1915 that due recognition be given to Negro artists in the United States.[228] And this movement had been aided by a growing interest in African Negro sculpture which as early as 1907 had inspired Picasso in the experiments leading to the development of cubism and other phases of the modern movement in art. Interest in the arts of the Negro has also been fostered by the increasing vogue for jazz, which at times has been praised by communists, among others, as an important American folk art. However, among communists the party line has varied in its point of view toward jazz, depending on the attitude toward folk art prevailing within the Soviet Union at the given time, on the prevailing party line toward minorities and the race problem, and on the attitude of Russia toward the United States.

In Russia itself, American jazz had first become widely known in 1925 when a small jazz band made up of American Negroes visited Moscow. With the extreme proletarianization of art under the first Five Year Plan, jazz fell into disfavor as a "bourgeois" product, but was revived in 1932 in connection with Stalin's new slogan, "Life is better, Life is gayer." In the middle thirties Russia even established a state jazz band. However, with the Nazi-Soviet pact of 1939, jazz began to decline once more; and under the anti-Americanism which has dominated Russian foreign policy since World War II, jazz has so completely lost official favor that the once enormously popular state jazz band has been abolished.

In those periods when jazz has been in favor in Russia, or else when the party line in the United States has especially sought to foster "Self-Determination in the Black Belt," the American Communist Party has usually upheld jazz either as a Negro "folk" art, or as a product of a minority downtrodden under "capitalism." During the 1930's, after the revival of jazz in Russia at the end of the first Five Year Plan, the party line in this country usually made a distinction between those aspects of jazz regarded as Negro folk music, and therefore considered good, and the more "commercial" varieties of jazz, which were looked upon as "capitalistic," and therefore bad. A somewhat different line has prevailed since World War II, with jazz now regarded as derived from the music of a laboring people, the American Negroes, and as representing a struggle led by Negro musicians to liberate music from the conditions imposed upon it by an evil "monopolized commodity production system." Bebop has been thought to show this contradiction and struggle within jazz in a

[228] See J. A. Porter, *Modern Negro Art* (New York, 1943), p. 98. Du Bois, besides being a founder of the N.A.A.C.P., was its director of publications and research from 1910 until 1934, and its director of special research from 1944 until 1948 when he was asked to resign at a time when he was active in behalf of Henry Wallace and of the Progressive Party. See Shirley Graham, "Why Was Du Bois Fired," *Masses & Mainstream*, Vol. 1, No. 9 (Nov. 1948), pp. 15-26; also Wilson Record, *The Negro and the Communist Party* (Chapel Hill, N.C., 1951), especially p. 264, note.

heightened form—as possessing "rich imaginative and inventive . . . qualities" on the one hand, and yet as also tending toward mere "barren
formalistic experiment" because of the conditions of modern life under
capitalism. But even at its worst, bebop is said to have the great advantage
of encouraging whites to collaborate with Negroes.[229]

According to some authorities on Negro art, it was the Federal Art
Project of the W.P.A. which gave many Negro artists their first real
chance to work on an equal basis with white men.[230] Certainly some of
the artists' organizations founded during the period of the New Deal
gave particularly strong support to the campaign for equal rights for
Negro artists. This was notably true of the Artists' Union, whose magazine,
Art Front, published articles on the problems of race, nationality, and
art, including one by the well-known art historian and critic, Meyer
Schapiro. In this article Schapiro subscribed to the more or less Marxian
view that social class rather than race or nation in the last analysis
determines "the conception of what is or should be American."[231]

One of the chief problems which faced the New Deal was the question
as to how far the federal government should enter the field of housing.
As everyone knows, the New Deal eventually encouraged government-
subsidized housing as the only way of securing adequate shelter for the
economically lowest third of the nation. However, so powerful was the
American tradition of private initiative in the building industry, so strong
the general opposition to "the government in business," that the only way
in which sufficient public support could be gained for housing legislation
was by putting it before the people not on its merits as a housing program
but as giving employment to workmen in the building trades.

For some time during the New Deal the communists were silent on the
housing question, both because they opposed Roosevelt until late in
1935, and because "orthodox" Marxians, following Engels, have ordinarily
opposed any alleviation of the workers' lot in an effort to avoid possible
postponement of the proletarian revolution. However, in September 1936,
the *Communist*, then the most authoritative party magazine in this country, finally came out in support of a housing program in an effort to win
working-class support and thereby gain control of the whole program.

The government-subsidized housing erected under the New Deal was

---

[229] For jazz in Russia see Jelagin, *op.cit.*, especially pp. 255ff. The party line in this
country is reflected in Sidney Finkelstein's discussion of jazz and bebop in "What
About Bebop?" *Masses & Mainstream*, Vol. 1, No. 7 (Sept. 1948), pp. 68-76; also
his book, *Jazz: a People's Music* (New York, 1948).

[230] Porter, *op.cit.*, p. 127.

[231] Meyer Schapiro, "Race, Nationality and Art," *Art Front*, Vol. 2, No. 4 (Mar.
1936), pp. 10-12. For Schapiro's views on art as an expression of class also see his
previously cited article in the *Marxist Quarterly*, "Nature of Abstract Art," especially
p. 88.

mostly of two chief types, both of which were derived ultimately from European prototypes originally developed, in part at least, under socialist influence, mainly because socialists were among the first to become interested in the housing problem. One of the two was that superblock type of row house oriented to the sun, and placed on the extra large city-block upheld in the various writings of the Fabian socialist, Raymond Unwin. As already indicated, this type of housing had been further developed in Austria and in Germany—both by socialists and by liberals such as Gropius—especially during the period of the Weimar Republic when social democracy had been particularly strong (Figs. 30 and 31). In the United States it has been much used for government-subsidized urban housing, such as the Williamsburg development in Brooklyn (Fig. 60), built in 1936-1937 under the Emergency Housing Division of the Public Works Administration but financed through private contracts. And more recently some of the principles—but some only—underlying this type of housing have been followed in real-estate developments built under private auspices, including Stuyvesant Town in Manhattan, erected after World War II by the Metropolitan Life Insurance Company.

The other variety of housing much used by the New Deal was the English garden city, "invented" by Ebenezer Howard and fostered by Fabianism and guild socialism. The actual buildings of the garden cities laid out under the New Deal (Fig. 61) show, however, some influence from German architecture of the International Style. These garden cities of the New Deal were also partly inspired by an earlier American garden city, Radburn, New Jersey, designed in 1929 under the influence of the English examples and like them built under private auspices. The garden-city type of government-built housing is best exemplified by the "Greenbelt" towns, four of which were projected, and three—Greenbelt, Maryland (Fig. 61), Greendale, Wisconsin, and Greenhills, Ohio—were carried out. Promoted by Rexford Tugwell as head of the Resettlement Administration primarily on the grounds of making work for building trades, they actually were in large part built by P.W.A. labor. Tugwell himself warmly believed in the ideas of Ebenezer Howard, while Clarence Stein, the able architect of Radburn who also served as adviser for the Greenbelt towns, is an avowed disciple of Howard and of Raymond Unwin, and likewise acknowledges the inspiration of his friend Lewis Mumford.

Although the Greenbelt towns followed the precedent of the English garden cities in being run as cooperatives, in them one of the most essential elements of the English garden city—namely, local industry—was not planned for. The result was that the towns almost inevitably became housing not for workingmen and their families but for members of the white-collar class with sufficient means to be able to commute to work in the nearest city. And with the return of prosperity and the decline of the New Deal, American suspicion of any business not conducted by individual private initiative once more increased in strength, so that in 1947 the cooperative stores at Greenbelt were being sharply assailed as monopolistic. But though not as yet wholeheartedly accepted by the entire American public, the new contributions to town planning made at Radburn and at the Greenbelt towns have exerted great influence abroad, and particularly in social democratic Sweden, communist Poland, and socialist Britain. Even in the United States more planned communities of this general type are being laid out under private initiative than is commonly supposed. Many of them are built or underwritten by great insurance companies as a form of investment—for example, Fresh Meadows (on Long Island in the outskirts of New York) and Park Forest (near Chicago), both begun in 1946.

The world-wide depression that gave rise to the New Deal in this country was, of course, also largely responsible for bringing the Nazis to power in Germany, and consequently for the migration of so many German artists to other countries including the United States. Because of their exaggerated nationalism, the Nazis violently opposed all modern abstract art, including the International Style in architecture, as being insufficiently national and Germanic. Thus some varieties of art important during the mildly socialistic Weimar Republic were now most sharply attacked. As already mentioned, the famous Bauhaus, like other centers of modern art in Germany, was closed as "bolshevistic" and "degenerate," in spite of the historical fact that the so-called "bolshevistic" art which it encouraged had long been proscribed in Soviet Russia itself.

It was during this period that several leading members of the Bauhaus group left Germany, notably Walter Gropius, Ludwig Mies van der Rohe, László Moholy-Nagy, and also Joseph Albers, Marcel Breuer, and Herbert Bayer. After only a brief stay in England, Gropius was called to Harvard, where he became chairman of the department of architecture in the Graduate School of Design, and where he called Breuer to join him for a time. Mies van der Rohe was made chairman of the department of architecture at Illinois Institute of Technology (then called Armour Institute); while Moholy-Nagy became the first head of the New Bauhaus in Chicago (later refounded and renamed the Institute of Design), of which he was still director at the time of his death in 1946. It will be recalled that Moholy-Nagy, with Albers, was responsible for developing at the Bauhaus a pedagogical method based in part on Russian constructivism, though with any specifically Russian or communist content omitted. This method of teaching he brought with him to the New Bauhaus and the Institute of Design at Chicago; and to a lesser degree,

741

also, it has been introduced at Harvard by Gropius, at Black Mountain College and Yale by Joseph Albers, and by Mies van der Rohe at the Illinois Institute of Technology with which the Chicago Institute of Design has now combined.

Most of the modern artists who left Germany when the Nazis were gaining power, and who migrated to the United States, are not socialists in any formal or active political sense even though often artistically radical. This is now true even of the painter George Grosz who, although he had participated in leftist political agitation in Germany immediately after World War I, had withdrawn from politics in the thirties after he came to this country to live. Nevertheless, many of these German architects and artists, like Gropius, regard themselves as stimulated by the artistic tradition of William Morris (who, it will be remembered, subscribed to some of the social and political principles of Marxism, though not to its materialism) so that they too believe in the close relationship of art to life, and thus to economic and social problems. However, their approach to such problems—like that of Morris himself—has usually had an ethical basis rather than the fundamentally economic basis characteristic of Marxism.

Of these émigré artists, Moholy-Nagy has exerted an especially strong influence on modern art in the United States, mainly through his books. We have already seen how as a youth in Hungary after World War I, Moholy-Nagy had come to consider himself a social, as well as an artistic, revolutionary, but his revolutionary art had been disapproved by the Hungarian Communist Party as too abstract and individualistic. Yet in spite of his almost anarchistic revolutionary individualism, Moholy-Nagy, like most other members of the Bauhaus group, was always deeply interested in social improvements and admired all who worked for social reform. That he regarded Marx and Lenin merely as two of those who had sought such reform is indicated in one of his books published in this country in which he wrote: "Under the pressure of new needs openminded resolute individuals emerged with fervent hopes for a better social order and for which they were ready to fight and sacrifice. . . . From the encyclopedists and Voltaire and Rousseau, the way led to Fourier, Proudhon, Marx, Bakunin, Kropotkin, Lenin. . . ." Nor did Moholy-Nagy limit himself to the socialists, anarchists, and communists just cited but went on to include in this list of social reformers scientists such as Einstein and Pavlov; several nonsocialist musicians, writers, and architects (including Gropius, Le Corbusier, and Frank Lloyd Wright); and several painters (among them Kandinsky, Picasso, the Russian suprematist Malevich, and the Dutch artist Mondrian).[232]

[232] László Moholy-Nagy, *Vision in Motion* (Chicago, 1947), p. 61.

Nevertheless, in certain respects Moholy-Nagy's point of view resembled that of Marx and apparently reflected in an indirect way the influence of Marxism. Like Marx, he maintained that "the so-called 'unpolitical' approach of art is a fallacy," and insisted that "the artist has a formative ideological function."[233] Like Marx, he attacked capitalism as a system imposed on labor, without plan in its social aspects, and with the end of squeezing out profits to their limit. Like Marx, again, he deplored the separation of fine and applied art and held that technological progress, in art as in everything else (Fig. 32), should be exploited for the benefit of all people and all peoples. But although he subscribed to the Marxian concept of the revolution, Moholy-Nagy—like the anarchist Bakunin, whom he greatly admired—sharply differed from Marx in his concept of the nature of the revolution. For he wholeheartedly agreed with Bakunin's statement that "a revolution must be social, not political,"[234] insisting that "the revolutionist should always remain conscious that the class struggle is, in the last analysis, not about capital, nor the means of production, but in actuality it concerns the right of an individual to a satisfying occupation, work that meets the inner needs, a normal way of life, and a real release of human powers."[235] In short, Moholy-Nagy rejected the primarily economic and political basis of Marxian materialism for an emphasis on the freedom of the individual now, rather than in some future classless society, a point of view also in sharp opposition to the authoritarian "democratic centralism" of Soviet Russia and of the Communist Party. And it was a point of view not only in sympathy with the anarchism of Bakunin or Kropotkin and the socialism of William Morris, but also with the individualism of the American democratic tradition. It is interesting to note in this connection that Moholy-Nagy's regard for democratic individualism seems to have increased during his years in the United States, doubtless as a result of the influence of the American environment upon him.[236]

Moholy-Nagy has been dealt with at length in this chapter primarily because of his sympathy with some aspects of anarchism and socialism, and because through his writings and teaching he has exerted such unusually wide influence on the arts of design in the United States. It must be remembered, however, that while other influential members of

[233] *Ibid.*, p. 29.   [234] Sibyl Moholy-Nagy, *Moholy-Nagy*, p. 234.
[235] L. Moholy-Nagy, *The New Vision* (New York, 1938), p. 16.
[236] See Moholy-Nagy, *Vision in Motion*, p. 48, where he interprets the word democracy, as he says, "in its essential original meaning, culminating in the philosophy of the best of the American revolutionaries, such as Jefferson, Paine and Whitman." While it is true that these great Americans have also been glorified by communists, particularly during the Popular Front, as exemplifying "democracy" in the Russian sense of the word, Moholy-Nagy's admiration for them seems to have been based on their individualism as well as on their democratic spirit.

743

the Bauhaus group have largely shared Moholy-Nagy's views in regard to design, many of them have not agreed with his political ideas. For example, we have seen that the political views of Walter Gropius, the founder of the Bauhaus, are those of a liberal and democrat who in art stresses the kind of cooperation and collective effort previously found in the medieval guild system and the ideas of William Morris. So important to Gropius is this kind of cooperation that the firm of eight American architects of which he is a member is actually called the Architects Collaborative, and all eight are considered to be on an entirely equal footing.

Clearly, then, while some aspects of Moholy-Nagy's philosophy could appeal to American democratic individualism, the point of view of Walter Gropius and other former members of the Bauhaus staff could in major respects appeal to that equalitarianism which is also such an important factor in the American tradition. It is thus not surprising that the Bauhaus group has been able to exert so profound an influence on the arts and on the education of artist and architect in the United States. Moreover, the theories of design held by the group have been fostered in the field of art criticism by the popularity in this country of the writings and lectures of Herbert Read, the famous English anarcho-socialist critic of art and literature. For like the Bauhaus, Read reflects in many ways the influence not only of William Morris but of constructivism as well; and his theory of art education has even been described by a friend as "based on a frank acceptance of the principles of the Bauhaus school to which he is attached by a natural predisposition."[237]

Because all of these men have to a considerable degree been interested in the social aspects of art and architecture they could be particularly influential during the 1930's when the depression had brought the United States to a new consciousness of social problems. At the same time, the cosmopolitanism of many of their theories of art could appeal to the increasing number of Americans who were becoming convinced that only through international cooperation can aggressor nations be controlled and further world wars prevented. Also the close attention that they have paid to solving local climatic problems in architecture could prove attractive to American regionalists. In thus appealing to American audiences on several different grounds, these artists, architects, and critics have been able to exert an enormous influence on American art and art education. And through the medium of their principles and beliefs perhaps the strongest indirect influence of some aspects (but some aspects only) of Marx's critique of capitalism has affected the art of the United States.

[237] See E. H. Ramsden, "Herbert Read's Philosophy of Art," in Herbert Treece, ed., *Herbert Read, an Introduction to His Work by Various Hands* (London, 1944), p. 48.

Yet because their social awareness, their collectivism, is fundamentally artistic rather than economic or political, they cannot justly be called Marxians. And because these men—whether socialists or liberals or simply artists—do not stress any specifically nationalistic spirit in art, they are far from having any basic sympathy for the variety of Marxism most powerful today, the relatively nationalistic Russian Marxism characteristic of Stalin and his followers including those communists in the United States who follow the Communist Party line.

Thus it is clear that attacks on *all* "modern" art as "Communistic" or "Socialistic"—attacks like that leveled by Representative Dondero of Michigan in a series of speeches delivered before the House in 1949[238]—cannot be accurate: the problem is not so simple as all that. For one thing, such attacks too often forget that before World War II many thoroughly patriotic Americans, disturbed by the rising power of nazism, joined organizations of the Popular Front which only later were to be considered subversive. Similarly, during World War II many loyal Americans, including many artists, considered it patriotic to admire the Russian stand and counterattack against the Nazis, and therefore innocently joined organizations to forward Russian-American friendship, some of which, however, were under communist control. Still other Americans, simply interested in fostering honest liberalism, joined groups later said to have been taken over by communist sympathizers, groups such as the Independent Citizens Committee of the Arts, Sciences and Professions, of which Mrs. Franklin D. Roosevelt was a member for a time. This committee, founded in 1944 as the Independent Voters Committee of Arts and Sciences to support the reelection of President Roosevelt, closely followed the Communist Party line and ended up

[238] For Dondero's speeches see the *Congressional Record*, Mar. 11, 1949, pp. 2364-65; Mar. 25, 1949, pp. 3297-98; May 17, 1949, pp. 6487-90; Aug. 16, 1949, pp. 11811-14. In his speech of August 16, Dondero attacked nonacademic art as communistic in the following words: "The human art termites, disciples of multiple 'isms' that compose so-called modern art, [are] boring industriously to destroy the high standards and priceless traditions of academic art. . . ." He went on to accuse all defenders of modern art of upholding the "party-line." Mr. Dondero apparently knew that the "isms" to which he objected were attacked by Lenin as early at 1920 and largely expelled from Russia, and that Stalin has continued to attack them as "formalistic" or "mechanistic."

For replies to Dondero, made by Representatives Plumley of Vermont and Javits of New York, see the *Congressional Record* for June 16, 1949, and August 23, 1949. In March 1950 the directors of the Museum of Modern Art in New York, the Institute of Contemporary Art, Boston, and the Whitney Museum of American Art, New York, issued "A Statement on Modern Art" in which they declared, "We . . . reject the assumption that art which is esthetically an innovation must somehow be socially or politically subversive, and therefore un-American. We deplore the reckless and ignorant use of political or moral terms in attacking modern art. We recall that the Nazis . . . and . . . the Soviets suppressed modern art. . . . and that Nazi officials insisted and Soviet officials still insist upon a hackneyed realism saturated with nationalistic propaganda."

among the backers of Henry Wallace. By that time many of the original noncommunist members had already resigned.[239] For American opposition to the communists had enormously increased, partly as a result of evidence uncovered by the House Committee on Un-American Activities in 1947, and especially as a result of communist activities in Greece, Italy, and France, and of the communist coup in Czechoslovakia early in 1948. On July 20, 1948, eleven of the leaders of the Communist Party were arrested by the F.B.I. and indicted under the Smith Act, passed in 1940, for conspiring to teach the overthrow of the United States government by force or violence. And on June 20, 1951 a year after the beginning of communist aggression in Korea, twenty-one additional leading communists were indicted under the same act. Among them was V. J. Jerome, the head of the cultural commission of the party.

For the purpose of counteracting this change in the American attitude, in 1948 the Kremlin had begun to place a renewed emphasis on propaganda for world peace, and communists began to foster a whole series of "peace congresses" in various parts of the world. In so doing, they were at first able to secure the support of a considerable number of liberals, including American liberals. The earliest of these congresses, held at Wroclaw, Poland (formerly Breslau, Germany) in August 1948, was attended by an American delegation, which included representatives of the arts who joined in praising Russian "peace" policies while attacking "American imperialism and its plans for war." Among the later congresses was one known as the Cultural and Scientific Conference for World Peace, which met in New York under the sponsorship of the National Council of Arts, Sciences and Professions in March 1949. This was on the eve of the Atlantic Pact against which the communist peace drive was partly directed. Among those who sponsored the conference were such famous noncommunists as Thomas Mann and Albert Einstein. One of the speakers was the left-wing American painter, Philip Evergood; another was Shostakovich, who attended as a member of a large Soviet Russian delegation. Some of the foreign delegates, including the Mexican painter Siqueiros, were prevented from attending because the Department of State refused them visas on the grounds that they were active members of a Communist party.[240]

One aspect of this campaign for peace was the World Peace Appeal, or so-called "Stockholm peace petition," which was circulated for signa-

[239] See Budenz, *Men without Faces*, p. 219, also Billy Rose's column, "Pitching Horseshoes," *New York Herald Tribune*, Feb. 24, 1950, p. 19. According to Rose, Mrs. Roosevelt was herself responsible for the decline of the committee when she resigned and attacked it after discovering that it had been taken over by communist sympathizers.

[240] *New York Times*, Mar. 24, 1949, p. 3.

tures in many countries and which Secretary of State Dean Acheson attacked as Moscow-inspired. The principal clearinghouse and distributor for the petition in the United States was the Peace Information Center, headed by W. E. B. Du Bois, the widely-known Negro whom we have already mentioned for his activities in fostering Negro art and artists. In August 1950 the Peace Information Center and its officers, including Du Bois, were instructed by the Department of Justice to register as foreign agents, and in February 1951 were indicted by a federal grand jury for failing to do so.[241]

Among the numerous American endorsers of the World Peace Appeal, many of them noncommunists, were Rockwell Kent, the painter, and the noted Negro singer, Paul Robeson, as well as no less than five Protestant bishops.[242] In the summer of 1950 the Department of State refused to validate the passports of both Kent and Robeson. Kent was accused of violating passport regulations on a trip abroad earlier in the year, a trip which had included a visit to Moscow with a delegation representing the World Committee of Peace Partisans, denounced by the Department of State as a communist-line organization. When told of the invalidation of his passport, Kent is reported to have said, "Anything that the Communists say about peace sounds good to me," and "I would work for peace with anyone, Communists or non-Communists."[243]

Paul Robeson (who had decided in the middle 1930's that the Negro had a better chance of advancing under Russian communism than in the United States) had also participated in the peace campaign from the beginning, and at home and abroad had repeatedly assailed the Marshall Plan, the Atlantic Pact, and the American defense of Korea. In November 1950 a communist-line World Peace Congress in Warsaw divided its International Peace Prize for Arts between Robeson and Picasso.[244] Robeson had once said, "It is unthinkable that [American Negroes] would go to war on behalf of those who have oppressed us for generations" against a country, the U.S.S.R., "which in one generation has raised our people to the full dignity of mankind."[245]

[241] *New York Herald Tribune*, Aug. 25, 1950, p. 5, and Feb. 10, 1951, p. 1. See also W. E. B. Du Bois, "I Take My Stand," *Masses & Mainstream*, Vol. 4, No. 4 (Apr. 1951), pp. 10-16. Later in 1951 the defendants were acquitted.

[242] *New York Herald Tribune*, Aug. 25, 1950, p. 5.

[243] See *Time*, Aug. 28, 1950, p. 17; *New York Herald Tribune*, Aug. 19, 1950, p. 3, and Mar. 4, 1950, pp. 1 and 6. In 1951, while a witness before the New York Supreme Court, Kent was asked if he believed that the only way social error could be remedied was through communism. He replied "If you mean, do I believe in Russian communism for America, I do not. I do believe in socialism. . . ." See the *New York Herald Tribune*, April 4, 1951, p. 19.

[244] See *Time*, Dec. 4, 1950, p. 38.

[245] *Ibid.*, Aug. 14, 1950, p. 12. In 1949 the House Committee on Un-American Activities listed Robeson as affiliated "with from fifty-one to sixty Communist-front

However, while it is certainly true that some of the American artists who participated in the peace petition, as well as in other activities discussed above, have either been members of the Communist Party or fellow travelers, it is important to remember that many others have been neither party members nor sympathetic to the party. In short, it cannot be too strongly emphasized that the artistic radicalism or liberalism which leads some American artists to sympathize with radicals in other fields may at times have a thoroughly American—if often naive—basis. For often it is an expression of a characteristically American spirit of individualistic nonconformity and thus of private enterprise.[246]

In conclusion, then, one can truthfully say that because a work of art is an expression of life, it necessarily in some degree reflects the conscious or unconscious philosophy of life of the individual artist (or group of artists) who produces it. But it cannot be denied that this philosophy in turn is in part necessarily affected by the environment and social beliefs of the artist. Consequently, in spite of sharp differences all the varieties of socialism share many of the same beliefs, so that the artists who subscribe to these different kinds of socialism have much in common in their approach to art: as might be expected, they tend to emphasize those kinds of art which seem to lend themselves to social expression and social usefulness. Yet, however interested in social problems they may appear to be, great artists are, almost by definition, unique individuals whose creative individuality does not easily lend itself to any form of economic or political collectivism. And it must also be remembered that the great majority of artists, when left to themselves, are not politicians of any kind, but just artists. Thus revolutionary art and revolutionary politics are frequently dissociated to a very considerable degree—they may or may not be combined in the same person—although (to repeat) radicalism

organizations": see the *New York Times*, Apr. 19, 1949, p. 6. He is a contributing editor of *Masses & Mainstream*.

[246] See Peyton Boswell's editorial, "A Plea for Tolerance," *Art Digest*, Vol. 23, No. 17 (June 1, 1949), p. 7. One might add that this frequent spirit of nonconformity, and hence of private enterprise, in the arts has often been looked upon with considerable suspicion by American private enterprise in business through fear of being accused of harboring radicals such as Communist Party members or fellow travelers. A possible case in point is that of actress Jean Muir, who in the summer of 1950 was paid off and dropped from a television show as a "controversial person" by the sponsor of the show in spite of Miss Muir's insistence that she is an anticommunist. Her name had been listed in a booklet, *Red Channels*, published under the aegis of the weekly newsletter, *Counterattack*. *Red Channels* "purports to catalogue radio and television personalities who have allegedly been sympathetic to Communist-front organizations." The dismissal of Miss Muir was denounced by the Council of Actors Equity Association, the A.F.L. theatrical union, which at the same time " 'unequivocally' condemned Communism and Fascism." See the *New York Herald Tribune*, Sept. 13, 1950, p. 17.

in art often predisposes the artist to regard radical social doctrines favorably.

Even in the Marxian view, however, there is no necessary one-to-one relationship between the development of the economic foundation of society and the ideological superstructure which rests upon it and which includes art. Art and economics and politics do not necessarily have to develop equally in the same society, or for that matter in the same human being. Hence although it is often easy to distinguish the arts of economic and political radicals from those of conservatives (who, unlike both radicals and liberals, prefer the status quo to either revolutionary or evolutionary change), it is, as we have seen, frequently difficult to distinguish between the kinds of art admired by radicals and those admired by socially-minded liberals. Historically, liberalism and socialism have tended to overlap, as they overlapped in the life of William Morris or even in the history of the Bauhaus, with the result that it has been relatively easy for socialists and many liberals to influence one another in the arts and to do so both consciously and unconsciously.

As this chapter has sought to show, by implication at least, this question of the relation of radicalism in art to social radicalism is also part of a problem which every artist has to face, the problem of achieving adequate originality while still retaining an adequate relationship with his fellow men. For if the artist is not artistically radical at all, his work may well lack the element of significant originality and individuality fundamental to all worthwhile art. If, on the contrary, he is so radical that no one can understand or appreciate his work—if, in short, his art lacks every kind of social significance—not only will artistic survival become difficult or impossible for him but he will fail (as socialists insist) to take his proper place in society. Yet if political radicalism leads him instead to devote his art *entirely* to fostering social aims so that works of art are nothing but a means to nonartistic ends, art then becomes nothing but a kind of propaganda. Each different form of society has its own particular dangers for the arts, and this tendency to reduce art to sheer propaganda, to sheer social utility, is the chief danger to which the arts of a socialist society may succumb, as developments in Soviet Russia have so clearly indicated. However, one must add in fairness that, with all its limitations, it is a tendency which in theory causes art to be considered an official necessity in the Soviet Union, and not a mere unessential luxury, as it is so often regarded in the United States.

It is true that in this country from early colonial times to the present, radical movements of a socialist nature have always been endemic, primarily because tendencies toward equalitarianism have always been characteristic of American democracy as they have also to some degree been characteristic of all forms of socialist theory. But in spite of the more-or-less equalitarian spirit of American democracy, socialism has never been able to gain in any direct way a really strong place in American civilization and art because American individualism has customarily been so suspicious of anything that might smack of collectivistic regimentation. Moreover, the Marxist belief in the class struggle and the triumph of the proletariat has never been very widely accepted in the United States, where so many of those whom Marx has labeled proletarians do not ordinarily think of themselves as members of any class, but if pressed to do so are likely to say that they consider themselves part of the middle class. As a result, very few of the varieties of socialism which have been found in the United States have originated there. And the few native groups which, like the Oneida Community, have adopted a communistic existence independent of foreign influence have usually been compelled to withdraw from ordinary American society and to adopt a communal way of life at least partly against their will, and mainly because their neighbors objected to some of their customs.

For all these reasons, from the seventeenth century to at least the middle of the twentieth century, socialist influences on art, as on other aspects of life in the United States, have been chiefly indirect. In this indirect way they have had considerable importance. But even indirectly they have ordinarily been strong only when some of the aims, ideals, and needs of the American democratic tradition have happened to coincide with some of the principles characteristic of socialism. Thus in the art of the United States, as in other aspects of American life, any imported socialist content has usually been retained only when it reinforces already existing American tendencies. Otherwise, except for the art of small, if vociferous, socialist and communist minorities, the socialist and especially the Marxian content has customarily been dropped out. Usually in the American version of an imported socialist style either there is little or no content other than that which may reside directly in the very nature of the medium and of the form given to that medium, resulting in what Russian Marxism today decries as formalism, or else—as is so often the case—the socialist content has been modified in a characteristically American direction.

Yet as is so often implied in this book, it cannot be said with truth that there is any *single* direction which can be called truly American. And American art helps to document this fact by indicating the existence in the United States of an ever prevailing yet ever varying tension between individualism *and* equalitarianism, a tension in which, unlike most socialism, the individual is considered primary *now* and not merely in some future society. The author believes that in this very tension (which socialist criticism helps to keep vital, and which in important respects is also not unrelated to the Christian tradition) lies hope for further efforts to overcome both the economic injustices that frequently accompany irresponsible individualism, and the bureaucratic or technocratic tyranny so often characteristic of large-scale collectivism. It is this tension, in short, which may offer particular hope for achieving a higher degree of individual and social justice not only in American life but throughout the world.

ACKNOWLEDGMENTS

The author wishes to thank the publishers, institutions, and individuals who granted permission to reproduce illustrations used in this chapter. The sources of the illustrations are as follows: FIG. 1, from Philip B. Wallace, *Colonial Churches and Meeting Houses* (New York: Architectural Book Publishing Co., 1931), p. 117; FIG. 2, from Edward D. Andrews, "Communal Architecture of the Shakers," *Magazine of Art*, Vol. 30, No. 12 (Dec. 1937), p. 712; FIG. 3, from the *Peg Board*, Vol. 4, No. 3 (June 1936), p. 65; FIG. 4, from Edward D. and Faith Andrews, *Shaker Furniture* (New Haven: Yale University Press, 1937), Pl. 27; FIG. 5, from Edward D. Andrews, *The Gift to Be Simple* (New York: J. J. Augustin, 1940), Fig. 6, opp. p. 36; FIG. 6, from *Leslie's Popular Monthly* (1885), but reproduced from Edward D. Andrews, *The Gift to Be Simple*, Fig. 16, opp. p. 100; FIG. 7, from Charles Nordhoff, *The Communistic Societies of the United States* (New York: Harper and Brothers, 1875), opp. p. 40; FIG. 8, from the *American-German Review*, of the Carl Schurz Memorial Foundation, Vol. 7, No. 1 (Oct. 1940), p. 7; FIG. 9, from Richard F. Burton, *The City of the Saints* (New York: Harper and Brothers, 1862), frontispiece; FIG. 10, from *American Architect and Building News*, I (Feb. 12, 1876), preceding p. 53; FIG. 11, photo. courtesy of Ewing Galloway; FIG. 12, from Pierrepont Noyes, *My Father's House* (New York: Farrar and Rinehart, 1937), frontispiece; FIG. 13, from an article by Isaac G. Reed in *Frank Leslie's Illustrated Newspaper* (1870), but reproduced from Frederick B. Adams, Jr., *Radical Literature in America* (Stamford, Conn.: Overbrook Press, 1939), p. 25; FIG. 14, from M. R. Werner, *Brigham Young* (New York: Harcourt Brace and Co., 1925), opp. p. 350; FIG. 15, from the *Cooperative Magazine and Monthly Herald*, No. 1 (Jan. 1826), but reproduced from George B. Lockwood, *The New Harmony Movement* (New York: D. Appleton, 1905), opp. p. 70; FIG. 16, from Walter Creese, "Fowler and the Domestic Octagon," *Art Bulletin*, Vol. 28, No. 2 (June 1946), p. 97, Fig. 22; FIG. 17, from the lithograph *Un Phalanstère* by Arnoux, which accompanied Victor Considérant's *Description du Phalanstère* (2nd ed., Paris, 1848); FIG. 18, from Jules Prudhommeaux, *Icarie et son fondateur Étienne Cabet* (Paris: Édouard Cornély & Cie., 1907), opp. p. 588; FIG. 19, from an old print reproduced in George B. Lockwood, *op.cit.*, opp. p. 210; FIG. 20, photo. courtesy of the *Red Bank* [N.J.] *Register*; FIG. 21, from W. R. Lethaby, *Philip Webb and His Work* (Oxford: Oxford University Press, 1935), opp. p. 4; FIG. 22, from Catherine Bauer, *Modern Housing* (Boston and New York: Houghton Mifflin Co., 1934), Pl. 8-C; FIG. 23, from *Moderne Bouwkunst in Nederland*, No. 1 (Rotterdam: W. L. & J. Brusse N.V., 1932), p. 24; FIG. 24, from Tony Garnier, *Une Cité industrielle* (Paris: Vincent, 1917), Pl. 64; FIG. 25, from George Grosz, *Das Gesicht der herrschenden Klasse*, Kleine revolutionäre Bibliothek, Band IV (Berlin: Malik-Verlag, 1921), Pl. 19; FIG. 26, from H. Bayer, W. Gropius, I. Gropius, eds., *Bauhaus, 1919-1928* (New York: Museum of Modern Art,

1938), p. 203; Fig. 27, from Philip C. Johnson, *Mies van der Rohe* (New York: Museum of Modern Art, 1947), p. 37; Fig. 28, from Walter Gropius, *The New Architecture and the Bauhaus* (New York: Museum of Modern Art, n.d.), Pl. 7; Fig. 29, from *ibid.*, Pl. 5; Fig. 30, from Bauer, *op.cit.*, Pl. 1-A; Fig. 31, from *ibid.*, p. 179; Fig. 32, from László Moholy-Nagy, *The New Vision* (4th rev. ed., New York: Wittenborn, Schultz, Inc., 1947), p. 44, Fig. 23; Fig. 33, from Alfred H. Barr, Jr., *Cubism and Abstract Art* (New York: Museum of Modern Art, 1936), Fig. 98; Fig. 34, from El Lissitzky [L. M. Lissitsky], *Russland* (Vienna: Anton Schroll and Co., 1930), Abb. 38; Figs. 35-43, photos. courtesy of Sovfoto; Fig. 44, courtesy of the Museum of Fine Arts, Boston; Fig. 45, supplied by Department of Art and Archaeology, Princeton University; Fig. 46, from Gerald H. Crow, *William Morris, Designer* (London: The Studio, 1934), p. 101; Fig. 47, from Bertram G. Goodhue, *A Book of Architectural and Decorative Drawings* (New York: Architectural Book Publishing Co., 1914), p. 112; Fig. 48, from the *Comrade*, Oct. 1903; Fig. 49, from John Ames Mitchell, *The Silent War* (New York: Life Publishing Company, 1906), opp. p. 200; Fig. 50, courtesy of the Whitney Museum of American Art; Fig. 51, from the *Masses*, Sept. 1917, p. 7; Fig. 52, from the *Liberator*, Apr. 1918, p. 1; Fig. 53, Collection of the Museum of Modern Art, New York, gift of A. Conger Goodyear; Fig. 54, from Diego Rivera, *Portrait of America* (New York: Covici, Friede, 1934), text by Bertram D. Wolfe, copyright 1934 by Bertram D. Wolfe, used by permission of Crown Publishers; Fig. 55, from Justino Fernández, *José Clemente Orozco* (Mexico City: Libreria de Porrua Hnos. y Cia., 1942), Pl. 67, Fig. 63; Fig. 56, Collection of the Museum of Modern Art, New York; Fig. 57, from James J. Sweeney, *Alexander Calder* (New York: Museum of Modern Art, 1943), p. 23; Fig. 58, from J. L. Martin, B. Nicholson, N. Gabo, eds., *Circle* (London: Faber and Faber, 1937), Pl. 15; Fig. 59, from Peyton Boswell, *Modern American Painting* (New York: Dodd, Mead and Co., 1940), opp. p. 83, courtesy of *Life* magazine and of the artist; Fig. 60, from Werner Hegemann, *City Planning and Housing* (New York: Architectural Book Publishing Co., 1938), Vol. 3, p. 141, Fig. 1024; Fig. 61, from Lewis Mumford, *The Culture of Cities* (New York: Harcourt Brace and Co., 1938), opp. p. 452.

Index to Volume 1

ASNOVA (Association of New Architects [U.S.S.R.]), 685n, 690n
Abbott, Leonard D., 716n
Abendblatt, 259n, 310
Abolitionism, 431
Abramovitch, Raphael, 362
Academy of Architecture (U.S.S.R.), 704
Acheson, Dean, 747
Acton, John, 217, 219
Adams, Brooks, 268, 419
Adams, Henry, 268, 412, 419
Adonai-Shomo community, 193
Agar, Herbert, 364n, 607
Agee, James, 607
Agitprop, 354-355
Agrarian League, 230
Alabyan, K., 704, 704n
Albers, Josef, 668, 669, 741
Alfaro Siqueiros, David, *see* Siqueiros, David Alfaro
Alinsky, Saul, 352n
All-Russian Society of Proletarian Architects, *see* WOPRA
Allen, Devere, 370, 371n, 378
Allen, Frederick Lewis, 347n
Altgeld, John, 262
Altman, Jack, 371n, 382, 383, 384, 392n, 394
Alvarez del Vayo, Julio, 362
Amalgamated Clothing Workers, 310, 329, 381
Amana, 127; and art, 626-628
America First Committee, 394
American Alliance for Labor & Democracy, 313
American Artists' Congress, 619n, 724, 736, 736n
American Economic Review, 469
American Fabian, 271
American Fabian Society, 208, 271
American Federation of Labor, 223, 242, 243, 245, 248-256, 275, 276, 285, 286, 331, 333, 357, 373; early Marxist orientation, 491n; early theory of the state, 496; and socialism, 252-256; strategy, 497
American Federationist, 252, 253
American Labor Alliance, 338; *see also* United Communist Party (1920)
American Labor Party (1919-1920), 331
American Labor Party (N.Y.), 357, 383, 384, 384n, 388-389, 391
American Labor Union, 254, 276, 277

American League for Peace and Democracy, 360
American Negro Labor Congress, 737
American Peace Mobilization, 396
American Plan, 330
American Railway Union, 260, 261, 263, 305
American Socialist, 315, 316
American Socialist Quarterly, 371n
American Student Union, 360, 360n, 382
American Union of Associationists, 205
American Workers Party, 385-386
American Writers' Congress, 1st (1935), 616-617; 2nd (1937), 617-618; 3rd (1939), 618
American Youth Congress, 360, 361
Americans for Democratic Action, 123, 403
Ameringer, Oscar, 300, 306n, 307, 520, 572
Amter, Israel, 339n
Anabaptism, 38, 40, 218
Anarchism, 63, 79n, 82-83, 139, 199, 208, 219, 233, 237-238; abolition of the state, 496; compared with socialism, 7; communist anarchism, 7-8, 10-11; communitarian anarchism, 198-201; individualist anarchism, 7, 10
Anderson, H. Dewey, 545n
Anderson, Maxwell, 473
Anderson, Sherwood, 354, 364n, 365, 607
Andrews, Edward D., 624n
Andrews, Faith, 624n
Andrews, Stephen Pearl, 200
Anthony, Saint, 113
Antinomianism, 141
Antonelli, Étienne, 83n
Anvil, 354
Appeal group (Socialist Party), 384
Appeal to Reason, 259, 270, 313, 604
Applegarth, Robert, 60
Aquinas, Thomas, Saint, 28-30, 34, 108
Aragon, Louis, 616, 618
Araquistain, Luis, 362n
Aristotle, 28
Arnold, George B., 186, 204
Aron, Raymond, 223n, 398n
Art and socialism, 623-751; in America, 705-751; in England, 650-654; in Germany, 654-669; in Soviet Union, 669-705; Art Nouveau, 658; Bauhaus, 660-669; city planning, 653-654; housing, 646, 653-654, 657, 667; International Style, 664-668; Marxist art theory, 636-

650; "die neue Sachlichkeit," 659-660; organicism, 643-644; utopianism, 625-636
Art Front, 736, 739
Art Young's Quarterly, 718
Artistic idealism, 690
Artists' and Writers' Congress (1941), 619n, 736n
Artists' Cooperative (U.S.S.R.), 703
Artists' Creative Union (U.S.S.R.), 704
Artists' Union, 736, 739
Arvin, Newton, 354, 620
"Ash-can School," 715, 729
Association of New Architects (U.S.S.R.), *see* ASNOVA
Associationism, *see* Fourierism
Atlantic Pact, 747
Attlee, Clement, 92-93
Auden, W. H., 123
Augustine, Saint, 106-107, 118
Aveling, Eleanor Marx, 651

Babel, Isaac, 355n
Babeuf, François N., 3n, 35, 37, 46, 118, 160
Bacon, Francis, 38, 430
Bacon, Roger, 108
Bailey, Gilbert F., 183n
Baker, Charles, 316
Baker, Ray Stannard, 272
Bakewell, Benjamin, 169
Bakunin, Mikhail, 7, 10, 63, 207, 219, 233-234, 235, 742; on revolution, 743
Ball, John, 30
Ballou, Adin, 173n, 178, 199, 200
Baran, Paul, 469
Barbusse, Henri, 359
Barmby, John G., 3n
Barmine, Alexander, 363n
Barnave, Antoine P. J. M., 40, 48
Barnes, J. Mahlon, 252, 281, 491
Baron, Murray, 371n
Barr, Alfred H., Jr., 659n, 679n
Barton, Bruce, 347
Barzun, Jacques, 50n
Basil, Saint, 113
Bates, Issacher, 134
Bauer, Otto, 375
Bayer, Herbert, 669, 741
Baykov, Alexander, 482n
Beard, Charles A., 268, 374n, 474
Bebel, August, 65, 374
Bechhofer, C. E., 80n
Beck, F., 363n
Becker, Carl, 364n
Becker, Lazar, 366
Becker, Maurice, 717, 719, 720, 721, 736

Bedacht, Max, 345, 345n, 397n
Beer, Max, 3n, 44, 45n, 47
Behrendt, Walter C., 656n
Behrens, Peter, 661n, 665
Bellamy, Edward, 220, 229, 260, 262, 264n, 269-271, 476, 603, 653
Bellamyite Nationalism, *see* Nationalism, Bellamyite
Belloc, Hilaire, 80
Bellows, George, 716, 716n, 717, 718
Beluze, Jean, 189
Benedict, Saint, 36
Beneš, Eduard, 618
Benét, William Rose, 607
Benham, G. B., 294
Benn, Ben, 716n
Bennett, William F., 315
Benson, Allan, 311, 312
Bentham, Jeremy, 160
Bentley, Elizabeth, 358n
Benton, Thomas H., 364n, 730, 730n
Berdyaev, Nikolai A., 113
Berger, Victor, 244, 261, 263, 264, 277, 278, 283, 285, 287, 293, 294, 296, 296n, 306n, 307, 311, 313n, 316, 317, 323, 326, 370n, 377, 401, 490
Berkman, Alexander, 239n, 288n, 316, 716n
Berlage, Hendrik P., 657
Bernard, Luther L., 546n
Bernard, Saint, 107
Bernieri, Camillo, 362
Bernstein, Eduard, 70-73, 377, 491
Berry, George, 333
Besant, Annie, 76
Bessie, Alvah, 619n
Bestor, Arthur E., Jr., 3n, 5n, 161n, 175n, 633n
Beveridge, Albert, 266
Bible, 24, 171
Bible communism (Oneida), 146-148
Biddle, George, 734n, 736
Biemiller, Andrew J., 371n, 378, 403
Bilbo, Theodore, 291
Billings, Henry, 729
Billings, Warren K., 316
Bimba, Anthony, 358
Birkbeck, Morris, 163
Bismarck, O. E. L., 65, 65n, 654
Bittelman, Alexander, 345n-346n
Black International, *see* International Working People's Association (Anarchist)
Blake, William J., pseud., *see* Blech, William J.
Blanc, Louis, 231
Blanshard, Paul, 369, 371, 371n, 373

Blast, 316, 354
Blatchford, Robert, 262
Blatchly, Cornelius C., 161, 193
Blech, William J. (William J. Blake, pseud.), 643n
Bliss, William D. P., 264n, 271
Blitzstein, Marc, 363
Bloor, Ella Reeve, 345
Blum, Léon, 94
Boas, Franz, 436
Bober, Mandell M., 471
Bodin, Jean, 31
Böhm-Bawerk, Eugen von, 463
Böhme, Jakob, 127
Bohn, Frank, 295, 313, 498
Boisguillebert, P. le P., 69
Bolshevik Revolution, 318-319; and American writers, 605
Bolshevism, 83-85, 318, 327, 335; political theory, 225-228; *see also* Communism (Russian)
Bonald, Louis de, 118
Bonar, James, 478n
Bordiga, Amadeo, 367
Boston Investigator, 181
Boswell, Peyton, 748n
Bouck, William, 333
Boudin, Louis B., 290, 320, 335, 420, 423, 462
Bourdelle, Antoine, 696
Bourne, Randolph, 718
Boyle, James, 142
Brady, Robert A., 469
Brainerd, David, 141
Brandeis, Louis D., 268
Bray, John Francis, 45
Bremer, Fredrika, 189n, 203n
Brenan, Gerald, 362n
Brenner, Anita, 362n
Brethren of the Common Life, 36
Brethren of the Free Spirit, 113
Breton, André, 724, 724n
Breuer, Marcel, 669, 741
Brewster, J. M., 130n
Bridges, Harry, 357, 396
Bridgman, Percy, 364n
Briefs, Goetz A., 216n
Brinnin, Malcolm, 607
Brinton, Christian, 716n
Brisbane, Albert, 175-180, 182, 184, 188, 193, 194, 195, 195n, 196, 197, 203, 205, 206, 207, 420
Brissenden, Paul, 279, 280n
Brodsky, Isaac, 689
Brook Farm, 175, 183-184, 192, 199, 201, 602
Brooke, A., 200

Brookhart, Smith W., 307
Brooks, Van Wyck, 289, 618, 718
Brookwood Labor College, 385
Brophy, John, 352n
Brotherhood of Locomotive Firemen, 260
Brotherhood of the Co-operative Commonwealth, 208, 260, 263
Brotherhood of the New Life, 193
Broun, Heywood, 371, 395
Browder, Earl, 112, 340, 341, 345, 345n, 349-350, 356, 357n, 358, 382, 396-397, 616, 691, 698, 710, 722, 732
Brown, Ford Madox, 652
Brown, Irving, 390
Brown, Milton W., 719n
Brown, Paul, 161, 164, 165, 167, 168, 168n, 170-172, 173-174, 174n, 193, 195-196, 199, 200, 203
Brown, Solyman, 191
Brownson, Orestes, 174, 192
Bruce, Andrew A., 303n
Bryan, William Jennings, 243, 262, 267, 282
Budenz, Louis F., 358n, 385-386, 398n, 670n, 694n, 727n
Büchner, Friedrich, 433
Bukharin, Nikolai, 319, 345, 362, 432, 447, 682-683, 693; in U.S., 320; on art, 686-688
Bullard, Arthur, 313
Burck, Jacob, 721
Burger, William T., 721n
Burke, Fielding, 354
Burke, Kenneth, 617, 618
Burley Community, 208
Burliuk, David, 679, 723
Burnham, James, 385
Burns, Emile, 111n
Burritt, Elihu, 179
Bush, Charles D., 307n
Byzantine style, 674

C.I.O., 357-358, 383, 384n, 389-390
C.I.O. News, 357
Caballero, Francisco Largo, *see* Largo Caballero, Francisco
Cabell, Branch, 347
Cabet, Étienne, 15, 156, 158-159, 160, 167, 189, 631, 634
Cade, Jack, 30
Cadman, S. Parkes, 347
Cahan, Abraham, 310, 377n
Cairnes, John Elliot, 75
Calder, Alexander, 730-731
Caldwell, Erskine, 354
Calhoun, Arthur W., 291n
Calmer, Alan, 609n

Calverton, Victor F., 374n, 609
Calvinism, 116-117, 129
Campanella, Tommaso, 36, 681
Campbell, Alexander, 129
Cannon, James P., 338, 340, 341, 344, 345n-346n, 366, 366n, 385, 386-388, 683
Cantwell, Robert, 354, 620
Capitalism; historical development, 30-35; Marxist analysis, 57-58; utopian analysis, 33-35
Carey, Henry C., 239
Carey, James F., 257, 274, 283n
Carlson, Oliver, 374n
Carlyle, Thomas, 75
Carpenter, Edward, 657
Carr, Edward H., 49n, 234n, 455n, 702n, 733n
Cathari, 113
Cedarvale community, 195n
Celesta community, 193
Celibacy, 113
Centers, Richard T., 545n
Central Committee on Arts (U.S.S.R.), 704
Ceresco Phalanx, see Wisconsin Phalanx
Chamberlain, John, 271, 363n, 364n, 617
Chambers, Whittaker, 358n, 398n
Chanin, Abraham, 730n
Channing, W. H., 184, 194, 195, 205
Chaplin, Charlie, 726
Chartism, 44, 61
Chase, Stuart, 374n
Chase, Warren, 181-183, 194, 203
Cheltenham community, 189
Chen, Jack, 646n, 704n
Chernyshevsky, Nikolai G., 672
Chicago Daily Socialist, 282, 299, 312
Choisy, Eugène, 117
Christensen, Parley, 331
Christian Church, 131
Christian Commonwealth colony, 264n
Christian socialism, 7, 12, 44, 122-123, 263, 270, 312, 650, 655, 705
Christian Socialist, 12n
Church Association for the Advancement of the Interests of Labor, 119
Church Social Union, 119
Claflin, Tennessee, 234
Clarity group (Socialist Party), 384, 388, 389, 394
Clarkson Phalanx, 194
Class struggle, 42, 57-59, 62, 68, 73, 76, 78-79, 110, 122, 173, 174, 205, 206, 208, 281, 287, 438, 462, 474, 494; Bernstein's view, 71; critique of the Marxist theory, 534-543

Class Struggle, 320, 322
Classical realism, 696
Classless society, 44
Clay, James Arrington, 200
Clayton Act, 302
Clement, Travers, 517n, 546n
Clermont Phalanx, 182, 193, 207
Cleveland Citizen, 278
Cloverdale Colony, 190
Clutton-Brock, Arthur, 653
Coates, Robert, 363
Codman, John T., 173n
Coeur d'Alene strike, 242, 261
Coldwell, Joseph, 324
Cole, George D. H., 80, 81
Cole, Henry, 656n
Coleman, Glenn, 717, 719
Coleman, McAlister, 262n, 352n, 371n
Collins, Frederick L., 482n
Collins, John A., 172, 199, 203
Colonization, 259, 263, 271
Colquhoun, Patrick, 46
Combe, George, 176
Cominform, see Communist Information Bureau
Coming Nation, 259, 270
Comintern, see International, Third (Communist)
Commission to inquire into the charges made against Leon Trotsky in the Moscow trials, see Dewey Commission
Committee for a Third International, 338
Committee for Cultural Freedom, 364
Committee for Industrial Organization, see C.I.O.
Committee on Un-American Activities, see United States, Congress, House, Committee on Un-American Activities
Common Sense, 362
Commons, John R., 177n, 183n, 198n
Communalism, 26, 33
Communia (Iowa), 159
Communism, 96; Aquinas' views, 29; compared with communist anarchism, 7-8; and democratic society, 225-228; feudal communism, 28; history of term, 3-6; political tactics of, 225-228; primitive communism, 34; primitive Christian communism, 24; and religion, 112; see also Socialism
Communism (Russian), 4-5, 8; economic development, 87-90; history, 82-90; Left opposition, 681-686, 690-693; N.E.P., 350n; Right opposition, 681-683, 686-693; see also Bolshevism
Communism (U.S.), 311; factionalism, 334-345; front technique, 331, 359-361;

and government agencies, 357-358; history, 334-345; and labor unions, 352, 357; literary theory, 608-610; Popular Front tactics, 355-361; splinter groups, 365-369; "third period" tactics, 350-355; and writers, 606-620; *see also* Communist Party (U.S.)
Communist (Communist Party), 446, 709, 739
Communist (Alcander Longley, ed.), 207
Communist Club (N.Y.), 234
Communist Information Bureau, 90, 96
Communist International, *see* International, Third (Communist)
Communist International, 350n, 612
Communist Labor Party (1919), 324, 335
Communist League, 55, 60
Communist League of Struggle, 366
Communist Manifesto, 4, 12-14, 49-51, 55, 57-60, 335, 645
Communist Party (German), 86
Communist Party (Russian), 4; Zinoviev-Stalin faction, 343; *see also* Bolshevism; Communism (Russian)
Communist Party (U.S.), 9, 14, 111-112, 210, 294, 324, 334, 337, 375, 384, 445, 446, 448, 492-493, 670, 698, 699, 732, 736, 746; and art, 708-714; front technique, 343; history, 338-345, 350-365; and labor unions, 397; Marxist-Leninist theory, 466-468; opportunism, 492-493; organization, 324, 550-552; Popular Front tactics, 502; position on jazz, 738; recent period, 395-399; the revolution, 494; unity negotiations with Socialist Party, 382; *see also* Communism (U.S.)
Communist Party Opposition 345, 725n
Communist Political Association, 396, 554
Communist World, 334
Communitarianism, Christian, 8, 11, 15, 35-36, 104, 112-115, 127-151, 155, 172-173, 546-547; and art, 625-630; cause of failure, 150-151; *see also* Utopian socialism; entries under specific movements, e.g., Shakerism
Communitarianism, liberal, 8, 15, 155-211, 546-547; and Americanization, 190-204; and art, 630-636; European background, 156-161; and Marxism, 204-211; J. H. Noyes's criticism, 147-148; *see also* Utopian socialism; entries under specific movements, e.g., Owenism
Complex marriage, 114-115, 144-145
Comrade, 312, 707, 708
Comte, Auguste, 109, 195, 269, 419
Conciliators (Communist Party), 340

Condorcet, 109, 412, 419
Conference for Progressive Labor Action, 385
Conference for Progressive Political Action, 298, 327, 332-333
Congress of Industrial Organizations, *see* C.I.O.
Conroy, Jack, 354, 617
Considérant, Victor, 188, 189, 189n, 636
Constructivism, 668, 675, 676, 678-680, 683, 685, 690n, 723, 730-731, 741, 744
Continental Congress of Workers and Farmers, 372
Cooke, Alistair, 358n
Cooke, Joseph J., 183
Coolidge, Calvin, 329, 332
Cooper, James Fenimore, 602
Cooper, Peter, 232, 236
Co-operative Magazine, 3
Cooperative movement, 44, 61, 63-64, 81, 207, 208, 230; consumers', 10, 73, 75, 77, 265; producers', 10, 73, 231, 265
Corey, Lewis (before 1925 known as Louis Fraina), 320, 321, 324, 334, 346n, 448, 494n, 517n, 522, 540n
Corning community, 189-190
Coughlin, Charles E., 305, 383n
Counts, George S., 364n, 648n
Courbet, Gustave, 674, 706
Covarrubias, Miguel, 719
Cowley, Malcolm, 354, 363, 616, 618, 620
Cox, Jesse, 294
Coxey, Jacob, 243
Coxey's army, 261
Craftsman, 706
Cram, Ralph Adams, 707n
Crane, Walter, 707
Critics Group, 714
Croly, Herbert, 268, 292, 313
Cromwell, Oliver, 114
Crook, Wilfrid H., 79n
Cross, Whitney R., 178n
Cubism, 668, 674, 676, 679, 699, 738
Cumberland Presbyterianism, 131
Cumbie, Tad, 306
Cunningham, William, 307n
Curran, Joe, 357
Curti, Merle E., 179n
Czolgosz, Leon, 239n

Dada, 616, 666-667, 668, 679, 725
Dahir, James, 654n
Daily Worker, 344, 346n, 358n, 386n, 397n, 710, 711, 713, 721, 722, 735
Dali, Salvador, 724
Dana, Charles A., 194, 198, 205, 207

Dana, Henry W. L., 617
Daniel, Franz, 371n, 383, 390
Darcy, Sam, 397n
Darrow, Clarence, 262, 313, 716n
Darwin, Charles, 171, 435
Darwinism, 150
Davidson, Jo, 717
Davidson, Percy E., 545n
Davies, Arthur B., 716, 717
Davies, J. E., 89n
Davis, Andrew Jackson, 193
Davis, Elmer, 364n
Davis, John W., 332
Davis, Stuart, 363, 717, 721, 729, 736
Dawson, William H., 63
Debo, Angie, 306n
Debs, Eugene V., 220, 244, 246, 257, 259, 275, 276, 277, 288, 293, 294, 298, 306, 308, 311, 370, 377, 423, 491, 520; and Bellamy, 270; and Bolshevism, 326-327; death, 334; early career, 260-263; and I.W.W., 254, 278-280; on 1900 campaign, 267; on Socialist Party tactics, 284-285; on working-class affiliation, 294-295; on World War I, 316-317; personal characteristics, 299-302; presidential campaigns, 274, 278, 280-282, 288-289, 326, 331; and Social Democratic Party, 264; views on labor party, 282-283
Debs, Kate (Mrs. E. V.), 300n, 316
Debs, Theodore, 264n
De Caux, Len, 357
Deets, Lee E., 569
Dehn, Adolf, 719, 720
De Leon, Daniel, 241, 242, 243, 252, 257, 258, 265, 273, 420, 423, 439, 497; career, 244-245; dual unionism, 253; and I.W.W., 278-280; Nationalist affiliation, 270; theories, 246-248
Dell, Floyd, 316, 604, 605
Delson, Max, 382, 384
Delson, Robert, 370n, 384, 393
De Man, Henri, see Man, Henri de
Democratic centralism, 9, 87, 227, 551-552, 671
Democratic Federation (British), 650
Democratic Party, 177, 198, 267, 291, 304, 335, 357, 373, 403
Democratic socialism, 9, 66-67, 77, 82, 95-96, 547-549
Dengel, P., 612
Descartes, René, 31, 159
Destler, Chester M., 461n
Deutsch, Babette, 618
Deutscher, Isaac, 702n
Deutscher Werkbund, 661n-662n

Dewey, John, 313, 363, 363n, 364, 369, 424, 448, 510, 721
Dewey Commission, 363, 721
Dial, 329, 718
Dialectical materialism, 11-12, 57n, 109-110; and Brisbane, 206; see also Economic interpretation of history
Dialectics, 714
Dicey, A. V., 42n
Dictatorship of the proletariat, 58n, 110
Dies, Martin, 360n
Diggers, 114
Dimitrov, Georgi, 356, 356n
Disciples of Christ, 129
Dittmann, Wilhelm, 328
Dix, Otto, 660n
Dobb, Maurice, 470
Dodd, Bella, 397n
Doesburg, Théo van, 679
Dombrowski, James, 120n, 260n, 264n, 270
Dominic, Saint, 107
Donatello, 31
Dondero, George A., 745, 745n
Donnelly, Ignatius, 243, 603
Dorfman, Joseph, 265n, 273, 473, 473n
Dos Passos, John, 300, 347, 348, 354, 354n, 362, 364n, 365, 607, 616, 620
Douglas, Dorothy W., 546n
Douglas, Paul, 315, 369
Dreiser, Theodore, 301, 374n, 605, 607, 618, 726
Drob, Judah, 517n
Drucker, Peter, 48, 50
Dual unionism, 253-254, 352
Dubinsky, David, 372, 383
Du Bois, William E. B., 737, 747
Duclos, Jacques, 346n, 396, 698
Dühring, Eugen, 16
Dunayevskaya, Raya, 469
Duncan, James, 161n
Dunlavy, John, 131
Dunne, William F., 339, 345n-346n, 397n
Dupee, Fred, 613
Durant, Will, 716n
Duranty, Walter, 355n
Dutt, R. Palme, 351n
Dwight, John S., 184, 192, 194, 196
Dynamo, 354

E.P.I.C. movement, 304, 373, 595
Eastman, Max, 290, 296, 312, 313n, 316, 338, 355n, 364n, 419, 424, 604, 607, 610-611, 681n, 715n, 717
Eberlein, Hugo, 323
Ebert, Friedrich, 328, 660

Ebon, Martin, 112n
Economic interpretation of history, 40, 42, 48-49, 67-68, 71-72, 76, 122, 462, 470, 474; Fourierist, 205-206; see also Dialectical materialism
Edel, Abraham, 535n
Edger, Henry, 195, 200
Edman, Irwin, 364n
Edwards, A. S., 294
Edwards, George, 391
Edwards, George S., 360n
Edwards, Jonathan, 130
Einstein, Albert, 746
Eisenstein, Sergei M., 726, 729
Eisler, Gerhart, 346n, 727
Eisler, Hanns, 727
Eliot, T. S., 604, 713
Ellis, Fred, 721
Ely, Richard T., 120, 270, 472, 472n
Emerson, Ralph W., 422, 601
End Poverty in California, see E.P.I.C. movement
Engdahl, J. Louis, 316, 326, 338
Engels, Friedrich, 41, 49, 56n, 68, 72, 251, 295n, 432; and art, 712; and Communist League, 55; on American prospects, 215; on factionalism in U.S., 244; on isolation of S. L. P., 248; on socialism in England, 74-75; social evolution, 436-437; see also Communist Manifesto, Marxism
Engle, Paul, 607
Enoch, Abner, 204
Ephrata community, 127, 191, 601; and art, 626-628
Epstein, Melech, 310n
Equalitarian Society, 368n
Equality community, 208
Erasmus, 171
Ercoli, M. (Togliatti), 356n
Erffa, Helmut von, 679n
Erfurt Congress (1891), 65
Ernst, Morris L., 364n
Esenin, Sergei A., 355n
Etzler, John A., 192n, 194, 601
Eugenics movement, 150
Evangelical revivalism, 128-132, 140, 145, 174, 306
Evans, Frederick, 139, 140, 628
Evans, George Henry, 230, 239
Evergood, Philip, 721, 729, 746
Evolutionary socialism, 4-5, 44, 76-77, 81, 119, 439-440, 493-494; immediate demands, 500; see also Revisionist socialism
Expressionism, 674

Fabian socialism, 9, 12, 70, 74-78, 80, 652-653, 740
Fairchild, James H., 203
Fairchild, Mildred, 542n
Faris, Ellsworth, 334n
Farmer-Labor Party (1920), 331
Farmer-Labor Party (1924), 331-332, 333
Farmer-Labor Party (Minnesota), 331, 383n
Farmer-Labor Political Federation (Wisconsin), 384, 389
Farmer-Labor Reconstruction League, 307
Farrell, James T., 354n, 365, 605, 617, 620
Fascism, 86, 91, 350, 355, 605, 617
Fast, Howard, 397
Fearing, Kenneth, 607, 620
Federal Art Project (Works Progress Administration), 734, 739
Federal Theater Project, 736
Federation of Soviet Architects, 704
Feiba Peveli community, 165
Feigenbaum, Benjamin, 294
Feininger, Lyonel, 660, 669
Fellenberg, Philip E. von, 157
Fellowship of Reconciliation, 386n, 400
Fellowship of Socialist Christians, see Frontier Fellowship
Ferrer Center, 716
Ferrer Guardia, Francisco, 716
Ferri, Enrico, 432
Feuerbach, Ludwig, 433
Fichte, Johann G., 654
Field, B. J., 366-367
Fighting Worker, 367n
Fine, Nathan, 258n
Finkelstein, Sidney, 699n, 712-714, 721
Fischer, Louis, 395
Fischer, Ruth, 326n, 356n, 727n
Fisher, Dorothy Canfield, 364n
Fiske, John, 436
Fitzgerald, F. Scott, 347, 348
Fitzpatrick, John J., 331
Fletcher, R. S., 195n
Flynn, Elizabeth Gurley, 716n
Folk art, 701-703, 731-732
Foner, Philip, 295
Forbes, Allyn B., 603
Forestville Community, 167
Formalism (artistic), 672-673, 684-685, 690, 693, 698, 700, 711, 713
Foster, William Z., 112n, 333, 340, 341-345, 353-354, 698, 709, 710
Fourier, Charles, 4, 5n, 33, 46, 118, 156, 157-158, 159, 161, 198, 215, 412, 414, 631, 742

Fourierism, 4, 155, 159, 175-188, 207, 208; and art, 631-636; and Marxism, 205-207; and political theory, 198-201
Fourth International, 367n
Fowler, Orson Squire, 632
Fowlie, Wallace, 725n
Fraenkel, Osmund K., 290
Fraina, Louis, *see* Corey, Lewis
Francis, Saint, 107
Frank, Waldo, 354, 361, 363, 374n, 615, 617, 718, 719
Franklin Community, 166, 201, 204
Fraticelli, 36
Frazier, Lynn, 303, 305, 307
Free Enquirer, 173
Freeman, Joseph, 320n, 605, 607, 611-612, 614, 617-618, 680n, 719n, 720n
Freese, Arnold, 371n
Freewill Baptism, 130, 133
Freiheit, 239n
"French turn," 367, 386
Fretageot, Marie D., 164, 165
Freud, Sigmund, 203n
Fréville, Jean, 675n
Frey, William, 195n
Froissart, Jean, 30n
Frontier Fellowship, 122-123
Frost, Robert, 619
Fruitlands, 201
Fülöp-Miller, René, 648n
Functionalism, 674, 676, 687, 690n
Furriers Union, 310
Furuseth, Andrew, 302
Futurism, 674, 680, 684, 685, 722

Gabo, Naum, 675n, 679, 730-731
Gabriel, Ralph, 421
Garden-city movement, 653-654, 740
Garland, Hamlin, 605
Garnier, Tony, 658-659
Garrison, K. C., 581n
Garrison, William Lloyd, 114, 147, 166, 175
Gary, Elbert, 329
Gates, Theophilus R., 142
Gauthier, Maximilien, 666n
Gaylord, W. R., 312
Geddes, Patrick, 718
Gellert, Hugo, 717, 719, 721
Gellhorn, Martha, 617
General German Labor Association (N.Y.), 234
General strike, 219
George, Harrison, 346n, 397n
George, Henry, 77, 239-241, 650
Georgian style, 629, 635
Gerber, Julius, 324

Germer, Adolph, 316, 390n
Ghent, William J., 296, 312, 334
Gideonse, Harry D., 364n
Giedion, Siegfried, 656n
Gilbert, John, 203n
Gilruth, R. A., 173n
Ginger, Ray, 260n, 262
Ginzburg, Moises, 676, 689, 690n
Gitlow, Benjamin, 290n, 322, 324, 333, 335, 338, 340n, 345, 345n, 366, 688, 718n; on internal struggles in Communist Party, 338-340
Gladden, Washington, 117
Glassberg, Benjamin, 325
Glintenkamp, H. J., 717
Godin, W., 363n
Godwin, Parke, 194, 198, 207, 420
Godwin, William, 171
Goebel, George, 283n, 287, 294, 499n
Gold, Michael, 354, 395, 605, 607, 620, 688, 710, 719n
Goldenweiser, Alexander A., 436
Goldman, Emma, 239n, 288n, 716n
Goldwater, Robert J., 679n
Gollancz, Victor, 395
Gompers, Samuel, 223, 229, 234, 248-256, 270, 275, 279, 333, 496n; career, 249-250; his conservative syndicalism, 491-492; pure and simple unionism, 251
Good Morning, 718
Goodhue, Bertram G., 707
Goodman, Paul, 653n
Goodman, Percival, 653n
Goose Caucus (Communist Party), 339-341
Gorkin, Julián, 724n
Gorky, Maxim, 695n, 696, 706, 727n
Gothic Revival style, 629, 635, 651, 652, 653, 707
Goudy, Frederic W., 707
Gouldner, Alvin W., 549n
Graham, James D., 380
Graham, Shirley, 738n
Grand Prairie Community, 183n
Grand Prairie Harmonial Institute, 193
Grant, E. P., 195n
Gray, John, 47, 157, 165
Great Awakening, 129
Greek Revival style, 629, 635
Greeley, Horace, 175, 178, 180, 184, 194, 195n, 198, 431
Green, Calvin, 413n, 420
Green, John, 390
Green Corn Rebellion, 305-308
Greenback Labor Party, 236
Greenback Party, 207, 232

Greenberg, Hayim, 215n
Greene, William A., 198
Gregory, Horace, 607
Gridley affair, 297-298
Grimké, Frederick, 419
Gronlund, Laurence, 208, 229, 259, 260, 262, 270
Gropius, Walter, 660-669, 679, 740, 741, 742, 744
Gropper, William, 719, 721, 729, 736
Grosse, Edward, 250
Grosz, George, 659, 719, 742
Group Theatre, 354
Grünberg, Carl, 3n
Guesde, Jules, 65
Guild socialism, 10, 12, 15, 80-82, 652, 740
Gusev, S., 351
Guthrie, William B., 32n

Haase, Hugo, 328
Haile, Margaret, 294
Halévy, Élie, 45n
Hall, Charles, 44, 48
Hall, William, 47
Hallgren, Mauritz, 347n
Halper, Albert, 354
Halperin, S. William, 351n
Hamilton, Alexander, 478
Hamlin, Talbot, 676n
Hammersmith Socialist Society, 651
Haney, Lewis H., 471
Hanford, Ben, 278
Hansson, Per Albin, 94
Hapgood, Hutchins, 716n
Hapgood, Powers, 352n, 383, 390
Harap, Louis, 712, 713
Harbinger, 183, 184, 632
Hardie, Keir, 261
Harding, Warren G., 346
Hardman, Jacob B. S., 329n, 385-386
Hardy, Jack, 358
Harington, James, 40, 48
Harmon, John, 169
Harmonial Brotherhood, 193
Harriman, Job, 245, 273, 274, 286, 287, 294
Harring, Harro, 203
Harris, Thomas L., 193
Harrison, Hubert H., 716n
Hart, Henry, 616
Hartlaub, G. F., 660n
Hartley, David, 171
Hausenstein, Wilhelm, 686n
Havel, Hippolyte, 716n
Hawkins, Richmond L., 195n
Hawthorne, Nathaniel, 602

Hayden, Sterling, 727
Hayes, Max S., 254, 273, 278, 294, 331, 491
Haymarket affair, 238
Haywood, William D., 257, 278-280, 285, 287, 288, 289, 290, 295n, 298, 316, 491, 496n, 497, 498
Hearnshaw, Fossey J. C., 39n
Hearst, William Randolph, 271, 311, 315
Heath, Frederic, 264, 271, 294
Hecker, Isaac, 192
Hegel, Georg W. F., 57, 57n, 206, 430, 654
Hegelianism, 13n, 109, 435
Heiden, Konrad, 355n
Heimann, Eduard, 86n, 122
Heinzen, Karl, 239n
Heller, Helen West, 716n
Hellman, Lillian, 620
Hemingway, Ernest, 361, 362n, 604, 606, 617, 618, 620
Henderson Bay community, 265n
Hendrick, Burton J., 272
Henri, Robert, 715-716, 716n, 717
Henson, Francis, 377, 390
Herbst, Josephine, 607
Herrick, Robert, 605
Herron, George D., 122, 257, 264n, 273, 312
Herzen, Alexander, 233
Hewitt, Abram S., 241
Hexter, J. H., 34n
Hickey, Tom, 287
Hicks, Elias, 162n
Hicks, Granville, 348n, 350, 354, 395, 609, 614, 617
Higgins, Eugene, 706, 717
Hilferding, Rudolf, 256, 326n, 328, 463n, 485n
Hillman, Sidney, 372, 383, 390
Hillquit, Morris, 229, 244, 244n, 245, 257, 258, 273, 275, 282, 285, 294, 297, 297n, 311, 314, 317, 317n, 323, 325, 326n, 332, 369, 370, 401, 423, 463, 490; and A.F.L., 254; death, 377; N.Y. mayoralty campaign, 314-315, 319; on propaganda tactics, 284; on the socialist state, 515-516; opposition to, in Socialist Party, 371-372; theoretical orthodoxy, 327-328; views on labor party, 283
Himes, Joshua V., 175
Hinds, William A., 192n
Hindus, Maurice, 355n
Hirsch, David, 249
Hiss, Alger, 358n
Historical evolution, 44-45, 56, 67-68

Hitchcock, H.-R., 730n
Hitler, Adolf, 86, 112, 221, 228n, 480
Hoan, Dan, 371, 380, 381, 401, 403n, 481n, 490
Hobbes, Thomas, 32, 48, 171, 430
Hobson, Samuel G., 80
Hodgskin, Thomas, 45, 47, 48, 50, 455
Hollingsworth, Leta, 580
Holton, Harriet, 143
Home community, 208
Homestead strike, 242
Hook, Sidney, 222n, 351n-352n, 354, 364, 385, 419, 423-424, 448, 520, 522, 527n
Hope, Henry R., 658n
Hopedale Community, 178, 199, 204
Hopkins, Charles Howard, 120
Horta, Victor, 658n
Housing, 739-741
Howard, Ebenezer, 653-654, 740
Howard, Sidney, 354, 364n
Howe, Irving, 390n
Howell, Robert B., 307
Howells, William Dean, 270, 603, 705
Hubbard, Elbert, 707
Hughan, Jessie Wallace, 283n, 461n
Hughes, Charles Evans, 330
Hughes, Langston, 354, 618
Hughley, J. Neal, 122
Huizinga, Johan, 30n
Humanitarianism, 136, 431
Humboldt, Charles, 609n, 610n, 615
Hume, David, 171
Humphries, Rolfe, 607
Hunt, William Morris, 706
Hunter, Robert, 282, 297n, 312
Huntingdon, F. D., 119
Hutcheson, William, 333
Hutchinson, John, 171
Hutterite Brethren, 38
Hylan, John F., 314-315
Hyndman, Henry, 76, 657

I.W.W., 10, 254, 276, 278-280, 285, 289, 316, 491, 494, 497; Chicago faction, 280; Detroit faction, 280
Icarianism, 155, 158-159, 189-190, 204; and art, 631-636; and Marxism, 207-208
Immediate demands, 220, 274, 287, 499-500; De Leon on, 247
Independent Citizens Committee of the Arts, Sciences and Professions, 745
Independent Labour Party (Great Britain), 491
Index of American Design, 734
Individualism, 41-42
Industrial Communists (1919), 337

Industrial Workers of the World, see I.W.W.
Ingerman, Sergius, 319
Instrumentalism, 424
Integral Phalanx, 180, 204
Intercollegiate Socialist Society, 312
International, First, 7, 60-63, 189, 207, 233, 461; in U.S., 234-235
International, Second (Socialist), 66, 248, 327, 461
International, Third (Communist), 66, 86, 91, 319, 323, 325, 326, 328, 345, 492, 494; program, 85-87; shifts in tactics, 1919-1945, 350n; 7th world congress, 355-356
International, Fourth (Trotskyist), 388
International Bureau of Revolutionary Artists, 703-704
International Ladies' Garment Workers' Union, 310, 373, 381
International News, 367n
International Socialist Review, 282, 288, 296, 298-299, 315, 319, 461n, 462, 463, 707-708
International Style, 664-668, 676, 680, 683, 690-691, 701, 730, 731, 740
International Trade Union Educational League, 341
International Workers Order, 735
International Working Men's Association (1864-1878), see International, First
International Working People's Association (Anarchist), 237
Isaacs, William, 369n
Ise, John, 469
Iskra, 368
Italian Left Fraction of Communism, 367

Jacotot, Joseph, 158
Jakira, Abraham, 339n
James, William, 422, 448
Jarrett, Bede, 24, 28
Jászi, Oscar, 3n, 566n
Jazz, 738-739
Jefferson, Thomas, 161, 358, 743n
Jelagin, Juri, 693n
Jennings, Robert L., 163, 166, 201
Jerome, Victor J., 395, 711, 713, 746
Jewish Daily Forward, 278 310, 315, 369, 371, 377n, 381
Joachim of Floris, 108
John Reed Club, 709
Johnson, Magnus, 307
Johnson, Philip C., 730n
Jonas, Alexander, 294
Jones, Alfred Winslow, 545n

Jones, Ellis O., 312
Jones, Joe, 721
Jones, (Mother) Mary, 312
Jones, Owen, 656n
Jones Family, 306
Josephson, Matthew, 354, 616
Joyce, James, 713
Jules, Mervin, 729
Juridical socialism, 16-17

Kallen, Horace M., 374n, 736n
Kamenev, Lev B., 362, 683, 688, 693
Kampffmeyer, Paul, 65n
Kandinsky, Wassily, 660, 679, 679n, 742
Karsner, David, 262n, 334
Katterfeld, L. E., 339n
Kautsky, Karl, 38, 59n, 63n, 72-73, 215, 262, 326n, 327, 374, 379, 432; criticism of Bolsheviks, 91
Kazin, Alfred, 347n
Kearny, Denis, 236n
Keep, Arthur, 258, 259n
Keinard, Benjamin F., 259n
Keller, Helen, 290
Kemp, Harry, 716n
Kendal Community, 167, 168, 194, 195, 201
Kent, Rockwell, 716n, 721, 735, 747
Ker, William Balfour, 708
Keracher, John, 335
Kerr, Charles, 461n
Ketteler, Baron Wilhelm E. von, 655
Keynesianism, 479
Khachaturyan, Aram, 700
Kilpatrick, William H., 364n
Kingsley, Charles, 75, 650
Kinmont, Alexander, 419
Kirby, Georgianna Bruce, 189n, 192n
Kirk, Kenneth E., 113n
Klee, Paul, 660
Klingender, Francis D., 711
Knights of Labor, 236, 238, 245; *Journal*, 245
Koestler, Arthur, 362n, 398, 615
Kollontay, Alexandra, 320
Kollwitz, Käthe, 659
Komroff, Manuel, 716n
Korsh, Karl, 528n
Kreuger, Maynard, 371n, 389, 399
Kriege, Herman, 177n, 230-231, 240
Kroeber, Alfred L., 436
Kropotkin, Petr, 7, 10, 653, 657, 742
Krupskaya, Nadezhda, 686n
Kruse, William F., 316
Krzycki, Leo, 378, 389
Kuczynski, Jurgen, 216n

Kukryniksi, The, 624
Kunitz, Joshua, 611

Labor exchange bank, 231
Labor theory of value, 69, 71-72
Labour Party (British), 78, 332; recent program, 92-94
Labriola, Antonio, 215, 432
La Follette, Robert M., 307, 332-334
La Follette seamen's act, 302
La Guardia, Fiorello, 373
Laidler, Harry W., 39n, 57n, 70n, 448, 494n, 546n
Lamarckism, 196
La Monte, Robert R., 477
Land reform, 231, 239-241, 249
Landauer, Carl, 469
Lange, Oscar, 469
Langer, William, 305
Lanier, Lyle H., 619n
Largo Caballero, Francisco, 362, 388
Larkin, James, 322, 324
Lash, Joseph P., 360n, 382
Laski, Harold J., 37, 50, 86, 395
Lasky, Victor, 358n
Lassalle, Ferdinand, 12, 64, 233, 476, 654
Lassalleanism, 207, 250;
Lasser, David, 382
Lasswell, Harold, 300n
Laurrell, Karl Ferdinand, 250
Lawson, John Howard, 607
Lawson, Thomas, 272
Lazarus, Marx E., 191n
League for a Revolutionary Workers Party, 367
League for Independent Political Action, 369
League for Industrial Democracy, 370
League for Peace and Democracy, 396
League of American Writers, 361, 617-618, 736n
League of Professional Groups for Foster and Ford, 364n
Le Corbusier (pseud. of C. É. Jeanneret-Gris), 665, 676, 690, 742
Lee, Algernon, 294, 314, 370, 377-378, 381
Lee, Ann, 113, 114, 132-135, 413
Left, 354
Left Front, 354
Left Review, 354
Lehman, Herbert, 391
Lemke, William, 305
Lenin, Vladimir I., 4, 5n, 9, 13, 16, 86, 91, 110n, 246, 293, 295n, 319, 379, 233-236

432, 605, 645n, 648, 742; Bolshevik Revolution, 318-319; death, 88; and De Leon, 246n; 1918 letter to American workers, 322-323; on art, 677-678, 680-681; on final stage of communism, 110; on political tactics, 226-228; and Social Democratic Labor Party, 83; theory of art, 670-672; united front tactic, 343
Leninism, 492
Leninist League, 368
Lens, Sidney, 352n
Leo Frank case, 301
Leontief, Wassily, 469
Leraysville Phalanx, 180, 191, 204
Lerner, Abba, 522
Le Rossignol, J. E., 471
Leroux, Jules, 190
Leroux, Pierre, 159, 190
LeSeur, Arthur, 303n
Levelers, 114
Levine, Louis, 79n
Lewis, Alfred Baker, 394
Lewis, John L., 249, 329, 333, 352n, 373, 390
Lewis, Lena Morrow, 283n
Lewis, Sinclair, 364n, 605
Liberator, 322, 611, 718-719, 723
Lie, Trygve, 56
Liebknecht, Karl, 65, 318, 663
Life, 708
Lifshitz, Mikhail, 714
Lilienthal, David E., 482, 733
Lin, Mousheng H., 161n
Lincoln, Abraham, 358
Lindbergh, Charles, 394
Lindeman, E. C., 355n
Lindgren, Edward I., 322, 339n
Lindsay, Alexander D., 26
Linton, William J., 705
Lippmann, Walter, 290, 292, 313
Liquidators (Communist Party), 339-340
Lissitsky, El [L. M.], 679, 730
Literature and socialism, 601-620
Lloyd, Henry Demarest, 262, 271-272, 298
Lloyd, William Bross, 296n
Locke, John, 32, 46, 48, 118, 159, 171
Locomotive Firemen's Magazine, 261
Lodge, Nucia, 648n
London, Jack, 257, 295, 312, 603, 705
London, Kurt, 681n
London, Meyer, 257, 257n, 294, 311, 317, 370n
Long, Huey, 383n
Longley, Alcander, 172, 173n, 196, 207

Longuet, Jean, 326n
Lore, Ludwig, 320, 335, 343, 344, 345n-346n, 385, 683
Los Angeles Times, 280n, 285
Lovestone, Jay, 339, 340, 341, 344, 345, 345n, 384n, 390, 609n, 688
Lovestoneites, see Communist Party Opposition
Lovett, Robert Morss, 605, 611
Lowenfeld, Henry, 398n
Lowie, Robert H., 436
Löwith, Karl, 108-109, 118n
Lozowick, Louis, 684n, 719, 720, 721, 736
Lubetkin, B., 685n
Luks, George, 715
Lumpkin, Grace, 354, 620
Lumpkin, Katharine Du Pre, 546n
Lunacharsky, Anatoly V., 671n, 678
Lundberg, Ferdinand, 364n
Lundy, Benjamin, 166
Lunn, George R., 292
Lurçat, André, 676n
Lusk committee, 324
Luther, Martin, 115-117
Luxemburg, Rosa, 226, 319, 323, 663
Lynd, Helen M., 545n
Lynd, Robert S., 545n
Lyons, Eugene, 353n, 359, 364n, 618n

Mably, Gabriel B. de, 33, 40
McAdoo, William G., 332
McBee, Alice E., 173n
McBride, John, 252
McCabe, Joseph, 716n
McCarthy, Joseph R., 397
McCarthy, Mary, 614
McCartney, Frederic O., 294
McCartney, James, 489n
McClure, Samuel S., 272
McClure's Magazine, 272
McDaniel, Osborne, 195n
MacDonald, Duncan, 331, 333
Macdonald, Dwight, 402n, 614, 693n
MacDonald, J. Ramsay, 79n, 308, 326n
McDowell, Arthur, 392n, 394
Macedonia Cooperative Community, 173
Macfadyen, Dugald, 654n
McGlynn, Edward, 241
McGuire, P. J., 249, 252, 270
Machiavelli, Niccolò, 31
McIlwain, C. H., 28n
MacIver, Robert M., 527n, 546n
McKay, David, 332n
McKenney, Ruth, 397n
McKinley, William, 267
M'Knight, James, 168, 168n, 201n, 204

MacLean, John P., 132n
MacLeish, Archibald, 361, 606, 607, 617, 620
McLevy, Jasper, 381, 402, 403n, 490, 589
Maclure, William, 164-165, 171, 171n, 172, 173, 204
Macluria community, 165, 204
McNamara case, 285
McNemar, Richard, 131
Macy, Matthew, 169
Madison, Charles A., 474n
Magil, Abraham B., 613, 710
Mainstream, 710, 711
Malevich, Kazimir S., 742
Maltz, Albert, 607, 710, 726
Man, Henri de, 657n
Manesca, Jean, 178
Mann, Thomas, 618, 746
Mannheim, Karl, 24, 155, 194
Manuilsky, Dmitri Z., 351
Marcantonio, Vito, 396n, 619n
Marinetti, Filippo T., 674
Markham, Edwin, 716n
Marlboro Association, 199
Marlen, George (pseud. of George Spiro), 368n
Marshall Plan, 747
Martel, Harry, 713
Martin, Homer, 390
Martov, Yuly O., 83
Marty, André, 362
Marx, Karl, 8, 45, 58n, 118, 222n, 231, 295n, 379, 432, 605, 653, 742; and American socialism, 420; and art, 625, 712; and Communist League, 55; authorship of *Critique of the Gotha Programme*, 5n; class theories, 223n; dictatorship of the proletariat, 8; expulsion of Weitling, 159; and First International, 61-63, 74; on American prospects, 215; on classical art, 639-641; on single tax, 240; theory of art, 670-672; theory of surplus value, 68-70; see also *Communist Manifesto*
Marxism, 4, 7, 12-14, 16-17, 44; absolute determinism, 439-442; and American communitarianism, 204-211; and American economic thought, 468-473; and American intellectuals, 348-350; and art, 636-751; Austro-Marxism, 375-376, 491; concept of property, 541-542; contrasted with Revisionism, 72-73; and Darwinism, 435; De Leon's contribution, 246-248; dialectical method, 446-447; dialectics in nature, 445-446; economic theory, 456-460; and Fabianism, 75-77; and history, 13-14; industrial

bureaucratization, 542-543; influence on Christian socialists, 122; introduction to America, 231, 233-235; its evolutionary approach, 435-439; its criticism of Social Gospel, 120; on nature of man, 432-435; organicism, 442-445; philosophical basis, 429-451; political types, 490-493; and religion, 109-112; sociological economics, 527-534; terminology, 5n; theoretical bases, 66-70; theory of stratification, 534-543; and utopian socialism, 127
Marxist, 367n
Marxist Workers League, 368
Masses, 289-290, 312, 313n, 315, 316, 322, 604, 610-611, 708, 715, 717, 718, 723
Masses & Mainstream, 607, 609, 615, 710, 713, 714, 720-721, 726, 737
Massing, Hede, 346n, 398n
Masters, Edgar Lee, 301
Materialistic interpretation of history, *see* Economic interpretation of history
Mather, Frank J., Jr., 706n
Matisse, Henri, 699
Matles, James, 357
Matthews, Joseph B., 359-360, 371n, 377
Maurer, James, 402n, 572
Maurice, Frederick D., 75, 650, 657
Maxwell, S. A., 303n
May, Henry E., 119
Mayakovsky, Vladimir V., 355n, 675
Meacham, Joseph, 132, 133, 137
Mead, Margaret, 569n
Mechanistic functionalism, 672-673, 689, 690
Meilakh, Boris, 700n
Melcher, Marguerite, 132n
Melnikov, K. C., 676
Melville, Herman, 268, 602
Mencken, Henry L., 280n, 605
Mendelsohn, Erich, 676n
Menger, Anton, 16-17
Mensheviks, 83-85, 318
Mercantilism, 33
Merriam, Frank F., 374
Merton, Robert K., 527n, 547n
Mesmerism, 150
Methodism, 129, 131
Meunier, Constantin, 684
Meyer, Hannes, 662, 665, 667, 676, 676n, 691
Meyerhold, Vsevolod E., 693
Mienov, Karl, 368
Mies van der Rohe, Ludwig, 660, 662, 663-666, 669, 679, 741
Milinis, ———, 676, 689

Militants (Socialist Party), 370-371, 374-376, 378-384, 386-388, 394
Mill, John Stuart, 75, 77, 455
Millay, Edna St. Vincent, 605, 607
Millennialism, 45, 106, 110, 129, 130, 132, 133, 138, 140, 175, 192, 218, 420; intermillennialism, 134-136, 140-141, 150; premillennialism, 134-135, 140, 150
Millennium, 7, 11, 108
Miller, Ernest C., 173n
Miller, Louis, 294
Miller, Samuel, 419
Miller, William, 130, 175
Millet, Jean F., 706
Millinery Workers Union, 310, 381
Mills, Walter Thomas, 303n, 306
Milwaukee Leader, 309, 315
Milwaukee Vorwärts, 263
Minor, Robert, 345, 717, 718, 721, 722
Mins, Leonard E., 61n
Minton, Bruce, 397n
Miró, Joan, 731
Mitchell, John Ames, 708
Mitchell, John Purroy, 315
Mitchell, Wesley Clair, 364n
Modern Monthly, 714
Modern Quarterly, 362
Modern School, 716
Modern School, 716n
Modern Times community, 200
Modigliani, Giuseppe E., 326n
Moholy-Nagy, László, 668-669, 679, 719n, 741, 742-744
Moleschott, Jacob, 433
Molly Maguires, 235
Molotov, Vyacheslav M., 694
Mondrian, Piet, 668, 731n, 742
Monetary reform, 231, 249, 262
Mooney, Tom, 316
Moore, Gwyn, 581n
Moore, Henry T., 581
Moravian Anabaptism, 36, 38
More, Thomas, 30, 33-37, 40, 50, 51, 109
Morelly, 33, 40
Morgan, Lewis, 436
Morgan, Thomas J., 252, 282n, 294
Morley, Henry, 36n
Mormonism; and art, 628-630
Morris, William, 12, 15, 17, 80, 220, 650-654, 655, 656, 657-658, 658n, 666, 706, 707, 718, 742, 744
Morse, John D., 726n
Moscow Art Theater, 728
Moscow trials, 361, 362-364, 613, 721; and American writers, 607
Moses, Robert, 733

Most, Johann, 238, 239n
Mountain Cove community, 193
Moyer-Haywood-Pettibone case, 278-279
Muckrakers, 271-272
Münster Anabaptism, 36
Münsterberg, Hugo, 565
Münzenberg, Willi, 359
Muir, Jean, 748n
Mukhina, Vera, 696
Mumford, Lewis, 615, 651n, 718, 736, 740
Murphy, Frank, 390-391
Murray, Orson S., 172, 199
Murray, William, 308
Muscovite baroque style, 701
Museum of Modern Art, New York, 730-732
Mussolini, Benito, 86
Muste, A. J., 121, 122, 385-386
Muthesius, Hermann, 661n-662n
Mutual criticism, 148-149
Myaskovsky, Nikolai Y., 700
Myers, Gustavus, 268

Nashoba community, 166
Nation, 329, 395
National Association for the Advancement of Colored People, 737
National Association of Manufacturers, 481n
National Council of Arts, Sciences and Professions, 746
National Labor Union, 232, 234
National Maritime Union, 397n
National Miners Union, 352n
National Negro Congress, 737
National Party, *see* Greenback Labor Party
National Rip-Saw, see *Social Revolution*
National Youth Administration, 361
Nationalism, Bellamyite, 208
Naturalism, 706
Nauvoo community (Icarian), 189
Nazi-Soviet pact, *see* Soviet-German pact
Nazism, 86, 99, 111, 363, 374-376, 665
Nechayev, Sergei, 234
Neef, Joseph, 165, 172
Negrete, Rosario, 367
Negrín, Juan, 362
Neo-Calvinist socialism, 122-123
Neo-Classicism, 684
Neoliberal socialism, 522
Neoplasticism, 668, 731n
Neue Zeit, 70, 319, 461n
New Appeal, see *Appeal to Reason*
New Dance, 354

New Deal, 221, 265, 372, 383, 390, 450, 465, 479, 486, 655; and art, 732-736
New Democracy, 234
New Harmony community, 163-169, 173, 189, 194, 201, 204
New Harmony Gazette, 166, 170, 173
New International (Socialist Propaganda League), 320
New Leader, 289n, 362, 381
New Llano community, 208
New Masses, 606, 607, 608n, 611, 612, 613, 615, 616n, 710, 711, 712, 714, 719-721, 735, 737
New Moral World, 157
New Republic, 292, 313, 329, 395
New School for Social Research, New York, 729-730
New Theatre, 354
New Times, 670n
New Workers' School, New York, 725n
New York Call, 283, 295n, 309, 311, 313, 315
New York Society for Promoting Communities, 161
New York Tribune, 175, 178, 179, 181, 183, 184, 261
New Yorker Volkszeitung, 243, 258
Newcomb, Charles K., 192
Newcomb, Simon, 472
Newhouse, Edward, 354, 607
Newton, Isaac, 159, 171
Nichols, Thomas L., 209n
Niebuhr, H. Richard, 117, 121
Niebuhr, Reinhold, 122, 380, 381-382, 394, 448, 522
Niemeyer Soares, Oscar, 666
Nietzsche, Friedrich W., 657
Nin, Andrés, 362
Nisbeth, Hugo, 190n
Non-Partisan League, 292, 303-305
Nordhoff, Charles, 546n
Norris, Frank, 605
Norris, George W., 307, 369, 482
North American Committee to Aid Spanish Democracy, 387
North American Phalanx, 184-189, 204, 207
Northampton Association, 183, 194, 199, 201, 204
Novembergruppe, 660, 679
Novy-Mir, 682
Noyes, John Humphrey, 114, 115, 140-150, 172n, 192n, 193, 546n, 601, 624, 630
Nussbaum, Frederick L., 27n
Nye, Gerald, 305, 307
Nygaardsvold, Johan, 94

Oberlin, J. F., 157
Oberman, Karl, 460n
Odets, Clifford, 354, 620
Odger, George, 60
Oehler, Hugo, 367
O'Hare, Kate Richards, 306, 323
Ohio Phalanx, 183n
Olgin, Moissaye J., 616
Olivier, Sidney, 76
Olney, Richard, 261
Olson, Ruth, 730n
One Big Union Club, 368n
One-Mentian Community, 199
Oneal, James, 289, 296, 319, 325, 370n, 371
Oneida Community, 7, 145-150, 193, 546, 547; and art, 628-630
Oneida Perfectionism, 11, 114-115, 127, 140-150; doctrine, 141-143
Operationalism, 434
Orage, Alfred R., 80
Orozco, José, 723, 724, 729-730, 734n
Ortega y Gasset, José, 399
Orvis, John, 193, 195n, 208
Osborn, Frederic J., 654n
Osthaus, Karl E., 658n
Otis, Brooks, 470
Otis, Harrison Grey, 280n
Overstreet, Harry A., 364n
Owen, Robert, 3, 15, 33, 35, 43-48, 118, 156-157, 159, 160, 161-173, 193, 198, 204, 230, 231, 631, 634, 653
Owen, Robert Dale, 173-174, 193
Owen, William, 163
Owenism, 4, 155, 157, 161-174, 178, 194, 199, 207; and art, 631-636; and political theory, 198-201

Pacifism, 139
Page, Charles H., 474n
Page, Kirby, 370
Page, Myra, 354
Paine, Thomas, 171, 358, 743n
Palmer, A. Mitchell, 330, 605
Palmer raids, 330
Panken, Jacob, 378
Paris Commune, 63, 207
Parker, Barry, 654
Parker, Robert A., 624n
Parker, Theodore, 195
Parkes, Henry B., 471
Parks, Larry, 727
Parliamentarism, 62
Parrington, Vernon L., 114n, 474
Parrington, Vernon L., Jr., 229
Parrot, Louis, 712n
Parsons, Albert R., 236, 238

Parsons, Lucy, 278
Partisan Review, 354, 612-614, 709, 714
Partisans of Peace, 712n
Party Builder, 289
Party Organizer, 353
Paternalism, 26
Patterson, Joseph Medill, 257n, 296n
Peace Information Center, 747
Pears, Sarah, 169
Pears, Thomas, 163, 169
Pears, Thomas C. Jr., 169n
Pease, Edward R., 76n
Pelham, Caroline C., 170n
Pelham, William, 163, 169, 196n
Penty, Arthur J., 80, 653
People, 257, 258
People's World, 397n
Pepper, John, 341, 343, 345n
Perfectionism, 112-115, 129, 132, 139, 141-144, 147, 149, 171, 172, 192, 200; Antinomian, 142; *see also* Oneida Perfectionism
Perkins, Frances, 383, 732n
Perlman, Selig, 216, 276n
Perry, Arthur L., 472
Perry, Ralph Barton, 364n
Pestalozzi, Johann H., 157
Peters, J., 549n
Peters, Paul, 607
Peterson, Jacob, 166, 166n, 204
Petty, William, 69
Pevsner, Nikolaus, 656n, 679
Phillips, Wendell, 177n
Phillips, William, 613
Photo-naturalism, 689
Picasso, Pablo, 675, 699, 712, 730, 738, 742, 747
Pieck, Wilhelm, 356, 356n
Pietism, 127
Pigou, Arthur C., 455
Pilnyak, Boris, 355n
Pinchot, Amos, 331
Plato, 24, 36, 104, 565
Plekhanov, Georgy V., 447, 712, 714
Point Hope Community, 200
Political Action Committee, 304, 335
Political Affairs, 699, 700, 711, 713
Poole, Ernest, 312, 705, 726
Poor, Henry Varnum, 734
Popular Front, 350n, 354-355, 606, 692, 709, 732, 737; in literature, 617-619
Popular Tribune, 188
Populism, 207, 245, 262, 291, 431
Porter, James A., 738n
Porter, Paul, 380n, 384, 392, 394
Portinari, Candido, 731
Positivism, 150, 434

Postgate, Raymond W., 84n
Potter, Henry Codman, 119
Powderly, Terence V., 245, 270
Poyntz, Juliet Stuart, 345n-346n
Pragmatism, 434
Prairie Home Community, 194, 199
Pravda, 683, 692, 693, 695n, 697, 699, 700, 712
Pressman, Lee, 357, 358n
Profintern, 342
Progress, 135, 141, 419-420; and art, 644-646
Progressive Labor Party (N.Y.), 241
Progressive Party, 397
Prokofyev, Sergei, 700
Proletarian Party (1920), 335, 338
Proletarian Socialist Party, *see* Industrial Communists (1919)
Proletarischer Magid, 310
Proletarskaya Revolyutsiya, 691
Proletcult, 354-355, 677, 678n, 688, 689, 692, 709, 710
Proudhon, Pierre Joseph, 7, 35, 198, 706, 742
Psychological sources of socialism, 559-562; clientele, 579-583; closure tendencies, 574-579; "conversion," 586-589; motivation, 583-586; need and frustration, 562-565; obstacles, 590-598; value, conflict, and power, 565-570; varieties of behavior, 570-579
Puech, Jules L., 42n, 46n
Pullman strike, 242, 261
Pulte, J. H., 195
Pushkin, Aleksandr S., 696
Putney Community, 142-145

Quakerism, 132, 141, 194, 199
Quarterly Journal of Economics, 477
Quill, Michael, 357

Radek, Karl, 362
Rahv, Philip, 608n, 612-615
Railway Times, 262
Ralston, Walter, 610n
Ramsden, E. H., 744n
Ramsey, David, 609n
Rand, Carrie, 312
Rand School, 312, 325, 379
Randall, Benjamin, 130
Rappites, 113, 114, 127, 161, 162, 163, 601; and art, 626-628
Raritan Bay Association, 187, 204
Rauschenbusch, Walter, 400
Ray, Man, 716n
Ray, Marcel, 660n
Read, Herbert, 653, 656, 725n, 744

Realism, 674; *see also* Socialistic realism

Reckitt, Maurice B., 80n

Record, Wilson, 788n

Redfield, Abraham, 721

Reed, John, 296, 312, 323, 324, 335, 604, 610

Reed, Louis S., 252n

Reese, Maria, 356n

Reform, 460

Regenerator, 199

Rein, Mark, 362

Reiss, Marvin, 713

Religious socialism, 7, 99-123, 431, 522; *see also* Christian socialism; Communitarianism, Christian; Utopian socialism; entries under specific movements, e.g., Shakerism

Renaissance style, 673

Republican Party, 177, 209, 267, 304

Reunion, Texas, 636

Reuther, Walter, 390-391

Revisionist socialism, 70-73; U.S., 448-450

Revivalism, 178

Revolution, 460

Revolutionary Age, 320

Revolutionary Policy Committee, 376-377, 384, 390

Revolutionary socialism, 4-5, 79, 84-85, 119, 440, 549-553

Revolutionary tactics, 62

Revolutionary Workers League, 367-368, 386

Rhodes, George, 403

Ricardo, David, 44, 46, 48, 69

Rieve, Emil, 372

Ripley, George, 195

Ripley, Sophia, 192

Rivera, Diego, 723, 724-726, 734, 734n

Robeson, Paul, 397, 747

Robinson, Boardman, 717, 718, 723

Robinson, Elizabeth, 203n

Robinson, Reid, 357

Robsjohn-Gibbings, T. H., 679n

Rochester, Anna, 352n

Rockefeller, John D., 262

Roe, Daniel, 165

Rogers, Kathryn, 300n

Rogge, O. John, 397

Rogin, Leo, 469, 479n

Rohe, Ludwig Mies van der, *see* Mies van der Rohe, Ludwig

Rohland, Paul, 716n

Rolland, Romain, 359

Rollins, William, 354

Roosevelt, Eleanor (Mrs. F. D.), 361, 745

Roosevelt, Franklin D., 112, 221, 356, 357, 372, 381, 383, 389, 390n, 478, 482, 486, 732, 734

Roosevelt, Theodore, 241, 271, 288, 315

Roosevelt, Theodore, Jr., 333

Rorty, James, 354, 364n

Rose, Billy, 746n

Rosenberg, Harold, 222n

Rosenfeld, Paul, 718

Roskolenko, Harry, 617

Ross, Edward Alsworth, 363n

Rousseau, Jean Jacques, 118, 160, 171, 198, 200, 210, 742

Rubin, Barnard, 713

Rudas, Ladislaus, 446n

Rukeyser, Muriel, 607, 620

Rummager, 338

Rummagers' League, *see* Industrial Communists (1919)

Ruskin, John, 75, 650, 651, 651n, 656, 658, 705, 718

Ruskin Community, 259

Russell, Charles Edward, 272, 288, 303n, 312, 313n, 314, 716n

Russo-German pact, *see* Soviet-German pact

Ruthenberg, Charles, 314, 316, 321, 324, 340, 341, 342-344, 345n

Rykov, Aleksei I., 362

SASS (Section of Architects of Socialist Construction [U.S.S.R.]), 689n

Sabine, George H., 37n, 40

Sacco, Nicola, 330

Sacco-Vanzetti case, 726

St. John, Vincent, 279, 497

Saint-Simon, Claude, 33, 45, 118, 159, 175, 412, 413

Salter, John T., 403n

Samson, Leon, 450

Sánchez, Salazar, Leandro A., 724n

Sanger, Margaret, 290

Sanial, Lucien, 251, 258n, 313

Saposs, David J., 250n, 385

Saunders, Charles, 499n

Sawyer, Charles H., 706n

Schapiro, Meyer, 666n, 681n, 736, 739

Scheidemann, Philipp, 328

Scheler, Max, 298, 302

"Schismatics," 131

Schlesinger, Benjamin, 491

Schlesinger, Rudolf, 692n

Schlüter, Hermann, 294, 460n

Schmalenbach, Fritz, 660n

Schmeckebier, Laurence E., 724n

Schmidt, Johann K., *see* Stirner, Max, pseud.

Schneider, David, 352n
Schneider, Isidor, 605, 607, 615-616, 617
Schopenhauer, Arthur, 411
Schulze-Delitzsch, F. H., 63, 64
Schumpeter, Joseph A., 348, 469n, 528n
Schurz, Carl, 309
Science & Society, 470
Scientific socialism, 5, 43, 44
Screen Writers' Guild, 726
Seaver, Edwin, 354, 617
Section of Architects of Socialist Construction (U.S.S.R.), see SASS
Seidel, Emil, 288
Seidman, Joel, 352n
Seligman, Edwin R. A., 68n, 470
Semper, Gottfried, 656, 666
Senior, Clarence, 370n, 375n, 383n
Serge, Victor, 362n, 587
Seven Arts, 717-718
Shachtman, Max, 344, 366n, 368, 683
Shahn, Ben, 726, 736
Shakerism, 7, 11, 112-113, 114, 127, 128, 132-140, 142, 143, 146, 161, 162, 189, 202, 601; and art, 626-628; and democracy, 139-140; social and political theory, 136-140; view of history, 135-136
Shambaugh, Bertha M. H., 627n
Shannon, Martha, 706n
Shapiro, Theodore, 370n
Share-the-Wealth movement, 373
Shaw, George Bernard, 76, 77, 255, 652
Sheean, Vincent, 361, 395, 607, 618
Shipkov, Michael, 362n
Shipstead, Hendrik, 307
Shostakovich, Dmitri, 693, 700, 746
Shuster, George N., 364n
Sillen, Samuel, 609, 612, 619n, 710, 711, 713
Simkhovitch, V. G., 471
Simons, Algie M., 274, 280, 282, 312, 461n, 463, 499n
Simpson, Herman, 258n
Sinclair, Upton, 272, 304, 312, 361, 371n, 373-374, 383n, 595, 604, 605, 607, 705, 716n, 726
Single tax, 239-240
Siqueiros, David Alfaro, 723-724, 746
Sismondi, J. C. L. de, 69
Sissman, Peter, 294
Skaneateles community, 172, 204
Skelton, Oscar D., 471
Skidmore, Thomas, 230
Sklar, George, 607
Sloan, John, 715, 716n, 717, 719, 729
Slobodkin, Henry, 312
Smith, Adam, 32, 46, 47, 48, 171

Smith, Alfred E., 333
Smith, Bernard, 609, 719n
Smith, Edwin S., 358, 358n
Smith, J. Allen, 268
Smith Act, 346n
Smolnikar, Andreas B., 192n, 193-194
Social Democracy of America, 244, 257, 260, 263
Social Democracy Red Book, 271
Social Democratic Federation 388, 392, 490; revisionist tendencies, 450
Social Democratic Herald, 278, 294
Social Democratic Labor Party, see Communism (Russian)
Social Democratic Party (Danish), 94
Social Democratic Party (German), 70, 86, 95, 461
Social Democratic Party (Norwegian), 94
Social Democratic Party (Swedish), 94
Social Democratic Party of America, 229, 258, 264-267, 271, 274; immediate demands, 265-266
Social Democratic Party of North America, 235
Social Democratic Workingmen's Party (German), 64-65
Social Democratic Workingmen's Party (U.S.), 461
Social Gospel, 264n
Social Gospel movement, 117, 119-121
Social legislation, 302
Social Party of New York, 234
Social Reform Association, 231
Social Reform Unity, 180
Social Revolution (formerly National Rip-Saw), 315
Socialism: and art, see Art and socialism; causes of failure, 217-228; criticism of communism, 91; early history, 23-51; history in U.S., 127-151, 155-211, 215-405; history of term, 3-6; recent history, 55-96; religious history, 99-123; types, 3-17; see also Christian socialism; Communism; Communitarianism, Christian; Communitarianism, liberal; Democratic socialism; Evolutionary socialism; Fabian socialism; Guild socialism; Juridical socialism; Neo-Calvinist socialism; Neoliberal socialism; Religious socialism; Revisionist socialism; Revolutionary socialism; Scientific socialism; State socialism; Utopian socialism
Socialism (Belgian), 94
Socialism (Czechoslovakian), 94-95
Socialism (French), 94-95
Socialism (Swiss), 94

Socialism (U.S.): and agrarian radicalism, 303-308; causes of failure, 450-451, 483-486, 543-546; clientele, 553-556, 579-583; evaluation, 402-405; and governmental policy, 477-483; history, 127-151, 155-211, 215-405; its peak in U.S., 267-268; psychological aspects, 559-598; sociological aspects, 525-556; its theory of history, 409-425; types, 546-553; and unionism, 223-225; utopian spirit, 215-217; and war, 502-504
Socialism and capitalism, 46-51, 68-70
Socialism and democracy, 77, 149, 418-425, 450-451, 511-512, 728-741
Socialism and individualism, 23-26, 30-35, 42, 416-417
Socialist Appeal, 387
Socialist Call, 379
Socialist International, *see* International, Second (Socialist)
Socialist Labor Party, 14, 207, 208, 251, 252, 253, 257, 258n, 263, 265, 274, 293, 337n-338n, 368-369, 448, 461; capture of the state, 496; distinctive doctrine, 490; early history, 236-249; factions, 243-244; immediate demands, 500-501; Kangaroos, 245-246, 258; strategy, 497
Socialist Labor Party (Cincinnati), 244
Socialist League (British), 651
Socialist Party (Italy), 95
Socialist Party (New York), 333
Socialist Party (U.S.), 9, 14, 246, 248, 257, 266, 461; capture of the state, 496; causes of decline, 291-293; commercialism, 298-299; and communism, 319-327; decline, 302-328; doctrinal diversity, 490-491; economic theory, 464-465; factionalism, 273-278, 369-382, 384-388; foreign-language federations, 308-311, 321, 323, 327; formation, 257; history, 273-278; immediate demands, 372, 499; internal problems, 293-302; its dilemma, 220-222; labor-party issue, 388-389; and labor unions, 389-391; and Nazism, 393-394; 1920 nomination, 331; Popular Front, 384; recent history, 369-384, 386-394, 399-402; revisionist tendencies, 450; the revolution, 494; strategy, 497; strength in 1912, 465n; and syndicalism, 498; unity negotiations with Communist Party, 382; wooed by communists, 356; and World War I, 308-309, 311-318; and World War II, 392-394
Socialist political theory: central problems, 509-518; the movement, 504-506; the new social order, 506-509; or-

ganicism, 517-518; on proletarian dictatorship, 514-517; the revolution, 493-495; the socialist state, 513-517; socialists in the existing order, 495-504
Socialist Propaganda League, 319, 320
Socialist Sentinel, 379n
Socialist Trades and Labor Alliance, 245, 253
Socialist Unity Party (German), 95
Socialist Voice, 379n
Socialist Workers Party, 346n, 388, 493
Socialistic Labor Party, *see* Socialist Labor Party
Socialistic realism, 695-697, 698, 699, 701, 702-703, 711
Solomon, Charles, 380
Sombart, Werner, 24, 215-217
Somerville, John, 689n
Sorel, Georges, 219, 653, 674
Sorge, Friedrich, 234, 235, 240, 248, 251, 420, 461
Sorokin, Pitirim A., 527n
Sovereigns of Industry, 208
Soviet Art, 690n
Soviet-German pact, 350n, 618, 720; its effect on American communists, 395-396; and American writers, 607-608
Soyer, Moses, 721n, 729
Soyer, Raphael, 721, 729
Spaak, Henri-Paul, 56
Spanish Civil War, 361-362, 387-388, 617
Spargo, John, 282, 286, 297n, 312, 420, 706, 708, 715
Spark, 368
Spartacism, 336
Spear, Charles A., 194
Spear, John Murray, 172, 193, 194
Speer, William, 131n
Spencer, Herbert, 269, 436
Spencer, Niles, 736
Spengler, Joseph J., 469
Spengler, Oswald, 412
Spinoza, Baruch, 171
Spiritual Franciscans, 29
Spiritualism, 138-139, 192
Stachel, Jack, 345, 345n-346n, 382
Stalin, Joseph, 4, 16, 84n, 295n, 318, 671, 675n; address on unionism, 1929, 352; consolidation of power, 88, 345, 350; influence on art, 681-705; Soviet expansion in Eastern Europe, 90; on Soviet planning, 482n; "troika," 362
Stalinism, 493; and art, 688-705
Stamm, Tom, 367
State capitalism, 9, 12, 87, 654, 732
State socialism, 9, 12, 87, 654
Stearns, Harold, 347

Stedman, Seymour, 294, 324
Steffens, Lincoln, 272, 348, 716n
Stein, Clarence, 740
Steinbeck, John, 610n, 620
Stephens, Uriah, 236
Stetler, Henry G., 402n, 554
Steunenberg, Frank, 279
Stewart, Donald Ogden, 361, 617
Stickley, Gustave, 706
Stirner, Max, pseud. (Johann K. Schmidt), 657
Stockholm peace petition, see World Peace Appeal
Stoicism, 104-106, 171
Stokes, J. G. Phelps, 257n, 290, 295, 313
Stokes, Rose Pastor, 313
Stolberg, Benjamin, 357n, 363n
Stone, Barton W., 131
Stone, Irving, 300n
Stone, Nahum I., 252n, 294
Stowe, Leland, 618
Strachey, John, 395
Strand, Paul, 363
Strasser, Adolph, 235, 249, 252
Street, George Edmund, 652
Strong, Anna Louise, 355n
Sumner, William Graham, 419, 478n
Sunrise Community, 208
Suprematism, 668, 674
Surplus value theory, 68-70, 71, 76, 457, 464, 475
Surrealism, 724-725, 731
Swedenborgianism, 191, 193
Sweeney, James J., 717n, 730n
Sweezy, Paul M., 528n
Sylvania Phalanx, 180
Sylvis, William, 232
Symes, Lillian, 546n
Syndicalism, 10, 44, 78-79, 146, 177, 219, 233, 276, 280, 491; abolition of the state, 496; and orthodox socialism, 79; strategy, 497
Syndicalist League of North America, 341

Taborites, 36
Taft, M. H., 294
Taft, Philip, 276n
Taggard, Genevieve, 607
Tarbell, Ida, 272
Tatlin, V., 675, 679, 683
Taussig, Frank W., 472
Taut, Bruno, 676n
Tawney, Richard H., 26, 28
Taylor, Nathaniel W., 141
Technocracy, 373
Tennessee Valley Authority, 481-483, 733

Thälmann, Ernst, 351n
Thalheimer, August, 336
Theatre Collective, 354, 709
Theatre of Action, 354
Theatre Union, 354
Thelen, Mary Frances, 109n
Thomas, Norman, 121, 225n, 333, 334, 364n, 369-375, 382, 388-389, 394, 399-402, 423, 442, 448, 516n, 522
Thompson, Carl D., 312
Thompson, Dorothy, 364n
Thompson, William, 47, 157, 455
Thoreau, Henry David, 10, 200, 601, 657
Thorndike, Edward L., 582
Tillich, Paul, 122
Tito, Marshal (Josif Broz), 90, 695n
Toledano, Ralph de, 358n
Tolstoy, Leo, 657
Tom Watson's Magazine, 301
Torgler, Ernst, 356n
Tory socialism, 44
Townley, Arthur C., 303-304
Townsend movement, 373
Toynbee, Arnold J., 293
Trachtenberg, Alexander, 290n, 325, 712
Trade Union Educational League, 342, 551
Trade Union Unity League, 352, 551
Trade unionism, 62, 75, 77, 81, 286; and politics, 332-333; see also entries under specific unions
Trager, Frank, 382
Trautmann, William, 279
Tresca, Carlo, 346n, 363n
Trevelick, Richard, 236
Trilling, Lionel, 348n
Troeltsch, Ernst, 116n, 117
Trotsky, Leon, 215, 295n, 319, 432, 609n, 687; and art theory, 682-686; assassination attempt, 724; controversy with Stalin, 88; Dewey commission, 363, 721; in U.S., 320, 319n-320n; on art, 623; on democratic centralism, 227; on Hillquit, 319; on Moscow trials, 363; and Rivera, 724; supported by Cannon and Shachtman, 344; supported by L. Lore, 343
Trotskyism, 14
Trotskyism (U.S.), 366, 384-388, 494, 708; and American writers, 605-606; and art, 714-715
Trumbull Phalanx, 180
Tucker, Irwin St. John, 316
Tugwell, Rexford, 740
Tukhachevsky, Mikhail N., 363
Turati, Filippo, 326n
Turgot, A. R. J., 109

Turner, Frederick Jackson, 243n, 471, 474
Tyler, Gus, 384, 388, 394
Tzara, Tristan, 725

Underwood, Samuel, 169
Unitarianism, 431
United American Artists, 619n, 736, 736n
United Auto Workers, 335, 390
United Communist Party (1920), 336, 338
United Crafts of Eastwood, 706
United Electrical Workers, 397
United Hebrew Trades, 244
United Labor Party, 239-241
United Labor Party of Chicago, 239
United Mine Workers, 308, 331, 352n
United Office and Professional Workers Union, 382
United Society of Believers in Christ's Second Appearing, see Shakerism
United States, Congress, House, Committee on Un-American Activities, 358n, 360n, 726-727, 732, 735, 736, 746
United States, Resettlement Administration, 740
United Toilers of America (1922), 338, 339
Universalism, 129
Untermann, Ernest, 299, 312, 463
Unwin, Raymond, 653, 654, 667, 740
Utopian socialism, 5, 13, 31, 42, 43, 44-48, 56, 155-211, 431; and art, 625-636; literature, 601-603; later influence of, 229-231; and religion, 100-109, 118-119; religious, 127-151; see also Communitarianism, Christian; Communitarianism, liberal; Religious socialism
Utopian Society, 373
Utopianism, 229, 705

Valley Forge community, 165, 194
Van Doren, Carl, 361
Van Patten, Philip, 237
Vanzetti, Bartolomeo, 330
Vayo, Julio Alvarez del, see Alvarez del Vayo, Julio
Veblen, Thorstein, 268, 448, 469; and Marxism, 473-477
Velde, Henry van de, 657-658, 660-661
Venable, Vernon, 412n, 733n
Veronesi, Giulia, 659n
Vico, Giambattista, 411
Victorian Mansard style, 630
Villard, Oswald Garrison, 369
Viollet-le-Duc, Eugène E., 657n
Vladeck, B. Charney, 371
Vlag, Piet, 604

Vlassov, A. V., 697, 700
Vogt, Hugo, 258, 258n
Vogt, Karl, 433
Vollmar, George von, 70
Voltaire, F. M. A. de, 742
Vorwärts, 257, 258n
Voyce, Arthur, 662n, 677n

WOPRA (All-Russian Society of Proletarian Architects), 685n, 690n
Wadleigh, Julian, 358n
Wagenknecht, Alfred, 316, 321, 339n
Waite, David H. ("Bloody Bridles"), 243
Waldensians, 29, 113
Waldman, Louis, 370, 377-378, 379, 381
Walker, Francis A., 472
Wallace, Henry, 397, 746
Wallas, Graham, 76
Walling, William English, 282, 290, 295, 311, 312, 424, 448, 463, 479n, 520, 716n
Walton, J. C., 307
Ward, Harry F., 122, 355n, 360
Ward, Lester F., 269, 419, 436, 474
Warren, Josiah, 167, 185, 195n, 196, 198, 199-200, 207, 635
Water Cure Journal, 182
Waton, Harry, 324
Watson, A. M., 194
Watson, Tom, 301
Wattles, James O., 163
Wattles, John O., 193
Wayland, Julius A., 259-260, 270
Weatherwax, Clara, 354
Weaver, James B., 243, 245, 267
Webb, Beatrice, 76, 79n, 87n
Webb, Philip, 652
Webb, Sidney, 76, 77, 79n, 87n
Weber, Max, 218, 225n, 405, 544n
Weber, Max (painter), 721
Wechsler, James, 360n
Weisbord, Albert, 366, 367
Weitling, Wilhelm, 159, 231, 240
Weld, C. H., 142
Wells, Seth Y., 413n
Werth, Alexander, 700n
Wesley, John, 141
Western Federation of Miners, 254, 276, 278, 279, 308
Western Labor Union, 254, 276
Wetter, Gustavo A., 685n
Weydemeyer, Joseph, 231, 460
Weyl, Walter, 268, 313
Wheeler, Burton K., 394
Whig Party, 177, 198, 209
Whitaker, C. H., 707n
White, Harry D., 358n

Whitman, Walt, 743n
Wickey, Harry, 716n
Wicks, Harry M., 339
Widick, B. J., 390n
Willey, Basil, 118
Williams, Albert R., 89n
Williamson, John, 555n
Wilshire, Gaylord, 299
Wilshire's Magazine, 299
Wilson, Edmund, 42n, 46, 49n, 50n, 318n, 349, 354, 354n, 365, 615
Wilson, J. Stitt, 298 312-313
Wilson, William, 302
Wilson, Woodrow, 268, 288, 291, 292, 302, 311, 312, 313n, 316, 317, 329
Winstanley, Gerrard, 33, 35, 37, 38-39, 40, 114
Winwar, Frances, 618
Wisconsin Phalanx (Ceresco), 178, 180-181, 187, 204
Witness, 143
Witt, Nathan, 358
Wolfe, Bertram D., 324, 522n, 702n
Wolff, Adolph, 716n
Wolman, Leo, 330n
Woodcock, Leonard, 394
Woodhull, Victoria, 234
Woodrow Wilson Independent League, 312
Woodward, C. Vann, 301n
Work, John M., 274n
Workers Alliance, 382
Workers Challenge, 339
Workers Communist League, 366
Workers Council, 338
Workers Dance League, 709
Workers Defense Conference of New England, 338; *see also* United Toilers of America
Workers Laboratory Theatre, 354
Workers League, 338
Workers Monthly, 719

Workers Music League, 709
Workers Party (Communist), 333, 338-341; *see also* Communist Party (U.S.)
Workers Party (Trotskyist), 367-386
Working Class Union, 306
Workingmen's Party of New York, 230
Workingmen's Party of the United States, 236
Workmen's Circle, 310
World Committee of Peace Partisans, 747
World Peace Appeal, 746-747
World Tomorrow, 370
Wortis, Joseph, 725n
Wortis, Rose, 382
Wright, Chester M., 313
Wright, Frances, 163, 166, 173
Wright, Frank Lloyd, 742
Wright, Lucy, 137
Wright, Richard, 354n, 365, 620

Yellow Springs community, 165, 191
Yofan, Boris M., 697, 704n
Young, Art, 708, 717, 718, 719, 721
Young, Brigham, 629, 630
Young, Mahonri, 717
Young, Marguerite, 607
Young Communist League, 375, 551
Young People's Socialist League, 316, 375, 582
Youngs, Benjamin S., 135, 420

Zack, Joseph (Kornfeder), 368n
Zam, Herbert, 382, 384
Zetkin, Klara, 677n
Zhdanov, Andrei, 672, 693n, 699, 700, 700n
Zigrosser, Carl, 716n
Zinoviev, Grigory, 84n, 326, 336, 337, 350n, 362, 683, 688, 693
Zoar Separatists, 113, 114
Zola, Émile, 674
Zorach, William, 736